You're Busy so We're Bite-Sized

✓ **Complete Each Lesson in 30-45 minutes**

✓ **Video, Text, Assessment in Each Lesson**

✓ **Mobile App that Syncs Automatically with the Online Course**

✓ **Always Know Exactly Where You Stand**

✓ **Lesson Progress and Mastery Metrics**

Your Plan to Pass is Waiting

If you fail to plan, then plan to fail. Wiley's Exam Planner is at the heart of why 9 out of 10 pass using our system.

- ✔ **Enter Your Exam Date**
- ✔ **Enter Your Weekly Study Hours**
- ✔ **See 700 Lessons Scheduled to the Day**

You Can Do This!

> ""

> ""

efficientlearning.com/resources

Wiley CPAexcel® Exam Review

STUDY
GUIDE

JULY 2017

REGULATION

Wiley CPAexcel® Exam Review

STUDY
GUIDE

JULY 2017

REGULATION

Gregory Carnes, Ph.D., CPA
Marianne M. Jennings, J.D.
Robert A. Prentice, J.D.

Wiley Efficient Learning™

Contents

About the Authors

CPAexcel® content is authored by a team of accounting professors and CPA Exam experts from top accounting colleges such as the University of Texas at Austin (frequently ranked the #1 accounting school in the country), California State University at Sacramento, Northern Illinois University (frequently ranked in the top 10 in its peer group and top 20 overall), and the University of North Alabama.

Professor Craig Bain
CPAexcel® Author, Mentor, and Video Lecturer
Ph.D., CPA
Northern Arizona University: Franke College of Business, Professor and Accounting Area Coordinator

Professor Allen H. Bizzell
CPAexcel® Author, Mentor, and Video Lecturer
Ph.D., CPA (inactive)
Former Associate Dean and Accounting Faculty, University of Texas (Retired)
Associate Professor, Department of Accounting, Texas State University (Retired)

Professor Gregory Carnes
CPAexcel® Author and Video Lecturer
Ph.D., CPA
Raburn Eminent Scholar of Accounting, University of North Alabama
Former Dean, College of Business, Lipscomb University
Former Chair, Department of Accountancy, Northern Illinois University

Professor B. Douglas Clinton
CPAexcel® Author and Video Lecturer
Ph.D., CPA, CMA
Alta Via Consulting Professor of Management Accountancy, Department of Accountancy, Northern Illinois University

Professor Charles J. Davis
CPAexcel® Author
Ph.D., CPA
Professor of Accounting, Department of Accounting, College of Business Administration, California State University—Sacramento

Professor Donald R. Deis Jr.
CPAexcel® Author and Video Lecturer
Ph.D., CPA, CFE
TAMUS Regents Professor and Ennis & Virginia Joslin Endowed Chair in Accounting, College of Business,
    Texas A&M University—Corpus Christi
Former Director, School of Accountancy, University of Missouri—Columbia
Former Professor and Director, Accounting Ph.D. Program, Louisiana State University—Baton Rouge

Professor Emeritus Marianne M. Jennings
CPAexcel® Author and Video Lecturer
J.D.
Professor of Legal and Ethical Studies, W.P. Carey School of Business, Arizona State University

Professor Robert A. Prentice
CPAexcel® Author and Video Lecturer
J.D.
Ed and Molly Smith Centennial Professor In Business Law and Distinguished Teaching Professor, J.D.
    McCombs School of Business, University of Texas—Austin

Professor Pam Smith
CPAexcel® Author and Video Lecturer
Ph.D., MBA, CPA
KPMG Professor of Accountancy, Department of Accountancy, Northern Illinois University

Professor Dan N. Stone
CPAexcel® Author and Video Lecturer
Ph.D., MPA, CPA (inactive)
Gatton Endowed Chair, Von Allmen School of Accountancy, University of Kentucky

Professor Donald Tidrick
CPAexcel® Author and Video Lecturer
Ph.D., CPA, CMA, CIA
Deloitte Professor of Accountancy, Northern Illinois University
Former Associate Chairman, Department of Accounting, Director of Professional Program in Accounting and Director of the
    CPA Review Course, University of Texas at Austin

About the Regulation Professors

Professor Gregory Carnes is Dean of the College of Business and Raburn Eminent Scholar of Accounting at the University of North Alabama. He was former Dean of the College of Business at Lipscomb University in Nashville, Tennessee, and former Department Chair and Crowe Chizek Professor of Accountancy at Northern Illinois University. He taught partnership taxation and taxation of compensation and benefits in NIU's Masters of Science in Taxation Program. Professor Carnes has published approximately 25 articles in journals such as the *Journal of Economic Psychology; Journal of the American Taxation Association; Advances in Taxation; The Journal of International Accounting; Auditing, and Taxation; The Tax Adviser; Taxation for Accountants; Taxation for Lawyers;* and *The CPA Journal.* He is a contributing author for the *South-Western Federal Taxation* series, popular textbooks used in university taxation courses. He has served as President of the Accounting Program Leadership Group and President of the North Alabama Society of CPAs chapter. He is a member of the AICPA, the Alabama Society of CPAs, the American Accounting Association, and the American Taxation Association. He has also provided professional tax training for national accounting firms and the AICPA.

Professor Carnes received his Ph.D. from Georgia State University, his M.S. (Tax Specialization) from the University of Memphis, and his B.S. (Accountancy) from Lipscomb University. He previously taught at Louisiana State University, and worked for Ernst & Young in Nashville, Tennessee.

Professor Marianne Jennings is an Emeritus Professor of Legal and Ethical Studies in Business at the W.P. Carey School of Business at Arizona State University. She was named professor of the year in the College of Business in 1981, 1987, 2000, and 2010 and was the recipient of a Burlington Northern teaching excellence award in 1985.

Professor Jennings has authored hundreds of articles in academic, professional and trade journals. She was given best article awards by the institute of Internal Auditors and the Association of Government Accountants in 2001 and 2004.

Currently she has six textbooks and monographs in circulation. The ninth edition of her textbook, *Case Studies in Business Ethics,* and the 11th edition of her textbook, *Business: Its Legal, Ethical and Global Environment,* were published in January 2017. Her first textbook, *Real Estate Law,* had its 11th edition published in 2016. Her text, *Anderson's Business and the Legal Environment,* had its 23rd edition published in 2016.

Professor Robert A. Prentice is the Ed and Molly Smith Centennial Professor of Business Law at the University of Texas at Austin and has taught both UT's and other CPA courses for 15 years. He created a new course in accounting ethics and regulation that he has taught for the last decade. Professor Prentice has written several textbooks, and many major law review articles on securities regulation and accountants' liability, and has won more than 30 teaching awards.

Welcome to Regulation

Welcome to Regulation (REG)! This "lesson" is an important step in your journey to CPA exam success. This series of videos will introduce you to your professors, provide guidance in the planning, application, and registration process. In addition, there are videos that provide an overview of the exam structure, time management hints, effective study strategies, and tips on how to maximize your points. Perhaps most important, the last video is a gentle reminder of how important it is to take care of you.

Business Law

The scope of material in the Regulation—Business Law Section that is fair game under the AICPA content guidelines has been changed significantly but is still vast (10%–20%). Cover all the material in each subject area as thoroughly as possible, but use the new learning objectives to help you stay focused on the big picture so that you can easily compartmentalize the minutiae. Regulation topics areas have a great deal of detail. All these details are fair game for the exam questions. Going over the material just once is inadequate to fully master it. For many of you, some of these subject areas will be completely new learning experiences. Whether the subject area is new to you or you studied it in college, take the lessons one at a time and in 30-minute increments. Then take the time to go back and review. If you try to master all the details in huge blocks of study time, you will not conquer the material. Do a little each day. Then go back and use the tools again to get more familiar with those concepts. When you are able to sit down and write your own outline or flow chart of each area, without referring back to the text, the flash cards, or the video, you have reached a point of mastery.

In addition, I recommend the following:

A. Review the Overview for each general subject area. The Overview gives you my opinion of where to emphasize your study.

B. Read the lesson text and view the video—go over the examples in the text and videos carefully.

C. Go through all of the questions available to you. The more questions you do, the more knowledge you have about question patterns, and the more you will realize that certain themes are repeated with different fact patterns. If you do not understand a particular question, use the discussion forum to post the question and ask for more explanation on the area. Also, going through the mentored discussions often clears up areas that are not familiar to you and can prevent you from spending too much time on one question or issue.

D. The exam does more than test in each subject area. The exam includes questions that have cross-over material. For example, it is not unusual for an exam question to cover issues of bankruptcy along with UCC Article 9 secured transaction questions. Often the answer for a question will require you to combine contracts formation with an issue related to suretyship. The materials include many of these combined topic questions. These questions are the best form of review because they require mastery of more than one area and integration of the materials.

~ Professor Marianne M. Jennings

Federal Taxation

The challenge in the tax area is that there are so many topics that can be tested. However, once a topic is chosen for the test, the question asked is usually somewhat basic. So make sure you know the foundational concepts very well and do not be as concerned about the complex areas.

When you take the exam, you will be working problems, so that is what you must practice. Do not just read the problems and the solutions. That will not prepare you. Work as many problems as you possibly can.

~ Professor Gregory A. Carnes

Ethics, Professional Responsibilities, and Federal Tax Procedures

In the REG section, I am initially responsible for the 10%–20% of REG that is devoted to Ethics, Professional Responsibilities, and Federal Tax Procedures.

First, this material covers the professional responsibilities (and liabilities) of tax professionals, derived in detail from the AICPA's Statements on Standards for Tax Services (SSTSs). These were rewritten and reorganized in 2010. Particular attention should be paid to SSTS No. 1 and to the fact that it is subordinate to conflicting Internal Revenue Code Guidelines. The other SSTSs are heavily based on common sense, fortunately. Other important guidelines for tax professionals come from the IRS's rules of practice contained in Circular 230 and civil and criminal provisions that apply to tax return preparers (TRPs) and others contained in the Internal Revenue Code (IRC).

Second, this material covers licensing and disciplinary systems, the standards state boards of accountancy impose for those who wish to qualify for a CPA license, and the grounds upon which those licenses might be taken away. Disciplinary processes are also covered. These are not necessarily logical, but must be learned.

Third, this material covers the common law malpractice theories (negligence, breach of contract, fraud) that might be the basis for lawsuits against accountants and also addresses federal statutory liability of accountants, including RICO and the Foreign Corrupt Practices Act. In real life, and hopefully on the exam, the most important part of this material for CPAs is the part that deals with potential negligence liability to third parties (non-clients, such as lenders, suppliers, and investors) who have relied on audited financial statements. There are several different tests for how widely a careless auditor's liability extends, with the most popular version being the Restatement's "limited class" test.

In the REG section, I am also responsible for the Government Regulation of Business and Business Structure (Selection of a Business Entity) portions of Business Law (which comprises 10%–20% of REG).

Much important material is contained in these sections.

Government Regulation of Business is divided into two sections—federal securities regulation and all other federal regulation. That division alone should tell you how important securities regulation is.

Federal Securities Regulation can itself be subdivided (largely) into the part based on the Securities Act of 1933 (that governs the initial sale of securities in the primary markets) and the part based on the Securities Exchange Act of 1934 (that governs the trading of securities in the secondary markets). Over the years, the CPA Exam has emphasized the definition of a "security," the Regulation D exemptions for registration, and the differences between the 1933 Act's Section 11 (a negligence-based statute that punishes false statements in the audited financial statements contained in registered public offerings) and the 1934 Act's Section 10(b) (an intent-based statute that punishes fraudulent statements of any type when securities are being bought and sold). Although an accountant's potential liability under Section 11 and Section 10(b) have long received much attention on the exam, recent disclosed questions indicate that the 1933 Act's Section 12(a)(1) and 12(a)(2) and the 1934 Act's Section 18(a) have received attention as well. The JOBS Act of 2012 made some significant changes to the 1933 Act material. What is an EGC? What is crowdfunding?

Other Federal Laws and Regulations—The material in this section has traditionally not received as much attention as the securities laws have, although it covers a wide range of federal regulatory matters, including labor law, employment law, and antitrust law. It might pay to give special attention to new content areas recently added to the course content specifications, including copyrights, patents, and money laundering.

The *Business Structure* portion of the Business Law materials has been moved to REG from BEC and completely reorganized. The most important part is probably the introductory material, which will give you the basics of all the major forms of business organization—partnership, corporation, LLP, LLC, and so on. The former organizational pattern focused on a particular form of organization (such as a partnership or an LLC) and then ran through its features (formation, operation, termination, powers, financial structure, rights, powers, etc.) before moving on to the next form. Now the content specifications indicate that we should focus on the features (formation, operations, termination, powers, financial structure, etc.) and within those sections compare and contrast the various forms of organization. This material is organized consistently with the new content specifications, but a great way to study would be to develop your own outline that reorganizes the material within each form of organization.

~ Professor Robert Prentice

Ethics, Professional Responsibilities, and Federal Tax Procedures

Ethics and Responsibility in Tax Practice

Regulations Governing Practice before the IRS

After studying this lesson, you should be able to:

1. Recall the regulations governing practice before the IRS.

2. Apply the regulations governing practice before the IRS to a specific scenario.

I. Introduction

A. Circular 230 contains the IRS's rules of practice governing CPAs and others who practice before the agency. The government may censure, fine, suspend, or disbar tax advisors from practice before the IRS if they violate Circular 230's standards of conduct. "Practicing" entails primarily preparing and filing documents, and communicating and meeting with IRS representatives on behalf of a taxpayer.

B. Subpart A of Circular 230 sets forth rules governing authority to practice before the IRS. Most importantly, Section 10.3 provides that "[a]ny certified public accountant who is not currently under suspension or disbarment from practice before the Internal Revenue Service may practice before the Internal Revenue Service by filing with the Internal Revenue Service a written declaration that he or she is currently qualified as a certified public accountant and is authorized to represent the party or parties."

C. Who may practice before the IRS? As long as they are not under suspension or disbarment:

1. Attorneys

2. CPAs

3. Enrolled agents

4. Enrolled actuaries (enrolled by the Joint Board for the Enrollment of Actuaries), but their practice is generally limited to issues related to qualified retirement plans

5. Enrolled retirement plan agents, but their practice is limited to issues related to employee plans and to IRS forms in the 5300 and 5500 series

D. Practice before the IRS

1. Practice before the IRS includes all matters connected with a presentation to the IRS or any of its officers or employees related to a taxpayer's rights, privileges, or liabilities under laws or regulations administered by the IRS.

2. These presentations include, but are not limited to:

   a. Preparing documents

   b. Filing documents

   c. Corresponding and communicating with the IRS

   d. Rendering written advice with regard to transactions having a potential for tax avoidance or evasion

   e. Representing a client at conferences, hearings, and meetings

3. A power of attorney (Form 2848) is required for an individual to represent a taxpayer before the IRS.

E. Subpart B of Circular 230 contains the substantive rules that govern tax practitioners, including CPAs. Our discussion will focus on those rules.

F. Subpart C spells out sanctions for violations. Subpart D contains procedural rules for disciplinary proceedings.

II. Substantive Provisions

A. Furnishing Information—A practitioner must *promptly* submit to the IRS any records or information that its agents and officers request properly and lawfully, "unless the practitioner believes in good faith and on reasonable grounds that the records or information are privileged." In other words, Section 10.20 requires prompt cooperation with all IRS requests for information.

B. Client's Omission—What if you learn that your client has not complied with the laws or made an error or omission on a tax return? Consistent with AICPA ethics guidelines, Section 10.21 requires the practitioner to promptly notify the client of the error and its potential consequences, but the practitioner need not notify the IRS of the error and may not do so without the client's permission.

C. Due Diligence and Reliance on Others—Practitioners must exercise *due diligence* in all aspects of their tax practice, including preparing tax returns and making representations to the IRS. Section 10.22 allows a practitioner to rely on the work product of others, if the practitioner used reasonable care in engaging, supervising, training, and evaluating them, although Sections 10.34 and 10.37 contain a couple of slight limitations on this reliance.

D. Delays—Practitioners may not *unreasonably* delay the prompt disposition of any matters before the Service. Stalling tactics are strongly discouraged by Section 10.23.

E. Assistance from the Disbarred—What if your former partner violated regulations and has been disbarred by the IRS? She still needs a job and wants to continue to do the same work as before, but have you sign off on everything since you are still in good standing. Section 10.24 provides that a practitioner should not knowingly accept even indirect assistance from any person disbarred or suspended from practice by the IRS.

F. Practice by Former IRS Agents—The IRS is concerned about abuses by former IRS agents who might try to exploit their former position when they leave the Service. Therefore, Section 10.25 contains extensive rules meant to prevent conflicts of interest, such as IRS employees going into private practice and working on cases they had knowledge of when they worked for the government. For example, if IRS agent Fred worked on a matter involving taxpayer Stan within one year before he left the IRS, he could not join an accounting firm and represent Stan in that matter within two years of leaving the Service. Fred should not use his knowledge or influence in assisting or representing Stan in IRS proceedings during that two-year period.

G. Notaries—A practitioner must not act as a notary public with respect to matters before the IRS in which he or she is involved or interested (Section 10.26).

H. Fees

    1. Unconscionable fees—No practitioner may charge an *unconscionable fee* for representing a client before the IRS.

    2. Contingent fees—The rest of Section 10.27 relates to contingent fees, providing that a practitioner *may not* charge a contingent fee for providing services before the IRS, with three exceptions. A contingent fee may be charged:

        a. For services rendered in connection with an IRS *examination or challenge* to either (i) an original tax return or (ii) an amended return or claim for refund when they were filed within 120 days of receiving a written notice of examination or written challenge to the original exam

        b. Where a claim for refund is filed solely in connection with determination of statutory interest or penalties

        c. When the accountant is representing the client in judicial proceedings

        In these three situations, the threat that the tax practitioner and client will play the "audit lottery" (taking an aggressive position because it is unlikely that the Service will substantively examine it) is small.

    3. PCAOB—Remember that the PCAOB believes that a public company auditor is not independent from an audit client if it offers that client any services on a contingent fee basis.

I. **Return of Client Records**—What if you have fired the client, or the client has fired you? You still have the client's tax records, but perhaps the client has not paid you. You don't want to give the client's records back until you are paid. Section 10.28 instructs the practitioner to promptly return any and all records needed for the client to comply with federal tax obligations. The practitioner may keep a copy. The rule specifies that the existence of a fee dispute does not change this obligation but recognizes that if applicable state law permits retention in the case of a fee dispute, the practitioner need return only those records that must be attached to the taxpayer's return. However, the rule further provides that the practitioner "must provide the client with reasonable access to review and copy any additional records of the client retained by the practitioner under state law that are necessary for the client to comply with his or her Federal tax obligations." The rule broadly defines "records of the client," but states that" [t]he term does not include any return, claim for refund, schedule, affidavit, appraisal or other document prepared by the practitioner . . . if the practitioner is withholding such documents pending the client's performance of its contractual obligation to pay fees with respect to such document."

J. **Conflicts of Interest**—Section 10.29 provides that practitioners should not represent a client before the IRS if to do so would create a *conflict of interest*.

    1. Such a conflict exists if the representation of one client would be adverse to that of another, or if there is a significant risk that the representation of one client would be *materially limited* by the practitioner's responsibilities to another client.

    2. Notwithstanding the existence of a conflict of interest, however, practitioners may represent a client if they:

        a. Reasonably believe that they can provide competent and diligent representation to the client;

        b. The representation is not prohibited by law; *and*

        c. The affected client gives *informed* consent in writing. Practitioners should keep the consents on file for at least three years.

K. **Solicitation**—Section 10.30 contains several limitations on solicitation of clients. Among others, false advertising is, of course, prohibited. But practitioners may publish accurate written schedules of fees and hourly rates.

L. **Check Negotiation**—A practitioner who prepares tax returns may not endorse or otherwise negotiate any check issued to a client by the IRS, according to Section 10.31.

M. **Practicing Law**—Tax accountants, typically, learn quite a bit of tax law, but nothing in Circular 230 is meant to authorize persons who are not members of the bar to practice law (Section 10.32).

N. **Best Practices**—Section 10.33 sets forth **best practices** for tax advisers, including:

    1. Communicating clearly with the client regarding the terms of the engagement, including the purpose, use, scope, and form of the advice

    2. Establishing the facts, determining which facts are relevant, evaluating the reasonableness of assumptions or representations, relating the applicable law to the relevant facts, and arriving at a conclusion supported by the law and the facts

    3. Advising the client regarding the import of the conclusions reached, including whether taxpayers may avoid accuracy-related penalties if they rely on the advice;

    4. Acting fairly and with integrity when practicing before the IRS

    5. Exercising any firm supervisory powers to ensure that firm employees act in accordance with best practices

O. **Tax Return Standards**—Section 10.34 instructs practitioners not to willfully, recklessly, or through gross incompetence sign a tax return or claim for refund that the practitioner knows or reasonably should know contains a position that: (1) lacks a reasonable basis; (2) is an unreasonable position as defined by the Internal Revenue Code (Section 6694(a)(2)); or (3) is a willful attempt to understate the tax liability or a reckless or intentional disregard of IRC rules. Nor should a practitioner advise a client to take such unreasonable positions.

1. Additionally, practitioners should not advise clients to take "frivolous" positions on documents filed with the IRS.

2. Practitioners must inform clients of penalties reasonably likely to be imposed with respect to positions taken.

3. Practitioners may generally rely in good faith on information provided by their clients but may not ignore inconsistent information in their personal knowledge or other red flags that might appear.

P. Competence—Practitioners must be competent, meaning that they possess "the appropriate level of knowledge, skill, thoroughness, and preparation necessary." Section 10.35 indicates that they may acquire competence by studying the relevant law or consulting with experts.

1. **Compliance procedures**—Section 10.36 provides that practitioners who have or share principal authority and responsibility for overseeing a firm's tax practice may be sanctioned if they either (a) willfully, recklessly, or through gross incompetence fail to take reasonable steps to assure that the firm has adequate procedures in place to ensure that all members and employees are complying with Circular 230 or (b) know or should know that a member or employee is not complying with Circular 230, but through willfulness, recklessness, or gross incompetence fail to take prompt corrective action. The obvious purpose of this provision is to prevent those officials at the top of an accounting firm from placing all the blame for inappropriate tax shelter or other activity on lower-ranking members of the firm. The provision is an exception to Section 10.22's provision that allows a practitioner to rely on the work product of others if the practitioner used reasonable care in engaging, supervising, training, and evaluating them.

2. **Other written advice**—Section 10.37 provides that tax practitioners may give written advice if the practitioners:

   a. Base the advice on reasonable factual and legal assumptions;

   b. Reasonably consider all relevant facts and circumstances that the practitioners know or reasonably should know;

   c. Use reasonable efforts to identify and ascertain relevant facts;

   d. Do not rely on others' representations if to do so would be unreasonable;

   e. Relate applicable law and authorities to facts; *and*

   f. Do not take into account the possibility that a tax return will not be audited, that an issue will not be raised on audit, or that an issue will be settled.

III. Penalties and Procedures

A. Subpart C of Circular 230 sets forth the rules and penalties for disciplinary proceedings.

1. As a general notion, Circular 230 authorizes the IRS to punish any tax professional who is incompetent, disreputable, violates the Treasury Department's rules of practice or with intent to defraud willfully and knowingly misleads or threatens the person being represented.

2. Section 10.50 empowers the IRS to impose a monetary penalty on practitioners who have violated practice rules. The maximum penalty equals 100% of the gross income derived from the conduct and may be added to other penalties, such as suspensions and censures. It may also be added to the 50% penalty of gross income authorized by 26 U.S.C. Section 6694, meaning that the penalty could theoretically be up to 150% of the income derived from an engagement.

3. Section 10.51 lists numerous acts of incompetence or disreputable conduct that are sanctionable under Section 10.50, including:

    a. Conviction of any crime under federal tax laws

    b. Conviction of any crime involving dishonesty or breach of trust

    c. Conviction of any state or federal felony that would render one unfit to practice before the IRS

    d. Giving false or misleading information to tax officials

    e. Soliciting employment in violation of Section 10.30

    f. Willfully evading taxes

    g. Being disbarred or suspended from practice as a CPA or an attorney;

    h. Contemptuous conduct before the IRS

B. The remainder of Subpart C, as well as Subchapter D, contains sections setting forth the procedures governing the process when the IRS takes disciplinary action against tax practitioners.

IRC Code and Regulations Related to Tax Return Preparers

After studying this lesson, you should be able to:

1. Recall who is a tax return preparer (TRP).

2. Recall situations that would result in federal TRP penalties.

3. Apply potential TRP penalties given a specific situation.

I. Introduction

A. The Internal Revenue Code (IRC) has many provisions that related solely or largely to *tax return preparers* (*TRPs*). Some also apply to tax advisors. This section surveys those provisions.

II. Who is a tax return preparer (TRP)?

A. **Definition**—A TRP, generally speaking, is "any person who prepares for compensation, or who employs one or more persons to prepare for compensation, all or a substantial portion of any return of tax or any claims for refund of tax" under the IRC.

B. **Coverage**—This provision covers not only federal income tax returns but also federal estate and gift tax returns, employment tax returns, and excise tax returns.

C. **Requirements**—People are TRPs if they:

1. Are paid

2. To prepare, or retain employees to prepare,

3. A substantial portion

4. Of any federal tax return or refund claim.

D. **Subtypes**—Assume Smith is preparing an income tax return for a client and brings in his partner, Kahn, who is an expert whose advice Smith uses to complete a major portion of the return. Smith signs the return. He is a *signing TRP*. Although Kahn contributed substantially to completion of the return, he did not sign it and is therefore a *nonsigning TRP*.

1. **Signing TRPs** are individual TRPs who bear "primary responsibility" for the overall accuracy of the return or claim for refund (Smith in our example).

2. **Nonsigning TRPs** are those other than the signing TRP who prepare all or a substantial portion of a return or claim for refund (Kahn in our example).

Example
Assume that Company A has just completed a major transaction and hires attorney Al to provide legal advice that is directly relevant to a determination of a significant entry on Company A's tax return. If Al does not prepare any other portion of the return and is not the signing TRP, he would be considered a nonsigning TRP.

E. **Substantial Portion**—The signing TRP is always responsible for a substantial portion of the return. But what about nonsigning TRPs? If Kahn (to return to our example) evaluates a corporate taxpayer's just-completed transaction and concludes that it entitles the taxpayer to take a large deduction, he has prepared a "substantial portion" unless the deduction involves either:

1. Less than $10,000, *or*

2. Less than $400,000, which is also less than 20% of the gross income indicated on the return.

Examples

1. Kahn opines that the taxpayer may take a deduction of $300,000 on a return reflecting $26 million in gross income. Kahn would not be a nonsigning TRP because, although $300,000 is a lot of money in most settings, it is not a "substantial portion" of a return featuring $26 million in gross revenue.

2. Sal prepares a schedule for Max's Form 1040, reporting $4,000 in dividend income, and gives written advice about Schedule A, which results in a claim of a medical expense deduction totaling $5,000. Sal does not sign the tax return, so she is not a signing TRP. Nor is she a nonsigning TRP, because the total amount of the deductions is less than $10,000.

F. **Not a TRP**—People are not TRPs merely because they:

1. Furnish typing, reproducing, or other mechanical assistance

2. Prepare as a fiduciary a return or claim for refund for any person

3. Prepare taxes as part of a Volunteer Income Tax Assistance (VITA) or a Low Income Tax Clinic (LITC) program, but only for returns prepared as part of that program

4. Prepare a return with no explicit or implicit agreement for compensation, even if the person receives an insubstantial gift, return service, or favor

5. Prepare a return or claim for refund of the employer (or of an officer or employee of the employer) by whom he or she is regularly and continuously employed

Example

Accountant Nguyen intends to electronically submit Company B's tax return on its behalf. However, Company B asks Nguyen whether it should treat a substantial number of its workers as employees or as independent contractors. Nguyen renders her advice and is paid for it. Nguyen then receives employment tax information from B and files B's return using that information. Here, Nguyen is a TRP, which she would not have been had she not rendered the advice but only transmitted the return electronically on B's behalf.

G. **Additional Clarification**

1. When there are multiple people working on a return, the one who is primarily responsible for the position giving rise to an understatement is the TRP punishable under these provisions.

2. If it is unclear who is responsible, the person with overall supervisory responsibility for the return or for the position will be the TRP.

3. A TRP with respect to one return is not considered a TRP with respect to another return merely because entries on the first return affected the second return *unless* the entry reported on the first return is directly reflected on the second return and constitutes a substantial portion of it.

Example

Joe is the sole TRP of a partnership income return for the ABC Partnership. Tim is a partner, and the partnership revenue from ABC constitutes 80% of his income most years. Joe is a TRP regarding Tim's individual return.

III. **Civil Penalties Imposed on TRPs**

A. **Understatement of Taxpayer's Liability**—Section 6694 of the IRC imposes civil penalties on TRPs for understatement of their clients' taxes.

B. Subsection (a) punishes understatement due to unreasonable positions.

1. An undisclosed position is "unreasonable" if there is *no substantial authority* (*<40% chance* of being sustained) for the position.

    a. "Substantial authority" is an objective standard requiring that the weight of authorities supporting the claimed position is substantial in relation to the weight of authorities opposing it.

    b. Tax practitioners tend to think of "no substantial authority" as there being <40% chance of the position being sustained in challenged before the IRS.

  2. If a position is *disclosed*, then it is "unreasonable" if there is no *reasonable basis* for the position

    a. Because disclosure calls the IRS's attention to the position and makes it clear that the taxpayer is not trying to "sneak" it by, a more lenient standard is applied in determining "unreasonableness."

    b. Tax practitioners tend to think of a position as having "no reasonable basis" if there is <20% chance of it being sustained if challenged.

  3. If the position relates to a *tax shelter*, it is "unreasonable" unless it is *more likely than not* (*MLTN*) (>*50% chance*) that the position will be sustained.

  4. The maximum civil fine per violation under Subsection (a) is the *greater* of $1,000 or 50% of the income derived by the TRP with respect to the return.

  5. **Reasonable cause defense**—No penalty applies if the TRP had "reasonable cause" (an objective standard) for the position and acted in "good faith" (a subjective standard).

C. Subsection (b) of 6694 imposes harsher punishments for willful or reckless understatements.

  1. The penalty for a willful or reckless understatement is the *greater* of $5,000 or 75% of the income derived by the TRP with respect to the claim (per violation).

  2. **Example**—TRP fabricates deductions or ignores information provided by taxpayer.

  3. **Good faith defense applies**—For example, the taxpayer might provide false information to the TRP which appears to be genuine and accurate.

D. **Disclosure Provisions**—Section 6695 punishes TRPs for, among other things:

  1. Failure to furnish copy of return to taxpayer

  2. Failure to sign return and show own identity

  3. Failure to furnish identifying number to the IRS

  4. Failure to keep a copy of the return

  5. Failure to file correct information returns

  6. Negotiation of check made out to the taxpayer (other than to deposit the full amount into the taxpayer's bank account)

  7. Failure to be diligent in determining eligibility for the earned income tax credit and the child tax credit

E. **Abusive Tax Shelters**—Section 6700 punishes TRPs and others who promote abusive tax shelters when they:

  1. Organize or participate in the sale of a shelter; *and*

  2. Either:

    a. Knowingly or recklessly make a materially false statement that affects tax liability, *or*

    b. Engage in a gross overvaluation (2X actual value) of property.

F. **Aiding and Abetting the Understatement of Tax Liabilities**—TRPs and others can be liable under 26 U.S.C. 6701 for aiding and abetting an understatement of tax liability.

  1. In order to be liable, the TRP must:

    a. Aid, assist, procure, or advise in preparation or presentation of any portion of any return or other document;

    b. Know or have reason to know that it will be used in matters arising under tax law; *and*

    c. Know that if the return or document is so used, an understatement of the tax liability of another person will result.

  2. Liability can be imposed even if the taxpayer does not have knowledge of or consent to the understatement.

  3. Merely furnishing typing, reproducing, or other mechanical assistance with respect to a document does not constitute having aided and abetted the preparation of that document.

G. Confidentiality—Subject to obvious exceptions for court orders, peer reviews, and the like, 26 U.S.C. 6713 penalizes TRPs if they:

  1. Disclose any information furnished to them in connection with preparation of a return, *or*

  2. Use any such information for any purpose other than to prepare the return.

H. Injunctions—In addition to civil fines, Section 7407 authorizes the IRS to enjoin TRPs from violating the Internal Revenue Code.

  1. TRPs may be enjoined from:

    a. Violating Section 6694 (understatement of tax liability) and 6695 (disclosure requirements);

    b. Misrepresenting education or experience as a TRP, or eligibility to practice before the IRS;

    c. Guaranteeing payment of any tax refund or allowance of any tax credit; *or*

    d. Engaging in any other fraudulent or deceptive conduct that substantially interferes with the proper administration of tax laws.

  2. These narrow injunctions for specific violations can pave the way for a broad injunction that bars people from serving as TRPs at all if they have continually or repeatedly violated these rules.

  3. Section 7408 provides similar injunctive authority relating to wrongdoing in connection with tax shelters and reportable transactions.

IV. Criminal Provisions—The IRC also contains criminal provisions to punish TRPs and others for various tax-related wrongs. In a criminal case, the burden of proof is on the government to establish the crime beyond a reasonable doubt, whereas the burden of proof in civil cases is a mere preponderance of the evidence.

A. Tax Evasion—26 U.S.C. Section 7201 punishes tax evasion and is applied very broadly.

  1. This provision has been used to prosecute, among other wrongs:

    a. Failure to file a return

    b. Falsifying income

    c. Falsifying amounts that reduce taxable income

  2. To secure a conviction, the government must prove:

    a. An affirmative act constituting an attempt to evade or defeat payment of a tax;

    b. Willfulness; *and*

    c. Existence of a tax deficiency.

B. Tax Fraud—26 U.S.C. 7206 punishes fraud and false statements by TRPs and others, criminalizing (among other wrongs):

  1. Willfully making and subscribing to any document made under penalty of perjury that the CPA does not believe to be true as to every material matter

2. Willfully aiding the preparation of any tax-related matter that is fraudulent as to any material matter

3. Removing or concealing a client's property with intent to defeat taxes

C. Most criminal tax prosecutions are brought under Sections 7201 or 7206, but other criminal provisions include:

1. Willful failure to file a return, supply information, or pay a tax (Section 7203)

2. Willful failure to collect or pay over a tax (Section 7202)

3. Fraudulent returns, statements, or other documents (Section 7207)

4. Attempts to interfere with the administration of Internal Revenue laws, such as by threatening or misleading IRS agents (Section 7212)

5. Unauthorized disclosure of taxpayer information (with obvious exceptions for court orders, peer reviews, etc.) (Section 7213)

6. Willful disclosure or use of confidential information learned while preparing a tax return (Section 7216)

7. Conspiracy to commit any offense or fraud against the United States, including tax offenses (18 U.S.C. Section 371)

8. Aiding and abetting tax fraud (18 U.S.C. Section 2)

Licensing and Disciplinary Systems

After studying this lesson, you should be able to:

1. Understand and explain the role and authority of the state boards of accountancy.

I. Role of State Boards of Accountancy

A. Authority
State boards of accountancy license CPAs and can prohibit non-CPAs from performing attest functions. State boards also license (and punish) CPA firms.

1. It is only state boards that can grant CPA licenses and only state boards that can take them away.

2. While the AICPA and state societies of CPAs cannot grant or take away CPA licenses, they can grant membership, take away membership, and punish members by suspensions, etc. The AICPA's authority in this regard is covered in the AUD materials.

3. The AICPA has developed the Uniform Accountancy Act (UAA) to provide states with a model to regulate CPAs. Most states have adopted some or all of the UAA, ensuring that most state rules for CPAs are identical or at least similar to AICPA rules. The rules of state societies of CPAs also, naturally, substantially follow AICPA rules.

B. Licensing
To qualify to be licensed as a "certified public accountant," one must meet several requirements. In most states, three steps are the key and may be accomplished in any order:

1. **Education**

   a. "BA + 30" (150 hours of college education, including a bachelor's degree);

   b. Professional ethics course (required by many states); *and*

   c. Continuing professional education—Once certification is gained, there are also continuing professional education requirements.

2. **Examination**

   a. Pass the Uniform CPA Exam.

3. **Experience**

   a. How long? One year of professional experience (but at least 2,000 hours).

   b. In what areas? In accounting, attest, management advisory, financial advisory, tax or consulting areas and may be while working for any employer (accounting firm, corporation, government agency, etc.).

C. Attest-Related Functions

1. One needs a CPA license to perform attest-related functions:

   a. Any audit or other engagement to be performed in accordance with SAS (Statements on Auditing Standards)

   b. Any review of a financial statement to be performed in accordance with SSARS (Statements on Standards on Accounting and Review Services)

   c. Any examination of prospective financial information to be performed in accordance with SSAE (Statements on Standards for Attest Engagements)

   d. Any engagement to be performed in accordance with the standards of the PCAOB

D. Nonattest Services

1. One does not need a CPA license to perform such nonattest services as:

    a. Preparation of tax returns

    b. Management advisory services (consulting)

    c. Preparing financial statements without issuing a report thereon

E. Discipline—State boards may revoke CPA licenses and impose other penalties (such as fines) for such acts as:

1. Fraud or deceit in obtaining a certificate

2. Cancellation of a certificate in any other state for disciplinary reasons

3. Failure to comply with requirements for renewal

4. Revocation of the right to practice before any state or federal agency, including the PCAOB

5. Dishonesty, fraud, or gross negligence in performance of services or failure to file one's own income tax returns

6. Violation of professional standards

7. Conviction of a felony or any crime involving fraud or dishonesty

F. Reciprocity—Most states are now an active part of the "UAA Mobility" project supported by the AICPA and the National Association of State Boards of Accountancy (NASBA). When fully implemented, accountants from one state will be able to represent clients in another state without obtaining a license from or paying a fee to the latter state's accountancy board.

II. Role of AICPA

A. Professional Ethics Division

1. Investigates violations of AICPA Code and sanctions minor cases

B. Joint Trial Board

1. Hears more serious cases

2. Has power to acquit, admonish, suspend, or expel

3. Initial decisions are made by a panel whose actions are reviewable by the full trial board, whose decisions are conclusive

C. Automatic expulsion from the AICPA without a hearing results when a member has been convicted or received an adverse judgment for:

1. Committing a felony;

2. Willfully failing to file a tax return;

3. Filing a fraudulent tax return on own or client's behalf; *or*

4. Aiding in preparing a fraudulent tax return for a client.

Rationale for automatic expulsion
If a member has already been convicted or received an adverse judgment, then there has already been an opportunity for the member to have a full-blown criminal or civil trial. Consequently, it would be a waste of resources to have a second hearing, and summary punishment is justified.

D. Revocation of certificate by a state board of accountancy also leads to automatic expulsion.

E. Joint Ethics Enforcement Program (JEEP)

1. The AICPA and most state CPA societies have agreements to split the handling of ethics complaints. The JEEP can handle violations across state lines with a single investigation, hearing, and punishment.

2. Typically, the AICPA handles:

    a. Matters of national concern

    b. Matters involving more than one state

    c. Matters in litigation

3. The individual states handle the rest.

> **Note**
> Public accounting firms and their members are heavily regulated by the Securities and Exchange Commission (SEC) and the Public Company Accounting Oversight Board (PCAOB). Their rules are covered in other lessons in these materials. Among many other requirements, these agencies require accountants to have state-issued CPA licenses in order to be authorized to audit public companies.

Federal Tax Practice and Procedures

Substantiation and Disclosure of Tax Positions

> **After studying this lesson, you should be able to:**
>
> 1. Summarize the requirements for the appropriate disclosure of a federal tax return position.
>
> 2. Identify situations in which disclosure of federal tax return positions is required.
>
> 3. Identify whether substantiation is sufficient given a specific scenario.

I. Introduction

    A. The Internal Revenue Code is lengthy and complex, so it is unsurprising that even when acting in good faith, taxpayers may find themselves in situations where they clash with the IRS regarding whether certain income is taxable, certain deductions are allowed, and the like.

    B. Therefore, the IRC has provisions that attempt to punish unreasonable actions by taxpayers and to protect good faith attempts at compliance with federal tax law. The Supreme Court once wrote that "the [tax] law is complicated, accounting treatment of various items raises problems of great complexity, and innocent errors are numerous. . . . It is not the purpose of the law to penalize frank differences of opinion or innocent errors made despite the exercise of reasonable care." [Spies v. U.S. (1943)]

    C. Requiring *disclosure* and *substantiation* of various positions is one important aspect of the IRS approach.

II. The IRC imposes (in Section 6662) a 20% penalty on various types of underpayments, including:

    A. Underpayments attributable to *negligence or disregard* of rules or regulations.

    B. Any *substantial understatement* of income tax.

        1. An "understatement" in this category is reduced by the amount attributable to any item where:

            a. The relevant facts affecting the tax treatment are adequately *disclosed* (typically on a Form 8275 or 8275R), *and*

            b. There is a "reasonable basis" (≥20% chance of being sustained) for the tax treatment.

        2. Disclosure is important here because an *undisclosed* position must be supported by "substantial authority," which requires a ≥40% chance of being sustained.

> **Example**
> Juan's tax preparer tells Juan that he can make a plausible claim to a particular deduction that will greatly reduce his taxes this year. A landmark case provides precedent for the claim, though the facts of the case are sufficiently different from Juan's that there's only a one-third chance that the position will be sustained. Juan and his TRP should disclose the position on Form 8275. Even if it is rejected, the 20% understatement penalty will not be incurred because there's more than a 20% chance of approval. Therefore, the amount of understatement will be reduced by the amount at stake in this deduction. Absent disclosure, the 20% penalty would have been applied once the deduction was rejected because it was not supported by substantial authority (≥40% chance of approval).

III. Reasonable Cause and Good Faith Defense (Section 6664)—No Section 6662 penalty is imposed if (a) there was "reasonable cause" for the underpayment and (b) the taxpayer acted with "good faith." (This defense obviously overlaps with the provision in Section 6662 that reduces an understatement where facts are disclosed and there is a reasonable basis for the tax treatment.)

A. Reasonable Cause

1. Definition—The exercise of ordinary care

2. Judged objectively

3. Examples of reasonable cause:

   a. Reliance on tax adviser *and/or*

   b. Reliance on advice of IRS employee.

4. Standards of belief:

   a. **Undisclosed position**—"Substantial authority" (≥40% chance of being sustained)

   b. **Disclosed position**—"Reasonable basis" (≥20% chance of being sustained)

B. Good Faith

1. Definition—Honesty of purpose

2. Judged subjectively

3. Examples:

   a. Reliance on erroneous W-2, with no red flags to indicate its inaccuracy.

   b. Reliance on erroneous advice of tax adviser where:

      i. Adviser was given all facts and circumstances;

      ii. Advice was not based on unreasonable assumptions; *and*

      iii. If the advice was that a regulation was invalid, the position was adequately **disclosed**.

Example

A taxpayer, being unfamiliar with tax law, hired and followed the advice of a practicing attorney in the area. The attorney's advice was erroneous, and the court disallowed a business expense deduction. However, the court did not impose a penalty because the taxpayer was able to establish:

- The adviser was a competent professional;

- Taxpayer provided necessary and accurate information; *and*

- Taxpayer actually relied in good faith on adviser's judgment.

   c. Notice again the important role that disclosure plays in this defense.

Example

Nina tells her TRP that she would like to take a particular deduction that would have a significant impact on her return's bottom line. After research, the TRP tells Nina that the deduction is barred by a particular IRS regulation and that, although there is some controversy about the matter, there is only a one-third chance that a court would overturn the regulation if Nina challenged it. Nina should disclose the position. If it is rejected, as it likely will be, she can still claim a reasonable cause/good-faith defense in response to any attempt to impose an underpayment penalty because her position had a reasonable basis.

IV. Disclosure and Substantiation

A. **Introduction**—Taxpayers have to pay penalties under Section 6662 because of their negligent conduct or because they have taken positions that are inappropriate.

1. Disclosure can help avoid liability by demonstrating that the taxpayer was acting in good faith and not trying to pull a fast one or otherwise sneak a position past the IRS.

2. Substantiation can help avoid liability by establishing entitlement to a claimed position and also indicating good faith by a taxpayer who is trying to get things right.

B. **Disclosure**—When a taxpayer takes a position contrary to an IRS regulation, the underpayment penalty does not apply, according to Treasury Regulation 1.6662–3, if:

1. The position is *disclosed* on "a properly completed and filed *Form 8275–R*";

2. The position represents a "good-faith challenge" to the validity of the regulation; *and*

3. The taxpayer has:

   a. A "reasonable basis" (≥ 20% chance of being sustained) for the position, *and*

   b. Kept adequate books and records or otherwise substantiated items properly.

C. **Substantiation**—As noted, accuracy-related penalties may be imposed for underpayments caused by negligence, which include:

1. Failure to keep adequate books and records.

   a. In general, the law does not require any specific type of record; taxpayers may choose any suitable system that clearly establishes the necessary facts.

   b. Deductions that are often questioned include:

      i. Home office deductions

      ii. Vehicle mileage

      iii. Gifts to clients

      iv. Food and entertainment

   c. Records that should be retained:

      i. All tax returns for the previous seven years

      ii. All records that pertain to a return for the previous three years

      iii. Other records, no matter how old, that would be needed to support a tax position on a subsequent return

2. Failure to substantiate items that gave rise to the underpayment.

   a. Among others, taxpayers are required to substantiate:

      i. **Charitable contributions**—The taxpayer must have a receipt for large donations to a charitable organization. Donations ≥ $250 must be documented with a receipt. Donations > $5,000 generally require a qualified appraisal.

      ii. **Business use of an automobile**—The taxpayer must track the miles driven for business use in a timely kept log.

3. Good faith provides a defense to even a failed effort.

Example
A taxpayer kept a log of contract labor expenses. The court held that the log was not sufficiently detailed to meet the legal standards and therefore disallowed the claimed deduction. However, the court also held that the log represented a good-faith effort to meet the standards and therefore did not impose the 20% underpayment penalty.

Taxpayer Penalties

After studying this lesson, you should be able to:

1. Recall situations that would result in taxpayer penalties relating to federal tax returns

2. Calculate taxpayer penalties relating to federal tax returns.

I. Introduction

A. The Internal Revenue Code (IRC) has several provisions that punish taxpayers for negligence, noncompliance, and even intentional fraud.

B. The penalties are both civil (burden of proof = preponderance of the evidence) and criminal (burden of proof = beyond a reasonable doubt.

C. The tax code recognizes that tax law is very complicated and therefore is not aimed at punishing taxpayers who have made diligent, good faith efforts to comply with the law.

II. Late Filing Penalties—The IRC (Section 6651) imposes penalties for late filing or failure to file as well as late payment of tax.

A. Late Filing or Failure to File

1. Penalty is 5% of the net tax due per month (up to 25% of unpaid taxes).

Example
Mary files her income tax form two months after the deadline. She owes $10,000 in tax. She must now pay the $10,000 in tax plus a $1,000 penalty [2 (months) × (5%) × $10,000 = $1,000].

2. If the failure to file is fraudulent, the penalty becomes 15% per month (up to 75% of unpaid taxes).

Example
Mary fraudulently fails to file her tax form but is caught by the IRS and does so two months after the deadline. She owes $10,000 in tax. She must now pay the $10,000 in tax plus a $3,000 penalty [2 (months) × (15%) × $10,000 = $3,000].

B. Late Payment of Tax

1. Penalty is 0.5% of the net tax due per month (up to 25%).

Example
Mary files her tax form in a timely manner but does not pay her tax until two months after it is due. She owes $10,000 in tax. She must now pay the $10,000 in tax plus a $100 penalty [2 (months) × (.5%) × $10,000 = $100].

Notes
1. The failure to file penalty is 10 times the size of the failure to pay penalty in order to encourage taxpayers to file, even if they are financially strapped.
2. For any month to which both the late filing and late payment penalties apply, the late filing penalty is reduced by the late payment penalty so that the maximum is 5% per month (up to 25%).
3. For returns filed more than 60 days after the due date (taking into account extensions granted), the minimum penalty is (in 2016) the lesser of $135 or 100% of the unpaid tax.
4. Taxpayers who have requested an extension by the due date and paid at least 90% of taxes owed will not face a failure-to-pay penalty.
5. A "reasonable cause" defense applies (example: serious illness strikes on the eve of the filing deadline).

III. Understatement Penalties—The key statute (26 U.S.C. 6662) imposes an accuracy-related 20% penalty on taxpayers for the following underpayments:

A. Underpayments attributable to **negligence** or **disregard** of rules or regulations.

    1. "Negligence" is "any failure to make a reasonable attempt to comply with" the rules.

        a. Negligence may include, among many other things: failure to keep adequate books and records and to otherwise substantiate items that gave rise to the understatement.

Example
Failing to include on an income tax return the income shown on a W-2 or 1099 and waiting until the last minute to file and in haste making numerous errors on return

        b. The statute focuses on two interrelated aspects:

            i. **Taxpayer conduct**—Did the taxpayer make reasonable attempts to get it right? Sophisticated taxpayers may be held to a higher standard, but even unsophisticated taxpayers may be viewed as negligent if they failed to consult a tax professional.

            ii. **Taxpayer positions**—A taxpayer position that lacks a "reasonable basis" may be attributed to negligence.

        c. A reasonable cause/good faith defense exists under Section 6664 and is discussed below.

        d. Disclosure of a position that is negligently taken is *not* a defense.

    2. "Disregard" may be negligent, reckless, or intentional.

        a. Negligent and reckless disregard largely overlap with the "negligence" provision of the statute.

        b. Intentional disregard may be problematic but is not necessarily wrongful just because the taxpayer takes a tax position that is ultimately found to be erroneous. A "good-faith" mistake of law provides a defense.

        c. Disclosure of a position on a Form 8275 or 8275-R may provide a defense to any penalty for intentional disregard if the position has a reasonable basis and the taxpayer has kept adequate books and records to properly substantiate necessary items.

B. Any Substantial Understatement of Income Tax

    1. For individuals, a "substantial understatement" is one that exceeds *the greater of*:

        a. 10% of the tax, *or*

        b. $5,000.

Example
Ted's correct tax amount is $10,000, but Ted reported only $6,000. Ted's understatement of $4,000 is less than the *greater* of the two standards ($5,000) and therefore is *not* a "substantial understatement."

    2. For non–Subchapter S corporations, a "substantial understatement" is one that exceeds the *lesser* of:

        a. 10% of the tax (or, if greater, $10,000), *or*

        b. $10 million.

Example
ABC Corporation's correct tax amount is $100,000, but it reported only $60,000. ABC's understatement is $40,000. That understatement does not exceed $10 million, but it does exceed the lesser standard of 10% of the tax ($10,000), which in this instance is equal to $10,000. Therefore, this is a "substantial understatement."

3. An "understatement" is reduced by the amount attributable to either:

   a. Any item for which there is or was "substantial authority" for the claimed tax treatment.

      i. "Substantial authority" is an objective standard requiring that the weight of authorities supporting the claimed position is substantial in relation to the weight of authorities opposing it.

      ii. Tax practitioners tend to think of "no substantial authority" as there being <40% chance of the position being sustained if challenged before the IRS.

      iii. Authorities that count include, among others, the IRC, regulations, revenue rulings and procedures, court cases, and congressional intent as reflected in committee reports.

   b. Any item if:

      i. The relevant facts affecting the tax treatment are adequately *disclosed* (typically on a Form 8275 or 8275R); *and*

      ii. There is a "reasonable basis" for the tax treatment.

         a. Because disclosure calls the IRS's attention to the position and makes it clear that the taxpayer is not trying to sneak it by, a more lenient standard is applied in determining "unreasonableness."

         b. Tax practitioners tend to think of a position as having "no reasonable basis" if there is <20% chance of it being sustained if challenged.

4. However, an understatement is *not* reduced under these rules if the transaction involved is a "tax shelter," defined as:

   a. A partnership or other entity,

   b. Any investment plan or arrangement, *or*

   c. Any other plan or arrangement, if a *significant purpose* of the partnership, entity, plan, or arrangement is the "avoidance or evasion" of income tax.

      i. Note: However, Section 6664 does provide a reasonable cause/good-faith exception that applies even to tax shelters.

      ii. The defense applies to tax shelters only if there is authority giving rise to a good faith believe that it is "more likely than not" (MLTN) (>50% likelihood) that the position taken will be sustained.

C. There are also penalties for other wrongs that are litigated much less frequently, including: for substantial valuation misstatements, for substantial estate or gift tax valuation understatements, for claimed tax benefits by reason of a transaction lacking economic substance, and others. For some of these categories, the penalty is 40% of the underpayment, rather than merely 20%.

IV. Reasonable Cause and Good Faith Defense (Section 6664)

A. No Section 6662 penalty is imposed if (a) there was "reasonable cause" for the underpayment and (b) the taxpayer acted with "good faith."

1. **Negligence or disregard**—Although the reasonable cause/good-faith defense apparently applies to understatements due to negligence or careless disregard of the rules, if the taxpayer was not negligent, she will not usually need the defense; if she was negligent, the defense usually will not succeed.

2. **Substantial understatement**—Therefore, the defense applies primarily in cases of substantial understatements where it largely overlaps with the provision of Section 6662 providing that any understatement is reduced by amounts for which there was "substantial authority" or *disclosed* positions for which there was a "reasonable basis."

B. **Reasonable Cause**

   1. Definition—The exercise of ordinary business care and prudence

   2. Judged objectively

   3. Examples of reasonable cause:

      a. Reliance on tax adviser

      b. Reliance on advice of IRS employee

      c. Death or illness of taxpayer or close family member

      d. Unavoidable destruction of records or place of business

   4. Belief requirement for reasonable cause related to tax positions:

      a. **Undisclosed position**—"Substantial authority" (≥40% chance)

      b. **Disclosed position**—"Reasonable basis" (≥ 20% chance)

      c. **Tax shelter position**—"More likely than not" (>50% chance)

C. **Good Faith**

   1. **Definition**—Honesty of purpose.

   2. Judged subjectively.

   3. Examples:

      a. Reliance on erroneous W-2, with no red flags to indicate its inaccuracy.

      b. Reliance on erroneous advice of tax adviser where:

         i. Adviser was given all facts and circumstances;

         ii. Advice was not based on unreasonable assumptions; *and*

         iii. If the advice was that a regulation was invalid, the position was adequately disclosed.

V. **Disclosure and Substantiation**—As noted in the previous lesson, disclosure and substantiation of positions taken can help establish the reasonable cause/good faith defense.

VI. Obviously there is no reasonable cause or good-faith defense when a taxpayer attempts to commit fraud. A 75% (of the portion of underpayment) civil penalty applies to fraudulent underpayments (26 U.S.C. 6663).

A. When the underpayment is allegedly fraudulent, the 75% penalty applies to the return's *entire* understatement, unless the taxpayer can establish that parts of it were not attributable to fraud.

VII. **Criminal Tax Culpability**—Taxpayers who willfully attempt to avoid paying taxes that they rightfully owe are subject to criminal punishment under the following provisions, among others:

A. **Tax Evasion**—26 U.S.C. Section 7201 punishes tax evasion and is applied very broadly.

    1. This provision has been used to prosecute, among other wrongs:

        a. Failure to file a return

        b. Falsifying income

        c. Falsifying amounts that reduce taxable income

    2. To secure a conviction, the government must prove:

        a. An affirmative act constituting an attempt to evade or defeat payment of a tax;

        b. Willfulness; *and*

        c. Existence of a tax deficiency.

    3. Maximum punishment for individuals: fine of $100,000 and/or 5 years in jail.

B. **Tax Fraud**—26 U.S.C. Section 7206 punishes fraud and false statements by taxpayers and others, criminalizing (among other wrongs):

    1. Willfully making and subscribing to any document made under penalty of perjury that the taxpayer does not believe to be true as to every material matter

    2. Willfully aiding the preparation of any tax-related matter that is fraudulent as to any material matter

    3. Removing or concealing property with intent to defeat taxes

Sources of Tax Authority and Research

After studying this lesson, you should be able to:

1. Identify key sources of legislative, administrative, and judicial authority.

2. Describe the process used for creating new tax statutes in Congress.

3. Weight sources of authority in determining relevance for specific tax issues.

4. Summarize the tax research process and key issues for communicating results.

I. **Types of Tax Authority**

   A. There are two types of authority: primary and secondary. Primary authority consists of the original sources of the law, whereas secondary authority is commentary on tax law such as treatises, journals, and commentaries provided by editorial services.

   B. Primary authority comes from each of the three branches of the federal government.

      1. Legislative authority

      2. Administrative authority

      3. Judicial authority

II. **Legislative Authority**—Authority from Congress

   A. Sources of statutory authority include:

      1. The Constitution, as all tax laws must be consistent with the provisions of the Constitution such as the 16th Amendment authorizing an income tax

      2. Internal Revenue Code Statutes (cited as IRC §351)

      3. Treaties

      4. Committee Reports of the House Ways and Means Committee, Senate Finance Committee, and the Joint Conference Committee

   B. The Internal Revenue Code (IRC) is the codification of the tax laws promulgated by Congress.

III. **Administrative Authority**—Authority from the Treasury Department and Internal Revenue Service. While there are many types of pronouncements issued by the Internal Revenue Service, the most significant are as follows. (Examples are provided for how each authority is cited.)

   A. **Treasury Regulations**—(Treas. Reg. §1.351-1). Regulations are published in the Federal Register and later in the Internal Revenue Bulletin.

      1. Regulations are organized in a sequential system with numbers preceding and following a decimal point. The numbers preceding the decimal point indicate the type of regulation or applicable area of tax law to which they pertain, while the numbers immediately following a decimal point indicate the Internal Revenue Code section being interpreted. Some of the more common prefixes include:

Number	Type
1	Income Tax
20	Estate Tax
25	Gift Tax
301	Administrative and Procedural Matters
601	Procedural Rules

2. Regulations can be classified as:

   a. Legislative—These regulations have almost as much weight as the statute (IRC), since Congress has authorized the Treasury to develop regulations dealing with a specific issue.

   b. Interpretative—These regulations are written under the general mandate given to Treasury to develop regulations to interpret the laws legislated by Congress.

   c. Procedural—These regulations apply to procedural issues such as the information required to be submitted, the process for submission, etc.

3. Regulations can also be classified as:

   a. Proposed—Regulations must be issued as proposed regulations for at least 30 days before becoming final, although they may exist in a proposed form for many years. Proposed regulations do not have the effect of law, but they do provide an indication of the IRS's view on a tax issue.

   b. Temporary—These regulations do have the effect of law but only for three years. Temporary regulations are usually issued when taxpayers need immediate guidance on a substantive matter of the law.

   c. Final regulations—Proposed or temporary regulations can later be issued as final regulations which have the effect of law until revoked.

B. **Revenue Rulings**—(Rev. Rul. 2009-12)

   1. Do not have as much weight as regulations

   2. Are limited to a given set of facts

   3. Deal with more specific issues than regulations

C. **Private Letter Rulings**—(PLR 200948009)

   1. Request by the taxpayer for the IRS to provide the tax consequences on a specific set of facts

   2. Transaction cannot have been completed by the taxpayer for the request to be made.

   3. Precedent applies only to the taxpayer making the request. However, PLRs can be used by other taxpayers to establish "substantial authority" for penalty purposes.

   4. IRS does not have to provide a ruling on the request.

D. **Revenue Procedures** (Rev. Proc. 2008-23)—These provide internal management practices of the IRS.

E. **Technical Advice Memoranda**—(TAM 201003016)—These are requested by the IRS field agents during an audit. They apply only to the affected taxpayer.

F. Other sources of authority include notices, announcements, and general council memoranda.

IV. Judicial Authority

A. **Courts of Original Jurisdiction**—Any tax dispute not resolved between the taxpayer and the IRS that goes to court must begin in a court of original jurisdiction.

   1. U.S. Tax Court

      a. Hears only tax cases.

      b. One court, but the 19 judges travel in smaller groups throughout the country to hear cases. For certain issues all judges may hear the case.

      c. Taxpayer does not have to pay deficiency before trial as long as a petition is filed in a timely manner.

      d. Jury trial is not available.

      e. The IRS has adopted an *acquiescence policy* for regular Tax Court decisions that it loses. *Acquiescence* indicates that the IRS will follow the decision in future situations, involving similar facts and issues. *Nonacquiescence* indicates that the IRS will not follow the decision and can be expected to litigate in situations involving similar facts and issues.

    f. Decisions of the Tax Court are appealed to U.S. Court of Appeals. As a matter of policy known as the *Golsen Rule*, the Tax Court will follow the law of the circuit to which a case is appealable.

  2. U.S. District Courts

    a. Jury trial is possible.

    b. Must pay deficiency first and then sue the IRS for a refund

    c. Judges are not tax specialists since all types of legal matters are tried.

    d. Many different district courts throughout the country

  3. U.S. Court of Federal Claims

    a. There is only one court in Washington, D.C.

    b. Must pay deficiency first and then sue the IRS for a refund

    c. 16 judges, who are not tax specialists, since all types of legal matters are tried

    d. Jury trial is not available.

  4. U.S. Tax Court—Small Cases Division

    a. $50,000 or less

    b. No appeal

B. Appellate Courts

  1. U.S. Court of Appeals

    a. Hears appeals from Tax Court and District Court.

    b. 11 circuits plus the District of Columbia Circuit.

    c. District court must follow the decision/precedent of the Circuit Court of Appeals for the circuit in which the District Court is located.

    d. Tax Court will follow previous decisions in the Circuit that will have jurisdiction on appeal (*Golsen rule*).

Definition
Precedent: The courts must follow previous decisions for future cases with the same controlling set of facts.

---

  2. U.S. Court of Appeals for the Federal Circuit—Hears appeals from the U.S. Court of Federal Claims.

C. U.S. Supreme Court

  1. Hears very few tax cases

  2. Highest court in the United States

V. Weighting of Authority

A. Legislative authority is weighted in the following order. Barring certain exceptions (e.g., constitutional issues), Congress has the last word on what the Federal tax law should be.

  1. The highest source of tax authority is the U.S. Constitution.

  2. The next highest source is the Internal Revenue Code.

  3. If a treaty exists with a foreign country, the provisions of the treaty control the tax consequences of a transaction.

B. Administrative Authority

1. Legislative regulations have almost as much weight as the IRC itself.

2. Other types of regulations have very significant authority within the context of administrative authority.

3. Revenue Rulings are the next highest source of authority.

4. Private Letter Rulings apply only to the taxpayer who requested the ruling.

C. Judicial Authority—The weighting of a judicial decision depends on:

1. Level of court

2. Legal residence of the taxpayer

3. Whether the IRS has acquiesced to the decision (meaning that the IRS has indicated that it will follow the decision in the future)

4. The date of the decision

5. Whether later decisions have concurred with opinion

VI. Research Process—The following steps should be followed when researching a tax issue:

A. Identify all relevant facts.

B. Clearly state problem to be solved.

C. Locate applicable tax authority.

D. Evaluate the relevance of the authorities.

E. Determine alternative solutions.

F. Determine most appropriate solution.

G. Communicate results.

VII. Communicating Research—A research memorandum should include the following key procedures:

A. Document all relevant facts.

B. Clearly describe the issue investigated.

C. Report conclusions.

D. Summarize rationale and authorities that support conclusions.

E. Summarize key authorities used in research.

Tax Practice and Procedure

After studying this lesson, you should be able to:

1. Describe the key steps in the audit process used by the Internal Revenue Service

2. Apply the statute of limitations to determine the audit time period for the IRS.

3. Summarize the most important steps in the appeals process when the taxpayer and the IRS do not agree.

4. List the key documents that provide standards of tax practice for CPAs and indicate the significant standards.

I. Audit Process

A. The audit process begins with a review of returns for error and matching information from W-2s, 1099s, and so on. This review is applied to all tax returns.

B. All returns are classified by type such as individual, corporation, partnership, fiduciary, and so on.

C. Each return is given a score from formulas that are part of the Discriminate Function System (DIF). The DIF score is used to determine which returns to review for possible audit.

D. Audits may be conducted in an IRS office or in the field. Simple audits may be handled through written correspondence.

E. A taxpayer may appoint qualified individuals to represent him or her before the IRS, usually a CPA, attorney, or enrolled agent.

F. The IRS has the power to summon the taxpayer's records and witnesses to testify.

G. IRS reports its findings in an *Income Tax Examination Changes Report*.

H. Disagreements between the taxpayer and the IRS may arise from questions of fact or from questions of law.

I. The IRS will take positions consistent with its administrative sources of the tax law.

J. The taxpayer and the IRS can negotiate until the issues are resolved.

K. If the taxpayer agrees to the audit changes proposed in the *Revenue Agent's Report* (RAR), he or she cannot pursue tax relief through the appeals process or through the Tax Court. However, note that a signed agreement binds the IRS and taxpayer with regard to only items in the agreement.

L. Nevertheless, once the deficiency is paid, the taxpayer can later pursue a claim for refund through the U.S. District Court or U.S. Claims Court.

M. If agreement is not reached through the audit process, the taxpayer will receive a copy of the RAR and a **30-day letter**.

N. The IRS encourages the taxpayer to agree to the RAR or request an appellate conference. However, the taxpayer is not required to respond.

O. If the IRS issues a **no change report** after an audit, the IRS generally cannot reopen the examination unless fraud or other similar misrepresentation is involved.

II. Appeals Process

A. To appeal, a written protest must be filed with the request for an appellate conference.

B. The protest must explain the taxpayer's position for each issue and provide the support on which the taxpayer is relying for questions of law.

C. The IRS is not required to grant an appeal in all cases.

D. In general, new issues may not be raised by the IRS during the appeal.

E. The appellate conference itself is informal when contrasted to a judicial proceeding.

F. If the case is settled, a Form 870-AD is signed, which means that the case will not be reopened unless there is a significant mathematical error or fraud.

G. If a taxpayer does not respond to the 30-day letter or does not reach agreement in the appeals process, a 90-day letter is issued.

H. The **90-day letter** is significant in that this is the time that the taxpayer has to file a petition with the Tax Court. If the petition is not filed in a timely manner, the taxpayer's only judicial recourse is through a U.S. District Court or a U.S. Claims Court, both of which require the deficiency to be paid before the judicial process can begin.

I. Once a petition has been filed with the Tax Court, the IRS cannot issue a notice of deficiency until the court's decision in the matter has been finalized.

III. Other Practice Issues

A. An offer in compromise may be agreed to by the IRS, which allows a taxpayer to settle a tax liability for less than the actual amount owed.

B. The IRS may request the taxpayer to extend the statute of limitations period. While not required to do so, a refusal to extend usually will lead the IRS to assess a tax deficiency.

C. Any communication that would be privileged between a taxpayer and an attorney is also privileged between a taxpayer and any person who is authorized to practice before the IRS.

D. This privilege does **not** apply to criminal tax matters or to corporate tax shelters.

IV. Signing a Return

A. A taxpayer must sign a tax return for it to be complete. Both spouses must sign a joint return. This creates joint and several liability for each spouse, which means that the IRS can collect the entire tax liability from either spouse.

B. A refund cannot be issued unless the return is signed.

C. A taxpayer can use an electronic signature to sign a return that is e-filed.

   1. The taxpayer needs a personal identification number (PIN) to file electronically.

   2. For a married filing jointly return, both spouses need PINs.

   3. A taxpayer can self-select/enter a PIN or have the tax practitioner generate/enter a PIN for him/her.

   4. Note that if a return is filed electronically, no forms or paper need to be mailed to the IRS, not even W-2s.

D. A parent or guardian can sign a child's return as the child's representative.

E. A tax return is signed under the penalty of perjury. If a taxpayer knowingly signs a false tax return, the taxpayer can be subject to civil and/or criminal penalties. See the "Compliance Responsibilities" lesson for more detail.

F. The tax preparer must also sign the tax return and provide a PIN. Failure to do so results in a $50 penalty to the tax preparer for each failure (maximum of $25,000 in any calendar year). The penalty applies separately to the failure to sign and failure to provide a PIN.

V. Standards of Practice

A. Circular 230 describes the rules that one must meet to be eligible to practice before the IRS. The term "practice" in this case relates to representing a client before the IRS. It does not include the preparation of tax returns.

B. In general, only CPAs, attorneys, and enrolled agents can practice before the IRS. Exceptions to this rule include individuals who are employees or officers of an entity. Limited exceptions are also made for registered tax return preparers.

C. Circular 230 provides numerous rules for the standard of conduct that must be met by those who practice before the IRS, including that an individual must:

    1. Advise a client of any noncompliance

    2. Exercise due diligence in representations

    3. Not charge an unconscionable fee

    4. Submit requested records to the IRS

D. CPAs are also subject to:

    1. AICPA's Code of Professional Conduct.

    2. AICPA's Statements on Standards for Tax Services.

VI. Rules Governing Authority to Practice under Circular 230

A. Who May Practice before the IRS—(Individuals may not be under suspension or disbarment.)

    1. Attorneys

    2. CPAs

    3. Enrolled agents

    4. Enrolled actuaries enrolled by the Joint Board for the Enrollment of Actuaries. However, practice is generally limited to issues related to qualified retirement plans.

    5. Enrolled retirement plan agents. However, practice is limited to issues related to employee plans and to IRS forms in the 5300 and 5500 series.

B. Practice before the IRS

    1. Practice before the IRS includes all matters connected with a presentation to the IRS or any of its officers or employees related to a taxpayer's rights, privileges, or liabilities under laws or regulations administered by the IRS.

    2. These presentations include but are not limited to:

        a. Preparing documents

        b. Filing documents

        c. Corresponding and communicating with the IRS

        d. Rendering written advice with regard to transactions having a potential for tax avoidance or evasion

        e. Representing a client at conferences, hearings, and meetings

    3. A power of attorney (Form 2848, *Power of Attorney and Declaration of Representative*) is required for an individual to represent a taxpayer before the IRS.

Compliance Responsibilities

After studying this lesson, you should be able to:

1. Describe the filing requirements and filing deadlines for individual and business returns.

2. Calculate accuracy-related penalties for taxpayers.

3. Apply preparer penalties for tax preparers.

4. Define levels of confidence for tax positions.

I. **Filing Requirements**—All taxpayers who have income in excess of a predetermined limit must file an income tax return.

    A. In general, an individual must file an income tax return if his gross income exceeds the standard deduction plus personal exemptions.

        1. This includes the additional standard deduction for one who is age 65 or over (but not the additional deduction for one who is blind). One is considered 65 on the day before her 65th birthday. So if one turns 65 on January 1, *2018* she would be considered 65 on December 31, *2017*, and therefore for the *2017* tax year.

> **Example**
> Alvin files as married filing jointly and is age 67. His wife is 59 years old. Their standard deduction (for 2017) is $12,700 + $1,250 (over age 65) = $13,950. Their personal exemptions are $8,100 ($4,050 × 2). Alvin and his wife do not need to file a return unless their gross income exceeds $22,050 ($13,950 + $8,100).

        2. Taxpayers must also file a return if net self-employment income exceeds $400 during the tax year.

> **Note**
> *The filing requirement includes the standard deduction and the increment for age 65, but does not include the increment to the standard deduction for blind taxpayers.*

II. **Penalties**—Penalties are imposed on taxpayers under four circumstances. First, a penalty is imposed if the taxpayer fails to file a required tax return. Second, a penalty is imposed if the taxpayer fails to make adequate tax payments during the year (underpayment). Third, a penalty if imposed if the taxpayer fails to pay the tax reflected on the tax return (delinquency). Finally, a penalty is imposed if the taxpayer files an inaccurate tax return.

    A. **Nonfiling Penalty**—A nonfiling penalty is imposed on taxpayers (who must file a return) if the return is not filed by the due date.

        1. The penalty for late filing is 5% per month (or a portion thereof) of the tax due with the return.

        2. The maximum penalty is 25% of the tax due, and the minimum penalty (due if tax is not paid within 60 days of the due date) is the lesser of $210 *(2017)* or the amount of the tax due. If the minimum tax applies and is greater than the maximum tax, then the minimum tax must be paid.

> **Note**
> *No penalty is imposed if no tax is due with the return, or the taxpayer is eligible for a refund.*

        3. If the failure to file is fraudulent (intentional), the penalty is increased to 15% per month up to a maximum of 75% of the tax due with the return.

    B. **Underpayment Penalty**—An underpayment penalty is imposed for failure to remit taxes during the year (i.e., on the required estimated payment dates).

> **Definition**
> *Tax Underpayment:* The difference between the tax due and the amount of tax paid on or before the filing of the return plus credits.

1. Required tax payments for individuals

   a. Taxes are remitted during the year through withholding or, if withholding is insufficient, through estimated tax payments. Taxpayers must make estimated payments (on the 15th of April, June, September, and January) if the amount of tax owed is at least $1,000 after subtracting withholding and credits.

   b. No penalty is imposed if the tax due with the return is less than $1,000.

   c. No penalty is imposed if the tax payments during the year were:

      i. At least 90% of current year taxes, *or*

      ii. 100% of last year's taxes. If the taxpayer's AGI exceeds $150,000, then tax payments during the year must be at least 110% of last year's taxes.

   d. The penalty can also be avoided if the annualization exception is met. For this exception the actual income for each quarter is computed, and then each estimated tax payment is based on that income computation.

2. Required corporate tax payments

   a. Estimated tax payments are due (if annual tax payments are at least $500) on 4/15, 6/15, 9/15, and 12/15 for a calendar-year corporation.

   b. There is no estimated tax underpayment penalty if the payments are at least equal to the lower of:

      i. 100% of current year's tax, *or*

      ii. 100% of the preceding year's tax.

      iii. The penalty can also be avoided if the annualization exception is met.

   c. A corporation with $1 million or more of taxable income in any of its three preceding tax years can use the preceding year's tax exception only for its first installment. The other installments must be based on the current year's tax to avoid penalty.

   d. If a taxpayer had a net operating loss in the previous tax year, the previous year's tax liability exception cannot be used to avoid anv underpayment penalty.

Example
TP remitted $8,000 in withholding this year, but his total income tax is $10,000. Hence, $2,000 is due with TP's return. TP will be subject to an underpayment penalty unless his total income tax paid in the preceding year was no more than $8,000 (if his AGI was less than $150,000).

---

3. Annualization method

   a. The annualization exception can be used by individuals and corporations.

   b. The amount due with an installment is:

      i. The tax due for the months ending before the due date of the installment, less

      ii. The amount required to be paid for previous installments.

   c. Different exceptions can be used for different installments. For example, the 100% of previous year's tax might be used for the first quarter, and the annualization method for the second quarter.

   d. If a taxpayer determines that the installment under the annualized income method is less than the required installment under the regular method, any reduction in a required installment is recaptured by increasing the amount of the next required installment by the amount of the reduction.

Example
The tax due under the annualization method for the first six months of the year is $50,000. Estimated payments and withholding before the second quarter payment are $32,000. Therefore, the required installment for the second quarter is $18,000 ($50,000 − $32,000).

C. **Nonpayment Penalties (and Interest)**—Are imposed if the taxes shown on the return are not paid on the filing date.

1. Interest on late payments starts on the due date for filing and is calculated using the Federal short-term interest rate.

2. Any tax due must be paid at the time of filing, or else a penalty of 0.5% of the underpayment is imposed per month or portion thereof (up to 25% in total).

Example
TP paid a tax of $1,000 25 days after filing his return. In addition to interest on the underpayment, TP owes $5 ($1,000 × .005) as a delinquency penalty.

3. If both the nonpayment penalty and the non-filing penalty are imposed, the maximum penalty is limited to 5% of the tax due per month.

4. Neither the nonfiling nor the nonpayment penalties are imposed if the taxpayer has a **reasonable cause** for failing to file or failing to pay.

Definition
Reasonable Cause: A cause outside the control of the taxpayer and not due to neglect, such as irregularities in mail delivery, death or serious illness, unavoidable absence, or disaster. A taxpayer, generally, has the burden of proving that a failure was due to reasonable cause.

Example
The taxpayer failed to file a timely return and pay taxes because his records were destroyed in a fire. This excuses both penalties, but not the interest on the underpayment.

D. **Accuracy Penalties**—Additional penalties may be imposed if the taxpayer underpays the actual tax because of an **inaccurate position** taken on a tax return.

Definition
Inaccurate Position: This occurs when a taxpayer disregards the tax rules without reasonable cause.

1. A penalty of 20% of the tax due to the inaccuracy is imposed if the inaccurate position is due to negligence. The penalty is waived if the taxpayer had a reasonable basis for the position taken.

2. A penalty of 20% of the tax due to the inaccuracy is imposed if the taxpayer **substantially understates** the tax. This penalty is waived if there was substantial authority for the position taken, or if the position was adequately disclosed on the tax return. The substantial authority standard is less stringent than the more likely than not standard, but more stringent than the reasonable basis standard.

> **Definition**
> *Negligence:* An intentional disregard of rules and regulations without intent to defraud.

> **Definition**
> *Substantial Understatement:* For individuals, a substantial understatement results when the additional tax due exceeds the greater of $5,000 or 10% of the total tax on the return. For corporations, a substantial understatement results when the understatement exceeds the lesser of 10% of the tax required to be shown on the return (or $10,000 if that is greater) or $10 million.

3. A penalty is imposed if there is a substantial or gross overstatement of the value or basis of any property. The penalty is 20% of the tax understatement for a **substantial misvaluation** and 40% for a gross misvaluation.

> **Definitions**
> *Substantial Misvaluation:* This occurs if the property is stated at 150% or more of the correct amount.
>
> *Gross Misvaluation:* This occurs if the property is stated at 400% or more of the correct amount.

4. The penalty for fraud is 75% of underpayment and an addition of 50% of the interest due on the underpayment.

> **Definition**
> *Fraud:* A deliberate action by the taxpayer to conceal, misrepresent, or deceive tax authorities about a tax deficiency.

III. **Preparer Penalties**—Penalties may also be imposed on tax preparers. Note that you may want to review Section VI below before continuing to reference definitions of key terms used in this section.

A. These penalties apply to all tax return preparers, including preparers for estate, gift, employment, excise, and exempt organization returns.

B. A tax return preparer who prepares a return or refund claim that includes an **unreasonable position** must pay a penalty of the greater of $1,000 or 50% of the income derived by the preparer for preparing the return.

1. There is an exception to this rule if the position was disclosed and there is a reasonable basis for it. However, this exception applies to reportable transactions and tax shelters only if the position has a **more likely than not** chance of being sustained.

2. The reasonable cause and good faith exceptions apply.

> **Definition**
> *Unreasonable Position:* A position is unreasonable if it does not have substantial authority.

C. If the understated tax liability is due to an unreasonable position and the preparer **willfully attempts** to understate the tax liability or recklessly or intentionally disregards rules or regulations, the penalty is the greater of $5,000 or 75% of the income earned by the tax preparer for preparing the return or claim.

D. Additional penalties may be imposed on preparers for:

1. Not signing returns done for compensation ($50 per failure; maximum of $25,500 per year; 2017)

2. Not providing a copy of the return for the taxpayer ($50 per failure; maximum of $25,500 per year; 2017)

3. Not keeping a list of returns filed ($50 per failure; maximum of $25,500 per year; 2017). The same penalty applies for not keeping a list of tax return preparers hired to prepare returns.

4. $510 (2017) for each instance of endorsing or negotiating a refund check.

5. Failure to provide the taxpayer's identifying number on the return ($50 per failure; maximum of $25,500 per year; 2017)

6. A preparer can be fined $510 (2017) per failure if he or she does not exercise due diligence in determining if a taxpayer is eligible for the earned income credit, child tax credit, or American Opportunity tax credit.

7. Providers may not base their fees on a percentage of the refund amount or compute their fees using any figure from tax returns.

E. Tax preparers are subject to penalties related to **knowingly** or **recklessly** disclosing tax return information. If a tax preparer uses or discloses tax return information without the client's explicit, written consent, each violation could result in a fine of up to $1,000, one year imprisonment, or both. Exceptions are provided for disclosures related to quality or peer reviews.

IV. **Summary of Terminology for Penalties**

A. Not frivolous = Not patently improper

B. Reasonable basis = At least one authority that has not been overruled (Treas. Reg. Sec. 1. 6662-3(b))

C. Substantial authority = More than a reasonable basis (approximately 40%)

D. More likely than not = More than 50% chance of succeeding

V. **Uncertain Tax Positions**—Corporations that have at least $10 million of assets and uncertain tax positions have to file Schedule UTP if the corporation or a related party has issued audited financial statements. Disclosure requirements include a concise description of each UTP ranked by the current year's relative magnitude based on the financial statement reserve.

VI. **IRS Registration**—Individuals preparing federal tax returns for compensation must register with the IRS and receive a PTIN (Paid Preparer Tax Identification Number).

Legal Duties and Responsibilities

Common Law Duties and Liabilities to Clients and Third Parties

After studying this lesson, you should be able to:

1. Summarize the tax return preparer's common law duties and liabilities to clients and third parties.

2. Identify situations that result in violations of the tax return preparer's common law duties and liabilities to clients and third parties.

Part One: Liability to Clients

I. Introduction

    A. Many malpractice lawsuits against accountants are based on various "common law" causes of action created by the courts over the years and often modified by legislatures. A high percentage of malpractice lawsuits against CPAs involve tax errors.

    B. The common law duties discussed in this lesson are owed to clients and third parties, and the focus is the impact that wrongdoing has on them. Breaches of common law duties can also breach state and/or federal statutes. For example, a tax accountant who defrauded a client by selling her a bogus tax shelter might well simultaneously violate various state and federal anti-fraud statutes discussed in other lessons.

    C. The most significant common law theories that will be covered in this lesson are:

        1. Breach of contract

        2. Negligence

        3. Fraud

    D. Note that a breach of contract action is based on breach of an agreement between two parties, whereas tort actions (such as negligence and fraud) are based on a duty (not to be careless and not to mislead) that the courts have imposed on accountants as a matter of public policy.

II. Breach of Contract

    A. Although client malpractice actions against tax accountants usually are brought in tort as negligence (and occasionally fraud) claims, breach of contract claims are common as well.

    B. Many courts, in an attempt to reduce the amount of litigation by eliminating duplicative theories, hold that:

        1. If the accountant did not do the job at all (e.g., Sam took the client's fee but never prepared or filed the tax return), he should be sued for breach of contract.

        2. But if the accountant did the job but did it carelessly (e.g., CPA May miscalculated the taxes, causing the client to pay a large tax penalty), she should be sued in negligence rather than for breach of contract.

    C. Other courts allow a breach of contract action in either case (after all, May also breached the contract by not performing satisfactorily). This distinction can be important, because there are differences in the two theories. For example:

        1. A breach of contract (BOK) theory often has a longer statute of limitations (four or even six years) than does a negligence cause of action (two years, typically).

        2. Comparative negligence ("Hey, the plaintiff was careless also and therefore should not recover from me for my carelessness or at least should have his recovery reduced") is typically not a defense in a BOK suit, as it is in a negligence suit.

D. **Elements of a Breach of Contract Suit**—To win a breach of contract lawsuit, a plaintiff must prove the following four elements:

1. Existence of an enforceable contract;

   a. While some agreements must be in writing to be enforceable, most do not, so breach of an oral contract is typically actionable.

   b. Obligations may be *expressly* spelled out (orally or in writing) but may also be *implied*. The law reads into professional contracts the obligation to perform to a professional standard.

2. Plaintiff client complied with contractual obligations;

   a. If the client, for example, promised to pay 50% of the agreed-upon fee in advance but then failed to do so, it would be unreasonable to require the accountant to do the taxes for free.

3. Defendant accountant breached the contract; and

   a. The breach may be intentional but need not be for this element to be satisfied.

Example
CPA Franny was very busy. She tried absolutely as hard as she could but couldn't file timely tax returns for client Tina. She has breached her contract with Tina, notwithstanding exerting her best efforts.

   b. Examples of breach:

      i. Accountant failed to complete the tax return as promised.

      ii. Accountant filed the tax return late.

      iii. Accountant filed the tax return filled with errors.

      iv. Accountant gave faulty tax planning advice to client.

4. Damages were caused by the breach.

   a. Plaintiffs may recover "compensatory" damages to compensate them for losses they sustained because of the breach. Such damages usually are not recoverable unless they were reasonably foreseeable at the time the contract was made.

   b. Punitive damages are not recoverable in BOK claims.

E. **Burden of Proof**

1. The burden of proof in most civil cases, including breach of contract and negligence cases, is the "preponderance of the evidence" standard, meaning that plaintiff need only establish that alleged facts are more likely true than not true (>50%).

F. **Defenses to Breach of Contract Claims**

1. **Statute of limitations**

   a. To prevent the uncertainty caused by memories fading and documents being lost, the law requires lawsuits to be filed reasonably promptly.

   b. Although there is considerable variation from state to state, in many states the statute of limitations is:

      i. Oral contract: two years from breach; *or*

      ii. Written contract: four years from breach.

2. **Justifiable breach**

   a. Sometimes a client's misconduct justifies an accountant's breach, precluding liability.

    b. Examples:

        i. Client refuses to provide accountant with the documents necessary to complete the tax return.

        ii. Client provides accountant with incomplete, inaccurate, or misleading information.

        iii. Client informs accountant that it will not pay her bill as promised.

        iv. Client's CFO was incompetent, undermining the reliability of the client's financial information. Accountant agreed to do the following year's tax return only on condition that the CFO be replaced. The client promised to do so but then did not. The accountant would be justified in refusing to complete the tax return.

  3. **Substantial performance**—If an accountant's breach of contract is major, she is not entitled to recover her fee and will be liable for damages. But if the breach is minor, she will be entitled to recover her fee, but minus damages to plaintiff caused by the breach.

III. Negligence

  A. **Elements of a Cause of Action for Professional Negligence**—In order to win a negligence malpractice case, a plaintiff must prove the following four elements by a preponderance of the evidence:

    1. Defendant accountant owed a *duty of care* to the client plaintiff.

      a. A contract between an accountant and a client typically includes a promise by the accountant to fulfill all professional responsibilities in a careful manner, but the law implies such a duty even if it is not spelled out in the engagement letter.

    2. Defendant *breached* the standard of care.

      a. The essence of a negligence claim is carelessness, not intentional wrongdoing.

      b. Accountants are not expected to be perfect but are expected to meet the standards of their profession in the relevant field—audit, tax, consulting, and so on. Auditors, for example, cannot detect all frauds but should catch those that a reasonably competent auditor would detect. Courts often say that accountants should act with the "skill and knowledge normally possessed by accountants in good standing in similar communities."

      c. The standard of care can be raised above that of the "reasonable" accountant by:

        i. An accountant being a specialist;

        ii. An accountant holding self out has having special expertise; *or*

        iii. A contractual provision in which the accountant promises a higher duty of care.

      d. Remember that in many jurisdictions, failure to do the job at all is remediable by a breach of contract action while doing a bad job is remediable only by a negligence action. Other jurisdictions allow both a breach of contract and a negligence lawsuit in a case where the accountant did the job but did it carelessly.

      e. **Examples of negligent breach**

        i. D carelessly neglects to file tax return on time.

        ii. D carelessly fails to file documentation needed to support a tax position.

        iii. D carelessly researches a tax issue and therefore erroneously advises the client to take a position that results in a substantial penalty.

        iv. D carelessly fails to consider tax return options that would save the client substantial tax liability.

        v. D carelessly advises a client to sell a business at a loss, but the transaction does not generate the tax savings promised.

3. The breach *proximately causes* an injury.

   a. Proximate causation has two parts:

      i. Factual ("but for") causation, meaning that the courts can say that "but for" the accountant's breach of the duty of due care, the loss would not have occurred; and

      ii. Legal ("proximate") causation, meaning that the injury was a reasonably foresee result of the breach.

   b. Proximate cause can be disrupted by an act or event that was beyond the control of and unforeseeable to the defendant (an "independent intervening cause").

4. Plaintiff client suffers *damages*.

   a. Plaintiffs are entitled to recover "compensatory damages" to compensate them for losses caused by the accountant's carelessness.

   b. But no "punitive damages" are allowed in negligence cases as they sometimes are in cases of intentional torts in order to punish defendants for intentional wrongdoing.

Example
Accountant Ji carelessly researches a tax issue and convinces client Pam to take a tax position that the tax court later rules to be frivolous. Pam has to pay back taxes of $20,000 and a penalty of $5,000. Pam sues Ji in negligence. Pam will not recover the $20,000, for she owed that money and would have had to pay it even if Ji had done everything right. But his carelessness caused her to pay the unnecessary $5,000 penalty, so Pam can recover that amount to compensate her for her loss. But Pam may not recover any punitive damages from Ji.

B. **Defenses**

1. **Statute of limitations**

   a. The SOL in most jurisdictions is two years from when the plaintiff knew or should have known of the right to sue. If the lawsuit is filed after that deadline, it will be dismissed.

2. **Comparative negligence**

   a. If the plaintiff was also careless and that carelessness contributed causally to the loss, the plaintiff's recovery will generally be reduced and perhaps even barred altogether (if plaintiff's carelessness exceeds 50%).

> **Note**
> *Including a disclaimer of liability in an engagement letter ("Tax accountant will not be liable to be a plaintiff for careless errors made.") will **not** serve as a defense to a negligence claim (nor to a breach of contract or fraud claim).*

C. **Negligent Misrepresentation**

1. In many jurisdictions, courts recognize causes of action for both negligence and negligent misrepresentation. Because many negligence lawsuits against accountants are based on statements they have made while giving tax advice or rendering audit opinions, negligent misrepresentation lawsuits are commonly brought against accountants.

2. **Elements of a cause of action.** The elements of a negligent misrepresentation claim are very similar to those of a straight negligence claim and typically lead to the same results. One common formulation requires the plaintiff to prove all of the following elements:

   a. Defendant is in the business or profession of supplying information.

      i. Accountants are, of course, in such a profession.

   b. Defendants provided false information for the guidance of others in their business transactions.

      i. CPAs working as tax advisers or TRPs, as auditors, or as consultants might do this.

    c. Plaintiff relies on the information.

        i. If there is one significant difference between the typical negligence cause of action and the negligent misrepresentation cause of action, it is this requirement of reliance.

    d. Proximate causation; and

        i. As with regular negligence, this requires proof of both factual and legal causation.

    e. Damage to plaintiff.

IV. Fraud

  A. The essence of fraud is intentional (or at least reckless) wrongdoing, as contrasted to mere carelessness, which is the essence of a negligence claim.

  B. The basic elements of a fraud claim are the same everywhere, but they are often packaged in different ways. A common formulation of the elements requires the plaintiff to prove:

    1. Defendant accountant made a false representation of fact (or omitted to state a fact in the face of a duty to do so).

      a. Opinions are not facts, so a false statement of opinion is not generally a basis for a fraud claim, even if intentionally made.

      b. However, a false statement of **expert** opinion is deemed tantamount to a representation of fact.

Example
If A sells his car, telling B that the car gets 50 miles per gallon when, in fact, it gets only 25, this is a false statement of fact, and B can sue A for fraud. If A sells B his car, telling B "I really love this car" when, in fact, A hates the car, B cannot sue for fraud because A stated merely an opinion (even though it was a false one). However, when an accountant issues a professional opinion—for example, by certifying financial statements as accurate or by opining as to whether there is a reasonable basis for a tax position—the statement carries more weight than a normal opinion by virtue of an accountant's expertise. It is treated as tantamount to a statement of fact and is actionable if fraudulent.

    2. The misrepresented (or omitted) fact was material.

      a. A minor error is often not actionable, even if the result of an intentional misstatement.

Example
A tax professional fills out a tax form by intentionally rounding a number up by $37. In most settings, that inaccuracy would be insignificant and therefore immaterial and therefore not actionable.

    3. The defendant accountant *knew* or *recklessly disregarded* the falsity.

      a. Knowledge (scienter) = *actual fraud.*

Example
A famous rock singer gave his money to D, an accountant, to invest. The accountant gave the singer monthly reports indicating that the money was being invested wisely and profitably. In fact, D had invested the money in several ventures that he himself operated, and most of it had been lost. The monthly reports were mostly fictitious. This is a clear case of actual fraud on the part of the accountant.

b. Reckless disregard or gross negligence = *constructive fraud*.

Example

Accountant D was hired to issue an audit report for ABC Co. When he appeared to begin the job, ABC's CEO handed him a finished audit report to sign. D signed it, hoping that it was accurate. It was not. D was liable for constructive fraud. He hoped that the report was accurate, but he had no reasonable grounds to believe that it was. He recklessly disregarded the truth.

4. The defendant accountant intended to and did induce plaintiff's reasonable reliance on the misstatement or omission; and

Example

Defendant auditor certified ABC Company's financial statements as accurate, knowing that they were not and being able to reasonably foresee that lenders and investors would likely rely on those statements in making financial decisions. In such a case, the auditor's intent to induce reliance would be clear.

5. The false statement (or omission) proximately caused damages to the plaintiff.

    a. Plaintiffs who can prove fraud can recover both:

        i. Compensatory damages, *and*

        ii. Punitive damages, which are rendered to both to punish the defendant for intentional wrongdoing and to deter the defendant and others from acting fraudulently in the future.

C. Whereas the burden of proof in most civil lawsuits, including those for breach of contract and negligence, is the preponderance of the evidence standard, it is a serious thing to accuse others of fraud. In most states, the burden of proof is raised slightly, requiring plaintiffs to prove their claims by "clear and convincing evidence," often defined as evidence that is substantially more probable to be true than not and that gives rise to a firm belief as to its factuality in the mind of the trier of fact."

D. **Defenses**—Because a plaintiff's carelessness is not nearly as bad as a defendant's intentional fraud, there is no comparative negligence or comparative fault defense to a fraud claim. However, there is at least one significant defense:

1. Statute of limitations

    a. The statute of limitations for fraud claims varies from state to state, but it is common to require plaintiffs to sue within four years of when they did or should have discovered the fraud.

E. Fraud, unlike mere negligence and breach of contract, often also constitutes a crime and is punishable under a wide array of state and federal statutes forbidding tax fraud, securities fraud, bank fraud, and so on.

Differences between Fraud and Negligence Causes of Action	Fraud	Negligence
Plaintiff must prove bad intent or recklessness	Yes	No
Plaintiff must prove carelessness	No	Yes
Plaintiff must prove proximate cause	Yes	Yes
Plaintiff can recover compensatory damages	Yes	Yes
Plaintiff can recover punitive damages	Yes	No
Comparative negligence is a defense	No	Yes
Burden of proof on plaintiff	Clear and convincing evidence	Preponderance of the evidence

Part Two: Liability to Third Parties

I. Breach of Contract

A. Normally only the parties to a contract are allowed to sue for its breach.

B. However, third parties sometimes may sue if they were *intended* beneficiaries of the contract.

C. Types of Beneficiaries

    1. Intended beneficiaries (can sue)

        a. Creditor beneficiaries

Example

Tam agrees to paint Dax's house. Dax agrees to pay Tam $1,000. Tam owes his creditor, Purdle, $1,000. Tam and Dax agree that Dax will pay the $1,000 to Purdle. If Tam paints Dax's house and Dax does not pay the $1,000 to Purdle, Purdle may sue Dax for breach of contract as an intended creditor beneficiary.

        b. Donee beneficiaries

Example

Tam agrees to paint Dax's house. Dax agrees to pay Tam $1,000. Tam wishes to give his nephew Purdle a $1,000 gift, so he and Dax agree that Dax will pay the $1,000 to Purdle. If Tam paints Dax's house and Dax does not pay the $1,000 to Purdle, Purdle may sue Dax for breach of contract as an intended donee beneficiary.

    2. Incidental beneficiaries (cannot sue)

Example

Tam agrees to paint Dax's house. Dax agrees to pay Tam $1,000. Pong, Dax's next-door neighbor is pleased because Dax's house is an eyesore and a new paint job for Dax's house may raise Pong's property value. Tam breaches the contract and does not paint Dax's house. Dax may sue, but Pong may not. Tam and Dax did not intend to benefit Pong (though they would have incidentally). Pong is a mere incidental beneficiary and cannot successfully sue on this contract to which he was not a party.

D. Tax Cases

Examples

1. Mary and Larry hired CPA Dean to give them tax advice for setting up a trust to benefit their children, Ed and Molly. Dean did so, but after Mary and Larry died, a new CPA looked at the documents and realized that Dean had made many mistakes that cost the trust (and therefore its beneficiaries, Ed and Molly) a lot of money because the trust was liable for substantial federal tax payments that could have been avoided. Dean argued that Ed and Molly were not parties to the contract he had with their parents, but the court allowed them to sue for its breach as intended donee beneficiaries of the contract

2. Sam and Pam were partners in various real estate ventures, some of which were not going well. Sam owed Pam $4 million. They signed a settlement agreement which featured as a critical part a $1 million tax refund that Pam thought Sam could recover. They agreed that Sam would hire CPA Smith to prepare the tax return and pay the refund to Sam's lawyer, Jones, who would convey the money to Pam. Sam did hire Smith. Smith knew of the settlement agreement. However, when the tax refund came, Smith conveyed the checks to Sam instead of Jones. Sam took the money and left the country. Pam sued Smith for breach of the contract he had with Sam. Though Pam was not a party to the contract, she was allowed to sue as an intended creditor beneficiary.

E. Audit Cases

1. When auditors breach their engagement letter by erroneously certifying financial statements indicating that a company is in good financial shape when it is not, creditors and investors often lose money. When these third parties attempt to sue for damages they sustained because of the breach, the issue of whether they are intended beneficiaries of the engagement letter arises.

2. In general, unless the engagement letter specifically states that a particular creditor or investor is to receive a copy of the audit report (or there is some other written acknowledgment by the auditor of the third party's legitimate reliance on the report), such third parties will not be allowed to sue as third-party beneficiaries.

II. Negligence

A. When accountants are careless in providing tax, audit, consulting, or other services, they generally will be held liable to one or a limited class of nonclients where the accountant knows:

1. The information being supplied to the client will be given to, or is for the benefit and guidance of, this limited class of third persons, *and*

2. The information will influence those third parties in a specific transaction or type of transaction.

B. **Audit Cases**—The case law in this area has developed primarily in the context of audit cases where third-party investors or creditors sued auditors who had carelessly certified their clients' inaccurate financial statements.

Example
Trejo audited ABC Co. and carelessly certified financial statements that greatly inflated ABC's value. Soon thereafter, ABC decided to put itself up for sale, and XYZ bought ABC after examining the audited financial statements. After XYZ completed the purchase, it realized that the financial statements were inaccurate and that it had overpaid for ABC. XYZ sued Trejo for negligence but lost because it was not foreseeable to Trejo that XYZ would rely on the financial statements because ABC was not yet for sale at the time he completed the audit.

C. Tax Cases

Examples

1. Sam and Pam were partners in various real estate ventures, some of which were not going well. Sam owed Pam $4 million. They signed a settlement agreement in which Sam promised to pay Pam a $1 million tax refund that he was entitled to. They also agreed that Sam would hire CPA Smith to prepare the tax return and pay the refund to Sam's lawyer, Jones, who would convey the money to Pam. Sam did hire Smith. Smith knew of the settlement agreement. However, when the tax refund came, Smith carelessly conveyed the checks to Sam instead of Jones. Sam took the money and left the country. Pam sued Smith for negligence (as well as breach of the contract). Smith denied that he owed any duty of care to Pam, who was not his client. But because Sam knew that Pam would be relying on his actions, he was held to owe her a duty of care.

2. CPA Dolan carelessly recommended a tax position to his client, Fanny. Fanny told her neighbor, Dipson, about the tax strategy, and Dipson tried it on his own return. The IRS rejected the position as being without any reasonable basis, and Fanny was hit with tax penalties. She sued Dolan for negligence and won. Dipson also sued Dolan for negligence; he lost. Dolan could not have reasonably foreseen that Dipson would also rely on his advice so he owed Dipson no legal duty of care.

3. CPA Willis joined with others to promote a tax shelter involving worthless coal rights. Willis issued a tax opinion concluding that the IRS would allow the deduction of large advance royalty payments. He and the other principals did not disclose that most of the money invested would go into their pockets. Plaintiff Pym was one of the investors who, based on the opinion, bought into the tax shelter. He lost a lot of money when the shelter was declared bogus by the IRS. Pym was allowed to sue Willis because he was part of a limited class of people to whom Willis supplied the negligently researched tax opinion knowing that they would rely on it to make the investment decision.

III. Fraud

A. Because fraud, being intentional or at least reckless, is more blameworthy than mere carelessness, courts tend to allow a wider range of third parties to recover from accountants who have acted fraudulently than from accountants who have been merely negligent.

B. The traditional rule has been that fraudsters are liable not just to clients but to everyone they can *reasonably foresee* will rely on their fraudulent acts or statements. However, some courts are uncomfortable with the potentially broad scope of the "reasonable foreseeability" standard and allow recovery only if there was some *special reason* for the defendant to believe that the particular plaintiff would rely on the false representations or omissions.

Example

Evy audited Bank One. A few months after she issued the audit report, Bank One started to negotiate a merger with Bank Two, and Evy agreed to allow the audit report to be included in the proxy document that would go to the shareholders in each bank who would vote on the merger. The financial statements made Bank One look very solid, which led Simon to invest in Bank Two, which would be strengthened by the merger, it appeared. After the merger, it turned out that Evy had recklessly (rising to the level of fraud) blown the audit and Bank One was not in good financial shape. The newly merged entity failed, and Simon lost a lot of money. While it was arguably reasonably foreseeable to Evy that an investor in Simon's position might rely on the financial statements of Bank One to invest in Bank Two, the court refused to find Evy liable to Simon in fraud absent her having information that there was an "especial likelihood" that he would rely on the audit report. However, there is an extremely strong argument that she did have information that there was an "especial likelihood" that the existing shareholders of Bank One and Bank Two, to whom the proxy materials would be sent, would rely. Evy should be liable to them if they can prove the elements of a fraud claim even in a jurisdiction requiring a special reason. In jurisdictions applying the "reasonable foreseeability" standard, Evy would likely be liable to Simon as well.

Privileged Communications, Confidentiality, and Privacy Acts

In today's high-tech information age, safeguarding client confidential information must be an extremely high priority for all CPAs. This section examines three aspects of that subject matter: confidentiality responsibilities, communication privileges, and privacy statutes.

After studying this lesson, you should be able to:

1. Summarize the rules regarding privileged communications as they relate to tax practice.

2. Identify situations in which communications regarding tax practice are considered privileged.

I. **Privileged Communications**

  A. **Introduction**—There are two broad types of privileges.

  1. **Testimonial privileges**—Classic privileged communications include attorney-client, doctor-patient, and priest-penitent. Where applicable, the protected party (client, patient, penitent) can prevent the party who received the protected communications (attorney, doctor, priest) from testifying.

  2. **Work product privilege**—This privilege typically prevents one party in a lawsuit from learning the other side's attorney's strategies for litigation.

  B. **Accountant-Client Testimonial Privilege**

  1. The federal courts have refused to recognize an accountant-client testimonial privilege.

  2. The state courts have refused to recognize a common law accountant-client testimonial privilege.

  3. Approximately 15 states have statutorily recognized an accountant-client privilege. In those states, remember:

    a. The privilege belongs to the client, not to the accountant;

    b. The privilege can be waived by the client, either expressly or through voluntary and knowing disclosure of the relevant information;

    c. Waiver of the privilege as to part of the communication is waiver as to all; *and*

    d. The privilege applies only in state court, where state procedural rules apply.

  C. **Tax Practitioners' Privilege**

  1. Section 7525 of the Internal Revenue Code extends a modest testimonial privilege to clients of all tax advisers authorized to practice before the IRS, including accountants. However, the privilege has several exceptions and has been construed narrowly by the courts.

  2. **Exceptions**—The privilege does not apply to:

    a. Criminal matters;

    b. Matters not before the IRS or federal courts in cases brought by or against the United States;

    c. Tax advice on state or local matters; *or*

    d. Written advice in connection with promotion of a tax shelter.

  3. **Construed narrowly**—Courts have not been uniform in their construction or application of the Section 7525 tax practitioners' privilege, but many have held that:

    a. It does not apply to information communicated to the practitioner solely for the purposes of facilitating tax return preparation.

    b. It merely extends to tax practitioners the same privilege accorded in the attorney-client relationship.

    c. Legal advice is protected, but not general accounting advice.

    d. The exceptions to the privilege are to be broadly construed.

D. Accountant's Working Papers

    1. Working papers are the notes, evidence, computations, and so on that accountants accumulate when doing professional work for their clients.

    2. These working papers belong to the accountants, absent express agreement to the contrary.

    3. Accountants must keep working papers confidential absent:

        a. Client consent to disclosure, *or*

        b. An enforceable government subpoena.

II. Confidential Communications

A. General Rule—According to the AICPA Code of Professional Conduct, absent client consent, a CPA shall not disclose confidential information disclosed by clients.

B. Exceptions—Recognized exceptions include:

    1. GAAP calls for disclosure

    2. An enforceable subpoena or summons has been issued

    3. An ethical examination is being conducted

    4. A peer review requires disclosure

    5. Disclosure is to other firm members on a "need-to-know" basis

C. Miscellaneous Rules

    1. CPAs may utilize outside computer services to process tax returns, as long as there is no release of confidential information.

    2. CPAs may reveal the names of clients without client consent, unless such disclosure releases confidential information.

    3. In divorce proceedings, a member who has prepared joint returns for the couple should consider both of them to be clients for purposes of requests for confidential information relating to tax returns. If given conflicting instructions, the CPA should consider the legal implications of disclosure with an attorney.

    4. Outsourcing and offshoring place a responsibility on the member who sends business, such as tax return preparation, to outside firms or to foreign shores (1 million U.S. tax returns per year are prepared in India) to ensure the confidentiality of clients' tax information.

D. Internal Revenue Code Provisions—As noted elsewhere in these materials, the IRC has several provisions dealing with confidentiality, including:

    1. Section 6713, which imposes a civil penalty for each unauthorized disclosure or use of tax information by a tax return preparer; *and*

    2. Section 7216, which imposes a criminal fine and potential imprisonment for knowingly or recklessly:

        a. Disclosing any information obtained in connection with the preparation of a return *or*

        b. Using such information for any purpose other than to prepare or assist in preparing a return.

E. Violations—Violation of confidentiality obligations is also grounds for a civil malpractice lawsuit by a client.

III. Privacy Acts

A. Introduction—In addition to the provisions referred to above, other privacy provisions relevant to the accountant-client relationship should not be ignored.

B. Generally Accepted Privacy Principles—Voluntary guidelines that the profession developed to assist accounting firms in establishing procedures and policies that will protect clients' information in their possession from hackers and others. There are 10 broad principles.

1. **Management**—An accounting firm should define, document, communicate, and assign accountability for its privacy policies and procedures.

2. **Notice**—An accounting firm should provide notice about its privacy policies and procedures and identify the purpose for which any personal information about clients is collected, used, retained, and disclosed.

3. **Choice and consent**—An accounting firm should describe the choices available to clients and obtain implicit or explicit consent with respect to the collection, use, and disclosure of personal information.

4. **Collection**—An accounting firm should collect personal information only for the purposes identified in the notice described above.

5. **Use, retention, and disposal**—An accounting firm should limit the use of personal information to the purpose identified in the notice and for which the client has provided consent.

6. **Access**—Firms should provide clients with access to their personal information for review and update.

7. **Disclosure to third parties**—Accounting firms should disclose information to third parties only for the purposes identified in the notice and only with the client's implicit or explicit consent. Accountants remain ultimately responsible for ensuring that this information is kept confidential.

8. **Security for privacy**—Accounting firms should protect personal information against unauthorized access, as identity theft is a growing problem.

9. **Quality**—Accounting firms should maintain accurate, complete, and relevant personal information for the purposes identified in the notice.

10. **Monitoring and enforcement**—The accounting firm should monitor compliance with its privacy policies and procedures and have procedures to address privacy-related inquiries, complaints, and disputes.

C. E-Mails—Some states require accountants to encrypt e-mails that contain clients' personally identifiable information, and several other states are considering this requirement.

D. Reasonable Measures—Some states also have statutes requiring firms, such as accounting firms, which have possession of individuals' social security numbers, to take reasonable measures to preserve the confidentiality of those numbers, including by taking precautions against identity theft.

E. Section 7216—As noted in the Tax Return Preparer (TRP) discussion elsewhere in these materials, Section 7216 of the IRC imposes criminal penalties for unauthorized disclosure or use of taxpayer information.

1. This provision applies not just to TRPs but to anyone who assists in preparing a return or provides auxiliary services in connection with return preparation regardless of whether they are paid.

2. The IRS does allow TRPs to use tax return information "for the purpose of providing other legal or accounting services to the taxpayer." For example, when the tax law changes, an accountant could use client tax return information to identify affected taxpayers for purposes of informing them about the change.

3. The IRS allows tax return preparers to use client information for purposes of sending newsletters to clients containing tax, general business, or economic information but not for purposes of soliciting business other than tax return preparation services.

4. A TRP may generally disclose to its insurance carrier tax return information considered necessary for obtaining and maintaining a professional liability insurance policy.

F. **Section 6713**—As noted in the TRP materials, Section 6713 imposes civil fines for:

1. Disclosure of any information furnished in connection with preparation of a federal tax return *and/or*

2. Use of such information for any purpose other than to prepare the return

G. **Bank Secrecy Act and Foreign Bank Accounts**

1. Under the Bank Secrecy Act (BSA), taxpayers have an obligation to report foreign bank accounts (FBAR).

2. Evidence indicates that only about 30% of such accounts are currently being reported, and the IRS has ratcheted up enforcement.

3. While FBAR penalties are aimed primarily at the taxpayer, a TRP who, perhaps not fully understanding the FBAR rules, checked the "No" box in answering the question as to whether the client has a foreign financial account might be punished under Internal Revenue Code provisions such as:

   a. Section 6694 (Understatement of a Taxpayer's Liability)

   b. Section 7201 (Criminal Attempt to Evade or Defeat Tax)

   c. Section 7206 (Criminal Fraud and Making False Statements)

Business Law

Agency

Types of Agency Relationships and Creation

After studying this lesson, you should be able to:

1. List the types of agency relationships and explain the differences.

2. Define an agency relationship and tell who the parties are.

3. Explain how an agency relationship is created and list the requirements for creation.

4. Discuss how agency relationships are terminated and the requirements for termination of all types of authority.

I. Agency Relationship and Parties

A. One party designates another to act on his, her, or its behalf.

Examples

1. A corporation authorizes its CEO to negotiate a merger.

2. A storeowner hires a clerk to receive payments and sell goods.

3. A college athlete hires a professional sports agent to represent him in negotiations with professional sports teams.

B. **Two Parties**—There are two parties in an agency relationship—principal and agent.

Definitions

Principal: The party who delegates authority to another in order to accomplish a task or consummate a transaction.

Agent: One who acts on a principal's behalf to accomplish a task or consummate a transaction for the principal.

II. Types of Agents

A. **Special Agent**—One authorized to conduct a single transaction or series of related transactions on the principal's behalf.

Examples

1. A real estate agent is authorized to sell only the principal's house.

2. The executor of an estate (principal) hires an estate liquidating company (special agent) to sell all the personal property for the estate.

3. A bankruptcy trustee (principal) hires a company (special agent) to liquidate the assets of a company in Chapter 7 bankruptcy.

B. **General Agent**—One authorized to conduct all necessary personal or business transactions for the principal.

Example
A restaurant owner (principal) who owns a restaurant in another city hires a manager (general agent) to run that restaurant. Such as agent could hire and fire employees, purchase supplies, and deal with health inspectors as examples of the types of authority such a manager would have.

C. Universal Agent—One authorized to do all acts that can be legally delegated to an agent.

Example

A soldier (principal) who is to be stationed abroad for three years appoints his sister (universal agent) to handle all his business affairs during his absence.

D. Power of Attorney

Definition

Power of Attorney: A formal written creation of an agency relationship that lists the authority granted.

1. A power of attorney must be signed by the principal (but need not be signed by the agent to be valid).

2. A power of attorney is generally construed narrowly.

E. Independent Contractor—An independent contractor is someone who acts on behalf of a principal, but that principal does not control the agent's day-to-day activities, and the scope of the independent contractor is limited.

Examples

1. You hire a lawyer to create a living trust for you. The lawyer is working for you on that limited activity, but you do not control the lawyer's work hours or have liability for the conduct of the lawyer toward third parties. (See the "Tort Liability of Agents and Principals" lesson for more information about the unique limitations of independent contractors.)

2. You hire a CPA firm to conduct an audit of your business income. The firm is an independent contractor.

III. Creation of an Express Agency Relationship

A. An actual agency relationship consists of two types of authority: express and implied authority.

B. Requirements for the Creation of an Express Agency Relationship

1. A writing or record is not generally required for a valid agency relationship, except when the contract that the agent is entering into is under the Statute of Frauds. (See the "Contracts" lessons for more information on the Statute of Frauds.)

   a. The contract the agent is authorized to enter into must be in writing under the Statute of Frauds, such as a real estate contract.

   b. The agency relationship cannot reasonably be completed within one year.

2. **Capacity of the agent**

Example

A minor agent can bind an adult principal, and vice versa (although the minor agent can quit at any time and the minor principal can disaffirm any contract negotiated by the adult agent). As a practical matter, using a minor may not show the best business judgment, but the CPA Exam has, in the past, had questions that required you to distinguish between the need for capacity of the principal vs. no requirement of capacity on the part of the agent.

3. **Consideration**—An agency relationship can be created with or without consideration and is called a gratuitous agency relationship. However, an agent who serves without consideration in a gratuitous agency can quit at any time.

C. Accompanying Implied Authority that Goes with Express Authority

1. When a principal creates an express agency relationship, the agent holds whatever authority is provided for in the agreement.

2. In addition, the agent has whatever authority is customary for his or her position—whatever authority can be implied because of the position.

Example
An apartment manager has the implied authority to receive rent, make minor repairs around the apartment building, and have tenants sign lease agreements because those types of actions are customary for most apartment managers.

IV. Creation of an Apparent Agency Relationship

A. Apparent Agency—This is an agency relationship in which the agent does not have an express agreement but still has authority to act as an agent for a principal because of the appearance of having that authority.

Example
Agent is not an employee of Principal but, in the presence of Principal, Agent tells X that she is such an employee. If Principal does not object, X may justifiably assume that Agent is indeed an employee of Principal and enforce subsequent contracts negotiated by Agent against Principal.

B. Lingering Apparent Agency—This type of agency exists when the principal fires an agent (ends the actual or express agreement), but the agent continues to act as an employee. The agency continues until properly terminated. (See the "Contract Liability of Agents and Principals" lesson for more discussion of the liabilities of the parties in this type of agency relationship.)

Example
XYC Corporation sells its custom-home division to Randy Eggerton, a former VP of XYZ. Eggerton continues to use office space at XYZ and even uses XYC's custom home plans and letterhead. By not stopping Eggerton from using its name and office space, XYZ has allowed Eggerton to remain as an agent.

C. Agency by Estoppel or Ostensible Authority—For the purposes of the exam, this agency relationship is another form of apparent authority agency that is created when the principal acts as if another is his or her agent.

V. Creation of an Agency Relationship by Ratification

A. In this situation, the agent does not have express, implied, or apparent authority, but he or she enters into a contract on behalf of an assumed principal. The principal is not bound, but ratification gives the principal a choice.

B. If another enters into a contract for you without authority, you, as the principal, can choose to be bound by the agreement.

Example
Hollywood Star P hires Ace Talent to handle public relations for her. Ace Talent books a personal appearance for Hollywood Star P. P need not honor the contract, but she could decide to do so for goodwill or because the publicity is so good.

Authority of Agents and Principals

After studying this lesson, you should be able to:

1. Explain the types of authority an agent can have.

2. Explain ratification.

3. Discuss how agency relationships are terminated and the requirements for termination of all types of authority

I. Creation of Actual Authority of Agents

A. When a principal creates an express agency relationship, the agent holds whatever authority is provided for in the agreement.

B. In addition, the agent has whatever authority is customary for his or her position—whatever authority can be implied because of the position.

Example
An apartment manager has the implied authority to receive rent, make minor repairs around the apartment building, and have tenants sign lease agreements because those types of actions are customary for most apartment managers.

II. Creation of an Apparent Agency Relationship

A. **Apparent Agency**—This is an agency relationship in which the agent does not have an express agreement but still has authority to act as an agent for a principal because of the appearance of having that authority.

Example
Agent is not an employee of Principal but in the presence of Principal, Agent tells X that she is such an employee. If Principal does not object, X may justifiably assume that Agent is indeed an employee of Principal and enforce subsequent contracts negotiated by Agent against Principal.

B. **Lingering Apparent Agency**—This type of agency exists when the principal fires an agent (ends the actual or express agreement), but the agent continues to act as an employee. The agency continues until properly terminated (see the "Contract Liability of Agents and Principals" lesson for more discussion of the liabilities of the parties in this type of agency relationship).

Example
XYZ Corporation sells its custom-home division to Randy Eggerton, a former VP of XYZ. Eggerton continues to use office space at XYZ and even uses XYZ's custom-home plans and letterhead. By not stopping Eggerton from using its name and office space, XYZ has allowed Eggerton to remain as an agent.

C. **Agency by Estoppel or Ostensible Authority**—For the purposes of the exam, this agency relationship is another form of apparent authority agency that is created when the principal acts as if another is his or her agent.

III. Creation of an Agency Relationship by Ratification

A. In this situation, the agent does not have express, implied, or apparent authority, but he or she enters into a contract on behalf of an assumed principal. The principal is not bound, but ratification gives the principal a choice.

B. If another enters into a contract for you without authority, you, as the principal, can choose to be bound by the agreement.

Example

Hollywood Star P hires Ace Talent to handle public relations for her. Public relations would include responding to the press, doing press releases, and helping with press conferences. However, a public relations agent does not have the authority to contract for Star P. However, Ace Talent does sign a contract for Star and books a personal appearance for Star P. Star P need not honor the contract but she could decide to do so for goodwill or because the publicity is so good.

Duties of Agents and Principals

After studying this lesson, you should be able to:

1. List the duties of the principal to the agent.

2. Explain the duties of the agent to the principal.

3. Discuss the requirements of the agent's fiduciary duty to the principal.

4. Describe the duties of both parties upon termination of the agency relationship.

I. Duties of Principal to Agent

A. To Comply with Agency Agreement—As with any other contract, a principal must follow the terms of the agency contract.

Example
Paula Prentice (principal) hired Alex Reger (agent) to serve as her driver for two years. Prentice agreed to pay Reger $1,500 per month for that period. As the principal, Prentice has the duty to pay Alex the $1,500 per month compensation that he was promised under the agency agreement.

B. To Reimburse Reasonable Expenses—The principal must reimburse the agent for expenses incurred in carrying out the agency agreement.

1. Absent contrary agreement, the principal is responsible for expenses the agent incurs in reasonably performing his or her activities on the principal's behalf.

Example
Alyssa (agent) is a truck driver who delivers furniture for Pruitt's Furniture Store (principal). While doing deliveries for Pruitt, Alyssa uses all of her gas and refills the truck with gasoline so that she can complete the deliveries. Absent agreement to the contrary, Pruitt should reimburse Alyssa for the expense.

II. Duties of the Agent to the Principal—Fiduciary Relationship

A. Fiduciary Duty

1. The agency relationship is a fiduciary relationship.

2. Because an agent is a fiduciary, the agent owes a supreme duty of loyalty to his or her principal. The agent cannot make a profit at the principal's expense.

Example
Rand Turner is the trainer for Cheshire Farms. Rand does not have an exclusive arrangement with Cheshire, and he also trains for Hillsbrook Farms. Rand arranged to have Cheshire sell two of its mares to Hillsbrook for a discounted price. Rand had already prenegotiated the sale of those mares by Hillsbrook to a third party for twice the amount Hillsbrook paid to Cheshire. Rand breached his fiduciary duty because he profited on the second sale without disclosing to Cheshire that the second sale, for twice the amount, was already pending.

B. Duty to Follow Instructions (Duty of Obedience)—The agent should follow the principal's instructions unless those instructions call for illegal or immoral acts.

C. Reasonable Care—The agent should discharge all responsibilities carefully and is theoretically liable in negligence to the principal for damage caused by carelessness.

Example
An agent hired by an estate to sell the personal property of the estate should make sure that the buyers have the ability to pay for those goods.

D. Accounting—The agent has a duty to provide the principal with an accounting for all funds of the principal.

E. The agent should always keep any of the principal's funds in the agent's custody separate from agent's own funds and should always be able to tell the principal exactly where the funds are located.

F. Duty of Disclosure—The agent should immediately inform the principal of any important information that the principal would want to know.

Example
Agent, a sales representative, learns that a long-established credit customer is on the brink of bankruptcy. Agent should inform principal so that principal can evaluate whether to continue selling to the customer on credit.

G. Duty of Loyalty—As a fiduciary, an agent acts in the best interest of the principal and does not make profits on transactions at the principal's expense.

    1. No competition—Agents' duty of loyalty means that they cannot compete with their principals.

Example
Agent (accountant) Arisiphons tax business away from his or her accounting firm (the principal) by telling small clients to come to his or her house on weekends where he or she will do their taxes for much less than the firm charges.

    2. No conflict of interest

Example
Agent is a buyer for a major retailer and begins buying goods from a company that the agent had established in a friend's name.

    3. No appropriation of business opportunities

Example
Two partners, Alex and Annie, are in the oil and gas business, and one learns of a fabulous oil and gas opportunity in Mexico. He or she invests in that opportunity for himself or herself only.

    4. No disclosure of confidential information

Example
Agent learns trade secrets, such as customer lists and preferences, while working for principal. Agent should not sell or give those trade secrets to anyone.

Misconception
Many believe that trade secrets can be disclosed and used for the agent's benefit unless the agent has signed a covenant not to compete. This is erroneous. The common law of agency imposes a duty of nondisclosure of confidential information that extends beyond the existence of the agency relationship regardless of whether the agent has signed a restrictive covenant. Even in those states that do not recognize covenants not to compete as valid, there is protection for the trade secrets of principals.

III. Duties of the Parties upon Termination—Agency relationships require special steps on the part of principals and agents when the relationship terminates in order to be certain third parties are not affected adversely.

    A. Termination of Agency Relationships by Act of the Parties.

        1. Termination by fulfillment—An agency relationship is terminated when the conduct authorized under the agency relationship is complete.

> **Example**
> Paul Purcell hired Alice Anderson (agent), a real estate broker, to sell his home. Once Alice has found a buyer and the sale closes, Paul's agency relationship with Alice terminates.

        2. Termination by lapse of time—If an agency relationship is restricted in length and the authorized length of time ends, then the agency relationship ends.

> **Example**
> Most real estate listing agreements, in which a homeowner (principal) hires a real estate broker (agent) to sell her house, are limited in length to 90 days. When the 90 days have ended, the listing agreement also ends.

        3. Termination by a specified event—An agency relationship established to accomplish an event ends when that event is done.

> **Example**
> A wedding planner (agent) hired to negotiate contracts for venues, cakes, flowers, etc, for a wedding has no further authority once the wedding takes place.

        4. Termination by mutual agreement—An agency relationship ends when the principal and agent agree that they wish to end their relationship.

> **Example**
> When a company (principal) and an advertising agency (agent) agree that they no longer wish to work with each other, they have reached a mutual agreement, and the agency will no longer have the authority to negotiate ad contracts for the company.

        5. Termination by unilateral act of one party—("You're fired" or "I quit")—When the principal or agent fails to perform the duties under the agency agreement, the agency relationship ends, just as in the case of any breach of contract.

> **Example**
> Paula Prentice (principal) hires Alex Reger (agent) to serve as her driver for two years. Prentice agrees to pay Reger $1,500 per month for that period. Either Prentice or Reger can end the relationship at any time. However, the termination of the agency does not resolve the underlying issues of damages for breach of contract to the other party.

          a. Exception to the grounds for termination—A principal cannot (i.e., has neither the right nor the power to) terminate an *agency coupled with an interest.*

          b. An agency coupled with an interest is a unique agency relationship, created by a writing, that gives the agent some interest vested in the property that is the subject matter of the agency relationship.

Example

Pat Page (principal) borrows $5,000 from Alice Akers. To secure the loan, Pat grants Alice a security interest (a property interest for the sole purpose of securing a debt—see the UCC Article 9 lessons) in Pat's antique store inventory. To protect her status as a lender, Alice inserts in the agreement a provision whereby Pat makes Alice his agent for the sale of the inventory in the event that Pat defaults on the loan. Since Alice has an interest in the subject matter of the agency (the inventory), the arrangement is an agency coupled with an interest, and Pat cannot terminate Alice's authority to sell without Alice's consent. Of course, if Pat repays the loan, then Alice will no longer have an interest in the subject matter and the agency will terminate.

B. Termination by Act of Parties—Terminates *only* express and implied authority, not apparent authority.

1. Principal has a duty to notify third parties about the termination in order to halt the agent's authority.

2. Agent has a duty to honor the termination and not use apparent authority to continue benefiting from the relationship.

3. Lingering apparent authority that exists after termination by act of the parties can be ended as follows:

    a. Actual notice to third parties that the agent no longer has authority

    b. Constructive notice—Publication or general mailings that indicate the agency relationship has been terminated

C. Termination by Operation of Law

1. Termination by death of either principal or agent

    a. Death of the principal means that there is no longer a party to the contract.

    b. Death of the agent speaks for itself.

2. Termination by insanity of the principal

    a. The insanity of the principal means that there is no party with capacity (see the "Contracts— Defenses to Formation" lesson for more information on capacity) to enter into contracts.

    b. As a result, the agency terminates by the way the law operates.

Example

Pam Poly hires Arnold Ashforth to sell Pam's house. Pam dies. The agency terminates at the moment of Pam's death.

3. Termination by bankruptcy

    a. Bankruptcy of the principal is another event that can trigger an operation-of-law termination of an agency, if the principal's bankruptcy would cause the agent to realize that P would no longer wish A to enter into transactions on P's behalf.

    b. Bankruptcy of the agent terminates an agency relationship only if the agent's bankruptcy would impair A's ability to act as an agent.

Example

Anissa (agent) has been working as the on-site leasing agent for Premiere Properties' (principal) apartment complex, Las Sendas. Premiere has declared bankruptcy. Anissa can continue with the day-to-day activities of Las Sendas, including signing leases and accepting rent. If, however, Anissa had been hired by Premiere to sell off some of its properties, the bankruptcy means that further sales would not be proper until the trustee has a chance to determine creditor rights and property transfers. (See the Bankruptcy lessons for more discussion of the rights of parties once bankruptcy is declared.)

4. **Termination by change of law**—As with all contracts, if the law makes the conduct of the agent or the subject matter of the contract illegal, the agency relationship ends. (See the "Contracts—Defenses to Formation" lesson for more discussion of the effect of illegality on a contract.)

 Examples

1. Alan is hired to buy a dog race track for Peter, and dog racing is declared illegal.

2. Chiquita Banana hires a mercenary group to provide protection for its employees in Colombia. The U.S. government passes a law that makes it illegal for U.S. companies to compensate groups that are listed as terrorist groups by the U.S. Department of Justice. Chiquita's agency relationship with the group terminates.

5. **Termination by circumstances such as loss or destruction of subject matter**—The loss or destruction of the property that is the subject matter of the agency relationship terminates the agency relationship.

Example

Anna is hired by Pepe to sell Pepe's warehouse, which is destroyed by a tornado before she can sell it. Anna's agency relationship ends because the subject matter is destroyed.

D. Termination by operation of law ends ALL authority: express, implied, and apparent. The duty of notice does not apply because the law has ended the agency relationship.

Contract Liability of Agents and Principals

After studying this lesson, you should be able to:

1. Describe the authority and liability of agents with regard to contracts entered into with third parties.

2. Describe the authority and liability of principals for contacts entered into on their behalf by their agents.

I. **Contract Relationships of Principals, Agents, and Third Parties**—The liability of the principal and agent to third parties for contracts and the ability of third parties to enforce contracts against principals and agents depend on two factors: the type of authority the agent had and whether the principal was disclosed to the third party.

II. **Liability of a Disclosed Principal**

   A. **Disclosed Principal**—In this situation, the third party is aware that the agent is acting for a principal and the third party knows who that principal is.

   Example
   A sports agent who is negotiating a contract for an NBA free agent is an example of a disclosed principal situation. The third party (the team) knows the identity of the player and knows that the sports agent is authorized to act on his behalf.

   B. **Disclosed Principal with Actual Authority (Express or Implied)**—In this situation, the principal *only* is liable to the third party.

   Examples

   1. Antique dealer (agent) is hired by an estate executor (principal) to sell an armoire from the estate. The executor placed the requirements with the agent on price for the armoire. The agent discloses the executor's name to the buyer (third party), explains her role, and negotiates a sale of the armoire for $1,700. The executor thinks the price is too low and refuses to honor the contract. The buyer can require the executor to convey title to the armoire, and the executor is liable for damages to the buyer for failure to deliver. The antique dealer has no liability to the buyer even if the executor breaches the contract.

   2. Principal hires agent to sell principal's house for at least $90,000. The express authority is for the agent to find a buyer to buy the house for $90,000. Agent finds a ready, willing, and able buyer for $100,000. The principal is bound to sell the house to the buyer because the agent had express authority to sell the house.

      MISCONCEPTION: Note, this is an agency to SELL the house, not list the house. An agency relationship to list (market the house and bring offers) does not include the authority to enter into contracts. In listing agreements, there is no implied authority for the real estate agent to actually contract and sell.

   3. Principal hires agent to manage principal's restaurant. Principal does not spell out agent's authority. The law implies that agent has the authority customarily exercised by managers of comparable businesses in the area (this is implied authority), which likely includes the authority to hire and fire employees, to open bank accounts, to purchase supplies, to sell to customers, etc.

   4. Principal instructs agent to deliver a truckload of furniture to a customer. The truck has a flat tire as the delivery is being made. Although principal did not instruct agent to do so, agent has the authority to replace the tire if it is incidental (necessary) to completion of the assigned task.

   5. When principal is out of town, a flash flood threatens his retail store. The manager of the store (agent) incurs substantial bills in a good-faith effort to protect the store from the flooding, even though agent has never been expressly authorized to do so by principal. Principal would be liable for payment of these funds because agent exercised emergency authority.

III. Disclosed Principal with Apparent Authority—There must always be a disclosed principal under apparent authority because the authority exists due to the principal holding out someone as an agent.

A. In this situation, the principal *only* is liable to the third party, but the agent is also liable to the principal for acting as an agent without express or implied authority.

B. Apparent Authority—Even if the agent lacks express or implied authority (both being types of "actual authority"), the principal may still be liable for contracts negotiated by the agent if:

1. Principal held agent out as principal's agent; that is, a third party reasonably believed that the agent worked for the principal and had the authority to enter into contracts;

2. Agent acted within scope of apparent authority; *and*

3. Third party reasonably relied on the appearance in entering into a contract.

Examples

1. Principal and principal's brother work together running a construction firm that builds single-family homes, townhomes, and custom homes. Principal's brother wants to take the custom-home contracts and operate his own building company that focuses on custom homes only. Principal agrees to transfer all the pending custom home contracts to his brother. Principal's brother continues to use office space in the principal's building, shows customers the floor plans with principal's name on them, and uses his old business cards that reflect the principal's business. If principal's brother does not finish the homes or absconds with the deposits for new homes, the principal would be liable for allowing his brother to continue to appear to be a part of his business.

2. Agent has been a traveling sales representative for principal for 10 years. Principal then fires agent for dishonesty. Agent goes to long-time customer X who has not heard of the firing and negotiates a contract to sell principal's goods to X and accepts a down payment, which he then steals. X can bind principal to the contract because it appeared to X that agent still had authority to work for principal. The terminated agent has what is known as lingering apparent authority, or authority that comes from the failure to let third parties know that the agent no longer works for you.

C. Terminating Agent's Authority—The means for terminating an agency relationship depends on the type of authority. (See also the "Duties of Agents and Principals" lesson for more information.)

1. **Terminating actual authority**—To effectively terminate an Agent's actual authority, the Principal must end the relationship. Termination of the relationship ends all actual authority, including express and implied authority.

2. **Terminating apparent authority**—The termination of actual authority ends express and implied authority, but not apparent authority. In the previous example about the terminated sales agent, first the principal should have given direct notice (phone, mail, or e-mail) to all of agent's regular customers that agent no longer worked for principal. Second, the principal should have given constructive notice to all potential customers by publishing in a newspaper of general circulation a notice that the agent no longer worked for the principal. In the principal's brother example, the principal would need to collect all the old business cards and building plans and structure and label the office so that customers would understand that his brother's business is different from his business.

3. **Limitation—operation of law agency terminations**—When agency relationships end by operation of law, as when the principal dies, such a termination ends all actual and apparent authority. The notice procedures discussed above are required in cases of termination of the agency by act of the parties; "You are fired," or "I quit."

D. Liability of Disclosed Principal—Agent has no Actual or Apparent Authority—In this situation, the agent only is liable to the third party; the principal has NO liability.

Example
Alex goes to a new town and represents to a hotel manager that he is there to book the hotel for the upcoming convention of the National Association of Realtors (NAR). Alex presents no authority, the manager does not check with the NAR, and the manager reserves the hotel for the NAR. The NAR is not liable to the hotel for the deposits and damages for no convention, but Alex is (if the hotel can find Alex!).

IV. Contract Liability of Partially Disclosed, and Undisclosed Principals under Actual Authority

A. Partially Disclosed Principals—If an agent is acting for a principal under actual authority, but does not identify the principal, then both the principal and the agent are liable to the third party. Real estate agents disclose that they are acting for a buyer but do not want the seller to know who the buyer is because the seller might increase the price if the buyer is a wealthy individual or a developer. The agent's principal would be unable to obtain a fair price for the property if the seller knew his or her identity.

Example
Agent negotiates to buy a house on behalf of a principal but does not tell the seller (the third party) who the principal is. Both the agent and the principal are liable to the seller (the third party) for damages if the agent, acting with authority, agrees to purchase the house but then the principal refuses to go through with the contract. A contract entered into with authority on behalf of a principal is the same as a contract that the principal actually enters into on his or her own. As a result, the undisclosed principal is liable on the contract along with the agent. Of course, the agent can identify the principal if the seller/third party pursues the claim for breach of the contract and would be entitled to reimbursement from the principal if the agent ends up paying the seller the damages.

B. Undisclosed Principals—If an agent with actual authority does not disclose to a the third party the fact that he or she is acting on behalf of a principal, and the third party believes the agent is acting on his or her own behalf, the agent and principal are *both* personally liable on the contract. However, the agent can identify the principal (unless there was an agreement of confidentiality), and the third party can choose to pursue the principal for any damages. The agent is entitled to reimbursement from the principal if the agent has to pay the third party any damages.

Example
Agent negotiates to buy a house on behalf of a principal but tells the seller that she is buying for herself.

Be sure to distinguish between the third party's right to enforce the contract and the liability of the agent and principal to the third party.

In the undisclosed principal situation, the agent is functionally a party to the contract and may enforce it against the third party. If the agent reveals the identity of the principal or the principal decides to disclose his or her identity, then the principal can enforce the contract against the third party.

The principal could face three situations under which the third party can refuse to perform for the previously undisclosed principal. If the third party has already performed the contract for the agent, then the third party is not required to perform the same contract again for the principal; and—if the contract is the type that cannot typically be assigned (e.g., it calls for personal service by the agent) or the third party's decision was based on the agent's personal credit standing, judgment, or skill and those factors were the bases for the third party contracting with the agent, then the third party can refuse to perform.

Tort Liability of Agents and Principals

After studying this lesson, you should be able to:

1. Discuss when agents and principals are liable for the torts committed by agents.

2. Diagram the tort liability between and among principals, agents, and third parties.

I. **Agent's Liability**—Agents are liable for the torts they commit.

> **Misconception**
> Many people believe that agents are not liable for the torts they commit if they were ordered to commit the torts by their boss. However, the agents *are* liable notwithstanding their obedience to their boss's instructions. We are always liable for our own torts, regardless of whom we were working for at the time.

II. **Principal's Liability through Conduct**

    A. A principal is liable for his or her agent's torts if the agent was doing as the principal instructed or ordered.

> **Example**
> Principal tells agent that X owes him money and agent should beat on X until she pays. If the agent does so, the principal is liable for assault and battery because she directed the commission of the tort.

    B. A principal is liable if the principal hires an agent who is not qualified to perform the job assigned (sometimes called negligent entrustment).

> **Example**
> Principal owns a construction company and entrusts agent, a high school student without a driver's license, with a large dump truck. Agent drives the vehicle carelessly and causes injury to X. X can recover from principal because principal negligently entrusted the truck to an agent incapable of handling it.

    C. A principal is liable for the torts of the agents if the principal failed to supervise properly (tort of negligent supervision).

> **Example**
> Principal hires agent who has a known history of violence as a door-to-door sales representative. While on a sales call, agent assaults a customer in the customer's home. Principal is generally liable for not supervising the agent.

    D. A principal is liable for the torts of the agent if the principal was negligent in hiring the agent (failure to screen agent applicants properly) and/or negligent in retention (i.e., the principal had reports of negligent conduct by the agent but took no action to stop those actions or terminate the agent).

Examples

1. Principal hires agent as a truck driver without checking agent's driving record, which would have disclosed multiple arrests for DUI. Agent causes an accident while driving under the influence. Principal is liable for negligent hiring.

2. Principal hires agent as a truck driver. Agent has a good driving record but later develops a drinking problem of which the principal is aware. Agent causes an accident while driving under the influence. Principal is probably liable for negligent retention.

III. Principal's Liability for Negligent Torts of the Agent or Acts of the Agent

A. Vicarious Liability—Even if the principal has not done anything wrong personally, he may be vicariously liable under the doctrine of *respondeat superior*.

B. Requirements for Vicarious Liability

1. **Existence of a master-servant relationship**— *Respondeat superior*, meaning, "let the master answer," is a doctrine based on a master-servant relationship between the principal and agent. A master-servant relationship is determined by the ability of the principal to control the activity of the agent. This relationship is different from an independent contractor relationship.

Example

If ABC Welding hires Lawyer X from the XYZ law firm to handle its commercial litigation, X is an independent contractor. If ABC Welding hires X as its general counsel, X is in a master-servant relationship. If X is an independent contractor, ABC does not have vicarious liability for X's torts, even when X is driving to depositions for ABC. However, if X is a general counsel for ABC, ABC would have liability for X's torts when he is driving to depositions on ABC litigation.

a. **Agent is a servant**—The key to determining whether the agent is a servant for whose torts the principal is liable or an independent contractor for whose torts the principal usually is not liable is this question: Does P have the right to control the method and manner of A's work?

    i.   If the answer is yes, then it is a master-servant relationship.

    ii. If the answer is no, then it is an independent contractor relationship.

b. **Additional factors**—In determining whether an agent is a servant or an independent contractor:

    i.   Does A work regular hours for P (e.g., 9–5)?

    ii. Does P provide A's tools?

    iii. Is A paid by the hour or week rather than by the job?

    iv. Is P A's major source of income rather than being simply one of A's many customers?

        1. If the answer is yes, then it indicates a master-servant relationship.

        2. If the answer is no, then it indicates an independent contractor relationship.

2. **Scope of Employment**—"Scope of employment" means that the agent (in the master-servant relationship) commits the tort while the agent is doing something for the principal.

a. The principal is less likely to be held liable for an agent's intentional torts than for an agent's mere negligence because it is more likely that the agent is not acting within the scope of employment when committing intentional torts. However, if the agent is authorized to commit the tort or motivated in any important way by a desire to serve the principal, then the principal is liable.

Note
Remember also that when an intentional tort is committed by an agent and the principal was aware or should have known that the agent had a tendency to commit those kinds of torts, the principal is liable (negligent hiring and negligent supervision).

Examples

1. Agent is a bouncer at Principal's bar. X, a customer, walks in and Agent exclaims: "That's the guy who stole my girlfriend!" Agent beats up X. Principal is not liable because Agent acted for purely personal motives.

2. Agent is a bouncer at Principal's bar. X, a customer, becomes unruly. Agent uses excessive force in ejecting X, even though Principal has warned Agent to be careful. X is seriously injured and sues Principal. Principal is probably liable.

    b. **Within authority**—An agent will be held to have acted within the scope of employment when committing the tort if these three questions are answered affirmatively:

        i. Was this the type of work agent was hired to do?

        ii. Did it occur substantially within normal time and space limitations?

        iii. Was it done to serve the principal in some way?

            a. While delivering furniture for his employer, P Furniture Co., Agent carelessly drives the truck through a stop sign injuring X. P is liable to X.

            b. While on vacation from his job at P Furniture Co., Agent carelessly drives his family car through a stop sign injuring X. P is not liable to X.

Example
If an administrative assistant takes her car and goes to the bank for the company with which she works (the Principal), the company is liable for the torts the administrative assistant (the Agent) commits while on her way to and from the bank. If the administrative assistant runs a red light during this journey, she is liable for any injuries that her running the red light causes, but the company is also liable for those injuries.

    c. **Deviations from the scope** of employment will not alter the principal's liability if:

        i. They are minor; *or*

        ii. After deviation, A is returning and "reasonably close" to the point of departure.

        iii. **Frolic and detour**—Agent is completing personal tasks while working on principal's business—no liability for principal during the frolic and detour.

        iv. **Return from frolic and detour**—Agent gets back to the business of the principal after personal business is complete; liability returns.

Examples

1. While delivering furniture for his employer, P Furniture Co., Agent leaves the highway to get a soda at a fast food restaurant that he spotted just off the highway. Agent drives his car carelessly in the fast food restaurant's parking lot and injures customer X. P is liable to X.

2. While delivering furniture for his employer, P Furniture Co., Agent leaves the highway to visit an old friend several miles away. After the visit, Agent is returning to the highway in order to complete the delivery and carelessly causes an accident on the on-ramp injuring X. P is liable to X.

> **Misconception**
> Many people believe that a principal cannot be liable unless he or she has done something morally blameworthy. However, a completely innocent principal can have the best motives in the world and be very careful but may still be liable for his or her agents' torts within the scope of authority. The rationale is based in part on the notion that the principal profits when the agent does things right and therefore should incur the costs when the agent errs. The rationale is also based in part on a natural desire to compensate the innocent victims of the agent's torts.

    v. When "extra-hazardous activity" is involved (e.g., use of explosives, radioactive material, etc.), then the principal has strict liability, even in the case of an independent contractor.

> **Example**
> Principal wishes to implode a downtown office building to make way for new construction and he or she hires the independent contractor A Construction Co. If A botches the job, Principal is liable.

    vi. Where a statute imposes a "nondelegable duty" (e.g., the duty of a railroad to maintain railroad crossings, the duty to repossess cars without breach of the peace).

Contracts

Introduction and Classification

Applicable Laws

After studying this lesson, you should be able to:

1. Explain the two sources of contract law and when they apply to particular contracts.

2. Describe what a contract is.

3. Explain why which source of contract law governs is important for determining the rights of the parties.

I. Sources of Contract Law

> **Definition**
> *Contract:* An agreement supported by consideration between two or more persons with competent capacity for a legal purpose.

A. **Sources of Contract Law**—The two sources of contract law are common law and Article 2 of the Uniform Commercial Code (UCC), also known as "Sales." The common law began its formulation in England through court decisions. In the United States, that body of law has continued to be refined and supplemented by court decisions throughout the fifty states. For purposes of the exam, common law is the view of the majority of the states on particular contract issues. Some common law has been codified by individual states into their statutes, but the exam focuses on the common law majority view and the UCC.

B. **Distinctions between the UCC Article 2 and Common Law**

1. The two sources govern different types of contract subject matter (see "Application" discussion).

2. The UCC is codified in statutory form and common law (for exam purposes) is the law developed in judicial decisions on contracts.

> **Note**
> *The UCC is a form of codified commercial law that was developed by business people, lawyers, and legal experts to create a system of consistent contract principles across state lines. All states, except for Louisiana, have adopted Article 2 of the UCC.*

> **Definition**
> *Statute:* An act of a legislature that declares, proscribes, or commands something; a specific law, expressed in writing.

3. Common law requires more details and precision than does UCC Article 2 for formation, terms, and damages.

4. The UCC Article 2 requires less detail than common law does from the parties to a contract and has terms that apply if the parties fail to agree on those terms. In addition, the UCC Article 2 has more flexibility than common law does when it comes to formation and performance. The goal of UCC Article 2 is to provide efficient ways for businesses to form contracts and deal expeditiously with issues that develop during performance.

> **Note**
> *Answers to exam questions are different depending on whether the subject matter of the contract is governed by UCC or common law. Be sure you know which types of contracts are under UCC and which are under common law. Study this section carefully.*

II. Application of Common Law vs. UCC

A. UCC Article 2 applies to contracts that involve the sale of goods.

    1. What constitutes a good? Goods are tangible personal property, such as cars, clothes, books, iPads, livestock, groceries, and trees and crops that the seller has already harvested.

    2. What types of contracts involve both the sales of goods and providing services? These are called blended contracts.

    3. If a contract involves providing both goods and services, then the UCC applies if the purpose of the contract is primarily the sale of the goods. If, however, the primary purpose of the contract is the installation of the goods, it is governed by common law.

Examples

1. A burglar alarm system involves the purchase of alarms, wire, and monitors. However, the buyer wants the alarm installed and functioning. The contract is a service contract and governed by common law.

2. A company agrees to rebind a school district's already owned textbooks. While goods are involved, the contract is for the service of binding. If the school district contracts to purchase rebound books, the contract is governed by the UCC because the purchase of books is the purchase of goods.

B. Common law applies to service and real estate contracts.

    1. Contracts for employment, agency agreements, lawn service contracts, car washes, and medical care are all examples of service contracts.

    2. Real estate contracts include leases, mortgages, liens, and contracts for the sale and purchase of real estate.

Examples

1. You contract with an artist to paint a portrait of you for a Christmas present. Is this a contract for a good—the finished portrait—or a contract for a service—the painting of the portrait? Obviously, the predominant feature of the contract is the artist painting (service) your portrait.

2. You order food to be cooked at a restaurant. Are you purchasing the cooking (preparation) of the food or the food itself? Here the food itself is the predominant feature and a sale of goods. See UCC 2-314(1).

C. When a contract involves both realty and the sale of goods, use the UCC (UCC 2-107) and common law for the sale of the appliances in a home.

Examples

1. Minerals, oil, gas, or structures on earth to be moved are considered goods if they are to be severed by the seller; if severed by the buyer, real estate law governs.

2. Sales of growing crops or timber are the sale of goods regardless who severs.

3. "Things" attached but not deemed fixtures, which can be severed without material harm to realty, are goods.

Example
A contract for the sale of a home is governed by common law (real estate). A contract hiring a real estate broker is also governed by common law (services). A contract for the sale of a mobile home by a manufacturer is governed by the UCC.

Exam Tip
Caution: Before answering any questions about contracts on the CPA Exam, first determine whether the subject matter is UCC or common law. There are differences between the two sources of laws and applying the wrong law will result in choosing one of the available answers that is correct for the WRONG source of law. Look at the subject matter of the contract and ask, "Am I under the UCC or am I under common law?"

D. Article 2 applies to merchants and nonmerchants alike—Certain sections apply only when a seller, buyer, or both are **merchants**.

Types of Contracts

I. **Types of Contracts**—Contracts are identified and described in various ways based on their characteristics. The characteristics and names used are not all mutually exclusive. The following are major concepts associated with contracts. A given contract may fall into more than one of the following types.

  A. **Express Contract**—A contract formed wholly by oral and/or written words.

  Example
  Over the phone, I offer to sell you my personal computer for $400. Later in the day, you send me a fax accepting my offer. The combination of the oral offer (phone) and the written acceptance (fax) creates an express contract. (Whether the contract is required to be in writing will be covered under the Statute of Frauds.)

  B. **Implied or Implied-in-Fact Contract**—A contract formed, at least in part, based on the conduct of the parties or based on the factual circumstances.

  Examples
  1. You call a tax accountant and inquire how much the accountant charges to prepare a tax return. The fee charged is given by the receptionist who answered your call. The next day, you drop off your canceled checks, W-2 forms, and other information at the accountant's office. The accountant prepares your return. Your conduct in dropping off the tax materials and the conduct of the accountant in preparing the tax return create an implied-in-fact contract.

  2. When you go to the doctor, not all of the payment terms and costs are clear; however, there is a basic understanding that you will pay for the services the doctor renders. Some urgent care clinics have moved away from implied contracts to express contracts, as they require patients to sign an agreement to pay before treatment and require a deposit or credit card prior to beginning treatment. These medical care providers have decided to move away from implied contracts to express contracts.

  C. **Quasi-Contract or Implied-in-Law Contract**—A contract imposed by the courts or by law when some performance has gone forward, even though there is no express or implied contract. The law creates a quasi-contract for the parties to prevent unjust enrichment of one party by the other.

  Example
  A political campaign staff member goes to a copy center store to order posters for her candidate. She asks the copy center employee to run 500 copies of the poster. When the campaign staffer leaves the campaign, the posters are picked up by another staff member who directs the copy center to talk to someone else on the campaign staff. Those at campaign headquarters were not aware of the terms of the poster production so they refuse to pay without a written agreement. As a result, the copy center is not paid. The copy center would still be entitled to payment because allowing the campaign to place the large order, use the posters, and not pay would be unjust enrichment. There is no written agreement, but the cost to the copy center is great, and the campaign benefited by having the posters to use.

D.   Bilateral Contract—A type of contract in which both sides make a promise. A promise is made by one party to the contract in exchange for a promise from the other party to the contract.

Example
Most contracts are bilateral contracts. The car dealership offers to sell you a car in exchange for your promise to make monthly payments for four years. The bank offers to lend you $150,000 for the purchase of a home in exchange for your promise to grant the bank a mortgage and make monthly payments on the mortgage loan.

E.   Unilateral Contract—A type of contract in which one side makes a promise in exchange for an action or performance from the other side.

Example
"Mow my yard, and I will pay you $50." You mow the yard and complete the performance. The yard owner is required to pay you the $50 in exchange for the act of mowing the yard.

"Drive my car from New York to San Francisco, and I will pay you $1,000." If you get the car to San Francisco, you collect the $1,000. The action or performance of mowing the yard or driving the car is given in exchange for the promise to pay.

F.   Executed Contract—A contract that has been fully performed by both parties to that contract.

Example
I offer to sell you my watch for $200. You accept, and we exchange the watch for $200 cash. Since the contractual obligations of both parties have been completed, it is now an executed contract.

G.   Executory Contract—A contract that has not yet been fully performed by the involved parties

Example
I offer to sell you my watch for $200 with the payment and transfer of the watch to take place in 10 days. You accept. Since no performance has taken place, but a valid contract has still been formed, it is called an executory contract.

H.   Partially Executed Contract—A contract that has been performed in part (i.e., one side has performed the contractual obligation). Rights of the parties under executed and executory contracts are different. You can find additional information on those differences in the statute of frauds discussion.

Example
If, for example, in the watch sale agreement, the buyer pays the seller the sales price of $200 but the seller has not yet delivered the watch, the contract is a partially executed contract because one side has performed but the other has not. In construction contracts, the building may be complete, but the owner has not yet paid because of loan processing time. The contract is partially executed, as the contract has been executed on the part of the contractor but not on the part of the landowner, who has not yet paid.

I.   Valid Contract—A contract that has been legally formed and meets all necessary requirements for formation. (For formation requirements, see the "Formation—Offer and Acceptance" lesson.)

J. **Void Contract**—A contract that lacks a legal purpose or is in violation of the law. A void contract cannot be enforced by the courts because enforcement would violate public policy and encourage illegal conduct. Also, contracts entered into by those who have been declared incompetent are void.

Example
You and I agree that if I pay you $10,000, you will burn down a certain building. Since the performance required under the contract is arson (i.e., a crime), not for a legal purpose, the contract is void. When movie characters say "There is a contract out on his life," you now know that they are incorrect. A contract for murder for hire is void.

K. **Voidable Contract**—An otherwise valid contract that can be set aside because one party has protection under the law and the right, by choice, to be relieved of liability under the contract. Examples of these include contracts that involve fraud in formation or one of the parties lacked the required capacity to form contracts.

Example
I offer to sell you a Picasso painting that I know is a fake for $100,000. You accept. Due to my fraud, you are relieved of any liability under this contract.

L. **Unenforceable Contract**—An otherwise valid contract that cannot be enforced because of a statutory or other legal defense. An unenforceable contract is one that the courts will not enforce, but such a contract still can be honored by the parties if they choose.

Example
I orally offer to sell you my real property for $125,000. You accept. This contract is unenforceable because it is not in writing, as required by the Statute of Frauds. (See text discussion of "Statute of Frauds.") The courts cannot enforce the agreement because there is a legal defense of a lack of writing. However, if buyer and seller choose to honor their oral agreement, the courts do not prohibit them from doing so.

Formation

Offer and Acceptance

After studying this lesson, you should be able to:

1. List all the elements required for the valid formation of a contract.

2. List how an offer can be terminated.

3. Explain the type of language needed for a valid acceptance.

4. Describe the timing rules for when an acceptance is effective.

5. Explain the requirements for the creation of a valid offer.

6. Describe what happens in formation when there are additional or differing terms in an acceptance of an offer.

I. Parties to a Contract

Definitions

Offeror: Party who makes the offer.

Offeree: Party with the right to accept the offer.

II. Requirements for the Formation of a Contract

   A. Offer

   B. Acceptance

   C. Consideration (see next lesson on "Consideration")

   D. No defenses (see lessons on "Contracts: Formation" and "Defenses to Formation")

III. Requirements of a Valid Offer

   A. Present Intent—Offer (and acceptance) must be made with serious intent (objective intent).

      1. Objective intent is measured by a reasonable person's interpretation of the acts, language of the parties, and the circumstances surrounding the transaction.

      2. Humor, anger, and context are used to determine intent.

Example

A business owner who is having a tough day writes in an e-mail, "Today has been so bad that I'd sell this business in a heartbeat to anyone with $50,000 in cash." Circumstances and language indicate that there is no intent to contract.

      3. Advertisements usually are not offers but rather an invitation to the reader to make an offer. An advertisement that is a unilateral offer meets the requirements.

Examples

1. Ad in newspaper from a clothier: "Dresses 50% off marked price." This is not an offer; it is inviting the reader to come to the store and offer to buy a dress for 50% of the marked price.

2. Ad by a dog owner: "I offer a $100 reward to the person who returns to me my lost dog Lasso (description)." The ad is a unilateral offer that will result in people who read it to look for the dog, thus, expending effort and time. It is a valid offer.

4. Present intent requires that the parties do something more than preliminary negotiations.

   a. **Price lists**—Invite a buyer to offer to purchase at the seller's listed prices (usual notation: "price subject to change"). Price lists are not offers but invitations to buyers to offer to buy at that price.

   b. **Solicitation of bids**—A solicitation invites bids (offers) to perform certain duties. The bid is the offer; the solicitation is not an offer.

   c. **Auctions**—The seller, through an auctioneer, invites bids (offers) from prospective buyers. The buyer, not the seller, is the offeror.

   d. **Negotiations**—Expressions of possible offers or future offers are not valid offers.

   e. **Inquiries about buying or selling**—"Would you consider selling your car for about $3,000?"

   f. Announcement of future plans

Example
"I might consider selling it for the right amount of cash."
"When I am ready to retire, I will be selling my business."
"I will be mailing out an offer to sell my car next month."

B. **Definite Terms**—Terms of the offer must be definite enough to cover the legal minimums for formation (same for acceptance).

   1. Under common law, definite and certain terms require identification of the parties, the subject matter, the price stated, and the time for performance.

   2. **UCC Article 2**—Article 2 relaxes the requirements of certainty and the definiteness of the terms. The UCC Article 2 requires only that the offer identify the subject matter (and quantity if more than one is being sold). Article 2 has a series of sections that supply any missing terms, including price, time of performance, delivery, and payment terms. "I will sell you some Rolex President watches" is not enough for an offer under the UCC but, "I will sell you one hundred Rolex President watches" is sufficient.

      a. **Open price term**—A reasonable or market price at the time of delivery will apply, or if price is to be fixed by either party, good faith is required in doing so—UCC 2-305.

      b. **Open payment term**—Payment is due at time and place buyer is to receive the goods—UCC 2-310.

      c. **Open quantity**—Quantity is to be set by output (of seller's factory) or need (All that the buyer needs (called Outputs or Requirements Contracts. These are valid because there is good faith and past measurements to rein in bad faith.

Misconception
A contract under the UCC requires a quantity to be enforceable. There is a UCC exception for output and requirements contract ("I will buy all the heating oil that I require for the winter," or "I will sell you all of my factory output.") The quantity is determined by past history of needs and factory production. So, a certain type of contract can be formed under the UCC without a specific quantity.

      d. **Open place of delivery term**—Delivery is at seller's business or, if the seller does not have a place of business, at seller's residence—UCC 2-308.

Misconception
Buyer Green is from New Orleans and Seller Smith is from Dallas. Smith offers to sell Green a watch for $100. Green accepts Smith's offer. The contract is silent as to the place of delivery, so delivery is at the buyer's place in New Orleans.

In absence of agreement, delivery is at Smith's residence in Dallas. Green is required to "pick up" the watch or be in breach of contract.

    e. **Open time for contracted performance**—In absence of agreement, it is a reasonable time—UCC 2-309.

C. **Communication of Offer**—The offer must be communicated by the offeror or authorized agent and received by the offeree or authorized agent.

Example
BonTon's CEO writes a letter offer to an MBA graduate offering her a position as director of credit at the store. However, the CEO never mailed the letter. There is no offer for the MBA to accept because it was never communicated. Even if the CEO's assistant found the letter in the CEO's desk and told the MBA of the letter, there is no power of acceptance unless and until the CEO communicates the offer or authorizes its communication to the MBA.

IV. Termination of Offers

A. **Revocation**—general rule—An offer can be revoked at any time prior to acceptance.

    1. Revocations are effective when they are received so they must be communicated.

    2. Revocation must be received prior to acceptance by the offeree. (See discussion below for timing rules on acceptance).

    3. Timing of acceptance

Example
Jane offers to sell Jim her textbook for $50. That evening, Jane changes her mind and mails Jim a letter of revocation. The next morning, Jim accepts Jane's offer. That afternoon, Jane's letter of revocation is received. Jane's revocation was not effective until received in the afternoon. Jim's acceptance in the morning binds Jane to the contract.

B. **Revocation of Irrevocable Offers—Options and Merchant's Firm Offers**

    1. **Options**—Options are unique in that they are offers that are part of a contract for time. Offeror and offeree have a separate contract for time. Offeree gives consideration (see the "Consideration" lesson), generally money, in exchange for the offeror's promise to keep the offer open (no revocation or lapse) for a specified period. Offeror must keep the offer open for the period specified for offeree who paid for it. The phrase "She has an option contract" is legally accurate because an option is an agreement that allows offeree's time to make a decision on whether to enter into the contract.

Example
A seller of land has offered to sell a parcel of land to a school district. The school district is not sure whether it wants to buy this tract but does not want the seller to be able to withdraw the offer. The school district offers the seller $5,000 if the seller will keep the offer open for three months. If the seller agrees and accepts the payment, the school district has an option and the seller must keep the offer open (not sell to someone else) for three months.

    a. The offeror cannot withdraw the offer during the option period.

    b. The offeree has the right to accept the offer during the option period but is not required to accept.

    c. The offeree's rejection during the option period does not end the option. The offeree has the right to that offer during the full option period.

2. **Firm offers**—UCC Article 2 has its own form of options called a merchant's firm offer.

    a. The requirements for and the effect of a merchant's firm offer are that it:

        i. Is made by a merchant (a merchant is defined, for purposes of the exam, as someone who is in the business of selling the goods that are the subject matter of the contract, e.g., Best Buy is a merchant of televisions; Home Depot is a merchant of lumber).

Definition

Merchant: A person who deals in goods of the kind being sold, or a person who holds himself or herself out as having knowledge or skill specific to the purchases or goods involved in the transaction.

Examples

Merchant (deals in goods of the kind being sold)

Manufacturer of washing machines

Retail seller of washing machines

Farmer who regularly sells crops

University that sells used and obsolete equipment five times a year

Merchant (holds self out as having knowledge or skill by occupation)

Restaurant owner who purchases a large oven for the restaurant

Computer division of the IRS that buys a new computer

University purchasing department that purchases chemistry laboratory equipment

---

        ii. The offeror states that it will be kept open or gives **assurance** that the offer will not be withdrawn for a stated period of time. (The maximum length is three months unless there is consideration.) If no time is given, the offer is kept open for a reasonable time (an amount of time determined by the nature of the goods). Produce firm offers that are left open-ended could be just days long whereas firm offers for computers that are left open could be up to three months long.

        iii. The offer is in a **signed writing (record)**—UCC 2-205.

Example

Green, a retail seller of TVs, offers in a letter to purchase 500 Model X TVs from Vision Inc. (a manufacturer of TVs) at the current Vision Inc. price list. In the letter, Green states that time is of the essence and that the offer is good for only 30 days from the date of the letter and will not be withdrawn during that time. A week later, Green decides to withdraw the offer and mails a revocation of the offer. Even if Vision receives the letter of revocation, Vision can accept Green's offer and bind Green to a contract during the 30-day period. Green's offer as a merchant, in a letter as a signed writing, gave Vision assurance that the offer would not be withdrawn for 30 days. Thus, Green made a firm offer, which was irrevocable without payment of consideration for the 30-day period, and Green cannot legally revoke the offer.

---

        iv. Does not require consideration

        v. Once these elements are present, the offeree holds an irrevocable offer (despite no consideration) for the time stated in the firm offer (or if none is stated, for a reasonable period) but no longer than three months—UCC 2-205.

        vi. If the parties want an offer for the sale of goods to remain open longer than three months, then there must be consideration, just as with option contracts under common law.

> **vii.** If the offeror is a nonmerchant, the rules for common-law options apply, and there must be consideration.

> **viii.** A valid firm offer is just like a common-law option; it cannot be revoked, and it ends only upon the expiration of the stated time or three months, whichever is shorter.

Examples

1. A rain check is an example of a merchant's firm offer. If a store runs out of an advertised product, it will give customers who ask for that product a rain check, which is something in writing that gives the customer the right to purchase the product at the sale price for the time provided on the rain check. The rain check time is its expiration date, such as "Good through 12/31/2017."

2. Sue owns a retail TV store. Sue, by a signed letter, offers to purchase from Adam, a TV manufacturer, 50 TVs at Adam's catalog price. Her letter states that her offer would remain open and not be withdrawn for 60 days. Sue's offer is irrevocable without having to pay consideration for the stated 60 days. If Sue had stated a six-month period (rather than 60 days), her offer would be irrevocable only for three months. After this period, she could revoke her offer at any time.

C. Rejection—An offer is terminated, at any time prior to acceptance, by the offeree saying or writing something as simple as "Terms are not acceptable," "No thank you," or "Funds for purchase are not available at this time."

1. An inquiry is not a rejection. Asking "Would you consider a lower price?" is not a rejection (see above for a discussion of inquiries not being offers).

2. A rejection is effective when it is received.

D. Counteroffer—General Rule—A counteroffer made at any time prior to acceptance is a form of rejection. A counteroffer is made when the offeree responds with changed terms. The determination of whether the offeree has made a counteroffer is controlled by whether the subject matter is under common law or UCC.

1. A counteroffer is not only a rejection of the original offer by the offeree but also a new offer that makes the original offeree an offeror.

2. Conditional acceptance is also a form of a counteroffer. A conditional acceptance is never acceptance but rather a counteroffer under both the UCC and the common law. Conditional acceptances usually are spotted through the use of prepositional phrases, such as "but I must," "on the condition that," or "provided that." These terms present in the offeree's response indicate conditional acceptance and, therefore, counteroffer.

> **Note**
> *Common law follows the mirror-image rule. That is, acceptance must be absolute, unequivocal, and unqualified. Any variation in the terms results in a counteroffer and rejection. UCC Article 2 rules are less rigid. (See the UCC discussion of additional terms that follows.)*

Example
David offers to sell his textbook to Doris for $60. Doris responds, "I would not buy your textbook for $60 but I will offer to pay you $50 for it." This is a counteroffer because Doris has made it conditional with the word "but," and David's offer for $60 is terminated. Doris has made a counteroffer to David to buy his book for $50. If Doris responded, "I will buy your textbook for $60, but I must take delivery right now," she has still made a conditional acceptance that is a counteroffer and a rejection even though she has agreed to pay the price.

E. Termination of Offers through Lapse of Time by Operation of Law

1. Lapse of time—**general rule**—An offer automatically terminates at the end of a stated period for its existence, or, if no period is stated, it terminates after a reasonable period has lapsed.

> **Note**
> *An offer that states that it will be kept open for a stated period can still be revoked at any time prior to acceptance unless it is a firm offer or option.*

Example
Sally sends an offer to a real estate investor and offers to sell her house for $121,000 cash, stating that the offer will be kept open for 90 days. Sally sends another letter to the investor on Day 15 that states "Never mind. Have decided to stay in my house and not sell." The offer is revoked. It is irrevocable only if the real investor pays for the 90-day period.

2. **Termination of Offers by Operation of the Law**—Certain events terminate an offer by law.

   1. **Death or insanity of the offeror or offeree**—The exception is options. Because options are separate contracts to hold an offer open, they do survive the death of the offeror.

   2. **Destruction of the specific subject matter of the offer—general rule**—If the specific object of the offer is destroyed prior to acceptance, the offer terminates automatically (perishes) with the destruction. If the items that are destroyed are fungible goods or commodities, the general rule does not apply because the offeror can easily obtain the same product to deliver to the offeree.

   3. **Illegality of the subject matter**—Sometimes the subject matter of the contract becomes illegal to sell. For example, in the United States, it is illegal to sell toys that contain paint with lead. When lead paint was discovered on toys manufactured in China, all offers that toy companies had made for selling toys made in China were terminated by operation of law due to illegality.

V. Acceptance of an Offer

A. **Unilateral Offer—General Rule**—Acceptance takes place upon completion (total performance) of the act required by the offer. Generally, no notice to the offeror is required, unless such is required by law (see UCC 2-206(2)) or the offeror would have no means to know that the act has been completed. For example, if a painter painted a second home for someone who does not live there year-round, the owner would require notice because the owner would have no way of knowing the house painting is done.

B. **Acceptance by Shipment of Goods**—A seller can form a contract through action, that is, shipment of goods—UCC 2-206(1)(b).

   1. The seller delivers conforming goods (goods that fulfill the buyer's order or offer) to a carrier.

   2. The seller can also accept an offer by promising to ship promptly.

   3. If the seller is shipping goods that are different from what the buyer ordered or offered to buy (i.e., nonconforming goods), the seller must notify the buyer **before** shipping that the shipment is offered only as an accommodation. If the seller ships *without advance notification* of the nonconforming goods, then there is an acceptance and automatic breach at the same time.

C. **Bilateral Offer—General Rule**—Acceptance (promise) must be absolute, unequivocal, unconditional, and communicated to the offeror.

   1. **Language of acceptance**—Determination of acceptance is controlled by whether the UCC Article 2 or common law applies. Before answering any question on acceptance, be sure to ask **whether the** contract is governed by the UCC or common law. Then apply the appropriate rules for acceptance according to the source of law that governs the contract.

      a. **Common law and the mirror-image rule** (noted earlier in discussion of rejection and counteroffer)—**Acceptance must be absolute, unequivocal, and unconditional, or it is treated as a counteroffer, not an acceptance.**

      Under common law, which applies to contracts involving real property and services (employment), any deviation in the terms of acceptance from those in the offer constitutes a counteroffer, not an acceptance.

      > **Exam Tip**
      > *It is rare to find any exam that does not have a question on either the language or the timing issues in offer and acceptance.*

> **Example**
>
> Sally makes a written offer to buy a house for $121,000 from Bill. Bill reviews the offer and is fine with the price, closing date, and payment terms. However, Bill wants to take the Tuff Shed from his backyard with him when he moves. Bill writes back, "Will sell on your terms. Tuff Shed is not included." The Tuff Shed may seem like an immaterial and negotiable item, but Bill has made a counteroffer and rejection because under the mirror-image rule under common law, the acceptance contains different terms.

2. **UCC Article 2 and Language of Acceptance**—UCC 2-207—Modifies the common law based on a definite expression of acceptance. A definite expression of acceptance followed by additional terms may or may not form a contract with the additional terms. (Review the "Formation—Offer and Acceptance" lesson and remember that whether the terms become a part of the contract depends on whether the parties are merchants and whether the terms are material, whether the offer is limited, and whether the offeror objects upon receiving the additional terms.)

> **Study Tip**
>
> Remember that conditional acceptance is never acceptance, under either UCC or common law. If an offeree uses language such as "I'll take it but . . . ," "I'll take it provided that . . . ," "I'll take it but I must . . . ," or "I'll take it on the condition that . . . ." there is a conditional acceptance. Conditional acceptance is never acceptance, it is a counteroffer. On the exam, watch for those prepositions in attempted acceptances (e.g., *but, provided, if, and only if*).

   a. For both merchants and nonmerchants, a definite expression of acceptance (not conditional acceptance) that does not change any terms results in a contract.

   b. For nonmerchants, if there is a definite statement of acceptance (not conditional acceptance) followed by some additional terms, a contract is formed, but without the additional terms.

   c. For merchants, if there is a definite statement of acceptance (not conditional acceptance) followed by additional terms, there is a contract WITH the additional terms UNLESS

   i. The additional terms are material, such as a waiver of warranties.

   ii. The offer specifically states, "This offer is limited to these terms." In this situation, a contract is formed, but without the additional terms in the acceptance.

   iii. The offeror objects within a reasonable time after receiving the acceptance to the additional terms.

> **Examples**
>
> 1. A seller offers to sell to the buyer 5,000 pounds of a "specific type" of chicken at 50 cents per pound. The buyer responds "I accept your offer for 5,000 pounds as certified by a public scale weight certificate the specific type of chicken at 50 cents per pound." Since this is a sale of goods (chicken), and the buyer gave a definite expression of acceptance ("I accept") without conditional assent to the modification, a contract is formed even though the buyer's acceptance with additional terms (public weight certificate) modified the terms of the seller's offer.
>
> 2. In the sale of 5,000 pounds of chicken in example #1, with the offeree's additional terms of a public scale weight certificate, since both parties are obviously merchants, the contract is formed on the offeree's (buyer's) terms unless the seller objects with notice to the buyer within a reasonable time. If the seller does object, the contract is formed on the seller's terms (delivery without a required public scale weight certificate).

3. Steib is a merchant of ribbon. Bold offers, "I will buy 50 spools of grosgrain blue ribbon for $4.39 per spool." Steib responds, "Will send ribbon. No warranty on color." The two have a contract *without* the warranty waiver because a warranty waiver is a material term.

Same parties but Bold adds, "This offer is limited to these terms." Steib responds, "Will send ribbon. Terms are 2/10/ net 30." The two have a contract for the ribbon with those payment terms because these types of terms are immaterial. The two have a contract for the ribbon *without* those payment terms because despite the fact that these types of terms are immaterial, the offer was expressly limited, and that controls all terms proposed after that—whether material or immaterial.

Same parties but Bold offers, "I will buy 50 spools of grosgrain blue ribbon for $4.39 per spool." Steib responds, "Will send ribbon. Terms are 2/10/ net 30." Bold e-mails back within two hours, "No, the terms on payment are not acceptable." The two have a contract without the payment terms because Bold objected in a timely manner.

If we changed the examples and made Bold and Steib nonmerchants, then there would be a contract for the ribbon without the additional terms in all three examples.

3. Timing of an acceptance—If sent by an authorized medium, the acceptance is effective, that is, a contract is formed when the offeree delivers the acceptance to the authorized medium—even if it is never received by the offeror.

    a. An authorized medium is the same or faster method of communication used by the offeror if no method is specified in the offer. If a means of acceptance is specified in the offer, the only authorized means is that specified means. If the offeree uses the authorized means, once the acceptance to a mail-authorized offer is dropped in a mailbox, there is acceptance of the offer, regardless of any delays or nondelivery. Often called the mailbox rule, this timing applies only to acceptance communication and not to offers, counteroffers, rejections, or revocations. Offers, counteroffers, rejections, and revocations are effective only when actually received.

    b. If the offer has an authorized means that is expressly specified as the means of acceptance and the offeree uses a means other than the means specified, it is considered a counteroffer and rejection because the offeree has violated the terms of the offer and the mirror-image rule.

    c. If the offer has no authorized means specified and the offeree sends acceptance by an unauthorized means, such as using a slower method of communication than that used by the offeror, then the acceptance is effective only when received by the offeror.

> **Note**
> *Under common law, the same method of communication is often required. The CPA Exam tends to avoid the split on the common law rule (some states follow the same means of communication requirement and other states allow the same or faster) by using problems in which the same or stipulated means are used for acceptance.*

Example
On May 1, Mary sends John a letter offering to sell her condo. John receives the offer on May 2. On May 3, Mary sends John a letter withdrawing her offer. On May 4, John sends a properly addressed letter with correct postage to Mary accepting her offer. On May 5, John receives Mary's letter of revocation. Mary does not receive John's letter of acceptance because of the destruction of the mail sack with the letter in it. Mary and John have a contract formed on May 4 when John used mail (implied authorization under all three of the above requirements) as the medium for acceptance. Mary's letter of revocation was not effective until received, which was after John had accepted.

    d. Silence—general rule—Silence generally is not an acceptance.

Consideration

After studying this lesson, you should be able to:

1. Explain what consideration is and why it is a requirement for forming a valid contract.

2. List the exceptions for the requirement of consideration and give examples of these exceptions.

I. **Consideration/Legal Detriment**—Consideration is required, along with offer and acceptance, for the formation of a contract.

> **Definition**
> *Consideration*: Consists of the benefit promised by the offeror (promisor) and the legal detriment promised or performed by the offeree (promisee). In a bilateral contract, both the offeror and offeree are promisors (those making a promise) and promisees (those receiving the promise). Both sides must have benefit and detriment for valid consideration to be present and the detriment on one side induces the detriment on the other side. The exchange of the detriment is bargained for by the parties.

   A. **Legal Detriment**—Often defined as doing what you are free not to do and not doing what you are free to do.

   You don't have to buy a car, but if you contract to buy one, your detriment is giving up the money.

   Likewise, you don't have to settle a lawsuit, but if you do settle it, giving up the right to have the case fully litigated is your detriment.

   Detriment is giving up money, rights, property, time—just think of what each side is giving up for what it wants under the contract.

   If you don't give anything up, you don't have detriment and are thereby missing the element of consideration, ergo, no contract.

> **Example**
> For example, you can't get more money for what you are already obligated to do. If you contract to do an audit for $15,000, you can't come back and say, "Oh, wow. I really underestimated the work—I am gonna need more money here." You have no new detriment. However, if you came back and said, "I think we are going to need to take a look at another factory as part of this *audit*," *that would mean something is* required in your professional opinion that was not in the original scope. If the client agrees, there is new detriment and you could be paid money for it because you have the detriment of an additional factory visit.

   1. **Consists of something of legal value**—Legal value can be measured by dollars and/or market value. An agreement for one side to purchase a Trek bicycle for $300 has the legal value detriment of $300 on one side in exchange for a bicycle that is worth $300 on the market. Legal value can, however, be giving up the right to file suit for damages. A promise not to file a suit against another has legal value—it is not doing what you are free to do. When two parties settle claims based on a car accident, each side is giving up the right to go to court and have a determination of damages that could be more or less than the settlement. Giving up that right to a lawsuit is legal detriment. When you buy a car you pay money—you are doing something you are free not to do, which is pay your money to the seller for the car.

> **Example**
> Sam negligently runs over Jim causing injury. Sam promises in writing that if Jim will not sue Sam in tort (negligence), Sam will pay Jim for all medical costs plus $10,000. Jim's agreement (forbearance to file a tort suit) is consideration to contractually obligate Sam to pay all of Jim's medical costs plus $10,000.

2. **Consists of a legally sufficient amount (adequacy of consideration)**—Courts do not generally examine the amount of consideration as long as it is actually exchanged. There can be differences in values on each side because the value of the promises is not the key—what is controlling is whether the value promised is legally sufficient so as not to be considered a gift. This element distinguishes gifts from contracts.

Example
If your grandmother says, "Come to my house tonight and I will give you my car," you do not have legally sufficient detriment because your grandmother is not giving you the car because you came over. She is giving you the car out of love; it is a promise to make a gift and, thus, not enforceable as a contract.

B. **Bargained-for Exchange**—This element of consideration means that the promise induces the detriment on each side. You are willing to sign the deed for title to your house because the buyer is willing to pay you $121,000.

Example
Mary's offer to purchase Jim's accounting text for $50 and his acceptance constitute consideration. The text and $50 both have legal value, the book and the $50 are both legally sufficient to show that this is not a gift, and Mary's promise to pay $50 induces Jim's promise to transfer the book and vice versa. The bargained-for action of detriment and benefit is the basis of the contract.

II. Preexisting Duty and Consideration

Definition
Preexisting Duty: A preexisting duty is one that exists under a valid contract or perhaps by law. A preexisting legal duty is an enforceable obligation.

A. **General Rule**—You cannot obtain more detriment from the other party in order to perform what you are already legally obligated to do. You are not entitled to more payment (consideration) for what you are already legally obligated to do. An example of a legal obligation for which you are not entitled to more money relates to law enforcement officials. Police officers cannot collect rewards for catching a criminal because they have a legal obligation to do so as part of their work.

The modification of a COMMON LAW contract requires additional consideration on BOTH sides; otherwise, the modification is not a valid contract because it is missing the required element of consideration.

Example
Able contracts to build you a home for $350,000 according to a set of specific plans and specifications. Later, Able tells you that he will lose money building your house and that he will complete the house only if you agree to pay him an additional $5,000. You agree. This agreement to pay $5,000 is without consideration and it is unenforceable. Able gave up nothing of legal value for the $5,000, as he was already legally obligated to build the same house for $350,000. Even if you agreed in writing to pay the $5,000, the agreement would not be a contract because it is missing the element of consideration. You would have offer and acceptance, but there is no contract because there must be additional consideration given by both sides. Your $5,000 is not enough to have the second agreement be a contract. Able would have to agree to do something more to be legally entitled to that price increase.

Under the UCC, parties to a contract are not required to agree to a modification, but if they do agree, additional consideration is not required, as long as the modification is made in good faith and not through duress. The modification of a contract under the UCC does not require additional consideration.

Example

Jake and Jonas have a contract for Jake to buy 600 roof flashing kits. Jonas has had a price increase of $2.54 per kit. Jonas explains what has happened to Jake. Jake cannot get a better price from any other dealer and agrees to pay $2.54 extra per kit. There is additional detriment on Jake's part, but not on the part of Jonas. Nonetheless, under the UCC, the two have a valid contract.

B. Exceptions to Preexisting Duty Rule

1. **Rescission and new contract**—The mutual rejection by both parties to a contract of their existing contract (rescission) and then making a new one ($355,000 to build the house above). The consideration consists of both sides giving up their rights under the original agreement in exchange for a new one. They are doing what they do not have to do in waiving those original contract rights.

2. **UCC modification for contracts for the sale of goods**—Under the UCC, the parties are permitted to, in good faith, modify their contracts even without additional consideration (detriment) on both sides (UCC 2-209(1)). The parties are not required to agree to a modification, but if they do agree and the subject matter is UCC, then the modification is enforceable despite the lack of consideration. The modification must also be in good faith. That is, one side cannot threaten the other side to stop performing on the contract unless there is a modification. No one *must* agree to a modification to an existing contract. However, if they do agree to a modification under the UCC, the modification is enforceable despite the lack of new consideration.

> **Note**
> The common law and UCC rules for modification are very different. Once again, always determine the subject matter of the contract and then determine whether the contract is under UCC or common law so that you can apply the different principles and reach the correct solution.

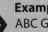

Example

ABC Gas Inc. has a requirement contract to furnish Green Industries with all the gas it needs to run its plants for 10 years at 50 cents per cubic foot of gas. Exploration and transportation costs will triple in the next three years, and ABC is starting to lose money on the contract. The current market price is 80 cents per cubic foot. ABC and Green agree in writing to raise the price of the gas supplied to Green to 60 cents per cubic foot for the rest of the term of the contract. Even though no consideration is given by ABC for the increase in price, the 60-cent price is now binding on both parties.

Example

Clara's Cookies has a supply contract with Clarence's Chips for Clarence's to furnish chocolate and butterscotch baking chips to Clara's at a price of $2.29 per pound. Clarence and Clara have their supply contracts run for one year and they have been doing business with each other for 10 years. An increase in gasoline prices has hit Clarence's business model (one that involves personal delivery to ensure that the chips do not melt) particularly hard. Clarence asks Clara if he can increase the price per pound to $2.30. Clara does not have to agree to the price increase, but, if she does, the increase is enforceable even though Clarence has no additional legal detriment and Clara does. Because the contract is under UCC, this modification without additional consideration is valid and enforceable.

III. Consideration in UCC Requirements and Output Contracts

A. **UCC Requirements Contract**—The type of contract is one in which a buyer agrees to purchase all that he needs for his home or business from the seller. The quantity is left open, but under the UCC this type of agreement is enforceable in order to allow businesses and buyers to operate on an as-needed basis.

Example
A homeowner who heats with propane gas or oil agrees to purchase all that she needs to heat her home for the winter. She does not know the amount she will need because the temperature for the winter will control that. She might need very little fuel, or she might need a great deal. But, her open-end quantity contract is still supported by consideration under the UCC.

B. **UCC Output Contract**—The contract is one in which a seller agrees to sell all that it produces to a particular buyer. Under the UCC, this type of open-end quantity agreement is a valid contract that is supported by consideration if the contract is based on an established production or ability to produce by the seller and the seller is required to sell its production to the buyer.

IV. Consideration in Accord and Satisfaction

Definition
Accord and Satisfaction: An accord is an agreement to waive legal rights and release another party from legal obligations. Satisfaction is the actual payment of the amounts agreed to in the accord. The detriment on both sides of an accord is both parties agreeing to do something they are not legally required to do (settle a claim) or not doing what they could legally do (bring a lawsuit to recover on their rights).

A. **Liquidated Debts and Accord and Satisfaction**—A liquidated debt is one in which the amount due and owing is clear to both parties.

Example
Charlie owes Fred $5,000 plus 5% interest, and the amount is to be paid in monthly payments over a two-year period. Charlie cannot write "Payment in full" on his 20th monthly check and have the debt discharged. He does not have detriment; only Fred would. If, however, Charlie negotiated with Fred and agreed to pay a lesser amount four months early and Fred agreed, then the "payment in full" would be the accord and Fred cashing the check would be the satisfaction because Charlie paid the full amount early and Fred got the use of his money earlier than he was entitled to have it.

Misconception
The parties to a liquidated debt can always agree to an early pay-off, and it is valid if there is detriment on both sides. If debtor owes creditor $5,000 on May 1 and debtor offers to pay creditor $4900 on March 1, there is consideration because creditor gets his money early and debtor gets to pay less.

B. **Unliquidated Debts and Accord and Satisfaction**—An unliquidated debt is one in which the parties acknowledge that money is due and owed, but they disagree on the amount. An agreement (accord) between the two parties on an amount and then payment of that amount is an accord and satisfaction because both are giving up their right to have the amount due determined by a court. "Payment in full" placed on a check for an unliquidated debt would serve to discharge the debt.

Examples
1. Sam negligently runs his car into the rear of John's car. Sam, in a signed writing, promises to pay John $1,000 if John will release Sam from any further property liability due to the accident. This accepted release by John is binding and bars John from any further recovery. Sam is giving up his right to have a court determine his level of liability and John is giving up the right to have the court possibly determine that his damages are greater than $1,000.

2. Joe, in his most recent will, leaves all of his assets to his son, Able, and nothing to his two married daughters who both were unaware of Joe's heart condition. It is learned that Able had not informed his sisters of their dad's condition and Joe has told friends that Able had said that his daughters did not care about him. The daughters have indicated they would contest the will. Able and his sisters agree that if the sisters do not contest the will, he will give each $15,000 from monies he will receive under the will. This (giving up the legal right to contest the will for $15,000) is a covenant not to sue (contract) and enforceable.

3. Jim borrows $100 from Joan payable back without interest. Jim sends to Joan a check clearly marked as "payment in full" for $90. Such an action would not serve to discharge the debt. Jim owes Joan $100, the debt is liquidated, and Joan can still legally pursue recovery of $10 from Jim.

4. Jim contracts to purchase from Joan a new file cabinet for $250. Upon delivery, Jim discovers that the cabinet is scratched. Jim tenders to Joan a check clearly marked "payment in full" for $200. Joan has no idea as to the cost of damage due to the scratches. She can avoid the issue and return the check (no accord), but if she cashes it (since reasonable persons could disagree as to the cost of damage), the purported debt is canceled because their agreement on what to do about the defective file cabinet (the scratch) is open for debate. It could cost $50 to fix it or $10 or something greater. The amount due is not liquidated even though the original purchase price was because they are now dealing with goods not delivered as promised. Joan does not have to accept the $200, but once she does, Jim's obligation is satisfied.

V. Past Consideration—A promise to pay for an act already completed is without (not bargained-for) consideration.

Example
An employer states, "In consideration of the 20 years of loyal service you have given the company, I promise to pay you $10,000." The promise is unenforceable because it is for an event that has already taken place.

VI. Exceptions to the Consideration Requirement

Definition
Estoppel: A legal principle that bars a party from denying or alleging a certain fact owing to that party's previous conduct, allegation, or denial.

A. **Promissory Estoppel**—A promise, which induces another party to rely on that promise and results in the party materially changing their position, estops the other party from refusing to honor that promise based on a claim of no valid consideration.

Example
Jim pledges (promises) $50,000 to the church to add a childcare room to the church. In reliance (induces church to change its position) thereon, the church contracts for the addition (changes substantially their position). In the interest of justice, the church can hold Jim to his pledge denying his claim that his pledge lacked consideration.

B. **Promises Barred by the Statute of Limitations**—The statute of limitations is the time the law imposes by statute for bringing a suit to enforce legal rights. For example, the general statute of limitations under the UCC is four years. Parties to a contract have four years from the time the contract is formed or from the time of the breach (depending on the reason for the suit) to enforce their rights. Once that time allowed under the statute passes, the contract is unenforceable. If, however, the party who owed money on that contract agrees to pay the amount due, the renewed promise to pay is enforceable because the party is agreeing to do something he was not required to do by law since the statute of limitations discharged the debt. Although the detriment is one-sided, these agreements are enforceable.

C. **Promises to Pay Debts Discharged in Bankruptcy**—A debtor need not assume responsibility for debts that could be discharged in bankruptcy, but if those debts are exempted from discharge prior to the discharge order, their payment can be enforced.

Writing and Records: The Statute of Frauds

After studying this lesson, you should be able to:

1. List the types of contracts that must be evidenced by a record in order to be enforceable.

2. Describe the exceptions to the Statute of Frauds.

3. Define the parol evidence rule and how courts interpret the terms in contracts evidenced by a record.

4. Explain the requirements for a record of a contract.

I. **The Statute of Frauds**—Originally, at common law, called the Statute for the Prevention of Frauds and Perjuries, this law (codified in most states) requires certain types of contracts to be in writing (be evidenced by a record, as discussed below) to be enforceable. The types of contracts that must be in writing are those that people are most likely to lie about in order to secure the benefit. If the Statute of Frauds requires a contract to be in writing and it is oral, then it is unenforceable. (See the "Introduction and Classification" lesson for discussion of the types of contracts.)

II. **Types of Contracts that Must Be in Writing under the Statute of Frauds**

   A. Guaranty of debt contracts

   B. Contracts involving an interest in real property

   C. Contracts impossible to perform within one year of formation

   D. Contracts for the sale of goods priced at $500 or more

   E. Promises of executors for personal liability for debts of the estate

> **Caution**
> Once again, determine the subject matter of the contract in order to determine which Statute of Frauds provision might apply. If you have goods, only the $500 or more provision applies.

III. **Contracts that Promise to Pay the Debt of Another**

   A. A contract that promises to pay the debt of another must be in writing under the Statute of Frauds:

   1. This requirement does not apply to original promises (i.e., where you borrow money for yourself and agree to repay that money); although such an agreement might be under another provision of the Statute of Frauds—see diagram that follows.

   2. A promise to pay the debt of another is illustrated by the following example that is shown in the triangle diagram: "If PD does not pay and is in default, then I (G) will pay." This is a collateral promise—the party who is promising to pay the debt of another is not the original promisor for the loan.

> **Note**
> If you own a business and are guaranteeing a loan to that business, it is not a promise to pay the debt of another. It is an original promise. For example, if A and B are general partners and A agrees to personally guarantee a loan to the partnership, it is not a promise to pay the debt of another. It is an original promise and need not be in writing. On the exam, this type of problem has appeared, where you are tested not only on your knowledge of the Statute of Frauds but also on your knowledge of individual and personal liability under certain business structures.

> **Definition**
> *Guarantor:* A person who guarantees to pay for someone else's debt if he or she should default on a loan obligation.

Example

Able is a commission agent selling Peter's products. Peter has a rule that his agents only sell to customers for cash. Able knows she can sell more, and thus make more commissions, if she can also sell to customers on credit. Able orally contracts with Peter allowing Able to sell to customers on credit, and if any customer does not pay when due, she agrees she will pay Peter. Some customers who were sold Peter's products on credit fail to pay Peter. Peter demands that Able pay.

Question: Does the Able-Peter contract allowing Able to sell on credit come under the Statute of Frauds?

Answer: Yes. It is a contract (formed by words) between a guarantor (Able) and a creditor (Peter) creating a secondary debt obligation. Able is liable only if customer, the principal debtor, fails to pay. In order to enforce the guaranty by Able, Peter must have a written agreement (record) signed by Able.

IV. Contracts Involving an Interest in Real Property

A. **General Rule**—Any contract involving an interest in real property, to be enforceable, must be in writing (unless one of the exceptions in B, below, applies), including:

   1. Real property purchase contracts

   2. Leases of real property (exceptions in most states apply to leases less than one year in length)

   3. Real property mortgages

   4. Easements

   5. Creation of any other real property interests

   6. Real estate broker contracts

B. **Exception to Writing Requirement for Real Property Rule**—This exception applies when the parties have behaved in such a way and provided evidence beyond their own words that there was some kind of contract relationship between them. The partial performance exception requires the following:

   1. Payment of some part or all of the purchase price has been made.

   2. The buyer in possession of the land by living there (residential) or proceeding to develop it (commercial land); *and*

   3. The buyer has made valuable improvements. In some situations, the possession is simply whatever possession is necessary for making the improvements. Courts are looking for some proof beyond one person's word against another's.

Example

Mary orally contracts to purchase Jim's house and lot. Mary sends Jim a check for 5% of the purchase price, which Jim cashes. The closing (passage of deed and payment) will not take place for two months. Mary's lease has expired, and Mary and Jim agree that Mary can move in to the house and pay Jim a rental payment. Mary moves into the house, plants a number of trees, and adds a deck to the back porch. Just before closing, Jim is offered $20,000 more than Mary's purchase price. Jim tenders return of Mary's down payment and claims the oral contract is unenforceable.

Question: Does this contract come under the Statute of Frauds?

Answer: Yes. A purchase of real property contract is an interest in real property.

Question: Can Jim successfully claim that the oral contract is unenforceable under the Statute of Frauds?

Answer: No. The partial performance rule applies (in all states) because there was a payment, possession, and valuable improvements, which will not allow Jim to use the Statute of Frauds as a defense to the contract.

Question: What if only the payment had been made (no possession or valuable improvement)?

Answer: This exception requires more than just payment to apply. Without more than payment, the exception does not apply.

V. Contracts that Cannot be Performed within One Year of Formation—General Rule

A. Any contract that is objectively impossible to perform within one year from the date of contract formation (date of acceptance) without breaching the terms must be in writing or have written evidence of it to be enforceable.

B. If the contract *could* be performed within one year, it need not be in writing to be enforceable. For example, ABC orally agrees to do an internal controls audit for XYZ Company. ABC does not know how long the audit will take. The oral agreement is valid because the audit could be done in less than a year. However, if ABC accepts a three-year engagement to do internal control audits each year, that contract must be in writing to be enforceable.

C. The one-year mark is measured from the date of acceptance; the time frame is not just the period of performance. For example, suppose Helen agrees to perform a nine-month consulting contract with Framery Inc., to run from June 1, 2011 until March 31, 2012. Helen agrees to do so on February 1, 2011. While the contract term is less than a year, Helen's acceptance is longer than a year out from completed performance so the agreement must be in writing.

D. The Statute of Frauds does not prevent parties who have oral agreements from honoring them. Also, if the parties have behaved as if there is an underlying contract, then the courts will not allow unjust enrichment. In other words, an executory contract that is oral and required to be in writing cannot be enforced. However, if a contract is executed or partially executed, the courts will not punish the parties for falling short of the Statute of Frauds and will require payment, for example, for work already performed. For example, if ABC Corporation hired Bryce to complete a 14-month consulting contract for $140,000 in salary and a $20,000 bonus for on-time completion, the contract should be in writing. However, if Bryce completed the consulting agreement, ABC still would owe the bonus because the contract is executed.

VI. Contracts for the Sale of Goods—Statute of Frauds Rules

A. Any contract for the sale of goods priced at $500 or more must be in writing or record (memorandum), or an applicable exception— UCC 2-201(1)(2)(3).

> **Note**
> You must determine whether the subject matter of the contract is under common law or UCC before you answer questions about whether the contract must be in writing in order to be enforceable. The rules for written contracts are different under UCC and common law.

    1. With the passage of the E-sign law, all states are required to accept electronic and fax communications as evidence of a written agreement.

    2. The writing requirement is now referred to as a "record" because a writing includes the E-sign forms of communication. When these materials use the term "writing" or "written agreement," they are including "record," which can be electronic as in an e-mail, a click agreement, a faxed document, or a PDF agreement.

Caution

Do not mix together the provisions of the Statute of Frauds. The UCC **Statute of Frauds** applies only to contracts for the sale of goods. So, a contract for the purchase of an option in real estate for $450 must be in writing because it is a real property interest. But a contract for the sale of a refrigerator for $450 need not be in writing because it is covered by the UCC. The amount of the purchase price is irrelevant for real property contracts, which are covered under common law **Statute of Frauds** provisions. Under UCC, the amount involved determines whether the contract must be in writing.

B. **Exceptions to the UCC General Statute of Frauds Rule**—UCC-201(2)(3)

1. **Merchant's confirmation memorandum—between merchants (only)**—If two merchants have an oral agreement that must be in writing under the UCC Statute of Frauds, that writing requirement is met through a process referred to as a merchant's confirmation memorandum. If one merchant sends the other merchant a written confirmation, and the other, after receipt, does not object in writing within 10 days, the oral contract is enforceable by either party even though only one party actually signed the memorandum. The memorandum can be given via letter, e-mail, or fax.

Examples

1. ABC is an auto parts store. ABC orders by phone $10,000 worth of parts from Auto Warehouse. Auto Warehouse immediately sends ABC a fax covering the contract made on the telephone. ABC receives the fax and reads it. Twelve days later, ABC learns it can buy all of the parts it ordered from another parts warehouse company for $9,500. ABC calls Auto Warehouse and tells Auto Warehouse not to ship the parts because it is claiming the Statute of Frauds as a defense. ABC and Auto Warehouse have an enforceable contract, even though it is an oral contract, for the sale of goods priced at $500 or more because both parties are merchants and Auto Warehouse sent by fax a written confirmation of the oral contract, which ABC read. Since ABC did not object to the contents of the written confirmation within 10 days of receipt, the oral contract is fully enforceable by Auto Warehouse.

2. S and B have an oral agreement for the sale of 500 pounds of T-bone steak at a price of $7.89 per pound. S sends B 200 pounds of T-bone steak, and B resells the steaks. B is liable for that amount of their agreement (200 × $7.89), but courts will not enforce the remainder of their alleged oral agreement. Likewise, if B sends S a check for 200 pounds of T-bone steaks (200 × $7.89) and S cashes the check, S must deliver 200 pounds of T-bone steak, but the remaining 300 pounds under their alleged oral agreement cannot be enforced.

2. **Specially manufactured goods**—Goods that a seller cannot resell in his/her ordinary course of business are special-ordered goods. An oral contract for special ordered-goods is enforceable if the seller has substantially begun performance, or has made an irrevocable commitment to do so, before the buyer cancels the order claiming the Statute of Frauds. An order for a custom-made suit would be an example.

3. **Admission under oath**—Any admission under oath (deposition, interrogatory, signing of answer, or on the stand during trial) that an oral contract was made removes the Statute of Frauds as a defense.

4. **Performance by buyer**—If the buyer takes possession or makes a payment accepted by the seller, the Statute of Frauds is removed (oral contract enforced), at least to the quantity accepted or paid for.

Examples

1. Green, owner of ABC Television, orally offers to sell Red a TV for $600. Later, Red calls Green and accepts Green's offer. Later still, Red changes his mind and does not wish to buy the TV. Because Red has not signed a written contract for the sale of goods priced at $500 or more, and Red has neither taken possession of nor made a payment for the TV, Red can claim the Statute of Frauds, and Green cannot enforce the oral contract against Red.

2. By telephone, Joan orders 300 backpacks from Bertha's Backpacks at a price of $20 each, to be delivered on the first of each month over the next three months in lots of 100. After Joan sends a check for the first 100 backpacks (which Bertha cashes), Bertha refuses to deliver the backpacks because she says the contract needed to be in writing to be enforceable. The contract can be enforced for the first 100 backpacks. Likewise, if Bertha delivered 100 backpacks and Joan accepted them, she would be required to pay for those 100 backpacks. However, neither situation would allow either party to demand performance for the full 300 backpacks, only for what has been paid for or for what has been delivered and accepted.

VII. Requirements for a Valid Writing/Record of a Contract—A record is tangible evidence of the existence of an oral contract. If the record meets all the standards and includes the necessary information, the requirements of the Statute of Frauds are met.

   A. Signature (authentication) of the party to be held liable on the oral contract.

   B. Exception—Merchant's confirmation memorandum allows one party's signature to bind both parties (both are merchants) to the agreement.

   C. A writing/record need not be in one document or formal. E-mails, letters, and faxes can be grouped together to establish the written/record requirement for a valid contract.

VIII. Interpretation of Terms in Contracts

   A. Meanings of Terms—Terms are assumed to have their ordinary meaning; if technical, their technical meaning.

   B. Ambiguities—Any ambiguity will be construed against the party who drafted the contract.

   C. No Contradictions—Under the UCC (UCC 2-202), a written contract can be explained, but not contradicted, by usage of trade, course of performance, or course of dealing.

IX. Parol Evidence Rule and How It Affects Contracts

   A. The parol evidence rule applies to fully integrated contracts. A fully integrated contract is one that is complete and unambiguous.

   1. Ambiguous terms—If the record of a contract has ambiguities, it is not fully integrated, and parol evidence can be introduced only to clean up the ambiguity.

   2. Obvious clerical or typographical error—In reducing oral contract into a record, parol evidence can be used for obvious typos and clerical errors because, again, it is not fully integrated.

   3. Incomplete contracts—Parol evidence can be admitted to "fill in" the gaps because an incomplete contract is not a fully integrated contract.

   4. Contract defenses—The parol evidence rule does not prohibit the introduction of evidence that shows a defense to formation, such as fraud or duress.

   B. Under the parol evidence rule, a fully integrated contract (one that is complete, unambiguous, and without defenses in formation) cannot be contradicted, varied, or altered by evidence of the parties' prior negotiations, prior agreements, or contemporaneous oral agreements. Once the parties reduce their agreement to a record, they are bound by those terms and cannot use the courts to rewrite their agreement. Without this rule, courts would always be dealing with who said what and when and whether what they said should be part of the contract. Remember the parol evidence rule by thinking, "If what you wanted is not in the contract but promised as an aside in negotiations, you can't bring that up later and expect to get it."

> **Example**
> Tenant leased a commercial warehouse from Landlord for three years. Landlord orally agreed to replace the elevator in the warehouse but did not want to put the replacement clause in their written agreement. Landlord didn't want other tenants to know and begin demanding new elevators. The lease agreement is fully integrated. If Landlord does not replace the elevator, Tenant cannot enforce the agreement because it was not part of the contract.

C. Exceptions to the Parol Evidence Rule

1. **Subsequent modification**—If the parties to a contract later agree to modify their contract, evidence of the modification is admissible. If the modification is required to be in writing, the parties will need that record as proof of the modification.

2. **Defenses to the formation of the contract**—Oral evidence can be introduced to show any of the defenses to formation (covered in the "Defenses to Formation" lesson). For example, if the seller used fraud or mistake or duress to get acceptance by the buyer, then the buyer can have evidence admitted to show that there is no valid contract.

Defenses to Formation

After studying this lesson, you should be able to:

1. Explain what happens when one party has a defense to the formation of a contract.

2. Define "fraud" and "misrepresentation," and explain their effect on a contract.

3. Describe the circumstances that would lead to duress being present in the formation of a contract.

4. Define "undue influence," and explain its effect on a contract.

5. List the defenses to formation of a valid contract.

6. Explain what capacity to form a contract is, and discuss the forms of incapacity. Explain what happens under each type of incapacity when it is present during formation.

7. Explain the two types of contracts that are void, i.e. lack legal purpose and discuss what happens when a contract is void.

8. Describe the types of mistakes and which ones result in a contract being rescinded.

I. **Five Types of Defenses to Formation**—Some actions during the formation stage of a contract result in the creation of defenses to formation of a valid contract. Offer, acceptance, and consideration must occur in a forthright atmosphere in which the parties agreed on a contract based on full and accurate information. If that voluntary and open atmosphere did not exist, there is a defense to the formation. The following are types of defenses that can be used to invalidate the formation of a contract (under both the UCC and common law):

   A. **Mistake**

   B. **Fraud** (also called fraud in the inducement) or misrepresentation

   C. **Duress**

   D. **Undue Influence**

   E. **Illegality**

II. **The Types of Capacity Required for Formation of a Contract**

   A. Each party must be of legal age (minors are limited in the types of valid contracts they can make).

   B. Each party must have the mental capacity to enter into a contract and mental capacity includes being free from a level of intoxication that results in mental incapacity.

III. **Age Capacity Requirement—Minors**

   A. **General Definition of a Minor**—In most states and for most contracts, a minor is any person under the age of 18. A minor is not prohibited by law from entering into contracts, except for contracts that are illegal (e.g., contracts for liquor or cigarettes). However, the law does provide protections for minors who do enter into contracts based on the public policy of protection of those who may not have developed the judgment or experience to enter into fairly negotiated contracts.

   B. **Minor's Right to Disaffirm**—A minor who enters into a contract has the right to disaffirm the contract and avoid liability at any time before reaching majority and for a reasonable time thereafter. The contract is voidable at the minor's option. When a contract is voidable, it can be set aside by one of the parties by choice. If the minor wants to honor the contract, the minor can do so—the contract is not void because a minor is involved. The contract may or may not be performed—at the minor's option.

   C. **How a Minor Disaffirms**—If a minor wishes to avoid liability (disaffirm), the minor must show intent to do so and must return any consideration derived from the contract that the minor still possesses or controls.

D. **Inability to Return Consideration**— The minor does not lose the right to disaffirm despite an inability to return the consideration. If the minor does not possess or control the consideration, the minor still has the right to disaffirm the contract. The minor need only return what he or she still has left of the consideration. If all a minor has left of a car that he or she purchased is a hubcap, the minor can return the hubcap and be entitled to recoup any money paid to the seller. The minor is entitled back any consideration that he or she has paid and cannot be held further on the contract.

E. **Exceptions to the Minor's Right to Disaffirm—Necessities**

   1. To be a contract of necessity, the following criteria must be met:

   a. It must be an item of necessity (e.g., food, clothing, shelter, etc.).

   b. It must be in value of what the minor is accustomed (standard of living).

   c. Minor must not be under the care of a parent or guardian.

   2. If all three criteria are met, the minor may disaffirm the contract but the minor is liable for the reasonable value of the goods used. Note: The contract remains voidable because of the lack of capacity but the courts allow recovery by the seller on the basis of reasonable value, not necessarily the negotiated contract price.

F. **Ratification**—Any minor's contract that is ratified by the minor after reaching the age of majority (now an adult), results in the minor being fully liable.

   1. **Express ratification**—The minor notifies the other party that he or she intends to honor the contract after reaching the age of majority.

   2. **Implied ratification**—The minor continues to perform on the contract beyond reaching the age of majority and what would be a reasonable time for disaffirming.

Example

Able, a minor age 17, is fully supporting his way through college (parents deceased). Able leases an apartment from Sue for one year with rental payments of $400 per month. Able makes five payments, turns 18, and makes one more payment before Able and Sue have a dispute followed by Able turning the apartment back to Sue upon moving. What are the possible claims and results of liability for Able?

Possible Results

If Able can disaffirm (within a reasonable time after becoming 18), Able (by majority rule) is entitled to the return of all six payments made to Sue and has no further liability (remaining six months' rent).

If a court determines that this is a contract for a necessity, Sue can keep the six payments made (reasonable value based on use) but cannot collect for the remaining six months' rent.

IV. The Requirement of Mental Capacity

A. **Mentally Incompetent Persons—General Rule**—Contracts made by a mentally incompetent person, but before a court has adjudged that person incompetent, are voidable by the person (the same as with a minor) during the period of incompetency and for a reasonable time after regaining his or her competency. To avoid liability, however, the mentally incompetent party must be able to return the consideration received under the contract. If the contract is made after the person has been adjudged incompetent by the court, the contract is void (the contract cannot be enforced by either side. A person who is declared incompetent can contract validly only if the contract is entered into by the incompetent's legal guardian, who is appointed at the declaration of incompetency), not voidable. Laws on necessity and ratification on voidable contracts after regaining competency are the same as for a minor.

B. **Intoxicated Persons and Capacity—General Rule**—Any person who becomes intoxicated can avoid any contract (the contract is voidable) made while intoxicated if the intoxication was to such an extent that the person did not understand the binding nature of the contract and did not understand what was actually being conveyed or purchased by the terms of the contract. The person must be so drunk that their state is one of being mentally incompetent (not yet court adjudged) at the time the contract was made in order to have the contract be voidable. Courts are generally stricter on restitution for contracts voidable by intoxication.

V. Types of Mistakes

A. Unilateral Mistake—General Rule—If only one of the parties makes a mistake, the mistake is binding on the mistaken party, unless:

1. The other party knows or should know of the mistake *or*

2. The mistake is material and obvious, as when there is a transposition of numbers, e.g., $501.20 vs. $5012.00. If the mistake is immaterial, e.g., $501.20 vs. $502.10, then the mistake is binding *or*

3. The error was due to a mathematical calculation (addition, subtraction, division, or multiplication) and the mistake was made inadvertently and not through gross negligence.

Example
Jim is going to offer to sell Mary his laptop computer for $550. That evening when Jim is typing up his offer to Mary, he inadvertently types the price at $500 rather than $550. Upon receiving Jim's letter, Mary writes back a simple "I accept" message.

Question: Do Jim and Mary have a contract?

Answer: Yes.

Question: What is the price in the contract?

Answer: Even though Jim intended to sell Mary the laptop computer for $550, he made a unilateral mistake, which Mary did not know had been made. Thus, the mistake falls on Jim and the contract is for $500.

Question: Would your answer be different if Jim had typed $5.50?

Answer: Yes, because here Mary would know Jim had made a mistake and such cannot be held against Jim.

B. Bilateral (Mutual) Mistake—General Rule—If both parties are mistaken and the mistake is one that involves the identity, existence, or quantity of the subject matter, the contract cannot be enforced by either party.

Example
John and Mary have negotiated an agreement for Mary to purchase John's office building for $787,000. Unbeknownst to both of them, the office building (which is located in another city) has burned down following a gas pipe explosion. Both parties are mistaken as to the existence of the subject matter and have the defense of mistake to the contract.

VI. Innocent Misrepresentation

A. Elements

1. Deception about the subject matter of a contract that involves facts or promises of performance.

2. The misrepresentation must be based on fact-based statements, not sales puffing (the use of superlatives to describe products or property).

   a. Expert opinions on the contract subject matter are statements of facts (e.g., an audit opinion or an appraisal).

   b. The opinions of nonexperts are treated in the same manner as puffing, (e.g., a non-accountant who says, "This company's earnings are on track.")

Statements of Fact	Puffing
"These bottles are made of 100% recycled materials."	"These bottles mean you are helping the environment."
"These shirts are 100% cotton."	"These shirts are soft and comfortable."
"You will lose two pounds per week on this diet."	"You will feel and look better on this diet."
"This ranch gets 41 inches of rain per year."	"This ranch gets plenty of water."

3. The deception involves something material: Would the information affect the party's decision to enter into the contract? In all of the above examples, the information is material.

4. One party has relied on the deception. Parties in negotiations are permitted to rely on the factual representations and promises of performance made by the other parties.

B. **Damages**—The basic difference between fraud and innocent misrepresentation is intent and for innocent misrepresentation the remedy is usually limited to rescission.

VII. Fraud (Fraud in the Inducement)

A. **Elements**

1. Just as with misrepresentation, the deception involves a material fact about the contract subject matter.

2. Just as in misrepresentation, one party has relied upon and been deceived by the other party's false representations.

3. Intentional deception is the factor that distinguishes misrepresentation from fraud.

Example
Jill is selling her home to Tanner. Tanner has required a termite inspection as a condition precedent (see the "Performance: Defining Performance and Breach" lesson for more information on conditions precedent) to closing on the purchase of the home. The first termite inspection by AAA Termite, Inc. results in a report that finds termites in the house. Jill does not turn the report over to Tanner; instead, she hires BBB Termite, Inc. to do a second inspection. BBB's report concludes that the house is clean, no termites. Tanner is pleased with the BBB report and closes on the house. Shortly after moving in, Tanner sees what he believes to be termite tracks. Tanner happens to call AAA, and AAA discloses the report. Because Jill withheld the AAA report from Tanner, there is intentional deception, not misrepresentation. The defense of fraud or fraudulent misrepresentation applies here.

If Jill hired BBB first and BBB found no termites even though there were termites, then there would be misrepresentation. Jill did not intend to mislead Tanner; she just hired a company that missed finding the termites.

B. **Damages**—If all three elements are present, the deceived party is entitled to damages (including punitive damages) or can rescind (cancel) the contract. Fraud in formation is one of the few times that punitive damages are available in contract suits.

VIII. Undue Influence

A. Undue influence arises when there is a special relationship, often called a confidential relationship, whereby one party, because of this relationship, can exercise undue influence over the free will of the other in rendering decisions. Examples include lawyer/client; priest/parishioner; child/elderly parent.

B. Undue influence exists when there is a relationship of trust and dependence and one party takes advantage of the other party because of the dependence.

C. Contracts entered into under undue influence are voidable. The party who is unduly influenced is able to set aside the contract if he or she wishes to do so.

Example
A sister, upon whom a disabled brother heavily relies for his care, talks her brother into contracting to sell his only asset, his house, to her at 50% of its market value. This relationship of dependence allowed the sister to overcome her brother's free will and, thus, the brother can set aside this contract or sale.

IX. Duress

A. Duress is a defense when one party in the formation stage is deprived of his or her free will or choice for entering into the contract.

B. Forms of Duress

1. Physical force or threat of physical force (that rise to level of criminal assault or battery) to the party or to their family. When there is this level of duress, the contract is void. The contract cannot be enforced. However, there need not be actual physical force; the threat of physical force still constitutes duress.

2. Threats to disclose private information

3. Economic pressure—if a party does not enter into a contract the other party threatens to ruin his or her business

Example
An employer threatens to fire and have an employee "blacklisted" in an industry the employer controls unless the employee contracts to sell the employer mineral rights to a piece of land the employee has just purchased. This threat of economic sanctions, loss of job, plus not being able to work and apply his or her industry skills to earn a living, is economic duress.

X. Illegality

A. Contracts in Violation of Statutes—Contracts in violation of a statute are void. There may be offer, acceptance, consideration, and capacity, but if the subject matter is illegal, the contract is void, which means that neither side can enforce the agreement.

1. Usury—This means charging a higher interest rate than permitted by law (maximum rate). Contracts for usurious loans are void. The remedy may be the entire contract is void, the interest is void, or the interest charged above the usurious rate is void.

2. Gambling contracts—These contracts are illegal and void but payment of the gambling debt may be only voidable.

3. Licensing statutes—If the purpose of the licensing law is mainly revenue generation, the contract with the unlicensed person may be enforceable. If the purpose is to regulate public welfare (e.g., a doctor or lawyer), the contract with the unlicensed person is null and void.

Example
Real estate agents are required to be licensed in all states in which they are working. Even if an unlicensed agent has a listing agreement in writing, there will be no commission paid nor will the listing contract be enforced by the courts because the licensing statutes are qualification statutes. To allow unlicensed agents to collect commissions would defeat the public purposes of having knowledgeable and trained agents.

B. Contracts Contrary to Public Policy—Contracts may be void not because they violate a statute but rather because enforcing them would undermine public policy goals and standards.

1. Unconscionable contracts or clauses in consumer contracts.

Example
A consumer credit contract under which the consumer is never able to repay the seller for the goods because the payments are spread among all the contracts instead of paying off the debt one item at a time to provide the consumer with some paid-off debts. It would be unconscionable to impose such a credit payment standard.

2. **Exculpatory clauses**—A clause in a contract, that disclaims any liability regardless of fault.

Example
A clause in a sale of goods contract that eliminates all liability for personal injuries caused by a product is void.

3. **Contracts in restraint of trade**—Covenants-not-to-compete.

   a. A covenant-not-to-compete is enforceable if it is:

      i. Ancillary—a part of a larger contract *and*

      ii. Reasonable in restraint in length of time and geographic scope

Example
Charles contracts to sell his Italian restaurant to Susan. In the contract is a clause that prohibits Charles from starting an Italian restaurant in the city for six months. This is probably an enforceable covenant-not-to-compete because it is ancillary—part of the sale of business contract and the restraint is reasonable in length and geographic scope.

   b. A covenant that is too broad in time or geographic scope can be modified by the court so as to make it valid. For example, five years can be reduced to 18 months and a covenant covering an entire state can be changed to a particular county. Often called "blue penciling," the court draws its limitations in order to protect the need for some form of restriction. Blue penciling saves an overly broad covenant-not-to-compete and gets rid of its illegality.

Performance: Defining Performance and Breach

After studying this lesson, you should be able to:

1. Explain the doctrine of substantial performance and how it discharges performance.

2. List the circumstances under which the obligations of performance under a contract are discharged and how discharge occurs.

I. **When Is Performance Due?** A contract is a legal obligation to perform a given promise. However, implied in every contract are certain conditions that must transpire for performance to occur. Likewise, the duty to perform can be discharged if other conditions occur. The presence or absence of conditions controls the duty to perform the promises under a contract.

   A. **Types of Conditions for Performance**

   1. **Precedent**—A precedent condition is something that must be present or occur before a party has a duty to perform.

   Example
   Jane signs a contract for the purchase of her first home. The condition precedent for the purchase is that she must qualify for a home mortgage loan at a rate not to exceed 6%. If Jane cannot secure financing, the condition precedent is not met and Jane is not required to perform under the contract.

   2. **Subsequent—A condition subsequent is something that must be present or occur after a duty to perform has arisen.** This condition subsequent must be present in order to hold a party liable on the contract, i.e., required to complete the contract duties.

   Example
   A fire policy has a provision, that requires the policyholder to submit a proof of loss by filing with the insurer, within 60 days after the fire, in order for the policyholder to recover for the fire loss. The requirement of the filing of a proof of loss after the fire to receive payment for the fire loss covered by the policy is a condition subsequent. If the condition subsequent of filing a proof of loss (also known as a proof of claim) is not met, then the insurer is discharged of its duty to perform, i.e., pay the insured for the loss.

   3. **Concurrent**—Each party's duty to perform under a contract is dependent upon the other party's absolute duty to perform at the same time. All contracts have some form of condition concurrent.

   Example
   A buyer of oranges promises to pay for the oranges only upon seller's delivery. The seller's duty to deliver is conditioned upon the buyer's tender or payment, and buyer's duty to tender or pay is conditioned upon seller's tender or delivery of the oranges.
   You also do the same thing when you are checking out at the grocery store. You and the store have conditions concurrent of payment and the store bagging the groceries for you to take with you as it passes title. (See the lesson on "Passage of Title and Risk of Loss" for more information on the passage of title.)

   B. **Discharge of Duty to Perform**—When is your duty to perform under a contract discharged? There are several types of actions, events, and legal provisions that provide a discharge for your contract duties.

   1. **Discharge by failure of conditions**—If the condition precedent does not occur, then the duty to perform is discharged.

Examples

1. DTR public accounting firm agrees to perform an audit of the Xanadu Publishing House, Inc. within six months of the signing of the engagement letter. An implied condition precedent is Xanadu giving DTR access to its records so that DTR can conduct the audit. If Xanadu never provides access to those records, DTR's duty to perform never arises because it cannot complete an audit without access to records and the ability to question employees. DTR would be discharged from its obligations under the audit agreement for the failure of the condition precedent.

2. If an author failed to complete a manuscript by the deadline provided in the publishing agreement, the author would be in breach of contract. However, the publisher must file suit within the statute of limitations (generally four years for breach of contract) in order to recover the advance paid to the author under the contract for the manuscript. If the publisher does not file suit within the four years, then the author's duty to return the advance is discharged.

2. **Discharge under the UCC**—Assurances and problems between contracting and performing

   a. At times, problems arise between the time the parties have their contractual obligations related to purchase and sale of goods and the actual delivery of the goods (performance of the contract). Article 2 has specific rights and steps for the parties during this interim period.

   b. **Heading off nonperformance with assurances**—The goal of Article 2 is to have the parties do all that is possible to get the contract performance completed. To do that, both buyers and sellers have the right of assurance and the duty of cooperation.

      i. Right of assurance—If a party has "reasonable grounds" to believe that the other party will not perform as contracted, he or she may demand in writing that the other party give adequate assurance of due performance—UCC 2-609. If the party does not provide reasonable assurance as demanded within 30 days, this failure is a repudiation of the contract and can be treated as an anticipatory breach.

         a. Once a party is entitled to and demands reasonable assurance, that party can suspend performance without liability until he or she receives the assurance requested.

         b. Reasonable grounds for insecurity depend on the facts. Between-merchants commercial standards may be used.

         c. The actions of assurance that can be requested also depend on the facts, and, again, between-merchants commercial standards can be used.

Example

Smith Inc. has contracted to buy a specific piece of equipment from ABC. Smith believes that if it runs this piece of equipment at a certain speed, it will increase Smith's productivity by 5%. Smith learns from another buyer (Green) who has previously purchased a similar piece of equipment from ABC that, although Green seldom ran the equipment at that speed, whenever Green did do so, the equipment broke down. ABC's literature had indicated the equipment could be run at a variety of speeds including the speed Smith anticipated running the equipment.

Question:
Is Green's experience sufficient (reasonable) grounds for Smith to believe that ABC's equipment will not perform as contracted?

Answer:
Most probably, yes.

Question:
What can Smith do before the equipment is delivered?

Answer:
In writing, ask for reasonable assurances that the equipment will perform as contracted and for protection if it does not.

Question:
What are reasonable requests for assurance that Smith could seek?

Answer:
Smith could ask for express warranties, money-back guaranty, or, perhaps, even replacement equipment if such is available. The point is that ABC must satisfy Smith's insecurity, as long as it is reasonable.

Example
Smith has two contracts with ABC. One is to sell ABC 100 washing machines with delivery on May 1 with ABC's payment to be made on or before June 1. The second is to sell ABC 100 dryers with delivery on July 1 with ABC's payment to be made on or before August 1. The washers are timely delivered and accepted by ABC. On June 15, Smith still has not been paid despite two phone calls requesting payment. Smith has reasonable grounds to ask for some assurance for payment of the dryers to be delivered on July 1. Smith, in writing, can demand reasonable assurance (perhaps the washing machine payment plus some other dryer payment, such as cash on delivery). Pending ABC's assurance, Smith can suspend the delivery of the dryers without liability and, if assurance is not forthcoming within 30 days, treat the dryer contract (washer contract already breached) as breached.

II. UCC Performance—Rights to determine performance

A. Determining Performance under the UCC—Inspection—Upon delivery of the goods, the buyer has the right of inspection.

    1. Unless agreed to the contrary or provided under Article 2 (i.e., a C.O.D. shipment does not allow buyers the right of inspection before payment), a buyer has a right, before paying for the goods, to inspect the goods at any reasonable time, place, or manner— UCC 2-513.

    2. Inspection need not be immediate. The buyer may receive the goods on a busy Friday afternoon and is not required to inspect them at that time—the buyer would have a reasonable time (at least through Monday) to conduct the inspection.

    3. Inspection allows the buyer to open boxes, examine goods, and even conduct tests to see if the goods meet the buyer's needs that were specified in the contract.

    4. On COD deliveries, the buyer must pay before the carrier will turn over the goods, but the buyer does not lose the right of inspection. The COD payment does not waive that right. However, the seller will have the buyer's money, and COD makes it more difficult to get the seller to correct any problems. The buyer, however, does not accept by making the payment on a COD delivery.

B. Determining Performance under the UCC—Right of rejection

    1. Under Article 2, the seller has an obligation to deliver goods that conform to the contract specifications. This requirement is sometimes called the "perfect tender rule."

    2. If the seller delivers goods that fall short of the contract requirements in any way (the shortfall need not be material because the perfect tender rule requires 100% compliance with the contract terms, including the correct goods, the correct color, and the correct amount), then the buyer has the following options:

        a. Reject the entire shipment;

        b. Accept the entire shipment; *or*

    c. Accept any commercial unit and reject the rest. A commercial unit is determined by industry practices and custom for the particular good involved in the contract. For example, candy is often shipped in bags of one gross—144 pieces. The buyer would reject a shipment of candy by the bag, not by individual pieces of candy. The purpose of rejection in commercial unit is to reduce confusion with partial packages and the breaking up of units.

Example

Seller's contract calls for delivery of 100 cases of carrots. Seller tenders to the buyer 200 cases of carrots, a nonconforming goods tender. The buyer could reject the entire 200 cases, accept the 200 cases paying for the additional 100 cases, or accept 100 cases and reject the other 100 cases.

---

    3. For information on the seller's obligations for delivery and proper contract for carriage, refer to the "Passage of Title and Risk of Loss" lesson.

C. **Determining UCC Performance—Buyer's Responsibilities for Rejection of Nonconforming Goods**—UCC 2-601

    1. To reject and pursue remedies, the purchaser must do so properly:

        a. Rejection must be within a reasonable time after tender of or delivery—UCC 2-602.

        b. Rejection is not effective until known by seller—UCC 2-602.

        c. Specific reasons for rejection should be given. If not given, buyer cannot pursue remedies if seller could have cured, or if seller made a request in writing for a written statement of reasons—UCC 2-605.

        d. If buyer has possession of the nonconforming goods, the buyer must act as a bailee (use reasonable care over the goods)—UCC 2-602. If buyer is a merchant, buyer must follow any of seller's reasonable instructions at seller's cost (buyer's reimbursement) concerning the disposition of the nonconforming goods—UCC 2-603.

        e. If the goods are perishable or threaten to rapidly decline in value, buyer must make a reasonable effort to sell, and he or she is entitled to reimbursement for all costs in caring for and selling the goods, plus a 10% sales commission, out of the proceeds of the sale—UCC 2-603.

        f. If seller does not give buyer instructions (and the goods are not perishable or rapidly declining in value), buyer can store the goods for seller's account (storage charge), reship back at seller's expense, or sell the goods deducting costs and sales commission from the proceeds—UCC 2-604.

D. **UCC Performance—Seller's Rights upon Rejection**

    1. The reason that the buyer is required to follow certain steps in rejecting goods is because Article 2 provides sellers with the opportunity to fix or "cure" the problems that the buyer has found upon inspection of the goods.

    2. **Fixing nonperformance—right to cure**—A seller who tenders nonconforming goods may still have the ability to cure and not be in breach of contract. Sometimes there is a casualty, partially or completely, to identified goods, or the seller is able to perform once the seller is made aware of the error.

        a. **Cure—UCC 2-508**

            i. If a seller tenders delivery of nonconforming goods prior to the contract date, and buyer rejects the goods, the seller can, with notice, indicate an intent to cure (i.e., fix whatever problem the buyer has pointed out as the reason for rejection). The seller always has until the time that contract performance is due to get conforming goods to the buyer who has rejected the initial delivery.

Example

Contract terms call for the seller to deliver, on or before June 1, 100 model Z washing machines. On May 16, the seller tenders 100 model A washing machines, and the buyer rejects the shipment. The buyer sends the seller a fax stating that the seller made an error and the nonconforming shipment has been rejected. The seller immediately sends the buyer a fax apologizing for the error and tells the buyer that a corrected shipment will be made in two days. The seller has now shown an intent to cure and if the washing machines are delivered before June 1, the seller is not liable for breach of contract.

    ii. Sometimes the seller tenders nonconforming goods to the buyer, but it is a tender that a reasonable buyer would be expected to accept (does not require a money allowance, but frequently this is the case). If the buyer rejects the reasonable tender, the seller, with notice of intent to cure, can tender conforming goods to the buyer within a reasonable period (even if after the contracted date of delivery) without being in breach.

Example

Contract terms call for seller's delivery of 100 model Z tape recorders at $800 per unit on or before June 1. On May 25, seller discovers that, due to a computer error, seller does not have 100 model Z tape recorders in stock but does have model A tape recorders, which sell for $950 per unit. On May 29, sellers tenders 100 model A tape recorders but only invoices buyer at $825 per unit price. Because of budget limitations, buyer rejects the model A tape recorders. If the seller notifies buyer that a corrected shipment will be made and such is tendered within a reasonable time (even after June 1), seller has made a cure of the contract delivery, is not in breach, and buyer must accept and pay for the goods.

E. UCC Performance—Substituted Performance—UCC 2-614(1)

    1. If, without fault of the seller, the agreed facilities or type of contract carrier is not available or delivery is impractical but a commercially reasonable substitute carrier is available, seller must use substitute carrier and buyer must accept delivery and pay. (Usually, any additional costs incurred by buyer must be borne by the seller.)

Example

Contract terms call for shipment via ABC Truck Lines. ABC Truck employees are on strike and no other drivers will cross the picket line. If XYZ Railroad is available and a reasonable substitute, seller must ship by this rail carrier and such shipment is not a breach of contract.

F. UCC—When Is There Acceptance or Actual Performance?

    1. Acceptance occurs under UCC 2-606 when any of the following have occurred:

        a. After opportunity to inspect the goods, buyer notifies seller either that the goods are conforming or that buyer will accept even if nonconforming goods. Payment for the goods in and of itself is not acceptance

        b. If buyer fails to reject the goods after inspection or after a reasonable opportunity to do so

        c. Buyer engages in any act that is inconsistent with seller's ownership (such as knowingly using nonconforming goods)

2. When can a buyer revoke acceptance?

   a. Under the following conditions, a buyer can revoke his or her previous acceptance—UCC 2-608:

      i. Buyer was given reasonable assurance seller would cure a nonconforming shipment, and cure has not taken place.

Example

A buyer orders 100 barrels of Brand 52 cleaning solvent. The seller delivers Brand 50 cleaning solvent, a weaker but still usable solvent. The seller tells the buyer to use what it can of the Brand 50 solvent and an immediate corrected Brand 52 shipment (cure) will be made. The buyer's use of the Brand 50 cleaning solvent is technically an acceptance. If, however, the seller does not immediately deliver the corrected Brand 52 solvent, the buyer can revoke his or her acceptance and hold the seller liable for breach (same as if the original nonconforming shipment had been rejected).

      ii. Seller has assured buyer that goods are conforming, and it is later discovered that goods are nonconforming.

Example

A buyer orders 20 cardboard boxes of red pens. Each cardboard box has 100 small boxes with a dozen pens in each. The cardboard boxes arrive with the words "Green Pens" on each cardboard box. Without opening the boxes, the buyer calls the seller and tells the seller of the "Green Pen" notation. The seller assures the buyer that the labeling is a mistake and inside the cardboard boxes are red pens. The buyer stores the cardboard boxes and pays the seller for the pens. When the buyer opens the cardboard boxes six months later, the buyer discovers that there are, in fact, only green pens inside, not the red pens that the seller had assured the buyer. In this case, the buyer can revoke the acceptance.

3. The nonconformity was difficult to detect.

Example

Buyer purchases a backup generator. Buyer has no facility to test the generator and stores it. Six months later, the original generator malfunctions, and when the backup generator is placed into service, buyer discovers it is defective. Buyer can revoke its earlier acceptance of the generator.

4. Revocation timing—Revocation must take place within a reasonable time of discovery or time in which the buyer should have discovered the defect, and revocation is not effective until the seller has notice of it.

Performance: Discharge of Performance

After studying this lesson, you should be able to:

1. Describe how performance is completed.

2. List the circumstances under which the obligations of performance under a contract are discharged and how discharge occurs.

I. **Discharge of Duty to Perform**—When is your duty to perform under a contract discharged? Several types of actions, events, and legal provisions provide a discharge for your contract duties.

 A. **Discharge by Failure of Conditions**—If the condition precedent does not occur, then the duty to perform is discharged.

 Examples

 1. DTR public accounting firm agrees to perform an audit of the Xanadu Publishing House, Inc. within six months of the signing of the engagement letter. An implied condition precedent is Xanadu giving DTR access to its records so that DTR can conduct the audit. If Xanadu never provides access to those records, DTR's duty to perform never arises because it cannot complete an audit without access to records and the ability to question employees. DTR would be discharged from its obligations under the audit agreement for the failure of the condition precedent.

 2. If an author failed to complete a manuscript by the deadline provided in the publishing agreement, the author would be in breach of contract. However, the publisher must file suit within the statute of limitations (generally four years for breach of contract) in order to recover the advance paid to the author under the contract for the manuscript. If the publisher does not file suit within the four years, then the author's duty to return the advance is discharged.

 B. **Discharge by Agreement or Party Action**

 1. **Release**—A release is a discharge of a party's obligations under a contract. A release usually must be in writing; it must be given voluntarily and in good faith; and it usually requires consideration.

 2. **Waiver**—A waiver by the nonbreaching party is a relinquishment of rights related to the other party to a contract and his or her breach.

 3. **Mutual rescission**—A mutual rescission is an enforceable mutual agreement to discharge all contract obligations and restore the parties to their precontract positions.

 Example
Able contracts with you to sell her accounting book for $70. Later, both of you change your mind about the sale, and you both agree to cancel the contract. This is mutual rescission. If you already paid the $70, then Able must return to you the $70 paid upon agreement of mutual rescission.

 C. **Discharge by Novation**—By agreement between the original parties to a contract and through a valid subsequent contract, a new party is substituted for one of the original parties, thereby discharging the duties of the parties under the original contract.

 Example
Son Able will not be able to pay the debt on a loan from West Bank when it comes due. Able's mother, Sue Able, and West Bank agree that if West Bank will release Son Able and provide a 30-day extension, Sue will pay the loan. In this novation, Son Able is discharged (released) from the loan, terminating the old contract, and a new contract is created by substituting Sue as the debtor. Notice that all parties must agree to a novation—the original parties to the agreement as well as the new third party who is being substituted through the novation.

D. Discharge by Accord and Satisfaction—This is an agreement whereby the original contract can be satisfied either by completion of the original performance or by a different performance. (See also the "Consideration" lesson.)

Example
Green owes you $5,000 due on May 1. On April 20, Green tells you he is not sure he can pay you the $5,000 but, if not, offers to deed to you a lot Green owns. You agree (which is the accord). On May 1, Green can satisfy the debt by either paying you $5,000 or by transfer of the deed to the lot.

E. Discharge by Operation of Law

1. **Statute of limitations**—If a suit for breach of contract is not filed in a court of law or equity within a statutory period of time, the nonbreaching party is barred from pursuing a remedy. This effectively discharges the contract. The statutory periods of time vary from state to state and depend on the type of contract. For the sale of goods, it is a four-year period from date of cause of action, but this period can be reduced to one year by agreement (see UCC 2-725). The time period for the statute of limitations starts when the cause of action arises. For example, the statute of limitations on a sales contract would run from the time the seller failed to deliver the goods.

2. **Bankruptcy decree**—Most obligations of a bankrupt debtor can be fully discharged by a decree in bankruptcy. (See the "Prebankruptcy Options and Introduction to Bankruptcy" and "Bankruptcy Process" lessons for more information on dischargeable and nondischargeable debts.)

3. **Discharge by impossibility or impracticability of performance**—This type of discharge of performance occurs when it has become objectively impossible for the contract obligations to be completed.

4. **Discharge by death or insanity** of the contract is an automatic discharge of the contract.

Example
For $500, Able contracts with Sue to sing at her party on Friday. On Thursday, Able dies. Because one party is no longer alive, this contract is objectively impossible to perform, discharging the contract.

5. **Discharge by destruction of the specific subject matter** of the contract is an automatic discharge of the contract.

Example
Able contracts to sell you her boat *Flying Cloud*. Before she can deliver the boat specified, the boat is destroyed through no fault of Able. This contract is automatically discharged at the time of destruction.

6. **Discharge by illegality**—If legal changes occur that now render the contract illegal, the contract is automatically discharged upon the change in the law.

Example
You have a contract with Able to build an apartment complex on your lot. Before construction, but after the contract has been formed, laws are changed so that only single residences may be built.

7. **Discharge by commercial impracticability**—For the UCC doctrine of commercial impracticability to apply, the failed performance must meet an objective standard and not be merely more difficult to perform. Extreme difficulty or cost may meet the objective standard test.

Examples

1. Able contracts to move hazardous waste 10 miles through a city to a hazardous waste site for $50 per load ($5 per mile). The city now prohibits hazardous waste to travel through the city. The only other safe route to the site is around a series of mountains for a distance of 300 miles. The new cost to travel far exceeds the contracted price per load. This contract would probably now be rendered commercially impractical.

2. Able has a contract to sell peanuts to Planter's Inc. Able's peanut crop is destroyed. There are peanuts available on the open market, but buying the peanuts would cost Able much more than the price Planter's is paying. The additional cost would not be commercial impracticability because, objectively, peanuts are available to satisfy the contract. Able could get around such an issue by contracting to sell the output from his peanut farm. If the crop is destroyed, it is objectively impossible for him to sell his output, and his duty would be discharged.

F. Discharge by Performance

1. Each party has completed the obligations negotiated under the terms of the contract. With some contracts, performance is easily determined: The seller either delivered the food for the catered lunch or did not. With other contracts, the complexity of the contract or the time required makes performance a more difficult question.

Example

Able contracts to sell Baker his car for $2,000. Able delivers his car to Baker, and Baker gives Able $2,000. The fully performed contract discharges both parties. A contract is automatically discharged when both parties fully perform.

2. **Doctrine of substantial performance**—Some contracts are complex in terms of determining whether performance has occurred, such as in the construction of a home. There can be variations from the contract, and the builder can still be paid as long as there is substantial performance. "Substantial performance" means that any deviation from the terms was done in good faith and for practical purposes (i.e., whatever was substituted is just as good as the original plan).

Example

Specifications for the building of a house call for Kohler plumbing fixtures. The contractor installs American Standard, a comparable-value fixture. Unless the contract payment was conditioned on installation of only Kohler plumbing fixtures, the specification is a promise and the installation of a comparable fixture is substantial performance rather than a material breach.

3. **Contracts that require personal satisfaction**—If a condition is precedent, it requires the actual satisfaction or approval for discharge of the contract.

Examples

1. The President of the United States hires you as an artist to paint his or her official portrait to his or her personal satisfaction. This is a condition. Any real dissatisfaction causes a failure of the condition and no liability for the president.

2. Smith is hired to clean the lobby of an office building to the personal satisfaction of the building manager. This is merely a promise for satisfaction, and a reasonable person test would be used to see if substantial performance had been achieved. If so, there is no material breach even if the building manager claims dissatisfaction.

4. **Discharge by material breach**—If one party has materially breached the contract, the other side is no longer obligated to perform and the other party's duties under the contract are discharged. A material breach is one in which the nonbreaching party's circumstances are affected by the other party's breach. For example, an airline catering firm that fails to deliver meals on time for flights has materially breached that supply contract because there is no way to obtain other sources of food in those circumstances.

5. **Discharge by Anticipatory Repudiation**—If one party indicates that it will not perform on the contract in advance of the performance date, the other party is excused from further performance. The non-breaching party can wait until the due date for performance, the party can bring suit for breach, and/or find substitute performance.

Passage of Title and Risk of Loss

After studying this lesson, you should be able to:

1. List and define all the terms used in shipping goods.

2. Describe when title passes from the seller to the buyer.

3. Explain why passage of title is a significant event in a sales-of-goods transactions.

4. Describe when risk of loss passes from the seller to the buyer.

5. Explain why passage of risk of loss is significant to both buyers and sellers.

6. Discuss the rights of third parties in title.

I. General Background on Title and Risk of Loss

A. Title and risk of loss under UCC Article 2 have very detailed and nuanced rules.

> **Misconception**
> In the sale of goods, title and risk of loss always pass at the same time. This statement is incorrect because (1) the parties can expressly determine the exact moment when title and risk of loss pass and the two can differ; and (2) even in absence of agreement, UCC Article 2 has rules that can have title and risk of loss pass at the same time in one situation and at different times in another situation.

B. Passage of title is found in **UCC 2-401**. Passage of risk of loss is found in **UCC 2-509**.

II. Identification—Prerequisite to passage of title and risk of loss

A. Before any interest in goods (title or risk of loss) can pass from a seller to a buyer, the goods must be in **existence** and **identified** to the contract—UCC 2-105(2).

B. General Rule on Identification—For goods in existence at the time the contract is entered into, identification occurs at the time the parties enter into the contract. If, for example, you are buying goods that have to be altered, they are not technically in existence at the time of the contract. A suit that you are having altered is not in existence at the time of the contracting. Once the goods are in existence, that is, alterations for you have been completed, then title can pass because the goods are identified.

C. Fungible Goods—Fungible goods are those that either cannot be distinguished because of homogenous qualities or are so mixed together that they cannot be distinguished by individual units (e.g., grains, fruit, cases of canned goods). Identification occurs when the goods are shipped, marked, or otherwise designated for the buyer (i.e., set aside in the warehouse). (See the "Remedies" lesson to also understand how identification is important in determining the remedies available to buyer and seller in cases of manufactured and fungible goods.)

D. Future Goods—For goods to be manufactured, such as when a company is manufacturing rocking chairs for a furniture store, identification occurs when those rocking chairs are shipped, marked, or otherwise designated for the buyer.

Examples

1. Green has 1,000 cases of peas in the warehouse, and Beyer has contracted to purchase 100 cases. Since the goods are fungible, the 100 cases must be identified (marked or separated from the mass) before title or risk of loss can pass.

2. Green and Smith have deposited wheat in a silo. Green's deposit is 5,000 bushels and Smith's deposit is 10,000 bushels. Smith sells 2,000 bushels to Beyer. The wheat is fungible (mixture of like kind goods with intent to become tenant-in-common owners) and is identified under the contract when it is shipped, marked, or otherwise designated for Beyer. Until then the risk remains with the sellers, Green and Smith. If the wheat were destroyed, the loss would be prorated based on ownership (pro rata shares).

Exam Tip
This is a key issue on the exam. First determine whether there are shipment terms in the language the exam provides for you, then determine risk of loss and title. Many questions in the past have focused on the distinction in passage of title and risk of loss in shipment vs. non-shipment contracts.

E. Once goods are in existence and identified, title and risk of loss can pass at the time the parties **expressly agree** or, if there is no agreement, they pass according to UCC Article 2 rules (covered in the following section).

III. **Delivery Terms**—How and when risk of loss and title pass depend on the shipping/delivery terms in a contract.

A. **FOB—(free on board)**—Place of shipment (seller's city, business, or warehouse, or "ship point."). Title and risk of loss pass upon **delivery (possession) of conforming goods to the carrier**—UCC 2-319(1)(a), 2-509(1)(a).

Example
Seller contracts to sell 100 personal laptop computers to Buyer at a given price with the FOB being the seller's warehouse via ABC Truck Lines. Until ABC Truck Lines picks up the 100 laptop computers, risk is on the seller. Once ABC Truck Lines has possession of the 100 laptop computers, the risk of loss is on the buyer.

B. **FAS (Free Alongside Vessel)**—Place of shipment. Title and risk of loss pass on seller's delivery of conforming goods alongside the vessel in the manner usual in that port or on a dock designated and provided by the buyer—UCC 2-319(2).

C. **CIF (Cost, Insurance, Freight)**—Title and risk of loss pass from seller to buyer when the seller delivers (possession) identified conforming goods to the carrier, obtains a negotiable bill(s) of lading covering transportation to a named destination, procures an insurance policy, and forwards to buyer all documents—UCC 2-320(2)(a).

D. **C&F (Cost and Freight)**—This follows the same rule as in CIF, except procurement of an insurance policy is not required on seller's part.

E. **COD (Cash on Delivery)**—This term requires the buyer to pay cash upon tender of the goods. If goods are shipped COD, then the timing of the buyer's right to inspection is affected (see **the** "Performance" lesson).

IV. **Passage of Title—REMEMBER**—When title passes is important for purposes of determining the rights of third parties with respect to the buyer and seller. For example, suppose that the IRS is about to levy a lien on the buyer's property. If the buyer has a contract that is FOB place of shipment and the goods are in transit, the IRS can seize the goods. If, however, the contract was FOB place of destination, title to the goods still rests with the seller during transit. The IRS cannot seize the goods from the seller's warehouse or from the carrier. Title does not pass until the goods are tendered at their destination.

A. Determine whether the contract is a delivery (shipment) or non-delivery (non-shipment) contract.

> **Note**
> *You must be sure that identification has occurred regardless of whether the contract is delivery or nondelivery. Without identification, title cannot pass.*

   1. In the absence of an agreement, delivery is at the seller's place of business or, if the seller has none, at the seller's residence. In other words, without an agreement, no delivery is provided for under Article 2.

   2. Passage of title occurs at different times depending on whether the contract is nondelivery or delivery.

B. Passage of Title in Nondelivery (Nonshipment) Contracts

   1. Determine whether there is a document of title involved with the goods and the contract.

   2. If there is no document of title, title passes at the moment the contract is made. Note that in nonshipment contracts for goods, identification and passage of title occur at the same time.

   3. If there is a document of title, and the document of title is nonnegotiable, then title passes to buyer upon buyer's receipt of the document—UCC 2-401(3)(a).

   4. If there is a document of title, and the document of title is negotiable, then title passes to the buyer upon the buyer's receipt of the document—UCC 2-401(3)(a), 2-509(2)(a).

C. Passage of Title in Delivery (Shipment) Contracts

   1. If delivery is FOB place of shipment or FOB seller's place of business, warehouse, or residence, then title passes at the time and place of shipments or when the goods are delivered to the carrier.

   2. If delivery is FOB place of destination or FOB buyer's city, business, warehouse, or residence, then title passes upon the seller's tender of conforming goods at place of contract destination—UCC 2-509(1)(b).

       a. Tender is the key—A proper tender is the seller's holding out to the buyer the goods in a reasonable manner, for a reasonable time, to allow the buyer to take possession of the goods—UCC 2-503(1). "Tender" means the goods have arrived, they are available for the buyer to pick up, and the buyer has been notified that the goods are there and available for pickup.

> **Examples**
>
> **1.** Bradford, a buyer in Norfolk, owes $210,000 to the IRS. The IRS has obtained a lien that allows it to seize any real and personal property owned by Bradford. Sanford, a seller from Los Angeles, has agreed to ship 100 cases of plastic travel bottles to Bradford. The shipment term is FOB Norfolk. The 100 cases of plastic travel bottles have arrived at the loading dock at Norfolk, and Bradford's receiving department has been notified. The IRS seizes the 100 cases of travel bottles from the loading dock. Bradford objects on the grounds that the bottles still belong to Sanford, that title has not yet passed, and that the IRS could not seize the goods. Bradford is incorrect. The 100 cases had been tendered and title passed to Bradford. The IRS could seize the goods.
>
> **2.** Change the situation a bit to understand FOB place of shipment. Suppose that Sanford is the party subject to an IRS lien and Sanford is shipping the 100 cases to Bradford under an FOB Los Angeles contract. The IRS seizes the 100 cases at Norfolk. This time Sanford objects, claiming it was too late for the IRS to seize the goods. Sanford is correct. Title passed to Bradford when the goods were delivered to the carrier in Los Angeles. The IRS could not seize the 100 cases as property belonging to Sanford because title had already passed.

D. Delivery "Ex-Ship"—Title and risk of loss do not pass until the ship arrives at a port of destination and not until the goods leave the ship's "tackle" or are otherwise properly unloaded. This is the converse of a delivery FAS, previously described—UCC 2-322.

E.   Delivery—If a contract merely calls for the seller to deliver at the buyer's destination and there are no other delivery terms, title passes from the seller to the buyer upon tender of conforming goods at buyer's destination—UCC 2-509(1)(b).

V.   Passage of Risk of Loss

A.   Remember—The goods must be identified or risk of loss cannot pass.

B.   Passage of Risk of Loss in Nondelivery Contracts

   1.   Determine whether the contract is a delivery or nondelivery contract. Unless the parties provide for shipment/delivery, there is no delivery provided under Article 2.

   2.   Determine whether the seller is a merchant or nonmerchant.

   a.   If seller is a merchant, risk of loss does not pass until buyer actually gets possession. For example, when you buy a sofa at The Room Store but agree to pick it up yourself, you do not assume the risk of loss until that sofa is in the back of your pickup truck.

   b.   If seller is a nonmerchant, risk of loss passes upon seller's tender of the goods to the buyer. If you buy a sofa at a garage sale and leave to go get your truck to pick it up, the risk of loss has already passed to you. If the sofa is destroyed while you are procuring your truck, you absorb the loss.

   3.   REMEMBER—In most cases the determination of risk of loss is important because it controls which of the parties' insurers will be responsible for reimbursement for the loss.

C.   Passage of Risk of Loss when There is Delivery (Shipment Contract)

   1.   If delivery is FOB place of shipment (or ship point) or FOB seller's place of business, warehouse, or residence, then the risk of loss passes at the time the goods are delivered to the carrier.

   2.   If delivery is FOB place of destination or FOB buyer's place of business, warehouse, or residence, then the risk of loss passes at the time of tender.

D.   Passage of Risk of Loss when There is a Negotiable Document of Title and No Delivery—Risk of loss passes to the buyer upon the buyer's receipt of the document—UCC 2-401(3)(a).

Example
Able Corp. sells 500 boxes of copy paper to Green company. The 500 boxes were shipped to the Fox Warehouse Co. earlier, and Fox issued to Able a negotiable warehouse receipt representing the 500 boxes. Able indorses and delivers the warehouse receipt to Green at 4:00pm on Friday. During the weekend, the warehouse burns down and the 500 boxes are completely destroyed. Green suffers the loss because risk of loss passed to Green upon Green's receipt of the negotiable document of title.

E.   Passage of Risk of Loss when There is no Delivery and a Nonnegotiable Document of Title—Risk of loss passes to buyer after receipt of the document and buyer has had a reasonable time to present the document, to receive the goods, or to give directions to the bailee.

Example
Able Corp. sells 500 boxes of copier paper to Green Company. The 500 boxes were shipped to the Fox Warehouse Co. earlier, and Fox issued a nonnegotiable warehouse receipt representing the 500 boxes. The warehouse is only open Monday through Friday from 7:30 am to 4:30 pm On Friday at 4:00 pm, Able delivers the warehouse receipt to Green. Over the weekend, the Fox warehouse burns down, and the 500 boxes are completely destroyed. Able suffers the loss because, although Green had title, risk of loss would not pass until Green has had a reasonable time to present the document to Fox or to give directions to the bailee Fox. Most courts would hold that 30 minutes is not a reasonable length of time and the risk of loss over the weekend was still with Able.

F. Passage of Risk of Loss when the Goods are Held by a Third Party (Bailee, Warehouseman, Someone Other than Seller) and There is No Document of Title—Risk of loss passes to the buyer when the bailee acknowledges the buyer's right to the possession of the goods. The risk of loss, in effect, passes upon the equivalent of tender by the warehouseman.

> **Example**
> Seller contracts to deliver 1,000 cases of beans to the buyer FOB buyer's warehouse. The beans are shipped by ABC Truck Lines. The truck arrives at buyer's warehouse at 1:00 pm on Monday. Buyer cannot unload the truck until Tuesday morning and asks the carrier to leave the truck at the buyer's warehouse dock until it is unloaded in two hours on Tuesday morning. Carrier agrees. During the night, through no fault of the buyer, the beans are destroyed by fire. The risk of loss has passed to the buyer, and the buyer must pay the seller for the beans. This is a destination delivery contract, and the seller's tender by the carrier began at 1:00 pm on Monday. This was a holding out to the buyer in a reasonable manner and, certainly, if the truck could be unloaded in two hours, the load was held out (the entire afternoon) for a reasonable time to enable buyer to take possession. Risk passed to the buyer Monday afternoon.

G. Summary of Rules on Passage of Title and Risk of Loss

Delivery Situations	Delivery Terms	Law
Delivery by shipment	Ship, FOB origin or seller's place of business—FAS, CIF, C&F	Title and risk of loss pass to buyer upon carrier's **possession** of conforming goods.
Delivery to destination	Deliver, FOB buyer's place of business—delivery exship	Title and risk of loss pass to buyer upon **tender** of conforming goods to the buyer.
Delivery by seller without physical movement of the goods	Delivery without a document of title	Title passes to buyer upon **formation** of the **contract**. Risk of loss passes to the buyer (a) upon the buyer's **receipt** of the goods if the seller is a merchant or (b) upon the seller's **tender** of the goods if the seller is a nonmerchant.
	Delivery with a document of title—nonnegotiable document	Title passes upon buyer's **receipt** of the document. Risk of loss passes to buyer after buyer receives the document **and a reasonable time has lapsed**.
	Delivery with a document of title—negotiable document	Title **and** risk of loss pass upon buyer's **receipt** of the document.

VI. Effect of Breach on the Passage of Title and Risk of Loss (Nonconforming Goods)

A. If goods are nonconforming due to **seller's breach** and the buyer has a right to reject the goods, risk of loss does not pass to the buyer until the defects are cured or buyer accepts goods despite their nonconformity—UCC 2-510 (1). The buyer does not hold the risk of loss for nonconforming goods in his/her possession or for their return to the seller.

B. In addition, if the goods are accepted and acceptance is revoked, risk of loss goes back to the seller to the extent that the buyer's insurance did not cover the loss—UCC 2-510 (2).

C. If the **breach is due to fault of the buyer** and risk has not passed, risk shifts immediately to the buyer for a commercially reasonable period after seller learns of the breach, but only to the extent not covered by seller's insurance—UCC 2-510 (3).

D. Breach affects risk of loss, but not title. Title passes according to the rules **despite** the breach.

VII. Special Issues in Title and Risk of Loss

    A. Sale on Approval—Until the buyer accepts the goods, **title and risk of loss remain with seller**. Cost of proper return (rejection of offer) falls on the seller—UCC 2-327 (1). Buyer can accept by:

        1. Due notification ("I accept")

        2. Failure to reject within the time of trial period (keeps goods beyond trial period)

        3. Doing any act inconsistent with seller's ownership. (Buyer takes home lawn mower to try it out for two weeks. During the two weeks, buyer mows 15 yards for fees.)

    B. Sale or Return—An actual sale with title, risk of loss, and possession with the buyer subject to the condition that buyer can restore title and risk upon the seller by a proper return of the goods. Cost of return is on the buyer. Failure to timely return finalizes the sale—UCC 2-327(2). The UCC treats a consignment as a sale or return.

VIII. Third-Party Rights and Title

    A. Article 2 has special provisions to deal with situations in which a third party is affected by title issues related to the conduct of the original parties to the contract (i.e., when there is some problem with perfect title as it relates to a third party).

    B. The problems result from there being an innocent third party known as a bona fide purchaser (BFP) for value, defined by Karl Llwelyn (the main author of the UCC) as "a pure heart and an empty head." In third-party right issues, who has the best title: the original owner or the BFP?

    C. Rights of a BFP when Void Title Has Been Transferred—A void title cannot be passed to anyone. The original owner has the best title—UCC 2-403 (1).

Example
Thomas, a thief, steals your bicycle and sells it to Smith. Smith has no knowledge that Thomas is not the owner or that the bike has been stolen. You discover Smith has the bike. You are entitled to return of your bicycle from Smith because Thomas had a void title (no title) to pass to Smith. Smith, however, can legally recover from Thomas if Smith can find Thomas.

    D. Rights of a BFP when There Is a Voidable Title—A title, that even though passed to a buyer, can be recovered. There is one exception—if the buyer in turn passes title to a BFP— UCC 2-403(1).

Example
Mary is a minor who contracts to sell her bicycle to an adult, Jim, for $250. Mary transfers the bicycle and title to Jim. Since Mary is a minor, Jim receives a voidable title, and Mary can disaffirm the sale and recover her bicycle. If Jim sells the bicycle to Judy (a BFP for value) before Mary disaffirms the sale, Mary can still disaffirm the contract with Jim but cannot recover the bicycle from Judy. Judy's title is absolute and cuts off Mary's voidable title.

IX. Rights of a BFP with Entrusting of Goods

    A. Entrusting of goods to a **merchant** (person who deals in goods of that kind) by a buyer gives the merchant the power to transfer all rights (including title) to a buyer in the ordinary course of business—UCC 2-403(2)(3).

> **Example**
>
> Harry took his TV set to ABC TV Inc. for repairs. ABC sells both used and new TVs. The set is repaired but, by mistake, is sold to a customer of ABC without knowledge of Harry's ownership rights. Since ABC is a merchant (in the business of selling used TVs), ABC passed good title to Harry's set to the customer, and Harry cannot recover the set from the customer. ABC has committed a tort of conversion, however, and is liable to Harry in a civil suit.

B. When entrusting goods to a **nonmerchant**, delivery is a mere bailment. Unless the original owner has given some indicia of ownership to the bailee to lead a buyer to believe that the bailee either is the owner or has authority to sell, there can be no passage of title (treat as a void title).

Remedies

Types of Remedies

After studying this lesson, you should be able to:

1. List the types of remedies available under common law and UCC.

2. Discuss when the types of remedies are available.

3. Discuss the limits of the types of remedies.

I. **Remedies for Breach**

A. **Types of Remedies**

1. **Damages**—Monetary recovery

a. **Nominal**—There is a breach but no financial loss has been suffered. Court awards a nominal amount ($1 or some other small amount).

b. **Compensatory**—These are all costs or loss actually suffered and proved caused by the breach.

c. **Incidental damages**—Incidental expenses are incurred by the nonbreaching party due to the breach and would include things such as lawyer's fees for recovering for the breach. (See UCC 2-715(1).)

d. **Consequential damages**—These include any foreseeable loss known by the breaching party (UCC 2-715(2)). These types of damages include penalties for delay in performing a contract because a party has been tardy in delivering goods or performance on a contract. To recover consequential damages, the breaching party must be aware that time is of the essence in the performance of the contract.

> **Examples**
>
> 1. Able contracts to purchase 100 transmissions for $40,000 from Sallar Inc. The transmissions are to be installed in custom-made recreational vehicles to be driven in the mountains. Delivery is to be on or before May 1. On April 20, Sallar tells Able that Sallar cannot deliver on time. Able immediately, with notice to Sallar, purchases the transmissions from Green Inc. on the open market at a price of $42,000. Able can collect from Sallar all expenses incurred in the making of the new contract, such as additional shipping charges and those incurred from Sallar's breach, such as delays in his work, and the actual increase in price of $2,000.
>
> 2. Able contracts with Sallor Inc. to deliver on or before May 1 parts for a special oil field valve that Able is making for Oiltax. Able's contract with Sallor specifically states "time is of the essence" and "any delay in our production and delivery will result in Able paying Oiltax liquidated damages of $1,000 per day." Sallor does not deliver on time, and by the time that Able can purchase the parts elsewhere, the delivery to Oiltax is five days late. Here Able can recover from Sallor not only all expenses and the increased parts price purchase costs but also the foreseeable liquidated damages ($5,000) caused by Sallor's breach.

e. **Punitive damages**—Damages awarded to punish a wrongdoer. Punitive damages are rarely given in breach of contract cases, with the example often used on the exam being in the case of fraud in the inducement in formation of the contract. (See "Defenses to Formation" for more information on this topic.)

f. **Liquidated damages**—The parties agree in their contract that a specific sum is to be paid in the event that the contract is breached. Liquidated damage provisions are enforceable as long as (a) at the time of formation of the contract, it is apparent that damages would be difficult to estimate in the event of breach, and (b) the amount stated is a reasonable sum estimate. The provision cannot be constituted as a penalty. (See UCC 2-718.)

Example

Able has agreed to construct a 100-unit apartment complex for Green. The completion date is agreed to be May 1 or earlier. Since Green will be preleasing the apartments with one-year leases to begin on May 1, it is agreed to include a liquidated damage clause to cover breach of lease actions and costs incurred in housing by the affected tenants if the apartments are not completed on time. The liquidated damage amount is based on average occupancy for new apartment buildings when first available in the community, and the estimate that at least 70% of the tenants would require substitute housing and storage. This is broken down on a daily basis to create the liquidated damage amount per day for late construction. This clause probably would be enforceable because of the difficulty in estimating damages and the reasonable amount per day.

B. Mitigation of Damages—When a breach takes place, the law usually imposes on the nonbreaching party the duty to take actions to mitigate (reduce) the amount of damages owed. Some states require such in breach of real estate lease cases.

Example

Able has a one-year lease with Green for $1,000 per month. After six months, Able breaches the lease and abandons the property. If mitigation is required, Green must use reasonable means to find and lease the property to a suitable tenant. Able is still liable for any difference and, if no tenant can be found, for the balance of the lease.

C. Remedies in Equity

1. **Specific performance**—Requiring the other party to perform the contract; available when there are rare goods (antiques) or for buyers of land (land is unique).

    a. If the object of the contract is unique and damages are inappropriate as a remedy, by court order, the nonbreaching party (usually a buyer) can force the breaching party to perform the contract. This is not applicable to personal service contracts.

Example

Able contracts to sell his lake lot to Green for $10,000. Able now has a better offer and refuses to deed the lot to Green. Because land is unique (no two parcels have the same legal description) and damages would hardly satisfy Green, who wants the lot, specific performance is an appropriate remedy.

2. **Rescission and restitution**—In rescission, the parties, in effect, go back to their corners and are restored to the same positions they were in before the contract was entered into. (See discussion of misrepresentation in the "Defenses to Formation" lesson for more information).

    a. Rescission is the undoing of a contract to return the parties to their original position. Generally, both parties must make restitution (i.e., returning anything each has received). As a remedy, this is where one party is in breach and the nonbreaching party with notice rescinds the contracts. (Remember that in mutual rescission, there is no breach but discharge of the contract.) The breaching party must restore the nonbreaching party to his or her original position, but the nonbreaching party cannot retain the benefits that he or she has received as unjust enrichment.

3. **Reformation**—A contract rewritten to address an issue that affects the parties. Reformation is used by the court to correct an imperfectly expressed contract. It is applied most often to correct clerical errors and errors in reducing a valid oral contract into a written form, or to make a covenant-not-to-compete reasonable in time or area—all to reflect the true intentions of the parties.

4. **Quasi-contract recovery**—Remedy given when there is no contract. (See the discussion of types of contracts in the "Introduction and Classification" lesson.) It is a remedy to give a reasonable value benefit to one party and avoid an unjust enrichment received by the other party.

> **Example**
> Able has a one-year $50,000 employment contract with Green. The contract contains an option to cancel clause "at any time," which renders the one-year contract unenforceable because of a lack of consideration. Able works for 15 days and is dismissed for no reason. Although there was no one-year contract for $50,000, Able has given Green valuable services. Green must pay Able a sum equal to the reasonable (market) value of those services. Not to be required to do so would give Green an unjust benefit.

Formulas for Damages

After studying this lesson, you should be able to:

1. List the types of remedies available for breach of contract.

2. List the types of damages and explain when they are available for recovery.

I. **UCC Remedies—Sellers**

A. **Identify Goods to the Contract**—The seller can set aside the goods for the contract. If the seller is still in the process of manufacturing the goods when the buyer repudiates the contract or fails to respond to assurances, the seller can proceed to complete the manufacturing and resell the finished product rather than sell the unfinished goods as scrap (UCC 2-704). The seller can then proceed with the other remedies discussed below.

B. **Withhold Delivery**—If the buyer has repudiated the contract, failed to provide assurances, or is insolvent, the seller can demand full payment in cash and withhold delivery if the assurances or payment are not given—UCC 2-702, 2-703(a). The seller can then proceed with the other remedies discussed below.

C. **Cancel and/or Rescind Contract**—If the buyer is not performing or has failed to provide assurances, the seller can cancel or rescind the contract. The seller must notify buyer of cancellation promptly and either proceed with remedies below or, if rescission is chosen, seller is entitled to be indemnified to return to the original position before the contract was made—UCC 2-703(f).

   1. Returning to the original position in cases of cancelations may require that the seller be given lost profits—the amount that the seller could have made had the goods been manufactured and sold. This remedy is available because the seller set aside its factory time for production.

   2. These are special UCC remedies.

D. **Resell Goods**

   1. The sale must be conducted in a reasonably commercial manner (public or private sale).

   2. The seller must always give the buyer notice of private and public sale (except for perishable or rapidly declining value goods).

   3. The sale must be conducted at a reasonable time and place.

   4. If the goods are specially manufactured and cannot be resold, the seller's remedy is the full contract price.

> **Note**
> **Important:** *Any profit goes to seller, but if there is a deficiency (proceeds of sale do not cover breach and sales costs plus contract price), seller is entitled to the amount not obtained through sale (i.e., to obtain a deficiency judgment against the buyer)—UCC 2-706.*

E. **Sue for Breach of Contract**—Used mostly if breach takes place before delivery or buyer improperly rejects goods.

   1. Measure of damages is difference between market price at time and place of tender and the unpaid contract price plus incidental (costs of breach) damages—UCC 2-708.

   2. The statute of limitations for bringing suit for breach of contract under the UCC is four years from the time the breach occurs. The parties can agree to a period of less than four years, but cannot agree to have less than a one-year statute of limitations.

   3. For breach of warranty, the statute of limitations begins to run when the goods are tendered to the buyer.

F. **Retain Buyer's Deposit**—Where the seller justifiably withholds delivery of goods and the buyer has made a deposit or payment and there is no liquidated damage clause, the seller may keep $500 or 20% of the purchase price, whichever is less.

G. **Remedies for Seller if Goods Are in Transit**—Neither seller nor buyer has possession—UCC 2-705.

1. **If buyer is insolvent** (not paying debts when due or in ordinary course of business, or insolvent under the Bankruptcy Act), the seller (upon buyer's repudiation) can stop any quantity shipped and can also recover goods from the buyer within 10 days after delivery. In addition, if the buyer misrepresents solvency within 90 days prior to delivery of goods on credit, there are no time limits on the seller's ability to recover the goods. Note that the rights for the seller to reclaim the goods when there is insolvency continue through delivery to the buyer (with the time limitations noted for insolvency events).

> **Example**
> Stratford sold 300 flat-screen TVs to Kelvinator Appliance on a line of credit. There were rumors in the retail appliance industry that Kelvinator was struggling financially. Stratford demanded assurances from Kelvinator that it would be able to pay for the TVs. Kelvinator sent an audited financial statement to Stratford on September 1 that indicated Kelvinator was in good financial condition and had a steady cash flow. Stratford shipped the 300 TVs to Kelvinator on October 1. While the TVs were in transit, Kelvinator filed for bankruptcy (on October 14). Stratford would occupy a position of priority above Kelvinator's secured creditors because of the misrepresentation of solvency, even though the goods would be reclaimed after 10 days. There is no time limit on a seller's right to reclaim the goods when there is a misrepresentation of solvency.

2. **If the buyer is not insolvent**—The seller can stop large shipments (carloads, truckloads, planeloads of goods). While we allow sellers to stop any size shipment for insolvency (to prevent having the seller lose the goods when there can be no payment), we only allow stoppage of large shipments for other reasons because large shipments are easier to track and stop. Stopping any size shipment for any reason would result in a slowing of commerce.

> **Note**
> *This detailed concept, on insolvency and the recovery of goods, has been tested on the exam a number of times. See the "Distribution of Debtor's Estate" lesson for further illustrations of this priority of sellers.*

> **Example**
> Contract calls for seller's delivery of five cases of peas to buyer's place of business. The five cases are loaded on ABC Truck carrier's truck. The truck is also hauling products from five other sellers. Buyer repudiates the contract claiming that seller's peas are of poor quality. Seller cannot stop the goods in transit because buyer's repudiation is not due to insolvency and the shipment (five cases) is not a truckload.

3. Seller can **stop shipment** at any time (under the insolvency and repudiation rules just discussed). Until buyer actually takes possession of the goods, there is a negotiation to buyer of a negotiable document of title or notification by a third party such as a warehouseman or carrier (see the "Passage of Title and Risk of Loss" lesson for more information) to the buyer that the goods are available for pickup.

H. **Remedies for Seller if the Buyer Has Possession**

1. If buyer received the goods on credit while insolvent, seller may reclaim the goods within 10 days of receipt by buyer. Remember, if there has been misrepresentation of insolvency, then the 10-day time limitation does not apply.

2. Seller can seek to recover damages noted—the compensatory damages of the contract purchase price plus any incidental damages incurred because of the buyer's failure to pay.

II. **UCC Remedies: Buyer**

A. **Remedies when the Seller Fails to Deliver the Goods**

1. **Cancel and rescind with notice**—The contract is rescinded by the buyer with the effect of restoring both buyer and seller back to the positions they would have been before entering the contract—UCC 2-711.

2. **Cover**—Permits the buyer to make a reasonable substitute purchase (e.g., on the open market) in good faith and within a reasonable time. The buyer can then recover the difference between the cost of cover and the contract price plus incidental damages (costs of breach) and consequential damages (foreseeable loss) less expenses saved in consequence of the seller's breach—UCC 2-712. (See the "Remedies" lesson in the "Contracts" section for discussion of incidental and consequential damages.)

3. **Sue for breach of contract**—The buyer can treat the nondelivery as a breach of contract and pursue a lawsuit to recover damages. The damages can include the difference between the market price at the time that the buyer learned of the breach (this time is changed to place of tender if goods are rejected or time of revocation of acceptance and at place of arrival) and contract price plus incidental and consequential damages—UCC 2-713.

4. **Specific performance**—Available when the goods are unique, or in other proper circumstances such as where the remedy to cover is not available (e.g., rare goods, antiques). Specific performance is available for land under common law but is rare under UCC Article 2. Rarely will specific performance be granted where damages are appropriate as a remedy—UCC 2-716.

Example

Seller agrees to sell to buyer an original painting by Picasso. Later, seller refuses to deliver the painting even though buyer has tendered fully the contract price. Buyer can in a court in equity file an action for specific performance (painting is unique—one of a kind) requiring the seller to transfer the painting to buyer.

5. **Replevin**—If seller refuses to tender delivery of identified goods to the buyer, and the buyer cannot cover, the buyer can file a suit in equity requiring the seller to deliver the goods to the buyer—UCC 2-716(3). Replevin is also rare and would occur in those types of contracts where cover is not possible.

B. **Remedies for Buyers if the Seller Tenders Nonconforming Goods—(Buyer Rejects)**

1. Some remedies that are available to buyers in the case of seller nondelivery are also available to buyers when sellers ship nonconforming goods, including:

   a. Cancellation

   b. Cover (*cover* means that the buyer goes out and finds substitute goods for what the seller failed to deliver or as a substitute for the wrong goods the seller delivered. If the seller was to deliver three-speed blenders, the buyer can go out and purchase substitute blenders to cover the breach by the seller. If all the buyer can find in the short time afforded for cover is five-speed blenders, that would be considered reasonable cover).

   c. Treat as breach of contract and pursue suit for damages

   d. Replevin possible for substituting for goods that are damaged or not delivered if the goods meet the equitable standards of uniqueness

2. Seek substitute goods (cover) for those damaged or nonconforming goods that have been rejected.

3. Buyer may also keep the goods and recover damages for the value of the goods as delivered and as they should have been (i.e., seller has delivered nonconforming goods); a price reduction for damages is typical.

   a. **If buyer accepts nonconforming goods**—The buyer can with notice pursue the following remedies (notice is important because failure to give notice bars buyer from any remedies)—UCC 2-607(3)(a).

      i. **Recover ordinary damages**—Incurred in the ordinary course of business and in a proper case receive incidental and consequential damages—UCC 2-714(1).

ii. **Recover for breach of warranty**—Buyer can recover the difference between the value of the goods accepted and the value the goods would have been, had they been as warranted (unless special circumstances show proximate damages of a different amount) plus, if appropriate, incidental and consequential damages—UCC 2-714(2).

Example

An accounting firm purchases a computer warranted to be a $40,000 value for $30,000. Upon delivery, the computer (although usable) is found to be worth only $20,000 due to a defect. Unless special circumstances would show proximate damages of a different amount, the buyer should recover $20,000, the difference between the value as warranted, $40,000, and the value of the computer as delivered, $20,000.

iii. **Deduction of damages from purchase price (the "self-help" remedy)**—Buyer can deduct all or any part of the damages from the price still due and payable to the seller—UCC 2-717. Buyer should note clearly to seller that the amount tendered is in "Full Accord and Satisfaction" or "Payment in Full," and seller's acceptance of the deducted amount is full satisfaction of the debt.

Example

Buyer has contracted for 10 new file cabinets priced at $300 each. The new file cabinets are tendered but two are scratched, though still fully usable. With notice, Buyer can accept all 10 file cabinets and tender to the seller a check for $2,900 ($50 per scratched cabinet deduction to cover refinishing costs) and a letter, indicating clearly on both the check and the letter that the check is intended as final payment and it is in full accord and satisfaction of the contract price. If Seller cashes the check, Buyer has fully paid and has no further liability.

4. **Liquidated damages**—The parties by agreement in the contract can predetermine the amount of damages in case of a future breach. The amount must be reasonable in anticipation of what the actual loss would be. This is useful if there would be difficulties in the proof of loss and other adequate remedies probably would not be available. If the court holds the amount to be a penalty, the liquidated damage provision is void. If valid, the parties are limited to the liquidated damages stated— UCC 2-718.

Example

Seller agrees to deliver certain inventory to Buyer, knowing that failure to deliver on time could result in Buyer having to shut down or limit production at its factory. Seller and Buyer agree that for every day Seller delays in making delivery, it will cost Buyer a loss of somewhere between $4,000 and $8,000. The contract contains a liquidated damage clause of $5,000 per day for each day's late delivery. This is a liquidated damage clause and is valid because it appears to be a reasonable amount in expectation of Buyer's loss, the proof of loss would be difficult to ascertain, and no other adequate remedy would be available.

5. **Buyer can seek recovery of payment**—If buyer makes a payment and seller is or becomes insolvent within 10 days of receipt of the payment and the goods are identified (see "Passage of Title and Risk of Loss" lesson), then buyer can tender the balance owed and is entitled to the goods—UCC 2-502.

Third-Party Rights

After studying this lesson, you should be able to:

1. Explain the requirements for creating a valid assignment and/or delegation.

2. Describe the rights of the parties in an assignment and/or delegation.

3. Define a third-party beneficiary relationship.

4. List the types of third-party beneficiary relationships and explain the rights of the parties.

5. List and give examples of the types of third-party contractual relationships.

I. **General Rule**—Unless a party is in privity (a party thereto) of contract, that party (called a third party) has no enforceable rights to or obligations under the contract. However, contract law does provide for certain types of third-party relationships that do give rights under the contract to third parties.

II. **Assignments and Delegations**

    A. **Terminology**

        1. **Rights**—Rights (or the benefits under a contract) can be assigned. For example, a contractor who owes money to Home Depot can assign his payment from a customer to Home Depot so that he can pay off his Home Depot bill. (See the "Consideration" lesson for discussion of benefits.)

        2. **Duties**—Duties are the detriment under a contract, and they can be delegated. For example, XYZ Corporation may be getting out of the business of home dry-cleaning pickup and delivery, but it still has contracts with 45 customers. XYZ can delegate the duties to ABC Company, a small local dry cleaner, to complete performance under the contracts. (See the "Consideration" lesson for discussion of both benefit and detriment as elements of consideration.)

        3. **Assignment and delegation parties**

            a. **Assignor**—Party (usually one of the original contracting parties) who makes the assignment (the contractor in the above example)

            b. **Assignee**—Party to whom rights are assigned (Home Depot in the above example)

            c. **Delegator**—Party who makes the delegation (XYZ Company in the above example)

            d. **Delegatee**—Party to whom the duties are delegated (ABC Company in the above example)

            e. **Obligor**—Name given to party in the contract for the party's detriment; every party to a contract has an obligation—the duty to perform; in a contract for the sale of a car, the buyer is the obligor for payment and the seller is the obligor for delivery of the car

            f. **Obligee**—Name given to party in the contract for the party's benefit; every party to a contract has a benefit; in a contract for the sale of a car, the buyer is the obligee for the car and the seller is the obligee for the money to be paid for the car

    B. **Assignments**

        1. Any right can be assigned or delegated unless an exception applies.

        2. The assignment of rights is a contract separate from the original agreement.

3. **Assignment exceptions**

    a. **Prohibited by contract terms (anti-assignment clause).**

Example
In a typical term lease, the lease contract terms do not allow the tenant to assign the lease without the landlord's consent. Most fire insurance policies prohibit assignment of the policy without the insurer's consent, but the policyholder can assign a money claim for a loss sustained covered by the policy.

    b. **Prohibited by statute**

Example
Future Social Security or workers' compensation benefits, in many states future wages, and some rights that are intended only for a particular person, such as alimony or child support, are not assignable by statute.

    c. **Prohibited by personal contracts**—Contracts unique to the person receiving services.

Example
You contract to tutor Green's children after observing them. Green assigns her right to your services to Hope for the tutoring of her children. This assignment is prohibited without your consent because Hope's children may have different needs or temperaments.

    d. **Prohibited due to increased material risks to the obligor**

Example
Green owns a restaurant and has a fire insurance policy (contract) with ABC Insure. Green cannot assign the policy to Able to cover a restaurant that Able owns on the other side of the city without ABC Insure's consent. The reason is that ABC Insure's policy was made based on risks assumed on ABC's evaluation of Green's circumstances. Able's circumstances and resulting risks could be quite different and thus could substantially increase ABC's risks.

C. **Delegations**—Duties under a contract can be delegated unless

    1. **Contract terms prohibit delegation**

Example
Green wants to have her products locally delivered to her customers' front porches. Any local delivery carrier can make these deliveries. Green contracts with ABC Del Inc. to make her deliveries and places in the contract that the contract cannot be delegated to any other carrier. This clause prohibits delegation.

    2. **Contract is based on the personal skill of the obligor (personal services contracts)**—Or a special trust has been placed in the obligor.

Example
You hire a famous heart specialist to perform a heart transplant. This doctor cannot delegate the surgery to any other doctor—even one with equal skills—because your contract was made dependent upon this doctor's skill and the trust that you have placed in him or her.

3. **Contract performance will materially vary from that expected by obligee**

Example
Green contracts with Smith to clean a surface by use of sandblasting. Green delegates the duty to Able who specializes in cleaning the same type of surface with hot water. Even though the result is the same, Green's expectation of sandblasting is materially different from that of hot water.

D. **Rights of the Parties upon Assignment—(Applies Equally to Delegation)**

1. An assignee (delegate) can acquire no better rights than those possessed by the assignor (delegator) (but can acquire lesser rights); the third party steps into the shoes of the original contracting party.

2. An assignment is not binding on the other party to the contract until the obligor has notice of the assignment:

   a. Between two assignees to the same contract, the one with the most rights is the one who

      i. Is first in time of assignment (U.S. rule) *or*

      ii. Is first to give notice of the assignment (English rule).

   b. Until given notice, the original party to the contract can discharge the contract by completing performance to the assignor.

Examples
1. John owes Jane $100. Jane assigns her right to the money to Sam. Until John has notice of the assignment, John can discharge his obligation by payment to Jane. If John has notice, John can only discharge the debt by payment to Sam. If Jane had also assigned, the next day after her assignment to Sam, the payment to Mary, and Mary gave John notice, as between Sam and Mary's priority, it depends on whether the U.S. rule (Sam gets priority by first in time) or the English rule (Mary gets priority by first to give notice) applies.

2. Jane has her mortgage through Fourth Second Bank. Fourth Second Bank assigns Jane's mortgage to CDO Mortgage Company. Neither Fourth Second Bank nor CDO Mortgage notifies Jane of the assignment. Jane continues to pay Fourth Second Bank. Jane has completed her monthly obligations by continuing to pay Fourth Second, and she is not required to pay CDO Mortgage until she knows of the assignment.

3. Any defenses that the original contracting party had now belong to the third-party assignee (delegate). Likewise, any defenses waived by the original party to the contract remained waived with respect to the third party.

Example
ABC Appliance store contracts to sell Jones a TV, Model X, for $1,450. Jones, through fraud, gives ABC false credit information. ABC is to make delivery at the end of the week on Friday. On Wednesday, ABC discovers that it had sold its last Model X TV earlier. ABC assigns its contract for delivery and sale to XYZ Appliance who has Model X TVs in stock. On Thursday, ABC learns of the fraud and notifies XYZ. ABC's defense of fraud (avoid the contract) is also a defense available to XYZ, which does not have to deliver the TV set to Jones.

4. An assignment does not waive or eliminate the contract rights of the original party to the contract. Unless released, the assignor remains liable to the other contracting party. If the assignee (delegatee) fails to perform the obligations under the contract, the assignor (obligor) is still responsible.

Caution: The only way an assignor can be released is if the original party to the contract agrees to a release. A novation is required to substitute parties to a contract. A novation requires the assent of both original parties to the contract as well as the assent of the substituted party. This concept of novation is often tested on the exam.

Example
Assume a tenant is allowed to assign the balance of a five-year lease with a landlord to an assignee. Unless the assignor (tenant) is released by the landlord, the assignor is still liable for any default by the assignee. Therefore, if the new tenant fails to pay rent, the original tenant remains liable for it. If, however, the landlord and tenant execute a novation, the assignee is substituted under the lease and the tenant is released from liability. A novation requires that all three parties agree to the substitution and release of the assignor (the original tenant).

III. Third-Party Beneficiary Contracts

A. Types of Third-Party Beneficiaries

1. **Donee (intended) beneficiary**—The contract must be made for the direct benefit of the beneficiary and the donee's rights must be given in the contract (i.e., the donee beneficiary has a legal right to what is given by the two parties to the contract).

Example
You contract with ABC Life Insurance Company for a $25,000 policy on your life with your spouse as the named beneficiary. The named beneficiary has no rights in the policy until you are dead. At that time, the life insurance company must honor its contract with you by paying the benefits according to the terms of your policy. Both the named beneficiary and your estate have the right to enforce the agreement against the insurance company upon your death. However, the beneficiary would not have the right to recover from your estate if the life insurance company did not pay.

2. **Creditor beneficiary**—There must be a debtor-creditor relationship, and the debtor must make a contract that befits the creditor with a third person.

Examples
1. ABC is the mortgagee (creditor/mortgage lender) on a home owned by Green (debtor). Green contracts to sell the home to Able (third person), with Able agreeing to assume the mortgage (become personally liable to make payments to ABC). Although ABC is not a party to the purchase contract, ABC is a creditor beneficiary and can enforce mortgage payments against Able. Creditor beneficiaries can enforce their rights against both parties to the contract.

2. You have a medical insurance policy and require emergency room treatment at a hospital. The hospital is a creditor beneficiary of your insurance policy because you owe the hospital for the emergency room treatment even if your insurance does not pay. The hospital has the right to bring suit to collect from either the insurance company or you because the hospital is one of your creditors.

3. **Incidental beneficiary**—A third party who receives an unintended benefit has no legal rights in a contract between two parties.

> **Example**
> A contractor has a contract with the city to build a swimming pool in a small neighborhood park. The swimming pool will increase the value of the homes in the neighborhood. The contractor breaches the contract. The city decides not to sue. The homeowners wish to file suits against the contractor as a beneficiary of the contractor-city contract. Since the homeowners are only incidental beneficiaries, they have no legal rights in the contractor-city contract. Incidental beneficiaries have no rights of enforcement against either party to the original contract.

Debtor-Creditor Relationships

Rights, Duties, and Liabilities of Debtors, Creditors, and Guarantors

Suretyship—Introduction, Creation, and Types

After studying this lesson, you should be able to:

1. Explain the type of surety and guaranty relationships and their purpose.

2. Describe the rights of co-sureties, and show how their shares of liability in the event of a default are computed.

3. Define all the terminology used for the rights of the parties in a surety relationship.

4. Define and distinguish the guarantor of collection.

5. Describe how a surety relationship is created.

I. **Introduction**

   A. **Definitions and Terms**

      1. A guarantor or a surety is someone who agrees to stand liable for a debt of another. A guaranty or suretyship is a way for a creditor to have another form of backup for payment of the obligation owed. A surety or guarantor can be in addition to any collateral the debtor might pledge to the creditor.

   B. **The Parties**

      1. Creditor

      2. Principal debtor

      3. Surety or guarantor

 Example
A surety or guarantor is liable to the creditor for the debt of the principal debtor. Frank owes money to June. Dallan agrees to serve as a surety for Frank. Frank is the principal debtor. June is the creditor, and Dallan is the surety or guarantor.

   C. In a straight surety or guaranty relationship, the surety or guarantor must pay the creditor when the debt is due (unless there has been a discharge of the debt). The creditor can turn to the surety or guarantor for payment.

   D. In a guarantor of collection relationship, the guarantor is responsible for the debt only after the principal debtor has defaulted because the guarantor is secondarily liable. A guarantor of collection does not pay until the creditor has exhausted other options for collection from the debtor. A release of a debtor from the debt obligation can create a discharge when there is a guarantor of collection vs. a surety (See "Suretyship—Rights of Parties and the Discharge and Reaffirmation Agreements" lesson.)

Exam Tip
The exam tends to use the terms "surety" and "suretyship" when dealing with most issues related to this topic. For the most part, the exam is testing the straight surety relationship. The exam has moved away from using the terms "guaranty" and "guarantor." If the terms "guarantor" and "guaranty" are used alone (with no qualifying language), then they equate with surety and suretyship. If the exam is addressing an issue related to the differing order of liability for a guarantor of collection, the term "guarantor of collection" is used. The exam uses this approach to avoid confusion regarding use of the term "guarantor." Most questions use only the terms "suretyship," "surety," and "co-surety."

II. Creation

A. Because the suretyship relationship is one in which a third party agrees to stand liable for the debt of another, the suretyship contract (or a written memo) must be in writing and signed by the surety (guarantor) for it to be enforceable against the surety.

B. **Consideration Is Not Required**—A surety relationship is created even when the surety is not compensated. However, certain differing rights result when there is a compensated vs. an uncompensated surety (See the "Suretyship—Rights of Parties" lesson).

C. **Creation of a Multiple Surety Relationship**

1. Creditors can request that the debtor provide more than one surety.

2. Creditors can ask for a subsurety. A subsurety is a surety for the surety, a party who agrees to be liable to the creditor if the principal debtor and the first surety fail to pay. A creditor cannot turn first to a subsurety. The creditor must approach subsureties in the order in which they agreed to stand liable.

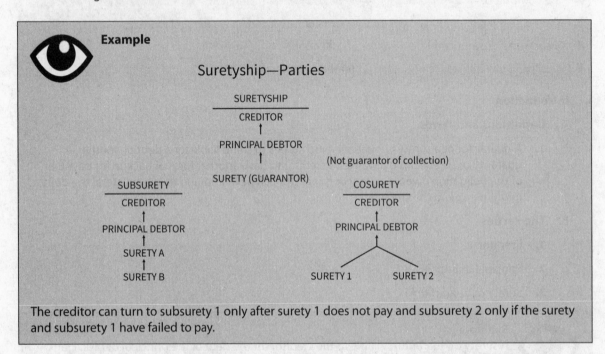

Example

Suretyship—Parties

SURETYSHIP

CREDITOR
↑
PRINCIPAL DEBTOR
↑
SURETY (GUARANTOR)

(Not guarantor of collection)

SUBSURETY

CREDITOR
↑
PRINCIPAL DEBTOR
↑
SURETY A
↑
SURETY B

COSURETY

CREDITOR
↑
PRINCIPAL DEBTOR
↑
SURETY 1   SURETY 2

The creditor can turn to subsurety 1 only after surety 1 does not pay and subsurety 2 only if the surety and subsurety 1 have failed to pay.

3. A creditor could ask for more than one surety on the same level of liability, known as co-sureties. Co-sureties agree to stand jointly and severally liable to the creditor for the principal debtor.

a. Co-sureties can be sureties for the full amount of the debt.

b. Co-sureties can be sureties for certain percentages of the debt.

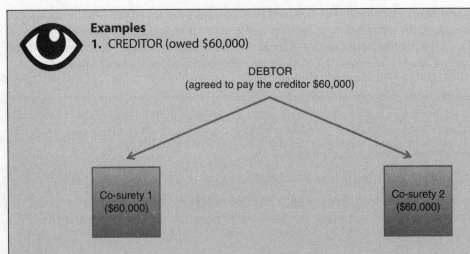

Examples

1. CREDITOR (owed $60,000)

DEBTOR
(agreed to pay the creditor $60,000)

Co-surety 1
($60,000)

Co-surety 2
($60,000)

The creditor can turn to one or both of the sureties for payment. If one surety has to pay the full amount due, then the other co-sureties are liable for paying their share (see right of contribution in the "Suretyship—Rights of Parties" lesson).

2. CREDITOR (owed $60,000)

DEBTOR (agreed to pay the creditor $60,000)

Rights of co-sureties when one surety is in bankruptcy. Suppose that a debtor owes the creditor $60,000. The debtor has three sureties, as follows:

Surety 1	Surety 2	Surety 3
$30,000	$45,000	$15,000

Surety 3 has declared bankruptcy. The debtor has defaulted and still owes $45,000. To determine how much Surety 1 and Surety 2 owe, you simply take Surety 3's pledged amount out of the denominator and continue to use the surety's share as the numerator. Our original denominator was $90,000. With Surety 3 out in bankruptcy, the denominator is now $75,000, and Surety 1 owes 30000/75000 and Surety 2 owes 45000/75000.

Surety 1 = 2/5 × 45,000 or $18,000
Surety 2 = 3/5 × 45,000 or $27,000

Suppose in Example 2 diagrammed above that co-surety 1 has declared bankruptcy. The same facts apply—the debtor owes $45,000 to the creditor and has defaulted. To find the liability of the two remaining sureties, simply change the denominator from $60,000 to $40,000. The numerator remains the same. Co-surety 2 owes $20,000/$40,000 or $22,500. Co-surety 3 owes the same since Co-sureties 2 and 3 are sureties for the same amount. However, a surety is NEVER required to contribute more than what was originally pledged. So, Surety 2 and Surety 3 each owe $20,000.

Be sure to know how to do these computations for surety liability, both with and without a surety bankruptcy.

4. **Rights of creditors and sureties on amount paid toward principal debt**—In the absence of an agreement, the contribution of each co-surety (if the principal debtor does not pay) is determined on a pro rata basis computed by a ratio of the proportionate maximum liability of each co-surety to the total amount that all co-sureties have pledged to stand liable.

Formula

(Max Liability of Co-surety / Total Max. Liability of All Co-sureties) × Amount Paid by Co-surety

Seeking Contribution = Amount of Contribution Entitlement

Example 2 from previous example: 3 co-sureties with $20,000 pledged

The principal debtor has defaulted. The creditor is still owed $45,000. Each of the co-sureties is liable for $20,000/$60,000, or one-third of the amount due. Each would be required to pay $15,000 of the remaining debt.

Suppose that there were two co-sureties, one for $45,000 and one for $15,000, and the debt remaining after the principal debtor's default is $45,000. Again, the maximum amount each co-surety would pay would be 15,000/60,000, or 1/4 and 45,000/60,000, or 3/4. Therefore, the $15,000 surety would pay $11,250 and the $60,000 surety would pay the remaining $34,750.

Example

Able, Baker, and Carl are co-sureties on a $50,000 debt owed by Daniel. Able's maximum liability is $10,000, Baker's maximum liability is $16,000, and Carl's maximum liability is $24,000. Daniel is in default and still owes $40,000. The creditor collects the full amount from Carl, and Carl seeks rights of contribution from Able and Baker. Carl has these rights because Carl has paid more than his proportionate share. Using the formula above:

Able: $10,000/$50,000 × $40,000 = $8,000

Baker: $16,000/$50,000 × $40,000 = $12,800 which means Carl's proportionate share owed is:

$24,000/$50,000 × $40,000 = $19,200

Suretyship—Rights of Parties

After studying this lesson, you should be able to:

1. Describe the rights of the debtor upon full payment of the debt.

2. Describe the rights of the creditor upon the debtor's default.

3. Explain the duties that creditors have on the repossession and sale of collateral.

4. Explain how proceeds from the sale of collateral are distributed.

I. **Rights of the Creditor when the Principal Debtor Defaults**

    A. Generally, upon a principal debtor's default, the creditor has several choices in terms of how to proceed to collect the amount due:

        1. Proceed against the principal debtor personally and/or the debtor's property.

        2. Proceed against the surety personally according to the surety contract.

        3. Proceed against collateral of the debtor held either by the creditor or the surety. Creditor can sell the collateral to satisfy the debt and default costs, and any balance must be turned over to the principal debtor.

II. **Rights of the Surety or Guarantor**

    A. **Exoneration**—This equitable right permits a surety to petition the court to order the creditor by court decree to exhaust recovery against the principal debtor before holding the surety liable.

Example
Phillip is in default on a guaranteed loan made by West Bank. Phillip has numerous assets, but these are located in another state. Evans, the surety, has most of her assets tied up (such as in long-term CDs) to the extent that if she is required to pay now, she will suffer severe financial losses. Under these circumstances, Evans could petition a court of equity for exoneration, which the court may grant.

    B. **Reimbursement and Indemnity**—Whenever the surety has fully or partially fulfilled the debtor's obligation to the creditor, the surety has a right to seek reimbursement from the principal debtor.

        1. Right of reimbursement covers all costs that the guarantor has incurred because of surety agreement.

        2. If principal debtor has a defense against paying the creditor, the surety's right of reimbursement is correspondingly reduced.

    C. **Subrogation**—Upon payment, the surety succeeds to any rights the creditor has (stands in the shoes of the creditor). These include the following.

        1. Creditor's rights against the principal debtor, including right to file a claim in bankruptcy

        2. Creditor's rights to the principal debtor's collateral held by the creditor or the surety

        3. Creditor's rights against third parties (e.g., those who damage the principal debtor's collateral held by the creditor)

        4. Creditor's rights against a co-surety

Example
Evans has guaranteed a loan made to Phillips by West Bank. West Bank has in its possession collateral owned by Phillips, of which some has been damaged due to the negligence of a third party, Green. Phillips files for bankruptcy and the bankruptcy court, upon West Bank's petition, allows West Bank to collect from Evans.

Question: What are Evans's rights in this situation?

Answer: Evans has the right of subrogation. This allows Evans to file West Bank's creditor's claim against Phillips's bankruptcy estate, to sue Green for damage to the collateral due to Green's negligence, and to take possession of any remaining collateral held by West Bank.

D. **Right of Contribution**—Applies when two or more sureties or guarantors are liable on the same obligation to the same creditor and, upon debtor's default, one co-surety pays more than his or her proportionate share of the obligation. The right of contribution entitles this co-surety to recover the amount paid above his or her share owed from the other co-surety.

1. **Generally**—Co-sureties are jointly and severally liable. They can become co-sureties by contract, can be bound as co-sureties for different amounts, and can become co-sureties even without knowledge of each other's existence. (See the "Suretyship—Introduction, Creation, and Types" lesson for a discussion of allocation of amounts.)

2. **Release of co-surety**—If the creditor releases a co-surety without the other co-sureties' consent (or reserving rights in the release in the remaining co-sureties), the remaining co-sureties' liability is released to the extent that the right of contribution cannot be obtained.

3. **Reimbursement**—If a co-surety is fully reimbursed, there is no right of contribution.

4. **Collateral**—In absence of agreement, co-sureties are entitled to share in proportion to their liability of a debtor's collateral in the hands of the creditor or acquired by a surety after the co-suretyship relationship was created.

III. **Defenses of the Parties—Events that *Do Not* Release or Discharge the Surety from Liability**—There are certain events than can occur as the principal debtor, the creditor, and the surety perform their obligations and exercise their rights. This section covers the events that do not result in a release of a surety.

A. **Insolvency of the Principal Debtor**—Problems with the principal debtor's ability to pay is the reason for the surety's agreement.

B. **Bankruptcy of the Principal Debtor**—Financial problems that the debtor might experience are among the reasons for having a surety agreement.

C. **Fraud or Misrepresentation by the Debtor**—The debtor fraudulently misrepresents his financial status in order to convince the surety to act as a surety for the debtor's obligation to the creditor. Unless the creditor participated with the debtor in perpetrating the fraud, the surety is not released because of the fraud. The surety has the usual contract defenses and resulting damage rights against the debtor, but the surety must still pay the obligation to the creditor.

D. **Principal Debtor's Incapacity**

Example
Daniel is the minor son of Emily, and Emily is the surety of a loan West Bank made to Daniel. Daniel, being a minor, has legally disaffirmed his liability on the loan. Although West Bank cannot hold Daniel liable, Emily cannot escape her surety liability by claiming her son's minority as a defense.

E. **Death of the Principal Debtor**—The death of the principal debtor does not discharge the surety. The surety is there as a backup for payment to the creditor when unforeseen events occur.

F. **Release**—Release by the creditor of the principal debtor, without the surety's consent and with the creditor reserving rights against the surety, does not result in a release of the surety. However, when there is a guarantor of collection vs. a surety, there is a release of the guarantor of collection because the guarantor agreed to pay only after the creditor exhausted all means of collection against the debtor.

G. **Changes or Modification**—Changes or modification of the loan terms when there is a compensated surety.

> **Example**
> Phillips wants a loan to start a restaurant. West Bank will not make the loan to Phillips unless she can secure a satisfactory surety. Evans, a financial entrepreneur, agrees with Phillips to be a surety if Phillips will turn over to Evans 5% of all gross proceeds for three years. Phillips agrees and the guaranteed loan contract is made with West Bank. Later, Phillips and West Bank make a material, binding modification of the loan without Evans's consent. Upon Phillips's default, because Evans is a compensated surety, Evans can escape surety liability only to the extent of loss Evans can prove he suffered due to the modification. The key here is that the modification must affect the ability to collect the amount due.

H. The creditor's failure to give the surety notice of the principal debtor's default does not result in a discharge. Unless the creditor agreed to give notice of the default, the creditor is not required to do so. The creditor is entitled to payment from the surety when there is default.

I. Failure of the creditor to first resort to the collateral in order to satisfy the debt does not result in a discharge of the surety because it is the creditor's choice as to proceed against the surety, the collateral, or through litigation against the principal debtor.

IV. Defenses of the Parties—Events that *Do* Result in the Release of the Surety

A. **Principal Debt Paid**—Once the principal debtor has satisfied his obligation to the creditor, the surety is released from the suretyship obligation.

B. **Surety's Incapacity**—Note that in some states a minor does not have capacity to contract as a guarantor or surety.

C. **Guarantor's Discharge Decree in Bankruptcy**—With certain exemptions discussed in the bankruptcy lessons, bankruptcy discharges all the debts of the bankrupt's estate, including surety obligations.

D. **Statute of Limitations Expires**—All contractual obligations are enforceable only if actions to enforce them are brought within the statute of limitations that applies to contracts. In a surety relationship, the statute of limitations for the creditor begins on the date upon which the surety's liability kicked in (i.e., when the creditor had the right to turn to the surety for payment).

E. **Fraud or Misrepresentation by the Creditor**—A surety is released from payment obligations to the creditor if the creditor participated with the principal debtor in committing fraud or misrepresentation that resulted in the surety's willingness to sign as a surety for the principal debtor. To be released for this reason, the surety must be able to show that the principal debtor and the creditor were in cahoots to use false information to convince the surety to act as a surety.

> **Example**
> Creditor, by fraud, induces a principal debtor to incur a large debt guaranteed by Jones for the purchase of land from the creditor, which later proves to be worthless. The principal debtor can avoid the loan due to the creditor's fraud. Jones also can avoid his/her payment as a surety because of the creditor's fraud on the principal debtor.
>
> **Note**: This is different from the debtor defrauding the surety.

F. **Release**—Release of the principal debtor without the guarantor's consent is also a release from liability of the guarantor. Collateral of the principal debtor held by either the creditor or the guarantor can still be used by the creditor to satisfy the debt.

G. **Refusal of Principal Debtor's Tender**—If the principal debtor tenders payment to the creditor under a surety contract, and the creditor refuses the proper tender, the surety is completely discharged from liability.

> **Note**
> If the creditor, in the release to the principal debtor, reserved rights against the guarantor, this is no longer a release but a covenant not to sue, which does not discharge the guarantor from liability.

> **Note**
> The principal debtor is not discharged if the proper tender is refused, but the surety is discharged and the principal debtor is not liable for future interest or other charges.

Example
Peter has a loan from West Bank that is fully guaranteed by Susan. Peter sends a check for the full amount of the debt, including interest, to West Bank. Peter has more than sufficient funds on deposit to cover the check and the check clearly states that payment is in full accord and satisfaction of the loan. However, a bank officer mistakenly believes that the amount of the check is insufficient to cover both the principal and interest owed and sends the check back to Peter. Under these circumstances (proper tender refused), Susan is discharged from her surety liability and only Peter remains liable to West Bank.

H. **Material Alteration by Creditor**—When there is an uncompensated surety, any material alteration of the written loan or surety contract, such as the amount of the debt, by the creditor is a complete discharge of the surety's liability. The material alteration release includes situations in which the creditor substitutes a different principal debtor. A surety contract is personal to the principal debtor, and there cannot be substitution or assignment without consent of the surety. Without consent, the surety is released from liability.

I. **Creditor's Failure to Disclose**—A creditor's failure to disclose material facts that affect the risks of liability to a prospective surety is, in most states, presumed to be the defense of fraud and permits the guarantor to disaffirm the surety contract (complete discharge of liability).

Examples
1. Peter seeks a loan from West Bank. After a careful credit analysis, West Bank denies the loan because of two factors that West Bank feels would make the loan too risky to make. The next day, Peter goes to West Bank with a prospective surety, Gloria, a wealthy customer of the bank. Gloria tells West Bank that if it will make the loan to Peter, she would sign a surety contract. In this case, if West Bank is willing to make the loan with Gloria as surety, the bank must tell Gloria of the material risk factors that caused it to deny the loan. Failure to do so is presumed fraud, and this allows Gloria, at any time, to disaffirm her surety liability.

Note: To avoid a violation of privacy, West Bank must have Peter's permission for disclosure.

2. Gloria is the mother of Phillip, and she has guaranteed a loan made to Phillip by West Bank. Later, Phillip and West Bank, without Gloria's consent, raise the amount of the loan's interest rate and extend the loan period. This is a binding (with consideration) and material modification of the loan contract. Since Gloria is a gratuitous (uncompensated) guarantor, this modification completely discharges her surety liability.

3. Evans is a gratuitous guarantor on a loan made to her daughter by West Bank. The loan is due in one month. Without Evans's consent, her daughter and West Bank agree to extend the loan period for one month without interest or other fees charged. After the one month, the daughter goes into default. It is not a change in the loan terms, it is simply an extension of time for the original terms (immaterial). The extension made no difference in amount due or even the ability of the debtor to pay. We discharge guarantors/sureties when they are affected by a change–that is, collateral is released, loan is restructured. But an added month on a loan that is already due does not change the loan contract in amount, interest, or terms.

J. **Changes and Modifications where There Is an _Uncompensated Surety_**—A material and binding modification of the loan contract made between the principal debtor and the creditor without the consent of the surety results in a release of the uncompensated surety.

K. **Surrender or Impairment of Debtor's Collateral**—If the creditor surrenders the debtor's collateral held in the creditor's possession without the consent of the surety or commits acts that impair the value of the collateral, the surety is discharged to the extent of loss suffered by the surety due to the surrender or impairment. The surety's obligation is reduced only by the amount of the collateral lost or released.

> **Example**
> West Bank made a $100,000 loan to Phillip with Phillip transferring to West Bank 5,000 shares of stock (value $25,000) and having Evans as a surety. Later, without Evans's consent, West Bank releases back to Phillip the 5,000 shares. Upon Philip's default, Evans's surety liability on the $100,000 surety will be reduced by the value of the shares released to Phillip (or $25,000).

L. **Special Release for Guaranty of Collections**—Any failure of the creditor to give the guarantor of collection proper notice of the principal debtor's default, or any material delay in attempting to collect first from the principal debtor, discharges the guarantor of collection from liability to the extent of loss suffered by such failure.

   1. Remember: A guaranty of collections is different from a surety or a simple guaranty so this failure to give notice is different from an ordinary guaranty relationship where the failure to give notice does not result in a release.

M. **Statute of Frauds**—Surety contracts must be in writing. A surety is always released from liability under an oral suretyship agreement.

N. **Statute of Limitations**—Surety contracts must be enforced within the time limits set for bringing suit under contracts.

Article 9—UCC Secured Transactions

Introduction and Creation of Security Interests

> **After studying this lesson, you should be able to:**
>
> 1. Explain why a security interest is important for creditors.
>
> 2. Describe the forms of collateral available under Article 9.
>
> 3. List the requirements for the creation of a security interest.
>
> 4. List and define the terms in Article 9 security interests.

I. Importance and Application

- **A.** Creditors want additional security if the debtor defaults.

  - **1.** An Article 9 security interest gives the creditor the right to specific collateral that the debtor owns, or has rights in, in order to satisfy the debt.

  - **2.** Article 9 also gives creditors a way to have priority to that collateral, through a step known as perfection of the security interest.

- **B.** Article 9 of the UCC is the uniform law that governs the rights of creditors and debtors for security interests in personal property and fixtures.

- **C.** Article 9 security interests apply to personal property or fixtures including goods, documents, instruments, general intangibles, chattel paper, and accounts), agricultural liens, sales of accounts, chattel paper, and promissory notes, and commercial consignments of $1,000 or more—UCC 9-109.

  - **1.** Transactions excluded from secured transactions law (other laws apply):

    - **a.** Landlord's liens

    - **b.** Mechanic's liens

    - **c.** Artisan's liens

    - **d.** Assignment of wage

    - **e.** Tort claims (see discussion of commercial tort claims below)

    - **f.** Insurance (except proceeds from policies covering covered collateral)

    - **g.** Judgments

    - **h.** Leases

    - **i.** Real estate mortgages

II. Basic Terminology

- **A.** **Definitions**—Important for creation and perfection by filing

> **Definitions**
>
> *Secured Party:* The creditor who has a security interest in the debtor's collateral. Can be a seller, or lender, or a buyer of accounts or chattels—UCC 9-102(a)(72).
>
> *Debtor:* The "person" who owes payment or other performance of the secured obligation—UCC 9-102(a)(28).
>
> *Security Interest:* The interest in the collateral (personal property, fixtures etc.), that secures payment or performance of an obligation—UCC 1-201(37).
>
> *Security Agreement:* An agreement that creates or provides for a security interest—UCC 9-102(a)(73).
>
> *Collateral:* The personal property or intangible interest that is the subject of the security interest—UCC 9-102(a)(12).
>
> *Financing Statement:* Referred to as a UCC-1 form, this instrument usually is filed to give public notice to third parties of the secured party's security interest—UCC 9-102(a)(39).

B. Collateral Definitions and Classifications

1. Tangible goods

Definitions

Consumer Goods: Used or bought primarily for personal, family, or household purposes—UCC 9-102(a)(23).

Equipment: Used or bought primarily for use in a business, and not part of inventory or farm products—UCC 9-102(a)(33).

Farm Products: Crops (including aquatic goods) and livestock, or supplies produced in a farming operation such as ginned cotton, milk, eggs, maple syrup, etc.—UCC 9-102(a) (34).

Inventory: Held by a person for sale under a contract of service or lease, or raw materials held for production and work in progress—UCC 9-102(a)(48).

Fixtures: Personal property that become so attached or so related to realty that an interest in them arises under real estate law—UCC 9-102(a)(41).

Accessions: Personal property that is so attached, installed, or fixed to other personal property (goods) that they become part of the goods (other personal property) (e.g. installing a compact disk tape recorder, radio in an automobile—UCC 9-102(a)(1).

2. Intangibles

Definitions

Chattel Paper: A writing or writings (records) that evidences both a security interest in goods and/or software used in goods and a monetary obligation to pay—such as a security agreement, or a security agreement and a promissory note.

Instrument: A negotiable instrument (e.g., check, note, CD, or draft) or other writing that evidences a right to the payment of money and is not a security agreement or lease, but a type that can ordinarily be transferred (by endorsement if necessary) by delivery—UCC 9-102(a)(47).

Account: Any right to receive payment for any property (real or personal) sold, leased, licensed, assigned, or otherwise disposed of, including intellectual licensed property; services rendered or to be rendered, such as contract rights; incurring surety obligations; policies of insurance; use of a credit card; winnings of a government sponsored or authorized lottery or other game of chance; health-care-insurance receivables (defined as an interest or claim under a policy of insurance to payment for health-care goods or services provided)—UCC 9-102(a)(2), (a)(46).

Deposit Account: Any demand, time savings, passbook, or similar account maintained with a bank—UCC 9-102(a)(29).

Agricultural Lien: A nonpossessory statutory lien on a debtor's farm products—UCC 9-102(a)(5).

Commercial Tort Claim: A claim arising out of a tort in which the claimant is an organization, or arose in the course of a claimant's business or profession, and does not include damages for death or personal injury—UCC 9-102(a)(13).

General Intangibles: Any personal property other than goods, accounts, chattel paper, deposit accounts, commercial tort claims, investment property, letter of credit-rights, documents, instruments, and money (i.e., oil royalties, copyrights, patents, etc.)—UCC 9-102(a)(42).

3. Payment intangibles—General intangibles under which the principal debtor's obligation is to pay money (such as a loan without an instrument or chattel paper)—UCC 9-102(a) (61).

4. Software is a good, if the software is so embedded in a computer that it is considered a part of the computer; if it is independent from the computer or a good, it is a general intangible—UCC 9-102(a)(44), (a)(75).

III. Creation of Security Interest

A. Requirements for a Security Interest to Attach—UCC 9-203

1. A writing

   a. Unless the collateral is in the possession of the secured party, there must be a written or authenticated security.

   b. The writing must be signed or authenticated by the debtor. (Authenticated includes any agreement or signature inscribed on a tangible medium or stored in an electronic or other retrievable medium—UCC 9-102(a)(7)(69).)

   c. The security agreement must describe the collateral. Revised Article 9 (which is covered on the exam) also gives examples of what constitutes a sufficient description of the collateral—UCC 9-108(b)—such as "specified listing, category, quantity, UCC defined collateral, etc." and states that supergeneric descriptions, such as "all the debtor's assets," or "all the debtor's personal property," or words of similar import are not a sufficient description. See UCC 9-108(c).

2. The secured party must give the debtor something of value (such as a binding commitment to extend credit, or security, or satisfaction of a preexisting debt, or consideration to support a simple contract)—UCC 1-201(44). Note: The creation of a security interest does not require consideration because a security interest can be given in order to secure a present debt and still be valid.

3. The debtor must have "rights" in the collateral.

   a. A debtor may be advanced a credit line by a creditor with the creditor taking a security interest in the equipment the debtor is buying with the credit line. Suppose that debtor and creditor sign the credit line agreement and security agreement (which meet all of the requirements listed above) on December 1. The equipment is to be delivered FOB seller's place of business on December 15. The security agreement will attach on December 15 when the seller identifies the goods (i.e., ships, marks, or otherwise designates or sets aside the equipment for or to the debtor/buyer).

B. When these three requirements are *all* met, the security interest attaches, which means that the creditor has rights in the collateral, including the right to repossess the collateral in the event the debtor defaults.

Misconception 1: To create a security interest for the secured party, there must be a written security agreement and the agreement must be signed by both the debtor and secured party. Both of these statements are incorrect. A security interest can be created by the secured party taking possession of the collateral under a security agreement, and if the security agreement is in writing or authenticated, only the debtor's authentication is required to create the security interest.

Misconception 2: The debtor must be the "owner" (have title) of the collateral before the secured party can have a security interest in the collateral. For example, suppose that the debtor has given a security interest in goods that are to be manufactured. Once those goods are identified under the contract, the debtor has rights in them, and the security interest attaches even though title will not pass until later.

C. Rights of the Creditor upon Security Interest Attachment

1. Creditor has the right to repossess the collateral (see the "Rights of Secured Parties and Debtors" lesson).

2. Creditor can sell the repossessed collateral (see the "Rights of Secured Parties and Debtors" lesson).

3. Creditor is a secured creditor and has priority over other unsecured creditors (see the "Priorities in Security Interests" lesson).

4. Creditor has priority in bankruptcy above unsecured creditors (see the "Distribution of Debtor's Estate" lesson).

5. Creditor has the right to perfect the security interest in order to stand first in line among secured creditors (see the "Priorities in Security Interests" lesson).

Perfection of Security Interests

After studying this lesson, you should be able to:

1. Define perfection and explain its purpose.

2. List the ways a creditor can obtain perfection.

I. What Is Perfection?

> **Definition**
>
> *Perfection*: A means by which a secured party gains priority to a debtor's collateral over other third parties who also claim to have an interest in the same collateral. Types of third parties who may claim a conflicting interest are unsecured creditors, other secured parties (unperfected) including lien holders, perfected secured parties, trustees in bankruptcy, and purchasers of the collateral.

II. Methods of Perfection—Filing; Possession; Automatic; and Temporary

A. Filing

1. **What is filed?**—Either a UCC-1 form or the security agreement.

2. **Filing requirements**—UCC 9-502

   a. A filing must state names of both the debtor (for registered organizations, estates, and trusts, the sufficiency of the debtor's name must meet certain criteria—UCC 9-503(a) and secured party.

   b. There are two different standards for financing statements versus security agreements. The standards for financing statements can be generic—UCC 9-504. The standards for security agreements require specificity—UCC 9-108.

   > **Note**
   > *Debtor's signature is not required as long as there is authentication by the debtor and a uniform national form is provided in UCC 9-521. In addition, addresses of the debtor and secured party must be stated or the filing officer will reject the filing because these addresses will prove to be critical for the notifications required for priorities—UCC 9-516b(4)(5), 9-520(a) (see the "Priorities in Security Interests" lesson).*

   c. A filing must contain a description of the collateral subject to the security interest. The description can be a generic description, such as "all assets" or "all personal property." For land-related security interests, a legal description of the land is required and the security interest is filed in real property records—UCC 9-504.

3. **Where is it filed?**

   a. **Filing location for perfection**—For all classifications of collateral, except those listed below or where perfection is limited to possession, or control, or specified in a statute, perfection is known as a central filing or in the designated offices for filing in the state where the debtor is located—UCC 9-301.

   b. **Exceptions**

      i. For fixtures, timber to be cut, and collateral to be extracted (such as oil, coal, gas, minerals) filing is in the jurisdiction where the collateral is located and the filing must include a description of the realty—UCC 9-301(3)(4), 9-502(b).

      ii. For possessory security interests, perfection (and priority) is in the jurisdiction where the collateral is located—UCC 9-301(2).

      iii. For certificated securities perfection is where the security certificate is located, but for uncertificated securities it is the location of the issuer—UCC 9-305(a)(1) (2).

4. **Timing issues with perfection**

   a. **When can a financing statement be filed?**

      i. Before a security agreement is made or a security interest attaches;

      ii. Before debtor authorization is required—UCC 9-502(d), 9-509; *or*

      iii. Before the authentication of a security agreement constitutes the debtor's authorization for the filing of a financing statement—UCC 9-509(b).

   b. Perfection occurs upon communication (allows electronic filings, if so authorized) of a financing statement (or security agreement) and tender of the filing fee to the filing officer—***OR***—acceptance of the financing statement by the filing officer—UCC 9-516(a).

      i. A filing is effective even if filing officer refuses it unless, generally—UCC 9-516(d):

         a. The proper filing fee is not tendered.

         b. The name of the debtor is not provided (which would prevent indexing).

         c. The record filing is communicated in an unauthorized (as set by the filing offices) medium.

         d. Where required, there is not a sufficient description of the realty—UCC 9-516(b).

5. **Time of perfection**

   i. **Financing statement**—Can be filed before a security agreement is made or a security interest attaches, but debtor authorization is required—UCC 9-502(d), 9-509, and the financing statement is not effective until all requirements are met (i.e., authentication and attachment). Authentication of a security agreement constitutes the debtor's authorization for the filing of a financing statement—UCC 9-509(b).

   For example, creditor files a financing statement on November 1 for a security interest in inventory of the debtor. They have agreed to the Article 9 financing arrangements and the paperwork is complete, but the debtor has not signed the paperwork. Debtor signs the paperwork on November 15. The perfection is not effective until November 15—all requirements for attachment must be met for the financing statement to be effective.

   ii. **Security interest**—Is perfected upon communication (allows electronic filings, if so authorized) of a financing statement (or security agreement) and tender of the filing fee to the filing officer ***OR*** acceptance of the financing statement by the filing officer—UCC 9-516(a) (see above for list of requirements for effective filing).

   iii. Generally, a person (such as the debtor) can file a correction statement if it is believed that the original financing statement is inaccurate or wrongfully filed, but this correction does not affect the effectiveness of the initial financing statement—UCC 9-518.

B. **Filed financing statement** is effective for five years from date of filing and can be extended for another five years if a continuation statement is filed (only) during the six-month period prior to the expiration of the five-year period—UCC 9-515.

> **Example**
> The five-year period for a perfected (by filing) security interest will expire on December 1. If the secured party wants to extend its perfection for another five years, the secured party must file a continuation statement at anytime from June 1 to December 1 (the six months before the expiration). Should the secured party file the continuation before the six-month window, the continuation would not be effective and its perfection would expire on December 1.

III. Perfection by Possession

1. **Generally**—Article 9 requires filing for perfection, but it also allows perfection by either possession or another method of perfection—UCC 9-310, 9-312(a), 9-313. For example, instruments (whether negotiable or nonnegotiable) can be perfected by filing or possession.

> **Note**
> *For public finance transactions or manufactured home transactions, the effective period is 30 years—UCC 9-515(b).*

2. **Possession**

   a. Creditor has physical possession of the goods.

   b. Pawn of goods is possession.

   c. Transfer of instruments or chattel paper from debtor to creditor is transfer of possession.

   d. *Field warehousing*—The creditor has an agent at the debtor's place of business (warehouse), and the creditor's agent's signature is required before the buyer can sell, pledge, or do anything with the goods subject to the field warehousing arrangement that might affect the creditor's rights and/or priority in those goods.

3. **Special rules on possession and perfection**

   a. **Letter of credit rights**—Perfection is by control unless it is a supporting obligation—UCC 9-308(d), 9-312(b)(2). Control means that the debtor cannot do anything with regard to the letter of credit without the approval of the creditor. (Although documents of title and letters of credit are no longer on the exam, they could be referenced under Article 9 as a form of collateral.)

   b. **Electronic chattel paper**—Perfection is by filing or control unless it is a supporting obligation—UCC 9-310(a), 9-313(a), 9-314(a).

   c. **Deposit accounts**—Used as original collateral; can be perfected only by control—UCC 9-312(b)(3).

   d. **Money**—Can be perfected only by possession—UCC 9-312(b)(3).

   e. *Investment property* (such as securities, security accounts, security entitlements, etc.)—May be perfected by filing—UCC 9-312(a)—or control—UCC 9-314. For priority purposes, perfection by control prevails over perfection by filing—UCC 9-328(1).

IV. Automatic Perfection—Perfection is automatic upon creation of the security interest (no filing or possession required). Applies only in a few situations. Two most important are:

1. A purchase money security interest (PMSI) in consumer goods—UCC 9-309(1).

   a. Consumer goods are goods used or bought primarily for personal, family, or household purposes—UCC 9-102(a)(23).

   b. PMSI is created when the interest is taken or retained by the seller of the collateral to secure the price—UCC 9-103(a)(2). In other words, the creditor is advancing the funds for the purchase of the collateral.

> **Note**
> *Although there can be PMSI security interests in inventory and equipment, the special protections discussed here apply only to PMSIs in consumer goods.*

 Example
Beyer wants to purchase a large-screen TV from Sallor TV Inc. for $1,500. Beyer pays $200 down and signs a security agreement giving Sallor TV a security interest in the set being purchased until the balance of $1,300 is paid. Sallor has a PMSI.

c. This special perfection rule has a practical basis. If every consumer credit purchase had to have a filed, perfected financing statement, the records would be impossible to manage.

d. The creditor need not be the merchant seller of the collateral. A bank can be an automatically perfected PMSI creditor if the debtor does indeed buy the goods that are listed in the security agreement.

> **Example**
> Beyer wants to buy a large-screen TV from Sallor TV Inc. Beyer goes to West Bank seeking a loan to buy the set. West Bank loans Beyer the money and Beyer signs a security agreement giving West Bank a security interest in the to-be-purchased TV set. If Beyer does purchase the set, West Bank has a PMSI in the set. (Note: If Beyer purchases a large refrigerator-freezer instead of the TV, West Bank would be an unsecured creditor.)

2. Other forms of collateral subject to automatic perfection are:

a. A sale of payment intangibles;

b. A sale of promissory notes;

    i. An assignment of health-care-insurance receivables to the health care provider; *and*

    ii. Supporting obligations, such as letter-of-credit rights, secondary obligations (guarantees, etc.) that support payments on accounts, chattel paper, instruments, general intangibles, etc.—UCC 9-308(d), 9-309.

3. Temporary Perfection—UCC 9-312(e)(f)(g)

1. There is temporary perfection **without filing or possession for certificated securities, negotiable documents, and instruments if new value is given**

a. For 20 days from creation of the security interest by authenticated security agreement;

b. Applicable only to certificated securities, negotiable documents, and instruments if new value is given.

2. If perfected by possession—Remains perfected for 20 days without a filing:

a. For goods in possession of a bailee or a negotiable document where the secured party makes the goods or documents available to the debtor for sale, exchange, loading, shipping, etc.

b. For a certificated security or an instrument where the secured party delivers the security certificate or instrument to the debtor for sale, exchange, collection, presentation, etc.

c. Need to take action for post-20-day period in order to retain perfection.

3. When a debtor moves out of state—(debtor moved to a new jurisdiction)—UCC 9-316.

a. If collateral is perfected in one jurisdiction (e.g., in state A) and the debtor moves into another jurisdiction (state B), the perfected secured party (state A) has priority over a subsequent perfected secured party in the new jurisdiction (state B) for a period of four months (or for the period of time remaining under the original perfection, whichever is earlier) from the date the debtor changes his/her location into the new jurisdiction (state B). Where there is a transfer of the collateral to another debtor, who then becomes the debtor and is located in another jurisdiction, the priority period is one year—UCC 9-316(a)(3). If the perfected secured party in the original jurisdiction perfects in the new jurisdiction within the four-month period, its priority continues until the perfection expires.

Example
West Bank has a perfected security interest in Wisconsin on Able's equipment. (Able is a sole proprietorship located in Wisconsin.) Able has built a new plant in Illinois and on May 1, without West's consent, transfers some of the equipment from the Wisconsin plant to the Illinois plant and installs the equipment with some newly purchased equipment there. On June 1, Able gets a loan from East Bank in Illinois putting up all the Illinois plant equipment as collateral. Before making the loan, East Bank had checked for prior filings on the equipment in Illinois. If Able goes into default to both West Bank and East Bank on August 1, West Bank has priority over East Bank as to the equipment moved to Illinois because West Bank's perfection in Wisconsin still has priority over the equipment transferred to the Illinois plant until September 1.

4. Automatic perfection in proceeds

a. **Proceeds**—UCC 9-315—Not only does a security interest continue in the collateral even after its sale or exchange, but it also applies to any proceeds (usually payments) payable to the debtor from the sale or destruction (assuming an insurance policy with the debtor as beneficiary) of the collateral. If perfection by filing includes proceeds, perfection also gives the secured party priority to proceeds. If proceeds are not perfected by filing, priority extends only for 21 days after the debtor's receipt unless the secured party perfects the proceeds by filing within the 21-day period.

Example
West Bank has a filed perfected security interest in all of Ralph's TV present inventory, any after-acquired inventory, and the proceeds from any of these TVs. Able purchases a TV from Ralph signing a security agreement in which she is to make monthly payments. Ralph goes into default to West Bank. Although West Bank cannot repossess the TV sold to Able (Able is a buyer in the ordinary course of business), West Bank is entitled to the monthly payments by Able as proceeds.

V. Rights of Secured Parties on Filing for Perfection

A. **Release**—A secured party can release all (used as a termination statement) or part of any collateral described in the filing thereby terminating its security interest in that collateral. Record of the release is by filing a uniform amendment form—UCC 9-512, 9-521(b).

B. **Assignment**—A secured party can assign all or any part of the security interest to a third-party assignee, and the assignee can become the secured party of record if the assignment is filed by use of a uniform amendment form—UCC 9-514, 9-521(a).

C. **Amendment**—If debtor and secured party so agree, the filing can be amended (as by adding new collateral if authorized by the debtor) by filing a uniform amendment form that indicates by file number the initial financing statement—UCC 9-512(a). The amendment does not extend the time period of perfection, but, if the amendment adds collateral, the perfection date (for priority purposes) for the new collateral begins only at date of the filing of the amendment—UCC 9-512(b)(c).

D. **Information Request**—Any person, such as a prospective creditor, can request from the filing officer "information" on previously filed security interests of a specific debtor. For a fee, a certificate or copies of the previous filings can be furnished—UCC 9-523(c), 9-525(d).

Priorities in Security Interests

After studying this lesson, you should be able to:

1. Explain the rights of the multiple creditors when there is attachment and when there is perfection.

2. Determine who has priority and in what order when there are multiple creditors.

I. General Rules

A. A perfected secured party's interest has priority over the following parties—UCC 9-317, 9-322:

   1. **Unsecured creditors**—Perfected secured creditor vs. unsecured creditor: Perfected secured creditor has priority.

   2. **Unperfected secured parties**—Perfected secured party vs. unperfected secured party: Perfected secured creditor has priority.

   3. **Lien creditors**—perfected secured creditor vs. lien creditor: First to attach has priority. If the perfected secured party perfected before the lien attached, the perfected secured party has priority. If the lien attached prior to perfection, the lien creditor has priority.

   4. **Judgment creditors**—Perfected secured creditor vs. judgment creditor: First to attach has priority. If the perfected secured party perfected before the judgment lien attached, the perfected secured party has priority. If the judgment lien attached prior to perfection, the lien creditor has priority.

   5. **Trustees in bankruptcy**—See priority rules in the "Distribution of Debtor's Estate" lesson.

II. Priority of Perfected Secured Parties over Buyers

A. **Buyers in the Ordinary Course of Business**—A buyer in the ordinary course of business takes free of a secured party's security interest, even if it is perfected, and buyer knows of the security interest at time of sale—UCC 9-320(a). Perfected secured creditor vs. buyer in the ordinary course of business: Buyer in the ordinary course of business wins and gets the goods/collateral.

Definition

Buyer in the Ordinary Course of Business: A buyer who buys goods from a merchant (a seller who deals in goods of that kind)—UCC 1-201(9).

B. **Buyer Not in the Ordinary Course of Business**—Perfected secured party vs. buyer not in the ordinary course of business: Perfected secured party takes priority because buyers not in the ordinary course of business need to check for creditors' interests before buying in less-than-ordinary transactions.

C. **Buyer Not in the Ordinary Course of Business**—Secured creditor vs. buyer not in the ordinary course of business: Buyer will have priority unless the buyer is aware of the creditor's secured interest.

Examples

1. West Bank has a perfected security interest in a tractor owned by a farmer. After the harvest season, the farmer sells the tractor to a farm implement dealer (one who sells and buys used and new tractors). The farmer goes into default, and West Bank claims priority to the tractor purchased by the farm implement dealer. The farm implement dealer claims it is a buyer in the ordinary course of business because it buys and sells used tractors. Here, West Bank has priority because the farm implement dealer is *not* a buyer in the ordinary course of business. The reason is the farmer (the seller) does not regularly sell tractors; thus, the farmer does not deal in goods of that kind.

---

2. On July 8, Ace, a refrigerator wholesaler, purchased 50 refrigerators. This comprised Ace's entire inventory and was financed under an agreement with Rome Bank that gave Rome a security interest in all refrigerators on Ace's premises, all future acquired refrigerators, and the proceeds of sales. On July 12, Rome filed a financing statement that adequately identified the collateral. On August 15, Ace sold one refrigerator to Cray for personal use and four refrigerators to Zone Co. for its business. Because Ace is a wholesaler, the purchase made by Zone, although for use in its business, was still a purchase in the ordinary course of business. All buyers in the ordinary course of business are protected.

D. Buyer Not in the Ordinary Course of Business of Consumer Goods—A buyer not in the ordinary course of business of consumer goods will prevail over a previously perfected secured party by attachment (automatically; without filing) if the buyer can prove the four requirements—UCC 9-320(b)(e). If the buyer cannot establish all four of these requirements, the perfected secured party has priority.

1. Buyer must give *value* to the seller-debtor;

2. Buyer must *not know* of secured party's security interest;

3. Buyer must buy for *personal use* (as consumer goods); *and*

4. Buyer must buy *before* the *secured party perfects by filing*.

> **Note**
> *A consumer seller/ creditor's automatically perfected security interest gives that seller/creditor over all other creditors, but the failure to file makes that seller/creditor subject to the buyer who is not even needed here because of the rules in the ordinary course of business.*

Example
Beyer purchases a large-screen TV for personal use from Ralph's TV store. Beyer cannot pay the full purchase price and, upon making a down payment, signs a security agreement giving Ralph a security interest in the set purchased. Ralph has a perfected PMSI without a filing (perfection by attachment). Later, while still making payments to Ralph, Beyer sells the set to her next-door neighbor, Sally Hawks. Hawks is not a buyer in the ordinary course of business. Due to some financial reverses, Beyer goes into default to Ralph's TV store. If Hawks did not know of Ralph's security interest at the time of sale and Hawks purchased the TV as a consumer good (for her personal, family, or household use), Ralph cannot repossess the set from Hawks. Had Ralph's TV store perfected its security interest (also) by filing before the sale to Hawks, it could have repossessed the TV from Hawks to satisfy the balance of Beyer's debt.

E. Buyers of Negotiable Instruments, Documents, or Securities—Buyers who are HDCs of instruments, holders to whom a negotiable document has been duly negotiated, or BFPs of securities have priority over a previously perfected security interest—UCC 9-330(d), 331(a).

III. Priority between Two Perfected Security Interests in the Same Collateral

A. General Rule—Priority between two perfected secured parties in the same debtor's collateral, including agricultural liens unless a state statute states otherwise, is first in time of perfection is first in priority right—UCC 9-322(a)(1).

B. Exceptions

1. Inventory—A PMSI in a debtor's inventory will have priority over a previously perfected non-PMSI providing these two events take place before the debtor takes possession of the collateral.

a. The PMSI secured party perfects; *and*

b. The PMSI secured party sends (and the non-PMSI party receives) written notice of the PMSI—UCC 9-324(b). This requirement is why addresses are required in the financing statements. The filed financing statement is where creditors obtain names and contact information so that they can exercise their priority rights under Article 9.

Example
Ralph's TV Inc. has a cash flow problem. On May 1, Ralph secures a loan from West Bank putting up Ralph's entire present inventory and any inventory thereafter acquired. This is a non-PMSI, and West Bank properly perfects its security interest with a filing on that same date. On August 1, Ralph learns that the store can purchase 100 TV sets directly from one of its suppliers, Inter TV. Ralph cannot pay cash but does pay 20% of the purchase price as a down payment and signs a security agreement giving Inter TV a security interest in the 100 TV sets that Ralph is purchasing. Delivery of the 100 TV sets is to be on or before September 1. Inter TV has a PMSI. On August 2, Inter TV perfects its security interest with a proper filing and on August 20 sends West Bank a fax, which is received, notifying West Bank of Inter TV's security interest. If Ralph goes into default to both West Bank and Inter TV, Inter TV would have priority over West Bank's after-acquired collateral interest in the 100 sets purchased by Ralph. This is because Inter TV has a PMSI properly perfected, and West Bank was sent and it received written notice of Inter TV's security interest prior to Ralph's possession of the 100 TV sets.

2. **Collateral other than inventory**—For any other types of collateral, a PMSI will have priority over a previously perfected non-PMSI provided that if the PMSI secured party perfects before or within 20 days after debtor takes possession of the collateral. No notice is required—UCC 9-324(a).

Example
Cross, a manufacturer, has a cash flow problem and on May 1 secures a loan from West Bank putting up all of its equipment currently owned and equipment it thereafter acquires as collateral. West Bank properly perfects its non-PMSI that same date. On July 1, Cross purchases a new piece of equipment from Equip Inc. Cross cannot pay cash but does pay 20% of the purchase price down and signs a security agreement giving Equip Inc. a PMSI in the new piece of equipment to be delivered on August 1. If Equip Inc. perfects its security interest by the August 1 delivery, or within 20 days thereafter, Cross takes possession (assuming Cross is in default) and would have priority over West Bank's prior perfected security interest.

3. **Software**—Applies only to a purchase-money security in software if used in goods subject to a purchase-money security interest. Priority is determined the same as if the goods are inventory (if the goods are inventory), or if not as if the goods are other than inventory—UCC 9-103(c), 9-324(f).

IV. Perfection and the Floating Lien

A. **Floating Lien Concept**—The floating lien concept allows the (perfected) secured party to have a security interest in collateral not in existence at time of its creation. The floating lien applies to payments made on sale or destruction or exchange of the collateral, to future advances of funds, and to commingled goods, and even continues when collateral is moved into a different jurisdiction. In short, a perfected secured party could have a single security interest in raw materials to be used in the manufacture of goods, and this interest would continue during the manufacturing process to the finished goods, during shipment to another state jurisdiction, and to the proceeds from the sale or exchange of these goods.

B. **Floating Lien Types**

1. **After-acquired collateral clauses**—A security agreement can provide not only for a security interest in the currently collateral of the debtor, but it can also be applied to any collateral the debtor acquires in the future—UCC 9-204. (This includes consumer goods when given as additional collateral if debtor acquires rights in them within 10 days after the secured party gives value.)

Example
West Bank has a perfected security interest in the present and after-acquired inventory of a retailer. The retailer purchases for cash some new inventory. West Bank's prior perfection also applies to the new inventory just purchased.

2. **Future advances**—A perfected security interest in collateral of the debtor can also be applied to future loans made by the perfected secured party using the same collateral as security without a new perfection for the new loans—UCC 9-204.

Example
On May 1, West Bank has a perfected security interest (for a loan of $200,000) in $1 million worth of the debtor's collateral. The security agreement includes a future advance clause that allows the debtor to borrow up to $400,000 using the same $1 million dollars of collateral. On August 1, the debtor borrows $100,000 from East Bank, giving East Bank a security interest in the same collateral. East Bank is treating its loan like a second mortgage. On September 1, the debtor, through the future advance clause, borrows another $200,000 from West Bank. West Bank does not perfect this loan. On October 1, the collateral has rapidly depreciated in value to $400,000, and the debtor goes into default on all three loans. In this case, because of the future advance clause, West Bank is entitled to the full $400,000 even though its last loan was subsequent to East Bank's $100,000 loan.

Rights of Secured Parties and Debtors

After studying this lesson, you should be able to:

1. Describe the rights of the debtor upon full payment of the debt.

2. Describe the rights of the creditor upon the debtor's default.

3. Explain the duties that creditors have on the repossession and sale of collateral.

4. Explain how proceeds from the sale of collateral are distributed.

I. **Creditor's Options upon Debtor Default**

    A. Upon debtor's default, the secured party can proceed under the UCC or can proceed with any existing judicial remedy. For example, a creditor could simply file a suit to reduce debt to judgment and levy on the debtor's nonexempt property—property other than the collateral, or garnish, etc.—UCC 9-601.

    B. **Creditor's Right to Require the Debtor to Assemble the Collateral**—If the security agreement so provides, the secured party can require the debtor to assemble the collateral upon debtor's default and place the collateral at a location reasonably convenient to both parties—UCC 9-609(c).

    C. **Creditor's Right to Render Collateral Unusable**—Upon default, the secured party can, without removal of the collateral, render the collateral unusable (not damaged) to the debtor—UCC 9-609(a). (Some states prohibit this.)

Example
A lumber sawmill owner is in default, and the secured party has a security interest in the huge machine that saws timber into lumber. Under this law, the secured party could remove the saw blades from the machine, rendering the machine unusable.

    D. **Creditor's Right to Pursue the Self-Help Remedy of Repossession**

        1. Upon debtor's default, the secured party is entitled to take peaceful possession of the collateral without the use of judicial process—UCC 9-609(b).

        2. The UCC does not define "peaceful possession." The general rule is that if the secured party can take possession without committing any of the acts listed below, the collateral has been taken peacefully.

            a. Trespass onto realty;

            b. Assault and/or battery; *or*

            c. Breaking and entering.

    E. **Creditor's Right to Pursue Judicial Process**—If the collateral cannot be taken peacefully or secured party does not wish to try, the secured party can secure possession through a judicial petition and hearing—UCC 9-609(b)(1), (c).

    F. **Creditor's Rights on Disposal of the Repossessed Collateral**

        1. **Keep collateral**—In full or partial satisfaction of the debt (always with debtor's consent)—UCC 9-620(a)(1),(c). In order to keep the collateral, the following steps are required:

            a. Secured party sends notice to the debtor and junior security interests, who gave notice of their claim or have filed a statutory security interest—UCC 9-620(a), 9-621; *and*

            b. The secured party has not received notification or objection from any of the above parties within 20 days after notice was sent.

2. **When the creditor must sell the collateral**—If the collateral is consumer goods and 60% or more of the purchase price (or debt if the collateral was not fully financed by the creditor) has been paid, the creditor must sell it—UCC 9-620(e).

3. **Creditor's right to sell collateral**—Secured party can always sell—UCC 9-610(a).

   a. **Time requirement for sale**—If objection is received or the secured party must sell, the secured party must dispose of the collateral within 90 days after taking possession.

   b. Otherwise the secured party can be held liable for tort of conversion or, if the collateral is consumer goods, for any loss and an amount not less than the credit service charge plus 10% of the principal amount of the debt, or the time price differential plus 10% of the cash price—UCC 9-620(f), 9-625(c).

   c. **Reasonable manner**—The UCC only requires that sale, lease, or license be conducted in a commercially reasonable manner—UCC 9-602(7), 9-603, 9-610(a).

   > **Note**
   > *The reason notice is not required in consumer goods transactions is because there might not be financing statements filed on the goods that would let the creditor know who the junior lienholders are. PMSIs are perfected without filing, so the selling creditor would have no way of determining all the junior lien holders in the transaction.*

      i. Sale can be public or private.

      ii. Secured party must give debtor notice of time and place of disposition, and, except for consumer goods junior lien holders who have given notice of their claims (Notice is not required if collateral is perishable, rapidly declining in value, or to be sold on a recognized market.), to junior lien holders of record 10 days before notification date. (Contents of notification are stated—UCC 9-613 for commercial transactions and UCC 9-614 for consumer transactions.)

      iii. Disposition must be at a reasonable time and place.

      iv. Secured party can disclaim disposal warranties.

      v. Secured party can "buy" if a public sale, goods are sold on a recognized market or one where there are widely distributed price quotations—UCC 9-610, 9-611.

   d. **Distribution of proceeds**

      i. **Expenses** incurred by secured party in repossession, keeping, and resale;

      ii. **Balance of debt** owed to the secured party;

      iii. **Junior lien holders** who have made written demands;

      iv. **Debtor** (unless the collateral is accounts or chattel paper, then to secured party unless, to the contrary, provided to the debtor in the security agreement)—UCC 9-608(a), 9-615(a).

   e. If the secured party receives noncash proceeds from the disposition, the secured party is required to make a value determination and apply this value in a reasonably commercial manner—UCC 9-608(a)(3), 9-615(c). The amount received from a disposition does not in and of itself give grounds that the sale was not conducted in a reasonable manner; however, the price may suggest the need for judicial scrutiny—UCC 9-627(a) (but see Official Comments 10 to UCC 9-610 and Comment 6 to UCC 9-615).

   f. **Creditor's rights to collect deficiency of sale funds from debtor**—Unless the collateral is accounts, chattel paper, payment intangibles, or promissory notes, if the proceeds are insufficient to cover the expenses and balance of the debt, the secured party is entitled to a deficiency judgment, which enables the secured party to get a writ to levy on other property (nonexempt) of the debtor. If the collateral is accounts, chattel paper, payment intangibles, or promissory notes, the secured party is entitled only to a deficiency judgment, if it is provided for in the security agreement—UCC 9-615(d)(e).

g. If there is failure of the secured party to conduct the disposition in a reasonable manner or to give proper notice, the deficiency of the debtor is reduced to the extent such failure affected the price received at the disposition—UCC 9-627(a)(3).

h. **Debtor's right of redemption**—If the secured party is not allowed to keep the collateral in possession in full satisfaction of the debt, the debtor or any other secured party has a right of redemption and by doing so can regain possession of the collateral until there is a sale—UCC 9-623.

   i. **Waiver**—The debtor can waive the compulsory requirement of the secured party to dispose and the debtor's right of redemption only after default—UCC 9-624.

II. **The Soldiers and Sailors Civil Relief Act (1940) (as amended 2012)**—Prohibits a secured party (whose security interest has been previously created) from repossession if the debtor (in default) has enlisted or has been called into active duty in the military after the security interest was created. This protection does not apply if the debtor is in the active military service at the time the security interest is created. This prohibition from repossession extends the entire period the debtor is in active service and can extend up to six months thereafter.

Misconception
Upon a debtor's default, only the secured party with priority has rights to the debtor's collateral.

This is incorrect because junior lien holders who have given the secured party written notice of their claims are entitled to notice (except for consumer goods) if the secured party wants to keep the collateral in full satisfaction of the debt and can object forcing a sale. If there is a sale, the secured party must turn over to junior lien holders any proceeds remaining after the expenses of default and balance of debt owed the secured party are satisfied.

Bankruptcy and Insolvency

Prebankruptcy Options, and Introduction to and Declaration of Bankruptcy

After studying this lesson, you should be able to:

1. List the options for creditors who have a nonpaying debtor.

2. Describe how a bankruptcy begins and who can begin the process.

3. Explain the differences between voluntary and involuntary bankruptcy.

4. Discuss the structure of each type of bankruptcy.

5. Describe the purpose of liens and the process of foreclosure.

6. Discuss the process of a creditor obtaining a judgment and how the judgment is executed for collection of the debt through attachment and garnishment.

7. Explain the options for creditor agreements, such as composition and assignment, to try to avoid debtor declaration of bankruptcy.

8. Discuss a debtor's rights for wrongful declaration of bankruptcy.

I. **When the Debtor Does Not Pay—Options for Creditors**

A. Creditors may execute rights under Article 9 secured transactions and/or suretyship agreements or under the Fair Debt Collections Practice Act (FDCPA) to try to collect the debt. Under the FDCPA, the Creditor may:

1. Not talk to the debtor once the debtor has a lawyer.

2. Contact third parties to obtain information about the debtor;

3. File suit for collection;

4. Not harass the debtor or call during certain time periods. Creditors may foreclose on liens.

Definitions

Bailee's Lien: A bailee, such as a warehouse company, a common carrier, or an innkeeper, has a right to compensation (by contract) or reimbursement (for expenses incurred in the keeping of the bailed property). To enforce this right of payment from the bailor, the bailee has a lien on the bailed property and can sell the property to satisfy the lien.

Artisan's Lien (sometimes referred to as a worker's lien): A contract bailee who improves or repairs bailed property to increase its value. Failure of bailor to pay as contracted allows the bailee to place a possessory lien on the bailed property, and the bailee, with proper notice, can sell the property to satisfy the lien.

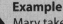

Example

Mary takes her car to Jim's Auto Shop to have some major repairs. A sign and a notice above her signature authorizing the repairs states clearly "All Repairs Are for Cash Payment." Mary authorizes Jim to repair the car for an estimate of $900. When she comes to pick up her repaired car, she does not have sufficient cash to pay the $900 repair bill. Jim refuses to give Mary her car until she tenders $900 in cash. Jim has met both criteria above to create an artisan's lien on the car. Following any statutory procedure, he may sell the car and deduct from the proceeds the cost of sale, costs suffered due to default, and the $900. Any balance would be turned over to Mary.

B. Relationship of Liens to Other Creditor Security Interests—In most states, an artisan's lien has priority over a previously perfected statutorily filed lien (such as a filed UCC-1 financing statement under Article 9).

> **Example**
> To purchase a tractor, farmer John signed a security agreement with West Bank and put up the tractor as security for the loan. West Bank has properly perfected its security interest by filing a UCC-1. Later, Farmer John takes the tractor to I.M. Implement and has some engine repairs made. All repairs are for cash. Having fallen on hard times, farmer John cannot pay cash for the repairs and is in default to West Bank. In this case, even though West Bank's lien is first in time, it is a filed lien and I.M. Implement's artisan's lien, being a possessory lien, has priority over West Bank's perfected secured interest. I.M. Implement can "foreclose on its lien," and satisfy all of its costs and repair charges from the proceeds before West Bank has any entitlement.

C. Obtain a Judgment against the Debtor and Execute that Judgment

1. **Attachment**—An action taken by a creditor for a court-ordered seizure for the taking into custody the debtor's nonexempt property prior to the creditor getting a judgment.

2. **Writ of execution**—After receiving an unsatisfied judgment, a creditor can seek from the court a writ to levy (possess and sell) on nonexempt property of the debtor. The order usually directs the sheriff or an official of the court to seize and sell the nonexempt property.Misconception

Misconception
The term "judgment proof" is a misnomer. With a proper claim, the plaintiff can almost always get a judgment. The problem is collecting the amount of the judgment. Many believe this is easy if the debtor has assets. The problem is that frequently many of the assets of individuals are exempt from collection of a judgment. Assets such as homesteads, cars, household furniture and appliances, farm animals, cemetery plots, clothing, books, and even tools of one's trade are exempt and not subject to a writ of execution. Thus, instead of being "judgment proof," it might be better to use the term "execution proof."

3. **Garnishment**—A court order requiring third parties (garnishees) to deliver a debtor's property held in their possession, or to pay debts they owe to the debtor to the creditor to satisfy a debt or judgment.

   a. Property typically garnished includes:

      i. Bank accounts

      ii. Wages—The garnishment of wages is usually limited by federal or state law to 25% of take-home pay. (Only two states prohibit garnishment of wages, except for child support.) An employer must pay to the court 25% and 75% to the debtor and employee, respectively. Some states permit continuous garnishments (i.e., one court order covers all wages owed by a particular employer without the creditor having to file for each period the wage is paid). An employer cannot discharge an employee because of a garnishment.

   b. Cannot garnish certain payments such as Social Security, and employers cannot fire an employee because of garnishment.

D. Other Creditor Collection Methods

1. **Composition of creditor's agreements**—A contract between the debtor and his or her creditors whereby the creditors agree to discharge the debtor's debts upon a payment (usually a lesser sum).

   a. Creditors who do not contract are not bound by the composition agreement.

   b. The advantage, however, of composition agreements is an immediate payment and it avoids costs and delay of bankruptcy proceedings; plus, many times the payments made exceed those a creditor would receive through bankruptcy.

2. **Setting aside fraudulent conveyances**—Transfers by a debtor of property to a third party, by gift or contract, done to defraud creditors can be set aside. In these cases, title reverts to the debtor subject to remedies of the creditors.

Example
Creditor Smith is about to get a judgment against debtor Jones, whose major nonexempt asset is a boat. Just before the judgment is issued, Jones transfers the boat to his 10-year-old son as a gift. This transfer is made strictly with the intent to deny Smith a writ to levy execution on Jones's boat, thus to defraud Smith. Smith can have title of the boat to the son set aside and then secure a writ of execution and levy on the boat.

3. **Assignment for the benefit of creditors**—This usually involves an insolvent debtor who voluntarily transfers certain assets to a trustee or assignee. The trustee or assignee liquidates the assets and tenders a payment on a pro rata basis in satisfaction of that debt to each creditor.

   a. The amount of property turned over to the trustee or assignee, and thus pro rata share, is entirely at the discretion of the debtor.

   b. Creditors can accept or reject amount tendered.

      i. Referred as a "cram-down" or "take-it-or-leave-it" choice of the creditor.

      ii. Acceptance by the creditor is a complete discharge of the debt.

      iii. Rejection eliminates a creditor's right to the property assigned, but creditor can then pursue other remedies including involuntary bankruptcy petition against debtor.

Example
Debtor Smith has come upon difficult financial times, and his 20 creditors are not willing to accept a lesser sum in a creditors' composition agreement. Smith's debts amount to $100,000. Smith turns over to a trustee (Jones) $20,000 worth of property and instructs Jones (for a fee) to sell the property and prorate the proceeds among his 20 creditors. Jones sells the property and then on, a pro rata basis, offers each creditor a sum. Creditors who accept the lesser sum discharge their debt. If all creditors accept the sums offered by Smith, the entire $100,000 in debt is discharged. If none of the creditors accept or only some do so, Smith could petition himself into bankruptcy.

II. Before You Begin to Study Bankruptcy

Study Tips
Advice for studying bankruptcy—The text is detailed for those who want or need some in-depth knowledge, and the law on bankruptcy is complicated. Add to this the fact that the percentage of the value of the subject area on the exam been reduced substantially but the content coverage has even been expanded with the enactment of the 2005 Bankruptcy Act, and you have a dilemma: How much time should you spend on detail when there will only be a few questions on the exam?

Even if you limit your study to the basics under the nine recommendations listed next, there is a lot to chew. Good luck.

A. **Do not memorize numerical amounts in the text.** You will never remember them, and the amounts change every three years. If you feel you need to know a few numerical amounts, consider these:

   1. The amount of the debt required for the filing of an involuntary Chapter 7

   2. The monetary limits for the filing of Chapter 12 and Chapter 13 petitions

   3. The maximums for the categories in priority of payment (distribution of liquidated estates)

B. Know the five different petition filing chapters—7, 9, 11, 12, and 13—who cannot file under each, and the requirements for filing under each.

C. **Generally**, know what a debtor is required to file beside the petition to commence the bankruptcy proceedings.

D. Know what **basically** constitutes the debtor's estate, including gifts, etc., acquired after petition is filed.

E. **Generally**, know what the federal exemptions are and, if the debtor elects the state exemptions, what the limitation is on the homestead equity amount.

F. Know what constitutes a **preference** for trustee avoidance of the transfer.

G. Know a **summary** of the order of priorities among creditors. Note that on unsecured creditors, the top priority is domestic support obligations and tax claims are low priority.

H. Know what debtors or debts will **not be discharged**. For example, partnerships and corporations cannot get a Chapter 7 discharge; only one Chapter 7 discharge is possible every eight years; there is no discharge for domestic support obligations, student loans, and generally due to conduct of the debtor.

I. Know the **requirements** of reaffirmations.

Note: The three types of bankruptcy emphasized most often on the exam are Chapters 7, 11, and 13.

Note

The law on bankruptcy is constantly changing for a number of reasons. First, the 1994 amendments to the Bankruptcy Act created a Bankruptcy Review Commission of nine members to review and make recommendations for possible yearly legislative reform. The passage of the Bankruptcy Abuse Prevention and Consumer Protection Act of 2005 referred to as the Bankruptcy Reform Act of 2005 resulted in substantial changes in bankruptcy filing and administration. Second, beginning on April 1, 1998, and every three years thereafter, almost all dollar amounts will be adjusted automatically to reflect the Consumer Price Index rounded off to the nearest $25. The text in the bankruptcy lessons has the April 1, 2016 adjustment figures and the Bankruptcy Reform Act of 2005 (including the most recent three-year adjustments).

The CPA Exam is less concerned with assessing your memorization of these numbers than with assessing your knowledge of the fact that they exist and how to use them.

III. Commencement of Bankruptcy—Types of Bankruptcy (*Very Important*)

    A. There are **five** types of bankruptcy. (The three emphasized on the exam are 7, 11, and 13.)

        1. **Chapter 7**—Referred to as **"straight bankruptcy"** or **liquidation**

            a. Permits **voluntary and involuntary petitions**

            b. Permits individuals and businesses to file

                i. Under the 2005 reforms, consumers generally cannot go directly to a Chapter 7 liquidation bankruptcy.

                ii. Consumer must establish that they do not have the means to repay their debt.

                iii. Known as the "means" test, this test is a formula that takes the debtor's monthly income, subtracts out allowable expenses provided for under the bankruptcy law, and then determines whether the debtor has the means to pay off his or her debts.

                iv. Consumers can be held responsible for bankruptcy abuse if they do not qualify under the means test.

                v. If there has been bankruptcy abuse, both the consumer and the consumer's lawyer can be held liable for costs.

            c. Trustee is appointed. (Note: Some questions on the exam deal with whether a trustee is required under the various chapters.)

    d. Not eligible for Chapter 7:

        i. Railroads

        ii. Domestic insurance companies

        iii. Savings banks

        iv. Savings and loans

        v. Cooperative banks

        vi. Certain SBA entities

2. **Chapter 9**—Allows for the adjustment of debts of an insolvent municipality—a rehabilitation of municipalities, defined as any political subdivision, public agency, or instrumentality (includes any taxing unit) of a state.

    a. Permits **voluntary petitions** by the municipality

    b. This chapter is rarely addressed on the exam.

3. **Chapter 11**—Allows for the **reorganization** of a debtor to pay debts—a rehabilitation of a debtor.

    a. Permits **voluntary and involuntary petitions**

    b. Allows companies to restructure and be discharged from certain debts

    c. Generally, no trustee

    d. Reorganization plan approved by half of the creditors with two-thirds of the total claims (includes shareholders)

    e. Court must approve.

    f. Savings and loans, banks, insurance companies are not eligible for Chapter 11.

4. **Chapter 12**—Allows for the **adjustment of debts of a family farmer and family fisherman**—a rehabilitation of a person (including a corporation or a partnership) who meets **the definition of a family farmer or fisherman** (rarely tested on the exam).

    a. Permits only **voluntary petitions** by the family farmer or family fisherman.

5. **Chapter 13**—Allows for the adjustment **of debts of an individual with regular income**—a rehabilitation of only individuals (not partnerships or corporations) with limited total secured and unsecured debt amounts.

    a. Permits only **voluntary petitions**

    b. Less than $394,725 in unsecured and less than $1,184,200 in secured debt

    c. Always has a trustee

    d. Applies only to individuals (debt limits)

    e. Debtor's plan

    f. Court confirmation

    g. Three to five years for plan—discharged if payment is made

> **Note**
> **IMPORTANT!** *Prior to commencement of a filing, the clerk of the bankruptcy court is required to give consumer debtors detailed notice of each chapter available under which they may proceed. The clerk also must provide informational materials on the types of services available from credit counseling agencies.*

IV. Requirements for Bankruptcy

  A. Chapter 7 (Voluntary)

    1. Any **person** (individual, partnerships, or corporations) may voluntarily petition themselves into a Chapter 7 bankruptcy (spouse can jointly file).

2. Exceptions to Chapter 7 eligibility:

   a. Banks

   b. Savings (buildings) and loan associations

   c. Credit unions

   d. Railroads

   e. Insurance companies

   f. Governmental units (usually);

   g. Small business investment companies licensed by the Small Business Administration

3. **Special consumer debtor requirements**—Before debtors (consumers) can file a petition, they must receive credit counseling from an approved nonprofit agency within 180 days prior to the date of filing.

B. **Chapter 7**—Involuntarily petition into a Chapter 7 bankruptcy

1. Same persons eligible as under voluntary Chapter 7 declaration **except:**

   a. All of the above exclusions from a voluntary Chapter 7 petition

   b. Nonprofit (not for profit) corporations

   c. **Farmers** (those that receive 80% or more of gross income from a farming operation and family farmers who meet that definition under a Chapter 12 bankruptcy)

2. **Requirements for creditors' involuntary petitions of a debtor into bankruptcy**

   a. If the debtor has **12 or more unsecured creditors with noncontingent claims,** the petition must be signed by three or more of these creditors whose aggregate claims are $15,775 or more;

   b. If the debtor has less than **12 unsecured creditors with noncontingent claims,** the petition requires only one (more can sign) of these creditors with an aggregate debt of $15,775 or more to sign the involuntary petition.

3. **Debtor's challenge involuntary petitions**—Requires creditors to prove:

   a. Debtor has not been paying debts as they become due; *or*

   b. Debtor's property has been placed in receivership, or debtor has made an assignment for the benefit of creditors within 120 days of the filing of the involuntary petition.

   c. Notice that the standard for involuntary bankruptcy is not proving that liabilities are greater than assets that is, insolvency in the accounting sense is not the test for the validity of an involuntary petition. The standard is the inability to pay debts as they become due.

> **Note**
> *If a court dismisses the creditor's petition due to the debtor's successful challenge, the bankruptcy court can assess all costs against the petitioners (including reasonable attorney fees and any damages). If the petition was filed in bad faith, recovering could include punitive damages. This would also be a form of bankruptcy abuse.*

V. Effect of Bankruptcy Petition

A. Upon the filing of a **voluntary petition** or the filing or **granting of an involuntary petition**, the court will grant an **order for relief** or a stay.

B. Order for relief or stay means that creditors must stop collection and all pending credit proceedings (lien foreclosure; judicial liens, etc., as discussed in the earlier sections of this lesson) are stayed (stopped), and the debts and payments will be handled through the bankruptcy court.

C. This sets in motion proceedings that lead to the discharge of the debtor's debts.

D. Upon filing of an involuntary petition, and following the determination that the debtor is insolvent (with insolvency being defined as the inability to pay debts as they become due), the order for relief is entered.

E. Some proceedings are not affected by the order for relief or stay including paternity determinations, child support hearings, and marriage dissolutions.

Bankruptcy Process

After studying this lesson, you should be able to:

1. List the responsibilities of the debtor upon a bankruptcy filing.

2. Summarize the duties of the trustee in bankruptcy.

3. Describe what property is included in the bankrupt's estate, including the meaning of the 180-day limitation.

4. Discuss what types of claims are valid.

5. Explain how a bankruptcy trustee can set aside payments and security interests as voidable preferences and the time limits for doing so.

6. Describe what constitutes a fraudulent conveyance by a debtor prior to declaration of bankruptcy.

7. List the property exemptions from the debtor's bankruptcy estate.

I. **Overview**—At this point, either the voluntary petition has been accepted by the bankruptcy court or the involuntary petition has been held to be valid. No matter how the parties got into bankruptcy court, the court follows a similar process in handling the debtor's estate. The steps outlined here occur **after** the order for relief has been entered (see lesson on "Prebankruptcy Options and Introduction to and Declaration of Bankruptcy").

II. **Debtor's Obligation to Provide Information**

A. The debtor is required to **file** the following (under oath and signed as being complete and accurate).

 1. List of all creditors with addresses and amounts owed;

 2. Schedule of assets and liabilities;

 3. Schedule showing current income and expenses;

 4. Statement of financial affairs;

 5. Statement of intention to retain or surrender any property (which secures a consumer debt), and to specify property claimed exempt from bankruptcy proceedings;

 6. Certificate from an approved credit-counseling agency (for consumers);

 7. Statement of the amount of monthly income itemized to show how the amount is calculated;

 8. Copy of debtor's federal income tax return for most recent year prior to filing; *and*

 9. Proof of payments received from employers during last six months.

 The debtor is also required to cooperate fully and to respond truthfully during examinations by the trustee or creditors, to appear at all hearings, and to surrender to trustee all property, books, and records subject to the bankruptcy proceedings. Failure by the debtor is grounds for denial of discharge of debts.

B. Failure to cooperate may also be grounds for the court to dismiss the bankruptcy petition.

III. **Appointment of the Trustee and Initial Duties**

A. In those proceedings where a trustee is required (Chapter 7) and after an order for relief is entered, the trustee (a government-appointed official) takes charge of the process that must be followed under the jurisdiction of the bankruptcy court.

B. Basic **trustee duties** include:

1. Collecting the debtor's property

2. Accounting for all property received and making a final report to account for the administration of the debtor's estate

3. Investigating the financial affairs of the debtor to determine what valid debts exist and whether the debtor has been involved in transferring property improperly to provide certain creditors with preferences or to hide property

4. Furnishing information and reports concerning the debtor's estate

5. Providing notice information to domestic support creditors

IV. Collection of Assets—The Debtor's Estate—Debtor's estate includes:

A. All tangible and intangible property—(all legal and equitable interests) of the debtor held at the time the bankruptcy proceedings began.

B. The following **after-acquired property** that the debtor acquired within 180 days after the petition is filed:

1. Property by **inheritance or gift**

2. Property by **divorce, separation, or property settlement**

3. **Beneficiary proceeds from a life insurance policy**

C. Any property appreciation, income, etc., from existing property but excludes withholdings for employee benefit plan contributions.

D. Property reacquired by trustee's avoidable powers such as preferences, fraudulent transfers, transfer by mistake, under duress, etc. (See the "Distribution of Debtor's Estate" lesson.)

V. Property that Is Exempt from Bankrupt's Estate

A. Only **individuals**, not partnerships or corporations, **can claim** exemptions.

B. Two lists of exemptions: state and federal. Congress has authorized states to limit exemptions to those of the state, and a majority of the states have done so. However, if the homestead is acquired within three and a half years preceding the date of filing, the maximum state homestead equity exempted is $160,375 and the debtor must have domiciled in the state for two years.

C. For the other states, the debtor can choose either the state or the federal exemptions below:

1. The debtor's interest in a homestead used as a residence up to a value of $47,350 (states exemptions vary significantly—up to $160,375)

2. The debtor's interest in a motor vehicle up to $3,775

3. The debtor's interest up to $600 per item in household furnishings (includes one computer, one television, one videocassette recorder, and educational materials and equipment, but excludes items such as works of art, antiques over $575 in value, electronic entertainment equipment with a fair value of over $575, appliances, wearing apparel, animals, crops, or musical instruments that are owned primarily for personal uses, subject to a total of $12,625 for all such)

4. The debtor's interest in any kind of property ("wildcard" exemption) up to a limit of $1,250 plus up to $11,850 of any unused homestead exemption

5. Any unused portion of the homestead exemption, subject to a limit of $11,500

6. The debtor's interest in implements, tools, or professional books used in his or her trade, not to exceed $2,375 in value

7. Any unmatured life insurance policies owned by the debtor (except for credit life policies) plus interests in accrued dividends and interest up to $12,625

8. Professionally prescribed health aids

9. The debtor's right to receive various government benefits, such as unemployment compensation, social security, veteran's benefits, etc.

10. The debtor's right to receive various private benefits, such as alimony, child support, pension payments, disability benefits, etc.

11. The right to receive damages for bodily injury up to $23,675

12. The debtor's interest in jewelry that is owned primarily for personal purposes up to a total of $1,600

VI. Bringing Transferred Property Back into the Bankruptcy Estate

A. The trustee has the power to set aside transfers of the debtor's property.

B. These set-asides of transfers of property by the debtor are called voidable preferences.

1. Trustee can set aside transfers due to the usual contract defenses, such as **duress, mistake, undue influence**, **failure of consideration**, **debtor's incapacity**, etc.

Example
The debtor was a minor at the time of transfer. The debtor, now in bankruptcy, still has the right to disaffirm the transfer due to his or her minority. The trustee can set aside this transfer.

2. Trustee can set aside fraudulent transactions. Note that there are no time limits here when fraud is involved.

Example
Debtor, three days before the filing for bankruptcy, transfers a boat (nonexempt property) to his daughter retaining possession and use, and converts nonexempt property into cash, buying a $100,000 life insurance annuity contract. The debtor already has substantial amounts of life insurance. Both the transfer of the boat and the purchase of the $100,000 policy can be set aside and become property subject to the bankruptcy proceedings.

3. Trustee can set aside any transfer of property of the estate made by the debtor **after the debtor became subject to the bankruptcy proceeding**, except those made with permission of the trustee or the court.

4. Trustee can set aside any transfer that results in a **legal or voidable preference**.

   a. There are two types of legal or voidable preferences: those for creditors and those for insiders. Note: Time lengths vary for the two different categories.

   b. **Elements for all transfers by debtors to creditors**

   i. A transfer of **debtor's property to a creditor**;

   ii. For an **antecedent or preexisting debt**;

   iii. Made within **90 days of the filing of the petition**;

   iv. Made while the debtor was insolvent (insolvency presumed for any transfer made within 90 days of the petition being filed).

   c. **Elements for all insiders**

   i. An insider is an individual or business that has a close relationship with the debtor. For example, a relative, a partner, a corporation (board of directors of which the debtor is a member or as an officer of the corporation);

   ii. A transfer of debtor's property to an insider;

iii. For an antecedent or preexisting debt;

iv. Made within **one year** from date **of the filing of the bankruptcy petition**;

v. Made while the debtor was insolvent. There is a presumption of insolvency for any transfer made during the **90-day window** that precedes the date of filing of the petition. To set aside a transfer made during the one-year period beyond the 90-day window, the trustee must actually **prove that the debtor was insolvent at the time of transfer**.

> **Note**
> *A fraudulent transfer is a fraudulent transfer, and those types of transfers can be set aside as well, just by showing that the transfer was done for the purpose of circumventing going through the bankruptcy process.*

C. EXCEPTIONS—to the trustee's authority to do a set–aside

1. A **contemporaneous exchange** between the debtor and a creditor for new value.

Example
Debtor retailer purchased new inventory and paid two days later in cash.

OR

Debtor purchases new inventory to be delivered on May 1 with the seller-creditor taking a **PMSI** in the new inventory to be delivered. If the secured seller-creditor perfects its security interest within **20 days after the debtor takes possession**, the security interest is not a preference.

2. The payment of a debt incurred in the ordinary course of business or financial affairs of the debtor.

Example
Debtor pays its utility bills upon receipt.

3. A **consumer debtor's payment** of up to $6,225 is not a preference.

4. Payments for **paternity, alimony, maintenance, and child support** are not preferences.

VII. Creditors' Meetings

A. The first creditors' meeting is called by the U.S. Trustee on behalf of the court (not less than 10 days nor more than 40 days from the order for relief). The judge does not attend.

B. Creditors—May elect a permanent trustee by majority vote if at least 20% of total unsecured claims filed are in attendance. If not, the trustee is appointed (usually the interim trustee).

C. Debtor—Is usually required to appear and may under oath be examined about his or her assets and any matter relevant to a discharge. Failure to answer truthfully is grounds for denial of discharge.

Distribution of Debtor's Estate

After studying this lesson, you should be able to:

1. Take a list of available property and allowable claims and distribute the property to the creditors according to statutory priorities.

2. Develop a list for the order of distribution of the bankrupt's estate and include limits on the priority for each level in the priority list.

I. **Determining the Debtors: The Filing of a Proof of Claim**—Any creditor, equity security holder, co-debtor, surety, or guarantor may file proof of any legal claim or interest on behalf of a creditor, or trustee.

   A. **Time for Filing**—Determined by rules of bankruptcy procedure. (Must be filed within 90 days from first meeting of creditors. Same for Chapter 12 and Chapter 13 bankruptcies.) Taxing and governmental units have 180 days.

   B. All legal obligations of the debtor are claims—Thus, there is no need to prove a claim. This includes **disputed and unliquidated claims** for which the court may estimate value.

II. **Trustee's Evaluation of Claims**—Any claim filed is deemed allowed unless a party in interest objects. Generally, the following claims will be disallowed, at least to the amount held unenforceable:

   A. Claims unenforceable due to fraud, usury, being illegal (unconscionable), failure of consideration, etc.;

   B. For **unexpired leases of the debtor**, the trustee can:

      1. Assume and perform the lease;

      2. Assume and assign or sublease; *or*

      3. Reject the lease (if not assumed within 60 days, lease is rejected).

III. **Distribution of Estate**

   A. **Perfected Secured Parties**—Perfected secured parties have priority to the collateral or proceeds over general creditors and the trustee. Unperfected secured parties are secured creditors who have rights in the collateral, but not above the rights of perfected secured parties. Once the collateral is sold and the perfected secured parties paid from the proceeds, the remaining unperfected secured creditors drop down into the general creditor category for their unpaid balances due.

      1. If the security agreement so provides, the secured party has priority in the collateral to cover costs of default plus reasonable attorney fees.

      2. If there is insufficient collateral or value to cover the perfected secured creditor debt entitlement, the creditor can file a claim as a general creditor. Any amount that exceeds the secured creditor's entitlement is available for general creditor distribution. The secured creditor has priority only for the amount provided by the collateral. Once that is received, the creditor takes his or her position with the other unsecured general creditors and other secured but unperfected creditors who have no collateral to satisfy their debt (because the perfected, secured parties have first rights of claim on that collateral).

> **Note**
> *The priorities of distribution for the bankrupt's estate are tested frequently on the exam. You will need to know the order of this list for priorities for distribution. When there are insufficient proceeds to cover any particular group, the funds are prorated among the members of that group, and subsequent groups receive nothing. The bankruptcy trustee keeps going down the priority list for distribution until reaching a point of insufficiency for that class of creditor. At that point, the remaining funds are prorated and the distribution is complete with the inevitable result that some creditors receive nothing from the bankruptcy estate because it was insufficient to satisfy all creditors.*

Example

West Bank is a perfected secured party on a loan balance of $10,000 with a security interest in $14,000 of the debtor's equipment. The debtor is in default. West Bank has repossessed the equipment and stored it for $500 pending its sale. West Bank also has $1,000 in attorney fees due to debtor's default. If the equipment is sold for $11,000 by either the debtor or trustee, assuming West Bank's security agreement also covers default costs and attorney fees, West Bank would receive the entire $11,000 and would have to file a claim as a general creditor for $500.

B. **Claims for Domestic Support Obligations**—Such as child support and alimony.

C. **Administrative Costs**—Including all the costs and expenses of the bankruptcy proceedings. Trustee, attorney, appraisal, and accountant fees fall into this category.

D. **Claims Arising in the Ordinary Course of Business**—After bankruptcy petition is filed but before the order of relief is entered (involuntary bankruptcy proceeding). If an involuntary petition has been filed but the trustee has not yet been appointed (such as when the debtor challenges the involuntary petition), any expenses incurred by the debtor in the ordinary course of business from date of filing to the appointment of the trustee or order of relief (called "gap creditors" or "interim"). The reason for this priority is so that the debtor is not shut down in the time it takes to get the bankruptcy process moving forward.

> **Example**
> Three creditors whose aggregate unsecured, noncontingent claims are $50,000 sign an involuntary petition putting Elizabeth, sole owner of a clothing store, into bankruptcy. Elizabeth immediately challenges the petition. A hearing is held two weeks later when the court rules in favor of the creditors, an order of relief is issued, and a trustee is appointed. During the two-week period, Elizabeth has continued to do business and has incurred debts to ABC Wholesale Clothes and XYZ Janitorial Services. When distribution of Elizabeth's estate takes place, ABC and XYZ will be third in line of general creditors to be paid.

E. **Employee Wages**—Employee claims for back wages, salaries, or commissions (including vacation, severance, sick leave, and other benefits) but limited to those earned within 180 days of the filing of the petition or cessation of business (whichever is first) to a maximum amount of $12,850.

1. **IMPORTANT**—Any amount of back wages, etc., owed, regardless of when owed or amount owed above the $12,850 during the 180-day period, is still a claim but for priority purposes goes to the last category—general creditors.

> **Example**
> Clara is employed as the manager of a clothing store. She is paid $5,000 per month. The clothing-store owner suffers financial reverses and, based on promises, Clara manages the store for four months without pay. The owner now goes into a Chapter 7 bankruptcy. Clara will file a claim for her entire $20,000 owed in back salary, with $12,850 (earned during the last 180 days) as a priority. The remaining $7,150 will be treated as a last general creditor priority. If Clara had worked one month without pay, quit, and the owner continued to manage the store for nine months, before she shut down the business and filed for bankruptcy, Clara would get employee priority only for what was earned within the 180-day period (up to the $12,850 maximum). For what was earned outside the 180 days (the one month before she quit and three of the nine months following and the excess above $12,850), Clara would have a claim as a general creditor.

F. **Contributions to Employee Benefit Plans**—Any claim for contributions to an employee benefit plan arising from services performed within 180 days before the filing of the petition or cessation of business (whichever comes first) up to $12,850 per employee (less the aggregate amount paid to employees under the fourth priority above). Any amount above the maximum is treated as a general creditor claim.

G. **Claims of Farm Producers and Fishermen**—Against debtors who own or operate grain storage facilities or fish storage or processing facilities, farm producers and fishermen can use up to the amount of $6,325 per creditor. Any amount above is treated as a general creditor claim.

H. **Consumer Creditors**—Those buyers who deposit or prepay for the purchase, lease, or rental of goods or services for personal, family, or household use up to an amount of $2,850 per creditor. Any amount above $2,850 is treated as a general creditor claim.

> **Example**
> John contracts with a yard fertilizer and maintenance company to mow his home yard weekly and fertilize it eight times during the coming year. The price is $3,000 less 10% if paid in advance. John pays $2,700 to the company. Before any services are performed, the company goes into Chapter 7 bankruptcy. John has a priority claim of $2,700 if there are funds remaining for this category and, if not, he has a general creditor priority claim of $150.

I. **Claims of Governmental Units for Various Taxes**—These are subject to time limits that vary on the type of tax.

J. **Claims for Death or Personal Injury**—Claims resulting from operation of a vehicle or vessel because debtor was intoxicated from use of alcohol, drugs, or other substances.

K. **All General Unsecured Creditors**

L. **If any Amount is Left, it Goes to the Debtor**

> **Example**
> Knox operates an electronics store as a sole proprietor. On April 5, year 1, Knox was involuntarily petitioned into bankruptcy under the liquidation provisions of the Bankruptcy Code. On April 20, a trustee in bankruptcy was appointed and an order for relief was entered. Knox's nonexempt property has been converted to cash, which is available to satisfy the following claims and expenses as may be appropriate:
>
> *Claims and Expenses*
>
> | | |
> |---|---|
> | Claims by Dart Corp. (one of Knox's suppliers) for computers ordered on April 6, year 1, and delivered on credit to Knox on April 10, year 1 | $20,000 |
> | Fee earned by the bankruptcy trustee | $15,000 |
> | Claim by Boyd for a deposit given to Knox on April 1, year 1, for a computer Boyd purchased for personal use but that had not yet been received by Boyd | $1,500 |
> | Claim by Noll Co. for the delivery of stereos to Knox on credit. The stereos were delivered on March 4, year 1, and a financing statement was properly filed on March 5, year 1. These stereos were sold by the trustee with Noll's consent for $7,500 for their fair market value | $5,000 |
> | Fees earned by the attorneys for the bankruptcy estate | $10,000 |
> | Claims by unsecured general creditor | $1,000 |
>
> The cash available for distribution includes the proceeds from the sale of the stereos.
>
> What amount will be distributed to the trustee as a fee if the cash available for distribution is $15,000?
>
> a. $6,000
> b. $9,000
> c. $10,000
> d. $15,000
>
> Secured creditors go first with the $5,000. Then you have $25,000 TOTAL administrative expenses for lawyers and trustees, and the trustees are $15,000 of that, so you take the $15,000/25,000 × the $10,000 remaining and 3/5 of $10,000, which is $6,000.

Discharge and Reaffirmation Agreements

After studying this lesson, you should be able to:

1. List the reasons a debtor can be denied a discharge.

2. List the debts that a debtor cannot have discharged in bankruptcy.

3. Describe the types of consumer debts that cannot be discharged.

4. Explain what reaffirmation agreements are and the requirements for them to be enforceable.

I. **Generally**—After the estate has been distributed, the court will grant the debtor a discharge decree (at a hearing), that releases the debtor from further liability of his or her debts. This decree is revocable for one year.

II. **Conditions under which Discharge May Be Denied**

    A. A **partnership** or **corporation cannot get a discharge decree** under Chapter 7 (can under other chapters), **only individuals can**.

    B. **A debtor will be denied a discharge** if he or she received a discharge within eight years before the filing of the current petition.

    C. **Grounds for Denial**—Any of the following acts by the debtor is a ground for denial of the discharge decree:

        1. Any intentional concealment, distribution, or transfer of assets or records to the detriment of creditors or the trustee (without justification);

        2. Any fraudulent claims, statements, oaths, or receipt or transfer of property;

        3. Any refusal to obey lawful orders, failure to file required or requested tax documents, failure to testify after grant of immunity, or explain loss or deficiency of assets; *or*

        4. Failure of debtor to complete the required consumer education course.

    D. **Consumer Debts** (can be rebutted by debtor)

        1. Any consumer debt incurred within 90 days of filing of petition (order of relief) of more than $675 to a single creditor for luxury goods or services;

        2. Any cash advance more than $950 by the debtor using a credit card or other open-ended consumer credit if incurred within 70 days of the filing of the petition (order of relief).

III. **Debts Not Discharged (by Statute) under Any Circumstances—(the most important ones)**

    A. **Unpaid Taxes (Two Years)**—Includes charges incurred to pay U.S. taxes (Taxes due at least three years prior to filing bankruptcy are discharged. Taxes due within two years of the filing of bankruptcy are NOT discharged.)

    B. **Debts**—Incurred through fraud, larceny, or embezzlement (i.e., obtaining money by false pretenses)

    C. **Judgments for Willful and Malicious Injuries** (i.e., something more than an accident or negligence)

    D. **Debts Incurred (Judgments) as a Result of Driving while Intoxicated**

    E. **Unscheduled Debts** (those not listed by the debtor upon filing of bankruptcy and not actually known to trustee)—See the "Bankruptcy Process" lesson.

    F. **Alimony, Maintenance, and Child Support**

    G. **Debts Resulting from fraud as a Fiduciary (Embezzlement)**

    H. **Fines and Penalties**—Payable to a governmental unit

I. **Student Loan Debts or Benefits** (exception if debtor can demonstrate undue hardship)

J. **Sarbanes-Oxley Bonuses and Incentives** awarded to executives of companies based on fraudulent financial statements—Their obligation to repay these amounts cannot be discharged

K. **Consumer Debts**—Debts incurred within 90 days of the bankruptcy filing by the debtor of $675 or less are exempted from this nondischarge. Anything that you spend over the $675 on luxury goods would be a nondischargeable debt—you would still owe that amount to that creditor.

IV. Tax Claims Discharged—If trustee requests a tax audit (determination of unpaid taxes) and the taxing authority does not notify the trustee within 60 days that the audit has been commenced, or if the audit is not completed within 180 days, both the trustee and debtor are discharged from tax liability.

V. Reaffirmations—Agreements between a debtor and creditor that a debt will not be discharged in bankruptcy.

A. Rules for a Reaffirmation to Be Enforceable

1. The agreement must be entered into prior to the granting of the discharge decree in bankruptcy;

2. The agreement must be signed and filed with the court;

3. If debtor is represented by an attorney, no hearing or court approval is required if the attorney files an affidavit or declaration that the debtor has been fully advised of the legal consequences of the agreement and such is not a hardship on the debtor or the debtor's family. If not represented by an attorney, a hearing and approval is required; *and*

4. The agreement must include a statement for debtor's right to rescind the agreement at any time prior to the discharge decree being granted or within 60 days of the filing of the agreement, whichever is later. This statement must be clearly and conspicuously stated.

B. The Bankruptcy Reform Act of 2005—Reaffirmation

1. If debtor's monthly income less debtor's monthly expenses is less than scheduled payments on reaffirmed debt, a rebuttable presumption of discharge due to hardship is presumed. To rebut (because the debtor wishes to pay the reaffirmed debts), the debtor can file a written explanation, and debtor's attorney must certify that in his or her opinion, the debtor is not unable (i.e., is able) to make the payments on the reaffirmed debts.

2. The debtor must receive several disclosures before signing a reaffirmation. These disclosures include notice that debtor is not required to affirm any debt; notice that liens on secured property (such as real estate mortgages and liens on cars) will remain in effect even if debt is not reaffirmed; state the amount of debt affirmed with rates of interest and when payments begin; and state the right to rescind. These disclosures must be signed by the debtor, certified by the debtor's attorney, and filed with the court with the reaffirmation agreement.

Government Regulation of Business

Federal Securities Regulation

Defining a "Security"

The first step in mastering securities regulation is logically to understand what a "security" is. The definition is rather broad.

After studying this lesson, you should be able to:

1. Understand which instruments and arrangements are treated as "securities" by the law and therefore come within the scope of securities regulation.

I. **Definition**

   A. The statutory definition (1933 Act) contains a laundry list, plus catch-all terms, broadly defining a **security** to mean:

   > "Any note, stock, treasury stock, bond, debenture, evidence of indebtedness, certificate of interest or participation in a profit-sharing agreement, collateral-trust certificate, pre-organization certificate of subscription, transferable share, **investment contract**, voting-trust certificate, certificate of deposit for a security, fractional undivided interest in oil, gas, or other mineral rights, any put, call, straddle, option, or privilege on any security, certificate of deposit, or group of index of securities (including any interest therein or based on the value thereof), or any put, call, straddle, option, or privilege entered into on a national securities exchange relating to foreign currency, or, in general, any interest or instrumentality common known as a 'security,' or any certificate of interest or participation in, temporary or interim certificate for, receipt for, guarantee of, or warrant or right to subscribe to or purchase, any of the foregoing."

   B. The 1934 Act's definition is quite similar.

      1. A share of corporate stock is the prototypical security. It is always a security and any other investment interest that seems to share most of its features, especially an investment of money to be managed by others with an expectation of profit, is probably a security.

II. **The Investment Contract**—The most important of the catch-all categories is the investment contract.

   A. Elements of an investment contract:

      1. Investment of money

      2. In a common enterprise

      3. With an expectation of profit

      4. To be earned primarily by the actions of others

Example
Promoters seeking to develop an orange grove could have incorporated and sold stock in the corporation to raise funds. Instead, they sold the actual trees to investors. If an investor put in 1/20th of the money, then he was deemed owner of 1/20th of the trees. All oranges were tended, harvested, and sold by the promoters. The owner of 1/20th of the trees would receive 1/20th of the profits. Although the promoters insisted that they were selling trees, the court held that they were actually selling "securities" in the form of an investment contract. The investors invested money in a common enterprise (if the weather was good all could profit; if there was a serious freeze, all investors would lose money). They did so hoping to make money primarily by the planting, cultivating, harvesting, and marketing efforts of the promoters.

III. Key Distinctions to Remember

A. Passive investors need legal protection more than investors who are actively involved in the enterprise and their investments are more likely to be deemed securities.

Examples

1. General partners invest money in a common enterprise (the partnership business) with an expectation of profit. However, because they are general partners, they can protect themselves by being actively involved in the enterprise. General partnership interests usually are not securities.

2. Limited partners invest money in a common enterprise (the partnership business) with an expectation of profit. Additionally, because they must sit on the sidelines in order to protect their limited liability and may not take an active role in directing the enterprise, they, unlike general partners, hope to profit by the efforts of others (the general partners). Limited partnership interests usually are securities.

B. A transaction involving an investment purpose is more likely to create a security than a transaction involving a purpose of consumption.

Example
A loans $50,000 to B so that B can start a business. B signs a note promising to pay the money back with interest. This is more likely to be a security than if B had borrowed the money (and signed the note) in order to buy a luxury boat that he wanted to cruise around in during his spare time.

The Registration Process

After studying this lesson, you should be able to:

1. Understand the background reasons for requiring companies to register securities with the SEC.

2. List the basic registration exemptions that exist.

3. Comprehend the traditional rules that govern the registration process.

4. Understand the recent reforms to the process and be able to explain what a WKSI and an FWP are.

I. **Requirements and Basic Procedure**

   A. **The 1933 Act's Requirements Cover**

      1. Initial public offerings, wherein companies sell to the general investing public for the first time

      2. Seasoned offerings, wherein public companies print and sell new securities to the public

      3. Secondary offerings, wherein persons controlling or closely affiliated with public companies sell their securities under circumstances where it is appropriate to treat the transaction as if it were being made by the company itself

   B. **Basic Procedure**

      1. Issuer files registration statement with SEC.

      2. Issuer waits 20 days for SEC approval, during which time preliminary "red herring" prospectus is disseminated, and oral offers and limited types of written offers can be made.

      3. Registration statement is deemed "effective" and sales can begin.

II. **The Distribution Process for Securities Is Similar to That for Products**

   A. **Product**—Manufacturer–Wholesaler–Retailer–Customer.

   B. **Security**—Issuer–Underwriter–Broker–Investor.

III. **Basic Legal Framework**

   A. **The Process Breaks down into Three Periods**:

      1. The prefiling period, before the registration statement is filed with the SEC;

      2. The waiting period, after the issuing company has filed but before the SEC has given permission for selling to begin (the effective date);

      3. The post-effective period.

   B. **During the Prefiling Period**—A company can neither offer to sell securities nor sell them.

   C. **During the Waiting Period**—A company may make oral offers and certain types of written offers but cannot sell the securities.

   D. **Elaboration**—During the waiting period, oral offers are permitted along with certain specified types of written offers, most importantly:

      1. The preliminary or "red herring" prospectus, and

      2. The "tombstone" ad, a black-bordered advertisement usually placed in the *Wall Street Journal* that would contain only:

         a. The name of the issuer;

         b. The full title of the security and the amount being offered;

         c. A brief description of the company's business;

         d. The price range of the security;

      e. The name of the managing underwriter;

      f. The contemplated date of the issuance; and

      g. A few other minor items.

    3. Both the red herring prospectus and the tombstone ad will contain cautionary words that they constitute neither offers to sell nor solicitations of offers to buy and that no binding contract can be entered into until after the registration statement becomes effective.

  E. **During the Post-Effective Period**—An issuer may both offer and sell the securities.

IV. Contents of Registration Statements—The registration statements include, among other items:

  A. Financial Statements audited by independent CPA

  B. Names of issuer, directors, officers, underwriters, etc.

  C. Risks

  D. Description of issuer's business

  E. Description of security and intended use for proceeds

V. Disclosure to Investors—Much of the registration statement's contents go into the prospectus, a part of the registration statement that must be delivered to buyers.

  A. The preliminary ("red herring") prospectus is used during the waiting period, but cannot be used thereafter; it contains most of the information that the final prospectus will contain, except for information such as the final price to be charged and fees to underwriters that cannot be determined until the effective date.

  B. The final prospectus is used after the effective date.

  C. The final prospectus must be delivered to investors before, or along with, the purchased securities (or written confirmation of purchase).

  D. The final prospectus may be supplemented by written advertising material called "free writing" that is not permissible during the waiting period.

VI. SEC Review

  A. **Theoretically**—The SEC reviews the registration statement during a 20-day waiting period and the registration statement becomes effective on the 20th day after filing.

  B. **Fact**—The SEC usually does not review the registration statements of seasoned issuers and often allows them to "accelerate" their registration statements and sell before the theoretical 20-day waiting period has expired. When the SEC does review registration statements, such as for all companies going public for the first time, it usually takes much longer than 20 days, typically 60–80 days. Nonetheless, the AICPA tests the theoretical legal framework rather than the actual practice.

  C. **Key point**—The SEC does not review the merits of the securities being offered nor make any guarantees to investors as to the quality of the securities. Issuers can sell the worst securities imaginable so long as they fully disclose how bad they are. Nor does the SEC guarantee the thoroughness and accuracy of the registration materials. When it allows a registration statement to become effective, the SEC is simply indicating that it has not found anything wrong with the disclosures contained therein. Nothing prevents the SEC from finding problems later and acting on them.

VII. Shelf Registration—Before shelf registration, a company that had two or more offerings in a relatively short time frame would have to go through the entire registration process for each offering, which was very duplicative and wasteful. The SEC realized that this was somewhat wasteful and began allowing the largest 2,000 or so companies to file a single registration statement that would cover the securities they expected to sell during the next three years. Then, whenever an advantageous "market window" presented itself, these firms could pull the securities "off the shelf" and begin selling them within just a day or two.

VIII. Securities Offering Reform Program (SORP)

A. In December 2005, through the Securities Offering Reform Program (SORP), the SEC expanded the "shelf registration" concept to what might be considered "company registration." The largest firms, which are widely followed in the marketplace, are allowed to file a registration statement covering three-year periods. They can then largely ignore the traditional rules covering permissible activities in prefiling and waiting periods. The notion is that these firms are so widely followed in the market every day that a registration statement really does not add much in the way of meaningful information. Therefore, they can talk about their companies and even their companies' stock, largely without restriction.

B. Two particular concepts should be noted.

1. **First**—The SORP rules divide issuers into several categories, the largest of which are called *well-known seasoned issuers* (WKSIs—pronounced "wicksees"). These are firms that have been reporting regularly to SEC for at least a year, (b) eligible to use Form S-3 or F-3, and (c) have either (i) $700 million of worldwide public common equity float, or (ii) have issued $1 billion of registered debt in the previous three years. These firms make up only 30% of listed firms but they control 95% of listed firms' assets. It is only these firms that are allowed to take full advantage of the new SORP rules, although more limited benefits flow to many smaller issuers.

2. **Second**—It is important to know the concept of a *free writing prospectus* (FWP). Traditionally, after the effective date, firms were allowed to supplement the final prospectus with additional literature called "free writing." WKSIs are now allowed to use additional material (FWPs) at any time with few restrictions other than the material usually has to be filed with the SEC. Some of the other categories of issuers are allowed to use FWPs on a more restricted basis (typically only after filing a registration statement).

C. The JOBS Act of 2012, which will be discussed in subsequent lessons, made additional significant changes to the traditional registration process, primarily by allowing firms that declare themselves to be *emerging growth companies* (EGCs) to receive certain breaks from the traditional rules.

Exempt Transactions and Securities

Because registration is expensive and time-consuming, companies seeking to raise capital would generally prefer to avoid it. They may avoid it if they sell exempt securities or sell nonexempt securities through exempt transactions. This lesson addresses exempt securities.

After studying this lesson, you should be able to:

1. Identify securities that are exempt from SEC registration rules.

2. Understand the basic rules that can exempt certain offerings from the SEC registration process.

3. Understand the motives and benefits for issuers of qualifying for these exemptions.

4. Comprehend that these are exemptions from the registration process but not from the antifraud rules.

5. Understand the (subordinate) role of state securities regulations (blue sky laws) in the overall securities regulatory scheme.

I. **Exempt Securities.** These types of securities are exempt from SEC registration requirements.

  A. **Bank and Government Securities**

    1. **Rationale**—Bank and government securities are heavily regulated by other federal and state laws.

    2. **Limitation**—Public utilities are not exempt.

  B. **Short-Term Notes**—Commercial notes (not notes for investment purposes) are exempt if carrying maturity of less than nine months.

  C. **Charitable Organizations' Securities**—Nonprofit educational, religious, benevolent, fraternal, or charitable organizations.

  D. **Others**

    1. Regulated savings and loans

    2. Federally regulated common carriers

    3. Receivers or trustees in bankruptcy (with court approval)

    4. Insurance and annuity policies (but not regular securities issued by insurance companies)

      a. **Limitation**—Regular securities issued by insurance companies are not exempt.

Example
Prudential Insurance Co. sells annuities. These carry many of the same characteristics of securities but are exempt from registration. Prudential Insurance Co. decides to have a public offering of its own securities to raise capital. This transaction is not exempt from registration on grounds that the offeror is an insurance company.

    5. Domestic governmental organizations

II. **Exempt Offerings**

  A. **Three Major Types**—Congress has authorized three major types of transaction exemptions wherein the securities need not be registered with the SEC even though they are not exempt securities.

    1. **"Small offering" exemptions** (authorized by Sec. 3(b) of the 1933 Act)

      a. **Rationale**—These offerings need not be regulated because of the relatively small threat to the public posed by a small offering.

Example
Regulation A, and Rules 504 and 505 of Regulation D

2. **Private placement exemptions** (authorized by Sec. 4(2) of the 1933 Act)

   a. **Rationale**—These offerings need not be regulated because of the sophisticated nature of offerees who can protect themselves.

   b. **Key concept**—Accredited Investors (AIs) who can look out for themselves and therefore do not need the protection of the 1933 Act's disclosure provisions, include: millionaires; persons who make $200,000/yr (or $300,000/yr with spouse); institutional investors; insiders of the issuer; and charitable, educational, or religious organizations worth at least $5 million. The SEC is currently considering amending its definition of an "accredited investor," in part to account for inflation.

Example
Rule 506 of Regulation D

3. **Intrastate offering exemptions** (authorized by Sec. 3(a)(11) of the 1933 Act)

   a. **Rationale**—These offerings need not be federally regulated because they happen primarily inside a single state's borders and can be adequately regulated by that state.

Example
Rule 147 under Section 3(a)(11) of the 1933 Act

B. **Characteristics of Key Transaction Exemptions**

   1. **Rule 504 of Regulation D**

      a. **Nature of issuer**—Rule 504 can be used mostly by small companies, not by 1934 Act reporting companies or investment companies.

      b. **Limit on amount**—Rule 504 can be used to raise only $1 million in any 12-month period.

      c. **Manner of offering**—General solicitation and advertising are not allowed unless either (a) the securities are registered under a state law requiring public filing and delivery of a substantive disclosure document to investors before sale, or (b) the securities are issued under a state law exemption that permits general solicitation, as long as sales are made only to accredited investors.

      d. **Purchaser requirements**—There are no such requirements; Rule 504 securities may be sold to anyone.

      e. **Information requirements**—There are none.

      f. **Filing requirements**—The issuer need only file a Form D with the SEC within 15 days of the first sale of securities under the exemption. Even failure to comply with this requirement will not disqualify the offering from the exemption, but the SEC may prevent the issuer from using Reg D again in the future.

      g. **Resale restrictions**—Resale is restricted unless the conditions mentioned for the manner of offering are met. If resale is restricted, the initial buyer must find its own exemption, which generally requires holding the securities for six months or a year before reselling them.

   2. **Rule 505 of Regulation D**

      a. **Nature of issuer**—Cannot be used by investment companies or companies that have recently been in trouble with the SEC ("bad boys").

      b. **Limit on amount**—Can be used to raise only $5 million in any 12-month period.

      c. **Manner of offering**—Cannot use general solicitation or advertising, unless sell only to AIs.

    d. Purchaser requirements—Can sell to an unlimited amount of accredited investors but no more than 35 unaccredited investors.

    e. Information requirements—Same as Rule 506.

    f. Filing requirements—Form D within 15 days.

    g. Resale restrictions—To prevent easy circumvention of the rule's restrictions, the shares' resale is restricted for **six months or** a year and the issuer must take steps to ensure that buyers know that they are restricted, such as by printing a legend on the securities.

3. Rule 506 of Regulation D

    a. Nature of issuer—Cannot be used by companies that have recently been in trouble with the SEC ("bad boys").

    b. Limit on amount—None.

    c. Manner of offering—Cannot use general advertising or solicitation, unless sell only to AIs.

    d. Purchaser requirements—Can sell to an unlimited number of accredited investors but no more than 35 unaccredited investors. Furthermore, all of the unaccredited investors must either be "sophisticated" in their own right or act through "purchaser representatives" who have the skill to evaluate the investments for them.

    e. Information requirements—No particular information must be disclosed if sales are exclusively to accredited investors, but if some sales are made to unaccredited investors, there are certain minimal disclosure requirements. The more funds are raised, the higher the disclosure requirements.

    f. Filing requirements—Form D within 15 days.

    g. Resale restrictions—To prevent easy circumvention of the rule's restrictions, the shares' resale is restricted for **six months or** a year and the issuer must take steps to ensure that buyers know that they are restricted, such as by printing a legend on the securities.

4. Regulation A (also known as Reg A+ after recent amendments)

    a. Nature of issuer—Cannot be used by 1934 Act reporting companies, investment companies, non-Canadian foreign issuers, or "bad actors."

    b. Limit on amount

        i. Tier 1—$20 million in 12-month period

        ii. Tier 2—$50 million in 12-month period

    c. Manner of offering—Unique "testing the waters" provision allows offeror to make some preliminary offers to determine whether there is sufficient interest in the securities and to cancel the offering completely without violation if there is not.

    d. Offeree and purchaser requirements

        i. Tier 1: None

        ii. Tier 2: Nonaccredited individual investor cannot buy stock constituting more than 10% or greater of his or her annual income or net worth (unless the stock is also listed on a national stock exchange). Nonaccredited firm cannot buy more than 10% of the greater of annual revenue or net assets.

    e. Information requirements

        i. Tier 1: Offering circular, 2 years unaudited F/S

        ii. Tier 2: Offering circular, 2 years audited F/S, *and* limited periodic reporting to SEC

    f. Filing requirements

        i. Tier 1: Simplified Form 1-A and offering circular

        ii. Tier 2: Simplified Form 1-A, offering circular, and 2 years audited F/S.

g. **Resale restrictions**—None

h. **Other**—Tier 2 offerings are exempt from state blue sky review, though states' regulators may continue to require mere "notice" filings and to punish fraud in connection with such offerings.

Type of Offering	Nature of Issuer	Limit on Amount	Manner of Offering	Offeree and Purchase Requirements	Information Requirement	Filing Requirement	Resale Restrictions
Reg. A	No '34 Act reporting companies, investment companies, non-Canadian foreign issuers, or "bad actors"	Tier 1: $20m/12 mo. Tier 2: $50m/12 mo.	"Testing the waters" permitted before filing Form 1-A	Tier 1: no requirements Tier 2: non-accredited individual investors can't buy stock worth more than 10% or greater of annual income or net worth	Tier 1: offering circular Tier 2: 2 yrs audited F/S, limited periodic reporting to SEC	Tier 1: simplified Form 1-A and offering circular Tier 2: simplified Form 1-A, offering circular, and 2 yrs audited F/S	None
Rule 147	Issuer must be organized and doing business in-state (80% test) and use 80% of proceeds in state	No limit	No limit, but must be intrastate	All offerees must be state residents	None	None	Limited to other residents for 9 mo.

5. **Rule 147 Intrastate Offering**

a. **Nature of issuer**—Issuer must be organized and doing business in the state in which it plans to do the offering. To be safe, should meet "80%" test, including having at least 80% of its assets in-state, making 80% of its revenue in-state, and using 80% of the proceeds of the offering in-state.

b. **Limit on amount**—No limit.

c. **Manner of offering**—No limitation, except that the offering must stay intrastate.

d. **Offeree and purchaser requirements**—All offerees and purchasers must be in-state residents; offer to even one out-of-state resident can disqualify the exemption.

e. **Information requirements**—None.

f. **Filing requirements**—None.

g. **Resale restrictions**—For nine months can resell only to other residents of the state.

C. **The Exemptions in Table Form**

1. **The exemptions in table form—Reg. D**

Type of Offering	Nature of Issuer	Limit on Amount	Manner of Offering	Offeree and Purchaser Requirements	Information Requirement	Filing Requirement	Resale Restrictions
Rule 504	No. '34 Act reporting companies or investment companies	$1m/ 12m o.	No general solicitation or advertising*	No requirements	None	Form D w/ in 15 days of first date	Restricted resale*
Rule 505	No "bad boys" or investment companies	$5m/ 12m o.	No general advertising or solicitation**	35 non-AIs unlimited AIs	None if all AIs. If sell to non-AIs, disclosure requirement varies with whether issuer is reporting company and amount of offering.	Form D	Restricted; take reasonable care to prevent resale
Rule 506	No "bad boys"	No limit	No general advertising or solicitation**	35 non-AIs unlimited AIs, but all non-AIs must be "sophisticated" or act through "purchaser reps"	Same as 505	Form D	Same as 505

* Under Rule 504, the limitations on general solicitation and resale are lifted if either (a) the securities are registered under a state law requiring public filing and delivery of a substantive disclosure document to investors before sale, or (b) the securities are issued under a state law exemption that permits general solicitation and advertising, so long as sales are made only to AIs.
** Can use general solicitation if sales are to only AIs.

D. **Key Point**—Reg A, Reg D, and Rule 147 are issuer exemptions. Additionally, Section 4(1) exempts everyone except issuers, brokers, and underwriters so that "Joe Blow" investors can resell their shares at any time without registering (unless they are "restricted resale" shares).

III. Blue Sky Laws

A. **Preempted Regulations**—Much state regulation, except for anti-fraud rules, was preempted by Congress in 1996.

1. The National Securities Markets Improvement Act (NSMI) preempts state regulation of "covered" securities, including:

   a. Those listed on any national exchange

   b. Those issued by registered investment companies

   c. Those sold to "qualified purchasers"

   d. Those sold pursuant to federal exemptions authorized by Sec. 4(2) (e.g., Rule 506)

2. The NSMI did not preempt state regulation of securities issued under Sec. 3(b), so issuers selling pursuant to Regulation A and Rules 504 and 505 must still follow individual blue-sky laws, but the JOBS Act of 2012 preempts state regulation of Reg A offerings if they are made only to "qualified purchasers."

B. **Merit Regulation**—In particular, the NSMI ends state "merit regulation" whereby states could prevent sale of securities if they thought the sale would endanger investors. The federal philosophy is to bar sale only if information provided to investors is inadequate or misleading.

C. **The NSMI Allows States to Continue to**

1. Enforce antifraud statutes; *and*

2. Require "notice" filing.

Misconception
Many people do not realize that these exemptions are simply exemptions from registration, not from federal antifraud rules. Therefore, if in the course of an exempt offering an issuing company makes any misrepresentations, it can be sued by the SEC or by investors.

The JOBS Act of 2012

After studying this lesson you should be able to:

1. Explain the rationale underlying passage of the JOBS Act of 2012.

2. Explain the key provisions of the JOBS Act of 2012.

3. Demonstrate how the JOBS Act of 2012 fits into the overall scheme of federal securities regulation.

I. The JOBS Act of 2012

A. Introduction

1. The JOBS Act is not really a "jobs" act. It is a securities law that amended federal law with the goal of making it easier for small companies to raise capital with the hope that this would eventually lead to job creation.

2. The acronym stands for: Jumpstart Our Business Startups.

3. The Act did five major things, which we will study:

   a. Created a new category of firms called *emerging growth companies* (EGCs) that can go public via an initial public offering (IPO) yet avoid most of the burdens of being public for five years

   b. Encouraged "crowdfunding"

   c. Increased the Regulation A exemption's ceiling from $5 million to $50 million

   d. Allowed firms doing private placements to engage in general solicitation and advertising in situations where they could not do so before

   e. Changed the definition of a "public company" in order to allow firms to grow bigger before being forced to go public and thereby be saddled with all the regulatory burdens that go with that status

B. Emerging Growth Companies (EGCs)

1. Until JOBS was passed, companies that held IPOs immediately became "public companies" or "reporting companies" that had to file continuous financial reports with the SEC (10-Ks, 10-Qs, 8-Ks) and meet many other expensive regulatory requirements. Hoping to lower small firms' regulatory costs substantially, this provision allowed relatively small firms to declare themselves EGCs and then go public but delay complying with all these regulatory burdens for a period of five years.

2. To be an EGC, a firm must meet the following criteria:

   a. Have less than $1 billion in annual gross revenues during its most recently completed fiscal year,

   b. Have been publicly traded for less than five years,

   c. Have a public float of less than $700 million, *and*

   d. Have not issued $1 billion in non-convertible debt in the prior three-year period.

3. An issuer will remain an EGC until the last day of the fiscal year following its five-year anniversary of its IPO or until the EGC fails to meet the EGC criteria, whichever occurs first. During that time, it is not a reporting company and will bear substantially fewer regulatory burdens than public companies traditionally have.

4. Among other benefits firms that declare themselves EGCs enjoy are:

   a. Include only two years (instead of three years) of audited financial statements in its equity IPO registration statement.

    b. Reduced disclosure requirements regarding their executives' pay.

    c. Right to submit to the SEC a draft equity IPO registration statement for confidential **review** prior to a public filing. This allows firms to get SEC guidance before they go public without their competitors getting a chance to examine the filed information as happens in regular IPOs. However, any submission, as amended, must be filed publicly with the SEC no later than 21 days before the issuer starts conducting roadshows for the offering.

    d. Exempt for five years from complying with:

        i. Section 404(b) of the Sarbanes-Oxley Act regarding the auditor attestation report of the company's internal control over financial reporting (still need SOX 404(a) certifications by CEO & CFO)

        ii. New PCAOB rules requiring things like mandatory audit firm rotation, unless the SEC determines that such rules are necessary and in the public interest

        iii. Various executive compensation provisions, including: (1) the say-on-pay vote requirement that gives shareholders the right to cast an advisory vote on top executives' pay, (2) the advisory vote on golden parachute payments requirement, and (3) the requirement to disclose the relationship between executive compensation and the financial performance of the company

5. JOBS also allows more publicity regarding a company that is going public than has traditionally been allowed. It eliminated key restrictions on publishing analyst research and on communications between securities analysts, investment bankers, management, and prospective investors while an EGC's IPO registrations are underway. For example, investment bank analysts may now publish research reports on EGCs while their IPO registration statements are pending, even if the banks are members of the underwriting syndicate.

6. Note that foreign companies can be EGCs and that there is no requirement that an EGC actually create any jobs to take advantage of these provisions. It is estimated that 90% of companies going public will qualify for EGC status.

C. Crowdfunding

1. *Crowdfunding* is a process by which entrepreneurs and business owners can use the Internet to raise capital, typically from large numbers of people who invest small amounts with little federal regulation.

2. JOBS allows firms to raise up to $1 million in a 12-month period from individual investors through the Internet, subject to certain requirements and limitations. Before JOBS, these companies couldn't offer securities (ownership interests) due to federal securities laws and were therefore limited to giving out t-shirts and the like in exchange for donations.

3. Although JOBS allows crowdfunding, Congress was sufficiently concerned about frauds against unsophisticated investors that it imposed several major limitations. Plus, the SEC will issue additional rules that may further constrain use of this new mechanism for small firms to raise capital.

4. With crowdfunding, investors will likely find it easier to invest in small companies, but they will receive less disclosure than under previous rules and will not be able to transfer the shares they buy for at least a year after purchase (other than transfers to the issuer, an accredited investor, or to family members upon death or divorce).

5. Other requirements for use of the crowdfunding exemption from registration are:

    a. Foreign companies (that can be EGCs) cannot use the crowdfunding exemption.

    b. The crowdfunding exemption is capped at $1 million in any 12-month period.

    c. To minimize the potential damage that might occur if a fraudster used crowdfunding, the JOBS act limits the amount any single investor can invest in all crowdfunded investments (not just in a single company) in any year to an amount not to exceed:

        i. The greater of $2,000 or 5% of the investor's annual income or net worth if both of these are less than $100,000, *and*

       ii. 10% of the investor's annual income or net worth not to exceed $100,000 if the investor's annual income or net worth is $100,000 or more.

   d. Investors can invest only through a broker or a "funding portal" that is registered with the SEC and FINRA. So, instead of regulating the company raising funds, Congress provides some level of investor protection by registering the entities through which the companies raise money. The funding portal or broker must:

       i. Provide investors with information regarding risk of investment loss and risk of investing in start-ups

       ii. Do due diligence by obtaining background checks and securities enforcement regulatory history for officers, directors, and 20% securities owners of the issuer

       iii. Ensure that proceeds put into escrow and given to issuers only when the targeted offering amount is obtained and permit investors to cancel commitments

   e. Companies must make certain disclosures that vary with the amount of funds they raise through crowdfunding:

       i. If a company raises $100,000 or less it is required to file only its most recent tax return, if any, and financial statements certified by the company's CEO.

       ii. If a company raises between $100,000 and $500,000, it must also have the financial statements reviewed by an independent public accountant.

       iii. If a company raises between $500,000 and $1 million, the financial statements must be audited.

   f. Companies raising capital through crowdfunding may not compensate promoters, finders, or lead generators for providing the broker or funding portal with the personal identifying information of any potential investor.

   g. There is a "bad actor" prohibition that bans certain issuers that have been in legal trouble.

   h. State securities laws are preempted and may not block crowdfunding.

D. General Solicitation

  1. In recent years, most firms have been raising their money not through IPOs but through private offerings of $1 million or less, typically with 30 or so investors, pursuant to Regulation D. Reg D contains restrictions on advertising and other general solicitations and JOBS relaxes those restrictions with the goal of giving more clarity to the rules and more freedom to issuers. In search of investors, firms may cast a wide net, so long as they throw the minnows back into the pond. The JOBS Act substantially relaxes the ban on general solicitation by:

   a. Eliminating the ban so long as all purchasers of the securities in an offering are "accredited investors" (millionaires, big institutional investors, etc.) under Regulation D, and

   b. Requiring the issuer to take "reasonable steps" to confirm the accredited investor status of all such investors.

E. Regulation A and Mini-IPOs

  1. Regulation A has been a hybrid between a private placement and an IPO. It has allowed firms to raise money by filing a stripped down offering document yet evading most traditional IPO requirements regarding publicity limitations in a sort of "mini-IPO." Regulation A even allows companies to "test the waters" by approaching investors to see if they would be interested in buying its shares and having the right to abandon the offering if investor interest is insufficient. This would be illegal "jumping the gun" under traditional rules.

  2. However, Regulation A had a ceiling of $5 million in any given year and most issuers did not view that amount to be worth going to the trouble of trying to get SEC approval for their offering document. Plus they had to go through state blue sky review, which was often slow and difficult.

  3. The JOBS Act raises the ceiling to $50 million, leading some to call it "Regulation A+."

4. State blue sky regulation is preempted, but only if the shares are listed on a national exchange or sold only to "qualified purchasers" (to be defined by the SEC).

F. Private Company Flexibility and Growth Act

1. In 2012, Facebook was approaching 500 shareholders because it had issued shares to many of its employees as compensation. Because firms became "public companies" (or "reporting companies") when they had an IPO or reached 500 shareholders and $10 million in assets, Facebook was facing all the burdens of being a public company without enjoying the benefits of an IPO. Therefore, it held an IPO, even though it didn't really want to.

2. The JOBS Act gives companies such as Facebook more control over when they go public by (a) raising the shareholder count ceiling from 500 to a maximum of either 2,000 persons in total or 500 persons who are not "accredited investors," and (b) excluding from the count investors who became shareholders through the issuer's employee compensation plan and investors who bought through crowdfunding.

Liability Provisions—1933 Act

The 1933 Act contains three explicit liability provisions—Sec. 11, Sec. 12(a)(1), and Sec. 12(a)(2). For exam purposes, Sec. 11 is the key. It is based upon common law fraud provisions, but dramatically relaxes some of the requirements of a common law fraud claim in a pro-plaintiff way.

After studying this lesson, you should be able to:

1. Understand the basic liability provisions of Section 11.

2. Understand the basic liability provisions of Section 12(a)(1).

3. Understand the basic liability provisions of Section 12(a)(2).

I. **The 1933 Act**—Because the 1933 Act focuses on the initial sale of securities, accountants' liability arises primarily due to inaccurate audited financial statements contained in the registration statement that must be filed with the SEC (unless an exemption applies). The Securities and Exchange Commission (SEC) can bring civil actions alleging 1933 Act violations, and injured investors can also bring lawsuits for civil damages.

II. **Three Primary Causes**—There are three primary causes of action for violation of 1933 Act provisions:

    A. **Sec. 11**—Remedies misleading statements and omissions contained in the registration statement as of its effective date.

    B. **Sec. 12(a)(1)**—Remedies violations of Sec. 5.

        1. Offering a security before filing a registration statement

        2. Selling a security before the registration statement becomes effective

        3. Selling a security without providing a prospectus

        4. Providing a prospectus that does not comply with Sec. 10 requirements

    C. **Sec. 12(a)(2)**—Remedies misstatements or omissions in the initial sale of securities that occur outside the registration statement.

        1. Until 1996, 12(a)(1) and 12(a)(2) were known as 12(1) and 12(2), respectively.

    D. Section 11 is the most important of these provisions, but here are a few things to keep in mind regarding Section 12(a)(1):

        1. Accountants are deemed "experts" with special responsibility.

        2. Only "sellers" of securities are liable under Secs. 12(a)(1) and 12(a)(2), so unless accountants "solicit" sales, they should not be liable under those sections.

Examples

1. Only "sellers" of securities are liable: ABC Accounting Firm certifies financial statements included in a registration statement. The financial statements are materially inaccurate. Additionally, the issuer sent out prospectuses that did not conform to Sec. 10 requirements. ABC may well be liable under Sec. 11 as an expert, but it will not be liable under Sec. 12(a)(1) if all it did was certify the financial statements.

2. Only "sellers" of securities are liable: ABC Accounting Firm was asked by its tax clients for investment advice. ABC advised the clients to invest in a company that was owned in large part by partners of ABC. The clients lost a large amount of money and sued ABC under Sec. 12(a)(2). The clients were able to win because ABC's partners had gone beyond their role as accountants and actually solicited investments by the clients.

III. Elements that Plaintiffs Must Prove to Win a Sec. 11 Claim

A. A false statement or omission of fact appeared in a registration statement.

    1. The accounting firm is liable only for that part of the registration statement (financial statements) that it prepared.

Examples

1. ABC Accounting Firm certifies the financial statements for a registration statement filed by XYZ Computer Co. The financial statements are accurate but some of the textual portion of the registration statement describing XYZ's business history is inaccurate. ABC is not liable for these inaccuracies.

2. Chapter 1: ABC Accounting Firm certifies the financial statements for a registration statement filed by XYZ Computer Co. The financial statements are accurate as of the effective date of the registration statement, but soon thereafter, the company suffers severe business reverses. The financial statements no longer accurately reflect XYZ's status. ABC cannot be liable under Sec. 11 for these problems.

B. The misstatement or omission was **material**.

Example

ABC Accounting Firm certifies the financial statements for a registration statement filed by XYZ Computer Co. The financial statements indicate that XYZ's earnings in the previous year were $3.2 million, when really they were only $3.18 million. The $20,000 error is probably immaterial to any investor's decision and ABC is not liable for the inaccuracy.

C. Plaintiff bought securities that were issued under the defective registration statement.

    1. Need not be first purchaser, but must be able to "trace" shares to registration statement

Examples

1. ABC Accounting Firm certifies the financial statements for a registration statement filed by XYZ Computer Co., a company going public for the first time. The financial statements are materially inaccurate and Joe, who bought his shares from Sam, sues ABC under Sec. 11. Joe can maintain the action despite not being the first purchaser. Because XYZ has just gone public for the first time, these shares were necessarily issued under the defective registration statement.

2. Chapter 1: ABC Accounting Firm certifies the financial statements for a registration statement filed by XYZ Computer Co., a company that went public a few years ago and is now making this seasoned offering. The financial statements are materially inaccurate. Joe read about the offering in the paper, called his broker, and said that he wanted to buy $10,000 worth of XYZ shares. Unless Joe can prove that the shares he bought were issued under the defective registration statement and were not previously issued shares, he cannot recover under Sec. 11.

D. Plaintiff suffered damages.

IV. Defenses for Accountant Under Sec. 11

A. Due Diligence

    1. Elements of Due Diligence:

        a. Reasonable investigation

        b. Reasonable basis

        c. Good faith belief

    2. Special burden on accountants who are "experts." Other individual defendants are allowed to rely upon "expertised portions" of registration statement.

Note
A Sec. 11 plaintiff need not prove that the accountant defendant (or any other defendant) acted in bad faith with what the law calls scienter. Indeed, a Sec. 11 plaintiff need not even prove that the accountant defendant (or any other) acted negligently. Negligence is the standard under Sec. 11, but the burden of proof is upon the defendant accountant to prove that he or she did not act negligently.

3. The issuing company itself has no due diligence defense; it is strictly liable for errors in the registration statement.

Example
ABC Accounting Firm certifies the financial statements for a registration statement filed by XYZ Computer Co. Notwithstanding the fact that ABC ensured that GAAP and GAAS were complied with and that ABC believed in good faith that the financial statements were accurate, it turns out that they contained materially misleading errors. Injured investors sue ABC, XYZ, and XYZ's officers and directors. ABC and all of XYZ's officers and directors who believed the financial statements were accurate have due diligence defenses and will not be liable. However, XYZ itself has no due diligence defense nor do any of its officers and directors who knew, or should have known, that ABC was making errors.

4. Lack of Reliance by P

Example
ABC Accounting Firm certifies the financial statements for a registration statement filed by XYZ Computer Co. The financial statements were materially erroneous, a fact that was later discovered and reported in the newspaper. Joe bought XYZ shares after having read the newspaper articles. Joe could not recover against ABC under Sec. 11 because he did not rely on the false statements.

5. Alternative Causation

Example
ABC Accounting Firm certifies the financial statements for a registration statement filed by XYZ Computer Co. The financial statements were materially erroneous. The price of XYZ stock dropped 15% following the announcement of the errors. However, the entire stock market declined an average of 15% during this same time frame, and computer stocks declined, on average, even more. ABC has a very good chance of convincing a jury that the decline in XYZ shares was not caused by the errors it made in certifying the financial statements.

6. Statute of Limitations: P Must Sue:

1. Within one year from when s/he discovered (or should have discovered) the false statements or omissions

   a. Inquiry notice: If P is put on notice that there is a problem, most courts start the one- year period running; they do not wait until P knows the full dimensions of the problem.

2. Within three years after the security was bona fide offered to the public (usually the effective date)

Example
On May 1, year 1, XYZ Computer Company's registration statement became effective. ABC Accounting Firm had certified the financial statements contained therein. In June of year 1, rumors began to circulate that XYZ had been claiming revenue from sales that were not final. Several financial publications published articles regarding these rumors. In August of year 2, investors filed a Sec. 11 lawsuit against ABC and XYZ seeking to prove that the financial statements contained in the registration statement had been materially misleading. Because the plaintiffs had been put on notice of the potential errors in June year 1, yet they waited 14 months to file the lawsuit, they are probably barred by the statute of limitations. They filed within the three-year of the offering deadline but missed the one-year of notice deadline.

B. Damages under Sec. 11

A. Defendants, including accountants, are jointly and severally liable under Sec. 11, except for:

   1. Outside directors (who are only severally liable), and

   2. Underwriters (whose liability is capped at the amount of securities they underwrote).

Example

ABC Accounting Firm certifies the financial statements for a registration statement filed by XYZ Computer Co. The financial statements were materially erroneous. Investors sued for $1,000,000. Defendants included ABC, XYZ, Sam (XYZ's CEO), Ed (an outside director on XYZ's board), and Big Chief Co., an underwriter that handled $100,000 of the offering. A jury found Ed to be 5% at fault because he had ignored some red flags indicating that the financial statements were inaccurate. All other defendants were also held to be potentially liable. Ed's maximum liability is $50,000 because he is an outside director. Big Chief's maximum liability is $100,000 because that is the amount of the offering that it underwrote. All of the other defendants, including the accounting firm, could be held liable for the full $1,000,000 if their co-defendants are insolvent.

B. Calculation of Sec. 11 Damages

   1. First, calculate the "amount paid," which is the lesser of:

   a. The amount actually paid by P; *or*

   b. The price at which the security was offered to the public.

Example

LMN Corp. files a registration statement and sells its stock to the public at $18/share. On the second day of public trading, P buys on the secondary market at $20/share. The "amount paid" is $18/share.

   2. Apply the proper formula

   3. When P sells the shares prior to filing suit:

Damages = "Amount paid" – Sale price

Example

P bought LMN shares at $10/share, the public offering price. After disclosure of errors in the financial statements contained in the registration statement, LMN shares dropped to $6/share. P sold at that price and soon thereafter filed a Sec. 11 lawsuit against Longhorn and its auditor. At the time the lawsuit was filed, LMN shares were trading at $4/share. P won the suit. Damages would be $4/share.

   4. When P still owns the shares at the time of judgment:

Damages = "Amount paid" – Value at "time of suit"

Example

P bought LMN shares at $10/share, the public offering price. After disclosure of errors in the financial statements contained in the registration statement, LMN shares dropped to $6/share. LMN shares were trading at $7/share on the day that P filed a Sec. 11 suit against LMN and its auditor. The shares were trading at $4/share on the day a jury rendered a verdict in favor of P against Ds. Damages would be $3/share.

5. When P sells the shares during the litigation at a price higher than the price "at time of suit," price:

> Damages = "Amount paid" – Sale

 Example
P bought LMN shares at $10/share, the public offering price. After disclosure of errors in the financial statements contained in the registration statement, the price of LMN shares dropped to $5/share on the day that P filed a Sec. 11 suit against LMN and its auditor. During the course of suit, the market rallied and P sold the shares at $9/share. LMN shares were trading at $4/share on the day a jury rendered a verdict in favor of P. P's damages would be $1/share.

6. When P sells during litigation at a price lower than the price "at time of suit":

> Damages = "Amount paid" – Value "at time of suit"

 Example
P bought LMN shares at $10/share, the public offering price. After disclosure of errors in the financial statements contained in the registration statement, P filed a Sec. 11 suit against LMN and its auditor. On the day suit was filed, LMN shares were trading at $7/share. During the lawsuit, P sold the shares for $2/share. A jury later returned a verdict for P. P's damages would be $3/share.

7. **Key point**—Punitive damages are not allowed under Sec. 11 or any other federal securities law provision.

C. Charts Summarizing 1933 Act Civil Liability

A. Elements of Recovery

Cause of Action?	Wrongful Act?	Scienter?	Reliance?	Causation?	Damage?	Potential Ds
Sec.11	Misleading statement or omission in RS	No; nor must P prove negligence	No, but must be able to "trace" shares to defective RS	No	Yes	Issuer and its insiders, underwriters, auditors, and other experts. Privity not necessary.
Sec.12(a)(1)	Illegal offer or sale (usually sale w/o registration where no exemption applies)	No; virtual strict liability	Same as Sec.11	No	Yes	All "sellers"—those who transfer title or who "solicit" the transaction. Privity not necessary.
Sec.12(a)(2)	Misleading statement	No; nor must P prove negligence	Same as Sec.11	No	Yes	Same as Sec.12(a)(1)

B. Defenses

Cause of Action	Statute of Limitations	Due Diligence	No Reliance by P	Alternate Causation
Sec.11	1 yr. from date misstatement was or should have been discovered and 3 yrs. from first bona fide offer to public.	Yes; all Ds except issuer	Yes, if P knew of error or 12-mo. earnings statement sent	Yes
Sec.12(a)(1)	1 yr. from date of violation and 3 yrs. from first bona fide offer to public	No, but Rule 508 protects unintentional and incidental violation of Reg.D.	No	No
Sec.12(a)(2)	1 yr. from date misstatement was or should have been discovered and 3 yrs. from sale to P	Yes	Yes, if P knew of error	Yes

Purposes, Requirements, and Provisions of the 1934 Act

The average company files a registration statement under the 1933 Act only once every nine years or so. If 1933 Act registration statements were the only source of public information about companies, investors would be in trouble. The 1934 Act is aimed at ensuring that the more important companies deliver a stream of steady information to the investing public via annual reports, quarterly reports, etc.

After studying this lesson, you should be able to:

1. Understand the wide coverage and great importance of Section 10(b).

2. Comprehend the essence of Section 10(b)'s liability provisions.

3. Comprehend the essence of Section 18(a)'s liability provisions.

4. Understand the essential purposes and basic provisions of the 1934 Securities Exchange Act.

5. List the key documents that make up the 1934 Act's periodic disclosure system.

I. **Regular Disclosure**—Provide regular disclosure by major companies even when they are not raising capital by filing registration statements.

II. **Punish Fraud**—In communications regarding the purchase and sale of securities of corporations of any size.

   A. Corporate disclosure cases

   B. Insider trading cases

III. **Created SEC**—This Act created the Securities and Exchange Commission to enforce all federal securities laws. Among other things, the SEC:

   A. Enforces the 1933 Act's registration and anti-fraud provisions

   B. Enforces the 1934 Act's continuous disclosure and anti-fraud provisions

   C. Registers and regulates broker-dealers

   D. Registers and regulates investment advisers

   E. Enforces rules regarding proxy solicitations and tender offers

   F. Enforces criminal provisions of the federal securities laws by investigating fraud and referring cases to the Department of Justice for prosecution.

IV. **Disclosure Requirement Under the 1934 Securities Exchange Act**

   A. **Who Are Reporting Companies that Must File Documents Regularly with SEC?**

      1. All companies whose shares are traded on national exchanges, such as the NYSE

      2. All companies that have registered their shares with the SEC, unless they have fallen below the following thresholds:

         a. 300 shareholders; or

         b. 500 shareholders and less than $10 million in total assets for each of the last three fiscal years.

      3. Even companies that have not registered with the SEC if they have more than **$10 million** in assets and more than **2,000 shareholders** in a single class

      4. A company that made a registered public offering during the year

      5. **OTC (over the counter)** "Bulletin Board" companies

      6. Remember that under the JOBS Act of 2012, firms that declare themselves to be Emerging Growth Companies (EGCs) need not comply with these filings for five years after their **initial public offering** (or until they no longer comply with the EGC requirements)

B. What Documents Must They File?

1. An initial registration form—(Form 10) disclosing such information as:

    a. Names of officers and directors

    b. Nature of business

    c. Financial structure of firm

    d. Bonus and profit-sharing provisions for officers and directors

2. Continuous disclosure forms

    a. 10-Ks—annual reports (containing certified F/S)

    b. 10-Qs—quarterly reports (F/S need not be certified)

    c. 8-Ks—interim reports covering important developments to be filed within four business days of when the development occurs

C. Other 1934 Act Filing Requirements

1. Concentrations of shares (Section 13(d))

    a. Any one individual (or group working in concert) who acquires 5% of a class of equity securities of a 1934 Act reporting company must within 10 days file a Schedule 13D, disclosing:

        i. The purpose of the purchase;

            (a) The key question is whether they are merely investing in the company or have acquired this block of shares as a prelude to takeover.

        ii. Amount and source of funds; *and*

        iii. Name and background of acquirer.

    b. Purpose of requirement—To alert shareholders to potential changes in control of their corporations.

2. Tender offers

    a. If an acquirer makes a tender offer to shareholders of a target corporation for control of the target, the 1934 Act imposes substantial filing requirements on both parties.

    b. Acquirer filings must disclose much the same information required by Schedule 13D and should include a discussion of plans for change if the acquisition succeeds.

    c. Target filings must include the target management's position regarding whether target shareholders should tender their shares or resist the takeover.

    d. Purpose of requirement—So that shareholders of target corporation can make an informed judgment as to whether they should tender or retain their shares.

3. Proxy solicitations (Section 14)

    a. Virtually all reporting companies must solicit proxies from shareholders in order to achieve the necessary quorum to hold their state law mandated annual meetings to elect directors and special meetings to approve transactions that shareholders are entitled to vote on, including mergers.

    b. The 1934 Act mandates that such solicitations must be accompanied by proxy statements containing SEC-mandated disclosures including:

        i. All material facts about matters to be voted on;

        ii. Extensive background on nominees if it is a board of directors' election; *and*

        iii. Extensive information on the advantages and disadvantages of a transaction if it is a special election for matters such as mergers or sale of major assets.

    c. All issuer proxy statements must include two years' audited F/S.

4. **Insider trading**

    a. Section 16(a) of the 1934 Act provides that three classes of persons must disclose their transactions in their own company's stock:

        i. Officers;

        ii. Directors; *and*

        iii. Holders of at least 10% of the company's registered equity securities.

            (a) Rationale—These three categories of persons have significant control over their company and could abuse it by engaging in insider trading; disclosure of their trades to the world should minimize any abuses.

            (b) In addition to filing with the SEC an initial report regarding their holdings when they attain the status of officer, director, or 10% holder, these persons must report any significant transactions in their company's shares within two days of the transaction.

    b. If a reporting company's officers, directors, or 10% holders do not comply with the Section 16(a) reporting requirements, the company itself must disclose these violations in its proxy statements and Form 10-Ks.

    c. Section 16(b) of the 1934 Act provides that any officer, director, or 10% holder must disgorge any profits derived from "shortswing" transactions in their company's stock. Actual use of inside information is irrelevant to Section 16 liability.

        i. **A "short-swing" transaction** occurs almost any time the insider buys within six months of selling or sells within six months of buying.

> **Example**
> If a director of A Corp. buys 100 A shares on July 1 for $60 and sells 100 A shares on December 10 for $70, a "short-swing" profit of $1,000 has been gained and must be disgorged.

    D. Any **intentionally misleading statement** in any of these 1934 Act documents is actionable.

V. Section 10(b) and Rule 10b-5 of the 1934 Act—Apply to all securities, no matter how big or small the company is, whether it is registered or unregistered with the SEC, and whether an initial offering or secondary trading is involved. The Sarbanes-Oxley Act of 2002 made some important changes to the 1934 Act.

    A. Key Points

        1. If there is a false statement in a registration statement, such as erroneous financial statements certified by an accounting firm, plaintiffs can sue under both Section 11 of the 1933 Act and Section 10(b) of the 1934 Act. However, whereas the standard of liability under Section 11 is mere negligence (and the burden of proof is on the defendant), the standard of liability under Section 10(b) is scienter (bad intent) and the burden of proof is upon the plaintiff.

        2. The SEC can bring civil charges alleging violations of Section 10(b) and injured investors can also bring civil suits for damages.

VI. What Plaintiffs Must Prove to Win a 10b-5 Claim

    A. False Statement or Omission of Material Fact

    B. Scienter by Defendant

        1. "Recklessness" is sufficiently similar to bad intent to satisfy the requirement.

> **Example**
> *Recklessness*
> ABC Accounting Firm certified the financial statements of XYZ Computer Co. that were included in XYZ's 10-K filing with the SEC. ABC did not comply with GAAP. Indeed, it cut corners in several respects and ignored several "red flags." Nonetheless, ABC thought the financial statements might be accurate and truly hoped that they were. ABC's actions are sufficiently reckless that, if the financial statements turn out to be materially inaccurate, ABC probably will be liable under Section 10(b).

    2. Unlike under Section 11, mere negligence will not suffice.

C. Reliance by Plaintiff

    1. Omission case—Plaintiff need not prove reliance.

        a. In an omission case, plaintiff is not claiming that any affirmative lies were told, only that material facts were omitted.

> **Example**
> *Omission*
> ABC Accounting Firm certified the financial statements of XYZ Computer Co. that were included in XYZ's 10-K filing with the SEC. ABC did comply with GAAP. However, XYZ had some unusual financial considerations not covered by GAAP that, when omitted, rendered the financial statements materially misleading. Plaintiff investors suing under Section 10(b) and Rule 10b-5 would not have to prove reliance for it is very difficult to prove that you relied on something that was hidden from you.

    2. Active misrepresentation case—Plaintiff must prove reliance.

        a. May satisfy by proof of "fraud on the market"—That is, by P showing that although s/he did not read the particular false statement (i.e., a faulty financial statement contained in a 10-K), market professionals did, and their reaction established a market price on which P relied when purchasing the securities.

> **Example**
> *Active Misrepresentation*
> ABC Accounting Firm certified the financial statements of XYZ Computer Co. that were included in XYZ's 10-K filing with the SEC. The financial statements reported earnings of $10 million. This was surprisingly good news, and the stock market reacted by boosting XYZ's share price by $10 per share. It turned out that the financial statements were inaccurate, overstating XYZ's earnings by 50%. Plaintiff investors under Section 10(b) need not show that they read the 10-K in order to sue. Rather, they relied on the accuracy of the market price as established by the professional analysts and institutional investors who did read the 10-K and whose activities largely establish the market price. The investors were indirectly misled.

D. Causation

    1. Transaction causation—To establish transaction causation, plaintiff must show that the false statements or omissions caused him to enter into the transaction (overlaps reliance element).

> **Example**
> Sam bought ABC shares from his girlfriend who had just become a stockbroker and was assigned the task of pushing ABC shares. It turns out that ABC's financial statements as contained in its most recent 10-K were inaccurate. Because Sam had not read those financial statements and did not really care what they said—he was buying to help out his girlfriend—he cannot establish transaction causation. Whatever misstatements were in the financial statements are not what caused him to buy the shares.

2. **Loss causation**—To establish loss causation, plaintiff must show that the false statements or omissions are what actually caused his financial loss; alternative causation may doom P's claim.

Example
Seeking a tax shelter, Paul wished to invest in an oil and gas limited partnership. He invested in ABC LP. Unfortunately for Paul, the entire oil and gas industry crashed just after he invested, and he lost lots of money. He sued ABC, proving that ABC had not disclosed that its promoters were not entirely honest and not very experienced in the oil and gas business. Paul may be able to show transaction causation ("I would not have bought ABC shares had I known the truth."), but he cannot show loss causation. Even if he had not invested in ABC, he would have invested in another oil and gas limited partnership and would have lost money there due to the industry-wide crash.

3. The fraud occurred in connection with a purchase or sale of securities.

   a. P must have bought or sold shares in order to have "standing" to sue.

Example
Connection with a Purchase or Sale of Securities
A has held ABC shares since Year 1. He proves that after he bought the shares, defendant officers and directors of ABC manipulated its shares for their own personal goals, causing its value to drop. Shares A bought in Year 1 at $30/share are now worth only $20/share. Nonetheless, A cannot successfully sue under Section 10(b) because he cannot prove that he bought or sold shares in connection with the false statements. He merely held the same shares.

   b. SEC can always sue without purchasing or selling, unlike investors suing for damages.

E. **Damages—Assuming plaintiff was a buyer who complains that she paid too much because of fraud:**

   1. **If P still owns shares**—Measure is amount paid minus market value at time of suit.

   2. **If P has sold shares**—Measure is amount paid minus sale price.

   3. **Punitive damages**—Are not allowed on any federal securities law theory, including 10(b).

VII. Section 10(b) Defenses

A. **Statute of Limitations**—Plaintiff must sue:

   1. Within two years of when the fraud was or should have been discovered, *and*

   2. Within five years of the fraud.

Example
Statute of Limitations
On May 1, Year 1, XYZ Computer Company's registration statement became effective. ABC Accounting Firm had certified the financial statements contained therein. In June of Year 2, rumors began to circulate that XYZ had been claiming revenue from sales that were not final. Several financial publications published articles regarding these rumors. In August of Year 4, investors filed a Section 10(b) lawsuit against ABC and XYZ, seeking to prove that the financial statements contained in the registration statement had been materially misleading. Because the plaintiffs had been put on notice of the potential errors in June of Year 2, yet they waited 26 months to file the lawsuit, they are probably barred by the statute of limitations. They filed within the five-year violation deadline but missed the two-year notice deadline.

B. Fraudulent or Reckless Conduct by Plaintiff

Example

Plaintiff is an officer of XYZ Computer Corp. and buys some of its shares. The shares plummet in price when it is learned that XYZ's most recent 10-K contained inaccurate financial statements. Plaintiff sues XYZ's accounting firm, ABC, under Section 10(b). ABC may avoid liability if it can prove that plaintiff, as an officer of XYZ, was in a position to see red flags that should have alerted him as to XYZ's troubles.

VIII. Chart Summarizing Section 10(b) Elements

Cause of Action or Omission	Section 10(b)
Misstatement	Yes
Materiality	Yes
Scienter	Yes (recklessness will suffice)
Causation	Yes, transaction (lie made me trade) and loss (lie caused stock price decline) both needed
Reliance	Omission: No Active mispresentation: Yes, but can satisfy by "fraud on the market"
Privity	No
Damages	Yes

IX. Section 18(a)

A. Although Section 10(b) is the most significant antifraud provision of the 1934 Securities Exchange Act, accountants are occasionally sued under Section 18(a) as well.

B. The statute reads, in part:

"Any person who shall make or cause to be made any statement in any application, report, or *document filed* pursuant to [this Act], which statement was at the time and in light of the circumstances under which it was made false or misleading with respect to any material fact, shall be liable to any person (not knowing that such statement was false or misleading) who, *in reliance upon such statement, shall have purchased or sold a security at a price that was affected by such statement, for damages caused by such reliance, unless the person sued shall prove that he acted in good faith and had no knowledge that such statement was false or misleading.*" (Emphasis added)

C. Among the key points to remember regarding Section 18(a) are:

1. It applies only to false statements in "filed documents"—documents filed with the SEC. Thus, it would not remedy false statements in press releases or interviews with the press. However, accountants often certify financial statements that are filed with the SEC and therefore become potentially liable under Section 18(a).

2. The courts have interpreted Section 18(a) to require plaintiffs to establish "eyeball reliance," that they saw, read, and believed the false statements. Because most investors do not read most documents that are filed with the SEC, this requirement definitely limits the usefulness of the provision to plaintiffs. The "fraud on the market" theory of reliance that is so important in Section 10(b) litigation is not available to plaintiffs suing under Section 18(a).

3. Section 18(a) assumes liability if filed documents contain materially false statements, and it shifts the burden of proof to defendants, such as accountants, to establish that they "acted in good faith and had no knowledge that such statement was false or misleading."

4. As with Section 10(b), privity of contract (as direct contractual relationship) is not an element of the right to sue. Therefore, investors may file Section18(a) lawsuits against accountants who did not buy or sell securities but who certified materially inaccurate financial statements that are filed with the SEC.

D. **Courts Hold that Plaintiffs Establish a Prima Facie Case for Recovery by Showing:**

1. Defendant made or caused to be made a false or misleading statement or omission;

2. In a filed document;

3. Materiality;

4. Plaintiff's purchase or sale of securities;

5. Plaintiff's "eyeball" reliance;

6. Causation; *and*

7. Damages.

E. **Key Defenses that Can Be Established by Defendant**

1. D acted in good faith and without knowledge that the statement was false or misleading; *and*

2. Statute of limitations (plaintiffs must sue both within one year of discovering the facts constituting the cause of action and within three years of when the cause of action accrued (which is upon plaintiff's purchase or sale).

Criminal Liability

The SEC has the authority to refer to the Department of Justice for criminal prosecution ANY intentional violation of ANY provision of the 1933 or 1934 Acts.

After studying this lesson, you should be able to:

1.   Understand that an intentional violation of any provision of the 1933 or 1934 Act is a crime.

I.   **1933 Securities Act**

   A.   Accountants are liable for any "willful" violation of any provision of the 1933 Act.

   B.   Penalties: Up to $10,000 fine and/or five years in jail

II.   **1934 Securities Exchange Act**

   A.   Accountants are liable for any "willful" violation of any provision of the 1934 Act.

   B.   Penalties: Up to $2,500,000 fine and/or 20 years in jail (up to $25 million fine if defendant is a firm).

   C.   These criminal penalties are cumulative; they may be imposed on top of the civil liability discussed elsewhere.

   D.   The SEC cannot bring criminal charges itself; rather, it refers these cases to the Department of Justice, which actually files and prosecutes the cases, often based on evidence provided by the SEC.

III.   **Sarbanes-Oxley Criminal Provisions**

   A.   SOX added several criminal provisions to the U.S. Code that accountants must be aware of.

   B.   Although it was already a crime to intentionally violate any provision of the 1933 and 1934 securities acts, Congress added a new securities fraud provision to the U.S. criminal code, 18 U.S.C. Sec. 1348, that is not as complicated as Section 10(b) and may eventually become nearly as important (although that certainly has not yet happened). That provision reads:

   1.   "Whoever knowingly executes, or attempts to execute, a scheme or artifice shall be fined under this title, or imprisoned not more than 25 years, or both."

      a.   To defraud any person in connection with any security of (a public company); *or*

      b.   To obtain, by means of false or fraudulent pretenses, representations, or promises, any money or property in connection with a class of (a public company).

   C.   In addition, SOX contains several criminal provisions for document retention and destruction that are covered elsewhere in these materials. They look like this:

   1.   **Willful failure to retain audit and review workpapers**—SOX also creates a new federal crime punishing a "knowing and willful" failure to retain audit or review work papers for a period of **five years** by up to 10 years in jail and a fine. (Sec. 802, codified at 18 U.S.C. §1520). The five-year period is functionally overridden by a different SOX provision that requires public company auditors to retain their working papers for seven years.

   2.   **Destruction of records**—SOX creates a new federal crime relating to destruction of records involved in *any* federal governmental matter or bankruptcy, making it a crime punishable by fine, imprisonment up to 20 years or both to "knowingly alter, destroy, mutilate, conceal, cover up, falsify, or make a false entry in any record, document, or tangible object with intent to impede, obstruct, or influence the investigation or proper administration of any matter within the jurisdiction of any department or agency of the United States or any case filed under (the Bankruptcy Code.)" (Sec. 802, codified at 18 U.S.C. §1519)

      a.   This statute is meant to eliminate any technical requirement that a subpoena already be issued or a proceeding be imminent before it is improper to destroy documents the government wants.

      b.   It goes well beyond audit-related documents.

3. **Corrupt tampering with documents to be used in an official proceeding**—SOX also creates a new federal crime for tampering with documents to be used in an official proceeding, providing that any person who "corruptly" (1) alters, destroys, mutilates, or conceals a record, document or other object, or attempts to do so, with the intent to impair the object's integrity or availability for use in an official proceeding, or (2) otherwise obstructs, influences, or impedes any official proceeding, or attempts to do so, shall be fined or imprisoned up to 20 years or both. The attempt to do these acts is also a crime. (Sec. 1102, codified at 18 U.S.C. §1512)

Other Federal Laws and Regulations

Employment Tax

Another key part of our country's social safety net is unemployment compensation...a temporary bridge of support for those who have involuntarily lost their jobs. As with many areas of the law, this one is mandated by the federal government, but substantial responsibility to administer the system is placed upon the states.

After studying this lesson, you should be able to:

1. Identify situations where accountants and other individuals may become personally liable for income taxes that their firms have not withheld and paid over to the federal government.

2. Identify when people qualify for Social Security benefits.

3. Explain how the Federal Insurance Contributions Act (FICA) works to fund Social Security and Medicare (but not Medicaid).

4. Explain how FICA works for self-employed individuals under the Self-Employed Contributions Act (SECA).

5. Explain how the Federal Unemployment Tax Act (FUTA) works.

I. **Payroll Taxes**

   A. To help ensure that employees' federal income taxes are paid, most employers must withhold federal income tax from employees' wages and deposit them with the federal government.

   B. Liability for failure to remit. Failure to withhold the taxes and remit them to the federal government may lead to a penalty of 100% of the tax not paid being imposed on any **responsible person** who **willfully fails** to pay the tax. 26 U.S.C. Sec. 6672.

      1. Who is a "responsible person"? The statute imposes liability on "any person required to collect, truthfully account for, and pay over any tax" who willfully fails to do so. There may be more than one "responsible party." Some courts hold that the key is whether the person had the "actual authority or ability," given his or her role within the corporation, to pay the taxes owed. In determining who is potentially liable to pay this penalty out of their own pocket, most courts look at seven factors, none of which is alone determinative:

         a. Is the person an officer or director?

         b. Does the person own part of the company?

         c. Is the person active in management of day-to-day affairs?

         d. Does the person have the ability to hire and fire?

         e. Does the person have discretion to decide which, when, and in what order debts or taxes will be paid?

         f. Does the person exercise control over daily bank accounts and disbursement records?

         g. Does the person have check-signing authority?

      2. When are CPAs "responsible persons"? Accountants have been held to be "responsible persons" when they cosigned a corporation's checks as representative of third parties and when they exercised a third party's authority to choose which creditors the corporation should pay. Accountants have been held *not* to be responsible persons where:

         a. They were bookkeepers who were neither officers nor managed day-to-day affairs of the firm.

         b. They performed part-time accounting duties with check-writing authority, but were not officers and wrote checks only as directed by superiors.

         c. They performed financial services and had signatory power for checks, but in practice signed checks only as directed by superiors.

         d. Their authority ran solely to preventing double payment of invoices.

3. What is "willful failure?"

  a. Conduct that is accidental or inadvertent is not willful.

  b. However, willful need *not* include an intent to defraud the government.

  c. Willfulness in this context means the awareness of the obligation and a conscious and voluntary payment to someone else with funds that should have been used to pay the tax owed.

4. Example. If ABC Co. lacks funds to both withhold taxes and pay its employees and its CFO chooses not to withhold taxes so that the ABC can make its payroll that month, the CFO is acting willfully and is potentially personally responsible to pay those taxes to the federal government if the ABC cannot do so.

II. Federal Insurance Contributions Act (FICA): Social Security and Medicare

A. **Social Security**—Social security benefits are aimed primarily at partially replacing earnings for workers who retire. Qualified individuals receive monthly benefits after they retire.

  1. A "fully insured" worker is entitled to payments that will vary in amount to account for inflation.

     a. To be "fully insured," one must work a minimum of 40 quarters (10 years) during which he or she pays social security (FICA) taxes into the system.

     b. For most of Social Security's existence, workers were entitled to full retirement benefits at age 65. However, for reasons of fiscal solvency, the "full benefits" threshold has been changed and is sliding later and later. For example, someone born in 1937 or before was entitled to full benefits at age 65. Someone born in 1938 was entitled to full benefits at age 65 and two months. Someone born between 1943 and 1954 is, or will be, entitled to full benefits at age 66. Someone born after 1960 will be entitled to full benefits at age 67. If people retire early, they will receive discounted benefits. For example, if Sally was born after 1960 and retires "early" at age 62, she will receive only 70% of the full monthly benefit payments. If she retires at 65, she will receive only 86.7% of the full monthly benefits.

     c. In addition to these pension benefits, "fully insured" workers earn survivor benefits for their widow or widower and dependents and disability benefits for themselves and their family.

  2. A "currently insured" worker is contributing to the Social Security system but has not yet contributed for 40 quarters. Such a worker is eligible for:

     a. Limited survivor benefits (usually limited to dependent minors or those caring for dependent minors);

     b. Disability benefits; *and*

     c. Lump sum death benefits.

B. **Medicare**—Medicare covers much of the costs of hospitalization and medical benefits of insured workers (and their spouses) who are 65 and older. It can cover younger disabled workers in some cases.

C. **How are Social Security and Medicare funded**

  1. The Federal Insurance Contributions Act (FICA) imposes social security tax on:

     a. Employers

     b. Employees

     c. The Self-Employed (under the Self-Employed Contributions Act Tax)

2. The FICA tax applies only to that compensation that is deemed "wages."

   a. "Wages" includes: salary, commissions, bonuses, fees, tips, fringe benefits, and other forms of active income.

   b. "Wages" excludes: reimbursed employee expenses, interests on bonds owned, dividends on stock owned, investment income, and other forms of passive income.

3. Features of FICA:

   a. Rates are generally the same for employer and employees, who share responsibility.

   b. Rates change from time to time. In 2016, the rate is 7.65% of the employee's wages, which is allocated 6.2% for Social Security and 1.45% for Medicare.

   c. Social Security taxes are paid on only a base amount of income that is adjusted periodically for inflation (up to $118,500 in 2016). Medicare taxes are not similarly capped. Example: If Ted made $130,000 in 2016, his last $11,500 would not be subject to Social Security tax but would be subject to Medicare tax.

   d. Note: FICA taxes fund Medicare, but not Medicaid, which is paid for out of general government revenues.

4. Employers' responsibilities under FICA:

   a. Pay own share

   b. Withhold employee's equal share and remit it to the federal government in a timely fashion

   c. Pay employee's share if fail to withhold it

   d. Furnish employee with a written statement of wages paid and contributions withheld

   e. Supply taxpayer identification numbers when filing returns

5. Employers' rights under FICA:

   a. Collect employee's share from employee (though employer may voluntarily pay employee's share and deduct that amount as additional compensation, making it taxable to the employee

   b. Deduct as a business expense the contributions made on its own behalf to FICA

6. Additional Medicare Tax (AMT). In order to help fund the expansion of Medicare and other healthcare benefits, the Affordable Care Act (ACA) imposed a 0.9% Medicare surtax on top of the existing 2.9% tax.

   a. The surtax is withheld and paid over to the government by the employer, but the employer does *not* contribute to this tax. Unlike with the regular FICA taxes, the employer does not match employee contributions under the AMT.

   b. The AMT applies only to relatively wealthy individuals, applying only to earnings over the following thresholds:

      • $200,000 for a single taxpayer

      • $250,000 for joint filers

      • $125,000 for a married taxpayer filing separately

   c. Example. A single taxpayer with an income of $300,000 would pay a 1.45% Medicare tax on the first $200,000 (with that amount being matched by an employer contribution, and a 2.35% tax on the remaining $100,000 (with the employer's contribution being remaining at 1.45%).

III. Self-Employed Contributions Act (SECA) Tax

A. Self-employed persons must pay not only their federal income tax on taxable earnings but also Social Security and Medicare taxes on their own self-employed taxable earnings.

    1. Self-employed income includes net business profits and director's fees.

    2. Self-employed income does *not* include gifts.

B. Features of the Self-Employed Contributions Tax:

    1. The self-employed can deduct 50% of FICA from taxes.

    2. Because a self-employed person does not have an employer to match his or her contribution, the base rate for most = FICA rate for employer and employee combined (15.3% in 2016)

        a. But remember that for higher earners, the Additional Medicare Tax (AMT) may raise the Medicare portion of this tax by 0.9% above certain levels of income.

    3. Base rate is reduced by any "wages" earned from third parties during the year, because of the FICA paid on those wages.

        a. IRS Example: If in 2016 Joe's wages are $78,000 and he has $40,700 in self-employed income, his employer will withhold 7.65% and pay another 7.65% in FICA taxes on the $78,000. Joe must then pay 15.3% on the first $40,500 in self-employed earnings. That takes him to the $118,500 cap. He need not pay any more Social Security tax, but must pay the 2.9% (1.45% employer's share plus 1.45% employee's share) Medicare tax on the remaining $200 in earnings. In this example, Joe does not make enough money for the AMT to apply.

IV. Federal Unemployment Tax Act (FUTA)

A. Purpose—Provide unemployment compensation benefits to workers who lose jobs and cannot find new ones

B. Mechanism:

    1. Federal unemployment tax (currently 6%)—Must be paid by employer who employs persons covered by this act.

        a. Deductible by employer (who pays it), not by employee (who does not).

    2. State unemployment tax—Must also be paid by employer

        a. State tax is credited against employer's federal tax up to a maximum amount of 90% of the federal tax.

        b. State tax may go up or down depending on claims against employer.

        c. Additional credit against federal tax is created by good claims record.

Example
ABC Co. has an excellent record and under its state's system is entitled to pay unemployment tax of only 4% as contrasted to the general state rate of 5%. ABC is entitled to take a credit of 5% against the federal unemployment tax rate of 6%.

    3. Taxable amount: Only the first $7,000 paid to each covered employee is taxable under FUTA, though many states require that the state tax be paid on a higher amount.

    4. The maximum federal rate fluctuates, but was 6.0% in 2016 with a maximum state offset credit of 5.4%, so many employers pay a federal tax of only 0.6% (on $7,000) after receiving credit for the state unemployment tax they pay.

5. Thought federally-mandated, the system is administered primarily by the states.

6. Employers must file if they pay $1,500 or more in wages during any calendar quarter, or have at least one full-time, part-time, or temporary employee during at least 20 different weeks during the year.

C. Coverage is Mandatory for Qualifying Employees

1. Employees usually must have worked for a minimum specified period and earned a minimum amount of wages to be eligible for benefits. These requirements vary from state to state.

D. Eligibility for benefits usually requires (in addition to the minimum employed period and minimum wages noted above) that the employee:

1. Was terminated involuntarily.

	Eligible	Not Eligible
Fired because of business reverses.	x	
Quit because of boredom with job.		x
Fired because of refusal to accept transfer to new department.		x
Fired for embezzling from client.		x
Laid off because of temporary decline in boss's contracts.	x	
Seasonal worker paid on yearly basis (e.g., baseball player).		x
Quit due to sexual harassment by co-employees.	x	
Fired because of carelessness on the job.	x	
Fired for repeatedly and vehemently arguing with boss.		x
Quit because firing was imminent and didn't want bad mark on record.		x

Example
Employer and employee got into a screaming match. The employee stalked toward the door, stopped and then turned around. The employer told him: "Keep on walking." This was held to be a termination, so the employee was entitled to recover unemployment compensation. If the employer had kept quiet, it probably would have been a "voluntary quit" and the employee would not have been entitled to unemployment compensation.

2. Is currently available for and looking for work, *and*

	Eligible	Not Eligible
Refused suitable job offer		x
Has not looked for new job		x
Enrolled full time in school		x
Is taking a few night school classes	x	

3. Is not receiving disqualifying income

	Eligible	Not Eligible
Receiving disability benefits		x
Receiving pension income		x
Receiving holiday, vacation, and back pay from earlier job		x

Affordable Care Act

This lesson explains and analyzes important provisions of the Affordable Care Act.

After studying this lesson, you should be able to:

1. Summarize important provisions of the ACA, such as the employer mandate and the individual mandate.

2. Identify violations of the ACA.

3. Determine which companies are subject to the employer mandate.

4. Calculate the coverage of basic ACA plans.

5. Calculate various new taxes imposed by the ACA.

I. **Introduction**—In 2010, Congress enacted the Affordable Care Act (ACA) (also called the Patient Protection and Affordable Care Act (PPACA) and sometimes Obamacare). Before the ACA, most Americans had health care coverage either through insurance provided by their employers or through government programs such as Medicare, Medicaid, and CHIP (Children's Health Insurance Program). But approximately 15% of Americans (40 million or so people) lacked such coverage. The ACA was enacted to cover many of those people and is the most significant legislative change in the health care field since Medicare and Medicaid were enacted in 1965. The ACA is 2,000 pages long, and 20,000 pages of regulations have been issued to implement it. This lesson summarizes the most important features of the hugely complicated ACA, which is being implemented in stages (and litigated endlessly).

II. **Quick Summary**—The government says, in part, that the ACA "eliminates pre-existing conditions, stops insurance companies from dropping you when you are sick, protects against gender discrimination, expands free preventative services and health benefits, expands Medicaid and CHIP, improved Medicare, requires larger employers to insure their employees, creates a marketplace for subsidized insurance providing tens of millions of individuals, families, and small businesses with free or low-cost health insurance."

III. **Extensions of Coverage**—The ACA has many provisions that extended health care coverage to more people and improved the quality of coverage for many who are already covered.

   A. **Coverage of Preexisting Conditions**—Before the ACA, people who had diabetes, cancer, or many other preexisting conditions often found it very difficult to obtain health care insurance. The ACA prohibits insurance companies from denying coverage on grounds of preexisting conditions. Nor may companies eliminate benefits, refuse to renew coverage, or otherwise discriminate on those grounds.

   B. **No Dropping Coverage Because of Illness**—Before the ACA, people who became ill and therefore especially needed health care coverage often saw that coverage eliminated. Someone who had bought a health insurance policy and paid premiums might still be dropped because, for example, the insurer reexamined the insured's application and detected unintentional mistakes or minor omissions. The ACA prohibits insurance companies from canceling coverage for reasons other than failure to pay or fraud. A policy cannot be canceled just because the insured became sick.

   C. **Eliminating Gender (and Other) Discrimination**—Women use more health care services than men, on average, in part because they can become pregnant. Before the ACA, insurers could deny coverage to women or charge them more on grounds of gender. The ACA prohibits this.

   1. The ACA also prohibits other forms of discrimination by allowing insurance companies to take into account only these factors when setting premium rates:

      a. **Age**—Because elderly people use more services than younger people (but they cannot be charged more than three times what younger people are charged for the same plan)

b. **Geographic location**—Because medical care is more expensive in New York City than it is, for example, in rural Kansas

c. **Tobacco use**—Because people who smoke will generally have more health problems than those who do not

d. **Individual versus family coverage**—Because a family of four will obviously tend to be use more health services than will a single individual

D. **Extending Coverage for Children**—Under the ACA, parents who purchase family insurance plans may provide coverage for their adult children under age 26, even if the children are married, financially independent, not living with their parents, and/or entitled to purchase health insurance at their own work.

E. **Minimizing Out-of-Pocket Expenses**—Total annual out-of-pocket expenses—including deductibles but not including the cost of insurance premiums—for plans under the ACA were $6,850 for an individual plan and $13,700 for a family plan in 2016. (Those numbers, and most others used in the ACA, are inflation-adjusted annually and therefore may be higher when you read this. They might also be altered by specific policies.) Once these limits are met, all covered costs will be paid by the insurer. Plans with higher premiums typically carry lower out-of-pocket maximums.

1. **Example**—Assume Sam, an unmarried man, needs surgery that will entail $30,000 in allowable costs. Sam's insurance plan has a deductible of $1,500 and a coinsurance payment of 20%. Sam pays the first $1,500, the amount of his deductible. His coinsurance cost would be $5,700. So, Sam's total costs would be $7,200, but his out-of-pocket maximum under his insurance plan happens to match the $6,850 maximum for plans sold in the ACA Marketplace in 2016. Sam's insurance company will pay all covered costs above $6,850 and any additional covered care for the rest of the year.

F. **Eliminating Lifetime Limits**—Before the ACA, insurance companies often placed caps on the total dollar amount they would spend on an individual. A person who contracted a disease that was chronic and very expensive to treat could be denied coverage after a while. The ACA eliminates such lifetime dollar limits (as well as annual dollar limits) but only for "essential health benefits."

1. An abortion, dental care, and elective cosmetic surgery are not "essential health benefits" under the ACA.

2. But the term "essential health benefits" is broadly defined to include these 10 items:

   a. Outpatient services (including diagnosis, observation, consultation, treatment, intervention, and rehabilitation services)

   b. Emergency services

   c. Hospitalization

   d. Maternity and newborn care

   e. Mental health and substance use disorder services

   f. Prescription drugs

   g. Rehabilitative services and devices

   h. Laboratory services

   i. Preventive and wellness services

   j. Pediatric services

G. **Medicaid Expansion**—The ACA expanded eligibility and federal funding for Medicaid by enabling states to extend Medicaid coverage to all legal residents 65 and older or with an income up to 133% of the poverty line. Because most poor children are covered by CHIP plans, the goal was to increase coverage for poor adults. However, the Supreme Court held that states had the option not to participate in this expansion, and many states chose not to for various fiscal and political reasons.

IV. Employer Mandate—When the ACA was enacted, approximately half of Americans received their health coverage via employer insurance plans. To ensure that employer coverage continued, the ACA required "Applicable Large Employers" (ALEs) to either (a) offer "minimum essential coverage" to at least 95% of their full-time employees and their dependents up to age 26, or (b) pay a tax penalty (known as the employer shared responsibility fee). This requirement is known as the employer mandate. Before the ACA, approximately 90% of these large companies were already offering health care coverage.

A. What is an ALE?—It is a firm that has employed an average of at least 50 full-time equivalent employees (FTEs) on average business days during the preceding year.

B. What about small employers?—Small employers do not pay the shared responsibility fee. They qualify for various levels of employer tax credits to help them afford to offer coverage to employees.

C. How are FTEs calculated?—A firm's FTEs are comprised of (1) actual full-time employees (employees who work at least 30 hours a week) and (2) part-time employees who work less than 30 hours a week but more than 120 days per year. Part-time employees are cumulated into FTEs by dividing the total number of hours they work in a week by 30.

    1. Example—ABC Co. tries to reduce its number of full-time employees by cutting Sam's and Tina's hours from 30 per week to 20 per week and hiring Tinh to work 20 hours a week to make up for Sam's and Tina's reduced workload. However, the three of them now work, cumulatively, 60 hours per week. When that number is divided by 30, it indicates that Sam, Tina, and Tinh constitute two FTEs. While ABC has not reduced its FTE total and is therefore still an ALE if it has more than 50 FTEs, because coverage is required only for full-time employees, ABC has reduced the number of workers to whom it must offer coverage.

D. Who are dependents?—Surprisingly, perhaps, spouses are not considered dependents, so coverage need not be offered to spouses. It must be offered only to employees and nonspousal dependents, primarily children. Stepchildren and foster children are excluded.

E. What is "minimum essential coverage"?

    1. With few exceptions, the employer must offer a group plan.

    2. Coverage must be affordable, costing less than 9.5% of the employee's income.

    3. Coverage must provide "minimum value." (The employer covers at least 60% of the cost.)

        a. Bronze level—Employer covers at least 60% of cost of covered services.

        b. Silver level—Employer covers at least 70% of cost of covered services.

        c. Gold level—Employer covers at least 80% of cost of covered services.

        d. Platinum level—Eemployer covers at least 80% of covered services.

    4. Coverage must be equivalent of the ACA Marketplace's Bronze benefit package, which includes, as mentioned, no gender discrimination, no exclusion for preexisting conditions, no yearly or lifetime limit on coverage for essential benefits, deductible and out-of-pocket maximums, and coverage of the 10 essential health benefits.

F. What is the tax penalty (employer shared responsibility fee)?

The fee is triggered if at least one employee does not receive qualifying coverage, shops on the ACA Marketplace (Internet sites operated by either the state or the federal government where individuals and small businesses can compare policies and rates and perhaps qualify for government subsidies), and is eligible for a federal premium subsidy.

    1. If the employer did not offer coverage to workers as required, the penalty in 2016 was a flat $2,000 per full-time employee (excluding the first 30 employees).

    2. If only a few workers were not covered, or if that coverage did not meet minimum value standards, the fine in 2016 was $3,000 per full-time employee *who received cost assistance* (but never more than $2,000 per full-time employee minus the first 30).

3. Note that while the responsibility to provide coverage takes into account an employer's total number of FTEs, the fees imposed are based on number of full-time workers, not FTEs.

4. **Example**—ABC Co. has 300 employees, 100 of whom work at least 30 hours per week. ABC does not offer health insurance coverage to any of its employees. At least one of ABC's full-time employees buys coverage on the ACA Health Insurance Marketplace and qualifies for federal support. ABC would owe $140,000 (100 full-time employees – 30 employee exclusion × $2,000).

5. **Example**—ABC has 300 employees, 100 of whom work at least 30 hours per week. ABC offers health insurance coverage to all its employees. Under ABC's plan, full-time employee Bill has to pay 15% of his income for his coverage (exceeding the 9.5% ceiling). Instead of accepting ABC's coverage, Bill goes to the ACA Marketplace to buy more affordable alternative coverage and qualifies for federal support. ABC would owe $3,000.

G. Disclosures

1. Firms must disclose the cost of health coverage (the cost to both the employer and the employee) on each employee's Form W-2 (though this does not mean that the coverage is taxable).

2. ALEs must provide Form 1095-C to covered employees and file both 1095-C and Form 1094-C with the IRS.

   a. **Purpose**—The information disclosed on these forms enables the IRS to determine the employers that are required to offer minimum essential coverage to all their full-time employees but are not doing so.

   b. **Penalty**—ALEs that fail to file may be penalized up to $260 for each failure to file, with the total penalty capped at $6 million annually.

3. Non-ALE entities that provide minimum essential coverage to individuals (including health insurance issuers, self-insured employers, and government agencies) must provide Form 1095-B to insureds and file 1095-B and 1094-B with the IRS.

   a. **Purpose**—Form 1095B informs individuals of their coverage (and the individuals may use this form to demonstrate that they have met the individual mandate).

   b. **Penalty**—Entities that fail to file these forms are subject to general reporting penalty provisions under IRS Section 6721 (failure to file correct information returns) and Section 6722 (failure to furnish correct payee statement). The maximum penalty under each provision is $250 per violation up to a maximum of $3,000,000 per year.

4. ACA Health Insurance Marketplaces (discussed below) that enroll individuals in qualified health plans file Form 1095-A with the IRS to indicate they have provided coverage to individuals and deliver the form to individuals to give them proof of insurance.

IRS Form	Purpose
Form 1095-C	ALEs provide employees proof of insurance
Form 1094-C	ALEs file to transmit Forms 1095-C to IRS
Form 1095-B	Insurers provide enrollees proof of insurance
Form 1094-B	Insurers file to transmit Form 1095-B to IRS
Form 1095-A	Health Insurance Marketplaces transmit form to IRS and provide purchasers proof of insurance

V. Individual Mandate—Insurance works best if risk is spread over a large pool of people. Younger and healthier people often do not spend their money on health insurance, but it is very expensive for insurance companies to cover only older, less healthy people. So, the ACA requires individuals either to pay to obtain coverage or to pay a tax (also known as a shared responsibility payment civil penalty). This is the "individual mandate."

A. Most individuals already have health coverage that counts as "minimum essential health coverage" and meets the ACA's requirements via their employer's plan, Medicare or Medicaid, CHIP, the Veteran's Administration, or TRICARE (which offers insurance to active members of the military). Individuals not covered should buy qualifying health insurance from either a private insurer or through one of the ACA's Health Insurance Marketplace (see below). The ACA provides tax credits and subsidies so that low- and middle-income individuals can afford coverage.

B. **Several categories of individuals are exempt from the individual mandate, including:**

1. Prisoners

2. Members of an Indian tribe

3. Undocumented immigrants

4. People without insurance for less than three months during the year

5. People with income below the threshold for filing a federal income tax return (in 2016: $10,300 for individuals and $20,600 for married couples filing jointly)

6. People who have to pay more than 8% of their income for health insurance (after taking into account employer contributions and tax credits)

7. Those who oppose having coverage on religious grounds

C. **Penalty Amount**—For those who are required to buy coverage and do not, the fee or penalty is the *greater* of either:

1. A *per person* amount of $695 per adult and $347.50 per child, capped at $2,085 per family (in 2016), *or*

2. A *percentage of income* amount of 2.5% of household income, capped at the total yearly premium for the national average price of a Bronze plan sold through the ACA Marketplace).

   a. **Example**—The IRS proposes an example with Jim, who is unmarried with no dependents and an income of $40,000. He has not purchased minimum essential coverage. The maximum *per person* fee is $695 in 2016. Calculating *percentage of income*, $40,000 minus $10,150 (the tax filing threshold for individuals) leaves $29,850. When that number is multiplied by 2.5%, it yields $746.25. According to the IRS, the annual national average premium for a Bronze plan was $2,448. Because Jim's percentage-of-income fee is less than the national average, the latter does not apply. Jim's percentage-of-income calculation, $746.25, is greater than $695, so that is his fee.

   b. **Example**—The IRS proposes a second example with a married couple, Eduardo and Julia, who have two dependent children and a household income of $70,000. They have not purchased minimum essential coverage. The *per person* fee would be $2,085 (two adults at $695 each, plus two children at $347.50 each). This number is exactly equal to the cap for this approach. Calculating *percentage of income*, $70,000 minus $20,300 (the tax filing threshold for married couples filing jointly) leaves $49,700. When multiplied by 2.5%, this yields $1,242.50. According to the IRS, the annual national average premium for a Bronze plan that covers the family was $9,792, which is much greater than $1,242.50 and therefore does not apply. Because $2,085 (the family's per person fee) is greater than $1,242.50 (the family's percentage-of-income fee), Eduardo and Julia would owe $2,085.

VI. **ACA Health Insurance Marketplace**—As noted earlier, Americans not covered by employers' plans, Medicare or Medicaid, CHIP, the Veterans Administration, or TRICARE (which offers insurance to active members of the military) may buy policies from private insurance companies or the new ACA Marketplace. Each state has the option to set up its own marketplace, but the majority failed to do so, and the federal government may (and did) step in to operate such a marketplace in more than 30 states. The Marketplace is a one-stop, online location at HealthCare.gov where applicants may shop, compare options, and enroll in an insurance plan while determining whether they are eligible for federal tax credits, subsidies, or discounts that will help them cover their insurance costs.

A. The Marketplace offers plans of different levels (Bronze, Silver, Gold, and Platinum). Even the lowest level (Bronze), though, must provide minimum benefits, minimum protections, and minimum value.

B. People who are not offered affordable, qualifying coverage by employers may qualify for cost assistance on the ACA Marketplace based on their income. Nearly 90% of Americans who have bought through the Marketplace received financial assistance of some type, averaging in 2015 approximately 72% of the total cost of the policy.

VII. Revenue-Raising Provisions—The ACA annually provides around $100 billion in subsidies to low- and middle-income Americans to help them pay for their new coverage. It also provides employer tax credits, marketplace subsidies, and expands Medicaid and CHIP. How does it pay for these things? In addition to the money raised through the employer mandate and individual mandate, the ACA helps to pay for all its benefits by imposing a series of taxes and fees, including the following:

A. Medical Care Expense Tax Deduction—The ACA saves the government money by restricting taxpayers' ability to deduct unreimbursed medical and dental expenses for themselves and for their families from their individual income taxes. Most important, the threshold for taking such deductions was raised for most taxpayers from 7.5% of adjusted gross income (AGI) to 10%. (For people 65 and older, this increase was delayed until 2017.)

1. Medical and dental expenses that may be deducted (if they accumulate to more than 10% of AGI) include, among others:

   a. Payments for the diagnosis, cure, mitigation, treatment, or prevention of disease

   b. Payments for treatments affecting any structure or function of the body

   c. Prescription medicines or insulin

   d. Doctor-ordered medical exams, X rays, and lab services

   e. Qualified long-term care services

   f. Medical treatment at a facility for drug or alcohol addiction

   g. Medical aids such as eyeglasses, hearing aids, braces, and wheelchairs

   h. Artificial teeth

   i. Ambulance service

2. Medical and dental expenses that are *not* deductible and therefore do not count toward the 10% level include, among others:

   a. Over-the-counter drugs

   b. Funeral expenses

   c. Toiletries

   d. Most cosmetic surgery (unless necessary to improve a deformity)

   e. Nicotine patches

   f. Maternity clothes

   g. Health club dues

   h. Life insurance premiums

   i. Illegal drugs or operations

   j. Teeth whitening

   k. Veterinary fees

3. **Related rules**

   a. The expenses must be itemized on a Schedule A to be deductible.

   b. The amount of insurance premium paid by a taxpayer's employer does not count toward the threshold, though those paid by the taxpayer are deductible.

   c. Any medical expenses paid with pretax dollars (via a Flexible Spending Account [FSA] where a tax benefit is already enjoyed) cannot be claimed toward the itemized deduction.

   d. Expenses must have been paid in the taxable year.

> **Example**
> Middle-age Rick and Rosa have an AGI of $200,000 and $50,000 in uninsured medical expenses. Their deduction is limited to that portion of their expenses that exceeds 10% of their $200,000 AGI. Therefore, they may deduct only $30,000 of their $50,000 in medical expenses. Before the ACA, Rick and Rosa could have deducted that portion of their expenses that exceeded 7.5% of their $200,000 AGI; in other words, they could have deducted $35,000 of their $50,000 in medical expenses.

B. **Medicare Surtax** (also known as Net Investment Income Surtax and as the Unearned Income Medicare Contribution Tax)—The ACA imposes a 3.8% surtax on net investment income (NII) of individuals and estates and trusts above a certain level.

   1. The Medicare NII surtax falls primarily on the relatively wealthy, because it applies only to investment income earned by individuals with AGIs above these levels (in 2016):

      a. $200,000 for a single taxpayer

      b. $250,000 for joint filers

      c. $125,000 for a married taxpayer filing separately

   2. Investment income includes:

      a. Capital gains

      b. Dividends from stocks

      c. Interest from bonds or loans

      d. Royalties

      e. Gains from the sale of investment real estate

      f. Rents

   3. Investment income does *not* include:

      a. Wages

      b. Social Security benefits

      c. Unemployment compensation

      d. Life insurance proceeds

      e. Active trade or business income

   4. The Medicare surtax on NII does not apply to any amount of gain that is excluded from AGI for regular income tax purposes, such as the first $250,000 ($500,000 for married couples) of gain recognized on sale of a principal residence.

   5. The taxable amount subject to the 3.8% surcharge is the *lesser* of:

      a. Net investment income, *or*

      b. The excess of AGI over the AGI thresholds.

6. **Example**—If a single filer has active income of $170,000 and NII of $100,000, then the 3.8% tax should be paid on $70,000 of income. The excess of AGI over the AGI threshold is $70,000 versus the NII of $100,000. Because the tax applies to the lesser of these two amounts, it would be 3.8% of $70,000, or $2,660.

7. **Example**—Dave and Carol are married and file a joint return. Each earns $175,000. They also have $40,000 in investment income. Their AGI is over the threshold of $250,000 by $100,000, so they will owe 3.8% of the lesser sum of $40,000, or $1,520.

C. **Medical Device Excise Tax**—The ACA imposes a 2.3% excise tax on sales of certain medical devices. The manufacturer or importer is responsible for paying the tax.

D. **Additional Medicare Tax**—The ACA imposes a 0.9% Additional Medicare Tax (AMT) on wages and self-employment income above a certain amount (e.g., $200,000 for a single taxpayer, $250,000 for joint filers, and $125,000 for a married taxpayer filing separately). Employers are required to withhold this surtax from employees' paychecks but need not match it. This tax also falls primarily on the relatively wealthy. But passive investment income is excluded.

1. **Example**—Maria, an unmarried taxpayer, earned wages of $190,000 and had $50,000 in passive income. She need not pay the 0.9% AMT, because her earned income was less than the $200,000 threshold for unmarried individual filers. However, her AGI is $240,000, so she must pay the 3.8% Medicare Surtax on unearned income. That calculation is the lesser of her AGI over the threshold ($240,000 – $200,000 – $40,000) or the amount of unearned income ($50,000). So, Maria owes zero AMT, but $1,900 (3.8% of $50,000) in Medicare Surtax.

E. **The Cadillac Tax**—So-called Cadillac Plans are employer-sponsored plans that provide generous benefits that exceed predetermined threshold amounts. The ACA imposes a 40% excise tax (the "Cadillac tax") on these excess benefits and is scheduled to go into effect in 2020. The tax will be deductible by the employer.

Worker Classification Laws and Regulations

This lesson describes and explains the ways in which workers may be classified—primarily as either employees or independent contractors—and the consequences thereof.

After studying this lesson, you should be able to:

1. Classify various workers as either employees or independent contractors.

2. Explain the consequences of workers being placed into these differing classifications.

3. Identify violations of federal rules and their consequences.

I. Introduction

A. Workers can be either employees or independent contractors.

   1. To be precise, we might use the term "common law employee" in order to distinguish most employees from that category known as "statutory employee" that is discussed later in this lesson.

   2. Independent contractors are often referred to as freelancers, consultants, contactors, temps, specialists, project workers, and so on.

B. The classification matters for several reasons, including many related to federal taxation.

C. If Sally is a common law **employee**, her employer:

   1. Must withhold income tax and her portion of FICA (social security and Medicare) taxes;

   2. Is responsible for paying FICA and FUTA taxes on Sally's wages; *and*

   3. Must give Sally a Form W-2, showing taxes withheld.

D. If Sally is a common law **employee**, she:

   1. May deduct unreimbursed employee business expenses (if she itemizes and they constitute more than 2% of her adjusted gross income).

E. However, if Sally is an **independent contractor**, the business that hires her:

   1. May be required to give Sally a Form 1099-Misc (Miscellaneous Income) to report what it has paid to her.

F. If Sally is an **independent contractor**, Sally:

   1. Is responsible for paying her own income tax and self-employment (SE) tax (covering social security and Medicare);

   2. May need to make estimated tax payments during the year to cover her tax liabilities; *and*

   3. May deduct business expenses on Schedule C of her tax return.

Who Pays Federal Taxes?

Sally performs work for ABC Co. Who must pay these taxes?	If Sally is an independent contractor	If Sally is an employee
Income tax	Sally	ABC Co.
Social security	Sally	ABC Co. (its share and Sally's)
Medicare	Sally	ABC Co. (its share and Sally's)
FUTA	N/A	ABC Co.

G. Reasons a principal might prefer a worker to be labeled an "independent contractor" rather than an "employee" include that the principal is:

1. Not liable to withhold and pay over worker's income tax

2. Not liable to pay FUTA taxes

3. Not liable to pay its share and to withhold and pay over worker's share of FICA taxes (for social security and Medicare) and AMT (Additional Medicare Tax)

4. Not liable to pay overtime and minimum wages under the Fair Labor Standards Act (FSLA)

5. Not liable for employee discrimination under the Civil Rights Act of 1964, which protects employees against discrimination of the basis of race, gender, religion, color, and national origin

6. Not liable for failure to provide leave and reinstatement under the Family Medical Leave Act (FMLA)

7. Less likely to be liable to third parties for injuries caused by workers' torts

H. Fun Facts

1. The government estimates that more than 3 million employees are misclassified as independent contractors.

2. These misclassifications cost the government more than $100 billion annually in underpayment of employment, FICA, and FUTA taxes.

3. Therefore, the government, particularly the IRS and the Department of Labor, are active in bringing misclassification lawsuits. In 2013, DOL investigation led to payment of more than $80 million in back wages for more than 100,000 misclassified employees.

II. Distinguishing between Employees and Independent Contractors

A. Many courts hold that workers are employees if their principals "control" or have the power to control the method and manner of their work, but independent contractors if not. This common law "control test" typically is supplemented by many additional factors, such as whether or not the worker (a) is generally on the job 40 hours a week, (b) works primarily for this principal, (c) uses the principal's tools, and (d) earns most of his or her income from this principal. The more of factors (a) to (d) that are present, the more likely the worker is an employee rather than an independent contractor.

B. The IRS uses an 11-part version of the common law test that looks at (a) behavioral control (two factors), (b) financial control (five factors), and (c) the type of relationship between the parties (four factors) to distinguish between employees and independent contractors. No single factor is conclusive.

1. **Behavioral control**

   a. **Instructions**—The more instructions given as to when and where to work, what tools or equipment to use, what assistants to hire, where to purchase supplies, what sequence to follow, and so on, the more likely that control is being exercised and the worker is an employee.

   b. **Training**—Independent contractors typically use their own methods. If they are trained in the principal's methods, workers are more likely to be employees.

2. **Financial control**

   a. **Unreimbursed business expenses**—Although employees often have unreimbursed business expenses, this is more commonly a characteristic of independent contractors.

   b. **Worker's investment**—Often, though not always, an independent contractor will tend to have a significant investment in the tools or facilities she uses to perform services for another. Employees are much less likely to make such investments.

   c. **Availability to market**—Independent contractors often advertise and in other ways seek to provide services to others in the marketplace.

   d. **Form of payment**—Employees are typically paid by the hour, week, or year. Independent contractors are more often paid a flat fee for the particular job.

   e. **Worker profit or loss**—Independent contractors typically have a chance to make a profit (or loss) from a job. Employees generally do not.

3. **Type of relationship**

   a. **Written contracts**—If the parties have a written contract describing the worker as either an employee or an independent contractor, this may be indicative in a close case. But such a writing will be ignored if its characterization is clearly inconsistent with other factors because substance is more important than form.

   b. **Benefits**—Independent contractors tend to provide their own medical plan, disability insurance, pension plan, and related benefits. If the business provides these to the worker, the worker is more likely an employee.

   c. **Permanency**—Independent contractors typically are hired to complete a particular task. The longer a relationship lasts or is envisioned to last, the more likely it is an employer-employee relationship.

   d. **Regular business of company**—If the worker provides services that are an integral part of the company's business, that worker is more likely an employee. If the services provided are more of a one-off for the company or tangential to its primary business, that worker is more likely an independent contractor.

Summary of IRS Test for Common Law Employees vs. Independent Contractors

Factor	Indicates employee status	Indicates independent contractor
Behavioral		
Company gives lots of instructions	Yes	No
Company trains worker in its methods	Yes	No
Financial		
Worker has few unreimbursed business expenses	Yes	No
Worker invests little in tools or facilities	Yes	No
Worker does not try to sell services to others in the market	Yes	No
Worker paid by the hour or week	Yes	No
Worker has no chance to profit from job other than collecting salary	Yes	No
Relationship		
Written contract describes worker as independent contractor	No	Yes
Worker provides own medical benefits, pension, etc.	No	Yes
Worker hired only to complete a particular task	No	Yes
Worker's services not part of company's regular business	No	Yes

III. Consequences of Misclassification

   A. **Consequences**—If an employee is miscategorized as an independent contractor without a "reasonable basis," several adverse consequences may follow for the employer. Employees may file complaints and lawsuits, and both the IRS and the Department of Labor (DOL) may become involved because the IRS wants to ensure that employers pay their legal share of taxes and the

DOL wants to ensure that workers who are truly employees receive their rights under various employment laws enacted over the years.

1. Employer may be liable for failing to withhold and pay state and federal payroll taxes.

2. Employer may be liable for failing to make matching FICA payments to cover Social Security and Medicare contributions.

3. Employer may be liable for back overtime and minimum wages under FLSA as well as fined (even criminally for "willful" violations).

4. Employer may be liable for missed FUTA contributions.

5. Employer may be liable for wrongfully excluding the worker from benefit plans provided to employees.

B. **Specific Fines**

1. **Unintentional**—If a misclassification is unintentional, the following penalties, among others, may be imposed:

   a. A $50 fine for each Form W-2 that should have been filed.

   b. Penalties of 1.5% of wages for income taxes that were not withheld, plus 40% of the FICA taxes that should have been withheld from the employee and 100% of the employer's matching FICA contribution.

   c. A 0.5% penalty on the unpaid tax liability for each month up to 25% of the total tax liability.

2. **Intentional or fraudulent**—If a misclassification is intentional or fraudulent, the IRS may impose penalties up to:

   a. 20% of all wages paid; *and*

   b. 100% of both the employer's and the employees' FICA taxes.

   c. Criminal penalties of up to $1,000 per misclassified worker and one year in jail are also possibilities.

C. **Safe Harbor**—Section 530(a) of the Revenue Act of 1978 provides a "safe harbor" allowing companies to classify workers as "independent contractors" even though the 11-part test indicates they are employees, so long a "reasonable basis" for the classification exists. A "reasonable basis" may derive from any one of the following:

1. The classification is consistent with industry practice,

2. A previous IRS or court ruling found the workers to not be employees, *or*

3. An IRS ruling or opinion letter supports the classification.

D. **Statutory Employees**—Certain workers are treated as employees for FICA purposes (social security and Medicare taxes), even though they may appear to be independent contractors under the 11-part control test, so long as they fall into one of the four following categories *and* meet one of the three following tests.

1. **Fourstatutory employee categories**

   a. **Drivers**—A driver who distributes beverages (other than milk) or meat, vegetables, fruit, or bakery products; or who picks up and delivers laundry or dry cleaning, if the driver is the company's agent or is paid on a commission basis.

   b. **Life insurance agents**—A full-time life insurance sales agent whose principal business activity is selling life insurance or annuity contracts, or both, primarily for just one company.

   c. **Home workers**—An individual who works at home on materials or goods that the business supplies and that must be returned to the business or someone the business names, if the business also furnishes specifications for the work to be done.

   d. Salespeople—A full-time traveling or city salesperson who works on a business's behalf and turns in orders to the business from wholesalers, retailers, contractors, or operators of hotels, restaurants, or other similar establishments. The goods sold must be merchandise for resale or supplies for use in the buyer's business operation, and the work performed must be the salesperson's principal business activity.

2. Three conditions

   a. The service contract states or implies that substantially all the services are to be performed by the worker personally.

   b. The worker does not have a substantial investment in the equipment and property used to perform the services.

   c. The services are performed on a continuing basis for the same business.

3. Note

   a. Though FICA taxes must be withheld from these statutory employees, federal income taxes need not be. Therefore, such workers are less expensive for an employer than are common law employees, though they are more expensive than independent contractors.

   b. FUTA taxes need be paid only for drivers and salespeople (categories a and d above), and not for life insurance agents and home workers (categories b and c).

4. The following table summarizes the tax treatment of various statutory employees.

Statutory Employees and Tax Payments

Type of Statutory Employee	If three conditions exist—worker to perform services personally, worker lacks substantial investment, services performed on continuing basis—then even if worker is an independent contractor, employer must withhold.
Delivery drivers	FICA: yes Income tax: no FUTA: yes
Life insurance agents	FICA: yes Income tax: no FUTA: no
Home workers	FICA: yes Income tax: no FUTA: no
Salespeople	FICA: yes Income tax: no FUTA: yes

E. Statutory Nonemployees—Three categories of workers are treated as self-employed independent contractors for *all* federal income tax purposes, even though the common law test or the IRS test might indicate that they are employees of others.

1. Licensed real estate agents, including real estate appraisers, if (a) they are paid on the basis of sales or output rather than number of hours worked, and (b) written contacts provide that they will not be treated as employees for federal income tax purposes.

2. Direct sellers who meet the two requirements of the previous paragraph (paid by output not hours worked and written contract specifying they won't be treated as employees for federal income tax purposes) if they fall into any of the three following groups:

   a. Persons engaged in selling consumer products in the home or place of business other than in a permanent retail establishment;

b. Persons engaged in selling consumer products to any buyer on a buy-sell basis, a deposit-commission basis, or any similar basis prescribed by regulations, for resale in the home or at a place of business other than a permanent retail establishment; *or*

c. Persons engaged in the trade or business of delivering or distributing newspapers or shopping news (including any services directly related to such delivery or distribution).

3. **Companion sitters** are individuals who furnish personal attendance, companionship, or household care services to children, the elderly, or the disabled.

    a. Companion sitters who are not employees of a companion sitting placement service are treated as self-employed for all federal tax purposes.

    b. A person in the business of placing companion sitters will not be treated as an employer of the sitter if that person does not receive or pay the salary or wages of the sitters and is compensated by the sitters or the persons who employ them on a fee basis.

4. The following table summarizes the rules governing when statutory nonemployees are treated as self-employed.

For Statutory Nonemployees to Be Treated as Self-Employed

Type of Worker	Must be paid by output, not hours?	Must have written contract indicating they are employees?	Must not be employee of placement service?
Real estate agent	Yes	Yes	N/A
Direct seller	Yes	Yes	N/A
Companion sitter	N/A	N/A	Yes.

Business Structure

Selection and Formation of Business Entity and Related Operation and Termination

Selection of a Business Entity

After studying this lesson, you should be able to:

1. Describe the basic features of important forms of business entities, such as partnerships, corporations, and LLCs. Identify the type of business entity that is best described by a given set of non-tax-related characteristics.

2. Understand the advantages and disadvantages of the different forms of business entity when compared and contrasted with one another.

I. Introduction

A. Businesses may be structured in numerous ways to attain various benefits. Ranging from a simple sole proprietorship (one-owner business) to large multinational corporations, firms are structured to gain various operational efficiencies and competitive advantages.

B. Business organizations date back to ancient times. Many early forms resembled today's partnerships. This form works well for small businesses, but is not optimal for accumulating large amounts of capital. Because general partners are personally liable for all of their firm's debts, so they generally wish to do business only with close friends and relatives whom they know and trust.

C. Eventually, **limited liability** was invented for the corporate form, which encouraged investors to take more risks with their money, because the most they could lose was their investment in the enterprise.

D. While corporations have the advantage of limited liability, but they suffer the comparative detriment of **double taxation** in that the firm pays corporate income tax on its earnings and then its shareholders pay individual income tax on the dividends they are paid from corporate profits. Partnerships, in contrast, enjoy single, pass-through taxation. Although the partnership files an informational return, it pays no income tax. For parties forming business organizations today, minimizing taxes is typically a major concern. Comparative taxation of various forms of business entities is discussed only briefly in this and following lessons, because major coverage comes in the taxation lessons.

E. For most of the 1900s, the major forms of business organization in the United States were corporations, general partnerships, *joint ventures*, limited partnerships, and sole proprietorships. However, around 1990, states began authorizing the creation of new forms of business organizations to encourage economic development. These organizations allow entrepreneurs and investors to enjoy both limited liability and single taxation without leaving even a single person exposed to general liability. The first form of these organizations was called the limited liability company (LLC). LLCs were made popular by IRS decisions to allow these new entities to elect ("check- the-box") partnership taxation, even though they embodied so many corporate characteristics that could have subjected them to double taxation under previous law.

F. Then "copycat" business forms were created to spread this "limited liability + single taxation" formula to the general partnership form through *limited liability general partnerships* (LLPs) and even to the limited partnership form through *limited liabilitylimited partnerships* (LLLPs).

G. Most accounting firms today are either LLPs or LLCs.

H. Although it appears not to be covered on the exam because they are not mentioned in the references to the REG section in the AICPA's content specifications for the exam, remember that, today many states are trying to encourage social entrepreneurs by making it easier to raise money for business models that emphasize social impact over profit. The two most popular types are L3Cs, authorized under Treasury Regulation 1.501(c)(3) and Benefit Corporations (B-Corps).

II. Types of Business Organization

A. **Sole Proprietorship**—A single-owner business. The firm's liabilities and assets belong solely to their owner. Its profits and losses belong to the sole owner. The sole proprietorship is not a separate legal or taxable entity. Unlimited personal liability puts the sole proprietor's personal assets at stake if the business loses money. Nothing need be filed with the state to launch a sole proprietorship. If Matt starts a cupcake catering business out of his home and takes no formal legal action to organize in another form, his business will be deemed a sole proprietorship. If Matt starts a cupcake catering business out of his home and takes no formal legal action to organize in another form, his business will be a sole proprietorship.

B. **General Partnership**—An association of two or more persons to carry on as co-owners of a business for profit. If Matt finds that his cupcakes often show up at catered dinners along with Adelita's salads, he may propose to Adelita that they join forces to offer a catering service with a full menu and to split the profits. If Matt and Adelita take no formal legal action to organize in another form, their new business will be a general partnership. If the partnership suffers financial reverses, Matt and Adelita are both potentially responsible to pay its debts out of their own individual pockets. If the business makes a profit, it will "pass through" to Matt and Adelita for income tax purposes. Whether distributed or not, profits are allocated and taxable directly to the partners. Although previous law treated partnerships as merely an aggregation of partners, current law generally recognizes partnership as an entity for most purposes.

C. **Joint Venture**—Term often used to denote a one-shot general partnership-type relation. Thus, if Matt and Adelita join forces to provide an ongoing full-menu catering business, they have a general partnership. However, if they agreed to work together to provide full-menu service for just a single, big dinner, they might be said to have formed a joint venture. Joint ventures are governed by general partnership law, so the distinction between the two is generally unimportant for legal purposes.

D. **Limited Partnership**—A partnership with at least one general partner and at least one limited partner. It is distinguished from a general partnership in that its limited partners give up some of the general management rights that partners in a general partnership would have in exchange for **the** limited liability enjoyed by shareholders of a corporation. **The limited partnership is a seperate legal entity. If** Matt and Adelita need financing for their new catering business, they might ask their wealthy friend, Jess, to become an investor. Jess does not intend to be active in the business and certainly does not wish to become generally liable for the debts of the catering business. If certain legal steps are taken, a limited partnership can be formed that will protect Jess from liability and thereby encourage him to invest his capital. However, if Jess takes an active role in managing the firm, he will forfeit his limited liability regarding those who see his activities and believe him to be a general partner. It bears repeating that a limited partnership must have at least one general partner who will be generally liable for the firm's obligations, though the general partner can be a corporation rather than an individual.

E. **Limited Liability Partnership (LLP)**—A relatively new form of business organization that carries greater protection from liability than exists in either general or limited partnerships. **The LLP** was created primarily to protect professionals, such as accountants, physicians, and attorneys, from undue malpractice liability arising from the errors of their partners. Thus, if Tad and Todd are CPAs who practice as general partners, Tad is personally liable for any malpractice committed by Todd. An LLP form can shield Tad from personal tort liability caused by Todd's malpractice. In LLPs, partners are generally liable only for (a) their own malpractice, and (b) the malpractice of those they directly supervise. Most (but not all) state provisions also protect partners from personal liability for LLP *contractual* obligations. In exchange for providing this extensive liability protection, many states require LLPs to carry minimum levels of malpractice insurance to help ensure that clients harmed by malpractice will have a viable remedy.

F. **Limited Liability Limited Partnership (LLLP)**—A relatively new form of business organization that allows the general partner(s) of a limited partnership to enjoy limited liability, just like limited partners. It places the burden on third parties who deal with LLLPs to protect themselves contractually because, absent contractual protection, they will not be able to dip into the pockets of either limited partners or general partners to be compensated for the firm's debts. All a limited partnership needs to do to elect to be an LLLP is to include a one-line statement to that effect in its certificate of limited partnership. **Although** the other forms of organization mentioned in this lesson are ubiquitous, as of 2016, only about 26 states had authorized LLLPs. Note that both general and limited partners in such partnerships will remain liable for the consequences of torts they personally commit while conducting partnership business. No form of business organization shields people from personal liability for the torts they personally commit.

G. **Corporation**—An artificial legal entity. Its owners (shareholders) typically enjoy limited liability. The creation of the notion of an artificial legal entity in order to encourage people to invest in others' business ideas is one of the great advances in Western legal thought. Kay may buy General Motors stock because she is secure in the notion that even if General Motors goes bankrupt, she will not be liable for its obligations. Her potential loss is limited to the amount she invested when she bought GM stock. Typically, corporations are theoretically burdened by double taxation, meaning they pay corporate income tax on their profits, and then when they distribute their gains to shareholders in the form of dividends, these shareholders pay individual income tax on their dividend income. By intelligent tax planning, however, there are ways to minimize the impact of double taxation.

H. **Subchapter S Corporation**—A corporation that can eliminate the double taxation that regular corporations (called Subchapter C corporations) face by meeting certain requirements of Subchapter S of the Internal Revenue Code, including having no more than 100 shareholders who unanimously agree to choose Subchapter S status.

I. **Professional Corporation (PC)**—A corporation formed pursuant to special statutory accommodations that typically aim at allowing accountants, doctors, lawyers, and some other professionals to gain some of the benefits of the corporate form, particularly various advantages related to offering benefits to employees. Typically, the shareholders in PCs enjoy limited liability (except for their own malpractice, of course), but are subject to double taxation. The corporation is a legal entity, separate and apart from its shareholders. PCs have lost popularity with the creation of LLPs (mentioned earlier) and LLCs (see the next paragraph). But because a PC can choose Subchapter S status, this form of organization survives.

J. **Limited Liability Company (LLC)**—A relatively new form of business organization that allows owners of businesses to gain the liability-limiting advantages of the corporate form while enjoying the single, pass-through tax benefits of the partnership form of business. LLCs may elect to be taxed as if they were Subchapter S corporations. Although most very large businesses are corporations and the corporate form probably remains the most important type of business organization, more LLCs are formed in the United States every year than any other form of business organization.

III. **Advantages and Disadvantages**

A. **Sole Proprietorships**

1. **Advantages**

a. **Total control**—The owner needs answer to no other owner; he or she may make all decisions. Other persons, such as creditors, might, of course, have something to say about how the business is run.

b. **Simplicity**—No formal documents need be filed to form a sole proprietorship, although even a sole owner of a business ultimately will have to deal with legal formalities such as tax forms, licenses to undertake a particular activity, and permission to do business in foreign jurisdictions.

c. **Taxation**—All income from the business accrues to the sole owner who is responsible for paying the individual income taxes on that amount.

2. **Disadvantages**

a. **General liability**—The owner is the business and the business is the owner in a sole proprietorship. Therefore, the owner is personally liable for any debts incurred by the business.

B. General Partnerships (GPS) (and Joint Ventures)

1. Advantages

a. Pass-through taxation—Partnerships enjoy single taxation because the partnership entity pays no taxes (although it files an informational return). Rather, partnership income passes through to the individual partners who pay individual income tax on their share.

b. Simplicity—No formal documents need be filed to form a general partnership. If two persons associate with the goal of carrying on as co-owners of a business for profit, the law will treat their relationship as a general partnership regardless of whether they have filed any legal documents. They may, however, file such documents if they choose and generally should do so to clarify the nature of their rights and responsibilities. A partnership that will last more than a year should put the partnership agreement in writing so it will be enforceable under the statute of frauds.

2. Disadvantages

a. General liability—All general partners are personally liable for the obligations of the business. Thus, if Sal and Pal each put $100,000 into a partnership, but it lost all that money and $100,000 more, Sal and Pal could each be personally liable for the extra $100,000 in losses.

C. Limited Partnerships (LPs)

1. Advantages

a. Pass-through taxation—Like general partnerships, limited partnerships enjoy single taxation.

b. Limited liability for the limited partners exists, so long as they do not take part in the management of the firm.

2. Disadvantages

a. Formality—Legal documents must be filed with a state office (typically the secretary of state, or perhaps the State Corporation Commission) in order to form a limited partnership. The firm's name must reflect its limited partnership status, as by using the term "Ltd" or "LP."

b. Authority—A limited partner must forfeit the right to manage the business in order to be entitled to limited liability. In truth, the law does allow a fair amount of direct involvement in the business (e.g., as employee, lender, guarantor) for a limited partner without imposing general liability.

c. General liability—A limited partnership must have at least one general partner who will be generally liable to creditors for the obligations of the partnership. However, that general partner can be a corporation whose artificial entity will shield any individual owners from personal liability for business debts.

D. Limited Liability Partnerships (LLPs)

1. Advantages

a. Pass-through taxation—Like partnerships, LLPs enjoy single taxation.

b. Limited liability—Like limited partners, LLPs are not liable for the general obligations of the partnership, although they typically remain liable for the tort liabilities generated by their own actions and the actions of those they supervise. Therefore, if Todd and Tad are partners in a CPA LLP and Todd commits malpractice, Tad will not be personally liable for that wrong. Tad is liable only for torts that he and the employees in the firm whom he supervises commit. In most states (full-shield states), this protection extends to the firm's tort *and contract* obligations. In some states (partial-shield states), the protection extends only to tort obligations, so that Todd and Tad would be personally liable for the firm's contractual debts. And, remember that in any state (and with any form of business organizations), a third-party, such as a lender, might require Todd and Tad to contractually bind themselves *as individuals* to pay firm's debts before the third-parties will lend money to the firm or otherwise do business with it.

    c. Authority—LLPs may be actively involved in managing the partnership without forfeiting the limited liability that partners in an LLP generally enjoy. This is a distinct advantage over the traditional limited partnership form.

2. Disadvantages

    a. Formality—Legal documents must be filed with a state office (typically the secretary of state) in order to form an LLP.

    b. Insurance requirement—In many states firms must maintain a minimum level of liability insurance (e.g., $1 million) in order to entitle partners to liability protection.

    c. Selectivity—Usually state statutes limit LLPs to particular professions, such as accountants, architects, and lawyers.

E. Limited Liability Limited Partnerships (LLLPs)

1. Advantages

    a. Pass-through taxation—Like all partnerships, LLLPs enjoy single taxation.

    b. Limited liability—As in limited partnerships, limited partners enjoy limited liability. Furthermore, in LLLPs, even general partners enjoy limited liability. (Remember, neither general nor limited partners in LLLPs may escape liability for torts they personally commit.)

2. Disadvantages

    a. Only about 25 states authorize the formation of LLLPs, and therefore there are questions as to how an LLLP authorized in one state will be treated if it does business in a state that does not recognize LLLPs.

    b. Limited partners generally have little say in how the business is run, just as in a limited partnership.

3. Formality—Legal documents must be filed with a state office (typically the secretary of state) in order to form an LLLP. However, a limited partnership can easily become an LLLP by simply amending its filing with the state to so indicate.

F. Corporations

1. Advantages

    a. Limited liability—All shareholders are entitled to limited liability, but two things should be kept in mind. First, occasionally rare circumstances exist that justify "piercing of the corporate veil" (making shareholders pay corporate debts from their own pockets). Second, especially with small corporations third parties may refuse to loan money to a corporation or to sell to it on credit unless its owners co-sign or otherwise guarantee the obligation, in which case the benefit is more theoretical than real. To repeat, this is equally true of LPs, LLPs, and LLLPs, of course.

    b. Legal personality—The corporation is viewed as a legal entity, separate and apart from its owners. It can own property, enter into contracts, and do pretty much any legal act that an individual can. This was formerly a distinct advantage over partnerships, which were viewed as mere aggregations of their owners. But modern partnership law increasingly treats partnerships in all their manifestations (GPs, LPs, LLPs, etc.) as entities for many purposes. This is true of LLCs.

    c. Perpetual duration—A traditional advantage of the corporate form has been its perpetual duration. The corporate entity is viewed as a separate legal entity, so it can last for a long, long time. If the five owners of ABC Corporation stock are all killed in a plane crash, ABC Corporation keeps on going in legal contemplation. Its new owners are the heirs of the five deceased owners. Under older laws, partnerships are dissolved upon the death or departure of individual partners so this is an important advantage for corporations. Under more modern partnership laws, however, arranging for partnerships to survive the death or departure of partners is generally easy.

2. Disadvantages

    a. Double taxation—The corporation is subject to corporate income tax, and shareholders are subject to individual income tax liability on dividends and other distributions. Therefore, double taxation has traditionally been viewed as a disadvantage of the corporate form. With proper tax planning, however, the effect of this disadvantage can be minimized.

    b. Formality—Legal documents must be filed with a state office (typically the Secretary of State) in order to form a corporation.

G. Subchapter S Corporations

    1. Advantages

        a. Limited liability—Subchapter S shareholders enjoy limited liability.

        b. Single taxation—Subchapter S corporations do not pay income tax, thereby avoiding double taxation.

    2. Disadvantages

        a. Formality—Legal documents must be filed with a state office (typically the Secretary of State) in order to form a Subchapter S corporation.

        b. Individual taxation—Corporate profits are considered as if they were distributed to shareholders, so an S-Corporation shareholder might be taxed on income he or she has never received, whereas a C-corporation shareholder is taxed on dividends only when these are actually received.

        c. Subchapter S requirements—To take advantage of the tax benefit offered by Subchapter S, a corporation must meet certain requirements, including:

            i. It is a domestic corporation;

            ii. All shareholders must consent to the S-Corporation election;

            iii. The firm can have no more than 100 shareholders, although all members of a family can be treated as a single shareholder;

            iv. All shareholders must be individuals, estates, certain exempt organizations, or certain trusts; and

            v. The corporation has only one class of stock (i.e., all outstanding shares confer identical rights to distribution and liquidation proceeds).

H. Limited Liability Companies

    1. Advantages

        a. Pass-through taxation—LLCs enjoy the single taxation of a partnership without having to meet the criteria required for Subchapter S status. (However, LLCs may choose to be taxed as corporate entities if they so desire.)

        b. Limited liability—All LLC members enjoy limited liability without forfeiting management rights as limited partners would have to.

    2. Disadvantages

        a. Formality—Legal documents must be filed with a state office (typically the Secretary of State) in order to form an LLC.

Formation

After studying this lesson, you should be able to:

1. Summarize the processes for formation of various business entities.

I. Formation

A. Sole Proprietorships

    1. No formal filing with the state is required for the creation of sole proprietorships.

    2. However, to do business, a sole proprietorship, like other forms of organization, may need to acquire a tax number and a license to, for example, sell fresh produce or operate a restaurant or provide plumbing services.

B. General Partnerships—No formal filing is required to create a general partnership either. All that is needed is an intention by two or more people to enter into a relationship that the law deems a partnership, which is generally co-ownership of a business for the purpose of making profit.

    1. Governing law—General partnerships are governed by the Revised Uniform Partnership Act (RUPA).

    2. RUPA is functionally a form contract that provides default rules in case partners in a general partnership have not formed a partnership agreement as to all issues.

    3. By agreement, partners may vary most RUPA provisions to meet their business needs, but they may not prejudice the rights of third parties. For example, partners Pat and Nat may vary their rights in the partnership by agreement, but they may not successfully agree that they do not have to pay the money they owe to third parties.

    4. A written partnership agreement is always a good idea, but this is not required unless the partnership is to last for a specified period longer than one year.

    5. Although no written filing is required, partners may file a *Statement of Partnership Authority* with the secretary of state. This document is often useful in dealing with third parties who might wish to know, for example, which partners' signatures need to be on a document of sale for the partnership to be bound.

C. LPs, LLPs, LLLPs, and LLCs

    1. A filing with a state agency, typically the secretary of state, generally is required to form the other forms of business organizations discussed in this section—limited partnerships (LPs), Limited Liability Partnerships (LLPs), Limited Liability Limited Partnerships (LLLPs), and Limited Liability Companies (LLCs), as well as corporations. These filings are analogous to a corporation's articles of incorporation.

    2. Governing law

        a. Limited partnership law is generally governed by the Revised Uniform Limited Partnership Act (RULPA). (Nearly half of the states have adopted the more recent 2001 Uniform Limited Partnership Act, which has significant differences from RULPA, but the ACIPA's blueprint for the exam does not list 2001 ULPA as a reference, so this lesson focuses on RULPA.)

        b. Although most states have enacted their own idiosyncratic version of an LLC statute, meaning that there is great variety in LLC laws from state to state, a revised model act does exist—the Revised Uniform Limited Liability Company Act (RULLCA).

        c. LLPs are generally provided for within states' RUPA or RULPA provisions.

        d. LLLPs are generally provided for within RULPA or 2001 ULPA. To become an LLLP, all the organizers need do is to state such an election in their filing of a certificate of limited partnership with the state.

D. Corporations

1. Many states have adopted some version of the Revised Model Business Corporation Act (RMBCA) to govern the operation of corporations formed there.

2. The Delaware Corporate Code is a model for many other states' corporate laws.

3. RMBCA requires that those forming a corporation file articles of incorporation that must include the following data:

   a. Corporate name (indicating corporate status by use of "Corp.," "Inc.," etc.);

   b. Number of authorized shares;

   c. Address of the initial registered office of the corporation and the first registered agent at that address; *and*

   d. Names and addresses of the incorporators.

4. The general process for forming a corporation includes:

   a. Filing articles of incorporation with the secretary of state;

   b. Holding an organizational meeting in which a board of directors is elected, and the contracts entered into by promoters are adopted or rejected;

   c. Drafting and adopting by-laws to govern the inner workings of the firm; *and*

   d. Obtaining certificates of authority to do business in other jurisdictions. Corporations are viewed as "domestic" corporations in the state in which they are formed and as "foreign" corporations in other states where they may wish to do business.

5. **Promoters and their contracts**—Before a corporation is officially formed, it often needs to hire employees, rent office space, and buy equipment, among others. A promoter is a person who takes the initiative to found and organize a business, often by doing such acts.

   a. Because of their unique position, promoters may take advantage of others and therefore have been held to owe a fiduciary duty of loyalty to:

      i. The proposed corporation;

      ii. Other promoters; *and*

      iii. Contemplated investors.

   b. Promoters are usually forbidden from profiting at all from pre-incorporation contracts (even if the contract is fair to the corporation) unless they:

      i. Make full disclosure to an independent board of directors and gain their approval; *or*

      ii. Make full disclosure to all original shareholders and gain their approval.

   c. Promoter liability on pre-incorporation contracts.

      i. Promoters are liable on the contracts they negotiate on the prospective corporation's behalf unless the contract clearly and explicitly indicates that the third party is looking only to the corporation for performance.

      ii. Even if the corporation is formed and adopts the contract, the promoter remains liable, absent a novation (an express release from the third party).

   d. Corporation liability on promoters' contracts. A corporation is liable on contracts negotiated by its promoters if it comes into existence and adopts the contract:

      i. Expressly (e.g., via the board of directors' resolution), *or*

      ii. Impliedly (e.g., via knowing and voluntary acceptance of the benefits of the contract).

   e. Right to enforce—Once it adopts the promoter's contracts, the corporation has the right to enforce them against third parties.

Operations: Nonfinancial Factors

> **After studying this lesson, you should be able to:**
>
> **1.** Summarize the nonfinancial operational features for various business entities.

I. Operations

A. Sole Proprietorships—The sole owner of a sole proprietorship makes all important decisions or delegates these decisions to someone of his or her choosing.

B. General Partnerships

1. *Absent agreement to the contrary*, all partners have equal rights in the management and conduct of business affairs. *As Tim acts to advance the business of the RST Partnership, he is an agent acting on behalf of his principals—Ron, Sam, and the partnership itself.*

> **Example**
>
> If A and B each contributed $50,000 to form ABC partnership, and C contributed $200,000, the partners might agree to give C more votes than A and B. Absent agreement to the contrary, however, each partner will have an equal vote notwithstanding their unequal financial contributions.

2. *Absent agreement to the contrary*, majority vote governs all ordinary course-of-business matters.

> **Example**
>
> A, B, and C are partners. A and B vote to borrow money from the bank. C votes against. A and B prevail. The loan is valid and C is potentially liable to repay it along with A and B, even though C voted against the transaction.

3. *However*, unanimity is needed to take actions contrary to the partnership agreement or to take action regarding "extraordinary matters," which might include such actions as:

    a. Admitting a new partner to the partnership

    b. Assigning partnership property

> **Example**
>
> Creditor X is owed money by ABC partnership. X wishes to have the partnership assign its trucks to X so that X can sell them to raise money to pay ABC's debt. Partners A, B, and C must all agree.

    c. Disposing of goodwill; *or*

> **Example**
>
> A, B, and C own an ice cream store with the name "ABC Creamery." X wishes to buy the store and to operate it under the name "ABC Creamery." All partners must agree to the sale.

    d. Doing any other act *that* would make it impossible to carry on the ordinary business of the partnership.

Example
A, B, and C own a furniture store in a small town. There is only one building in town suitable for housing the business. D wishes to buy the building. A, B, and C, must unanimously agree to sell.

4. A key legal issue is whether a partnership is an entity separate from its owners. RUPA states that a partnership is an entity distinct from the partners (owners) in some cases.

    a. The assets of a partnership are treated as those of the business unit.

    b. Title to real property may be acquired in the partnership's name.

    c. Each partner is considered a fiduciary of the partnership.

    d. Each partner is considered an agent of the partnership.

    e. The partnership may sue and be sued in its own name. Therefore, a judgment against the partnership is not a judgment against the partner.

5. In other ways, a partnership is treated as an aggregate of the individual partners.

    a. Unlike a corporation, a partnership lacks continuity of existence.

    b. No person can become a partner without consent of all the partners. Therefore, the transferee of a partnership interest, unlike the transferee of shares in a corporation, does not become an owner without the consent of the existing partners.

    c. Debts of a partnership are ultimately the debts of the individual partners.

    d. A partnership is not subject to regular federal income tax. Instead, taxable income is determined at the individual level.

C. Limited Partnerships, LLPs, and LLLPs

1. In these forms of limited partnerships, one or more general partners make management decisions, whereas limited partners generally sit on the sidelines playing the role of passive investors.

2. As noted elsewhere, if limited partners in limited partnerships (not LLLPs) leave the sidelines and become actively involved in the control of the limited partnership, they may forfeit their limited liability as to creditors who rely on their apparent role as general partners.

D. Corporations

1. Shareholders elect directors; directors select officers; and officers make the day-to-day decisions needed to operate the corporation. This is often called the corporate pyramid, with shareholders at the base, directors in the middle, and officers at the top.

2. In small corporations, the same people may of course be the primary shareholders, directors, and officers.

3. **Piercing the corporate veil:** Corporations are distinct legal entities, so their obligations typically are not visited upon their shareholders personally. In other words, the most a shareholder can lose when investing in a corporation is the amount he or she spent to purchase the shares. If Ford Motor Corporation went bankrupt tomorrow, its shareholders might lose their investment, but unlike general partners in a general partnership, they would not be personally liable for any outstanding obligations of Ford. However, when small, closely held corporations are involved, courts sometimes "pierce the corporate veil" and reach into shareholders' pockets to satisfy corporate obligations. This act would be unusual but can happen when courts believe such is necessary to prevent the corporate form from being used to defeat public convenience, justify wrong, protect fraud, or defend crime.

4. **Factors**—The following considerations (usually in combination) may induce a court to pierce the corporate veil:

   a. Commingling of funds and other assets of the corporation with those of individual shareholders

   b. Diversion of the corporation's funds or assets for the personal use of shareholders

   c. Failure to maintain the necessary corporate formalities

   d. Failure to adequately capitalize the corporation for the reasonably foreseeable risks of the enterprise

   e. Use of the corporation as a mere shell or conduit to operate a single venture or some particular aspect of the business of an individual shareholder

   f. Absence of separately held corporate assets

   g. Formation and use of the corporation to assume the existing liabilities of another person or entity

E. **Limited Liability Companies**

1. LLCs may be operated in one of two primary ways:

   a. **Member-managed or (owner-managed)**—LLC members may choose to run the business themselves, as if they were general partners (unlike general partners, however, they enjoy limited liability).

   b. **Manager-managed**—LLC members may also choose to delegate managerial powers to one or more members or non-members.

2. The choice of one of these forms and a number of other decisions regarding the operations of the LLC can be set forth in an "operating agreement" that should be filed with the secretary of state along with the articles of organization. LLC members are given great freedom to operate the firm as they choose pursuant to the operating agreement, which can dictate finances and organization, set forth percentages of interests, allocation of profits and losses, members' rights and duties, and so on.

3. Remember that although there is a revised uniform act for LLCs (RULLCA), relatively few states have adopted it. Most states have adopted their own version of an LLC law, meaning that legal uniformity is greatly lacking across the nation.

4. In virtually every state, one person may form an LLC. Only a few states prohibit single-member LLCs.

5. An LLC is a legal entity that can do business, sue, open a bank account, and so on, in its own name.

6. Courts are much less likely to "pierce the veil" of an LLC because LLCs have so many fewer formalities they are supposed to follow. Still, it may happen if there is no true distinction between the LLC and its owners or if the members operate the LLC fraudulently or begin with inadequate capitalization.

Financial Structure

After studying this lesson, you should be able to:

1.   Summarize the financial operation features for various business entities.

I.   **Introduction**—Because all the partnership forms (GPs, LPs, LLP, LLLPs) automatically allocate income to partners or members and can elect single (passthrough) taxation, the more complicated financial issues tend to relate to corporations. Therefore, this section discusses primarily corporation law pursuant to the RMBCA. However, this section begins with a discussion of general partnership rules on important financial matters that may generally be deemed to apply to other forms of partnerships. It concludes with a brief description of LLC issues relating to financial structure.

II. **Partnerships—Financial Structure**

   A. **Capital Accounts**

   1.   Under RUPA, each partner is deemed to have an account that is:

   a.   Credited with an amount equal to the money plus the value of any other property, net of the amount of any liabilities, the partner contributes to the partnership, and the partner's share of the partnership profits;

   b.   At the same time, this account is charged with an amount equal to the money plus the value of any other property, net of the amount of any liabilities, distributed by the partnership to the partner and the partner's share of partnership losses.

   2.   Partners are to be reimbursed for payments made and indemnified for liabilities incurred in the ordinary course of the partnership business.

Example
An emergency arises and partner Sandy pays $10,000 out of her own pocket in order to preserve partnership property worth many times that amount. Sandy is entitled to be reimbursed from partnership funds.

   3.   Partners are to be reimbursed for advances to the partnership made beyond agreed capital contributions. These are loans and the partners are creditors generally on par with outside creditors.

   4.   As noted elsewhere, absent agreement to the contrary, partners equally share profits and losses. If they have agreed to a non-equal sharing of profits but have not made any provision for the sharing of losses, losses will be shared in proportion to profits.

   B. **Interest**

   1.   Under RUPA, partners, absent agreement to the contrary, should receive interest on advances made to the partnership beyond the amount of capital they agreed to contribute.

   C. **Right to Profits**

   1.   Absent agreement to the contrary, profits and losses are to be equally shared by the partners.

Example
A contributes $100,000 to a partnership with B, who contributes $10,000. Although the partners have made unequal contributions, absent agreement to the contrary they will equally share profits.

   2.   If the partners agree to share profits in some proportion other than equally, but make no agreement regarding losses, losses will be shared in the same proportion as profits.

> **Example**
> A, B, and C are partners. A contributed more to the partnership than B and C, so the partners agree that A will receive 50% of the profits and B and C will each receive 25%. The partners never even consider losses. Unfortunately, the business does not go well and the partnership loses $200,000. A is responsible for 50% of the losses, and B and C are responsible for 25% each.

3. Note that RULPA provides for limited partnerships that profits will be divided as providing in writing in the partnership agreement. Absent such an agreement, they will be divided according to capital contributions made and not returned.

D. Distributions in Kind

1. Partners have no right to receive, and may not be required to accept, a distribution in kind (rather than in cash).

> **Example**
> Sam dissociates from a partnership and the remaining partners wish to continue the partnership and buy out Sam's interest. Calculations indicate that Sam is owed $50,000. The partners would like to give him a partnership tractor that is worth $50,000. Sam would prefer cash. Sam is entitled to insist on cash, even though it might inconvenience the partnership.

III. Corporate Financial Structure and Shareholder Distributions—Introduction and Definitions

A. Types of Corporate Securities—There are several types of corporate securities.

1. **Equity securities**

   a. **Common stock**—The owners of common stock are the true owners of a corporation. They bear the most risk and have the most to gain. They have the right to vote for directors, to share pro rata in the profits of the corporation when paid out as dividends and to share in the surplus of assets over liabilities, if any, when the corporation dissolves.

   b. **Preferred stock**—Preferred shareholders may have economic rights that are superior to those of common shareholders in terms of either dividend rights or assets upon dissolution. Preferred shareholders are entitled to have their preferences respected. Preferred shares are usually cumulative, meaning that if the board chooses not to declare any preferred dividends in a given year, the right to receive them accumulates and in a subsequent year the board must pay both that year's preferred dividends and those that have cumulated unpaid **before any dividends are paid on common shares**. There is no right to payment of preferred dividends. There is only a right to be preferred to common shares if dividends are paid. If there's no money for dividends, then there's no money for dividends. However, if there is SOME money for dividends, holding preferred shares is good because you will be in line ahead of the common shareholders if insolvency threatens. If the preferred shares are noncumulative, no arrearages arise from one year's non-declaration and nonpayment. Once dividends are declared, the receiving shareholders are unsecured creditors of the corporation for that amount until they are actually paid.

   c. **Treasury stock**—Common stock that, once issued to shareholders, has now been repurchased by the corporation is called treasury stock. Such stock is often distributed to shareholders pro rata as a **share dividend**.

2. **Debt securities**—These are issued to creditors who, functionally, loan money to the corporation. They are not shareholders and do not have the rights to vote, to inspect, etc. that belong to shareholders. However, like other lenders and unlike common shareholders, they do have the right to be repaid and to be paid specified interest whether the corporation is prospering or not. There are three main types of debt securities:

    a. **Notes**—Short-term unsecured debt instruments

    b. **Debentures**—Long-term unsecured debt instruments

    c. **Bonds**—Debt instruments secured by corporate property

B. Other Terms

1. **Redeemable**—Redeemable shares must be repurchased by the corporation under specified conditions and at specified prices if the shareholder so desires.

2. **Callable**—Shares that are redeemable at the corporation's option.

3. **Convertible**—Debt securities that are convertible to equity securities at specified ratios at the request of the holder.

4. **Warrants, rights, and options**—Legal entitlements to purchase equity (not debt) securities at a specified price and time at the request of the holder. Until exercised, these entitlements carry no dividend, inspection, or other rights.

C. Consideration—Shares should not be simply given away, as it would undermine corporate fiscal soundness and invite fraud. Therefore, shares must be issued only in exchange for consideration that meets both quality and quantity tests.

1. **Quality tests**

    a. Traditionally, proper consideration included only money paid, services performed, and property received.

    b. Traditionally, improper consideration included unsecured promissory notes, promises to perform future services, and promises to transfer property.

    c. However, the modern trend is to recognize as valid consideration: "Any tangible or intangible benefit to the corporation, including cash, promissory notes, services performed, contracts for services to be performed, or other securities of the corporation,"

        i. The board of directors can adequately protect the corporation by issuing shares only where there is a good chance it will benefit the corporation because the promissory notes will probably be paid, the services will probably be performed, etc.

2. **Quantity tests**

    a. **Par Value**—This means **face value**.

        i. The RMBCA has abolished the concept, but its use persists in many states.

        ii. The issuance of **no par** is also permitted.

        iii. Par value is not always a gauge of a corporation's solvency, because watered stock (stock issued in exchange for consideration that is less than the par value of the shares) is sometimes issued.

        iv. In states that still require that consideration be at least equal to the par value, corporations use **nominal** par value (typically a very low value) to preserve maximum flexibility to issue shares in exchange for at least the par value.

    b. Today, if stock is issued for less than par (in states where that concept is still recognized) or less than the authorized (by the board of directors) purchase price, then the liability to creditors and other stockholders may be placed upon:

        i. The board who allowed the sale;

        ii. The buyer who paid too little; *and*

        iii. Transferees of the original buyer who both know that he or she paid too little and who pay too little themselves.

c. **Valuation of consideration received**

    i. **General rule:** Absent a showing of bad faith, the board's valuation of consideration received in exchange for stock is presumptively valid.

Example
The board of directors of ABC Corporation wishes to purchase a tract of land from X so that it can build a factory thereon. X likes ABC's prospects and wishes to receive 10,000 ABC shares as the sale price for the land rather than cash. The board authorizes the transaction. Disgruntled shareholder Z challenges the transaction on grounds that the shares issued to X were worth more than the land received from X. To prevail, Z must prove not only that the land was worth less than the shares but also that the directors acted in bad faith.

D. **A Primary Purpose of Most Corporations**—To provide income for owners through a stream of dividend payments

    1. **Types of dividends**

        a. Cash

        b. Stock

            i. A **stock dividend** might be issued by a corporation that has no readily available funds for cash dividends. Such a dividend does not reduce the assets in the corporate till nor transfer anything but paper to shareholders. Typically, shareholders are issued one new share for each 50 or so that they already hold.

            ii. Related is the **stock split**, which involves a greater increase in outstanding shares than does a stock dividend. Typically, shareholders are issued two or three shares for each one that they already hold. Again, the transaction has no effect on the net worth of the corporation, which has no more or fewer assets. Only paper has been transferred to the shareholders.

            iii. **Difference: Dividend and Split.** The primary difference between a stock dividend and a stock split is an accounting difference. In a stock split, a division of the shares of stock, not of the earnings or profits of the corporation, takes place without any change in or impingement upon the existing status on the corporate books of the earned surplus and capital accounts. However, in a stock dividend, an addition of shares of stock and a division of, at least, some of the earnings or profits of the corporation take place, with such division being reflected on the corporate books by an irreversible allocation of corporate funds from the earned surplus to the capital account.

        c. Property

Example
One company in England that operates a crematorium occasionally delivers a certificate for a free cremation as a dividend to its shareholders. More typically, property dividends are in the form of shares of stock of other corporations that the distributing corporation has acquired.

        d. To be proper, dividends must be paid:

            a. Only out of legally available funds; and

            b. Only in accordance with applicable preferences.

e. *Repurchase of shares has the same effect as a dividend payment (taking money out of the corporate treasury and putting it into shareholders' pockets) and must meet the same solvency standards.*

f. A distribution may not be made by a corporation if:

    a. After giving effect to the distribution, the corporation would be insolvent; or

        i. Key is **bankruptcy solvency**: Can the corporation meet its debt obligations as they come due?

    b. The distribution exceeds the **surplus** (defined as the "excess of the net assets of a corporation over its stated capital") of the corporation.

        i. Key is **equity solvency**: Do the corporation's assets exceed its liabilities?

g. **Board discretion**

    a. **General rule**—The board of directors' decision to pay or not pay dividends and the choice of amounts is presumed legitimate.

    b. **Exception**—To overcome this presumption and to force a board to pay more dividends, shareholders must prove that:

        i. The board acted in bad faith; *and*

        ii. Funds to pay dividends existed in a legally available source.

IV. LLC Financial Structure

A. The key LLC financial provisions tend to reflect comparable corporate (or partnership, occasionally) provisions.

B. Contributions to an LLC, as with a corporation or partnership, may be made in cash, property or services.

C. Obligations to contribute to an LLC are not excused by death, disability, or inability to perform and are enforceable by the creditors of the LLC who have relied upon them.

Examples

1. If member A agrees to contribute $50,000 to an LLC but dies before doing so, A's estate is liable to pay the amount.

2. If an LLC operating agreement describes member A's contribution of $50,000 to the LLC and A does not actually contribute that amount, creditor X of the LLC who loaned it money based on the belief that that amount had been contributed by A could force A to make the contribution.

D. Like corporations, LLCs may not make distributions to members if after doing so the firm would be insolvent (either in the sense that it cannot pay its bills as they come due or in the sense that its total liabilities exceed its total assets).

    1. Reasonable compensation for present or past services or payments made in the ordinary course of business under bona fide benefits or retirement plans are not "distributions" for this purpose. Therefore, an LLC could pay a reasonable salary to a member without complying with this solvency limitation.

    2. If a distribution is improperly made, the member or non-member managers who approve it are personally liable to creditors, as are members who receive distributions they know to have been improperly made. Liability is limited to the amount above what could have been properly distributed.

E. If an LLC commits to make a distribution to members but does not make the distribution, the members become general, unsecured creditors of the LLC for purposes of that amount.

F. Profits are shared as agreed in the operating agreement. If the operating agreement does not address this issue, then profits are shared in accordance with members' capital accounts (Contribution + Profits allocated – Losses allocated – Distributions).

Organization	How are Profits Shared?
Sole Proprietorship	100% to owner
General Partnership	As agreed in partnership agreement; if agreement as to losses only, then share profits the same as losses; if no agreement, share equally
Limited Partnership	As agreed in partnership agreement; if not addressed, share according to capital contributions made and not returned
C Corporation	100% to corporation
S Corporation	To shareholders in accordance with percentage of stock ownership (per-share, per-day method)
LLC	As agreed in the operating agreement; if not addressed then in accordance with capital account (Contribution + Profits allocated – Losses allocated – Distributions)

Example

The board of directors authorizes the issuance of 10,000 shares of $1 par value stock for $20/share. The board allows 1,000 shares to be sold to Sue for $10/share. Sue sells 500 of the shares to Sam for $10/share. She sells the other 500 shares to Ace for $10/share. Sam knows that Sue did not pay the authorized sale price; Ace does not know it. If creditors of the corporation go unpaid, they may sue the board and Sue for $10,000 and Sam for $5,000 (the total recovery cannot exceed $10,000). Ace, however, is not liable because he did not know that Sue did not pay the authorized price.

Note

Treasury stock may be purchased at less than the par value; if the company's share prices have dropped since the shares were originally issued, that may be the only way the company can resell them.

Termination

After studying this lesson, you should be able to:

1. Summarize the processes for terminating various business organizations.

I. Termination

A. Sole Proprietorships

1. A sole proprietorship naturally terminates when the sole owner dies or otherwise departs the business. The owner may terminate the business at any time he or she chooses to do so.

B. General Partnerships

1. The process to end a partnership may be governed by the partnership agreement. If it is not, the Revised Uniform Partnership Act (RUPA) provides a scheme that consists of dissociation, dissolution, and winding up (also known as liquidation). The partners' management rights (except with regard to winding up) terminate at the end of the partnership.

2. Under RUPA, the fact that partners are added to or removed from the partnership does not automatically lead to the dissolution of the partnership (as was formerly the case).

   a. Rather, the causes of "dissociation" of a partner from the partnership include:

      i. Notice of a partner's express will to dissolve the partnership

      ii. Death of a partner

      iii. Bankruptcy of a partner

      iv. Expulsion of a partner under the terms of the partnership agreement

      v. Occurrence of an event stipulated in the partnership agreement as causing dissociation

3. RUPA lists a few situations in which a partnership *must* be wound up; in all other situations, a buyout of a partner must occur. Thus, a partner's dissociation (through death, bankruptcy, etc.) must lead to either a buyout by the remaining partners or the dissolution of the partnership. The former (buyout) is preferred over the latter (dissolution) so that the business may continue.

4. If dissolution does not occur, the partnership shall purchase the interest of the dissociating partner at the amount that would have been distributable to the dissociating partner from his or her partnership account if, on the date of dissociation, the assets of the partnership were sold at the greater of liquidation or going-concern value (offset by damages caused if the dissociation was wrongful).

5. RUPA provides a 90-day "cooling off" period between dissolution and liquidation in order to give the parties an opportunity to negotiate an amicable buyout.

6. In winding up the partnership business, creditors (including partners) must be paid first. If there are insufficient assets to pay off creditors, then the partners (including the estates of the deceased partners) will have to contribute to the partnership to satisfy the obligations. If funds are left over after paying creditors, then the partnership shall make a distribution to partners in amounts equal to any excess of credits over charges in their partners' accounts.

C. Limited Partnerships, LLPs, and LLLPs

1. The process of dissociation, winding up, and liquidation (termination) for the various forms of limited partnerships (including LLPs and LLLPs) is sufficiently similar to that of general partnerships that it need not be separately treated.

2. The departure of a limited partner will not result in the dissolution of a limited partnership, and the departure of a general partner need not do so either with proper planning.

D. Corporations

1. Corporations may be voluntarily dissolved upon the approval of their directors and shareholders.

   a. Typically, a majority of directors vote to propose dissolution and a majority of shareholders vote to approve the proposal.

2. Corporations may be involuntarily dissolved *administratively* by the secretary of state for such reasons as:

   a. Failure to pay franchise taxes;

   b. Failure to file annual reports; *or*

   c. Failure to properly establish and maintain a registered agent or office.

3. Corporations may be involuntarily dissolved *judicially* in:

   a. An action by the attorney general, where:

      i. The corporation fraudulently obtained approval for its articles of incorporation, *or*

      ii. The corporation has abused its legal authority.

   b. An action by *shareholders*;

      i. If management is deadlocked;

      ii. If those controlling the corporation are acting in an illegal or oppressive way, such as by looting the corporation or wasting its assets; *or*

      iii. If the shareholders are deadlocked and cannot elect directors.

   c. In an action by creditors if:

      i. The creditor's claim has been reduced to judgment, the execution on the judgment returned unsatisfied, and the corporation is insolvent; *or*

      ii. The corporation has admitted in writing that the creditor's claim is due and owing and the corporation is insolvent.

4. **Liquidation**—After dissolution, the corporate business and affairs must be wound up and liquidated.

   a. The directors have a duty to "discharge or make reasonable provision" for claims. They must then distribute assets to shareholders.

   b. Directors will not be liable to claimants with regard to claims barred or satisfied if they have complied with the Revised Model Business Corporation Act's (RMBCA's) statutory procedures for:

      i. Giving notice to known claimants;

      ii. Publishing notice of dissolution;

      iii. Requesting that other claimants present their claims; *and*

      iv. Obtaining appropriate judicial determinations (e.g., of the amount of collateral needed for payment of contingent claims, claims reasonably expected to arise after dissolution, or claims not yet made).

5. Other major organic changes (in addition to dissolution) include sale of all or substantially all of a corporation's assets (not in the ordinary course of business) and mergers or consolidations with other corporations. Shareholder interests are protected in such transactions that can so fundamentally alter their interests by:

   a. **Procedures**—Directors owing a fiduciary duty must propose and shareholders must approve in a vote; and

   b. **Appraisal rights**—Dissenting shareholders may request that their shares be purchased at a court-valued rate pursuant to their appraisal rights (also called dissenters' rights).

6. **LLCs**

1. LLC law varies more from state to state than do most other forms of business organization. However, the process commonly follows the dissociation-winding up-termination approach of RUPA for general partnerships.

2. Among the events that cause a person to be dissociated as a member from an LCC, according to RULLCA, are the following:

   a. The person gives notice of express will to withdraw;

   b. An event causes dissolution based on the operating agreement;

   c. The person is expelled pursuant to the operating agreement;

   d. The person dies; *and/or*

   e. The person is a corporation, partnership, or other organization that has been dissolved.

3. Among the events that cause the LLC to dissolve, according to RULLCA:

   a. An event caused dissolution based on the operating agreement

   b. Consent of all members

   c. Passage of 90 consecutive days during which the company has no members

   d. Court order, upon application of a member, dissolving the LLC on grounds that the conduct of its activities is unlawful or that carrying on the company's activities is not "reasonably practicable" in conformity with the operating agreement

   e. Court order, upon application of a member, dissolving the LLC on grounds that those in control of the company are illegally or fraudulently acting or are oppressively behaving to harm the applicant

4. RULLCA contains detailed provisions regarding winding up of an LLC's business by gathering together its assets and paying its obligation to creditors (including members who are creditors). If any surplus remains, it should be distributed to (a) each person whose contributions have not been repaid; if any money remains, it should be distributed to (b) members and dissociated members in equal shares.

Rights, Duties, Legal Obligations, and Authority of Owners and Management

Rights and Duties

After studying this lesson, you should be able to:

1. Summarize the rights, duties, and legal obligations of owners and management.

2. Identify the rights, duties, and legal obligations of owners or management given a specific scenario.

I. **General Partnerships**

   A. **Absent agreement to the contrary partners are entitled to:**

      1. Equal management rights; *and*

      2. Have their capital contribution repaid and to equally share in profits.

   B. **Partnership property belongs to the partnership.** *RUPA states: "Property acquired by a partnership is property of the partnership and not of the partners individually."* Property purchased with partnership assets is presumed to be partnership property. Partners do not own any specific partnership property directly or individually. It is owned by the partnership as a legal entity. Partners are entitled to use or possess partnership property, but only on behalf of the partnership.

   Examples

   1. Sam is entitled to use a partnership truck for partnership purposes, but not to move his sister's furniture on a weekend (unless his partners agree).

   2. Sue owes money to Fred. Sue is a partner in the STD partnership. Sue may not assign partnership property to Fred in order to satisfy her debt to him. Sue may assign her partnership interest to Fred, but this does not make him a partner or give him partnership rights in any way. It only allows him to collect payments the other partners choose to make that Sue would be entitled to as a partner.

   C. Creditors of individual partners may not seize partnership property to satisfy the individual debts of partners. Rather, they may go to court to obtain a *charging order* in which the judge orders the other partners to pay any distribution due to the debtor partner to that partner's creditor instead. Creditors of an individual partner may even purchase that partner's partnership interest at auction, but they gain only the right to receive distributions due the partner. They do not become real partners for any purpose (voting, access to information, etc.).

   D. As noted elsewhere, general partners are *not* entitled to compensation for work performed for the partnership, except for "reasonable compensation" rendered in winding up the business of the partnership.

   E. Partners may veto the admission of potential new partners because new partners may be added only upon the unanimous consent of the existing partners. This is often called the right of *delectus personae*.

   F. **Information Rights**

      1. Partners and their agents are entitled access to partnership books and records during ordinary business hours.

      2. Each partner and the partnership shall furnish to partners and their legal representatives:

         a. **Without demand**—Any information concerning the partnership's business and affairs reasonably required for the proper exercise of partners' rights;

         b. **Upon demand**—Any other partnership information reasonably requested.

G. Right to an Accounting—May be invoked by a partner. An accounting is a judicial proceeding to provide a comprehensive and effective settlement of all partnership affairs. An auditor or other court appointee conducts the accounting with oversight by the court. The accounting makes a final determination of the monetary value of each partnership interest.

H. Standards of Conduct—The only fiduciary duties a partner owes to the partnership and other partners are the:

1. *Duty of loyalty*, which includes:

   a. Accounting for any benefit derived;

   b. Avoiding conflicts of interest; *and*

   c. Refraining from competing with the partnership business.

2. *Duty of care*, which includes refraining from engaging in grossly negligent or reckless conduct, intentional misconduct, or a knowing violation of the law.

I. Naturally, in a limited partnership the general partners who manage the firm owe these duties of care and loyalty to the passive limited partners.

II. Limited Partnerships, LLPs, and LLLPs

A. Limited Partnerships

1. **General partners**—In LPs, general partners have essentially the same rights and responsibilities as do general partners in general partnerships.

2. **Limited partners**—In LPs, limited partners have many of the same rights as general partners in general partnerships, but they may not take part in managing the business of the partnership without imperiling their limited liability status. They are supposed to act more as passive investors, as shareholders do in public corporations.

   a. That said, limited partners can do the following without losing their limited liability:

      i. Vote on any matter as authorized by the partnership agreement

      ii. Inspect and copy the partnership records

      iii. Obtain financial information, tax returns, and other partnership information if just and reasonable

      iv. Assign their partnership interest

      v. Receive the fair value of the partnership interest upon withdrawal

   b. Typically, the financial risk (liability) of a limited partner who does not participate in management and control of the business is limited to the partner's investment in the partnership. However, a limited partner may incur personal liability for the firm's debts if:

      i. No limited partnership certificate was filed, *or*

      ii. The certificate contained a false statement.

B. LLPs

1. Partners in an LLP have roughly the same rights and duties as partners in a general partnership.

2. The significant difference between an LLP and a general partnership is that partners in an LLP are not liable for the torts of other partners—only for their own and those of the people they supervise. And in many states, partners in an LLP are also sheltered from personal liability for partnership contractual obligations.

C. LLLPs

1. Partners in an LLLP have roughly the same rights and duties as partners in a limited partnership.

2. The key difference between an LLLP and a limited partnership is that even general partners may enjoy limited liability in an LLLP, whereas in a limited partnership, there must be at least one person or entity that bears general liability.

III. Corporations

A. Shareholders have few duties (although controlling shareholders sometimes are held to owe fiduciary duties not to abuse minority shareholders), but they have several important rights. They do **not** have the right to manage the day-to-day affairs of the corporation. Instead, their influence is more indirect. But they do have many key rights, including the right to:

1. Vote for corporate directors

2. Inspect corporate records for proper purposes at proper times and in proper locations

    a. Inspection must be in good faith and for a proper purpose, including:

        i. Corporate financial condition

        ii. The propriety of dividends

        iii. Mismanagement of the corporation

        iv. The names and addresses of other shareholders

    b. Improper purposes include to:

        i. Harass management

        ii. Discover trade secrets

        iii. Gain a competitive advantage

        iv. Develop a mailing list for sale or for similar use

3. Have their financial priorities respected (e.g., if they hold preferred shares, their preferences should be respected);

4. Receive notice of, and vote on proposals for major organic changes in the corporation, such as significant amendments to the articles of incorporation, dissolution, mergers with other companies, or sale of major corporate assets. Shareholders may also exercise **appraisal rights** (the right to have their shares purchased by the corporation at a fair price determined by judicial proceeding) when they dissent from major organic changes.

5. File direct lawsuits against the corporation or its officers and directors for injuries done to them specifically, and derivative lawsuits for injuries done to all shareholders in their capacity as shareholders.

    a. Before filing a derivative suit, shareholders usually must make a demand on the board of directors that the corporation bring suit, unless such a demand is obviously futile. Only if such a demand is not complied with may the shareholder proceed to file the derivative suit.

6. Exercise preemptive rights to buy their proportional share of new issuances of securities in order to maintain their relative voting strength in the corporation (although articles of incorporation often eliminate these rights).

B. Directors have several important duties, including:

1. **Duty of attention**—"Directors must direct." They must not be mere figureheads, meaning that they should, at a minimum:

    a. Attend most board meetings

    b. Gain a basic familiarity with the company's business

    c. Study the company's financial statements

2. **Duty of care**—Directors are not expected to be perfect, but must act:

    a. In good faith

    b. With the care of an ordinarily prudent person in a like position

    c. In a manner reasonably believed to be in the best interests of the corporation

3. **Duty of loyalty**—Directors owe a fiduciary duty to shareholders. They must be loyal to the corporation and its shareholders, meaning:

   a. They should avoid conflicts of interest.

   b. The transactions between a director and the corporation are not automatically void but will be carefully scrutinized. Such transactions are permitted if (1) they are approved by an affirmative majority of disinterested directors, (2) they are approved by a majority of knowledgeable shareholders, or (3) they are "fair" to the corporation.

   c. They should respect the *corporate opportunity doctrine* by not appropriating for themselves business opportunities that rightfully belong to the corporation.

C. **Directors' Rights**

1. **Right to rely**—Directors have the right to rely on the reports of officers and other directors unless they have some reason to be suspicious.

2. **Business judgment rule**—Courts are not business experts, so they normally do not second-guess the business decisions of directors or officers. Rather, they apply the "business judgment rule," which states: "In the absence of a showing of bad faith on the part of the directors or of a gross abuse of discretion, the business judgment of the directors will not be interfered with by the courts. The acts of directors are presumptively acts taken in good faith and inspired for the best interests of the corporation, and a minority stockholder who challenges their bona fides of purpose has the burden of proof."

3. **Liability protection**—Under the business judgment rule, directors (and officers) will not be held liable for mistaken judgments and actions so long as they acted in good faith with an intent to benefit the corporation. Additionally, most states allow shareholders to amend articles of incorporation to eliminate director (and officer) liability for errors of judgment or even carelessness (although not for acts of fraud or dishonesty).

4. **Right to profit**—Directors have the opportunity to breach their fiduciary duty to the corporation by profiting in transactions with it. But such transactions are not automatically improper, and they may be perfectly legitimate so long as a majority of directors, who are fully informed and disinterested, approve the transaction *and* the transaction is fair to the corporation. This is true even if the conflicted director's presence is accounted for in ensuring that a quorum was present for the meeting and the conflicted director voted for the transaction.

D. **Officers**

1. Officers run the day-to-day operations of the corporation under the supervision of the board of directors, so they are very powerful and have the opportunity to abuse that power.

2. Officers are constrained by the same duties of care and loyalty that constrain directors.

IV. **Limited Liability Companies**

A. Whether an LLC is managed by members or by non-member managers, those managing the firm generally owe duties of care and loyalty to the (other) members.

B. Despite the fact that LLCs are generally intended to be more "contractarian" in nature (e.g., governed by the agreement of the members rather than by default statutory provisions), *the* RULLCA prohibits an operating agreement from totally eliminating the duty of loyalty, the duty of care, or any other fiduciary duty.

C. The RULLCA also provides that the members in an LLC shall consistently discharge their duties under the act and under the operating agreement with contractual obligations of "good faith and fair dealing."

D. However, the RULLCA also provides that those duties that would typically be owed by either members managing the firm or managers managing the firm may be limited in various ways if the limitations are not "manifestly unreasonable." For example, the operating agreement may:

1. Identify specific types of activities that do not violate the duty of loyalty

2. Alter the duty of care, except to authorize intentional misconduct or knowing violation of law

3. Eliminate a member or manager's liability to the LLC for money damages, except for such actions as breach of the duty of loyalty, intentional infliction of harm on the firm, or intentional violation of criminal law

E. Additionally, courts protect members by:

1. Allowing them to escape an operating agreement by convincing a court that its provisions are "manifestly unreasonable;" *and*

2. Providing a judicial remedy dissolving an LLC if the managers or members controlling the firm are guilty of "oppressive conduct" directly harmful to a member.

F. The business judgment rule will generally apply when managers' good faith business decisions are challenged.

Authority of Owners and Managers

After studying this lesson, you should be able to:

1. Summarize the authority of owners and management.

2. Identify the authorities of owners or management given a specific scenario.

I. Partnerships

    A. Agency Law—In partnerships, agency law tends to govern regarding the authority of partners to bind the partnership.

    B. General Principles—As a general rule, agency law provides:

        1. An act of a partner for apparently carrying on in the ordinary course the partnership business binds the partnership, unless (a) the partner had no authority to act for the partnership in the particular matter and (b) the person with whom the partner was dealing knew or had received notification that the partner lacked authority.

        2. An act of a partner that is not apparently for carrying on in the ordinary course the partnership's business binds the partnership only if the act was authorized by the other partners.

    C. A partner binds both the partnership and the other partners if he or she acts with:

        1. Actual authority (expressed or implied); *or*

        2. Apparent authority, which cannot exist where:

            a. The third party knows of a partner's lack of authority, *or*

            b. The partner's action is one that requires unanimity, such as an agreement to admit a new partner.

    D. Ratification—An act lacking both actual and apparent authority may still bind a partnership that ratifies the action expressly or by knowingly accepting the benefits of the agreement.

    E. Tort Liability—Consistent with agency law, partnerships are generally liable for the torts committed by their partners or other agents within the scope of their employment or authority.

        1. **Intentional torts**—A partnership is usually liable if a partner commits an intentional tort while trying to advance partnership interests, even if he or she does so in a wrongful way.

        2. **Misapplication of funds**—The Revised Uniform Partnership Act (RUPA) imposes virtually strict liability on a partnership for the misapplication of money received by the partnership "in the course of its business." Between the innocent partners who had nothing to do with the misapplication and the innocent customer or client of the partnership, RUPA provides that the innocent customer or client deserves the most protection.

        3. **Joint and several liability**—Under RUPA, contract and tort liability are typically joint and several, meaning that a creditor may sue any general partner and hold that partner completely liable without suing the others. However, RUPA usually provides that the assets of the partnership must be exhausted before the partnership creditor proceeds against the individual assets of the general partners.

        4. **Late arrivers**—If a general partner joins an existing partnership, he or she is personally liable for all subsequently-incurred debts, but is liable for preexisting debts only out of his or her partnership contribution.

II. **Corporations**

    A. The Corporate Pyramid—The corporation is typically viewed as a pyramid. Shareholders are passive investors whose input into corporate management is their vote for directors. Directors then set overall corporate policy and select officers. Officers are at the top of the pyramid, making the day-to-day decisions that bind the firm.

B. **Directors**—Most state corporate codes provide that "the business and affairs of a corporation shall be managed under the supervision of a board of directors." Directors have broad authority to:

1. Borrow money

2. Sell corporate property

3. Hire and fire officers and other employees

4. Declare or refuse to declare dividends

5. Make or refuse to make other distributions to shareholders

6. Set the salaries of employees, officers, and even themselves

7. Propose for shareholder approval:

   a. Sale of major corporate assets

   b. Mergers or consolidations with other firms

   c. Dissolution

   d. Amendments to the articles of incorporation

C. **Officers** run the firm's day-to-day operations and typically have various types of authority to bind the firm, including:

D. **Express Authority, Derived from:**

1. Articles of incorporation

2. By-laws

3. Directors' resolutions

4. Statutes

E. **Implied Authority, Derived by Virtue of their Offices**—The general trend is to find broad authority inherent in the offices of CEO, CFO, and so on, but in questionable situations the other party may always demand a board of directors resolution to provide proof of express authority. Of course even top officers would not have authority to bind the corporation in truly extraordinary transactions, such as mergers, sales of major corporate assets, and borrowing unusually large sums of money.

F. **Ratification**—Even if an officer acts without either express or implied authority, the board of directors could always bind the corporation by ratifying the contracts.

III. Limited Liability Companies (LLCs)

A. The operating agreement should indicate whether the LLC will be member-managed or manager-managed. Absent provision to the contrary, an LLC is assumed to be member-managed.

B. If member-managed, an LLC will operate much like a general partnership:

1. Each member has equal rights in management.

2. Ordinary business issues are decided by majority vote.

3. Acts outside the ordinary course of business require unanimous approval.

4. The operating agreement may be amended only with the consent of all members.

C. If manager-managed, an LLC will operate much like a limited partnership, with the managers assuming the role of a general partner:

1. Except as otherwise provided in the Revised Uniform Limited Liability Company Act (RULLCA), matters related to the activities of the company will be exclusively decided by the managers.

2. Managers have equal rights in the management and conduct of the firm.

3. Issues arising in the ordinary course of business are decided by a majority vote of the managers.

4. The consent of all managers is required to engage in extraordinary transactions, such as the sale of all or substantially all firm property, approval of a merger, or amendment of the operating agreement.

5. Managers may be removed at any time, with or without cause, by a majority vote of the members.

D. Whereas partnership law generally provides for "statutory apparent authority," indicating that a partnership will generally be bound whenever a general partner acts to carry on the business of the partnership in the usual way, RULLCA provides to the contrary—that "a member is not an agent of the limited liability company solely by reason of being a member." An LLC may be manager-managed, so "statutory apparent authority," which still exists in several individual states' LLC statutes, has been eliminated in RULLCA.

E. The vast majority of interactions between LLCs and third parties will involve LLC employees; general agency law will govern these transactions, and no surprises should occur.

F. An LLC, like a general partnership, may (but need not) file a statement of authority with the state that expressly spells out the managerial authority of its managers (whether they are also members or not).

Federal Taxation

Introduction to Tax Review

I. **Federal Taxation Content**—The AICPA provides a brief listing of the subject areas that are considered for inclusion in the tax portion of the Uniform CPA Exam.

   A. **AICPA Outline—The AICPA provides an outline of the tax contents (and their approximate weights) for the REG portion of the exam.** The formatting shown for this outline is as shown in the AICPA Blueprint specifications.

The Regulation Section is divided into the following five areas:

Area I Ethics, Professional Responsibilities and Federal Tax Procedures	10–20%
Area II Business Law	10–20%
Area III Federal Taxation of Property Transactions	12–22%
Area IV Federal Taxation of Individuals	15–25%
Area V Federal Taxation of Entities	28–38%

The tax materials cover areas III, IV, and V. Area I is included in the Business Law area.

Overview of Tax Content Areas

Area III covers the federal income taxation of property transactions and topics related to federal estate and gift taxation.

Area IV covers the federal income taxation of individuals from both a tax preparation and tax planning perspective.

Area V covers the federal income taxation of entities including sole proprietorships, partnerships, limited liability companies, C corporations, S corporations, joint ventures, trusts, estates and tax-exempt organizations, from both a tax preparation and tax planning perspective.

Detail of Tax Content Areas (The numbers are keyed to the lesson outline below to show you the area this topic is covered in the material)

I. **Federal Taxation of Property Transactions**

   A. **Acquisition and Disposition of Assets**

   1. Basis and holding period of assets (2)

   2. Taxable and nontaxable dispositions (6, 7)

   3. Amount and character of gains and losses, and netting process (including installment sales) (2, 3, 4, 11)

   4. Related party transactions (including imputed interest) (7)

   B. **Cost Recovery (Depreciation, Depletion and Amortization)** (5)

   C. **Estate and Gift Taxation**

   1. Transfers subject to gift tax (27)

   2. Gift tax annual exclusion and gift tax deductions (27)

   3. Determination of taxable estate (28)

II. **Federal Taxation of Individuals (Including Tax preparation and Planning Strategies)** (25)

   A. **Gross Income (Inclusions and Exclusions) (Includes Taxation of Retirement Plan Benefits)** (8, 9, 10, 12, 13, 14)

   B. **Reporting of Items from Pass-Through Entities** (11)

   C. **Adjustments and Deductions to Arrive at Adjusted Gross Income and Taxable Income** (15, 16, 17, 18, 19, 20, 21)

   D. **Passive Activity Losses (Excluding Foreign Tax Credit Implications** (21)

E. Loss Limitations (9, 21)

F. Filing Status and Exemptions (22, 23)

G. Computation of Tax and Credits (26)

H. Alternative Minimum Tax (24)

III. Federal Taxation of Entities

    A. Tax Treatment of Formation and Liquidation of Business Entities (37, 38, 42, 52, 53)

    B. Differences Between Book and Tax Income (Loss) (31)

    C. C Corporations

        1. Computation of taxable income (including alternative minimum taxable income), tax liability, and allowable credits (30, 31, 32, 33, 34, 51)

        2. Net operating losses and capital loss limitations (30, 32)

        3. Entity/owner transactions, including contributions, loans, and distributions (29, 36)

        4. Consolidated tax returns (35)

        5. Multijurisdictional tax issues (including consideration of local, state, and international tax issues) (39, 40)

    D. S Corporations

        1. Eligibility and Elections (47)

        2. Determination or ordinary business income (loss) and separately stated items (48)

        3. Basis of shareholder's interest (48)

        4. Entity/owner transactions (including contributions, loans, and distributions (49)

        5. Built-in gains tax (49)

    E. Partnerships

        1. Determination or ordinary business income (loss) and separately stated items (43)

        2. Basis of partner's interest and basis of property contributed to partnership (42)

        3. Partnership and partner elections (42)

        4. Transactions between a partner and the partnership (including services performed by a partner and loans) (44)

        5. Impact of partnership liabilities on a partner's interest in a partnership (42)

        6. Distributions of partnership assets (45)

        7. Ownership changes (46)

    F. Limited Liability Companies (42, 53)

    G. Trusts and Estates

        1. Types of trusts (50)

        2. Income and deductions (50)

        3. Determination of beneficiary's share of taxable income (50)

    H. Tax Exempt Organizations

        1. Types of organizations (41)

        2. Obtaining and maintaining tax exempt status (41)

        3. Unrelated business income (41)

II. Course Structure—To facilitate preparation for the CPA Exam, the review materials are divided into the following sections and lessons:

III. Exam Preparation—The AICPA provides a brief outline of the skills candidates should possess for the exam.

A. AICPA-Indicated Tasks—In addition to demonstrating knowledge and understanding of these topics, candidates are required to demonstrate the skills required to apply that knowledge in providing tax preparation and advisory services and performing other responsibilities as certified public accountants. To demonstrate such knowledge and skills, candidates will be expected to demonstrate the following skill levels:

Evaluation: The examination or assessment of problems, and use of judgment to draw conclusions.

Analysis: The examination and study of the interrelationships of separate areas in order to identify causes and find evidence to support inferences.

Application: The use or demonstration of knowledge, concepts or techniques.

Remembering and Understanding: The perception and comprehension of the significance of an area utilizing knowledge gained.

B. AICPA-Recommended Publications—The AICPA recommends that candidates study the following publications:

1. Internal Revenue Code of 1986, as amended, and Regulations
2. Treasury Department Circular 230
3. Other administrative pronouncements regarding federal taxation
4. Case law on federal taxation
5. Public Law 86-272
6. Uniform Division of Income for Tax Purposes Act (UDITPA)
7. Current federal tax textbooks

> **Note**
> *It is certain that a thorough examination of the Internal Revenue Code and Regulations will prepare a candidate for the exam. Unfortunately, most of us have other things to do over the next 20 years. The CPAexcel® materials are designed to help you focus on the tax issues that we feel are most likely to be tested on the exam since you will not have time to review the publications listed here.*

C. Advice for Preparation

1. Use review materials strategically.

   a. Use review material to organize preparation for thorough coverage.

   b. The review materials can be used to briefly review familiar topics (refresh the memory) or focus on new material.

   c. Use review problems and questions as a mechanism for calibrating study efforts.

   d. Watch the multimedia portions of the review course, then read all text materials, and finally complete all problems.

2. **Keep the ultimate objective in mind**—To pass the exam. Study topics strategically.

   a. Tax topics constitute only 60%–80% of the REG portion of the exam. Integrate the study of taxation with an overall strategy on the REG. This strategy minimizes the risk that a poor score on one topic will cause a failure on this portion of the exam.

Example
A risky strategy is to ignore a topic because of a relatively strong understanding of other topics in the same part of the exam. This strategy is risky because the topical coverage is approximate and it may be difficult to score high enough in one topic to offset a poor score in another topic.

b. The initial time invested in understanding new topics may have a higher payoff than additional time invested in perfecting comprehension in other topics.

Example
If individual taxation is relatively clear, but corporate taxation is confusing, a good strategy would be to concentrate on corporate topics. A relatively superficial understanding of corporate topics could result in immediate gains because some of the questions on corporate topics are likely to be relatively easy.

D. Preparation for Tax Questions

1. No essay questions will be given on the tax portion of the exam.

   a. Tax questions are objective and will likely have unambiguous answers. Hence, the questions will probably avoid uncertain interpretations of the law.

Example
The determination of whether an activity qualifies as "hobby" is quite uncertain because this determination is based on numerous factors. Hence, objective questions are unlikely to ask about the determination of hobby status.

---

   b. "Nitpicking" questions are likely because details are unambiguous.

Example
While the determination of hobby status is uncertain, the hobby loss presumption is unambiguous. A profit in three of five consecutive years results in the presumption that an activity is not a hobby. Hence, a question is more likely to be asked about this detail rather than the more ambiguous determination of hobby status.

---

2. **How much detail should be studied?**—There are over 2,000 pages in the Internal Revenue Code, so it is difficult to say. A few suggestions follow:

   a. The scope of the exam is limited to the law in effect as of six months before the beginning of the testing period in which you take the exam. More recent changes should be ignored.

   b. Besides changes in the law, the tax code is replete with transition rules (temporary rules existing until a change in the law becomes permanent). Questions about temporary changes are unlikely, but questions about phase-in rules are possible.

   i. Note that in recent years many new tax provisions have been passed that are intended to be in effect for only one or two years. Only the temporary changes that are the most important have been included. However, note that the likelihood that these provisions will be tested is not as high as for other material due to their temporary status.

   c. **A focus on specific numbers is also unlikely because there are too many specific numbers in the law and many are indexed to change each year.** Any figure that is indexed to inflation does not have to be memorized. These figures are included in the materials so you will be aware of them, but generally include a date after the number to indicate the year for that particular number (e.g., exemption amount is $4,050 (2017)).

   i. **Examples of important phase-out amounts that are not indexed for inflation are:**

   1. Contributions to Coverdell Savings Accounts (*Taxation of Retirement Plans*): Contributions to a Coverdell Education Savings Account are limited to $2,000 per beneficiary, per year. The contribution is phased out proportionately if the taxpayer's AGI exceeds $190,000 for married filing jointly (a $30,000 range) or $95,000 for single taxpayers (a $15,000 range).

2. **$25,000 Loss Deduction for Rental Real Estate** (*Limitations on Business Deductions*): The exception is phased out for taxpayers with an AGI over $100,000 at the rate of 50% ($1 of deduction for each $2 of AGI over $100,000).

3. **Child Tax Credit** (*Personal Tax Credits*): The credit is phased out for married taxpayers with AGI in excess of $110,000 ($75,000 for unmarried). The credit is reduced $50 for each $1,000 (or portion) over the trigger AGI amount.

4. **American Opportunity Tax Credit** (*Personal Tax Credits*): The credit is phased out ratably for single taxpayers with AGI in excess of $80,000 ($160,000 in the case of a joint return). The credit is phased out over a $10,000 range ($20,000 for joint return) and, thus, is completely gone when AGI reaches $90,000 ($180,000 joint return).

3. Remember to work as many problems as you can. Do not just read the problems and then read the solutions. On the exam you will have to WORK the problems, and the best way to improve on that skill is to work, work, work as many problems as you can.

4. The most important tax forms that you should be familiar with are included in the videos and in the appropriate lessons. You do not need to memorize anything other than the form/schedule number and the general type of information reported on the form. You may be given a short portion of a form to complete. If so, input the information requested on each line of the form based on the tax law you learned in the lessons.

IV. Test-Taking Tips

A. Educated guesses are a critical part of an exam strategy. An "educated" guess is made by eliminating all incorrect alternatives and then using general concepts (or principles) to select between the remaining alternatives.

Example

A question several years ago asked if a taxpayer is entitled to deduct jury pay that the taxpayer had to give to his employer because the employer paid the employee during the time the employee spent on a jury. There is an obscure provision that covers this situation, but who would have studied it (given its obscurity)? An educated guess would be a deduction for adjusted gross income because the employee must include the jury pay in income, but should not be taxed on it because he or she was forced to remit it to his or her employer. An itemized deduction would have not been fair because the limits placed on these deductions might have caused the employee to be taxed on the jury pay.

B. Should you anticipate specific topics (e.g., new provisions)? With the exception of a few disclosed questions, the exams have been closed since 1996. The questions on disclosed exams indicate that exams do not stress new provisions, perhaps because of the ambiguity involved with the application of new law.

C. The AICPA examines the validity of proposed questions by including "trial" questions on the exam. These questions are not scored, but they are interspersed with actual test questions. Hence, an inability to answer some tax questions should not be cause for concern—These questions could be trial questions.

D. **Advice for Exam Performance**

1. Stay cool and do not be hasty.

2. Budget your time.

3. Eliminate alternatives.

4. Use your common sense.

5. Think positively and be confident.

Property Transactions

Sales and Dispositions of Assets

After studying this lesson, you should be able to:

1. Classify an asset as ordinary, capital, or Section 1231.

2. Compute the realized gain/loss from a property transaction.

3. Apply the basis rules for gifts and compute the gain/loss from the sale of gifted assets.

4. Determine the proper tax basis for assets converted from personal use to business use.

I. **Categories of Assets**—Assets can be divided into three mutually exclusive categories: ordinary, Section 1231, and capital.

   A. **Ordinary Assets**

      1. Inventory and accounts/notes receivables are ordinary assets.

      2. Depreciable property used in a trade/business and realty that have been owned for a year or less are ordinary assets.

      3. Generally, copyrights and musical, artistic, and literary works are ordinary assets if held by the person who created the work. A composer can elect to have his or her musical work treated as a capital asset.

   B. **Section 1231 Assets**—Depreciable property used in a trade/business and realty that have been owned for more than one year are Section 1231 assets.

   C. **Capital Assets**

      1. Capital assets do not include the items listed above as ordinary and Section 1231 assets.

      2. *Most other types of property, including property held for investment use and personal use, are capital assets.* Goodwill of a corporation is also a capital asset. Patents are usually treated as capital assets.

   D. **Acquired property can also be divided into the following four categories:**

      1. Real property

      2. Personal property

      3. Intangible assets

      4. Natural assets

II. **Sales and Dispositions**

   A. **A realized gain or loss** must be computed any time there is a sale or disposition of property.

      1. The term **sale or disposition** includes sales, exchanges, trade-ins, casualties, condemnations, thefts, and retirements.

      2. Realized gain or loss is computed as follows:

> Amount realized
> – Adjusted basis
> ---
> Realized gain/Loss

   B. **Computing amount realized is a four-step process:**

      1. Cash received; *plus*

      2. Fair market value of any property and services received; *plus*

3. *Liabilities assumed by the buyer; reduced by debts of buyer assumed by seller; minus*

4. Selling expenses.

Example

Property with a $10,000 mortgage and a basis of $15,000 is sold for $10,000 cash, and buyer assumes the mortgage. The amount realized is $20,000, and the gain is $5,000.

C. **Adjusted Basis**—This equals the cost or other acquisition basis of the property,

1. *Plus capital improvements (not repairs),*

2. Minus depreciation, amortization, and depletion.

3. Cost includes any liabilities or expenses connected with the acquisition.

D. A **recognized gain/loss** is the amount of realized gain/loss that is included in the taxable income of the taxpayer.

III. **Special Basis Issue**

A. **Basis Issues for Gifts**

1. If property is gifted to a taxpayer, the donee's basis is:

a. **Gain basis** = adjusted basis of the donor.

b. **Loss basis** = lower of:

i. Fair market value (FMV) at date of gift, or

ii. Adjusted basis of the donor.

c. **Depreciable basis** = gain basis.

d. The basis is **increased** for the portion of any **gift tax paid** by the donor due to appreciation in the property:

$$\text{Adjustment to basis} = \frac{\text{Unrealized appreciation}}{\text{(FMV at data of gift} - \text{Annual exclusion)}} \times \text{Gift tax paid}$$

> **Note**
> Not all realized gains/losses will be recognized. If not recognized, they are either excluded or deferred. The recognized gain/loss will never exceed the realized gain/loss. Assume that all realized gains/losses are recognized unless you are aware of a tax law that provides otherwise.

> **Note**
> Only losses of sales from investment and business assets are deductible. Hence, while personal assets are capital assets, losses of these assets are not deductible.

Example

Tom received a gift of property with an FMV of $104,000 and an adjusted basis of $74,000. The donor paid a gift tax of $18,000 on the transfer. Tom's basis for the property would be $80,000 determined as follows:

$$\$74{,}000 \text{ basis plus } \left[\$18{,}000 \text{ gift tax} \times \frac{(\$104{,}000 \text{ FMV less } \$74{,}000 \text{ basis})}{(\$104{,}000 \text{ FMV less } \$14{,}000 \text{ exclusion})}\right] = \$80{,}000$$

B. **Tax Effects of Basis for Gifts**

1. A **gain** is recognized only if the donee sells property for more than the gain basis.

2. A **loss** is recognized only if the donee sells property for less than the loss basis.

3. If the property is sold by the donee for an amount in-between the gain and loss basis, **no gain or loss is recognized**.

> **Note**
> The gain and loss basis differs only when the FMV of the property is less than its basis. The law allows a built-in gain to be transferred to another individual, but does **not** allow a transfer of a built-in loss.

Example

TP receives a used auto from his father as a gift. The father bought the auto for $10,000 several years ago and the auto is worth $15,000 at the time of the gift. TP will take his father's basis ($10,000) in the auto.

If the father had a basis of $20,000 in the auto, in TP's hands the auto would have a gain basis of $20,000 and a loss basis of $15,000. Loss can only be recognized to the extent that the auto is sold for less than $15,000. Gain can only be recognized to the extent that the auto is sold for more than $20,000. If the automobile is sold for an amount between $15,000 and $20,000, no gain or loss is recognized.

C. Holding Period of Gifted Property

1. If the **gain basis** is used to compute realized gain or loss, the holding period of the property for the donee **includes the holding period of the donor**.

2. If the **loss basis** is used, the holding period of the donee **begins on the date of the gift**.

Examples

1. X purchased property on July 14, 2017, for $10,000. X made a gift of the property to Z on June 10, 2018, when its FMV was $8,000. Since Z's basis for gain is $10,000, Z's holding period for a disposition at a gain extends back to July 14, 2017. Since Z's $8,000 basis for loss is determined by reference to FMV at June 10, 2018, Z's holding period for a disposition at a loss begins on June 11.

2. In year 1, Dylan Coile bought a diamond necklace for her own use at a cost of $10,000. In year 10, when the fair value was $12,000, Dylan gave this necklace to her daughter, Hannah. No gift tax was due or paid on the gift of the necklace.

   Hannah's holding period for the gift:

   A. Starts in year 10.

   B. Starts in year 1.

   C. Depends on whether the necklace is sold by Hannah at a gain or at a loss.

   D. Is irrelevant because Hannah received the necklace for no consideration of money or money's worth.

The correct answer is B (starts in year 1). Because fair value ($12,000) at the date of the gift is more than the donor's adjusted basis ($10,000), the donor's adjusted basis of $10,000 is the donee's basis for gain and basis for loss. Thus, because the donor's adjusted basis is also the donee's basis, the holding period of the donee includes the holding period of the donor.

D. Inheritances—Basis and Holding Period

1. The basis of property acquired from a decedent is the fair market value at the date of death, or the FMV on the alternate valuation date (six months after the date of death) if that date is selected by the executor as the valuation date.

2. Holding period is deemed to be long-term.

Note
These rules prevent a nondeductible personal loss from being converted into a business loss.

Example
Ann received 100 shares of stock as an inheritance from her uncle Henry, who died January 20, 2018. The stock had an FMV of $40,000 on January 20, and an FMV of $30,000 on July 20, 2018. The stock's FMV was $34,000 on June 15, 2018, the date the stock was distributed to Ann.

If the alternate valuation is not elected or if no estate tax return is filed, Ann's basis for the stock is its FMV of $40,000 on the date of Henry's death. If the alternate valuation is elected, Ann's basis will be the stock's $34,000 FMV on June 15 (the date of distribution) since the stock was distributed to Ann within six months after the decedent's death.

3. The FMV rule is not applicable to appreciated property acquired by the decedent by gift within one year before death if such property then passes from the donee-decedent to the original donor or donor's spouse. The basis of such property to the original donor (or spouse) will be the adjusted basis of the property to the decedent immediately before death.

Example
Son gives property with FMV of $40,000 (basis of $5,000) to terminally ill father within one year before father's death. The property is included in father's estate at FMV of $40,000. If property passes to son or son's spouse, basis will remain at $5,000. If passed to someone else, the property's basis will be $40,000.

E. Property Converted from Personal to Investment/Business Use

Gain basis = Adjusted basis
Loss basis and depreciable basis = Lower of (1) adjusted basis or (2) FMV at date of conversion

Capital Gains and Losses

After studying this lesson, you should be able to:

1. Distinguish between long-term and short-term gains and losses.

2. Identify collectibles and be able to apply their special capital gain rules.

3. Net capital gains and losses in the proper order.

4. Summarize the differences in the capital gain/loss rules for individuals and corporations.

I. **Eligibility**—Only a "sale or disposition" of a "capital" asset is eligible for capital gains netting.

> **Definition**
> *Capital Assets:* Include all assets except inventory, accounts receivable, depreciable assets and realty used in a business, creative works (in the hands of the creator), or certain miscellaneous assets (such as government publications or obligations). Self-created musical works are treated as capital assets even though these are creative works.

A. Investment assets and personal use assets are capital assets. Common capital assets include stocks, bonds, real estate, and goodwill of a corporation.

II. **Long Term versus Short Term**—Each capital gain and loss is classified according to whether the asset is long term or short term.

A. Long-term assets are those held over one year.

B. **Definition**—The holding period begins and ends on the date title passes. The holding period for stocks and securities acquired by purchase begins on the trade date that the stock or security was acquired, and ends on the trade date on which the stock or security was sold or exchanged.

C. For transactions where the basis of a new asset is determined by the basis of an old asset, the holding period of the old asset "tacks" onto the holding period of the new asset.

> **Example**
> TP's pickup was destroyed in a storm and he replaced it with a similar pickup. If TP elected to defer the gain as an involuntary conversion, then the holding period of the old pickup will tack onto the holding period for the new pickup.

D. There are automatic holding periods for nonbusiness bad debts (short term) and inheritances (long term).

E. If a taxpayer has short-term capital gains **distributions**, from a mutual fund, these are reported and taxed as ordinary income. That is, these are not included in the netting process described below—they are always taxed as ordinary income.

> **Misconception**
> *Losses on the sale of personal use assets are not deductible despite the fact that these assets are capital assets.*

F. For a lease that is a capital asset, the holding period is determined by the length of the lease.

III. **Netting Process—Individuals and Corporations**

A. **Approach for Netting Process:**

1. Short-term gains and short-term losses are netted against each other to get net short-term gain or net short-term loss.

2. Long-term gains and long-term losses are netted against each other to get net long-term gain or net long-term loss.

3. If the first two steps result in two net positions of the opposite signs (i.e., one is a gain and one is a loss), they are netted against each other (yields net capital gain or net capital loss). If net short-term and net long-term signs are the same, they maintain their separate character (i.e., do not net any further).

Individuals' Treatment of Net Capital Gain or Capital Loss	
Net capital gain treatment summarized	
Net Capital Gain Result	**Treatment**
1. All long term	Tax rate is 15% (0% for taxpayers in the 15% or 10% tax brackets) and 20% for taxable income that is in the 39.6% bracket for ordinary income.
2. All short term	Taxable in full as ordinary income.
3. Part long term and part short term	For short-term portion, taxable in full as ordinary income. For long-term portion, same as #1 above.
Net capital loss treatment summarized	
Net Capital Loss Result	**Treatment**
4. All long term	Annual deduction limit of $3,000 ($1,500 for married filing separately taxpayers); portion not used to generate deduction carried over indefinitely.
5. All short term	Annual deduction limit of $3,000 ($1,500 for married filing separately taxpayers); excess carried over indefinitely.
6. Part long term and part short term	Deduct short-term first toward $3,000 ($1,500 for married filing separately taxpayers) annual deduction limit; any remaining portion of annual limit can be made up of long-term capital loss (LTCL). Excess loss is carried over indefinitely. Deduct short-term first, long-term second. Annual deduction limited to taxable income. Cannot carry loss back (must carry forward).

IV. Rules for Individuals

A. If the combination of net short-term and net long-term gains and losses is negative, then individuals can deduct this **net capital loss** up to $3,000 per year. The deduction is for AGI and is limited to taxable income.

1. Any excess capital loss for an individual can be carried forward, indefinitely, but cannot be carried back. Short-term capital losses are used first, and then long-term capital losses.

2. If an individual dies with unused capital losses, these cannot be transferred to his estate (but can be used in the year of death subject to regular limitations).

B. The losses that are subject to the carryforward retain their character as short-term or long-term in future years. Long-term capital losses that have been carried forward offset capital gains in the following order:

1. Capital gains taxed at 28%

2. Capital gains taxed at 25%

3. Capital gains taxed at 20% (or 15% for some taxpayers)

Definition

Net Capital Loss: Occurs if a net loss results from combining net short-term gains and losses with net long-term gains and losses.

Example

An individual has a $4,000 STCL and a $5,000 LTCL for 2016. The $9,000 net capital loss results in a capital loss deduction of $3,000 for 2016, while the remainder is a carryover to 2017. Since $3,000 of the STCL would be used to create the capital loss deduction, there is a $1,000 STCL carryover and a $5,000 LTCL carryover to 2017. The $5,000 LTCL carryover would first offset gains in the 28% group.

C. If the combination of net short-term and net long-term gains and losses results in long-term capital gain, then this is labeled "net capital gain." If the combination results in short-term capital gain this is taxed as ordinary income.

D. **Net capital gain** is the portion of capital gain net income (if any) that is eligible for a reduced tax rate.

Example

This year TP realized a net short-term gain of $5,000 and a net long-term loss of $3,000. TP's capital gain net income of $2,000 is comprised of net short-term gains and, accordingly, is taxed at the regular income tax rates. There is no net capital gain in this instance to tax at preferential rates.

E. Note that even though qualified dividend income is taxed at the same tax rate as long-term capital gain, the dividend income is not included in the netting process for capital gains and losses.

V. Individuals—Preferential Tax Rates—The special tax treatment accorded a net capital gain for individual taxpayers is a lower tax rate.

A. The tax calculation is done by computing the regular tax on income without the net capital gain plus the preferential tax rate times the net capital gain.

B. The preferential tax rate depends on the composition of the net long-term gain.

1. Net capital gain is taxed at a **maximum** rate of 20% for taxpayers whose ordinary income is taxed at the 39.6% rate. If the taxpayers regular tax rate is 15% or lower, then the maximum tax rate on long-term capital gains is 0%. For all other taxpayers the rate is 15%.

2. 3.8% net investment income tax

a. A 3.8% net investment income tax applies to taxpayers whose modified AGI exceeds $250,000 if married filing jointly and $200,000 if single or head of household. The 3.8% tax applies to the lesser of (a) net investment income, or (b) the excess of AGI over the AGI thresholds. Capital gains are included in net investment income, so the highest tax rate on regular capital gains is 23.8% (20% + 3.8%). These AGI thresholds are not indexed for inflation.

Note
Unless provided otherwise, assume throughout this course that the 15% rate applies to capital gains rather than higher rates.

b. Net investment income (NII) includes income from:

i. Interest, dividends, annuities, rents, and royalties, unless such income is derived from a trade/business activity

ii. Other passive income

iii. Gain from the sale of assets generating such income

iv. Reduced by deductions allocated to this income

Example
A single filer has active income of $160,000 and net investment income (NII) of $100,000. The 3.8% tax will be paid on $60,000 of income. The excess of AGI ($260,000) over the AGI threshold ($200,000) is $60,000 versus the NII of $100,000. Because the tax applies to the lesser of these two amounts, it will be 3.8% of $60,000, or $2,280.

3. Net capital gain attributable to straight-line depreciation claimed on real estate is taxed at a maximum rate of 25%.

4. Net capital gain from "collectibles" is taxed at a maximum rate of 28%.

Definition
Collectible: A tangible personalty such as coins, art, and antiques purchased for investment purposes. Gold and silver are also classified as collectibles subject to the 28% rate.

Example
In 2017, TP has a 25% marginal tax rate on regular taxable income. He realized the following gains:

$9,000 gain on the sale of art held five years.

$20,000 gain on the sale of securities held 15 months.

$15,000 gain on the sale of securities held three years.

$7,000 gain on the sale of long-term rental realty attributable to depreciation.

The $9,000 gain is taxed at a maximum of 28%, while the $15,000 and the $20,000 gains are taxed at a maximum of 15%. The $7,000 gain is taxed at a maximum rate of 25%.

C. Special rules exist for netting losses against various categories of long-term gains.
   1. Capital losses offset capital gains in the following order:

   1. Capital gains taxed at 28%
   2. Capital gains taxed at 25%
   3. Capital gains taxed at 20%/15%

Examples

1. In 2017, TP has a net short-term capital loss of $20,000. He has also realized a net long-term gain of $50,000 that comprises the following net gains and losses:

$10,000 gain on the sale of coins held three years.

$25,000 gain on the sale of securities held three years.

$15,000 gain on the sale of realty (attributable to depreciation).

TP has a net capital gain of $30,000. The short-term capital loss first offsets the gain on the collectibles, and then offsets $10,000 of the gain attributable to depreciation. Hence, the net capital gain of $30,000 comprises a $5,000 gain taxed at 25% (the realty) and a $25,000 gain taxed at a maximum rate of 15%.

2. In 2017, TP has a net long-term gain of $20,000 comprised of the following capital gains and losses:

$5,000 loss on the sale of coins held three years.

$15,000 gain on the sale of securities held three years.

$10,000 gain on the sale of realty (attributable to depreciation) held four years.

The long-term capital loss from the collectibles first offsets part of the long-term gain attributable to depreciation. Hence, the net long-term gain of $20,000 comprises $5,000 gain taxed at 25% (the realty) and a $15,000 gain taxed at a maximum rate of 15%.

Summary of Preferential Long-Term Capital Gain Rates (Individuals)

Ordinary Income Rate	Regular LTCG Rate	Maximum Rate for 25% Gain	Maximum Rate for Collectible Gain	Could 3.8% NII Tax Apply?
10%	0%	10%	10%	No
15%	0%	15%	15%	No
25%	15%	25%	25%	No
28%	15%	25%	28%	Possibly
33%	15%	25%	28%	Likely
35%	15%	25%	28%	Yes
39.6%	20%	25%	28%	Yes

Note: The preferential rates are the maximum rates that will be applied to a source of income. If the ordinary income rate for the taxpayer is less than the preferential rate, then the ordinary rate is used to tax the long-term capital gain.

D. Tax Computation

1. The tax on net long-term capital gains is computed after the non-long-term capital gain potion of taxable income has been taxed.

2. As shown in the chart above, each net long-term capital component is taxed at the lower of the regular tax marginal rate or the capital gains rate that applies to that component.

Example

TP has the following income:

Gain from stock sale taxed at maximum of 15%	$12,000
Ordinary income	$20,000

The $20,000 is taxed first using the individual tax table. The $12,000 net capital gain is then taxed. Note that the $20,000 of ordinary income places the taxpayer in the 15% tax bracket, so the net capital gain is taxed at 0%.

If TP had $60,000 of ordinary income, which would place him in the 25% bracket, the net capital gain would be taxed at 15%.

E. Personal Casualty and Theft Gains and Losses—Gains and losses from casualties and thefts of property held for personal use are separately netted, without regard to the holding period of the converted property.

1. If gains exceed losses (after the $100 floor for each loss), then all gains and losses are treated as capital gains and losses, short term or long term, depending upon holding period.

Example

An individual incurred a $25,000 personal casualty gain, and a $15,000 personal casualty loss (after the $100 floor) during the current taxable year. Since there was a net gain, the individual will report the gain and loss as a $25,000 capital gain and a $15,000 capital loss.

2. If losses (after the $100 floor for each loss) exceed gains, the losses (1) offset gains, and (2) are an ordinary deduction from AGI to the extent in excess of 10% of AGI.

Example

An individual had AGI of $40,000 (before casualty gains or losses), and also had a personal casualty loss of $25,000 (after the $100 floor) and a personal casualty gain of $15,000. Since there was a net personal casualty loss, the net loss will be deductible as an itemized deduction of [$25,000 − $15,000 − (10% × $40,000)] = $6,000.

F. Special Situations—Some special rules exist for certain capital gains and losses.

1. For gains and losses incurred by partnerships and S corporations, the determination of the maximum tax rate is made at the entity level.

2. Special rules apply for preferred stock issued by financial institutions and sold to the federal government as part of the economic stabilization process. Gain from the sale of this specific type of preferred stock is treated as ordinary income.

3. **Qualifying small business stock**

    a. Gains from the sale of qualifying small business stock by noncorporate taxpayers are eligible for a 100% exclusion.

    b. **Qualifying small business stock** is stock of a small business corporation (less than $50 million in capital) held for more than five years.

    c. The maximum gain eligible for the exclusion for each qualifying stock is the greater of 10 times the taxpayer's basis in the stock or $10 million in aggregate.

    d. The exclusion percentage was lower than 100% for stock purchased in the following time periods:

        i. 50%—before February 18, 2009.

Study Tip
Note that the date of purchase of the stock, not the date of sale, determines whether the 50%, 75%, or 100% exclusion will potentially apply in the future.

ii. 75%—after February 17, 2009 and before September 28, 2010.

Example

ABC Corporation, a qualified small business corporation, issued 100 shares of stock to TP for $20,000 on March 1, 2011. On September 25 of 2017, TP sold the stock for $300,000 and realized a gain of $280,000. Since the stock was held for more than five years the gain is eligible for this special treatment. The gain eligible for the exclusion cannot exceed the greater of $200,000 (10 times TP's basis) or $10 million. Hence, 100% of the qualifying gain of $280,000 is excluded from income.

Note that if the stock had been issued on March 1, 2010, only 75% of the gain ($210,000) would be excluded from income. The remaining gain ($70,000) is taxed at ordinary income rates, but the rate will not exceed 28%.

G. Section 1244 Stock

1. Special rules also apply for Section 1244 stock sold by individuals. Gains from the sale of Section 1244 stock are treated as regular long-term capital gains, but losses are treated as ordinary losses (maximum characterized as ordinary is $100,000 for married filing jointly and $50,000 for others).

2. Section 1244 stock is stock of a domestic small business corporation meaning that the capital receipts of the corporation do not exceed $1,000,000 at the time the stock is issued. Also, at least 50% of the corporation's gross receipts have to be generated from sources other than investment income during the previous five tax years.

3. Additionally, the seller of the stock had to be the original holder of the stock for Section 1244 to apply.

4. If a Section 1244 loss creates a net operating loss, that NOL can be carried forward to future years.

VI. If a nondealer, noncorporate taxpayer subdivides real property into at least two lots for resale, the gain from the sale of the lots will be treated as capital gain as long as the taxpayer had held the property for at least five years and no substantial improvement had been made to the lots by the taxpayer. All gain on the first five lots sold will be capital gain. For all lots sold over five, 5% of the selling price will be treated as ordinary income.

VII. Options—Special rules apply, if a taxpayer incurs a loss on an option which he holds to buy or sell property due to the lapse of the option:

A. If the optioned property would have been a capital asset in the taxpayer's hands, the loss is a capital loss.

B. If the optioned property would be a Section 1231 asset in the taxpayer's hands, the capital gain/ordinary loss rules for Section 1231 assets applies.

C. If the optioned property would have been an ordinary asset in the taxpayer's hands, the loss is an ordinary loss.

VIII. Rules for Corporations

A. Corporations use the same netting process but can only use a "net capital loss" to offset capital gain net income. That is, no deduction is allowed if the net capital loss exceeds net capital gains.

B. However, the loss can be used in other tax years. Net capital losses are carried over as short-term capital losses, and these losses are carried back three years and forward five years.

C. For corporations, all capital gains, both short-term and long-term, are taxed at the regular ordinary income rates. Corporations do not have a preferential tax rate for long-term capital gains. One exception is that corporations can tax gain from sales of timber held more than 15 years at a maximum rate of 23.8%.

Examples

1. This year ABC Corporation began operations and realized taxable income of $36,000. ABC also recognized the following gains and losses.

Short-term capital gains	$8,500
Short-term capital losses	($4,500)
Long-term capital gains	$1,500
Long-term capital losses	($3,500)

Question: What is ABC corporation's taxable income?

Answer: ABC is taxed on $38,000, which comprises ordinary income of $36,000 and $2,000 of short-term capital gains. Net short-term capital gains are $4,000 and net long-term capital losses are ($2,000). These are netted again to produce the $2,000 short-term capital gains.

2. A corporation has a NLTCL of $8,000 and a NSTCG of $2,000, resulting in a net capital loss of $6,000 for 2017. The $6,000 NLTCL is not deductible for 2017 but is first carried back as a STCL to 2014 to offset capital gains. If not used up in 2014, the STCL is carried to 2015 and 2016 and then forward to 2018, 2019, 2020, 2021, and 2022 to offset capital gains in those years.

VII. Information on Sales of Capital Assets

A. Proceeds from the sale of stocks facilitated by a broker are reported to the taxpayer on Form 1099-B. The form includes the date of sale and acquisition, sales price, basis, and tax withheld.

B. Sales of real estate, including a principal residence, are reported to the taxpayer on Form 1099-S.

C. Sales of capital assets are reported on Form 8949 and the totals are then transferred to Form 1040 Schedule D.

1. Capital gains and losses are reported by the taxpayer on Schedule D.

2. Short-term capital gains and losses are reported in Part II and long-term gains and losses in Part III. Capital loss carryforwards are also included.

3. Note that capital gain distributions from mutual funds (reported on Form 1099-DIV) are reported as long-term gains on Schedule D. If a mutual fund distributes short-term capital gain, that is shown as dividend income on Form 1099-DIV.

4. Part III works through the netting process of capital gains and losses.

Section 1231 Assets

After studying this lesson, you should be able to:

1. Identify Section 1231 assets.

2. Define Section 1245 and Section 1250 assets.

3. Compute depreciation recapture on the sale of Section 1231 assets.

4. Net Section 1231 gains and losses properly and determine the tax treatment.

5. Apply the lookback rule to the sale of Section 1231 assets.

Tax Form for This Lesson: Form 4797 (available for download and printing from the lesson overview of your software).

I. Section 1231—Section 1231 is designed to provide capital gain treatment to a net gain generated from transactions involving involuntary conversions and the disposition of business assets.

    A. The scope of Section 1231 is determined by the nature of the asset and the type of disposition.

        1. Section 1231 applies to the sale or exchange of "Section 1231" assets.

Definition

Section 1231 Assets: Assets used in a business and held for over 12 months (long-term). Section 1231 assets include realty and depreciable property but exclude capital assets, inventory, accounts receivable, copyrights, and government publications.

        2. Section 1231 also applies to all involuntary conversions of business assets.

    B. Recapture for Individuals

        1. Section 1245 recapture—Section 1245 property is all depreciable property other than buildings.

            a. All depreciation is subject to the recapture rules, regardless of the method used, to the extent of recognized gain.

            b. Section 1245 recapture is the lesser of gain recognized or all depreciation taken.

            c. Section 1245 treats gain on property disposed of as ordinary income to the extent depreciation was taken. No recapture is required if the property is disposed of at a loss. The taxpayer simply treats the gain amount, up to the amount depreciated, as ordinary income instead of long-term capital gain. Gain in excess of the recaptured amount is treated as Section 1231 gain.

            d. If the property is disposed of at a recognized loss, the loss is a Section 1231 loss. Thus, no depreciation is recaptured.

            e. Depreciation includes cost recovery, depreciation, Section 179 immediate expensing, first-year bonus depreciation, and amortization of Section 197 intangibles.

            f. For buildings owned by individuals, "unrecaptured Section 1250 gains" recharacterizes gains on realty as eligible for a special (25%) tax rate to the extent of accumulated straight-line depreciation.

        2. Section 1250 recapture—Section 1250 recapture applies to buildings (depreciable real property).

            a. Applies only when an accelerated depreciation method is used and property is sold at a gain. Note that accelerated depreciation is not available for real property placed into service in 1987 or later.

    b. Also does not apply when property is disposed of at a loss.

    c. Section 1250 of the Internal Revenue Code treats gain in an amount equal to the excess of accelerated depreciation taken over straight-line depreciation as ordinary income. This excess is known as additional depreciation.

    d. The lower of additional depreciation or recognized gain is ordinary income. The excess gain, if any, is Section 1231 gain.

3. General exceptions to Sections 1245 and 1250

    a. Gifts (recapture potential carries over to donee).

    b. Death (recapture potential is eliminated; does not carry over to one who inherits the property).

    c. Charitable transfers (potential recapture reduces charitable contribution deduction).

    d. Certain tax-free exchanges (i.e., like-kind and involuntary conversion). (Recapture potential carries over to the property received in the exchange.) Realized gain is recognized to the extent of boot received (like-kind exchange) or amount not reinvested (involuntary conversion).

4. Shortcuts

    a. Recapture does not recharacterize losses.

    b. Gains on the sale of land held long-term in a business are always 1231 gains since land is not depreciable.

    c. Gains on the sale of business personalty held long-term are ordinary income, unless sold for an amount greater than the original purchase price.

Definitions

Section 1245 Recapture: Refers to depreciable personalty (assets other than buildings).

Section 1250 Recapture: Applies to depreciable real estate (buildings).

Examples

1. ***Section 1245 recapture, all gain is ordinary***—TP sells a machine held long-term with an original cost of $10 and accumulated depreciation of $7. If the machine is sold for $5, then TP will have a realized gain of $2 (TP's adjusted basis is $3). TP would characterize this gain as ordinary to the extent of accumulated depreciation. Hence, the entire gain is taxed as ordinary income.

2. ***Section 1245 recapture, appreciation in asset taxed as Section 1231 gain***—TP sells a machine held long-term in the trade with an original cost of $10 and accumulated depreciation of $7. If the machine is sold for $14, then TP will have a realized gain of $11. TP would characterize this gain as ordinary to the extent of accumulated depreciation ($7). Hence, $7 of gain will be taxed as ordinary income and the remaining $4 of gain will be Section 1231 gain.

3. ***Section 1250 recapture and 25% Rate***—TP sells a building held long-term in the trade with an original cost of $100 and accumulated depreciation of $45. If the building is sold for $120, then TP will have a realized gain of $65 (TP's adjusted basis is $55). This gain would be taxed as a Section 1231 gain, but $45 of the gain would be taxed at a rate of 25% (assuming all depreciation is straight-line depreciation) whereas the remaining $20 of gain would be eligible for a rate of 15% (0% for lower bracket taxpayers).

4. Assume the following facts for a Section 1245 depreciation recapture:

   Equipment
   Original cost—$100,000
   Accumulated depreciation—$55,000 (used *accelerated depreciation*)

Sales price—$110,000

Amount realized (sales price)		$110,000
Original cost	$100,000	
Less: Depreciation taken	55,000	
Equals: Adjusted basis		45,000
Equals: Recognized and realized gain		$65,000
Section 1245 gain		$55,000*
(Ordinary income)		
Section 1231 gain		$10,000**
Equals: Total recognized gain		$65,000

*Lesser of $65,000 (recognized gain) or $55,000 (all depreciation taken).

**Plug amount: $65,000 (recognized gain) minus $55,000 (Section 1245 gain recaptured amount).

Note: All of this is identical for individuals, corporations, partnerships, and trusts and, generally, estates.

5. Assume the same facts as used for the Section 1245 depreciation recapture example (#4 above) along with the following additional facts. The asset is a building and straight-line depreciation was $40,000.

Note: Straight-line depreciation was not used, but we must know what it would have been if it had been used.

Original cost	$100,000	
Less: Depreciation taken	55,000	
Equals: Adjusted basis		$45,000
Amount realized (sales price)		$110,000
Less: Adjusted basis		45,000
Equals: Recognized (realized) gain		$65,000
Section 1250 gain (ordinary income)		$15,000*
Plus: Section 1231 gain		50,000**
Equals: Total recognized gain		$65,000

*Lesser of $65,000 (recognized gain) or $15,000, additional depreciation taken ($55,000 accelerated depreciation minus $40,000 straight-line depreciation).

**Plug amount: $65,000 recognized gain minus $15,000 section 1250 gain recaptured amount. Note that $40,000 of this $50,000 gain is taxed at a maximum rate of 25%.

Note

All of this is identical for individuals, corporations, partnerships, and trusts and, generally, estates (except C [regular] corporations will have additional recapture under Section 291 of the Internal Revenue Code which is part of [i.e., in addition to] Section 1250 recapture and not in lieu of Section 1250 recapture). (See next text for a brief discussion of Section 291.)

C. Recapture for Corporations

1. For Section 1245 property (personalty), the rules for a corporation are the same as for an individual.

2. For Section 1250 property (buildings) for corporations, the accumulated depreciation claimed in excess of straight-line depreciation is subject to being recaptured as ordinary income.

3. Section 291 recapture also applies to corporations. Section 291 depreciation recapture applies only to buildings, and is computed as follows:

> Section 1245 recapture IF the property had been Section 1245 property
>
> Less: The actual Section 1250 recapture
>
> Excess amount
> × 20%
>
> Section 291 recapture

4. The 25% rate on straight-line depreciation for buildings does not apply to corporations.

    a. Section 291 recapture for C corporations is part of (i.e., in addition to) Section 1250 recapture and is *not* in lieu of Section 1250 recapture.

Example of Section 1250 Property for Corporations

Assume the same facts as in example #5 above except that the seller is a corporation.

Original cost	$100,000
Less: Depreciation taken	55,000
Equals: Adjusted basis	$45,000
Amount Realized (sales price)	$110,000
Less: Adjusted basis	45,000
Equals: Recognized (realized) gain	$65,000
Section 1250 gain (ordinary income)	23,000*
Plus: Section 1231 gain	42,000**
Equals: Total recognized gain	$65,000
Section 291 Recapture Formula:	
Ordinary income under Section 1245	$55,000
Less: Ordinary income under Section 1250	(15,000)
Equals: Excess ordinary income under	$40,000
Section 1245 over and above Section 1250	
Times: Section 291 percentage	× 20%
Equals: Amount of ordinary income recapture under Section 291	$8,000

*Lesser of $65,000 (recognized gain) or $15,000 (additional depreciation taken of $55,000 accelerated depreciation minus $40,000 straight-line depreciation) plus Section 291 recapture of $8,000 ($15,000 + $8,000 = $23,000).

**Plug amount: $65,000 (recognized gain) minus $23,000 (Section 1250 gain – recaptured amount).

D. **Netting**—All Section 1231 gains and Section 1231 losses are netted.

1. The combining of Section 1231 gains and losses is accomplished in **two steps.** First, net all casualty and theft gains and losses on property held for more than one year.

    a. If the losses exceed gains, treat them all as ordinary losses and gains and do not net them with other Section 1231 gains and losses.

    b. If the gains exceed losses, the net gain is combined with other Section 1231 gains and losses.

    c. To the extent that Section 1231 gains exceed Section 1231 losses, the net gain is treated as a long-term capital gain.

    d. If Section 1231 losses exceed Section 1231 gains, the loss is deductible as an ordinary loss (subject to a lookback limit during the previous five years).

    e. The lookback provision states that the net Section 1231 gains must be offset by net Section 1231 losses from the five preceding tax years that have not previously been recaptured. To the extent of these losses, the net Section 1231 gain is treated as ordinary income.

Examples

1. Taxpayer Z has net Section 1231 gain of $20,000 in 2017. In 2016 she had net Section 1231 gain of $10,000 and net section 1231 loss of $25,000 in 2015. In 2016 the $10,000 gain is taxed as ordinary income since there were Section 1231 losses of $25,000 in the previous year. In 2017, $15,000 of the gain is taxed as ordinary income and the remaining $5,000 is taxed as Section 1231 gain. The Section 1231 loss of $25,000 in 2015 was recaptured in 2016 ($10,000) and 2017 ($15,000).

2. Taxpayer has a gain of $10,000 from the sale of land used in his business, a loss of $4,000 on the sale of depreciable property used in his business, and a $2,000 (noninsured) loss when a car used in his business was involved in a collision. The net gain or loss from casualty or theft is the $2,000 loss. The net casualty loss of $2,000 is treated as an ordinary loss and not netted with other Section 1231 gains and losses. The $10,000 gain is netted with the $4,000 loss resulting in a net Section 1231 gain of $6,000, which is then treated as a long-term capital gain.

E. **Summary of Gains and Losses on Business Property**—The treatment of gains and losses (other than personal casualty and theft) on property held for more than one year is summarized in the following **four steps:**

1. Separate all recognized gains and losses into four categories

   a. Ordinary gain and loss

   b. Section 1231 casualty and theft gains and losses

   c. Section 1231 gains and losses other than by casualty or theft

   d. Gains and losses on capital assets (other than by casualty or theft)

> **Note**
> *Items b and c are only temporary classifications. All gains and losses ultimately will receive ordinary or capital treatment.*

2. This step deals with depreciation recapture. Any gain (casualty or other) on Section 1231 property is treated as ordinary income to extent of Section 1245, 1250, and 291 depreciation recapture.

3. This step deals with gains and losses from casualties and thefts. After depreciation recapture, any remaining Section 1231 casualty and theft gains and losses on business property are netted.

   a. **If losses exceed gains**—The losses and gains receive ordinary treatment

   b. **If gains exceed losses**—The net gain is combined with other Section 1231 gains and losses in #4 below.

4. This step deals with other Section 1231 gains and losses and any net casualty/theft gains from #3. Any remaining Section 1231 gains and losses (other than by casualty or theft) are combined with any net casualty or theft gain from #3 above.

   a. **If losses exceed gains**—The losses and gains receive ordinary treatment

   b. **If gains exceed losses**—The net gain receives LTCG treatment (except ordinary income treatment to extent of nonrecaptured net Section 1231 losses for the five most recent tax years)

F. **Sales Reporting**—Sales of business property, including depreciation recapture, are reported on Form 4797, *Sales of Business Property*.

Section 1231 Assets—Cost Recovery

After studying this lesson, you should be able to:

1. Differentiate between realty and personalty.

2. Utilize the MACRS depreciation rules for realty including the mid-month convention.

3. Apply the MACRS depreciation rules to personalty including the half-year and mid-quarter convention.

4. Compute Section 179 expense for qualifying assets.

5. Identify listed assets and applicable limitations for computing depreciation.

6. Calculate amortization for intangible assets.

Tax Form for This Lesson: Form 4562 (available for download and printing from the lesson overview of your software).

I. **Depreciation**—Depreciation deductions are allowed for assets used to produce income, but the deductions must be calculated using cost recovery rules.

> **Note**
> *The MACRS tables always include the appropriate convention (half-year, midmonth, mid-quarter) for the period the asset is purchased, but not for the period the asset is sold. If computing depreciation using the formula instead of the table, the appropriate convention must always be applied to the formula. When using the MACRS tables, the percentage in the table is always multiplied by the asset's original cost.*

A. **Cost Recovery Rules**—Cost recovery is computed under a uniform method using the class life period (MACRS). The IRS provides tables (MACRS Tables) that show the percentage of the asset's cost basis that can be depreciated each year, based on the asset's classification. Depreciation can also be computed using the appropriate depreciation formula, rather than the MACRS table. For example, 200% declining balance method uses 2 times the straight-line rate to multiply by the asset's adjusted basis (e.g., 40% for 5-year property [2 × 100%/5 years]).

1. Only business property and income-producing property (e.g., rental real estate) is depreciable. Property used for personal purposes and investment assets are not depreciable.

> **Example**
> TP invests in a large stock portfolio. She has a computer that is used solely for managing her stock portfolio. While the stocks that she owns are not depreciable since they are investment assets, the computer can be depreciated to offset any income from the investment activity.

2. 200% declining balance or 150% declining balance is used for personalty; straight line is used for realty

   a. Definitions—**Realty** is land and other assets affixed thereto (buildings). **Personalty** is any tangible asset that can be moved (not fixed to land).

3. Recovery for personalty is computed as though assets are purchased at midyear (midyear convention), while recovery for realty uses a mid-month convention. For personalty, depreciation is allowed for half of the year in which it is purchased, regardless of when it is purchased. For realty, depreciation is allowed for half of the month in which it is purchased, regardless of the date it is purchased during the month.

> **Example**
> TP purchased machinery and a building on August 4, 2017. The machinery will be depreciated for 6 months in 2017 and the building will be depreciated for 4.5 months (.5 for August and 4 for September through December).

   a. In the year of purchase, these conventions are already incorporated into the percentages provided in the MACRS tables so no adjustment is necessary to the numbers from the tables.

4. *While there are numerous class lives for personalty, some of the more common are:*

   a. 3 years—Certain manufacturing tools and tractor units for use over the road; race horses

   b. 5 years—Automobiles, light trucks, computers, certain assets used in high-technology manufacturing, office equipment, rental appliances, furniture, carpets, etc., but excluding office furniture and fixtures

   c. 7 years—Most equipment, machinery, office furniture, and fixtures (also the default category for unspecified-class property)

   A 200% declining balance method is used for these classes. Land improvements are included in the 15-year class and are depreciated using the 150% declining balance method.

5. The cost of **leasehold improvements** made by a lessee generally must be recovered over the MACRS recovery period of the underlying property without regard to the lease term. *Qualified leasehold improvement property* (i.e., an improvement to the interior portion of nonresidential real property), *qualified restaurant property, and qualified retail improvement property* are recovered over a 15-year recovery period using the straight-line method and half-year convention (unless the mid-quarter convention applies). Upon the expiration of the lease, any unrecovered adjusted basis in abandoned leasehold improvements is treated as a loss.

6. Residential realty (apartments, houses, duplexes, etc.) is depreciated over a 27.5-year straight line. Nonresidential realty is depreciated over a 39-year straight line.

7. A disposition of the asset follows the appropriate midyear or midmonth convention. Note that for the year of sale these adjustments are not included in the MACRS tables because it is not known in what year the asset will be sold. Thus, the numbers from the tables must be adjusted as described above.

> **Note**
> *Personal property also has 10-year, 15-year, and 20-year property classes.*

Example
TP sells machinery and a building on March 3, 2017. The machinery is eligible for 50% of the depreciation that would have been permitted if the asset had not been sold. For the realty the taxpayer is allowed 2.5 months depreciation (2 for January–February and .5 for March) for 2017.

---

8. **Bonus depreciation**

   a. Bonus depreciation of 50% is allowed for new qualifying property placed in service in 2015 to 2017.

   b. Bonus depreciation applies unless the taxpayer elects not to do so. Qualifying property is new tangible property with a recovery period of less than or equal to 20 years, computer software, and qualified improvement property. Qualified improvement property is improvements to the interior of nonresidential property that is made after the building is placed in service.

   c. A taxpayer can elect not to use bonus depreciation for a class of property (in which case the election applies to the whole class). The bonus depreciation is allowed for both regular and AMT purposes. No AMT depreciation adjustment is required for any property that uses bonus depreciation.

Example
During August 2017, a taxpayer purchases new 5-year MACRS property for $2,000. The additional first-year depreciation would be $2,000 × 50% = $1,000. Regular MACRS deprecation for 2017 using the 200% declining-balance formula and the half-year convention would be ($2,000 − $1,000) × 2/5 × ½ = $200. As a result, the total deduction for this property for 2017 would be $1,000 + $200 = $1,200.

---

9. A mid-quarter convention is used for all new personalty (instead of the midyear convention) if more than 40% of personalty acquired during the year is purchased in the last quarter of the year. One-half quarter depreciation is allowed for the quarter the asset is purchased and one-half quarter for the quarter the asset is sold.

Example

In January 2017, a calendar-year taxpayer purchased used machinery for $10,000. In December 2017, the taxpayer purchased additional used machinery for $30,000. All machinery was assigned to the 5-year, 200% class. No other depreciable assets were purchased during the year. Since the machinery placed in service during the last three months of the year exceeded 40% of the depreciable basis of all personal property placed in service during the taxable year, all machinery must be depreciated using the mid-quarter convention. The taxpayer may claim 3½ quarters depreciation on the machinery acquired in January ($10,000 × 40% × 3.5/4 = $3,500) and only ½ quarter of depreciation for the machinery acquired in December ($30,000 × 40% × .5/4 = $1,500).

On August 1 of this year TP purchased and placed into service an office building costing $264,000 including $30,000 for the land.

Question: What is TP's MACRS deduction for the office building?

Answer: $234,000 is straight-line depreciated over 39 years, but TP is only entitled to 4.5 months (note that a half month is allowed for August using the mid-month convention) this year. Hence, the cost recovery is $2,250 this year.

B. **Section 179 Election**—There is a Section 179 election to expense a limited amount of tangible **personalty** if used in a trade activity. It is not available for income-producing property (i.e., rental property) or real property (i.e., real estate).

Note that Section 179 expensing is taken into account before bonus depreciation for years that permitted bonus depreciation. Off-the-shelf computer software also qualifies under Section 179, as does qualified leasehold property, qualified restaurant property, and qualified retail improvement property. Air conditioning and heating units also qualify.

1. The maximum amount expensed in any year is limited to the lesser of business income or $510,000 for 2017 ($500,000 for 2016).

2. The Section 179 expense cannot exceed the income from the business, reduced for all expenses except Section 179. Any election to expense in excess of the business income limit is carried forward (indefinitely) and used in a year when income is sufficient.

3. The Section 179 election is phased out (dollar for dollar) if qualified assets purchased exceed $2,030,000 for 2017 ($2,010,000 for 2016).

4. A carryforward is not allowed if the Section 179 deduction is reduced due to the excess purchase provision.

5. The taxpayer can revoke the Section 179 election in later years as long as the return is still eligible to be amended.

6. If property for which Section 179 has been collected is converted to nonbusiness use, the Section 179 and MACRS deductions claimed in excess of what would have been allowed if Section 179 had not been elected must be recaptured as income.

Examples
1. TP purchased $2,070,000 (2017) of tangible assets for use in his trade. The Section 179 limit of $510,000 is reduced by $40,000 ($2,070,000 − $2,030,000) to $470,000. There is no carryforward of the amount that is phased out.

2. TP, a self-employed taxpayer, had business income of $15,000 in 2017 prior to deductions associated with cost recovery. This year TP purchased equipment for $25,000.

   Question: What is TP's deduction under the election to expense the cost of the machinery?

   Answer: TP can elect to expense $25,000, but the deduction is limited to the business income of $15,000. The remaining $10,000 can be carried forward indefinitely and expensed in future years when there is sufficient business income.

3. TP, a self-employed taxpayer, purchased equipment in 2017 for $2,100,000.

   Question: What portion of the cost may TP elect to treat as an expense rather than as a capital expenditure?

   Answer: Since $2,100,000 exceeds the $2,030,000 trigger by $70,000, the overall limit of $510,000 is reduced to $440,000 ($510,000 − $70,000).

4. For this problem, assume a taxpayer acquired the following personal property in 2017 to be used in trade or business and has elected the Section 179 deduction. This is the only personal property acquired during the year by the taxpayer:

   New equipment (5-year property class): $610,000

   Recovery period: 5 years

   Taxable income: $1,500,000

The Section 179 deduction and depreciation deduction for this property are computed as follows:

Note: Because taxable income before the Section 179 deduction is more than the maximum annual Section 179 deduction of $510,000, the taxable income limitation does not apply.

Because more than $510,000 of personal property was acquired during the year, the dollar limitation applies as shown below:

Amount of personal property acquired	$610,000
Minus: Maximum Section 179 write-off	−510,000
Remaining cost of equipment	$100,000

The first year bonus depreciation for new equipment is as follows:

Basis of equipment	$100,000
Times: Bonus first-year depreciation	× 50%
First-year bonus depreciation	$ 50,000
Times: Statutory percentage	× 20%*
Year 1 normal depreciation	$10,000

* Equipment is 5-year property: Year 1 percentage, from Internal Revenue Service MACRS cost recovery table.

Thus, the total first year deduction for the property for the year is $510,000 + $50,000 + $10,000 = $570,000.

Assuming a 35% tax bracket, this equates to a savings of $199,500 in taxes ($570,000 deduction × 35%). In the end, the cost to the business for the new equipment was really $410,500 ($610,000 − $199,500 savings).

C. **Alternatives to MACRS**—The taxpayer can elect several alternatives to MACRS.

   1. Straight line can be used for personalty over the MACRS life of the asset. The same MACRS lives and conventions are retained for this method.

2. The alternative depreciation system (ADS) provides for straight line (for tangible personal property, straight line or 150% declining balance can be used) over an extended life. ADS straight line must be used for computing earnings and profits, and for listed property not used more than 50% for business purposes.

D. **Luxury Auto Limits**—Autos are subject to an annual ceiling on recovery.

1. Special rules limit the amount of depreciation that can be claimed on a passenger automobile (GVW of 6,000 pounds or less). However, these limits are adjusted annually for inflation, so the exact dollar limits do not need to be memorized for the exam. For 2017, first-year depreciation is limited to $3,160 ($3,560 for trucks and vans). If bonus depreciated is elected, these amounts are increased in 2017 by $8,000 to $11,160 ($11,560 for trucks and vans).

2. Trucks, vans, and SUVs (and any other vehicle) that weigh more than 6,000 pounds are exempt from the luxury automobile rule. However, for these heavier vehicles, the Section 179 election is limited to $25,000 (assuming 100% business use). Regular MACRS rules apply for the remaining basis.

3. The limits mentioned above assume 100% business/investment use (applies to Section 179 also). For mixed-use autos, the limit is multiplied by the percentage of business/investment use.

4. Similar restrictions apply to vehicles leased for business use.

Examples

1. A taxpayer can claim first-year cost recovery of $3,160 (2017) for an auto costing $30,000. However, if the taxpayer uses the auto 30% of the time for personal purposes, then the taxpayer can only claim recovery of $2,212 ($3,160 × 70%).

2. An individual purchased a new automobile and places it in service during 2017. If the first-year depreciation limit otherwise would be $3,160, if bonus depreciation is elected, it is increased by $8,000 so that the maximum depreciation for 2017 would be $11,160.

E. **Listed Property**—Must pass business use test.

Definition

Listed Property: Includes assets, such as computers and vehicles, that are commonly used for both business and personal purposes. Cell phones are not included as listed property.

1. To use regular MACRS rules, the business use of listed assets must exceed 50% of total use.

2. For purposes of this test, business use is limited to use in the trade/business or for the convenience of the employer. That is, investment use is not considered for meeting the 50% test.

3. Failure to meet the business use test means cost recovery is limited to straight line (ADS). However, both the business and investment use of the asset may be depreciated. ADS depreciation must be used for the entire depreciable life of the asset, even if the 50% test is met in future years. Additionally, if the 50% test is failed in the current year but accelerated depreciation had been taken in previous years, the excess depreciation from prior years must be recaptured.

Examples
1. In Year 1 and Year 2 a computer is used 60% for business use. The 200% declining balance method is used for Years 1 and 2. In Year 3 the business use percentage is 45% and investment use is 12%. For Year 3, ADS straight-line depreciation must be used because the 50% test has been failed, but 57% of the asset's basis can be depreciated. Excess depreciation over straight-line from Years 1 and 2 must be recaptured in Year 3. Additionally, the asset must be depreciated using ADS for the remainder of its depreciable life.

Comprehensive Example
A new five-year asset is purchased in March 2017 for $660,000. This is the only asset purchased by this calendar-year company in 2017. The property is eligible for both bonus depreciation and Section 179 expensing. Note: Section 179 expensing is taken into account before bonus depreciation. Cost recovery is computed as follows:

Section 179 expense	$510,000	
Remaining basis	$150,000	($660,000 − $510,000)
Bonus %	× 50%	
Bonus depreciation	$ 75,000	
Remaining basis	$ 75,000	($660,000 − $510,000 − $75,000)
MACRS %	× 20%	
MACRS expense	$ 15,000	

Total Depreciation:

Section 179	$510,000
Bonus	75,000
MACRS	15,000
	$600,000

II. Amortization and Depletion

A. Depletion—Natural resources are subject to straight-line depletion.

1. Depletion is allowed on timber, minerals, oil, and gas, and other exhaustible natural resources or wasting assets.

2. There are two basic methods to compute depletion for the year:

   a. Cost method divides the adjusted basis by the total number of recoverable units and multiplies by the number of units sold (or payment received for, if cash basis) during the year.

      i. Adjusted basis is cost less accumulated depletion (not below zero).

Example
Land cost $10,050,000 of which $50,000 is the residual value of the land. There are 1,000,000 barrels of oil recoverable. If 10,000 barrels were sold, cost depletion would be ($10,000,000 × 1,000,000 barrels) × 10,000 = $100,000.

   b. Percentage method uses a specified percentage of gross income from the property during the year.

      i. Deduction may not exceed 50% of the taxable income (before depletion) from the property.

      ii. May be taken even after costs have been recovered and there is no basis

      iii. May be used for domestic oil and gas wells by "independent producer" or royalty owner; cannot be used for timber

      iv. The percentage is a statutory amount and generally ranges from 5% to 20% depending on the mineral.

B. Amortization Rules

1. Most **acquired intangible assets** are to be amortized over a 15-year period, beginning with the month in which the intangible is acquired. (The treatment of self-created intangible assets is not affected.) Section 197 applies to most intangibles acquired either in stand-alone transactions or as part of the acquisition of a trade or business.

2. An amortizable Section 197 intangible is any qualifying intangible asset which is acquired by the taxpayer and which is held in connection with the conduct of a trade or business. Qualifying intangibles include goodwill, going concern value, workforce, information base, know-how, customer-based intangibles, government licenses and permits, franchises, trademarks, and trade names.

3. Certain assets qualify as Section 197 intangibles only if acquired in connection with the acquisition of a trade or business or substantial portion thereof. These include covenants not to compete, computer software, film, sound recordings, videotape, patents, and copyrights.

4. Certain intangible assets are expressly excluded from the definition of Section 197 intangibles including many types of financial interests, instruments, and contracts; interests in a corporation, partnership, trust, or estate; interests in land; professional sports franchises; and leases of tangible personal property.

5. No loss can be recognized on the disposition of a Section 197 intangible if the taxpayer retains other Section 197 intangibles acquired in the same transaction or a series of transactions. Any disallowed loss is added to the basis of remaining Section 197 intangibles and recovered through amortization.

6. **Amortization** is allowed for several special types of capital expenditures.

   a. Pollution control facilities can be amortized over 60 months if installed on property that was placed in operation prior to 1976. The pollution control investment must not increase output, capacity, or the useful life of the asset.

   b. Patents and copyrights may be amortized over their useful life.

      (1) 17 years for patents; life of author plus 50 years for copyrights

      (2) If become obsolete early, deduct in that year

   c. Research and experimental expenses may be amortized over 60 months or more. Alternatively, may be expensed at election of taxpayer if done so for year in which such expenses are first incurred or paid.

   d. Intangible assets for which the Code does not specifically provide for amortization are amortizable over their useful lives.

C. Organization and Start-Up Expenses

1. Expenses incurred in connection with the **organization of a corporation**.

2. $5,000 of these expenses may be deducted, but the $5,000 is reduced by the amount of expenditures incurred that exceed $50,000. Expenses not deducted must be **capitalized and amortized** over **180 months** (unless an election is made not to do so), beginning with the month that the corporation begins its business operations. Election must be filed with first corporate tax return.

3. Same rules apply **for start-up costs**. Start-up costs are expenditures that would be deductible except that the corporation has not yet started its trade or business operation.

4. **Typical organizational expenses** are legal services incident to organization, accounting services, organizational meetings of directors and shareholders, and fees paid to incorporate. They must be incurred before the end of the taxable year when the business begins (but they do not have to be paid, even if on a cash basis).

5. Costs of issuing and selling stock (**syndication expenses**) must also be capitalized, but cannot be amortized.

III. Reporting—Depreciation and Amortization are reported on Form 4562, *Depreciation and Amortization*. See the following MACRS tables.

MACRS Tables

Table 1. General Depreciation System

> Applicable Depreciation Method: 200% Declining Balance Switching to Straight Line
> Applicable Recovery Periods: 3, 5, 7 years
> Applicable Convention: Half-year

Depreciation Rate (%) Based on Recovery Year and Recovery Period

Recovery Year	Recovery Period (years)		
	3	5	7
1	33.33	20.00	14.29
2	44.45	32.00	24.49
3	14.81	19.20	17.49
4	7.41	11.52	12.49
5		11.52	8.93
6		5.76	8.92
7			8.93
8			4.46

Table 2. General Depreciation System

> Applicable Depreciation Method: 200%
> Declining Balance Switching to Straight Line
> Applicable Recovery Periods: 3, 5, 7 years
> Applicable Convention: Mid-quarter (property placed in service in first quarter)

Depreciation Rate (%) Based on Recovery Year and Recovery Period

Recovery Year	Recovery Period (years)		
	3	5	7
1	58.33	35.00	25.00
2	27.78	26.00	21.43
3	12.35	15.60	15.31
4	1.54	11.01	10.93
5		11.01	8.75
6		1.38	8.74
7			8.75
8			1.09

Table 3. General Depreciation System

Applicable Depreciation Method: 200%
Declining Balance Switching to Straight Line
Applicable Recovery Periods: 3, 5, 7 years
Applicable Convention: Mid-quarter (property placed in service in second quarter)

Depreciation Rate (%) Based on Recovery Year and Recovery Period

Recovery Year	Recovery Period (years)		
	3	5	7
1	41.67	25.00	17.85
2	38.89	30.00	23.47
3	14.14	18.00	16.76
4	5.30	11.37	11.97
5		11.37	8.87
6		4.26	8.87
7			8.87
8			3.33

Table 4. General Depreciation System

Applicable Depreciation Method: 200%
Declining Balance Switching to Straight Line
Applicable Recovery Periods: 3, 5, 7 years
Applicable Convention: Mid-quarter (property placed in service in third quarter)

Depreciation Rate (%) Based on Recovery Year and Recovery Period

Recovery Year	Recovery Period (years)		
	3	5	7
1	25.00	15.00	10.71
2	50.00	34.00	25.51
3	16.67	20.40	18.22
4	8.83	12.24	13.02
5		11.30	9.30
6		7.06	8.85
7			8.86
8			5.53

Table 5. General Depreciation System

Applicable Depreciation Method: 200%
Declining Balance Switching to Straight Line
Applicable Recovery Periods: 3, 5, 7 years
Applicable Convention: Mid-quarter (property placed in service in fourth quarter)

Depreciation Rate (%) Based on Recovery Year and Recovery Period

Recovery Year	Recovery Period (years)		
	3	5	7
1	8.33	5.00	3.57
2	61.11	38.00	27.55
3	20.37	22.80	19.68
4	10.19	13.68	14.06
5		10.94	10.04
6		9.58	8.73
7			8.73
8			7.64

Table 6. General Depreciation System—Residential Real Estate

Applicable Depreciation Method: Straight Line
Applicable Recovery Period: 27.5 years
Applicable Convention: Mid-month

Depreciation Rate (%) Based on Recovery Year and Recovery Period

Recovery Year	Month Placed in Service in First Recovery Year											
	1	2	3	4	5	6	7	8	9	10	11	12
1	3.485	3.182	2.879	2.576	2.273	1.970	1.667	1.364	1.061	0.758	0.455	0.152
2	3.636	3.636	3.636	3.636	3.636	3.636	3.636	3.636	3.636	3.636	3.636	3.636
3	3.636	3.636	3.636	3.636	3.636	3.636	3.636	3.636	3.636	3.636	3.636	3.636
4	3.636	3.636	3.636	3.636	3.636	3.636	3.636	3.636	3.636	3.636	3.636	3.636
5	3.636	3.636	3.636	3.636	3.636	3.636	3.636	3.636	3.636	3.636	3.636	3.636
6	3.636	3.636	3.636	3.636	3.636	3.636	3.636	3.636	3.636	3.636	3.636	3.636
7	3.636	3.636	3.636	3.636	3.636	3.636	3.636	3.636	3.636	3.636	3.636	3.636
8	3.636	3.636	3.636	3.636	3.636	3.636	3.636	3.636	3.636	3.636	3.636	3.636
9	3.636	3.636	3.636	3.636	3.636	3.636	3.636	3.636	3.636	3.636	3.636	3.636
10	3.637	3.637	3.637	3.637	3.637	3.637	3.636	3.636	3.636	3.636	3.636	3.636
11	3.636	3.636	3.636	3.636	3.636	3.636	3.637	3.637	3.637	3.637	3.637	3.637
12	3.637	3.637	3.637	3.637	3.637	3.637	3.636	3.636	3.636	3.636	3.636	3.636
13	3.636	3.636	3.636	3.636	3.636	3.636	3.637	3.637	3.637	3.637	3.637	3.637
14	3.637	3.637	3.637	3.637	3.637	3.637	3.636	3.636	3.636	3.636	3.636	3.636

(continued)

Recovery Year	Month Placed in Service in First Recovery Year											
	1	2	3	4	5	6	7	8	9	10	11	12
15	3.636	3.636	3.636	3.636	3.636	3.636	3.637	3.637	3.637	3.637	3.637	3.637
16	3.637	3.637	3.637	3.637	3.637	3.637	3.636	3.636	3.636	3.636	3.636	3.636
17	3.636	3.636	3.636	3.636	3.636	3.636	3.637	3.637	3.637	3.637	3.637	3.637
18	3.637	3.637	3.637	3.637	3.637	3.637	3.636	3.636	3.636	3.636	3.636	3.636
19	3.636	3.636	3.636	3.636	3.636	3.636	3.637	3.637	3.637	3.637	3.637	3.637
20	3.637	3.637	3.637	3.637	3.637	3.637	3.636	3.636	3.636	3.636	3.636	3.636
21	3.636	3.636	3.636	3.636	3.636	3.636	3.637	3.637	3.637	3.637	3.637	3.637
22	3.637	3.637	3.637	3.637	3.637	3.637	3.636	3.636	3.636	3.636	3.636	3.636
23	3.636	3.636	3.636	3.636	3.636	3.636	3.637	3.637	3.637	3.637	3.637	3.637
24	3.637	3.637	3.673	3.637	3.637	3.637	3.636	3.636	3.636	3.636	3.636	3.636
25	3.636	3.636	3.636	3.636	3.636	3.636	3.637	3.637	3.637	3.637	3.637	3.637
26	3.637	3.637	3.637	3.637	3.637	3.637	3.636	3.636	3.633	3.636	3.636	3.636
27	3.636	3.636	3.636	3.636	3.636	3.636	3.637	3.637	3.637	3.637	3.637	3.637
28	1.970	2.273	2.576	2.879	3.182	3.485	3.636	3.636	3.636	3.636	3.636	3.636
29	0.000	0.000	0.000	0.000	0.000	0.000	0.152	0.455	0.758	1.061	1.364	1.667

Like-Kind Exchanges and Involuntary Conversions

Two common areas for which gains and losses may not be recognized are like-kind exchanges and involuntary conversions.

After studying this lesson, you should be able to:

1. Assess whether an exchange qualifies as a like-kind exchange.

2. Compute the deferred gain/loss for a like-kind exchange.

3. Determine how the receipt of boot affects the recognition of gain from an exchange.

4. Evaluate the tax basis of the asset received in the exchange.

5. Appraise whether an event qualifies as an involuntary conversion.

6. Compute the recognized gain/loss from an involuntary conversion.

7. Calculate the basis in the new asset that replaced the converted asset.

Tax Form for This Lesson: Form 8824 (available for download and printing from the lesson overview of your software).

I. Like-Kind Exchanges

A. Overview—The deferral provision for direct (like-kind) exchanges is an example of deferral provisions governing transactions for which significant economic changes have not occurred for the taxpayer due to the transaction. In a classic direct exchange, the taxpayer simply exchanges one asset for another, like-kind asset. **Losses are never recognized** from a like-kind exchange. **Recognized gain is the lesser of:**

1. Realized gain; *or*

2. Boot received.

 Examples

1. Joan Reed exchanged commercial real estate that she owned for other commercial real estate plus cash of $50,000. The following additional information pertains to this transaction:

Property given up by Joan Reed:

Fair value	$500,000
Adjusted basis	$300,000

Property received by Joan Reed:

Fair value	$450,000

What amount of gain should be recognized in Joan Reed's income tax return for the exchange?
A. $200,000
B. $100,000
C. $50,000
D. $0

The correct answer is C ($50,000). Recognized gain is the lesser of (1) realized gain of $200,000 or (2) boot received ($50,000).

Realized gain: $500,000 fair value of property received ($450,000 + Voot received of $50,000) – $300,000 (adjusted basis of property given up) equals $200,000. The deferred gain is $150,000.

2. Land held for investment with a basis of $10,000 was exchanged for other investment real estate with an FMV of $9,000, an automobile with an FMV of $2,000, and $1,500 in cash. The realized gain is $2,500. Even though $3,500 of boot was received, the recognized gain is only $2,500 (limited to the realized gain). The basis of the automobile (unlike property) is its FMV of $2,000 while the basis of the real estate acquired is $9,000 ($10,000 + $2,500 gain recognized – $3,500 boot received).

B. Rules are **mandatory**, not elective.

C. **Qualifying Property**—Qualifying property must be exchanged.

    1. Only business and investment property qualifies for deferral.

> **Definitions**
>
> *Business Property*: Any property used in a business or held for investment. In contrast, property held for other reasons is referred to as personal use or "personal" property.
>
> *Realty*: Land and any property attached thereto (i.e., buildings).
>
> *Personalty*: Tangible property that is not realty.

> **Example**
> An apartment building is realty, but a truck is personalty.

    2. Nonqualifying property includes the following:

        a. Inventory

        b. Partnership interests

        c. Stocks, bonds, and notes

        d. Certificates of trust or beneficial interest

        e. Other securities or evidence of indebtedness or interest

    3. The property received in the exchange must be "like-kind" property.

> **Definition**
> *Like-Kind Property*: This property has the same general character as the property given up.

        a. In general, all realty is considered like-kind. So, the exchange of land for an office building is like-kind.

        b. Personalty is divided into broad asset classes, and assets must be within the same class to be like-kind. Examples of asset classes are office furniture, fixtures, and equipment; computer equipment; automobiles; and light-duty trucks. However, an exchange of real property for personalty is NEVER considered like-kind.

        c. Business property can be exchanged for investment property.

> **Example**
> An exchange of a pickup truck for a dump truck may qualify as a like-kind exchange. However, an exchange of an apartment building for a barge cannot be like-kind, because it is an exchange of realty for personalty.

        d. Property located outside the United States will not qualify as like-kind when exchanged for property located inside the United States.

        e. There are special rules that apply to like-kind exchanges when like-kind property is acquired from related taxpayers.

        f. **Exchange of insurance policies**—No gain or loss is recognized on an exchange of certain life, endowment, and annuity contracts to allow taxpayers to obtain better insurance.

D. **Holding Period**—Holding period of like-kind property surrendered tacks on to the holding period of like-kind property received.

II. Like-Kind Exchanges and the Receipt of Boot—The receipt of boot triggers gain recognition.

Definition
Boot: Nonqualifying property received by the taxpayer.

A. Cash and nonqualifying (not like-kind) property are considered boot.

B. Mortgage relief is treated as boot received if the taxpayer's mortgage that is assumed is greater than the mortgage that the taxpayer assumes on the new property he or she is receiving. However, if the taxpayer assumes a larger mortgage than he or she gives up, this excess reduces his amount realized, but it does not reduce other boot received.

Examples

1. A owns investment land with an adjusted basis of $50,000, FMV of $70,000, but which is subject to a mortgage of $15,000. B owns investment land with an adjusted basis of $60,000, FMV of $65,000, but which is subject to a mortgage of $10,000. A and B exchange real estate investments with A assuming B's $10,000 mortgage and B assuming A's $15,000 mortgage. The computation of realized gain, recognized gain, and basis for the acquired real estate for both A and B is as follows:

	A		B
FMV of real estate received	$65,000		$70,000
+ Liability on old real estate assumed by other party (boot received)	15,000	(1)	10,000
Amount realized on the exchange	$80,000		$80,000
– Adjusted basis of old real estate transferred	–50,000		–60,000
– Liability assumed by taxpayer on new real estate (boot given)	–10,000	(2)	–15,000
Gain realized	$20,000		$5,000
Gain recognized (1) minus (2)	$5,000		$–
Basis of old real estate transferred	$50,000		$60,000
+ Liability assumed by taxpayer on new real estate (boot given)	10,000		15,000
+ Gain recognized	5,000		—
– Liability on old real estate assumed by other party (boot received)	—		
	–15,000		–10,000
Basis of new real estate acquired	$50,000		$65,000

2. Assume the same facts as above except that the mortgage on B's old real estate was $6,000 and that A paid B cash of $4,000 to make up the difference. The tax effects to A remain unchanged. However, since the $4,000 cash cannot be offset by the liability assumed by B, B must recognize a gain of $4,000 and will have a basis of $69,000 for the new real estate.

C. Boot does **not** cause realized losses to be recognized.

D. The basis of like-kind property received can be computed as follows:

FMV of property received
– Postponed gain
+ Postponed loss
Basis of like-kind property

1. Basis of non-like-kind property received is the property's FMV, since gain has been recognized to that extent.

> **Example**
> **Question:** Leker exchanged a van that was used exclusively for business and had an adjusted tax basis of $20,000 for a new van. The new van had an FMV of $10,000, and Leker also received $3,000 in cash. What was Leker's tax basis in the acquired van?
>
> **Answer:** Leker has a realized loss on this exchange of $7,000 ($13,000 amount realized—$20,000 adjusted basis). He received $3,000 of boot, but boot does not cause realized losses to be recognized. Therefore, the recognized loss is zero and the postponed loss is $7,000. Leker's basis in the acquired van is its FMV ($10,000) plus the postponed loss ($7,000), or $17,000.

III. Involuntary Conversions

A. Overview—The involuntary conversion of property resulting in a realized gain is eligible for deferral.

1. This deferral provision does not apply to losses. Note that losses are recognized as casualty losses.

2. Applies to business, investment, and personal use property.

3. The deferral provision governing involuntary conversions applies when a gain is generated because an asset is destroyed, stolen, or condemned.

4. Taxpayers may elect to defer gains if the proceeds from the conversion are reinvested in similar property within a reasonable period of time. Hence, after reinvesting in similar property, the taxpayer has no wherewithal to pay the tax, and in addition, no disposition of substance has occurred.

5. If property is converted directly into property similar or related in service or use, complete nonrecognition of gain is mandatory. The basis of replacement property is the same as the property converted.

6. **Eligible for deferral**

   a. Definition of involuntary conversion.

> **Exam Tip**
> Note, that while the deferral rules for like-kind exchanges are mandatory, the rules for involuntary conversions are elective. Also, gains and losses are deferred under the like-kind exchange rules, while only gains are deferred for involuntary conversions.

> **Definitions**
> *Involuntary Conversion*: The result of the destruction (complete or partial), theft, seizure, casualty (an unexpected, unavoidable outside influence like a storm, fire, or shipwreck, or condemnation of property); or sale or exchange under *threat or imminence* of condemnation of the taxpayer's property (*eminent domain*).
>
> *Condemnation*: A taking by the government. An imminent threat of condemnation is considered sufficient to trigger an involuntary conversion.

   b. Gains from conversion of any kind of property are eligible for deferral (not just business property; personal use property qualifies also).

7. **Defer gain**—If the taxpayer replaces the converted property with similar property, he or she may elect to defer gain from the transaction.

   a. **Replacement property**

      i. The replacement property must be similar or related in the service or use made by the taxpayer.

> **Note**
> *Gains are eligible for deferral because of an involuntary conversion, but losses are recognized (e.g., not postponed).*

Definition

Similar or Related in the Service or Use: The end use of the replacement property must be similar to the use of the converted property. The determination of whether replacement property qualifies is similar to the process for determining if property qualifies as like-kind. However, this test is generally narrower than the like-kind test, because the properties must also have similar end uses.

    b. **Replacement time period**

        i. The replacement must be made within two years from the *end* of the tax year in which the gain is realized.

        ii. The replacement period is extended to three years if the conversion was a condemnation of business realty. The replacement period can also be extended with IRS permission, or if the area of the conversion is declared a disaster area.

        iii. If property is not replaced within the time limit, an amended return is filed to recognize gain in the year realized.

    c. Excess proceeds over replacement cost causes recognition of gains.

Amount realized from conversion

− Adjusted basis of old property

Realized gain/loss

Amount realized from conversion

− Cost of replacement property

Recognized gain, limited to realized gain

    d. **Adjusted basis**

        i. The adjusted basis of the new property is its cost reduced by any deferred gain.

Examples

1. TP's pickup was destroyed in a storm. The pickup has an adjusted basis of $2,000, and TP received $4,500 in insurance proceeds. Thus, TP realized a gain of $2,500 from the conversion of the pickup. If TP only spends $4,300 on a similar pickup within the replacement period, then TP will recognize $200 of gain (the amount of proceeds that were not reinvested). The adjusted basis of the new pickup will be $2,000 ($4,300 − $2,300).

2. Taxpayer had unimproved real estate (with an adjusted basis of $20,000) that was condemned by the county. The county paid Taxpayer $24,000, and Taxpayer reinvested $21,000 in unimproved real estate. $1,000 of the $4,000 realized gain would not be recognized. Taxpayer's tax basis in the new real estate would be $20,000 ($21,000 cost − $1,000 deferred gain).

3. Assume the same facts as #2 except the taxpayer reinvested $25,000 in unimproved real estate. None of the $4,000 realized gain would be recognized. Taxpayer's basis in the new real estate would be $21,000 ($25,000 cost − $4,000 deferred gain).

    e. **Holding Period**—Holding period of the converted property carries over to the qualified replacement property.

Other Nonrecognition Transactions

This lesson covers several areas for which recognized gains or losses are either excluded or deferred.

After studying this lesson, you should be able to:

1. Determine when and how the wash sale rules defer the recognition of losses.

2. Define related parties and apply the loss disallowance rules.

3. Use the ownership and usage tests to determine who is eligible to exclude gains from the sale of a principal residence.

4. Compute the recognized gain/loss from the sale of a principal residence.

Tax Forms for This Lesson: Form 6252 (available for download and printing from the lesson overview of your software).

I. Other Loss Disallowances

A. **Overview**—There are three common provisions that mandate deferral of losses because of opportunities to manipulate taxes. The first, wash sales, are losses from the sales of securities that often occur near year-end. The second provision governs losses from the sale of business/investment property to related parties. In both cases, there is an attempt to recognize a loss without giving up control of the underlying asset. The third area relates to short sales of assets.

B. **Wash Sales**—Losses from the sale of securities are not recognized if similar securities are purchased within 30 days of the sale.

Definition

Wash sale: A sale that results from the purchase of "substantially identical" stock or securities within a 30-day window around the sale date.

1. The taxpayer takes an adjusted basis in the new securities equal to the cost plus the deferred loss from the wash sale.

2. Holding period of the new stock or securities includes the holding period of the old stock or securities.

> **Note**
> Note that the wash sale rules apply only to losses, not to gains.

 Example
TP sold 100 shares of XYZ stock on December 22 for $1,200. The stock had an adjusted basis of $2,000, and TP realized a loss of $800. If TP purchased 100 shares of XYZ on January 15 of the next year for $1,400, the loss on the December 22 sale would be deferred as a wash sale. The stock held by TP would have a basis of $2,200 ($1,400 plus $800).

> **Note**
> The "repurchase" of a security can occur either before or after sale of the original security—the 30-day period is a window centered on the sale date. The repurchase period is 61 days, the day of sale plus 30 days before and after this day.

C. **Losses—Related Parties**

1. Losses from sales of business/investment property to related parties are not recognized. Note that losses from the sale of personal use property are never recognized.

Definition

Related Parties: Included in the definition of related parties are the following:

- Members of a family (spouse, children, grandchildren/descendants, parents, brothers and sisters, and grandparents/ancestors).
- An individual and a corporation in which the individual owns, directly or indirectly, more than 50% in value of the corporation's outstanding stock.
- A partner and a partnership in which the partner owns, directly or indirectly, more than 50% of the capital interests or profits interests in such partnership.
- Beneficiaries of estates and trusts can also be treated as related parties.

a. Deferred losses create a "right of offset" which can be used to reduce a gain upon the ultimate sale of the property to an unrelated taxpayer. However, the right of offset cannot create a loss, nor make a loss greater.

> **Note**
> *In-laws are not considered related parties, although they are eligible to be claimed as dependents; nor are aunts and uncles related parties.*

b. **Holding period**—of the original buyer does not include the holding period of the seller; it begins on the date of purchase of property from a related party.

2. **Payments to Related Parties**

a. An accrual method C corporation is effectively placed on the cash method of accounting for purposes of deducting accrued interest and other expenses owed to a related cash method payee. No deduction is allowable until the year the amount is actually paid.

b. This rule applies for partners and S corporation shareholders who own any interest in a partnership or S corporation (e.g., even 1%).

Examples

1. A calendar-year corporation accrues $10,000 of salary to an employee (a 60% shareholder) during 2017 but does not make payment until February 2018. The $10,000 will be deductible by the corporation and reported as income by the employee-shareholder in 2018.

2. TP sold stock to S, his brother, for $1,000. TP had an adjusted basis in the stock of $2,500, but cannot deduct the realized loss of $1,500 because S is a related party. S takes a basis in the stock of $1,000. If S eventually sells the stock to an unrelated third party for $1,800, S can offset the $800 gain with $800 of the deferred loss. The remainder of the deferred loss ($700) is not recognized.

D. **Short Sale**

1. A "short sale" of appreciated stock held by the taxpayer is treated as constructive sale on the date of the short sale.

> **Note**
> *The related party rules are not applicable to the sale of personal use property because these losses are not deductible under any circumstances. The only time a loss on personal use property is deductible is if the disposition qualifies as a personal casualty.*

Definition

Short Sale (also called "selling short against the box"): A transaction where the taxpayer borrows and sells shares identical to those already owned. This transaction has the effect of eliminating the taxpayer's risk of loss and opportunity for gain potential.

2. The short sale rule causes taxpayers to recognize gains on any short sales even if the sale was not closed through the purchase of additional stock or the delivery of shares previously owned. This rule is referred to as "marking to market," because the gain is measured by the value of the shares at the end of the year.

3. The short sale rule also requires taxpayers to defer losses. Losses are deferred until the short position is actually closed.

II. Sale of Principal Residence

A. Overview—The law provides for an exclusion of gains from a principal residence once every two years. No need to report on income tax return unless gain is not fully excluded.

1. A single taxpayer may exclude realized gains up to $250,000 if the **ownership and use tests** are met.

2. Married couples filing jointly can exclude up to $500,000 on the sale of a residence if:

   a. **Either**—The taxpayer or spouse meets the **ownership test**.

   b. **Both**—The taxpayer and spouse meet the **use test**.

   c. For single and married taxpayers, during the two-year period ending on the date of the sale, neither the taxpayer nor spouse excluded gain from the sale of another home (**frequency limit**).

Example
TP, a single taxpayer, sold his residence. He had an adjusted basis in the residence of $55,000 and received $415,000 on the sale before commissions. If TP paid sales commissions of $10,000, then he realized a gain of $350,000 on the sale. TP may be eligible to exclude $250,000 of the gain. The remaining gain ($100,000) would be taxed as a capital gain.

   d. Any depreciation taken must be recaptured on the sale (e.g., the gain attributed to the portion of the home depreciated as an office). As long as the business portion is not a separate building, the gain does not need to be allocated between the business and personal portions of the residence.

Example
Ron sold his principal residence during 2017 for a gain of $20,000. He used one room of the residence for business and deducted $1,000 of depreciation in 2016. Although Ron meets the ownership and use tests to exclude residence sale gain from income, he can exclude only $20,000 – $1,000 = $19,000 from income. The remaining $1,000 of gain is taxable and must be included in gross income.

   e. If the sale occurs not later than two years after the death of a spouse, the surviving spouse may exclude $500,000 of gain. Note, that the rules in "a" and "b" must have been met at the date of death of the deceased spouse for this provision to apply.

Example
TP has owned and occupied his residence for the past seven years. In January of this year, TP married S who moved into TP's residence. Immediately prior to the marriage, S sold her residence and excluded the gain. In June, TP and S sold TP's residence. TP qualifies for the exclusion, but S violates the frequency test. Nonetheless, TP can elect to exclude $250,000 of gain on the sale.

   f. The exclusion will not apply to the extent that the property was not used as a principal residence during a portion of the five-year testing period. For example, if during the five-year window the property is rented as a vacation home for two years and then used as a residence for three years, 40% of the gain (two years/five years) cannot be excluded from income. This limitation does not apply if the nonqualified use occurs *after* the home was used as a principal residence.

Example
On January 2, 2012, Diane buys a residence for $400,000 and uses it as rental property for two years, claiming $30,000 of depreciation deductions. On January 2, 2014, Diane converts the property to her principal residence. She moves out on January 11, 2016, and sells the property for $700,000 on January 2, 2017, resulting in a gain of $700,000 − $370,000 = $330,000.

The $30,000 of gain that is attributable to depreciation deductions must be included in income. Of the remaining $300,000 of gain, 2 years/5 years × $300,000 = $120,000 of gain is allocated to nonqualified use and is not eligible for exclusion. Since the remaining gain of $300,000 − $120,000 = $180,000 does not exceed the maximum exclusion ($250,000), Diane can exclude a total of $180,000 of gain from gross income. As a result, Diane must include $330,000 − $180,000 = $150,000 in gross income. Finally, note that the period from January 11, 2016, to January 2, 2017, is after she last used the home as her principal residence so it is not a period of nonqualified use.

B. Ownership and Use Tests

1. The residence must be owned and used by the taxpayer as a principal residence for at least two of the preceding five years (ownership and use tests).

    a. The amount of time need not be continuous (e.g., ownership and use must only total 730 days during the previous five years).

    b. Short or temporary absences (e.g., vacations) are ignored and use is imputed for taxpayers who are institutionalized (e.g., unable to care for themselves). Additionally, an individual can suspend the running of the five-year test period if serving in the uniformed services, Foreign Service, Peace Corps, or intelligence community.

    c. For married taxpayers, either spouse can meet the ownership test, but both must meet the use test. If only one spouse meets the use test, then that spouse can only claim a $250,000 exclusion.

    d. Special rules apply to divorced taxpayers.

        i. If a residence is transferred to a taxpayer incident to a divorce, the time during which the taxpayer's spouse or former spouse owned the residence is added to the taxpayer's period of ownership.

        ii. A taxpayer who owns a residence is deemed to use it as a principal residence while the taxpayer's spouse or former spouse is given use of the residence under the terms of a divorce or separation.

    e. A taxpayer's period of ownership of a residence includes the period during which the taxpayer's deceased spouse owned the residence so long as the taxpayer does not remarry before date of sale.

Example
TP has owned and occupied his residence for the past five years. In January of this year, TP married S who moved into TP's residence. In June, TP sold his residence. TP qualifies for the ownership and use test, but S violates the use test. Hence, TP can elect to exclude a maximum of $250,000 of gain on the sale.

C. Other Unforeseen Circumstances

1. If a residence is sold prematurely due to changes in employment or health (or other unforeseen circumstances such as a natural disaster, multiple births, or change in wedding plans), then the **maximum** amount of the exclusion is prorated based upon the number of qualifying months (ownership or use) divided by two years (or the equivalent in months or days). The qualifying months are the lesser of the number of ownership/use months or the number of months since the last sale.

> **Example**
> TP has owned and occupied his residence for the past 18 months. TP was transferred across the country and subsequently sold his residence for a gain of $200,000. TP does not qualify for the exclusion because he has not owned and occupied his residence for two years. Nonetheless, because of the change in employment TP can elect to exclude up to 75% (18/24) of the maximum ($250,000) from the sale. In this situation, TP can exclude $187,500 of the gain ($12,500 will be a taxable gain).

D. Note that the 3.8% tax on net investment income can apply to gain from the sale of a principal residence, but this is unusual since any capital gain up to $250,000 (single) or $500,000 (married) is excluded from taxation if the primary residence is sold. Overall, this means that this tax will not apply to most taxpayers who sell their homes. However, if taxpayers sell their primary home, and the income threshold is met, and capital gains exceed $250,000 for individuals or $500,000 for married couples, the excess realized gain is taxed at 3.8%. A home sale may also result in a capital gain that increases a taxpayer's AGI for purposes of calculating the limits noted above.

> **Example**
> Mary and Joe have a combined salary of $300,000. They sell their house for $1.4 million, earning a capital gain of $900,000. Their AGI is $300,000 plus $400,000 ($900,000 capital gain minus the $500,000 exclusion) for a total of $700,000. Their AGI exceeds the $250,000 threshold by $450,000. Their net investment income is $400,000 ($900,000 − $500,000 exclusion). The lower of the net investment income or excess AGI is $400,000. The additional tax on net investment income is: $400,000 × 3.8% = $15,200.

Federal Taxation of Individuals

Income

Gross Income—General Concepts and Interest

Two common areas for which gains and losses may not be recognized are like-kind exchanges and involuntary conversions.

After studying this lesson, you should be able to:

1. Use judicial doctrines to determine income for applicable transactions.

2. Assess the tax effects of interest bearing financial instruments.

3. Compute the tax consequences of the receipt of dividends.

Tax Form for This Lesson: Form 1040 Schedule B (available for download and printing from the lesson overview of your software).

I. **In this lesson we begin covering the first part of the income tax formula: gross income. The entire formula is as follows:**

	Gross income
Minus:	Deductions for AGI
	Adjusted gross income
Minus:	Greater of (1) standard deduction or (2) itemized deductions, and
Minus:	Personal and dependency exemptions
	Taxable income
Times:	Tax rate
	Income tax liability
Plus:	Other taxes
	Total tax
Minus:	Credits
Minus:	Prepayments
	Taxes due (or refund)

II. **General Rules**

   A. In general, income is broadly defined, so any realized increases in wealth should be assumed to be included in income unless the tax law provides for a specific exclusion or deferral.

   B. Taxable income differs from accounting income. The purposes of these sets of rules are different so do not confuse them.

   C. Income is not limited to cash receipts. Bartering can also produce income, as can the receipt of property or services in return for services rendered. Bartering is the exchange of property or services. The fair market value of the property or services received must be included in income.

   D. If a taxpayer unexpectedly finds property that she can legally keep, this has increased her net worth and the fair market value of the property is included in her income.

III. **Judicial Concepts**—The courts have constructed several special rules to address income recognition in unusual circumstances.

   A. **Constructive Receipt**—Constructive receipt requires a *cash basis taxpayer to include the value of property in income in the period in which the right to (or control of) the property is acquired.* The income is not constructively received if substantial restrictions exist on the taxpayer's use of the funds. For example, if the taxpayer would have to forfeit future bonuses to receive the funds then a substantial restriction exists.

Example
TP received a check on December 28 for services this year. He must recognize the income because he has control over the property (the check).

B. **Tax Benefit Rule**—The tax benefit rule requires a taxpayer to include an expense reimbursement in income if the expense was deducted in a prior period and the deduction reduced the taxpayer's taxable income.

Example
TP deducted a $200 business expense last year, but because of limitations the deduction only reduced his taxable income by $120. This year a client reimbursed $150 of the original expense. TP must include $120 of the reimbursement in his income this year.

C. **Claim of Right Doctrine**—The claim of right rule requires the taxpayer to include property in income in the period in which an apparent claim to the property materializes.

1. A later repayment of the property (because the claim was not valid) generates a deduction, but does not influence the earlier recognition of the income.

Example
Last year TP was paid a $100 bonus, but this year TP's employer discovered an error and required TP to repay $90 of the bonus. TP should include the $100 bonus in his income last year and claim a $90 deduction for the repayment this year.

D. **Assignment of Income Doctrine**—Income is taxed to the individual who earns the income, even if the taxpayer directs that the funds be paid to someone else. Income cannot be assigned for tax purposes to someone other than the party that earned it.

Example
X owns a building and assigns the rents to Y. The rents remain taxable to X, even though the rents are received by Y.

IV. **Interest Income**

A. **General Rules**

1. Interest is included in income when received (cash basis) or accrued (accrual basis).

2. Common sources of taxable interest that individuals often have are:

a. United States Treasury notes and bonds

b. Federal and state tax refunds

c. Mortgages

3. Special imputed interest rules apply to obligations purchased at a discount or a premium.

4. Prepaid interest income is always taxed when received.

B. **Bond Premiums**—Premiums occur when the amount paid for the bond is more than its face value.

1. If a taxpayer buys a taxable bond at a premium:

a. An election can be made to amortize the premium.

b. The amortization reduces the basis of the bond.

      c. The amortization offsets the interest income from the bond.

      d. The amortized bond premium is computed using the constant yield to maturity method.

   2. For tax exempt bonds, taxpayers must amortize premiums, but no deduction is available.

C. Bond Discounts—Discounts occur when the amount paid for the bond is less than its face value. This difference is known as the discount but basically represents interest income that should be recognized in the future.

   1. Individuals amortize bond discounts (as interest income).

   2. Original issue discounts must be amortized using the effective interest rate method.

Definition

Original Issue Discount: A loan made that requires a payment at maturity exceeding the amount of the original loan. This additional payment is a discount and constitutes interest. These obligations are often non-interest bearing.

Example

TP purchased a zero coupon (non-interest bearing) obligation for $8,000. It will mature at $10,000 in five years. The $2,000 difference is not a capital gain, but is interest income that must be recognized.

D. Short-Term Discounts—These are taxed at maturity as ordinary income for cash basis taxpayers. They are reported as earned for accrual basis taxpayers.

   1. A short-term obligation has a maturity of one year or less.

   2. This rule also applies to original issue discounts for short-term government bonds.

   3. In order to defer recognition of the discount, the interest cannot be withdrawn or made available without penalty.

E. Series EE Bonds—Interest on Series EE bonds is not paid annually but when the bond matures. The interest is not included in income until maturity unless the taxpayer elects to include the annual increases in the value of the bond as income each year. If the election is made it applies to all future years also. Interest on series EE *savings bonds can be excluded at maturity or when redeemed if the taxpayer uses the proceeds to pay higher education expenses in the year of redemption.*

   1. The exclusion is available if the owner of the bond is at least 24 years old (the bond must not be held in a child's name).

   2. The interest is excluded in proportion to the educational expenses (tuition and fees) of the taxpayer, spouse, or dependent that are not reimbursed by scholarships.

   3. The exclusion is phased out for 2017 when modified AGI exceeds $78,150 ($117,250) for single (filing jointly) status. The phaseout is proportionate over a range of $15,000 ($30,000 for married-jointly).

Examples

   1. During 2017, a married taxpayer redeems Series EE bonds receiving $6,000 of principal and $4,000 of accrued interest. Assuming qualified higher education expenses total $9,000, accrued interest of $3,600 ($9,000/$10,000 × $4,000) can be excluded from gross income.

2. Assume the joint return of the married taxpayer in the above example has modified AGI of $137,250 for 2017. Excess AGI is $20,000 ($137,250 – $117,250). The reduction would be ($20,000/$30,000) × $3,600 = $2,400. Thus, of the $4,000 of interest received, a total of $1,200 could be excluded from gross income.

V. Municipal Interest—Interest on state or local governmental obligations and obligations of a possession of the United States is excluded.

 A. The exclusion does not extend to some special types of municipal bonds, such as "arbitrage" bonds. An arbitrage bond is a bond for which any portion of the proceeds are reasonably expected to be used to acquire higher yielding investments.

 B. The exclusion does not mean that interest on municipal bonds cannot be used in other tax calculations, such as in the computation of the alternative minimum tax or the exclusion of social security benefits.

> **Note**
> *If the state or local bond is sold at a gain, such gain is taxable. Losses are also deductible. The character of the gain/loss is capital since bonds are an investment asset.*

 C. For bonds issued after February 17, 2009, or in 2010, certain issuers can elect for the bonds to be treated as Build America Bonds. These are municipal bonds but the election means that the interest on the bonds will be included in income, and the holder will receive a tax credit equal to 35% of the interest.

VI. Interest-Free and Below-Market Loans

 A. If the interest charged for a loan is less than the current market rate (which is based on the Applicable Federal Rates published monthly by the IRS), then special rules may apply. In general, it is assumed that the borrower pays the current market rate of interest to the lender. The borrower will have interest expense and the lender interest income for this hypothetical payment.

  1. The lender is then assumed to make a payment to the borrower equal to the hypothetical payment (since the payment was not actually made). The tax consequences to the borrower for this deemed payment are:

   a. Compensation income if the borrower is an employee.

   b. Dividend income if the borrower is a shareholder.

   c. A gift in most other circumstances.

  2. Interest using the applicable federal rate is compounded every six months.

Examples

1. Beth works for Publishing, Inc. and receives a $100,000 non-interest bearing loan from Publishing. Assume that the current market rate of interest is 10%. Beth is assumed to pay interest of $10,000 ($100,000 × 10%) to Publishing. The deductibility of this interest is governed by the specific rules related to interest deductions. Publishing recognizes $10,000 of interest income. Since Beth is an employee, she is also deemed to receive $10,000 of compensation income (subject to payroll taxes).

2. Parents make a $200,000 interest-free demand loan to their unmarried daughter on January 1, 2017. Assume the average federal short-term rate is 3% for 2017. If the loan is outstanding for the entire year, the daughter is treated as making a $6,045 ($200,000 × 3% × 1/2) + ($203,000 × 3% × 1/2) = $6,045) interest payment on 12/31/17, which is included as interest income on the parents' 2017 tax return. Note that interested is compounded every six months. The parents are treated as making a $6,045 gift to their daughter on 12/31/17. (Note that the gift will be offset by annual exclusions totaling $28,000 (for 2017) for gift tax purposes [2 × $14,000] as discussed.)

 B. Several types of loans are exempt from the below-market rules:

  1. In general loans are excluded if the loan amount does not exceed $10,000 and the borrower does not use the proceeds to purchase investment assets.

  2. If the amount of the loan does not exceed $100,000 and there is not a tax-avoidance motive, the deemed interest paid by the borrower is limited to the borrower's investment income on the loan proceeds. The investment income is deemed to be zero if $1,000 or less.

VII. Interest Reporting

A. Interest is reported on Lines 1 through 4 of Form 1040 Schedule B. Schedule B must be used if either interest or dividends exceed $1,500. Otherwise they are reported only on Form 1040.

B. If total interest or dividends exceed $1,500, then Part III must be completed related to foreign accounts.

C. Interest is reported to the taxpayer on Form 1099-INT.

Gross Income—Other Inclusions

After studying this lesson, you should be able to:

1. Delineate the tax effects of payments related to a divorce.

2. Calculate the tax consequences of payments received for damages and related to insurance benefits.

3. Determine the income recognized from annuity payments.

I. **Wages**—Wages are reported on Form W-2 and are included in income in the year received.

II. **Tip Income**

    A. Only tips received as cash, or on debit and charge cards, must be reported to the employer for purposes of paying and withholding payroll taxes. Tips only have to be reported to the employer if they are greater than or equal to $20 for a month (but all tips must be included in taxable income). Tips can be reported to the employer on Form 4070A or a similar statement and must be signed by the employee. They must be reported by the 10th day of the following month, or the next day after the 10th that is not a Saturday, Sunday, or legal holiday.

    B. A daily tip record should be kept so tips can be reported to the employer and on the tax return.

III. **Alimony**—Alimony is taxed to the recipient and the payor is granted a deduction ("for AGI"). In this way, the income is only taxed once to the ultimate recipient. Payments to a former spouse that do not qualify as alimony are treated as a division of property: nontaxable to the recipient and nondeductible by the payor.

    A. **Alimony**—Alimony is taxable to the one receiving the payments and deductible by the one making the payments. To qualify as alimony, the payments must be:

> **Note**
> *It is permissible for alimony to terminate before the spouse's death; it just cannot extend beyond death.*

        1. **Required** by decree or written agreement and not characterized as something other than alimony;

        2. Made in **cash**;

        3. Paid to or on behalf of **former spouse;**

        4. **Terminate** upon death of recipient; *and*

        5. Payor and payee cannot be members of the same **household**.

    B. **Child Support**—Child support is not taxable to the one receiving the payments and is **not deductible** by the one making the payments.

    C. **Property Transfers**—to a former spouse under a divorce decree are **not a taxable event**. The transferor's basis in the property transfers to the transferee.

    D. If the required amount of child support and alimony are not received, payments are first assumed to be child support.

    E. Special front-loading rules require recapture of deductions and income if alimony payments decline more than $15,000 over the first three years after the divorce.

Example
The following alimony payments are made: Year 1, $100,000; Year 2, $80,000; and Year 3, $45,000. The alimony recapture is computed as follows:

A. The excess of the Year 2 payments over the Year 3 payments ($80,000 − $45,000 = $35,000) is $20,000 above $15,000. This is the first recapture amount.

B. Next, reduce the Year 2 payments by the $20,000 from step A, producing $60,000 ($80,000 – $20,000).

C. The Year 2 payments (now $60,000) plus the Year 3 payments ($45,000) equals $105,000. Divide $105,000 by 2 to obtain $52,500.

D. The excess of the Year 1 payments over $52,500 is $47,500 ($100,000 – $52,500 = $47,500) which is $32,500 above $15,000. This is the second recapture amount. The total recapture amount is $20,000 from step A plus $32,500 from step D, which equals $52,500.

IV. Income from Community Property

A. Community property law divides income into separate property and community property.

  1. Separate property consists of assets owned before marriage or acquired by gift or inheritance while married.

  2. Community property is property acquired during a marriage unless by gift or inheritance.

B. Allocation of Income

  1. Depending on the state, income from separate property may be either separate property (Idaho, Louisiana, and Texas) or community property (Alaska, Arizona, California, Nevada, New Mexico, Washington, and Wisconsin). If community property, each spouse is taxed on 50% of the income. If separate property, the income is reported by the spouse who owns the property.

  2. Personal service income is usually community property.

V. Damages

A. Personal Injuries—Damages for physical injury or physical sickness are excluded.

  1. If an action has its origin in a physical injury or physical sickness, then all damages therefrom (other than punitive damages) are excluded (e.g., damages received by an individual on account of a claim for loss due to a physical injury to such individual's spouse are excludible from gross income).

  2. Damages (other than punitive damages) received on account of a claim of wrongful death and damages that are compensation for amounts paid for medical care (including medical care for emotional distress) are excluded.

  3. Emotional distress is not considered a physical injury or physical sickness. No exclusion applies to damages received from a claim of employment discrimination, age discrimination, or injury to reputation (even if accompanied by a claim of emotional distress).

  4. Punitive damages generally must be included in gross income, even if related to a physical injury or physical sickness.

Definition
Compensation for physical injuries: Any payment that compensates for damages due to a physical injury or illness. As long as the action generating a payment is due to a physical injury or illness, then all damage payments received, except for punitive damages, are excludible from income. This is the case even if the injured party is being reimbursed for lost wages.

B. Attorney's fees and costs recovered as part of a judgment must be included in income if the underlying recovery is included in gross income.

C. Income from a wrongly incarcerated individual for loss of liberty, lost income, pain and suffering, and other physical and emotional injuries is excluded from income.

Example

TP was in an accident caused by Smith. TP received $1,000 to compensate him for medical expenses, $5,000 for emotional distress due to injury, and $2 million for punitive damages. TP is taxed on $2 million but not on the compensation for expenses or emotional distress (it was due to a physical injury).

VI. Income in Respect of a Decedent (IRD)

A. IRD is income that the decedent had **earned before his death**, but had **not yet recognized** as income because of his method of accounting.

B. IRD must be included in the gross income of the person who receives it, and it has the same character as it would have had if the decedent had recognized it.

C. Some common examples of IRD are **accrued income, accrued interest** on U.S. savings bonds and on savings accounts, and **dividends** for which the record date was before the date of death.

VII. Jury Duty Pay—Jury duty pay is includible in income. If the jury pay is given to the juror's employer then a deduction for AGI is received to offset this income.

VIII. Unemployment Compensation—This amount is taxable.

> **Note**
> If a taxpayer receives a judgment or settlement as a result of a discrimination suit, the damages received typically are included in gross income. Attorney's fees and other costs incurred as part of the suit are deductible for AGI, limited to the amount of the proceeds that are included in income.

> **Note**
> Unemployment compensation is taxable because it is a replacement for wages.

Gross Income—Exclusions

This lesson explains the most important exclusions from gross income for taxpayers.

After studying this lesson, you should be able to:

1. Apply rules to determine receipts that can be excluded from income if the proper requirements are met, such as prizes and awards, scholarships, and life insurance benefits received.

2. Distinguish between gifts and inheritances and determine the basis and holding period rules for each.

3. Identify the types of debt forgiveness that can be excluded from income.

4. Compute the tax consequences of the receipt of social security benefits.

I. Prizes and Awards

A. The **fair market value** of these items must be included in income.

B. Prizes or awards can be **excluded** if they are for civic, **artistic, educational, scientific, or literary achievement** and the recipient is:

   1. Selected without action on his/her part;

   2. Not required to perform services; *and*

   3. If the amount is paid directly to a tax-exempt or governmental organization.

II. Scholarships

A. Amounts received as scholarships can be **excluded** from income to the extent that the funds are used by a degree seeking student for **tuition, fees, books, supplies**, and equipment required for courses.

B. Amounts received for room and board are treated as **earned income**.

C. Payments received by a student under a comprehensive student work-learning-service program at a college or university are excluded from income if participation in the program is required.

III. Life Insurance Proceeds

Note
If the payments from the university are in return for services rendered, the amounts are taxable as wages, even if the services are a condition for receiving the degree, or required of all candidates for the degree.

A. Proceeds of life insurance received due to the death of the insured are excluded from income. Life insurance proceeds are generally subject to estate tax at the time of the decedent's death. Hence, subjecting the beneficiary to income taxation upon receipt of the proceeds would constitute a double tax on the proceeds.

   1. The exchange/sale of a life insurance policy for the cash surrender value is treated like a sale and the proceeds in excess of the cost are income.

   2. One exception to this rule is the surrender of a policy or sale of a policy by a terminally ill taxpayer. Accelerated death benefits from a life insurance policy can be excluded from income if the insured taxpayer is terminally or chronically ill. Terminally ill means that a physician has certified that death is likely to occur in 24 months or less. Chronically ill means that the individual cannot perform some common daily activities (e.g., eating, bathing).

B. A life insurance policy purchased (from the insured or the owner of the policy) for consideration is treated like an asset and the proceeds in excess of the cost are income.

Example

TP owned a life insurance policy on his spouse, but was short of cash. He sold the policy for $100 to B, an unrelated individual. Upon the death of TP's spouse, B received $500 from the life insurance company. B will be taxed on $400 of income ($100 is return of capital). If TP had not sold the policy, then TP would have received $500 tax-free.

Able was the owner and beneficiary of a $30,000 life insurance policy on Baker. Able sold the policy for $10,000 to Carr, who subsequently paid $6,000 of premiums. If Baker dies, Carr's gross income from the proceeds of the life insurance policy would total $30,000 – ($10,000 + $6,000) = $14,000.

IV. Gifts and Inheritances—Gifts and inheritances are taxed under the Federal Estate and Gift Tax law. To avoid the double taxation of these transfers, their value is excluded from the income of the recipient.

   A. Gifts—Gifts are excluded if the purpose of the transfer was detached generosity (no quid pro quo or consideration was expected in return for the transfer).

   B. Income—Income accrued up to time of gift is still taxed to the donor, whereas income accruing after the gift is taxed to recipient (donee).

V. Forgiveness of Debt

   A. Generally, the forgiveness of debt results in income to the borrower unless the forgiveness is a gift, or the forgiveness is related to a bankruptcy proceeding.

   B. If the taxpayer is bankrupt or insolvent, the debt forgiveness is not taxable.

      1. However, the taxpayer must reduce tax attributes such as net operating losses (NOLs), credit carryovers, and then the basis of property. The taxpayer can elect to reduce the basis of property first rather than other tax attributes.

      2. The amount excluded from income must be applied to reduce tax attributes in the following order:

         a. Net operating loss (NOL) for taxable year and loss carryovers to taxable year

         b. General business credit

         c. Minimum tax credit

         d. Capital loss of taxable year and carryovers to taxable year

         e. Reduction of the basis of property

         f. Passive activity loss and credit carryovers

         g. Foreign tax credit carryovers to or from taxable year

      3. Instead of reducing tax attributes in the above order, a taxpayer may elect to first reduce the basis of depreciable property.

   C. A taxpayer that is insolvent, but not bankrupt, can exclude forgiveness of debt only to the extent of the insolvency.

> **Note**
> *Whether an item is a gift depends on the intent of the donor, not the intent of the donee. For example, S rakes the leaves in T's yard as a gesture of kindness, but T decides to pay her $20 for her work. Even though S did not expect to be paid, S has $20 of income because T's intent was to pay him for the services he rendered.*

Example

UNA, Inc. has assets of $500,000 and debts of $750,000. Therefore, their insolvency is $250,000. If creditors forgive $400,000 of debt, the first $250,000 will be excluded from income. The remaining $150,000 will be included as income. UNA will reduce other tax attributes for the $250,000 of excluded income.

D. For cancellation of debt on real property used in a trade or business, no income is recognized even if the taxpayer is not bankrupt or insolvent. However, the taxpayer must reduce the basis of the property by the amount of forgiven debt.

E. For discharges of indebtedness on a taxpayer's principal residence in connection with a debt restructure or foreclosure in 2007–2016, up to $2 million of debt relief may be excluded from income. This provision has not been extended to 2017. This debt is limited to indebtedness to acquire, construct, or substantially improve a principal residence. Thus, home equity loans, whose proceeds are not used for these purposes, are not included in this exclusion.

VI. Social Security Benefits—Generally, SSB are not included in income. However, if the taxpayer's provisional income (PI) exceeds a specified amount, up to 85% of the benefits may be included in income.

PI = AGI + Tax-exempt interest + 50% (SSB)

The following base amounts (BA) must be used:

	BA1	BA2
Married taxpayers filing jointly	$32,000	$44,000
Married taxpayers that file	$ 0	$ 0
All other taxpayers	$25,000	$34,000

If PI exceeds BA1 but not BA2, then the taxable amount of SSB is the lesser of:

$50\% \times SSB$

$50\% \times (PI - BA1)$

If PI exceeds BA2, then the taxable amount of SSB is the lesser of:

$.85 \times SSB$, or

$.85 \times (PI - BA2)$, plus the lesser of

amount included based on first formula, or

$4,500 (unless married filing jointly, then $6,000).

VII. Foster Child Payments—Payments are excluded from income if they are for reimbursement for expenses incurred to care for the foster child.

VIII. Welfare Payments—Welfare payments received from governmental entities are not included in income.

> **Note**
> If PI is less than $25,000, then none of the SSB is included in income.

IX. Worker's Compensation—Worker's compensation payments are excluded from income since these are paid due to a physical injury on the job.

X. Rental value of parsonage or cash rental allowance for a parsonage is excluded by a minister.

Taxation of Items from Business Entities

After studying this lesson, you should be able to:

1. Compute the tax on dividend distributions from a corporation

2. Report the tax items flowing from a partnership or S corporation on Form 1040

3. Compute the income from a sole proprietorship on Schedule C

4. Report the income from farming operations on Schedule F

Tax Forms for This Lesson: Form 1040 Schedules B, C, E and F; Schedule K-1 for partnership and S corporation; Form 1099-DIV

This lesson reviews the taxation of income distributions/flow from business entities such as corporations, partnerships, and S corporations. The computation of income from the entities is covered in other lessons. The focus of this lesson is on the taxation of the income to the owner.

I. **Dividends on Stock**—Generally, distributions of cash or property to shareholders is taxed as dividend income if the distribution is made from the corporation's retained earnings (called **earnings and profits (E&P)** for tax purposes).

Definition
Dividend: To the extent of earnings and profits, any distribution of cash or property from a corporation to its shareholders is a dividend.

A. The **value** of the property received in a dividend is the amount included in income to the extent the dividend is paid from earnings and profits.

   1. Determining the taxability of dividends is a three-step process:

      a. Dividend income to the extent of earnings and profits;

      b. Then a reduction in the basis of the stock;

      c. Once the basis is exhausted, the excess is capital gain.

   2. Earnings and profits are the tax version of retained earnings.

   3. Dividends are taxed to cash-basis taxpayers in the period in which the property is made available (typically when received).

B. **Qualified Dividend Income**

   1. Qualified dividend income is taxed at the same rates as long-term capital gains for individuals. It is not taxed (0%) if the taxpayer is in the 10% or 15% bracket. For higher tax brackets, dividend income is taxed at 15% or 20%. To qualify for this lower rate, the dividend must be received from a domestic corporation or a foreign corporation whose stock is tradable on an established U.S. securities market. If the stock was held for 60 days or less during the 121-day period beginning 60 days before the ex-dividend date, then the dividend does not qualify for this lower rate.

   2. A 3.8% net investment income tax applies to taxpayers whose modified AGI exceeds $250,000 if married filing jointly and $200,000 if single or head of household. The 3.8% tax applies to the lesser of (a) net investment income, or (b) the excess of AGI over the AGI thresholds. Dividends are included in net investment income, so the highest tax rate on qualified dividend income is 23.8% (20% + 3.8%). These thresholds are not indexed for inflation.

C. Stock dividends on common stock are not taxable as long as the dividend is proportionate (same percentage for all shareholders). A stock dividend or split requires the taxpayer to adjust the basis of the stock's new number of shares.

Examples

1. TP owns 40 shares in XYZ Corporation purchased at a cost of $10 per share ($400 total). TP received an additional 10 shares as a stock dividend. He has realized no income and his shares now have a basis of $8 each ($400 divided by 50 shares).

2. T owns 100 shares of XYZ Corp. common stock that was acquired in 2010 for $12,000. In 2016, T received a nontaxable distribution of 10 XYZ Corp. preferred shares. At date of distribution the FMV of the 100 common shares was $15,000, and the FMV of the 10 preferred shares was $5,000. The portion of the $12,000 basis allocated to the preferred and common shares would be

$$\text{Preferred} = \frac{\$5,000}{\$20,000}\ (\$12,000) = \$3,000$$

$$\text{Common} = \frac{\$15,000}{\$20,000}\ (\$12,000) = \$9,000$$

D. To be nontaxable, the stock dividend must be paid to **common** stockholders. Either common or preferred stock can be paid to common stock shareholders. A stock dividend paid to **preferred** stockholders is always taxable.

E. An option to receive cash in lieu of stock (whether or not exercised) triggers recognition of dividend income.

F. Distributions from mutual funds are usually characterized as either ordinary dividends or capital gains. All ordinary dividends are treated as dividend income and the mutual fund will indicate if any of these are qualified dividends taxed at lower rates. All capital gain distributions are treated as long-term capital gains.

G. Dividend Reporting

1. Dividends are reported on Lines 5 through 6 of Form 1040 Schedule B. Schedule B must be used if either interest or dividends exceed $1,500. Otherwise they are reported only on Form 1040.

2. If total interest or dividends exceed $1,500 then Part III must be completed related to foreign accounts.

3. Dividends are reported to the taxpayer on Form 1099-DIV.

II. Income or Loss from Rents and Royalties, Partnerships, and S Corporations.

A. Rents and Royalties

1. Rents and royalties are fully taxable after deducting appropriate expenses. Net rents and royalties are reported on Schedule E Supplemental Income and Loss of Form 1040.

2. If the taxpayer reports on an accrual basis, rental revenues are taxable in the earlier of either the period earned or the period received. Prepaid collections of rents and royalties, including nonrefundable deposits, are reported immediately.

3. Refundable security deposits are included if and when the taxpayer claims the right to keep amounts received due to a failure of the depositor to live up to the terms of the agreement.

4. In calculating net rents and royalties, certain items may be deducted.

   a. *As to rents*, deductions include depreciation, taxes, insurance, and other ordinary and necessary expenses. If the taxpayer occupies a portion of the rental property, only the portion of costs applicable to the portion rented can be deducted in arriving at net rental income. The costs related to the owner-occupied portion are not deductible as rental expenses but may qualify as itemized deductions (e.g., property taxes, mortgage interest, et cetera).

    b. *As to royalties*, deductions include ordinary and necessary expenses. Royalty owners of natural resources may use percentage depletion.

B. Income from Partnerships (Including Limited Liability Companies) and S Corporations

1. Partnerships and S corporations, examples of pass-through entities, are not subject to income taxation. The tax treatment of the activities of these entities flows through to the individual owner(s).

2. A partner's share of income from a partnership, whether a limited partnership or a general partnership and whether distributed to the partner or not, is reported to the partner on Form K-1, *Partner's Share of Income, Deductions, Credits, etc.*, prepared along with the partnership return. The partner's share of ordinary income is reported by the partner on Schedule E of Form 1040.

3. A stockholder's share of S corporation earnings, regardless of whether it was distributed to the shareholder or not, is reported to the shareholder on Form K-1, *Shareholder's Share of Income, Deductions, Credits, etc.*, prepared along with the S corporation return. The shareholder's share of ordinary income is reported by the shareholder on Schedule E of Form 1040.

4. The corporation or partnership's ordinary income, capital gains, deductions, and credits retain their separate character when they flow from the entity to the owner.

5. Every partner/S shareholder will receive a Schedule K-1 which details the tax implications of the partnership to the partner. In determining the partner's share of partnership income (loss), the partnership must identify ordinary business income (loss) as well as separately stated items.

6. Ordinary business income (loss) includes all partnership income or loss that does not need to be separately stated. Items that have alternative tax treatments are separately stated. That is, if an item can be treated differently by a taxpayer, depending on the taxpayer's circumstances, then it needs to be separately stated. The most common separately stated items include short- and long-term capital gains (losses), charitable contributions, and dividend/interest income.

7. Limitations on passive activity losses are discussed in the "Limitations on Business Deductions" lesson. Other limitations are discussed in the partnership and S corporation material.

III. Sole Proprietorships

A. Net business income and losses are reported on Schedule C of Form 1040 as part of an individual's gross income.

B. Business Income

1. Business income includes gross profit (Gross sales receipts – Cost of goods sold = Gross profit).

2. Business income also includes the fees of a sole proprietor such as a CPA or an attorney performing professional services.

3. Board of directors' fees are also considered self-employment income.

4. Business income is reduced by business expenses and expenses for business use of home to arrive at net profit or loss on Schedule C, *Profit or Loss from Business*, of Form 1040.

C. Business Expenses and Deductions

1. Business expenses may be deducted if they are directly related to the business and are ordinary and necessary. Business expense deductions are deductions for adjusted gross income but are not reported separately on the Form 1040 because they are reported net with business income. Schedule C (similar to an income statement) contains the income and expense items, and net profit.

IV. Farming Income and Expenses

A. A farming business involves the cultivating of land or raising or harvesting of any agricultural or horticultural commodity. It does not include contract harvesting, or the buying or reselling of plants or animals grown or raised by another person.

B. An individual engaged in farming must file Schedule F (Form 1040), *Farm Income and Expenses*. Additionally, a farmer must also file Schedule SE in order to compute self-employment tax on farm earnings. Completing Schedule F for farming is similar to completing a Schedule C which is used by sole proprietors. Partnerships engaged in farming must file Form 1065, while corporations engaged in farming must file the appropriate Form 1120.

C. The income and expenses from farming are generally treated in the same manner as the income and expenses from any other business. Similarly, the general rules that apply to all cash and accrual taxpayers also apply to farming businesses.

1. A cash-basis farmer who receives insurance proceeds as a result of the destruction or damage to crops may elect to include the proceeds in income for the year after the year of damage if the farmer can show that the income from the crops would normally have been reported in the following year.

2. Income from the sale of a crop is normally reported in the year of sale. However, if the farmer has pledged all of part of the crop production to secure a Commodity Credit Corporation loan, the farmer may elect to report the loan proceeds as income in the year received rather than reporting income in the year the crop is sold. The amount reported as income becomes the farmer's basis for the crop and is used to determine gain or loss upon the sale of the crop.

3. A farmer may generally deduct soil and water conservation expenditures that are consistent with a conservation plan approved by a federal or state agency. However, the deduction is annually limited to 25% of the farmer's gross income from farming. Excess expenses can be carried over for an unlimited number of years subject to the 25% limitation in each carryover year.

    a. Expenses related to the draining of wetlands or to land preparation for the installation of center pivot irrigation systems may not be deducted under this provision.

    b. Land clearing expenses must be capitalized and added to the farmer's basis in the land.

Example

A farmer had gross income from Farm A of $25,000 and gross income from Farm B of $19,000 for the current year. During the year the farmer spent $16,000 on Farm B for soil and water conservation expenditures under a plan approved by a state agency. For the current year, the farmer's deduction of the $16,000 of soil and water conservation expenditures would be limited to ($25,000 + $19,000) × 25% = $11,000.

4. Cash-basis farmers can generally deduct prepaid feed costs in the year of payment if the deduction does not materially distort income. However, no deduction is allowed for advance payments for feed, seed, fertilizer, or other supplies to the extent such prepayments exceed 50% of total deductible farming expenses (excluding the prepaid items).

Example

During December 2017, a calendar-year farmer purchased a 6-month supply of feed for $6,000 and also purchased $2,000 of seed to be used in the subsequent spring planting season. The farmer's other farm expenses totaled $9,000. In this case the farmer's 2017 deduction for prepaid feed and seed would be limited to 50% × $9,000 = $4,500.

5. The cost of most tangible personal property used in a farming business cannot be depreciated under the 200% declining-balance method, but instead is generally recovered using the MACRS 150% declining-balance method over a five-year recovery period.

6. An individual engaged in farming can elect to determine current year tax liability by averaging, over the previous three years, all or part of his/her current-year income from farming.

Accounting Methods and Periods—Individuals

I. Tax Accounting—Tax accounting consists of specialized rules for realizing and accounting for income. The accounting rules also apply to expenses, but these rules are described in detail in the section covering deductions. Like financial accounting, the rules used to determine taxable income are premised upon ascertaining net income. Unlike conservative financial accounting rules, the tax rules treat ambiguous circumstances **liberally**, by assuming income is recognized. Thus, the tax rules are normally structured to recognize a larger, rather than smaller, tax liability.

II. Realization

> **Definition**
> *Realization:* The event that triggers the taxation of income. Like realization for financial accounting, realization is difficult to define precisely.

  A. Realized income is presumed to be taxable.

  1. Realization generally occurs when a transaction results in the receipt of property or a right capable of valuation.

  2. Income cannot be realized or recognized if the property received by the taxpayer is not susceptible of valuation. For example, a taxpayer may not be able to value a promise to pay for property based upon future events.

  B. Return of capital is not income.

  1. Receipts are not recognized as income to the extent the receipts represent the cost of goods or the cost of property sold.

> **Definition**
> *Return of capital:* The cost of goods or the cost of property sold.

>
> **Example**
> SH purchases $10,000 of Motorola stock, and later sells the stock for $13,000. SH is allowed to recover her cost/capital of $10,000 before realizing income. Therefore, her realized income is $3,000 ($13,000 – cost basis of $10,000).

  C. Specific Exceptions—Congress has enacted specific exceptions for untaxed (unrecognized) income.

  1. Nonrecognition provisions may exclude income from taxation or merely defer taxation of the income until a later period.

  2. Each type of unrecognized income may be subject to specific, unique limits.

> **Definition**
> *Gross income:* The amount of realized income after eliminating deferred and excluded income.

D. Corollary—Expenses are Presumed Nondeductible.

1. Nondeductible expenses do not influence taxable income.

2. Congress only authorized deductions for a list of specific expenses.

3. Similar to nonrecognition provisions, each type of deduction may be subject to specific, unique limits.

III. Accounting Methods and Periods

A. *An individual's income is reported on Schedule C.* Methods of accounting available to report income are *cash, accrual,* and *hybrid.* Individuals always report on the *calendar year-end.*

B. **Accrual Method**—The accrual method for taxes is very similar to financial accounting, but exceptions to accrual are usually income increasing.

1. For tax purposes, unearned (prepaid) income is recognized in the year received, rather than the year earned.

2. To the extent that accrued expenses are deductible, the deduction can be claimed in the period in which the liability becomes certain (all events test).

3. Dividends are included in gross income in the year received under both the cash and accrual methods.

4. Generally no advance deduction is allowed for accrual method taxpayers for estimated or contingent expenses; the obligation must be "fixed and determinable."

C. **Cash Method**—The cash method of accounting recognizes income (and expenses) in the year in which payment is received (or paid).

1. This rule only addresses the timing of income (and expense), not whether income has been realized.

2. Under the cash basis, a taxpayer has no accounts receivable because no accounting entry is made for sales on account (no property has been received).

3. Prepaid expenses are prorated for cash basis taxpayers if recognition of the total expense in the current year would distort taxable income.

> **Note**
> *A cash basis taxpayer does not need to reduce property to cash to trigger income recognition.*
>
> *A cash basis taxpayer cannot write off accounts receivable but can write off a loan. No entry is made for sales on account, but a loan requires an entry (debit loan receivable and credit cash).*

D. **Special Inventory Rules**

1. In general, business with inventories must use the accrual method to report purchases (cost of goods sold) and sales. This method is known as the hybrid method of accounting if other accounts are kept using the cash basis.

2. Taxpayers whose annual gross receipts do not exceed $1 million can also use the cash method for purchase and sales accounts. The test is satisfied for a prior year if the average annual gross receipts for the previous three-year period do not exceed $1 million. Once the test is failed, the entity must use the accrual method for all future tax years.

3. Taxpayers whose annual gross receipts exceed $1 *million,* but are less than $10 million can use the cash method for purchase and sales accounts if their primary business is delivering services (not manufacturing, wholesale, or retail) and they are not a corporation.

4. **Manufacturers and retailers**

    a. Manufacturers and certain retailers and wholesalers are required to use the **uniform capitalization method** to capitalize all the direct and indirect costs allocable to property they produce and for property bought for resale. These costs are then allocated to ending inventory and property sold during the year, which usually results in an increase in the basis of the inventory.

b. Property is produced if the taxpayer constructs, builds, installs, manufactures, develops or improves property.

c. Exceptions to the uniform capitalization method include: small personal property dealers (those with $10 million or less in gross receipts during the preceding three years); long-term contracts; costs incurred in certain farming businesses and in raising and harvesting crops and timber; certain creative expenses and personal property; intangible drilling and development costs; natural gas acquired for resale; and research and experimental expenditures.

5. Costs required to be capitalized:

    a. Costs required to be capitalized under the uniform capitalization rules include direct materials and direct labor, and virtually all indirect production (such as utilities, repairs, rent, depreciation) costs must be capitalized for tax purposes.

    b. Marketing, selling, advertising, and distribution expenses are not required to be capitalized under the uniform capitalization rules. General and administrative expenses also do not have to be capitalized.

    c. Storage costs are required to be capitalized to the extent that they can be traced to an off-site storage or warehouse facility. Those storage costs attributed to an on-site facility are not required to be capitalized.

    d. Interest must be capitalized if the debt is incurred or continued to finance the construction or production of real property, property with a recovery period of 20 years, property that takes more than two years to produce, or property with a production period exceeding one year and a cost exceeding $1 million.

6. Costs can be allocated between ending inventory and cost of goods sold using FIFO, LIFO, weighted average, or specific identification. However, LIFO can be used only if it is also used for financial reporting. During a period of rising prices, LIFO produces a higher cost of goods sold and lower taxable income.

7. Taxpayers can value inventory at the lower of cost or market unless they are using LIFO (in which case cost must be used). Market is defined as replacement cost or reproduction cost.

IV. Changes in Accounting Methods

1. Once a taxpayer has selected a particular method of accounting it cannot be changed without the consent of the IRS.

2. In general, any adjustment to income required due to a voluntary change in accounting method is spread over four years beginning with the year of change. A voluntary change includes changing from an incorrect to a correct method. If the adjustment is less than $25,000, the taxpayer can include all income in the year of change.

3. If the change in accounting method is initiated due to an IRS examination, any positive adjustment to income is included in the earliest tax year under examination.

V. Prepaid Items

A. Prepaid Interest, Rents, and Royalties—Are usually taxed when received. Lease deposits are not income when received if they can be returned to the lessee at the end of the lease term. They are taxed when the lessor receives an unrestricted right to them.

B. The taxpayer can elect to include prepaid service income in gross income when received. However, under the deferral method the taxpayer only has to include the payments in gross income in the year of receipt if they are also included in the taxpayer's financial statements. The remaining payments are taxed in the following year (even if not yet earned). The deferral rule also applies to payments received by hotels and other venues where significant services are provided to the lessee.

C. Revenue from the advanced payment of goods can be deferred until earned as long as the same reporting method is used for financial accounting.

D. Prepaid dues and subscriptions are reported over the membership or subscription period.

E. Leasehold Improvements—The fair value of leasehold improvements is income to the landlord if the improvements are made in lieu of rent.

Example
In 2017, a landlord signed a five-year lease. During 2016, the landlord received $5,000 for that year's rent and $5,000 as advance rent for the last year (2021) of the lease. All $10,000 will be included in income for 2017.

VI. The **installment method** applies to gains (not losses) from the disposition of property where at least one payment is to be received after the year of sale. The installment method does not change the character of the gain to be reported (e.g., ordinary, capital, etc.), and is required unless the taxpayer makes a negative election to report the full amount of gain in year of sale.

A. The installment method **cannot be used** for property held for sale in the ordinary course of business (except time-share units, residential lots, and property used or produced in farming) and cannot be used for sales of stock or securities traded on an established securities market.

B. The amount to be reported in each year is determined by the formula

$$\frac{\text{Gross profit}}{\text{Total contract price}} \times \text{Amount received in year}$$

1. Contract price is the selling price reduced by the seller's liabilities that are assumed by the buyer, to the extent not in excess of the seller's basis in the property. The gross profit percentage is the Gross profit/Contract price.

Examples
1. Taxpayer sells property with a basis of $80,000 to buyer for a selling price of $150,000. As part of the purchase price, buyer agrees to assume a $50,000 mortgage on the property and pay the remaining $100,000 in 10 equal annual installments together with adequate interest.

The contract price is $100,000 ($150,000 – $50,000); the gross profit is $70,000 ($150,000 – $80,000); and the gross profit ratio is 70% ($70,000 × $100,000). Thus, $7,000 of each $10,000 payment is reported as gain from the sale.

2. Assume the same facts as above except that the seller's basis is $30,000. The contract price is $120,000 ($150,000 – Mortgage assumed but only to extent of seller's basis of $30,000); the gross profit is $120,000 ($150,000 – $30,000); and the gross profit ratio is 100% ($120,000/$120,000). Thus, 100% of each $10,000 payment is reported as gain from the sale. In addition, the amount by which the assumed mortgage exceeds the seller's basis ($20,000) is deemed to be a payment in the year of the sale. Since the gross profit ratio is 100%, all $20,000 is reported as gain in the year the mortgage is assumed.

2. Any depreciation recapture under Sections 1245, 1250, and 291 must be included in income in the year of sale. The amount of recapture included in income is treated as an increase in the basis of the property for purposes of determining the gross profit ratio. The remainder of gain is spread over installment payments.

Example
Baxter sells equipment with an adjusted basis of $50,000 to a buyer for $50,000 cash plus a $50,000 interest-bearing note to be paid next year. The equipment had originally cost $90,000, and Baxter had deducted depreciation of $40,000 on the equipment. Baxter realizes a gain of $100,000 – $50,000 = $50,000 on the installment sale and must immediately recognize gain to the extent of Section 1245 depreciation recapture of $40,000, which is not eligible for installment reporting. The gross profit ratio is determined after adding the $40,000 of recapture to the $50,000 of adjusted basis, resulting in a gross profit ratio of 10% [$100,000 – $90,000) / $100,000]. As a result, the $40,000 of depreciation recapture plus 10% × $50,000 cash payment = $5,000 must be recognized this year, while the remaining 10% × $50,000 = $5,000 of gain will be recognized next year when payment on the note is received.

3. Installment obligations arising from non-dealer sales of property used in the taxpayer's trade or business or held for the production of rental income (e.g., factory building, warehouse, office building, apartment building) are subject to an interest charge on the tax that is deferred on such sales to the extent that the amount of deferred payments arising from all dispositions of such property during a taxable year and outstanding as of the close of the taxable year exceeds $5 million. This provision does not apply to installment sales of property if the sales price does not exceed $150,000, to sales of personal use property, and to sales of farm property.

4. A disposition of the installment obligation will trigger recognition of the deferred gain. The entire gain will be recognized immediately if the installment note is sold or otherwise encumbered. The installment obligation (note receivable) must have a market interest rate or else a portion of the gain will be treated as imputed interest.

VII. Expenses

A. Expenses are deemed paid under the cash basis when charged to a credit card.

B. The accrual method must be used to expense inventory sold unless average gross receipts are less than $1 million.

C. For prepaid expenses related to a business under the cash method, an immediate deduction can be taken when paid as long as the benefits from the expenditure do not extend beyond the earlier of:

1. 12 months after benefits first begin *or*

2. The end of the year after the year in which the payment was made.

3. If the 12-month rule is not met, the deduction must be spread over the period for which the expenses apply.

Examples

1. On December 1, 2016, a calendar-year taxpayer pays a $10,000 property insurance premium with a 1-year term that begins on February 1, 2017. The amount paid must be capitalized and is not deductible for 2016 because the benefit attributable to the $10,000 payment extends beyond the end of the taxable year following the taxable year in which the payment is made. The premium will be deductible over the period to which it relates.

2. Assume the same facts as in the last example, except that the policy has a term beginning on December 15, 2016. The 12-month rule applies to the $10,000 payment because the benefit attributable to the payment extends neither more than 12 months beyond December 15, 2016 nor beyond the end of the taxable year following the taxable year in which the payment is made. Thus, the taxpayer is not required to capitalize the payment and may deduct the $10,000 payment in 2016.

D. Notwithstanding the above, prepaid interest must always be amortized over the life of the loan.

E. Under the accrual method of accounting, there are times when it is not clear when economic performance has occurred. Therefore, the following rules have been established:

1. If there is an obligation to **perform** services or goods in the future (i.e., repairs), the deduction does not occur until the goods or services are provided.

2. If there is an obligation to **pay** for future goods or services, the deduction does not occur until the recipient has received the goods or services.

3. The taxpayer can only deduct refunds, rebates, awards, prizes, provision of warranty work or service contracts, taxes, and insurance premiums when actually paid.

4. If the expenditure is a recurring item, and economic performance occurs within 8½ months after the close of the tax year (or when the return is filed if earlier), then the expenditure generally can be deducted in the year incurred.

5. Vacation pay and bonuses are deducted only if paid within 2½ months after the close of the tax year.

F. Capital Expenditure versus Repair

1. It is sometimes difficult to determine whether a cost should be capitalized as part of the property or expensed as a repair. Expenditures that increase the value of the property or substantially increase the property's useful life are capitalized. Costs are also capitalized if the expenditure adapts the property to a new or different use.

2. Costs are deducted as repairs if they maintain the normal operating condition of the asset but do not increase its value or lengthen its life.

Example
TP paints the outside of a factory building. This expenditure would be deducted as a repair, unless it was included as part of a renovation of the entire property.

3. Costs incurred to place an asset in service are capitalized as part of the cost of the property. This includes taxes that are paid as part of the acquisition and the costs of removing unwanted property.

4. Small costs that are not material are expensed as an administrative convenience. Examples include items such as pencils, pens, paper, waste baskets, and so on.

G. IRS regulations provide guidance on the decision to capitalize or expense a particular expenditure.

1. All costs that are incurred in acquiring or producing a unit of property (UOP) are included in its cost, except for employee compensation and overhead costs. The cost includes all related expenditures incurred before the date the asset is placed in service, even of these expenditures would be repairs if incurred after placed in service.

2. A single UOP includes all components that are functionally interdependent. Thus, a building includes the walls, floors, ceilings, roof, windows, doors, electrical systems, plumbing, heating and air systems, and so on. The major exception to this rule is that if a component is treated separately for depreciation purposes, then it will not be grouped into another UOP.

3. The cost of a UOP includes costs incurred to obtain a clean title and investigation costs.

4. The taxpayer can elect to capitalize employee compensation and overhead costs (can elect separately or for both). The election can be made for particular acquisitions.

5. Taxpayers can elect under the de minimis safe harbor election to expense outlays for lower-cost items. The election is irrevocable. This safe harbor applies if the taxpayer:

   a. Has written procedures in place at the beginning of the tax year that provide for the expensing of amounts below a specified dollar amount or that have a useful life of 12 months or less;

   b. Also expenses the items for its accounting/book records; *and*

   c. Insures that items costing more than $5,000 are capitalized ($2,500 if the company does not have acceptable (generally meaning audited) financial statements).

6. The de minimis safe harbor election cannot be made for inventory, land, and certain types of spare parts.

7. Routine maintenance to keep UOPs operating efficiently (such as testing, cleaning, inspecting, and replacing parts) is expensed. To be routine, it must be expected that the expenditure will be needed more than once during the asset's life.

8. An expense cannot be treated as routine maintenance if:

   a. It improves a UOP (treated as a betterment);

   b. A loss has been deducted against the property's basis or the basis has been reduced as part of a sale/exchange;

    c. The asset has deteriorated to a point that it could not be used and the expenditures restore the UOP to an operating condition;

    d. It is to adapt a UOP to a new or different use; *or*

    e. It is for maintenance, improvement, or repair of network assets or certain spare parts.

9. A cost is treated as a betterment if it:

    a. Enlarges or increases the capacity of a UOP *or*

    b. Materially increases the productivity, efficiency, or quality of the UOP.

10. Qualifying small taxpayers (those with $10 million or less average annual gross receipts in the three preceding tax years) can deduct improvements made to an eligible building property (one with an unadjusted basis of $1 million or less). The new safe harbor election applies only if the total amount paid during the tax year for repairs, maintenance, improvements, and similar activities performed on the eligible building does not exceed the lesser of $10,000 or 2% of the building's unadjusted basis.

11. Qualifying small taxpayers (including businesses with less than $10 million in assets) may elect to make these changes in accounting methods on a cut-off basis. This allows the new accounting method to be used solely for amounts paid or incurred, and dispositions, in taxable years beginning after 2013. Since prior years are not affected, no adjustment to income is needed for the change. If elected, these taxpayers will not be required to file Form 3115, *Application for Change in Accounting Method*.

Taxation of Employee Benefits

This lesson describes the income implications of benefits that employers often provide their employees.

After studying this lesson, you should be able to:

1. Determine the tax consequences of insurance benefits received from employers.

2. Assess the tax effects of the receipt of other fringe benefits from employers.

3. Compute the income recognized from the receipt and exercise of stock options.

Any benefit received by an employee is included in gross income unless there is a specific provision that excludes the benefit.

I. Insurance Benefits Received

A. Benefits from Taxpayer-Purchased Policies—Health and disability insurance proceeds are excluded if the taxpayer paid the premiums.

1. Benefits under a policy purchased by the taxpayer are excluded even if payments are a substitute for lost wages.

B. Benefits from Employer-Purchased Policies

1. If the employer paid the premium for disability insurance, then proceeds from the disability policy are taxed to the recipient.

2. Health insurance proceeds may be excluded if the taxpayer's employer paid the premiums. In this case, medical expense reimbursements are excluded:

   a. As long as the expenses reimbursed are for qualified medical expenses (thus, if the reimbursement exceeds the qualified expenses then the excess is income), *or*

   b. If payment is received for loss of (or the use of) a body part or permanent disfigurement.

   c. These exclusions apply for the employee and the employee's spouse and dependents.

C. In certain cases, members of the armed forces who were injured while performing combat duty do not have to include disability payments in income.

D. Benefits received from long-term care policies are excluded from income up to $360 per day in 2017, but excess amounts over this limit are not included if the funds were used for actual long-term care services.

Example
TP was disabled last year. TP's provided-employer health insurance paid his medical expenses of $50,000 and paid TP $40,000 for the wages TP lost while he was disabled. TP may exclude the $50,000, but TP is taxed on the disability proceeds of $40,000 because the employer paid the insurance premiums.

Disability Insurance Summary

- Premiums paid by taxpayer—**not** deductible

- Premiums paid by taxpayer's employer—**excluded** from taxpayer's income; deductible by employer

- Benefits received by the taxpayer from a policy paid for by the taxpayer—**excluded** from income

- Benefits received by the taxpayer from a policy paid for by the employer—**included** in income

II. Fringe Benefits

A. **Life Insurance Premiums**—Those paid by an employer are excluded on the basis of group-term life insurance.

   1. The limit on this exclusion is the amount of premiums necessary for a $50,000 face value group-term policy.

   2. For amounts over $50,000, the insurance benefits are taxable based on the rates in an IRS table. The rates are based on the age of the taxpayer.

   3. Note that this exclusion applies only to term life insurance policies. If an employer pays premiums on a whole-life insurance policy for an employee the value of those premiums are included in income.

Example
UT, Inc. provides life insurance for its employees equal to their annual compensation. T's annual compensation is $80,000 and the includible income per $1,000 of coverage is $1.20 per month (T is 42 years old).

T can exclude payments for the first $50,000 of coverage from income. She is taxed on the excess coverage of $30,000 ($80,000 – $50,000). She has 30 excess increments ($30,000/1,000) each of which is taxed at $1.20 per month, so her income inclusion is $432 (30 × $1.20 × 12).

B. **Employer-Purchased Health and Long-Term Care Plans**

   1. **Health insurance premiums**—Those paid by an employer are excluded.

      a. **Corollary**—Self-employed individuals can deduct 100% of health insurance premiums paid for coverage of self, spouse, and dependents. However, the deduction cannot exceed the taxpayer's net earnings from self-employment.

   2. Employer paid premiums for disability insurance plans and long-term care policies are also excluded from income.

   3. Employer paid premiums for wage continuation insurance are included in income, because a wage continuation plan is not considered to be a health plan.

   4. Group health plans and health insurance issuers providing dependent coverage of children generally must continue to provide coverage of children until age 26.

C. **Personal Expenses Paid by Employer**—If an employer pays the expenses of an employee, the payment is income to the employee because it is compensatory in nature.

Example
In lieu of additional salary, an employer makes a $200 car payment for an employee. The $200 payment is income to the employee.

D. **Food and Lodging**—The value of food and lodging provided by employer to employees is excluded from the income of the employee if the following conditions are met.

   1. The provision must be for the convenience of the employer meaning that the food and lodging must be provided for a noncompensatory reason. For example, a hospital may provide free meals in the hospital's cafeteria for doctors so they will be on call in case an emergency occurs.

   2. Employer-provided meals must be provided in kind (i.e., not cash for meals) on the employer's premises.

   3. The employer must require the employee to accept lodging as a condition of employment for it to be excluded from income. It must also be provided on employer's premises.

Example
EE employs TP as a manager of a motel. EE provides lodging worth $2,000 to TP in order to keep TP on call in case of complaints. TP may exclude the value of the lodging if EE requires that TP accept the lodging as a condition of employment.

E. Working Condition—Fringe benefits are excluded from the employee's income.

    1. A working condition benefit is a benefit provided by the employer that would be deductible (as an employee business expense) if the employee had instead paid the expense.

Example
T is an attorney and his law firm reimburses him for his dues to the American Bar Association and his subscription to the *National Law Review*. These reimbursements are excluded from income as working condition fringe benefits

F. De Minimis Fringes—Are excluded because these benefits are small in value and infrequent. Examples include occasional use of the copy or fax machine, typing services, and free coffee provided in the office.

G. No Additional Cost Services—Are excluded benefits when provided to employee, their spouses, or dependents.

    1. These benefits are those provided by employers at no substantial additional cost, such as plane tickets provided to airline employees when there are empty seats.

    2. For businesses with more than one line of business (e.g., operating a hotel and a rental car service), the exclusion only applies for services provided in the business line that the employee works in.

> **Note**
> *Exclusion applies only to services provided by employers, not to products given to or sold at a discount to employees. If an employee is allowed to take groceries home that have met their expiration date, the value of the groceries would not be excluded since they are a product and not a service.*

H. Employee Discounts—These are excluded if the discount is not excessive (except on realty and marketable securities).

    1. The discount is limited to 20% of the value of services.

    2. The limit on the discount for purchases of merchandise is the average gross profit percentage for the employer.

Example
T is employed at an office supply store and is allowed to buy a computer that cost the store $900 (offered for sale at $1,300) for $1,000. Since T is paying at least the store's cost, the discount does not exceed the gross profit and is excluded from income.

If the store also provides shipping services for customers, and T is allowed to ship items at a 50% discount, the portion of the discount that exceeds 20% of the value of the services is included in T's income.

I. Nominal Gifts—The value of nominal gifts to employees is excluded up to $25 per employee, as long as the gifts are not cash or gift certificates.

Example
TP is employed by a grocery store that provides all employees with a complimentary turkey for Thanksgiving. If the value of the turkey is less than $25, then the gift is excluded by TP.

J. Safety and Length of Service Achievement Awards—Are excluded from income and are subject to a limit of $400 if not a qualified plan, and $1,600 if part of a qualified plan.

1. The award will be taxed if it is made in cash.

2. The award can be given only because of length of service or safety records.

3. The award can be given no more than once every five years.

K. Transportation and Parking—Employer reimbursements for mass transit transportation ($255 per month) and parking ($255 per month) are excludible up to the limits shown in 2017.

L. Reimbursement for commuting with a bicycle can be excluded up to $20 (not indexed for inflation) per month. Qualified expenses include the purchase, repair, and storage of the bike if it is regularly used for commuting to work.

Example
TP is employed by a firm that provides all employees with monthly parking passes. If the value of the parking benefit is less than $255 per month (2017), then this benefit is excluded by TP.

M. Other Special Benefits—"Qualified" benefits provided by employer may be excluded, including:

1. Employees can **exclude** (up to $5,000; $2,500 if married filing separately) from gross income the value of **child and dependent care services** provided by the employer, if the services are provided so that the **employee can work**.

2. Employees can exclude (up to $5,250) from gross income the value of assistance provided by the employer **for undergraduate and graduate tuition, fees, books, and supplies.**

3. Employees can **exclude** from gross income up to $13,570 (in 2017) of **expenses incurred to adopt a child**, if these expenses are reimbursed by the employer. The exclusion is **phased-out** at AGI levels between $203,540 and $243,540 in 2017.

4. If the adoption expenses are not reimbursed by the employer, the taxpayer receives a **nonrefundable credit** for qualified adoption expenses up to the same $13,570 limit per child.

5. Employer reimbursement of moving expenses are excluded, but only if the moving expenses would have been deductible by the employee if he or she had paid for them.

6. Use of athletic facilities provided at a location owned or leased by the employer are excluded. This benefit applies to the employee, the employee's spouse and dependents as well as retirees.

7. Employer-provided retirement advice is excluded.

8. Qualified tuition reduction by nonprofit educational institutions is excluded and applies to the following: the employee; the employee's spouse and dependents; and undergraduate education, except for graduate students who receive tuition waivers for serving as a graduate assistant.

9. Benefits paid to the family of a deceased employee are included in income.

10. **Flexible Spending Accounts (FSAs)** are accounts set up by employers to allow their employees to contribute a portion of their salary (pretax funds) to an account. The funds in the account must be used during the tax year to pay for specific expenses of the taxpayer. Specifically, accounts can be created to pay medical, dependent care, or adoption expenses. One drawback of an FSA is that any funds not used by the end of the tax year (may be extended to 2½ months after year-end at option of employer) are forfeited by the employee.

11. Contributions by the employer to state unemployment insurance funds are not taxable to the employee.

N. Discrimination Rules

1. Most of the fringe benefits discussed in this lesson cannot discriminate against non–highly compensated employees. That is, the benefit cannot be extended to only those who are highly compensated.

2. If a benefit is discriminatory, then the highly compensated employees are taxed on the fair market value of the benefit. Non–highly compensated employees are not taxed on the value if it is otherwise excludible.

3. The discrimination rules do not apply to the following fringe benefits (so highly compensated employees would not have to include the value in income):

    a. Health insurance premiums (as long as plan is not self-insured)

    b. Working condition fringe benefits

    c. Transportation and parking fringe benefits

    d. Lodging on the employer's premises

O. **Accountable Plans**—When employees are reimbursed for business expenses, the determination if this is taxable depends on whether the employee has an accountable plan.

1. If employee business expenses are reimbursed under an accountable plan, then the reimbursement is not taxable (for FICA or income tax) and the employee gets no deduction for the expense. Technically, the tax law requires the reimbursement to be included as income and the employee's deduction is for AGI. Since this always nets to zero, the IRS allows the income and deduction to not be reported.

2. If the expenses are reimbursed, but not under an accountable plan, the reimbursement must be included in income (for FICA and income tax) and the deduction is a 2% miscellaneous itemized deduction.

3. For a plan to be accountable:

    a. It must substantiate all expenses to be reimbursed; *and*

    b. Excess reimbursements must be returned to the employer.

P. **Cafeteria Plans**

1. Under a cafeteria plan, an employee can choose between cash and certain "qualified benefits."

2. Cash is treated as wages.

3. Qualified benefits are tax-free benefits if they would have been tax-free if not offered through a cafeteria plan.

4. Qualified benefits include:

    a. Benefits/coverage under accident or health plans

    b. Long-term or short-term disability coverage

    c. Group-term life insurance coverage

    d. Dependent care assistance programs

    e. Section 401(k) plans

    f. Contributions through health savings accounts

    g. Adoption assistance

III. **Stock Options**

A. **Key Dates for Stock Options**

1. **Grant date**—Date the option is granted to employee.

2. **Exercise date**—Date that the option is exercised and the stock is purchased.

3. **Sale date**—Date that the stock is sold.

B. **Nonqualified Stock Options**

1. No income is recognized when the option is granted.

2. On the exercise date, the employee-recognized ordinary income is equal to:

> (FMV of stock − Exercise price) × # of shares exercised.

    a. The employer receives a salary deduction for this same amount.

    b. The employee has a basis in the stock equal to its FMV on the exercise date. When the stock is later sold, this basis is used in computing the gain/loss from the sale..

C. Incentive Stock Options—No income is recognized (except for AMT) when the option is **granted or exercised**. The consequences when the stock itself is later sold vary:

> **Note**
> *For an ISO, the exercise price cannot be less than the FMV of the stock on the grant date.*

    1. The gain on sale is LTCG if acquired stock is:

        a. Held more than one year; *and*

        b. Not sold until after two years from the date the option was granted.The employer does not receive a deduction.

D. If these requirements are not met, the option is treated like a **non-qualified stock option**:

> **Note**
> *Even the tax effects are like those for an NQSO; the timing of the income recognition still takes effect on the date the stock is sold, not the exercise date.*

    a. The gain on the stock sale is ordinary income and the employer receives a deduction equal to the stock's FMV on the exercise date over the exercise price;

    b. The difference in the FMV on the sale date and the FMV on the exercise date is capital gain or loss.

Summary of Tax Effects of Stock Options		
	Incentive Stock Option	Nonqualified Stock Option
Grant date	None	None
Exercise date	None (except for AMT)	Ordinary income
Sale date	Ordinary income/capital gain (AMT reverses)	

E. The corporation receives a deduction only for the ordinary income portion.

IV. Readily Ascertainable Value

    1. If a nonqualified stock option has a **readily ascertainable value** on the grant date, the recipient is taxed on the FMV of the option at that time. In that case, there are no other tax consequences until the stock is sold. That is, there are no income tax consequences on the exercise date.

    2. To have a readily ascertainable value, generally the option must be traded on an active market. Note that if the recipient cannot trade the option because of a restriction from the employer (which is often the case) then the option's value is considered to be zero on the grant date.

Taxation of Retirement Plans

After studying this lesson, you should be able to:

1. Identify common types of retirement plans including IRAs.

2. Delineate the key differences between traditional and Roth IRAs.

3. Determine the tax consequences of payments made to different types of retirement plans.

4. Assess the income effects of distributions from retirement plans.

I. **Retirement Savings**—Contributions made by an employer (and sometimes the contributions by an employee) to a "qualified" retirement plan are not subject to tax until the contributions are withdrawn from the plan.

    A. **Qualified Pension Plans**—Contributions of salary to "qualified" pension plans are deferred until distributions are made from the pension.

        1. For a plan to be "qualified," it must meet nondiscriminatory, funding, vesting, and certain participation/coverage requirements.

        2. Early withdrawals (before age 59½) trigger a penalty in addition to the taxation of the withdrawal.

        3. Employees can also make elective deferrals into certain qualified plans and the deferred amounts are not subject to current taxation. The most common type of elective deferral plans are 401(k)s, SIMPLE plans, 457 plans and 403(b) plans. More explanation of these plans is provided below.

    B. **Individual Retirement Accounts (IRAs)**—The income earned on contributions made to an individual retirement account is not subject to tax in the current year. The taxation of these contributions varies according to the type of the account—traditional, Roth, or educational.

    C. **Traditional IRAs**—Provide a deduction for eligible contributions.

        1. **Contributions**—The limit on any IRA contribution (deductible or nondeductible) is $5,500 (2017), or compensation (an additional $1,000 catch-up contribution is allowed for taxpayers over the age of 50). Hence, for a married couple, the limit on IRA contributions is $11,000, or combined compensation. Excess contributions are subject to a 6% excise tax each year until withdrawn.

        2. **IRA deductions**—If the taxpayer is not a participant in a qualified pension plan, the IRA contributions can be deducted for AGI. IRA contributions can also be deducted by taxpayers who are active participants in qualified plans, but this deduction is phased out proportionately over a $10,000 range ($20,000 if married filing jointly) if the taxpayer's modified AGI exceeds the limit below.

Definition
Modified AGI: Modified AGI is generally computed as: AGI + IRA deduction + Domestic production activities deduction + Student loan interest + Foreign earned income exclusion and housing cost exclusion + Exclusion for employer-provided adoption assistance

---

Taxable years beginning in	Joint Returns Phase-Out range
2017	$99,000 – $119,000

Taxable years beginning in	Single Taxpayers Phase-Out range
2017	$62,000 – $72,000

Example
TP is a single taxpayer who has modified AGI of $64,000. This year (2017), TP is covered by a qualified pension plan, and he made a $5,500 contribution to an IRA. Because of the phase-out, TP loses 20% ($1,100) of the IRA deduction ([$64,000 − $62,000]/$10,000). Hence, TP deducts $4,400 ($5,500 − $1,100) of the IRA contribution. The remaining $1,100 is a nondeductible contribution.

3. Note that the phase-out of the IRA deduction is always rounded up to the nearest $10, and the minimum deduction is $200 if the entire deduction is not phased out.

4. A married taxpayer who is not an active participant can deduct contributions even if the taxpayer's spouse is an active participant. However, this deduction is phased out proportionately over a $10,000 range if the joint modified AGI exceeds $186,000 in 2017.

5. Taxpayers who cannot deduct IRA contributions can nonetheless defer the income earned by nondeductible IRA contributions to traditional IRAs. Nondeductible contributions to traditional IRAs are reported on Form 8606. The taxpayer's basis in the IRA is computed on this form.

6. IRA contributions must be made by the original due date of the return, April 15, to be deductible for the previous tax year.

D. Roth IRA—Contributions are not deductible.

1. The limit on contributions to a Roth IRA is the same as those to a traditional IRA (compensation of $5,500, or $6,500 for those 50 or older [$11,000 if married filing jointly]) without consideration of the rule about participation in a qualified pension. The limit on Roth contributions is coordinated with other IRAs so that combined contributions to all IRAs cannot exceed these limits.

2. Covered contributions to a Roth IRA are phased out proportionately if the taxpayer's modified AGI for 2016 exceeds $186,000 for married filing jointly (a $10,000 range) or $118,000 for single taxpayers (a $15,000 range).

E. Conversion of a Traditional IRA to a Roth IRA—A traditional IRA can be converted to a Roth IRA, but this is a taxable event.

1. The taxpayer must recognize gain at the time of the conversion to the extent that the conversion amount exceeds the tax basis in the IRA.

2. The same rules apply to conversions of 401(k) plans into Roth plans.

F. Coverdell Education Savings Account—Contributions to a Coverdell Education Savings Account (formerly Education IRA) are not deductible, but income may not be subject to tax.

1. A Coverdell Education Savings Account must be established exclusively to pay higher education costs (tuition, fees, books, and room and board reduced by tax-free scholarships and similar payments, including elementary and secondary school expenses) for a beneficiary who is under age 18 (unless a special-needs student).

2. Contributions to a Coverdell Education Savings Account are limited to $2,000 per beneficiary, per year. The contribution is phased out proportionately if the taxpayer's AGI exceeds $190,000 for married filing jointly (a $30,000 range) or $95,000 for single taxpayers (a $15,000 range).

II. Retirement Distributions

A. Withdrawals from a "Traditional" IRA—Are taxed as income in the year of withdrawal.

1. If the taxpayer has made nondeductible contributions to the IRA, then withdrawals are prorated between the total nondeductible contributions and the remaining balance in the account (because the taxpayer has basis for the nondeductible contributions). The portion of withdrawals that constitute nondeductible contributions is not subject to tax.

2. Withdrawals from a traditional IRA may be subject to a penalty tax of 10%. This tax is not imposed if the taxpayer is disabled or age 59½. Withdrawals are also exempt from the penalty when they are used for death or disability expenses or

   a. Made in the form of certain periodic payments,

   b. Used to pay medical expenses in excess of the allowable percentage of AGI,

   c. Used to purchase the health insurance of an individual who is unemployed for at least 12 weeks,

   d. For first-time home buyer expenses (limited to $10,000),

   e. Distributed for qualified higher education expenses,

   f. Levied by the IRS, *or*

   g. Made by individuals called or ordered to active military duty.

3. Withdrawals from a traditional IRA must begin when the taxpayer reaches age 70½.

4. Up to $100,000 of distributions from an IRA will be tax-free if contributed to a charitable organization by an individual age 70½ or over.

5. If a taxpayer receives a distribution from an IRA that would be subject to the 10% penalty, the taxpayer can deposit the funds into another eligible retirement plan within 60 days and avoid the penalty. In such a case the distribution would also not be included in income.

B. **Withdrawals from a Roth or Coverdell Education Savings Account**—May be tax exempt.

   1. Withdrawals of contributions from a Roth IRA are not taxed as income. Withdrawals are assumed to be from contributions first, rather than prorated between contributions and accrued income.

   2. Withdrawals of income accumulated in a Roth IRA are not taxed as income if the distribution occurred five years or more from the date of the initial contribution, and if it is made on or after an individual attains age 59½. Withdrawals of income are also not taxed if used to pay for the taxpayer's death or disability expenses or if used for first-time home buyer expenses or certain education expenses.

   3. Withdrawals of contributions of income from a Coverdell Education Savings Account are not subject to tax if used to pay higher education expenses, or rolled into a Coverdell Education Savings Account for a member of the beneficiary's family.

   4. Taxpayers may waive the exclusion for withdrawals from a Coverdell Education Savings Account if they prefer to claim the Hope/Lifetime credits for the educational expenditures.

   5. If a withdrawal (or a portion of a withdrawal) from a Coverdell Education Savings Account is not used for education expenses, then the withdrawal is prorated between total contributions and accumulated income. The portion of the withdrawal that constitutes income is subject to tax plus the 10% penalty tax.

   6. Withdrawals from a Roth IRA are reported on page 2 of Form 8606.

C. **Distribution Rules from Qualified Plans**

   1. Most taxpayers do not have any basis in their qualified retirement plans, so all distributions are taxable. Basis is not received for employer contributions that are not taxed and for employee contributions that are deducted on the employee's tax return.

   2. If a taxpayer made a contribution of his own funds to the plan and did not receive a deduction for the contributions (e.g., after-tax funds were used), basis is received for these contributions.

   3. If a taxpayer has basis in the retirement plan, then the annuity rules are used to determine the taxable portion of each payment.

      a. Each payment is part income/part return of capital.

      b. Excluded Portion = (Cost of Annuity/Expected Return) × Annual Payment.

    c. Expected return is annual annuity amount multiplied by life expectancy determined by the IRS table.

    d. Exclusion ratio stays the same until the entire cost is fully recovered; additional payments are fully taxable.

    e. If the annuitant dies before the total cost is recovered, the unrecovered cost is a deduction on the taxpayer's final return.

Example

Mr. Kitten purchased an annuity contract for $50,000 from the XYZ Company on March 31, Year 1. He is to receive $1,000 per month starting April 1, Year 1 and continuing for life. He has a life expectancy of 10 years as of March 31, Year 1. Mr. Kitten's reportable annuity income for Year 1 is:

Cost of Annuity ($50,000) / Expected Return (120 months × $1,000 = $120,000) × Pmt. ($9,000) = $3,750

Includible Amount = $9,000 − $3,750 = $5,250

---

    4. The total retirement annuity and the taxable portion of the annuity are reported on Form 1040 each year.

    5. Withdrawals from a qualified plan may be subject to a penalty tax of 10%. This tax is not imposed if the taxpayer is at least age 59½. Withdrawals are also exempt from the penalty when:

        a. Used for death or disability expenses,

        b. Made in the form of certain periodic payments, or

        c. Used to pay medical expenses in excess of the applicable percentage of AGI.

D. Tax on Excess Accumulations

    1. Distributions from qualified plans must begin by the "required beginning date" and the payment each year must be at least equal to the required minimum distribution.

    2. If the required distribution is not made, a tax equal to 50% of the required distribution not made must be paid.

    3. The required beginning date is by April 1 of the later of:

        a. the year the taxpayer reaches age 70½ or

        b. the year the employee retires.

III. Special Retirement Plans—Self-employed taxpayers may make deductible contributions to special retirement plans.

    A. Qualified plans for self-employed individuals are called Keogh or HR 10 plans. These plans have the same limits as pension plans, except the maximum percentage limit is based upon self-employment earnings. For 2017, contributions are limited to the lesser of $54,000 or 100% of earned income. Earned income equals net earnings from self-employment less 50% of the self-employment tax less the allowable Keogh contribution.

    B. Section 457 plans may be offered by state and local governments and tax-exempt organizations. Employees may defer up to $18,000 in 2017.

    C. A 401(k) plan allows voluntary employee contributions to reduce taxable salary up to a maximum of $18,000, plus $6,000 catch-up for those aged 50 and over (2017). A 403(b) plan is similar to a 401(k) plan but is offered by education institutions. The same limits apply for 403(b) plans.

    D. A simplified employee pension (SEP) is a plan where the employer may contribute to a SEP-IRA for each employee. Contributions can be limited to employees who (a) are at least 21 years old, (b) have performed service for the employer during at least three of the last five years, and (c) have received compensation from the employer of at least $600 in 2017.

1. Contributions can be discretionary, but must be a uniform percentage of compensation for each employee.

2. Contributions must be 100% vested at all times.

3. Contributions for 2017 to an employee's SEP-IRA are excludable from the employee's income to the extent they do not exceed the lesser of:

   a. 25% of the employee's compensation; or

   b. $54,000.

4. To take a deduction for contributions for a particular year, the contributions made for that year must be made by the due date (including extensions) of the employer's income tax return for that year.

E. Employers establishing a SIMPLE IRA plan make either matching or nonelective contributions. Like SEPs, a SIMPLE IRA plan allows an employer to make contributions toward its employees' retirements, subject to higher limits than those applicable to IRA contributions, without having to deal with the complex compliance and reporting rules that apply to qualified retirement plans.

   1. The limit for SIMPLE plans is $12,500 for 2017.

   2. SIMPLE IRA plans are available to employers with 100 or fewer employees that receive at least $5,000 of compensation in the prior calendar year. However, employers who have established a SIMPLE IRA plan but who no longer qualify because they exceed the 100-employee limit have a two-year grace period under which they can continue to maintain the plan.

F. Employers may create a Roth 401(k) for their employees. Similar to Roth IRAs, after-tax dollars are contributed to these plans, but all distributions from these plans are tax-exempt.

IV. Section 529 Plans

A. These plans are used to save for college expenses through a vehicle that allows the earnings to be excluded from gross income.

B. Contributions are not deductible, and a beneficiary must be specified for the plan. States typically allow lifetime contributions of as much as $250,000 to the plan.

C. Earnings in the plan are tax-deferred.

D. Distributions from the plans are excluded from income to the extent that the distribution is used to pay for tuition, fees, books, etc., and reasonable room and board costs. Distributions not used for a qualified purpose are subject to income taxation and a 10% penalty.

V. ABLE Accounts

A. ABLE accounts were created to encourage individuals and families to set aside funds to support individuals with disabilities or who are blind to help them maintain their quality of life and health.

B. No deduction is allowed for contributions. Assets can be accumulated tax-free and distributions are not taxable if used to pay disability related expenses.

C. Nonqualified distributions are taxable and subject to a 10% penalty.

D. Each disabled person is limited to one ABLE account and total annual contributions by all individuals to any one ABLE account is limited to $14,000 (2017). Aggregate contributions are subject to the state limit for Section 529 accounts.

E. Eligible individuals must have become blind or disabled before turning 26 and must be entitled to benefits under the Supplemental Security Income (SSI) or Social Security Disability Insurance (SSDI) programs.

F.   If an eligible individual dies, any amounts remaining in the account are subject to income tax on investment earnings, but not to the 10% penalty.

VI. Nonqualified Deferred Compensation Plans

A.   If compensation is deferred but not under a qualified plan, the compensation is taxed currently unless the provisions of Section 409A are met. In general, the employee must agree to defer the compensation before the beginning of the tax year in which the compensation will be earned. At the time of deferral, the employee must specify when the compensation will be paid in the future.

B.   If the provisions of Section 409A are not met, then in addition to the compensation being taxed in the year earned, an excise tax equal to 20% of the compensation must also be paid. Interest is also charged on the underpayment at the underpayment rate plus 1%.

C.   The business that has the responsibility for paying the deferred compensation cannot deduct it until the year that the employee recognizes the compensation as income

Deductions

Deductions—Basic Principles

After studying this lesson, you should be able to:

1. Classify activities as related to trade/business, investment, or personal activities.

2. Apply deductibility rules for each activity type.

3. Recognize expenditures that are not deductible when certain provisions are met.

4. Determine when prepayments are deductible.

I. **General Rules**

   A. Deductions can be divided into two broad categories: **deductions for AGI** and **deductions from AGI** (i.e., itemized deductions).

   B. Activities/transactions can be divided into three mutually exclusive categories:

   1. Personal

   2. Trade/business

   3. Investment

   C. Expenses related to one's **personal activities cannot be deducted** unless specifically provided for in the IRC (e.g., charitable contributions, mortgage interest).

   D. Expenses related to **trade or business activities** are deductible if they are related to the business operations and are **ordinary, necessary, and reasonable**.

   E. Expenses related to **investment activities** or other activities that produce income are deductible if **ordinary, necessary, and reasonable**. Expenses related to the **management or maintenance of property** and in connection with the **determination of any tax** are deductible.

> **Definitions**
>
> *Ordinary and Necessary*: Interpreted to mean the nature of the expenditure is customary and appropriate under the circumstances.
>
> *Reasonable*: Interpreted to mean that an expenditure cannot be extravagant in amount.

II. **Disallowed Deductions**—There are several expenditures for which a deduction is prohibited.

   A. No personal expenses are deductible unless specifically allowed, including personal legal expenses (unless the legal expense relates to tax planning or tax preparation services).

   B. Expenditures benefiting more than one period must be capitalized rather than expensed.

   C. No expenses can be deducted if the expenditure is against public policy. Payments in violation of public policy are not necessary and not deductible. Examples include bribes, fines, and penalties. Expenses of operating an illegal drug business are not deductible. However, cost of goods sold can be deducted for an illegal drug business. The ordinary, necessary, and reasonable expenses of operating other illegal businesses are permitted (as long as the expense itself is not against public policy).

D. No expenses can be deducted if the expense is used to generate tax-exempt income. Thus, a taxpayer (whether an individual or a business) may not deduct life insurance premiums in which the taxpayer is directly or indirectly the beneficiary. However, an employer may deduct the group term life insurance premiums if the insured employee or his/her beneficiaries would receive the insurance proceeds.

E. Lobbying expenses at the state and federal level; deductions are permitted at the city and county government level.

F. For publicly traded companies, executive compensation for the CEO and the four other most highly compensated officers that exceeds $1 million per person is not deductible unless the income is based on a performance-based compensation plan.

G. Specific disallowed deductions from previous exams include life insurance premiums, funeral expenses, and disability insurance premiums.

Deductions for AGI

After studying this lesson, you should be able to:

1. Distinguish between deductions for AGI and deductions from AGI.

2. List the most common deductions for AGI and summarize the deductibility requirements, particularly for moving expenses and student loan interest.

Tax Forms for This Lesson: Form 1040 and Schedules C, E, and F (available for download and printing from the lesson overview of your software).

I. **Types of Deductions**—Because the tax laws only allow the deduction of certain specific expenses, it is necessary to identify qualifying expenditures. Each deduction is classified as either for AGI or from AGI. This lesson focuses on deductions for AGI.

Definition
AGI: This acronym refers to "adjusted gross income." AGI is calculated by subtracting deductions for AGI from gross income.

II. **Deductions for AGI**

    A. Deductions for AGI primarily consist of business-related expenses. These deductions are subject to few(er) limits than itemized deductions.

    B. **Business Expenses**—Associated with a "trade" are deductible for AGI.

Definition
Trade: An activity with a continuous level of profit seeking, such as in the case of a self-employed taxpayer who depends on the activity for his or her livelihood.

        1. Deductions for AGI are often claimed on separate forms where the deductions serve to directly offset the income generated by the activity.

    Example
Trade expenses offset trade income directly on Schedule C, whereas rental expenses offset rental revenues on Schedule E.

        2. Expenses associated with rental and royalty activities are deducted "for" AGI whether or not the activity is considered a trade.

    C. **Nonbusiness Deductions**—There are several major categories of *non-business deductions, which are deducted for AGI.*

        1. Alimony payments (discussed in the lesson "Gross Income—Other Inclusions")

        2. Half of the self-employment taxes paid by self-employed taxpayers

        3. 100% of the medical insurance premiums (not exceeding self-employment income) paid by a self-employed taxpayer (including spouse, children under age 27, and dependents) for taxpayers (and spouse) who are not eligible to participate in an employer subsidized health plan

            a. The same applies for premiums paid for long-term care insurance by self-employed individuals who are not eligible to participate in an employer subsidized long-term care plan.

4. Moving expenses

5. IRA (Keogh) contributions and other contributions to self-employed retirement plans (discussed in the lesson "Taxation of Retirement Plans")

6. Interest on student loans

7. Contributions to Health Savings Accounts (discussed in the lesson "Taxation of Retirement Plans")

8. Attorney's fees and court costs for discrimination suits

9. Penalty for early withdrawal of savings

10. Domestic production activities deduction (discussed in the lesson "Special Corporate Deductions")

11. Other deductions for AGI include forfeited interest on premature withdrawals, repayment of jury pay, and expenses associated with reforestation, clean fuels, and performing artists

12. Qualified higher education expenses

13. Certain educator expenses

III. **Moving Expenses**—To be deductible, moving expenses must be associated with a job change or a first job.

   A. The new job location must add 50 miles to the old commute to justify deduction.

   B. The taxpayer must be active in a new job for a substantial period after the move.

Definition

Substantial Period of Employment: For an employee, this is 39 weeks during the next 12 months. A self-employed taxpayer must meet this requirement, as well as an additional requirement of 78 weeks during the next 24 months. This requirement is waived if it is not met because of death, disability, involuntary separation without cause, or transfer for the benefit of the employer.

   C. Qualifying expenses for the move are limited to reasonable amounts paid to move possessions and transportation costs (not meals) for taxpayer and others residing with the taxpayer. If a personal automobile is used, transportation costs are computed at 17 cents per mile (2017). The cost of storing and insuring possessions while being moved is deductible, limited to any consecutive 30-day period after the possessions are moved from the former residence (and before they are delivered to the new residence).

   D. The following expenses are not deductible as moving expenses:

   a. Meals

   b. Cost of selling old or purchasing new home

   c. Car license/registration costs

   d. Driver's license fees

   e. House hunting costs (pre- or post-move)

   f. Travel costs to former home

   g. Temporary living costs in new location

Example

TP was transferred from New York to Florida by his employer. TP incurred the following expenses:

Lodging and travel while moving	$1,000
Pre-move house hunting	$1,200
Costs of moving personal effects	$1,800

What is the deductible moving expense if TP is employed full-time? Assuming TP meets the employment test after the move, then $2,800 can be deducted for AGI.

IV. Student Loan Interest—Interest paid on student loans is deductible.

Definitions

Student Loan: Is one whose proceeds are used to pay "qualifying" educational expenses of the taxpayer, his or her spouse, or dependents (at the time of the expenditure).

Qualifying Educational Expenses: Include tuition, fees, and room and board reduced by educational exclusions (scholarships, education IRAs, education savings bonds, etc.).

    A. The deduction is limited to $2,500 of interest that is not otherwise deductible.

    B. The deduction is phased out in 2017 proportionately for married taxpayers with an AGI in excess of $135,000 over a range of $30,000 ($65,000 for unmarried over a range of $15,000).

    C. If the parent claims the student as a dependent, the parent can deduct the interest, even if the student paid it. If the student pays the interest and is not a dependent, then the student deducts the interest on her return.

V. Qualified Higher Education Expenses Are Deductible.

Definition

Qualified Higher Educational Expenses: Defined the same as expenses under the Hope credit: tuition and academic fees required for enrollment or attendance at a post-secondary educational institution by the taxpayer, spouse, and/or dependents.

    A. The deduction is limited to $4,000 of otherwise nondeductible expenses reduced by other tax-free benefits (such as scholarships or Coverdell Education Savings Account distributions). The deduction cannot be claimed for a student if the Hope or Lifetime credit has been claimed with respect to that same student.

    B. The deduction is permitted for taxpayers with a modified AGI that does not exceed $65,000 ($135,000 for joint returns). If AGI exceeds these amounts, a deduction of $2,000 is permitted if AGI does not exceed $80,000 ($165,000 for joint returns). If AGI exceeds these higher limits, then no deduction is allowed.

VI. Educator Expenses—An individual who is a teacher in grades kindergarten through grade 12 can deduct, as a deduction for AGI, up to $250 for expenses related to books, equipment, and supplies that are used in the classroom. Professional development expenses also qualify if they relate to the subject matter being taught. Any excess over $250 is a 2% miscellaneous itemized deduction.

VII. Health Savings Accounts

    A. Qualified taxpayers can contribute funds to a health savings account and receive a deduction for AGI in the year the contributions are made. In 2017, annual contributions are limited to $3,400 for singles and $6,750 for families. Distributions must be used exclusively for qualified medical expenses. (Health insurance premiums are not qualified.)

B. Amounts distributed from a health savings account to pay qualified medical expenses of the account beneficiary are not includible in income. Nonqualified distributions are included in gross income and subject to a 20% penalty. Medicine and drugs are qualified only if they are prescription drugs or insulin.

C. To qualify, a taxpayer must be covered only under a high-deductible health plan and may not be entitled to benefits under Medicare. In 2017, a high-deductible health plan must have a deductible of at least $1,300 ($2,600 for family coverage), and annual out-of-pocket expenses cannot exceed $6,550 ($13,100 for family coverage).

Itemized Deductions—Medical, Taxes, Interest

After studying this lesson, you should be able to:

1. Compute the standard deduction for taxpayers including special additions if certain requirements are met.

2. Identify allowable medical expenses and compute deductible medical expense.

3. Delineate between the types of taxes that are and are not deductible.

4. Apply the detailed rules for determining the deduction for home mortgage interest.

5. Calculate the deduction for investment interest.

Tax Form for This Lesson: Form 1040 Schedule A (available for download and printing from the lesson overview of your software).

I. **Itemized Deductions (from AGI)**—Itemized deductions consist primarily of non-trade business expenses (employee and investment expenses) and a few personal expenses that can be deducted. These deductions are subject to individual limits, and in the aggregate must exceed the standard deduction before any benefit will be realized.

    A. **Personal Itemized Deductions**—Six types of personal expenses may be itemized.

        1. Medical expenses

        2. Interest

        3. Taxes

        4. Charitable contributions

        5. Casualty losses

        6. Miscellaneous deductions

    B. All itemized deductions are reported on Form 1040 Schedule A by the taxpayer.

II. **The Standard Deduction**—The standard deduction may be claimed in lieu of *itemized deductions*.

    A. Standard deduction amounts vary according to filing status (2017) and are indexed for inflation.

Single	$6,350
Head of household	$9,350
Married—jointly	$12,700
Married—separate	$6,350

    B. An additional amount is added to the standard deduction if either the taxpayer or his or her spouse is (1) age 65 or over or (2) blind. In 2017, the amount of the addition is $1,550 for unmarried and $1,250 for married taxpayers. These amounts are indexed for inflation.

    C. Taxpayers choose to itemize if aggregate itemized deductions (after application of limits specific to each individual type of deduction) exceeds the standard deduction.

    D. Spouses filing separately must file consistently (if one elects to itemize, both must itemize).

III. **Medical Expenses**

    A. Uninsured medical expenses are eligible for deduction if the total expense exceeds a limit based upon AGI.

Definition
Medical Expense: Any expenditure for the care, prevention, cure, or treatment of disease or bodily function. It is deductible for the taxpayer, spouse, and dependent (gross in come and joint return tests do not apply for this purpose).

B. Expenses must exceed 10% of AGI to be deductible.

C. Deductible items include dental, medical, and hospital care; prescription drugs; equipment such as wheelchairs, crutches, eyeglasses, hearing aids, contacts; transportation for medical care; medical insurance premiums; qualified long-term care expenses and insurance; alcohol and drug rehabilitation; weight-reduction programs if as part of medical treatment; stop-smoking programs and prescription drugs for nicotine withdrawal.

> **Note**
> *Medical expenses are the only itemized deductions allowed for payments made on behalf of someone other than the taxpayer (i.e., dependents).*

D. Nondeductible items include funeral, burial, and cremation expenses; nonprescription drugs (except insulin); bottled water; toiletries; cosmetics; health spas; unnecessary cosmetic surgery.

E. Nursing home expenses qualify if the primary reason for being there is for medical reasons.

F. Capital expenditures may qualify if (1) incurred based on the advice of a physician, (2) the facility is primarily used by the patient alone, and (3) the expense is reasonable. Cost is fully deductible in year incurred. An expense can only be taken to the extent that it exceeds the increase in the value of the property.

G. Qualifying automobile expenses are actual expenses or 17 cents (2017) per mile.

H. Lodging is deductible up to $50 per night; also applies for someone required to travel with a patient. No deduction is allowed for meals, unless part of treatment program.

I. Medical expenses are not deducted until paid, and not until the year in which treatment is received, unless prepayment is required by provider.

> Qualified Medical Expenses
> − Reimbursements from Insurance
> − <u>10% of AGI</u>
> = Deductible Medical Expense

Example
Ralph and Alice Jones, both age 37, who have adjusted gross income of $60,000, paid the following medical expenses: $3,900 for hospital and doctor bills (above reimbursement), $1,250 for prescription medicine, and $1,600 for medical insurance. The Joneses would compute their medical expense deduction as follows:

Prescribed medicine	$1,250
Hospital, doctors	3,900
Medical insurance	1,600
	$6,750
Less 10% of AGI	−6,000
Medical expense deduction	$750

IV. Taxes—Property taxes and income taxes imposed by state, local, or foreign governments can be deducted as an itemized deduction. For cash basis taxpayers, the taxes are deductible in the year paid or withheld.

A. Personal Income Taxes—Imposed by state, local, or foreign governments are deductible.

B. Federal Taxes, Death, Excise, and Sales Taxes—In general, are not deductible.

C. Property Taxes—Imposed on personal-use property owned by taxpayer are deductible as an itemized deduction.

1. Property taxes on property used for business purposes can be deducted as a business expense.

2. Property taxes do not include special assessments unless these assessments are for repair or maintenance of the property, or imposed for interest payments.

3. Personal property taxes based on the value of the property (ad valorem) are deductible.

4. Special assessments are not deductible.

5. Fees and licenses (dog, automobile, hunting and fishing, etc.) are not deductible.

D. Taxes are deducted in year withheld or paid, even if payment relates to a different tax year.

E. The following taxes are not deductible for individuals:

1. Federal income taxes

2. Federal, state, or local estate or gift taxes

3. Social security and other federal employment taxes paid by employee (including self-employment taxes)

4. Social security and other employment taxes paid by an employer on the wages of an employee who only performed domestic services (i.e., maid, etc.)

V. Interest

A. Home Mortgage Interest—Interest paid on debt secured by a personal residence can be deducted as an itemized deduction.

1. Interest paid on debt relating to the taxpayer's principal place of abode and second home is eligible for deduction.

   a. Interest on a maximum of $1 million of acquisition indebtedness can be deducted if the debt was used to purchase, construct, or improve the residence.

   b. Interest on the lower of (1) $100,000 or (2) the equity in the home (FMV – other mortgages) can be deducted regardless of how the proceeds of the debt were used.

> **Note**
> *Taxpayers can elect to deduct state and local sales taxes instead of state and local income taxes. If this election is made, the amount of sales taxes can be determined by using actual receipts or by using a table provided by the IRS. The table includes state sales taxes only so an adjustment is required to add local sales taxes. Taxpayers may also add to the table amount sales taxes on major purchases such as cars, motorcycles, motor homes, SUVs, trucks, boats, and airplanes.*

Example
Allan purchased a home for $380,000, borrowing $250,000 of the purchase price that was secured by a fifteen-year mortgage. In 2017, when the home was worth $400,000 and the balance of the first mortgage was $230,000, Allan obtained a second mortgage on the home in the amount of $120,000, using the proceeds to purchase a car and to pay off personal loans. Allan may deduct the interest on the balance of the first mortgage acquisition indebtedness of $230,000. However, he can deduct interest on only $100,000 of the second mortgage as qualified residence interest because it is considered home equity indebtedness (i.e., the loan proceeds were not used to acquire, construct, or substantially improve a home). The interest on the remaining $20,000 of the second mortgage is nondeductible personal interest.

2. Points can be deducted if paid by taxpayer in the year of purchase or improvement of the residence.

Definition

Points: Compensation paid to a lender solely for the use or forbearance of money. Fees paid for services do not qualify as points.

---

    a. Points paid for refinancing are considered prepaid interest that must be amortized over life of loan.

    b. Premiums for qualified mortgage insurance related to acquisition indebtedness on a qualified residence are treated as qualified mortgage interest. This deduction phases out if AGI exceeds $100,000. 10% of the deduction is lost for each $1,000 of AGI, or portion thereof, which exceeds $100,000.

B. Investment Interest Expense—Is limited to net investment income (investment income less investment expenses).

    1. Investment income includes interest, dividends, rents, royalties, and annuities if not derived from a trade/business, a passive activity, or a real estate activity for which there is active participation.

    2. Net capital gain attributable to the sale of investment property and qualified dividend income is not included in investment income unless the taxpayer elects to do so. If the taxpayer elects to include this as investment income, this gain must be taxed at ordinary income rates, rather than the preferential capital gain rates.

    3. Investment expenses are expenses related to the production of investment income. Note that investment expenses are included in computing net investment income only to the extent that they are deductible after application of the 2% phaseout rule for itemized deductions. 2% expenses other than investment expenses are applied against the phaseout first.

Examples

1. Assume a taxpayer has the following items of income and expense for 2017:

Interest income	$15,000
Net long-term capital gain	18,000
Investment interest expense	25,000

The taxpayer's deduction for investment interest expense is generally limited to net investment income ($15,000) for 2017 unless the taxpayer elects to include a portion of the net LTCG in the determination of the investment interest expense limitation. If the taxpayer elects to treat $10,000 of the net LTCG as investment income, all of the taxpayer's investment interest expense will be deductible. But by doing this, $10,000 of the net LTCG will be taxed at ordinary tax rates, leaving only the remaining $8,000 of net LTCG to be taxed at preferential rates.

2. TP has adjusted gross income of $100,000 and investment expenses of $3,200. There are no other 2% expenses. The investment expenses of $3,200 are deducted only to the extent they exceed $2,000 (2% × $100,000), resulting in a $1,200 deduction. Therefore, when computing net investment income, only $1,200 of investment expenses are included in the computation.

---

    4. Disallowed investment interest is carried over to future years.

C. Personal Interest—That which includes credit card interest, car loan interest, and interest on income tax underpayments, is not deductible.

D. Other Interest Rules

    1. Prepaid interest must be allocated to the years to which the payments relate. Accrual basis taxpayers deduct interest ratably over the life of the loan. Mortgage prepayment penalties are deductible as interest.

    2. Not deductible if related to the production of tax-exempt income.

Itemized Deductions—Other

After studying this lesson, you should be able to:

1. Identify permissible charitable contribution deductions.

2. Apply limitations for certain types of contributions including carryover rules.

3. Determine whether an event qualifies as a casualty.

4. Compute the casualty loss deduction for personal use property and business property.

5. Identify which miscellaneous deductions are subject to the 2% rule.

6. Assess when phaseout of itemized deductions is applicable and compute phaseout.

I. **Charitable Contributions**—An itemized deduction is allowed for contributions of cash or property to qualified charities.

 A. **Charitable contributions must be made to qualified donees (recipients).**

 1. Public (A) charities are government subdivisions, hospitals, churches, schools, and similar institutions operated for religious, scientific, educational, or charitable purposes.

 2. Private (B) charities include fraternal orders, cemetery companies, and private foundations operated for religious, scientific, educational, or charitable purposes.

 3. Political organizations do not qualify as charities.

 4. Qualified charities must be domestic organizations. However, a domestic organization can conduct its charitable activities in a foreign country.

 B. **Contributions can include cash or property, but not services.**

 1. All contributions must be reduced by any value or benefit received by the taxpayer.

 2. For **LTCG** property:

 a. **FMV** is deductible.

 b. This deduction is limited to **30% of AGI**.

 c. The 30% of AGI limitation for capital gain property can be removed if the taxpayer elects to deduct the FMV reduced by the appreciation in the property.

 d. The deduction is limited to the adjusted basis of tangible personal property if the charitable organization does not use the property in a manner that is related to its tax-exempt purpose.

 e. For contributions of tangible personal property exceeding $5,000, if the donee organization sells the property within three years of contribution, the taxpayer must recapture (in the year of sell) the deduction to the extent it exceeded the basis of the property. This recapture can be avoided if the donee organization certifies that the property had been used for an exempt purpose and that this use was substantial.

 f. Special rules exist for charitable contributions of qualified conservation property, which is a contribution of a qualified real property interest exclusively for conservation purposes, and the donee is prohibited from making certain transfers of the property. These contributions are deductible up to 50% of AGI (100% for qualified ranchers and farmers) and excess contributions can be carried over for 15 years.

 3. **All Other Property**

 a. The deduction is the fair market value of the property reduced by ordinary income or short-term capital gain that would be recognized if the property was sold.

 b. **Ordinary income property** includes ordinary income due to depreciation recapture.

Example

Taxpayer owns machinery with a fair market value of $25,000 and adjusted basis of $15,000. Depreciation claimed is $7,000. If the machine was sold, the total gain would be $10,000 ($25,000 – $15,000), of which $7,000 would be recaptured as ordinary income. If this property was contributed to a qualified charitable organization, the deduction would be $18,000 ($25,000 – $7,000).

    c. If the fair market value of the property is less than its adjusted basis, the deduction is limited to the fair market value.

4. Unreimbursed costs (including $0.14/mile; not indexed for inflation) can be deducted.

5. For contributions of clothing and household goods, the value of these contributions can be deducted only if the items are in good used condition or better. Deductions may be disallowed for contributions of clothing or household items with minimal value, such as used socks or undergarments. This rule does not apply if the value of a single item exceeds $500 and a qualified appraisal is attached.

6. Up to $100,000 of distributions from an IRA will be tax-free if contributed to a charitable organization by an individual age 70 or over. This contribution will also not be subject to the 50% or 30% limitations.

7. A taxpayer who makes a payment to or for the benefit of a college or university and is thereby entitled to purchase tickets to athletic events is allowed to deduct 80% of the payment as a charitable contribution. Any payment that is attributable to the actual cost of tickets is not deductible as a charitable contribution.

8. A taxpayer may deduct as a charitable contribution up to $50 per school month of unreimbursed expenses to maintain a student in the 12th grade or lower in a taxpayer's home, if this is pursuant to a written agreement with a qualified charity.

C. Written records of the contribution are required.

1. No deduction is allowed for a single contribution of **$250 or more** unless the donor has **written acknowledgment** of the amount and purpose of the contribution from the donee organization. A canceled check is not sufficient.

2. Contributions of cash are not deductible unless the donor has a canceled check, credit card statement, or written statement from the charity.

3. For property valued at more than $500, a description of the property must be provided.

4. A qualified appraisal is required for donations of property worth more than $5,000.

5. For property valued at more than $500,000, the qualified appraisal must be attached to the tax return.

6. The requirements for property valued at more than $5,000 and $500,000 do not apply to cash, intellectual property, inventory, publicly-traded securities, and qualified vehicles.

7. Tax reporting

    a. Noncash charitable contributions are reported on Form 8283.

    b. Section A is for property valued at $5,000 or less. Section B is for property valued at more than $5,000.

D. Rule for Contributions of Autos, etc.—If an auto, boat, or airplane with a claimed value of more than $500 is donated, and the donee sells the vehicle without significant use of the vehicle, the deduction is limited to the gross sales proceeds from the sale of the vehicle. The donee organization must provide substantiation of this amount for the donor to attach to the return.

E. Deduction Limitations—*Limitations of the aggregate contribution deduction are based on AGI.*

1. Deduction is limited to 50% of AGI for aggregate contributions of cash combined with contributions of property.

2. Deduction for contributions of capital gain property to public ("A") charities is limited to 30% of AGI (ignoring cash contributions).

3. Deduction for contributions of capital gain property to private ("B") charities is limited to 20% of AGI (ignoring cash contributions).

4. Contributions in excess of the limits carryforward five years.

5. The 50% limitation is applied before the 30% limitations. The 30% limitation is applied before the 20% limitation.

Example

Ben's adjusted gross income is $50,000. During the year he gave his church $2,000 cash and land (held for investment more than one year) having a fair market value of $30,000 and a basis of $22,000. Ben also gave $5,000 cash to a private foundation to which a 30% limitation applies. Since Ben's contributions to an organization to which the 50% limitation applies (disregarding the 30% limitation for capital gain property) exceed $25,000 (50% of $50,000), his contribution to the private foundation is not deductible this year. The $2,000 cash donated to the church is deducted first. The donation for the gift of land is not required to be reduced by the appreciation in value, but is limited to $15,000 (30% × $50,000). Thus, Ben may deduct only $17,000 ($2,000 + $15,000). The unused portion of the land contribution ($15,000) and the gift to the private foundation ($5,000) are carried over to the next year, still subject to their respective 30% limitations.

Alternatively, Ben may elect to reduce the value of the land by its appreciation of $8,000 and not be subject to the 30% limitation for capital gain property. In such case, his current deduction would be $25,000 ($2,000 cash + $22,000 land + $1,000 cash to private foundation), but only the remaining $4,000 cash to the private foundation would be carried over to the next year.

F. **Nondeductible** contributions include contributions to/for/of

1. Civic leagues, social clubs, and foreign organizations

2. Communist organizations, chambers of commerce, labor unions

3. The value of the taxpayer's time or services

4. The use of property, or less than an entire interest in property

5. Blood donated

6. Tuition or amounts in place of tuition

7. Payments to a hospital for care of particular patients

8. "Sustainer's gift" to retirement home

9. Raffles, bingo, etc. (but may qualify as gambling loss)

10. Fraternal societies if the contributions are used to defray sickness or burial expenses of members

11. Political organizations

12. Travel, including meals and lodging (e.g., trip to serve at charity's national meeting), if there is any significant element of personal pleasure, recreation, or vacation involved

II. **Casualty Losses**—Casualty losses involving personal assets are eligible for deduction if the total unreimbursed loss exceeds a limit based upon AGI. Casualty losses of business assets are deducted as business losses.

A. A casualty loss is calculated by subtracting the adjusted basis of the damaged property from any insurance proceeds.

Definition

Casualty: A sudden, unexpected event damaging or destroying an asset. A casualty includes the theft of an asset.

B. Losses **not deductible** as casualties include

1. Losses from the breakage of china or glassware through handling or by a family pet.

2. Disease, termite, or moth damage.

3. Expenses incident to casualty (temporary housing, etc.).

4. Progressive deterioration through a steadily operating cause and damage from normal process. Thus, the steady weakening of a building caused by normal or usual wind and weather conditions is not a casualty loss.

5. Losses from nearby disaster (property value reduced due to location near a disaster area).

6. Loss of future profits from, for example, ice storm damage to standing timber that reduces the rate of growth or the quality of future timber. To qualify as a casualty, the damage must actually result in existing timber being rendered unfit for use.

> **Note**
> *Any type of property can generate a casualty loss. However, a casualty of business property qualifies as a business loss. Hence, only casualty losses of personal assets are deducted as itemized deductions.*

C. **Amount of Casualty Loss**—For purposes of calculating the casualty loss, the adjusted basis of the damaged property is limited to the lesser of the adjusted basis or the decline in the value of the asset due to the casualty.

1. This limit does not apply to the complete destruction of a business asset.

2. The loss is deducted in the year that the casualty occurs or the theft is discovered.

D. For personal casualty losses, the deduction is computed as follows:

> Lower of decline in FMV or AB of property
>
> Insurance Reimbursements
>
> − $100 per casualty
>
> − <u>10% × AGI</u>
>
> <u>Casualty loss deduction</u>

Example

Frank Jones's lakeside cottage, which cost him $13,600 (including $1,600 for the land) on April 30, 1991, was partially destroyed by fire on July 12, 2017. The value of the property immediately before the fire was $46,000 ($24,000 for the building and $22,000 for the land), and the value immediately after the fire was $36,000. He collected $7,000 from the insurance company. It was Jones's only casualty for 2017, and his AGI was $20,000. Jones's casualty loss deduction from the fire would be $900, computed as follows:

Value of entire property before fire	$46,000
Value of entire property after fire	36,000
Decrease in fair market value of entire property	$10,000
Adjusted basis (cost in this case)	$13,600
Loss sustained (lesser of decrease in FMV or adjusted basis)	$10,000
Less insurance recovery	−7,000
Casualty loss	$3,000
Less $100 floor	−100
Loss after $100 floor	$2,900
Less 10% of AGI	−2,000
Casualty loss deduction	$900

E. **If a gain results from the casualty** (insurance reimbursement exceeds property's adjusted basis), then all casualty gains and losses are netted. Note that this netting is done before the 10% of AGI reduction. A net casualty gain is treated as a capital gain.

Example
An individual incurred a $5,000 personal casualty gain and a $1,000 personal casualty loss (after the $100 floor) during the current taxable year. Since there was a net gain, the individual will report the gain and loss as a $5,000 capital gain and a $1,000 capital loss.

F. **If losses (after the $100 floor for each loss) exceed gains**, the losses (1) offset gains and (2) are an ordinary deduction from AGI to the extent **in excess of 10% of AGI.**

Example
An individual had AGI of $40,000 (before casualty gains and losses) and also had a personal casualty loss of $12,000 (after the $100 floor) and a personal casualty gain of $3,000. Since there was a personal casualty net loss, the net loss will be deductible as an itemized deduction of [$12,000 − $3,000 − (10% × $40,000)] = $5,000.

G. Appraisal fees (to determine fair market value) are a 2% miscellaneous itemized deduction.

III. Miscellaneous Itemized Deductions—Certain business-oriented expenses are not associated with trade activities but are, nonetheless, deductible as itemized deductions. These deductions are referred to as miscellaneous itemized deductions. Some of these expenses are subject to the 2% of AGI limitation, while others are merely added with other itemized deductions.

A. Operation of the 2% of AGI Floor Limitation

1. The floor limit is applied by subtracting 2% of AGI from the aggregate amount of the deductions subject to the floor.

2. Any excess deductions over the floor are included with other itemized deductions.

Example
TP has an AGI of $100,000 and miscellaneous itemized deductions subject to the 2% floor of $3,500. TP can include $1,500 of these deductions with his other itemized deductions.

B. There are five major types of miscellaneous deductions subject to the 2% floor.

1. Employee business expenses not reimbursed under an accountable plan. If reimbursed under an accountable plan, then these expenses are deducted for AGI.

   a. Expenses include job hunting in the same trade or business, specialized clothing used on the job if not suitable for wearing at other times, and other necessary expenses related to one's role as an employee.

2. Investment expenses (not royalty or rental expenses)

3. Tax return preparation expenses

4. Home office expenses of an employee

5. Hobby expenses

C. Other miscellaneous itemized deductions subject to the floor include appraisal fees to determine casualty loss and legal fees to procure alimony.

D. There are several types of deductions **not** subject to the 2% floor.

   1. Repayments previously included in income under the claim of right doctrine

   2. Remaining basis of terminated annuity

   3. Gambling losses to extent of winnings

   4. Other miscellaneous deductions not subject to the floor include work expenses of handicapped taxpayers, estate taxes related to income in respect of a decedent, short sale expenses, and expenses relating to cooperative housing corporations.

IV. Overall Limitation on Itemized Deductions

A. Taxpayers whose AGI exceeds a threshold must reduce the total amount claimed for itemized deductions. The threshold (2017) is:

Married filing jointly	$313,800
Head of Household	$287,650
Single	$261,500

B. The reduction is 3% of the amount of AGI in excess of the threshold.

C. Itemized deductions **not** subject to the phase-out are medical expenses, investment interest expenses, casualty and theft losses, and gambling losses.

D. The reduction is the lower of:

   1. 3% × (AGI – Threshold), or

   2. 80% × (Taxes + Home mortgage interest + Charitable contributions + 2% Miscellaneous deductions).

Example

H and W are calendar-year married taxpayers filing a joint return for 2017. The couple has AGI of $803,900 and $25,000 of itemized deductions consisting of $15,000 taxes, $6,000 of contributions, and $4,000 of mortgage interest. The couple's total itemized deduction of $25,000 is reduced by $14,703 to $10,297. The reduction amount is the smaller of (a) or (b) computed as follows:

a. 3% of excess AGI: $14,703 [3% of $490,100 (i.e., $803,900 AGI less $313,800 threshold)].

b. 80% of otherwise allowable itemized deductions: $20,000 (i.e., 80% of $25,000).

Allowable itemized deductions is $10,297 ($25,000 – $14,703).

Employee Business Expenses

After studying this lesson, you should be able to:

1. Define accountable plans and contrast tax effects for accountable versus non-accountable plans.

2. Compute deductible travel and entertainment expenses.

3. Evaluate the education expenses that are deductible as a business expenses.

Tax Form for this Lesson: Form 2106 (available for download and printing from the lesson overview of your software).

I. Accountable Plans

A. If employee business expenses are reimbursed under an accountable plan, then the reimbursement is not taxable (for FICA or income tax) and the employee gets no deduction for the expense. Technically, the tax law requires the reimbursement to be included as income and the employee's deduction is for AGI. Since this always nets to zero, the IRS allows the income and deduction to not be reported.

B. If the expenses are reimbursed, but not under an accountable plan, the reimbursement must be included in income (for FICA and income tax), and the deduction is a 2% miscellaneous itemized deduction.

C. If the expenses are not reimbursed by the employer, the employee's deduction is a 2% miscellaneous itemized deduction.

D. For a plan to be accountable:

    1. Must substantiate all expenses to be reimbursed, and

    2. Excess reimbursements must be returned to the employer.

    3. Per diem reimbursements at a rate not in excess of the federal per diem rate and mileage rate per mile are deemed to satisfy the substantiation requirement if the employee provides the time, place, and business purpose of expenses.

> **Exam Tip**
> *How should you answer a question about the deductibility of employee business expenses included under an accountable plan? The context of the question is important. For example, if the question says that the reimbursement has been included in income, then the deduction is for AGI. If the question states that the reimbursement is not included in income, then there is no deduction. The key is that this should have no effect on AGI.*

II. Travel Expenses—Deductions for cost of travel are limited to trips with a business purpose.

A. **The Cost of Transportation**—Is deductible when the primary purpose is business.

    1. Commuting between the taxpayer's residence and the place of business is never deductible. However, travel from one job or work area to a second job or work area is deductible. Also, travel from home to a "temporary work location" is deductible if the assignment is short-term in nature.

    2. The amount and purpose of the transportation must be substantiated.

    3. Transportation costs include direct costs (airfare, tolls, gas, depreciation of a vehicle, insurance, etc.), or a mileage rate of 53.5 cents (2017) can be claimed for auto use. If the mileage rate is used, the only costs added to this amount are for parking and tolls.

B. **Meals and Lodging Expenses**—Can be claimed when the taxpayer is "away from home" overnight.

Definitions

Away from Home Overnight: Means the trip is of sufficient duration to require the taxpayer to rest.

Home: The taxpayer's principal place of business. If the taxpayer is assigned to a new location for an indefinite period of time or for more than a year, the "tax home" shifts to the new location. Thus, there would be no travel expenses to this location. Rather, this would now be commuting to the new business home.

1. The cost of meals is reduced by 50%. This reduction applies not just when traveling, but also when entertaining. The 50% reduction rule will not apply if:

   a. The full value of the meal or entertainment is included in the recipient's income or excluded as a fringe benefit.

   b. An employee is reimbursed for the cost of a meal or entertainment. (The 50% reduction rule applies to the party making the reimbursement.)

   c. The cost is for a traditional employer-paid employee recreation expense (e.g., a company Christmas party).

   d. The cost is for samples and other promotional activities made available to the public.

   e. The expense is for a sports event that qualifies as a charitable fund-raising event.

   f. The cost is for meals or entertainment sold for full consideration.

2. For business travel that is mixed with personal travel, the travel to the location is deductible only if more than 50% of the total days are business days. If the 50% test is met, all of the transportation costs to the location are deductible. If not met, then none of the transportation costs are deductible. If Friday and Monday are both business days, then the weekend can also be counted as business days.

3. There are limited circumstances when lodging can be deducted even when not "away from home." For example, a national professional association may have its annual meeting in the city where this employer has its business. If an employer requires an employee to stay overnight at the conference hotel, the lodging is deductible if all the following are met:

   a. The employee is required to stay overnight.

   b. The lodging does not exceed five days and does not occur more than once per quarter.

   c. The employee is required to participate in the event that necessitates the overnight stay.

   d. The lodging is not lavish or extravagant.

4. Even if these requirements are not met, the lodging is deductible if incurred for a valid business reason. For example, a professional football team may stay at a local hotel the night before home football games to prepare for the game. This would be a valid business reason for a deduction.

C. **Other Travel-Related Limits**—Include the following:

   1. Travel cannot be a form of business education (e.g., a French teacher travels to France).

   2. The cost of a companion is deductible if the companion is an employee of the taxpayer or serves some legitimate business purpose.

   3. No deduction is allowed for travel to "investment" seminars.

   4. Significant restrictions are placed on deductions for conventions and seminars held on cruise ships or in foreign countries.

III. **Entertainment**—Deductions for the cost of entertainment are closely regulated and limited to 50% of expenditures.

A. Business must be conducted in association with the entertainment or be directly related to the operations of the business.

1. Entertainment must involve a person with a business relation (e.g., customer, client, employee, partner, etc.).

2. A substantial discussion must occur.

3. The discussion must either occur before, during, or after the entertainment on the same business day.

4. No deductions for facilities or club dues.

5. Dues to clubs organized for pleasure or recreation are not deductible. Dues for public service clubs (e.g., Kiwanis), professional organizations, and trade associations are deductible.

6. The deduction for tickets to an entertainment activity is limited to the face value of the ticket (before the 50% disallowance).

7. **Business gifts are limited to $25 per donee**, per year.

B. Contemporaneous written records are required. The record must establish the cost, time, activity, relationship, and business purpose of the entertainment.

C. The cost of deductible meals and entertainment is reduced by 50% (to represent the personal enjoyment of the taxpayer). No reduction is made when the entertainment is provided to employees as compensation, or if provided as a means of advertising or marketing.

Example
TP provided a Florida vacation to his highest volume salesperson this year. TP can deduct the entire cost of the vacation because it is compensation to the employee.

IV. Education Expenses

A. Education expenses are **not deductible** if:

1. To **meet minimum standards** of a current job or

2. To **qualify the taxpayer for a new trade or business**

B. Education expenses are **deductible** if:

1. To **maintain or improve existing skills** required in a current job or

2. To **meet the requirements of an employer** or imposed by law to retain employment status

> **Note**
> *No deduction is allowed for CPA review courses. Sorry!!*

Example
Law school tuition cannot be deducted because it is required to qualify for a new profession (even if the taxpayer never intends to practice as a lawyer).

V. Employee Business Expenses Are Reported on Form 2106

A. Vehicle expenses are computed in Part II of the form and then transferred to Part I.

B. Total employee business expenses are computed in Part 1 and are then transferred to Schedule A as 2% miscellaneous itemized deductions.

C. Form 2106EZ can be used if no reimbursements are received by the employer and if the standard mileage rate is used for vehicle expenses.

Deductions—Losses and Bad Debts

After studying this lesson, you should be able to:

1. List the type of losses deductible for tax purposes.

2. Define worthless assets and related tax consequences.

3. Differentiate between business bad debts and non-business bad debts and apply related tax rules.

4. Compute net operating loss for an individual taxpayer.

I. **Losses**—Losses on the disposition of business assets can generally be deducted, but the deduction of losses from the disposition of personal (nonbusiness) assets is prohibited.

   A. **Deductible Losses**—These are generated with the disposition of business assets.

   1. A disposition occurs with a sale, exchange, or worthlessness of an asset.

   2. The disposition of personal assets will not generate deductible losses unless the disposition qualifies as a personal casualty.

Definition
Business Asset: An asset used in a trade, held for investment, or used by an employee in an employment capacity. A personal asset is an asset used for a motive other than profit seeking (e.g., a personal reason).

---

   3. An asset that is used partially for business purposes and partially for personal purposes is generally treated as two distinct assets based upon the proportion of time the asset is used for each purpose.

   B. **Requirements for Deducting the Cost of Worthless Securities**

   1. In general, the security must be totally worthless (no residual value).

   2. A worthless asset is treated as being sold for nothing on the last day of the year.

   3. The character of the loss is usually capital. However, if the loss is incurred by a corporation on its investment in an affiliated corporation (80% or more ownership), the loss is generally an ordinary loss.

II. **Bad Debts**—These are deductible if the loan is made in a trade activity.

   A. Loans can only be deducted using a direct write-off method.

   B. Business loans can be deducted to the extent that the loan is partially worthless.

   C. Nonbusiness bad debts are also deductible.

> **Note**
> *A cash basis taxpayer can deduct losses from worthless loans, but not losses generated by the failure of customers to pay for sales on account. A cash basis taxpayer never establishes a basis for an account receivable (sale on account), whereas a basis for a direct loan is created with the transfer of cash.*

Definition
Nonbusiness Bad Debt: Any bona fide loan that is not made in a trade capacity, but has a bona fide profit motive.

---

   1. Whether a loan is bona fide or a disguised gift, depends on facts such as whether interest is charged and collateral is required.

   2. Nonbusiness bad debts are deductible as short-term capital losses in the year of complete worthlessness (no partial worthlessness is allowed).

III. Limitations on Deduction of Losses

A. Losses on the disposition of trade assets are subject to the netting rules under 1231, and losses on investment assets are subject to the netting rules for capital assets. In general, these netting procedures allow deductible losses to offset gains without limit.

B. If capital losses exceed capital gains, then this "net capital loss" is subject to a $3,000 deduction limit for individuals. No deduction is allowed for net capital losses for corporations.

C. Special rules apply if Section 1244 qualifying small corporation stock is sold at a loss or becomes worthless (losses are deductible up to $100,000 as ordinary losses, but gains are still taxed as capital gains). The individual selling the stock must be the original holder of the stock. To qualify as Section 1244 stock, the total capitalization of the corporation cannot exceed $1,000,000 at the time the stock is issued.

IV. Net Operating Losses

A. NOLs must be carried back to the two preceding tax years (beginning with the second prior year) unless an election is made in the year of the NOL to forgo the carryback. The carryover period is 20 years.

B. NOLs are only allowed for business losses and casualty losses. Any nonbusiness losses or expenses must be added back to the taxable loss to determine the NOL. The IRS has stated that losses from rental activity are business losses for purposes of computing the NOL.

C. The net operating loss of a corporation is, in general, equal to its taxable loss for the tax year. A corporation is allowed to include the dividends that received deduction in computing its net operating loss.

D. For an individual, the following cannot create an NOL:

    1. Personal exemptions

    2. Standard deduction or itemized deductions (except for casualty loss), and other nonbusiness deductions in excess of nonbusiness income

    3. Excess of nonbusiness capital losses over nonbusiness capital gains (limited to $3,000)

    4. An NOL deduction from another year

E. In the year to which the NOL is being applied, the NOL is a deduction for AGI for an individual and a regular business deduction for a corporation. For an individual, any deductions that were based on AGI for the carryback year must be recomputed except for the charitable contribution deduction.

Example

George, single with no dependents, started his own delivery business and incurred a loss from the business for 2017. In addition, he earned interest on personal bank deposits of $1,800. After deducting his itemized deductions for interest and taxes of $9,000, and his personal exemption of $4,050, the loss shown on George's Form 1040 was $20,850. George's net operating loss would be computed as follows:

Taxable income		$(20,850)
Nonbusiness deductions	$9,000	
Nonbusiness income	−1,800	7,200
Personal exemption		4,050
Net operating loss		$(9,600)

Limitations on Business Deductions

After studying this lesson, you should be able to:

1. Identify hobby losses and apply related limitations on deductibility.

2. Determine the deductibility of expenses related to a home office.

3. Distinguish among the three different types of vacation homes for tax purposes and determine deductible expenses for each.

4. Define passive losses and apply limitations on deductibility.

I. Hobby Losses

A. Hobby expenses may be deducted if the hobby generates revenue.

Definition
Hobby: An activity that is not primarily profit-oriented because it is primarily undertaken for personal enjoyment.

1. The expenses from this activity are deductible, but only to the extent the activity generates revenues. In other words, no hobby loss (expenses in excess of revenue) is deductible.

B. To avoid the hobby designation, the taxpayer must produce evidence that there is a real profit motive in conducting the activity.

Example
TP is a wealthy doctor who also owns a ranch in Colorado. TP only visits the ranch during the summer when he uses it to conduct recreational activities. If the ranch is not operated at a profit, then expense deductions are limited to the revenue produced by the ranch.

C. The deductions associated with a hobby are limited to the revenue generated by the activity.

1. Expenses can only be deducted as "2% miscellaneous" itemized deductions. Expenses not allowed due to insufficient income do not carry over to future tax years.

2. The limitation is imposed by deducting expenses in the following order:

   a. Interest and taxes (fully deductible as itemized deductions)

   b. Cash expenses

   c. Depreciation

Examples
1. TP paints landscapes in the mountains during his summer vacations. This year, TP incurred $400 in airfares and lodging, but only sold $50 in paintings.

Question: How much can TP deduct?

Answer: TP can deduct hobby expenses up to the amount of hobby income. In this case, TP can deduct $50 as a miscellaneous itemized deduction subject to the 2% of the AGI limit.

2. Glenn is an engineer who races a Formula Three car as a hobby. This year Glenn received a salary of $97,000 from his employer and won $3,000 in various car races while incurring $9,000 of out-of-pocket expenses in his racing hobby. Glenn must include the $3,000 of prizes in his gross income, raising his AGI to $100,000. His $9,000 of hobby expenses are only deductible to the extent of $3,000. Assuming that Glenn itemizes his deductions but has no other miscellaneous itemized deductions, his hobby expenses would result in a deduction of $3,000 − (2% × $100,000) = $1,000.

D. The burden of proving a lack of profit motive can be shifted to the IRS.

    1. When the activity generates a profit in three out of five consecutive years, the IRS must prove the taxpayer has no profit motive in conducting the activity.

    2. If there are losses in at least three of the previous five years, the taxpayer has the burden to prove that the activity is a business.

II. Business Use of the Home—Deductions associated with a home office or the rental of a personal residence are subject to special limits.

    A. Home Office Expenses—These can be deducted for a portion of a residence used as an office.

        1. Business use of the office must be exclusive and regular.

        2. The office must be a principal place of business.

        3. If the office is not a principal place of business, then it can still qualify if it is used as the ordinary place for meeting clients or for the administration of the business (There is no other fixed location used for substantial administration).

        4. If the taxpayer is an employee, then the office must be used for the convenience of the employer.

        5. Expenses must be allocated between the portion of the dwelling used as residence and the office.

            a. The IRS provides a simplified method for computing the home-office deduction, which is multiplying the allowable square footage by $5. The maximum square footage under this method is 300, limiting the deduction to $1,500.

        6. Office deductions are limited to income after non-office expenses. Office deductions are applied toward income in the same order as the hobby loss limit (mortgage interest and real estate taxes, cash expenses, depreciation), but excess deductions carry forward and can be used in future years when business income is sufficient.

Examples

    1. TP, a self-employed taxpayer, uses one fourth of his or her apartment exclusively and regularly as an office. TP conducts business only at this location. This year TP received fees of $5,000 and paid rent, utilities, etc., on the apartment of $8,000.

Question: What amount may TP deduct in conjunction with the home office?

Answer: TP may deduct one-fourth of the rent ($2,000) for AGI. This will be reported on Schedule C with other business income and expenses.

    2. Taxpayer uses 10% of her home exclusively for business purposes. Gross income from her business totaled $750, and she incurred the following expenses:

	Total	10% Business
Interest	$4,000	$400
Taxes	2,500	250
Utilities, insurance	1,500	150
Depreciation	2,000	

Since total deductions for business use of the home are limited to business gross income, the taxpayer can deduct the following for business use of his home: $400 interest; $250 taxes; $100 utilities and insurance; and $0 depreciation (operating expenses such as utilities and insurance must be deducted before depreciation). The remaining $50 of utilities and insurance, and $200 of depreciation can be carried forward and deducted in future years subject to the same restrictions.

    B. Vacation Home Expenses—These occur when a personal residence is rented.

        1. If rented for less than 15 days a year, it is treated as a **personal residence**. Rent income is excluded and mortgage interest and property taxes are deductible on Schedule A.

2. If rented for 15 days or more, and if it is not used for personal purposes for **more than the greater of 1) 14 days or 2) 10% of the total days rented**, it is treated as **rental property**. All rent is taxable, net of all regular rental expenses, prorated for the percentage of rental days only. A rental loss is allowable.

3. If rented for 15 days or more, and if it is used for personal purposes for **more than the greater of 1) 14 days or 2) 10% of the total days rented**, it is treated as **personal/rental property**. All regular expenses are prorated as above for rental days, but a rental loss is not allowed. Expenses must be deducted in the same order as for a hobby.

Examples

1. TP owns a duplex. He rents one side of the duplex and lives in the other side. The rental was occupied all year and TP received $7,200 in rent. This year TP paid real estate taxes of $6,400, fire insurance of $600, and TP paid $800 to have the rental painted.

Question: If depreciation on the entire duplex is $5,000, how much will the rental increase TP's adjusted gross income?

Answer: TP's AGI will increase by $400. The $7,200 of revenue will be offset by $3,200 in taxes, $300 in insurance, $800 of maintenance, and $2,500 of depreciation (deducted in that order).

2. Taxpayer rents her condominium for 120 days for $2,000 and uses it herself for 60 days. The rest of the year it is vacant. Her expenses are

Mortgage interest	$1,800
Real estate taxes	600
Utilities	300
Maintenance	300
Depreciation	2,000
	$5,000

Taxpayer may deduct the following expenses:

	Rental expense	Itemized deduction
Mortgage interest	$1,200	$600
Real estate taxes	400	200
Utilities	200	--
Maintenance	200	--
Depreciation	--	--
	$2,000	$800

Taxpayer may not deduct any depreciation because her rental expense deductions are limited to rental income when she has personal use of the condominium in excess of the 14-day or 10% rule.

III. **At Risk**—Loss deductions incurred in a trade or business, or in the production of income, are limited to the amount a taxpayer has "**at risk**."

A. Applies to all activities except the leasing of personal property by a closely held corporation (5 or fewer individuals own more than 50% of stock).

B. Applies to individuals and closely held regular corporations.

C. Amount "at risk" includes

1. The cash and adjusted basis of property contributed by the taxpayer, *and*

2. Liabilities for which the taxpayer is personally liable; excludes nonrecourse debt.

D. For real estate activities, a taxpayer's amount at risk includes "qualified" nonrecourse financing secured by the real property used in the activity.

    1. Nonrecourse financing is qualified if it is borrowed from a lender engaged in the business of making loans (e.g., bank, savings and loan) provided that the lender is not the promoter or seller of the property or a party related to either; or is borrowed from or guaranteed by any federal, state, or local government or instrumentality thereof

    2. Nonrecourse financing obtained from a qualified lender who has an equity interest in the venture is treated as an amount at risk, as long as the terms of the financing are commercially reasonable

    3. The nonrecourse financing must not be convertible, and no person can be personally liable for repayment.

E. Excess losses can be carried over to subsequent years (no time limit) and deducted when the "at risk" amount has been increased.

IV. Passive Activity Losses—Losses from passive activities can offset only passive income. Passive losses cannot offset portfolio income or income from active businesses.

    A. The expenses and revenues from **passive activities** are combined (netted) and the expenses in excess of revenue (the passive loss) are suspended.

Definitions

Portfolio Income: Investment income such as interest, dividends, capital gains, and royalties.

Passive Activity: A profit-seeking activity in which the taxpayer does not materially participate in its management.

---

    1. Material participation means being involved in the operation of the activity in a continuous, substantial way. Two specific ways to meet this requirement are to work more than 500 hours in the activity, or to work more than 100 hours if no other individual works more than 100 hours.

    2. All limited partners and most rental activities are considered passive without regard to the taxpayer's participation. Exceptions to this rule are allowed for car rentals, hotels, golf courses, and other activities where the average rental time is seven days or less, or 30 days or less if significant personal services are provided by the owner in connection with the rental.

Example

An individual taxpayer reports the following items for the current year:

Ordinary income from partnership A, operating a movie theater in which the taxpayer materially participates	$70,000
Net loss from partnership B, operating an equipment rental business in which the taxpayer does not materially participate	(9,000)
Rental income from building rented to a third party	7,000
Short-term capital gain from sale of stock	4,000

What is the taxpayer's adjusted gross income for the year?

    A. $70,000

    B. $72,000

    C. $74,000

    D. $77,000

Solution

The correct answer is $74,000. The taxpayer must include the ordinary income of $70,000 from partnership A as well as the $4,000 short-term capital gain from the sale of stock. The $7,000 of rental income is passive income that must be reported but can be offset by passive activity losses, if any. In this case, the $9,000 net loss from partnership B is considered a passive activity loss, and $7,000 of this loss can be used to offset the passive activity income of $7,000. The remaining $2,000 of passive activity loss would be carried forward to offset passive activity income in the next tax year, if any. It can be carried forward indefinitely but cannot be carried back.

3. Real estate professionals are excepted from the limit. A real estate professional must perform more than 50% of his or her personal services in trades or businesses involving real property, and must perform more than 750 hours of services in real property trades or businesses in which he or she materially participates.

Note
The passive loss rules apply to individuals, estates, trusts, personal service corporations, and closely held C corporations.

B. **Rental Real Estate**—An exception to the limitation of passive losses exists for taxpayers who actively manage rental reality.

Definition

Active Participation: Occurs for taxpayers who own at least 10% of the property and significantly participate in decision-making. This is a much easier benchmark to meet than material participation.

1. An active manager can deduct a maximum loss of $25,000 per year.

2. The exception is phased out for taxpayers with an AGI exceeding $100,000 at the rate of 50% ($1 of deduction for each $2 of AGI exceeding $100,000).

Example
TP has an AGI of $130,000 and is an active manager in rental realty. If the rental activity generates a loss of $20,000, TP is limited to a deduction of $5,000 ($20 − [($130 − 100) × 50%]).

C. Suspended losses become deductible in later years if income is generated or the activity is sold.

D. **Credits** from passive activities can be used only to offset the tax liability attributable to passive activity income.

1. Excess credits are carried forward indefinitely (subject to limited carryback during the phase-in period).

2. Excess credits (unlike losses) cannot be used in full in the year in which the taxpayer's entire passive activity interest is disposed of. Instead, excess credits continue to be carried forward.

3. Credits allowable under the passive activity limitation rules are also subject to the general business credit limitation.

Individual Tax Issues

Personal and Dependency Exemptions

After studying this lesson, you should be able to:

1. Determine if one is a dependent under the qualifying child rule.

2. Assess if one is a dependent under the qualifying relative rule.

3. Apply the multiple support agreement criteria.

4. Evaluate the dependency status for children of divorced payments.

5. Determine when phaseout of exemptions is applicable and compute phaseout.

I. **Personal Exemptions**—Most taxpayers can claim an exemption in computing taxable income on their own return. The 2017 exemption amount is $4,050.

    A. No personal exemption can be claimed for a taxpayer (or spouse) who is claimed as a dependent by another taxpayer.

        1. Personal exemptions include the taxpayer and spouse if married filing jointly.

        2. A personal exemption can be claimed on the taxpayer's final return even if the taxpayer or spouse dies during the tax year.

        3. If spouses file married filing separate then typically each spouse claims a personal exemption on his/her own return. Note that if one spouse has no gross income and no one else has claimed him/her as a dependent, the other spouse can claim him/her as an exemption on the married filing separate return.

        4. A full exemption is allowed even if birth or death occurred during the year.

II. **Dependency Exemptions**—The tests for a dependency exemption are applied on the last day of the year, or the last day the dependent was alive (if the dependent died during the year). One must meet all tests to claim an individual as a dependent.

> **Definition**
> *Dependency Exemptions:* Flat deductions allowed for individuals (other than the taxpayer) who satisfy several specific tests.

    A. One can qualify as a dependent as either a **qualifying child** or a **qualifying relative**.

    B. **A Qualifying Child**—Can be claimed as a dependent if the following tests are met:

        1. **Relationship test**—The dependent must be a natural child, stepchild, adopted child, foster child, sibling, step-sibling, or a descendant of any of these. Note, that this definition includes brothers, sisters, nieces, and nephews.

        2. **Residence test**—The dependent must have the same principal place of abode as the taxpayer for more than one half of the tax year. Note, that one could live with several individuals who potentially qualify to claim the individual as a dependent (mother, aunt, grandfather) at the same time.

        3. **Age test**—The dependent must be under the age of 19 at the end of the tax year, or under 24 if a full-time student for at least five months of the tax year. The qualifying child must also be younger than the taxpayer claiming the QC as a dependent. There is no age limitation if the individual is permanently and totally disabled.

        4. **Joint return test**—A dependent cannot file married-jointly.

            a. A dependent can file jointly to obtain a refund (the dependent is not required to file according to gross income level). Otherwise, a married-jointly taxpayer will not qualify as a dependent despite passing all of the other tests.

5. **Citizenship/residency test**—A dependent must be a citizen or resident of the U.S., or a resident of Canada or Mexico.

6. **Not self-supporting test**—To be claimed as a dependent, the individual must not have provided more than 50% of his or her own support.

7. **Other requirements**—In addition to the above, a qualifying child must be younger than the taxpayer who is claiming the child as a dependent. Also, if a parent is qualified to claim the child as a dependent but declines, no other individual can claim the individual unless that individual's AGI is higher than that of any parent.

C. **Tie-Breaker Rules**—If more than one individual qualifies to claim the potential dependent, the following rules apply:

1. If one individual is a parent, the parent claims the exemption. If a parent is eligible to claim the qualifying child, the parent cannot allow another eligible individual to claim the child unless the eligible individual has a higher AGI for the tax year than the AGI of any other person eligible to claim the child.

2. If both individuals are parents and they do not file a joint return, the parent with whom the child resided the longest during the tax year claims the exemption.

3. If same as 2. and the child lives with both parents at the same time, the parent with the highest AGI claims the exemption.

4. If none of the individuals is a parent, the taxpayer with the highest AGI claims the exemption.

D. **The Qualifying Relative Rule**—This rule defines relative very broadly, including all common relatives except for cousins. Stepparents, stepsiblings, and in-laws also qualify. The term also includes any person who lives in the taxpayer's home for the entire tax year. A person temporarily absent for vacation, school, or sickness or indefinitely confined in a nursing home meets the member of household test.

A qualifying child cannot also be a qualifying relative. In addition to the relationship test, the following tests must be met to claim a qualifying relative as a dependent:

1. **Support test**—The taxpayer must provide more than 50% of the dependent's total support. The multiple support agreement provision continues to apply.

> **Definition**
> *Support:* Includes food, clothing, value of lodging, medical, education, recreation, and certain capital expenses.
>
> Excludes services provided by the taxpayer, life insurance premiums, funeral expenses, nontaxable scholarships, and income and social security taxes paid from a dependent's own income.

a. The support test traces the source of the funds used to pay for necessities.

b. *Support does not include unused* sources of funds of dependent. For example, elderly parent receives Social Security that is deposited in her bank account and *not used* for her care is not included as support.

c. Scholarships do not count as support.

2. **Gross income test**

a. The dependent's gross income must be less than the exemption amount for the year ($4,050 for 2017). Gross income is defined as only the income that is taxable.

> **Note**
> *A child under the age of 19 can receive significant amounts of income and not violate the support test. The income would not violate the support test if it was not used to pay for necessities (e.g., the income was placed in savings).*

Example

A child of the taxpayer (under age 19) earned $5,000 this year and received a scholarship that paid tuition of $8,000. If the child uses the funds from wages for necessities, the child will still satisfy the support test if the taxpayer provides at least $5,001 of necessities (5,001/10,000 > 1/2).

  b. There are **two exceptions** to this test. These apply for a child/stepchild or for an adopted or a foster child:

    i. That is **under the age of 19** at the end of the tax year. or

    ii. That is **under 24** at the end of the tax year and is **a full-time student** for at least five months during the tax year.

  c. Joint return test—Same as above.

  d. Citizenship/residency test—Same as above.

III. **Other Dependency Rules**—There are situations in which individuals may be supported but not meet all tests for a dependency exemption. In two circumstances, multiple support agreements and divorced parents, the law provides for a dependency exemption despite the technical violation of one or more of the tests.

> **Note**
> *A dependent cannot claim others as a dependent. Additionally, the dependent's social security number must be listed on the return for the exemption to be claimed.*

  A. **Multiple Support Agreements**—Allow a group of taxpayers who (together) support an individual more than 50%.

    1. Except for the support test, each individual in the group would otherwise be eligible to claim the individual as a dependent.

    2. The taxpayer claiming the exemption provides over 10% but less than half of the support.

    3. A written agreement allocates the dependency exemption to a member of the group. All members providing more than 10% of the support must sign.

Example

TP lives alone and has no income. TP is supported by the following people:

	Support	Percent
A (an unrelated friend)	$2,400	40%
B (TP's sister)	2,400	40%
C (TP's son)	720	12%
D (TP's son-in-law)	480	8%

Question: Under a multiple support agreement, who is eligible to claim TP as a dependent?

Answer: Either B or C may claim a dependency exemption for TP (A is not related and D did not provide at least 10% of the total support).

  B. **Divorced Parents**—An exception applies for children who are supported by parents who have been divorced or legally separated for the last six months of the year.

    1. The parent with custody (over half the year) is entitled to dependency exemption in the absence of any written agreement.

    2. The custodial parent can waive the exemption to the other parent by signing Form 8332. The non-custodial parent must attach this form to the return to claim the exemption.

C. When the taxpayer and spouse file separate returns, the taxpayer only may take an exemption for the spouse when the spouse has no gross income and was not claimed as a dependent on another taxpayer's income tax return.

IV. Phaseout of Exemptions—Exemptions are subject to a phaseout for wealthy taxpayers. The phaseout is triggered by a high AGI, and the amount of the phaseout is determined through a stepwise increment.

A. The AGI trigger for the phaseout varies by filing status.

Filing Status	AGI—Beginning of Phaseout (2017)	AGI Above Which Exemption Fully Phased Out (2017)
Married Jointly	$313,800	$436,300
Head of Household	$287,650	$410,150
Single	$261,500	$384,000

B. Two percent of total exemptions are lost for each $2,500 increment (or portion) above the trigger AGI.

1. Each $2,500 increment is called a **step**. Each step is rounded upward and multiplied by 2%. This percentage is then multiplied by the total amount of exemptions claimed, and the product is added to taxable income.

Example
A single taxpayer has AGI that is $48,500 over the trigger. This is 19.4 steps ($48,500/$2,500). The total steps are rounded up to 20 and each step results in a loss of 2% of the exemptions. In other words, the taxpayer will lose 40% of his exemptions. If the taxpayer claimed a personal exemption of $4,050 (2016), the phaseout will be $4,050 × 40% or $1,620.

2. Shortcut—All exemptions are phased out when AGI is $122,501 over the trigger ($122,501 divided by $2,500 results in 50 steps). Since each step results in a 2% reduction, 100% of the exemptions are lost.

Example
TP is a single taxpayer who claims two personal (dependency) exemptions. If TP's

AGI exceeds the phaseout trigger by $25,300, what portion of the exemptions is subject to a phaseout?

TP's AGI is $25,300 over the trigger, and this translates into 11 steps ($25,300/$2,500). Hence, TP would lose 22% of the exemptions.

Filing Status

Filing status determines the tax rate to be applied to taxable income. In addition, each filing status has a unique standard deduction. The determination of filing status occurs at year-end (or the death of the taxpayer or spouse). As an aside, it is important to note that most taxpayers are required to calculate their tax using a **tax table** instead of the tax rate schedule.

After studying this lesson, you should be able to:

1. Determine the proper filing status and use it to compute taxable income.

2. Evaluate whether head of household status is required.

3. Apply the requirements to determine if surviving spouse status is available.

4. Compute taxable income for a dependent on another return applying special rules.

5. Apprise whether a child is subject to the kiddie tax, and compute tax liability.

Tax Form for This Lesson: Form 1040 (available for download and printing from the lesson overview of your software).

I. **Married Filing Jointly**—Married taxpayers are treated to wider tax brackets if they choose to file under married-jointly. This election generally means that any tax liability is joint and several. Joint status may be elected by a married couple.

   A. Marital status is determined on the last day of the year, or the last day the taxpayer is alive.

   B. A spouse can avoid joint liability when income is omitted from a joint return if the spouse qualifies as an **innocent** spouse (the spouse has no reason to know of an omission from income and the error can be attributed to the other spouse).

   C. **Abandoned Spouse**—An abandoned spouse is a married taxpayer who is allowed to file as though they are unmarried. An abandoned spouse may file as a head of household. The following requirements must be met:

      1. The taxpayer's spouse has not lived in the home for the last six months of the calendar year.

      2. The taxpayer must provide more than half the cost of maintaining a home for self and a dependent child.

> **Definition**
> *Child*: A descendant of the taxpayer (e.g., son, daughter, or grandchild), or a stepchild, adopted child, or foster child.

   D. An election can be made to treat a nonresident alien spouse as a U.S. resident for income tax and wage withholding purposes. So married filing jointly can be elected by an individual who is married to a nonresident alien.

II. **Married Filing Separate**—Others, who are married, must file as married-separate.

   A. Married filing separately requires that the spouses divide income and expenses (according to ownership).

   B. Special rules also apply to prevent taxpayers from receiving benefits from filing separately. For example:

      1. If one spouse itemizes, the other spouse must itemize deductions also.

      2. Neither spouse can claim the earned income credit.

3. Neither spouse can claim the child and dependent care credit.

4. Neither spouse can claim an education credit.

5. An expense or credit is not allowed for adoption expenses.

6. The deduction for net capital losses is limited to $1,500 (rather than $3,000).

III. **Surviving Spouse**—Taxpayers, who are not married, may nonetheless qualify for a more advantageous tax rate schedule if they are a surviving spouse. A surviving spouse is also known as a qualifying widow(er).

A. A **surviving** spouse may use the married-joint rates for two years after the taxpayer's spouse has died. Filing status is Qualifying Widower with Dependent Child. To qualify as a surviving spouse, the taxpayer must provide more than half of the cost of maintaining the household (rent, mortgage interest, taxes, home insurance, repairs, food, utilities, etc.) for a dependent child, a stepchild, or an adopted child. The child's principal place of abode must be with the taxpayer.

> **Note**
> *In determining whether the child is a dependent, the three rules normally used to determine dependency status are ignored: (1) the joint return test; (2) the gross income test for qualifying relatives; and (3) the rule that a dependent cannot also have dependents.*

IV. **Head of Household**—Head of household status represents a de facto family for certain single taxpayers.

A. The taxpayer must provide more than half of the cost of maintaining the household for a qualifying child or a qualifying relative (a nonrelative living in the home for the entire tax year does not qualify). If one is a dependent due to a multiple support arrangement, that also does not qualify. This home must be the qualifying child's or qualifying relative's principal residence for more than half of the tax year.

> **Note**
> *A taxpayer whose spouse dies in the current tax year is usually eligible to file married-joint in the current year regardless of surviving spouse status. The surviving spouse exception applies to the following two tax years during which the taxpayer will use the married-joint rates (despite the absence of a spouse).*

B. Note that a girlfriend/boyfriend or a child of a girlfriend/boyfriend cannot be a qualifying relative for purposes of the head of household test since non-relatives living in the home for the entire tax year do not qualify.

C. Two exceptions to these rules:

1. If the **qualifying child** (defined same as for exemption rules) is an unmarried son, daughter, or grandchild, the child need not qualify as a dependent. A custodial parent who has released the exemption to the other parent can still file as head of household even though a dependency exemption was not claimed (assuming all other requirements are met). The noncustodial parent cannot file as head of household.

2. If the **qualifying relative** is a parent, the parent need not live with the taxpayer, but the taxpayer must provide more than 50% of the cost of maintaining the parent's home.

V. **Single**

A. Everyone who is unmarried and does not qualify for surviving spouse or head of household must file single—the default filing status.

B. Shortcut—A taxpayer who resides with a dependent child is most likely to be eligible for some special tax treatment, such as abandoned or surviving spouse status.

VI. **Overview of Standard Deduction**—The standard deduction is an automatic deduction that reduces the taxable income of most taxpayers.

A. Taxpayers can elect to deduct standard deduction in lieu of itemized deductions, and the amount varies by filing status.

Filing Status	2017 Standard Deduction
Married Individuals Filing Joint Returns and Surviving Spouses	$12,700
Heads of Households	$9,350
Unmarried Individuals (Other than Surviving Spouses and Heads of Households)	$6,350
Married Individuals Filing Separate Returns	$6,350

1. **Shortcut**—To determine most amounts (limits, cutoffs, etc.) for a taxpayer filing married-separately, divide the amount for married-joint in half.

Study Tip
For most tax items that vary based on filing status, married taxpayers receive higher amounts than single taxpayers. However, this is not the case for the additional standard deduction.

B. Special adjustments are made to the standard deduction in two instances.

1. Taxpayer (or spouse if filing jointly) is blind or reaches age 65 at year-end.

   a. In this instance, the standard deduction determined above for 2017 is increased by $1,250 if the taxpayer who is blind, or at least is age 65, is married or is a surviving spouse. Otherwise, the amount of the additional standard deduction is $1,550. Note, that if a taxpayer is 65 and blind, she would receive two additional standard deductions.

   b. These additions do not apply to dependents.

VII. Special Rules for Dependents on Another Return—A taxpayer claimed as a dependent by another is entitled to a "mini" standard deduction and no personal exemption. Amounts are indexed for inflation.

A. The "mini" standard deduction is $1,050 (2017).

1. A dependent can earn a regular standard deduction by earning income. The amount of the standard deduction is the greater of the mini standard deduction or earned income plus $350 (2017) (limited to the regular standard deduction).

Example
TP is claimed as a dependent on her parents' return. This year TP received interest of $1,200 and wages of $2,200. TP is eligible for a standard deduction of $2,550, $2,200 + $350 (2017).

Definition
Earned Income: Income generated by personal services (wages, self-employment income, etc.) as opposed to income generated by property (interest, dividends, etc.).

VIII. Kiddie Tax—The so-called kiddie tax is designed to discourage taxpayers from giving income-generating property to children in order to have the income taxed at the child's low tax rates.

A. The kiddie tax includes all children who are under 18. It also includes children who are 18, or between 19 and 23 who are full-time students, if their earned income does not exceed 50% of their total support for the year. Note that if a child would have his 19th birthday on January 1, he is assumed to turn 19 on the preceding December 31 (same applies for other ages). The tax is reported on Form 8615.

1. Taxable income for the child is divided into net unearned income and other income.

2. Net unearned income is taxed at the parent's tax rate, while other income is taxed at child's tax rate. If the parents are divorced, in general the tax rate of the custodial parent is used.

3. The parents can elect to report the child's income on their tax return and pay the tax if all the following conditions are met. The election is made by attaching Form 8814.

   a. The child is under age 19, or 24 if a full-time student.

   b. The child's income is only from interest, dividends, and capital gain distributions.

   c. The child's gross income is less than $10,000.

   d. The child is not filing a joint return.

   e. No estimated payments, back-up withholding, or prior year refunds can be applied to the tax.

B. Net unearned income is computed by reducing unearned income. Amounts are indexed for inflation.

1. Taxpayers who don't itemize subtract $2,100 from unearned income (2017).

2. Taxpayers who itemize subtract $1,050 plus itemized deductions allocated to unearned income (2017).

C. Taxation examples:

Examples	One	Two	Three
Unearned Income	$2,250	$500	$3,000
Earned Income	250	800	6,100
	2,500	1,300	9,100
Standard Deduction	(1,050)	(1,150)	(6,350)
Personal Exemption	0	0	0
Taxable Income	$1,450	$150	$2,750
Taxed at Parent's Rate (Unearned Income > $2,100)	$150	$0	$900
Taxed at Child's Rate	$1,300	$150	$1,850

Alternative Minimum Tax and Other Taxes

After studying this lesson, you should be able to:

1. Compute self-employment tax.

2. Calculate the alternative minimum tax for individual taxpayers.

3. Identify the most common adjustments and preferences when computing the AMT.

Tax Form for This Lesson: Form 6251 (available for download and printing from the lesson overview of your software)

I. Self-Employment Tax—The SE tax and the social security tax (OASDI) operate in tandem. Each tax consists of two parts, a retirement rate and a health insurance rate. The retirement rate is capped by a maximum amount of wages and income subject to the tax. If the tax is imposed on wages exceeding the maximum (e.g., the taxpayer changed jobs), then the excess tax can be claimed as a refund.

A. SE Tax—The SE tax consists of two parts imposed at twice the OASDI tax rate.

1. The first part of the SE rate (social security) is 12.4% on the first $127,200 (2017) of SE income (the ceiling).

2. If wages are earned in addition to SE income, then the ceiling is reduced by the wages subject to OASDI.

3. The second part of the SE rate (Medicare) is 2.9% on all SE income (no ceiling).

Example
TP earned $29,600 in wages and $103,600 in self-employment income. While all $133,200 is subject to the 2.9% tax, only $97,600 ($127,200 – $29,600 for 2017) of the SE income is subject to the 12.4% tax ($29,600 has already been subjected to FICA).

B. The SE tax is imposed on income from self-employment.

1. Self-employment income is gross income from self-employment less deductions associated with the activity. SE income includes director's fees.

   a. The distributive share from a partnership/LLC is self-employment income if the partner is a material participant in the business. The distributive share from an S corporation is never included in self-employment income.

> **Note**
> *The deductible business expenses incurred by self-employed taxpayers are deductible for AGI.*

2. The last step in calculating the tax is to multiply self-employment income by 92.35% (or reduce it by 7.65%).

3. Self-employment income × 92.35% must exceed $400 for the SE tax to be assessed.

4. **Reminder**—One-half of the SE tax is deductible for AGI.

Examples
1. TP is a self-employed cash-basis taxpayer who recorded the following this year:

Receipts	$45,000
Dividends (investments)	300

Cost of sales	22,000
Other operating expenses	4,500
State business taxes	950
Federal self-employment tax	1,400

Question: What is TP's net earnings from self-employment?

Answer: $17,550 is SE earnings (the dividends are not earned and the self-employment tax is not deductible in calculating net earnings).

2. TP is a cash-basis self-employed repairman with gross receipts of $20,000 this year. Over the year TP paid the following:

Repair parts	$2,500
Listing in Yellow Pages	2,000
Estimated federal income taxes	1,000
Business long-distance phone calls	400
Charitable contributions	200

Question: What is TP's net self-employment income?

Answer: $15,100 ($20,000 – $2,500 – $2,000 – $400). Note that the charitable contributions are deducted on Schedule A.

3. TP, a retired corporate executive, earned consulting fees of $9,000 and director's fees of $4,000 this year.

Question: What is TP's gross income from self-employment this year?

Answer: $13,000

Example
A taxpayer has self-employment income of $50,000. The reduction is $50,000 × 7.65% = $3,825, resulting in *net earnings from self-employment* of $50,000 – $3,825 = $46,175 and a self-employment tax of $46,175 × 15.3% = $7,065. In computing adjusted gross income, the taxpayer is allowed to deduct 50% × $7,065 = $3,533.

C. **Nanny Tax**—Taxpayers who employ domestic workers, must withhold and pay FICA if cash wages exceeds $2,000 (2017).

D. Self-employment taxes are reported on Form 1040 Schedule SE.

1. There is a long-form and short-form Schedule SE.

2. Most taxpayers can use the short-form unless:

a. Wages plus self-employment income exceeds the annual wage base limitation for social security taxes *or*

b. The taxpayer works as a minister, pastor, etc.

II. Payroll Taxes

A. Social security tax of 6.2% is levied on the first $127,200 of wages in 2017.

B. Medicare tax of 1.45% is levied on all wages paid.

C. The social security and Medicare tax is matched by the employer.

III. Hospital Insurance Tax—An additional .9% hospital insurance tax applies to wages as follows:

    A. Joint filers with wages > $250,000.

    B. Single and head of household filers with wages > $200,000.

    C. Self-employment income above these limits.

    D. This tax applies only to employees, not to employers.

IV. Alternative Minimum Tax

    A. The alternative minimum tax (AMT) is a separate tax system that calculates a broader tax base by modifying taxable income for both individuals and corporations. These modifications generally serve to increase taxable income by adding items of income not recognized by regular tax and disallowing deductions that do not necessarily represent economic outlays. The AMT applies only to taxpayers whose net regular liability is less than the tentative tax calculated under the broad AMT rules. This outline covers the individual AMT. The formula shown below follows Form 6251, which is the form for reporting the AMT.

Formula for Computing the AMT

Regular taxable income

± Adjustments

+ <u>Preferences</u>

AMT income

− <u>Exemption</u>

AMT base

× <u>Rate</u>

Tentative minimum tax before foreign tax credit

− <u>Certain credits (see discussion below)</u>

Tentative minimum tax

− <u>Regular tax liability</u>

<u>AMT (if positive)</u>

    B. **Adjustments**—AMT adjustments are specific adjustments that can either increase or decrease taxable income when alternative minimum taxable income is computed. These adjustments often represent income or deductions used to defer the taxation of economic income. Hence, many (but not all) of these adjustments are merely timing differences that will reverse in future periods.

> **Note**
> *There is no difference between AMT cost recovery and regular cost recovery for real property. Different methods are required only for personalty.*

        1. The AMT adjustment applies to MACRS 3-, 5-, 7-, and 10-year property that is depreciated using the 200% declining-balance method. For AMT, the 150% declining-balance method is used over the MACRS life.

> **Exam Tip**
> *Questions focusing on the accelerated portion of cost recovery will likely give the total amounts for the regular tax and the AMT. You will use this information to compute the AMT adjustment for depreciation.*

            a. Note that no AMT adjustments are required for assets purchased in 2008 to 2017 that use bonus depreciation. For more information on bonus depreciation see the "Section 1231 Assets—Cost Recovery" lesson.

        2. **Percentage of completion contract** income over completed contract income.

3. For itemized deductions:

   a. The phaseout of itemized deductions is subtracted from taxable income (i.e., phaseout does not apply for AMT).

   b. No deduction is allowed for taxes (it must be added back to taxable income).

   c. Two percent miscellaneous deductions are not allowed.

   d. Home mortgage interest is deductible only if the loan proceeds are used to acquire or improve the home.

4. Personal and dependency exemptions and the standard deduction (if used) are added back.

5. The compensation element on the exercise date for an incentive stock option.

6. Installment method may not be used by dealers.

C. **Preferences**—These always increase AMT income. The most common preference items for individuals are:

1. Tax-exempt interest on private activity bonds has been a preference item for many years, but a few recent exceptions have been enacted.

   a. For bonds issued after July 30, 2008, the interest on tax exempt housing bonds is not treated as a preference item if the bonds are for low-income housing developments, mortgage bonds, or mortgage bonds for veterans.

   b. For any private activity bonds issued in 2009 and 2010, the interest earned from these bonds will *not* be included as AMT income.

2. Percentage depletion in excess of cost basis on certain mineral properties.

3. **Qualifying Small Business Stock (QSBS)**

   a. For QSBS that was purchased before September 28, 2010, the general rule for this preference item is that 7% of the gain excluded from income under the qualified small business stock provision (see the "Capital Gains and Losses" lesson for more detail) is a preference item for the AMT. Gain is excluded only if the stock was held for more than five years.

   b. Gain on the sale of qualified small business stock that was acquired after September 27, 2010, and is sold more than five years after the purchase date will not be subject to the AMT. This gain is also completely excluded from regular tax.

D. **AMT exemption**—Taxpayers are entitled to an AMT exemption of $84,500 if married filing jointly ($54,300 if not married) in 2017.

1. The exemption is subject to a phaseout triggered by AMTI over $160,900 if married, $120,700 if single (2017).

2. The phaseout rate is 25% of the amount of AMTI over the trigger.

3. For children subject to the kiddie tax, the AMT exemption cannot exceed the sum of the child's earned income plus $7,500 (in 2017).

Example
For a married taxpayer with AMTI of $256,900, the phaseout is triggered because AMTI exceeds the $160,900 trigger. This taxpayer is $96,000 over the trigger which means that $24,000 of the exemption will be lost ($96,000 × 25%).

4. The AMT has two tax brackets, 26% and 28%.

E. Tax Credits

1. The foreign tax credit is allowed for the AMT, as are all nonrefundable personal credits, including:

   a. Child tax credit

   b. Adoption credit

   c. American Opportunity and Lifetime Learning (education) tax credits

   d. Low-income saver's credit

   e. Residential energy efficient property credit

   f. Nonbusiness energy property credit

   g. Credit for the elderly and disabled

   h. Child and dependent care credit

2. The preferential rates on capital gains are available for a net capital gain when calculating the AMT tentative tax.

3. Taxpayers pay the greater of the tentative minimum tax (before credits) or regular tax (before credits).

4. The amount of AMT paid, which is due to timing differences between regular taxable income and AMTI, creates an *AMT credit* that can be used to offset regular tax liability (but not below the tentative minimum tax for a given year) in future years. The AMT credit can be carried forward indefinitely.

Tax Planning Strategies for Individuals

After studying this lesson, you should be able to:

1. Determine the marginal tax rate for a taxpayer.

2. Choose appropriate acceleration or deferral of selected tax items based on changes in rates.

3. Explain common tax planning strategies.

4. Describe planning strategies for the alternative minimum tax.

I. Using Tax Rates in Tax Planning

    A. Marginal tax rate is the rate that should be used for decision making.

Definition

Marginal Tax Rate: The amount of taxes that will be paid on the next dollar of taxable income or that will be saved on the next dollar of deduction.

Example

T is in the 35% tax bracket and itemizes on her tax return. She plans to make a charitable contribution of $1,000 to her alma mater on December 31. The net cost of this contribution to T is $650, since she will save $350 in taxes ($1,000 × Marginal tax rate of 35%) because the contribution is deductible.

    B. If rates are increasing in the future, accelerate income and defer deductions.

    C. If rates are decreasing in the future, accelerate deductions and defer income.

    D. Differences in tax rates over time present opportunities for tax planning. These differences can happen for several reasons.

        1. Differences due to changing tax brackets based on change in taxable income

Example

B is in the 10% tax bracket in Year 1 but expects to be in a 25% tax bracket in Year 2.

B should adopt tax strategies that will accelerate income into Year 1 or defer deductions into Year 2. If he accelerates $10,000 of income into Year 1, his tax savings will be $1,500 ($10,000 × (25% − 10%)).

        2. **Differences due to the time value of money**—Note in this example that if the time of value of money is considered, the savings is less than $1,500 since he must pay the $1,000 of taxes ($10,000 × 10%) in Year 1 rather than in Year 2. If he could earn 5% on these funds then he forgoes interest income of $50 ($1,000 × 5%). His net cash savings is $1,450 ($1,500 − $50).

        Caution: Do not consider the time value of money on the exam unless you are specifically directed to do so in the instructions

        3. **Differences due to statutory changes in rates across years**

Example

C is in the 40% tax bracket in Year 1, but Congress has decreased her tax bracket to 35% for Year 2. C should adopt tax strategies that will accelerate deductions from to Year 1 or defer income to Year 2. If she defers income of $100,000 until Year 2, her tax savings will be $5,000 ($100,000 × (40% − 35%)).

4. Shifting income to lower-bracket taxpayers is also a viable strategy.

Example
Mother is in a 50% tax bracket and her 25-year-old son is in a 10% tax bracket. Mother gifts $100,000 of bonds paying 8% interest to Son. The $8,000 of interest income will be taxed at the son's 10% rate, a savings of $3,200 for the family ($8,000 × (50% − 10%)).

5. Differences based on character of income also present planning opportunities (e.g., long-term capital gain versus ordinary income).

Example
Assume that long-term capital gains are taxed at 20% and ordinary income at 40%. Taxpayers should consider strategies to convert ordinary income into long-term capital gains. If taxpayer D sells stocks at a gain of $3,000 that have been owned for 11 months, the gain is taxed as ordinary income at the 40% rate (assuming there are no capital losses to net this against). If D had held the stocks for more than one year, the gain would be taxed at 20%.

6. Differences based on jurisdiction (e.g., U.S. tax rates versus foreign tax rates).

7. The effective income tax rate for a taxpayer is the federal income tax liability for the year divided by taxable income. This rate should not be used for tax planning, but it does provide an estimate of the overall income tax burden for a taxpayer.

8. Comparing the rate on tax-free bonds to the rate on taxable bonds. The relationship between the rates is computed as follows:

Taxable rate × (1 − Marginal tax rate) = Tax-free rate

For example, a 10% taxable bond is equivalent to a tax-free bond that yields 8.5% for a taxpayer at the 15% marginal tax rate [10% × (1 − 0.15) = 8.5%].

II. **Tax Strategies**—Common tax strategies that may be helpful for solving problems on the exam include:

A. Avoid income by choosing nontaxable fringe benefits over taxable salary.

Example
Taxpayer F earns a salary of $75,000 per year but does not receive health insurance benefits from his employer. Since health insurance is a tax-free fringe benefit, F should consider having his employer pay his $5,000 of health insurance premiums and reduce his salary to $70,000. This will reduce his taxable salary by $5,000.

B. Defer income by meeting rules such as like-kind exchange rules.

C. Maximize contributions to retirement plans.

D. Recognize capital gains if capital losses have already been recognized which can offset the gains.

Example
Taxpayer W has $30,000 of capital losses and no capital gains for the current tax year. W will be able to deduct net capital losses of $3,000. If W can generate $27,000 of capital gains, these gains will be offset by the unused capital losses so that no additional tax liability will be due on account of these gains.

E. Generate passive income to offset unused passive losses.

F. Insure that carryforward amounts are used before they expire (e.g., charitable contributions, net operating losses).

III. Tax Planning for the AMT

A. Taxpayers should adopt planning strategies to avoid the individual AMT.

    1. Reduce adjustments and preferences that increase AMT income, such as certain types of tax-exempt interest and income from the exercise of incentive stock options.

    2. Consider the deductions that are not allowed for AMT purposes, and minimize those in years when one is subject to the AMT, especially itemized deductions such as:

        a. No deduction is allowed for taxes.

        b. There is no allowance for 2% miscellaneous deductions.

        c. Home mortgage interest is deductible only if the loan proceeds are used to improve the home.

B. If the individual AMT cannot be avoided, it may be advantageous to accelerate income into the AMT year since it will be taxed at a maximum rate of 28%. However, a level of income will eventually be reached where the taxpayer is no longer subject to the AMT but to the regular income tax rates, which may be higher than 28%. Income should be accelerated until this level of income is reached.

IV. Tax Planning for Charitable Contributions

A. Gifting appreciated property to a charity avoids recognizing the appreciation as income.

Example
Taxpayer Z has owned stock for four years that has a basis of $30,000 and fair market value of $100,000. If Z sells the stock, she will recognize a long-term capital gain of $70,000. If Z contributes the stock to a charity, she will receive a deduction of $100,000 and will avoid recognizing the appreciation of $70,000 as taxable gain.

B. Loss property should not be gifted because the loss is not recognized. Rather, the asset should be sold so the loss can be recognized. The cash from the sale can then be contributed to a charity.

V. Other Tax Planning Strategies—Tax planning should not be done in isolation; instead it should be a part of a taxpayer's overall financial goals and integrated with nontax considerations. Three general tax planning strategies involve (1) the timing of income and deductions, (2) the shifting of income and deductions between taxpayers, and (3) the conversion of the character of income and deductions.

A. **Timing**—The tax accounting period in which an expense is deducted or in which income is recognized affects the real tax savings or cost because of the time value of money. A simple tax planning strategy would be to accelerate a tax deduction to an earlier period while deferring the recognition of income to a later period.

    1. **Installment sale**—A taxpayer may want to structure the casual sale of an asset so that at least one payment is received in the year(s) following the year of sale. By using the installment method and spreading the gain over multiple years, the taxpayer's gain will be deferred and may be taxed in lower brackets

    2. **Net operating loss**—A taxpayer should carefully consider whether to carry back an NOL or elect to forgo the carryback period. A taxpayer may want to carry the loss forward only if she anticipates being in a higher marginal tax bracket in carryforward years.

    3. **Casualty loss**—If a casualty loss is sustained in a presidentially declared disaster area, the taxpayer may make an election to deduct the loss in the year preceding the year in which the loss was incurred in order to obtain a more immediate tax benefit for the loss deduction.

    4. **Medical expenses**—Because of the 10% of AGI threshold for deducting medical expenses, taxpayers often are unable to take a deduction for unreimbursed medical expenses. However, it may be possible to take a medical expense deduction if the expenses are bunched into one year. Medical expenses generally are deductible when paid but can be deducted in the year charged to a credit card.

5. **Itemized deductions**—If a taxpayer's total itemized deductions are approximately the same as the standard deduction, a taxpayer may benefit from bunching itemized deductions into a year in which the taxpayer intends to itemize, with the intention of taking the standard deduction in the following year. By alternating standard deduction and itemized deductions years, the taxpayer may be able to maximize deductions over a multiyear time frame.

6. **Alternative minimum tax**—If a taxpayer is not subject to AMT in 2017 but expects to be in 2018, she may accelerate expenses that are not deductible for AMT into 2017. For example, the taxpayer might consider paying off home equity debt since the interest expense is usually not deductible for AMT purposes. Alternatively, if the taxpayer expects to pay an AMT in 2017 but not in 2018, he might consider accelerating ordinary and short-term capital gain income into 2017 while deferring expenses not deductible for AMT into 2018 (e.g., state and local income taxes, real estate taxes, miscellaneous deductions in the 2% category).

7. **Short-term capital gain**—If a taxpayer has short-term capital gains (which are taxed at ordinary income tax rates), he might consider selling capital assets that will generate capital losses in order to offset the short-term capital gain. Taxpayers are allowed to deduct up to $3,000 of net capital loss against ordinary income each year, with any net capital loss in excess of $3,000 carried forward to future years.

8. **Estimated tax**—An exception that can be used to avoid an underpayment penalty for the current year is for a taxpayer to make estimated payments and withholdings that in total are at least equal to 100% (110% if prior year AGI was greater than $150,000) of the tax liability for the prior year. Income tax withholdings are considered paid equally throughout the year, even if the taxes are withheld near the end of the year. Taxpayers who anticipate that taxes for the current year are underpaid might consider adjusting withholdings for the remainder of the year to avoid the underpayment penalty.

B. **Income and Deduction Shifting**—This planning strategy seeks to take advantage of the differences in tax rates between taxpayers or between taxing jurisdictions. The goal is to shift income from high-tax-rate to low-tax-rate taxpayers or jurisdictions and to shift deductions from low-tax-rate to high-tax-rate taxpayers or jurisdictions.

1. **Children**—Parents can reduce their family's income tax by shifting income that would otherwise be taxed at higher rates to their children whose income is taxed at lower rates. Even if the kiddie tax applies, the first $2,100 (2017) of unearned (e.g., interest) income will be taxed at the child's rates. Additionally, if the child has no earned income (e.g., wages), the child's unearned income will be partially offset by a limited basic standard deduction of $1,050 (2017).

2. **Gift tax exclusion**—A taxpayer interested in family wealth planning may want to consider the annual gift tax exclusion when gifting appreciated assets to family members. There is an annual $14,000 (2017) exclusion per donee for gifts of a present interest. This means that up to $14,000 of gifts can be given to a donee without making a taxable gift. Additionally, if the appreciated assets are given to family members not subject to the kiddie tax who are in the lowest two brackets, the capital gain on sale of the assets will be taxed at a 0% rate as opposed to a 15% or 20% rate if sold by the parents.

3. **Section 529 plan**—A Section 529 educational savings plan could be established for a child or grandchild. Using a special election, a taxpayer could currently fund up to five years of annual exclusions into the plan without making a taxable gift. This would permit up to $70,000 (2017) to be deposited into a child's Section 529 plan where the principal would grow tax deferred, and later distributions used for the child's college costs would be exempt from tax.

C. **Conversion**—This planning strategy involves converting ordinary income that would be taxed at regular rates into income that will be taxed at a preferential rate. Additionally, this strategy might be applied to convert deductions that would be subject to limitations into ordinary deductions that are deductible without limitation.

1. **Qualified dividends**—A taxpayer may want to consider replacing investments generating interest income taxed at regular rates with stocks paying qualified dividends that are taxed at a reduced rate of 15% or 20%, or possibly 0% if the taxpayer is in the 10% or 15% bracket. In

order to qualify for the reduced rate, the underlying stock on which a dividend is paid must be held for at least 61 days during the 121-day period beginning 60 days before the ex-dividend date (91 days of the 181-day period for preferred stock).

2. **Passive activities**—A taxpayer may be able to increase participation in what would otherwise be a "passive activity" in order to classify the activity as an active business activity whose losses are currently deductible. Alternatively, a taxpayer might be able to decrease participation in a profitable business activity in order to classify the income as passive activity income that could then be sheltered by losses generated from other passive activities.

VI. **Planning for Tax Losses**—The following loss limitations will also likely appear on the exam.

A. **Capital Loss—Individuals**—Limited to $3,000 per year against ordinary income or $1,500 for married filing separately taxpayers assuming no capital gains. Any remaining excess amount can be carried forward.

B. Business bad debts can be fully deducted in the year of partial or total worthlessness as an ordinary business loss.

C. **Net Operating Losses**

1. Net operating losses and loss carryforwards are offset against income items.

2. Net operating losses may be carried back two years and carried forward 20 years.

D. **Losses from Loans between Related Parties**

1. Treated as either gifts or as bad debts, usually nonbusiness, depending on the facts and circumstances.

2. Need to determine if a bona fide debtor-creditor situation existed and that the transaction was not in reality a gift. The existence of an agreement, interest, payments, and so on will indicate a loan. If deemed a gift, no deduction is allowed for bad debt.

E. **Losses on Stock**

1. **Worthless securities**—Worthless securities in a corporation are generally deemed sold for $0 on the last day of the tax year.

   a. Such securities are usually treated as a capital loss, yielding a $3,000 ($1,500 for married filing separately taxpayers) maximum deduction per year.

   b. Thus, if a single taxpayer had a $60,000 investment in stock that became worthless, it would take 20 years at $3,000 per year to fully deduct the capital loss (assuming no capital gains during these years).

2. **Losses on Section 1244 stock** (small business stock)

> **Definition**
> *Section 1244 Stock*: Stock in a corporation with total capitalization of $1 million or less.

   a. This rule (special loss treatment) applies only to the original shareholder of the stock, whether individuals or partnership shareholders, and is not available to corporate shareholders.

   b. Section 1244 applies to the *sale or exchange of stock at a loss as well as to stock that is still held but becomes worthless*.

   c. *For purposes of Section 1244 only*, the basis of Section 1244 stock to the shareholder is fair value when fair value is less than the adjusted basis of property exchanged for the stock.

   d. **Basic rule**—Losses on Section 1244 stock are treated as an ordinary loss (and thus fully deductible) up to a maximum of $50,000 ($100,000 for married filing jointly taxpayers) per year. Any excess loss is a capital loss, thus yielding a $3,000 ($1,500 for married filing separately) maximum deduction per year.

Tax Credits

Personal Tax Credits

After studying this lesson, you should be able to:

1. Determine when personal tax credits are allowable and list necessary requirements.

2. Compute the following tax credits: (1) child credit, (2) education credits, (3) dependent care credit.

3. Distinguish between refundable and non refundable credits.

Tax Credit Categories

Personal Credits:

Child Tax Credit

Saver's (IRA) Credit

Education Tax Credits

Dependent Care

Adoption Expense Credit

Elderly Credit

Alternative Motor Vehicle Credit

Residential Energy Efficient Property Credit

Foreign Tax Credit

General Business Credits:

Research and Development

Rehabilitation

Miscellaneous

Refundable Credits:

Earned Income

Child Credit (partially refundable)

American Opportunity/Hope Credit (partially refundable)

Health Coverage Tax Credit

I. **Order of Credits**—Credits are applied against the tax liability in a predetermined order.

    A. The order of applying credits against tax is determined by the nature of the credit:

        1. Personal (i.e., nonrefundable) credits are limited to gross tax, and there is no carryover of any excess.

        2. The general business credit is limited to a percentage of gross tax after personal credits, and any excess carries over (back one year and forward 20 years).

        3. Refundable credits (see list above) are applied last because these credits have no limit based upon tax (any excess, or a portion of the excess, is refunded to the taxpayer).

    B. **AMT**—See the "Alternative Minimum Tax and Other Taxes" lesson for discussion of credits for the AMT.

II. **Personal Credits**—Personal credits are allowed for a number of activities deemed socially desirable.

    A. **Child Credit**—A $1,000 Child Credit is allowed for each **qualifying child (as defined under the dependency rules)** *under the age of 17.*

        1. Qualifying children's names and Social Security numbers must be included on the return.

        2. The credit is phased out for married taxpayers with AGI in excess of $110,000 ($75,000 for unmarried). The credit is reduced $50 for each $1,000 (or portion) over the trigger AGI amount. These amounts are not indexed for inflation.

> **Example**
> TP is married (filing jointly) with two dependent children under the age of 17. This year TP has an AGI of $123,500. TP will be able to claim a credit of $1,300 because TP's gross credit of $2,000 is reduced by $700 (14 × $50).

        3. The additional child tax credit is refundable to the extent of 15% of the taxpayer's earned income in excess of $3,000. *For a taxpayer with three or more qualifying children, the credit is the greater of this amount or the excess of his Social Security taxes for the tax year over his Earned Income Credit for the year.* Combat pay is treated as earned income for purposes of computing this refundable credit, even though combat pay is not taxable. *Taxpayers electing to exclude foreign income or housing benefits are not eligible for the refundable portion of the credit.*

        4. A taxpayer who erroneously claims the child credit due to intentional disregard of the rules is ineligible to claim the credit for a period of two tax years. If the credit is claimed due to fraud the period is extended to 10 years.

III. **Education Credits**

    A. The American Opportunity Tax Credit (AOTC) is allowed up to a maximum of $2,500 per year for each eligible student.

        1. The credit is computed as 100% of the first $2,000 and 25% of the next $2,000 of qualified educational expenses.

        2. Qualified educational expenses are nondeductible tuition and academic fees (reduced by tax-free benefits, such as scholarships) incurred during a student's first **four years** of postsecondary education. The expenses must relate to an academic period beginning in the current tax year, or the first three months of the next tax year. Course materials are also included.

        3. A qualifying student includes the taxpayer, spouse, or any dependent of the taxpayer enrolled at least half time in an institution of higher education. To be eligible, the student must be enrolled in a degree program.

        4. The credit is phased out ratably for single taxpayers with AGI in excess of $80,000 ($160,000 in the case of a joint return). The credit is phased out over a $10,000 range ($20,000 for joint return) and, thus, is completely gone when AGI reaches $90,000 ($180,000 joint return).

        5. The credit can be claimed against the AMT, and 40% of the credit is refundable.

    B. **Lifetime Learning Credit**—Is allowed up to a maximum of $2,000 per taxpayer per year.

        1. The credit is computed as 20% of $10,000 of qualified educational expenses incurred for the taxpayer, spouse, or dependent.

        2. Qualified educational expenses are nondeductible tuition and academic fees (reduced by tax-free benefits, such as scholarships) incurred by a taxpayer. Materials and textbooks are qualified expenses only if required to be purchased from the university (this differs from the AOTC). The expenses must be for post-secondary education, but need not relate to a degree program. Student does not need to be at least half-time for expenses to qualify.

3. The Lifetime Learning Credit is phased out ratably for single taxpayers with an AGI for 2017 in excess of $56,000 ($112,000 in the case of a joint return) and is phased out over a $10,000 range ($20,000 for married-jointly).

4. The AOTC credit, the Lifetime Learning Credit, and distributions from educational IRAs are **mutually exclusive** in that an educational expenditure can never simultaneously qualify for more than one benefit (i.e., no "double dipping").

Example

TP spent $3,000 in tuition for his first year in postsecondary education. He was reimbursed $500 through a tax-exempt scholarship, and he recorded AGI of $20,000. TP can use the unreimbursed tuition of $2,500 to claim a $2,125 AOTC credit (100% of $2,000 and 25% of $500).

a. **Shortcut**—The two credits differ in the percentage applied to calculating the credit (100% and 25% for the AOTC versus 20% for the Lifetime), the total expenses eligible for the credit ($4,000 per year for the AOTC versus $10,000 total for the Lifetime), and the type of expenses covered by the credit (first four years of postsecondary education in a degree program for the AOTC versus any postsecondary education for the Lifetime). The AOTC applies per student ($2,500 per student), whereas the Lifetime Learning Credit applies per tax return (maximum $2,000 credit per year).

Examples

1. Alan paid qualified tuition and related expenses for his dependent, Betty, to attend college. Assuming all other relevant requirements are met, Alan may claim either an American Opportunity credit or lifetime learning credit with respect to his dependent, Betty, but not both.

2. Cathy paid $2,000 in qualified tuition and related expenses for her dependent, Doug, to attend college. Also during the year, Cathy paid $600 in qualified tuition to attend a continuing education course to improve her job skills. Assuming all relevant requirements are met, Cathy may claim the American Opportunity credit for the $2,000 paid for her dependent, Doug, and a lifetime learning credit for the $600 of qualified tuition that she paid for the continuing education course to improve her job skills.

3. The facts are the same as in example #2, except that Cathy paid $4,500 in qualified tuition and related expenses for her dependent, Doug, to attend college. Although an American Opportunity credit is available only for the first $4,000 of qualified tuition and related expenses paid with respect to Doug, Cathy **cannot** add the $500 of excess expenses to her $600 of qualified tuition in computing the amount of her lifetime learning credit.

4. Ernie has one dependent, Frank. During the current year, Ernie paid qualified tuition and related expenses for Frank to attend college. Although Ernie is eligible to claim Frank as a dependent on Ernie's federal income tax return, Ernie does **not** do so. Therefore, assuming all other relevant requirements are met, Frank is allowed an education credit on Frank's federal income tax return for his qualified tuition and related expenses paid by Ernie, and Ernie is not allowed an education credit with respect to Frank's education expenses. The result would be the same if Frank had paid his qualified tuition expenses himself.

C. **A "Saver's Credit"**—Is allowed for voluntary contributions to IRA and qualified retirement accounts.

1. The credit is a maximum of $1,000 (in addition to any exclusion or deduction that would otherwise apply) and is based upon IRA contributions (Roth or Traditional).

2. The taxpayer must be 18 or older, not a full-time student, nor claimed as a dependent on another return, and cannot receive a distribution from the account.

3. No credit is allowed for taxpayers with an AGI (2017) in excess of $62,000 ($46,500 for head of household and $31,000 for single taxpayers).

4. Qualifying taxpayers multiply IRA contributions by 50%, 20%, or 10% depending on the level of AGI (indexed for inflation).

Examples

1. TP is married (filing jointly) and has an AGI of $23,500. If TP contributes $2,000 to an IRA, TP will be able to claim a credit of $1,000 (50% × $2,000) because TP's AGI is below $37,000 (the cut-off level for 50% for married-jointly in 2017). This credit is in addition to a $2,000 IRA deduction.

2. TP is single and has an AGI of $12,000. If TP contributes $3,000 to a Roth IRA, TP will be able to claim a credit of $1,000 (50% × $3,000, limited to a maximum of $1,000) because TP's AGI is below $18,500 (the cut-off level for 50% for single in 2017).

IV. **Dependent Care Credit**—The dependent care credit is designed to provide a tax credit for a portion of the expenses incurred for caregiving while the taxpayer is employed.

  A. To be eligible for the credit, a person needing care must live with the taxpayer for more than half the year.

   1. A qualifying child or dependent under the age of 13 automatically qualifies (the child can violate the gross income test and still qualify for care).

   2. Other dependents or a spouse will also qualify if they are incapable of self-care (physical or mental disability). This individual must live in the same household as the taxpayer for more than half of the tax year.

  B. Expenditures for household services and care are required for the credit.

   1. Care can be given within the home, but the caregiver cannot be a dependent relative or child of the taxpayer.

   2. The taxpayer must be employed and earn at least as much as the amount of the expenses. If married, then the taxpayer must file jointly (unless abandoned) and the spouse must also be employed.

   3. Income is imputed to a full-time student (at least five months per year) or a spouse incapable of self-care ($250 per month for one child; $500 per month for more than one).

   4. Other rules include:

      a. Expenses for a child below kindergarten qualify; expenses for before or after school care of a child in kindergarten or higher grade may qualify.

      b. Full amount paid for day camp or similar programs, even if the program specializes in a particular activity.

      c. Summer school and tutoring programs are education and do not qualify.

      d. Sick child centers may qualify for either the credit or a medical expense, but not as both.

      e. For boarding school, amounts paid for food, lodging, clothing, and education must be separated from amounts paid for other goods or services.

      f. Additional cost of providing room and board for a caregiver may qualify if expenses are in addition to normal household expenses.

      g. Cost of overnight expense does not qualify.

      h. Expenses incurred during the specific time of day that the taxpayer was looking for a job also qualify.

C. The credit is calculated by multiplying the qualifying expenditures by the appropriate credit percentage.

    1. The credit percentage begins at 35% if an AGI is less than $15,000, and is reduced by 1% for each $2,000 increment (or part) in an AGI above $15,000. The minimum dependent care credit is 20%.

        a. Shortcut—Taxpayers with an AGI over $43,000 will receive the minimum dependent care credit of 20%.

    2. The maximum amount of expense eligible for the credit is $3,000 ($6,000 if more than one individual qualifies for care) or, if lower, earned income (of the lesser-earning spouse if married).

Examples

    1. TP is a single parent with a 10-year-old child at home. This year TP earned $8,000 and paid $2,000 for the care of the child while TP worked. TP qualifies for a dependent care credit of $700 ($2,000 × 35%).

2. TP is a self-employed taxpayer who pays $3,000 for the after-school care of his or her dependent nine-year-old child. TP has an AGI of $86,000.

Question: What amount of the expenses is eligible for the childcare credit?

Answer: For one dependent, the maximum eligible amount is $3,000 or earned income. The credit percentage in this case would be 20%.

V. Adoption Credit

A. The adoption credit is allowed for adoption expenses.

    1. Reasonable expenses up to $13,570 (2017) associated with an adoption qualify for the credit.

    2. A $13,570 (2017) adoption credit is available for children with special needs regardless of actual expenses.

    3. The credit is phased out for taxpayers with an AGI (2017) in excess of $203,540, and is completely phased out for taxpayers with modified adjusted gross income of $243,540.

    4. The credit is limited to the regular tax liability, but any excess credit is carried forward for five years.

B. Qualified adoption expenses incurred or paid during a tax year prior to the year in which the adoption is finalized may be claimed as a credit in the tax year following the year the expense was incurred. Adoption expenses incurred during the year the adoption becomes final or in the year following the finalization of the adoption are claimed in the year they were incurred. Qualified adoption expenses are taken into account in the year the adoption becomes final and include all reasonable and necessary adoption fees, court costs, attorney fees, and other expenses that are directly related to the legal adoption by the taxpayer of an eligible child. However, expenses incurred in carrying out a surrogate parenting arrangement or in adopting a spouse's child do not qualify for the credit.

VI. Credit for the Elderly and the Disabled

A. Eligible taxpayers are those who are either (1) 65 or older or (2) permanently and totally disabled.

    1. Permanent and total disability is the inability to engage in substantial gainful activity for a period that is expected to last for a continuous 12-month period.

    2. Married individuals must file a joint return to claim the credit unless they have not lived together at all during the year.

    3. Credit cannot be claimed if Form 1040A or 1040EZ is filed.

B. Credit is **15%** of an initial amount reduced by certain amounts excluded from gross income and AGI in excess of certain levels. The amount of credit is limited to the amount of tax liability.

    1. Initial amount varies with filing status.

        a. $5,000 for single or joint return where only one spouse is 65 or older

        b. $7,500 for joint return where both spouses are 65 or older

        c. $3,750 for married filing a separate return

        d. Limited to disability income for taxpayers under age 65

    2. Reduced by annuities, pensions, Social Security, or disability income that is excluded from gross income.

    3. Also reduced by 50% of the excess of AGI over:

        a. $7,500 if single;

        b. *$10,000 if joint return;*

        c. $5,000 for married individual filing separate return.

Example

H, age 67, and his wife, W, age 65, file a joint return and have adjusted gross income of $12,000. H received Social Security benefits of $2,000 during the year. The computation of their credit would be as follows:

Initial amount		$7,500
Less: Social Security	$2,000	
50% of AGI over $10,000	1,000	3,000
Balance		4,500
		× 15%
Amount of credit (limited to tax liability)		$675

VII. Motor Vehicle Credits

    A. Alternative Motor Vehicle Credit

        1. An income tax credit is available for **qualified fuel cell vehicles**. This is a new vehicle propelled by power derived from one or more cells that convert chemical energy directly into electricity by combining oxygen with hydrogen fuel.

        2. The alternative motor vehicle credit is also allowed against the AMT.

    B. Credit for New Qualified Plug-in Electric Drive Motor Vehicles

        1. A credit is also allowed for purchases of **new** qualified plug-in electric drive motor vehicles. The credit is limited to $5,000 for most passenger cars and trucks, but can go as high as $7,500 for large commercial vehicles. This credit phases out based on the number of vehicles sold during the year.

        2. A similar credit is allowed for new qualified plug-in electric drive two-wheeled motorcycles. This credit is limited to the lower of 10% of the cost or $2,500.

VIII. Earned Income Credit (EIC)—The earned income credit is a complex method of mitigating employment taxes for low income taxpayers. This is a refundable credit.

    A. The credit is generated by earning income.

        1. The credit percentage increases if the taxpayer maintains a home with qualifying children. The credit percentage is 7.65% for no qualifying children, 34% for one qualifying child, 40% for two qualifying children, and 45% for three or more qualifying children.

2. The credit is phased out based on earned income or AGI (if greater) exceeding a threshold that also depends upon the number of qualifying children.

   a. **Qualifying child** is defined as it is for the dependency exemption rules; that is, a natural child, stepchild, adopted child, foster child, sibling, step-sibling, or a descendant of any of these. Note that this definition includes brothers, sisters, nieces, and nephews. The descendants must be under the age of 19, full-time students under 24, or permanently disabled dependents; the qualifying child must also be younger than the taxpayer.

   b. The qualifying child also must have lived in the taxpayer's home for more than half of the tax year in the United States.

   c. A qualifying child can only be used by one taxpayer to claim the EIC. If more than one person qualifies to claim the qualifying child, the tie breaker rules are similar to those used for dependency exemptions. Note that the individual who claims the qualifying child as a dependent must be the same individual who claims the EIC. (One exception is if the custodial parent waives the exemption, the custodial parent retains the right to claim the EIC.)

3. The credit is disallowed if disqualified income, such as interest, dividends, tax exempt interest, and other investment income exceeds $3,450 (2017). A taxpayer who erroneously claims the earned income credit due to intentional disregard of the rules is ineligible to claim the credit for a period of two tax years. If the credit is claimed due to fraud the period is extended to 10 years.

4. The most common sources of earned income that qualify for the credit are wages, salaries, tips, and earnings from self-employment. Combat pay can also be included as earned income. Taxable disability payments from an employer plan qualify as earned income until the taxpayer reaches normal retirement age.

5. A taxpayer cannot claim the credit if she files as married filing separately.

6. The taxpayer must have been a U.S. citizen or resident alien for the entire tax year and must have a valid Social Security number to claim the credit.

B. Taxpayers between the ages of 25 through 64 without qualifying children are also eligible if they are not claimed as a dependent on another's return and lived in the United States for more than half the year.

C. Information on qualifying children for the earned income credit is reported on Form 1040 Schedule EIC. The amount of the credit is reported on page 2 of Form 1040.

D. A paid preparer must also complete Form 8867 which provides a checklist to insure that the preparer met all due diligence requirements for taking the EIC on the return. There is a $510 penalty for each failure to meet these requirements.

IX. Health Coverage Tax Credit

A. **The Individual Mandate**—Beginning in 2014, all individuals are required to buy insurance coverage.

   1. Naturally, there are several exceptions to "all." For example, the following categories of people are not penalized for not having health insurance:

      a. People who have to pay more than 8% of their income for health insurance (after taking into account employer contributions and tax credits)

      b. Members of an Indian tribe

      c. Incarcerated individuals

      d. Undocumented immigrants

      e. People without insurance for less than three months during the year

      f. People whose religion opposes reimbursement from an insurance policy

      g. People with family income below the threshold for filing a federal income tax return

    2. People meet the insurance requirement if they are covered through one or more of the following sources:

      a. A plan offered by an employer

      b. Medicare

      c. Medicaid or Children's Health Insurance Program (CHIP)

      d. The veterans' health program

      e. TRICARE (covering service members and their families)

      f. A grandfathered health care plan in existence before the ACA was enacted

      g. A policy purchased by a person through an ACA exchange that is at least Bronze level

    3. If people are not in the exempt categories and do not meet the requirement by purchasing insurance, then they are subject to a penalty (2017) of $695 per adult and $347.50 per child (up to $2,085 per family or 2.5% of family income, whichever is greater).

B. The Affordable Care Act provides a credit that is designed to make health insurance affordable to individuals with modest incomes who are not eligible for other qualifying coverage, such as Medicare, or eligible employer-sponsored health insurance plans. The credit is available for those whose income is between 100% and 400% of the federal poverty level and who do not otherwise have access to coverage. The credit is advanceable meaning that it can be used to reduce the monthly health care premium during the year. The credit is also refundable.

C. Employer Mandate

    1. Beginning in 2015, a large employer (i.e., at least 50 full-time equivalent employees) not offering coverage for all its full-time employees and their dependents, offering minimum essential coverage that is unaffordable, or offering minimum essential coverage of less than 60% of medical expenses, is required to pay a penalty. The annual tax penalty is $2,000 per full-time worker.

    2. Even if the employer offers health insurance, if any full-time employee is certified as having purchased health insurance through a state exchange and received a tax credit, such employers must then absorb a $3,000 per year tax penalty for each employee receiving the tax credit.

X. First-Time Homebuyers Credit

    A. In the past, a homebuyers credit was allowed for first-time homebuyers. This credit still has relevance in 2017 because in some cases it is subject to recapture. For purchases after April 8, 2008, and before 2009, the credit is unusual in that it must be repaid over 15 years on a straight-line basis beginning in the second tax year after the year in which the home is purchased. If sold during the 15-year period, the unrecaptured credit must be added to the tax liability. No repayment is required if the taxpayer dies. Since no interest is charged over the 15 years, the credit is essentially an interest-free loan.

XI. Energy Tax Credits

    A. Residential Energy Efficiency Property (REEP)— Individual taxpayers are allowed a credit for expenditures for installing certain energy-efficient property in the taxpayer's residence. The REEP credit allowed for a tax year equals the sum of:

        1. 30% of the qualified solar electric property expenditures; *plus*

        2. 30% of the qualified solar water heating property expenditures.

    B. Nonbusiness Energy Credit—This credit is 10% of the amount spent for energy efficiency improvements and residential energy property expenditures, with a lifetime limit of $500 (no more than $200 can be for windows). This credit expired at the end of 2016 and at the time of this writing has not been extended to 2017.

Estate and Gift Taxation

Federal Gift Tax

After studying this lesson, you should be able to:

1. Differentiate between gifts and inheritances.

2. List and define the different forms of joint ownership of property.

3. Identify the key exclusions from the gift tax.

4. Apply the gift splitting rules.

5. Compute the unified credit for gift purposes.

6. Summarize the gift tax formula including deductions.

Tax Form for this Lesson: Form 709 (available for download and printing from the lesson overview of your software).

I. Gifts and Inheritances—General Definitions

Definition
Gift: A transfer of property for less than adequate consideration.

A. Transfers, in a business context, are typically for consideration, meaning that they are taxable to the recipient/employee.

B. Transfers for love and affection or marriage are gratuitous.

C. A transfer during the life of the donor (an **inter vivos transfer**) *triggers a gift tax*.

D. A transfer at death (a *testamentary* transfer) triggers the estate tax.

E. The donor or decedent can only transfer their ownership interests and not the interests owned by others. In community property states (Texas and California, among others), property acquired during a marriage is owned one-half by each spouse.

    1. The recipient of a gift is called a **donee**, and the recipient of an inheritance is called an **heir**.

F. The donee or heir is secondarily liable for the transfer tax.

G. The decedent's will directs transfers after the death of the decedent.

H. When a taxpayer transfers property to a trust, the taxpayer has made two gifts, the income interest and the remainder interest (unless the donor retains one of these interests).

    1. The beneficiary of the income interest receives the income from the trust each year.

    2. The beneficiary of the remainder interest receives the property (corpus) of the trust when the trust terminates.

    3. The income and remainder interests are valued using actuarial tables provided by the IRS. The rate used in the valuation is 120% of the applicable Federal midterm rate (published by the IRS) for the month in which the transfer is made.

I. **Reminder**—Gifts and inheritances are not income to recipients. Under the income tax, most donees assume a carryover basis for a gift and the holding period "tacks" from the donor. For inheritances, the heir takes a step-up basis (the fair market value that was included in the estate) and the holding period is always long-term.

II. **The Transfer Must be Complete to be Treated as a Gift**

    A. The gift must be delivered to the donee.

    B. The donor must give up control of the property.

    C. The donee must accept the gift; the donee cannot disclaim or refuse the gift or it will be incomplete.

III. **Joint Ownership**—The creation of a joint ownership interest without equal consideration from each co-owner is considered a gift of the excess contribution to the owner making a smaller contribution. Joint ownership is determined under the law of each state, but typically **tenants in common** do not hold property with the right of survivorship. **Tenancy by the entirety** and **joint tenancy with the right of survivorship** hold property with the right of survivorship. **Right of survivorship** means that when one co-owner dies, the property immediately passes to the other co-owners.

    A. The creation of a joint interest without adequate consideration creates a gift regardless of the form of ownership (tenancy in common or joint tenancy).

    B. Transfers of cash to joint bank accounts do not constitute a complete gift until the donee withdraws the cash.

    C. A purchase of a savings bond held jointly in the name of the donee and the donor is not a complete gift.

    D. The creation of a joint interest with a spouse (with the right of survivorship) is not taxed because of the marital deduction.

Example

TP purchases real estate for $50,000 and this property is owned by TP and his son as tenants in common (one-half interest each). TP made a complete gift of $25,000 to his son. If TP had contributed $40,000 and the son contributed $10,000, then the amount of the gift would be $15,000 ($25,000 − $10,000).

    E. The termination of joint ownership may also trigger a tax, if the proceeds are not divided according to each owner's interest.

IV. **Exclusions from Gift Tax**—There are several important exceptions to the taxation of gifts, including the annual exclusion.

    A. Certain transfers are not considered gifts:

        1. Payment of another individual's medical or educational expenses (tuition and fees only) is not considered a gift. However, these payments must be made directly to the medical provider or the educational institution.

        2. Political contributions are not gifts.

        3. The satisfaction of an obligation is not a gift.

        4. Transfers to civic leagues and social welfare organizations; labor, agricultural and horticultural organizations; and business leagues are not gifts.

V. **Gifts—Summary**

    A. Gross gifts include the following:

        1. Cash and property transfers

        2. Debt forgiveness to family members

        3. Sales at bargain prices to family members

        4. Loans to family members at a bargain (below-market interest rates)

        5. Transfers of property into trust for the benefit of others

        6. Purchases of jointly owned real estate or securities if one co-owner contributes more than a fair proportionate share

B. The following are **not** considered to be gifts subject to the federal gift tax:

1. Donations of personal services

2. Transfers that can be revoked, such as placing assets in revocable trusts or placing cash into a joint bank account until the noncontributing owner actually withdraws funds. (When the noncontributing owner actually withdraws funds, a gift is now made.)

3. Payments to minor family members for food, shelter, clothing, and other reasonable support needs

4. Payments to an employee that in substance are compensation for personal services

5. Payments for education expenses or medical expenses paid on behalf of a donee, provided the payments are made directly to the educational institution or the medical provider

6. Payments for political contributions

7. Property settlements incident to divorce

Example
TP makes a $5,000 child support payment. This is not considered a gift if TP has the obligation to make child support payments.

C. **Annual Exclusion**—An "annual exclusion" of $14,000 (2017) eliminates modest gifts from the application of the gift tax.

1. The annual exclusion is applied per donee per year.

2. The annual exclusion only applies to a gift of a **present interest**. Thus, if the gift is made in trust and will not benefit the recipient currently, there is no exclusion allowed.

Definition
Present Interest: The right to income or to enjoy property currently. A gift to a minor in a trust is considered a present interest if the trustee has the ability to use the funds for the benefit of the minor before the age of 21 (such as for education, medical, etc), and any remaining funds will be distributed to the minor upon reaching age 21.

VI. Integration of Gift and Estate Tax—The federal gift tax and estate tax are coordinated in order to assure that all transfers are only subjected to one of the two transfer taxes. The transfer taxes are integrated so that taxable gifts affect the tax base for the estate tax.

A. The two transfer taxes—These were unified after 1976 and hence, special transition rules apply to transfers prior to 1976.

B. **Deductions**—For both the estate and gift taxes.

1. There is an unlimited marital deduction for transfers to a spouse.

2. There is an unlimited charitable contribution deduction for transfers to charity.

C. **Unified credit**—A unified credit provides that the first 5,490,000 (2017) of transfers from an estate and/or gifts will not trigger a tax liability

1. The unified credit applies to taxable transfers by gift or bequest to allow a minimum cumulative amount of tax-free transfers.

2. Because the unified credit applies to **taxable** transfers, it is not used to offset transfers eligible for a marital deduction (transfers to a spouse) or charitable deduction (transfers to a charity).

VII. Gift Splitting—In community property states, one-half of all property generally belongs to each spouse. Hence, a gift of community property is automatically split between the spouses. To equalize this effect, a gift-splitting election is available.

A. **The Purpose of a Gift-Splitting Election**—Is to equalize treatment of gifts by spouses with the treatment of gifts in a community property state.

1. The election is available each year.

2. The donor must be married at the time of the transfer.

B. **Under the Gift-Splitting Election**—A gift is split and treated as being given equally by both spouses.

1. The value of the gift is divided in two and each spouse is treated as making a gift.

2. Both spouses can use an annual exclusion for gifts of present interests. Note, that both spouses will need to file a gift tax return so that each can elect gift-splitting.

Example
TP is married to S and this year made a gift of $50,000 to his son. If TP and S elect to gift splitting, the $50,000 gift is treated as two $25,000 gifts to the son, one gift from TP and one from S. Each gift would be eligible for an annual exclusion of $14,000 (2017), so each spouse would have made a taxable gift of $11,000.

VIII. Deductions—Two important deductions are available in calculating the amount of taxable gifts.

A. **A Marital Deduction**—Is allowed for most gifts to a spouse.

1. Gifts of **terminable interests** generally do not qualify for the deduction.

Definition
Terminable Interest: An interest in property that terminates upon the death of the recipient. For example, a taxpayer who receives the right to occupy property for the duration of his life has received a terminable interest in that the taxpayer's rights terminate upon his death.

2. The deduction is unlimited in amount.

3. The amount of the deduction is the total gift less any excluded portion (if the annual exclusion applies).

4. The marital deduction does not apply for gifts to a spouse who is not a U.S. citizen, but an annual exclusion of $149,000 (2017) is permitted.

Examples
1. H and W became engaged in April, when H gave W a ring with a value of $50,000. In July H and W were married and H gave W a new car worth $75,000.

Question: What amount of annual exclusion may H claim?

Answer: H can claim $14,000 annual exclusion (2017) for the April gift and a $75,000 marital deduction for the new car. The remaining $36,000 for the ring is taxable since H and W were not married at the time of the gift.

2. TP gives Mrs. TP $60,000.

Question: What is the amount of the taxable gift?

Answer: TP can exclude the first $14,000 under the annual exclusion and then claim a marital deduction for the remaining $46,000. No taxable gift was made.

B. **A Charitable Contribution Deduction**—Is allowed for gifts to charitable organizations.

1. A charity is defined similarly to income tax (educational, scientific, religious organizations), but includes foreign charities and excludes cemeteries.

2. There is no limitation on the amount of the deduction.

Example
TP donated $60,000 to his church.

Question: What is the amount of the taxable gift?

Answer: TP can deduct all $60,000 for gift tax purposes because the church qualifies as a charity. No taxable gift was made.

IX. **Gift Tax Formula**—The gift tax calculation includes current gifts and past gifts. The purpose of adding gifts from previous periods is to use prior gifts to determine the gift tax rate (since the rates are progressive) on current gifts. To prevent double taxation of these gifts, the gift tax on prior taxable gifts (not the gift tax paid, but the amount of tax computed ignoring payments) is then subtracted from the total gift tax.

A. **The Federal Gift Tax Formula**

Gross gifts (cash plus FMV of property at date of gift)		$xxx
Plus: One-half of spouse's gifts to third parties if gift splitting elected		x
Less:		
One-half of gifts to third parties treated as given by spouse if gift splitting elected	$ x	
Annual exclusion (up to $14,000 per donee)	x	
Unlimited exclusion for tuition or medical expenses paid on behalf of donee	x	
Unlimited exclusion for gifts to political organizations	x	
Charitable gifts (remainder of charitable gifts after annual exclusion)	x	
Marital deduction (remainder of gifts to spouse after annual exclusion)	x	(xx)
Taxable gifts for current year		$ xx
Add: Taxable gifts for prior years		x
Total taxable gifts		$ xx
Transfer tax on total taxable gifts		$ xx
Less: Transfer tax on taxable gifts made prior to current year		(x)
Transfer tax for current year		$ xx
Transfer tax credit	$ xx	
Less: Transfer tax credit used in prior years	x	(x)
Net gift tax liability		$ xx

B. There are four steps to calculate the gift tax:

1. First, determine current taxable gifts (gifts reduced by exclusions and deductions).

2. Second, add previous taxable gifts and calculate the total gift tax.

3. Third, reduce the total gift tax by the gift tax computed on taxable gifts from previous periods using the current rates for the unified tax.

4. Fourth, reduce any remaining gift tax by the unused portion of the unified credit.

Note
The gift tax on previous gifts is computed using the current tax rate schedule and ignores the use of the unified credit. This amount does not represent the amount of gift tax paid in previous years.

C. **Filing requirements**—The requirement for filing a return is based upon the annual exclusion.

1. April 15 is the due date for gifts made in the prior year; no fiscal years are allowed.

2. The gift tax return (Form 709) is due if gifts exceed the annual exclusion or if a gift is made of a future interest.

3. No gift tax return is required if a gift to charity exceeds the annual exclusion, as long as the entire value of the transfer qualifies for a charitable contribution.

4. If the donor dies, the gift tax return for the year of death is due not later than the due date for filing the decedent's federal estate tax return (generally nine months after date of death).

> **Note**
> *The unused portion of the unified credit is used to reduce the total gift tax. The amount of unified credit used must be tracked from each period because the gift tax on previous periods ignores the amount of gift tax actually paid.*

X. **Integrated Review Problem**—For each situation, indicate whether the transfer of cash, the income interest, or the remainder interest is a gift of present interest (P), a gift of a future interest (F), or not a completed gift (N).

A. A created a $500,000 trust that provided his mother with an income interest for her life and his sister with the remainder interest at the death of his mother. A expressly retained the power to revoke both the income interest and the remainder interest at any time.

1. The income interest at the trust's creation.

   a. N—incomplete transfer due to power to revoke.

2. The remainder interest at the trust's creation.

   a. N—incomplete transfer due to power to revoke.

B. B created a $100,000 trust to provide her nephew with an income interest until he reaches age 45. When the trust was created, the nephew was age 25 and income distribution was to begin at age 29. The remainder interest, upon the nephew reaching age 45, goes to B's niece.

1. The income interest.

   a. F—no transfer to the nephew for four years.

C. C made a $10,000 cash gift to his son in May of this year and another gift of $12,000 in cash to his son in August of this year.

1. The cash transfers.

   a. P—$14,000 will be excluded (2017).

D. This year D transferred property worth $20,000 to a trust with the income to be paid to his 22-year-old niece. After the niece reaches age 30, the remainder interest is to be distributed to D's brother. The income interest is valued at $9,700 and the remainder interest is valued at $10,300.

1. The income interest.

   a. P—complete transfer because the niece is currently receiving the income. This is a gift of a present interest so the annual exclusion applies to it.

2. The remainder interest.

   a. F—the brother will not receive the gift for another eight years. This gift is a future interest so none of it is excluded by the annual exclusion.

E. E made a $40,000 cash gift to his uncle this year. E was married throughout the year and elected with his spouse to gift split.

1. The cash transfer.

   a. P—$28,000 will be excluded (2017).

F. This year F created a $1,000,000 trust, which provides his sister with an income interest for 10 years after which the remainder will pass to F's brother. F retained the power to revoke the remainder interest at any time. The income interest is valued at $600,000.

1. The income interest.

   a. P—complete transfer because the sister is currently receiving the income. This is a gift of a present interest so the annual exclusion applies to it.

2. The remainder interest.

   a. N—incomplete transfer due to power to revoke. There is no gift tax since it is not a completed gift.

Federal Estate Tax

After studying this lesson, you should be able to:

1. Define the gross estate and identify inclusions for the gross estate.

2. Compute the unified credit for estate tax purposes.

3. Summarize the estate tax formula.

4. Describe the applicability of the generation–*skipping tax to transfers at death.*

Tax Form for This Lesson: Form 706 (available for download and printing from the lesson overview of your software).

I. **Gross Estate**—The gross estate includes property owned by the decedent at death and certain property transfers.

Definition
Estate: A legal entity that comes into existence automatically at the death of a taxpayer (the **decedent). The executor** of the estate collects the assets of the decedent, pays the decedent's debts, and distributes the remaining assets to the beneficiaries according to the decedent's will or according to the state law governing inheritances. The estate exists for the period required by the executor to perform his or her duties.

A. **Property Owned by the Decedent**—Property owned at the date of death is included in the probate estate.

Definition
Probate Estate: This estate includes cash, stocks, and assets such as a residence, clothing, and jewelry. The probate estate is the collection of the decedent's possessions for legal purposes, whereas the gross estate is a measure of the value of these possessions for estate tax purposes.

B. **Property Transferred by the Decedent at Death**—Is also included in the gross estate.

1. Transfer of property occurs without probate through operation of law.

Example
Property held in joint ownership with right of survivorship passes to the survivor upon the death of the first owner. The interest held in this property by the decedent would be included in his or her gross estate.

2. Other forms of property that pass by operation of law include retained life estates, revocable gifts, transfers triggered by death (retirement benefits), and life insurance.

C. **Valuation of Property**—Property is included in the gross estate at the fair market value.

1. The valuation date is the date of death, or the executor can elect to have the property valued on an alternative valuation date.

Definition

Fair Market Value: This is a question of fact, but the standard is the amount that a willing buyer and willing seller would agree upon when both are in possession of all relevant information.

2. The alternate valuation date is six months after the date of death or on the date the property is disposed of (if earlier than six months after the date of death).

3. The election to use the alternate valuation date is only available if it causes gross estate and tax payable to decline.

4. An executor can elect to value certain realty used in farming or in connection with a closely held business at a **special use valuation**. The farm or business must continue to be used in that capacity for at least five years during the eight-year period after the date of death.

Definition

Special Use Valuation: Allows realty to be valued at a current use that does not result in the best or highest fair market value. This election is available when the business is conducted by the decedent's family, constitutes a substantial portion of the gross estate, and the property passes to a qualifying heir of the decedent. Decrease in value cannot exceed $1,120,000 for individuals dying in 2017.

II. **Specific Inclusions in Gross Estate**—Certain property transfers are included in the gross estate because the transfer could be used to avoid the estate tax.

   A. **Life Insurance**—Proceeds are included in the gross estate under either of two conditions.

      1. The decedent had incidents of ownership (e.g., the right to designate the beneficiary).

      2. The decedent's estate or executor is the beneficiary of the insurance policy.

   B. **Jointly Owned Property**—Is included in the gross estate.

      1. The value of the decedent's interest as a tenant in common is included in the gross estate.

      2. For jointly owned property by a husband and wife (right of survivorship or tenancy in the entirety), 50% of the value of the property will be included in the estate of the first spouse to die.

      3. For jointly owned property with the right of survivorship (unmarried owners), 100% of the property is included in the estate of the first owner to die. If it can be proven that the decedent did not pay 100% of the cost of property when originally purchased, then the amount included is the fair market value of the property multiplied by the percentage paid for by the decedent.

      Examples

      1. TP owns a one-half interest in property worth $100,000. The property was originally acquired for $20,000 and TP provided $5,000 (25%) of the price. If the property is held with the right of survivorship with a person other than TP's spouse, then TP's gross estate will only include $25,000. This is 25% of the value of the property, and this is equal to the portion of the purchase price provided by TP ($5,000/$20,000).

      2. Bob furnished 80% of the consideration to buy land and his friend Amy furnished the remaining 20%. The land was titled as joint tenants with right of survivorship.

Question: What amount is included in Bob's estate?

Answer: If Bob dies first, 80% of the value of the property (valued as of Bob's death) will be in Bob's gross estate. If Bob and Amy are husband and wife and Bob dies first, his estate will include 50% of the value of the property.

   C. **Retained Interests**—Property transferred where the decedent retained an interest or a power.

      1. A retained life estate or the retention of a power to alter, amend, or revoke a transfer are retained interests that cause the property subject to the power to be included in the gross estate.

Definition

Life Interest: An interest in property that is retained for the life of the transferor. For example, a life interest in a residence means that the residence can be occupied for the life of the owner even though the property itself has already been transferred to another individual.

2. The power to designate possession or enjoyment of property or income (including power created by another that can be exercised in the decedent's favor) will also cause the property to be included in the gross estate.

    a. A general power of appointment allows the taxpayer to designate property to herself, her creditors, or to others. Therefore, if the taxpayer dies while retaining the general power, the property subject to the appointment is included in her gross estate.

    b. A special power or appointment does not allow a taxpayer to designate property to him. Therefore, if the taxpayer dies while retaining the special power, the property subject to the appointment is not included in his gross.

Example
Donor transferred property in trust with income to self for life and property to go at donor's death to R (remainderman).

Question: What is included in the donor's estate upon his death?

Answer: The trust property will be in the donor's gross estate.

D. **Transfers within Three Years of Death**—Certain gifts within three years of death are included in the gross estate of the decedent.

    1. Transfers with retained interests, revocable transfers, and transfers of life insurance are included in the decedent's gross estate if the transfer is made within three years of death.

    2. The property is included at the date of death value.

    3. The gift tax paid on the gift is included in the estate for any gifts made within three years of death (this is the **gross up provision**).

Example
Two years ago TP transferred a life insurance policy on his life to S (his son), and paid gift tax on the transfer.

Question: When TP died this year, what was included in his estate?
Suppose that TP also transferred stock to S.

Answer: The value of the insurance and the gift tax paid on the transfer are included in T's gross estate. If TP had transferred stock, only the gift tax would be in his gross estate because TP did not retain any interest and the transfer was not completed by the death of the decedent.

E. **Summary—Gross estate** includes the fair market value (FMV) of all property in which the decedent had an interest at time of death.

    1. **Concurrently held property**

        a. If property was held by tenancy in common, only the FMV of the decedent's share is included.

        b. Include one-half the FMV of community property and one-half the FMV of property held **by spouses** in joint tenancy or tenancy by the entirety.

        c. Include one-half of FMV if the property held by two persons in joint tenancy was acquired by gift, bequest, or inheritance (one-third if held by three persons, etc.).

    d. If property held in joint tenancy was acquired by purchase by **other than spouses**, include the FMV of the property multiplied by the percentage of total cost furnished by the decedent.

  2. The FMV of transfers with retained life estates and revocable transfers are included in the gross estate.

  3. Include the FMV of transfers intended to take effect at death (i.e., the donee can obtain enjoyment only by surviving the decedent, and the decedent prior to death had a reversionary interest of more than 5% of the value of the property).

  4. Include any property over which the decedent had a **general power of appointment** (i.e., decedent could appoint property in favor of decedent, decedent's estate, or creditors of decedent or decedent's estate).

  5. Include the value of life insurance proceeds from policies payable to the estate and policies over which the decedent possessed an "incident of ownership" (e.g., right to change beneficiary).

  6. Include income in respect of a decedent.

  7. Include gifts of life insurance within three years of the decedent's date of death.

  8. Include gift tax paid on all transfers made within three years of death.

III. Marital Deduction—In order to avoid taxing a married couple's estate twice, a deduction is provided for a transfer or bequest to a surviving spouse.

  A. To qualify for the marital deduction, the spouse must receive property outright and be able to control its ultimate destination.

    1. Property that passes to the surviving spouse as a result of joint tenancy qualifies.

    2. Only the net value of property subject to mortgage qualifies.

    3. Property rights that are terminable do not qualify.

> **Definition**
> *Terminable Interest*: This interest fails due to a contingency or the passage of time. An example of a terminable interest is where the decedent grants the spouse the right to occupy a residence until such time as the spouse remarries.

    4. The deduction is unlimited in amount.

  B. **Qualified** terminable interest property **(QTIP)** will qualify for the deduction.

    1. An election is made to use the marital deduction for a transfer to a spouse of less than a complete interest in trust.

    2. The surviving spouse must receive all of the trust income annually (or more often) for life, but the decedent determines where the property goes at the surviving spouse's death.

    3. The property must be included in the surviving spouse's estate at its value when the survivor dies.

  C. No marital deduction is allowed for non-citizen spouses.

    1. An exception to this rule is a transfer to a **qualified domestic trust**, which assures estate tax imposition upon a non-citizen spouse's death.

>
> **Example**
> The decedent's will leaves property in trust with income to the surviving spouse for the duration of her life. At her death the property goes to the decedent's daughter by a previous marriage.
>
> **Question:** Is a marital deduction available for this property?
>
> **Answer:** The marital deduction may be elected on this transfer under the QTIP rules.

IV. Other Deductions—Deductions are allowed for expenses and losses because the taxable estate represents the net amount transferred to beneficiaries.

A. Debts of the Estate—These debts, for example mortgages and accrued taxes, are deductible.

B. Final Expenses—These expenses are deductible.

Example
Funeral expenses and administration expenses (e.g., attorneys' and accountants' fees) are examples. State death taxes paid are also deductible.

1. The executor has the option of deducting administration expenses on the estate tax return or the estate's income tax return. If deducting on the income tax return the executor must indicate that the deduction will not also be taken on the estate tax return.

C. Casualty and Theft Losses—Are deductible without any floor limitation.

1. The losses must be incurred during the administration of the estate.

2. The executor has option of deducting casualty and theft losses on the estate tax return or the estate's income tax return.

D. Charitable Contributions—Are deductible without any limitation.

1. The same charities as the gift tax (e.g., includes foreign charities, but excludes cemeteries).

V. Estate Tax Computation—The estate tax calculation uses the taxable estate increased by adjusted taxable gifts (post 1976). Including gifts results in a higher tax rate applied to the estate property. However, these gifts are not double taxed because gift taxes paid reduce the tax imposed on total transfers.

A. Four Steps—There are four steps to calculating the estate tax.

1. **First**—The taxable estate is increased by **adjusted taxable gifts** made after 1976.

Definition
Adjusted Taxable Gifts: Taxable gifts other than gifts already included in the gross estate. Adjusted taxable gifts are included at date of gift values.

Example
D had a taxable estate of $5,690,000 and had made adjusted taxable gifts of $800,000 that were not included in the estate. D did not pay any tax on the gifts because he used his unified credit to offset the gift tax.

Question: If the unified credit offsets $5,490,000 of taxable transfers (2017), how much of the estate will effectively be subject to the estate tax?

Answer: D's estate will owe tax on $1,000,000 ($5,690,000 plus $800,000 less $5,490,000).

2. **Second**—Apply current tax rates to total transfers. The maximum tax rate for 2017 is 40%.

3. **Third**—Reduce the tentative transfer tax by gift taxes paid or payable (at current rates) on post-1976 gifts.

4. **Fourth**—Subtract the unified credit and other credits.

5. **Credits against the estate tax**

   a. For 2017, the unified credit will eliminate the tax on a net estate of $5,490,000.

> **Note**
>
> The unified credit can be looked at in two equivalent ways. For an estate of $6,240,000 in 2017, if the entire unified credit equivalent of $5,490,000 is available, then only $750,000 of the estate is taxable. The tax due would be $300,000 since the estate is in the 40% bracket.
>
> On the actual estate tax return, for an estate of $6,240,000, the tax before the credit is $2,441,800. The unified credit is $2,141,800, which also results in a tax due of $300,000.

   b. Any unused credit from a spouse dying after 2010 may be used in the future by the surviving spouse. Note that an election to use the remaining credit must be made by filing Form 706 even if \the estate of the deceased would otherwise not require a return to be filed.

> **Example**
>
> Henry died in 2013 with a taxable estate of $2 million. An election is made on Henry's estate tax return to permit his wife, Wilma, to use his unused exclusion of $3.25 million. Wilma, who had not made any lifetime taxable gifts, dies in 2017 with a taxable estate of $9 million. The total applicable exclusion amount available to Wilma's estate will consist of her basic exclusion amount of $5.49 million plus the $3.25 million of Henry's unused exclusion amount, for a total exclusion of $8,740,000.

   c. There is a credit for tax on "prior transfers" to adjust for taxes on proximate deaths (deaths within 10 years).

   d. A credit is allowed for all or part of the death taxes paid to a foreign country.

   e. If property gifted before 1977 is included in the transferor's gross estate, a credit is allowed for any gift taxes paid on these gifts equal to the lesser of the gift tax paid or the estate tax attributable to this property.

B. **Filing Requirement**—The requirement for filing a return is based upon whether the gross estate exceeds the exemption equivalent.

   1. The estate tax is levied on the estate, but installment payments of estate taxes is available for closely held business interests.

   2. The estate tax return (form 706) is due nine months after date of death.

   3. An estate tax return must be filed if the gross estate plus adjusted taxable gifts equal or exceed the exemption equivalent.

C. The Federal Estate Tax Formula

Gross estate (cash plus FMV of property at date of death, or alternate valuation date)		$xxx
Less:		
Funeral expenses	$x	
Administrative expenses	x	
Debts and mortgages	x	
Casualty losses	x	
State death taxes	x	
Charitable bequests (unlimited)	x	
Marital deduction (unlimited)	<u>x</u>	<u>(xx)</u>
Taxable estate		$xxx
Add: Post-76 adjusted taxable gifts		<u>xx</u>
Total taxable life and death transfers		<u>$xxx</u>
Transfer tax on total transfers		$ xx
Less:		
Post-76 gift taxes (specially computed at estate tax rates in effect at time of death)	$x	
Transfer tax credit ($2,141,800 for 2017)	x	
Foreign death and prior transfer tax credits	<u>x</u>	<u>(x)</u>
Net estate tax liability		<u>$ xx</u>

VI. The Generation-Skipping Tax (GST)

Definition
Generation-Skipping Tax: A supplemental tax, **that prevents the avoidance of the transfer taxes by skipping one generation of recipients.**

A. Generation-skipping tax (GST) is triggered by the transfer of property to someone who is more than one generation younger than the donor or decedent (e.g., a grandparent transfers property to a grandchild, rather than a child).

B. The GST is not applicable to a transfer of property to someone who is more than one generation younger than donor or decedent, if the persons in the intervening generation are deceased (e.g., a transfer to a grandchild is not subject to the tax if the grandchild's parents are dead).

C. The GST is not widely applicable because most transfers qualify for an annual gift tax exclusion and each donor/decedent is entitled to a large aggregate exemption that is equal to the amount of the unified credit for the estate tax.

Example
Determine whether the transfer is subject to the generation-skipping transfer tax (A), the gift tax (B), or both taxes (C).

Question: TP's daughter, D, has one child, GD. This year TP made an outright gift of $8,000,000 to GD.

Answer: C. The GST is an addition to the gift tax because a generation (D) was skipped.

Federal Taxation
of Entities

Corporate Taxation

Formation of a Corporation

After studying this lesson, you should be able to:

1. Evaluate whether a corporate formation is eligible for deferral of gain/loss.

2. Compute the basis of stock held by shareholders and assets by corporation after formation.

3. Determine the holding period for stock and assets after the formation.

4. Calculate the effect of liability assumptions by the corporation on gain and basis.

I. **Recognition of Gain or Loss**—The recognition of gain or loss on a contribution of property in exchange for stock is determined by the ownership levels of the contributing shareholders.

II. **Deferral**—Deferral of gain and loss is required for members of the control club.

> **Definition**
> *Control Club*: The group of individuals who participate in a transfer of property to a corporation and are in control of the corporation immediately after the transfer.

    A. To be eligible for membership in the control club, property must be contributed (services rendered to the corporation is not property).

    B. The property must be transferred in exchange for stock.

> **Definition**
> *Stock*: Any equity interest (common and preferred) except that "nonqualified" preferred stock (NPS) is treated as boot. NPS is preferred stock that is expected to be redeemed within 20 years.

    1. Immediately after the transfer, the transferor(s) are in control, and control is defined as owning at least 80% of the voting and nonvoting stock.

    2. The receipt of boot (e.g., cash, short-term notes, securities, etc.) triggers gain but not loss.

    3. Note: In order to meet the 80% control test, shareholders who contributed services for their stock may also contribute a small amount of property so their stock ownership can contribute to meeting the 80% requirement. However, the IRS has ruled that the value of the property must be equal to at least 10% of the value of the services for the shareholder's stock ownership to be included.

    4. Existing shareholder contributes property so that the group will meet the 80% test. The value of the property contributed by the existing shareholder must be equal to at least 10% of the value of the stock owned by the existing shareholder before the new contribution can be included in the group.

    5. Any depreciation recapture potential transfers to corporation with the property.

> **Definition**
> *Boot*: Property received other than stock.

    C. If boot is received, the **gain recognized** to the shareholder is the lower of:

        1. **Realized gain** or

        2. The fair market value of the **boot received**

D. If stock is received in exchange for services:

    1. The transferor has **wage income** equal to the fair market value of the stock received (and basis in the stock equal to that amount).

    2. The **corporation has a salary expense deduction** (unless the services rendered were an organizational expense).

E. Reminder: The corporation does not realize any gain or loss on issuing stock.

III. Basis Issues—The *adjusted basis for qualifying property is a carryover basis.*

    A. The corporation takes an adjusted basis in the property from the transferor plus any gain recognized by the transferor.

    B. The corporation's basis in the property received is:

> Shareholder's basis in property + Gain recognized by shareholder

    C. The shareholder's stock takes the adjusted basis of the transferred property plus any gain recognized less any boot received.

    D. The shareholder's basis in the stock received from the corporation is:

> Basis of all property transferred to the corporation
>
> + Gain recognized by shareholder
>
> − Boot received by shareholder
>
> − Liabilities assumed by corporations

        1. Shortcut—A carryover basis is the fair value of the property less the gain deferred (or plus any loss deferred). This shortcut works only if the value of the property is known.

Example

TP contributes a building worth $200,000 to a corporation in exchange for 100% of the corporate stock. TP has an adjusted basis of $100,000 in the building, but the property is subject to a $25,000 mortgage. The corporation takes an adjusted basis of $100,000 in the building, but TP takes an adjusted basis of $75,000 in his stock.

Example

Individuals A, B, and C form ABC Corp. and make the following transfer to their corporation:

Item Transferred	A	B	C
Property—FMV	$10,000	$8,000	$–
Adjusted basis	1,500	3,000	–
Services rendered	–	–	1,000
Liability assumed by ABC Corp.	2,000	–	–
Gain or Loss to Shareholder			
Consideration received			
Stock (FMV)	$ 8,000	$7,600	$1,000
2-year note (FMV)	–	400	–
Liability assumed by ABC Corp.	2,000	–	–
Amount realized	$10,000	$8,000	$1,000
Adjusted basis of property	(1,500)	(3,000)	–
Realized gain/loss	$ 8,500	$5,000	$1,000
Gain recognized to shareholder	$500[a]	$400[b]	$1,000[c]
Basis of Stock to Shareholder:			
Basis of assets contributed	$ 1,500	$ 3,000	$ –
+ Gain recognized	500	400	1,000
– Boot received	–	(400)	–
– Liability relief	(2,000)	–	–
	$ 0	$ 3,000	$1,000
Basis of Property to Corp:			
Basis of assets contributed	$ 1,500	$ 3,000	$ –
+ Gain recognized	500	400	1,000
	$ 2,000	$ 3,400	$1,000

[a]Liability in excess of basis: $2,000 – $1,500 = $500
[b]Lower of recognized gain or boot received; assumes B elects out of the installment method
[c]Ordinary compensation income

E. Debt Assumption—A contribution of encumbered property requires that the transferor reduce the basis of the stock by the amount of debt assumed by the corporation.

F. Basis Adjustment for Loss Property

1. If the total basis of the property transferred by a shareholder is greater than the fair market value of the property, a basis adjustment is required to prevent the shareholders and the corporation from both benefiting from this unrealized loss. The downward basis adjustment is allocated proportionately among all assets contributed by the shareholder that had a built-in loss.

2. Note: If the shareholder and corporation elect, the shareholder's stock basis can be reduced rather than the corporation's assets.

Example
Amy transferred Lossacre with a basis of $6,000 (FMV of $2,000) and Gainacre with a basis of $4,000 (FMV of $5,000) to ABE Corp. in exchange for stock in a Section 351 transaction. Since the aggregate adjusted basis of the transferred property ($10,000) exceeds its aggregate FMV ($7,000), ABE's aggregate basis for the property is limited to $7,000. The required basis reduction of $3,000 would reduce ABE's basis for Lossacre to $3,000 ($6,000 – $3,000). Amy's basis for her stock would equal the total basis of the transferred property, $10,000.

Alternatively, if Amy and ABE elect, ABE's basis for the transferred property will be $6,000 for Lossacre and $4,000 for Gainacre, and Amy's basis for her stock will be limited to its FMV of $7,000.

IV. Debt Assumptions—Gain may be recognized in two circumstances if the corporation assumes the shareholders' debt.

    A. If the total liabilities assumed by the corporation exceed the total adjusted basis of property transferred by the shareholder, then gain must be recognized as follows:

Gain recognized = Liabilities assumed – Basis of property transferred

Example
Shareholder contributes property to a corporation with a fair market value of $100 and adjusted basis of $60. A liability of $70 is attached to the property and is assumed by the corporation. The shareholder recognizes a gain of $10 ($70 liability – $60 basis). The shareholder's basis in her stock is zero.

    B. If the debt was not incurred by the shareholder for valid business reasons, then the corporate assumption will cause ALL of the debt relief to be treated as boot. This will cause gain to be recognized, but only to the extent of the realized gain.

Example
Shareholder contributes property to a corporation with a fair market value of $100 and adjusted basis of $60. A liability of $50 is attached to the property and is assumed by the corporation. The liability was not incurred for a valid business reason. Therefore, the $50 debt is treated as boot. The realized gain is $40 ($100 amount realized – $60 basis). The recognized gain is $40, the lower of the boot ($50) or realized gain ($40). The shareholder's basis in her stock is $50 ($60 basis in property – $50 debt relief + $40 gain recognized).

V. Holding Period

    A. The Shareholder's Holding Period—For the stock may or may not include the amount of time the shareholder held the property just given to the corporation.

        1. Capital asset or Section 1231—Asset transferred to corporation—property holding period is tacked on to stock holding period.

        2. All other property—Holding period of property **does not tack** on. Holding period for stock begins on day after the transfer.

    B. The Corporation's Holding Period—In the property received **always includes** the period that the transferor held the property before the exchange.

VI. Debt vs. Equity—Corporate debt can be reclassified as equity, but this is a question of fact.

    A. Debt characteristics are important (instrument, collateral, interest, etc.).

    B. The corporation is not thinly capitalized (debt equity ratio too high).

    C. No gain or loss is recognized on the **issuance of debt**.

Example

Assume the following facts for a debt versus equity illustration:

A shareholder transfers $400,000 to a corporation. At the end of the first year of successful operations, the corporation distributes a $100,000 payment to the shareholder. This payment is a dividend.

If the transfer by the shareholder is all equity (i.e., stock), the effect of the $100,000 payment (dividend payment) to the shareholder is:

Effect on shareholder	**Effect on corporation**
Taxable income of $100,000	No deduction
(Dividends)	(Dividends are not deductible by corporation)

If the transfer by the shareholder is all debt (i.e., loan to the corporation), and if we assume $80,000 is principal and $20,000 is interest, the effect of the $100,000 payment to the shareholder is:

Effect on shareholder	**Effect on corporation**	**Taxable income of $20,000**
$20,000 deduction	(Interest income)	(Interest is deductible by corporation)

Principal is not deductible by the corporation or taxable to the shareholder.

VII. Capital Contributions and Corporation's Basis

    A. Definition—Capital contributions include money or property received by a corporation with nothing being given in return.

    B. Property Contributions

        1. By shareholders—There is no gain or loss to a corporation when shareholders contribute property. Shareholder's basis in stock is increased by basis of property contributed.

        2. By nonshareholders—There is no gain or loss to the corporation; basis to corporation in property contributed is zero.

    C. Money Contributions—The corporation must *reduce the basis* of *any property acquired with the money* during a 12-month period after the contribution was received. The reduction in the basis is equal to the amount of the money contribution. So, a contribution of $100, used toward the purchase of a $500 asset, would result in a basis in that asset of $400.

    D. Any *additional* money (money in excess of the amount of reduction in basis), after the 12-month period, is used to reduce the basis of existing property of the corporation. So, a contribution of $400, used to purchase an asset of $100, would result in an asset with a basis of zero and $300 of "excess" money, which would be used to reduce the basis of some other asset.

Corporate Income

After studying this lesson, you should be able to:

1. Identify personal holding companies and closely-held companies.

2. Reconcile book income to taxable income and describe the purpose of the M-1 and M-3.

3. Compute the net operating loss for a corporation and apply carryback/carryforward rules.

4. Utilize the corporate tax formula to compute taxable income.

Tax Form for This Lesson: Form 1120, Schedule M-3 (available for download and printing from the lesson overview of your software).

I. Corporate Tax Formula

The Corporate Income Tax Formula

Realized Income

less

Nonrecognition of Income:

Deferrals and Exclusions Cost of Goods Sold

equals

Gross Income

less

Deductions

equals

Taxable Income before Special Deductions

less

Special Deductions

equals

Taxable Income

times

Tax Rates equals **Gross Tax** less

Credits and Payments

plus

Other Taxes

equals

Net Tax

A. The corporate tax calculation is very similar to the formula used to calculate individual taxes. The general income and deduction rules for corporations are the same as those for individuals. For example, the NOL rules for individuals and corporations are generally the same.

> **Definition**
> *C Corporation*: A corporation subject to the corporate income tax is often referred to as a C corporation because the rules governing the corporate tax are contained in Subchapter C of the Internal Revenue Code.

B. The Corporate Formula—Is analogous to the individual formula.

    1. Expenses are generally deductible as business deductions (subject to the limits placed on business deductions, such as reasonable, ordinary, etc.).

    2. There are categories of special deductions subject to special limitations (see the lesson "Special Corporate Deductions" for more details).

    3. Deductible capital losses are offset against recognized capital gains, but there is no deduction for a **net capital loss**. Rather, a net capital loss is carried over (back three years/forward five years) to offset against capital gains in other years.

C. Special Rules

    1. Corporations can choose a fiscal year unless the corporation makes an "S" election or qualifies as a personal service corporation. Personal service corporations generally must use a calendar year-end.

> **Definition**
> *Personal Service Corporation*: A corporation whose principal activity is the performance of personal services performed by employees who own substantially all of the stock; for example, a medical corporation whose owners are also the doctors providing the medical services.

    2. Accrual accounting is **required** except for small corporations (gross receipts less than $5 million), certain personal service corporations, and S corporations. Recurring expenses, however, must be paid within 8 1/2 months of the fiscal year-end. Additionally, expenses to certain related taxpayers (e.g., cash-basis shareholders) can only be deducted when paid.

    3. Multiple tax brackets are not available for members of a "controlled group" (see the "Taxation of Related Corporations" lesson) or for personal service corporations (a flat 35% tax rate is employed).

    4. Passive loss rules

        a. Passive loss limits do not apply to corporations (except personal service corporations and certain "close" corporations).

        b. Closely held corporations can use passive losses to offset active corporate income but not portfolio income.

        c. Personal service corporations cannot offset passive losses against either active income or portfolio income.

> **Definition**
> *Closely Held Corporation*: A corporation is a closely held corporation if at any time during the last half of the taxable year more than 50% in value of its outstanding stock is owned, directly or indirectly, by or for not more than five individuals.

5. For tax years beginning after 2015, the due dates for corporate tax returns are as follows:

   a. For calendar year corporations, the due date is April 15. An automatic *six*-month extension is available to October 15.

   b. For corporations with a June 30 year-end, the due date is September 15. An automatic **seven**-month extension is available to April 15 of the following year.

   c. For all other corporations, the due date is the 15th date of the fourth month following the close of the tax year. An automatic **six**-month extension is available.

   Estimated corporate tax payments are required if the tax liability exceeds $500.

6. Corporations are subject to:

   a. Regular tax rates

Taxable income	Rate
$0–$50,000	15%
$50,001–$75,000	25
$75,001–$10 million	34
Over $10 million	35

   b. The less-than-34% brackets are phased out by adding an additional tax of 5% of the excess of taxable income over $100,000, up to a maximum additional tax of $11,750.

   c. The 34% bracket is phased out for corporations with taxable income in excess of $15 million by adding an additional 3% of the excess of taxable income over $15 million, up to a maximum additional tax of $100,000.

7. Certain personal service corporations are not eligible to use the less-than-35% brackets, and their taxable income is taxed at a flat 35% rate.

Examples

1. ABC, a calendar-year, accrual-basis corporation, received $10,000 of life insurance proceeds due to the death of its controller. ABC was the owner and beneficiary of this policy.

Question: What amount of taxable income do the proceeds generate?

Answer: None. Life insurance proceeds are excluded.

2. ABC, a calendar-year, accrual-basis corporation, paid $3,000 of insurance premiums on the life of its manager (ABC is the beneficiary of this $100,000 policy) and $4,000 of group term insurance premiums for the corporation's four employees (the employees' spouses are the beneficiaries of these $10,000 policies).

Question: What amount should ABC deduct for insurance premiums this year?

Answer: $4,000. The key man premiums are not deductible.

II. **Book Income versus Taxable Income**—Schedule M-1 is a reconciliation of book income to taxable income. Schedule M-1 reconciles to taxable income before the dividends received and net operating loss deductions. Corporations with total assets of $10 million or more are required to file schedule M-3, which provides much more detail than Schedule M-1.

A. Nondeductible expenses are **added** to book income (federal tax expense, net capital loss, expenses in excess of limits, etc.).

B. Income that is taxable but not included in book income is **added** to book income (e.g., prepaid income included in taxable income).

C. Nontaxable income that is included in book income is **subtracted** from book income (municipal interest, life insurance proceeds, etc.).

D. Deductions not expensed in book income are **subtracted** from book income (dividends received deduction, election to expense, etc.).

E. Schedule M-3 is divided into three sections.

   1. Part I provides certain financial information and reconciles worldwide consolidated net income on the book financial statements to book income for the entities included on the corporate tax return.

   2. Part II reconciles the book income computed in Part I to the taxable income shown on the Form 1120. For each reconciling item the effect due to permanent differences and timing differences must be shown.

   3. Part III provides a breakdown of the expense/deduction items that affect the reconciliation of book income to taxable income in Part II. This total is carried to Part II and combined with the income items listed in Part II.

   4. Certain large S corporations and partnerships must also file Schedule M-3.

Examples

   1. Book income of $100 includes a federal tax expense of $22 and municipal interest of $13. The two adjustments to taxable income are identical to reversing entries— add expense of $22 and subtract income of $13 to book income. Hence, taxable income is $109.

2. This year ABC Corporation, an accrual-basis, calendar-year corporation, reported book income of $380,000. Included in that amount was $50,000 of municipal bond interest, $170,000 for federal income tax expense, and $2,000 of interest expense on debt incurred to carry the municipal bonds.

Question: What amount should ABC report as taxable income on Schedule M-1 of Form 1120?

Answer: $502,000, as calculated by reducing book income by $50,000 and increasing it by $172,000.

3. This year ABC Corporation, a calendar-year, accrual-basis corporation, had a net book income of $100,000. Included in the computation were the following:

Provision for federal income tax	$26,000
Net capital loss	11,000
Key man insurance premiums	4,000

Question: What is ABC's taxable income?

Answer: $141,000—computed by adding these adjustments to book income.

4. This year ABC Corporation reported book income of $140,000. Included in that amount was $50,000 for meals and entertainment expense, and $40,000 for federal income tax expense.

Question: What amount should be reported as ABC's taxable income in the Form M-1 reconciliation?

Answer: $205,000—computed by adding back one-half of meals and all of federal taxes to book income.

III. Net Operating Loss—A net operating loss (NOL) is negative taxable income carried from other tax years.

    A. The carryover period is back two years and forward 20 years.

    B. Any carryover from a previous or prior year is not included in calculating the current year NOL (specific for each year).

    C. The current year carryover ignores carryovers created in other years. Multiple carryovers to one year are used in a FIFO order.

    D. Charitable contributions are not allowed in computing the NOL.

    E. NOL carrybacks can be reported on an amended return (Form 1120X), or Form 1139, *Corporation Application for Tentative Refund*, can be filed by the end of the tax year following the year of loss.

IV. Schedule M-2 of Form 1120 analyzes changes in a corporation's Unappropriated Retained Earnings per books between the beginning and end of the year.

Balance at beginning of year

Add: Net income per books

            Other increases

Less: Dividends to shareholders

            Other decreases (e.g., addition to reserve for contingencies)

Balance at end of year

Accounting Methods and Periods—Corporations

After studying this lesson, you should be able to:

1. Determine the proper tax year for a business entity.

2. Determine when the accrual method is required.

3. Apply the income reporting rules for long-term projects.

This lessons builds on the "Accounting Methods and Periods—Individuals" lesson. The principles for individuals also apply to business entities.

I. Accounting Periods

A. The term *taxable year* refers to a taxpayer's annual accounting period. *Annual accounting period* means the annual period that the taxpayer uses to compute income in keeping his books.

    1. Calendar year is a period of 12 months ending on December 31.

    2. Fiscal year is a period of 12 months ending on the last day of a month other than December.

    3. 52–53-week year is an annual period always ending on the same day of the week (e.g., last Sunday of a month, or the Sunday closest to the end of a month).

B. A business establishes an accounting period by filing its first tax return.

C. Rules for Adoption of Taxable Year

    1. *Corporation* that is a C corporation (other than a personal service corporation) may adopt any taxable year that it chooses. A *personal service corporation* generally must adopt a calendar year.

    2. *Partnership* is a pass-through entity and generally must use the same tax year as that used by its partners owning more than 50% of partnership income and capital. A different taxable year may be permitted if there is a substantial business purpose.

    3. *S corporation* is a pass-through entity and generally must adopt a calendar year. A different taxable year may be permitted if there is a substantial business purpose.

    4. *Estate* may adopt any taxable year for its income tax return that it chooses.

    5. *Trust* (other than charitable and tax-exempt trusts) must adopt a calendar year.

D. Substantial business purpose and IRS approval are generally required to **change a taxable year**. Taxpayers can request permission to change a year by filing Form 1128, Application for Change in Accounting Period, by the 15th day of the second month after the close of a short period.

    1. The business purpose requirement may be satisfied if the taxpayer is requesting a change to a natural business year. The business purpose test will be met if the taxpayer receives at least 25% of its gross receipts in the last two months of the selected year, and this 25% test has been satisfied for three consecutive years.

    2. The IRS may require that certain conditions be met before it approves a request for change (e.g., the IRS may require partners to switch to the same year as is being requested by the partnership).

E. Some changes in tax years require *no* approval.

    1. A corporation (other than an S Corporation) may change its year if its taxable year has not changed within the past 10 years ending with the calendar year of change; the resulting short period does not have an NOL; the corporation's annualized taxable income for the short period is at least 90% of its taxable income for the preceding year; and the corporation's status (e.g., personal holding company) for the short period is the same as the preceding year.

    2. A newly acquired subsidiary that will be included in a consolidated return must change its taxable year to the same year as used by its parent.

F. Taxable Periods of Less than 12 Months

1. If due to beginning or ending of taxpayer's existence, tax is computed in normal way (e.g., corporation is formed, or individual dies). The taxpayer's exemptions and credits are not prorated. In the case of a decedent, the income tax return can be filed as if the decedent lived throughout the entire tax year.

2. If the short period is due to a *change in taxable year*, taxable income generally must be *annualized*. However, a new subsidiary that has a short year because of being included in a consolidated return is not required to annualize.

   a. When annualizing, an individual cannot use the tax tables and must itemize deductions. Personal exemptions must be prorated.

   b. Taxable income is multiplied by 12 and divided by the number of months in short period.

   c. The tax is computed and multiplied by the number of months in the short period, then divided by 12.

Examples

Pearl Corp. is a C Corporation that has been using a fiscal year ending June 30. It changes to a fiscal year ending September 30 for 2017. Pearl must file a tax return for its fiscal year ending June 30, 2017, as well as a tax return for its short period beginning July 1, 2017, and ending September 30, 2017. Pearl determines that its taxable income for the short period ending September 30 is $30,000. Because Pearl's short period is the result of a change in taxable year, Pearl must annualize its taxable income for the short period and determine its tax as follows:

Taxable Income: $30,000 × 12 months/3 months = $120,000. Tax on $120,000 = $30,050. Tax for short period: $30,050 × 3 months/12 months = $7,513.

II. Tax Accounting Methods

A. Cash versus Accrual Accounting—In general, the following entities cannot use the cash method of accounting:

1. Regular C corporations

2. Partnerships that have regular C corporations as partners

3. Tax shelters (Note: The exceptions listed in item "B" below do **not** apply to tax shelters.)

Definition

Tax Shelter: An entity other than a C corporation for which ownership interests have been offered for sale in an offering required to be registered with Federal or State security agencies.

B. Notwithstanding the above, the following entities can use the cash method:

1. Any corporation (or partnership with C corporation partners) whose annual gross receipts do not exceed $5 million. The test is satisfied for a prior year if the average annual gross receipts for the previous three-year period do not exceed $5 million. Once the test is failed, the entity must use the accrual method for all future tax years.

2. Certain farming businesses

3. Qualified personal service corporations

> **Definition**
>
> *Qualified Personal Service Corporation:* A corporation that exists if (1) substantially all of the activities of the business consist of services in health, law, engineering, architecture, accounting, actuarial science, performing arts, or consulting; and (2) at least 95% of its stock is owned by the employees performing the services.

III. Long-Term Contracts

A. Special rules apply to recognize income for production projects that generally take more than one year to complete (e.g., aircraft, ships).

B. The general rule is that the percentage of completion method must be used to recognize income, so that the gross profit from the project is recognized over the time period that it takes to complete the project.

C. The completed contract method allows the gross profit from the project to be deferred until the year that the production process is complete. This method may be used by:

1. Those with $10 million or less in average gross receipts during the preceding three years if the project is expected to last no more than two years

2. Home construction contractors

3. A contract where less than 10% of the total costs relates to the actual construction of property on the land

Special Corporate Deductions

There are certain corporate deductions subject to special limitations.

After studying this lesson, you should be able to:

1. Differentiate organizational expenses, start-up costs, and syndication expenses.

2. Compute the deduction for organizational expenses and start-up costs.

3. Compute charitable contribution for corporations.

4. Calculate the dividends received deduction.

5. Determine the applicability of the domestic production deduction.

6. Apply the ordering rules for special corporate deductions.

I. Organizational, Start-Up, and Syndication Expenditures

A. Expenses incurred in connection with the organization of a corporation are organizational expenses. $5,000 of these expenses may be deducted, but the $5,000 is reduced by the amount of expenditures incurred that exceed $50,000. Expenses not deducted must be **capitalized**, and **amortized** over **180 months**, beginning with the month that the corporation begins its business operations, unless an election is filed not to do so.

1. Typical organizational expenses are legal services incident to organization, accounting services, organizational meetings of directors and shareholders, and fees paid to incorporate. They must be incurred before the end of the taxable year that business begins (but they do not have to be paid, even if on the cash basis).

B. An additional deduction is allowed using the same rules as above for start-up costs. Start-up costs are expenditures that would be deductible as regular operating expenses, except that the corporation has not yet started its trade or business operation so they do not meet the criteria for deductibility. For example, if a new restaurant pays waitresses while they are being trained, but before it opens for business, these salary payments are start-up costs.

C. Costs of issuing and selling stock are **syndication expenses**. They must also be capitalized, but cannot be amortized.

Example 1
A calendar-year corporation was organized and began business during 2017 incurring $4,800 or organizational expenditures. The corporation may deduct the $4,800 of organizational expenditures for 2017.

Example 2
A calendar-year corporation was organized during February 2017 incurring organizational expenditures of $6,000. Assuming the corporation begins business during April 2017, its maximum deduction for organizational expenditures for 2017 would be $5,000 + [($6,000 − $5,000) × 9/180] = $5,050.

Example 3
A calendar-year corporation was organized during February 2017 incurring organizational expenditures of $60,000. Assuming the corporation begins business during April 2017, its maximum deduction for organizational expenditures for 2017 would be $60,000 × 9/180 = $3,000.

II. Charitable Contributions—Can be deducted after the amortization of organizational expenditures.

A. Charitable Contribution Rules—Are the same as for individuals, with the following exceptions:

1. A corporation's contribution of inventory or depreciables or real property used in its trade or business to charities that use the property in a manner related to the exempt purpose and solely for the care of the ill, needy, or infants, or where the property is used for research purposes under specified conditions, is subject to special rules.

2. The deduction is the lower of:

AB of property + 50% × (FMV − AB),   or   2 × AB

3. This rule applies for contributions of "wholesome" food inventory by corporations and other businesses to charities that use the food in an appropriate manner. These contributions can also be deducted up to 15% of taxable income (instead of the regular 10% limit). Note that this rule applies to all businesses, not just corporations.

B. The corporation can elect to deduct accrued contributions if the contributions are actually paid in the first three-and-a-half months following the year-end.

C. The limit on the deduction is 10% of taxable income (before special deductions for charity, dividends received domestic production, and carryovers).

D. Any excess charitable contribution (above the 10% limit) carries forward for five years (there is no carryback).

Example

The books of a calendar-year, accrual method corporation for 2017 disclose net income of $350,000 after deducting a charitable contribution of $50,000. The contribution was authorized by the board of directors on December 24, 2017, and was actually paid on January 31, 2018. The allowable charitable contribution deduction for 2017 (if the corporation elects to deduct it when accrued) is $40,000, calculated as follows: ($350,000 + $50,000) × .10 = $40,000. The remaining $10,000 is carried forward for up to five years.

III. Dividends-Received Deduction—The dividends-received deduction (DRD) is a percentage (%) of domestic dividends.

A. To be eligible, the stock must be of a domestic corporation held over a 45-day window (90 days for preferred stock). This prevents dividend stripping. The DRD cannot be claimed by S corporations, personal service corporations, and personal holding companies.

B. The DRD percentage depends on the level of stock owned by the corporation.

1. **Shortcut**—If the corporation owns less than 20% of the stock of another corporation, then the dividends-received deduction (DRD) is 70% of the dividends received. If the corporation owns 80% or more, then the DRD is 100% of the dividends received. All ownership levels between these two extremes are entitled to an 80% DRD.

Note

If a consolidated tax return is filed when a parent owns at least 80% of the subsidiary, intercompany dividends are eliminated in the consolidation process and not included in consolidated gross income.

Ownership percentage	Deduction percentage
Less than 20%	70%
More than 20% but less than 80%	80%
80% or more	100%

C. The DRD is limited by taxable income (before the DRD), unless the DRD creates or adds to a net operating loss. For this limitation, calculate the corporation's taxable income before any net operating losses, any capital loss carrybacks, and the dividends-received deduction.

D. The following steps *are required* to compute the DRD:

1. Multiply dividends received by the deduction percentage.

2. Multiply taxable income before dividends-received deduction as calculated previously by the deduction percentage.

3. Subtract Step 1 from taxable income before dividends-received deduction.

4. If Step 3 yields a *negative* amount (i.e., loss), Step 1 is the dividends-received deduction.

5. If Step 3 yields a *positive* amount, the dividends-received deduction is the lower of Step 1 or Step 2.

Example
ABC corporation received $100 in dividends from a domestic corporation (ABC owned less than 20% of the stock). If ABC has taxable income (before the DRD) of $200, then the DRD is $70. If ABC has taxable income (before the DRD) of $90, then ABC is only entitled to a DRD of $63 (70% of $90).

Note
The dividends-received deduction is not limited by taxable income if the full dividends-received deduction creates or adds to a net operating loss. For example, suppose ABC corporation received $100 in dividends from a domestic corporation (ABC owned less than 20% of the stock). If ABC has taxable income (before the DRD) of $10, then the DRD is $70 because it exceeds taxable income and thereby creates a net operating loss (an NOL of $60).

Examples
1. A corporation has income from sales of $20,000, dividend income of $10,000, and business expenses of $22,000, resulting in taxable income before the DRD of $8,000. Since taxable income before the DRD ($8,000) is less than dividend income ($10,000), the DRD is limited to $8,000 × 80% = $6,400. As a result, taxable income would be $8,000 − $6,400 = $1,600.

2. In the previous example assume the same facts except that business expenses are $22,001, resulting in taxable income before the DRD of $7,999. Since the full DRD ($8,000) would create a $1 net operating loss ($7,999 − $8,000), the taxable income limitation does not apply and the full DRD ($8,000) would be allowed.

E. Additional limits are imposed on the DRD if debt is used to finance the investment in stock (DRD is limited to the proportion of dividends that are not financed by debt).

Example
P, Inc. purchased 25% of T, Inc. for $100,000, paying with $50,000 of its own funds and $50,000 borrowed from its bank. During the year P received $9,000 in dividends from T, and paid $5,000 in interest expense on the bank loan. No principal payments were made on the loan during the year. If the stock were not debt financed, P's DRD would be $9,000 × 80% = $7,200. However, because half of the stock investment was debt financed, P's DRD is $9,000 × [80% × (100% − 50%)] = $3,600.

F. The reduction in the DRD cannot exceed the interest deduction allocable to the portfolio stock indebtedness.

Example
Assume the same facts as in the previous example except that the interest expense on the bank loan was only $3,000. The reduction in the DRD would be limited to the $3,000 interest deduction on the loan. The DRD would be ($9,000 × 80%) − $3,000 = $4,200.

IV. Domestic Production Deduction (DPD)—Corporations engaged in production activities within the United States qualify for a deduction equal to 9% times the lower of (1) qualified production activity income or (2) taxable income. The DPD is reduced for the production of oil, gas, and related products.

A. Qualified production activity income is equal to:

   1. Gross receipts from domestic production less:

      a. Cost of goods sold, direct expenses allocated to this income, a prorated share of indirect expenses allocated to this income.

B. This deduction may not exceed 50% of the wages allocable to domestic production income.

Example
Hanover Company produces computer chips and has the following information:

Gross receipts from qualified production activities	$1,000,000
Related cost of goods sold	400,000
Direct costs related to receipts (not including wages)	200,000
Indirect costs related to receipts	100,000
W-2 wages related to receipts	100,000

40% of the indirect costs relate to the qualified production activities. Hanover Company's taxable income is $350,000.

Hanover's qualified production income is:

Gross receipts from qualified production activities:	$1,000,000
Related cost of goods sold	− 400,000
Direct costs related to receipts (not including wages)	− 200,000
Indirect costs related to receipts	− 40,000
W-2 wages related to receipts	− 100,000
	$ 260,000

Hanover's qualified production activities deduction is:

9% × the lower of (1) QPAI of $260,000

(2) Taxable income of $350,000

9% × $260,000 =$23,400.

Note that the QPAD cannot exceed 50% of the W-2 wages related to the qualified production income, which is $50,000 ($100,000 × 50%).

V. Casualty Losses—Treated the same as for an individual except

  A. There is no $100 floor.

  B. If property is completely destroyed, the amount of loss is the property's adjusted basis.

  C. A partial loss is measured the same as for an individual's nonbusiness loss (i.e., the lesser of the decrease in FMV, or the property's adjusted basis).

VI. Research and Development Expenditures of a Corporation (or Individual)—May be treated under one of three alternatives:

  A. Currently expensed in year paid or incurred

  B. Amortized over a period of 60 months or more if life not determinable

  C. Capitalized and depreciated over determinable life

VII. Insurance Premiums

  A. A corporation may deduct insurance premiums paid for casualty insurance, employee health or accident insurance, and life insurance coverage for its employees and their beneficiaries.

  B. Premiums paid on life insurance policies in which the corporation itself is the beneficiary are not deductible.

Example

Moss Corporation's Income Statement for 2017 showed the following expenses for life insurance premiums:

Group-term life insurance premiums paid on employees' lives with the employees' dependents as beneficiaries	$10,000
Term life insurance premiums paid on life insurance policy on the life of the president of Moss Corporation with Moss Corporation named as beneficiary	$7,000

On its 2017 tax return, how much should Moss Corporation deduct for life insurance premiums?

  A. $0

  B. $7,000

  C. $10,000

  D. $17,000

The correct answer is C ($10,000). The life insurance premiums paid on the life of the president of Moss Corporation are not deductible since the Moss Corporation is the beneficiary of the life insurance policy.

VIII. Ordering Rules for Corporate Deductions—The following expenses are deducted in a specific order because each one is limited to the amount of income after reducing taxable income by the prior deduction.

Corporate Tax Formula—Special Deductions

Gross Income

Less: Deductions (except charitable, dividends received, domestic production deduction, NOL carryback, capital loss carryback)

Taxable income for charitable limitation

Less: Charitable contributions (<= 10% of above)

Taxable income for Div. Rec'd deduction (however, note that NOL carryforwards are not allowed for computing the DRD limit)

Less: Dividends received deduction

Taxable income before carrybacks

Less: Domestic Production Deduction, NOL carryback, and STCL carryback

TAXABLE INCOME

Corporate Alternative Minimum Tax

After studying this lesson, you should be able to:

1. Determine whether the AMT rules apply to a particular corporation.

2. Compute the alternative minimum tax for corporations.

3. Identify the most common adjustments and preferences when computing the AMT.

4. Calculate the adjusted current earnings adjustment and its effect on AMTI.

I. **The Corporate AMT Formula**—Is very similar to the individual formula in that taxable income is modified by adding tax preferences and adding or subtracting adjustments to income. The tax is called an alternative tax because it is imposed in lieu of the regular tax when the AMT's "tentative" tax exceeds the regular tax.

II. **Small Corporation Exemption**—The AMT does not apply to small corporations, but other firms need to calculate the AMT to determine if it applies in any given year.

A. The **corporate AMT doesn't apply to small corporations meeting a gross receipts test.** The tentative minimum tax (TMT) is zero if the corporation's average annual gross receipts for all three-tax-year periods ending before the tax year do not exceed $7,500,000. If a corporation fails this test for any year, then it will be subject to the AMT for ALL future years.

B. The above gross receipts test is applied by substituting $5,000,000 for $7,500,000 for the first three-year-tax period (or portion thereof) of the corporation that's taken into account under the test. **For new corporations, the TMT is always zero for its first year of operations.** A corporation formed in *2016* would be subject to the following tests:

> 2017—Exempt from AMT for first year
>
> 2018—Testing period is 2017
>
> 2019—Testing period is 2017–2018
>
> 2020—Testing period is 2017–2019

Example
Zero Corp., a calendar-year corporation, was formed on January 2, 2014, and had gross receipts for its first four taxable years as follows:

Year	Gross receipts
2014	$4,500,000
2015	9,000,000
2016	8,000,000
2017	6,500,000

Zero is automatically exempt from AMT for 2014. It is exempt for 2015 because its gross receipts for 2014 do not exceed $5 million. Zero also is exempt for 2016 because its average gross receipts for 2014–2015 do not exceed $7.5 million. Similarly, it is exempt for 2017 because its average gross receipts for 2014 to 2016 do not exceed $7.5 million. However, Zero will lose its exemption from AMT for 2018 and all subsequent years because its average gross receipts for 2015 to 2017 exceed $7.5 million.

III. Adjustments and Preferences—Adjust taxable income (before NOL carryovers) for "tax preferences" and "adjustments" similar to individual formula.

    A. Preferences

> **Definition**
> *Tax Preferences:* Increase taxable income when computing alternative minimum taxable income (AMTI). They often represent economic income excluded from regular taxable income or excessive deductions.

1. **Tax-exempt interest**—On private activity bonds (net of related expenses). Interest from general obligation bonds is not added back. For any private activity bonds issued in 2009 and 2010, the interest earned from these bonds will not be included in AMT income.

2. **Excess of percentage depletion**—Deduction over property's adjusted basis.

3. The excess of intangible drilling costs using a 10-year amortization over 65% of net oil and gas income

    B. Adjustments

> **Definition**
> *AMT Adjustments:* Specific adjustments that can either increase or decrease taxable income when computing alternative minimum taxable income. These adjustments often represent income or deductions used to defer the taxation of economic income.

1. The AMT adjustment applies only to MACRS 3-, 5-, 7-, and 10- year property that is depreciated using the 200% declining balance method. For AMT, the 150% DBM is used over the MACRS life. Note, that no AMT adjustments are required for assets purchased in 2008–2017 that use bonus depreciation. For more information on bonus depreciation see the "Limitations on Business Deductions" lesson.

> **Note**
> *There is no difference between AMT cost recovery and regular cost recovery for real property. Different methods are required only for personalty.*

2. Differences in gain/loss between regular tax and AMT caused by **different bases in assets** (due to different depreciation methods). There is no difference between AMT cost recovery and regular cost recovery for real property. Different methods are required only for personalty.

3. Difference in **percentage-of-completion method income over completed contract method income**.

4. Add regular tax net operating losses in excess of AMT net operating losses.

5. The installment method cannot be used for sales of inventory-type items.

IV. Adjusted Current Earnings (ACE)—The adjustment for ACE is a recognition that the list of preferences and adjustments contained in the AMT formula was not all-inclusive. Congress addressed this problem by using the adjustments for calculating E&P as a basis for providing a better yardstick for comparing AMTI with economic income.

    A. A Positive ACE—Represents high pretax economic earnings.

1. To calculate ACE, modify AMTI by adding economic income and adjusting for timing differences analogous to E&P adjustments. Common adjustments are:

    a. Increase for life insurance proceeds less expenses related to policy

    b. Increase in municipal interest income less related expenses

    c. Increase for the 70% dividends received deduction (i.e., deduction is not allowed in ACE)

    d. Adjustment reflecting that installment sales method is not allowed for ACE

    e. Increase for intangible drilling costs

    f. Increase for organizational expense amortization

2. No adjustment is required in computing ACE for:

   a. Excess charitable contributions

   b. Net capital losses

   c. Penalties

   d. Disallowed travel and entertainment

   e. Federal income taxes

   f. 80% and 100% dividends received deduction

3. If ACE exceeds AMTI (before the ACE adjustment), then 75% of this difference is used as an adjustment for calculating AMTI.

4. Because of timing differences, ACE can also be a negative adjustment, but it is limited to a cumulative amount of prior positive adjustments.

ACE Computation Summary

AMTI before ACE Adjustment and NOL Deduction

Add:	Tax-exempt interest on municipal bonds (less expenses); except not interest on tax-exempt bonds issued in 2009 or 2010.
	Tax-exempt life insurance death benefits (less expenses)
	70% dividends-received deduction
Deduct:	Depletion using cost depletion method
	Depreciation using ADS straight-line method for all property (This adjustment eliminated for property placed in service after 1993.)
Other:	Capitalize organizational expenditures and circulation expenses.
	Add increase (subtract decrease) in LIFO recapture amount (i.e., excess of FIFO value over LIFO basis).
	Installment method cannot be used for non dealer sales of property.
	Amortize intangible drilling costs over five years.

Equals: ACE (Adjusted Current Earnings)

− Pre-ACE AMTI

Balance (positive or negative)

× 75%

ACE adjustment (positive or negative)

Example

Acme, Inc. has adjusted current earnings (ACE) of $100,000 and alternative minimum taxable income (before this adjustment) of $60,000. Since adjusted current earnings exceeds pre-ACE AMTI by $40,000, 75% of this amount must be added to Acme's AMTI. Thus, Acme's AMTI before exemption for the year is [$60,000 + ($40,000 × 75%)] = $90,000.

Exam Tip

When answering questions regarding the computation of ACE, you must determine whether the question is asking (1) how an item impacts ACE, or (2) if starting with taxable income, are the items added or subtracted to compute ACE. For example, the 100% dividends received deduction **reduces** ACE. But if the question starts with taxable income and asks what adjustment is required when starting with taxable income for the 100% DRD, **no adjustment** is required since the 100% DRD already reduced taxable income.

V. Other Items in Corporate AMT Formula—Special characteristics of the corporate AMT formula including the AMT NOL deduction and the corporate AMT exemption.

   A. The AMT NOL deduction is allowed for the carryover of net operating losses under the AMT in prior years, and is limited to 90% of AMTI (before NOL).

   B. The AMT exemption for corporations is $40,000, and it is phased out for AMTI over $150,000 (25% of the amount of AMTI over this trigger).

Example
ABC Corporation has AMTI of $250,000. ABC will be entitled to claim an exemption of $15,000 ($40,000 less 25% of $100,000).

   1. Shortcut—An exemption for the corporate AMT is completely phased out when AMTI equals $310,000. This is $160,000 over the phaseout trigger of $150,000, and this means that the entire $40,000 exemption is phased out (25% of $160,000).

   C. Corporations pay the greater of the tentative minimum tax or regular tax.

   D. The foreign income tax credit can reduce the AMT liability.

   E. An eligible small business (ESB) can also reduce its AMT liability by the research credit. An ESB's average gross receipts for the previous three years must not exceed $50 million. This provision applies to partnerships and sole proprietorships in addition to corporations.

VI. AMT Credit Limitation—In years that the AMT is paid, a credit (minimum tax credit) is generated that can be used in future tax years. The entire AMT amount is available for this credit. This credit is available in a year in which the tentative minimum tax is less than the regular tax. In those years, it can be used to reduce the regular tax but not below the amount of the tentative minimum tax for that year.

VII. Formula for Corporate AMT

	Regular taxable income before Net Operating Loss (NOL) deduction
+	Tax preference items
+(−)	Adjustments other than Adjusted Current Earnings (ACE) and NOL deduction
	Pre-ACE AMTI
+(−)	ACE adjustment (75% of difference between pre-ACE AMTI and ACE)
−	AMT NOL deduction (limited to 90% of pre-NOL AMTI)
	AMTI
−	Exemption ($40,000 less 25% of AMTI over $150,000)
	Alternative minimum tax base
×	20% rate
	Tentative AMT before foreign tax credit
−	AMT foreign tax credit
	Tentative minimum tax (TMT)
−	Regular income tax (less regular tax foreign tax credit)
=	Alternative minimum tax (if positive)

Penalty Taxes

After studying this lesson, you should be able to:

1. Compute the accumulate earnings tax.

2. Identify the acceptable reasons for accumulating income.

3. Determine the accumulate earnings credit.

4. Apply the income and ownership tests to determine the applicability of the personal holding company tax.

5. Summarize how dividends impact the applicability of both penalty taxes.

I. **Accumulated Earnings Tax**—Corporations are sometimes used to avoid high individual tax rates. For example, the first $25,000 of corporate taxable income is taxed at only 15%. This use of the corporate form to reduce tax rates only works if the income remains in the corporation. If the income is distributed as dividends, then it is subject to the individual tax and no tax savings is realized. The accumulated earnings tax is designed to mitigate this use of the corporate form. Unnecessarily high levels of accumulated taxable income trigger this penalty tax, and it operates by imposing a penalty tax on any undistributed income. Hence, the accumulated earnings tax can be avoided either by documenting business reasons for accumulating income, or by distributing income as dividends.

   A. An accumulated earnings tax of 20% is imposed on undistributed accumulated taxable income.

      1. Accumulated taxable income is computed by adjusting taxable income to reflect retained economic income.

      2. Dividend distributions reduce accumulated taxable income because income is not accumulated if dividends are paid out to shareholders.

      3. For purposes of the accumulated earnings tax, dividends include consent dividends and dividends paid within *three*-and-a-half months of year-end.

Definition
Consent Dividends: Hypothetical dividends that are treated as if they were paid on the last day of the corporation's taxable year. Since they are not actually distributed, shareholders increase their stock basis by the amount of consent dividends included in their gross income.

---

      4. Finally, an accumulated earnings credit is subtracted from any accumulation to represent the "reasonable" accumulation of earnings for business purposes.

Accumulated Earnings Tax Formula

Taxable Income

+ Dividends-received deduction

+ NOL deduction

− Federal and foreign income taxes

− Excess charitable contributions (over 10% limit)

− Net capital loss

− Net LTCG over net STCL (net of tax)

Adjusted taxable income

− Dividends paid within 3 1/2 months after close of tax year

− Consent dividends

− Accumulated earnings credit

Accumulated taxable income

× 20%

Accumulated earnings tax

B. **Adjustments**—There are six modifications made to taxable income to reflect economic accumulations of income.

1. Taxable income is reduced by (1) accrued income taxes, (2) excess charitable contributions, (3) net capital loss, (4) net capital gain after tax.

Definition

Excess Charitable Contributions: The amount of contributions to charity in excess of the corporate deduction limit (10% of taxable income).

a. **Shortcut**—The adjustments for net capital loss and net capital gain are mutually exclusive in that only one can occur in any given year. That is, either the corporation will have capital losses in excess of gains (a net capital loss) or vice versa (a net capital gain).

2. Taxable income is increased by adding back (5) the dividends-received deduction and (6) any net operating loss or capital loss carryovers.

C. **Accumulated Earnings Credit**—The accumulated earnings credit is the greater of two numbers related to earnings and profits.

1. One number is the amount of the current earnings and profits needed for the "reasonable needs" of the business.

Definition

Reasonable Needs of a Business: A question of fact, but they have been found to include amounts necessary to finance business expansion (actual or planned), to provide working capital, or to retire liabilities. Reasonable needs, however, do not include amounts retained for unrealistic needs or for loans to shareholders.

2. A flat $250,000 ($150,000 for service (e.g., health, law, accounting, engineering) corporations) less the accumulated earnings and profits at the close of preceding year.

Note
Since the credit is the greater of these two items, there is no maximum on the credit as long as reasonable business needs support it.

II. Personal Holding Company (PHC) Tax—Corporations are sometimes used to hold investments because corporations are entitled to deduct a portion of dividends received. Hence, taxable income will be less if dividends are received by a corporation rather than an individual. The personal holding company tax is designed to mitigate this use of the corporate form. This penalty tax is triggered by relatively high levels of investment income in a corporation and it operates by imposing a penalty tax on any undistributed income. Hence, the personal holding company tax can be avoided either by keeping investment income levels relatively low, or by distributing income as dividends.

Personal Holding Company Tax Formula

Taxable Income

+ Dividends-received deduction

+ Net operating loss deduction (except NOL of immediately preceding year allowed without a dividends-received deduction)

− Federal and foreign income taxes

− Charitable contributions in excess of 10% limit

− Net capital loss

− Net LTCG over NSTCL (net of tax)

Adjusted taxable income

− Dividends paid during taxable year

− Dividends paid within 3 1/2 months after close of year (limited to 20% of dividends actually paid during year)

− Dividend carryover

− Consent dividends

Undistributed PHC income

× **20%**

Personal Holding Company Tax

A. A PHC tax of 20% is imposed only on corporations qualifying as personal holding companies.

1. Banks, insurance, and finance companies are exempt from the tax because their business purpose is to manage investments.

2. The tax base for the PHC tax is taxable income adjusted to reflect retained economic income.

3. Like the accumulated earnings tax, the PHC tax can be avoided by paying dividends.

> **Note**
> *A corporation that passes the tests as a personal holding company may be subject to the PHC tax only if it also has undistributed PHC income.*

B. Income and Ownership Tests—A corporation is a personal holding company if it "passes" two tests: the income test and the ownership test.

1. The income test is met if personal holding company income constitutes 60% of adjusted ordinary gross income (AOGI).

Definitions

Personal Holding Company Income: This income includes taxable dividends, interest, and sometimes, rents, royalties, and personal service contracts.

Adjusted Ordinary Gross Income (AOGI): Gross income excluding capital and 1231 gains and reduced by expenses associated with the production of rent and royalty income.

2. The ownership test is met if more than 50% of the value of the stock is owned directly or indirectly by five or fewer individuals at any time during the last half of the year.

> **Definition**
> *Indirect Ownership*: Determined by stock "attribution" rules. These rules define ownership to include the stock held by an entity (the portion relating to a corporation, partnership, trust, or estate) or by family members (brothers and sisters, spouse, ancestors, and lineal descendants). An individual will not be considered to be the constructive owner of the stock owned by nephews, cousins, uncles, aunts, and any of his/her spouse's relatives.

    a. **Shortcut**—A corporation with 10 or more equal and unrelated shareholders would not be a PHC because it will not pass the ownership test.

C. **Adjustments**—PHC income is taxable income modified by five adjustments. The adjustments to taxable income are designed so that the tax base (undistributed PHC income) reflects retained economic income.

    1. Taxable income is reduced by (1) accrued income tax, (2) excess charitable contributions, and (3) net capital gain (after tax).

    2. Taxable income is increased by adding back (4) the dividends-received deduction and (5) the carryover for net operating losses from year prior to the previous year.

        a. **Shortcut**—The adjustments for the PHC are similar to those used for the accumulated earnings tax except that there is no adjustment for net capital losses and the adjustment for net operating loss carryovers does not include an NOL from the previous year.

D. **PHC Tax**—The PHC tax is imposed on undistributed PHC income.

    1. To reduce PHC income, dividends must be pro rata. (The dividends cannot be paid disproportionately.)

    2. For purposes of the PHC tax, dividends include dividends paid during the year, consent dividends, and dividends paid within 3½; months of year-end (limited to 20% of dividends actually paid during year).

    3. A deficiency dividend can also be paid to avoid the PHC tax.

> **Definition**
> *Deficiency Dividend*: A dividend expressly declared to avoid the tax and is paid within 90 days of tax imposition (the finding of a deficiency due to the PHC tax).

Taxation of Related Corporations

After studying this lesson, you should be able to:

1. Determine whether two or more corporations form an affiliated group.

2. Compute the applicable adjustments for consolidated taxable income.

3. Assess whether two or more corporations form a parent-subsidiary controlled group.

4. Evaluate whether two or more corporations form a brother-sister controlled group.

5. Identify the limitations placed on corporations that are members of a controlled group.

I. Overview—Corporations can be directly related through inter-corporate ownership or indirectly related through common shareholders.

II. Affiliated Groups—An "affiliated group" exists when one corporation owns **at least 80% of the voting power** of another corporation **and** holds shares representing at least 80% of its **value**. This test must be met on **every day of the year.**

Example
P corporation owns 80% of S corporation and 20% of X corporation. S owns 70% of X, but all other shares are held by unrelated individuals. P and S form an affiliated group. Because in aggregate P and S also own more than 80% of the stock of X, this corporation is also included in the affiliated PSX group.

Example
P Corp. owns 80% of the stock of A Corp., 40% of the stock of B Corp., and 45% of the stock of C Corp. A Corp. owns 40% of the stock of B Corp. A consolidated tax return could be filed by P, A, and B.

III. Elect to File—Eligible affiliated corporations can elect to file a consolidated return.

   A. Consolidating permits the corporations to eliminate intercompany profits and losses, allows the profitable corporation to offset its income against losses of another corporation, and permits net capital losses of one corporation to offset capital gains of another.

> **Note**
> Ownership of a corporation is determined by examining the amount of voting stock, as well as other classes of stock. To qualify as a parent, a corporation must own 80% or more of each class. Once a parent and subsidiary exist, then related corporations can be included in the affiliated group if the total ownership (including all corporations within the group) rises to 80% or more.

   B. Gains and losses on intercompany sales are deferred until disposition outside the group. These gains and losses will be recognized at the time of the eventual disposition outside the consolidated firm but the nature of the gain or loss is determined by the use of the property at the time of the intercompany sale.

   C. Foreign corporations, exempt corporations, S corporations, and insurance companies are not eligible to consolidate.

   D. The election to consolidate must be unanimous and it is binding on future returns (irrevocable) and creates a joint and several tax liability.

   E. The members of the group must conform their tax year to the parent's tax year.

F. Intercompany dividends are eliminated from consolidated taxable income.

G. The parent adjusts the basis of the stock of a consolidated subsidiary for allocable portion of income, losses, and dividends.

Example
Parent and Subsidiary file consolidated tax returns using a calendar year. During 2017, Subsidiary paid a $10,000 dividend to Parent. Also during 2016, Subsidiary sold land with a basis of $20,000 to Parent for its FMV of $50,000. During 2017, Parent sold the land to an unrelated taxpayer for $55,000.

The intercompany dividend is eliminated in the consolidation process and is excluded from consolidated taxable income. Additionally, Subsidiary's $30,000 of gain from the sale of land to Parent is deferred for 2016. The $30,000 will be included in consolidated taxable income for 2017 when Parent reports $5,000 of income from the sale of that land to the unrelated taxpayer.

IV. Controlled Groups—Controlled groups are **parent-subsidiary corporations, brother-sister groups, and certain insurance companies**.

A. A controlled group of corporations is entitled to one $250,000 accumulated earnings tax credit and is limited to taxable income in each of the first two brackets, as though the group were one corporation. A controlled group also receives only one Section 179 expense deduction and one AMT exemption.

Example
Rather than form a corporation that expects to generate $100,000 of taxable income, a taxpayer might try to form four corporations with $25,000 of taxable income each. This tactic would allow each corporation to be taxed at 15% instead of the higher tax rates imposed on taxable income over $25,000. However, the four corporations would form a controlled group and would only be eligible for one set of tax brackets that could be allocated among the group.

B. The following tests are applied on the **last day of the year**.

C. **Parent-Subsidiary**—The focus here is on corporate ownership. A parent-subsidiary controlled group exists if:

1. Stock possessing at least 80% of the **voting power** of all *classes of stock entitled to* **vote**, or at least 80% of the total **value** of shares of all *classes of stock* of each of the corporations, except the common parent, is owned by one or more of the other corporations, and

2. The **common parent owns** stock possessing at least 80% of the total combined voting power of all classes of stock entitled to vote, or at least 80% of the total value of shares of all classes of stock of at least one of the other corporations.

D. **Brother-Sister**—The focus here is on **individual ownership**. A brother-sister controlled group exists if:

1. Two or more corporations are owned by five or fewer persons (individuals, estates, or trusts):

    a. Who have a common ownership of more than 50% of the total combined voting powers of all classes of stock entitled to vote, or more than 50% of the total value of shares of all classes of stock of each corporation, and

    b. Who possess stock representing at least 80% of the total combined voting power of all *classes of stock entitled to vote*, or at least 80% of the total value of shares of all classes of each corporation.

    c. The 80% test does not apply for determining brother-sister corporations in some circumstances. These circumstances include determining corporate tax brackets, the accumulated earnings credit, and the minimum tax exemption.

Example
A, B, and C corporations are owned by X and Z (unrelated individuals) as follows:

	Corporations		
Individual	A	B	C
X	40%	30%	60%
Z	10%	65%	30%

A cannot be a member of a controlled group because it fails the control test (X and Z only own 50%). B and C both meet the total control test (80% or more by five or fewer individuals) and this group also passes the common ownership test (60%). X owns at least 30% of Corporations B and C, and Z owns at least 30% of both of these corporations. So the total common ownership that X and Z have in B and C is 60% (30% + 30%). The 50% common ownership test is met. Thus, BC is a controlled group!

Example

Individual shareholder	Corporations		Stock considered for 50% test
	W	X	
A	30%	20%	20%
B	5	40	5%
C	30	35	30%
D	15	5	5%
E	20	–	–
	100%	100%	60%

Corporations W and X are a controlled group since five or fewer individuals own more than 50% of each corporation when counting only identical ownership.

Also note that A, B, C, and D own at least 80% of Corporations W and X. E is not included in the 80% test since she did not own any stock in X.

Example

Individual shareholder	Corporations		Stock considered for 50% test
	Y	Z	
F	80%	5%	5%
G	10	90	10
H	10	5	5
	100%	100%	20%

Corporations Y and Z are not a controlled group since shareholders F, G, and H do not own more than 50% of Y and Z when counting only identical stock ownership.

Distributions from a Corporation

The calculation of earnings and profits is critical to determining whether a corporate distribution is a dividend (taxable to a shareholder) or a return of capital (tax-free up to the shareholder's basis). A distribution qualifies as a dividend if earnings and profits are positive. Hence, earnings and profits is the tax analog to retained earnings.

After studying this lesson, you should be able to:

1. Compute earnings and profits.

2. Differentiate how current and accumulated earnings and profits impact dividend income.

3. Calculate the tax effect of cash distributions to shareholder.

4. Determine the tax effects of property distributions to shareholder and corporation.

5. Evaluate the impact of distributions on earnings and profits.

I. **Earnings and Profits**—To properly classify distributions from a corporation, one must know the corporation's earnings and profits (E&P). To determine earnings and profits, taxable income must be adjusted to represent economic income. Hence, many of the adjustments will be very similar to the reconciling items used to adjust taxable income with book (accounting) income, except the direction of the change will be reversed.

   A. **Additions to Taxable Income**—Are made for exempt income or deductions that do not represent an economic outlay.

      1. Municipal interest and life insurance proceeds are added to taxable income because they are economic inflows excluded from taxable income.

      2. The dividends-received deduction does not represent an economic outlay, so it is added back to taxable income in computing E&P.

      3. Deductions claimed for carryovers from previous years (carryforwards) are added back to taxable income.

      4. Domestic production activities deduction

      5. Proceeds from corporate life insurance policy (less cash surrender value)

   B. **Some Expenditures are Not Deductible**—But represent economic outlays. These expenditures reduce taxable income in computing E&P.

      1. The amount of federal income tax (net of credits) reduces taxable income in computing E&P because it represents an economic outlay.

      2. Related party losses

      3. Penalties, fines, lobbying expenses, life insurance premiums for a "key" man, and the disallowed portion of meals and entertainment expenses

   C. **Some Modifications to Taxable Income**—Modifications are timing differences and can be positive or negative.

      1. The deferred portion of a gain from a current installment sale (but not other deferrals) is also added to taxable income because it represents an economic inflow. When the gain is recognized in later years, it reduces taxable income because it has already been included in E&P in the year of the sale.

      2. The amount of depreciation deducted in excess of straight-line is viewed as a form of deferral and it is added back to taxable income (like the installment gain, this is a timing adjustment that will reverse in later years). The Alternate Depreciation System (ADS) is used to compute depreciation for earnings and profits. See the "Section 1231 Assets—Cost Recovery" lesson for more details on ADS.

   3. Section 179 expense

   4. Net capital loss and the excess amount of charitable contributions

D. Distributions generally reduce E&P

   1. Cash distributions reduce E&P.

   2. Distributions of property reduce E&P by the greater of the value of the property or the adjusted basis and this amount is then reduced by any liabilities that are assumed by the shareholder.

   3. A distribution of **appreciated** property will first increase E&P by the amount of the gain recognized on the distribution.

   4. Distributions **cannot create a deficit** in E&P—only losses can create a deficit.

> **Note**
> *Distributions cannot create a deficit in E&P, but E&P can have a negative balance due to net operating losses (negative taxable income).*

> **Example**
> If Corporation Mouse distributes property with a FMV of $1,000 and a basis of $1,200 to shareholder Cat and Cat assumes a liability attached to the property of $300, E&P is reduced by $900 ($1,200 − $300).

II. Dividend Treatment—The taxation of distributions as dividend income to shareholders depends upon the earnings and profits (E&P) accumulated in the corporation prior to distribution. Distributions are:

A. Taxable as **dividend income** to extent of the shareholder's pro-rata share of **E&P**;

B. **Excess is tax-free** to extent of shareholder's **basis** in stock (and reduces the basis);

C. Remaining distribution amount is taxed as a **capital gain**;

D. Both current and accumulated E&P are used to determine whether a distribution is a dividend. There are four possible scenarios.

> **Definitions**
> *Current E&P:* That which is generated during the year (up to the year-end).
>
> *Accumulated E&P:* The amount on the first day of the year (ignoring current E&P).

   1. Scenario #1—If both current and accumulated E&P are negative, then distributions are a return of capital (tax-free up to adjusted basis—and then capital gain).

   2. Scenario #2—If both current and accumulated E&P are positive, then the distribution is taxed as a dividend. Distributions are first taken from current E&P by allocating E&P to each distribution, based on the amount of the distributions. If there is only one distribution during the year, then all of the current E&P is allocated to that distribution. Once current E&P is depleted, then distributions reduce accumulated E&P.

   3. Scenario #3—If current E&P is positive but accumulated E&P is negative, then a distribution is a dividend only to the extent of the current E&P.

   4. Scenario #4—If accumulated E&P is positive but current E&P is negative, then a distribution is a dividend to the extent of net E&P (accumulated E&P less an allocated portion of the deficit in current E&P) on the date of the distribution.

> **Exam Tip**
> *Questions about distributions from E&P will typically use year-end distributions or describe income as **earned ratably** throughout the year. This language simplifies the calculation of the E&P balance on the date of the distribution (necessary to determine whether the distribution is from current or accumulated E&P).*

E&P Status at Time of Distribution	*Accumulated E&P is negative*	*Accumulated E&P is positive*
Current E&P is negative	Scenario 1: Distributions are a return of capital	Scenario 4: Dividend income to extent of accumulated E&P after netting against deficit in current E&P
Current E&P is positive	Scenario 3: Dividend income to extent of current E&P	Scenario 2: Dividend income to extent of current E&P, then accumulated E&P

E. A deficit in current E&P is allocated ratably during the year based on time, even if there is only one distribution for the year.

Example
ABC Corp has a deficit in current E&P for the current year of $20,000. A distribution of $10,000 is made on April 1 and that is the only distribution for the year. One-fourth (90 days/365 days) of the current E&P is allocated to the distribution, or $4,932.

F. *If more than one distribution is made during the year a positive current E&P balance is* **prorated** *among the distributions based on the amount of the distributions.*

Example
A corporation has accumulated earnings and profits of $4,000 and current earnings and profits of $20,000. During the current year it distributes $15,000 to its common shareholders in March and another $15,000 to its common shareholders in October. The $20,000 of current earnings and profits are allocated pro rata to the two distributions, making $10,000 of the March distribution and $10,000 of the October distribution taxable as a dividend. The accumulated earnings and profits of $4,000 are then allocated to the March distribution. As a result, $14,000 of the March distribution and $10,000 of the October distribution are taxable as dividends.

G. Accumulated E&P is allocated in chronological order.

III. Property Distribution—Distributions of property (in-kind distributions).

A. The value of the property distributed (net of any debt assumed by the shareholder) is the amount eligible for dividend treatment.

B. The distribution of appreciated property causes the corporation to recognize gains (not losses) like a sale of the property.

Example
A corporation distributes property with an FMV of $10,000 and a basis of $3,000 to a shareholder. The corporation recognizes a gain of $10,000 – $3,000 = $7,000.

C. If the liability on the property exceeds the property's fair market value, the FMV is treated as being equal to the liability.

Example
A corporation distributes property with an FMV of $10,000 and a basis of $3,000 to a shareholder, who assumes a liability of $12,000 on the property. The corporation recognizes a gain of $12,000 – $3,000 = $9,000.

D. Amount distributed = FMV − Liabilities on property

E. Basis of the property to the shareholder is the fair market value.

F. **Constructive dividends** are also treated as distributions.

Definition

Constructive Dividend: A payment to a shareholder that, although not formally declared as a dividend, is regarded as a dividend. Property distributions to shareholders will often be treated as a constructive dividend.

Example

TP is the sole shareholder of Green Incorporated. This year, Green paid TP a salary of $200,000 when a reasonable amount of compensation for TP's services would have been $50,000. The excess salary ($150,000) is unreasonable compensation and is not deductible by Green. Instead, this amount is construed as a dividend payment to TP.

Comprehensive Example

Z Corp. has two 50% shareholders, Alan and Baker. Z Corp. distributes a parcel of land (held for investment) to each shareholder. Gainacre with an FMV of $12,000 and an adjusted basis of $8,000 is distributed to Alan, while Lossacre with an FMV of $12,000 and an adjusted basis of $15,000 is distributed to Baker. Each shareholder assumes a liability of $3,000 on the property received. Z Corp. must recognize a gain of $4,000 on the distribution of property to Alan but cannot recognize the loss on the distribution to Baker.

	Alan	Baker
Dividend ($12,000 − $3,000)	$9,000	$9,000
Tax basis for property received	12,000	12,000
Effect (before tax) on Z's earnings and profits:		
Increased by gain (FMV − Basis)	4,000	0
Increased by liabilities distributed	3,000	3,000
Decreased by greater of FMV or adjusted basis of property distributed	(12,000)	(15,000)
Net effect on earnings and profits	(5,000)	(12,000)

Corporate Redemptions and Liquidations

A corporation may engage in two types of transactions that can be viewed as a purchase of the stock held by a shareholder. A corporation may redeem stock by purchasing it from a shareholder. On the other hand, a corporation may dissolve and thereby cause the stock held by shareholders to be liquidated. Unfortunately, these transactions are not always treated as simple sales of stock because these transactions can also be structured to avoid taxes.

After studying this lesson, you should be able to:

1. Contrast the tax implications of dividends and redemptions.

2. Determine when a sale of stock to a corporation qualifies as redemption.

3. Compute the tax effects of redemption to shareholder and to corporation's earnings and profits.

4. Evaluate tax effects to shareholders of corporate liquidation.

5. Calculate effect of liquidation on corporate income, including disallowance of loss rules.

6. Identify requirements for a tax-deferred liquidation of a subsidiary.

I. **Redemptions**—A redemption of stock occurs when a corporation repurchases stock from a shareholder. The redemption is generally treated by the shareholder as a sale of the stock that will trigger recognition of gain or loss. However, a redemption of stock can also be structured to have the identical effect of a dividend distribution. Hence, the tax rules are constructed to assure that redemptions, which have the effect of a dividend, are taxed as dividends rather than sales of stock.

    A. There are two advantages of redemption treatment. First, the shareholder is able to offset stock basis against the redemption proceeds. Second, any resulting gain is treated as capital gain, which is often advantageous as compared to dividend income.

Example
TP owns 100 shares that constitute 100% of Blue Inc. This year, in lieu of a $100 dividend, Blue redeems oneshare of stock for $100. This redemption is essentially a disguised dividend because TP remains the sole shareholder of Blue after the redemption.

II. **Three Methods to Qualify**—In order for a redemption to be taxed as a sale, it must qualify under one of three circumstances:

    A. **First**—A redemption will be treated as a sale, if the distribution is **not essentially equivalent to a dividend (NEED)**.

Definition
Not Essentially Equivalent to a Dividend (NEED): This phrase has been interpreted to mean that there is a "meaningful" reduction in the shareholder's rights, including voting rights and rights to earnings.

        1. **Shortcut**—NEED is a question of fact that is very ambiguous.

    B. **Second**—A **substantially disproportionate** redemption will also qualify as a sale if the shareholder passes two tests: the **control** test and the **reduced interest test**.

Definitions
Control Test: The shareholder must own less than 50% of the voting shares after the redemption.

Reduced Interest Test: The shareholder must own less than 80% of the shares that were owned prior to the redemption.

Example
A owns 40 shares of XYZ corporation (one1-third of the outstanding stock), and the remaining 80 shares are owned by B. If XYZ redeems 10 of A's shares and 10 of B's shares, the redemption would not be substantially disproportionate for A. Although A owns less than 50% of XYZ shares after the redemption (30/100), his interest has only declined from 33% (40/120) to 30% (30/100). Thus, the redemption would not meet the reduced interest test because A's interest did not decline to 80% of the previous ownership level.

C. **Third**—A **complete termination** of the shareholder's interest in the corporation qualifies as a sale.

Definition
Complete Termination: The shareholder must surrender the stock owned directly.

1. For complete terminations, family attribution (but not entity attribution) can be waived with the execution of an agreement by the taxpayer to notify the IRS of any subsequent acquisitions of stock for the next 10 years.

2. In the agreement the taxpayer must agree to not acquire any stock interest in the corporation during the next 10 years. The taxpayer also cannot exercise managerial control over the corporation in any manner.

3. If this agreement is violated at any time during the 10 years then the waiver of the family attribution rules in the year of the sale is voided.

4. An inheritance of stock in the corporation will not violate the 10-year agreement.

Note
The scope of attribution rules is not uniform across various tax topics. For example, the attribution rules applying to redemptions is narrower than the attribution rules applying to the personal holding companies. The latter rules include siblings (brothers and sisters) who are not included for the redemption rules.

III. **Attribution**—For purposes of the redemption tests, the shareholder's interest includes stock owned directly and indirectly. Indirect or constructive ownership is determined through stock attribution rules.

A. **Family Attribution**

Definition
Family Attribution: Stock is owned by family members. It is defined to include spouse, children, grandchildren, and parents.

Example
XYZ corporation is owned equally by TP and his three children. Under the family attribution rules, TP is deemed to own all of the stock of the corporation while each child is only deemed to own TP's shares (no attribution between siblings).

B. **Entity Attribution—Corporations**

Definitions
Stock Attribution: A taxpayer is deemed to own stock held by other related taxpayers. There are two forms of attribution: attribution to/from an entity and attribution to/from family.

Entity Attribution: Stock owned by a corporation, partnership, trust, or estate is deemed to be owned by a taxpayer who is an owner or beneficiary of the entity. Additionally, stock owned by the owner or beneficiary may be deemed to be owned by the entity.

1. **Entity to owner**—A shareholder is only subject to entity attribution if the corporation is controlled by the shareholder (owning 50% or more of the value of the stock). In this case, the shareholder is deemed to own a proportionate interest (equal to the ownership interest) of the stock held by the corporation. If the shareholder owns less than 50% of the corporation, then none of the stock owned by the corporation is attributed to the shareholder.

2. **Owner to entity**—Stock owned by a 50% or greater shareholder is deemed to be owned in full (100%) by the corporation. If the shareholder owns less than 50% of the corporation, there is no attribution from the shareholder to the entity.

C. **Entity Attribution—Partnerships**

1. **Entity to owner**—Stock owned by a partnership is deemed to be owned by the partner based on her ownership interest in the partnership. Note this attribution applies to all partners, not just partners who own 50% or more.

2. **Owner to entity**—Stock owned by a partner is deemed to be owned in full by the partnership. Note that this attribution applies to stock owned by all partners, not just partners who own 50% or more.

D. **Entity Attribution—Estates and Trusts.** The attribution rules for estates and trusts are similar to the rules for partnerships.

Examples

1. A taxpayer owns a 10% interest in a partnership. If the partnership owns 100 shares of a corporation, then the partner is deemed to own 10 shares of the stock (10% of the stock held by a partnership).

2. TP owns 10% in Corporation A. If Corporation A owns 100 share of Corporation R, TP is not attributed any stock of Corporation R. However, if TP owns 60% of Corporation A, then TP would be deemed to own 60 shares (100 × 60%) of Corporation R.

IV. **Consequences to Corporation**

A. If the corporation distributes appreciated property as part of the redemption, the appreciation is recognized by the corporation. However, the loss in distributed assets that have declined in value is not recognized. If the property has been depreciated, the corporation may have to recognize Section 1245 or Section 1250 recapture.

B. The corporation must reduce its earnings and profits for redemptions. The reduction is the lower of 1) the redeemed stock's proportionate share of E&P, or 2) the amount of the redemption.

1. If the redemption is actually treated as a dividend, E&P is reduced by the greater of the FMV or adjusted basis of the property distributed, reduced by any liabilities attached to the property.

V. **Partial Liquidations**

A. A partial liquidation is treated as a sale by noncorporate shareholders, so it is a fourth method to qualify for redemption treatment. There are two tests for partial liquidations, one objective and one subjective.

Definition
Partial Liquidation: A contraction of the corporate business. Hence, the determination for sale treatment is made by looking for a contraction at the corporate level.

B. The objective test requires that the corporation must completely terminate a **qualifying business** and must continue to operate at least one qualifying business.

Definition
Qualifying Business: A trade conducted for five years prior to the determination.

C. To meet the subjective test, the distribution must qualify as not essentially equivalent to a dividend in that it results from a genuine contraction of the corporate business, and not just from the sale of excess inventory.

VI. Redemption Used to Pay Death Taxes

A. A redemption used to pay death taxes may also be treated as a sale under two conditions.

B. The death of a shareholder in a valuable closely-held corporation may result in significant death taxes. However, if the corporate stock is the primary asset of the estate, then a redemption may be necessary in order to pay the estate tax. If the stock held by the estate is treated as a sale, no additional tax is usually due because adjusted basis of stock is increased to FMV on date of death.

    1. The stock held by the decedent must be a large portion of the estate (35% of adjusted gross estate).

    2. The redemption is limited to the amount of federal and state death taxes and funeral and administrative expenses.

VII. Stock Distributions

A. Stock distributions are not taxable to the shareholder if there is no option to receive property in lieu of stock and there is no change in proportionate interests of the shareholders.

B. A **stock bailout** is treated as a dividend to the shareholder to the extent of earnings and profits at the time of the sale or redemption.

> **Note**
> *Not essentially equivalent to a dividend for purposes of a partial liquidation is different from the definition of NEED for redemptions. The former focuses on the source of the distribution at the corporate level, while the latter examines the effect of the distribution at the shareholder level. However, both definitions are similar in that they are very subjective tests.*

> **Definition**
> *Stock Bailout:* A distribution of nonvoting stock followed by sale (or redemption) of the stock by the corporation.

VIII. Complete Liquidations—A distribution in complete liquidation occurs with the dissolution of a corporation and the distribution of remaining assets. A complete liquidation is similar to a redemption in that the shareholders receive assets in exchange for canceling the shares of stock.

    A. Shareholders Recognize Gain or Loss—On the Liquidating Distribution

        1. The gain or loss is determined by subtracting the adjusted basis of the stock from the fair market value of the distribution, reduced by any taxes paid by the corporation for the liquidation.

        2. Any gain or loss recognized by the shareholder will generally be a capital gain or loss (depending on whether the stock is a capital asset). The related party rule that disallows losses on sales of assets between related parties does not apply.

        3. If the distributed property is subject to a liability, then the shareholder reduces the fair market value of the property by the amount of liabilities.

        4. The adjusted basis of the property received in the distribution is its fair market value on the date of distribution, reduced by any taxes paid by the corporation for the liquidation.

> **Example**
> TP received realty worth $100 in liquidation of XYZ corporation. TP had a basis of $25 in the XYZ stock and the realty was subject to a mortgage of $40. TP will recognize a gain of $35 because the net value received was $60 reduced by an adjusted basis of $25. TP will have an adjusted basis in the realty of $100.

B. A Corporation Will Recognize Gain or Loss—When It Makes a Liquidating Distribution.

1. The computation of the gain or loss is computed by subtracting the adjusted basis from the fair market value of the property distributed on the date of distribution.

2. The nature of the gain or loss depends on the nature of the asset distributed (ordinary, capital, or Section 1231).

3. If the distributed property is subject to a liability, then the fair market value of the property cannot be less than the amount of liabilities.

Example
As part of a corporation liquidation, Corporation T distributes land with an FMV of $50,000, adjusted basis of $20,000, and debt attached to the property of $65,000. Corporation T recognizes gain of $45,000 ($65,000 − $20,000).

4. Expenses incurred in the liquidation are deducted on the last corporate return.

Example
ABC corporation liquidated by distributing inventory worth $200 to its shareholders. If the inventory had an adjusted basis of $70, ABC would recognize ordinary income of $130 on the liquidation.

5. If the corporation realizes a loss on the distribution of property in complete liquidation to a shareholder owning more than 50% (including constructive ownership) in value of the corporation's stock, then the loss is not recognized if:

   a. The distribution of each asset is not pro-rata *or*

   b. The property distributed is disqualified property (i.e., property acquired by the liquidating corporation in a tax-free incorporation or as a contribution to capital during a five-year period ending on the date of the distribution).

6. Built-in losses will be disallowed on distributions of some disqualified property to any shareholder, if the principal purpose was to recognize loss by the corporation in connection with the liquidation.

   a. Such a purpose is presumed, if the transfer occurs within two years of the adoption of the plan of liquidation, unless a business purpose can be established.

   b. Any decline in value for the property after its contribution to the corporation results in a deductible loss to the liquidating corporation. Only the built-in loss at the time of contribution is disallowed.

   Note
   Under the related-party rule, all losses are disallowed. Under the non-related-party rule, only built-in losses are disallowed.

Example
A shareholder makes a capital contribution which includes property unrelated to the corporation's business with a basis of $15,000 and an FMV of $10,000 on the contribution date. Within two years the corporation adopts a plan of liquidation and sells the property for $8,000. The liquidating corporation's recognized loss will be limited to $10,000 − $8,000 = $2,000.

C. Subsidiaries—No Gain or Loss Is Recognized—On the liquidation of a subsidiary by the parent under two conditions. When a controlled subsidiary is liquidated, no real disposition of the assets has occurred. The assets have merely been transferred from one corporate pocket to another. The key to deferring gain and loss is the establishment of control and the timing of the liquidation.

1. First, the parent must own 80% of the voting stock and other stock of the subsidiary.

2. Second, the subsidiary must distribute its assets within the tax year (or within three years of the close of the tax year of the first distribution).

3. The parent corporation takes a carryover basis in the distributed assets and inherits the subsidiary's tax attributes.

4. Minority shareholders will recognize gain or loss on the liquidation.

Example

Parent Corp. owns 80% of Subsidiary Corp., with the remaining 20% of Subsidiary stock owned by Alex. Parent's basis in its Subsidiary stock is $100,000, while Alex has a basis for her Subsidiary stock of $15,000. Subsidiary Corp. is to be liquidated and will distribute: to Parent Corp. assets with an FMV of $200,000 and a basis of $150,000, and will distribute to Alex assets with an FMV of $50,000 and a basis of $30,000. Subsidiary has an unused capital loss carryover of $10,000. The tax effects of the liquidation will be as follows:

Parent Corp. will not recognize gain on the receipt of Subsidiary's assets in complete liquidation, since Subsidiary is an at least 80%-owned corporation. The basis of Subsidiary's assets to Parent will be their transferred basis of $150,000, and Parent will inherit Subsidiary's unused capital loss carryover of $10,000.

Alex will recognize a gain of $35,000 ($50,000 FMV – $15,000 stock basis) from the liquidation. Alex's tax basis for Subsidiary's assets received in the liquidation will be their FMV of $50,000.

Subsidiary Corp. will not recognize gain on the distribution of its assets to Parent Corp but will recognize a gain of $20,000 ($50,000 FMV – $30,000 basis) on the distribution of its assets to Alex.

Corporate Reorganizations

After studying this lesson, you should be able to:

1. Determine whether a corporate reorganization qualifies as a specific type of tax-deferred transaction.

2. Compute tax effects of a qualifying reorganization to acquiring and target corporations.

3. Evaluate tax effects of a qualifying reorganization to shareholders.

4. Identify the tax attributes that carryover with a qualifying reorganization.

I. **Acquisitions and Reorganizations**—Mergers, stock acquisitions, and asset acquisitions can all qualify for reorganization status if the shareholders of the acquired corporation receive sufficient equity from the acquiring corporations.

    A. **Type A Reorganization**

Definition

Type A Reorganization: A merger or consolidation under state law (called a statutory merger). Note that Target is exchanging its assets for Acquiring's stock. Once Target dissolves, the shareholders of Target own Acquiring stock.

1. In a merger, the acquired corporation (target) dissolves into another corporation (the acquiring corporation).

2. In a consolidation, both the acquired and the acquiring corporations dissolve into a new (surviving) corporation.

3. At least 50% of the consideration provided to Target by Acquiring must be stock in Acquiring.

4. The shareholders of the acquired firm can only defer gains and losses to the extent they receive equity of the acquiring corporation. Note, that both voting and/or nonvoting stock can be used in Type A reorganization.

5. Forms of payment that do not qualify as equity, are considered boot.

6. Acquiring must assume all of the liabilities of Target.

Definition

Boot: Property that does not qualify for nonrecognition. Boot triggers the recognition of gain, but not the recognition of losses.

Example

T corporation merges into B corporation. All T shareholders receive B stock in exchange for their T shares. T shareholders will defer gains and losses on the disposition of their T shares because this transaction qualifies as a reorganization. If B corporation transferred consideration other than voting stock in the acquiring firm, these payments would be considered boot. These payments would not disqualify the merger unless more than 50% of the consideration received by a majority of T shareholders consisted of received boot instead of equity (violation of continuity of interest requirement).

B. Type B Reorganization

Definition

Type B Reorganization: An acquisition of the stock of the target solely in exchange for voting stock of the acquiring firm. Acquiring exchanges its own stock for stock in Target. Target remains in existence, but it is now owned at least 80% by Acquiring. The former Target shareholders now own stock in Acquiring.

1. The acquiring firm must exchange its own voting stock (or that of its parent company) for the stock of the target. Note that the use of nonvoting stock will disqualify the transaction from being a tax-free B reorganization.

2. The acquiring firm must own at least 80% of the stock of the target firm (voting and all other classes of stock) after the most recent acquisition of stock. Note that 80% does not need to be acquired during this acquisition; rather, total ownership must be 80% after the transaction.

3. Any consideration other than voting shares in the acquiring corporation, will violate the requirements of the reorganization.

Example
B corporation offers B stock to the shareholders of T corporation. If 90% of the T shareholders exchanged their T shares for B shares, then these shareholders would defer any gains or losses on the disposition of their T shares.

C. Type C Reorganization

Definition

Type C Reorganization: An acquisition of "substantially all" of the assets of the target solely in exchange for voting stock of the acquiring firm. Note, that Target is exchanging its assets for Acquiring's stock. The shareholders of Target own Acquiring stock after the reorganization.

1. The target firm then distributes the stock and other assets to its shareholders.

2. **Substantially all of the assets** is defined by the IRS as 90% of net asset value and 70% of gross asset value.

3. The stock that Acquiring transfers to Target can be only voting stock and must be at least 80% of the consideration provided. Other consideration provided (i.e., boot) cannot exceed 20% of the total consideration provided by Acquiring.

   a. If liabilities attached to Target's assets are assumed by Acquiring, this liability relief is not considered as boot (and therefore not subject to the 20% test) unless other boot is also given. If other boot is also given, then the total amount of boot and liability relief cannot exceed 20% of the consideration.

Example
B corporation transfers B common stock to T corporation in exchange for all of T's assets. T then distributes the B stock to its shareholders. The shareholders of T would defer gains and losses on the cancellation of their T shares. The shareholders would have an adjusted basis in the B shares equal to their adjusted basis in the old T shares.

D. Type D Reorganization

Definition

Type D Reorganization: A divisive reorganization (not acquisitive) in that a corporation (the parent) divides by transferring assets to a subsidiary in exchange for subsidiary shares.

1. The parent then distributes the subsidiary shares to its shareholders (spin-off) or redeems P stock with the S stock (split-off). Alternatively, the parent could be liquidated into two new corporations (a split-up).

2. In all events, the parent corporation must receive and distribute control of the subsidiary in the exchange (80% of the voting and other classes of stock).

Example

P corporation creates a subsidiary, S corporation, and contributes an office building to S in exchange for all of the S shares. If P then distributes the S shares to its shareholders, this transaction would qualify as a spin-off. The shareholders of P would defer any gains and losses on the distribution and would allocate the adjusted basis of their P stock between their P shares and the S shares.

E. **Other Reorganizations**—Exist to defer gains and losses on specialized transactions.

1. E and F reorganizations are recapitalizations and nominal changes (such as changes in the name of the corporation or the state of incorporation).

2. G reorganizations are related to bankruptcy recapitalizations.

F. In addition to meeting the specific reorganization rules described above, tax-free reorganizations must meet the following judicial principles:

1. The transaction must be motivated by a valid **business purpose**.

2. The **continuity the of business enterprise test** requires that the acquiring corporation must (1) continue the historic business of the target corporation, or (2) use a significant portion of target's assets in the continuing business of acquiring corporation.

3. A merger only qualifies as a reorganization if the **continuity of interest requirement** is met. This test requires that a substantial amount of the consideration that Acquiring gives to Target must be stock in Acquiring. If at least 50% of the consideration is Acquiring stock then this test is definitely met, but the IRS has ruled that 40% can be sufficient also.

4. The **step transaction doctrine** permits multiple steps to be collapsed into a single step when the steps are so interdependent on one another that one would not have occurred without the other(s). Collapsing these steps may lead to a tax result other than that desired by the taxpayer.

II. **Deferral of Gains/Losses and Basis Issues**—Generally, a reorganization does not require income recognition at the **corporate level** (by either the target or the acquiring corporation).

A. **Acquiring Corporation**—In a reorganization, the acquiring corporation does not recognize gain or loss on the transfer of its stock for the acquired corporation.

1. An exception to this rule occurs if the acquiring corporation distributes appreciated property (in addition to stock). The appreciated property will trigger gain recognition to the acquiring corporation just as if the acquiring firm sold the assets.

2. The basis that the acquiring corporation takes in the assets received is:

Basis in property to Target + Gain recognized by Target

B. **Acquired Corporation**—In a reorganization, the acquired corporation does not generally recognize gain or loss.

1. A distribution of appreciated property to shareholders in connection with the acquisition will trigger gain recognition by the acquired corporation.

2. **Shortcut**—Whenever a corporation distributes appreciated property (property with a value in excess of adjusted basis), the corporation will recognize the gain. This applies regardless of whether the distribution is related to a reorganization, a redemption, or a liquidation.

C. **Shareholders**—No gain or loss is recognized to the shareholders of the corporations involved in a tax-free reorganization if they receive only stock in exchange for property of the acquiring organization.

   1. If shareholders receive other property in addition to stock, it is treated as ***boot*** and **gain is recognized equal to the lower of:**

      a. Boot received *or*

      b. Realized gain.

         i. Any gain recognized will be dividend income to the extent of the shareholder's proportionate share of Target's E&P. Any remaining gain is capital gain.

   2. The basis to the shareholder in the **stock received** is:

Basis in stock surrendered

\+ Gain recognized

− Boot received

Example
Pursuant to a merger of Corporation T into Corporation P, Smith exchanged 100 shares of T that he had purchased for $1,000 for 80 shares of P having an FMV of $1,500 and also received $200 cash. Smith's realized gain of $700 is recognized to the extent of the cash received of $200 and is treated as a capital gain. Smith's basis for his P stock is $1,000 ($1,000 + $200 recognized gain − $200 cash received).

III. **Tax Attributes**—The tax attributes of the target firm (such as net operating loss carryovers) survive in reorganizations.

Definition
Tax Attributes: The tax characteristics of the firm. The most common attributes are the adjusted basis of assets, the earnings and profits of the corporation, carryovers (including net operating loss, capital loss, and excess charitable contributions), accounting methods (including depreciation methods), and tax credit carryovers.

A. If the target firm disappears (in a merger or asset acquisition), then the acquiring corporation is entitled to the target's tax attributes.

Example
B acquires the assets of T in a merger, which qualifies as a reorganization. The adjusted basis of T's assets does not change even though the assets are now owned by B. In addition, the depreciation methods used on the T assets will continue to be used by B.

B. If the target survives as a subsidiary (e.g., after a stock acquisition), then the tax attributes stay with the target corporation. The acquiring firm can avail itself of a limited amount of the target's attributes through a consolidation with the target. The use of tax attributes by a surviving corporation or a parent is strictly limited through the application of complex provisions designed to limit tax incentives for corporate acquisitions.

C. Specific Limitations

1. Earnings and profit of the target firm carries over to Acquiring. However, if Target has a deficit in E&P, that deficit can be used to offset only future earnings of the combined companies (not past E&P of Acquiring).

2. An NOL of Target is limited as follows for Acquiring's first tax return after the reorganization:

(Income of Acquiring × # of days in year after transfer) / 365 days

Example

Corporation P (on a calendar year) acquired Corporation T in a statutory merger on October, 19, 2017, with the former T shareholders receiving 60% of P's stock. If T had an NOL carryover of $70,000 and P has taxable income (before an NOL deduction) of $91,500, the amount of T's $70,000 NOL carryover that can be deducted by P for 2017 would be limited to $91,500 × 73/365 = $18,300.

3. Additionally, if there is a significant change in the ownership of Target (generally > 50% over a three-year period) the amount of Target's NOL that can be used annually in all future years is strictly limited (Section 382 limitation) to:

FMV of Target's stock before the change × Long-term tax-exempt rate

Example

If T's former shareholders received only 30% of P's stock in the preceding example, there would be a more than 50 percentage point change in ownership of T Corporation, and T's NOL carryover would be subject to a Section 382 limitation. If the FMV of T's stock on October 19, 2017, was $500,000 and the long-term tax-exempt rate were 3%, the Section 382 limitation for 2016 would be ($500,000 × 3%) × (73/365 days) = $3,000.

Thus, only $3,000 of T's NOL carryover could be deducted by P for 2016. The remaining $70,000 – $3,000 = $67,000 of T's NOL would be carried forward by P and can be used to offset P's taxable income for 2017 to the extent of the Section 382 annual limitation (i.e., $500,000 × 3% = $15,000).

IV. Other Types of Acquisitions—The corporate tax consequences of a taxable acquisition (not a reorganization) depend upon the form of the acquisition.

A. **Subsidiaries**—If the acquiring firm purchases the stock of the target and operates the target as a **subsidiary**, then neither firm recognizes any gain or loss.

1. The tax attributes of the target survive, albeit trapped in the target firm.

2. The acquiring firm uses the purchase price of the target's shares as the adjusted basis of the subsidiary.

3. The adjusted basis of the target's assets does not change.

B. **Section 338 Elections**—Under certain conditions in a taxable stock purchase, the acquiring firm can elect to step up the basis of the target's asset to FMV.

1. This election, referred to as a 338 election, requires the recognition of any gain generated by the difference between the adjusted basis of the target's assets and the fair market value of the stock.

2. The benefit of the election (step up in the basis of the acquired assets) is generally less than the tax cost triggered by gain recognition. Hence, the election is rarely invoked.

C. **Taxable Mergers**—If the acquiring firm merges the target or acquires the assets of the target, then the target corporation recognizes gains and losses on the transfer of its assets.

1. The adjusted basis of the target's assets is their fair market value. Any excess purchase price is allocated to goodwill and amortized over 15 years.

Multijurisdictional Tax Issues

State and Local Taxation

After studying this lesson, you should be able to:

1. List most common taxes levied by state and local governments.

2. Define nexus and describe the process used to determine which states have jurisdiction to tax income.

3. Differentiate between business and nonbusiness income.

4. Describe the apportionment process for computing state income taxes.

I. **Types of State and Local Taxes**—State and local governments levy many different types of taxes. The most common are as follows:

   A. **Sales Taxes**

      1. Levied on tangible personal property and some services.

      2. Exemptions vary by state but usually include items bought for resale and that are used in manufacturing.

   B. **Use Taxes**—Levied on the use of tangible personal property that was not purchased in the state.

   C. **Property Taxes**

      1. *Ad valorem* taxes based on the value of real property (realty taxes) and personal property (personalty taxes).

      2. There are usually exemptions for certain types of property, including those for inventory.

      3. A few states also tax intangible property.

      4. Usually levied for property owned at a specific date.

   D. **Franchise Tax**

      1. Levied on the privilege of doing business in a state.

      2. Based on the value of the capital used in the jurisdiction (common stock, paid-in capital, and retained earnings).

   E. **Excise Tax**

      1. Levied on the quantity of an item or sales price.

         a. Examples include tax on gasoline, cigarettes, and alcohol.

      2. Can be charged to a manufacturer or consumer.

   F. **Unemployment Tax**

      1. Levied on taxable wages with a limit per employee (usually $7,000).

      2. Rate varies based on experience of employer.

   G. Incorporation fees are charged for incorporating in a state or registering to do business in a state.

II. **Jurisdiction to Tax**—Because many businesses conduct operations in more than one state, a significant issue is determining which states have the authority to levy a tax on a particular business.

Definitions

Domestic Corporations: Entities incorporated under the laws of a particular state.

Foreign Corporations: Corporations incorporated in another state.

A. Difficult to determine the degree of power to tax foreign corporations.

B. Supreme Court developed four tests to determine jurisdiction to tax (Complete *Auto Transit v. Brady*):

   1. Business activity must have substantial nexus with state.

   2. The tax must be fairly apportioned.

   3. The tax cannot discriminate against interstate commerce.

   4. The tax must be fairly related to services that the state provides.

C. Nexus for taxing a corporation's income does not exist if activity in the state is limited to:

   1. Soliciting sales of tangible personal property that are approved and shipped outside the state

   2. Advertising

   3. Determining reorder needs of customers

   4. Furnishing autos to sales staff

Definition

Nexus: The degree of the relationship that must exist between a state and a foreign corporation for the state to have the right to impose a tax. The application of nexus to state taxation is governed by Public Law 86-272. This law applies to sales of tangible personal property and does not apply to the sale of services or to the leasing or renting of property. Nexus is determined on a year by year basis.

Example

Corporation FLY's business domicile is in Texas and it sells widgets to wholesalers in Colorado. The orders are solicited, approved, and shipped from Texas. FLY does not have nexus with Colorado so the sales to Colorado wholesalers are not subject to taxation by Colorado.

D. The following types of activities are usually sufficient to establish nexus with a state (if these activities occur in the state):

   1. Approving/accepting orders

   2. Hiring/supervising employees other than sales staff

   3. Installation

   4. Maintaining an office or warehouse (an office maintained by an independent contractor does not establish nexus)

   5. Providing maintenance or engineering services

   6. Making repairs

   7. Investigating creditworthiness or collecting delinquent accounts

   8. Providing training for employees other than sales staff

III. State Income Tax Computation—A model law known as the Uniform Division of Income for Tax Purposes Act (UDIPTA) helps to minimize differences among state tax laws.

A. The starting point for computing state income taxes is federal taxable income, increased by adjustments such as (specific rules depend on state):

   1. Dividends received deduction

   2. Expenses related to interest earned on U.S. bonds

   3. State income taxes

    4. Depreciation in excess of that allowed for state

    5. Municipal interest taxed for state purposes

B. Decreased by:

    1. Federal income taxes paid

    2. Expenses related to municipal interest income

    3. Interest on U.S. bonds

    4. Depreciation in addition to that allowed for federal purposes

C. **Business versus Nonbusiness Income**—If more than one state has nexus to tax the income of a business entity then the income must be apportioned among the states. Designating income as business or nonbusiness is very required for this computation.

    1. Business income is apportioned among all the states in which the corporation does business.

    2. **Business income**—Is generally:

        a. Generated from business's regular operations (**transactional test**), *or*

        b. From the sale of property that is an integral part of the business (**functional test**).

    3. **Nonbusiness income**—Generally includes investment income and income from transactions not part of regular operations. Nonbusiness income is generally allocated to the state of incorporation.

    4. If investment income is generated by regular business operations it is business income.

Example
SMALL Company is domiciled in Oregon. SMALL has invested some of its excess cash reserves with a financial firm in North Carolina. The investment income earned from these investments is taxed in Oregon. Note that if the investment was part of SMALL's regular business operations then the income would be allocated to North Carolina.

D. Apportionment

    1. Business income is apportioned among the states in which it is earned based on apportionment factors such as sales, property, and payroll.

    2. In general, states have discretion to apply different tax rules to different types of income. The U.S. Supreme Court has allowed states great flexibility to choose an apportioning formula and to tax income of an interstate business.

    3. Some states use only one apportionment factor. Others vary in how they weight the factors.

    4. Different types of factors are used for financial institutions and service businesses.

    5. **Sales factor** is computed as:

Total sales in state / Total sales

        a. The state of sale is determined based on the point of delivery.

        b. If the business does not have nexus in the state of delivery then the sale is apportioned to the state where the sale originated.

    6. **Property factor** is computed as:

Average value of property in state / Value of all property

a. Property is limited to real property and tangible personal property, but does not include cash. It is valued at cost or book value depending on the state.

b. Property also includes leased property (usually valued at the annual lease times eight).

c. Property is included only if used in the production of business income.

7. **Payroll factor** is computed as:

> Compensation paid or accrued in state / Total compensation paid or accrued

a. Compensation includes fringe benefits if taxable under federal law.

b. Payments to independent contractors and paid into Section 401(k) plans are usually not included.

c. Compensation is included only if related to the production of business income.

Examples

1. Assume Multistate Corp. conducts business in several states and provided relevant information as follows:

Total	Total	State A
Sales	$4,000,000	$1,000,000
Average property	5,000,000	2,000,000
Compensation	1,000,000	200,000
Business taxable income before apportionment	500,000	

State A uses the UDITPA apportionment formula to compute state taxable income for Multistate Corp.'s business income. The sales factor for State A would be $1,000,000 / $4,000,000 = 25%. The property factor would be $2,000,000 / $5,000,000 = 40%. The compensation factor would be $200,000 / $1,000,000 = 20%. The apportionment factor would be (25% + 40% + 20%) / 3 = 28.33%. As a result, $500,000 × 28.33% = $141,667 of Multistate Corp.'s business income would be taxed by State A.

2. Assume State A in Example #1 gives double weight to the sales factor. The apportionment factor would be (25% + 25% + 40% + 20%) / 4 = 27.5%.

---

8. **The Uniform Division of Income for Tax Purposes Act (UDITPA)** is a model act adopted by the National Conference of Commissioners on Uniform State Laws (NCCUSL) and the American Bar Association to promote uniformity in state allocation and apportionment rules. Not all states have adopted this Act.

a. The Act provides that if income-producing activity occurs in more than one state, the receipts are assigned to the state where the greatest cost of performance was incurred.

b. Intangible assets are excluded from the property factor under the standard formula.

c. To promote fairness across states the Act provides the following:

> If the allocation and apportionment provisions of UDITPA do not fairly represent the extent of the taxpayer's business activity in the state, the taxpayer may petition for, or the tax administrator may require, with respect to all or any part of the taxpayer's activity, if reasonable:
>
> a. Separate accounting
>
> b. The exclusion of any one or more of the factors
>
> c. The inclusion of one or more additional factors that will fairly represent the taxpayer's business activity in this state
>
> d. The employment of any other method to effectuate an equitable allocation and apportionment of the taxpayer's income

IV. Filing Requirements for State Income Taxes

A. Filing approaches vary across states, including:

1. Each entity reports separately.

2. Affiliated corporations file a consolidated return.

3. Members of a unitary group combine their transactions on one return.

Example
LBJ Corporation owns 100% of LB and BJ Corporations. LBJ has business operations in TN and GA. LB has operations only in TN and BJ only in GA. Under separate entity reporting, LBJ and LB would file separate returns in TN, and LBJ and BJ would file separate returns in GA. If TN required the filing of consolidated returns then LBJ and LB would file a consolidated return in TN.

B. Unitary groups meet the definitional requirements of a specific state. Generally three requirement are evaluated to determine if entities should be combined, including unity of:

1. Ownership—more than 50%

2. Operations

3. Use—centralized management

C. Partnerships may be included in a unitary group.

D. Businesses may be included in a unitary group even if there is not nexus with a state.

E. Note that some states do not recognize the federal S Corporation election.

F. Some states also tax partnerships at the entity level.

Taxation of Foreign Income

I. General Rules

A. Treaties between the United States and other countries generally override the tax provisions in the U.S. tax law or foreign tax law.

B. Foreign taxpayers are usually taxed only on U.S. source income.

C. U.S. persons are taxed on all income earned anywhere in the world.

   1. A U.S. person includes a citizen or resident of the U.S., a domestic partnership or corporation, and any estate or trust other than a foreign estate or trust

   2. A U.S. corporation is subject to tax on its worldwide income, including the income of a *foreign branch*. In contrast, a U.S. corporation is generally not taxed on the net income of a *foreign subsidiary* corporation until the income is repatriated in the form of dividends to the parent corporation.

Example
A U.S. corporation's foreign subsidiary has $1,000 of earnings but makes no distributions to its U.S. parent during the year. The U.S. corporation is not taxed on the $1,000 of earnings of its foreign subsidiary.

II. Sourcing of Income and Deductions—Determining whether income is U.S. source or foreign source is critical for computing the federal income tax.

A. Earned income is foreign source if earned in a foreign country and U.S. source if earned domestically. This also includes employee benefits.

B. Unearned income is foreign source if received from a foreign resident or for property that is used in a foreign country.

C. Income from the sale of personalty is determined based on the residence of the seller, except:

   1. Inventory is sourced where title transfers.

   2. In the case of depreciable property, recapture is sourced where depreciation was claimed. Remaining gain is sourced where title transfers.

D. Income from the sale of intangibles is sourced where the amortization was claimed. Source of income from the use of intangible property is determined by the country in which the property is used.

E. Income from the sale or exchange of real property is sourced based on the location of the property. Source of income from the use of tangible real property is determined by the country in which the property is located.

F. Interest income is U.S. source if received from:

   1. U.S. government

2. Noncorporate U.S. residents

3. Domestic corporations

G. If a U.S. corporation receives 80% or more of its active business income from foreign sources over the previous three years then interest received from that corporation is foreign source.

H. Dividends from U.S. corporations are U.S. source and from foreign corporations are foreign source.

I. If a foreign corporation receives 25% or more of gross income from income connected with a U.S. business for the three previous tax years then dividends from that foreign corporation are U.S. source.

J. Deductions must also be allocated or apportioned as U.S. source or foreign source.

K. The IRS has the authority to change the allocation of income and deductions if it determines that the taxpayer's methods do not clearly reflect income.

III. Outbound Transactions

A. The transfer of assets from the United States to a foreign country may trigger income (depreciation recapture applies).

B. If assets are used in a trade or business outside the United States, gain is deferred unless the property is:

1. Inventory or unrealized receivables

2. Installments obligations

3. Foreign currency

IV. Controlled Foreign Corporations (CFC)

A. A CFC is a foreign corporation for which more than 50% of the voting power or value of stock is owned by U.S. shareholders (limited to those who own, directly and indirectly, 10% or more of the foreign corporation) on any day of the tax year of the foreign corporation.

Example
Bottom, Inc., a foreign corporation, is owned by eight U.S. shareholders. One shareholder owns 37% and the other seven shareholders own 9% each. Bottom is not a CFC because only one shareholder owns 10% or more and this shareholder does not own more than 50%.

If one of the smaller shareholders increases its ownership interest to 14%, then Bottom would be a CFC since the two shareholders owning 10% or more would own 51% of Bottom.

B. Certain types of income from a CFC are taxed to a U.S. shareholder as a constructive dividend, even if no actual distribution has occurred. This income is referred to as Subpart F income. The main types of income subject to this rule include:

1. Income that is not connected economically to the country in which the corporation is organized

2. Income from insuring the risk of loss from outside the county in which the corporation is organized

Example
Bottom, Inc. is a CFC for the entire tax year. Top, Inc., a U.S. based corporation, owns 75% of Bottom for the entire year. Both are calendar year corporations. Subpart F income is $50,000 and no distributions have been made. What is Top's constructive dividend for the tax year? $50,000 \times 75\% = \$37,500$.

V. Worldwide Income—Potential Double Taxation

A. U.S. taxpayers are taxed on all income earned anywhere in the world.

B. Three provisions mitigate the potential double taxation of this income:

   1. Foreign income taxes paid are an itemized deduction for individuals.

   2. Alternatively, a credit may be claimed for foreign taxes paid.

   3. Certain individuals can elect to exclude foreign-earned income.

C. The credit for foreign taxes paid is limited if the U.S. effective tax rate exceeds the foreign effective rate.

> Limit = U.S. tax on worldwide income × Foreign source taxable income / Worldwide taxable income

   1. Individuals must add personal exemptions to worldwide income.

   2. Excess foreign tax credits can be carried back one year and carried forward 10 years.

   3. Individuals who have only passive foreign income that does not exceed $300 ($600 for joint returns) can elect to be exempt from the foreign tax credit limitation.

   4. A foreign tax credit usually provides a greater benefit than a deduction. The deduction may be preferable when the foreign effective tax rate is high and foreign income, as compared to worldwide income, is small.

   5. In addition to the foreign taxes actually paid, a U.S. corporation that receives dividends from a *10% or more owned foreign corporation* (based on voting stock) is entitled to a deemed paid foreign tax credit for the foreign income taxes paid by that foreign corporation with respect to such dividends. A corporation taking the **deemed paid credit** must *gross-up* (increase) the amount of dividend income that it received by the foreign income tax paid on those dividends. The deemed paid credit is subject to the FTC limitation.

Example
A U.S. corporation receives a dividend of $75 from a wholly owned foreign subsidiary that has paid $25 of foreign income taxes on the earnings to which the dividend relates. The U.S. corporation's dividend income of $75 is grossed up by the $25 of foreign income taxes paid by its subsidiary, to $100. The U.S. corporation is then eligible for a foreign tax credit for the $25 of foreign income taxes that it is deemed to have paid.

D. Qualifying individuals must meet one of two tests to benefit from the foreign-earned income exclusion:

   1. During a continuous period that includes an entire tax year, the individual must be a bona fide resident of at least one foreign country.

   2. The individual must have a tax home in a foreign country and must have been present in one or more foreign countries for at least 330 days during any 12 consecutive months.

   3. Qualifying individuals can exclude:

     a. Foreign-earned income from personal services, limited to $102,100 in 2017.

     b. Employer-provided foreign housing income, limited to $14,294 (14% of the $102,100) for 2017. This exclusion is allowed only to the extent it exceeds 16% × $102,100, or $16,336.

     c. Taxpayers must file an election to take the exclusion, which is binding for future years until revoked.

     d. If a taxpayer was present in a foreign country for at least 330 days but less than the entire year, the exclusion is prorated on a daily basis (365-day year).

Example

J is a bona fide resident of a foreign country and is a U.S. citizen. For 2017, she receives a salary of $110,000 and interest income of $2,500. Of the earned income of $110,000, $102,100 may be excluded and the remaining $7,900 is taxed. The unearned income of $2,500 is not eligible for the exclusion and is taxable.

If J also receives employer-provided housing assistance of $20,000, this may be excluded to the extent it exceeds 16% of $102,100. The excess for J is $3,664 ($20,000 − $16,336). Note that the housing exclusion can never exceed $14,294 in 2017.

VI. Foreign Currency Gains and Losses

A. Foreign currency exchange gains and losses resulting from the normal course of business operations are ordinary.

B. Foreign currency exchange gains and losses resulting from investment or personal transactions are capital.

VII. Transfer Taxes

A. Taxpayers may use transfer pricing to manipulate the amount of income earned in the United States. Assume that BIG Corporation has manufacturing operations in the United States and in a foreign country, and that the U.S. entity sells its product to the foreign entity for the foreign entity to then use in its operations. Clearly, the sales price that BIG sets for the product will determine the amount of gain generated in the United States.

B. If the IRS determines that the price set by BIG does not clearly reflect income, the IRS has broad powers under Section 482 to reallocate income to insure that income is clearly stated.

Example

A U.S. Corporation sells its product to an independent third party as well as to its foreign subsidiary, each of whom operate as distributors of its product in a foreign market. The unit price charged the independent distributor is $200, while the unit price charged its foreign subsidiary is $125. If the U.S. corporation dealt with its subsidiary at "arm's length," then the unit price charged the foreign subsidiary would have been $200. The IRS may utilize Sec. 482 to allocate $75 of profit from the subsidiary to the U.S. corporation.

C. Because it may be difficult for a taxpayer to determine what price might be used by unrelated taxpayers dealing at arm's length, the IRS permits taxpayers to enter into an Advance Pricing Agreement (APA) with the IRS on the best method for determining arm's length prices for transfers between taxpayers owned or controlled by the same interests. Pursuant to an APA, a taxpayer and the IRS agree as to the transfer pricing method to be used to determine the transfer prices for specified transactions.

VIII. U.S. Taxation of Foreign Persons

A. Nonresident foreign persons generally are subject to U.S. tax on two categories of income: (1) *income that is effectively connected with a U.S. trade or business (ECI)*, and (2) certain passive types of U.S. source income commonly referred to as *fixed and determinable annual or periodical income (FDAP)*.

1. A foreign person's **income that is effectively connected with a U.S. trade or business (ECI)** is subject to tax at regular graduated income tax rates and deductions are allowed in computing the amount subject to tax. A trade or business generally is defined by case law as profit-oriented activities that are regular, substantial, and continuous. Effectively connected with a U.S. trade or business means that (1) the income is derived from assets held for use in the conduct of a U.S. business, and (2) the activity of the U.S. business was a material factor in the realization of the income. Under an income tax treaty, the U.S. may

instead agree to tax business profits of a treaty resident only if the profits are attributable to a permanent establishment (PE) in the U.S. A PE is a fixed place of business through which business is wholly or partially carried on. Simply maintaining storage facilities within the U.S. generally does not by itself amount to a PE.

2. Generally, a nonresident alien who performs personal services within the U.S. is considered to be engaged in a U.S. trade or business. However, the performance of personal services will not constitute a U.S. trade or business if (1) the nonresident alien is present in the U.S. for 90 days or less during the tax year, (2) the amount of compensation received for U.S. services is $3,000 or less, and (3) the nonresident alien works for either a foreign person who is not engaged in a U.S. trade or business, or the foreign office of a U.S. person.

3. **Fixed and determinable annual or periodical income (FDAP)** is generally subject to a 30% withholding tax that is applied to the gross amount of income with no deductions allowed. Withholding of tax occurs at the source of payment (i.e., the person paying the income is required to withhold the tax and remit it to the IRS). FDAP primarily is from passive, nonbusiness activities *including* such items as interest, dividends, rents, royalties, and annuities. FDAP generally *excludes* gain from the sale or exchange of real or personal property, and income that is excluded from gross income by U.S. persons. The 30% withholding tax rate may be reduced or even eliminated by an applicable income tax treaty.

IX. Transfers of Property to Foreign Corporations

A. Gain (but not loss) is generally recognized on the transfer of property by a U.S. person to a foreign corporation notwithstanding the deferral provision of Subchapter C that otherwise would apply. This prevents gains from escaping U.S. taxation and is accomplished by providing that a "foreign corporation" shall not be considered a corporation for purposes of the Subchapter C provisions (e.g., Sec. 351 transfer to a controlled corporation, Sec. 332 liquidation of a subsidiary, Sec. 361 transfer of property pursuant to a corporate reorganization).

Example
U.S. Corporation P owns property with a value of $1 million that has a zero tax basis. Corporation P transfers title to the property to its foreign subsidiary, Corporation S, in exchange for all of the stock of Corporation S. If Sec. 351(a) applied, no gain would be recognized on the transfer of the appreciated property to S. Thereafter, S could sell the property and recognize the gain. Assuming that S does not distribute its earnings to P and that Subpart F does not apply, the gain would escape U.S. taxation. However, since foreign Corporation S is not considered a corporation for purposes of applying Sec. 351, P's realized gain of $1 million on the transfer of property to S is recognized and subject to U.S. taxation.

B. The above recognition rule does *not* apply to any property transferred to a foreign corporation for use by such foreign corporation in the active conduct of a trade or business outside of the U.S. Exceptions requiring gain recognition apply to transfers of certain types of property that are likely to be promptly resold or are highly fungible such as receivables, copyrights, inventory, installment obligations, foreign currency or foreign-currency-denominated investments, and interests in leased property.

Tax-Exempt Entities

Tax-Exempt Organizations

After studying this lesson, you should be able to:

1. Summarize filing requirements for tax-exempt organizations.

2. Describe allowable activities for tax-exempt organizations.

3. Define unrelated business income and identify examples.

Tax Form for This Lesson: Form 990 (available for download and printing from the lesson overview of your software).

I. **Tax-Exempt Organizations**—Tax-exempt organizations include **charities, labor organizations, social clubs, pension and profit-sharing trusts, and private foundations**.

   A. **Exemption**

      1. An exempt organization (EO) may be in the form of a corporation or trust, and it must apply for and receive an exemption from taxation (Form 1023 or Form 1024).

      2. Most organizations must apply for exemption using Form 1023, Application for Recognition of Exemption Under Section 501(c)(3) of the IRC. However, a shorter application Form 1023-EZ, Streamlined Application for Recognition of Exemption Under Section 501(c)(3) of the IRC, can be used by organizations with assets of $250,000 or less and annual gross receipts of $50,000 or less. An organization utilizing Form 1023-EZ must submit the form and applicable user fee online. Form 1023-EZ cannot be used by foreign organizations, churches, schools, hospitals, and private foundations.

   B. **Filing Requirements**

      1. EO must file an information return (Form 990) if gross receipts exceed $50,000.

         a. This form reports income, expenses, and substantial contributors. It also must include total lobbying and political expenditures.

         b. Churches do not have to file Form 990.

         c. Form 990 must be filed on or before the 15th day of the fifth month after the close of the tax year. For tax years beginning after 2015, an automatic six-month extension is available.

         d. Form 990-EZ can be used unless gross receipts exceed $200,000 (or if total assets exceed $500,000).

      2. Most EOs that are not required to file an information return must file an annual electronic notice with the IRS (**Form 990-N**).

         a. This notice includes demographic information and justifies the continuing basis for tax-exempt status. The EO must also confirm that annual gross receipts are usually $50,000 or less.

         b. The groups that are exempt from the electronic notice requirement include churches, state institutions, and governmental units.

      3. EOs that do not meet these filing requirements for three consecutive years will lose their tax-exempt status.

      4. Most EOs must make their last three years' tax returns and their tax-exempt application available to interested parties.

C. Private Foundations

Definition
Private Foundations: Tax-exempt organizations that receive less than one-third of their annual support from their members and the general public.

1. Private foundations file Form 990-PF.

2. **Private foundations** are Sec. 501(c)(3) organizations other than churches, educational organizations, hospitals or medical research organizations operated in conjunction with hospitals, endowment funds operated for the benefit of certain state and municipal colleges and universities, governmental units, and publicly supported organizations.

    a. An organization is **publicly supported** if it normally receives at least one-third of its total support from governmental units and the general public (e.g., support received in the form of gifts, grants, contributions, membership fees, gross receipts from admissions, sales of merchandise, etc.)

    b. Private foundations may be subject to taxes based on investment income, self-dealing, failure to distribute income, excess business holdings, investments that jeopardize charitable purposes, and taxable expenditures. The initial taxes (with the exception of the tax on investment income) are imposed because the organization engages in prohibited transactions. Additional taxes are imposed if the prohibited transactions are not corrected with a specified period.

II. **Qualification**—To qualify as an EO the organization must operate exclusively for a tax-exempt purpose.

A. Many EOs are organized for religious, charitable, scientific, literary, or educational purposes; prevention of cruelty to children or animals; or promoting amateur sports activities.

B. Influencing legislation or political parties is not an acceptable purpose.

1. An excise tax of 5% is imposed on the lobbying expenditures of charitable organizations, and a 5% tax may also be imposed on organization managers who agreed to the expenditures.

2. However, Section 501(c)(3) organizations (e.g., charitable organizations) can participate in lobbying efforts if an election is made and lobbying expenditures do not exceed certain ceilings. This exception does not apply to churches and private foundations.

3. The **lobbying expenditures** cannot exceed the lower of:

    a. $1,000,000 *or*

    b. (20% × first $500,000 paid for exempt purposes) + (15% of the second $500,000) + (10% of the third $500,000) + (5% of any additional expenditures). "Paid" refers to the expenditures incurred in pursuing the tax-exempt activities.

4. The amount spent on grass-roots lobbying to **influence legislation** cannot exceed 25% of the amount determined by this formula.

5. If these limits are exceeded, a 25% excise tax is imposed on the excess expenditures. At certain excess levels a charity can lose its tax exemption.

Example
An organization's exempt purpose expenditures for the year are $3 million. If the organization makes the election, it may spend $300,000 ($100,000 (20% of $500,000) + $75,000 (15% of $500,000) + $50,000 (10% of $500,000) + $75,000 (5% of the remaining $1,500,000)) on lobbying for the year, and $75,000 (25% of $300,000) of that amount may be spent on grassroots lobbying.

C. A tax is imposed on non-permitted political expenditures equal to:

    1. 10% of the expenditure, charged to the organization, *and*

    2. 2.5% of the expenditure, charged to a manager who agreed to the expenditure (maximum of $5,000 per expenditure).

D. A tax-exempt organization can participate in a joint venture with a for-profit organization if the venture furthers a charitable purpose.

III. Unrelated Business Income—An EO is taxed on its unrelated business income (UBI).

  A. To be UBI, income must:

    1. Be from a business regularly carried on, *and*

    2. Be unrelated to the EO exempt purposes.

  B. A business is substantially related only if the activity contributes importantly to the accomplishment of the exempt purposes of the organization.

  C. Related income (meaning that the income is not subject to tax) includes:

    1. An activity where substantially all work is performed for no compensation

    2. A business carried on for the convenience of students or members of a charitable, religious, or scientific organization

    3. Sale of merchandise/stock received as contributions

    4. In general, investment income

    5. Rents received from real property

  D. Income from debt-financed property unrelated to the exempt function of the EO is UBI.

  E. Income from advertising in journals of the EO is UBI.

  F. UBI is taxed (only if it exceeds $1,000) at regular corporate rates if the organization is a corporation; at trust rates if it is a trust.

  G. Exempt organizations with **unrelated business income** must file Form 990-T, *Exempt Organization Business Income Tax Return*, if the organization has gross income of at least $1,000 from an unrelated trade or business. The obligation to file Form 990-T is in addition to the obligation to file Form 990. Additionally, Form 990-T may be required even though Form 990 is not required to be filed.

  H. An organization must make estimated tax payments if it expects its tax for the year to be more than $500.

IV. Disclosure Rules for Deductibility

  A. Not all tax-exempt entities qualify for deductibility of contributions. Those that do not qualify must disclose such in a conspicuous format in all fundraising solicitations.

  B. Charities eligible to receive tax-deductible contributions that receive contributions greater than $75 must inform the donor that her deduction is limited to the excess of the contribution over the value of the goods or services received from the charity.

Partnership Taxation

Formation and Basis

After studying this lesson, you should be able to:

1. Define partnerships for tax purposes and list the entities taxed as partnerships.

2. Differentiate the characteristics of general and limited partners.

3. Evaluate whether a partnership formation is eligible for deferral of gain/loss.

4. Compute the basis of interest held by partners and assets by partnership after formation.

5. Determine the holding period for partnership interest and assets after the formation.

6. Calculate the effect of liability assumptions by the partnership on gain and basis.

7. Determine the required year-end for partnerships.

I. **Introduction**—A business operated as a partnership is not recognized as a taxable entity under the income tax laws. Instead, the partners divide the income and expenses of the business and report their share on individual returns. The income is taxed to the owners regardless of distributions. Distributions are, in turn, treated as a return of capital. The distinction between partnerships and corporations is important because no tax is imposed on partnerships.

II. **Partnership Definition**

> **Definition**
> *Partnership*: An association of two or more taxpayers to operate a business that is not taxed as a corporation.

   A. An entity may be exempt from partnership rules if organized for investment purposes.

   B. A partnership must be an **association** of two or more taxpayers with the objective of making a profit. The existence of a partnership is a question of fact, but co-ownership and/or joint use of property does not necessarily constitute a partnership. There must be an active conduct of a business with the intent to share profits.

   C. Certain publicly traded partnerships (i.e., master limited partnerships) are taxed as corporations.

III. **Check-the-Box**—Under the "check-the-box" regulations, unincorporated entities may elect to be taxed as an association (corporation) or a partnership.

   A. Some associations are automatically taxed as corporations and are not eligible to make an election. These *per se* corporations include business entities formed under statutes that refer to the entities as incorporated.

   B. The default entity is a partnership when the business has more than two owners. This default rule typically applies to partnerships and limited liability companies. If an entity does not prefer the default rule, it can elect to be taxed as a corporation.

   C. If an entity has only one owner, then the default classification is that the entity is disregarded for federal income tax purposes. These entities can also elect to be taxed as a corporation.

   D. An election under the check-the-box regulations is effective if filed within the first 75 days of the tax year.

IV. General/Limited Partners

> **Definitions**
>
> *General partners:* Can participate in management and have joint and several liability for the partnership's debts. All partnerships must have at least one general partner.
>
> *Limited partners:* Are only liable up to their investment, but they cannot participate in management without losing their limited status.

A. A partnership loss will be a passive loss to a limited partner.

B. A partnership loss may be a passive loss to a general partner depending upon whether the partner meets the material participation test. See the "Limitations on Business Deductions" lesson for more detail.

C. Note that owners of limited liability companies are known as members and they also have limited liability.

D. Limited liability partnerships also usually filed as partnerships for federal tax purposes, unless the partners elect differently.

> **Note**
> *Without specific information (e.g., number of hours of activity for the partner), partnerships engaging in rental activities are most likely passive. See the "Limitations on Business Deductions" lesson for more detail.*

V. Partner Interests—Each partner owns a **capital interest and a profits** interest.

A. The capital-sharing ratio represents each partner's share of partnership capital.

B. Profit and loss (P&L) sharing ratios are each partner's share of profits and losses, respectively.

VI. Formations—The formation of a partnership does not trigger income, but requires that both the partners and the partnership calculate adjusted basis.

A. Contributions to a partnership are not taxable events, but require partners to calculate a substituted basis for their partnership interest.

B. **Deferred Gain or Loss**—Partners and partnerships recognize no gain or loss on contributions in exchange for a *partnership interest*.

   1. The control club used for corporate contributions is not relevant for partnerships since partnerships are taxed as conduits.

      a. Reminder—The **control club** is the 80% control requirement necessary to provide shareholders with deferral for contributions to a corporation.

   2. No distinction is made between an initial contribution and later additional contributions.

   3. No deferral is available for contributions to a partnership in exchange for property—deferral is only available for exchanges of property for a partnership interest.

C. **Exceptions Exist for Nonrecognition**

   1. Services contributed for a partnership interest create income in the amount of the value of the partnership interest (which also becomes the adjusted basis of the partnership interest).

> **Example**
> X received a 10% capital interest in the ABC Partnership in exchange for services rendered. On the date X was admitted to the partnership, ABC's net assets had a basis of $30,000 and a FMV of $50,000. X must recognize compensation income of $5,000, and would have a basis of $5,000 for the partnership interest.

   2. There is no deferral for contributions that are essentially disguised sales or attempts to diversify stock holdings.

Examples
1. There is no deferral of gain on appreciated stock contributed to an investment partnership.

2. TP contributes property ($100 FMV and basis of $20) to partnership PS in exchange for a 5% interest. Five days later, TP withdraws $100 cash. This is a disguised sale, and TP will recognize a gain of $80 on the "contribution" of the property.

VII. Basis Issues at Formation—Each partner calculates his or her personal adjusted basis (outside basis) in the partnership, and the partnership calculates the adjusted basis of the assets (inside basis) held by the partnership.

   A. Partnership—A partnership takes a carryover basis (the adjusted basis of the property in the hands of the partners) for contributed property.

> **Definition**
> *Inside Basis of Property:* The aggregate basis of assets in the hands of the partnership.

      1. Since the adjusted basis of contributed property carries over from the partners to the partnership, the holding periods and depreciation methods also continue unabated.

   B. Partner—Each partner takes a substituted basis in the partnership interest from the assets contributed to the partnership.

> **Definition**
> *Outside Basis of Property:* The adjusted basis of each partners' interest in the partnership.

VIII. Holding Period

   A. The holding period in the partnership interest includes the holding period of the contributed asset for contributions of capital assets and Section 1231 assets. For other assets, the holding period starts when the contribution is received by the partnership.

   B. The holding period that the partner has in the asset before contributed always transfers to the partnership, regardless of the type of asset contributed.

   C. The adjusted basis for contributions of services is the value included in the income of the partner.

   D. The adjusted basis for partnership interests purchased from existing partners or interests received as gifts or inheritances are determined like other assets (cost or carryover basis, respectively).

IX. Computation of Basis of Partnership Interest—Partners continually adjust their outside basis for partnership transactions, including the deduction of their share of partnership losses.

   A. Increases—*A partner's basis is increased by contributions of property, income, and increases in liabilities.*

      1. A partner's proportionate share of income includes gains and exempt income.

      2. A partner's proportionate share includes increases in liabilities (treated like a contribution).

   B. Decreases—*A partner's basis is decreased by distributions, expenses, and deemed distributions.*

      1. A partner's proportionate share of expenses, including deductions, losses, and nondeductible expenses (not capital expenditures)

      2. A partner's proportionate share of decreases in liabilities (deemed distributions)

Definition
Deemed Distribution: Occurs with any decrease in the partnership liabilities.

3. **Reminder**—A partner's basis in the partnership cannot be reduced below zero. If the net change in basis in the partnership interest due to debt being assumed by the partnership exceeds the total basis of the assets contributed, the partner must recognize gain equal to that excess to prevent negative basis from occurring.

Example
Partner R, a 25% partner, contributes property to the partnership with an adjusted basis of $20, FMV of $50, and a liability of $30 which the partnership assumes. R's basis is first increased by $20 for the basis of the property, then decreased by $30 for the debt assumption. However, since the partnership debt increased by $30, and R is responsible for 25% of the debt, or $7.50, his basis is increased by $7.50. The net effect on basis is a decrease of $2.50 (basis of $20 less $22.50 of debt shifted to other partners).

If R's basis before this contribution was $0, he would recognize $2.50 of gain to avoid negative basis. If R's basis before the contribution was $10, his ending basis would be $7.50 ($10 − $2.50).

C. **Debt Allocations—Changes in Liabilities Affect a Partner's Basis.**

1. An **increase** in the **partnership's liabilities** (e.g., loan from a bank, increase in accounts payable) increases each partner's basis in the partnership by each partner's share of the increase.

2. Any **decrease** in the **partnership's liabilities** is considered to be a distribution of money to each partner and reduces each partner's basis in the partnership by each partner's share of the decrease.

3. Any **decrease** in a partner's **individual liability** by reason of the assumption by the partnership of such individual liabilities is considered to be a distribution of money to the partner by the partnership (i.e., partner's basis is reduced).

4. Any **increase** in a partner's **individual liability** by reason of the assumption by the partner of partnership liabilities is considered to be a contribution of money to the partnership by the partner. Thus, the partner's basis is increased.

Example
The XYZ partnership owns a warehouse with an adjusted basis of $120,000 subject to a mortgage of $90,000. Partner X (one of three equal partners) has a basis for his partnership interest of $75,000. If the partnership transfers the warehouse and mortgage to Partner X as a current distribution, X's basis for his partnership interest immediately following the distribution would be $15,000, calculated as follows:

Beginning basis	$75,000
Individual assumption of mortgage	+ 90,000
	$165,000
Distribution of warehouse	−120,000
Partner's share of decrease in partnership's liabilities	− 30,000
Basis after distribution	$15,000

Assume that one of the other one-third partners had a basis of $75,000 immediately before the distribution. What would the partner's basis be immediately after the distribution to Partner X? The partner's basis would be $45,000 (i.e., $75,000 less one-third of the $90,000 decrease in partnership liabilities).

5. In the example above, we assumed that debt was allocated based on ownership percentage. This is usually a reasonable assumption for the CPA Exam. However, the debt allocation rules are actually much more complex than this.

    a. **Recourse debt**—For recourse debt, each partner's share of debt is measured by his or her economic risk of loss assuming a **constructive liquidation scenario** occurred. While this material is likely too complex for the exam, you should be aware that limited partners are not allocated any share of recourse debt.

    b. **Nonrecourse debt**—This is debt for which the lender's only recourse, in the event of default, is to take back the property. As above, the allocation of nonrecourse debt is likely too complex for the exam. However, you should be aware that nonrecourse debt is often allocated based on the partners' profit sharing ratios. Also, contrasted with recourse debt, both **general and limited** partners are allocated nonrecourse debt.

D. A partner's basis for the partnership is adjusted in the following order: (1) increased for all income items (including tax-exempt income); (2) decreased for distributions; and (3) decreased by deductions and losses (including nondeductible items not charged to capital).

> **Example**
> A partner with a basis of $50 for his partnership interest at the beginning of the partnership year receives a $30 cash distribution during the year and is allocated a $60 distributive share of partnership ordinary loss and an $8 distributive share of capital gain. In determining the extent to which the ordinary loss is deductible by the partner, the partner's partnership basis of $50 is first increased by the $8 of capital gain and reduced by the $30 cash distribution to $28, so that his deductible ordinary loss is limited to his remaining basis of $28.

E. **Summary**—See the following calculation of outside basis.

Beginning Basis		
Plus:		
		Contributions
Partner's share of:		Debt Increases
		Partnership Income
		Exempt Income
Less:		
Distributions:		Cash Distributions
		Property Distributions
Partner's share of:		Nondeductible Expenses
		Expenses and Losses
		Debt Decreases
Ending Basis		

X. **Capital Account**

A. While basis represents one's investment in a partnership for tax purposes, capital account represents the amount a partner should receive when the partnership is liquidated.

B. Basis and capital account are computed in a similar fashion, except:

1. Liabilities of the partnership do not affect the capital account.

2. The fair market value of contributions and distributions impact the capital account, rather than the tax basis.

XI. Permitted Tax Years—Partners report income in the year that the partnership tax yearends.

A. Since the partnership and the partners may not have the same year-ends, the partners only report income once the partnership closes its books at the partnership year-end.

Example

ABC is a partnership with a June 30 fiscal year-end. Partner A, however, has a calendar year-end. This year ABC earned $24,000 for the fiscal year and also earned an additional $9,000 from July through December. If A is an equal partner in ABC, he should report $8,000 of income this year (one-third of $24,000). A's share of the income from July through December will not be taxed until ABC closes its books next year.

B. Required Tax Year: The required tax year for the partnership is determined as follows:

1. Partnerships use the same year-end as its **majority** interest partner(s) (more than 50% capital and P&L).

Example

A partnership is formed by a corporation (which receives a 55% partnership interest) and five individuals (who each receive a 9% partnership interest). The corporation has a fiscal year ending June 30, while the individuals have a calendar year. The partnership must adopt a fiscal year ending June 30.

2. If the partnership has no single year for the majority, then the partnership uses same year-end as **all** of its principal partners (5% P&L interest or more).

3. If neither the majority interest nor principal partner test is met, the required tax year is determined by using the least aggregate deferral method. This method is computationally intensive, but determines the year-end which will provide the least amount of deferral for the entire partnership group.

C. If a partnership does not want to use the required tax year, the partners can elect a fiscal year-end (with IRS permission) if there is a business purpose; a natural business year can also be used.

Definition

Natural Business Year: A year in which 25% or more of the gross receipts occur in the last two months of the year (three consecutive years).

D. A second exception to the required tax year is that under Section 444 partnerships may elect a year-end with no more than three months of deferral, but a deposit with the IRS is required to compensate the government for the deferral benefits to the partners (only if the deferral benefit exceeds $500).

E. The **taxable year** of a partnership ordinarily **will not close** as a result of the death or entry of a partner, or the liquidation or sale of a partner's interest. But the partnership's taxable year closes as to **the partner** whose **entire interest** is sold or liquidated. Additionally, the partnership tax year closes with respect to a deceased partner as of date of death.

Example
A partner sells his entire interest in a calendar-year partnership on March 31. His pro rata share of partnership income up to March 31 is $15,000. Since the partnership year closes with respect to him at the time of sale, the $15,000 is includible in his income and increases the basis of his partnership interest for purposes of computing gain or loss on the sale. However, the partnership's taxable year does not close as to its remaining partners.

Example
X (on a calendar year) is a partner in the XYZ Partnership that uses a June 30 fiscal year. X died on April 30, 2017. Since the partnership year closes with respect to X at his death, X's final return for the period January 1 through April 30 will include his share of partnership income for the period beginning July 1, 2016, and ending April 30, 2017. His share of partnership income for May and June 2017 will be reported by his estate or other successor in interest.

F. Beginning in 2016, partnership returns are due on or before the 15th day of the third month following the year-end. Partnerships can extend their returns for six months from the due date, which is September 15 for calendar-year partnerships.

G. Any partnership that fails to file a timely return is liable for a monthly penalty equal to $200 (2017) times the number of persons who were partners during any part of the tax year, for each month (or partial month) that the return is not filed.

Flow-Through of Income and Losses

After studying this lesson, you should be able to:

1. Define separately stated items for flow-through purposes.

2. Compute partnership income and distributive share to partners.

3. Apply the loss limitation rules for partners.

Tax Form for this Lesson: Form 1065 and 1065K-1 (available for download and printing from the lesson overview of your software).

I. Allocations of Income

A. Items of income and expense are allocated from the partnership to partners. Partners include these items (known as their distributive share) on the return that includes the year-end of the partnership. Partners modify their adjusted basis in the partnership for these allocations.

B. **Allocations**—Partners receive a share of income or a (potentially different) share of loss, according to the *partnership agreement*.

   1. Any special allocation must pass a judgmental **substantial economic effect** test that ensures that partners with special allocations bear the economic burden or receive the economic benefit of the special allocation.

   2. If no special allocation is provided in the partnership agreement, then separately stated items are distributed in the same proportions as income and loss.

II. Distributive Share

A. Partnerships report a share of items of income and expense to each partner.

   1. Partnerships are **not** subject to tax, but report taxable income on Form 1065.

   2. Profits and losses are allocated to each partner based on each partner's profit and loss sharing ratio.

   3. Measuring and reporting partnership income involves a two-step process.

      a. All items of income, gain, deduction, loss, or credit that are required to be separately stated, or that are specially allocated, are removed from the partnership's ordinary income or loss determination process. Each partner's proportionate share of these items is reported on Schedule K-1.

      b. The remaining items are lumped together to produce the net ordinary income or loss, which is also proportionately reported to each partner.

   4. Partnerships report taxable income (ordinary income) and separately stated items to each partner on Schedule K-1.

Definition
Separately Stated Items: Any tax items (deductions, income, preferences, etc.,) that might affect partners differently—these items retain their character to the owners.

      a. Some common examples of separately stated items include:

         i. Capital gains and losses

         ii. Section 1231 gains and losses

       iii. Charitable contributions

       iv. Foreign income taxes

       v. Section 179 expense deduction

       vi. Interest, dividend, and royalty income

       vii. Interest expense on investment indebtedness

       viii. Net income (loss) from rental real estate activity

       ix. Net income (loss) from other rental activity

       x. Tax-exempt income

   b. Frequently encountered ordinary income and deductions (non-separately stated items) include

       i. Sales less cost of goods sold

       ii. Business expenses such as wages, rents, bad debts, and repairs

       iii. Deduction for guaranteed payments to partners

       iv. Depreciation

       v. Amortization (over 180 months) of partnership organization and start-up expenditures

       vi. Section 1245 and 1250, recapture

5. Capital withdrawals do not affect income.

6. The **character** of any gain or loss recognized on the disposition of property is generally determined by the nature of the property in the hands of the partnership. However, for contributed property, the character may be based on the nature of the property to the contributing partner before contribution.

   a. If a partner contributes **unrealized receivables**, the partnership will recognize ordinary income or loss on the subsequent disposition of the unrealized receivables.

   b. If the property contributed was **inventory** property to the contributing partner, any gain or loss recognized by the partnership on the disposition of the property within five years will be treated as ordinary income or loss.

   c. If the contributed property was a **capital asset,** any loss later recognized by the partnership on the disposition of the property within five years will be treated as a capital loss to the extent of the contributing partner's unrecognized capital loss at the time of contribution. This rule applies to losses only, not to gains.

7. Partnerships may use the cash basis of accounting unless the partnership is a "tax shelter" or at least one partner is a C corporation. Exceptions allow the cash method for farming and where the partnership (or corporate partner) is a small business (average annual gross receipts of $5 million or less for the three prior years ending with the current tax year).

8. Partnerships may elect to amortize organization and start-up costs.

   a. **Definition:** Organization costs relate to organizing the business so they will benefit the business for its entire life, the length of which cannot be estimated. Start-up costs are expenditures of a nature that would usually be deducted in the year incurred, but cannot be deducted since they were incurred before the business began operations (e.g., training costs for employees). Organizational expenses in the amount of $5,000 may be deducted, but the $5,000 is reduced by the amount of expenditures incurred that exceed $50,000.

   b. Start-up expenses in the amount of $5,000 may be deducted, but the $5,000 is reduced by the amount of expenditures incurred that exceed $50,000.

     c. Expenses not deducted must be capitalized and amortized over 180 months, beginning with the month that the corporation begins its business operations. An election can be made to not deduct or amortize the expenses.

     d. **Syndication** expenditures (cost of selling partnership interests) are capitalized and cannot be amortized.

9. Special simplified reporting (and IRS audit) rules exist for electing large partnerships (non-service partnership with over 100 partners).

10. General partners' distributive shares are subject to the self-employment tax, whereas limited partners' shares usually are not. However, guaranteed payments for both general and limited partners are subject to the self-employment tax.

B. Family Partnerships

1. If the business is primarily service oriented (capital is not a material income-producing factor), a family member will be considered a partner only if the family member shares in the management or performs needed services.

2. Capital is not a material income-producing factor if substantially all of the gross income of the business consists of fees, commissions, or other compensation for personal services (e.g., accountants, architects, lawyers).

3. A family member is generally considered a partner if the family member actually owns a capital interest in a business in which capital is a material income-producing factor.

4. Where a capital interest in a partnership in which capital is a material income-producing factor is treated as created by gift, the distributive shares of partnership income of the donor and donee are determined by first making a reasonable allowance for services rendered to the partnership, and then allocating the remainder according to the relative capital interests of the donor and donee.

Example
Dad is a half partner in a partnership where capital is a material income producing factor. Dad gives a 20% interest to his son. This year, the partnership earns $100 of income and Dad provides services worth $10. The son is allocated a partnership income of $18.

C. Loss Limitations

1. Partners can only deduct losses if all three of the following hurdles are passed (in this order):

     a. Partners must have enough basis to deduct the loss.

     b. Partners can deduct losses only to the extent of their at-risk amount. Generally, at-risk equals the partners' basis less the partner's share of nonrecourse debt. Qualified nonrecourse real estate financing is included in at-risk basis.

     c. If the loss is a passive loss, the partner can deduct the loss only to the extent of passive income. Limited partners' losses are passive by definition (for more information see the lesson "Limitations on Business Deductions").

2. Disallowed losses are carried over and used in future years when the remaining criteria are met.

Transactions with Partners

Despite the status of partnerships as conduit entities, arm's-length contracts between a partner and partnership are recognized for tax purposes.

After studying this lesson, you should be able to:

1. Define guarantee payments and apply flow-through rules for these payments.

2. Apply built-in gain/loss rules to sales of property contributed to partnerships.

3. Identify related party transactions involving partnerships that have special tax treatment.

I. **Guaranteed Payments**—Guaranteed payments are those made to partners without regard to partnership income.

    A. Partners are not employees of the partnership, but might receive guaranteed payments for services or capital investment.

    B. Guaranteed payments are ordinary income to the recipients at the partnership year-end.

    C. Guaranteed payments (for deduction purposes) reduce partnership income and thereby reduce each partner's distributive share of such income.

    D. Guaranteed payments are deemed to be paid to the partner on the last day of the partnership's tax year, regardless of when payment was actually made.

II. **Precontribution (Built-In) Gains and Losses**—*These are allocated back to the original contributing partners when the property is sold.*

Definition

Built-In Gain (or Loss) Property: Property that has appreciated (declined) in value at the time of its contribution to the partnership (the value of gain property is greater than its adjusted basis, whereas the value of loss property is less than its adjusted basis).

Misconception

There is no time limit on the allocation of the amount of built-in gains and losses from sales of property. A time limit (five years) applies to the characterization of these gains and losses as ordinary or capital. Another time limit (seven years) applies to the distribution of built-in gain property (to partners).

    A. The built-in gain or loss is allocated to the contributing partner up to the gain or loss realized on the sale.

    B. The character of the built-in gains and losses is generally determined by the use of the property by the partnership, with two exceptions.

        1. Sales of contributed ordinary income or loss property (e.g., inventory and accounts receivable) generate ordinary income or loss to the contributing partner. The characterization of income or loss as ordinary from a sale of inventory is limited to five years (five years after the property was contributed to the partnership). There is no time limit for the ordinary income characterization for accounts receivables.

            a. Note that **all** gain or loss on the sale is treated as ordinary if the above rule is met. It is not limited to the built-in gain or loss at the time of contribution.

Example

Partner A is an art dealer and a partner in ABC Partners, a consulting firm. A contributes a painting (he held as inventory) to ABC to decorate the ABC office (a Section 1231 asset). The painting has a FMV of $10,000 and an adjusted basis of $6,000. If ABC sells the painting within five years of the contribution, any gain or loss will be allocated to A (up to the built-in gain or loss) and will be characterized as ordinary income. Thus, if the painting is sold four year later for $11,000, the $5,000 gain ($11,000 − $6,000) is characterized as ordinary income. If ABC sells the painting after five years, then the $5,000 gain is Section 1231 gain. Note that in both cases, since the built-in gain was only $4,000 ($10,000 − $6,000), the first $4,000 of gain is allocated to Partner A. The remaining $1,000 of gain is allocated to A and the other partners based on their profit-sharing ratios.

2. Sales of contributed capital assets with built-in capital losses generate capital losses to contributing partners (again only for five years after the contribution). However, for built-in capital losses, the amount of loss that can be recharacterized as capital is limited to the built-in loss at the time the asset was contributed.

Example

Partner R contributes a capital asset to RST Partnership, which will be used by the partnership as inventory. The asset has a FMV of $10,000 and adjusted basis of $15,000. The built-in loss is $5,000 and, when this asset is sold, the first $5,000 of recognized loss will be allocated to R. If RST sells the asset three years later for $8,000, the recognized loss is $7,000. The first $5,000 of loss is allocated to R and the other $2,000 of loss is allocated to R and the other partners based on their loss-sharing ratios. The $5,000 loss allocated to R is a capital loss (since this was sold within five years), but the remaining $2,000 loss will be characterized based on how the partnership used the asset (Inventory = Ordinary loss). Note, that only the built-in loss is recharacterized as a capital loss.

III. Related Party Rules

A. If a person engages in a transaction with a partnership other than as a member of such partnership, any resulting gain or loss is generally recognized. However, if the transaction involves a **more than 50% owned partnership,** one of three special rules may apply. Constructive ownership rules apply in determining whether a transaction involves a more than 50% owned partnership. For this purpose, an individual's family includes brothers and sisters, spouse, ancestors, and lineal descendants.

1. **No losses** are deductible from sales or exchanges of property between a partnership and a person owning (directly or indirectly) more than 50% of the capital or profits interests in such partnership, or between two partnerships in which the same persons own (directly or indirectly) more than 50% of the capital or profits interests. A gain later realized on a subsequent sale by the transferee will not be recognized to the extent of the disallowed loss.

Examples

1. Partnership X is owned by three **equal** partners, A, B, and C, who are brothers. Partnership X sells property at a loss of $5,000 to C. Since C owns a more than 50% interest in the partnership (i.e., C constructively owns his brothers' partnership interests), the $5,000 loss is disallowed to Partnership X.

2. Assume the same facts as in the above example #1. C later resells the property to Z, an unrelated taxpayer, at a gain of $6,000. C's realized gain of $6,000 will not be recognized to the extent of the $5,000 disallowed loss to the Partnership X. Thus, C will recognize $1,000 gain.

2. A **gain** recognized on a sale or exchange of property between a partnership and a person owning (directly or indirectly) more than 50% of the capital or profits interests in such partnership, or between two partnerships in which the same persons own (directly or indirectly) more than 50% of the capital or profits interests, will be treated as **ordinary income** if the property is **not a capital asset** in the hands of the transferee.

3. No deduction for a payment to a partner can be claimed by an accrual partnership until the cash basis partner includes the payment in income. Note that this applies to all partners (not just those owning more than 50%).

IV. Partners are generally not considered to be employees for purposes of employee fringe benefits (e.g., cost of $50,000 of group-term life insurance, exclusion of premiums or benefits under an employer accident or health plan, etc.). The value of a partner's fringe benefits are deductible by the partnership as guaranteed payments and must be included in a partner's gross income.

Partnership Distributions

After studying this lesson, you should be able to:

1. Differentiate between nonliquidating and liquidating distributions.

2. Determine tax consequences for partners of nonliquidating distributions.

3. Compute tax consequences for partners of liquidating distributions.

4. Describe applicability of special rules to certain partnership distributions.

I. **Gain/Loss Deferral**—Partnerships generally do not recognize gains or losses on distributions.

   A. Partners can recognize gains on nonliquidating or liquidating distributions of cash. Cash distributed in excess of outside basis causes gain recognition.

   B. Nonliquidating distributions of property **never** trigger loss recognition, but losses may be recognized on a liquidating distribution.

II. **Nonliquidating (or Current) Distributions**

> **Definition**
> *Nonliquidating Distribution*: A distribution to a continuing partner, including a draw by the partner.

   A. Arm's-length sales to partners are not distributions.

   B. **Basis Effects**—For partners, non *liquidating distributions are a return of capital that reduces outside basis (in a specific order).*

      1. First, the partner's adjusted basis is allocated to cash distributions and cash deemed distributed (reductions in liabilities).

      2. Second, the partner's adjusted basis is allocated to distributions of unrealized receivables and inventory in an amount equal to the partnership's basis in these assets.

      3. Finally, the partner's adjusted basis is allocated to other assets distributed. Any deficiency in the partner's adjusted basis is allocated to properties with unrealized losses, and any excess basis is allocated to properties with unrealized gains.

> **Example**
> Casey had a basis of $9,000 for his partnership interest at the time that he received a nonliquidating partnership distribution consisting of $5,000 cash and other property with a basis of $3,000 and an FMV of $8,000. No gain is recognized by Casey since the cash received did not exceed his partnership basis. Casey's $9,000 basis for his partnership interest is first reduced by the $5,000 cash and then reduced by the $3,000 basis of other property, to $1,000. Casey will have a basis for the other property received of $3,000.

      4. Distributed property retains its inside basis (in the hands of the partner) unless the partner runs out of outside basis, then the inside basis of the property is reduced to the outside basis.

> **Example**
> Sara receives a current distribution from her partnership at a time when the basis for her partnership interest is $10,000. The distribution consists of $7,000 cash and Section 1231 property with an adjusted basis of $5,000 and a FMV of $9,000. No gain is recognized by Sara since the cash received did not exceed her basis. After being reduced by the cash, her partnership basis of $3,000 is reduced by the basis of the property (but not below zero). Her basis for the property is limited to $3,000.

5. If the distributed property consists of multiple assets, then the allocation of basis can be quite complex. A simple approach is to allocate the outside basis by the amount of the inside basis.

Example

Two parcels of inventory (Parcel A and Parcel B) are distributed to a partner in a nonliquidating proportionate distribution at a time when the partner has an outside basis of $12. Parcel A has an inside basis of $6 and Parcel B has an inside basis of $18. Each parcel is worth $20. In this situation, one-fourth [($6/($6 + $18) × $12] or $3 of the outside basis is allocated to parcel A. The remaining three-fourths of the outside basis ($9) is allocated to parcel B [$18/($6 + $18) × $12].

III. **Liquidating Distributions**—A liquidating distribution may result in gain or loss, and it requires the partner to transfer his or her outside basis to assets received from the partnership.

  A. A liquidating distribution occurs when the entire partnership is liquidated or the interest of one partner is redeemed.

   1. The distribution can be a series of transfers.

   2. The partnership, generally, does not recognize any gains or losses.

  B. **Basis Effect**—Liquidating distributions are treated as a return of capital and the partner's outside basis is substituted for the inside basis of distributed property.

   1. Like nonliquidating distributions, distributions of cash (and deemed distributions) trigger gain to the extent cash exceeds outside basis.

   2. Distributed property retains its inside basis, but this amount is adjusted (up or down) depending upon the outside basis of the partner. The calculation of this adjustment is complex and unlikely to be tested.

   3. Inventory and receivables must be distributed pro-rata (a non-pro-rata distribution will be disproportionate).

  C. **Loss Recognition**—Unlike nonliquidating distributions, partners can recognize losses on liquidating distributions, but only if two conditions are met:

   1. First, the distribution must consist only of cash, inventory, and unrealized receivables.

   2. Second, the outside basis of the partner's interest exceeds the sum of cash plus the inside basis of the receivables and inventory.

Examples

1. Day had a basis of $20,000 for his partnership interest before receiving a distribution in complete liquidation of his interest. The liquidating distribution consisted of $6,000 cash and inventory with a basis of $11,000. Since Day's liquidating distribution consisted of only money and inventory, Day will recognize a loss on the liquidation of his partnership interest. The amount of loss is the $3,000 difference between the $20,000 basis for his partnership interest and the $6,000 cash and the $11,000 basis for the inventory received. Day will have an $11,000 basis for the inventory.

2. Assume the same facts as in Example #1 except that Day's liquidating distribution consists of $6,000 cash and a parcel of land with a basis of $11,000. Since the liquidating distribution now includes property other than money, receivables, and inventory, no loss can be recognized on the liquidation of Day's partnership interest. The basis for Day's partnership interest is first reduced by the $6,000 cash to $14,000. Since no loss can be recognized, the parcel of land must absorb all of Day's unrecovered partnership basis. As a result, the land will have a basis of $14,000.

IV. **Retirement Distributions**

  A. Payments made in liquidation of the interest of a retiring or deceased partner are generally treated as partnership distributions made in exchange for the partner's interest in partnership property. Such payments generally result in capital gain or loss to the retiring or deceased partner.

B. However, payments made to a retiring or deceased general partner in a partnership in which capital is **not** a material income-producing factor must be reported as ordinary income by the partner to the extent such payments are for the partner's share of unrealized receivables or goodwill (unless the partnership agreement provides for a payment with respect to goodwill).

1. Amounts treated as ordinary income by the retiring or deceased partner are either deductible by the partnership (treated as guaranteed payments) or reduce the income allocated to remaining partners (treated as a distributive share of partnership income).

2. Capital is **not** a material income-producing factor if substantially all of the gross income of the business consists of fees, commissions, or other compensation for personal services (e.g., accountants, doctors, dentists, lawyers).

V. Special Issues—Complications are created by built-in gains, deemed distributions, and disproportionate distributions.

A. Deemed distributions (reductions in liabilities) are treated as cash distributions.

B. Distributions of marketable securities (up to the value of the securities less the partner's share of appreciation inherent in the securities) are treated as deemed distributions.

C. Distributions of built-in gain property to other partners (other than the partner who originally contributed the property) within seven years of the original contribution cause gain recognition.

VI. "Disproportionate" distributions of **hot assets** can also trigger income recognition.

Definitions

Hot Assets: Generate ordinary income or loss because the partner has not yet been taxed on accrued, but unrealized, income.

Disproportionate Distributions: Occur when ordinary income assets (inventory and receivables) are distributed to partners without regard to their proportionate ownership interests. Therefore, if a 12% partner receives 12% of the hot assets, then no special rules need to be applied because it is a proportionate distribution. **Most CPA Exam questions on this topic will be proportionate distributions**.

A. A distribution is disproportionate as to a partner's share of unrealized receivables or substantially appreciated inventory. Inventory is **substantially appreciated** if its FMV exceeds 120% of its basis.

1. Hot assets are inventory and unrealized receivables. For distributions, inventory has to be substantially appreciated (FMV > 120% × adjusted basis) for it to be classified as a hot asset.

   a. Unrealized receivables generally are receivables of cash basis taxpayers. Potential Section 1245 and Section 1250 recapture are also included as an unrealized receivable.

   b. Inventory is defined as any asset other than cash, capital assets, or Section 1231 assets.

2. The partner may receive more than the partner's share of these assets, *or*

3. The partner may receive more than the partner's share of other assets, in effect giving up a share of unrealized receivables or substantially appreciated inventory.

4. The partner may recognize gain or loss. The gain or loss is the difference between the FMV of what is received and the basis of what is given up. The gain or loss is limited to the disproportionate amount of unrealized receivables or substantially appreciated inventory that is received or given up. The character of the gain or loss depends on the character of the property given up.

B. The partnership may similarly recognize gain or loss when there is a disproportionate distribution with respect to substantially appreciated inventory or unrealized receivables.

Example

A, B, and C each own a one-third interest in a partnership. The partnership has the following assets:

	Adjusted Basis	FMV
Cash	$6,000	$6,000
Inventory	6,000	12,000
Land	9,000	18,000
	$21,000	$36,000

Assume that A has a $7,000 basis for his partnership interest and that all inventory is distributed to A in liquidation of his partnership interest. He is treated as having exchanged his one-third interest in the cash and the land for a two-thirds increased interest in the substantially appreciated inventory. He has a gain of $3,000. He received $8,000 (2/3 × $12,000) of inventory for his basis of $2,000 (1/3 × $6,000) in cash and $3,000 (1/3 × $9,000) of land. The gain is capital if the land was a capital asset. The partnership is treated as having received $8,000 (FMV of A's one-third share of cash and land) in exchange for inventory with a basis of $4,000 (basis of inventory distributed in excess of A's one-third share). Thus, the partnership will recognize ordinary income of $4,000.

VII. Optional Section 754 Adjustment to Basis of Partnership Property

A. On a distribution of property to a partner or on a sale by a partner of a partnership interest, the partnership may elect to adjust the basis of its assets to **prevent any inequities** that otherwise might occur. Once an election is made, it applies to all similar transactions unless the IRS approves revocation of the election.

B. Upon the **distribution of partnership property,** the basis of remaining partnership property will be adjusted for all partners.

1. Increased by

   a. The amount of gain recognized to a distributee partner, *and*

   b. The excess of the partnership's basis in the property distributed over the basis of that property in the hands of distributee partner.

2. Decreased by

   a. The amount of loss recognized to a distributee partner, *and*

   b. The excess of basis of property in hands of distributee over the prior basis of that property in the partnership.

Example

Day had a basis of $20,000 for his partnership interest before receiving a distribution in complete liquidation of his interest. The liquidating distribution consisted of $6,000 cash and inventory with a basis of $11,000. Since Day's liquidating distribution consisted of only money and inventory, Day will recognize a loss on the liquidation of his partnership interest. The amount of loss is the $3,000 difference between the $20,000 basis for his partnership interest, and the $6,000 cash and the $11,000 basis for the inventory received. Day will have an $11,000 basis for the inventory. If a Section 754 election were in effect, the basis of remaining partnership property would be increased by $3,000.

VIII. Integrated Review Problem—A, B, and C formed ABC partnership with the following contributions:

	Asset	Adjusted Basis	Fair Market Value	Interest
A	Cash	$40,000	$40,000	50%
B	Land	12,000	21,000	20%
C	Inventory	24,000	24,000	30%

A. The land was a capital asset to B and subject to a mortgage of $5,000, assumed by the partnership. Assume that this year the partnership breaks even, but decides to make distributions to each partner.

1. What is B's initial basis? $8,000 (12,000 − 5,000 + (20% × 5,000)).

2. What is C's initial basis? $25,500 (24,000 + (30% × 5,000)).

3. A nonliquidating cash distribution may reduce the recipient partner's basis below zero. False.

4. A nonliquidating distribution of unappreciated inventory reduces the recipient partner's basis in the partnership. True.

5. In a liquidating distribution of property other than money, where the partnership's basis of the distributed property exceeds the basis of the partner's interest, the partner's basis in the distributed property is limited to his or her predistribution basis in the partnership interest. True.

6. Gain is recognized by the partner who receives a nonliquidating distribution of property, where the adjusted basis of the property exceeds his basis in the partnership interest before the distribution. False.

7. In a nonliquidating distribution of inventory, where the partnership has no unrealized receivables or appreciated inventory, the basis of inventory that is distributed to a partner cannot exceed the inventory's adjusted basis to the partnership. True.

8. The partnership's nonliquidating distribution of encumbered property to a partner who assumes the mortgage does not affect the other partners' bases in their partnership interests. False.

Sales and Terminations

I. **Sales of Partnership Interests**—A sale of a partnership interest results in a gain or loss calculated in the manner used for other assets, using outside basis to compute the gain or loss. The portion of any gain or loss due to **hot assets** is not eligible for capital gain treatment.

   A. **Sales**

   1. The sale, exchange, or liquidation of a partner's entire interest closes the partnership's tax year for that partner, but not for other partners or for the partnership as a whole. The income for a partner that dies during the year passes to the partner for the portion of the year that he or she was alive.

   2. The selling partner's amount realized includes the buyer's assumption of the selling partner's share of the partnership liabilities.

Example
Miller sold her partnership interest to Carter for $150,000 cash, plus Carter's assumption of Miller's $60,000 share of partnership liabilities. The amount realized by Miller on the sale of her partnership interest is $150,000 + $60,000 = $210,000.

   B. **Hot Assets**

   1. If the partnership has hot assets at the time a partnership interest is sold, the selling partner must allocate a portion of the sale proceeds to these assets and recognize ordinary income.

   2. Hot assets are a) unrealized receivables (receivables of a cash basis taxpayer; includes depreciation recapture), and b) inventory.

Definition
Inventory: All assets other than cash, capital assets, and Section 1231 assets.

   3. The remaining sale proceeds are allocable to the selling partner's capital asset interest and result in a capital gain or loss.

Example
X has a 40% interest in the XY Partnership. Partner X sells his 40% interest to Z for $50,000. X's basis in his partnership is $22,000, and the cash-method partnership had the following receivables and inventory:

	Adjusted Basis	Fair Market Value
Accounts receivable	0	$10,000
Inventory	4,000	10,000
Potential Section 1250 recapture	0	10,000
	$4,000	$30,000

X's total gain is $28,000 (i.e., $50,000 – $22,000). Since the Section 1250 recapture is treated as "unrealized receivables" and the inventory is appreciated, X will recognize ordinary income to the extent that his selling price attributable to Section 751 items ($30,000 × 40% = $12,000) exceeds his basis in those items ($4,000 × 40% = $1,600), that is, $10,400. The remainder of X's gain ($28,000 – $10,400 = $17,600) will be treated as capital gain.

C. In addition to hot assets, if the partnership owns collectibles or has Section 1250 assets, these items may also impact the gain from the sale of a partnership asset. The selling partners gain will be taxed at 28% to the extent it is due to collectibles, and any unrecaptured Section 1250 gain will be taxed at 25%.

D. If a Section 754 election is in effect, then basis adjustments to partnership property may be needed. These basis adjustments benefit the new partner who purchased the partnership interest.

1. Upon the **sale or exchange of a partnership interest**, the basis of partnership property to the **transferee** (not other partners) will be

a. Increased by the excess of the basis of the transferee's partnership interest over the transferee's share of the adjusted basis of partnership property; *or*

b. Decreased by the excess of transferee's share of adjusted basis of partnership property over the basis for the transferee's partnership interest.

Example

Assume X sells his 40% interest to Z for $80,000 when the partnership balance sheet reflects the following:

XY Partnership

	Basis	FMV
Assets		
Accounts Receivable	$0	$100,000
Real Property	30,000	100,000
Capital		
X (40%)		$80,000
Y (60%)		120,000

Z will have a basis for his partnership interest of $80,000, while his share of the adjusted basis of partnership property will be only $12,000. If the partnership elects to adjust the basis of partnership property, it will increase the basis of its assets by $68,000 ($80,000 – $12,000) solely for the benefit of Z. The basis of the receivables will increase from 0 to $40,000 with the full adjustment allocated to Z. When the receivables are collected, Y will have $60,000 of income and Z will have none. The basis of the real property will increase by $28,000 to $58,000, so that Z's share of the basis will be $40,000 (i.e., $12,000 + $28,000).

II. Terminations—The termination of a partnership requires the closing of the partnership books.

A. Termination requires a closing of the partnership

1. Termination requires a closing of the partnership tax year.

2. Termination results in a deemed distribution of assets to the partners.

B. A partnership terminates for tax purposes if either of the following events occur:

1. No part of the business continues to be carried on by any partner in the partnership form.

III. Integrated Review Problem—A, B, and C formed ABC partnership with the following contributions:

	Asset	Adjusted Basis	Fair Market Value	Interest
A	Cash	$40,000	$40,000	50%
B	Land	12,000	21,000	20%
C	Inventory	24,000	24,000	30%

A. The land was a capital asset to B and subject to a mortgage of $5,000, assumed by the partnership. Assume that this year the partnership breaks even but decides to make distributions to each partner.

1. What is B's initial basis? $8,000 (12,000 − 5,000 + (20% × 5,000)).

2. What is C's initial basis? $25,500 (24,000 + (30% × 5,000)).

3. A nonliquidating cash distribution may reduce the recipient partner's basis below zero. False.

4. A nonliquidating distribution of unappreciated inventory reduces the recipient partner's basis in the partnership. True.

5. In a liquidating distribution of property other than money, where the partnership's basis of the distributed property exceeds the basis of the partner's interest, the partner's basis in the distributed property is limited to his predistribution basis in the partnership interest. True.

6. Gain is recognized by the partner who receives a nonliquidating distribution of property, where the adjusted basis of the property exceeds his basis in the partnership interest before the distribution. False.

7. In a nonliquidating distribution of inventory, where the partnership has no unrealized receivables or appreciated inventory, the basis of inventory that is distributed to a partner cannot exceed the inventory's adjusted basis to the partnership. True.

8. The partnership's nonliquidating distribution of encumbered property to a partner who assumes the mortgage does not affect the other partners' bases in their partnership interests. False.

S Corporation Taxation

Eligibility, Election, Termination

After studying this lesson, you should be able to:

1. List the tax characteristics of S corporations.

2. Determine if a corporation meets the eligibility requirements to elect S status.

3. Evaluate if election requirements have been met for a valid S election.

4. Assess if an S corporation election has been terminated.

I. **Legal Status**—The S election can only be made by a corporation, and the corporation retains its legal corporate status after the election.

    A. S corporations retain corporate status and their corporate characteristics when:

        1. Shareholders are not liable for corporate debt.

        2. Shares can be freely transferred.

        3. Shareholders can be employees (separation of ownership and management).

    B. **Tax Characteristics**—Unlike C corporations, S corporations act as conduits for taxable income.

        1. Like partners, S shareholders are taxed on portion of income or loss, regardless of distributions.

        2. There is no imposition of the corporate AMT, PHC, or accumulated earnings taxes. Individual (not corporate) tax preferences are allocated to shareholders.

        3. The adjusted basis of shareholders' stock is generally adjusted at year end.

        4. Shareholders recognize gains when the value of distributions (cash or property) exceeds the adjusted basis in the stock.

        5. Partners in a partnership are not eligible to benefit from many fringe benefit exclusions because partners who work for the partnership are not considered to be employees. This same rule applies to S corporation shareholders who own 2% or more of the S corporation.

        6. A 2% or greater S corporation shareholder can deduct premiums paid on health insurance policies issued in his or her own name as a deduction for AGI as long as the shareholder has earned income from the S corporation that exceeds the total of all premiums paid.

        7. Shareholders who work for the S corporation are employees who are subject to payroll taxes (social security and Medicare). However, the distributive share to shareholders is not subject to self-employment taxes.

    C. **Default Rules for S Corporations are the C Corporation Rules**—Despite conceptual similarity to partnerships, corporate rules serve as default rules for S corporations.

        1. There is no special provision for contributions of property to an S corporation. Hence, the "control club" rule prevails for nonrecognition.

        2. S corporations can elect to amortize organizational expenses.

        3. Distributions of property take an outside basis of FMV (rather than inside basis).

        4. Distributions of built-in gain or loss property do not have any special implications for the contributing shareholder.

        5. Distribution of appreciated property causes recognition of gain at the corporate level (passed through to shareholders).

6. There is no earnings and profits calculation because all earnings are taxed to shareholders, but a special calculation is necessary to distinguish Subchapter S earnings (called accumulated adjustments) from earnings and profits accumulated previously under Chapter C status.

II. **Eligibility Rules**—To qualify for an S election, a corporation must have the requisite ownership structure and be an eligible entity.

A. **Eligibility Entity**—The corporation must be an eligible entity.

1. Foreign corporations are not eligible.

2. Certain members of affiliated groups, parents of subsidiaries, financial institutions, and DISCs are not eligible (certain banks are eligible).

3. S corporations may own an 80% or more equity interest in a C corporation.

4. S corporations may own a **qualified** Subchapter S subsidiary.

Definition

Qualified Subchapter S Subsidiary: A corporation that meets all requirements for Subchapter S status and is owned 100% by a parent S corporation.

B. **Shareholder Requirements**—Shareholders must be eligible.

1. Nonresident aliens, C corporations, and partnerships are not eligible.

   a. **Shortcut**—An S corporation can be a parent corporation, but it cannot be a subsidiary of any corporation except another subchapter S corporation.

2. Estates (bankruptcy or testamentary) can be shareholders.

3. Trusts can be shareholders, if grantor or testamentary (two-year limit after transfer).

4. Special stock voting trusts and qualified S trusts can be shareholders (all beneficiaries are qualified and electing shareholders).

5. Small business electing trusts and exempt entities are allowed as shareholders.

C. **Shareholder Limit**—An eligible corporation can have no more than 100 shareholders.

1. All members of a family and their estates are treated as a single shareholder.

2. Each beneficiary of a shareholding trust is counted as a separate shareholder.

3. Co-owners of stock each count as one shareholder.

D. **Stock Requirements**—Only one class of stock is outstanding.

1. Shares that vary solely in voting rights are not considered two classes of stock.

2. Convertible debt does not violate the requirement unless and until it is converted into a second class of stock.

3. Unissued treasury stock does not violate the requirement.

4. A **safe harbor** exists for shareholder debt to prevent these securities from being interpreted as a second class of equity. The debt must be evidenced by a written promise that is not contingent or convertible. Short-term unwritten loans are sanctioned in amounts under $10,000.

III. **Election Requirements**—The shareholders of the corporation must make a qualifying election to obtain or revoke S status.

A. Unanimous consent of shareholders is required for election.

Note
In its initial year, a corporation must make the S election on or before the 15th day of the third month after commencing business.

1. The election is valid for the current year, if it is made on or before the 15th day of the third month (Form 2553).

2. An election that is ineligible for the current year is still valid for the next year (if the circumstance causing ineligibility is corrected).

3. All current shareholders (and past shareholders for the current year, up to date of election) must consent to election.

4. Both spouses must consent, if the stock is jointly owned.

B. Termination Requirements—Termination of the election can occur through three circumstances.

1. A voluntary termination occurs through a majority vote (a majority of all shareholders) specifying a prospective year or made before the 15th day of the third month for the current year.

   a. Also note, that if there is a greater than 50% change in the ownership of the S corporation, the new owners must affirm that they wish to continue to S election.

2. An involuntary termination occurs through a violation of an eligibility requirement, and this termination is effective on the date of the violation.

   a. **Reminder**—The IRS can waive an inadvertent termination.

Definition
Short Year: A tax year consisting of less than 12 months.

3. An involuntary termination can occur due to a violation of the limit on passive investment income exceeding 25% of gross receipts for three consecutive years (see discussion of S corporate taxes in the "Income and Basis" and "Distributions and Special Taxes" lessons). This termination is effective on the first day of the fourth consecutive year. This provision only applies if the S corporation has earnings and profits (from previous C corporation years) on its balance sheet.

Examples

For a calendar-year S corporation, a revocation not specifying a revocation date that is made on or before March 15, 2017, is effective as of January 1, 2017. A revocation not specifying a revocation date that is made after March 15, 2017, is effective as of January 1, 2018. If a revocation is filed March 11, 2017, and specifies a revocation date of July 1, 2017, the corporation ceases to be an S corporation on July 1, 2017.

A calendar-year S corporation with common stock outstanding issues preferred stock on April 1, 2017. Since its S corporation status terminates on April 1, it must file an S corporation tax return (Form 1120S) for the period January 1 through March 31 and a C corporation tax return (Form 1120) for the period April 1 through December 31, 2017. Both tax returns would be due by March 15, 2018.

Income and Basis

After studying this lesson, you should be able to:

1. Define separately stated items for flow-through purposes.

2. Compute S corporation income and flow-through allocations to shareholders.

3. Calculate adjusted basis of S corporation stock.

4. Apply the loss limitation rules for S corporation shareholders.

Tax Forms for This Lesson: Form 1120S and Form 1120SK-1 (available for download and printing from the lesson overview of your software).

I.   Operating Rules

A.   Required Year-End—Rather than pay the corporate tax, S corporations report income to shareholders on a year-end consistent with that of the shareholders.

B.   A Calendar Year-End—This is generally the default for S corporations.

1. S corporations can elect a fiscal year-end (with IRS permission) if there is a business purpose to the election. The most common business purpose is to elect a **natural business year**.

Definition
Natural Business Year: A year in which 25% or more of the gross receipts occur in the last two months of the year (three consecutive years).

2. S corporations may elect a year-end under Section 444 with no more than three months of deferral (a deposit with the IRS is required to compensate the government for the deferral benefits to the shareholders if the benefits exceed $500).

II. Reporting Operations—S corporations calculate taxable income (reported on Form 1120S) in a manner similar to partnerships (e.g., no personal deductions).

A.   S corporations may use the cash basis of accounting unless the corporation is a tax shelter.

B.   An S corporation reports taxable income (ordinary income) and separately stated items for each shareholder on Schedule K-1 whether or not any dividends were declared.

Definition
Separately Stated Items: Any tax items (deductions, income, preferences, etc.,) that might affect owners differently. These items retain their character to the owners and must, therefore, be reported separately for each owner.

C.   S corporations are not entitled to most special corporate deductions, such as the dividends-received deduction.

D.   S corporations do not pay alternative minimum tax, personal holding company tax, or accumulated earnings tax.

E.   S corporations make most of the tax elections (not shareholders), including the election to amortize organization and start-up costs.

F.   S Corporation returns are due on the 15th day of the third month after the close of the tax year. An automatic six-month election is permitted.

G. An S corporation that fails to file a timely return is liable for a monthly penalty equal to $200 (2017) times the number of persons who were shareholders during any part of the tax year, for each month (or partial month) that the return is not filed.

H. Health and accident insurance premiums and other *fringe benefits* paid by an S corporation on behalf of a more than 2% shareholder-employee are deductible by the S corporation as compensation and includible in the shareholder-employee's gross income on Form W-2.

I. Expenses and interest owed to any cash-method shareholder are deductible by an accrual-method S corporation only when paid.

Example

An accrual-method calendar-year S corporation accrues $2,000 of salary to a cash-method employee (a 1% shareholder) during 2017 but does not make payment until February 2018. The $2,000 will be deductible by the corporation in 2018 and reported by the shareholder-employee as income in 2018.

III. Flow-Through to Shareholders—Each shareholder reports income consistent with the period in which the corporate stock was held.

A. Each shareholder reports income and separately stated items according to pro-rata share of stock ownership.

1. If relative interests change during the year, each shareholder calculates the share of income on a daily basis.

2. To calculate the daily share of income prior to (or after) the change in shares, divide annual income (and separately stated items) by the number of days in the year. Next, multiply this amount by (1) number of days prior to (after) the change and (2) the percentage ownership interest.

Example

As of January 1 of this year, TP1 owned all 100 shares of ABC, a calendar year S corporation. On February 9th (the 40th day of this year), TP1 sold 25 shares to TP2. This year (365 days), ABC reported $73,000 in nonseparately stated income and made no distributions to shareholders. What amount of income should TP1 report from ABC?

TP1 should report income of $56,750 calculated using the daily income ($200 per day) for the 40 days TP1 owned 100% and 75% of the daily income for the 325 days after the sale. Note, that the seller is deemed to own the shares on the day of the sale.

3. If a shareholder's interest is completely terminated (death or sale), then the share can be calculated by closing the books as of the termination date (an **interim** close). However, all shareholders, including the departing shareholder, must agree to this treatment.

Example

As of January 1 of this year, TP1 owned half of the 100 shares of ABC, a calendar year S corporation. On February 9th TP1 sold all of his shares to TP2. This year (365 days) ABC reported $73,000 in ordinary income, that accrued ratably throughout the year, and a capital loss of $3,650, which occurred on June 30. What amount of nonseparately stated income should TP1 report from ABC?

Unless the shareholders elect an interim close, TP1 should report ordinary income of $4,000 ($200 per day for the 40 days TP1 owned 50%) and a capital loss of $200 ($10 per day for the 40 days TP1 owned 50%). If all the shareholders elect an interim close, then TP1 still reports the $4,000 of ordinary income (it accrued ratably). TP1 cannot, however, report any of the loss because it occurred after he sold his stock.

IV. Adjusted Stock Basis—Each shareholder has an adjusted basis in his S stock that must be modified by contributions, income, distributions, and expenses.

   A. First, contributions to capital increase the shareholder's adjusted basis.

   B. Second, the shareholder's share of income (including exempt income) increases the shareholder's adjusted basis.

   C. Third, distributions to the shareholder decrease the shareholder's adjusted basis.

   D. Fourth, the shareholder's share of loss (including nondeductible expenses) decreases the shareholder's adjusted basis.

Calculation of S Shareholder's Basis

Initial Basis

Plus: Additional Contributions

   Shareholder's share of: Corporate Income

   Exempt Income

Less: Distributions from AAA/OAA (in following order):

   Cash

   Inventory and receivables

   Other property

   Nondeductible Expenses

   Corporate Losses

   E. Stock basis is adjusted in the following order:

   1. Increased for all income items

   2. Decreased for distributions that are excluded from gross income

   3. Decreased for nondeductible, noncapital items

   4. Decreased for deductible expenses and losses

Example
An S corporation has tax-exempt income of $5,000 and an ordinary loss from business activity of $6,000 for calendar year 2017. Its sole shareholder had a stock basis of $2,000 on January 1, 2017. The $5,000 of tax-exempt income would pass through to the shareholder, increasing the shareholder's stock basis to $7,000, and would permit the pass-through and deduction of the $6,000 of ordinary loss, reducing the shareholder's stock basis to $1,000.

V. Loss Limitations—Loss deductions are limited in four ways.

   A. First, the adjusted basis of the stock limits loss deductions because a shareholder's basis cannot be reduced below zero.

Example
An S corporation had an ordinary loss from business activity of $6,000 and made a $7,000 cash distribution to its sole shareholder during calendar year 2017. The sole shareholder had a stock basis of $8,000 on January 1, 2017. The $7,000 cash distribution would be nontaxable and would reduce stock basis to $1,000. As a result, only $1,000 of the $6,000 ordinary loss would be allowable as a deduction to the shareholder for 2017. The remaining $5,000 of ordinary loss would be carried forward and deducted by the shareholder when there is stock or debt basis to absorb it.

B. Second, the adjusted basis of loans to the corporation by the shareholder can be used for loss deductions once the adjusted basis of the stock is exhausted. However, later increases in basis are used to restore the basis of the debt before basis of the stock.

    1. Debt basis is created when the shareholder loans his or her own funds to the S corporation.

    2. Once reduced, the basis of debt is later increased (but not above its original basis) by **net undistributed income**.

Example
An S corporation incurred losses totaling $50,000. Its sole shareholder (who materially participates in the business and is at-risk) had a stock basis of $30,000 and debt with a basis of $15,000. The shareholder's loss deduction is limited to $45,000. The losses first reduce stock basis to zero, then debt basis is reduced to zero. The excess loss of $5,000 can be carried forward and deducted when there is basis to absorb it.

Example
An S corporation incurred a loss of $20,000 for 2017. Its sole shareholder (who materially participates in the business and is at-risk) had a stock basis of $10,000 and debt with a basis of $15,000. The pass-through of the $20,000 loss would first reduce stock basis to zero, and then reduce debt basis to $5,000.

Assume that for 2018, the same S corporation had ordinary income of $10,000 and made a $4,000 cash distribution to its shareholder during the year. The first $4,000 of basis increase resulting from the pass-through of income would be allocated to stock in order to permit the $4,000 distribution to be nontaxable. The remaining basis increase (net undistributed income of $6,000) would restore debt basis to $11,000 (from $5,000).

C. Third, shareholders may only deduct losses to the extent they are "at risk" for investments in the corporation.

D. Fourth, passive loss limits may also limit loss deductions depending upon the nature of the corporate business and the shareholders' participation in management activities.

E. Unused losses (due to inadequate basis) are carried forward indefinitely (until the adjusted basis of the stock increases or the S election is revoked).

F. If an S corporation contributes appreciated property to a charitable organization, the corporation can deduct the fair market value of the property. However, S corporation shareholders can reduce their basis by only the contributed property's basis.

Example

This year S corporation, an S electing corporation, reported the following:

Gross income	$210,000
Business expenses	283,000
Charitable contributions	14,600

S has two shareholders: PW owns 10% of the stock, and M owns 90%. What amount should PW report this year from S?

S operated at a $73,000 loss, so PW should report $7,300 of loss and $1,460 of charitable contributions. Suppose that PW sold his stock 60 days after the beginning of the year. If PW sold his stock, then (absent a terminating election) the operating loss would be prorated on a daily basis. Hence, S incurred a daily loss of $200 ($73,000/365) and PW's share would be $1,200 ($200 × 60 × 10%). Likewise, the charitable contribution would be $240 ($40 × 60 × 10%).

Example

ABC, a calendar year S corporation, had an ordinary loss of $36,500 this year. TP owned 50% of ABC for the first 40 days of the year before selling the stock to an unrelated party. TP's basis in the stock was $10,000 and TP was a full-time employee of the corporation. What is TP's share of the loss this year?

The share of the loss is $2,000—calculated by multiplying TP's share (50%) of the daily loss ($100) times the number of days TP held the stock (40).

Distributions and Special Taxes

After studying this lesson, you should be able to:

1. Apply gain recognition rule to corporations for distribution of appreciated property.

2. Compute the tax effects of distributions to S corporation shareholders.

3. Define the accumulated adjustments account.

4. Apply built-in gains tax rule for conversions of C corporations to S corporations.

5. Calculate passive investment income tax.

I. **Distributions**—Distributions may trigger corporate gain, but normally represent a return of capital to shareholders.

   A. **Corporate Gain**—The corporation generates gains by distributing appreciated property.

      1. The gain is passed through to shareholders like other income.

> **Example**
> S Corporation distributes land to its sole shareholder. If the land has a value of $100 and an adjusted basis of $80 on the date of distribution, then S Corporation will recognize $20 of income on the distribution. No tax will be imposed on S Corporation. Instead, the gain will be passed through to the shareholder.

   B. **Shareholder Income if Corporation Has No E&P**—A distribution creates a gain to the shareholder if the distribution exceeds the shareholder's *adjusted basis in the stock*.

      1. The amount of a distribution is the amount of cash plus the **value** of any property distributed (less any debt on the property assumed by the shareholder).

      2. Distributions in excess of adjusted basis are taxed as gains from the sale of stock.

      3. **Shortcut**—Distributions in excess of adjusted basis will most likely be taxed as capital gains because stock will most likely be a capital asset in the hands of the shareholder (an asset held for investment).

   C. **Shareholder Income if S Corporation Has E&P**—Shareholders of S corporations with accumulated earnings and profits (E&P) from a previous status as a C corporation are subject to a complex distribution system.

      1. **Shortcut**—An S corporation that has **always** been an S electing corporation will not need to use an accumulated adjustments account unless and until the S election is terminated. In addition, an S corporation, that was previously a C corporation, will not need to use an accumulated adjustments account unless the corporation had earnings and profits from this prior period.

      2. Accumulated undistributed income generated during S status is recorded at the corporate level in the **accumulated adjustments account (AAA)**.

      3. AAA is adjusted in the same way as stock basis except (1) no adjustment is made for tax exempt income (and related expenses) and (2) AAA can be negative (only losses can reduce AAA below zero; distributions cannot create a deficit in AAA).

      4. OAA is the **other adjustments account** that tracks tax-exempt income earned by the corporation.

      5. **Order of distributions**

         a. Distributions follow this order:

            i. First tax-free from AAA (nontaxable; note that distributions from AAA also reduce stock basis)

      ii. Then from E&P (dividend income)

      iii. Next from stock basis, which is a tax-free return of capital

      iv. The remaining distribution is a capital gain

    b. An S corporation can make a **bypass election**, which allows the distribution to first come from E&P and then AAA.

6. Distributions from AAA reduce the balance of AAA (but distributions never reduce AAA below zero—only losses can accomplish this feat).

7. Distributions from AAA and OAA reduce the adjusted basis of the shareholder's stock.

> **Example**
> At the end of this year, ABC corporation (an electing S corporation) has AAA of $100 and E&P of $50. If ABC makes a distribution of $180 to its sole shareholder, the shareholder will report the first $100 as tax-free from the AAA account. Note that this $100 also reduces the basis in the stock. The next $50 is dividend income from the E&P account. The final $30 is a return of capital. If SH had a basis in his ABC stock immediately before the distribution of $120, he would report two sources of income: 1) dividend income of $50 for the distribution from the E&P account, and $10 capital gain (basis of $120 − $100 from AAA − $30 return of capital).

D. Distributions of cash during a minimum one-year period following termination of an S corporation election receive special treatment.

    1. Treated as a tax-free recovery of stock basis to the extent it does not exceed AAA balance.

    2. Since only cash distributions receive this special treatment, the corporation should not distribute property during this post-termination transition period.

II. Built-in Gains Tax—An S corporation can be subject to tax if the corporation sells property that contained a **built-in gain** at the time of the S election.

> **Definition**
> *Built-in Gain Property*: For purposes of a tax on an S corporation, appreciated property (value in excess of adjusted basis) as of the beginning of the first year of the S status.

A. Shortcut—A built-in gains tax is not imposed on a corporation that has always been an S electing corporation.

B. The tax is imposed at the highest corporate rate (35%) and is limited to the net amount of built-in gain at the time of election.

C. The tax can only be imposed for a period of 5 years after the S election is made.

D. In the year of the sell, if property is also sold that had built-in losses at the date of the S election, these built-in losses can offset the built-in gains.

E. The total built-in gain subject to this tax in any given year is also limited to the S corporation's taxable income for that year.

Example
ABC Corporation made an S election this year and, at the time of the election, it held property with a value of $100 and the basis of $80. ABC will be taxed on this $20 built-in gain (at the highest corporate rate) if the property is sold any time during the next 5 years.

For 2017, an S corporation has taxable income of $100,000, which includes a $40,000 long-term capital gain (LTCG) that is also a recognized built-in gain. Since its recognized built-in gain of $40,000 is less than its taxable income, its built-in gains tax for 2017 is $40,000 × 35% = $14,000. Since the built-in gain was a long-term capital gain, the built-in gains tax paid of $14,000 is treated as a long-term capital loss. As a result, a net long-term capital gain of $26,000 ($40,000 LTCG – $14,000 LTCL) passes through to shareholders for 2017.

III. **Passive Investment Income Tax**—An S corporation can be subject to the top corporate tax rate if the corporation reports excessive passive investment income and the corporation has E&P from prior status as a C corporation.

Definition
Passive Income: For purposes of the exam includes interest, dividends (except dividends from a subsidiary to the extent the subsidiary is conducting an active trade or business), royalties, and rents (unless substantial extra services are provided).

    A. Excessive passive income is passive income over 25% of gross receipts.

    B. The IRS may waive this tax if the corporation establishes that it made distributions within a reasonable time of discovering that E&P existed from a prior year.

Example
ABC Corporation made an S election this year and, at the time of the election, it had E&P. This year ABC will be subject to a tax on excessive passive income if it receives interest of $100 and no other revenue.

    C. **Shortcut**—A corporation that has never been a regular C corporation or does not have E&P from a prior period as a C corporation cannot be subject to the corporate tax on excessive net passive income.

IV. **LIFO Recapture**—A C corporation using LIFO that converts to S status must recapture the excess of the inventory's value using a FIFO cost flow assumption over its LIFO tax basis as of the close of its last tax year as a C corporation.

    1. The LIFO recapture is included in the C corporation's gross income, and the tax attributable to its inclusion is payable in four equal installments.

    2. The first installment must be paid by the due date of the tax return for the last C corporation year, with the three remaining installments due by the due dates of the tax returns for the three succeeding taxable years.

Fiduciary Taxation

Income Taxation of Fiduciaries

After studying this lesson, you should be able to:

1. Compute taxable income for fiduciaries.

   Identify items of income in respect of a decedent.

2. Define distributable net income.

3. Determine the effect of distributable net income on the income of the fiduciary and beneficiaries.

Tax Form for This Lesson: Form 1041 (available for download and printing from the lesson overview of your software).

I. **Fiduciaries**—Trusts and estates can be taxed on the income that accrues during the administration of the fiduciary. The trust/estate is taxed on income retained by the fiduciary and not distributed currently to beneficiaries. Income distributed to beneficiaries is reported as income during the beneficiary's tax year in which the estate year ends.

II. **Key Definitions**

Definitions

Trust: A legal entity created by transfer of property from a **grantor**. The purpose of the trust is to hold and administer property for **beneficiaries** according to the terms of the trust instrument. The trust exists for the period determined by the trust instrument and state law.

Terminable Interest: An interest that ends upon the occurrence of a contingency.

Remainderman: A person who receives property after a present interest is terminated.

Contingent Interest: An interest that is created upon the occurrence of a contingency.

III. **Income Concepts**

    A. **Single Taxation**—Income is taxed only once to either the fiduciary or the beneficiary.

        1. A distribution deduction for fiduciary prevents double taxation.

        2. Income taxed to beneficiaries retains its character (a conduit approach).

    B. **Income Computation**—Individual income tax rules generally apply to determining the taxable income for fiduciaries.

        1. Fiduciaries get a personal exemption depending on the type of fiduciary: $600 for estates, $300 for simple trusts and for complex trusts that distribute all of their income currently, and $100 for all other complex trusts.

Definitions

Simple Trust: A trust that (1) must distribute all income currently, (2) make no distributions of corpus currently, and (3) make no current charitable contributions. Any trust that does not qualify as simple must be complex.

Grantor Trust: A trust controlled by the grantor through retained powers or the possibility the property in the trust will revert to the grantor.

2. A trust may be simple in some years and complex in others.

3. Fiduciaries get no standard deduction, but can deduct interest, taxes, charitable contributions, and trustee's fees. Section 179 cannot be used by trusts or estates.

4. When income is distributed currently by the fiduciary, then the fiduciary acts as a conduit and the beneficiaries are taxed on the distributed income.

5. Investment advisory fees of nongrantor trusts and estates generally are subject to the 2% of AGI floor as miscellaneous itemized deductions, unless the fees are not "commonly incurred" by individuals.

   a. Costs that are unique to an estate or trust and not commonly incurred by an individual are not subject to the 2% of AGI floor. Costs not subject to the 2% of AGI floor include the costs of preparing the estate and generation-skipping transfer tax returns, fiduciary income tax returns, and the decedent's final individual tax return.

   b. Also, appraisal fees to determine the FMV of the decedent's assets as of date of death (or alternate valuation date), to determine the value for purposes of making distributions, or as otherwise required to properly prepare the estate or trust's tax returns are not subject to the 2% floor. Additionally, some fiduciary expenses are not subject to the 2% floor, including probate costs, fiduciary bond premiums, legal publication costs of notices to creditors or heirs, and the cost of certified copies of the decedent's death certificate.

6. The executor has the option of deducting administration expenses on the estate tax return or the estate's income tax return. If deducting on the income tax return the executor must indicate that the deduction will not also be taken on the estate tax return. The same option applies to casualty losses.

7. Capital losses offset capital gains, and a net capital loss of up to $3,000 can be deducted with the remainder carried forward.

8. Any unused capital loss and net operating loss (NOL) carryovers from the decedent's final Form 1040 are not allowed as deductions.

C. Administrative expenses can be deducted on the estate income tax return (Form 1041) if the estate irrevocably waives the right to take the deduction on the federal estate tax return (Form 706).

   1. Examples of administrative expenses are fiduciary fees, legal fees, accounting fees, and court costs.

   2. Administrative expenses may be divided between the estate income tax return and the federal estate tax return in any manner desired by the fiduciary (i.e., executor or administrator) of the estate, as long as a waiver is filed for the portion of the administrative expenses that are allocated to the estate income tax return.

D. Fiduciary accounting rules determine what can be disbursed.

   1. Receipts and disbursements of trusts and estates are categorized by the fiduciary instrument or state law as either belonging to income or corpus (principal).

Definition
Corpus: The principal or property in a trust or estate. The income earned on the principal is distinguished from the principal.

   2. Income and deductions are allocated among beneficiaries according to the trust instrument.

E. **Deduction for Distributions**

   1. Fiduciaries are entitled to deduct distributions of **income** to beneficiaries.

   2. Fiduciaries pay income taxes, including an alternative minimum tax (when applicable), if the fiduciary has **undistributed** taxable income.

IV. Distributable Net Income (DNI)

    A. Distributions of Income—Create a distribution deduction for the fiduciary.

        1. The distribution deduction cannot exceed the distributable net income.

Definition

Distributable Net Income (DNI): The amount of accounting "income" that's available to be distributed; typically capital gains belong to corpus and are not part of DNI.

---

        2. Property distributions are not generally treated as dispositions of assets, but instead as distributions of DNI.

        3. Beneficiaries are taxed on the receipt of distributions (to the extent of DNI).

        4. Beneficiaries report income for the beneficiary's tax year in which the estate's or the trust's year-ends.

    B. Calculation of DNI—Requires adjusting taxable income.

        1. Add back personal exemption, net tax-exempt income, and net capital loss.

        2. Subtract net capital gains allocable to corpus (keep net capital gains allocable to income beneficiaries or charity).

        3. For estates and complex trusts, there is a two-tier system of allocating income and deductions and a "throwback" rule to discourage tax avoidance by timing trust distributions.

Example

This year an estate reports $50k of capital gains (allocable to corpus), $100k of interest income, $25k of administrative expenses (allocable to income), and $12k of real estate taxes. Taxable income (before the distribution deduction) is $112,400 ($50,000 + $100,000 − $25,000 − $12,000 − $600). DNI is $63,000 calculated by adding back the personal exemption of $600 and subtracting out the net capital gains of $50k.

---

        4. Shortcut—To calculate DNI, subtract net capital gains from accounting income.

    C. Income Tax Formula for Fiduciaries

Gross Income

Less:

        Interest

        Taxes

        Business expenses

        Depreciation

        Charitable contributions

Less Distribution Deduction (maximum is DNI)

Less Personal exemption

Taxable Income

× Tax Rates

equals Gross Tax

Less credits

Plus additional taxes

Tax Payable

V. Procedural Rules

A. Trusts must use a calendar year, but estates may choose any year-end. Both must file by the 15th day of the fourth month after the year-end (if the 15th falls on the weekend or holiday, the due date is the next business day following the 15th). Beginning in 2016, an automatic extension of five and one-half months is allowed to file income tax returns for Form 1041.

B. Trusts must pay estimated income taxes, but estates need only pay estimated income taxes after their first two tax years of operation.

C. Fiduciaries must file an income tax return (Form 1041) if gross income exceeds $600, if the fiduciary has taxable income, or if a nonresident alien is a beneficiary.

D. The alternative minimum tax applies to estates and trusts and is computed in the same manner as for individuals. The AMT exemption for an estate or trust is $24,100 for 2017.

E. An estate or trust is subject to the 3.8% Medicare Contribution Tax on net investment income. The tax is imposed on the lessor of (a) an estate or trust's undistributed net investment income, or (b) the excess of an estate or trust's AGI over the dollar amount at which an estate or trust's highest income tax bracket begins.

> **Note**
> *Any estate tax paid due to the IRD is deductible as a miscellaneous itemized deduction (not a 2% itemized deduction) on the individual income tax return.*

VI. Income in Respect of a Decedent

Income in Respect of a Decedent—Income in respect of a decedent (IRD) occurs if a decedent was entitled to receive income at the date of death, but the income was not included in the decedent's final tax return. Hence, the income must be taxed as income to the estate (because it has not yet been subjected to any income tax) and also included on the estate tax return (because it is part of the property owned by the decedent at the time of death).

A. Income and expenses are reported on a decedent's final individual income tax return up to the date of death.

1. Income actually and constructively received through the date of death is included on the final return. When the decedent was on the cash basis, some income will not be received until after the date of death.

> **Definition**
> *Income in Respect of a Decedent*: Income earned by the decedent but not included in the decedent's final return.

> **Example**
> D died on July 10. D is a cash basis taxpayer who receives a paycheck at the end of each month. The paycheck covering the period up to July 10 is not received until the end of July. It will be income in respect of a decedent.

2. Deductible expenses paid through the date of death are properly claimed in the decedent's final return.

B. Income (or expenses) in respect of a decedent is taxed as income to the estate (or beneficiary if distributed).

> **Definition**
> *Expenses in Respect of a Decedent*: Deductible expenses paid after the date of death.

C. There is no step up in basis to fair market value for income in respect of decedent. This income has not yet been subject to income tax.

D. The income is included in **both** the estate income tax return and the estate tax return.

E. Accrued expenses paid after the date of death attributed to income in respect of a decedent are deducted on **both** the estate income tax return and the estate tax return.

F. Estates (or beneficiaries) that are taxed on income in respect of a decedent are entitled to deduct the estate tax on this property.

VII. Treatment of Simple Trust and Beneficiaries

A. Income is taxed to beneficiaries, not to trust.

B. Beneficiaries are taxed on the income required to be distributed (up to DNI), even though not actually distributed during the year.

C. Income passes through to beneficiaries retaining its characteristics (e.g., tax-exempt income passes through retaining its exempt status).

D. If multiple beneficiaries, DNI is prorated in proportion to the amount of required distribution to each beneficiary.

VIII. Treatment of Complex Trust and Beneficiaries

A. A two-tier income distribution system is used.

1. First tier: Distributions of the first tier are income amounts that are required to be distributed and include distributions that can be paid out of income or corpus, to the extent paid out of income.

2. Second tier: Distributions of the second tier are all other amounts that are actually paid during the year or are required to be paid.

B. DNI is first allocated to distributions in the first tier. Any remaining DNI is prorated to distributions in the second tier.

Example
A trust has DNI of $9,000. The trust instrument requires that $6,000 of income be distributed annually to Alan. Further, it permits distributions to Baker and Carr of income or corpus at the trustee's discretion. For the current year, the trustee distributes $6,000 to Alan, $4,000 to Baker, and $2,000 to Carr.

Since Alan's distribution is a first tier distribution, all $6,000 distributed is taxable to Alan. This leaves only $3,000 of DNI to be allocated to the second tier distributions to Baker and Carr. Since DNI would be allocated in proportion to the amounts distributed, $2,000 of Baker's distribution and $1,000 of Carr's distribution would be taxable.

Tax Credits

Business Tax Credits

> This lesson continues the discussion of tax credits from the earlier lesson, "Personal Tax Credits".
>
> **After studying this lesson, you should be able to:**
>
> 1. Determine when business tax credits are allowable and list necessary requirements.
>
> 2. Compute the foreign tax credit and its effect on the tax liability.

I. **Foreign Tax Credit**—The U.S. taxes income from all sources, including income from foreign countries. The purpose of this credit is to prevent double taxation of foreign income that is subject to income tax in the foreign jurisdiction.

    A. The credit is limited to the lower of the foreign tax paid, or the proportion of U.S. tax allocable to foreign sourced income (known as the foreign tax credit limitation).

        1. The proportion of U.S. tax allocable to foreign sourced income (foreign tax credit limitation) is determined by multiplying U.S. tax times the ratio of foreign taxable income to total taxable income.

Example
TP records 20% of his income from abroad. TP can claim a foreign tax credit in the amount of the lesser of his foreign tax paid or 20% of the U.S. tax paid.

        2. Excess foreign tax credits carryback one year and forward 10 years. The excess amount is the foreign taxes paid or accrued for a tax year that exceeds the foreign tax credit limitation.

    B. In lieu of a credit, a taxpayer can elect to mitigate foreign taxes in two other ways.

        1. Taxpayers can claim the foreign tax as an itemized deduction.

        2. Taxpayers can elect to exclude income earned (in excess of housing costs) while a bona fide resident in a foreign country. The exclusion is a maximum of $102,100 (2017; adjusted for inflation) if the taxpayer is physically present in the foreign country for at least 330 days in any 12 consecutive months.

Example
TP earned $99,000 from working 340 days in France in 2017. TP can exclude $95,107 (340/365 × $102,100) because he was in residence more than 330 days.

II. **General Business Credit**—The **general business credit** consists of a combination of credits designed to subsidize certain activities. While each credit is calculated independently, the combination of credits is subject to an overall limit.

    A. The overall credit is limited to "net regular" tax.

Definition
Net Regular Tax Liability: The regular tax less personal credits.

1. The limit is:

> Net regular liability
>
> plus AMT less nonrefundable credits (not including AMT credit)
>
> Less 25% of net regular liability over $25,000.

B. The upshot of the credit is that the business credit cannot offset all of the regular tax if the liability exceeds $25,000.

    1. Unused credits are carried back one year and then forward 20 years.

    2. Credits cannot reduce the regular liability below the "tentative" tax required to be paid under the alternative minimum tax.

Examples

TP has a net regular tax liability of $125,000 this year. TP has a general business tax credit of $70,000 and no other credits.

Question: What amount of general business tax credit is TP eligible to claim?

Answer: The maximum credit TP could claim would be $100,000 ($125,000 − ($125,000 − 25,000) × .25,000). Since he has a credit of only $70,000, he can claim the entire credit.

Question: What if TP also had a tentative minimum tax liability of $105,000?

Answer: If his tentative tax was $105,000, he could only reduce his regular tax liability to the amount of the tentative tax by claiming a maximum credit of $20,000, because the credit cannot reduce the regular tax liability below the tentative minimum tax for AMT purposes.

III. The Rehabilitation Credit—This is typical of the credits available under the general business credit. There are a number of other credits that are available for specific activities. Each credit has unique requirements and limits, but the rehabilitation credit is a good example.

    A. The rehabilitation credit percentage depends upon the type of expenditure.

        1. Expenditures to rehabilitate property placed in service before 1936 are eligible for a 10% credit.

        2. Expenditures to rehabilitate certified historic structure are eligible for a 20% credit.

    B. Qualifying expenditures are often used to adjust basis, and may be subject to recapture.

        1. The adjusted basis of the property is reduced by the amount of credit.

        2. Rehabilitation credit is recaptured if the building is held less than five years (the recapture rate is 20% per year).

IV. Small Employer Health Insurance Credit

    A. An eligible small employer (ESE) can claim a credit equal to 50% of its nonelective contributions for health insurance for its employees (25% for small tax-exempt employers).

    B. To be eligible for the credit, an ESE has to contribute at least 50% of the cost of the employee's insurance premiums under a contribution arrangement.

    C. The full amount of the credit is available only to an ESE with 10 or fewer full-time equivalent employees and whose employees have average annual full-time equivalent wages of less than $26,200 (2017). The credit is fully phased out once the number of full-time employees reaches 25 and/or the average wages reach $52,400 (2017).

D. For purposes of the credit, the owner of a business and specified relatives are not treated as employees (and thus, no credit is allowed for the employer contributions for the health insurance of those employees).

E. Any unused credits may be able to be carried back or carried forward.

V. Work Opportunity Tax Credit (WOTC)

A. This credit is calculated on the amount of wages paid per eligible employee during the first year of employment. The credit is 40% of qualified wages, with a maximum credit of $2,400.

B. The credit is elective.

C. The credit is targeted at certain employee groups, such as veterans and long-term unemployment recipients.

D. The WOTC reduces the deduction for wages.

VI. Research Credit

A. Incremental research expenditures are eligible for a 20% credit. The research must be conducted within the U.S. and does not apply to research for commercial production, surveys, or social science research.

B. Taxpayers may elect to use an alternative simplified research credit. This is equal to 14% of the excess of qualified research expenses over 50% of the average research expenses for the last three years.

C. An eligible small business (ESB) can also reduce its AMT liability by the research credit. An ESB's average gross receipts for the previous three years must not exceed $50 million.

D. No deduction is allowed for research expenditures used to compute the research credit.

VII. Low-Income Housing Credit

A. The amount of credit for owners of low-income housing projects depends on (1) whether the taxpayer acquires existing housing or whether the housing is newly constructed or rehabilitated, and (2) whether or not the housing project is financed by tax-exempt bonds or other federally subsidized financing. The applicable credit rates are the appropriate percentages issued by the IRS for the month in which the building is placed in service.

B. The amount on which the credit is computed is the portion of the total depreciable basis of a qualified housing project that reflects the portion of the housing units within the project that are occupied by qualified low-income individuals.

C. The credit is claimed each year (for a 10-year period) beginning with the year that the property is placed in service. The first-year credit is prorated to reflect the date placed in service.

VIII. Disabled Access Credit

A. A tax credit is available to an eligible small business for expenditures incurred to make the business accessible to disabled individuals. The amount of this credit is equal to 50% of the amount of the eligible access expenditures for a year that exceed $250 but do not exceed $10,250.

B. An *eligible small business* is one that either (1) had gross receipts for the preceding tax year that did not exceed $1 million, or (2) had no more than 30 full-time employees during the preceding tax year and (3) elects to have this credit apply.

C. *Eligible access expenditures* are amounts incurred to comply with the requirements of the Americans with Disabilities Act of 1990 and include amounts incurred for the purpose of removing architectural, communication, physical, or transportation barriers that prevent a business from being accessible to, or usable by, disabled individuals; amounts incurred to provide qualified readers to visually impaired individuals; and amounts incurred to acquire or modify equipment or devices for disabled individuals. Expenses incurred in connection with new construction are not eligible for the credit.

D. This credit is included as part of the general business credit; no deduction or credit is allowed under any other Code provision for any amount for which a disabled access credit is allowed.

IX. Empowerment Zone Employment Credit

A. The credit is generally equal to 20% of the first $15,000 of wages paid to each employee who is a resident of a designated empowerment zone and performs substantially all services within the zone in an employer's trade or business.

B. The deduction for wages must be reduced by the amount of credit.

X. Employer Social Security Credit

A. Credit allowed to food and beverage establishments for the employer's portion of FICA tax (7.65%) attributable to reported tips in excess of those tips treated as wages for purposes of satisfying the minimum wage provisions of the Fair Labor Standards Act.

B. No deduction is allowed for any amount taken into account in determining the credit.

XI. Employer-Provided Child Care Credit

A. Employers who provide child care facilities to their employees during normal working hours are eligible for a credit equal to 25% of qualified child care expenditures and 10% of qualified child care resource and referral expenditures. The maximum credit is $150,000 per year and is subject to a 10-year recapture rule.

B. *Qualified child care expenditures* include amounts paid to acquire, construct, and rehabilitate property that is to be used as a qualified child care facility (e.g., training costs of employees, scholarship programs, compensation for employees with high levels of child care training).

    1. To prevent a double benefit, the basis of qualifying property is reduced by the amount of credit, and the amount of qualifying expenditures that would otherwise be deductible must be reduced by the amount of credit.

Other Tax Issues

Tax Planning Strategies for Business Entities

> **After studying this lesson, you should be able to:**
>
> **1.** Explain common tax planning strategies for companies.
>
> **2.** Describe planning strategies for the alternative minimum tax.
>
> **3.** Understand common corporate tax planning strategies.

I. Tax Planning for the AMT

  A. Taxpayers should adopt planning strategies to avoid the corporate AMT.

    1. Reduce adjustments and preferences that increase AMT income, such as certain types of tax-exempt interest.

    2. Consider the deductions that are not allowed for AMT purposes and minimize those in years when one is subject to the AMT.

  B. If the corporate AMT cannot be avoided, it may be advantageous to accelerate income into the AMT year since it will be taxed at a maximum rate of 20%. However, a level of income will eventually be reached where the taxpayer is no longer subject to the AMT but to the regular income tax rates, which may be higher than 20%. Income should be accelerated until this level of income is reached.

  C. Alternative Minimum Tax—If a taxpayer is not subject to AMT in 2017 but expects to be in 2018, accelerate expenses that are not deductible for AMT into 2017. Also accelerate expenses into 2017 that would increase adjusted current earnings in 2018.

II. Tax Planning for Charitable Contributions

  A. Contributions of Inventory

    1. A corporation's contribution of inventory or depreciables or real property used in its trade or business to charities that use the property in a manner related to the exempt purpose and solely for the care of the ill, needy, or infants, or where the property is used for research purposes under specified conditions, is subject to special rules.

    2. The deduction is the lower of:

$$\text{AB of property} + 50\% \times (\text{FMV} - \text{AB}), \quad \text{or} \quad 2 \times \text{AB}$$

    3. This rule applies for contributions of "wholesome" food inventory by corporations and other businesses to charities that use the food in an appropriate manner. These contributions can also be deducted up to 15% of taxable income (instead of the regular 10% limit). Note that this rule applies to all businesses, not just corporations.

  B. The corporation can elect to deduct accrued contributions if the contributions are actually paid in the first three and a half months following the year-end.

III. Consideration of Nontax Factors in Tax Planning

  A. Tax effects should never be the only factors considered for a decision.

  B. Nontax factors must also be considered.

  C. It is possible that the alternative with the best tax outcome increases costs in other areas for the company.

D. The goal is to maximize after-tax income, not minimize taxes.

Example

Assume that a corporation is considering two alternative strategies. The revenue, tax savings, and nontax costs associated with each strategy is as follows:

	Marginal Revenue	Marginal Tax Savings	Marginal Nontax Costs
Strategy A	$100,000	($30,000)	$30,000
Strategy B	$100,000	($40,000)	$50,000

Note that the tax-minimizing strategy is Strategy B since it reduces taxes by $40,000 as compared to $30,000 for Strategy A. However, Strategy B increases tax costs by $50,000 which is $20,000 more than the $30,000 increase for Strategy A. The net change in marginal costs is zero for Strategy A and $10,000 for Strategy B, with revenue being the same ($100,000) for both. Therefore, the optimal strategy that maximizes after-tax income is Strategy A (net income is $100,000 for A and $90,000 for B), while the tax minimizing strategy is Strategy B.

IV. Other Tax Planning Strategies

A. Consider hiring children as employees as their wages will be taxed at a lower tax rate. Make sure that compensation is reasonable.

B. When forming a business entity, make sure that the rules are met to defer gains and losses.

C. For partnerships, increase basis in partnership interest with partnership debt so that additional losses can be used by partners on their tax returns.

D. For regular corporations, use tax-free fringe benefits to maximize benefits to employees/owners and their family members.

Business Entity Choice

After studying this lesson, you should be able to:

1. Identify **the legal structures for business entities**.

2. Describe the permissible tax entity forms for each business entity type under the check-the-box regulations.

3. Compare and contrast tax entity forms on key characteristics.

4. Explain the advantages and disadvantages of partnership status.

5. List the key similarities and differences of S corporations and partnerships.

I. **Legal Forms**—There are various legal forms that owners can choose for their business, each with certain tax and nontax advantages and disadvantages.

   A. Most common legal forms include:

      1. Sole proprietorships (not a separate entity)

      2. Corporations

      3. General partnerships

      4. Limited partnerships

      5. Limited liability companies

      6. Limited liability partnerships

      7. Business trusts

   B. These legal forms fall into one of the following tax classifications:

      1. Corporations (C and S)

      2. Partnerships

      3. Trusts

      4. Sole proprietorship (individual files on Schedule C)

   C. **Types of Partnerships**

      1. **General partnerships** exist when two or more partners join together and do not specifically provide that one or more partners is a limited partner. Since each general partner has unlimited liability, creditors can reach the personal assets of a general partner to satisfy partnership debts, including a malpractice judgment against the partnership even though the partner was not personally involved in the malpractice.

      2. **Limited partnerships** have two classes of partners, with at least one general partner (who has the same rights and responsibilities as a partner in a general partnership) and at least one limited partner. A limited partner generally cannot participate in the active management of the partnership and, in the event of losses, generally can lose no more than his or her own capital contribution. A limited partnership is often the preferred entity of choice for real estate ventures requiring significant capital contributions.

      3. **Limited liability partnerships** differ from general partnerships in that with an LLP, a partner is not liable for damages resulting from the negligence, malpractice, or fraud committed by other partners. However, each partner is personally liable for his or her own negligence, malpractice, or fraud. LLPs are often used by service providers such as architects, accountants, attorneys, and physicians.

      4. **Limited liability companies** that do not elect to be treated as an association taxable as a corporation are subject to the rules applicable to partnerships (a single-member LLC would

be disregarded as an entity separate from its owner). An LLC combines the nontax advantage of limited liability for each and every owner of the entity with the tax advantage of pass-through treatment and the flexibility of partnership taxation. The LLC structure is generally available to both nonprofessional service providers and capital-intensive companies.

5. **Electing large partnerships** are partnerships that have elected to be taxed under a simplified reporting system that does not require as much separate reporting to partners as does a regular partnership. For example, charitable contributions are deductible by the partnership (subject to a 10% of taxable income limitation), and the Section 179 expense election is deducted in computing partnership ordinary income and not separately passed through to partners. To qualify, the partnership must not be a service partnership or engaged in commodity trading, must have at least 100 partners, and must file an election to be taxed as an electing large partnership. A partnership will cease to be an electing large partnership if it has fewer than 100 partners for a taxable year.

II. **Check-the-Box Regulations**—Under the check-the-box regulations, unincorporated entities may elect to be taxed as an association (corporation) or a partnership.

A. Some associations are automatically taxed as corporations and are not eligible to make an election. These *per se* corporations include business entities formed under statutes that refer to the entities as incorporated. These entities are taxed as either S corporations or C Corporations.

1. *Per se* corporations include:

    a. Entities incorporated under state law

    b. Insurance companies

    c. State-chartered banks, if deposits are insured by FDIC

    d. Publicly-traded partnerships

    e. Specified foreign entities

2. Certain other entities (such as REITs, tax-exempt organizations, etc.) are also classified as corporations.

B. For entities not listed as *per se* corporations, the default options for the entity is a partnership when the business has more than two owners. This default rule typically applies to partnerships and limited liability companies. If an entity does not prefer the default classification, it can elect to be taxed as a corporation.

C. If an entity has only one owner, then the default classification is that the entity is "disregarded" for federal income tax purposes. These entities can also elect to be taxed as a corporation.

1. **Disregarded** means that the entity, while clearly a distinct entity for legal purposes, is ignored for federal income tax purposes.

2. An LLC owned 100% by an individual is treated as a sole proprietorship.

3. An LLC owned 100% by a corporation is treated as a division of the corporation on Form 1120.

D. An election under the check-the-box regulations is effective if filed within the first 75 days of the tax year.

E. An election can be changed after five years or with IRS permission.

F. A business trust is taxed as a trust on Form 1041.

III. **Tax Entities Can be Compared and Contrasted on the Following Characteristics**—(Note: Refer to the chart at the end of this lesson for a summary of this material.)

A. **Limited Liability**—Corporate shareholders and LLC members have limited liability, as do limited partners.

B. **Double Taxation**—The only entity subject to double taxation is C corporations. Income is taxed to the corporation and then a second time when paid to shareholders as a dividend.

C. Retain Income at Lower Current Tax Cost—The entity that may be able to retain income at a lower tax cost is the C corporation (this depends on the level of current tax rates for corporations and individuals). This is not possible with flow-through entities since income flows to the owners even if not distributed.

Example
Assume that the highest corporate/individual tax rate is 40%/70%. C corporations would pay tax at a 40% rate and retain the remaining income. Note that the second level of tax is avoided if dividends are not paid but the funds are used to expand the business. For LLCs, partnerships, and S corporations, the income would flow through to the owners and potentially be taxed at 70%.

D. Tax-Deferred Contributions—While both corporations and partnerships can be formed in such a manner that realized gains/losses are deferred, the rules are much more favorable for partnerships (and LLCs) since there is no 80% control test requirement for deferrals for partnerships.

E. Distributions—The distributions rules favor partnerships (and LLCs). Gain is recognized on partnership distributions only if the cash distributed exceeds the partner's basis in his or her partnership interest. If a corporation distributes appreciated property as a dividend, redemption, or liquidation, gain will be recognized to the corporation (for the appreciation) and potentially to the shareholder (double taxation) as well.

F. Owner Basis for Entity Level Debt—Only partners in a partnership and LLC members can increase their basis in their ownership interest for entity level debt. This benefits the partner/member since losses can be deducted on the owner's tax return only to the extent of basis in the ownership interest. This is the reason that partnerships are often used for tax shelters.

G. Fringe Benefits—Partners in a partnership are not eligible to benefit from many fringe benefit exclusions because partners who work for the partnership are not considered to be employees. This same rule applies to S corporation shareholders who own 2% or more of the S corporation.

IV. Characteristics of Partnerships

A. Advantages

1. Single taxation

2. **Flexibility**—Partners can allocate income, expenses, credits, and all other tax items in any manner as long as the allocation has substantial economic effect.

Example
Partners A and B agree to share income 50/50 for Year 1 but share losses 70/30. For Year 2 A and B change the income sharing ratio to 40/60. These allocations are permissible because of the flexibility afforded to the allocation of partnership income.

3. Basis increase for debt

4. Tax-deferred contributions/admissions

5. Distributions/withdrawals rarely produce gain to the partners

B. Disadvantages

1. Unlimited liability for general partners

2. Limited partners have limited management rights.

V. Comparison of Partnerships and S Corporations

A. Key Similarities

1. Both are flow-through entities with single taxation.

2. LLC members, limited partners, and S corporation shareholders have limited liability (but general partners do not),

3. Both have restrictions on the year-end that must be used for the entity.

B. Key Differences

1. Partners have flexibility with profit and loss sharing ratios. S corporations must allocate all tax items according to the percentage of stock owned by each shareholder.

2. The built-in gain rules that apply to partnerships do not apply to S corporations.

3. Income allocations from partnerships to general partners are subject to the self-employment tax. Income allocations from S corporations are not subject to the self- employment tax.

4. Partners receive a basis increase for partnership debt whereas S corporation shareholders do not.

Comparison of Business Entities					
Issue	C Corporation	S Corporation	Partnership	Multi-Member LLC	Sole Proprietorship
Limited liability	Yes	Yes	No—General Yes—Limited	Yes	No
Double taxation	Yes	No	No	No	No
Retain income at lower tax loss	Depends on relative tax rates	No	No	No	N/A
Tax-deferred contributions	Possibly—subject to control test	Possibly—subject to control test	Yes	Yes	N/A
Double taxation on distributions	Yes	Possibly	No	No	No
Owner's basis for entity level debt	No	No	Yes	Yes	N/A

Multiple Choice Questions

I. Ethics, Professional Responsibilities, and Federal Tax Procedures

Ethics and Responsibilities in Tax Practice

Regulations Governing Practice before the Internal Revenue Service

AICPA.120604REG

1. Under Treasury Circular 230, which of the following actions of a CPA tax advisor is characteristic of a best practice in rendering tax advice?

   A. Requesting written evidence from a client that the fee proposal for tax advice has been approved by the board of directors.
   B. Recommending to the client that the advisor's tax advice be made orally instead of in a written memorandum.
   C. Establishing relevant facts, evaluating the reasonableness of assumptions and representations, and arriving at a conclusion supported by the law and facts in a tax memorandum.
   D. Requiring the client to supply a written representation, signed under penalties of perjury, concerning the facts and statements provided to the CPA for preparing a tax memorandum.

AICPA.101157REG

2. Pursuant to Treasury Circular 230, which of the following statements about the return of a client's records is correct?

   A. The client's records are to be destroyed upon the submission of a tax return.
   B. The practitioner may retain copies of the client's records.
   C. The existence of a dispute over fees generally relieves the practitioner of responsibility to return the client's records.
   D. The practitioner does **not** need to return any client records that are necessary for the client to comply with the client's federal tax returns.

assess.AICPA.REG.ethics.230-0001

3. While preparing a tax return for a new client and reviewing the client's prior-year return, a CPA noticed an error made by the client's former tax preparer. According to Treasury Department Circular 230, which of the following is the CPA specifically required to do in this case?

   A. Contact the tax preparer who made the error and suggest that an amended return be prepared for the client.
   B. Inform the client of the error and insist that the return be amended.
   C. Inform the client of the error and advise of the consequences.
   D. Advise the client to contact the tax preparer of the prior-year return.

Internal Revenue Code and Regulations Related to Tax Return Preparers

AICPA.101155REG

4. Louis, the volunteer treasurer of a nonprofit organization and a member of its board of directors, compiles the data and fills out its annual Form 990, *Return of Organization Exempt from Income Tax*. Under the Internal Revenue Code, Louis is **not** considered a tax return preparer because:

   A. He is a member of the board of directors.
   B. The return does **not** contain a claim for a tax refund.
   C. He is **not** compensated.
   D. Returns for nonprofit organizations are exempt from the preparer rules.

AICPA.100991REG-SIM

5. Which of the following will not get CPA Sandy in trouble with the IRS?

   A. Failing to furnish copies of returns to her clients.
   B. Failing to sign returns she prepares and files.
   C. Failure to furnish her preparer's identifying number to her clients.
   D. Failure to keep copies of the returns she prepares.

Licensing and Disciplinary Systems

AICPA.100996REG-SIM

6. Which of the following can grant a CPA license?

   A. A state board of accountancy.
   B. The AICPA.
   C. The Securities Exchange Commission.
   D. All of the above.

AICPA.960502REG-BL

7. Which of the following bodies ordinarily would have the authority to suspend or revoke a CPA's license to practice public accounting?

A. The SEC.
B. The AICPA.
C. A state CPA society.
D. A state board of accountancy.

AICPA.081903REG-1D

8. When an ethics complaint carrying national implications arises, which entity typically handles it?

A. SEC.
B. PCAOB.
C. State CPA society.
D. AICPA.

Federal Tax Practice and Procedures

Substantiation and Disclosure of Tax Positions

sub.disc.tax.pos.002

9. Fitely hired a tax accountant whom his attorney recommended. The accountant, Tilder, recommended that Fitely take a particular tax position that resulted in an understatement of taxes and the IRS is now seeking to penalize Fitely. In order to establish a good faith defense against the 20% understatement penalty, which of the following does Fitely need to establish:

A. That Tiler was a competent professional.
B. That Fitely gave Tilder all necessary and accurate information.
C. That Fitely actually relied in good faith on Tilder's judgment.
D. All of the above.

sub.disc.tax.pos.003

10. Which of the following burdens of proof must be met when a disclosed position regarding a particular individual deduction is evaluated to determine whether it was taken in good faith.

A. ≥ 10% chance of being sustained
B. ≥ 20% chance of being sustained
C. ≥ 40% chance of being sustained
D. >50% chance of being sustained

sub.disc.tax.pos.001

11. Taxpayer Clegg would certainly like to take a particular deduction that is barred by an IRS regulation. However, after considerable research Clegg's tax attorney believes that there is a one-third chance that a court would overturn the regulation as invalidly promulgated by the IRS. What should Clegg do?

A. Take the deduction without disclosure.
B. Take the deduction, but disclose it.
C. Not take the deduction.
D. All of the above.

Taxpayer Penalties

aq.tax.pen.006_2017

12. Slim is considering taking an aggressive tax position on his income tax return. His experienced tax CPA has evaluated the position carefully and determined that there is a one in four chance that it will, if challenged, be sustained. What should Slim do?

A. Take the position but not disclose it.
B. Take the position and disclose it.
C. Not take the position.
D. All of the choices.

aq.tax.pen.005_2017

13. ABC Corporation, a Chapter C corporation, had a correct tax amount of $1,000,000 but reported only $800,000. There is no claim of fraud. Is this a "substantial understatement" that will subject ABC to the 20% understatement penalty?

A. Yes, and its penalty will be $40,000.
B. Yes, and its penalty will be $20,000.
C. Yes, and its penalty will be $10,000.
D. No.

aq.tax.pen.002_2017

14. Xina carelessly filed her taxes 10 months late. She owed $100,000 in taxes. What is Xina's late filing penalty?

A. $100,000
B. $75,000
C. $50,000
D. $25,000

Sources of Tax Authority and Research

AICPA.101091REG-SIM

15. Which of the following type of regulations cannot be cited as authority to support a tax position?

A. Legislative regulations.
B. Interpretive regulations.
C. Procedural regulations.
D. Proposed regulations.

AICPA.060811REG-P2-AR

16. In evaluating the hierarchy of authority in tax law, which of the following carries the greatest authoritative value for tax planning of transactions?

A. Internal Revenue Code.
B. IRS regulations.

C. Tax court decisions.

D. IRS agents' reports.

AICPA.101092REG-SIM

17. Which of the following courts is not a court of original jurisdiction?

A. United States Tax Court.

B. United States District Court.

C. United States Court of Appeals.

D. United States Court of Federal Claims.

AICPA.101093REG-SIM

18. All of the following are administrative sources of the tax law except:

A. Private letter rulings.

B. Technical advice memoranda.

C. Revenue rulings.

D. Committee reports.

AICPA.120713REG

19. Which Senate committee considers new tax legislation?

A. Budget.

B. Finance.

C. Appropriations.

D. Rules and Administration.

Tax Practice and Procedure

AICPA.120726REG

20. An IRS agent has just completed an examination of a corporation and issued a "no change" report. Which of the following statements about that situation is correct?

A. The taxpayer may **not** amend the tax return for that taxable year.

B. The IRS generally does **not** reopen the examination except in cases involving fraud or other similar misrepresentation.

C. The IRS may **not** reopen the examination.

D. The IRS may **not** examine any other tax return of the corporation for a period of one year.

AICPA.101119REG-SIM

21. Which of the following documents does NOT govern the conduct of a CPA who is engaged in providing tax services?

A. AICPA's Code of Professional Conduct

B. AICPA's Statements on Standards for Tax Services

C. Circular 230

D. Internal Revenue Service Audit Guides

AICPA.101118REG-SIM

22. If a taxpayer receives a *30-day letter* from the Internal Revenue Service, the taxpayer:

A. Must pay the tax deficiency or respond to the issues raised through written correspondence to the IRS within 30 days of the date of the letter.

B. May ignore the letter and take no action.

C. Must pay the tax deficiency or file a petition with the Tax Court within 30 days of the date of the letter.

D. Must pay the tax deficiency and file a petition with the District Court within 30 days of the date of the letter.

AICPA.921106REG-P2-AR

23. On April 15, 2016, a married couple filed their joint 2015 calendar-year return showing gross income of $120,000.

Their return had been prepared by a professional tax preparer who mistakenly omitted $45,000 of income, which the preparer in good faith considered to be nontaxable. No information with regard to this omitted income was disclosed on the return or attached statements.

By what date must the Internal Revenue Service assert a notice of deficiency before the statute of limitations expires?

A. April 15, 2022.

B. December 31, 2021.

C. April 15, 2019.

D. December 31, 2018.

AICPA.940518REG-AR

24. A calendar-year taxpayer files an individual tax return for 2015 on March 20, 2016. The taxpayer neither committed fraud nor omitted amounts in excess of 25% of gross income on the tax return.

What is the latest date that the Internal Revenue Service can assess tax and assert a notice of deficiency?

A. March 20, 2019.

B. March 20, 2018.

C. April 15, 2019.

D. April 15, 2018.

Compliance Responsibilities

AICPA.951116REG-AR

25. A civil fraud penalty can be imposed on a corporation that underpays tax by

   A. Omitting income as a result of inadequate recordkeeping.
   B. Failing to report income it erroneously considered not to be part of corporate profits.
   C. Filing an incomplete return with an appended statement, making clear that the return is incomplete.
   D. Maintaining false records and reporting fictitious transactions to minimize corporate tax liability.

AICPA.120729REG

26. Sam's year 2 taxable income was $175,000 with a corresponding tax liability of $30,000. For year 3, Sam expects taxable income of $250,000 and a tax liability of $50,000. In order to avoid a penalty for underpayment of estimated tax, what is the minimum amount of year 3 estimated tax payments that Sam can make?

   A. $30,000
   B. $33,000
   C. $45,000
   D. $50,000

AICPA.940520REG-AR

27. Which, if any, of the following could result in penalties against an income tax return preparer?

   I. Knowing or reckless disclosure or use of tax information obtained in preparing a return.
   II. A willful attempt to understate any client's tax liability on a return or claim for refund.

   A. Neither I nor II.
   B. I only.
   C. II only.
   D. Both I and II.

AICPA.950519REG-AR

28. Chris Baker's adjusted gross income on her 2016 tax return was $160,000. The amount covered a 12-month period. For the 2017 tax year, Baker may avoid the penalty for the underpayment of estimated tax if the timely estimated tax payments equal the required annual amount of

   I. 90% of the tax on the return for the current year paid in four equal installments.
   II. 100% of prior year's tax liability paid in four equal installments.

   A. I only.
   B. II only.

   C. Both I and II.
   D. Neither I nor II.

AICPA.010505REG-AR

29. A taxpayer filed his income tax return after the due date but neglected to file an extension form. The return indicated a tax liability of $50,000 and taxes withheld of $45,000.

   On what amount would the penalties for late filing and late payment be computed?

   A. $0
   B. $5,000
   C. $45,000
   D. $50,000

Legal Duties and Responsibilities

Common Law Duties and Liabilities to Clients and Third Parties

AICPA.930504REG-BL

30. A CPA's duty of due care to a client most likely will be breached when a CPA

   A. Gives a client an oral instead of written report.
   B. Gives a client incorrect advice based on an honest error of judgment.
   C. Fails to give tax advice that saves the client money.
   D. Fails to follow generally accepted auditing standards.

AICPA.930502REG-BL

31. A CPA will most likely be negligent when the CPA fails to

   A. Correct errors discovered in the CPA's previously issued audit reports.
   B. Detect all of a client's fraudulent activities.
   C. Include a negligence disclaimer in the CPA's engagement letter.
   D. Warn a client's customers of embezzlement by the client's employees.

AICPA.930503REG-BL

32. Which of the following elements, if present, would support a finding of constructive fraud on the part of a CPA?

   A. Gross negligence in applying generally accepted auditing standards.
   B. Ordinary negligence in applying generally accepted accounting principles.
   C. Identified third party users.
   D. Scienter.

Privileged Communications, Confidentiality, and Privacy Acts

AICPA.101044REG-SIM

33. Trego is a CPA. Under which of the following circumstances would it be permissible for Trego to share confidential client information?

   A. He has been hospitalized on April 14 and needs to share information with his partner, Tandy, who will complete a client's tax return before the April 15 deadline.
   B. A client has filed a complaint with the State Board of Accountancy about Trego's work, and he needs to show the Board confidential information to prove that he acted professionally throughout the engagement.
   C. None of the above.
   D. A and B.

AICPA.101047REG-SIM

34. Jetmore was surprised to learn how much income his tax client, Quantilco, Inc., was making. He thought that Quantilco's competitors might be interested in the information, so he sold it to one of them. When Quantilco found this out, it started investigating what consequences it might visit upon Jetmore. Which of the following is true?

   A. He may be sued civilly by the IRS.
   B. He may be prosecuted criminally by the Department of Justice.
   C. A and B.
   D. None of the above.

AICPA.101043REG-SIM

35. Which of the following are recognized exceptions that allow disclosure of confidential information?

   A. An enforceable subpoena has been served on the CPA.

   B. An ethical examination is being conducted regarding the CPA's conduct.
   C. A peer review is occurring.
   D. All of the above.

AICPA.101027REG-SIM

36. Lakin is a CPA whose client, Sublette, is being sued by a state government in state court for evasion of state income taxes. Sublette does not want Lakin to testify against him regarding information that Sublette communicated to Lakin. Which of the following is true in a state with a statutory version of the accountant-client testimonial privilege?

   A. Only Lakin can invoke the testimonial privilege.
   B. Sublette can invoke the privilege as to parts of the communications he had with Lakin, while asking Lakin to testify as to other parts.
   C. If the suit was in federal court, the state privilege would not apply even though the communication took place in the state.
   D. A and B.

AICPA.101095REG

37. In which of the following situations is there a violation of client confidentiality under the AICPA Code of Professional Conduct?

   A. A member discloses confidential client information to a court in connection with arbitration proceedings relating to the client.
   B. A member discloses confidential client information to a professional liability insurance carrier after learning of a potential claim against the member.
   C. A member whose practice is primarily bankruptcy discloses a client's name.
   D. A member uses a records retention agency to store clients' records that contain confidential client information.

II. Business Law

Agency

Types of Agency Relationships and Creation

AICPA.911113REG-BL

38. Orr gives North power of attorney. In general, the power of attorney

   A. Will be valid only if North is a licensed attorney at law.
   B. May continue in existence after Orr's death.

   C. May limit North's authority to specific transactions.
   D. Must be signed by both Orr and North.

AICPA.101007REG-SIM

39. Which of the following would **not** have capacity to create an agency relationship?

   A. An unincorporated association
   B. A corporation
   C. An individual
   D. A government agency

AICPA.920506REG-BL

40. A principal and agent relationship requires a

   A. Written agreement.
   B. Power of attorney.
   C. Meeting of the minds and consent to act.
   D. Specified consideration.

AICPA.130710REG

41. Which of the following conditions must be met to form an agency?

   A. An agency agreement must be in writing.
   B. An agency agreement must be signed by both parties.
   C. The principal must furnish legally adequate consideration for the agent's services.
   D. The principal must possess contractual capacity.

AICPA.910501REG-BL

42. Simpson, Ogden Corp.'s agent, needs a written agency agreement to

   A. Enter into a series of sales contracts on Ogden's behalf.
   B. Hire an attorney to collect a business debt owed to Ogden.
   C. Purchase an interest in undeveloped land for Ogden.
   D. Retain an independent general contractor to renovate Ogden's office building.

Authority of Agents and Principals

aq.auth.agent.prin.001_2017

43. The apparent authority of a partner to bind the partnership in dealing with third parties

   A. Will be effectively limited by a formal resolution of the partners of which third parties are aware.
   B. Will be effectively limited by a formal resolution of the partners of which third parties are unaware.
   C. Would permit a partner to submit a claim against the partnership to arbitration.
   D. Must be derived from the express powers and purposes contained in the partnership agreement.

aq.auth.agent.prin.002_2017

44. Bolt Corp. dismissed Ace as its general sales agent and notified all of Ace's known customers by letter. Young Corp., a retail outlet located outside of Ace's previously assigned sales territory, had never dealt with Ace. Young knew of Ace as a result of various business contacts. After his dismissal, Ace sold Young goods, to be delivered by Bolt, and received from Young a cash deposit for 20% of the purchase price. It was not unusual for an agent in Ace's previous position to receive cash deposits. In an action by Young against Bolt on the sales contract, Young will

   A. Win, because Bolt's notice was inadequate to terminate Ace's apparent authority.
   B. Lose, because Ace lacked any implied authority to make the contract.
   C. Lose, because Ace lacked any express authority to make the contract.
   D. Win, because a principal is an insurer of an agent's acts.

aq.auth.agent.prin.003_2017

45. Sol, an agent for May, made a contract with Simon that exceeded Sol's authority. If May wishes to hold Simon to the contract, May must prove that

   A. May ratified the contract before withdrawal from the contract by Simon.
   B. Sol was May's general agent even though Sol exceeded his authority.
   C. Sol believed he was acting within the scope of his authority.
   D. Sol was acting in the capacity of an agent for an undisclosed principal.

Duty of Agents and Principals

AICPA.900501REG-BL

46. Generally, an agency relationship is terminated by operation of law in all of the following situations, except the

   A. Principal's death.
   B. Principal's incapacity.
   C. Agent's renunciation of the agency.
   D. Agent's failure to acquire a necessary business license.

AICPA.950509REG-BL

47. Young Corp. hires Wilson as a sales representative for six months at a salary of $5,000 per month, plus 6% of sales.

   Which of the following statements is correct?

   A. Young does not have the power to dismiss Wilson during the six-month period without cause.
   B. Wilson is obligated to act solely in Young's interest in matters concerning Young's business.
   C. The agreement between Young and Wilson is not enforceable, unless it is in writing and signed by Wilson.
   D. The agreement between Young and Wilson formed an agency coupled with an interest.

AICPA.051148REG

48. Under the agent's duty to account, which of the following acts must a gratuitous agent perform?

	Commingle Funds	Account for the Principal's Property
A.	Yes	Yes
B.	Yes	No
C.	No	Yes
D.	No	No

AICPA.960503REG-BL

49. Which of the following statements represent(s) a principal's duty to an agent who works on a commission basis?

   I. The principal is required to maintain pertinent records, account to the agent, and pay the agent according to the terms of their agreement.
   II. The principal is required to reimburse the agent for all authorized expenses incurred, unless the agreement calls for the agent to pay expenses out of the commission.

   A. I only.
   B. II only.
   C. Both I and II.
   D. Neither I nor II.

AICPA.920509REG-BL

50. Ogden Corp. hires Thorp as a sales representative for nine months at a salary of $3,000 per month, plus 4% of sales.

   Which of the following statements is correct?

   A. Thorp is obligated to act solely in Ogden's interest in matters concerning Ogden's business.
   B. The agreement between Ogden and Thorp formed an agency coupled with an interest.
   C. Ogden does not have the power to dismiss Thorp during the nine-month period without cause.
   D. The agreement between Ogden and Thorp is not enforceable, unless it is in writing and signed by Thorp.

Contract Liability of Agents and Principals

AICPA.051141REG

51. Food Corp. owns a restaurant called The Ambers. The corporation president, T.J. Jones, hires a contractor to make repairs at the restaurant, signing the contract "T.J. Jones for The Ambers." Two invoices for restaurant repairs were paid by Food Corp. with corporate checks. Upon presenting the final invoice, the contractor was told that it would not be paid. The contractor sued Food Corp. Which of the following statements is correct regarding the liability of Food Corp.?

   A. It is not liable, because Jones is liable.
   B. It is not liable, because the corporation was an undisclosed principal.
   C. It is liable, because Jones is not liable.
   D. It is liable, because Jones had authority to make the contract.

AICPA.900504REG-BL

52. Able, as agent for Baker, an undisclosed principal, contracts with Safe to purchase an antique car. In payment, Able issues a personal check to Safe. Able cannot cover the check but expects Baker to give him cash to deposit before the check is presented for payment.

   Baker did not do so and the check was dishonored.

   Baker's identity became known to Safe.

   Safe may not recover from

   A. Baker, individually, on the contract.
   B. Able, individually, on the contract.
   C. Baker, individually, on the check.
   D. Able, individually, on the check.

AICPA.081943REG-2A.3

53. Easy Corp. is a real estate developer and regularly engages real estate brokers to act on its behalf in acquiring parcels of land. The brokers are authorized to enter into such contracts but are instructed to do so in their own names without disclosing Easy's identity or its relationship to the transaction. If a broker enters into a contract with a seller on Easy's behalf:

   A. The broker will have the same actual authority as if Easy's identity had been disclosed.
   B. Easy will be bound by the contract because of the broker's apparent authority.
   C. Easy will not be liable for any negligent acts committed by the broker while acting on Easy's behalf.
   D. The broker will not be personally bound by the contract, because the broker has express authority to act.

AICPA.931114REG-BL

54. Which of the following rights will a third party be entitled to after validly contracting with an agent representing an undisclosed principal?

    A. Disclosure of the principal by the agent.
    B. Ratification of the contract by the principal.
    C. Performance of the contract by the agent.
    D. Election to void the contract after disclosure of the principal.

AICPA.941117REG-BL

55. Bolt Corp. dismisses Ace as its general sales agent and notifies all of Ace's known customers by letter.

    Young Corp., a retail outlet located outside of Ace's previously assigned sales territory, had never dealt with Ace. Young knew of Ace as a result of various business contacts. After his dismissal, Ace sold Young goods, to be delivered by Bolt, and received from Young a cash deposit for 20% of the purchase price. It is not unusual for an agent in Ace's previous position to receive cash deposits.

    In an action by Young against Bolt on the sales contract, Young will

    A. Lose, because Ace lacked any implied authority to make the contract.
    B. Lose, because Ace lacked any express authority to make the contract.
    C. Win, because Bolt's notice was inadequate to terminate Ace's apparent authority.
    D. Win, because a principal is an insurer of an agent's acts.

Tort Liability of Agents and Principals

AICPA.081942REG-2A.3

56. Baker (P) leaves her two-month-old daughter, Summer, at the Ave Maria Child Care Center (D). Because Summer will not stop crying, one of D's employees, Davis, hits Summer's head against the corner of a shelf, causing major brain injury. Davis later pleads guilty to injury to a child and goes to jail. P sues D for Davis's tort. Which of the following is true?

    A. A principal is never liable for an agent's intentional tort.
    B. D is not liable, because Davis was not acting within the scope of employment – she was hired to help children, not to injure them.
    C. P will probably recover.
    D. Because Davis is only an employee, she cannot be liable.

AICPA.081940REG-2A.3

57. Seifert (P) is driving on a toll road in New York and exits. She throws her usual 50 cents into the basket and proceeds to drive away when she hears yelling. She quickly realizes that, on this day, she has driven beyond her usual exit and, therefore, owes more money. She is backing up to apologize and pay the difference when she is confronted by the toll collector, LaBelle, who has left the toll booth and repeatedly punches P in the face. P sues LaBelle's employer, the Turnpike Authority (D), for assault and battery. D proves that it has instructed its employees never to hit customers. Which of the following is true?

    A. D is not liable, because LaBelle acted against explicit instructions.
    B. The Authority is liable, because LaBelle was acting within the scope of his employment to benefit the Authority.
    C. Neither A nor B.
    D. A and B.

AICPA.931113REG-BL

58. Generally, a disclosed principal will be liable to third parties for its agent's unauthorized misrepresentations, if the agent is an

	Employee	Independent Contractor
A.	Yes	Yes
B.	Yes	No
C.	No	Yes
D.	No	No

AICPA.101011REG-SIM

59. Your client, Sanitary Dairies, Inc., employs Harold Stone as a milk-truck driver. Stone negligently runs the truck into the car of Ronald Green, injuring Green, his wife, and damaging Green's car. Stone is also injured in the collision. Which of the following is correct?

    A. If Stone had never had a previous accident, Sanitary Dairies would not be liable.
    B. Stone can avoid liability, because he was engaged in the performance of his principal's business.
    C. If Green is shown to have been contributorily negligent, he cannot recover for his injuries, or for the damage to the car.
    D. Stone is not entitled to receive worker's compensation.

Contracts
Introduction and Classification

Applicable Laws

AICPA.101009REG-SIM

60. Susan Worth has a lease for two years at the Bedford Arms apartment complex. Susan has the opportunity to study at Oxford for one year and has agreed to sublease her apartment to Karen Knight. Karen is to take over the lease on August 1, 2010, and finish the term of the lease, which ends May 31, 2011. Susan and Karen execute an agreement for the lease takeover. In January 2011, Karen misses her rent payment and then moves out of the apartment. The Bedford Arms owner wants to recover from Susan. This contract:

    A. Is governed by common law.
    B. Is governed by the UCC.
    C. Is governed by neither because it is not a lease.
    D. Any contract under the UCC.

aq.app.laws.001_2017

61. On March 13, Ike contracted with Turner for Turner to perform in Ike's club, exclusively, for four weeks beginning June 2 for $10,000 per week. Which of the following statements is correct?

    A. The contract is governed by the UCC.
    B. The contract is governed by common law.
    C. Turner's services are governed by common law, and the payment is governed by the UCC.
    D. Because the contract does not begin immediately, it is governed by the UCC.

aq.app.laws.002_2017

62. Janice Gwinn is having an in-floor vacuum system put in her new home. The cost of the components for the system and installation is $22,000. She has signed a contract with Jill's Permanent Vacuum Systems for that amount with installation to be completed as the phases of construction of the home proceed and allow. Which of the following statements is correct about this contract?

    A. Because the contract is one for the purchase of a vacuum, it is the sale of a good and is governed by the UCC.
    B. Because the contract involves real estate, it is governed by common law.
    C. Because the contract is a sale by a merchant, it is governed by the UCC.

    D. Because the contract is one predominantly for installation, it is governed by common law.

aq.app.laws.003_2017

63. Gwyneth's grandmother asks Gwyneth to come to her house on Tuesday evening for a visit and promised that Gwyneth would be glad that she came. Gwyneth did go to her grandmother's house on Tuesday evening, but she arrived late. Gwyneth's grandmother said, "Well, I was going to give you my car since I can't drive anymore, but since you cannot even show up on time, I have changed my mind."

    Which of the following statements is correct?

    A. There is no contract between Gwyneth and her grandmother for the car.
    B. There is a contract between Gwyneth and her grandmother, and it is governed by the UCC.
    C. There was a contract, but Gwyneth did not perform properly, so the grandmother can refuse to honor the contract.
    D. The contract is for Gwyneth's services in coming over and is governed by common law.

Types of Contracts

AICPA.111181REG

64. The text of the letter from Bridge Builders, Inc. to Allied Steel Co. is as follows:

    We offer to purchase 10,000 tons of No. 4 steel pipe at today's quoted price for delivery two months from today. Your acceptance must be received in five days.

    Bridge Builders intended to create a (an)

    A. Option contract.
    B. Unilateral contract.
    C. Bilateral contract.
    D. Joint contract.

AICPA.910516REG-BL

65. Kay, an art collector, promised Hammer, an art student, that if Hammer could obtain certain rare artifacts within two weeks, Kay would pay for Hammer's postgraduate education. At considerable effort and expense, Hammer obtained the specified artifacts within the two-week period. When Hammer requested payment, Kay refused. Kay claimed there was no consideration for the promise. Hammer would prevail against Kay based on

    A. Unilateral contract.
    B. Unjust enrichment.
    C. Public policy.
    D. Quasi contract.

AICPA.101010REG-SIM

66. Which of the following would be an example of an implied contract?

    A. John being treated by a doctor without first agreeing to the charges for the service.
    B. A contract between a real estate broker and a property owner.
    C. Any contract under the UCC.
    D. Any contract other than a contract for the sale of land.

Formation

Offer and Acceptance

AICPA.900512REG-BL

67. On September 27, Summers sent Fox a letter offering to sell Fox a vacation home for $150,000. On October 2, Fox replied by mail agreeing to buy the home for $145,000.

Summers did not reply to Fox.

Do Fox and Summers have a binding contract?

    A. No, because Fox failed to sign and return Summers' letter.
    B. No, because Fox's letter was a counteroffer.
    C. Yes, because Summers' offer was validly accepted.
    D. Yes, because Summers' silence is an implied acceptance of Fox's letter.

AICPA.920521REG-BL

68. On September 10, Harris, Inc., a new car dealer, placed a newspaper advertisement stating that Harris would sell 10 cars at its showroom for a special discount only on September 12, 13, and 14. On September 12, King called Harris and expressed an interest in buying one of the advertised cars.

King was told that five of the cars had been sold and to come to the showroom as soon as possible. On September 13, Harris made a televised announcement that the sale would end at 10:00 PM that night. King went to Harris's showroom on September 14 and demanded the right to buy a car at the special discount.

Harris had sold the 10 cars and refused King's demand. King sued Harris for breach of contract.

Harris's best defense to King's suit would be that Harris's

    A. Offer was unenforceable.
    B. Advertisement was not an offer.

    C. Television announcement revoked the offer.
    D. Offer had not been accepted.

AICPA.920522REG-BL

69. On April 1, Fine Corp. faxed Moss an offer to purchase Mos's warehouse for $500,000. The offer stated that it would remain open only until April 4 and that acceptance must be received to be effective. Moss sent an acceptance on April 4 by overnight mail and Fine received it on April 5.

Which of the following statements is correct?

    A. No contract was formed because Moss sent the acceptance by an unauthorized method.
    B. No contract was formed because Fine received Mos's acceptance after April 4.
    C. A contract was formed when Moss sent the acceptance.
    D. A contract was formed when Fine received Mos's acceptance.

AICPA.900514REG-BL

70. Opal offered, in writing, to sell Larkin a parcel of land for $300,000. If Opal dies, the offer will

    A. Terminate prior to Larkin's acceptance only if Larkin received notice of Opal's death.
    B. Remain open for a reasonable period of time after Opal's death.
    C. Automatically terminate despite Larkin's prior acceptance.
    D. Automatically terminate prior to Larkin's acceptance.

AICPA.921111REG-BL

71. On February 12, Harris sent Fresno a written offer to purchase Fresno's land. The offer included the following provision: "Acceptance of this offer must be by registered or certified mail, received by Harris no later than February 18 by 5:00 p.m. CST."

On February 18, Fresno sent Harris a letter accepting the offer by private overnight delivery service. Harris received the letter on February 19.

Which of the following statements is correct?

    A. A contract was formed on February 19.
    B. Fresno's letter constituted a counteroffer.
    C. Fresno's use of the overnight delivery service was an effective form of acceptance.
    D. A contract was formed on February 18 regardless of when Harris actually received Fresno's letter.

Consideration

AICPA.950520REG-BL

72. Grove is seeking to avoid performing a promise to pay Brook $1,500. Grove is relying on lack of consideration on Brook's part.

    Grove will prevail if Grove can establish that

    A. Prior to Grove's promise, Brook had already performed the requested act.
    B. Brook's only claim of consideration was the relinquishment of a legal right.
    C. Brook's asserted consideration is only worth $400.
    D. The consideration to be performed by Brook will be performed by a third party.

AICPA.921114REG-BL

73. Castle borrowed $5,000 from Nelson and executed and delivered to Nelson a promissory note for $5,000 due on April 30. On April 1, Castle offered, and Nelson accepted, $4,000 in full satisfaction of the note. On May 15, Nelson demanded that Castle pay the $1,000 balance on the note. Castle refused.

    If Nelson sued for the $1,000 balance, Castle would

    A. Win, because the acceptance by Nelson of the $4,000 constituted an accord and satisfaction.
    B. Win, because the debt was unliquidated.
    C. Lose, because the amount of the note was not in dispute.
    D. Lose, because no consideration was given to Nelson in exchange for accepting only $4,000.

AICPA.901121REG-BL

74. Which of the following requires consideration to be binding on the parties?

    A. Material modification of a contract involving the sale of real estate.
    B. Ratification of a contract by a person after reaching the age of majority.
    C. A written promise signed by a merchant to keep an offer to sell goods open for 10 days.
    D. Material modification of a sale of goods contract under the UCC.

assess.AICPA.REG.consideration-0036

75. Kelly owed Connor $500. Connor agreed to accept Kelly's microwave oven instead of the money. Kelly immediately delivered the oven to Connor. Which of the following terms correctly describes this agreement?

    A. Mutual rescission
    B. Accord and satisfaction

C. Novation
D. Material alteration

AICPA.920524REG-BL

76. In which of the following situations does the first promise serve as valid consideration for the second promise?

    A. A police officer's promise to catch a thief for a victim's promise to pay a reward.
    B. A builder's promise to complete a contract for a purchaser's promise to extend the time for completion.
    C. A debtor's promise to pay $500 for a creditor's promise to forgive the balance of a $600 liquidated debt.
    D. A debtor's promise to pay $500 for a creditor's promise to forgive the balance of a $600 disputed debt.

Writing and Records: The Statue of Frauds

AICPA.050903-REG

77. Kram sent Fargo, a real estate broker, a signed offer to sell a specific parcel of land to Fargo for $250,000. Kram, an engineer, had inherited the land. On the same day that Kram's letter was received, Fargo telephoned Kram and accepted the offer. Which of the following statements is correct under the common law Statute of Frauds?

    A. No contract could be formed because Fargo's acceptance was oral.
    B. No contract could be formed because Kram's letter was signed only by Kram.
    C. A contract was formed and would be enforceable against both Kram and Fargo.
    D. A contract was formed but would be enforceable only against Kram.

AICPA.130708REG

78. To which of the following transactions does the common law Statute of Frauds not apply?

    A. Contracts for the sale of real estate.
    B. Agreements made in consideration of marriage.
    C. Promises to pay the debt of another.
    D. Contracts that can be performed within one year.

Defenses to Formation

AICPA.921118REG-BL

79. Maco, Inc. and Kent contracted for Kent to provide Maco certain consulting services at an hourly rate of $20. Kent's normal hourly rate was $90 per hour, the fair market value of

the services. Kent agreed to the $20 because Kent was having serious financial problems. At the time the agreement was negotiated, Maco was aware of Kent's financial condition and refused to pay more than $20 per hour for Kent's services. Kent has now sued to rescind the contract with Maco, claiming duress by Maco during the negotiations. Under the circumstances, Kent will

A. Win, because Maco refused to pay the fair market value of Kent's services.
B. Win, because Maco was aware of Kent's serious financial problems.
C. Lose, because Maco's actions did not constitute duress.
D. Lose, because Maco cannot prove that Kent, at the time, had no other offers to provide consulting services.

AICPA.130705REG
80. Which of the following types of conduct renders a contract void?

A. Mutual mistake as to facts forming the basis of the contract.
B. Undue influence by a dominant party in a confidential relationship.
C. Duress through physical compulsion.
D. Duress through improper threats.

AICPA.130707REG
81. What type of conduct generally will make a contract voidable?

A. Fraud in the execution.
B. Fraud in the inducement.
C. Physical coercion.
D. Contracting with a person under guardianship.

AICPA.930521REG-BL
82. All of the following are effective methods of ratifying a contract entered into by a minor except

A. Expressly ratifying the contract after reaching the age of majority.
B. Failing to disaffirm the contract within a reasonable time after reaching the age of majority.
C. Ratifying the contract before reaching the age of majority.
D. Impliedly ratifying the contract after reaching the age of majority.

AICPA.920529REG-BL
83. If a buyer accepts an offer containing an immaterial unilateral mistake, the resulting contract will be

A. Void as a matter of law.
B. Void at the election of the buyer.

C. Valid as to both parties.
D. Voidable at the election of the seller.

Performance

Defining Performance and Breach

AICPA.010513REG-BL
84. Which of the following actions if taken by one party to a contract generally will discharge the performance required of the other party to the contract?

A. Material breach of the contract
B. Delay in performance
C. Tender
D. Assignment of rights

AICPA.050907-REG
85. When there has been no performance by either party, which of the following events generally will result in the discharge of a party's obligation to perform as required under the original contract?

	Accord and Satisfaction	Mutual Rescission
A.	Yes	Yes
B.	Yes	No
C.	No	Yes
D.	No	No

Discharge of Performance

AICPA.910523REG-BL
86. Maco Corp. contracted to sell 1,500 bushels of potatoes to LBC Chips. The contract did not refer to any specific supply source for the potatoes. Maco intended to deliver potatoes grown on its farms. An insect infestation ruined Maco's crop but not the crops of other growers in the area. Maco failed to deliver the potatoes to LBC. LBC sued Maco for breach of contract. Under the circumstances, Maco will

A. Lose, because it could have purchased potatoes from other growers to deliver to LBC.
B. Lose, unless it can show that the purchase of substitute potatoes for delivery to LBC would make the contract unprofitable.
C. Win, because the infestation was an act of nature that could not have been anticipated by Maco.
D. Win, because both Maco and LBC are assumed to accept the risk of a crop failure.

Passage of Title and Risk of Loss

SALE-0026

87. In deciding a controversy involving the question of who has the risk of loss, the court will look primarily to

   A. The intent of the parties manifested in the contract.
   B. The shipping terms used by the parties.
   C. Whether title has passed.
   D. The insurance coverage of the parties.

SALE-0030

88. On Monday, Wolfe paid Aston Co., a furniture retailer, $500 for a table. On Thursday, Aston notified Wolfe that the table was ready to be picked up. On Saturday, while Aston was still in possession of the table, it was destroyed in a fire. Who bears the loss of the table?

   A. Wolfe, because Wolfe had title to the table at the time of loss.
   B. Aston, unless Wolfe is a merchant.
   C. Wolfe, unless Aston breached the contract.
   D. Aston, because Wolfe had not yet taken possession of the table.

SALE-0017B

89. Cey Corp. entered into a contract to sell parts to Deck, Ltd. The contract provided that the goods would be shipped "FOB Cey's warehouse." Cey shipped parts different from those specified in the contract. Deck rejected the parts. A few hours after Deck informed Cey that the parts were rejected, they were destroyed by fire in Deck's warehouse. Cey believed that the parts were conforming to the contract. Which of the following statements is correct?

   A. Regardless of whether the parts were conforming, Deck will bear the loss because the contract was a shipment contract.
   B. If the parts were nonconforming, Deck had the right to reject them, but the risk of loss remains with Deck until Cey takes possession of the parts.
   C. If the parts were conforming, risk of loss does not pass to Deck until a reasonable period of time after they are delivered to Deck.
   D. If the parts were nonconforming, Cey will bear the risk of loss, even though the contract was a shipment contract.

Remedies

Types of Remedies

AICPA.920535REG-BL

90. Kaye contracted to sell Hodges a building for $310,000. The contract required Hodges to pay the entire amount at closing. Kaye refused to close the sale of the building. Hodges sued Kaye.

   To what relief is Hodges entitled?

   A. Punitive damages and compensatory damages
   B. Specific performance and compensatory damages
   C. Consequential damages or punitive damages
   D. Compensatory damages or specific performance

Formulas for Damages

CONT-0088

91. On June 1, year 1, Nord Corp. engaged Milo & Co., CPAs, to perform certain management advisory services for 9 months for a $45,000 fee. The terms of their oral agreement required Milo to commence performance any time before October 1, year 1. On June 30, year 2, after Milo completed the work to Nord's satisfaction, Nord paid Milo $30,000 by check. Nord conspicuously marked on the check that it constituted payment in full for all services rendered. Nord has refused to pay the remaining $15,000 arguing that, although it believes the $45,000 fee is reasonable, it had received bids of $30,000 and $38,000 from other firms to perform the same services as Milo. Milo endorsed and deposited the check. If Milo commences an action against Nord for the remaining $15,000, Milo will be entitled to recover

   A. $0 because there has been an enforceable accord and satisfaction
   B. $0 because the Statute of Frauds has not been satisfied
   C. $8,000 because $38,000 was the highest other bid
   D. $15,000 because it is the balance due under the agreement

Third-Party Rights

AICPA.921114REG-BL

92. Castle borrowed $5,000 from Nelson and executed and delivered to Nelson a promissory note for $5,000 due on April 30. On April 1, Castle offered, and Nelson accepted, $4,000 in full satisfaction of the note. On May 15, Nelson demanded that Castle pay the $1,000 balance on the note. Castle refused.

    If Nelson sued for the $1,000 balance, Castle would

    A. Win, because the acceptance by Nelson of the $4,000 constituted an accord and satisfaction.
    B. Win, because the debt was unliquidated.
    C. Lose, because the amount of the note was not in dispute.
    D. Lose, because no consideration was given to Nelson in exchange for accepting only $4,000.

AICPA.901121REG-BL

93. Which of the following requires consideration to be binding on the parties?

    A. Material modification of a contract involving the sale of real estate.
    B. Ratification of a contract by a person after reaching the age of majority.
    C. A written promise signed by a merchant to keep an offer to sell goods open for 10 days.
    D. Material modification of a sale of goods contract under the UCC.

AICPA.920524REG-BL

94. In which of the following situations does the first promise serve as valid consideration for the second promise?

    A. A police officer's promise to catch a thief for a victim's promise to pay a reward.
    B. A builder's promise to complete a contract for a purchaser's promise to extend the time for completion.
    C. A debtor's promise to pay $500 for a creditor's promise to forgive the balance of a $600 liquidated debt.
    D. A debtor's promise to pay $500 for a creditor's promise to forgive the balance of a $600 disputed debt.

AICPA.950520REG-BL

95. Grove is seeking to avoid performing a promise to pay Brook $1,500. Grove is relying on lack of consideration on Brook's part.

    Grove will prevail if Grove can establish that

    A. Prior to Grove's promise, Brook had already performed the requested act.
    B. Brook's only claim of consideration was the relinquishment of a legal right.
    C. Brook's asserted consideration is only worth $400.
    D. The consideration to be performed by Brook will be performed by a third party.

Debtor-Creditor Relationships

Rights, Duties, and Liabilities of Debtors, Creditors, and Guarantors

Suretyship: Introduction, Creation, and Types

AICPA.951128REG-BL

96. Which of the following rights does one cosurety generally have against another cosurety?

    A. Exoneration
    B. Subrogation
    C. Reimbursement
    D. Contribution

AICPA.910526REG-BL

97. Edwards Corp. lent Lark $200,000. At Edwards's request, Lark entered into an agreement with Owen and Ward for them to act as compensated co-sureties on the loan in the amount of $200,000 each.

    If Edwards releases Ward without Owen's or Lark's consent, and Lark later defaults, which of the following statements is correct?

    A. Lark will be released for 50% of the loan balance.
    B. Owen will be liable for the entire loan balance.
    C. Owen will be liable for 50% of the loan balance.
    D. Edwards's release of Ward will have no effect on Lark's and Owen's liability to Edwards.

AICPA.931125REG-BL

98. Nash, Owen, and Polk are co-sureties with maximum liabilities of $40,000, $60,000, and $80,000, respectively. The amount of the loan on which they have agreed to act as co-sureties is $180,000. The debtor defaulted at a time when the loan balance was $180,000. Nash paid the lender $36,000 in full settlement of all claims against Nash, Owen, and Polk.

   The total amount that Nash may recover from Owen and Polk is

   A. $0
   B. $24,000
   C. $28,000
   D. $140,000

AICPA.921126REG-BL

99. Ivor borrowed $420,000 from Lear Bank. At Lear's request, Ivor entered into an agreement with Ash, Kane, and Queen for them to act as co-sureties on the loan. The agreement between Ivor and the co-sureties provided that the maximum liability of each co-surety was: Ash, $84,000; Kane, $126,000; and Queen, $210,000. After making several payments, Ivor defaulted on the loan. The balance was $280,000.

   If Queen pays $210,000 and Ivor subsequently pays $70,000, what amounts may Queen recover from Ash and Kane?

   A. $0 from Ash and $0 from Kane.
   B. $42,000 from Ash and $63,000 from Kane.
   C. $70,000 from Ash and $70,000 from Kane.
   D. $56,000 from Ash and $84,000 from Kane.

AICPA.090593REG-II-C-1

100. Camp orally guaranteed payment of a loan Camp's cousin Wilcox had obtained from Camp's friend Main. The loan was to be repaid in 10 monthly payments. After making 6 payments, Wilcox defaulted on the loan and Main demanded that Camp honor the guarantee. Regarding Camp's liability to Main, Camp is

   A. Liable under the oral surety agreement because the loan would be paid within one year.
   B. Liable under the oral surety agreement because Camp benefited by maintaining a personal relationship with Main.
   C. Not liable under the oral surety agreement because Camp's surety agreement must be in writing to be enforceable.
   D. Not liable under the oral surety agreement because of failure of consideration.

Suretyship—Rights of Parties

AICPA.950527REG-BL

101. Wright cosigned King's loan from Ace Bank. Which of the following events would release Wright from the obligation to pay the loan?

   A. Ace seeking payment of the loan only from Wright.
   B. King is granted a discharge in bankruptcy.
   C. Ace is paid in full by King's spouse.
   D. King is adjudicated mentally incompetent.

AICPA.940524REG-BL

102. A party contracts to act as a surety for the collection of the debts of another. As a result of the suretyship agreement, which of the following statements is correct?

   A. The creditor may proceed against the surety without attempting to collect from the debtor.
   B. The surety agreement must be in writing.
   C. The surety may use any defenses available to the debtor.
   D. The creditor must be notified of the debtor's default by the surety.

AICPA.941131REG-BL

103. Ingot Corp. lent Flange $50,000. At Ingot's request, Flange entered into an agreement with Quill and West for them to act as compensated co-sureties on the loan in the amount of $100,000 each. Ingot released West without Quill's or Flange's consent, and Flange later defaulted on the loan.

   Which of the following statements is correct?

   A. Quill will be liable for 50% of the loan balance.
   B. Quill will be liable for the entire loan balance.
   C. Ingot's release of West will have no effect on Flange's and Quill's liability to Ingot.
   D. Flange will be released for 50% of the loan balance.

AICPA.941129REG-BL

104. Which of the following defenses would a surety be able to assert successfully to limit the surety's liability to a creditor?

   A. A discharge in bankruptcy of the principal debtor.
   B. A personal defense the principal debtor has against the creditor.
   C. The incapacity of the surety.
   D. The incapacity of the principal debtor.

AICPA.950526REG-BL

105. Green was unable to repay a loan from State Bank when due.

State refused to renew the loan unless Green provided an acceptable surety. Green asked Royal, a friend, to act as surety on the loan. To induce Royal to agree to become a surety, Green fraudulently represented Green's financial condition and promised Royal discounts on merchandise sold at Green's store. Royal agreed to act as surety and the loan was renewed. Later, Green's obligation to State was discharged in Green's bankruptcy. State wants to hold Royal liable.

Royal may avoid liability

A. If Royal can show that State was aware of the fraudulent representations.
B. If Royal was an uncompensated surety.
C. Because the discharge in bankruptcy will prevent Royal from having a right of reimbursement.
D. Because the arrangement was void at the inception.

Article 9 UCC Secured Transactions

Introduction and Creation of Security Interests

AICPA.941157REG-BL

106. Under the Secured Transactions Article of the UCC, which of the following requirements is necessary to have a security interest attach?

	Debtor has rights in the collateral	Proper filing of a security agreement	Value given by the creditor
A.	Yes	Yes	Yes
B.	Yes	Yes	No
C.	Yes	No	Yes
D.	No	Yes	Yes

AICPA.101170REG

107. Under the Secured Transactions Article of the UCC, which of the following statements is correct regarding a security interest that has not attached?

A. It is effective against the debtor, but not against third parties.
B. It is effective against both the debtor and third parties.
C. It is effective against third parties with unsecured claims.
D. It is not effective against either the debtor or third parties.

AICPA.120608REG

108. Under the Secured Transactions Article of the UCC, which of the following security agreements does NOT need to be in writing to be enforceable?

A. A security agreement collateralizing a debt of LESS than $500.
B. A security agreement where the collateral is highly perishable or subject to wide price fluctuations.
C. A security agreement where the collateral is in the possession of the secured party.
D. A security agreement involving a purchase money security interest.

AICPA.090595REG-II-E-3

109. Under the Secured Transactions Article of the UCC, all of the following are needed to create enforceable security interest except

A. A security agreement must exist.
B. The secured party must give value.
C. The debtor must have rights in the collateral.
D. A financing statement must be filed.

AICPA.921146REG-BL

110. Under the UCC Secured Transactions Article, when collateral is in a secured party's possession, which of the following conditions must also be satisfied to have attachment?

A. There must be a written security agreement.
B. The public must be notified.
C. The secured party must receive consideration.
D. The debtor must have rights to the collateral.

Perfection of Security Interests

AICPA.071203REG-BL

111. Jones lives in Oklahoma and is the owner of a large number of valuable antiques. Treasures Delight, located in Arkansas, is a seller of antiques. Treasures Delight is owned by Sally Delight. Delight offers to purchase all of the antiques owned by Jones paying 60% of the agreed price and, by agreement, signs a security agreement for the balance putting up her entire inventory as security. The security agreement provides for monthly payments. Which of the following is correct?

A. Since this is a purchase money security interest, Jones is automatically perfected without a filing.
B. Although this is a purchase money security interest, Jones must file to have a perfected security interest.

C. There is not a purchase money security interest because being antiques for resell classifies the collateral as inventory.

D. If Jones decides to file for perfection of his security interest, Jones would file a financing statement in Oklahoma.

AICPA.900549REG-BL

112. Sun, Inc., manufactures and sells household appliances on credit directly to wholesalers, retailers, and consumers.

Sun can perfect its security interest in the appliances without having to file a financing statement or take possession of the appliances if the sale is made by Sun to

A. Consumers.

B. Wholesalers that sell to buyers in the ordinary course of business.

C. Retailers.

D. Wholesalers that sell to distributors for resale.

AICPA.120609REG

113. Under the Secured Transactions Article of the UCC, which of the following items can usually be *excluded* from a filed original financing statement?

A. The name of the debtor.

B. The address of the debtor.

C. A description of the collateral.

D. The amount of the obligation secured.

AICPA071204REG-BL

114. Which of the following requires a filing for perfection?

A. A purchase money security interest in consumer goods.

B. A purchase money security interest in equipment.

C. A security interest in negotiable promissory notes.

D. None of the above.

AICPA.931159REG-BL

115. Grey Corp. sells computers to the public. Grey sold and delivered a computer to West on credit. West executed and delivered to Grey a promissory note for the purchase price and a security agreement covering the computer. West purchased the computer for personal use. Grey did not file a financing statement.

Is Grey's security interest perfected?

A. Yes, because Grey retained ownership of the computer.

B. Yes, because it was perfected at the time of attachment.

C. No, because the computer was a consumer good.

D. No, because Grey failed to file a financing statement.

Priorities in Security Interests

AICPA.931160REG-BL

116. Noninventory goods were purchased and delivered on June 15. Several security interests exist in these goods. Which of the following security interests has priority over the others?

A. Security interest in future goods attached June 10.

B. Security interest attached June 15.

C. Security interest perfected June 20.

D. Purchase money security interest perfected June 24.

AICPA.940552REG-BL

117. Under the UCC Secured Transactions Article, what is the order of priority for the following security interests in store equipment?

I. Security interest perfected by filing on April 15, 2016.

II. Security interest attached on April 1, 2016.

III. Purchase money security interest attached April 11, 2016, and perfected by filing on April 20, 2016.

A. I, III, II.

B. II, I, III.

C. III, I, II.

D. III, II, I.

AICPA.921149REG-BL

118. On July 8, Ace, a refrigerator wholesaler, purchased 50 refrigerators. This comprised Ace's entire inventory and was financed under an agreement with Rome Bank that gave Rome a security interest in all refrigerators on Ace's premises, all future acquired refrigerators, and the proceeds of sales. On July 12, Rome filed a financing statement that adequately identified the collateral. On August 15, Ace sold one refrigerator to Cray for personal use and four refrigerators to Zone Co. for its business.

Which of the following statements is correct?

A. The refrigerators sold to Zone will be subject to Rome's security interest.

B. The refrigerator sold to Cray will not be subject to Rome's security interest.

C. The security interest does not include the proceeds from the sale of the refrigerators to Zone.

D. The security interest may not cover after-acquired property even if the parties agree.

AICPA.940549REG-BL

119. Under the UCC Secured Transactions Article, which of the following after-acquired property may be attached to a security agreement given to a secured lender?

	Inventory	Equipment
A.	Yes	Yes
B.	Yes	No
C.	No	Yes
D.	No	No

AICPA.921147REG-BL

120. Under the UCC Secured Transaction Article, what is the effect of perfecting a security interest by filing a financing statement?

A. The secured party can enforce its security interest against the debtor.

B. The secured party has permanent priority in the collateral even if the collateral is removed to another state.

C. The debtor is protected against all other parties who acquire an interest in the collateral after the filing.

D. The secured party has priority in the collateral over most creditors who acquire a security interest in the same collateral after the filing.

Rights of Secured Parties and Debtors

AICPA.101012REG-SIM

121. A debtor purchased an LCD television from BestBuy for $1,000. BestBuy financed the transaction. With finance charges, the total cost of the financing is $1,200. After the debtor has paid $600, he defaults on the payment and BestBuy repossesses the TV. BestBuy has decided to keep the TV as a floor display model. The debtor believes it would be best if BestBuy sold the TV.

A. Under Article 9, BestBuy must sell the TV.

B. Under Article 9, BestBuy is not required to sell the TV.

C. Under Article 9, the debtor has no control over the creditor's actions once there has been a default.

D. Under Article 9, the decision to sell or retain is always within the discretion of the creditor.

AICPA.921150REG-BL

122. Under the UCC Secured Transactions Article, if a debtor is in default under a payment obligation secured by goods, the secured party has the right to

	Peacefully repossess the goods without judicial process	Reduce the claim to a judgment	Sell the goods and apply the proceeds toward the debt
A.	Yes	Yes	Yes
B.	No	Yes	Yes
C.	Yes	Yes	No
D.	Yes	No	Yes

AICPA.941160REG-BL

123. Under the Secured Transactions Article of the UCC, which of the following remedies is available to a secured creditor when a debtor fails to make a payment when due?

	Proceed against the collateral	Obtain a general judgment against the debtor
A.	Yes	Yes
B.	Yes	No
C.	No	Yes
D.	No	No

AICPA.940554REG-BL

124. Drew bought a computer for personal use from Hale Corp. for $3,000. Drew paid $2,000 in cash and signed a security agreement for the balance. Hale properly filed the security agreement. Drew defaulted in paying the balance of the purchase price. Hale asked Drew to pay the balance. When Drew refused, Hale peacefully repossessed the computer.

Under the UCC Secured Transactions Article, which of the following remedies will Hale have?

A. Obtain a deficiency judgment against Drew for the amount owed.

B. Sell the computer and retain any surplus over the amount owed.

C. Retain the computer over Drew's objection.

D. Sell the computer without notifying Drew.

AICPA.930550REG-BL

125. Under the UCC Secured Transactions Article, which of the following statements is correct concerning the disposition of collateral by a secured creditor after a debtor's default?

A. A good faith purchaser for value and without knowledge of any defects in the sale takes free of any subordinate liens or security interests.
B. The debtor may not redeem the collateral after the default.
C. Secured creditors with subordinate claims retain the right to redeem the collateral after the collateral is sold to a third party.
D. The collateral may only be disposed of at a public sale.

Bankruptcy and Insolvency

Prebankruptcy Options, and Introduction to and Declaration of Bankruptcy

AICPA.910529REG-BL

126. Unger owes a total of $50,000 to eight unsecured creditors and one fully secured creditor. Quincy is one of the unsecured creditors and is owed $6,000. Quincy has filed an involuntary bankruptcy petition against Unger under the liquidation provisions of Chapter 7 of the Federal Bankruptcy Code. Unger has been unable to pay debts as they become due. Unger's liabilities exceed Unger's assets. Unger has filed papers opposing the bankruptcy petition.

Which of the following statements regarding Quincy's petition is correct?

A. It will be dismissed because the secured creditor failed to join in the filing of the petition.
B. It will be dismissed because three unsecured creditors must join in the filing of the petition.
C. It will be granted because Unger's liabilities exceed Unger's assets.
D. It will be dismissed because Unger's debt to Quincy alone is less than the required limit to bring an involuntary petition.

AICPA.082053REG-II.C.I

127. Green is heavily in debt to numerous creditors. Green does have some assets, including an antique car that he drives in parades and to other functions. Green is looking for a method that will allow him to get out of debt without going into bankruptcy, and will allow him to continue to drive his antique car. Green sells the antique car to a friend living in another city at a price estimated at 70% of the car's actual value. The friend has agreed to allow Green to keep the car and use it as before the sale. Green then gets all other creditors, except Sharp, to sign an agreement that, upon selling all of his remaining non-exempt assets, and with an appropriate division of proceeds, they would release him from his debts. Which of the following is correct?

A. Since the vast majority of creditors signed the Composition of Creditor's Agreement, Sharp is also bound by the agreement.
B. The above agreement is called an Assignment for the Benefit of Creditors.
C. If Sharp cannot prove the transfer of the antique car as fraud-in-fact, Sharp has virtually no remedy available.
D. Sharp can pursue an action based on fraud-in-law to set aside the sale to Green's friend.

AICPA.910530REG-BL

128. A voluntary petition filed under the liquidation provisions of Chapter 7 of the Federal Bankruptcy Code

A. Is not available to a corporation unless it has previously filed a petition under the reorganization provisions of Chapter 11 of the Federal Bankruptcy Code.
B. Automatically stays collection actions against the debtor except by secured creditors.
C. Will be dismissed unless the debtor has 12 or more unsecured creditors whose claims total at least $5,000.
D. Does not require the debtor to show that the debtor's liabilities exceed the fair market value of assets.

AICPA.911128REG-BL

129. Which of the following statements is correct concerning the voluntary filing of a petition in bankruptcy?

A. If the debtor has 12 or more creditors, the unsecured claims must total at least $5,000.
B. The debtor must be insolvent.
C. If the debtor has fewer than 12 creditors, the unsecured claims must total at least $5,000.
D. The petition may be filed jointly by spouses.

AICPA.940523REG-BL

130. Which of the following methods will allow a creditor to collect money from a debtor's wages?

A. Arrest.
B. Mechanic's lien.
C. Order of receivership.
D. Writ of garnishment.

Bankruptcy Process

AICPA.990510REG-BL

131. Under the liquidation provisions of Chapter 7 of the Federal Bankruptcy Code, certain property acquired by the debtor after the filing of the petition becomes part of the bankruptcy estate.

An example of such property is

A. Municipal-bond interest received by the debtor within 180 days of the filing of the petition.
B. Alimony received by the debtor within one year of the filing of the petition.
C. Social Security payments received by the debtor within 180 days of the filing of the petition.
D. Gifts received by the debtor within one year of the filing of the petition.

AICPA.050902-REG

132. Under the Federal Bankruptcy Code, which of the following rights or powers does a trustee in bankruptcy not have?

A. The power to prevail against a creditor with an unperfected security interest.
B. The power to require persons holding the debtor's property at the time the bankruptcy petition is filed to deliver the property to the trustee.
C. The right to use any grounds available to the debtor to obtain the return of the debtor's property.
D. The right to avoid any statutory liens against the debtor's property that were effective before the bankruptcy petition was filed.

AICPA.931127REG-BL

133. The filing of an involuntary bankruptcy petition under the Federal Bankruptcy Code

A. Terminates liens on exempt property.
B. Terminates all security interests in property in the bankruptcy estate.
C. Stops the debtor from incurring new debts.
D. Stops the enforcement of judgment liens against property in the bankruptcy estate.

AICPA.911144REG-BL

134. On February 28, 2005, Master, Inc. has total assets with a fair market value of $1.2mn and total liabilities of $990,000.

On January 15, 2005, Master made a monthly installment-note payment to Acme Distributors Corp., a creditor holding a properly perfected security interest in equipment, having a fair market value greater than the balance due on the note. On March 15, 2005, Master voluntarily files a petition in bankruptcy under the liquidation provisions of Chapter 7 of the Federal Bankruptcy Code. One year later, the equipment is sold for less than the balance due on the note to Acme.

Master's payment to Acme could

A. Be set aside as a preferential transfer, because the fair market value of the collateral was greater than the installment-note balance.
B. Be set aside as a preferential transfer, unless Acme showed that Master was solvent on January 15, 2005.
C. Not be set aside as a preferential transfer, because Acme was oversecured.
D. Not be set aside as a preferential transfer if Acme showed that Master was solvent on March 15, 2005.

AICPA.921137REG-BL

135. On August 1, 2004, Hall files a voluntary petition under Chapter 7 of the Federal Bankruptcy Code.

Hall's assets are sufficient to pay general creditors 40% of their claims.

The following transactions occurred before the filing:

– On May 15, 2004, Hall gave a mortgage on Hall's home to National Bank to secure payment of a loan National had given Hall two years earlier. When the loan was made, Hall's twin was a National employee.
– On June 1, 2004, Hall purchased a boat from Olsen for $10,000 cash.
– On July 1, 2004, Hall paid off an outstanding credit card balance of $500. The original debt had been $2,500.

The National mortgage was

A. Preferential, because National would be considered an insider.
B. Preferential, because the mortgage was given to secure an antecedent debt.
C. Not preferential, because Hall is presumed insolvent when the mortgage was given.
D. Not preferential, because the mortgage was a security interest.

Distribution of Debtor's Estate

AICPA.901134REG-BL

136. On May 24, Knurl, an appliance dealer, files for bankruptcy under the provisions of Chapter 7 of the Federal Bankruptcy Code. A trustee is appointed and an order for relief is entered. Knurl's non-exempt property is converted to cash, which is available to satisfy the following claims and expenses:

Claim by Card Corp. (one of Knurl's suppliers) for toasters ordered on May 11, and delivered on credit to Knurl on May 15.	$50,000
Fee earned by the bankruptcy trustee.	$12,000
Claim by Hill Co. for the delivery of televisions to Knurl on credit. The televisions were delivered on April 9, and a financing statement was properly filed on April 10. These televisions were sold by the trustee, with Hill's consent, for $7,000, their fair market value.	$7,000
Fees earned by the attorneys for the bankruptcy estate.	$8,000

The cash available for distribution includes the proceeds from the sale of the televisions. What amount will be distributed to Card if the cash available for distribution is $50,000?

A. $23,000
B. $30,000
C. $31,000
D. $43,000

AICPA.901131REG-BL

137. In a voluntary bankruptcy proceeding under Chapter 7 of the Federal Bankruptcy Code, which of the following claims, filed within 90 days of the filing for bankruptcy, will be paid first?

A. Unsecured federal taxes.
B. Utility bills up to $1,000.
C. Voluntary contributions to employee benefit plans.
D. Employee vacation and sick pay up to $2,000 per employee.

AICPA.950532REG-BL

138. Dart Inc., a closely held corporation, is petitioned involuntarily into bankruptcy under the liquidation provisions of Chapter 7 of the Federal Bankruptcy Code. Dart contests the petition.

Dart has not been paying its business debts as they become due, has defaulted on its mortgage-loan payments, and owes back taxes to the IRS. The total cash value of Dart's bankruptcy estate after the sale of all assets and payment of administration expenses is $100,000.

Dart has the following creditors:

– Fracon Bank is owed $75,000 principal and accrued interest on a mortgage loan secured by Dart's real property. The property was valued at and sold, in bankruptcy, for $70,000.
– The IRS has a $12,000 recorded judgment for unpaid corporate income tax.
– JOG Office Supplies has an unsecured claim of $3,000 that was filed in timely fashion.
– Nanstar Electric Co. has an unsecured claim of $1,200 that was not filed in a timely fashion.
– Decoy Publications has a claim of $14,000, of which $2,000 is secured by Dart's inventory that was valued and sold, in bankruptcy, for $2,000. The claim was filed in a timely fashion.

Assume that the bankruptcy estate was distributed.

What total dollar amount would Fracon Bank receive on its secured and unsecured claims?

A. $70,000
B. $72,000
C. $74,000
D. $75,000

AICPA.950531REG-BL

139. Dart Inc., a closely held corporation, is petitioned involuntarily into bankruptcy under the liquidation provisions of Chapter 7 of the Federal Bankruptcy Code. Dart contests the petition.

Dart has not been paying its business debts as they become due, has defaulted on its mortgage-loan payments, and owes back taxes to the IRS. The total cash value of Dart's bankruptcy estate, after the sale of all assets and payment of administration expenses, is $100,000.

Dart has the following creditors:

– Fracon Bank is owed $75,000 principal and accrued interest on a mortgage loan secured by Dart's real property. The property was valued at and sold, in bankruptcy, for $70,000.
– The IRS has a $12,000 recorded judgment for unpaid corporate income tax.
– JOG Office Supplies has an unsecured claim of $3,000 that was filed in timely fashion.
– Nanstar Electric Co. has an unsecured claim of $1,200 that was not filed in timely fashion.
– Decoy Publications has a claim of $14,000, of which $2,000 is secured by Dart's inventory that was valued and sold, in bankruptcy, for $2,000. The claim was filed in timely fashion.

Assume that the bankruptcy estate was distributed.

What dollar amount would Nanstar Electric Co. receive?

A. $0
B. $800
C. $1,000
D. $1,200

AICPA.911145REG-BL

140. On February 28, 2005, Master, Inc. has total assets with a fair market value of $1.2mn and total liabilities of $990,000.

On January 15, 2005, Master made a monthly installment-note payment to Acme Distributors Corp., a creditor holding a properly perfected security interest in equipment having a fair market value greater than the balance due on the note. On March 15, 2005, Master voluntarily files a petition in bankruptcy under the liquidation provisions of Chapter 7 of the Federal Bankruptcy Code. One year later, the equipment was sold to Acme for less than the balance due on the note.

Which of the following statements correctly describes Acme's distribution from Master's bankruptcy estate?

A. Acme will receive the total amount it is owed, even if the proceeds from the sale of the collateral were less than the balance owed by Master.
B. Acme will have the same priority as unsecured general creditors, to the extent that the proceeds from the sale of its collateral are insufficient to satisfy the amount owed by Master.
C. The total proceeds from the sale of the collateral will be paid to Acme, even if they are less than the balance owed by Master, provided there is sufficient cash to pay all administrative costs associated with the bankruptcy.
D. Acme will receive only the proceeds from the sale of the collateral in full satisfaction of the debt owed by Master.

Discharge and Reaffirmation·Agreements

AICPA.941134REG-BL

141. Under the liquidation provisions of Chapter 7 of the Federal Bankruptcy Code, which of the following statements applies to a person who has voluntarily filed for and received a discharge in bankruptcy?

A. The person will be discharged from all debts.
B. The person can obtain another voluntary discharge in bankruptcy under Chapter 7

after three years have elapsed from the date of the prior filing.
C. The person must surrender for distribution to the creditors amounts received as an inheritance, if the receipt occurs within 180 days after filing the bankruptcy petition.
D. The person is precluded from owning or operating a similar business for two years.

AICPA.901133REG-BL

142. A claim will not be discharged in a bankruptcy proceeding if it

A. Is brought by a secured creditor and remains unsatisfied after receipt of the proceeds from the disposition of the collateral.
B. Is for unintentional torts that resulted in bodily injury to the claimant.
C. Arises from an extension of credit based upon false representations.
D. Arises out of the breach of a contract by the debtor.

AICPA.901132REG-BL

143. Chapter 7 of the Federal Bankruptcy Code will deny a debtor a discharge when the debtor

A. Makes a preferential transfer to a creditor.
B. Accidentally destroys information relevant to the bankruptcy proceeding.
C. Obtains a Chapter 7 discharge ten years previously.
D. Is a corporation or a partnership.

AICPA.970512REG-BL

144. Under the liquidation provisions of Chapter 7 of the Federal Bankruptcy Code, a debtor will be denied a discharge in bankruptcy if the debtor

A. Fails to list a creditor.
B. Owes alimony and child support payments.
C. Cannot pay administration expenses.
D. Refuses satisfactorily to explain a loss of assets.

AICPA.020505REG-BL

145. Under Chapter 7 of the Federal Bankruptcy Code, what affect does a bankruptcy discharge have on a judgment creditor when there is no bankruptcy estate?

A. The judgment creditor's claim is non-dischargeable.
B. The judgment creditor retains a statutory lien against the debtor.
C. The debtor is relieved of any personal liability to the judgment creditor.
D. The debtor is required to pay a liquidated amount to vacate the judgment.

Government Regulation of Business
Federal Securities Regulation

Defining a "Security"

AICPA.081944REG-2.D.1

146. Sam, a Harlingen business owner, sues a local shopping mall, accusing it of conspiring with a former partner of Sam's to put Sam out of business. Sam lacks resources to pay his lawyers and otherwise fund the lawsuit. Sternberg forms Plaintiff's Funding Corp. (PFC) and comes to Sam's aid. Sternberg and PFC induce ten people to put up $5,000 each to buy an 11% stake in the litigation. Sam uses the $50,000 to fund the lawsuit, which recovers $5.4mn. The ten investors were entitled to $594,000, but were never paid. They sued Sternberg and PFC for securities fraud. Defendants claimed that no "securities" were involved in this case. Which is true?

   A. The defendants are correct; there were no "securities" involved in this case.
   B. The investors should win; these were securities in the form of an "investment contract."
   C. These interests were securities, because they were stock-derivative option-equity contracts.
   D. None of the above.

AICPA.940538REG-BL

147. Under the Securities Exchange Act of 1934, which of the following types of instruments is excluded from the definition of "securities"?

   A. Investment contracts.
   B. Convertible debentures.
   C. Non-convertible debentures.
   D. Certificates of deposit.

AICPA.930530REG-BL

148. Which of the following is least likely to be considered a security under the Securities Act of 1933?

   A. Stock options.
   B. Warrants.
   C. General partnership interests.
   D. Limited-partnership interests.

AICPA.101171REG

149. Which of the following transactions is subject to registration requirements of the Securities Act of 1933?

   A. The public sale of stock of a trucking company regulated by the Interstate Commerce Commission.

   B. A public sale of municipal bonds issued by a city government.
   C. The issuance of stock by a publicly traded corporation to its existing shareholders because of a stock split.
   D. The public sale by a corporation of its negotiable ten-year notes.

AICPA.081945REG-2.D.1

150. Alliance Leasing Corp. locates and recruits more than 1,500 investors from all over the U.S. to invest in an enterprise that uses investor money to buy commercial office or kitchen equipment, that was then leased out to third-party lessees. Investors' funds are to be placed in special accounts at either Wells Fargo Bank or Merrill Lynch, and Alliance is to use the capital to "engage in a single or multiple transactions with a lessee." In several cases, Alliance bundles the leases together in packages of several million dollars each, which were purchased by institutional investors. The lease payments by the lessees are then to be paid to the investors on a monthly basis for two years, with a balloon payment at the end of the two-year period. Alliance represents that investors would earn a return of 14% per year (as would Alliance, which was splitting the profits with investors 50/50) and that the investment is "low risk." After Alliance goes bankrupt, investors sue its principals for securities fraud. Defendants claimed that no "securities" were involved. Which of the following is true?

   A. These interests are "securities."
   B. These interests are not securities, because the interests were not bought over an organized stock market.
   C. These interests are not securities, because there is no common interest.
   D. B and C.

The Registration Process

AICPA.920539REG-BL

151. Non-WKSI issuer World Corp. wants to make a public offering of its common stock. On May 10, World prepares and files a registration statement with the SEC.

   On May 20, World places a "tombstone ad," announcing that it was making a public offering.

   On May 25, World issues a preliminary prospectus and the registration statement becomes effective on May 30.

On what date may World first make oral offers to sell the shares?

A. May 10.
B. May 20.
C. May 25.
D. May 30.

AICPA.940532REG-BL

152. A preliminary prospectus, permitted under SEC regulations, is known as the

A. Unaudited prospectus.
B. Qualified prospectus.
C. "Blue-sky" prospectus.
D. "Red herring" prospectus.

AICPA.911136REG-BL

153. When a common stock offering requires registration under the Securities Act of 1933,

A. The registration statement is automatically effective when filed with the SEC.
B. The issuer would be acting unlawfully if it were to sell the common stock without providing the investor with a prospectus.
C. The SEC will determine the investment value of the common stock before approving the offering.
D. The issuer may make sales ten days after filing the registration statement.

AICPA.901139REG-BL

154. The registration requirements of the Securities Act of 1933 are intended to provide information to the SEC to enable it to

A. Evaluate the financial merits of the securities being offered.
B. Ensure that investors are provided with adequate information on which to base investment decisions.
C. Prevent public offerings of securities when management fraud or unethical conduct is suspected.
D. Assure investors of accuracy of the facts presented in the financial statements.

AICPA.940533REG-BL

155. A tombstone advertisement

A. May be substituted for the prospectus under certain circumstances.
B. May contain an offer to sell securities.
C. Notifies prospective investors that a previously offered security has been withdrawn from the market and is therefore effectively "dead."
D. Makes known the availability of a prospectus.

Exempt Transactions and Securities

AICPA.060652REG

156. Which of the following securities is exempt from registration under the Securities Act of 1933?

A. Municipal bonds.
B. Securities sold by a discount broker.
C. Pre-incorporation stock subscriptions.
D. One-year notes issued to raise working capital.

AICPA.930535REG-BL

157. Regulation D of the Securities Act of 1933

A. Restricts the number of purchasers of an offering to 35.
B. Permits an exempt offering to be sold to both accredited and non-accredited investors.
C. Is limited to offers and sales of common stock that do not exceed $1.5mn.
D. Is exclusively available to small business corporations as defined by Regulation D.

AICPA.910545REG-BL

158. Which of the following securities is exempt from the registration requirements of the Securities Act of 1933?

A. Common stock with no par value.
B. Warrants to purchase preferred stock.
C. Bonds issued by a charitable foundation.
D. Convertible debentures issued by a corporation.

AICPA.920544REG-BL

159. Data, Inc., intends to make a $375,000 common-stock offering under Rule 504 of Regulation D of the Securities Act of 1933. Data

A. May sell the stock to an unlimited number of investors.
B. May make the offering through a general advertising.
C. Must offer the stock for a period longer than 12 months.
D. Must provide all investors with a prospectus.

AICPA.082102REG-II.D.I

160. Which of the following transactions is subject to registration requirements of the Securities Act of 1933?

A. The public sale by a corporation of its negotiable ten-year notes.
B. The public sale by a charitable organization of 10-year bearer bonds.
C. The sale across state lines of municipal bonds issued by a city.
D. Issuance of stock by a publicly traded corporation to its shareholders, because of a stock split.

The JOBS Act of 2012

AICPA.120758REG-SIM

161. Sam is a multimillionaire. He invested $100,000 in Company A's crowdfunded venture. Later that year, he wanted to invest in Company B's crowdfunded venture. What is the largest amount Sam can invest in B's offering?

    A. $0
    B. $10,000
    C. $100,000
    D. $1,000

AICPA.120759REG-SIM

162. The JOBS Act allows general solicitation in a Reg D Rule 506 offering if the issuer takes "reasonable steps" to insure what?

    A. That it files a registration statement with the SEC within 15 days of its first sale.
    B. That it raises no more than $50 million in a single year.
    C. That it sells only to accredited investors.
    D. All of the above.

AICPA.120757REG-SIM

163. The maximum amount that a firm can raise through crowdfunding in a single year is:

    A. $1 million.
    B. $5 million.
    C. $10 million.
    D. Unlimited, so long as they sell only to accredited investors.

AICPA.120754REG-SIM

164. Under the JOBS Act, a foreign company cannot

    A. Be an EGC.
    B. Use the crowdfunding exemption.
    C. A and B.
    D. None of the above.

AICPA.120756REG-SIM

165. A qualifying firm that declares itself to be an EGC enjoys all the following benefits for up to five years after its IPO, except:

    A. Need not comply with SOX 404(b) requirement of audit for internal controls.
    B. Need not comply with new PCAOB rules.
    C. Reduced disclosure regarding executive compensation.
    D. Immunity from fraud liability.

Liability Provisions: 1933 Act

AICPA.930505REG-BL

166. To be successful in a civil action under Section 11 of the Securities Act of 1933, concerning liability for a misleading registration statement, the plaintiff must prove the

	Defendant's intent to deceive	Plaintiff's reliance on the registration statement
A.	No	Yes
B.	No	No
C.	Yes	No
D.	Yes	Yes

AICPA.920502REG-BL

167. Dart Corp. engages Jay Associates, CPAs, to assist in a public-stock offering. Jay audits Dart's financial statements and gives an unqualified opinion, despite knowing that the financial statements contain misstatements. Jay's opinion is included in Dart's registration statement.

Larson purchases shares in the offering and suffers a loss when the stock declines in value after the misstatements becomes known.

In a suit against Jay and Dart under the Section 11 liability provisions of the Securities Act of 1933, Larson must prove that

    A. Jay knew of the misstatements.
    B. Jay was negligent.
    C. The misstatements contained in Dart's financial statements were material.
    D. The unqualified opinion contained in the registration statement was relied on by Larson.

AICPA.911108REG-BL

168. Jay Associates, CPAs, gives an unqualified opinion on Nast Power Co.'s financial statements. Larkin bought Nast bonds in a public offering subject to the Securities Act of 1933. The registration statement filed with the SEC includes Nast's financial statements.

Larkin sues Jay for misstatements contained in the financial statements under the provisions of Section 11 of the Securities Act of 1933.

To prevail, Larkin must prove

	Scienter	Reliance
A.	Yes	No
B.	Yes	Yes
C.	No	No
D.	No	Yes

AICPA.931108REG-BL

169. Ivor and Associates, CPAs, audit the financial statements of Jaymo Corporation.

As a result of Ivor's negligence in conducting the audit, the financial statements include material misstatements.

Ivor was unaware of this fact. The financial statements and Ivor's unqualified opinion are included in a registration statement and prospectus for an original public offering of stock by Jaymo.

Thorp purchases shares in the offering. Thorp receives a copy of the prospectus prior to the purchase, but does not read it. The shares decline in value as a result of the misstatements in Jaymo's financial statements becoming known.

Under which of the following Acts is Thorp most likely to prevail in a lawsuit against Ivor?

	Securities Act of 1933, Section 11	Securities Exchange Act of 1934, Section 10(b), Rule 10b-5
A.	Yes	Yes
B.	Yes	No
C.	No	Yes
D.	No	No

AICPA.101159REG

170. In which of the following types of action, brought against a CPA who issues an audit report containing an unqualified opinion on materially misstated financial statements, may a plaintiff prevail without proving reliance on the audit report?

A. An action for common-law fraud.
B. An action for common-law breach of contract.
C. An action brought under Section 11 of the Securities Act of 1933.
D. An action brought under Rule 10b-5 of the Securities Exchange Act of 1934.

Purposes, Requirements and Provisions of the 1934 Act

AICPA.082101REG-II.D.I

171. What is the standard that must be established to prove a violation of the anti-fraud provisions of Rule 10b-5 of the Securities Exchange Act of 1934?

A. Negligence.
B. Intentional misconduct.
C. Criminal intent.
D. Strict liability.

AICPA.051135REG

172. Under the liability provisions of Section 18 of the Securities Exchange Act of 1934, for which of the following actions would an accountant generally be liable?

A. Negligently approving a reporting corporation's incorrect internal financial forecasts.
B. Negligently filing a reporting corporation's tax return with the IRS.
C. Intentionally preparing and filing with the SEC a reporting corporation's incorrect quarterly report.
D. Intentionally failing to notify a reporting corporation's audit committee of defects in the verification of accounts receivable.

AICPA.101150REG

173. Which defense must an accountant establish to be absolved from civil liability under Section 18 of the Securities Exchange Act of 1934 for false or misleading statements made in reports or documents filed under the Act?

A. Lack of gross negligence.
B. Exercise of due care.
C. Good faith and lack of knowledge of the statement's falsity.
D. Lack of privity with an injured party.

AICPA.081934REG-1E2

174. Ted buys Synchotic Corporation shares based on Synchotic's announcement of record earnings. But just a few days later, on July 1, 2010, Synchotic admits that its earnings had been artificially inflated via fraudulent earnings management. Its stock price drops dramatically that day, and Ted makes a significant loss. Ted wishes to bring a 1934 Act securities-fraud lawsuit against Synchotic. In terms of the statute of limitations, when must Ted bring his lawsuit?

A. Within one year of when he should have discovered the fraud or within three years of the fraud.
B. Within one year of when he should have discovered the fraud and within three years of the fraud.
C. Within two years of when he should have discovered the fraud or within five years of the fraud.
D. Within two years of when he should have discovered the fraud and within five years of the fraud.

AICPA.951111REG-BL

175. Under the anti-fraud provisions of Section 10(b) of the Securities Exchange Act of 1934, a CPA may be liable if the CPA acts

A. Negligently.
B. With independence.
C. Without due diligence.
D. Without good faith.

Criminal Liability

AICPA.081958REG-2.D.1

176. Turtle was audit partner on ABC Accounting's audit of Jemison Corporation. Turtle knew that the audit was ineptly performed, although he hoped (without much reason) that the financial statements were accurate. He certified them as such. Which of the following is true?

A. If a court decided that Turtle had acted willfully, he could be held criminally liable under the federal securities laws.
B. If a court decided that Turtle had acted negligently, he could be held criminally liable under the federal securities laws.
C. Both A and B.
D. None of the above.

AICPA.060654REG

177. Under the Securities Exchange Act of 1934, which of the following penalties could be assessed against a CPA who intentionally violates the provisions of Section 10(b), Rule 10b-5 of the Act?

	Civil liability of monetary damages	Criminal liability of a fine
A.	Yes	Yes
B.	Yes	No
C.	No	Yes
D.	No	No

AICPA.081957REG-2.D.1

178. Seimone, an auditor for the ABC accounting firm, learns that her audit client, Bupkis Co., is about to announce a record profit. She buys Bupkis shares in a fake name and profits upon the public announcement. Which of the following is true?

A. The SEC may bring civil charges against Seimone.
B. The SEC may bring criminal charges against Seimone.
C. A and B.
D. None of the above.

AICPA.081960REG-2.D.1

179. CPA Sobel engages in insider trading of the shares of an audit client. She is caught. The SEC brings a civil action and forces Sobel to give up her insider-trading profits and pay a civil fine of three times the amount of the profits. Sobel thought she had been punished sufficiently, but then the DOJ began an investigation. Which of the following is true?

A. DOJ cannot bring criminal charges because Sobel has been punished enough.
B. The DOJ can choose to bring criminal charges to supplement the SEC's civil action.
C. To bring criminal charges would amount to double jeopardy.
D. A and C.

AICPA.081959REG-2.D.1

180. Willful violations of which of the following acts can create the basis for federal criminal liability?

A. The 1933 Securities Act.
B. The 1934 Securities Exchange Act.
C. A and B.
D. None of the above.

Other Federal Laws and Regulation

Employment Tax

AICPA.951132REG-BL

181. Taxes payable under the Federal Unemployment Tax Act (FUTA) are

A. Calculated as a fixed percentage of all compensation paid to an employee.
B. Deductible by the employer as a business expense for federal income-tax purposes.
C. Payable by employers for all employees.
D. Withheld from the wages of all covered employees.

AICPA.901137REG-BL

182. The Federal Unemployment Tax Act (FUTA)

A. Requires both the employer and employee to pay FUTA taxes, although the amounts to be paid by each are different.
B. Does not apply to businesses with fewer than 35 employees.
C. Does not apply to employers that conduct business only in one state and employ only residents of that state.
D. Allows the employer to take a credit against the FUTA tax if contributions are made to a state unemployment fund.

AICPA.911133REG-BL

183. An unemployed CPA would generally receive unemployment compensation benefits if the CPA

A. Was fired as a result of the employer's business reversals.
B. Refused to accept a job as an accountant while receiving extended benefits.
C. Was fired for embezzling from a client.
D. Left work voluntarily without good cause.

Affordable Care Act

aq.aca.0007

184. Under his health care plan, Tran has a deductible of $1,200, a coinsurance of 20%, and an out-of-pocket limit that matches the federal maximum of $6,850 (in 2016). Tran has significant surgery for which his bill is $5,000, hospitalization for which his bill is $40,000, and home health care after he leaves the hospital which comes to $4,000. How much of the hospital bill will Tran pay, assuming he pays the three bills in the order mentioned?

A. $40,000
B. $6,850
C. $3,425
D. $4,890

aq.aca.0003

185. Income from which of the following is (are) deemed unearned income for purposes of the ACA's Medicare surtax on unearned income?

A. Stocks
B. Bonds
C. Capital gains
D. All of the above

aq.aca.0002

186. In 2013, thirty-something Tessa had an AGI of $75,000. She had some severe dental problems and paid her dentist $10,000 that was not covered by insurance. How much may Tessa deduct from her income tax form under the ACA?

A. $10,000
B. $7,500
C. $2,500
D. $4,375

Worker Classification Laws and Regulations

worker.law.reg.007

187. Which of the following professions might well be deemed *statutory employees* under the proper circumstances?

A. Lumberjacks.
B. Welders.
C. Farmers.
D. Life insurance agents.

worker.law.reg.001

188. Tim works alongside three other workers at ABC Co. They all do the same work. They all work 8-5 most days and are required to work occasionally in the evening or on a weekend. They are all paid on an hourly basis. The other three workers are labeled and treated as employees, but Tim signed a contract saying that he is an *independent contractor*. Later, litigation arose regarding Tim's status. Which of the following is **true**?

A. Because Tim signed the contract, he is indeed an independent contractor rather than an employee of ABC.
B. Signing the contract is not the most important factor in this scenario, but Tim is nonetheless an independent contractor.
C. A court will probably disregard the contract and hold that Tim is an employee.
D. Choices 1 and 2.

worker.law.reg.006

189. LMN Corporation classified many of its workers as independent contractors, but that classification became the subject of litigation and was determined to be erroneous. Which of the following does **not** support a safe harbor defense for LMN?

A. An opinion from its corporate counsel.
B. The classification is consistent with industry practice.
C. A previous IRS ruling found these workers to be independent contractors
D. An IRS ruling in a case involving JKL Co. found similarly situated workers to be independent contractors.

Business Structure Selection and Formation of Business Entity and Related Operation and Termination

Selection

AICPA.090615BEC-I-A

190. Under the Revised Uniform Limited Partnership Act, which of the following statements is correct regarding limited partnerships?

A. Limited partners may lose limited liability if they participate in management activities.
B. Limited partnerships may legally exist without filing a certificate of limited partnership.
C. Limited partners have the same rights, responsibilities, and authority as general partners.
D. Limited partners may contribute cash only and may not contribute services as their capital contributions.

AICPA.921101REG-BL

191. Which of the following statements is correct concerning the similarities between a limited partnership and a corporation?

A. Each is created under a statute and must file a copy of its certificate with the proper state authorities.
B. All corporate stockholders and all partners in a limited partnership have limited liability.
C. Both are recognized for federal income-tax purposes as taxable entities.
D. Both are statutorily permitted to exist in perpetuity.

AICPA.090609BEC-I-D

192. Which of the following forms of business generally provides all owners with limited liability, while avoiding federal taxation of income at the entity level?

A. A Subchapter C corporation.
B. A Subchapter S corporation.
C. Partnership.
D. Limited partnership.

AICPA.920515BEC-BL

193. Assuming all other requirements are met, a corporation may elect to be treated as an S corporation under the Internal Revenue Code if it has

A. Both common and preferred stockholders.
B. A partnership as a stockholder.
C. One hundred or fewer shareholders.
D. The consent of a majority of the stockholders.

AICPA.051144BEC

194. Which of the following statements describes the same characteristic for both an S corporation and a C corporation?

A. Both corporations can have more than 100 shareholders.
B. Both corporations have the disadvantage of double taxation.
C. Shareholders can contribute property into a corporation without being taxed.
D. Shareholders can be either citizens of the U.S. or foreign countries.

Formation

AICPA.051132BEC

195. Following the formation of a corporation, which of the following terms best describes the process by which the promoter is released from, and the corporation is made liable for, pre-incorporation contractual obligations?

A. Assignment.
B. Novation.
C. Delegation.
D. Accord and satisfaction.

AICPA.051133BEC

196. Under the Revised Model Business Corporation Act (RMBCA), which of the following items of information must be included in a corporation's articles of incorporation (charter)?

A. Name and address of each incorporator.
B. Nature and purpose of the corporation's business.
C. Name and address of the corporation's promoter.
D. Election of either C corporation or S corporation status.

AICPA.082088BEC-I.BEC.I.A

197. What type of business organization may generally be formed without filing an organizational document or certificate with a state-government agency or office?

A. A corporation.
B. A limited-liability company.
C. A general partnership.
D. A limited partnership.

AICPA.940511BEC-BL

198. Under the Revised Model Business Corporation Act (RMBCA), which of the following must be contained in a corporation's articles of incorporation?

A. Quorum voting requirements.
B. Names of stockholders.

C. Provisions for issuance of par and non-par shares.

D. The number of shares the corporation is authorized to issue.

Operations: Nonfinancial Factors

AICPA.082086BEC-I.BEC.I.B

199. Which of the following circumstances may permit the piercing of the corporate veil of a closely held corporation and therefore cause its shareholders to be held personally liable?

    I.   The corporation is thinly capitalized.

    II. The corporation borrows money from a shareholder without giving the shareholder a security interest in corporate assets.

A. I only.

B. II only.

C. Both I and II.

D. Neither I nor II.

AICPA.120601REG

200. Which of the following statements is correct regarding a limited liability company's operating agreement?

A. It must be filed with a central state agency.

B. It must be in writing.

C. It is designed to forestall and resolve disputes among the owners.

D. It is necessary for a limited liability company to exist.

AICPA.931120BEC-BL

201. The corporate veil is most likely to be pierced and the shareholders held personally liable if

A. The corporation has elected S corporation status under the Internal Revenue Code.

B. The shareholders have commingled their personal funds with those of the corporation.

C. An ultra vires act has been committed.

D. A partnership incorporates its business solely to limit the liability of its partners.

AICPA.080922BEC-1B

202. Elmo forms a corporation to run a retail store. He buys $100,000 worth of its stock, as does his mother. They are the only two shareholders. The store's location was not favorable and the business does not take off. Over the course of five years, Elmo slowly burns through the $200,000 in capital, as the store posts losses every year. Near the end of the sixth year, the corporation takes bankruptcy, leaving creditors on the hook for $40,000; they had delivered inventory to the store for which the corporation

had been unable to pay. The creditors sue Elmo and his mother personally. Given the facts presented, what should happen?

A. The court should pierce the corporate veil, because the store was obviously undercapitalized.

B. The court should pierce the corporate veil, because the creditors failed to have Elmo or his mother personally guarantee their extensions of credit.

C. The court should not pierce the corporate veil.

D. A and B.

AICPA.101002REG-SIM

203. Sal wishes to form a business entity that he will own and control all by himself. Which of the following is not a good choice for him?

A. Sole proprietorship.

B. General partnership.

C. LLC.

D. Corporation.

Financial Structure

AICPA.051140BEC

204. Which of the following decreases stockholder equity?

A. Investments by owners.

B. Distributions to owners.

C. Issuance of stock.

D. Acquisition of assets in a cash transaction.

AICPA.940513BEC-BL

205. To which of the following rights is a holder of a public corporation's cumulative preferred stock always entitled?

A. Conversion of the preferred stock into common stock.

B. Voting rights.

C. Dividend carryovers from years in which dividends were not paid, to future years.

D. Guaranteed dividends.

AICPA.101004REG-SIM

206. Ed, Fred, and Ned form the EFN general partnership. Ed and Fred each contribute $50,000 to start the business. Ned contributes $25,000. Ed and Fred both work 20 hours a week for the business, while Ned works 40 hours a week. After capital contributions are repaid, the firm starts turning a profit. The partners had not expressly agreed how those profits should be shared. Which of the following is true?

A. The profits should be shared equally.

B. Ed and Fred should receive more of the profits than Ned, because they put more capital into the partnership.

C. Ned should receive a greater share of the profits than Ed and Fred, because he is contributing more labor to the business.

D. None of the above.

AICPA.920519BEC-BL

207. Price owns 2,000 shares of Universal Corp.'s $10 cumulative preferred stock. During its first year of operations, cash dividends of $5 per share are declared on the preferred stock, but were never paid. In the second year, dividends on the preferred stock were neither declared, nor paid.

If Universal is dissolved, which of the following statements is correct?

A. Universal will be liable to Price as an unsecured creditor for $10,000.

B. Universal will be liable to Price as a secured creditor for $20,000.

C. Price will have priority over the claims of Universal's bond owners.

D. Price will have priority over the claims of Universal's unsecured judgment creditors.

AICPA.951118REG-BL

208. Which of the following statements is correct regarding the division of profits in a general partnership when the written partnership agreement only provides that losses be divided equally among the partners?

Profits are to be divided

A. Based on the partners' ratio of contribution to the partnership.

B. Based on the partners' participation in day-to-day management.

C. Equally among the partners.

D. Proportionately among the partners.

Termination

AICPA.940514BEC-BL

209. Under the Revised Model Business Corporation Act (RMBCA), a merger of two public corporations usually requires all of the following, except

A. A formal plan of merger.

B. An affirmative vote by the holders of a majority of each corporation's voting shares.

C. Receipt of voting stock by all stockholders of the original corporations.

D. Approval by the Board of Directors of each corporation.

AICPA.970503BEC-BL

210. Which of the following actions may be taken by a corporation's Board of Directors without stockholder approval?

A. Purchasing substantially all of the assets of another corporation.

B. Selling substantially all of the corporation's assets.

C. Dissolving the corporation.

D. Amending the articles of incorporation.

AICPA.941124REG-BL

211. The partners of College Assoc., a general partnership, decide to dissolve the partnership and agree that none of the partners will continue to use the partnership name.

Under the Uniform Partnership Act, which of the following events will occur on dissolution of the partnership?

	Each partner's existing liability will be discharged	Each partner's apparent authority will continue
A.	Yes	Yes
B.	Yes	No
C.	No	Yes
D.	No	No

Rights, Duties, Legal Obligations, and Authority of Owners, and Management

Rights and Duties

AICPA.930515REG-BL

212. Cobb, Inc., a partner in TLC Partnership, assigns its partnership interest to Bean, who is not made a partner. After the assignment, Bean asserts the rights to

I. Participate in the management of TLC.

II. Cobb's share of TLC's partnership profits.

Bean is correct as to which of these rights?

A. I only.

B. II only.

C. I and II.

D. Neither I nor II.

AICPA.920518BEC-BL

213. A corporate stockholder is entitled to which of the following rights?

A. To elect officers.

B. Receive annual dividends.

C. Approve dissolution.

D. Prevent corporate borrowing.

AICPA.080907BEC-1A1

214. Tilda, Max, and Boniface form an equal partnership that manufactures batteries for solar-powered cars. Unfortunately, their ambition exceeds their technology and the partnership is unable to pay several contractual obligations entered into in its name. A supplier, Sims Co., is owed $400,000 on materials it delivered to the partnership. Sims has sued and received a judgment against the three partners and the partnership. Sims should begin its quest to satisfy the judgment by proceeding against the assets of:

   A. Tilda.
   B. Max.
   C. Boniface.
   D. The partnership.

AICPA.951123BEC-BL

215. To which of the following rights is a stockholder of a public corporation entitled?

   A. The right to have annual dividends declared and paid.
   B. The right to vote for the election of officers.
   C. The right to a reasonable inspection of corporate records.
   D. The right to have the corporation issue a new class of stock.

AICPA.080911BEC-1A1

216. Mary buys an interest in the ABC accounting firm and thereby joins Adam, Betty, and Chen as an equal one-fourth partner. Mary thinks the firm's prices are a little high. When an acquaintance consults Mary about having the firm do her personal income tax return, Mary tells her: "Just come over to my house this weekend. I'll do the return for you and charge you only half of what my firm would charge." Which partnership duty, if any, has Mary breached?

   A. Duty of care.
   B. Duty of loyalty in the form of no competition
   C. Duty of loyalty in the form of no disclosure of confidential information.
   D. All of the above.

Authority of Owners and Managers

AICPA.951117REG-BL

217. Which of the following statements is (are) usually correct regarding general partners' liability?

   I. All general partners are jointly and severally liable for partnership torts.
   II. All general partners are liable only for those partnership obligations they actually authorized.

   A. I only.
   B. II only.
   C. Both I and II.
   D. Neither I nor II.

AICPA.910505BEC-BL

218. Davis, a director of Active Corp., is entitled to

   A. Serve on the Board of a competing business.
   B. Take sole advantage of a business opportunity that would benefit Active.
   C. Rely on information provided by a corporate officer.
   D. Unilaterally grant a corporate loan to one of Active's shareholders.

AICPA.082087BEC-I.BEC.I.D

219. The principle that protects corporate directors from personal liability for acts performed in good faith on behalf of the corporation is known as

   A. The "clean hands doctrine."
   B. The "full-disclosure rule."
   C. The "responsible person doctrine."
   D. The "business-judgment rule."

AICPA.930514REG-BL

220. On behalf of a general partnership that operates an appliance store, a partner, Locke, contracts to buy 15 stoves from Gage. Unknown to Gage, Locke was not authorized by the partnership agreement to make such contracts. Another partner, Vorst, refuses to allow the partnership to accept delivery of the stoves and Gage seeks to enforce the contract.

   Gage will

   A. Lose, because Locke's action was not authorized by the partnership agreement.
   B. Lose, because Locke was not an agent of the partnership.
   C. Win, because Locke had express authority to bind the partnership.
   D. Win, because Locke had apparent authority to bind the partnership.

AICPA.900507BEC-BL

221. In the absence of a specific provision in its articles of incorporation, a corporation's Board of Directors has the power to do all of the following, except

   A. Repeal the bylaws.
   B. Declare dividends.
   C. Fix the compensation of directors.
   D. Amend the articles of incorporation.

III. Federal Taxation of Property Transactions

Property Transactions

Sales and Dispositions of Assets

AICPA.130904REG

222. Simmons gives her child a gift of publicly-traded stock with a basis of $40,000 and a fair market value of $30,000. No gift tax is paid. The child subsequently sells the stock for $36,000. What is the child's recognized gain or loss, if any?

   A. $4,000 loss.
   B. No gain or loss.
   C. $6,000 gain.
   D. $36,000 gain.

AICPA.911130REG-P2-AR

223. Hall, a divorced person and custodian of her 12-year old child, filed her 2016 federal income tax return as head of a household. She submitted the following information to the CPA who prepared her 2016 return:

   1. The divorce agreement, executed in 2014, provides for Hall to receive $3,000 per month, of which $600 is designated as child support. After the child reaches 18, the monthly payments are to be reduced to $2,400 and are to be continued until remarriage or death. However, for the year 2016, Hall received a total of only $5,000 from her former husband. Hall paid an attorney $2,000 in 2015 in a suit to collect the alimony owed.
   2. In June 2016, Hall's mother gifted her 100 shares of a listed stock. The donor's basis for this stock, which she bought in 1985, was $4,000, and market value on the date of the gift was $3,000. Hall sold his stock in July 2016 for $3,500. The donor paid no gift tax.
   3. During 2016, Hall spent a total of $1,000 for state lottery tickets. Her lottery winnings in 2016 totaled $200.
   4. Hall earned a salary of $25,000 in 2016. Hall was not covered by any type of retirement plan, but contributed $2,000 to an IRA in 2016.
   5. In 2016, Hall sold an antique that she bought in 1995 to display in her home. Hall paid $800 for the antique and sold it for $1,400, using the proceeds to pay a court-ordered judgment.
   6. Hall paid the following expenses in 2016 pertaining to the home that she owns: realty

taxes, $3,400; mortgage interest, $7,000; casualty insurance, $490; assessment by city for construction of a sewer system, $910; interest of $1,000 on a personal, unsecured bank loan, the proceeds of which were used for home improvements. Hall does not rent out any portion of the home.

What was Hall's reportable gain or loss in 2016 on the sale of the 100 shares of stock gifted to her?

   A. $0
   B. $500 gain
   C. $500 loss
   D. $1,000 loss

AICPA.130911REG

224. For an individual business owner, which of the following would typically be classified as a capital asset for federal income tax purposes?

   A. Accounts receivable.
   B. Marketable securities.
   C. Machinery and equipment used in a business.
   D. Inventory.

AICPA.901128REG-P2-AR

225. Joe Hall owns a limousine for use in his personal service business of transporting passengers to airports. The limousine's adjusted basis is $40,000. In addition, Hall owns his personal residence and furnishings that together cost him $280,000.

Hall's capital assets amount to

   A. $320,000
   B. $280,000
   C. $40,000
   D. $0

AICPA.120702REG

226. Upon her grandfather's death, Jordan inherited 10 shares of Universal Corp. stock that had a fair market value of $5,000. Her grandfather acquired the shares in 1995 for $2,500. Four months after her grandfather's death, Jordan sold all her shares of Universal for $7,500. What was Jordan's recognized gain in the year of sale?

   A. $2,500 long-term capital gain.
   B. $2,500 short-term capital gain.
   C. $5,000 long-term capital gain.
   D. $5,000 short-term capital gain.

Capital Gains and Losses

AICPA.910546REG-P2-AR

227. A corporation's capital losses are

A. Deductible only to the extent of the corporation's capital gains.
B. Deductible from the corporation's ordinary income to the extent of $3,000.
C. Carried back two years and forward 20 years.
D. Forfeited if the corporation had no capital gains in the year in which the capital losses were incurred.

AICPA.130915REG

228. Summer, a single individual, had a net operating loss of $20,000 three years ago. A Code Sec. 1244 stock loss made up three-fourths of that loss. Summer had no taxable income from that year until the current year. In the current year, Summer has gross income of $80,000 and sustains another loss of $50,000 on Code Sec. 1244 stock. Assuming that Summer can carry the entire $20,000 net operating loss to the current year, what is the amount and character of the Code Sec. 1244 loss that Summer can deduct for the current year?

A. $35,000 ordinary loss.
B. $35,000 capital loss.
C. $50,000 ordinary loss.
D. $50,000 capital loss.

AICPA.020501REG-AR

229. Jackson, a single individual, inherits Bean Corp. common stock from his parents. Bean is a qualified small business corporation under Code Section 1244. The stock costs Jackson's parents $20,000 and has a fair market value of $25,000 at the parents' date of death. During the year, Bean declares bankruptcy and Jackson is informed that the stock is worthless.

What amount may Jackson deduct as an ordinary loss in the current year?

A. $0
B. $3,000
C. $20,000
D. $25,000

AICPA.970505REG-AR

230. How are a C corporation's net capital losses used?

A. Deducted from the corporation's ordinary income only, to the extent of $3,000.
B. Carried back three years and forward five years.
C. Deductible in full from the corporation's ordinary income.
D. Carried forward 15 years.

AICPA.910521REG-P2-AR

231. For a cash-basis taxpayer, gain or loss on a year-end sale of listed stock arises on the

A. Trade date.
B. Settlement date.
C. Date of receipt of cash proceeds.
D. Date of delivery of stock certificate.

Section 1231 Assets

AICPA.941134REG-AR

232. On January 2, 2012, Bates Corp. purchases and places into service seven-year MACRS tangible property costing $100,000. On December 31, 2016, Bates sells the property for $102,000, after having taken $47,525 in MACRS depreciation deductions.

What amount of the gain should Bates recapture as ordinary income?

A. $0
B. $2,000
C. $47,525
D. $49,525

AICPA.101126REG-SIM

233. The results of UNA Corporation's first six years of operations are presented below.

Year	Results of Operations.
1	Section 1231 losses of $50,000.
2	Section 1231 losses of $30,000.
3	Section 1231 gains of $75,000.
4	Section 1231 losses of $20,000.
5	Section 1231 losses of $30,000.
6	Section 1231 gain of $80,000

UNA corporation's year-six Section 1231 gain can best be characterized as

A. $80,000 Section 1231 gain.
B. $50,000 ordinary income; $30,000 Section 1231 gain.
C. $80,000 ordinary income.
D. $55,000 ordinary income; $25,000 Sec. 1231 gain.

AICPA.120732REG

234. Lobster, Inc. incurs the following losses on disposition of business assets during the year:

Loss on the abandonment of office equipment	$25,000
Loss on the sale of a building (straight-line depreciation taken in prior years of $200,000)	250,000
Loss on the sale of delivery trucks	15,000

What is the amount and character of the losses to be reported on Lobster's tax return?

A. $40,000 Section 1231 loss only.
B. $40,000 Section 1231 loss, $50,000 long-term capital loss.
C. $40,000 Section 1231 loss, $250,000 long-term capital loss.
D. $290,000 Section 1231 loss.

AICPA.101125REG-SIM

235. On August 22, 2016 Martha purchases a computer to use in her childcare business. She sells the computer on December 28, 2016 for $2,000 when the machine has an adjusted tax basis of $1,700. What is the amount and character of the gain on the sale?

A. $300 short-term capital gain.
B. $300 long-term capital gain.
C. $300 ordinary income.
D. $300 Section 1231 gain.

AICPA.950557REG-BL

236. Which of the following items is tangible personal property?

A. Share of stock.
B. Trademark.
C. Promissory note.
D. Oil painting.

Section 1231 Assets—Cost Recovery

AICPA.120730REG

237. As part of a business acquisition, on January 1, Fast, Inc. entered into a covenant not to compete with Swift, Inc. for a period of five years, with an option by Swift to extend it to seven years. What is the amortization period of the covenant for tax purposes?

A. 5 years.
B. 7 years.
C. 15 years.
D. 17 years.

AICPA.101135REG-SIM

238. ACE Landscaping purchased equipment for $3,000 in the current year that it plans to use 100% for business purposes. The equipment qualifies as 5-year property. The deprecation percentages provided in the MACRS tables are as follows:

Year 1	20.00%
Year 2	32.00%
Year 3	19.20%
Year 4	11.52%
Year 5	11.52%
Year 6	5.76%

On August 20 of Year 3 ACE sells the equipment for $1,800. The depreciation allowed for the equipment for Year 3 is (rounded to the nearest dollar):

A. $ 0
B. $173
C. $288
D. $575

AICPA.101108REG

239. On August 1, 2016, Graham purchases and places into service an office building costing $264,000, including $30,000 for the land. What was Graham's MACRS deduction for the office building in 2016?

A. $9,600
B. $6,000
C. $3,600
D. $2,250

AICPA.910550REG-P2-AR

240. Under modified accelerated cost recovery system (MACRS) depreciation for property placed in service after 1986,

A. Used tangible depreciable property is excluded from the computation.
B. Salvage value is ignored for the purposes of computing the MACRS deduction.
C. No type of straight-line depreciation is allowable.
D. The recovery period for depreciable realty is 27.5 years.

Like-Kind Exchanges and Involuntary Conversions

AICPA.090845REG

241. A heavy equipment dealer would like to trade some business assets in a non-taxable exchange. Which of the following exchanges would qualify as non-taxable?

A. The company jet for a large truck to be used in the corporation.
B. Investment securities for antiques to be held as investments.
C. A road grader held in inventory for another road grader.
D. A corporate office building for a vacant lot.

AICPA.910523REG-P2-AR

242. In a "like-kind" exchange of an investment asset for a similar asset that will also be held as an investment, no taxable gain or loss will be recognized on the transaction if both assets consist of

A. Convertible debentures.
B. Convertible preferred stock.

C. Partnership interests.

D. Rental real estate located in different states.

assess.AICPA.REG.like.exchange-0012

243. Dawson, Inc.'s warehouse (with an adjusted tax basis of $75,000) was destroyed by fire. The following year, Dawson received insurance proceeds of $195,000 and acquired a new warehouse for $167,000. Dawson elected to recognize the minimum gain possible. What is Dawson's basis in the new warehouse?

A. $47,000

B. $75,000

C. $139,000

D. $167,000

AICPA.901130REG-P2-AR

244. In 2016, Joan Reed exchanges commercial real estate that she owns for other commercial real estate, plus $50,000 cash. The following additional information pertains to this transaction:

Property given up by Reed.	
Fair market value.	$500,000
Adjusted basis.	$300,000
Property received by Reed.	
Fair market value.	$450,000

What amount of gain should be recognized in Reed's 2016 income-tax return?

A. $200,000

B. $100,000

C. $50,000

D. $0

AICPA.120745REG

245. Hogan exchanged a business-use machine having an original cost of $100,000 and accumulated depreciation of $30,000 for business-use equipment owned by Baker having a fair market value of $80,000 plus $1,000 cash. Baker assumed a $2,000 outstanding debt on the machine. What taxable gain should Hogan recognize?

A. $0

B. $3,000

C. $10,000

D. $11,000

Other Nonrecognition Transactions

AICPA.090838REG

246. Sands purchased 100 shares of Eastern Corp. stock for $18,000 on April 1 of the prior year. On February 1 of the current year, Sands sold 50 shares of Eastern for $7,000. Fifteen days later, Sands purchased 25 shares of Eastern for $3,750. What is the amount of Sand's recognized gain or loss?

A. $0

B. $500 loss.

C. $1,000 loss.

D. $2,000 loss.

AICPA.090847REG

247. Wynn, a single individual age 60, sold Wynn's personal residence for $450,000. Wynn had owned Wynn's residence, which had a basis of $250,000, for six years. Within eight months of the sale, Wynn purchased a new residence for $400,000. What is Wynn's recognized gain from the sale of Wynn's personal residence?

A. $0

B. $50,000

C. $75,000

D. $200,000

AICPA.120746REG

248. A married couple purchased their principal residence for $300,000. They spent $40,000 on improvements. After living in it for 10 years, the couple sold the home for $650,000 and paid $36,000 in real estate commissions. What gain should the couple recognize on their joint return?

A. $0

B. $ 60,000

C. $274,000

D. $310,000

AICPA.921118REG-P2-AR

249. Among which of the following related parties are losses from sales and exchanges not recognized for tax purposes?

A. Father-in-law and son-in-law.

B. Brother-in-law and sister-in-law.

C. Grandfather and granddaughter.

D. Ancestors, lineal descendants, and all in-laws.

AICPA.950504REG-AR

250. Conner purchases 300 shares of Zinco stock for $30,000 in 2001. On May 23, 2015, Conner sells all the stock to his daughter, Alice, for $20,000, its then fair market value. Conner realizes no other gain or loss during 2015. On July 26, 2016, Alice sells the 300 shares of Zinco for $25,000.

What is Alice's recognized gain or loss on her sale?

A. $0

B. $5,000 long-term gain.

C. $5,000 short-term loss.

D. $5,000 long-term loss.

IV. Federal Taxation of Individuals

Income

Gross Income—General Concepts and Interest

AICPA.940503REG-AR

251. During 2017, Kay received interest income as follows:

On U.S. Treasury certificates	$4,000
On refund of the prior year's federal income tax	$500

The total amount of interest subject to tax in Kay's 2017 tax return is

A. $4,500.
B. $4,000.
C. $500.
D. $0.

AICPA.931121REG-P2-AR

252. Charles and Marcia are married cash-basis taxpayers. In 2017, they had interest income as follows:

$500 interest on federal income tax refund

$600 interest on state income tax refund

$800 interest on federal government obligations

$1,000 interest on state government obligations

What amount of interest income is taxable on Charles and Marcia's 2017 joint income tax return?

A. $500
B. $1,100
C. $1,900
D. $2,900

AICPA.921116REG-P2-AR

253. In 2017, Clark filed Form 1040EZ for the 2016 taxable year. In 2017, Clark received a state income tax refund of $900 plus interest of $10, for overpayment of 2016 state income tax.

What amount of the state tax refund and interest is taxable in Clark's 2017 federal income tax return?

A. $0
B. $10
C. $900
D. $910

AICPA.951110REG-AR

254. In 2016, Stewart Corp. properly accrued $5,000 for an income item on the basis of a reasonable estimate. In 2017, after filing its 2016 federal income tax return, Stewart determined that the exact amount was $6,000.

Which of the following statements is correct?

A. No further inclusion of income is required as the difference is less than 25% of the original amount reported and the estimate had been made in good faith.
B. The $1,000 difference is includible in Stewart's income tax return.
C. Stewart is required to notify the IRS within 30 days of the determination of the exact amount of the item.
D. Stewart is required to file an amended return to report the additional $1,000 of income.

AICPA.931133REG-P2-AR

255. In 2016, Farb, a cash-basis individual taxpayer, received an $8,000 invoice for personal property taxes.

Believing the amount to be overstated by $5,000, Farb paid the invoiced amount under protest and immediately started legal action to recover the overstatement. In November 2017, the matter is resolved in Farb's favor, and he receives a $5,000 refund. Farb itemizes his deductions on his tax returns.

Which of the following statements is correct regarding the deductibility of the property taxes?

A. Farb should deduct $8,000 in his 2016 income tax return and should report the $5,000 refund as income in his 2017 income tax return.
B. Farb should not deduct any amount in his 2016 income tax return and should deduct $3,000 in his 2017 income tax return.
C. Farb should deduct $3,000 in his 2016 income tax return.
D. Farb should not deduct any amount in his 2016 income tax return when originally filed, and should file an amended 2016 income tax return in 2017.

Gross Income—Other Inclusions

AICPA.931124REG-P2-AR

256. John and Mary were divorced in 2016. The divorce decree provides that John pay alimony of $10,000 per year, to be reduced by 20% on their child's 18th birthday. During 2017, John paid $7,000 directly to Mary and $3,000 to Spring College for Mary's tuition.

What amount of these payments should be reported as income in Mary's 2017 income tax return?

A. $5,600
B. $8,000
C. $8,600
D. $10,000

AICPA.130912REG

257. Randolph is a single individual who always claims the standard deduction. Randolph received the following in the current year:

Wages	$22,000
Unemployment compensation	6,000
Pension distribution (100% taxable)	4,000
A state tax refund from the previous year	425

What is Randolph's gross income?

A. $22,000
B. $28,425
C. $32,000
D. $32,425

AICPA.090854REG

258. An individual received $50,000 during the current year pursuant to a divorce decree. A check for $25,000 was identified as annual alimony, checks totaling $10,000 as annual child support, and a check for $15,000 as a property settlement. What amount should be included in the individual's gross income?

A. $50,000
B. $40,000
C. $25,000
D. $0

AICPA.060804REG-AR

259. Porter was unemployed for part of the year in 2017. Porter received $35,000 in wages, $4,000 from a state unemployment compensation plan, and $2,000 from his former employer's company-paid supplemental unemployment benefit plan. What is the amount of Porter's gross income in 2017?

A. $35,000
B. $37,000

C. $39,000
D. $41,000

AICPA.911128REG-P2-AR

260. Hall, a divorced person and custodian of her 12-year old child, filed her 2017 federal income tax return as head of a household. She submitted the following information to the CPA who prepared her 2017 return:

1. The divorce agreement, executed in 2015, provides for Hall to receive $3,000 per month, of which $600 is designated as child support. After the child reaches 18, the monthly payments are to be reduced to $2,400 and are to be continued until remarriage or death. However, for the year 2017, Hall received a total of only $5,000 from her former husband. Hall paid an attorney $2,000 in 2017 in a suit to collect the alimony owed.

2. In June 2016, Hall's mother gifted her 100 shares of a listed stock. The donor's basis for this stock, which she bought in 2001, was $4,000, and market value on the date of the gift was $3,000. Hall sold her stock in July 2017 for $3,500. The donor paid no gift tax.

3. During 2017, Hall spent a total of $1,000 for state lottery tickets. Her lottery winnings in 2017 totaled $200.

4. Hall earned a salary of $25,000 in 2017. Hall was not covered by any type of retirement plan, but contributed $2,000 to an IRA in 2017.

5. In 2017, Hall sold an antique that she bought in 1995 to display in her home. Hall paid $800 for the antique and sold it for $1,400, using the proceeds to pay a court-ordered judgment.

6. Hall paid the following expenses in 2017 pertaining to the home that she owns: realty taxes, $3,400; mortgage interest, $7,000; casualty insurance, $490; assessment by city for construction of a sewer system, $910; interest of $1,000 on a personal, unsecured bank loan, the proceeds of which were used for home improvements. Hall does not rent out any portion of the home.

What amount should be reported in Hall's 2017 return as alimony income?

A. $36,000
B. $28,800
C. $5,000
D. $0

Gross Income—Exclusions

AICPA.081202REG-SIM

261. Blake, a single individual age 67, had a 2017 adjusted gross income of $60,000 exclusive of social security benefits. Blake received social security benefits of $8,400 and interest of $1,000 on tax-exempt obligations during 2017. What amount of social security benefits is excludable from Blake's 2017 taxable income?

    A. $0
    B. $1,260
    C. $4,200
    D. $8,400

AICPA.020503REG-AR

262. Fuller was the owner and beneficiary of a $200,000 life insurance policy on a parent. Fuller sold the policy to Decker, for $25,000. Decker paid a total of $40,000 in premiums.

    Upon the death of the parent, what amount must Decker include in gross income?

    A. $0
    B. $135,000
    C. $160,000
    D. $200,000

AICPA.081201REG-SIM

263. In 2017, Joan accepted and received a $10,000 award for outstanding civic achievement. Joan was selected without any action on her part, and no future services are expected of her as a condition of receiving the award. What amount should Joan include in her 2017 adjusted gross income in connection with this award?

    A. $0
    B. $ 4,000
    C. $ 5,000
    D. $10,000

AICPA.970501REG-AR

264. Klein, a master's degree candidate at Briar University, was awarded a $12,000 scholarship from Briar. The scholarship was used to pay Klein's university tuition and fees. Klein also received $5,000 for teaching two courses at a nearby college.

    What amount is includible in Klein's gross income?

    A. $0
    B. $ 5,000
    C. $12,000
    D. $17,000

AICPA.950501REG-AR

265. Which payment(s) is(are) included in a recipient's gross income?

    I. Payment to a graduate assistant for a part-time teaching assignment at a university. Teaching is not a requirement toward obtaining the degree.
    II. A grant to a Ph.D. candidate for his participation in a university-sponsored research project for the benefit of the university.

    A. I only.
    B. II only.
    C. Both I and II.
    D. Neither I nor II.

Taxation of Income from Business Entities

ITAX-0011B

266. Jack and Joan Mitchell, married taxpayers and residents of a separate property state, elect to file a joint return for 2017 during which they received the following dividends:

	Received by	
	Jack	Joan
Alert Corporation (a qualified, domestic corporation)	$400	$50
Canadian Mines, Inc. (a Canadian company)		300
Eternal Life Mutual Insurance Company (dividends on life insurance policy)	200	

Total dividends received to date on the life insurance policy do not exceed cumulative premiums paid. For 2017, what amount should the Mitchells report on their joint return as dividend income?

    A. $550
    B. $600
    C. $750
    D. $800

ITAX-0012B

267. During 2015, Karen purchased 100 shares of preferred stock of Boling Corp. for $5,500. During 2018, Karen received a stock dividend of ten additional shares of Boling Corp. preferred stock. On the date the preferred stock was distributed, it had a fair market value of $60 per share. What is Karen's basis in the ten shares of preferred stock that she received as a dividend?

    A. $0
    B. $500
    C. $550
    D. $600

TPRO-0014B

268. On July 1, 2011, Lila Perl paid $90,000 for 450 shares of Janis Corp. common stock. Lila received a nontaxable stock dividend of 50 new common shares in August 2017. On December 20, 2017, Lila sold the 50 new shares for $11,000. How much should Lila report in her 2017 return as long-term capital gain?

   A. $0
   B. $ 1,000
   C. $ 2,000
   D. $11,000

Accounting Methods and Periods—Individuals

AICPA.120606REG-SIM

269. Which of the following taxpayers may use the cash basis as its method of accounting for tax purposes?

   A. Partnership that is designated as a tax shelter.
   B. Retail store with $2 million in gross receipts.
   C. An international accounting firm organized as a partnership.
   D. Office cleaning corporation with average annual income of $8 million.

AICPA.090859REG

270. Dart, a C corporation, distributes software over the Internet and has had average revenues in excess of $20 million dollars per year for the past three years. To purchase software, customers key-in their credit card number to a secure web site and receive a password that allows the customer to immediately download the software. As a result, Dart doesn't record accounts receivable or inventory on its books. Which of the following statements is correct?

   A. Dart may use either the cash or accrual method of accounting as long as Dart elects a calendar year end.
   B. Dart may utilize any method of accounting Dart chooses as long as Dart consistently applies the method it chooses.
   C. Dart must use the accrual method of accounting.
   D. Dart may utilize the cash basis method of accounting until it incurs an additional $10 million to develop additional software.

AICPA.941140REG-AR

271. Under the uniform capitalization rules applicable to property acquired for resale, which of the following costs should be capitalized with respect to inventory if no exceptions are met?

	Marketing costs	Off-site storage costs
A.	Yes	Yes
B.	Yes	No
C.	No	No
D.	No	Yes

AICPA.951102REG-AR

272. Lake Corp., an accrual-basis calendar year corporation, had the following 2017 receipts:

2018 advanced rental payments where the lease ends in 2018	$125,000
Lease cancellation payment from a 5-year lease tenant	50,000

Lake had no restrictions on the use of the advanced rental payments and renders no services. What amount of income should Lake report on its 2017 tax return?

   A. $0
   B. $50,000
   C. $125,000
   D. $175,000

AICPA.921113REG-P2-AR

273. Unless the Internal Revenue Service consents to a change of method, the accrual method of tax reporting is mandatory for a sole proprietor when there are

	Accounts receivable for services rendered	Year-end merchandise inventories
A.	Yes	Yes
B.	Yes	No
C.	No	No
D.	No	Yes

Taxation of Employee Benefits

AICPA.921114REG-P2-AR

274. Under a "cafeteria plan" maintained by an employer,

   A. Participation must be restricted to employees, and their spouses and minor children.
   B. At least three years of service are required before an employee can participate in the plan.
   C. Participants may select their own menu of benefits.
   D. Provision may be made for deferred compensation other than 401(k) plans.

AICPA.010510REG-AR

275. Darr, an employee of Sorce C corporation, is not a shareholder. Which of the following would be included in a taxpayer's gross income?

A. Employer provided medical insurance coverage under a health plan.
B. A $10,000 gift from the taxpayer's grandparents.
C. The fair market value of land that the taxpayer inherited from an uncle.
D. The dividend income on shares of stock that the taxpayer received for services rendered.

AICPA.101122REG-SIM

276. Easel Co. has elected to reimburse employees for business expenses under a nonaccountable plan. Easel does not require employees to provide proof of expenses and allows employees to keep any amount not spent. Under the plan, Mel, an Easel employee for a full year, gets $400 per month for business automobile expenses. At the end of the year Mel informs Easel that the only business expense incurred was for business mileage of 12,000 at a rate of 30 cents per mile, the IRS standard mileage rate at the time. Mel encloses a check for $1,200 to refund the overpayment to Easel. What amounts should be reported in Mel's gross income for the year?

A. $0
B. $1,200
C. $3,600
D. $4,800

AICPA.130906REG

277. Johnson worked for ABC Co. and earned a salary of $100,000. Johnson also received, as a fringe benefit, group term-life insurance at twice Johnson's salary. The annual IRS-established uniform cost of insurance is $2.76 per $1,000. What amount must Johnson include in gross income?

A. $100,000
B. $100,276
C. $100,414
D. $100,552

Taxation of Retirement Plans

AICPA.931128REG-P2-AR

278. Davis, a sole proprietor with no employees, has a Keogh profit-sharing plan to which he may contribute 100% of his annual earned income.

For this purpose, "earned income" is defined as net self-employment earnings reduced by the

A. Deductible Keogh contribution.
B. Self-employment tax.
C. Self-employment tax and one-half of the deductible Keogh contribution.
D. Deductible Keogh contribution and one-half of the self-employment tax.

AICPA.911132REG-P2-AR

279. Hall, a divorced person and custodian of her 12-year old child, filed her 2016 federal income tax return as head of a household. She submitted the following information to the CPA who prepared her 2016 return:

1. The divorce agreement, executed in 2015, provides for Hall to receive $3,000 per month, of which $600 is designated as child support. After the child reaches 18, the monthly payments are to be reduced to $2,400 and are to be continued until remarriage or death. However, for the year 2016, Hall received a total of only $5,000 from her former husband. Hall paid an attorney $2,000 in 2016 in a suit to collect the alimony owed.

2. In June 2016, Hall's mother gifted her 100 shares of a listed stock. The donor's basis for this stock, which she bought in 1985, was $4,000, and market value on the date of the gift was $3,000. Hall sold her stock in July 2016 for $3,500. The donor paid no gift tax.

3. During 2016, Hall spent a total of $1,000 for state lottery tickets. Her lottery winnings in 2016 totaled $200.

4. Hall earned a salary of $25,000 in 2016. Hall was not covered by any type of retirement plan, but contributed $2,000 to an IRA in 2016.

5. In 2016, Hall sold an antique that she bought in 1995 to display in her home. Hall paid $800 for the antique and sold it for $1,400, using the proceeds to pay a court-ordered judgment.

6. Hall paid the following expenses in 2016 pertaining to the home that she owns: realty taxes, $3,400; mortgage interest, $7,000; casualty insurance, $490; assessment by city for construction of a sewer system, $910; interest of $1,000 on a personal, unsecured bank loan, the proceeds of which were used for home improvements. Hall does not rent out any portion of the home.

Hall's $2,000 contribution to an IRA should be treated as

A.   An adjustment to income in arriving at adjusted gross income.
B.   A deduction from adjusted gross income subject to the 2% of adjusted gross income floor.
C.   A deduction from adjusted gross income not subject to the 2% of adjusted gross income floor.
D.   Nondeductible, with the interest income on the $2,000 to be deferred until withdrawal.

AICPA.060805REG-AR

280.   A calendar-year individual is eligible to contribute to a deductible IRA. The taxpayer obtained a six-month extension to file until October 15 but did not file the return until November 1. What is the latest date that an IRA contribution can be made in order to qualify as a deduction on the prior year's return?

A.   October 15
B.   April 15
C.   August 15
D.   November 1

AICPA.090844REG

281.   A 33-year-old taxpayer withdrew $30,000 (pretax) from a traditional IRA. The taxpayer has a 33% effective tax rate and a 35% marginal tax rate. What is the total tax liability associated with the withdrawal?

A. $10,000
B. $10,500
C. $13,000
D. $13,500

AICPA.101139REG-SIM

282.   John invested $2,000 a year into his retirement plan from his before tax earnings (that is, he received a deduction for these contributions and was not taxed on the income). His employer contributed $3,000 a year to John's retirement fund. After 30 years of contributions, John retires and receives a distribution, which is not tax-free, of $350,000, the balance in his retirement fund. John must include what amount in gross income?

A. $0
B. $200,000
C. $260,000
D. $350,000

Deductions

Deductions—Basic Principles

AICPA.900532REG-P2-AR

283.   John Budd is the sole stockholder of Ral Corp., an accrual-basis taxpayer engaged in wholesaling operations. Ral's retained earnings at January 1, 2017, amounted to $1,000,000. For the year ended December 31, 2017, Ral's book income, before federal income tax, was $300,000. Included in the computation of this $300,000 were the following:

Dividends received on 500 shares of stock of a taxable domestic corporation that had 1,000,000 shares of stock outstanding (Ral had no portfolio indebtedness)	$ 1,000
Loss on sale of investment in stock of unaffiliated corporation (this stock had been held for two years; Ral had no other capital gains or losses)	(5,000)
Keyman insurance premiums paid on Budd's life (Ral is the beneficiary of this policy)	3,000
Group term insurance premiums paid on $10,000 life insurance policies for each of Ral's four employees (the employees' spouses are the beneficiaries)	4,000
Amortization of cost of acquiring a perpetual dealer's franchise (Ral paid $48,000 for this franchise on July 1, 2017, and is amortizing it over a 48-month period)	6,000
Contribution to a recognized, qualified charity (this contribution was authorized by Ral's board of directors in December 2017, to be paid on January 31, 2018)	75,000

On December 1, 2017, Ral received advance rental of $27,000 from a tenant for a three-year lease commencing January 1, 2017, to cover rents for the years 2018, 2019, and 2020. In conformity with GAAP, Ral did not include any part of this rental in its income statement for the year ended December 31, 2017.

What amount should Ral deduct for keyman and group life insurance premiums in computing taxable income for 2017?

A. $0
B. $3,000
C. $4,000
D. $7,000

AICPA.101136REG-SIM

284. Tom owns a fast-food restaurant which he reports as a sole proprietorship for tax purposes. Which of the following expenses is allowed as a deduction on Tom's Schedule C for the current year?

A. Wages of $20 per week to his 14-year-old daughter who cleans the restaurant on Saturdays.
B. Speeding ticket of $75 that he incurred while picking up supplies to bring to the restaurant.
C. A bribe of $200 to the city inspector charged with inspecting whether restaurants have met all city health requirements.
D. State income taxes paid during the year of $1,650.

AICPA.010504REG-AR

285. Mock operates a retail business selling illegal narcotic substances. Which of the following item(s) may Mock deduct in calculating business income?

I. Cost of merchandise
II. Business expenses other than the cost of merchandise

A. I only.
B. II only.
C. Both I and II.
D. Neither I nor II.

AICPA.941148REG-AR

286. A corporation's penalty for underpaying federal estimated taxes is

A. Not deductible.
B. Fully deductible in the year paid.
C. Fully deductible if reasonable cause can be established for the underpayment.
D. Partially deductible.

AICPA.940515REG-AR

287. On December 1, 2016, Michaels, a self-employed cash-basis taxpayer, borrowed $100,000 to use in her business. The loan was to be repaid on November 30, 2017. Michaels paid the entire interest of $12,000 on December 31, 2016.

What amount of interest was deductible on Michaels's 2017 income tax return?

A. $12,000
B. $11,000
C. $1,000
D. $0

Deductions For AGI

AICPA.010507-AR

288. Which of the following conditions must be present for a payment to qualify as deductible alimony?

I. Payments must be in cash.
II. The payments must end no later than the recipient's death.

A. I only.
B. II only.
C. Both I and II.
D. Neither I nor II.

AICPA.910526REG-AR

289. Dale received $1,000 in 2017 for jury duty. In exchange for regular compensation from her employer during the period of jury service, Dale was required to remit the entire $1,000 to her employer in 2017.

In Dale's 2017 income tax return, the $1,000 jury duty fee should be

A. Claimed in full as an itemized deduction.
B. Claimed as an itemized deduction to the extent exceeding 2% of adjusted gross income.
C. Deducted from gross income in arriving at adjusted gross income.
D. Included in taxable income without a corresponding offset against other income.

AICPA.120748REG

290. Cole earned $3,000 in wages, incurred $1,000 in unreimbursed employee business expenses, paid $400 as interest on a student loan, and contributed $100 to a charity. What is Cole's adjusted gross income?

A. $3,000
B. $2,600
C. $2,500
D. $1,600

AICPA.921105REG-P2-AR

291. Alex and Myra Burg, married and filing joint income tax returns, derive their entire income from the operation of their retail candy shop. Their 2017 adjusted gross income was $50,000. The Burgs itemized their deductions on Schedule A for 2017.

The following unreimbursed cash expenditures were among those made by the Burgs during 2017:

Repair and maintenance of motorized wheelchair for physically handicapped dependent child	$ 300
Tuition, meals and lodging at special school for physically handicapped dependent child in the institution primarily for the availability of medical care, with meals and lodging furnished as necessary incidents to that care State income tax	1,200
Self-employment tax	7,650
Four tickets to a theater party sponsored by a qualified charitable organization; not considered a business expense; similar tickets would cost $25 each at the box office	160
Repair of glass vase accidentally broken in home by dog; vase cost $500 in 2012; fair value $600 before accident and $200 after accident	90
Fee for breaking lease on prior apartment residence located 20 miles from new residence	500
Security deposit placed on apartment at new location	900

What amount should the Burgs deduct for moving expenses in their itemized deductions on Schedule A for 2017?

A. $0
B. $500
C. $900
D. $1,400

AICPA.120718REG

292. Davidson was transferred from Chicago to Atlanta. In connection with the transfer, Davidson incurred the following moving expenses:

Moving the household goods	$2,000
Temporary living expenses in Atlanta	400
Lodging on the way to Atlanta	100
Meals	40

What amount may Davidson deduct if the employer reimbursed Davidson $2,000 (not included in form W-2) for moving expenses?

A. $100
B. $120
C. $500
D. $520

Itemized Deductions—Medical, Taxes, Interest

AICPA.950508REG-AR

293. Matthews was a cash basis taxpayer whose records showed the following:

2016 state and local income taxes withheld	$1,500
2016 state estimated income taxes paid December 30, 2016	400
2016 federal income taxes withheld	2,500
2015 state and local income taxes paid April 15, 2017	300

What total amount was Matthews entitled to claim for taxes on her 2016 Schedule A of Form 1040?

A. $4,700
B. $2,200
C. $1,900
D. $1,500

AICPA.010501REG-AR

294. Carroll, an unmarried taxpayer with an adjusted gross income of $100,000, incurred and paid the following unreimbursed medical expenses for the year:

Doctor bills resulting from a serious fall	$ 5,000
Cosmetic surgery that was necessary to correct a congenital deformity	15,000

Carroll had no medical insurance and is 60 years old. For regular income tax purposes, what was Carroll's maximum allowable medical expense deduction, after the applicable threshold limitation, for the year?

A. $0
B. $10,000
C. $15,000
D. $20,000

AICPA.120701REG

295. An individual taxpayer earned $10,000 in investment income, $8,000 in noninterest investment expenses, and $5,000 in investment interest expense. How much is the taxpayer allowed to deduct on the current-year's tax return for investment interest expenses?

A. $0
B. $2,000
C. $3,000
D. $5,000

AICPA.940508REG-AR

296. The 2016 deduction by an individual taxpayer for interest on investment indebtedness is

    A. Limited to the investment interest paid in 2016.

    B. Limited to the taxpayer's 2016 interest income.

    C. Limited to the taxpayer's 2016 net investment income.

    D. Not limited.

AICPA.120727REG

297. Which of the following statements is correct regarding the deductibility of an individual's medical expenses?

    A. A medical expense paid by credit card is deductible in the year the credit card bill is paid.

    B. A medical expense deduction is allowed for payments made in the current year for medical services received in earlier years.

    C. Medical expenses, net of insurance reimbursements, are disregarded in the alternative minimum tax calculation.

    D. A medical expense deduction is NOT allowed for Medicare insurance premiums.

Itemized Deductions—Other

AICPA.970502REG-AR

298. Jimet, an unmarried taxpayer, qualified to itemize deductions. Jimet's adjusted gross income was $30,000 and he made a $2,000 cash donation directly to a needy family. Jimet also donated stock, valued at $3,000, to his church. Jimet had purchased the stock four months earlier for $1,500.

What was the maximum amount of the charitable contribution allowable as an itemized deduction on Jimet's income tax return?

    A. $0

    B. $1,500

    C. $2,000

    D. $5,000

AICPA.120749REG

299. Doyle has gambling losses totaling $7,000 during the current year. Doyle's adjusted gross income is $60,000, including $3,000 in gambling winnings. Doyle can itemize the deductions. What amount of gambling losses is deductible?

    A. $0

    B. $3,000

    C. $5,800

    D. $7,000

AICPA.120747REG

300. Carter incurred the following expenses in the current year: $500 for the preparation of a personal income tax return, $100 for custodial fees on an IRA, $150 for professional publications, and $2,000 for union dues. Carter's current year adjusted gross income is $75,000. Carter, who is not self-employed, itemizes deductions. What will Carter's deduction be for miscellaneous itemized deductions after any limitations in the current year?

    A. $0

    B. $ 750

    C. $1,250

    D. $2,750

AICPA.970504REG-AR

301. Deet, an unmarried taxpayer, qualified to itemize deductions.

Deet's adjusted gross income was $40,000 and he made a $1,500 substantiated cash donation directly to a needy family. Deet also donated art, valued at $11,000, to a local art museum. Deet had purchased the art work two years earlier for $2,000.

What was the maximum amount of the charitable contribution allowable as an itemized deduction on Deet's income tax return?

    A. $12,500

    B. $11,000

    C. $ 3,500

    D. $ 2,000

AICPA.950507REG-AR

302. Moore, a single taxpayer, had $50,000 in adjusted gross income for 2016. During 2016, she contributed $18,000 to her church. She had a $10,000 charitable contribution carryover from her 2016 church contribution.

What was the maximum amount of properly substantiated charitable contributions that Moore could claim as an itemized deduction for 2016?

    A. $10,000

    B. $18,000

    C. $25,000

    D. $28,000

Employee Business Expenses

AICPA.941131REG-AR

303. Banks Corp., a calendar year corporation, reimburses employees for properly substantiated qualifying business meal expenses. The employees are present at the meals, which are neither lavish nor extravagant, and the reimbursement is not treated as wages subject to withholdings.

    For 2017, what percentage of the meal expense may Banks deduct?

    A. 0%
    B. 50%
    C. 80%
    D. 100%

AICPA.120717REG

304. Nichol Corp. gave gifts to 15 individuals who were customers of the business. The gifts were not in the nature of advertising. The market values of the gifts were as follows:

5 gifts	@ $15 each
9 gifts	@ $30 each
1 gift	@ $100

    What amount is deductible as business gifts?

    A. $0
    B. $75
    C. $325
    D. $445

AICPA.101121REG-SIM

305. During the 2017 holiday season, Palo Corp. gave business gifts to 17 customers. These gifts, which were not of an advertising nature, had the following fair market values:

4 at	$10
4 at	$25
4 at	$50
5 at	$100

    How much of these gifts was deductible as a business expense for 2017?

    A. $840
    B. $365
    C. $140
    D. $0

AICPA.101120REG-SIM

306. Abe Architect owns his own architectural consulting firm. During the current year he incurred the following expenses related to meetings with clients and potential clients:

Meal expenses	$2,000
Dues to Five-Star Country Club	$5,000
Greens fee for playing golf with clients	$1,500
Tickets to Super Bowl (face value = $1,000)	$3,500

    What is the amount of deductible expenses for the current year related to these expenditures?

    A. $2,250
    B. $4,500
    C. $3,500
    D. $12,000

AICPA.990506REG-AR

307. Baker, a sole proprietor CPA, has several clients that do business in Spain. While on a four-week vacation in Spain, Baker took a five-day seminar on Spanish business practices that cost $700. Baker's round-trip airfare to Spain was $600. While in Spain, Baker spent an average of $100 per day on accommodations, local travel, and other incidental expenses, for total expenses of $2,800.

    What amount of educational expense can Baker deduct on Form 1040 Schedule C, *Profit or Loss From Business*?

    A. $ 700
    B. $1,200
    C. $1,800
    D. $4,100

Deductions—Losses and Bad Debts

AICPA.101123REG

308. Jason Budd, CPA, reports on the cash basis. In April 2016, Budd billed a client $3,500 for the following professional services:

Personal estate planning	$2,000
Personal tax return preparation	1,000
Compilation of business financial statements	500

    No part of the $3,500 was ever paid. In April 2017, the client declared bankruptcy, and the $3,500 obligation became totally uncollectible. What loss can Budd deduct on his tax return for this bad debt?

    A. $0
    B. $500
    C. $1,500
    D. $3,500

AICPA.911147REG-P2-AR

309. In the case of a corporation that is not a financial institution, which of the following statements is correct with regard to the deduction for bad debts?

   A. Either the reserve method or the direct charge-off method may be used, if the election is made in the corporation's first taxable year.
   B. On approval from the IRS, a corporation may change its method from direct charge-off to reserve.
   C. If the reserve method was consistently used in prior years, the corporation may take a deduction for a reasonable addition to the reserve for bad debts.
   D. A corporation is required to use the direct charge-off method rather than the reserve method.

AICPA.990507REG-AR

310. Destry, a single taxpayer, reported the following on his 2017 U.S. Individual Income Tax Return Form 1040:

Income:	
Wages	$5,000
Interest on savings account	1,000
Net rental income	4,000
Deductions:	
Personal exemption	$4,050
Standard deduction	6,300
Net business loss	16,000
Net short-term capital loss	2,000

What is Destry's net operating loss that is available for carryback or carryforward?

   A. $ 7,000
   B. $ 9,000
   C. $15,100
   D. $16,000

AICPA.910529REG-P2-AR

311. An individual's losses on transactions entered into for personal purposes are deductible only if

   A. The losses qualify as casualty or theft losses.
   B. The losses can be characterized as hobby losses.
   C. The losses do not exceed $3,000 ($6,000 on a joint return).
   D. No part of the transactions was entered into for profit.

AICPA.101124REG-SIM

312. For the year ended December 31, 2017, Sanchez had a net operating loss of $100,000. Taxable income for the earlier years, computed without reference to the net operating loss, was as follows:

Taxable Income	
2013	$90,000
2014	$80,000
2015	$50,000
2016	$40,000

If Sanchez makes no special election to waive the net operating loss carryback, what amount of net operating loss will be available to Sanchez for 2018?

   A. $ 0
   B. $ 10,000
   C. $ 60,000
   D. $ 100,000

Limitations on Business Deductions

AICPA.130920REG

313. Smith has an adjusted gross income (AGI) of $120,000 without taking into consideration $40,000 of losses from rental real estate activities. Smith actively participates in the rental real estate activities. What amount of the rental losses may Smith deduct in determining taxable income?

   A. $0
   B. $15,000
   C. $20,000
   D. $40,000

AICPA.120721REG

314. An individual taxpayer reports the following items for the current year:

Ordinary income from partnership A, operating a movie theater in which the taxpayer materially participates	$70,000
Net loss from partnership B, operating an equipment rental business in which the taxpayer does not materially participate	(9,000)
Rental income from building rented to a third party	7,000
Short-term capital gain from sale of stock	4,000

What is the taxpayer's adjusted gross income for the year?

A. $70,000
B. $72,000
C. $74,000
D. $77,000

AICPA.060808REG-P2-AR

315. Barkley owns a vacation cabin that was rented to unrelated parties for 10 days during the year for $2,500. The cabin was used personally by Barkley for 3 months and left vacant for the rest of the year. Expenses for the cabin were as follows:

Real Estate Taxes	$1,000
Maintenance and Utilities	$2,000

How much rental income (loss) is included in Barkley's adjusted gross income?

A. $0
B. $ 500
C. $ (500)
D. $(1,500)

AICPA.101104REG

316. Lane, a single taxpayer, received $160,000 in salary, $15,000 in income from an S Corporation in which Lane does not materially participate, and a $35,000 passive loss from a real estate rental activity in which Lane materially participated. Lane's modified adjusted gross income was $165,000. What amount of the real estate rental activity loss was deductible?

A. $0
B. $15,000
C. $25,000
D. $35,000

AICPA.120710REG

317. Brenda, employed full time, makes beaded jewelry as a hobby. In year 2, Brenda's hobby generated $2,000 of sales, and she incurred $3,000 of travel expenses. What is the proper reporting of the income and expenses related to the activity?

A. Sales of $2,000 are reported in gross income, and $2,000 of expenses are reported as an itemized deduction subject to the 2% limitation.
B. Sales of $2,000 are reported in gross income, and $3,000 of expenses are reported as an itemized deduction subject to the 2% limitation.
C. Sales and expenses are netted, and the net loss of $1,000 is reported as an itemized deduction NOT subject to the 2% limitation.
D. Sales and expenses are netted and deducted for AGI.

Individual Tax Issues

Personal and Dependency Exemptions

AICPA.940514REG-AR

318. Jim and Kay Ross contributed to the support of their two children, Dale and Kim, and Jim's widowed parent, Grant. For 2016, Dale, a 19-year old full-time college student who lives at home when not at college, earned $4,500 as a baby-sitter.

Kim, a 23-year old bank teller, earned $12,000. Kim provided more than 50% of her support during 2016. Grant received $5,000 in dividend income and $4,000 in nontaxable social security benefits.

Grant, Dale, and Kim are U.S. citizens and Grant and Dale were over one-half supported by Jim and Kay.

How many exemptions can Jim and Kay claim on their 2016 joint income tax return?

A. Two
B. Three
C. Four
D. Five

AICPA.060251REG-V-D

319. Sara Hance, who is single and lives alone in Idaho, has no income of her own and is supported in full by the following persons:

	Amount of Support	Percent of Total
Alma (unrelated friend)	$2,400	48
Ben (Sara's brother)	2,150	43
Carl (Sara's son)	450	9
Total	$5,000	100

Under a multiple support agreement, Sara's dependency exemption can be claimed by:

A. No one
B. Alma
C. Ben
D. Carl

AICPA.931136REG-P2-AR

320. Joe and Barb are married, but Barb refuses to sign a 2016 joint return. On Joe's separate 2016 return, an exemption may be claimed for Barb if

A. Barb was a full-time student for the entire 2016 school year.
B. Barb attaches a written statement to Joe's income tax return, agreeing to be claimed as an exemption by Joe for 2016.

C. Barb was under the age of 19.
D. Barb had no gross income and was not claimed as another person's dependent in 2016.

assess.AICPA.REG.person.exempt-0031

321. John earned $500,000 in his business during the current year, and his wife received investment income of $15,000. John provides more than half of the support of his widowed sister, who lives with John and earned $45,000 in salary. John also provides full support for his two children, an 18-year-old daughter and a 20-year-old son, who is a full-time college student. The family employs a live-in housekeeper and a live-in butler to assist them with their residence. What is the maximum number of personal and dependency exemptions that John and his wife are eligible to claim?

A. Two exemptions
B. Four exemptions
C. Five exemptions
D. Seven exemptions

AICPA.101117REG-SIM

322. Which of the following tests does NOT have to be met for Tom to claim a dependency exemption under the qualifying relative rule?

A. Age Test
B. Gross Income Test
C. Support Test (50% support from Tom)
D. Citizenship/Residency Test

Filing Status

AICPA.921110REG-P2-AR

323. For head of household filing status, which of the following costs are considered in determining whether the taxpayer has contributed more than one-half the cost of maintaining the household?

	Food consumed in the home	Value of services rendered in the home by the taxpayer
A.	Yes	Yes
B.	No	No
C.	Yes	No
D.	No	Yes

AICPA.101106REG

324. A taxpayer's spouse dies in August of the current year. Which of the following is the taxpayer's filing status for the current year?

A. Single.
B. Qualifying widow(er).
C. Head of household.
D. Married filing jointly.

AICPA.060319REG-AR

325. Parker, whose spouse died during the preceding year, has not remarried. Parker maintains a home for a dependent child. What is Parker's most advantageous filing status?

A. Single
B. Head of household
C. Married filing separately.
D. Qualifying widow(er) with dependent child.

AICPA.060810REG-AR

326. In which of the following situations may taxpayers file as married filing jointly?

A. Taxpayers who were married but lived apart during the year.
B. Taxpayers who were married but lived under a legal separation agreement at the end of the year.
C. Taxpayers who were divorced during the year.
D. Taxpayers who were legally separated but lived together for the entire year.

Alternative Minimum Tax and Other Taxes

AICPA.130918REG

327. Which of the following may **not** be deducted in the computation of alternative minimum taxable income of an individual?

A. Traditional IRA account contribution
B. One-half of the self-employment tax deduction
C. Personal exemptions
D. Charitable contributions

AICPA.120711REG

328. On their joint tax return, Sam and Joann had taxable income (AGI) of $150,000 and claimed the following itemized deductions:

Interest of $15,000 on a $100,000 home equity loan to purchase a motor home

Real estate tax and state income taxes of $18,000

Unreimbursed medical expenses of $15,000 (prior to AGI limitation)

Miscellaneous itemized deductions of $5,000 (prior to AGI limitation)

Both Sam and Joann are less than 65 years old. Based on these deductions, what would be the amount of AMT add-back adjustment in computing alternative minimum taxable income?

- A. $21,750
- B. $23,750
- C. $35,000
- D. $38,750

AICPA.120735REG

329. Farr, an unmarried taxpayer, had $70,000 of adjusted gross income and the following deductions for regular income tax purposes:

Home mortgage interest on a loan to acquire a principal residence	$11,000
Miscellaneous itemized deductions above the threshold limitation	$ 2,000

What are Farr's total allowable itemized deductions for computing alternative minimum taxable income?

- A. $0
- B. $ 2,000
- C. $11,000
- D. $13,000

AICPA.931137REG-P2-AR

330. The alternative minimum tax (AMT) is computed as the

- A. Excess of the regular tax over the tentative AMT.
- B. Excess of the tentative AMT over the regular tax.
- C. The tentative AMT plus the regular tax.
- D. Lesser of the tentative AMT or the regular tax.

AICPA.910533REG-P2-AR

331. An employee who has Social Security tax withheld in an amount greater than the maximum for a particular year, may claim

- A. Such expenses as either a credit or an itemized deduction, at the election of the employee, if that excess resulted from correct withholding by two or more employers.
- B. Reimbursement of such excess from his employers, if that excess resulted from correct withholding by two or more employers.
- C. The excess as a credit against income tax, if that excess resulted from correct withholding by two or more employers.
- D. The excess as a credit against income tax, if that excess was withheld by one employer.

Tax Planning Strategies for Individuals

AICPA.101086REG-SIM

332. Ms. Planner is in the 25% tax bracket and itemizes on her tax return. She plans to make a charitable contribution of $12,000 to her alma mater this year. The net cost of this contribution to T is:

- A. $0
- B. $3,000
- C. $9,000
- D. $12,000

AICPA.101087REG-SIM

333. Chris is in the 50% tax bracket in Year 1 but Congress has decreased his tax bracket to 30% for Year 2. Which of the following would be an appropriate tax planning strategy for Chris?

- A. Defer income until Year 2.
- B. Accelerate income into Year 1.
- C. Defer deductions until Year 2.
- D. Increase his estimated tax payments for Year 1.

AICPA.101088REG-SIM

334. Appropriate strategies for reducing the alternative minimum tax include all of the following except:

- A. Do not exercise incentive stock options.
- B. Make additional charitable contributions.
- C. Increase home mortgage interest on primary mortgage.
- D. Increase 2% miscellaneous itemized deductions.

AICPA.101089REG-SIM

335. Jose has owned stock for eight years that has a basis of $20,000 and fair market value of $100,000. Jose contributes the stock to a qualified charity. Which of the following is a proper tax consequence from this transaction?

- A. Jose has recognized gain of $80,000.
- B. Jose has a charitable contribution of $100,000.
- C. Jose has a charitable contribution of $80,000.
- D. Jose has a charitable contribution of $20,000.

AICPA.101090REG-SIM

336. Orleans has owned land as an investment for five years. His basis in the land is $70,000 and the land's current fair market value is $50,000. Which of the following statements is correct with regard to this land?

- A. If Orleans sells the land to his father he can deduct the $20,000 loss in the land.
- B. If Orleans gives the property to an unrelated friend he can deduct the $20,000 loss in the land.

C. Orleans should sell the land, recognize the $20,000 capital loss, and then gift the $50,000 cash from the sale to his friend.

D. If the land is sold to an unrelated party, the $20,000 loss cannot be recognized since the land is not depreciable.

Tax Credits

Personal Tax Credits

AICPA.101128REG-SIM

337. Mr. and Mrs. Alexander have two dependent children, one of whom (Cal) is a freshman in college during 2016. Tuition and fees paid for Cal during 2016 total $15,000. The Alexanders also paid $10,000 in 2016 for their 14 year old daughter, Kaitlin, to attend a private high school. The Alexanders file a joint tax return for 2016 and report adjusted gross income of $150,000. Cal is a full-time student and enrolled in a degree program. What is the Alexander's Hope/American Opportunity Tax Credit for 2016?

A. $ 0
B. $2,500
C. $5,000
D. $15,000

AICPA.101130REG-SIM

338. Which of the following statements is false with regard to the child and dependent care credit?

A. The caregiver cannot be a dependent relative or child of the taxpayer.

B. The credit percentage begins at 35% and phases out once AGI exceeds a certain threshold. As income increases the credit percentage is eventually reduced to zero.

C. The maximum amount of expense eligible for the credit is $3,000 ($6,000 if more than one individual qualifies for care).

D. A qualifying child or dependent under the age of 13 who lives with the taxpayer more than one-half of the tax year is a qualifying individual for purposes of claiming the credit.

AICPA.940517REG-AR

339. Which of the following credits can result in a refund, even if the individual had no income tax liability?

A. Credit for prior year minimum tax.
B. Elderly and permanently and totally disabled credit.
C. Earned income credit.
D. Child and dependent care credit.

AICPA.101105REG

340. Which of the following disqualifies an individual from the earned income credit?

A. The taxpayer's qualifying child is a 17-year-old grandchild.

B. The taxpayer has earned income of $5,000.

C. The taxpayer's five-year-old child lived in the taxpayer's home for only eight months.

D. The taxpayer has a filing status of married filing separately.

AICPA.921111REG-P2-AR

341. In 2016, to qualify for the child care credit on a joint return, at least one spouse must

	Have an adjusted gross income of $15,000 or less	Be gainfully employed/looking for work or a student when related expenses are incurred
A.	Yes	Yes
B.	No	No
C.	Yes	No
D.	No	Yes

Estate and Gift Taxation

Federal Gift Tax

AICPA.910540REG-P2-AR

342. On July 1, 2017, Vega made a transfer by gift in an amount sufficient to require the filing of a gift tax return. Vega was still alive in 2017.

If Vega did not request an extension of time for filing the 2017 gift tax return, the due date for filing was

A. March 15, 2018.
B. April 15, 2018.
C. June 15, 2018.
D. June 30, 2018.

AICPA.090848REG

343. George and Suzanne have been married for 40 years. Suzanne inherited $1,000,000 from her mother. Assume that the annual gift-tax exclusion is $14,000. What amount of the $1,000,000 can Suzanne give to George without incurring a gift-tax liability?

A. $14,000
B. $28,000
C. $500,000
D. $1,000,000

AICPA.120705REG

344. The answer to each of the following questions would be relevant in determining whether a tuition payment made on behalf of another individual is excludible for gift tax purposes EXCEPT:

A. Was the tuition payment made for tuition or for other expenses?
B. Was the qualifying educational organization located in a foreign country?
C. Was the tuition payment made directly to the educational organization?
D. Was the tuition payment made for a family member?

AICPA.090842REG

345. Which of the following payments would require the donor to file a gift tax return?

A. $30,000 to a university for a spouse's tuition
B. $40,000 to a university for a cousin's room and board
C. $50,000 to a hospital for a parent's medical expenses
D. $80,000 to a physician for a friend's surgery

Federal Estate Tax

AICPA.130905REG

346. What is the due date of a federal estate tax return (Form 706), for a taxpayer who died on May 15, year 2, assuming that a request for an extension of time is **not** filed?

A. September 15, year 2
B. December 31, year 2
C. January 31, year 3
D. February 15, year 3

AICPA.090831REG-SIM

347. H and W are married citizens. All of their real and personal property is owned as tenants by the entirety or as joint tenants with right of survivorship. The gross estate of the first spouse to die:

A. Includes only the property acquired by the deceased spouse.
B. Is governed by federal tax provisions rather than community property laws.
C. Includes one third of all real estate as the dower right of the first spouse to die.
D. Includes half of the value of all the property owned regardless of which spouse furnished the original consideration.

AICPA.090832REG-SIM

348. Ordinary and necessary administration expenses of an estate are deductible:

A. Only on the fiduciary income tax return.
B. Only on the estate tax return.
C. On the fiduciary income tax return if the estate tax deduction is waived.
D. On both the fiduciary income tax return and the estate tax return.

AICPA.090833REG

349. Under which of the following circumstances is trust property with an independent trustee includible in the grantor's gross estate?

A. The trust is revocable.
B. The trust is established for a minor.
C. The trustee has the power to distribute trust income.
D. The income beneficiary disclaims the property, which then passes to the remainderman, the grantor's friend.

AICPA.901140REG-P2-AR

350. Which one of the following is a valid deduction from a decedent's gross estate?

A. Expenses of administering and settling the estate.
B. State inheritance tax.
C. Income tax paid on income earned and received after the decedent's death.
D. Federal estate tax.

V. Federal Taxation of Entities

Corporate Taxation

Formation of a Corporation

AICPA.921119REG-P2-AR

351. Feld, the sole stockholder of Maki Corp., paid $50,000 for Maki's stock in 2008. In 2017, Feld contributed a parcel of land to Maki but was not given any additional stock for this contribution. Feld's basis for the land was $10,000, and its fair market value was $18,000 on the date of the transfer of title.

What is Feld's adjusted basis for the Maki stock?

A. $50,000
B. $52,000
C. $60,000
D. $68,000

AICPA.090851REG

352. Ames and Roth form Homerun, a C corporation. Ames contributes several autographed baseballs to Homerun. Ames purchased the baseballs for $500, and they have a total fair market value of $1,000. Roth contributes several autographed baseball bats to Homerun. Roth purchased the bats for $5,000, and they have a fair market value of $7,000. What is Homerun's basis in the contributed bats and balls?

    A. $0
    B. $5,500
    C. $6,000
    D. $8,000

AICPA.941152REG-AR

353. Adams, Beck, and Carr organized Flexo Corp. with authorized voting common stock of $100,000. Adams received 10% of the capital stock in payment for the organizational services that he rendered for the benefit of the newly formed corporation. Adams did not contribute property to Flexo and was under no obligation to be paid by Beck or Carr. Beck and Carr transferred property in exchange for stock as follows:

	Adjusted basis	Fair market value	% of Flexo stock acquired
Beck	5,000	20,000	20%
Carr	60,000	70,000	70%

What amount of gain did Carr recognize from this transaction?

    A. $40,000
    B. $15,000
    C. $10,000
    D. $0

AICPA.090839REG

354. In April, A and B formed X Corp. A contributed $50,000 cash, and B contributed land worth $70,000 (with an adjusted basis of $40,000). B also received $20,000 cash from the corporation. A and B each receives 50% of the corporation's stock. What is the tax basis of the land to X Corp.?

    A. $40,000
    B. $50,000
    C. $60,000
    D. $70,000

AICPA.930553BEC-P2-AR

355. In 2016, Stone, a cash basis taxpayer, incorporated her CPA practice. No liabilities were transferred. The following assets were transferred to the corporation:

Cash (checking account)	$ 500
Computer equipment Adjusted basis	30,000
Fair market value	34,000
Cost	40,000

Immediately after the transfer, Stone owned 100% of the corporation's stock. The corporation's total basis for the transferred assets is

    A. $30,000
    B. $30,500
    C. $34,500
    D. $40,500

Corporate Income

AICPA.951101REG-AR

356. In 2017, Starke Corp., an accrual–basis calendar-year corporation, reported book income of $380,000. Included in that amount was $50,000 municipal bond interest income, $170,000 for federal income tax expense, and $2,000 interest expense on the debt incurred to carry the municipal bonds.

What amount should Starke's taxable income be as reconciled on Starke's Schedule M-1 of Form 1120, *U.S. Corporation Income Tax Return*?

    A. $330,000
    B. $500,000
    C. $502,000
    D. $550,000

AICPA.130908REG

357. Azure, a C corporation, reports the following:

Pretax book income of $543,000.

Depreciation on the tax return is $20,000 greater than depreciation on the financial statements.

Rent income reportable on the tax return is $36,000 greater than rent income per the financial statements.

Fines for pollution appear as a $10,000 expense in the financial statements.

Interest earned on municipal bonds is $25,000.

What is Azure's taxable income?

    A. $528,000
    B. $543,000
    C. $544,000
    D. $559,000

AICPA.060813REG-P2-AR

358. Which of the following items should be included on the Schedule M-1, *Reconciliation of Income (Loss) per Books With Income per Return*, of Form 1120, *U.S. Corporation Income Tax Return*, to reconcile book income to taxable income?

A. Cash distributions to shareholders
B. Premiums paid on key-person life insurance policy
C. Corporate bond interest
D. Ending balance of retained earnings

AICPA.911149REG-P2-AR

359. Would the following expense items be reported on Schedule M-1 of the corporation income tax return showing the reconciliation of income per books with income per return?

	Interest incurred on loan to carry U.S. obligations	Provision for state corporation income tax
A.	Yes	Yes
B.	No	No
C.	Yes	No
D.	No	Yes

AICPA.941132REG-AR

360. For the year ended December 31, 2017, Kelly Corp. had net income per books of $300,000 before the provision for Federal income taxes. Included in the net income were the following items:

Dividend income from an unaffiliated domestic taxable corporation (taxable income limitation does not apply and there is no portfolio indebtedness)	$50,000
Bad debt expense (represents the increase in the allowance for doubtful accounts)	80,000

Assuming no bad debt was written off, what is Kelly's taxable income for the year ended December 31, 2017?

A. $250,000
B. $330,000
C. $345,000
D. $380,000

Accounting Methods and Periods—Corporations

AICPA.120606REG-SIM

361. Which of the following taxpayers may use the cash basis as its method of accounting for tax purposes?

A. Partnership that is designated as a tax shelter.
B. Retail store with $2 million in gross receipts.

C. An international accounting firm organized as a partnership.
D. Office cleaning corporation with average annual income of $8 million.

AICPA.120742REG

362. In calculating the tax of a corporation for a short period, which of the following processes is correct?

A. Divide current-year income by prior-year income, then multiply the result by prior-year tax.
B. Compute tax on short-period income, then multiply the result by 12 divided by the number of months in the short period.
C. Determine the average taxable income for the past three years, then multiply the result by the number of months in the short period divided by 12.
D. Annualize income and calculate the tax on annualized income, then multiply the computed tax by the number of months in the short period divided by 12.

AICPA.130923REG

363. The selection of an accounting method for tax purposes by a newly incorporated C corporation

A. Is made on the initial tax return by using the chosen method.
B. Is made by filing a request for a private letter ruling from the IRS.
C. Must first be approved by the company's board of directors.
D. Must be disclosed in the company's organizing documents.

AICPA.930542REG-P2-AR

364. Ace Rentals Inc., an accrual-basis taxpayer, reported rent receivable of $35,000 and $25,000 in its 2017 and 2016 balance sheets, respectively. During 2017, Ace received $50,000 in rent payments and $5,000 in nonrefundable rent deposits.

In Ace's 2017 corporate income tax return, what amount should Ace include as rent revenue?

A. $50,000
B. $55,000
C. $60,000
D. $65,000

AICPA.090859REG

365. Dart, a C corporation, distributes software over the Internet and has had average revenues in excess of $20 million dollars per year for the past three years. To purchase software, customers key-in their credit card number to a secure web site and receive a password that allows the customer to immediately download

the software. As a result, Dart doesn't record accounts receivable or inventory on its books. Which of the following statements is correct?

A. Dart may use either the cash or accrual method of accounting as long as Dart elects a calendar year end.
B. Dart may utilize any method of accounting Dart chooses as long as Dart consistently applies the method it chooses.
C. Dart must use the accrual method of accounting.
D. Dart may utilize the cash basis method of accounting until it incurs an additional $10 million to develop additional software.

Special Corporate Deductions

AICPA.951109REG-AR

366. If a corporation's charitable contributions exceed the limitation for deductibility in a particular year, the excess

A. Is not deductible in any future or prior year.
B. May be carried back or forward for one year at the corporation's election.
C. May be carried forward to a maximum of five succeeding years.
D. May be carried back to the third preceding year.

AICPA.120736REG

367. Robin, a C corporation, had revenues of $200,000 and operating expenses of $75,000. Robin also received a $20,000 dividend from a domestic corporation and is entitled to a $14,000 dividend-received deduction. Robin donated $15,000 to a qualified charitable organization in the current year. What is Robin's contribution deduction?

A. $15,000
B. $14,500
C. $13,900
D. $13,100

AICPA.060815REG-P2-AR

368. In the current year, Brown, a C corporation has gross income (before dividends) of $900,000 and deductions of $1,100,000 (excluding the dividends-received deduction). Brown received dividends of $100,000 from a Fortune 500 corporation during the current year.

What is Brown's net operating loss?

A. $100,000
B. $130,000
C. $170,000
D. $200,000

AICPA.940524REG-AR

369. Kisco Corp.'s taxable income for 2017 before taking the dividends received deduction was $70,000. This includes $10,000 in dividends from an unrelated taxable domestic corporation.

Given the following tax rates, what would Kisco's income tax be before any credits?

Partial rate table	Tax rate
Up to $50,000	15%
Over $50,000 but not over $75,000	25%

A. $10,000
B. $10,750
C. $12,500
D. $15,750

AICPA.900529REG-P2-AR

370. John Budd is the sole stockholder of Ral Corp., an accrual basis taxpayer engaged in wholesaling operations.

Ral's retained earnings at January 1, 2017, amounted to $1,000,000.

For the year ended December 31, 2017, Ral's book income, before federal income tax, was $300,000.

Included in the computation of this $300,000 were the following:

Dividends received on 500 shares of stock of a taxable domestic corporation that had 1,000,000 shares of stock outstanding (Ral had no portfolio indebtedness)	$1,000
Loss on sale of investment in stock of unaffiliated corporation (this stock had been held for two years; Ral had no other capital gains or losses)	(5,000)
Keyman insurance premiums paid on Budd's life (Ral is the beneficiary of this policy)	3,000
Group term insurance premiums paid on $10,000 life insurance policies for each of Ral's four employees (the employees' spouses are the beneficiaries)	4,000
Amortization of cost of acquiring a perpetual dealer's franchise (Ral paid $48,000 for this franchise on July 1, 2017, and is amortizing it over a 48-month period)	6,000
Contribution to a recognized, qualified charity (this contribution was authorized by Ral's board of directors in December 2017, to be paid on January 31, 2018)	75,000

On December 1, 2017, Ral received advance rental of $27,000 from a tenant for a three-year lease commencing January 1, 2017, to cover rents for the years 2018, 2019, and 2020. In conformity with GAAP, Ral did not include any part of this rental in its income statement for the year ended December 31, 2017.

What portion of the dividend revenue should be included in Ral's 2017 taxable income?

A. $150
B. $200
C. $300
D. $900

Corporate Alternative Minimum Tax

AICPA.941149REG-AR

371. Which of the following credits is a combination of several tax credits to provide uniform rules for the current and carryback-carryover years?

A. General business credit.
B. Foreign tax credit.
C. Minimum tax credit.
D. Enhanced oil recovery credit.

AICPA.910549REG-P2-AR

372. Foreign income taxes paid by a corporation

A. May be claimed either as a deduction or as a credit, at the option of the corporation.
B. May be claimed only as a deduction.
C. May be claimed only as a credit.
D. Do not qualify either as a deduction or as a credit.

AICPA.101131REG-SIM

373. Which of the following statements concerning tax credits is true?

A. The foreign tax credit is available for business entities, such as corporations, but not for individuals.
B. Unused general business credits are carried back two years and forward 20 years.
C. For the rehabilitation credit, expenditures to rehabilitate property placed in service before 1936 are eligible for a 20% credit.
D. The work opportunity tax credit is calculated on the amount of wages paid per eligible employee during the first year of employment. The maximum credit is $2,400 per eligible employee.

AICPA.990511REG-AR

374. Sunex Co., an accrual-basis, calendar-year domestic C corporation, is taxed on its worldwide income. In the current year, Sunex's U.S. tax liability on its domestic and foreign source income is $60,000 and no prior year foreign income taxes have been carried forward.

Which factor(s) may affect the amount of Sunex's foreign tax credit available in its current-year corporate income tax return?

	Income source	The foreign tax rate
A.	Yes	Yes
B.	Yes	No
C.	No	Yes
D.	No	No

AICPA.101129REG-SIM

375. The following information pertains to Wald Corp.'s operations:

Worldwide taxable income	$300,000
U.S. source taxable income	180,000
U.S. income tax before foreign tax credit	96,000
Foreign source taxable income	120,000
Foreign income taxes paid on foreign source taxable income	39,000

What amount of foreign tax credit may Wald claim?

A. $28,800
B. $36,600
C. $38,400
D. $39,000

Penalty Taxes

AICPA.910542REG-P2-AR

376. The accumulated earnings tax can be imposed

A. Regardless of the number of stockholders of a corporation.
B. On personal holding companies.
C. On companies that make distributions in excess of accumulated earnings.
D. On both partnerships and corporations.

AICPA.950523REG-AR

377. Edge Corp. met the stock ownership requirements of a personal holding company. What sources of income must Edge consider to determine if the income requirements for a personal holding company have been met?

I. Interest earned on tax-exempt obligations.
II. Dividends received from an unrelated domestic corporation.

A. I only.
B. II only.
C. Both I and II.
D. Neither I nor II.

AICPA.930555REG-P2-AR

378. Kari Corp., a manufacturing company, was organized on January 2, 2016. Its 2016 federal taxable income was $400,000 and its federal income tax was $100,000.

What is the maximum amount of accumulated taxable income that may be subject to the accumulated earnings tax for 2016 if Kari takes only the minimum accumulated earnings credit?

A. $300,000
B. $150,000
C. $50,000
D. $0

AICPA.941145REG-AR

379. Zero Corp. is an investment company authorized to issue only common stock.

During the last half of 2016, Edwards owned 450 of the 1,000 outstanding shares of stock in Zero. Another 350 shares of stock outstanding were owned, 10 shares each, by 35 shareholders who are neither related to each other nor to Edwards.

Zero could be a personal holding company if the remaining 200 shares of common stock were owned by

A. An estate where Edwards is the beneficiary.
B. Edwards's brother-in-law.
C. A partnership where Edwards is not a partner.
D. Edwards's cousin.

AICPA.951112REG-AR

380. Kane Corp. is a calendar year domestic personal holding company. Which deduction(s) must Kane make from 2016 taxable income to determine undistributed personal holding company income prior to the dividend-paid deduction?

	Federal income taxes	Net long-term capital gain less related federal income taxes
A.	Yes	Yes
B.	Yes	No
C.	No	Yes
D.	No	No

Taxation of Related Corporations

AICPA.930543REG-P2-AR

381. In 2017, Portal Corp. received $100,000 in dividends from Sal Corp., its 80%-owned subsidiary.

What net amount of dividend income should Portal include in its 2017 consolidated tax return?

A. $100,000
B. $80,000

C. $70,000
D. $0

AICPA.940523REG-AR

382. Tech Corp. files a consolidated return with its wholly-owned subsidiary, Dow Corp. During 2017, Dow paid a cash dividend of $20,000 to Tech.

What amount of this dividend is taxable on the 2017 consolidated return?

A. $20,000
B. $14,000
C. $6,000
D. $0

AICPA.941146REG-AR

383. With regard to consolidated tax returns, which of the following statements is correct?

A. Operating losses of one group member may be used to offset operating profits of the other members included in the consolidated return.
B. Only corporations that issue their audited financial statements on a consolidated basis may file consolidated returns.
C. Of all intercompany dividends paid by the subsidiaries to the parent, 70% are excludable from taxable income on the consolidated return.
D. The common parent must directly own 51% or more of the total voting power of all corporations included in the consolidated return.

AICPA.060817REG-AR

384. Jans, an individual, owns 80% and 100% of the total value and voting power of A and B Corps., which in turn own the following (both value and voting power):

Ownership		
Property	A Corp	B Corp
C Corp	80%	–
D Corp	–	100%

All companies are C corporations except B Corp., which had elected S status since inception. Which of the following statements is correct with respect to the companies' ability to file a consolidated return?

A. A, C, and D may file as a group.
B. A and C may not file as a group, and B and D may not file as a group.
C. A and C may file as a group, and B and D may file as a group.
D. A and C may file as a group, but B and D may not file as a group.

AICPA.900536BEC-P2-AR

385. In the consolidated income tax return of a corporation and its wholly-owned subsidiary, what percentage of cash dividends paid by the subsidiary to the parent is tax-free?

   A.   0%
   B.   70%
   C.   80%
   D.   100%

Distributions from a Corporation

AICPA.120752REG

386. Simon, a C corporation, had a deficit in accumulated earnings and profits of $50,000 at the beginning of the year and had current earnings and profits of $10,000. At year end, Simon paid a dividend of $15,000 to its sole shareholder. What amount of the dividend is reported as income?

   A. $0
   B. $ 5,000
   C. $10,000
   D. $15,000

AICPA.940525REG-AR

387. On January 1, 2017, Kee Corp., a C corporation, had a $50,000 deficit in earnings and profits. For 2017 Kee had current earnings and profits of $10,000 and made a $30,000 cash distribution to its stockholders. What amount of the distribution is taxable as dividend income to Kee's stockholders?

   A. $30,000
   B. $20,000
   C. $10,000
   D. $0

AICPA.090835REG

388. Fox, the sole shareholder in Fall, a C corporation, has a tax basis of $60,000. Fall has $40,000 of accumulated positive earnings and profits at the beginning of the year and $10,000 of current positive earnings and profits for the current year. At year end, Fall distributed land with an adjusted basis of $30,000 and a fair market value (FMV) of $38,000 to Fox. The land has an outstanding mortgage of $3,000 that Fox must assume. What is Fox's tax basis in the land?

   A. $38,000
   B. $35,000
   C. $30,000
   D. $27,000

AICPA.910545REG-P2-AR

389. Nyle Corp. owned 100 shares of Beta Corp. stock that it bought in 1993 for $9 per share. In 2017, when the fair market value of the Beta stock was $20 per share, Nyle distributed this stock to a noncorporate shareholder.

   Nyle's recognized gain on this distribution was

   A. $2,000
   B. $1,100
   C. $900
   D. $0

AICPA.090850REG

390. Webster, a C corporation, has $70,000 in accumulated and no current earnings and profits. Webster distributed $20,000 cash and property with an adjusted basis and fair market value of $60,000 to its shareholders. What amount should the shareholders report as dividend income?

   A. $20,000
   B. $60,000
   C. $70,000
   D. $80,000

Corporate Redemptions and Liquidations

AICPA.090826REG-SIM

391. What is the usual result to the shareholders of a distribution in complete liquidation of a corporation?

   A.   No taxable effect
   B.   Ordinary gain to the extent of cash received
   C.   Ordinary gain or loss
   D.   Capital gain or loss

AICPA.090825REG-SIM

392. A corporation was completely liquidated and dissolved this year. The filing fees, professional fees, and other expenditures incurred in connection with the liquidation are:

   A.   Deducted in full by the dissolved corporation.
   B.   Deducted in full by the shareholders of the dissolved corporation.
   C.   Treated as capital losses by the dissolved corporation.
   D.   Not deductible by the corporation or the shareholders.

AICPA.090827REG-SIM

393. How does a noncorporate shareholder treat the gain on a redemption of stock that qualifies as a partial liquidation of the distributing corporation?

A. Entirely as a capital gain
B. Entirely as a dividend
C. Partly as a capital gain and partly as a return of capital
D. Entirely as a tax-free transaction

AICPA.060503REG-SIM

394. S Corporation was a wholly-owned subsidiary of P Corporation. Both corporations were domestic C corporations. P received a liquidating distribution of property (worth $250 and a basis of $135) from S in cancellation of the stock. What amount of gain will P recognize if P had a basis of $100 in the S stock before the receipt of the property?

A. $ 0
B. $ 35
C. $150
D. $250

AICPA.970506BEC-AR

395. Elm Corp. is an accrual-basis, calendar-year C corporation with 100,000 shares of voting common stock issued and outstanding as of December 28, 2017.

On Friday, December 29, 2017, Hall surrendered 2,000 shares of Elm stock to Elm in exchange for $33,000 cash. Hall had no direct or indirect interest in Elm after the stock surrender. Additional information follows:

Hall's adjusted basis in 2,000 shares of Elm on December 29, 2017 ($8 per share)	$16,000
Elm's accumulated earnings and profits at January 1, 2017	25,000
Elm's 2017 net operating loss	(7,000)

What amount of income did Hall recognize from the stock surrender?

A. $33,000 dividend
B. $25,000 dividend
C. $18,000 capital gain
D. $17,000 capital gain

Corporate Reorganizations

AICPA.090824REG-SIM

396. P corporation acquired the assets of its wholly-owned subsidiary, S corporation, under a plan that qualified as a tax-free complete liquidation of S. Which of the following of S's unused carryovers may be transferred to P?

A. Excess charitable contributions.
B. Net operating loss.
C. Both of the above are transferred.
D. None of the above is transferred.

AICPA.950525BEC-AR

397. Jaxson Corp. has 200,000 shares of voting common stock issued and outstanding. King Corp. has decided to acquire 90% of Jaxson's voting common stock solely in exchange for 50% of its voting common stock and retain Jaxson as a subsidiary after the transaction.

Which of the following statements is true?

A. King must acquire 100% of Jaxson stock for the transaction to be a tax-free reorganization.
B. The transaction will qualify as a tax-free reorganization.
C. King must issue at least 60% of its voting common stock for the transaction to qualify as a tax-free reorganization.
D. Jaxson must surrender assets for the transaction to qualify as a tax-free reorganization.

AICPA.910543BEC-P2-AR

398. Pursuant to a plan of corporate reorganization adopted in July 2017, Gow exchanged 500 shares of Lad Corp. common stock that he had bought in January 2017 at a cost of $5,000 for 100 shares of Rook Corp. common stock having a fair market value of $6,000.

Gow's recognized gain on this exchange was

A. $1,000 long-term capital gain.
B. $1,000 short-term capital gain.
C. $1,000 ordinary income.
D. $0.

AICPA.090830REG-SIM

399. ABC has 200 shares of voting common stock outstanding. XYZ has decided to acquire 90% of the ABC stock solely in exchange for 50% of its voting stock. ABC will become XYZ's subsidiary after the transaction. Which of the following statements is true?

A. XYZ must acquire 100% of ABC for the transaction to qualify as a reorganization.
B. The transaction is a reorganization.
C. XYZ must issue at least 60% of its stock for the transaction to qualify as a reorganization.
D. ABC must surrender assets to XYZ to qualify as a reorganization.

Multijurisdictional Tax Issues

State and Local Taxation

AICPA.101074REG-SIM

400. Machine Corporation buys a business van in State V and pays 6% sales tax. The van is used in State W by Machine. State W has a 9% sales

tax. Because of this transaction, State W is likely to impose which of the following taxes on Machine?

A. Sales tax.
B. Income tax.
C. Use tax.
D. Franchise tax.

AICPA.101078REG-SIM

401. Clock Corporation owns 80%, 90%, and 100%, respectively, of its three subsidiaries, Lamp, Chair, and Table. The corporations have elected to file a consolidated tax return for U.S. federal income tax. The corporations have nexus as follows:

	Nexus
Clock	States M and N
Lamp	States M and N
Chair	State N
Table	States M and N

If a consolidated state income tax return is filed in State M, which corporations will be included in the return?

A. Clock
B. Clock and Table.
C. Clock, Lamp, and Table.
D. Clock, Lamp, Chair, and Table.

AICPA.101077REG-SIM

402. Callaway Company manufactures its products in State F and sells them in States F and G. Callaway's sales are as follows for the current year:

Sales shipped from State F to customers in State F	$10,000
Sales shipped from State F to customers in State G	40,000

Assume that Callaway has nexus in both states F and G. What is Callaway's State F sales factor for the current year?

A. 0%
B. 20%
C. 50%
D. 100%

AICPA.101076REG-SIM

403. Which of the following types of income would likely be considered "business income" for state income tax purposes?

A. Dividends from stock held as long term investments.
B. Gain from the sale of land that is not used in the taxpayer's regular business operations.

C. Rent received from corporate office space not used in the taxpayer's regular business operations.
D. Royalties from the licensing of a song that was produced as part of ordinary business operations.

AICPA.101075REG-SIM

404. Woods Corporation's federal taxable income for the current year is $250,000 which includes the following:

$15,000 of deducted state income taxes

$25,000 of interest income on United States Treasury Bonds

Woods also had $10,000 of interest from state and local bonds that it owns. Federal depreciation in excess of that allowed for state purposes was $7,000. Woods operates exclusively in State F, which does not tax income earned on federal obligations, taxes all municipal bond interest, and disallows a deduction for state income taxes. What is Wood's state taxable income?

A. $257,000.
B. $243,000.
C. $307,000.
D. $250,000.

Taxation of Foreign Income

AICPA.101072REG-SIM

405. Which one of the following types of income is **not** U.S.-source income?

A. Salary earned in the United States
B. Interest income on United States Treasury Bonds
C. Income from the sale of land located in Japan by a Japanese resident to a taxpayer whose residence is in the United States
D. Rents received from property located in the United States

AICPA.101070REG-SIM

406. Mr. Travel is a U.S. citizen who has been a resident of Spain for five years. In 2017, he has the following income from Spanish sources:

	Salary	Interest Income
Gross amount	$90,000	$20,000
Spanish income tax (20%)	(18,000)	(4,000)
Net cash received (80%)	$72,000	$16,000

The interest income was from a Spanish money market account. Mr. Travel also was provided housing from his employer that had a fair market value of $30,000 (not subject to Spanish tax). Total U.S.-source earned income for Mr.

Travel was $60,000. How much of the foreign taxes paid is eligible to be used in the foreign tax credit computation?

A. – $0 –
B. $ 4,000
C. $18,000
D. $22,000

AICPA.101069REG-SIM

407. Mr. Travel is a U.S. citizen who has been a resident of Spain for five years. In 2017, he has the following income from Spanish sources:

	Salary	Interest Income
Gross amount	$90,000	$20,000
Spanish income tax (20%)	(18,000)	(4,000)
Net cash received (80%)	$72,000	$16,000

The interest income was from a Spanish money market account. Mr. Travel also was provided housing from his employer that had a fair market value of $40,000 (not subject to Spanish tax). Total U.S.-source earned income for Mr. Travel was $60,000. What is Mr. Travel's minimum includible United States gross income from these transactions? The housing exclusion is $14,294 and foreign earned income exclusion is $102,100 in 2017.

A. $ 60,000
B. $105,706
C. $110,000
D. $200,000

AICPA.101073REG-SIM

408. Which of the following statements is incorrect?

A. Foreign currency exchange gains and losses resulting from the normal course of business operations are ordinary.
B. Foreign currency exchange gains and losses resulting from investment transactions are capital.
C. Foreign currency exchange gains and losses resulting from personal transactions are capital.
D. Foreign currency exchange gains and losses resulting from the normal course of business operations are capital.

AICPA.101071REG-SIM

409. ABC, Inc., has $120,000 U.S. source income, $80,000 of foreign source income, and $25,000 foreign taxes deemed paid. Assume that the U.S. income tax liability before the foreign tax credit is $61,250. ABC's foreign tax credit is

A. – $0 –
B. $24,500

C. $25,000
D. $61,250

Tax-Exempt Entities

Tax-Exempt Organizations

AICPA.101081REG

410. An organization that operates for the prevention of cruelty to animals will fail to meet the operational test to qualify as an exempt organization if

	The organization engages in insubstantial nonexempt activities	The organization directly participates in any political campaign
A.	Yes	Yes
B.	Yes	No
C.	No	Yes
D.	No	No

AICPA.101079REG

411. The organizational test to qualify a public service charitable entity as tax exempt requires the articles of organization to

I. Limit the purpose of the entity to the charitable purpose.
II. State that an information return should be filed annually with the Internal Revenue Service.

A. I only.
B. II only.
C. Both I and II.
D. Neither I nor II.

AICPA.101085REG

412. Which of the following activities conducted by a tax exempt organization will result in unrelated business income?

I. Selling articles made by handicapped persons as part of their rehabilitation, when the organization is involved exclusively in their rehabilitation.
II. Operating a grocery store almost fully staffed by emotionally handicapped persons as part of a therapeutic program.

A. I only.
B. II only.
C. Both I and II.
D. Neither I nor II.

AICPA.101084REG

413. The private foundation status of an exempt organization will terminate if it

A. Becomes a public charity.
B. Is a foreign corporation.

C. Does not distribute all of its net assets to one or more public charities.

D. Is governed by a charter that limits the organization's exempt purposes.

AICPA.101080REG

414. Which of the following exempt organizations must file annual information returns?

A. Churches.
B. Internally supported auxiliaries.
C. Private foundations.
D. Those with gross receipts of $50,000 or less in each taxable year.

Partnership Taxation

Formation and Basis

AICPA.950527REG-AR

415. Strom acquired a 25 percent interest in Ace Partnership by contributing land having an adjusted basis of $16,000 and a fair market value of $50,000. The land was subject to a $24,000 mortgage, which was assumed by Ace. No other liabilities existed at the time of the contribution.

What was Strom's basis in Ace?

A. $0
B. $16,000
C. $26,000
D. $32,000

AICPA.090853REG

416. A $100,000 increase in partnership liabilities is treated in which of the following ways?

A. Increases each partner's basis in the partnership by $100,000.
B. Increases the partners' bases only if the liability is nonrecourse.
C. Increases each partner's basis in proportion to their ownership.
D. Does **not** change any partner's basis in the partnership regardless of whether the liabilities are recourse or nonrecourse.

AICPA.911160FAR-P2-AR

417. The holding period of a partnership interest acquired in exchange for a contributed capital asset begins on the date

A. The partner is admitted to the partnership.
B. The partner transfers the asset to the partnership.
C. The partner's holding period of the capital asset began.
D. The partner is first credited with the proportionate share of partnership capital.

AICPA.931149REG-P2-AR

418. On June 1, 2017, Kelly received a 10% interest in Rock Co., a partnership, for services contributed to the partnership. Rock's net assets at that date had a basis of $70,000 and a fair market value of $100,000.

In Kelly's 2017 income tax return, what amount must Kelly include as income from transfer of partnership interest?

A. $7,000 ordinary income
B. $7,000 capital gain
C. $10,000 ordinary income
D. $10,000 capital gain

AICPA.931148REG-P2-AR

419. Pert contributed land with a fair market value of $20,000 to a new partnership in exchange for a 50% partnership interest. The land had an adjusted basis to Pert of $12,000 and was subject to a $4,000 mortgage, which the partnership assumed. What is the adjusted basis of Pert's partnership interest?

A. $10,000
B. $12,000
C. $18,000
D. $20,000

Flow-Through of Income and Losses

AICPA.130925REG

420. What is the tax treatment of net losses in excess of the at-risk amount for an activity?

A. Any loss in excess of the at-risk amount is suspended and is deductible in the year in which the activity is disposed of in full.
B. Any losses in excess of the at-risk amount are suspended and carried forward without expiration and are deductible against income in future years from that activity.
C. Any losses in excess of the at-risk amount are deducted currently against income from other activities; the remaining loss, if any, is carried forward without expiration.
D. Any losses in excess of the at-risk amount are carried back two years against activities with income and then carried forward for 20 years.

AICPA.901127REG-P2-AR

421. Don Wolf became a general partner in Gata Associates on January 1, 2017, with a 5% interest in Gata's profits, losses, and capital.

Gata is a distributor of auto parts. Wolf does not materially participate in the partnership business. For the year ended December 31, 2017, Gata had an operating loss of $100,000. In addition, Gata earned interest of $20,000 on a temporary investment. Gata has kept the principal temporarily invested while awaiting delivery of equipment that is presently on order. The principal will be used to pay for this equipment.

Wolf's passive loss for 2017 is

A. $0.
B. $4,000.
C. $5,000.
D. $6,000.

AICPA.911155REG-P2-AR

422. Which of the following limitations will apply in determining a partner's deduction for that partner's share of partnership losses?

	At-risk	Passive loss
A.	Yes	No
B.	No	Yes
C.	Yes	Yes
D.	No	No

AICPA.060823REG-AR

423. A partnership had four partners. Each partner contributed $100,000 cash. The partnership reported income for the year of $80,000 and distributed $10,000 to each partner. What was each partner's basis in the partnership at the end of the current year?

A. $170,000
B. $120,000
C. $117,500
D. $110,000

AICPA.090856REG

424. Dale was a 50% partner in D&P Partnership. Dale contributed $10,000 in cash upon the formation of the partnership. D&P borrowed $10,000 to purchase equipment. During the first year of operations, D&P had $15,000 net taxable income, $2,000 tax-exempt interest income, a $3,000 distribution to each partner, and a $4,000 reduction of debt. At the end of the first year of operation, what amount would be Dale's basis?

A. $16,500
B. $17,500
C. $18,500
D. $21,500

Transactions with Partners

AICPA.940529REG-AR

425. Guaranteed payments made by a partnership to partners for services rendered to the partnership, that are deductible business expenses under the Internal Revenue Code, are

I. Deductible expenses on the *U.S. Partnership Return of Income*, Form 1065, in order to arrive at partnership income (loss).
II. Included on schedules K-1 to be taxed as ordinary income to the partners.

A. I only.
B. II only.
C. Both I and II.
D. Neither I nor II.

AICPA.941157REG-AR

426. White has a one-third interest in the profits and losses of Rapid Partnership. Rapid's ordinary income for the 2017 calendar year is $30,000, after a $3,000 deduction for a guaranteed payment made to White for services rendered. None of the $30,000 ordinary income was distributed to the partners.

What is the total amount that White must include from Rapid as taxable income in his 2017 tax return?

A. $3,000
B. $10,000
C. $11,000
D. $13,000

AICPA.950529REG-AR

427. A guaranteed payment by a partnership to a partner for services rendered, may include an agreement to pay

I. A salary of $5,000 monthly without regard to partnership income.
II. A 25% interest in partnership profits.

A. I only.
B. II only.
C. Both I and II.
D. Neither I nor II.

AICPA.910559REG-P2-AR

428. Under the Internal Revenue Code sections pertaining to partnerships, guaranteed payments are payments to partners for

A. Payments of principal on secured notes honored at maturity.
B. Timely payments of periodic interest on bona fide loans that are not treated as partners' capital.
C. Services or the use of capital without regard to partnership income.
D. Sales of partners' assets to the partnership at guaranteed amounts regardless of market values.

AICPA.101114REG-SIM

429. Abe, Betsy, and Dan decide to form the equal ABD partnership at the beginning of Year One. Abe contributed depreciable assets that he has owned for five years that have a basis of $15,000 and a value of $20,000. Betsy contributed $20,000 cash. Dan contributed $12,000 in cash and land with a basis of $5,000 and a value of $8,000. How much income is allocated to Abe if

the partnership sells the assets contributed by Abe for $18,000?

A. $0
B. $1,000
C. $3,000
D. $5,000

Partnership Distributions

AICPA.951131REG-AR

430. Hart's adjusted basis in Best Partnership was $9,000 at the time he received the following nonliquidating distributions of partnership property:

Cash	$5,000
Land	
Adjusted basis	7,000
Fair market value	10,000

What was the amount of Hart's basis in the land?

A. $0
B. $4,000
C. $7,000
D. $10,000

AICPA.951132REG-AR

431. Stone's basis in Ace Partnership was $70,000 at the time he received a nonliquidating distribution of partnership capital assets. These capital assets had an adjusted basis of $65,000 to Ace, and a fair market value of $83,000. Ace had no unrealized receivables, appreciated inventory, or properties which had been contributed by its partners.

What was Stone's recognized gain or loss on the distribution?

A. $18,000 ordinary income.
B. $13,000 capital gain.
C. $5,000 capital loss.
D. $0.

AICPA.120739REG

432. As a general partner in Greenland Associates, an individual's share of partnership income for the current tax year is $25,000 ordinary business income and a $10,000 guaranteed payment. The individual also received $5,000 in cash distributions from the partnership. What income should the individual report from the interest in Greenland?

A. $5,000
B. $25,000
C. $35,000
D. $40,000

AICPA.900526REG-P2-AR

433. Hart's adjusted basis of his interest in a partnership was $30,000. He received a nonliquidating distribution of $24,000 cash plus a parcel of land with a fair market value and partnership basis of $9,000.

Hart's basis for the land is

A. $9,000
B. $6,000
C. $3,000
D. $0

AICPA.911154REG-P2-AR

434. The basis to a partner of property distributed "in kind" in complete liquidation of the partner's interest is the

A. Adjusted basis of the partner's interest increased by any cash distributed to the partner in the same transaction.
B. Adjusted basis of the partner's interest reduced by any cash distributed to the partner in the same transaction.
C. Adjusted basis of the property to the partnership.
D. Fair market value of the property.

Sales and Terminations

AICPA.900522REG-P2-AR

435. The personal service partnership of Allen, Baker & Carr had the following cash-basis balance sheet at December 31, 2016:

Assets

	Adjusted basis per book	Market value
Cash	$102,000	$102,000
Unrealized accounts receivable	–	420,000
Totals	$102,000	$522,000
Liability and Capital		
Note payable	$ 60,000	$ 60,000
Capital accounts:		
Allen	14,000	154,000
Baker	14,000	154,000
Carr	14,000	154,000
	$102,000	$522,000

Carr, an equal partner, sold his partnership interest to Dole, an outsider, for $154,000 cash on January 1, 2017. In addition, Dole assumed Carr's share of the partnerships liability. What was the total amount realized by Carr on the sale of his partnership interest?

A. $174,000
B. $154,000
C. $140,000
D. $134,000

AICPA.951133REG-AR

436. On January 3, 2017, the partners' interests in the capital, profits, and losses of Able Partnership were:

% of capital, profits and losses	
Dean	25%
Poe	30%
Ritt	45%

On February 4, 2017, Poe sold her entire interest to an unrelated party. Dean sold his 25% interest in Able to another unrelated party on December 20, 2017. No other transactions took place in 2017. For tax purposes, which of the following statements is correct with respect to Able?

A. Able terminated as of February 4, 2017.
B. Able terminated as of December 20, 2017.
C. Able terminated as of December 31, 2017.
D. Able did not terminate.

AICPA.120737REG

437. "Hot assets" of a partnership would include which of the following?

A. Cash
B. Unrealized receivables
C. Section 1231 assets
D. Capital assets

AICPA.931159REG-P2-AR

438. On December 31, 2017, after receipt of his share of partnership income, Clark sold his interest in a limited partnership for $30,000 cash and relief of all liabilities.

On that date, the adjusted basis of Clark's partnership interest was $40,000, consisting of his capital account of $15,000 and his share of the partnership liabilities of $25,000. The partnership has no unrealized receivables or substantially appreciated inventory.

What is Clark's gain or loss on the sale of his partnership interest?

A. Ordinary loss of $10,000
B. Ordinary gain of $15,000

C. Capital loss of $10,000
D. Capital gain of $15,000

AICPA.900523REG-P2-AR

439. The personal service partnership of Allen, Baker & Carr had the following cash basis balance sheet at December 31, 2015:

Assets

	Adjusted basis per book	Market value
Cash	$102,000	$102,000
Unrealized accounts receivable	–	420,000
Totals	$102,000	$522,000

Liability and Capital

Note payable	$ 60,000	$ 60,000
Capital accounts:		
Allen	14,000	154,000
Baker	14,000	154,000
Carr	14,000	154,000
	$102,000	$522,000

Carr, an equal partner, sold his partnership interest to Dole, an outsider, for $154,000 cash on January 1, 2016. In addition, Dole assumed Carr's share of the partnerships liability. What amount of ordinary income should Carr report in his 2016 income tax return on the sale of his partnership interest?

A. $0
B. $20,000
C. $34,000
D. $140,000

S Corporation Taxation

Eligibility, Elections, Terminations

AICPA.120750REG

440. Which of the following statements about qualifying shareholders of an S corporation is correct?

A. A general partnership may be a shareholder.
B. Only individuals may be shareholders.
C. Individuals, estates, and certain trusts may be shareholders.
D. Nonresident aliens may be shareholders.

AICPA.060256REG-AR

441. Which of the following is an eligibility requirement in 2017 to file a valid election to be taxed as an S corporation?

A. Must have no more than 75 shareholders, and a husband and wife who each own stock are counted as two shareholders.

B. Must have no more than 100 shareholders, and a husband and wife who each own stock are counted as two shareholders.

C. Must have no more than 100 shareholders, and a husband and wife who each own stock are counted as one shareholder.

D. Must have no more 75 shareholders, and a husband and wife who each own stock are counted as one shareholder.

AICPA.941144REG-AR

442. On February 10, 2017, Ace Corp., a calendar year corporation, elected S corporation status and all shareholders consented to the election. There was no change in shareholders in 2017. Ace met all eligibility requirements for S status during the preelection portion of the year.

What is the earliest date on which Ace can be recognized as an S corporation?

A. February 10, 2018
B. February 10, 2017
C. January 1, 2018
D. January 1, 2017

AICPA.900527REG-P2-AR

443. Which one of the following will render a corporation ineligible for S corporation status?

A. One of the stockholders is a decedent's estate.

B. One of the stockholders is a bankruptcy estate.

C. The corporation has both voting and nonvoting common stock issued and outstanding.

D. The corporation has 150 stockholders.

AICPA.910557REG-P2-AR

444. After a corporation's status as an S corporation is revoked or terminated, how many years is the corporation required to wait before making a new S election, in the absence of IRS consent to an earlier election?

A. 1
B. 3
C. 5
D. 10

Income and Basis

AICPA.941143REG-AR

445. As of January 1, 2017, Kane owned all the 100 issued shares of Manning Corp., a calendar year S corporation. On the 40th day of 2017, Kane sold 25 of the Manning shares to Rodgers. For the year ended December 31, 2017 (a 365-day calendar year), Manning had $73,000 in nonseparately stated income and made no distributions to its shareholders.

What amount of nonseparately stated income from Manning should be reported on Kane's 2017 tax return?

A. $56,750
B. $54,750
C. $16,250
D. $0

AICPA.120708REG

446. Which of the following items must be separately stated on Form 1120S, *U.S. Income Tax Return for a Corporation, Schedule K-1*?

A. Mark-to-market income
B. Unearned revenue
C. Section 1245 gain
D. Gain or loss from the sale of collectibles

AICPA.090858REG

447. An S corporation engaged in manufacturing has a year end of June 30. Revenue consistently has been more than $10 million under both cash and accrual basis of accounting. The stockholders would like to change the tax status of the corporation to a C corporation using the cash basis with the same year end. Which of the following statements is correct if it changes to a C corporation?

A. The year end will be December 31, using the cash basis of accounting.

B. The year end will be December 31, using the accrual basis of accounting.

C. The year end will be June 30, using the accrual basis of accounting.

D. The year end will be June 30, using the cash basis of accounting.

AICPA.130917REG

448. Carson owned 40% of the outstanding stock of a C corporation. During a tax year, the corporation reported $400,000 in taxable income and distributed a total of $70,000 in cash dividends to its shareholders. Carson accurately reported $28,000 in gross income on Carson's individual tax return. If the corporation had been an S corporation and the distributions to the owners had been proportionate, how

much income would Carson have reported on Carson's individual return?

A. $28,000
B. $132,000
C. $160,000
D. $188,000

AICPA.020504REG-AR

449. Stahl, an individual, owns 100% of Talon, an S corporation. At the beginning of the year, Stahl's basis in Talon was $65,000. Talon reported the following items from operations during the current year:

Ordinary loss	$10,000
Municipal interest income	6,000
Long-term capital gain	4,000
Short-term capital loss	9,000

What was Stahl's basis in Talon at year-end?

A. $50,000
B. $55,000
C. $56,000
D. $61,000

Distributions and Special Taxes

AICPA.120707REG

450. A sole proprietorship incorporated on January 1 and elected S corporation status. The owner contributed the following assets to the S corporation:

	Basis	Fair market value
Machinery	$ 7,000	$ 8,000
Building	11,000	100,000
Cash	1,000	1,000

Two years later, the corporation sold the machinery for $4,000 and the building for $110,000. The machinery had accumulated depreciation of $2,000, and the building had accumulated depreciation of $1,000. What is the built-in gain recognized on the sale?

A. $100,000
B. $ 99,000
C. $ 6,000
D. $0

AICPA.090852REG

451. Sandy is the sole shareholder of Swallow, an S corporation. Sandy's adjusted basis in Swallow stock is $60,000 at the beginning of the year. During the year, Swallow reports the following income items:

Ordinary income	$30,000
Tax-exempt income	5,000
Capital gains	10,000

In addition, Swallow makes a nontaxable distribution to Sandy of $20,000 during the year. What is Sandy's adjusted basis in the Swallow stock at the end of the year?

A. $60,000
B. $70,000
C. $80,000
D. $85,000

AICPA.101112REG

452. Beck Corp. has been a calendar year S corporation since its inception on January 2, 2007. On January 1, 2017, Lazur and Lyle each owned 50% of the Beck stock, in which their respective tax bases were $12,000 and $9,000. For the year ended December 31, 2017, Beck had $81,000 in ordinary business income and $10,000 in tax-exempt income. Beck made a $51,000 cash distribution to each shareholder on December 31, 2017. What was Lazur's tax basis in Beck after the distribution?

A. $1,500
B. $6,500
C. $52,500
D. $57,500

AICPA.931144REG-P2-AR

453. If an S corporation has no accumulated earnings and profits, the amount distributed to a shareholder

A. Must be returned to the S corporation.
B. Increases the shareholder's basis for the stock.
C. Decreases the shareholder's basis for the stock.
D. Has no effect on the shareholder's basis for the stock.

AICPA.020508REG-AR

454. Baker, an individual, owned 100% of Alpha, an S corporation. At the beginning of the year, Baker's basis in Alpha Corp. was $25,000. Alpha realized ordinary income during the year in the amount of $1,000 and a long-term capital loss in the amount of $3,000 for this year. Alpha distributed $30,000 in cash to Baker during the year.

What amount of the $30,000 cash distribution is taxable to Baker?

A. $0
B. $7,000
C. $4,000
D. $30,000

Fiduciary Taxation

Income Taxation of Fiduciaries

AICPA.990513REG-AR

455. Astor, a cash-basis taxpayer, died on February 3. During the year, the estate's executor made a distribution of $12,000 from estate income to Astor's sole heir and adopted a calendar year to determine the estate's taxable income. The following additional information pertains to the estate's income and disbursements for the year:

	Estate income
Taxable interest	$65,000
Net long-term capital gains allocable to corpus	5,000
Estate disbursements:	
Administrative expenses attributable to taxable income	14,000
Charitable contributions from gross income to a public charity made under the terms of the will	9,000

For the calendar year, what was the estate's distributable net income (DNI)?

A. $39,000
B. $42,000
C. $58,000
D. $65,000

AICPA.911139REG-P2-AR

456. Ordinary and necessary administration expenses paid by the fiduciary of an estate are deductible

A. Only on the fiduciary income tax return (Form 1041) and never on the federal estate tax return (Form 706).
B. Only on the federal estate tax return and never on the fiduciary income tax return.
C. On the fiduciary income tax return only if the estate tax deduction is waived for these expenses.
D. On both the fiduciary income tax return and on the estate tax return by adding a tax computed on the proportionate rates attributable to both returns.

AICPA.911125REG-P2-AR

457. Which of the following fiduciary entities are required to use the calendar year as their taxable period for income tax purposes?

	Estates	Trusts (except those that are tax exempt)
A.	Yes	Yes
B.	No	No
C.	Yes	No
D.	No	Yes

AICPA.090837REG

458. The Simone Trust reported distributable net income of $120,000 for the current year. The trustee is required to distribute $60,000 to Kent and $90,000 to Lind each year. If the trustee distributes these amounts, what amount is includible in Lind's gross income?

A. $0
B. $60,000
C. $72,000
D. $90,000

Tax Credits

Business Tax Credits

AICPA.101129REG-SIM

459. The following information pertains to Wald Corp.'s operations:

Worldwide taxable income	$300,000
U.S. source taxable income	180,000
U.S. income tax before foreign tax credit	96,000
Foreign source taxable income	120,000
Foreign income taxes paid on foreign source taxable income	39,000

What amount of foreign tax credit may Wald claim?

A. $28,800
B. $36,600
C. $38,400
D. $39,000

AICPA.990511REG-AR

460. Sunex Co., an accrual-basis, calendar-year domestic C corporation, is taxed on its worldwide income. In the current year, Sunex's U.S. tax liability on its domestic and foreign source income is $60,000 and no prior year foreign income taxes have been carried forward.

Which factor(s) may affect the amount of Sunex's foreign tax credit available in its current-year corporate income tax return?

	Income source	The foreign tax rate
A.	Yes	Yes
B.	Yes	No
C.	No	Yes
D.	No	No

AICPA.941149REG-AR

461. Which of the following credits is a combination of several tax credits to provide uniform rules for the current and carryback-carryover years?

A. General business credit.
B. Foreign tax credit.
C. Minimum tax credit.
D. Enhanced oil recovery credit.

AICPA.101131REG-SIM

462. Which of the following statements concerning tax credits is true?

A. The foreign tax credit is available for business entities, such as corporations, but not for individuals.
B. Unused general business credits are carried back two years and forward 20 years.
C. For the rehabilitation credit, expenditures to rehabilitate property placed in service before 1936 are eligible for a 20% credit.
D. The work opportunity tax credit is calculated on the amount of wages paid per eligible employee during the first year of employment. The maximum credit is $2,400 per eligible employee.

AICPA.910549REG-P2-AR

463. Foreign income taxes paid by a corporation

A. May be claimed either as a deduction or as a credit, at the option of the corporation.
B. May be claimed only as a deduction.
C. May be claimed only as a credit.
D. Do not qualify either as a deduction or as a credit.

Other Tax Issues

Tax Planning Strategies for Business Entities

AICPA.101087REG-SIM

464. Chris is in the 50% tax bracket in Year 1 but Congress has decreased his tax bracket to 30% for Year 2. Which of the following would be an appropriate tax planning strategy for Chris?

A. Defer income until Year 2.
B. Accelerate income into Year 1.

C. Defer deductions until Year 2.
D. Increase his estimated tax payments for Year 1.

AICPA.101086REG-SIM

465. Ms. Planner is in the 25% tax bracket and itemizes on her tax return. She plans to make a charitable contribution of $12,000 to her alma mater this year. The net cost of this contribution to T is:

A. $0
B. $3,000
C. $9,000
D. $12,000

AICPA.101088REG-SIM

466. Appropriate strategies for reducing the alternative minimum tax include all of the following except:

A. Do not exercise incentive stock options.
B. Make additional charitable contributions.
C. Increase home mortgage interest on primary mortgage.
D. Increase 2% miscellaneous itemized deductions.

AICPA.101089REG-SIM

467. Jose has owned stock for eight years that has a basis of $20,000 and fair market value of $100,000. Jose contributes the stock to a qualified charity. Which of the following is a proper tax consequence from this transaction?

A. Jose has recognized gain of $80,000.
B. Jose has a charitable contribution of $100,000.
C. Jose has a charitable contribution of $80,000.
D. Jose has a charitable contribution of $20,000.

AICPA.101090REG-SIM

468. Orleans has owned land as an investment for five years. His basis in the land is $70,000 and the land's current fair market value is $50,000. Which of the following statements is correct with regard to this land?

A. If Orleans sells the land to his father he can deduct the $20,000 loss in the land.
B. If Orleans gives the property to an unrelated friend he can deduct the $20,000 loss in the land.
C. Orleans should sell the land, recognize the $20,000 capital loss, and then gift the $50,000 cash from the sale to his friend.
D. If the land is sold to an unrelated party, the $20,000 loss cannot be recognized since the land is not depreciable.

Business Entity Choice

AICPA.120706REG

469. For which of the following entities is the owner's basis increased by the owner's share of profits and decreased by the owner's share of losses but is NOT affected by the entity's bank loan increases or decreases?

A. S corporation.
B. C corporation.
C. Partnership.
D. Limited liability company.

AICPA.990504REG-AR

470. Lane Inc., an S corporation, pays single coverage health insurance premiums of $4,800 per year and additional premiums of $7,200 per year for family coverage. Mill is a ten percent shareholder-employee in Lane. On Mill's behalf, Lane pays Mill's family coverage under the health insurance plan. What amount of insurance premiums is includible in Mill's gross income?

A. $0
B. $4,800
C. $7,200
D. $12,000

AICPA.060822REG-P2-AR

471. Which of the following is an advantage of forming a limited liability company (LLC) as opposed to a partnership?

A. The entity may avoid taxation.
B. The entity may have any number of owners.
C. The owner may participate in management while limiting personal liability.
D. The entity may make disproportionate allocations and distributions to members.

AICPA.060257REG-AR

472. Which of the following statements concerning S corporations is False?

A. S corporations must be incorporated under state law in the same fashion as C corporations.
B. S corporation shareholders are not liable for the debt of the corporation.
C. An S corporation can issue both voting and non-voting common stock.
D. S corporations are subject to the alternative minimum tax.

AICPA.060814REG-P2-AR

473. Which of the following types of entities is entitled to the net operating loss deduction?

A. Partnerships.
B. S corporations.
C. Trusts and estates.
D. Not-for-profit organizations.

Answers and Explanations

1. **Answer: C**

   Circular 230's section 10.33 recommends these steps as "best practices" for federal tax advisors.

2. **Answer: B**

   The IRS allows tax practitioners to retain *copies* of the client's records.

3. **Answer: C**

   Both Circular 230 and the Code of Professional Conduct tells CPAs who learn of such errors to inform the client of the error and advise the client of the consequences so that the client can make an informed decision regarding how to proceed.

4. **Answer: C**

   People are TRPs if (a) they are paid, (b) to prepare or retain employees to prepare, (c) a substantial portion, (d) of any federal tax return. Because Louis was not paid specifically to prepare the return, he does not satisfy the first requirement to be a TRP.

5. **Answer: C**

   Under current rules, Sandy must furnish the preparer's identifying number to the IRS but not to her clients.

6. **Answer: A**

   Only state boards of accountancy can grant a CPA license.

7. **Answer: D**

   While certain types of punishments may be meted out by the SEC, the AICPA, and state CPA societies, only a state board of accountancy truly has the power to revoke a CPA's license to practice public accountancy. Nonetheless, the SEC may, for example, prevent an accountant from appearing before it or doing any attest work for a public company.

   The AICPA may revoke an accountant's membership, as may a state CPA society. But only the state board of accountancy may revoke a license to practice.

8. **Answer: D**

   The AICPA handles ethical complaints with national implications.

9. **Answer: D**

   All choices are needed to establish the good faith defense.

10. **Answer: B**

    This "reasonable basis" standard applies to disclosed positions.

11. **Answer: B**

    With disclosure, Clegg can avoid an underpayment penalty even if the position is ultimately rejected because there is a reasonable basis (≥ 20% chance of approval) for it.

12. **Answer: B**

    Because this meets the "reasonable basis" test (≥20%), it can be taken if disclosed without courting an understatement penalty.

13. **Answer: A**

    This was a substantial understatement, because the $200,000 amount, while not exceeding $10,000,000, does exceed the lesser amount of 10% of the tax ($100,000) (which, in turn, exceeds $10,000). The penalty will be 20% × $200,000 = $40,000.

14. **Answer: D**

    The late filing penalty is capped at 25% of the amount of taxes owed ($100,000 × 25% = $25,000). Absent the cap, Xina would have owed $50,000.

15. **Answer: D**

    Proposed regulations do not have the effect of law, but they do provide an indication of the IRS's view on a tax issue.

16. **Answer: A**

    The Internal Revenue Code is the highest tax authority.

17. **Answer: C**

    The United States Court of Appeals hears appeals from the U.S. Tax Court and the U.S. District Court. It is not a court of original jurisdiction.

18. **Answer: D**

    Committee reports are legislative sources of authority which provide insight into the intention of the House Ways & Means Committee, Senate Finance Committee, and Joint Conference Committee.

19. **Answer: B**

    Tax legislation in the Senate begins in the Senate Finance Committee.

20. **Answer: B**

    After a "no change" report the IRS cannot reopen the examination unless the corporation has committed fraud.

21. **Answer: D**

    IRS Audit Guides provide guidance to revenue agents who are conducting audits but they do not govern the conduct of CPAs engaged in providing tax services.

22. **Answer: B**

    The taxpayer is not required to respond to a *30-day letter*, although if there is no response the IRS will follow with a *90-day letter*.

23. **Answer: A**

    The statute of limitations on asserting a notice of deficiency lasts for three years and begins on the date the return is filed. Returns filed early are viewed as being filed on the due date. If the amount of income omitted is greater than 25 percent of the income reported on the taxpayer's income tax return, the statute of limitations is extended to six years.

    The married couple in this case omitted $45,000 of income, which is more than 25 percent of the $120,000 reported on their joint income tax return.

    Hence, the statute of limitations on asserting a notice of deficiency in this case would end six years after the due date of the return—April 15, 2022.

24. **Answer: C**

    The Internal Revenue Service (IRS) is required to assess taxes within the assessment period. After the end of the assessment period, the IRS usually may not collect taxes. The assessment period begins on the day that the return is considered filed and last for three years after that date. Returns are considered filed on the last day of the filing period, even for returns filed early.

Hence, for a calendar-year taxpayer who filed an individual tax return for 2015 on March 20, 2016, the assessment period will end on April 15, 2019.

25. **Answer: D**

    A civil fraud penalty can be imposed on a taxpayer if the Internal Revenue Service (IRS) is able to show by a preponderance of evidence that the taxpayer had specific intent to evade a tax. After the IRS originally shows that fraudulent actions by the taxpayer have occurred, the taxpayer must prove that any tax underpayment was not attributable to fraudulent behavior. The civil fraud penalty amounts to 75% of the tax underpayment.

    Specific intent to evade taxes could be shown of a corporation that maintained false records and reported fictitious transactions to minimize corporate tax liability.

26. **Answer: B**

    No penalty is imposed if the tax payments during the year are at least 90% of current year taxes or 100% of last year's taxes. If the taxpayer's AGI exceeds $150,000, then tax payments during the year must be at least 110% of last year's taxes. $30,000 × 110% = $33,000.

27. **Answer: D**

    Disclosure or use of the information on a tax return can only be done with the written consent of the taxpayer. Absent the taxpayer's written consent, disclosure or use of the taxpayer's tax return information by a tax preparer makes the preparer subject to a penalty for knowingly or recklessly disclosing corporate tax information. Penalties also may be imposed on income tax preparers that willfully attempt to understate the tax liability on a return or refund claim.

    This response indicates penalties may be imposed against preparers that knowingly or recklessly disclose or use tax information obtained in preparing a return or willfully attempt to understate any client's tax liability on a return or claim for refund. Thus, it is correct.

28. **Answer: A**

    The required annual amount is usually the lower of 90% of the tax shown on the taxpayer's current year return or 100% of the tax shown on the taxpayer's prior year return. If the taxpayer's adjusted gross income exceeded $150,000 in the prior year and the taxpayer elects to base his/her required annual amount on the prior year, then the taxpayer would have to use 110% of the prior year's return.

Thus, Baker must base his required annual amount on 90% of the current year's tax liability or, since his adjusted gross income exceeded $150,000, 110% of the prior year's liability.

29. **Answer: B**

The late filing and late payment penalty is based upon the balance due. $50,000 owed less $45,000 withheld = $5,000 net due.

30. **Answer: D**

Due care refers to a CPA's duty to act as a reasonable accountant would when rendering services to a client. GAAS are, by definition, the standards that reasonable CPAs use. Failure to follow them is almost certainly a breach of the duty of due care.

31. **Answer: A**

A CPA is negligent when s/he fails to use the amount of care that a reasonable CPA would use. A reasonable CPA would likely correct errors that were discovered, and failure to do so would likely be negligent.

32. **Answer: A**

Fraud usually involves intentional deception. This question, however, asks about a close cousin of fraud constructive fraud. In a constructive fraud case, gross negligence (sometimes referred to as recklessness) acts as a substitute for intentional deception. Ordinary negligence or carelessness is not serious enough to act as a substitute for intent.

33. **Answer: D**

Two recognized exceptions to the confidentiality requirement are disclosure to other firm members on a need-to-know basis and disclosure during an ethics examination.

34. **Answer: C**

Both of the first two choices are potential consequences of breach of the duty of confidentiality when it involves taxpayer information.

35. **Answer: D**

A, B, and C all list recognized exceptions to the confidentiality obligation.

36. **Answer: C**

State privilege statutes apply only in the state courts in the particular state, not in federal court.

37. **Answer: C**

It is certainly possible that a client would not want it known that s/he was considering filing for bankruptcy. Therefore, members who practice in that area must be sensitive to that fact.

38. **Answer: C**

In general, power of attorney is the power to handle some or all of a person's affairs, depending on what a person wishes to grant. One may grant to another the power to do a few things, or the power to do everything.

39. **Answer: A**

An unincorporated association does not have capacity, because it is not an individual or an entity, and therefore has no contractual capacity.

40. **Answer: C**

One cannot become another's agent unless both sides agree and consent to the arrangement.

41. **Answer: D**

The principal must have the ability to enter into contracts.

42. **Answer: C**

There is no general requirement that an agency agreement be in writing in order to be enforceable, but this choice illustrates a case in which a writing is required. Some parts of the Statute of Frauds influence even agency agreements. If the agent will be dealing with real property, or making an agreement to act as an agent for over one year, the agreement must be in writing. Here, land is real property.

Note that the other parts of the Statute of Frauds do not apply to agency situations. If the agent will sell goods of over $500 in value, or will deal with suretyships, a spoken agreement is acceptable.

43. Answer: A

Apparent authority depends on how things appear to a third party dealing with the agent. Usually if it appears the agent was authorized, apparent authority will exist. If a partner's authority was expressly limited by a resolution and the third party knew of the resolution, apparent authority would not exist. The third party would know that the partner's authority was limited.

44. Answer: A

If an agent is terminated, a principal must give actual notice to old customers and published notice to new ones. Failure of the principal to give proper notice gives an agent apparent authority to make contracts with customers and subjects the principal to liability. Bolt failed to give published notice of Ace's termination, although 5t did give notice to old customers. Thus, Ace had apparent authority to make contracts with new customers who were aware that Ace was Bolt's agent. Young (a new customer) knew of Ace, and thus Bolt is liable because 5t's notice was inadequate

45. Answer: A

A principal is liable for contracts made by an agent on its behalf if the agent had some type of authority (actual or apparent). If the contract was unauthorized, the principal will be liable only if the principal ratifies. The principal must ratify prior to the third party's withdrawal from the contract. Thus, if May ratifies prior to Simon's withdrawal, Simon will be bound by the contract.

46. Answer: C

Except for an agency for a specific term and an agency coupled with an interest, either side may terminate the agency arrangement at will. Therefore, no operation of law is needed when an agent desires to renounce his authority.

47. Answer: B

Agents such as Wilson have a fiduciary duty of the utmost good faith and loyalty toward their principals. Failing to act in Young's interest is a clear violation of this duty.

48. Answer: C

C is the best answer, as agents have a duty not to commingle their funds with the principal's funds, and should account for the principal's property.

49. Answer: C

Agents owe many duties to principals. Principals owe only a few duties to their agents, but they are important. A principal must pay an agent whatever has been contracted. Paying according to the terms of an agreement necessarily encompasses maintaining pertinent records, so that the principal can properly account to the agent.

Also, a principal must reimburse an agent for all authorized expenses, unless the agreement calls for the agent to pay them. The presumption is that the principal will pay an agent's expenses incurred within the scope of authority, absent agreement to the contrary.

50. Answer: A

Thorp is an agent, as he has been hired to act on Ogden's behalf by representing it. A primary duty of an agent is one of loyalty—an agent must act in his principal's interests and not his own when participating in matters affecting the principal's business.

51. Answer: D

This is the best answer, because corporate presidents certainly have authority to bind the corporation to contracts for normal activities, such as these repairs.

52. Answer: C

The relationship between a drawer of a check and a payee is unrelated to that between an agent and principal. A principal is not responsible for the payment of an agent's personal checks.

53. Answer: A

This question mixes concepts of tort liability and contract liability. In terms of contract liability, actual authority is the same, no matter which type of an agency this is. Therefore, this is the correct answer.

54. Answer: C

Normally, an agent is not bound by a contract signed on behalf of his principal. However, this question illustrates the exception to the rule, because the principal is UNDISCLOSED. In such a situation, the agent can be made to honor the agreement.

55. Answer: C

If an agent has authority of some kind, he can bind a company to contracts he makes on their behalf. This is true even if the professional relationship has been terminated. Apparent authority may remain effective after a termination. To end all authority, a company must give appropriate notice to EVERYONE, not just to existing customers. The company must give PUBLICATION notice to all businesses of the termination. Otherwise, the dismissed agent retains the power to bind his ex-employer to contracts.

56. Answer: C

Because Davis was attempting to advance her employer's interest by maintaining order in the day-care center, even though she did so in a wrongful manner, her employer is liable. Therefore, this is the best answer.

57. Answer: B

This is an agent trying to do her job in order to benefit her boss, but doing so in a wrongful manner. Because she is within the scope of employment, albeit aiding the boss in a wrongful manner and likely in disregard of instructions, the boss is liable, so this is the correct choice.

58. Answer: B

A principal is liable for ALL AUTHORIZED misrepresentations, but not for all UNauthorized misrepresentations. In such a case, the principal is liable only if an employee makes the misrepresentation. For the record, an employee is a worker who tends to be paid wages or salary, has a long-term relationship with the principal, and is supervised by the principal.

59. Answer: C

This question brings in another aspect of law—negligence and the defense of contributory negligence, which is a bar to recovery if established.

60. Answer: A

Real property interests, including leases, are under common law.

61. Answer: B

Contracts for services are governed by common law.

62. Answer: D

Where there are mixed contracts (sale of both goods and services), we look to the price and the intent of the parties. The parts for such a system are small in comparison to the labor required for its installation throughout the construction process. Also, Janice does not just want vacuum parts. She wants the system installed.

63. Answer: A

A contract requires consideration, and this is a promise to make a gift, which cannot be consideration because there is love and affection underlying the gift but no detriment on Gwyneth's side.

64. Answer: C

The act of acceptance is not the act of performing the contract, which is what would be a unilateral contract. The act of acceptance is making a promise in exchange for the offer, which is also a promise.

65. Answer: A

This is a unilateral contract because it can only be accepted by performing an act. By the terms of the offer, Hammer cannot accept with a promise. Instead, Hammer has to do an act, which results in total performance of the contract. A unilateral contract is formed if the required action is completed. Here, by presenting Kay with the artifacts, Hammer has accepted the offer and formed a valid contract.

66. Answer: A

By going to the doctor, you have an implicit agreement to pay.

67. Answer: B

A counteroffer rejects the original offer. This is a counteroffer, because the terms differ from those in the original offer. For a contract involving real estate or almost anything other than a sale of goods, the "mirror image" rule is in place. If the response is not a mirror image acceptance of the offer, then it is a rejection. If it is accompanied by a new offer, it is a counteroffer.

68. Answer: B

This answer is correct as the best defense. The ad, as are most general business advertisements, is only "invitations to trade." An invitation to trade invites a party (here the buyer) to make an offer; it is not itself an offer.

69. **Answer: B**

Although most acceptances of bilateral offers are sent by an authorized medium and effective when sent by the authorized medium, the offeror can condition acceptance to not be effective until received. Therefore, regardless of the medium used, the acceptance must be received before the offer terminates by lapse of time. This offer terminated at midnight on April 4, and the acceptance was not received until April 5, after the offer was terminated.

70. **Answer: D**

An offer, unless irrevocable, IS terminated immediately upon the death of the offeror, and thus no contract could be formed.

71. **Answer: B**

Normally, under the mailbox rule acceptances are valid as soon as they are mailed. However, in this case we have an exception, because the offeror specified the method of acceptance (registered or certified mail) AND a time by which offeror had to actually receive the acceptance. By the terms of the offer, the acceptance was not sent as authorized and arrived late. Therefore, it is a counteroffer, which Harris may now accept or reject.

72. **Answer: A**

Past actions cannot count as consideration for current promises. For consideration to exist, a contract must be a bargained for exchange. If, for example, you took me to work yesterday, and I say today, "Because you gave me a ride yesterday, I promise to pay you $20," you cannot hold me to the promise. There is no consideration.

73. **Answer: A**

This answer is correct because although the amount of the debt is a certain amount ($5,000) and a liquidated debt, Castle offered a lesser sum ($4,000) 30 days before the debt was due as full satisfaction for the $5000 debt. This amount was accepted (accord) by Nelson. The giving-up of 30 days before payment was due is consideration and discharges the $5,000 debt.

74. **Answer: A**

A real estate contract cannot be modified unless additional or new consideration is given. Only UCC contracts for the sale of goods can be modified without new consideration.

75. **Answer: B**

When the parties agree to accept an alternative means of payment, which they do not have to do, both sides have given detriment and have created an accord. Once the microwave is delivered, there is satisfaction

76. **Answer: D**

To give consideration, a person must promise to do something new or something not already obligated to do. If the debt is rightfully disputed, a debtor is not under a preexisting obligation to pay the full amount. In offering to pay $500, the offeror is promising to do something he or she does not otherwise have to do - pay $500. This promise, then, is consideration that supports the forgiveness of the rest of the disputed debt.

77. **Answer: D**

This answer is correct because a contract for the sale of realty falls under the Statute of Frauds requiring a writing signed by both parties or a written memo signed by the party to be charged to be enforceable. Kram signed the letter and the contract is enforceable against Kram.

78. **Answer: D**

Only contracts that CANNOT be performed within a year must be in writing.

79. **Answer: C**

This answer is correct because for duress to be proved Kent would have to show that Maco's actions were threats that overcame Kent's free will forcing Kent into a contract at the $20 rate. Kent needed money and willingly agreed to the $20 rate. Although Maco benefited from the contract rate, it did not force Kent to enter into the $20 rate contract.

80. **Answer: C**

Physical threats do render a contract void.

81. **Answer: B**

This creates a voidable contract. If someone misrepresents information about the contract subject matter, you are free to go ahead with the contract or rescind it—it is voidable.

82. **Answer: C**

If someone enters into an agreement before reaching the age of majority, the contract is voidable. After reaching the age of majority, however, the person may ratify, or agree to be bound by, the contract either expressly or impliedly. This makes the contract fully valid and enforceable. Ratification cannot take place while the individual is still a minor. The minor does not have the capacity to ratify during the period of minority.

83. **Answer: C**

This answer is correct because the mistake is immaterial and has no effect on an otherwise valid contract. Therefore, the contract is enforceable by either party.

84. **Answer: A**

If a party is in material breach of a contract, the nonbreaching party is discharged from his or her performance of the contract

85. **Answer: A**

A is correct because two methods of discharge of the original contract are by accord (agreement to accept a different performance) and satisfaction whereby the substituted performance is performed, and mutual rescission, whereby both parties agree to the discharge of their obligations (mutual rescission).

86. **Answer: A**

The potatoes were not specifically identified goods at the time of contract formation and risk of loss had not passed to LBC. Thus, their destruction does not discharge Maco from its obligations. They still have a duty to provide substitute potatoes since some are available. If the goods had been specifically identified to come from Maco's farms in the contract, then they could escape their obligations.

87. **Answer: A**

This answer is correct because the UCC rules concerning risk of loss only apply if the parties have not allocated risk of loss in their contract.

88. **Answer: D**

This answer is correct because provided there is no agreement to the contrary and neither party is in breach, risk of loss will in the case of a merchant seller, pass to the buyer on physical receipt of the goods. In this situation, Aston Co., a merchant, will bear the loss of the table since Wolfe had not yet taken possession of it.

89. **Answer: D**

The UCC places risk of loss on the breaching party. Since Cey shipped nonconforming goods, it breached the contract and would have risk of loss until the nonconforming goods were accepted by the buyer or until the goods were cured by Cey. Since Deck rejected the goods and Cey did not cure the goods, risk of loss remained with Cey. Shipping terms have no bearing on risk of loss in this situation because the goods did not conform to the contract.

90. **Answer: D**

This answer is correct because Hodges has a choice of these remedies. Because the subject of the contract (realty) is unique (no two pieces of property with the same legal description) and damages are really inadequate because performance is more valuable than money damages, Hodges can file a petition for specific performance requiring Kaye to deed the property to Hodges. Hodges could elect instead to file a lawsuit for breach of contract and seek damages (for the loss of the bargain) actually sustained.

91. **Answer: D**

This answer is correct. A payment of less than the originally agreed-upon price will serve as complete discharge of an obligation under a contract only if there is a bona fide dispute as to the amount owed, and both parties agree to the lesser sum. In this case Milo and Nord had agreed upon a fee for services of $45,000; thus, this debt was liquidated since the amount was certain. And since Milo had completed the work to Nord's satisfaction, no bona fide dispute as to the amount owed arose; thus the debt remains liquidated, and Nord will be required to pay the full $45,000. The fact that Milo had endorsed and deposited the check which Nord had conspicuously marked as constituting payment in full is of no effect since the obligation was a liquidated debt, instead of an unliquidated debt.

92. **Answer: A**

This answer is correct because although the amount of the debt is a certain amount ($5,000) and a liquidated debt, Castle offered a lesser sum ($4,000) 30 days before the debt was due as full satisfaction for the $5000 debt. This amount was accepted (accord) by Nelson. The giving-up of 30 days before payment was due is consideration and discharges the $5,000 debt.

93. **Answer: A**

A real estate contract cannot be modified unless additional or new consideration is given. Only UCC contracts for the sale of goods can be modified without new consideration.

94. **Answer: D**

To give consideration, a person must promise to do something new or something not already obligated to do. If the debt is rightfully disputed, a debtor is not under a preexisting obligation to pay the full amount. In offering to pay $500, the offeror is promising to do something he or she does not otherwise have to do—pay $500. This promise, then, is consideration that supports the forgiveness of the rest of the disputed debt.

95. **Answer: A**

Past actions cannot count as consideration for current promises. For consideration to exist, a contract must be a bargained for exchange. If, for example, you took me to work yesterday, and I say today, "Because you gave me a ride yesterday, I promise to pay you $20," you cannot hold me to the promise. There is no consideration.

96. **Answer: D**

When two people act as a cosurety, neither can generally be held liable for an entire debt. Thus, when one cosurety, upon debtor's default, pays more than his or her proportional share, the cosurety can recover from the other cosurety the amount paid in excess of his or her share.

97. **Answer: C**

Since Edwards released one of the two sureties, the remaining surety is liable for only half of the entire debt. Until the release, Edwards could have collected the entire debt from either surety, and then that surety could have sued the other surety for half of that amount under the right of contribution. However, now Edwards can only collect 50% of the debt from Owen, because it has eliminated Owen's ability to collect anything from Ward.

98. **Answer: C**

When there are co-sureties, each has a right to a proportionate contribution from the others if a co-surety pays an unfair share of the debt. In this case, Nash's liability is 2/9 of the total liability among all co-sureties ($40,000 out of a total $180,000). She therefore should not pay more than 2/9 of any total settlement. She

has a right to recover $7/9 \times \$36,000$ from the others, or $28,000. More specifically, she will get $12,000 from Owen and $16,000 from Polk.

99. **Answer: B**

The total maximum amount that the sureties stand to lose is $84,000 + $126,000 + $210,000 = $420,000. If the loss is below the maximums, each co-surety is ultimately liable for a proportionate share of the total debt based on their maximum liability. For example, Queen will bear 50% of any loss because Queen is liable for $210,000 of the $420,000 total maximum, or 50%.

Here, after Ivor has paid in $70,000 toward his loan balance of $280,000, the loan balance stands at $210,000. The exact order of payments is not important; what is important is that at the end of the day all co-sureties pay their fair share. Since the debt balance is $210,000, and the maximum total the sureties stand to lose is $420,000, each surety will pay exactly 1/2 of their personal maximum liability. Since Queen paid the entire debt to begin with, Queen is able to recover half of Ash's maximum, or $42,000, and half of Kane's maximum, or $63,000.

100. **Answer: C**

If a guaranty is made by an express contract with the creditor, to be enforceable against the guarantor the guaranty contract must be in writing and signed by the guarantor. The only exception is the "main purpose" or "leading object" doctrine where the guarantor will benefit financially or economically. Thus, Camp cannot be held liable on the oral guaranty under the Statute of Frauds.

101. **Answer: C**

If the loan is repaid in full by any party, the obligations of those liable for repayment are discharged.

102. Answer: B

The Statute of Frauds requires a suretyship contract to be in writing unless the surety financially or economically benefits from making the surety agreement.

103. Answer: A

Co-sureties have rights against each other in the event that they are forced to pay more than their fair share. Here, Quill and West are equal co-sureties, because they are responsible for the same amount ($100,000). If Quill is initially forced by Ingot to pay the entire amount, it may, in a separate lawsuit, seek 50% of what it paid from West. Since West's release was not consented to by Quill, Quill retains its right of contribution against West.

104. Answer: C

When a surety loses capacity, the surety can usually avoid liability. Many legal obligations are therefore extinguished, including obligations taken on as a surety.

105. Answer: A

A creditor is required to disclose any known material facts to a surety before the surety signs a loan agreement, if such facts will substantially increase the surety's risks. When a creditor does not make such disclosures, the creditor has committed presumed fraud, and the surety may use this as a defense to repayment.

106. Answer: C

To create a security interest the creditor must give value, the debtor must have rights in the collateral, and the creditor must take possession of the collateral or obtain the agreement in a signed or authenticated writing by the debtor. Filing is not necessary to create an interest, it is only necessary to perfect an interest that has already been created.

107. Answer: D

For a security interest to attach, the following must be present:

Underlying debt/obligation; Either a security agreement or possession of the collateral by the creditor; and Debtor must have interest in the property. Until all three are present, the security interest does not attach.

108. Answer: C

Possession is nine tenths of the law, and under Article 9, possession is the security interest as well as perfection.

109. Answer: D

Unless the collateral is in the possession of the secured party, there must be a written or authenticated security agreement (describing the collateral), the secured party must give the debtor something of value, and the debtor must have rights in the collateral. Thus, A, B, and C are requirements to create an enforceable security interest. Perfection (by filing) is merely a means which gives third parties notice of the secured party's priority interest in case of debtor default and not a requirement to create the security interest.

110. Answer: D

A security interest gives the creditor a right to the debtor's interest in the collateral if the debtor does not repay the debt. The collateral is security for debt. If the debtor has no rights in the collateral, the creditor has no security interest.

111. Answer: B

The antiques are classified as inventory (collateral to be held for resell). Thus, although a purchase money security interest was created, being inventory, a filing is required for perfection.

112. Answer: A

One may perfect a security interest without filing if he or she has a purchase money security interest (PMSI) in consumer goods. This happens when the money to purchase the collateral is given as the basis of the security interest.

The collateral, however, must be in consumer goods and purchased by a consumer for personal, family, or household use for a PMSI to exist.

113. Answer: D

There need not be the amount of the debt reflected in the publicly filed financing statement. All that needs to be included is which collateral is subject to the security interest, not the value of the collateral or the debt.

114. Answer: B

Here, possession as a method of perfection is not practical, and, although it is a purchase money security interest, the collateral equipment is not covered by the automatic perfection rule. Thus, a filing is required.

115. **Answer: B**

Filing is not necessary to perfect this security interest, because Grey has a purchase money security interest (PMSI) in the computer to be used for personal use (a consumer good). A PMSI arises when a creditor extends credit that is used to purchase the collateral, as a consumer good, which is the computer in this security agreement. A PMSI is perfected automatically at the time the interest attaches.

116. **Answer: D**

Usually, the first security interest to be perfected has top priority. There is an exception, though, for a purchase money security interest, or a purchase money security interest. A purchase money security interest in noninventory collateral has priority if it is perfected before the debtor takes possession or within 20 days thereafter.

117. **Answer: C**

All perfected interests take priority over unperfected interests, regardless of when they arose, so II will be last. If more than one perfected interest exists, then the first to be perfected takes priority. Interests I and III are both perfected. The first is obviously perfected on April 15, 2004, and the third is not perfected by filing until April 20, 2004. An exception to the first in time is first in priority rule is when you have a PMSI in collateral other than livestock or inventory (here the collateral is store equipment) where a second in time of perfection takes place before or within twenty (20) days after the debtor takes possession of the collateral.

118. **Answer: B**

Even though the interest is perfected, Cray still gets to keep the refrigerator. A buyer in the ordinary course of business takes goods free from a security interest, even if the buyer has knowledge of the security agreement.

119. **Answer: A**

The debtor may give a security interest in either inventory or equipment that the debtor has rights to and the security agreement can also provide that this security interest applies to any inventory or equipment the debtor acquires in the future.

120. **Answer: D**

The secured party, in perfecting the security interest, gives notice to others of its superior claim to most others. There are exceptions. For example, those secured parties who acquire a purchase-money security interest in the collateral may take priority over a previously perfected nonpurchased money security if certain conditions are met.

121. **Answer: A**

The debtor has paid 60% of the PURCHASE PRICE, so BestBuy must sell the TV.

122. **Answer: A**

When a debtor defaults, the secured creditor may repossess the collateral on its own so long as the repossession is done without disturbing the peace. The secured party may use a court proceeding to have the amount of its claim reduced to a judgment and by a writ of execution levy on the nonexempt property of the debtor. Once the collateral has been recovered, the secured party may sell the goods in a commercially reasonable manner to recover the debt owed.

123. **Answer: A**

A secured creditor has a security interest in some collateral. If the debt is not repaid according to the agreement with the debtor, the secured creditor may peacefully repossess the collateral and either keep or sell the collateral to satisfy the debt. In the alternative, the creditor may sue the debtor for amounts owed, just as any other creditor can, and obtain a judgment against the debtor.

124. **Answer: A**

Remedies after a default are cumulative. If one method does not fully satisfy the debt, others may be sought. If the computer is repossessed and sold, and money is still owed, Hale may seek a deficiency judgment against Drew for the remainder.

125. **Answer: A**

As with most statutory-sanctioned sales (tax lien sales, judicial lien sales, etc.), a sale made by a secured party under Article 9 of the UCC, if made properly, passes good title free from any lien or security interest to the buyer. Until the sale the debtor or any other secured party has right of redemption. The sale can be public or private proceedings.

126. **Answer: D**

An involuntary petition may succeed if the aggregate unsecured claims of the petitioners equals or exceeds $13,425. Quincy's claim of $6000 alone does meet that limit.

127. Answer: D

Since Sharp did not sign the Agreement, he is not bound by it. To be an assignment for the benefit of creditors, Green would have to voluntarily transfer certain assets to a trustee or an assignee who, in turn, offers each creditor a pro rata payment. This not only did not happen, but the Agreement assured him that almost all of his debts would be cancelled. Although there may be fraud-in-fact on the sale of the antique car, it will be difficult to prove, since there was a substantial payment (70% of the car's estimated value) to a non-relative. What Sharp can prove is fraud-in-law, whereby, despite the sale, Green was allowed to possess and use the car as if the sale never took place. This gives Sharp the basis for an action of fraud-in-law; a presumption of fraud, which it is doubtful Green can rebut.

128. Answer: D

This is balance sheet insolvency, and the debtor does not have to make such a showing. So long as the debtor is not abusing the bankruptcy relief laws, the debtor may file for Chapter 7 protection.

129. Answer: D

Petitions are often filed by spouses jointly. Either may file alone, or they may file together.

130. Answer: D

This action, if ordered by a court, will deduct sums directly from a paycheck. State laws generally limit the amount that can be deducted to around 25% of a debtor's after-tax wages.

131. Answer: A

A debtor's estate in bankruptcy consists of all tangible and intangible property of the debtor held at the commencement of the bankruptcy proceedings. In addition, the estate consists of any after-acquired income from such property.

Therefore, interest from municipal bonds (held as part of the estate) also becomes part of the estate. Any gifts received within 180 days of the filing the petition also become part of the estate. All other payments received after the filing of the petition are not considered income from the existing debtor's (bankruptcy) estate.

Therefore, B and C are incorrect, because they are payments received after the filing of the petition, and are not considered income from the existing debtor's (bankruptcy) estate.

D is incorrect, because it is a gift received more than 180 days after the filing of the petition.

132. Answer: D

This answer is correct, because although the trustee can avoid some statutory liens (such as landlord's lien), the trustee cannot avoid all (key word is "any") statutory or common law liens (such as certain warehouse liens).

133. Answer: D

Once a bankruptcy petition is filed, the enforcement of any lien against this property is stopped pending a resolution through bankruptcy proceedings.

134. Answer: C

A payment is not preferential if it is not more than the creditor would have received in a bankruptcy proceeding. Since Acme has a perfected security interest, its rights are unaffected by the bankruptcy proceeding, and it retains the right to receive repayment of its debt without having the payments set aside.

135. Answer: B

A debtor who declares bankruptcy may not give one creditor better treatment than others. Any payment or security interest made to a particular creditor within 90 days of declaring bankruptcy is a preferential payment if the payment is made on an antecedent debt. An antecedent debt is one that existed at the time bankruptcy was declared.

136. Answer: A

All three of the other claims have a higher priority than the claim of Card. Card is a general creditor and comes last in the pecking order. All superior claims must be paid in full first, and then any leftovers will be paid to Card.

After $50,000 − $12,000 − $7,000 − $8,000, Card will receive only $23,000.

137. Answer: D

The bankruptcy establishes an order of priority for claims like these. After administrative expenses are paid, unpaid wages earned for 90 days prior to filing of the petition, up to $10,950 per employee, are paid; then, unpaid contributions to employee benefit plans, up to $10,950 per employee, are paid; then, taxes are paid; lastly, utility bills with the general creditors are paid.

138. Answer: C

Of the $100,000, the first $70,000 will go to Fracon Bank, as that money was generated by the sale of the house in which they had a security interest. This leaves Fracon with an additional $5,000 in general debt. The next $2,000 will similarly go to Decoy as money raised from the sale of their security interest. This leaves $28,000. The next $12,000 will go to the IRS to satisfy their recorded judgment, leaving $16,000. All taxes are paid before general creditors are paid. The final $16,000 is divided pro rata among remaining creditors, since there is not enough to pay all of them in full. However, all general creditors who have filed a claim in a timely fashion must be fully repaid before those who have not filed in a timely fashion are paid anything. So, we have $20,000 of total general creditors' claims, and $16,000 to pay them. Each will take 80% of their unsecured claims. Fracon will take 80% of $5,000, or $4,000. This will be added to the $70,000 already received, to get the total of $74,000.

139. Answer: A

Of the $100,000, the first $70,000 will go to Fracon Bank, as that money was generated by the sale of the house in which they had a security interest. The next $2,000 will similarly go to Decoy as money raised from the sale of their security interest. This leaves $28,000. The next $12,000 will go to the IRS to satisfy their recorded judgment, leaving $16,000. All taxes are paid before general creditors are paid. The final $16,000 is divided pro rata among remaining creditors, since there is not enough to pay all of them in full. However, all general creditors who have filed a claim in a timely fashion must be fully repaid before those who have not filed in a timely fashion are paid anything. Therefore, all cash will be used up before Nanstar collects anything.

140. Answer: B

If this sale does not generate enough to cover the entire debt, then Acme becomes a general creditor for that portion of the debt. A perfected secured creditor only has a special priority right to the security interest, or collateral. When the collateral has been disposed of, it must wait in line for further payments with everyone else.

141. Answer: C

After Chapter 7 liquidation proceedings begin, all non-exempt property at the time of the filing of the petition of the debtor becomes part of the distribution to creditors. In addition, some interests, including inheritances acquired by the debtor within 180 days of filing a voluntary petition, become a part of the debtor's estate for distribution.

142. Answer: C

Claims based on fraud or other intentional wrongdoing by the debtor will not be discharged. If a debtor commits fraud, that debtor cannot take advantage of the bankruptcy laws when it comes time to pay the defrauded party.

143. Answer: D

Corporations and partnerships may go through a Chapter 7 liquidation, but do not qualify for a general discharge from all remaining debts as natural persons do.

144. Answer: D

Generally, a bankrupt debtor, at the end of bankruptcy proceedings, will receive a discharge decree. Unless the debtor has committed an act such as fraud, intentional concealment of assets, refusal to explain the loss of assets, and the like, is a partnership or corporation, or the debtor has received a discharge decree within eight years of the current filing petition, the discharge decree will be granted. Here, the debtor has committed an act, has refused satisfactorily to explain a loss of assets, and as such will be denied a discharge decree in bankruptcy.

145. Answer: C

Unless the debtor has been denied a discharge decree owing either to an act of the debtor (such as fraud, intentional concealment of assets, and the like), or where, by statute, the debt is not discharged (such as in the case of unpaid taxes), the discharge decree releases the debtor from personal liability for debts owed to his or her creditors.

A judgment creditor's debt is dischargeable and therefore is not on the statutory list of non-dischargeable debts.

146. Answer: B

All the elements of an investment contract are present. There was an investment of money ($5,000 each) in a common enterprise (all would profit or lose, depending on how the lawsuit came out), with an expectation of profit ($594,000 in this case), to be derived primarily from the efforts of others (Sam and his attorney).

147. **Answer: D**

The 1934 Act governs securities. Securities represent either a right to assets or a corporation's indebtedness, while a certificate of deposit acknowledges that monies have been received and sets out terms for repayment in the future. A holder of a CD is not a creditor, because (s)he has not "loaned" money; (s)he has merely deposited it. Therefore, certificates of deposit do not fall within the scope of the 1934 Act.

148. **Answer: C**

When a person invests in an enterprise that is primarily managed by another, the investment will probably qualify as a security. In a general partnership, the partners themselves are in charge of management. Investments in such a venture are likely made only by the partner/managers themselves, and are unlikely to be classified as securities.

149. **Answer: D**

The 1933 Act applies to sales of securities, including stocks, bonds and notes that are issued for periods over nine months.

150. **Answer: A**

The court held that these were interests in the form of an investment contract, so this is the correct answer. There was an investment of money (by 1,500 investors) in a common enterprise (all parties would either make or lose money, depending on the outcome), with an expectation of profit (14% return) to be derived primarily by the actions of others (those bundling and administering the leases).

151. **Answer: A**

As soon as a registration statement is filed, ORAL offers may be made, as well as limited written advertising. The 20-day waiting period that exists applies to when the securities may actually be SOLD. Unless the SEC speeds up the approval process, no sale can take place for 20 days after the filing.

152. **Answer: D**

After a prospectus and registration statement have been filed with the SEC, there is a 20-day waiting period before stocks may be issued. During this time, a preliminary, or "red herring," prospectus may be issued to investors.

153. **Answer: B**

If a security is non-exempt and must register, then all investors must be given a prospectus.

This is true even if the investor is accredited. If anyone is entitled to a prospectus, then everyone is entitled to a prospectus.

154. **Answer: B**

The requirements force an issuer to give a prospectus to most investors, and to file a registration statement with the SEC. This will ensure that an investor can at least make an informed decision.

The SEC does not, however, guarantee success or evaluate the merits of an offering.

155. **Answer: D**

During the waiting period of 20 days immediately after registering with the SEC, tombstone ads may be placed. Tombstone ads are heavily restricted and may contain only limited information, such as the type of security and where a potential investor would acquire a now-available prospectus.

156. **Answer: A**

Governmental securities are exempt from registration under the 1933 Act.

157. **Answer: B**

Regulation D provides exemptions for offers that are limited. Private non-investment companies can offer up to $5mn in any one-year period as long as there are not more than 35 NON-ACCREDITED investors. There is no limit on accredited investors, such as banks and investment companies.

158. **Answer: C**

Any security issued by a charity, railroad company, farmers' co-operative, or bank is exempt from registering under the 1933 Act.

159. **Answer: A**

Rule 504 of Regulation D applies to small issues. If a company will issue $1mn or less in a one-year period, it qualifies for this exemption.

So long as Data is not an investment company, there are no further restrictions on offerings this small, except that they cannot be offered through general advertising, unless certain requirements are met. Data may make the offering to any number of any kind of investors.

160. **Answer: A**

Ten-year notes are securities and their public sale requires registration, absent the existence of an applicable exemption (such as under Regulation D).

161. Answer: A

$100,000 is the most someone can invest in crowdfunded ventures during the course of a single year.

162. Answer: C

General solicitation will be allowed under Rule 506 (and 505) Reg D offerings only if the issuer takes reasonable steps to insure that it sells only to accredited investors. If it does not engage in general solicitation, the issuer can sell to up to 35 unaccredited investors under Reg. D.

163. Answer: A

$1 million is the ceiling for the crowdfunding exemption.

164. Answer: B

Foreign firms cannot use the crowdfunding exemption.

165. Answer: D

Obviously even EGCs are not going to be allowed to commit fraud with impunity.

166. Answer: B

Section 11 states that if "any part of the registration statement...contained an untrue statement of material fact...any person acquiring such security...(may bring a civil lawsuit)." Showing an intent to deceive is unnecessary to win a civil lawsuit, as is a plaintiff's reliance on the false statement.

167. Answer: C

A Section 11 plaintiff does not have the burden of showing that defendants acted fraudulently or carelessly and need not establish reliance. The primary things that plaintiffs must show to win their Section 11 claims are that there was a material misstatement in the registration statement on the effective date; that they can trace their shares to that registration statement; and that they suffered damages.

168. Answer: C

The 1933 Act makes a plaintiff's job relatively easy. Plaintiffs need not establish either reliance or negligence to win a Section 11 case. The burden in both of these issues is on the defendants to prove that the plaintiff did not rely and that they acted with due diligence. Indeed, an issuing company cannot escape liability, even by showing due diligence - it is strictly liable for material misstatements in the registration statement that caused the plaintiff's losses.

169. Answer: B

The key fact here is that Ivor did not know of the error. It acted negligently, but not with bad intent (scienter). Absent bad intent, there can be no fraud and therefore no liability under Section 10(b) of the 1934 Act, which is an anti-fraud statute. However, defendants who are merely negligent are liable for materially false statements in a defective registration statement pursuant to Section 11 of the 1933 Act.

170. Answer: C

With minor exceptions, a plaintiff in a Section 11 suit need not provide reliance in order to prevail.

171. Answer: B

To be liable under Rule 10b-5 of the 1934 Act, a defendant must act intentionally. Courts hold that a defendant must act with scienter (intent) or "extreme recklessness" (which is similar to scienter) to be liable under 10b-5.

172. Answer: C

C is the best answer, because public corporations must file 10-Qs with the SEC and negligently false statements therein are remediable under Section 18.

173. Answer: C

Section 18(a) establishes a presumption of liability for false statements in filed documents, but allows defendants to escape liability if they prove that they "acted in good faith and had no knowledge that such statement was false or misleading."

174. Answer: D

This answer is correct because it uses the correct statute of limitations (2yr/5yr, rather than 1yr/3yr), and notes properly that the plaintiff must meet both deadlines.

175. Answer: D

This provision requires an untrue statement and an intent to defraud. Defenses include lack of knowledge that the statement was false and acting in good faith.

176. Answer: A

The federal securities laws' criminal provisions punish "willful" violations of the 1933 and 1934 securities acts.

177. Answer: A

Any intentional violation of any provision of the 1934 Act is a crime. It should also be noted that potential criminal penalties include jail time, as well as fines. In addition, such a violation certainly opens an accountant up to potential civil liability, because the courts have implied a private right to sue on behalf of investors injured by Section 10(b)/Rule 10b-5 violations.

178. Answer: A

The SEC may bring civil charges against Seimone.

179. Answer: B

It is common for the SEC to bring civil charges and then the DOJ to bring criminal charges in insider-trading cases.

180. Answer: C

Because both A and B are accurate, this is the best answer.

181. Answer: B

Businesses pay into a fund that is used to pay unemployment benefits. The monies put into this fund are tax deductible.

182. Answer: D

Many states run their own unemployment fund and require employers to make contributions to it. If such is the case, the employer does not have to pay more overall unemployment tax. The employer may credit the amounts paid to a state fund against contributions required by the federal government.

183. Answer: A

Unemployment compensation is given to persons who lose their jobs and are not fired for cause. If an employer changes or "downsizes" his business, the newly laid-off worker is generally eligible for benefits.

184. Answer: D

And here's why. Tran first pays for the surgery—$1,200 for the deductible and then the co-pay which is 20% × $3800 ($5,000 cost − $1,200 deductible) which is $760. So far, he has paid $1,960 ($1,200 + $760), which is less that the maximum. Then Tran turns to the hospital bill. His deductible has been exhausted, so he would pay, absent the ceiling, coinsurance of 20% of $40,000, or $8,000. However, this puts

him well over the maximum. He would pay only $6,850 (the maximum) minus $1,960 (the amount he has already paid), which comes to $4,890. The health insurer will pay the other $35,110 ($40,000 − $4,890). And it will pay the entire cost of the home health care ($4,000) and all of the rest of Tran's essential medical care expenses for the rest of the year.

185. Answer: D

Because A, B, and C are all recognized as unearned income for purposes of the ACA's Medicare surtax, this is the best answer.

186. Answer: C

Under the ACA, Tessa could deduct all expenses over $7,500 (the 10% threshold), which means a $2,500 deduction.

187. Answer: D

This profession is listed in the rules as potentially being a *statutory employee* if three conditions are met: the service contract states or implies that substantially all the services are to be performed by the worker personally, the worker does not have a substantial investment in the equipment and property used to perform the services; and the services are performed on a continuing basis for the same business.

188. Answer: C

The factors we know about (same work as employees, regular hours, required to work overtime, paid on an hourly basis) all point toward Tim being an employee.

189. Answer: A

This is the correct choice. It is good that LMN sought the opinion of its counsel, but this is not sufficient to support the safe harbor defense.

190. Answer: A

While limited partners may consult with the general partners, work for the partnership in a non-management capacity, guaranty its obligations and do a number of other things without forfeiting limited liability, they may not participate in management. They are granted limited liability and in exchange are expected to remain passive investors.

191. Answer: A

Both of these organizations require special steps in their creation. One of these steps is the filing of a certificate, usually with the Secretary of State.

192. Answer: B

If the requirements of a Subchapter S corporation are met, the corporate entity pays no federal income tax. All income is passed through to the shareholders. Although the shareholders enjoy limited liability, they do pay personal income tax on dividends received.

193. Answer: C

The maximum number of permissible Subchapter S corporation shareholders has risen over the years, from 35 to 75 to (now) 100.

194. Answer: C

C is the best answer, because shareholder contributions are not taxable in either form.

195. Answer: B

B is the best answer. The general rule is that promoters are liable on pre-incorporation contracts that they negotiate on the corporation's behalf.

When the corporation comes into existence and adopts the contracts, the general rule is that both the promoter and the corporation are now liable under them.

However, if the other party agrees to release the agent from liability and to look only to the corporation for satisfaction, then a novation has taken place.

196. Answer: A

The articles of incorporation must include (1) the name of the corporation; (2) the number of shares it is authorized to issue; (3) the street address of its registered office and the name of its agent at that address; and (4) the name and address of each incorporator.

197. Answer: C

A general partnership is formed when two people throw their fortunes together, intending to be co-owners of a business for profit. They need file nothing with the Secretary of State's office, although they may choose to do so.

198. Answer: D

The articles of incorporation must include (1) the name of the corporation; (2) the number of shares it is authorized to issue; (3) the street address of its registered office and the name of its agent at that address; and (4) the name and address of each incorporator.

199. Answer: A

Thin capitalization, which endangers the legitimate interests and expectations of third-party corporate creditors, particularly tort creditors, can be grounds for piercing the corporate veil.

200. Answer: C

This is the purpose of an LLC operating agreement, which is why it is a good idea that these be in writing and filed with the state (although this is not required).

201. Answer: B

The corporate veil is almost never pierced, and investors almost never lose more than their investment. Only when shareholders use a corporation for their own (usually fraudulent) personal use is there even a remote possibility that the veil will be pierced. When shareholders have heavily commingled personal funds and corporate funds, the rare exception to the rule may arise.

202. Answer: C

There is no evidence of commingling of funds, diversion of corporate assets, failure to maintain formalities, or any of the other factors that can induce a court to pierce the corporate veil. The mere fact that a business fails does not indicate that it was originally undercapitalized.

203. Answer: B

A partnership requires at least one other person or entity to be Sal's partner in ownership and management of the firm, so this is not a good choice.

204. Answer: B

B is the best answer, as distributions to owners reduce the corporate treasury and thereby decrease stockholder equity.

205. Answer: C

Cumulative preferred stock does not guarantee payment of a dividend in any particular year.

However, if required dividends are not paid in any given year, they must be "made up" in the current year before any common shareholders receive a dividend. It is the "cumulative" portion of the description that is key here—that is what gives the right to carryover payments.

The "preferred" portion gives the preference over common shareholders.

206. **Answer: A**

In the absence of agreement to the contrary, profits are to be shared equally among the partners.

207. **Answer: A**

Cumulative preferred stock gives the holder the right to payment of dividends before common shareholders are paid. It does not guarantee that dividends will be declared, but if dividends are declared, they must be paid.

Once a corporation declares dividends, the payments become corporate debt. Here, Price is owed $5 \times 2,000$ shares $= \$10,000$.

He is an unsecured creditor, because this debt has not been secured by a separate agreement that creates a security interest. His debt does not have priority over judgment creditors, bond owners, or secured creditors.

208. **Answer: C**

When there is no agreement to the contrary in a GENERAL partnership, profits are divided equally. They are divided according to percentage of contribution in a LIMITED partnership, if there is no agreement to the contrary.

209. **Answer: C**

Shareholders must be given only the exchange rights provided in the articles of share exchange. They are not automatically entitled to voting shares in the new corporation.

210. **Answer: A**

Shareholders have the right to vote on many important corporate changes, including amendments to the articles of incorporation, dissolution, sale of all or substantially all of the corporation's assets, and mergers and consolidations. Choices B, C, and D are all on this list. Choice A is, therefore, the correct answer. Often, one corporation can buy all or substantially all of the assets of another company without there being any large qualitative change in the life of the purchasing corporation. Therefore, when a large corporation gobbles up the assets of a smaller corporation, the shareholders of the large buyer do not have the right to vote on the transaction. There would be a much greater impact on the life of the selling corporation and its shareholders would therefore have the right to vote on the transaction.

211. **Answer: C**

Simply deciding to dissolve a partnership does not dissolve liability. If money is owed on contracts, tort judgments, or otherwise, the partners are still responsible for them. Apparent authority does continue after partners have decided to dissolve the partnership. Notice must be given to others (by contact for those with which the partnership has actually done business and by publication for everyone else) before apparent authority stops.

212. **Answer: B**

A partnership is like a marriage, in that partners do not have to be partners with anyone unless they want to be. A new partner cannot be added to a partnership without the unanimous consent of the existing partners. Unless someone getting an assignment is made a partner, (s)he will not have any management rights. The right to a share of profits, however, may be assigned. It is the only thing that is owned by each individual partner, and not collectively. Bean may receive Cobb's share of the partnership profits.

213. **Answer: C**

A shareholder does have this right. Unless there is a court order bringing about involuntary dissolution, shareholders will vote on the proposal.

214. **Answer: D**

Because a partnership creditor must proceed against the assets of the partnership first, this answer is correct.

215. **Answer: C**

Shareholders do have the right to a reasonable inspection of corporate records. Full inspection may be limited if a shareholder owns a small number of shares or has held his interest for only a short period of time.

216. **Answer: B**

By taking this potential client away from the business, Mary has breached the duty of loyalty by competing with the firm.

217. **Answer: A**

General partners are jointly and severally liable, or potentially liable, for an entire tort judgment against their firm. Their liability extends beyond acts they authorized. Even unauthorized acts can create liability for the general partners.

218. Answer: C

A director must make decisions for the corporation, such as deciding which policies will be followed and whether or not dividends will be declared. In so doing, a director must use reasonable business judgment to meet the standard of care required of him. This is not a duty to use perfect judgment.

If a director relies on information provided by corporate officers when he makes decisions, he has likely used reasonable business judgment. There is no need for directors to independently verify all information given to them.

219. Answer: D

Under the business-judgment rule, courts refuse to second guess the decisions of corporate directors (and officers) in most situations, because the judges realize that they themselves are not business experts. There are some recognized exceptions to the business-judgment rule, particularly where the corporate managers were in a conflict-of-interest situation when they acted.

220. Answer: D

As long as an agent has authority OF SOME KIND, he can bind the partnership to a contract.

Locke, as a general partner, is an agent. He does not have actual authorization to buy the stoves, so he does not have express authority to buy them. However, he DOES have apparent authority.

This arises when a third party (in this case Gage) reasonably believes that the agent has authority to make the order. It is clearly reasonable to think that a general partner in a kitchen equipment business is authorized to buy stoves. The contract will be enforceable against the partnership.

221. Answer: D

Amending the Articles is a major step and is beyond the powers of the directors. Shareholders must approve such a change.

222. Answer: B

The recipient of a gift has a gain basis and a loss basis in the asset received. The gain basis is the donor's adjusted basis ($40,000) and the loss basis is the lower of the fair market value or the adjusted basis ($30,000). If the asset is later sold for an amount in-between the gain and loss basis ($36,000 is in-between $40,000 and $30,000), no gain or loss is recognized.

223. Answer: A

A donee basis in property acquired by gift usually equals the donor's basis in the property plus the gift tax paid. However, if the fair market value of the gifted property at the time of the gift is less than the donor's basis in the property, the donee assumes the fair market value of the property at the time of the gift as its basis for computing losses. The donee still uses the donor's basis in the property plus the gift tax paid in computing gains.

As with this problem, using the fair market value of the property at the time of the gift as the property's basis in computing losses and the donor's basis in the property plus the gift tax paid in computing gains leads to instances where no gain or loss is recognized. This situation occurs when the donee assumes the fair market value of the property at the time of the gift for losses and sells the property for more than the fair market value assumed as the property's basis for computing losses but less than the donor's basis in the property plus the gift tax paid in computing gains.

When Hall received the stock as a gift from her mother, the fair market value of the stock ($3,000) was less than her mother's basis in the property ($4,000). Thus, Hall assumed the stock's fair market value at the time of the gift of $3,000 as her basis in the stock for computing losses and her mother's basis of $4,000 as her basis in the stock for computing gains. Hall sold the stock for $3,500. Using Hall's basis in the stock for computing losses of $3,000 indicates that she realized a gain of $500. However, using Hall's basis in the stock for computing gains of $4,000 indicates that she realized a loss of $500. Therefore, Hall would not recognize any gain or loss from the sale of the gifted stock.

224. Answer: B

Marketable securities are an investment that qualifies as a capital asset.

225. Answer: B

Capital assets are defined as all those assets held by the taxpayer, except for those listed in Code Section 1221. Those assets listed in Code Section 1221 include inventory, accounts receivable and depreciable property or real estate used in business.

Hall's limousine does not qualify as a capital asset, because it is depreciable property used in business. However, Hall's personal residence and furnishings qualify as capital assets, as they are not inventory, accounts receivable and depreciable property or real estate used in business.

Therefore, Hall's capital assets amount to $280,000.

226. **Answer: A**

Property bequeathed due to the death of the owner has a fair market value basis to the beneficiary, and a long-term holding period. Jordan's gain on the sale of the inherited stock is:

Amount Realized	$7,500
Adjusted Basis	(5,000)
Recognized Gain	$2,500

Even though Jordan has owned the stock for only four months her holding period is long-term since the stock was inherited.

227. **Answer: A**

Capital gains and losses are required to be classified as short-term (that is, those on assets held for one year or less) and long-term (that is., those on assets held for more than one year). Short-term capital gains are netted against short-term capital losses with the result of a net short-term capital gain or loss.

Similarly, long-term capital gains are netted against long-term capital losses to get the net long-term capital gain or loss. The net short-term capital gain or loss and the net long-term capital gain or loss are netted with the resulting capital gain net income, taxable income to the corporation.

Capital losses in excess of gains may not be used to reduce the taxable income of the corporation. The unused capital losses may be carried back for three years and carried forward five years.

This response states that a corporation's capital losses are deductible only to the extent of the corporation's capital gains.

228. **Answer: C**

Even though the NOL includes $15,000 ($20,000 × 3/4) of Section 1244 loss that can be combined with the current Section 1244 loss of $50,000, the maximum deduction for a given tax year is $50,000 for a Section 1244 loss ($100,000 if married filing jointly).

229. **Answer: A**

To quality for ordinary treatment, 1244 stock must be issued to the taxpayer for money or other property transferred by the taxpayer to the corporation.

230. **Answer: B**

A corporation sustaining a net capital loss shall carry back such net capital loss to each of the three taxable years preceding the loss year and carry over such net capital loss to each of the five taxable years succeeding the loss year.

231. **Answer: A**

The holding period for stocks and securities acquired by purchase begins on the trade date that the stock or security was acquired and ends on the trade date on which the stock or security was sold or exchanged.

Therefore, the gain or loss on a year-end sale of listed stock arises on the trade date.

232. **Answer: C**

The property sold by Bates Corp. is Section 1245 property and, as such, is subject to 1245 recapture. Section 1245 property includes all depreciable personal property (for example, equipment and machinery). Under Section 1245 recapture, gains are treated as ordinary income to the extent of depreciation or amortization taken on the property. The basis of Bates Corp.'s property at the time of the sale is $52,475—$100,000 purchase price, less $47,525 in depreciation. Hence, the corporation had a gain of $49,525. However, owing to Section 1245 recapture, the amount of depreciation allowed, $47,525, will be considered ordinary income and only $2,000 will be considered a gain.

233. **Answer: D**

The lookback provision states that the net Section 1231 gains must be offset by net Section 1231 losses from the five preceding tax years that have not previously been recaptured. To the extent of these losses, the net Section 1231 gain is treated as ordinary income. The $75,000 gain in Year 3 was recaptured as ordinary income by $50,000 of the Year 1 loss and $25,000 of the Year 2 loss. Note that $5,000 of the Year 2 loss remains unrecaptured. The $80,000 gain is recaptured as ordinary income to the extent of the $5,000 remaining Year 2 loss, $20,000 Year 4 loss, and $30,000 Year 5 loss for a total of $55,000. The remaining $25,000 gain is treated as a Sec. 1231 gain.

234. **Answer: D**

All of the assets sold are assets that have been used in a business and are therefore Section

1231 losses. Thus, all of the losses are Section 1231 losses and total $290,000.

235. **Answer: C**

Tangible assets that are used in a trade or business and owned for one year or less are ordinary assets. Since the computer was owned for slightly more than four months, the gain is classified as ordinary income.

236. **Answer: D**

The painting is obviously tangible, and it is the tangible thing ITSELF that has value. A promissory note may be a tangible piece of paper, but it is not the paper itself that has value. Only a right that the paper REPRESENTS has value. The same applies to a share of stock, which is represented by a stock certificate. Obviously, a trademark is an intangible property right.

237. **Answer: C**

The statutory amortization period for a covenant not to compete that is related to a business acquisition is 15 years.

238. **Answer: C**

The MACRS rules for personalty use the half-year convention which provides a deduction for one-half of the regular deprecation for the asset in the year it is sold. This, the depreciation for Year 3 is $3,000 × 19.2% × 1/2, or $288.

239. **Answer: D**

Under MACRS, the office building is considered non-residential real property. Land cannot be depreciated. Its class life is 39 years. MACRS requires that the straight-ine method be used to compute the depreciation of 39-year class life property. Therefore, the office building would be depreciated at a rate of $6,000 per year ([$264,000 building cost, less $30,000 cost of land]/39 years). However, the mid-month convention applies to 39-year class life property. This convention requires that, regardless of when realty is placed into service, it is considered to be placed into service at mid-month. Therefore, for August 2016 (the first month of service), Graham could deduct $250 (= $6,000/12 months × one-half of a month). For the period of September 2016 to December 2016 (the remainder of the tax year), Graham could deduct $2,000 (= $6,000 × 4/12 months). Hence, Graham's MACRS deduction for the office building in 2016 would be $2,250, the sum of the two periods.

240. **Answer: B**

Under MACRS, the property's depreciable basis as determined by Code Section 162 is used to compute the depreciation deductions, except that salvage values are considered to be zero. Hence, the salvage value is ignored for computing the MACRS depreciation deduction and, therefore, this response is correct.

241. **Answer: D**

An exchange will be non-taxable if it qualifies under the like-kind exchange rules. All realty is considered like-kind property. Since the building and the land are both realty, this qualifies as a non-taxable like-kind exchange.

242. **Answer: D**

Exchanges involving property held primarily for sale; stocks, bonds, notes and other securities; partnership interests; certificates trusts or beneficial interest; and evidences of indebtedness are not considered "like-kind" exchanges and, as a result, do not qualify for the non-recognition of gains or losses.

243. **Answer: B**

A fire qualifies as an involuntary conversion, and realized gain can be deferred since the old warehouse is replaced with a new warehouse.

Amount realized from conversion	$195,000
Adjusted basis of old property	(75,000)
Realized gain	$120,000
Amount realized from conversion	$195,000
Cost of replacement property	(167,000)
	$28,000

The recognized gain is $28,000, the lower of the realized gain or the amount realized that was not reinvested in the new warehouse. The deferred gain is $92,000 ($120,000 – $28,000).

The adjusted basis of the new property is its cost reduced by any deferred gain:

$167,000 – $92,000 = $75,000.

244. **Answer: C**

When a taxpayer exchanges property for "like-kind" property, no gain or loss is generally recognized. However, if boot is received, gain is recognized to the extent of boot received in the exchange. The exchanges of real estate for "like-kind" real estate qualify for non-recognition under the "like-kind" exchange rules.

Reed gave up real estate with an adjusted basis of $300,000. Reed received real estate with a fair market value of $450,000 and $50,000 in cash. Hence, Reed realized a gain of $200,000.

However, this gain is only recognized to the extent of the boot that Reed received, $50,000.

245. **Answer: B**

This is a qualified like-kind exchange because a machine was exchanged for equipment and Hogan's use for each is for business purposes.

Amount Realized:		
Equipment received	$80,000	
Cash	1,000	
Debt relief	2,000	
Total		$83,000
Adjusted Basis:		
Cost	$100,000	
Depreciation	(30,000)	
		(70,000)
Realized Gain		$13,000

Debt relief and the cash received are both considered to be boot received, which is a total of $3,000. The recognized gain is the lower of the realized gain, $13,000, or boot received, $3,000.

246. **Answer: C**

Sand's basis per share is $180 ($18,000/100 shares). Sand's realized loss on the 50 shares sold is $2,000 ($7,000 amount realized − $9,000 basis ($180 × 50 shares). This loss is not recognized under the wash sale rule if the same stock is repurchased within 30 days. Since only 25 shares were repurchased during the 30-day period, 50% (25 shares/50 shares) of the loss is not recognized. Therefore, $1,000 of the realized loss is recognized.

247. **Answer: A**

A taxpayer may exclude realized gains up to $250,000 ($500,000 if filing joint) on the sale of a residence if the residence has been owned and used by the taxpayer as a principal residence for at least two of the preceding five years. (Note that for the $500,000 exclusion both spouses must meet the use test, but only one must meet the ownership test). Wynn's realized gain is $200,000 ($450,000 amount realized − $250,000 adjusted basis), so all of this gain can be excluded.

248. **Answer: A**

The realized gain is computed as follows:

Amount Realized:		
Cash	$650,000	
Commission	(36,000)	
		$614,000
Adjusted Basis:		
Cost	$300,000	
Improvements	40,000	
		(340,000)
Realized gain		$274,000

Since this is a married couple that meets the ownership and use test they can exclude up to $500,000 of gain on the sale of a principal residence. Thus, none of the $274,000 gain is included in income.

249. **Answer: C**

Losses from sales and exchanges made by related parties are not recognized for tax purposes. A taxpayer's brothers and sister (whole and half blood), spouse, ancestors and lineal descendants are considered related parties. A taxpayer's in-laws are not considered members of his/her family.

This response correctly states that a taxpayer's ancestors and lineal descendants are considered related parties in respect to the taxpayer.

250. **Answer: A**

A taxpayer acquiring property through purchase or exchange from a person who sustained a loss on the transaction that was disallowed owing to related taxpayer rules realizes a gain on the sale or other disposition of the property only to the extent that the gain exceeds the amount of the disallowed loss. Alice acquired the Zinco stock from her father, who sustained a disallowed loss of $10,000 ($20,000 selling price, less $30,000 purchase price). Hence, Alice would have to realize a gain of more than $10,000 for her to recognize a gain, since she now has a right of offset of $10,000.

Alice purchased the stock from her father for $20,000 and sold the stock for $25,000 – realizing a gain of $5,000. Since Alice's realized gain is less than her father's right of offset, Alice does not recognize any gain on the sale of the stock.

251. **Answer: A**

Interest income received on U.S. Treasury certificates is not exempt from federal income tax. In addition, while federal income tax refunds are nontaxable, the interest received on the refund is taxable income.

Hence, the interest income on the U.S. Treasury certificates and on the refund of prior year's federal income tax is reported on Kay's 2015 tax return, putting the total amount of interest subject to tax in Kay's 2017 tax return at $4,500.

252. **Answer: C**

Refunds and recoveries attributable to a prior tax year are excluded from income to the extent that the amount does not reduce the amount of tax imposed for the earlier year. However, interest received on these refunds and recoveries is taxable interest income.

Thus, Charles and Marcia should include the interest received on the state and federal income tax refunds as interest income on their income tax return. In addition, Charles and Marcia should include the interest received on federal government obligations as taxable interest income on their income tax return because interest on these obligations is taxable. However, interest on state government obligations is tax-exempt income and, as a result, Charles and Marcia should not include interest income from these obligations on their income tax return.

Hence, Charles and Marcia should report $1,900 of interest income, the sum of the $500 interest on federal income tax refund, $600 interest on state income tax refund and $800 interest on federal government obligations.

253. **Answer: B**

Federal and state income tax refunds are excluded from a taxpayer's taxable income to the extent that the refund did not reduce the amount of tax for the earlier year. However, any interest earned on these refunds is considered taxable income.

Thus, Clark's state income tax refund is excluded from taxable income. However, the $10 in interest income from the refund is taxable income and, therefore, included on Clark's 2017 federal income tax return.

254. **Answer: B**

Under the accrual method of accounting, income is reported once all events to establish a taxpayer's right to receive the income have occurred and the amount can be determined with reasonable accuracy.

If an amount of income has been accrued on the basis of a reasonable estimate with the exact amount to be determined at a later date, any difference between the estimate and exact amount is to be included in income or deducted in the year when the exact amount can be determined.

255. **Answer: A**

Under the tax benefit rule, recoveries of taxes previously deducted by a taxpayer that were overpaid should be reported as income by the taxpayer in the year of recovery. The taxes subject to the tax benefit rule are: state income taxes; personal property taxes; real property taxes; state sales and use taxes; state corporation franchise taxes; stamp taxes; federal excise taxes; customs duties; and farmland preservation credits.

Farb's overstatement arose from personal property taxes, a tax subject to the tax benefit rule. Thus, Farb should deduct $8,000 in his 2016 income tax return and should report the $5,000 refund as income in his 2017 income tax return when the case is settled.

256. **Answer: B**

Alimony received by a taxpayer is included in that taxpayer's gross income and alimony paid by a taxpayer is deductible from that taxpayer's gross income. To be considered alimony, the payments must be made under a divorce or separation agreement. Payments to third parties (such as tuition, rent and mortgage) by the spouse paying alimony for the spouse receiving alimony receive the same treatment as cash payments.

John and Mary have a divorce decree stipulating $10,000 per year payments from John to Mary, but the amount decreases to $8,000 when their child reaches the age of 18 years. Due to this decrease, $2,000 of the $10,000 payment would be considered child support and, as a result, would not be reported by Mary as income. The remaining $8,000 would be considered alimony and, therefore, reported as income by Mary.

257. **Answer: C**

All of the items received are included in gross income except for the state income tax refund. Since Randolph always uses the standard deduction, no tax benefit is received when the state income taxes are paid. Therefore, the refund is not taxable.

258. **Answer: C**

Alimony is included in the recipient's income, but child support payments and property settlements are not.

259. Answer: D

Wages are included in gross income for the year in which they are received. Unemployment compensation is also included in gross income since it replaces income that would have been received if working. Therefore, the total amount included in gross income is $41,000.

260. Answer: D

Alimony paid under a divorce or a separation agreement is included as taxable income by the payee spouse and deductible by the payor spouse. Payments that are fixed as child support are not treated as alimony.

Thus, these payments are not included as taxable income by the payee spouse nor deductible by the payor spouse. If the payor spouse pays less than the amount specified as child support payments, the entire amount is treated as child support payments.

Hall's divorce agreement provides for $3,000 per month, of which $600 is designated as child support. Hence, Hall should have received $28,800 in alimony and $7,200 in child support. However, she only received $5,000, which is less than the $7,200 she should have received in child support. Therefore, the entire $5,000 would be considered child support and Hall would not report any alimony.

261. Answer: B

PI = AGI + tax-exempt interest + 50% (SSB)

PI = $60,000 + $1,000 + 50% (8,400) = $65,200.

Since PI ($65,200) exceeds Base Amount 2 ($34,000), then the taxable amount of SSB is the lesser of:

1. .85 × SSB ($8,400) = $7,140, or
2. .85 × [PI – BA2; $65,200 – $34,000) = $26,520, plus the lesser of
    1. amount included based on the 50% formula (50% × $8,400) = $4,200, or
    2. $4,500 (unless married filing joint, then $6,000), which provides $26,520 + $4,200 = $30,720 for part b of the formula.

Thus, the amount included in income is the lower of $7,140 or $30,720, so the amount excluded is $1,260 ($8,400 – $7,140).

262. Answer: B

Decker's cost basis is the $25,000 he paid for the policy plus the $40,000 he paid in premiums. $200,000 less $65,000 = $135,000.

263. Answer: D

Joan meets all of the requirements to exclude the gift from income, except that she accepted the award and received payment. Therefore, the FMV of the award, $10,000, is included in her income.

264. Answer: B

Since the scholarship was used to pay tuition and fees, none of it is taxable. For purposes of this section, a qualified scholarship is any amount received by an individual as a scholarship or fellowship grant (as defined in paragraph (c)(3) of this section), to the extent the individual establishes that, in accordance with the conditions of the grant, such amount was used for qualified tuition and related expenses

Amounts receive for teaching are taxable. Inclusion of qualified scholarships and qualified tuition reductions representing payment for services are taxable.

265. Answer: C

Gross income is the starting point in determining a taxpayer's tax liability. As a result, it is broadly defined. Gross income encompasses all income from all sources, including compensation for services, business income, interests, dividends, rents, and ordinary and capital gains.

Hence, both a payment to a graduate assistant for a part-time teaching assignment at a university and a grant to a Ph.D. candidate for his participation in a university-sponsored research project for the benefit of the university would be included in a taxpayer's gross income.

266. Answer: C

The amount of dividends would be ($400 + $50 + $300) = $750. The $200 dividend on the life insurance policy is not gross income, but is considered a reduction of the cost of the policy.

267. Answer: D

Generally, stock dividends are nontaxable, and a taxpayer's basis for original stock is allocated to the dividend stock in proportion to fair market values. However, any stock that is distributed on preferred stock results in a taxable stock dividend. The amount to be included in the shareholder's income is the stock's fair market value on date of distribution. Similarly, the shareholder's basis for the dividend shares will be equal to their fair market value on date of distribution (10 × $60 = $600).

268. Answer: C

After the stock dividend, the basis of each share would be determined as follows:

$$\frac{\$90,000}{450 + 50} = \$180 \text{ per share}$$

Since the holding period of the new shares includes the holding period of the old shares, the sale of the 50 new shares for $11,000 results in a LTCG of $2,000 [$11,000 − (50 shares × $180)].

269. Answer: C

Partnerships can use the cash method regardless of the amount of gross receipts as long as none of the partners are C corporations.

270. Answer: C

C corporations cannot use the cash method of accounting unless their average annual gross receipts for the previous three years do not exceed $5,000,000. Once the $5,000,000 test is failed the accrual method must be used for all future tax years. Since Dart has had revenues of more than $20 million for the last three years it must use the accrual method of accounting.

271. Answer: D

Manufacturers and certain retailers and wholesalers are required to use the uniform capitalization rules to capitalize direct and indirect costs allocable to property they produce and for property they purchase for resale. Marketing, selling, advertising, and distribution expenses are not required to be capitalized. Storage costs are required to be capitalized to the extent that they can be traced to an off-site storage or warehouse facility. Those storage costs attributed to an on-site facility are not required to be capitalized.

This response correctly indicates that marketing costs are not required to be capitalized and that costs attributable to off-site storage facilities are required to be capitalized.

272. Answer: D

For accrual-based taxpayers, items generally are included in gross income for the year in which the income is earned. However, for tax purposes, income is earned when (1) all the events have occurred to attach the taxpayer's right to receive the income and (2) the amount of income can be determined with reasonable accuracy. Cash based taxpayers report income when it is actually received or constructively received (i.e., in the taxpayer's control).

Since there are no restrictions on the advance lease payments or the lease cancellation payment and no services need to be rendered, Lake Corp. has a right to receive the advance lease payments and the lease cancellation payments in the current year. The payments also can be determined with reasonable accuracy. Hence, both the advance lease payments and the lease cancellation payments should be reported on Lake Corp.'s tax return.

This response includes both the advance lease payments and the lease cancellation payments in Lake Corp.'s taxable income.

273. Answer: D

Unless the IRS consents to a change of method, taxpayers are to use the accrual method of accounting for purchases and sales if inventories are used.

Accounts receivable for services rendered does not trigger the required use of the accrual method.

This response correctly indicates that accounts receivable for services rendered would not lead to the required use of the accrual method and that the use of inventories would trigger the required use of the accrual method.

274. Answer: C

Cafeteria plans allow employees to select from a menu of fringe benefits and cash and not include the value of the nontaxable benefits in their gross income. The requirements of cafeteria plans are:

1) All participants must be employees;
2) Participants may choose between two or more benefits composed of cash or qualified benefits;
3) Participants are required to make elections among the benefits;
4) The plan must be in writing and have certain specified information;
5) The plan may not provide participants with deferred income, except for under 401(k) plans.

This response states that under cafeteria plans participants may select their own menu of benefits.

275. Answer: D

Dividend income is taxable income.

276. Answer: D

Since this is not an accountable plan, all reimbursements are included in the employee's income ($400 × 12 months = $4,800) and all employee deductions will be 2% miscellaneous itemized deductions.

277. **Answer: C**

The first $50,000 of group-term life insurance provided by an employer is a tax-free fringe benefit. Johnson receives $200,000 of group-term life insurance, so $150,000 of this coverage is taxable. There are 150 units of $1,000 each of excess coverage, included in income at $2.76 for each unit. The income from the insurance coverage is $414 ($2.76 × $150). When the $414 is included with the $100,000 salary, gross income is $100,414.

278. **Answer: D**

For determining the amount of income that a self-employed individual may contribute to a Keogh profit-sharing plan, earned income is defined as net self-employed earnings less the deductible Keogh contribution and one-half of the self-employment tax.

279. **Answer: A**

Individual taxpayers not active in certain employer-sponsored retirement plans may deduct cash contributions to individual retirement accounts to the extent of the lesser of $5,500 or 100 percent of the taxpayer's gross income in 2016. Those taxpayers covered by employer-sponsored retirement plans may still take individual retirement account deductions subject to a phase-out based on their adjusted gross income.

No taxes are paid on the interest income earned on individual retirement accounts until the retirement savings are distributed. The individual retirement account deduction is an adjustment to income in arriving at adjusted gross income.

280. **Answer: B**

IRA contributions must be made by the original due date of the return (April 15) even if the return is extended.

281. **Answer: D**

The $30,000 distribution from the traditional IRA is taxable at the taxpayer's marginal tax rate for federal income tax purposes. In addition, since this is an early distribution (before age 59 ½) and none of the exceptions for early distributions are met, the distribution is also subject to a 10% penalty tax. Therefore, the $30,000 distribution will be taxed at a 45% rate (35% marginal tax rate + 10% penalty tax). Total tax liability is $13,500 ($30,000 × 45%).

282. **Answer: D**

John does not have any basis in his retirement account. He did not receive basis for his contributions because they were made from earnings that were not taxed. He did not receive basis for his employer's contributions since they were made from employer funds. Therefore, the entire $350,000 distribution is included in John's gross income.

283. **Answer: C**

A taxpayer may not deduct life insurance premiums in which the taxpayer is directly or indirectly the beneficiary. Hence, Ral Corp. may not deduct the $3,000 in keyman insurance premiums that it paid on Budd's life because the corporation is the beneficiary. However, a taxpayer may deduct the group term life insurance premiums if the insured employee or his/her beneficiaries would get the insurance proceeds. Thus, Ral Corp. may deduct the $4,000 in group term insurance premiums paid on the $10,000 life insurance policies for each of Ral Corp.'s four employees.

284. **Answer: A**

It is an ordinary and necessary expense to have the restaurant cleaned, and the $20 is reasonable.

285. **Answer: A**

No deduction or credit shall be allowed for any amount paid or incurred during the taxable year in carrying on any trade or business if such trade or business (or the activities which comprise such trade or business) consists of trafficking in controlled substances (within the meaning of schedule I and II of the Controlled Substances Act) which is prohibited by federal law or the law of any state in which such trade or business is conducted. However, a deduction is allowed for the cost of merchandise purchased.

286. **Answer: A**

Fines and penalties generally may not be deducted as a business expense, including those paid to the federal government. Hence, a corporation's penalty for underpaying federal estimated taxes is not deductible.

287. **Answer: B**

Cash-basis taxpayers report income when cash or property is actually or constructively received. There is no constructive receipt for deductions. Deductions for cash-basis taxpayers generally are taken when actually paid. However, for expenses covering 12 months or more, the deduction must be spread over the period for which the expenses apply. Thus, since the loan was to be repaid in 12 months, the deduction for the interest must be spread over the 12-month period.

Thus, to account for the period of December 1, 2016 to December 31, 2016, Michaels would have deducted $1,000 of the interest on her 2016 income tax return and $11,000 on her 2017 income tax return to account for the period January 1, 2017, to November 30, 2017.

288. **Answer: C**

Alimony payments you make under a divorce or separation instrument, such as a divorce decree or a written agreement incident thereto, are deductible if all of the following requirements are met:

1. You and your spouse or former spouse do not file a joint return with each other;
2. You pay in cash (including checks or money orders);
3. The divorce or separation instrument does not say that the payment is not alimony;
4. If legally separated under a decree of divorce or separate maintenance, you and your former spouse are not members of the same household when you make the payment;
5. You have no liability to make any payment (in cash or property) after the death of your spouse or former spouse; *and*
6. Your payment is not treated as child support.

289. **Answer: C**

If an employer requires jury pay to be remitted in exchange for regular compensation for the period the employee was performing jury duty, the employee may deduct the jury duty pay from her gross income as an adjustment arriving at adjusted gross income.

As Dale was required by her employer to remit the $1,000 in jury duty pay in exchange for regular compensation for the period the employee was performing jury duty, Dale should deduct the jury duty pay from her gross income in arriving at adjusted gross income.

290. **Answer: B**

The unreimbursed employee business expenses and charitable contribution are itemized deductions, so these do not affect the computation of adjusted gross income. AGI equals the $3,000 of wages less student loan interest of $400, or $2,600.

291. **Answer: A**

If an employee or a self-employed individual moves his/her residence due to a change of his/her principal place of work, reasonable expenses resulting from moving household goods and personal effects from the old residence to the new residence and from traveling from the old residence to the new residence may be deducted. To qualify for the deduction, the new job site must be at least 50 miles further away from the old residence than was the old principal job.

If the taxpayer was unemployed before the move, the job site must be at least 50 miles away from his/her old residence. In addition, the taxpayer must be employed full-time in the area of the new principal place of work for at least 39 weeks during the 12-month period following the move, or if self-employed, for at least 78 weeks in the 24-month period following the move with at least 39 of the 78 weeks in the 12-month period following the move.

Neither the $500 fee for breaking the lease on the prior apartment residence nor the $900 for the security deposit placed on the apartment at the new location may be deducted as moving expenses. They are not qualified expenses nor was the move work related or more than 50 miles.

Also note that the question asks to determine the moving expenses that are deducted on Schedule A. Moving expenses are deducted on Form 1040; they are not itemized deductions.

292. **Answer: A**

Qualified moving expenses are limited to the expenses for moving the household goods ($2,000) and lodging ($100). Meals are not deductible during a move and temporary living expenses are never deductible. The $2,100 of qualified expenses is reduced by the $2,000 reimbursement from the employer.

293. **Answer: C**

Certain state and local taxes are deductible as an itemized expense during the year in which the taxes were actually paid. Deductible taxes include income and real property. State and local fees are not deductible. Federal income taxes also are not deductible.

During 2016, Matthews paid $1,500 in state and local income taxes withholding and $400 in state estimated income taxes. Thus, she is entitled to claim $1,900 for taxes on her 2016 Schedule A of Form 1040. Matthew's 2016 state and local income taxes paid on April 15, 2017 will be deductible on her 2017 tax return because these taxes were not actually paid in 2016.

294. Answer: B

Total allowable medical expenses is $20,000. Only medical expenses in excess of 10% of AGI are allowable as a deduction. Carrol's AGI is $100,000 × .010 = $10,000. Total expenses of $20,000 − $10,000 = $10,000 deductible expenses.

295. Answer: B

Investment interest expense is deductible to the extent of net investment income. Net investment income is defined as investment income ($10,000) less noninterest investment expenses ($8,000), or $2,000. So, $2,000 of the $5,000 of investment interest expense is deductible as an itemized deduction. The remaining $3,000 is carried over, indefinitely, and deducted in a year that has sufficient net investment income.

296. Answer: C

A noncorporate taxpayer's deduction for interest on investment indebtedness is limited to the taxpayer's net investment income. Interest on investment indebtedness is interest paid or accrued that is allocable to property held for investment.

297. Answer: B

Medical expenses paid by an individual are deductible in the year paid.

298. Answer: B

$1,500 is correct. The $2,000 cash donated to a needy family is not deductible because the needy family is not a qualified charitable organization. The stock was purchased for $1,500 and not held for one year to be capital gain property, therefore the deduction for the stock is the fair market value of the stock ($3,000) less the short-term capital gain ($1,500) if the stock had been sold ($3,000 − basis of $1,500) = $1,500.

299. Answer: B

Gambling losses are deductible as a miscellaneous itemized deduction, but are limited to the gambling winnings of $3,000.

300. Answer: C

All of the expenses listed are allowed as 2% miscellaneous itemized deductions, which total $2,750. This amount is reduced by 2% of AGI ($75,000), which is $1,500. Thus, Carter's deduction is $1,250.

301. Answer: B

The $1,500 donation to the needy family is incorrect. The family is not a qualified charitable organization. Because the artwork was held over two years, it is capital gain property and Deet can use FMV of $11,000 for the value of his charitable contribution to the art museum.

302. Answer: C

An individual's charitable contribution to public charities may not exceed 50 percent of the individual's adjusted gross income. The 50 percent deduction ceiling applies to contributions made to:

1. Churches;
2. Educational institutions that maintain a regular faculty and curriculum;
3. Hospitals and medical schools;
4. Organizations supported by the government that hold property and/or investments for the benefit of a college or university;
5. Federal, state or local governmental units; and
6. Organizations normally receiving most of its support from the public or a governmental unit. The amount that exceeds the 50 percent deduction ceiling may be carried forward for 5 years.

Since Moore's charitable contributions were made to an organization (a church) qualifying for a 50 percent deduction ceiling, she may deduct up to $25,000, 50 percent of her adjusted gross income of $50,000. Moore may meet this ceiling by deducting the $18,000 that she contributed to her church in 2016 and carrying forward $7,000 of the $10,000 charitable contribution carryover from her 2015 church contribution.

303. Answer: B

Meals and entertainment expenses are limited to 50% of their total amount. For meals and entertainment expenses that an employee is reimbursed by his/her employer, the percentage limit applies to the employer. However, if the reimbursement is included in the employee's income, the percentage limits apply to the employee and not the employer. Food and beverage expenses are only deductible, if: (1) the expenses are not lavish or extravagant; (2) the taxpayer (or one of his employees) is present when the food or beverages were provided; and (3) the expense relates directly to the conducting of business.

Assuming that a Banks Corp.'s employee was present when the meals were provided and that the expenses were for a bona fide business purpose, the meals expense can be deducted because they were not lavish or extravagant. Since the corporation reimbursed its employees, Banks Corp. may deduct 50% of the meals expense.

304. Answer: C

The deduction for business gifts is limited to $25 per individual/customer who receives a gift. The total deduction is computed as follows:

5 × $15 =	$ 75
9 × $25 =	$225
1 × $25 =	$ 25
Total	$325

305. Answer: B

The deduction for business gifts is limited to $25 per donee per year. The deduction is computed as follows:

4 at $10		$40
4 at $25		100
4 at $50	limited to $25	100
5 at $100	limited to $25	125
	Total	$365

306. Answer: A

Dues are not deductible. All of the other expenses are deductible but subject to the 50% limitation for meals and entertainment. Note that the deduction for the Super Bowl tickets is limited to the face value of the tickets, before the 50% limitation. The allowable deduction is $2,250 (($2,000 + $1,500 + $1,000) × 50%).

307. Answer: B

When traveling outside the U.S. primarily for vacation (4 weeks total versus 1 week seminar), the cost of the trip is a nondeductible personal expense. Baker can deduct the registration fees for the business seminar and deduct the out of pocket expenses for the time that was directly related to the business seminar (1 week). 5 days × $100 per day plus $700 registration = $1200 of deductible education expense.

308. Answer: A

Since Budd reports on the cash basis he did not recognize income when the client was billed. Therefore, he has no basis in the receivable to deduct when it becomes uncollectible.

309. Answer: D

Corporations other than certain financial institutions are required to use the direct charge-off method in accounting for bad debts. Certain financial institutions are allowed to use the reserve method.

Under the direct charge-off method, corporations may claim a deduction once a specific business debt becomes partially or wholly worthless and a specific nonbusiness debt becomes wholly worthless.

310. Answer: A

$7,000 is correct.

Wages	$5,000
Interest on savings account	1,000
Net rental income	4,000
Net business loss	(16,000)
Net short-term capital loss	(2,000)
AGI	(8,000)
Deductions:	
Personal exemption	$4,050
Standard deduction	6,350
Taxable Loss	(18,400)

Adjustments to arrive at NOL carry back or carry forward (Use Form 1045, Schedule A for calculation purposes.)

$18,400	TAXABLE LOSS
Plus $4,050	Personal exemption, Destry cannot deduct his personal exemption.
Plus $5,350	Adjustment for deductions that are not connected to a trade or business or employment, such as the standard deduction of $6,300 reduced by the non-business income of $1,000 interests from savings.
Plus $2,000	Short term capital loss as adjusted by business capital gains and losses (–0–).
($7,000)	Correct carry back or forward

311. Answer: A

An individual's losses on transactions entered into for personal purposes are only deductible if the losses qualify as casualty or theft losses. If the losses originated due to a trade or business, individuals also may deduct losses originating from transactions entered into for profit.

312. Answer: B

The $100,000 NOL would first be carried back to 2015 and offset $50,000 of income. It would then be carried to 2016 and offset $40,000 of income. This would leave $10,000 of NOL ($100,000 – $50,000 – $40,000) to carryforward to 2018.

313. Answer: B

Since Smith actively participates in the rental real estate activity he can deduct up to $25,000 of rental losses. However, this deduction is reduced once modified AGI exceeds $100,000. Smith has $20,000 of excess AGI ($120,000 – $100,000) so he loses $10,000 ($20,000 × 50%) of the deduction. Of the $40,000 of losses, he can deduct $15,000 ($25,000 – $10,000). The remaining $25,000 of losses is suspended.

314. Answer: C

The loss from partnership B and the rental income are passive. Passive losses can only offset passive income, so the $9,000 loss offsets the $7,000 of rental income, but the net passive loss of $2,000 is not deductible. The ordinary income of $70,000 from partnership A and the $4,000 capital gain are taxable to produce a total AGI of $74,000.

315. Answer: A

Special rules apply to realty that is used for both personal and rental purposes. If the number of rental days is less than 14 then the property is treated as if it was used 100% for personal use. In that case, the rental revenue is ignored (i.e., does not have to be recognized).

The only items that can be deducted are real estate taxes and mortgage and these items must be reported on Schedule A.

Therefore, there is no rental income and no rental expenses.

316. Answer: B

Lane has $160,000 in active income, $15,000 of passive income, and $35,000 of passive losses. Note that the exception that allows deduction for up to $25,000 of rental real estate losses does not apply since Lane's modified AGI exceeds $150,000. The passive losses can only be deducted to the extent of passive income, so $15,000 is correct.

317. Answer: A

Income from a hobby is reported as other income on the front page of Form 1040. Deductions such as travel expenses are 2% miscellaneous itemized deductions, and expenses can be deducted only to the extent of revenues.

318. Answer: B

For a taxpayer to claim an individual as an exemption on his tax return, the individual must be a qualifying child or qualifying relative. Kim is not a qualifying child or a qualifying relative because she provides over 50% of her own support. Therefore, no one can claim her as a dependent.

Dale is a qualifying child and can therefore be claimed as a dependent. He meets the relationship, age, residence (lives at home for more than half the year; time at college counts as home), joint return, and citizen test.

Grant does not qualify as a qualifying relative because he fails the gross income test. His gross income exceeds the personal exemption amount for 2016 of $4,050.

Hence, Jim and Kay may take an exemption for Dale and, including themselves, take a total of three personal exemptions.

319. Answer: C

Ben has provided over 10% of Sara's support and all of the qualifying relative tests are met (gross income, joint return, citizen) except for the support test, but it is met through the multiple support agreement. The individuals as a group have provided over 50% of Sara's support.

320. Answer: D

When a joint return has been filed, personal exemptions may be taken for the taxpayer and spouse. However, when the taxpayer and spouse file separate returns, the taxpayer only may take an exemption for the spouse when the spouse has no gross income and was not claimed as a dependent on another taxpayer's income tax return.

321. Answer: B

There are two personal exemptions for John and his wife. Dependency exemptions are as follows:

Widowed sister: Fails the gross income test

Daughter: Meets age test so is a qualifying relative

Son: Meets age test since is a full-time college student and less than 24, so is a qualifying relative

Housekeeper: Does not indicate that John and wife provide more than 50% of supportButler: Does not indicate that John and wife provide more than 50% of support

322. **Answer: A**

The Age Test applies to the qualifying child rule but not the qualifying relative rule. The gross income, support, and citizenship/residency tests must all be met for the qualifying relative rule to be met.

323. **Answer: C**

For head of household filing status, the following costs are considered in determining whether the taxpayer has contributed more than one-half the cost of maintaining the household: rent; mortgage interest; taxes; insurance on the home; repairs; utilities; and food eaten in the home. The following costs may not be considered: clothing; education; medical treatment; vacations; life insurance; transportation; rental value of home owned by taxpayer; and the value of services provided by the taxpayer or a member of the taxpayer's household.

This response correctly indicates that the food consumed may be considered in determining whether the taxpayer has contributed more than one-half the cost of maintaining the household and that value of services provided by the taxpayer may not be considered.

324. **Answer: D**

In the year of death, the surviving spouse may always file as married filing jointly.

325. **Answer: D**

In the year that an individual's spouse dies, the spouse's filing status is married filing joint. For the two years after the year of death, the qualifying widow can continue to file as married filing joint if the taxpayer provides more than half of the cost of maintaining the household (rent, mortgage interest, taxes, home insurance, repairs, food, utilities, etc.) for a *dependent child* (step, adopted, foster also).

326. **Answer: A**

Whether taxpayers live together does not impact filing status. Marital status is determined on the last day of the tax year. Since the taxpayers were married as of the end of the tax year they may file married filing joint (note that they could also file married filing separately).

327. **Answer: C**

Personal exemptions cannot decrease AMT income.

328. **Answer: C**

The following amounts are added back to taxable income to compute AMT income:

Interest because proceeds were not used for principal residence	$15,000
Taxes	18,000
Medical expenses (no adjustment since 10% of AGI threshold applies for regular tax also)	–0–
2% miscellaneous itemized deductions (deducted $5,000 – (2% × $150,000) for regular tax)	2,000
Total add-back	$35,000

329. **Answer: C**

2% miscellaneous itemized deductions are not allowed for AMT purposes. Home mortgage interest is allowed as long as the loan proceeds were used to acquire or make capital improvements to a principal residence. Thus, the correct answer is $11,000.

330. **Answer: B**

The alternative minimum tax (AMT) ensures that all taxpayers share the tax burden fairly by preventing taxpayers with substantial income from avoiding significant tax liability. The AMT equals the excess of the tentative AMT tax over the regular tax.

331. **Answer: C**

An employee who has Social Security tax withheld in an amount greater than the maximum for a particular year, may claim the excess as a credit against income tax, if that excess resulted from correct withholding by two or more employers. An employee who had excess Social Security tax withheld from one employer should be reimbursed by the employer.

332. **Answer: C**

Her tax savings is $3,000 ($12,000 × 25%) since the contribution is deductible. Therefore, her net cost is $9,000 ($12,000 – $9,000).

333. **Answer: A**

Since his income tax rate is declining, he will save 20% on any income deferred from the 50% tax rate in Year 1 to the 30% tax rate in Year 2.

334. Answer: D

2% miscellaneous itemized deductions are not deductible for AMT purposes so increasing these will not reduce the AMT.

335. Answer: B

When long-term capital gain property is contributed to a qualified charity, the fair market value of the property can be deducted as a charitable contribution.

336. Answer: C

If Orleans gives the property to his friend, the $20,000 loss disappears since the friend's loss basis in the land will be its fair market value of $50,000. Therefore, Orleans should sell the land so he can recognize the loss. He can then contribute the cash from the sale to his friend.

337. Answer: B

The credit is computed as 100% of the first $2,000 and 25% of the next $2,000 of qualified educational expenses, for a total of $2,500. This credit does not begin phasing out in 2015 for married filing joint returns until AGI reaches $160,000. The credit applies only to post-secondary expenses so the tuition for Kaitlin does not qualify.

338. Answer: B

The credit percentage begins at 35% if AGI is less than $15,000, and is reduced by 1% for each $2,000 increment (or part) in AGI above $15,000. The minimum dependent care credit is 20%. Therefore, this statement is false.

339. Answer: C

Certain tax credits can result in a refund, even if the individual had no income tax liability. Tax credits resulting in a refund are credits for earned income, tax withheld, excess social security tax withheld, and excise tax for certain nontaxable uses of fuels and light weight diesel vehicles.

340. Answer: D

A married taxpayer must file as married filing jointly to qualify for the earned income credit.

341. Answer: D

Individual taxpayers with adjusted gross income of $15,000 or less may claim a child care credit for 35 percent of employment related expenses. The credit is reduced by one percent of the expenses for each $2,000 of adjusted gross income over $15,000, but is not reduced to less than 20 percent of the expenses.

This response correctly indicates at least one spouse does not need to earn $15,000 or less to claim the credit. Earning more than $15,000 does not make a taxpayer ineligible for the credit, it reduces the amount of the credit by decreasing the percentage of the expenses that may be claimed.

This response also correctly indicates that at least one spouse must be gainfully employed or looking for work to claim the credit.

342. Answer: B

Individual taxpayers making gifts that are not fully excludable due to the $14,000 annual exclusion for each gift are required to file a gift tax return, Form 709, by the April 15th of the year following the year the gifts were given by the donor. The required filing date differs, if the donor died during the year that the gifts were made.

343. Answer: D

An unlimited exclusion from the gift tax applies for gifts to spouses. Therefore, Suzanne can give the entire $1,000,000 to George and pay no gift tax.

344. Answer: D

Tuition payments can potentially be excluded from the gift tax if made for any individual. The exclusion is not limited to just family members so this information is not relevant.

345. Answer: B

There is an unlimited exclusion for education gifts if the tuition is paid directly to the educational institution. However, this exclusion is limited to tuition and does not apply to room and board. For 2017, $14,000 of the gifts to the cousin can be excluded from the gift tax, so the remaining $26,000 is subject to the gift tax. A gift tax return must be filed to reflect this transaction.

346. Answer: D

The due date of the estate tax return is nine months after the date of death.

347. Answer: D

For married individuals, half of the value of jointly owned property is always included in the estate of the first spouse to die.

348. Answer: C

Ordinary and necessary administration expenses of an estate are deductible on the fiduciary income tax return if the administrator of the estate waives the deduction on the estate tax return.

349. Answer: A

In general, once a trust is established and the taxpayer has transferred property to the trust, this property will not be included in the taxpayer's gross estate at death unless the taxpayer maintains ownership or control of the property. Since this trust can be revoked, the taxpayer still controls the property so at death the property will be included in his gross estate. Other conditions listed in the problem (trust for a minor, independent trustee can distribute income, disclaimer) do not cause the taxpayer to retain ownership in the property.

350. Answer: A

Administration and selling expenses may be claimed either as a deduction from the decedent's gross estate for estate tax purposes or as a deduction from the estate's taxable income for income tax purposes.

351. Answer: C

A shareholder's initial basis in the stock of a corporation is the amount the shareholder paid for the stock.

Thus, Feld's initial basis in the Maki Corp.'s stock is $50,000, the amount that Feld paid for the stock. Contributions of property to corporations results in the contributing shareholder's basis for the corporation's stock to increase by the amount of the shareholder's adjusted basis in the property. Thus, Feld's basis in the Maki Corp.'s stock increased by $10,000 due to Feld's property contribution.

Hence, Feld's adjusted basis for the Maki Corp. stock is $60,000, the sum of his initial $50,000 basis and the $10,000 adjusted basis of the contributed property.

352. Answer: B

When property is contributed to a corporation in exchange for stock, the corporation takes the same basis in the property that the shareholder had, increased by any gain recognized by the shareholder. Ames had a cost basis in the balls of $500 and Roth had a basis of $5,000 in the bats, so the total basis for Homerun is $5,500.

353. Answer: D

The transaction would qualify as a tax-free event for Carr because it would be considered to be a Section 351 transfer. Under Section 351, no gain or loss is recognized if the property is transferred solely for the exchange of stock of the corporation, if immediately after the transfer the transferring taxpayer or taxpayers have control over the corporation. Control is defined as owning at least 80% of corporation's voting stock and at least 80% of the corporation's other classes of stock.

Since Beck and Carr together own 90% of the corporation immediately after the transfer, the transaction would be a tax-free event for both taxpayers.

354. Answer: C

X Corp's basis in the land is B's basis in the land ($40,000) plus any gain recognized by B. B's recognized gain is the lower of (1) the realized gain, or (2) the boot received. The realized gain is $30,000 ($70,000 − $40,000). The boot received is the cash of $20,000. Thus, the gain recognized is $20,000. X Corp's basis in the land is $60,000 ($40,000 + $20,000).

B's amount realized is computed as follows: The corporation received cash of $50,000 and land of $70,000 for a total of $120,000. But it also gave $20,000 cash back to B as part of the formation. This is subtracted from above, so the net value of what the corporation received is $100,000. $100,000 × 50% = $50,000, so that is the value of the stock received by B. His amount realized is $50,000 + cash received of $20,000 = $70,000.

355. Answer: B

When a shareholder transfers property to a corporation, the corporation takes the shareholders basis in the property.

Stone's basis of the property transferred into the corporation was $30,500, the adjusted basis of the computer equipment ($30,000) plus the cash ($500).

Hence, the corporation's basis in the property also would be $30,500.

356. Answer: C

The purpose of Schedule M-1 of Form 1120, *U.S. Corporation Income Tax Return* is to reconcile book income (loss) with income per the return. Certain items need to be added to and subtracted from book income to reconcile with income per the tax return.

Federal income taxes; excess capital losses over capital gains; income subject to tax not recorded on the books; and expenses recorded on the books not deducted on the return must be added to book income. Income recorded on the books but not included on the return, including tax-exempt interest, and deductions on the return not charged against the books must be subtracted from book income.

This response correctly subtracts the tax-exempt municipal bond interest from and adds federal income tax and interest expense on the debt to carry the municipal bonds to book income.

357. **Answer: C**

Taxable income is computed as follows:

Pretax book income	$543,000
Excess depreciation	(20,000)
Prepaid rental income	36,000
Fines	10,000
Municipal interest income	(25,000)
Taxable income	$544,000

358. **Answer: B**

Premiums paid on key-person life insurance policies reduce book income but not taxable income, so this is a reconciling item for Schedule M-1.

359. **Answer: B**

The purpose of Schedule M-1 of Form 1120, *U.S. Corporation Income Tax Return* is to reconcile book income (loss) with income per the return. Certain items need to be added to and subtracted from book income to reconcile with income per the tax return. Federal income taxes; excess capital losses over capital gains; income subject to tax not recorded on the books; and expenses recorded on the books not deducted on the return must be added to book income. Income recorded on the books but not included on the return, including tax-exempt interest, and deductions on the return not charged against the books must be subtracted from book income.

Both the interest incurred on loan to carry U.S. obligations and the provision for state corporation income tax are deductible for GAAP. and for income tax purposes. Hence, since both of the expenses would be included in book income and in income per the return, there is no difference to reconcile and, as a result, neither expense would appear on the Schedule M-1 of Form 1120, *U.S. Corporation Income Tax Return*.

360. **Answer: C**

If a C corporation owns less than 20% of a domestic corporation, 70% of dividends received or accrued from corporation may be deducted. A C corporation owning 20% or more but less than 80% of a domestic corporation may deduct 80% of the dividends received or accrued from the corporation. Similarly, C corporation owning 80% or more of a domestic corporation may deduct 100% of the dividends received or accrued from the corporation. However, the dividend received deduction is limited to a percentage of the taxable income of the corporation, unless the corporation sustains a net operating loss. If the corporation has a net operating loss, the dividend received deduction may be taken without limiting the deduction to a percentage of the corporation's taxable income.

Since Kelly Corp. is not affiliated with the corporation paying the dividends, it owns less than 20% of the corporation paying the dividends and, as a result, may take a 70% (or $35,000) dividend received deduction. Bad debts are deductible with no percentage limitation. However, Kelly Corp. cannot take a deduction for its bad debt expense because no bad debt was actually incurred. Instead, the expense represents an increase in allowances for doubtful accounts. The corporation's bad debt expense must be added back to net income.

Hence, Kelly Corp.'s taxable income is $345,000—net income of $300,000 minus dividend received deduction of $35,000 and plus the bad debts expense of $80,000.

361. **Answer: C**

Partnerships can use the cash method regardless of the amount of gross receipts as long as none of the partners are C corporations.

362. **Answer: D**

If a corporation filed a short-year return for 3 month, the income for that period is first multiplied by 4 (12 months/3 months) to annualize the income for 12 months. The corporate tax liability is then computed on this amount for the full 12 months. That amount is the multiplied by 3/12 to prorate for the short tax year.

363. **Answer: A**

Accounting methods for a new corporation are made on the initial tax return.

364. Answer: D

Ace Corp. would report rent revenue of $65,000. Of this amount, $55,000 (the sum of $50,000 in rental payments and $5,000 in nonrefundable rent deposits) would be cash receipts. Ace Corp. is an accrual based taxpayer. Therefore, for tax purposes, income is earned when (1) all the events have occurred to attach the taxpayer's right to receive the income and (2) the amount of income can be determined with reasonable accuracy. With respect to rent receivable, the income must have been earned to record it as a receivable.

Hence, in calculating rent revenue, the $10,000 increase in rent receivable from 2016 to 2017 would have to be added to the corporation's cash receipts.

365. Answer: C

C corporations cannot use the cash method of accounting unless their average annual gross receipts for the previous three years do not exceed $5,000,000. Once the $5,000,000 test is failed the accrual method must be used for all future tax years. Since Dart has had revenues of more than $20 million for the last three years it must use the accrual method of accounting.

366. Answer: C

When a corporation's charitable contributions exceed the limitation for deductibility in a particular year (i.e., 10% of taxable income for the year), the excess may be carried over and deducted for five years. This response states the correct carryover period and is, therefore, correct.

367. Answer: B

Taxable income before dividends and contributions is $125,000 ($200,000 − $75,000). The 10% of taxable income limitation for C corporations uses taxable income BEFORE the dividends received deduction, which is $145,000. Thus, the charitable contribution limitation is $14,500 ($145,000 × 10%).

Taxable income before dividends	$125,000
Dividends	20,000
Taxable income before special deductions	$145,000
Charitable contributions	(14,500)
Taxable income after charitable deduction	$130,500
Dividends-received deduction	(14,000)
Taxable income	$116,500

368. Answer: C

Ignoring the dividend, Brown has a net operating loss (NOL) of $200,000. Brown must also include the $100,000 of dividends in income, reducing the NOL to $100,000. Brown also is permitted to take the dividends received deduction.

Since the dividend is received from a Fortune 500 corporation it is reasonable to assume that Brown owns less than 20% of the corporation, so the dividends received deduction is 70% of the dividends received, or $70,000. This increases the NOL to $170,000.

Note that the dividends received deduction is not limited to the taxable income of Brown since Brown has a loss before the dividends received deduction.

369. Answer: B

If a C corporation owns less than 20% of a domestic corporation, 70% of dividends received or accrued from corporation may be deducted. A C corporation owning 20% or more but less than 80% of a domestic corporation may deduct 80% of the dividends received or accrued from the corporation. Similarly, C corporation owning 80% or more of a domestic corporation may deduct 100% of the dividends received or accrued from the corporation. However, the dividend received deduction is limited to a percentage of the taxable income of the corporation, unless the corporation sustains a net operating loss. If the corporation has a net operating loss, the dividend received deduction may be taken without limiting the deduction to a percentage of the corporation's taxable income.

Since it is not otherwise noted, it is assumed that Kisco Corp. owns less than 20% of the domestic corporation. Hence, Kisco may deduct 70% (or $7,000) of the dividends received, giving taxable income of $63,000. Kisco's income tax on that amount of income is $10,750 – the sum of multiplying the first $50,000 of income by the tax rate of 15% and the remaining $13,000 of income by 25 percent.

370. Answer: C

Since Ral Corp. owns less than 20% of the domestic corporation that paid the dividends (500 shares of 1,000,000 total shares), it may take a 70% dividend received deduction for the dividends.

Hence, Ral Corp. would include $300 of its dividend revenue in its taxable income. If Ral Corp. owned 20 or more but less than 80%

of the domestic corporation, it could have deducted 80% of the dividends. Similarly, if 80% or more of the corporation was owned, 100% of the dividends would be deductible. Thus, this response is correct.

371. **Answer: A**

The general business credit is a combination of several tax credits that are computed separately under each under its own set of rules. The purpose of the general business credit is to combine these credits into a single amount to provide uniform rules for the current credits that may be taken to offset a taxpayer's tax liability.

In addition, the credit provides uniform rules for carryback-carryover years. The general business credit may be carried back for 1 year, then forward for 20 years. The general business credits are composed of the: investment credit; work opportunity credit; alcohol fuel credit; incremental research credit; low-income housing credit; disabled access credit; credit for producing electricity from specified renewable resources; enhanced oil recovery credit; Indian employment credit; employer Social Security credit; empowerment zone employment credit; orphan drug credit; and excise tax payments to the Trans-Alaska Pipeline Liability Fund credit.

372. **Answer: A**

Foreign income taxes paid by a corporation may be claimed either as a deduction or as a credit, at the option of the corporation. To minimize a corporation's tax liability, it is better to claim the credit for the foreign income taxes than to deduct the taxes.

The foreign tax credit allows for a dollar-for-dollar deduction from the corporation's tax liability, whereas the deduction is from taxable income.

373. **Answer: D**

The work opportunity tax credit is 40% of the first $6,000 of wages per employee, so the maximum credit is $2,400.

374. **Answer: A**

The income source is important because U.S. source income and foreign source income impact the computation of the foreign tax credit. The foreign tax rate impacts the computation because the foreign tax credit applies when the U.S. tax rate exceeds the foreign tax rate.

375. **Answer: C**

The foreign tax credit is the lower of:

1) foreign tax paid ($39,000), or
2) U.S. tax × foreign taxable income / worldwide taxable income

$96,000 × $120,000 / $300,000 = $38,400

376. **Answer: A**

The accumulated earnings tax is a tax imposed on corporations that accumulate earnings beyond reasonable amount. This tax was imposed to prevent corporations from accumulating earnings and profits with the purpose of avoiding income tax on its shareholders.

Any corporation accumulating earnings beyond the point of reasonable needs of the business is considered to have accumulated the earnings for the tax benefit of its shareholders, unless a preponderance of the evidence indicates otherwise. Only the shareholders of closely-held corporations would tend to have the power to retain corporate earnings for their benefit. As a result, the accumulated earnings tax tends to be applied more often to closely-held corporations.

However, the number of shareholders in a corporation is not a determining factor in imposing the tax. Hence, the accumulated earnings tax may be applied regardless of the number of shareholders in a corporation.

377. **Answer: B**

For the personal holding company (PHC) tests, interest earned on tax-exempt obligations is excluded from PHC income. PHC income consists of: dividends; interest; annuities; rents; mineral, oil and gas royalties; copyright and patent royalties; produced film rents; compensation for more than 25% use of corporate property by shareholders; amounts received under personal services contracts; and amounts received from estates and trusts.

Since only the dividends should be included, this response is correct.

378. **Answer: C**

The accumulated earnings tax is a penalty tax imposed on corporations that accumulates earnings and profits for the purpose of avoiding income tax for its shareholders. The accumulated earnings tax is equivalent to 20% of the corporation's accumulated taxable income.

Accumulated taxable income is composed of taxable income adjusted downward for federal income and excess profits taxes, charitable deduction in excess of the ceiling, net capital gains and losses, and taxes of foreign countries and U.S. possessions and upward for certain corporate deductions, net operating loss deduction and capital loss carryback or carryover.

When calculating the accumulated earnings tax, corporations are given a credit, the accumulated earnings credit, of $250,000 ($150,000 for certain service corporations) plus dividends paid within the first 2 1/2 months of the corporation's tax year less accumulated earnings and profits at the end of the preceding tax year.

Hence, the maximum amount of accumulated taxable income that may be subject to the accumulated earnings tax for 2016 if Kari Corp. takes only the minimum accumulated earnings credit is $50,000. This amount is composed of $400,000 in taxable income less both a downward adjustment of $100,000 for federal income taxes and the $250,000 accumulated earnings credit.

379. Answer: A

Domestic and foreign corporations satisfying the personal holding company stock ownership and income tests are personal holding companies. As such, the corporation will be subject a 15% penalty tax on undistributed personal holding company income. The stock ownership test is satisfied if, at some time during the corporation's tax year, 50% or more of the corporation's stock was directly or indirectly owned by five or fewer individuals.

An individual indirectly owns stock if it is owned by the individual's family or partner. Family includes the individual's brothers, sisters, spouse and lineal descendants and ancestors. An individual will not be considered to be the constructive owner of the stock owned by nephews, cousins, uncles, aunts, and any of his/hers spouses relatives. Constructive ownership also may exist if the individual is a partner in a partnership or the beneficiary of an estate that is a shareholder. The income test is satisfied if 60% or more of the corporation's adjusted ordinary gross income is personal holding company income.

With 450 shares, Edwards already directly owns 45% of Zero Corp.'s outstanding stock. If an estate where Edwards is the beneficiary owns the remainder of the corporation's 200 shares of stock, Edwards would directly or indirectly own 5% of the corporation. An ownership

exceeding the 50% direct or indirect ownership percentage is needed to satisfy the stock ownership test.

Hence, Zero Corp. could be a personal holding company if the remaining 200 shares were owned by an estate where Edwards is the beneficiary. Each response given to this question satisfies the stock ownership test for a personal holding company because, in each response, five or fewer individuals would own more than 50% of the corporation's stock. However, this response is the best as it concentrates over 50% ownership under the control of one individual.

380. Answer: A

Personal holding companies are required to pay taxes on their undistributed personal holding company income. Personal holding company income and undistributed personal holding company income differ. Undistributed personal holding company income is computed by adjusting taxable income, then subtracting the dividends paid deduction. Deductions are made from taxable income for federal and foreign taxes; charitable contributions (based on a higher percentage limitation than the 10% of income limitation imposed on corporations); and excess capital gains (i.e., any excess net long-term capital gain over net short-term capital loss for the tax year).

Corporate deductions for dividends received and any net operating loss deduction must be added back, and business expenses and depreciation exceeding rental income may have to be added back. Hence, both the federal income taxes and the net long-term capital gain should be deducted from taxable income by Kane in determining undistributed personal holding company income prior to the dividend-paid deduction.

381. Answer: D

A C corporation owning 80% or more of a domestic corporation may deduct 100% of the dividends received or accrued from the corporation. Owning 20% but less than 80% of a domestic corporation allows for an 80% deduction of dividends received or accrued from the corporation. An ownership percentage of less than 20% leads to a deduction of 70% of the dividends-received. However, the dividend received deduction is limited to a percentage of the corporation's taxable income, unless the corporation sustains a net operating loss. If the corporation has a net operating loss, the dividend-received deduction may be taken without limiting the deduction to a percentage of the corporation's taxable income.

Since Portal Corp. owns 80% of Sal Corp., Portal Corp. may deduct all of the dividends received from Sal Corp. and, as a result, have no dividend income.

382. **Answer: D**

When filing a consolidated return, the intercompany dividends between the parent and its subsidiaries are not taxable. To be permitted to file a consolidated return, the parent and its subsidiaries must be members of an affiliated group.

Corporations qualify as members of an affiliated group by having a common parent that directly owns at least 80% of the total voting stock and at least 80% of the total value of the stock in at least one other includible corporation. In addition, a minimum of one of the other includible corporations must own at least 80% in each of the remaining includible corporations. The primary advantages of filing a consolidated return are that: (1) intercompany dividends are excludable from taxable income; (2) losses of one affiliated member offset gains of another member; and (3) intercompany profits are deferred until realized.

383. **Answer: A**

The primary advantages of filing a consolidated return are that: (1) losses of one affiliated member offset gains of another member; (2) intercompany dividends are excludable from taxable income; and (3) intercompany profits are deferred until realized.

Since this response indicates that the operating losses of one group member may be used to offset operating profits of the other members, it is correct.

384. **Answer: D**

A and C are an affiliated group because A owns at least 80% of C and A is the parent company. B and D may not file a consolidated return because S corporations are not eligible to be in an affiliated group.

385. **Answer: D**

When filing a consolidated return, the intercompany dividends between the parent and its subsidiaries are not taxable. To be permitted to file a consolidated return, the parent and its subsidiaries must be members of an affiliated group. Corporations qualify as members of an affiliated group by having a common parent that directly owns at least

80% of the total voting stock and at least 80% of the total value of the stock in at least one other includible corporation. In addition, a minimum of one of the other includible corporations must own at least 80% in each of the remaining includible corporations. The primary advantages of filing a consolidated return are that: (1) intercompany dividends are excludable from taxable income; (2) losses of one affiliated member offset gains of another member; and (3) intercompany profits are deferred until realized. Hence, the dividends are fully deductible and this response is, therefore, correct.

386. **Answer: C**

When accumulated E&P is negative and current E&P is positive, distributions are treated as dividends to the extent of current E&P. Thus, $10,000 is reported as dividend income and the other $5,000 is a return of capital.

387. **Answer: C**

Corporate distributions to shareholders are taxable to the shareholder as dividend income to the extent earnings and profits, current and accumulated. Distributions in excess of earnings and profits are treated as returns of capital that are nontaxable except to the extent that the distribution exceeds the shareholders basis in the property.

Since Kee Corp. had current earnings of $10,000, the shareholders would be viewed as receiving $10,000 in dividend income. The remaining $20,000 of the distribution would be treated as a return of capital. Distributions are deemed to be paid from current earnings and profits and then from accumulated earnings and profits.

388. **Answer: A**

For dividends, the amount distributed is the fair market value of the property received less any liabilities assumed by the shareholder, or $35,000 ($38,000 − $3,000). Fox would have $35,000 of dividend income since earnings and profits is at least this amount. However, the basis in the property received as a taxable dividend is always the fair market value of the property, or $38,000.

389. **Answer: B**

Corporations recognize taxable gains but not losses from nonliquidating distribution of appreciable property to their shareholders. The transaction is viewed as if the corporation sold the property to its shareholders at its fair market value on the day of the distribution.

Hence, Nyle Corp. would recognize a gain of $1,100, the fair market value of the Beta stock (100 shares multiplied by $20 per share) less its basis in the stock (100 shares multiplied by $9 per share).

390. **Answer: C**

Dividend income must be reported for the distribution to the extent of Webster's current and accumulated earnings and profits ($70,000). The amount of the distribution is the cash of $20,000 plus the fair market value ($60,000) of the property distributed, or $80,000. This distribution is taxed as $70,000 of dividend income with the remaining $10,000 treated as a return of the shareholders' bases in their stock.

391. **Answer: D**

Shareholders of a distribution in complete liquidation of a corporation receive capital gain or loss treatment just as if they hold their stock.

392. **Answer: A**

Expenses related to a liquidation are deductible by the liquidating corporation.

393. **Answer: A**

Noncorporate shareholders treat the gain on a redemption of stock that qualifies as a partial liquidation of the distributing corporation as a capital gain, just as if they had sold their stock. Corporate shareholders receive dividend treatment on a partial liquidation.

394. **Answer: A**

If stock of a subsidiary is liquidated by its parent company, any realized gain on the transaction is, in general, not recognized. The realized gain to parent is $150 ($250 property received – $100 basis). The recognized gain is zero.

395. **Answer: D**

This answer is correctly calculated as follows: Cash received $33,000 less adjusted basis of $16,000 = $17,000 capital gain. Amounts received by a shareholder in a distribution in complete liquidation of a corporation shall be treated as in full payment in exchange for the stock. If property is received in a distribution in complete liquidation, and if gain or loss is recognized on receipt of such property, then the basis of the property in the hands of the distributee shall be the fair market value of such property at the time of the distribution.

396. **Answer: C**

Tax attributes of the subsidiary transfer to the parent after a tax-free liquidation of the subsidiary into the parent.

397. **Answer: B**

No gain or loss is recognized by a corporation that is a party to a qualified reorganization in which stock is exchanged solely for stock or securities of another corporation that is also a party to the reorganization.

As this reorganization is a Type B: Stock for Stock transaction, the reorganization is tax-free.

398. **Answer: D**

If taxpayer receives stocks or securities under a plan of reorganization from a corporation included in the reorganization, the taxpayer does not recognize a gain or loss from the transaction. However, if the taxpayer receives boot, the transaction is taxable up to the amount of the boot.

Since Gow received the Rook Corp. stock solely in exchange for his Lad Corp. stock under a plan of reorganization and did not receive any boot, the transaction would be tax-free for Gow.

399. **Answer: B**

The 80% control test is met since 90% of ABC's voting stock is being acquired. XYZ is using its voting stock as required for B reorganizations.

400. **Answer: C**

If property is purchased in one state but used in a different state, the state of use is likely to impose a use tax for the use of the property in its jurisdiction.

401. **Answer: C**

Only affiliated corporations that have Nexus with State M will be included in the state consolidated income tax return for State M.

402. **Answer: B**

$10,000/($10,000 + $40,000) = 20%.

403. **Answer: D**

Business income is generated from the business's regular operations, or from the sale of property that is an integral part of the business. Therefore, the royalty income could be business income

404. Answer: A

The starting point for computing state taxable income is $250,000. Adjustments are:

State income taxes	+ $15,000
Municipal interest income	+ $10,000
Excess federal depreciation	+ $7,000
U.S. Treasury interest income	−$25,000
State taxable income	$257,000

405. Answer: C

Income from the sale of personalty is determined based on the location of the property.

406. Answer: B

Since the $90,000 earned income was excludable from U.S. income the $18,000 in Spanish taxes is not eligible for the foreign tax credit. The $4,000 related to the interest income is eligible.

407. Answer: B

The $90,000 of salary is completely excluded. Foreign-earned income from personal services is excluded up to 102,100 in 2017. The housing is excludable to the extent it exceeds 16% × $101,100, or $16,336. This excess is $23,664 ($40,000 − $16,336). However, the housing exclusion may never exceed $14,294 in 2017, so the includible housing income is $25,706 ($40,000 − $14,294). The interest income is fully includible as is the U.S. source earned income of $60,000. Therefore, includible income is $25,706 + $20,000 + $60,000, or $105,706.

408. Answer: D

Foreign currency exchange gains and losses resulting from the normal course of business operations are ordinary, not capital.

409. Answer: B

$25,000, but not to exceed the foreign tax credit limitation of $80,000/($120,000 + $80,000) × $61,250 = $24,500.

410. Answer: C

Engaging in insubstantial nonexempt activities will not cause an exempt organization to lose its exempt status. However, exempt organizations are strictly prohibited from engaging in political campaigns and activities.

411. Answer: A

The charitable entity must affirm that its activities will be limited to its charitable purposes.

412. Answer: D

Neither activity produces unrelated business income because the activities generating the revenue relate to the tax-exempt purpose of the organization. (Articles were made as part of the rehabilitation process and the store was being operated for the purpose of creating a therapeutic process for the participants.)

413. Answer: A

A *private foundation* is a tax-exempt organization which receives less than one-third of its annual support from its members and the general public. Therefore, public charities that solicit broad public support do not meet this definition.

414. Answer: C

Private foundations must file Form 990-PF annually.

415. Answer: A

A partner's initial basis in a partnership is equal to the amount of cash that the partner contributed plus the partner's adjusted basis for property when contributed. If the partnership assumes indebtedness from the contributed property, the contributing partner's basis is reduced by the amount of indebtedness assumed by the other partners. Strom's basis in the contributed property was $16,000.

However, the property was subject to a $24,000 mortgage. Strom's partners assumed $18,000 of the mortgage, $24,000 multiplied by 75% (the percentage of the partnership not owned by Strom). Subtracting the $16,000 in liabilities assumed by the other partners, gives Strom a negative basis.

However, a partner's basis in the partnership's interest cannot be negative. Thus, Strom's basis in the partnership is zero.

416. Answer: C

Partners increase their bases in their partnership interests by their respective share of the partnership's debt, both recourse and nonrecourse.

417. **Answer: C**

   The holding period of a partnership interest acquired in exchange for a contributed capital asset begins on the date the partner's holding period of the capital asset began.

418. **Answer: C**

   When an individual contributes services to a partnership for a capital interest in the partnership, the individual reports taxable income equal to the fair market value of the transferred capital interest.

   Capital interests received are treated as guaranteed payments, which means the capital interest is viewed a salary payment and, as such, reported as ordinary income by the partner.

   Since the fair market value of the partnership's net assets is $100,000 and Kelly contributed services for a 10% interest in the partnership, Kelly must recognize $10,000 of ordinary income.

419. **Answer: A**

   A partner's initial basis in a partnership is equal to the amount of cash that the partner contributed plus the partner's adjusted basis for property when contributed. If the partnership assumes indebtedness from the contributed property, the contributing partner's basis is reduced by the amount of indebtedness assumed by the other partners.

   Pert contributed land with an adjusted basis of $12,000. However, the land was subject to a mortgage of $4,000, which was assumed by the partnership.

   Since Pert has a 50% interest, the other partners assumed $2,000 of the mortgage. Thus, Pert's adjusted basis in the partnership interest is $10,000, the $12,000 adjusted basis of the land contributed less the $2,000 of the mortgage assumed by the other partners.

420. **Answer: B**

   This is a true statement.

421. **Answer: C**

   Passive activity losses are the amount that total losses from passive activities exceed total gains from passive activities. The characterization of a partner's share of the partnership's income as passive or nonpassive depends on the partner's participation in the partnership's income earning activities.

Since Wolf did not materially participate in the partnership business, his share of the partnership's operating loss, $5,000, is considered a loss from a passive activity. Passive income does not include portfolio income.

As a result, Wolf's share of the $20,000 in interest income would not be passive. Therefore, since Wolf had no gains from passive activities to offset the loss from his share of the partnership's operating loss, Wolf would have a passive loss of $5,000, equal to his share of the partnership's operating loss.

422. **Answer: C**

   At-risk rules limit the amount of loss deductions from investment activities to the amount the taxpayer had at-risk. The amount that a taxpayer had at risk is the amount of cash and basis of property contributed to an activity. Borrowed amounts are considered to be at risk to the extent that the taxpayer is personally liable for repayment. At-risk rules do not apply to partnerships, but the rules do apply to the individual partners.

   Passive activity rules prevent the offsetting of nonpassive income with passive losses and credits from passive activities. Passive activity rules do not apply to partnerships, but the rules do apply to the individual partners.

   This response correctly indicates that at-risk and passive activity rules apply in determining a partner's deduction for that partner's share of partnership losses.

423. **Answer: D**

   Basis is computed as follows:

Contribution	$100,000
25% of income	20,000
Distribution	(10,000)
	$110,000

424. **Answer: C**

   Dale's basis is computed as follows:

Cash contributed	$10,000
Equipment debt (50%)	5,000
Taxable income (50%)	7,500
Tax-exempt income (50%)	1,000
Debt reduction (50%)	(2,000)
Distribution	(3,000)
Ending basis	$18,500

425. **Answer: C**

Guaranteed payments from a partnership for the services of a partner are treated as salary payments and, as a result, receive similar treatment under the Internal Revenue Code. Therefore, in contrast to provisions applying to other withdrawals of assets from partnerships by partners, guaranteed payments are deductible by the partnership. The deduction for guaranteed payments may create an ordinary loss for the partnership. Guaranteed payments are required to be reported separately from the partner's share of the partnership's income on the partner's K-1.

Thus, guaranteed payments made by a partnership to partners for services rendered to the partnership, that are deductible business expenses under the Internal Revenue Code, are deductible expenses on the *U.S. Partnership Return of Income*, Form 1065, in order to arrive at partnership income (loss) and included on schedules K-1 to be taxed as ordinary income to the partners.

426. **Answer: D**

Guaranteed payments to partners from their partnership for partnership services or capital are not treated as partnership distributions. Instead, the payments are treated as salary payments to employees or interest payments.

Hence, White would have to include the $3,000 guaranteed payment on his 2017 tax return. In addition, since partnerships are pass-through for tax purposes, White must include his share of the partnership's income on his tax return. White share of the partnership's income would be $10,000 ($30,000 in partnership income multiplied by White's 1/3 share in profits and losses).

Therefore, the total amount that White must include from Rapid Partnership as taxable income in his 2017 tax return is $13,000, the sum of the $3,000 in guaranteed payments made to White and White's share of the partnership's income.

427. **Answer: A**

Guaranteed payments from a partnership for the services of a partner are treated as salary payments and, as a result, are made without regard to the partner's share of the partnership's income.

Thus, a guaranteed payment by a partnership to a partner for services rendered may include an agreement to pay a salary of $5,000 monthly without regard to partnership income and may not include an agreement to pay 25% interest in partnership profits.

428. **Answer: C**

Under the Internal Revenue Code sections pertaining to partnerships, guaranteed payments are payments to partners for services or the use of capital without regard to partnership income.

Thus, guaranteed payments are treated similarly to salary payments to the partner, not as partnership distributions.

429. **Answer: C**

The realized gain on the sale of the assets is $3,000 ($18,000 – $15,000 basis in assets). Abe's built in gain on the contribution is $5,000. The amount of gain allocated to Abe is the lower of the realized gain or built-in gain, so $3,000 is the allocation.

430. **Answer: B**

A partner's basis in property received in a nonliquidating distribution is the same as the partnership's basis immediately before the distribution. However, the partner's basis in the property may not exceed his/her basis in the partnership less any cash received in the distribution.

Hart received property with a basis of $12,000 ($5,000 in cash plus the partnership's basis in the land of $7,000). However, his basis in the partnership interest is $9,000, so the basis in the property distributed must be limited to this amount. Since the distribution included $5,000 in cash, Hart's basis in the land is $4,000 ($9,000 – $5,000).

431. **Answer: D**

A partner receiving a distribution from a partnership usually does not recognize a gain or loss. Gains are recognized only to the extent the partner receives an amount of cash exceeding his/her adjusted basis in the partnership interest. Gains from property distributions other than cash are not recognized until the partner sells or disposes of the property. Therefore, Stone does not recognize any gain or loss from the distribution.

432. **Answer: C**

The partner must report $25,000 of ordinary income and the $10,000 guaranteed payment. The distribution does not generate additional income since the partner has sufficient basis to absorb it.

433. **Answer: B**

If a partner receives property from the partnership in a nonliquidating distribution, the partner assumes a basis in the property equal to the partnership's basis in the property immediately before the distribution. However, the basis assumed may not exceed the partner's interest in the partnership less any cash received in the distribution. The partnership's basis in the land distributed to Hart was $9,000. However, Hart would not assume this amount as his basis in the land because it exceeds his interest in the partnership less any cash received in the distribution. Thus, Hart's basis would be limited to $6,000, his interest in the partnership of $30,000 less the $24,000 of cash received.

434. **Answer: B**

The basis to a partner of property distributed "in kind" in complete liquidation of the partner's interest is the adjusted basis of the partner's interest reduced by any cash distributed to the partner in the same transaction.

435. **Answer: A**

In computing the amount realized from the sale of a partner's interest in the partnership, the partner must consider their share of the partnership's liabilities along with the cash or value of property received. Thus, Carr's share of the partnership's liabilities, $20,000 ($60,000 in total liabilities multiplied by Carr's one-third interest in the partnership), must be included in determining the amount realized by Carr.

Therefore, the total amount realized by Carr on the sale of his partnership interest is $174,000, the sum of the $154,000 in cash received and Carr's $20,000 share of the partnership's liabilities.

436. **Answer: B**

For tax purposes, a partnership terminates when it stops doing business as a partnership or 50% or more interest in partnership capital and profits is exchanged within 12 months. When the partnership's business and financial operations are continued by other members, there is a deemed distribution of assets to the remaining partners and the purchaser and a hypothetical recontribution of assets to a new partnership.

Since Poe sold her 30% interest on February 4, 2017, when Dean sold his 25% interest on December 20, 2017 over 50% of the partnership had been exchanged within 12 months. As a result, Able Partnership terminated on

December 20, 2017, the date that over 50% of the partnership's interest had been exchanged within past 12 months.

437. **Answer: B**

"Hot assets" for a partnership include ONLY inventory and unrealized receivables.

438. **Answer: D**

If a partner sells his/her interest in the partnership, the partner recognizes a capital gain equal to the amount that the payment exceeds the partner's adjusted basis in the partnership.

Clark's adjusted basis in the partnership is $40,000 immediately before the sale. The assumption of Clark's share of the partnership's liabilities is viewed as a distribution to Clark. Thus, Clark's adjusted basis must be reduced by the assumption of his share of the partnership's liabilities, putting his adjusted basis at $15,000. The payment of $30,000 received by Clark exceeds his adjusted basis of $15,000 by the amount of $15,000. Hence, Clark must recognize a capital gain of $15,000.

439. **Answer: D**

If a partner sells or exchanges his/her partnership interest and the partnership has either unrealized receivables or substantially appreciated inventory, the partner recognizes an ordinary gain to the extent that the amount realized by the partner due to the unrealized receivables or substantially appreciated inventory is greater than the partner's basis in the items.

When Carr sold his partnership interest in Allen, Baker and Carr, the partnership had unrealized receivables. The amount realized by Carr due to the unrealized receivables was $140,000, the partnership's total unrealized receivables of $420,000 multiplied by Carr's one-third ownership interest.

Carr does not have any basis in the unrealized receivables (indicating that none of the receivables have been collected). Hence, Carr must report an ordinary gain of $140,000, the $140,000 realized by Carr due to the unrealized receivables less Carr's basis in the receivables, which is zero.

440. **Answer: C**

Individuals, estates, and certain trusts may be shareholders in an S corporation.

441. **Answer: C**

The shareholder limit is 100 and members of the same family count as one shareholder.

442. **Answer: D**

Ace Corp.'s S election would be recognized as of January 1, 2017. An S election made by the 15th day of the 3rd month of the tax year is effective for that year. To be retroactive, the corporation had to be eligible on all days in the tax year prior to the day of the election and all persons that were shareholders before that day, but not on that day, must consent to the election.

443. **Answer: D**

To be eligible for S corporation status, a corporation must have 100 or less shareholders. All members of a family and their estates are treated as a single shareholder.

444. **Answer: C**

Once a corporation's S status is revoked or terminated, the corporation must wait five years before making a new S election, in the absence of IRS consent to an earlier election.

445. **Answer: A**

The amount of the nonseparately stated income from Manning Corp. that should be reported on Kane's 2017 tax return should be Kane's pro rata share of the corporation's income.

Since Kane owned 100% of Manning and sold a 25% share on the 40th day of Manning's tax year, Kane's portion of the income would be calculated with respect to 100% ownership for the first 40 days of the corporation's tax year and 75% ownership for the remainder of the tax year.

Kane's share of Manning's income from the first 40 days of the corporation's tax year would be $8,000 = 100% ownership × (40 days/365 days) × $73,000 in income. Kane's share of the corporation's income for the remainder of the year would be $48,750 = 75% ownership × (325 days/365 days) × $73,000 in income).

Hence, the amount of the nonseparately stated income from Manning Corp. that should be reported on Kane's 2017 tax return is $56,750 – the sum of $8,000 from the first 40 days and $48,750 from the remainder of the tax year.

446. **Answer: D**

Collectible gain is taxed at a maximum rate of 28% and can be offset with collectible losses, so it needs to be separately stated.

447. **Answer: C**

Once the S corporation completes the steps necessary to become a C corporation, it will be allowed to retain its June 30 year-end since C corporations are not subject to the tax-year limitations to which partnerships and S corporations are. However, C corporations cannot use the cash method of accounting unless their average annual gross receipts for the previous three years do not exceed $5,000,000. Once the $5,000,000 test is failed the accrual method must be used for all future tax years. Since this corporation has had revenues of more than $10 million it must use the accrual method of accounting.

448. **Answer: C**

The distributive share to Carson would be $400,000 × 40% = $160,000.

449. **Answer: C**

65,000 − 10,000 + 6,000 + 4,000 − 9,000 = 56,000. The question is asking how the municipal interest income effects basis as well as the effect of the net capital losses.

1. Stock purchases
2. Capital contributions
3. Nonseparately stated income items
4. Separately stated income items

Decreases
1. Nonseparately stated computed loss
2. Separately stated loss and deduction items
3. Distributions not reported as income by shareholder
4. Nondeductible expenses of corporation

Separately stated items.
Tax-exempt income
Capital gains and losses
Section 1231 gains and losses
Charitable contributions
Passive gains, losses, and credits
Portfolio income
Foreign income
Investment income and expense
Depletion
Section 179 expense

450. **Answer: D**

The built in gains tax applies only when an existing C corporation makes an S corporation election. The built in gains tax does not apply when a sole proprietorship makes an S election, so the correct answer is $0.

451. **Answer: D**

An S corporation shareholder increases/decreases her basis in the S corporation stock by her share of the corporation's income (taxable and nontaxable) and expenses (deductible and nondeductible). Distributions also reduce the stock basis. Sandy's basis is reduced to $40,000 for the distribution ($60,000 − $20,000) and is increased for all three income items for an ending basis of $85,000 ($40,000 + $30,000 + $5,000 + $10,000).

452. **Answer: B**

$6,500 is correct. His/her portion of income items of the corporation that are separately computed and passed through to shareholder, including tax-exempt income, increases the stock basis of each S corporation shareholder. Basis is calculated as follows:

Beginning Basis	$12,000
Plus 50% profits	40.500(81,000 × 50%)
Plus 50% exempt	5,000(10,000 × 50%)
Less distributions	(51,000)
Ending Basis	$6,500

453. **Answer: C**

A distribution from an S corporation that has no accumulated earnings and profits reduces the basis of a shareholder's stock. If the payment exceeds the shareholder's basis in the stock, it is viewed as a payment in exchange for stock.

454. **Answer: C**

Calculate basis in an S corporation as follows: The current basis of $25,000 is increased by the $1,000 of income to $26,000, then reduced for the distribution of $30,000 which would reduce the basis to $0 and produce a $4,000 gain. The $3,000 loss is suspended until there is more basis in the future.

If the amount of the distribution exceeds the adjusted basis of the stock, such excess shall be treated as gain from the sale or exchange of property.

455. **Answer: B**

$42,000 is correct as follows:

Taxable interest	$65,000
Estate disbursements	
Administrative expenses attributable to taxable income (2)	(14,000)
Charitable contributions from gross income to a public charity, made under the terms of the will (1)	(9,000)
Estate's distributable net income (DNI)	$42,000

1. An estate qualifies for a deduction for amounts of gross income paid or permanently set aside for qualified charitable organizations. The adjusted gross income limits for individuals do not apply. However, to be deductible by an estate, the contribution must be specifically provided for in the decedent's will. If there is no will, or if the will makes no provision for the payment to a charitable organization, then a deduction will not be allowed even though all of the beneficiaries may agree to the gift.

2. Expenses of administering an estate can be deducted either from the gross estate in figuring the federal estate tax on Form 706 or from the estate's gross income in figuring the estate's income tax on Form 1041. However, these expenses cannot be claimed for both estate tax and income tax purposes.

456. **Answer: C**

Ordinary and necessary administration expenses paid by the fiduciary of an estate are deductible either in computing the estate's taxable income for income tax purposes or in computing the decedent's taxable estate for estate tax purposes. For the deduction to be taken for income tax purposes, the estate tax deduction must be waived. This response correctly states that administration expenses are deductible on the fiduciary income tax return only if the estate tax deduction is waived for these expenses.

457. **Answer: D**

Estates may use either the calendar year or a fiscal year for its tax year. Trusts, except those that are tax-exempt, are required to use the calendar year for its tax year. This response correctly indicates that estates are not required to use the calendar year as its tax year and that trusts, except those that are tax-exempt, are required to use the calendar year.

458. **Answer: C**

The amount of income recognized by the beneficiaries is the lower of the amount distributed ($150,000) or distributable net income ($120,000). Thus, Kent and Lind will recognize income of $120,000. Since they received total distributions of $150,000, the income recognized is 80% ($120,000/$150,000) of the amount received. Thus, Lind's income is 80% × $90,000, or $72,000.

459. **Answer: C**

The foreign tax credit is the lower of:

1) foreign tax paid ($39,000), or
2) U.S. tax × foreign taxable income / worldwide taxable income

$96,000 × $120,000 / $300,000 = $38,400

460. **Answer: A**

The income source is important because U.S. source income and foreign source income impact the computation of the foreign tax credit. The foreign tax rate impacts the computation because the foreign tax credit applies when the U.S. tax rate exceeds the foreign tax rate.

461. **Answer: A**

The general business credit is a combination of several tax credits that are computed separately under each under its own set of rules. The purpose of the general business credit is to combine these credits into a single amount to provide uniform rules for the current credits that may be taken to offset a taxpayer's tax liability.

In addition, the credit provides uniform rules for carryback-carryover years. The general business credit may be carried back for 1 year, then forward for 20 years. The general business credits are composed of the: investment credit; work opportunity credit; alcohol fuel credit; incremental research credit; low-income housing credit; disabled access credit; credit for producing electricity from specified renewable resources; enhanced oil recovery credit; Indian employment credit; employer Social Security credit; empowerment zone employment credit; orphan drug credit; and excise tax payments to the Trans-Alaska Pipeline Liability Fund credit.

462. **Answer: D**

The work opportunity tax credit is 40% of the first $6,000 of wages per employee, so the maximum credit is $2,400.

463. **Answer: A**

Foreign income taxes paid by a corporation may be claimed either as a deduction or as a credit, at the option of the corporation. To minimize a corporation's tax liability, it is better to claim the credit for the foreign income taxes than to deduct the taxes.

The foreign tax credit allows for a dollar-for-dollar deduction from the corporation's tax liability, whereas the deduction is from taxable income.

464. **Answer: A**

Since his income tax rate is declining, he will save 20% on any income deferred from the 50% tax rate in Year 1 to the 30% tax rate in Year 2.

465. **Answer: C**

Her tax savings is $3,000 ($12,000 × 25%) since the contribution is deductible. Therefore, her net cost is $9,000 ($12,000 − $9,000).

466. **Answer: D**

2% miscellaneous itemized deductions are not deductible for AMT purposes so increasing these will not reduce the AMT.

467. **Answer: B**

When long-term capital gain property is contributed to a qualified charity, the fair market value of the property can be deducted as a charitable contribution.

468. **Answer: C**

If Orleans gives the property to his friend, the $20,000 loss disappears since the friend's loss basis in the land will be its fair market value of $50,000. Therefore, Orleans should sell the land so he can recognize the loss. He can then contribute the cash from the sale to his friend.

469. **Answer: A**

The owner's basis is increased for her
distributive share of profits and losses for
S corporations, partnerships, and limited
liability companies. However, owner's basis
is not affected by the debt of S corporations,
while it is for partnerships and limited liability
companies.

470. **Answer: D**

The cost of health and accident insurance
premiums paid on behalf of the greater than 2%
S corporation shareholder-employee (hereafter
referred to as "shareholder") is deductible by
the S corporation and reportable as additional
compensation to the shareholder. Note that the
problem indicates that "additional" premium
for family coverage is $7,200, so this must be
added to the $4,800 to get the total premium of
$12,000.

471. **Answer: C**

In an LLC, a member can participate in
management and have limited liability.
In a partnership, if a partner participates
in management she must be a general
partner, and general partners have
unlimited liability.

472. **Answer: D**

This statement is false. Since S corporation
income flows directly to the shareholders, the
corporation is not subject to the AMT.

473. **Answer: C**

Trusts and estates can carryback or carryforward
a net operating loss.

Task-Based Simulations

Ethics, Professional Responsibilities, and Federal Tax Procedures

Ethics and Responsibilities in Tax Practice

Internal Revenue Code and Regulations Related to Tax Return Preparers

Task-Based Simulation 1

Preparer's Responsibility		
	Authoritative Literature	
		Help

A CPA sole practitioner has tax preparers' responsibilities when preparing tax returns for clients.

Items 1 through 9 each represent an independent factual situation in which a CPA sole practitioner has prepared and signed the taxpayer's income tax return. For each item, select from the following list the correct response regarding the tax preparer's responsibilities. A response may be selected once, more than once, or not at all.

Answer List

P.   The tax preparer's action constitutes an act of tax preparer misconduct subject to the Internal Revenue Code penalty.

E.   The Internal Revenue Service will examine the facts and circumstances to determine whether the reasonable cause exception applies; the good faith exception applies; or both exceptions apply.

N.   The tax preparer's action does **not** constitute an act of tax preparer misconduct.

	(P)	(E)	(N)
1. The tax preparer disclosed taxpayer income tax return information under an order from a state court, without the taxpayer's consent.	○	○	○
2. The tax preparer relied on the advice of an advisory preparer to calculate the taxpayer's tax liability. The tax preparer believed that the advisory preparer was competent and that the advice was reasonable. Based on the advice, the taxpayer had understated income tax liability.	○	○	○
3. The tax preparer did not charge a separate fee for the tax return preparation and paid the taxpayer the refund shown on the tax return less a discount. The tax preparer negotiated the actual refund check for the tax preparer's own account after receiving power of attorney from the taxpayer.	○	○	○
4. The tax preparer relied on information provided by the taxpayer regarding deductible travel expenses. The tax preparer believed that the taxpayer's information was correct but inquired about the existence of the travel expense records. The tax preparer was satisfied by the taxpayer's representations that the taxpayer had adequate records for the deduction. Based on this information, the income tax liability was understated.	○	○	○
5. The taxpayer provided the tax preparer with a detailed check register to compute business expenses. The tax preparer knowingly overstated the expenses on the income tax return.	○	○	○
6. The tax preparer disclosed taxpayer income tax return information during a quality review conducted by CPAs. The tax preparer maintained a record of the review.	○	○	○

7. The tax preparer relied on incorrect instructions on an IRS tax form that were contrary to the regulations. The tax preparer was not aware of the regulations or the IRS announcement pointing out the error. The understatement was immaterial as a result of the isolated error. ○ ○ ○

8. The tax preparer used income tax return information without the taxpayer's consent to solicit additional business. ○ ○ ○

9. The tax preparer knowingly deducted the expenses of the taxpayer's personal domestic help as wages paid in the taxpayer's business on the taxpayer's income tax return. ○ ○ ○

Task-Based Simulation 1 Solution

Preparer's Responsibility

Authoritative Literature

Help

	(P)	(E)	(N)
1. The tax preparer disclosed taxpayer income tax return information under an order from a state court, without the taxpayer's consent.	○	○	●
2. The tax preparer relied on the advice of an advisory preparer to calculate the taxpayer's tax liability. The tax preparer believed that the advisory preparer was competent and that the advice was reasonable. Based on the advice, the taxpayer had understated income tax liability.	○	●	○
3. The tax preparer did not charge a separate fee for the tax return preparation and paid the taxpayer the refund shown on the tax return less a discount. The tax preparer negotiated the actual refund check for the tax preparer's own account after receiving power of attorney from the taxpayer.	●	○	○
4. The tax preparer relied on information provided by the taxpayer regarding deductible travel expenses. The tax preparer believed that the taxpayer's information was correct but inquired about the existence of the travel expense records. The tax preparer was satisfied by the taxpayer's representations that the taxpayer had adequate records for the deduction. Based on this information, the income tax liability was understated.	○	○	●
5. The taxpayer provided the tax preparer with a detailed check register to compute business expenses. The tax preparer knowingly overstated the expenses on the income tax return.	●	○	○
6. The tax preparer disclosed taxpayer income tax return information during a quality review conducted by CPAs. The tax preparer maintained a record of the review.	○	○	●
7. The tax preparer relied on incorrect instructions on an IRS tax form that were contrary to the regulations. The tax preparer was not aware of the regulations or the IRS announcement pointing out the error. The understatement was immaterial as a result of the isolated error.	○	●	○
8. The tax preparer used income tax return information without the taxpayer's consent to solicit additional business.	●	○	○
9. The tax preparer knowingly deducted the expenses of the taxpayer's personal domestic help as wages paid in the taxpayer's business on the taxpayer's income tax return.	●	○	○

Explanations

1. **(N)** A return preparer will be subject to penalty if the preparer knowingly or recklessly discloses information furnished in connection with the preparation of a tax return, unless such information is furnished for quality or peer review, under an administrative order by a regulatory agency, or pursuant to an order of a court.

2. **(E)** The reasonable cause and good faith exception applies if the return preparer relied in good faith on the advice of an advisory preparer who the return preparer had reason to believe was competent to render such advice.

3. **(P)** A return preparer will be subject to penalty if the preparer endorses or otherwise negotiates (directly or through an agent) any refund check issued to a taxpayer (other than the preparer) if the preparer was the preparer of the return or claim for refund that gave rise to the refund check.

4. **(N)** A return preparer may in good faith rely without verification upon information furnished by the client or third parties, and is not required to audit, examine, or review books, records, or documents in order to independently verify the taxpayer's information. If the IRS requires supporting documentation as a condition for deductibility, the return preparer should make appropriate inquiries to determine whether the condition has been met.

5. **(P)** A return preparer will be subject to penalty if there is a willful attempt in any manner to understate the tax liability of any taxpayer. A preparer is considered to have willfully attempted to understate liability if the preparer disregards information furnished by the taxpayer to wrongfully reduce the tax liability of the taxpayer.

6. **(N)** A return preparer will be subject to penalty if the preparer knowingly or recklessly discloses information furnished in connection with the preparation of a tax return, unless such information is furnished for quality or peer review, under an administrative order by a regulatory agency, or pursuant to an order of a court.

7. **(E)** Under these facts, a position taken on a return that is consistent with incorrect instructions does not satisfy the realistic possibility standard. However, if the preparer relied on the incorrect instructions and was not aware of the announcement or regulations, the reasonable cause and good faith exception may apply, depending upon the facts and circumstances.

8. **(P)** A return preparer will be subject to penalty if the preparer knowingly or recklessly discloses information furnished in connection with the preparation of a tax return, unless such information is furnished for quality or peer review, under an administrative order by a regulatory agency, or pursuant to an order of a court.

9. **(P)** A return preparer will be subject to penalty if there is a willful attempt in any manner to understate the tax liability of any taxpayer or there is a reckless or intentional disregard of rules or regulations. The penalty will apply if a preparer knowingly deducts the expenses of the taxpayer's domestic help as wages paid in the taxpayer's business.

Business Law

Agency

Tort Liability of Agents and Principals

Task-Based Simulation 2

Relationships		
	Authoritative Literature	
		Help

Situation

Lace Computer Sales Corp. orally contracted with Banks, an independent consultant, for Banks to work part-time as Lace's agent to perform Lace's customers' service calls. Banks, a computer programmer and software designer, was authorized to customize Lace's software to the customers' needs, on a commission basis, but was specifically told not to sell Lace's computers.

On March 15, Banks made a service call on Clear Co. to repair Clear's computer. Banks had previously called on Clear, customized Lace's software for Clear, and collected cash payments for the work performed. During the call, Banks convinced Clear to buy an upgraded Lace computer for a price much lower than Lace would normally charge. Clear had previously purchased computers from other Lace agents and had made substantial cash down payments to the agents. Clear had no knowledge that the price was lower than normal. Banks received a $1,000 cash down payment and promised to deliver the computer the next week. Banks never turned in the down payment and left town. When Clear called the following week to have the computer delivered, Lace refused to honor Clear's order.

Items 1 through 5 relate to the relationships between the parties. For each item, select from List I whether only statement I is correct, whether only statement II is correct, whether both statements I and II are correct, or whether neither statement I nor II is correct.

List I

A. I only
B. II only
C. Both I and II
D. Neither I nor II

		(A)	(B)	(C)	(D)
1.	I. Lace's agreement with Banks had to be in writing for it to be a valid agency agreement.	○	○	○	○
	II. Lace's agreement with Banks empowered Banks to act as Lace's agent.				
2.	I. Clear was entitled to rely on Banks' implied authority to customize Lace's software.	○	○	○	○
	II. Clear was entitled to rely on Banks' express authority when buying the computer.				
3.	I. Lace's agreement with Banks was automatically terminated by Banks' sale of the computer.	○	○	○	○
	II. Lace must notify Clear before Banks' apparent authority to bind Lace will cease.				
4.	I. Lace is not bound by the agreement made by Banks with Clear.	○	○	○	○
	II. Lace may unilaterally amend the agreement made by Banks to prevent a loss on the sale of the computer to Clear.				
5.	I. Lace, as a disclosed principal, is solely contractually liable to Clear.	○	○	○	○
	II. Both Lace and Banks are contractually liable to Clear.				

Task-Based Simulation 2 Solution

```
┌─────────────────┐
│ Relationships   │
│       ┌──────────────────────┐
│       │ Authoritative Literature │
│       │            ┌──────────────┐
│       │            │ Help         │
└───────┤            │              │
        └────────────┤              │
                     └──────────────┘
```

		(A)	(B)	(C)	(D)
1.	I. Lace's agreement with Banks had to be in writing for it to be a valid agency agreement.	○	●	○	○
	II. Lace's agreement with Banks empowered Banks to act as Lace's agent.				
2.	I. Clear was entitled to rely on Banks' implied authority to customize Lace's software.	●	○	○	○
	II. Clear was entitled to rely on Banks' express authority when buying the computer.				

(Continued)

	(A)	(B)	(C)	(D)
3. I. Lace's agreement with Banks was automatically terminated by Banks' sale of the computer. II. Lace must notify Clear before Banks' apparent authority to bind Lace will cease.	○	●	○	○
4. I. Lace is not bound by the agreement made by Banks with Clear. II. Lace may unilaterally amend the agreement made by Banks to prevent a loss on the sale of the computer to Clear.	○	○	○	●
5. I. Lace, as a disclosed principal, is solely contractually liable to Clear. II. Both Lace and Banks are contractually liable to Clear.	●	○	○	○

Explanations

1. **(B)** Statement I is incorrect because normally an agency agreement need not be in writing unless the agency contract cannot be completed in one year. Statement II is correct because Lace authorized Banks to be Lace's agent.

2. **(A)** Statement I is correct because Banks was given actual, express authority by Lace to perform Lace's customers' service calls and to customize Lace's software to the customer's needs. As an extension to this actual, express authority, Clear can also rely on what is customary and ordinary for such an agent to be able to do under implied authority. Statement II is incorrect because Banks did not have express authority to sell the computer. In fact, Banks was told not to sell Lace's computers.

3. **(B)** Banks breached his/her fiduciary duty to Lace and breached his/her duty to follow instructions when s/he sold the computer. This, however, does not automatically terminate their agreement. Statement II is correct because Banks had dealt with Clear before as Lace's agent. Therefore, Clear must receive actual notice to terminate the apparent authority.

4. **(D)** Statement I is incorrect because Banks had apparent authority to sell the computer even though Banks did not have actual authority to do so. Statement II is incorrect because Lace is bound by the contract with Clear. Any modification of the contract must be made by both parties to the contract, not just one.

5. **(A)** Statement I is correct because since Lace was a disclosed principal, only Lace, the principal, is liable under the contract to Clear, the third party. Banks, the agent, is not. For the same reason, statement II is incorrect.

Contracts

Formation: Offer and Acceptance

Task-Based Simulation 3

```
┌─────────────────┐
│ Contractual     │
│ Relationship    │
│      ┌──────────────────────────┐
└──────│ Authoritative Literature │
       │           ┌──────────────────────┐
       └───────────│ Help                 │
                   └──────────────────────┘
```

Situation

On December 15, Blake Corp. telephoned Reach Consultants, Inc. and offered to hire Reach to design a security system for Blake's research department. The work would require two years to complete. Blake offered to pay a fee of $100,000 but stated that the offer must be accepted in writing, and the acceptance received by Blake no later than December 20.

On December 20, Reach faxed a written acceptance to Blake. Blake's offices were closed on December 20 and Reach's fax was not seen until December 21.

Reach's acceptance contained the following language:

"We accept your $1,000,000 offer. Weaver has been assigned $5,000 of the fee as payment for sums owed Weaver by Reach. Payment of this amount should be made directly to Weaver."

On December 22, Blake sent a signed memo to Reach rejecting Reach's December 20 fax but offering to hire Reach for a $75,000 fee. Reach telephoned Blake on December 23 and orally accepted Blake's December 22 offer.

Items 1 through 7 relate to whether a contractual relationship exists between Blake and Reach. For each item, determine whether the statement is True or False.

	True	False
1. Blake's December 15 offer had to be in writing to be a legitimate offer.	○	○
2. Reach's December 20 fax was an improper method of acceptance.	○	○
3. Reach's December 20 fax was effective when sent.	○	○
4. Reach's acceptance was invalid because it was received after December 20.	○	○
5. Blake's receipt of Reach's acceptance created a voidable contract.	○	○
6. If Reach had rejected the original offer by telephone on December 17, he could not validly accept the offer later.	○	○
7. Reach's December 20 fax was a counteroffer.	○	○

Items 8 through 12 relate to the attempted assignment of part of the fee to Weaver. Assume that a valid contract exists between Blake and Reach. For each item, determine whether the statement is True or False.

	True	False
8. Reach is prohibited from making an assignment of any contract right or duty.	○	○
9. Reach may validly assign part of the fee to Weaver.	○	○
10. Under the terms of Reach's acceptance, Weaver would be considered a third-party creditor beneficiary.	○	○
11. In a breach of contract suit by Weaver, against Blake, Weaver would not collect any punitive damages.	○	○
12. In a breach of contract suit by Weaver, against Reach, Weaver would be able to collect punitive damages.	○	○

Items 13 through 15 relate to Blake's December 22 signed memo. For each item, determine whether the statement is True or False.

	True	False
13. Reach's oral acceptance of Blake's December 22 memo may be enforced by Blake against Reach.	○	○
14. Blake's memo is a valid offer even though it contains no date for acceptance.	○	○
15. Blake's memo may be enforced against Blake by Reach.	○	○

Task-Based Simulation 3 Solution

Contractual Relationship		
	Authoritative Literature	
		Help

		True	False
1.	Blake's December 15 offer had to be in writing to be a legitimate offer.	○	●
2.	Reach's December 20 fax was an improper method of acceptance.	○	●
3.	Reach's December 20 fax was effective when sent.	○	●
4.	Reach's acceptance was invalid because it was received after December 20.	○	●
5.	Blake's receipt of Reach's acceptance created a voidable contract.	○	●
6.	If Reach had rejected the original offer by telephone on December 17, he could not validly accept the offer later.	●	○
7.	Reach's December 20 fax was a counteroffer.	●	○

Explanations

1. **(F)** Although the final contract has to be in writing to be enforceable since performance of contract would take longer than a year, the offer itself can be oral.
2. **(F)** The offer specified that the acceptance must be in writing. Since Reach put the acceptance in writing and faxed it to Blake, this was a proper method of acceptance.
3. **(F)** Common law applies to this fact pattern since the contract does not involve a sale of goods. Reach's attempted acceptance stated $1,000,000 instead of $100,000 as contained in the offer. Reach's attempted acceptance thus was instead a counteroffer. Under both common law and the Uniform Commercial Code, offers, revocations, rejections, and counteroffers are valid when received.
4. **(F)** Blake's offer specified that the acceptance must be received no later than December 20. Reach's faxed acceptance was received in Blake's office on December 20 on the fax machine. Therefore, Blake did receive the fax on time even though it was not seen until the following day.
5. **(F)** Reach's attempted acceptance stated $1,000,000 instead of $100,000 as contained in the offer. Since the terms did not match, no contract was formed, voidable or otherwise.
6. **(T)** Since there is no firm offer or option contract, the rejection terminates the offer.
7. **(T)** Since the December 20 fax terms did not match the original offer's terms, it serves as a counteroffer that rejects the original offer and creates a new offer.

		True	False
8.	Reach is prohibited from making an assignment of any contract right or duty.	○	●
9.	Reach may validly assign part of the fee to Weaver.	●	○
10.	Under the terms of Reach's acceptance, Weaver would be considered a third-party creditor beneficiary.	●	○
11.	In a breach of contract suit by Weaver, against Blake, Weaver would not collect any punitive damages.	●	○
12.	In a breach of contract suit by Weaver, against Reach, Weaver would be able to collect punitive damages.	○	●

Explanations

8. **(F)** Parties may typically assign the contract right to receive money to another party.
9. **(T)** When parties have a right to receive money, they may validly assign all or a portion of this right to a third party.
10. **(T)** The terms of Reach's acceptance names Weaver as a third-party beneficiary to receive $5,000. Since the intent was to pay a debt owed by Reach to Weaver, this makes Weaver a creditor beneficiary.

11. **(T)** Punitive damages are not awarded for mere breach of contract cases such as this suit by Weaver against Blake.

12. **(F)** In a suit by Weaver against Reach, no punitive damages will be awarded since this would be only a breach of contract case.

	True	False
13. Reach's oral acceptance of Blake's December 22 memo may be enforced by Blake against Reach.	○	●
14. Blake's memo is a valid offer even though it contains no date for acceptance.	●	○
15. Blake's memo may be enforced against Blake by Reach.	●	○

Explanations

13. **(F)** Since the work would require two years to complete, the contract cannot be performed within one year and, therefore, must be in writing to be enforceable. The party to be charged must have signed the contract and Reach did not do this.

14. **(T)** An offer does not need to have a date for acceptance, in which case, the offer remains open for a reasonable time.

15. **(T)** Blake's signed memo sets forth an offer which was later accepted orally by Reach. This can be construed as enough written evidence to satisfy the Statute of Frauds. Because Blake, the party to be charged, signed the memo, it is enforceable against Blake by Reach.

Formation: Consideration

Task-Based Simulation 4

```
┌─────────────────────┐
│ Consideration       │
│     ┌───────────────────────┐
│     │ Authoritative Literature │
│     │         ┌──────────────────┐
│     │         │ Help             │
└─────┴─────────┴──────────────────┘
```

For each of the numbered statements or groups of statements select either A, B, or C.

Selections

A. Both parties have given consideration legally sufficient to support a contract.

B. One of the parties has not given consideration legally sufficient to support a contract. The promise, agreement, or transaction is generally not enforceable.

C. One of the parties has not given consideration legally sufficient to support a contract. However, the promise, agreement, or transaction is generally enforceable.

	(A)	(B)	(C)
1. Party S feels a moral obligation because Party F let S stay in his place for free when S attended college. S now promises to pay F for the past kindness.	○	○	○
2. F agrees to deliver all of the sugar that Company S will need in her business for the following year. S agrees to purchase it at the market price.	○	○	○
3. F does not smoke for one year pursuant to S's agreement to pay F $200 if she does not smoke for one year.	○	○	○
4. F dies, leaving a valid will that gives S $100,000.	○	○	○

(Continued)

	(A)	(B)	(C)
5. F is an auditor of XYZ Company. S is a potential investor of XYZ and offers to pay F $1,000 if F performs a professional, quality audit of XYZ Company. The $1,000 is in addition to the fee F will get from XYZ. F does perform a professional, quality audit.	O	O	O
6. F had agreed, in writing, to work for S for five years for $100,000 per year. After two years, F asks for a 20% raise. S first agrees, then later changes his mind. F, while not agreeing to additional duties or changing his position, wants to enforce the raise in salary.	O	O	O
7. S promised to pay F $1,000 if he crosses the Golden Gate Bridge on his hands and knees. F does so.	O	O	O
8. F promised to pay S $200 for a computer worth $2,000. S agreed to the deal.	O	O	O
9. F agreed to purchase all of the parts from S that S can produce in her business for the next six months. S also agreed.	O	O	O
10. S agreed to accept $1,000 from F for a $1,500 debt that is not disputed. S now wants the additional $500. Focus on the agreement to accept the lesser amount.	O	O	O
11. S agreed to accept $1,000 from F for a debt that S claims is $1,500 but F in good faith claims is $800. F agreed to the $1,000 initially, then decides he will pay only $800. Focus on the enforceability of the agreement for $1,000.	O	O	O
12. S agreed to donate $100 to F, a public charity.	O	O	O

Task-Based Simulation 4 Solutions

Consideration		
	Authoritative Literature	
		Help

	(A)	(B)	(C)
1. Party S feels a moral obligation because Party F let S stay in his place for free when S attended college. S now promises to pay F for the past kindness.	O	●	O
2. F agrees to deliver all of the sugar that Company S will need in her business for the following year. S agrees to purchase it at the market price.	●	O	O
3. F does not smoke for one year pursuant to S's agreement to pay F $200 if she does not smoke for one year.	●	O	O
4. F dies, leaving a valid will that gives S $100,000.	O	O	●
5. F is an auditor of XYZ Company. S is a potential investor of XYZ and offers to pay F $1,000 if F performs a professional, quality audit of XYZ Company. The $1,000 is in addition to the fee F will get from XYZ. F does perform a professional, quality audit.	O	●	O
6. F had agreed, in writing, to work for S for five years for $100,000 per year. After two years, F asks for a 20% raise. S first agrees, then later changes his mind. F, while not agreeing to additional duties or changing his position, wants to enforce the raise in salary.	O	●	O
7. S promised to pay F $1,000 if he crosses the Golden Gate Bridge on his hands and knees. F does so.	●	O	O
8. F promised to pay S $200 for a computer worth $2,000. S agreed to the deal.	●	O	O
9. F agreed to purchase all of the parts from S that S can produce in her business for the next six months. S also agreed.	●	O	O

	(A)	(B)	(C)
10. S agreed to accept $1,000 from F for a $1,500 debt that is not disputed. S now wants the additional $500. Focus on the agreement to accept the lesser amount.	○	●	○
11. S agreed to accept $1,000 from F for a debt that S claims is $1,500 but F in good faith claims is $800. F agreed to the $1,000 initially, then decides he will pay only $800. Focus on the enforceability of the agreement for $1,000.	●	○	○
12. S agreed to donate $100 to F, a public charity.	○	○	●

Explanations

1. **(B)** Party F gave S a gift in the past. S's promise to now pay for the usage is not enforceable because F's action is past consideration, and the contract needs consideration on both sides. Furthermore, S's feeling of a moral obligation does not create consideration.

2. **(A)** This is an example of a requirements contract. F has given consideration because s/he gave up the right to sell that sugar to someone else.

3. **(A)** F refrained from doing something which she had a right to do. This constitutes consideration.

4. **(C)** This is not enforceable under contract law because S does not give any consideration in return. It is enforceable, however, as a will, which does not require the elements of a contract such as consideration, but does require other formalities.

5. **(B)** F already had a preexisting legal duty to do a professional, quality audit of XYZ Company.

6. **(B)** F had a contract to work for S for five years for $100,000 per year. F is not giving any new consideration for the raise since during that five years, he already is obligated to complete the contract.

7. **(A)** F did something that he did not have to do in exchange for the agreed $1,000. This is a unilateral contract.

8. **(A)** F agreed to pay $200 and in exchange S agreed to sell the computer. Both have given consideration that is **legally** sufficient. Legally sufficient refers to the validity of the consideration, not the amount. Consideration does not have to be of equal value as long as it is legal consideration and bargained for.

9. **(A)** Both parties have given consideration for this output contract. F gave up the right to buy these parts elsewhere and S gave up the right to sell her output to someone else.

10. **(B)** F has a preexisting legal duty to pay the full $1,500. When S agreed to accept less, F gave up nothing. F still owes the remaining $500.

11. **(A)** In this case, both parties gave consideration. S, in agreeing to accept the $1,000, gave up the right to collect more of the disputed amount. F gave up the right to pay less of the disputed amount.

12. **(C)** Although the charity gave no consideration in exchange for the promised donation, the promise to donate to a charity is generally enforceable based on public policy reasons.

Performance: Passage of Title and Risk of Loss

Task-Based Simulation 5

Analysis

Authoritative Literature

Help

Situation

Angler Corp., a food distributor, is involved in the following disputes:

- On September 8, Angler shipped the wrong grade of tuna to Mason Restaurants, Inc. under a contract that stated as follows: "FOB Angler's loading dock." During shipment, the tuna was destroyed in an accident involving the common carrier's truck. Mason has refused to pay for the tuna, claiming the risk of loss belonged to Angler at the time of the accident.

- On October 3, Angler shipped 100 bushels of peaches to Classic Foods, Inc., a retail grocer. Because of a delay in shipping, the peaches rotted. Classic elected to reject the peaches and notified Angler of this decision. Angler asked Classic to return the peaches at Angler's expense. Classic refused the request, claiming it had no obligation to do so.
- On October 23, Angler orally contracted to sell Regal Fast-Food 1,500 pounds of hamburger meat for $1,500. Delivery was to be made on October 31. On October 29, after Angler had shipped the hamburger meat to Regal, Regal sent Angler the following signed correspondence:

    "We are not going to need the 1,500 pounds of meat we ordered on October 23. Don't ship."

Regal rejected the shipment and claimed it is not obligated to purchase the hamburger meat because there is no written contract between Angler and Regal.

Determine whether each of the numbered legal conclusions is Correct or Incorrect.

	Correct	Incorrect
1. When the accident happened, the risk of loss belonged to Angler.	○	○
2. If Angler had shipped the correct grade of tuna to Mason, the risk of loss would have been Angler's at time of the accident.	○	○
3. The contract between Angler and Mason was an FOB destination point contract.	○	○
4. Angler had title to the tuna at time of the accident since Angler shipped nonconforming goods.	○	○
5. Classic is required to return the peaches at Angler's expense per Angler's instructions.	○	○
6. Classic may throw the peaches away because they were rotted.	○	○
7. Since Classic elected to reject the rotted peaches, Classic may not also sue for damages.	○	○
8. Regal is not obligated to purchase the hamburger meat because there was no written contract between Angler and Regal.	○	○
9. The Uniform Commercial Code applies to the contract between Angler and Regal.	○	○
10. Regal's correspondence to Angler, dated October 29, satisfies the appropriate Statute of Frauds.	○	○
11. Angler should keep the hamburger until Regal finally accepts it and sue Regal for $1,500.	○	○
12. Assuming that all of the original facts are the same except that Regal never sent Angler the correspondence dated October 29, then Angler may hold Regal in breach of contract.	○	○
13. Assuming that all of the original facts are the same except that the contract was for $450, then Angler may hold Regal in breach of contract.	○	○
14. Assume that all of the original facts are the same except that Regal never sent Angler the correspondence and Angler shipped to Regal 800 pounds of the hamburger on October 29. Regal accepted the 800 pounds. Regal, then, on October 31 orally rejected the shipment for the remaining 700 pounds. Under these facts, the contract is enforceable against Regal for the 800 pounds but not the full 1,500 pounds.	○	○
15. Under the same facts found in 14. above, the contract is enforceable against Regal for the full 1,500 pounds.	○	○

Task-Based Simulation 5 Solution

Analysis

Authoritative Literature

Help

	Correct (C)	Incorrect (I)
1. When the accident happened, the risk of loss belonged to Angler.	●	○
2. If Angler had shipped the correct grade of tuna to Mason, the risk of loss would have been Angler's at time of the accident.	○	●
3. The contract between Angler and Mason was an FOB destination point contract.	○	●
4. Angler had title to the tuna at time of the accident since Angler shipped nonconforming goods.	○	●
5. Classic is required to return the peaches at Angler's expense per Angler's instructions.	●	○
6. Classic may throw the peaches away because they were rotted.	○	●
7. Since Classic elected to reject the rotted peaches, Classic may not also sue for damages.	○	●
8. Regal is not obligated to purchase the hamburger meat because there was no written contract between Angler and Regal.	○	●
9. The Uniform Commercial Code applies to the contract between Angler and Regal.	●	○
10. Regal's correspondence to Angler, dated October 29, satisfies the appropriate Statute of Frauds.	●	○
11. Angler should keep the hamburger until Regal finally accepts it and sue Regal for $1,500.	○	●
12. Assuming that all of the original facts are the same except that Regal never sent Angler the correspondence dated October 29, then Angler may hold Regal in breach of contract.	○	●
13. Assuming that all of the original facts are the same except that the contract was for $450, then Angler may hold Regal in breach of contract.	●	○
14. Assume that all of the original facts are the same except that Regal never sent Angler the correspondence and Angler shipped to Regal 800 pounds of the hamburger on October 29. Regal accepted the 800 pounds. Regal, then, on October 31 orally rejected the shipment for the remaining 700 pounds. Under these facts, the contract is enforceable against Regal for the 800 pounds but not the full 1,500 pounds.	●	○
15. Under the same facts found in 14. above, the contract is enforceable against Regal for the full 1,500 pounds.	○	●

Explanations

1. **(C)** Angler breached the contract by shipping nonconforming goods to Mason. Therefore, Angler retains the risk of loss until it cures or until Mason accepts the goods despite the nonconformity.
2. **(I)** This was an FOB shipping point contract so that the risk of loss would have passed over to the buyer upon delivery to the carrier.
3. **(I)** Because the terms were FOB the seller's loading dock, it was an FOB shipping point contract.

4. **(I)** Title and risk of loss do not necessarily pass to a buyer at the same time. In this case, risk of loss remained with the seller because of the shipment of nonconforming goods. However, title passed under the original terms despite the breach of contract.

5. **(C)** Classic is obligated to follow any reasonable instructions of the seller as a merchant who rejects goods, even nonconforming, under a contract.

6. **(I)** Classic must follow the reasonable instructions given by Angler to return the peaches at Angler's expense.

7. **(I)** Classic may also sue for any damages that were caused by the delay in shipping.

8. **(I)** Although the contract must be evidenced by a writing because it involved a sale of goods for more than $500, the correspondence that Regal sent to Angler on October 29 satisfies the writing requirement under the UCC Statute of Frauds. It indicated that a contract had been made. It was signed by Regal, the party to be charged, and it stated the quantity. The price was not needed in the correspondence.

9. **(C)** The Uniform Commercial Code applies because the contract was for a sale of goods (i.e., hamburger meat).

10. **(C)** The correspondence satisfies the UCC Statute of Frauds, which does not require that all terms be in writing.

11. **(I)** Angler should resort to an appropriate remedy such as reselling the hamburger to someone else in a commercially reasonable fashion. If Angler gets less than the original contract price, it may recover the difference from Regal.

12. **(I)** Since there was no writing to evidence the contract for $1,500, it is not enforceable.

13. **(C)** The contract need not be in writing because it was for less than $500.

14. **(C)** Since Angler shipped and Regal accepted a portion of the goods, the oral contract is enforceable up to the amount shipped and accepted. This is one of the exceptions in the UCC Statute of Frauds.

15. **(I)** The exception in the UCC Statute of Frauds allows the oral contract to be enforced up to the amount delivered and accepted or paid for.

Task-Based Simulation 6

Analysis		
	Authoritative Literature	
		Help

Situation

On February 1, Grand Corp., a manufacturer of custom cabinets, contracted in writing with Axle Co., a kitchen contractor, to sell Axle 100 unique, custom-designed, kitchen cabinets for $250,000. Axle had contracted to install the cabinets in a luxury condominium complex. The contract provided that the cabinets were to be ready for delivery by April 15 and were to be shipped FOB seller's loading dock. On April 15, Grand had 85 cabinets complete and delivered them, together with 15 standard cabinets, to the trucking company for delivery to Axle. Grand faxed Axle a copy of the shipping invoice, listing the 15 standard cabinets. On May 1, before reaching Axle, the truck was involved in a collision and all the cabinets were damaged beyond repair.

Items 1 through 5 refer to the above fact pattern. For each item, determine whether (A), (B), or (C) is correct.

	(A)	(B)	(C)
1. A. The contract between Grand and Axle was a shipment contract.	○	○	○
B. The contract between Grand and Axle was a destination contract.			
C. The contract between Grand and Axle was a consignment contract.			
2. A. The risk of loss for the 85 custom cabinets passed to Axle on April 15.	○	○	○
B. The risk of loss for the 100 cabinets passed to Axle on April 15.			
C. The risk of loss for the 100 cabinets remained with Grand.			

	(A)	(B)	(C)
3. A. The contract between Grand and Axle was invalid because no delivery date was stated.	○	○	○
B. The contract between Grand and Axle was voidable because Grand shipped only 85 custom cabinets.			
C. The contract between Grand and Axle was void because the goods were destroyed.			
4. A. Grand's shipment of the standard cabinets was a breach of the contract with Axle.	○	○	○
B. Grand would not be considered to have breached the contract until Axle rejected the standard cabinets.			
C. Grand made a counteroffer by shipping the standard cabinets.			
5. A. Axle is entitled to specific performance from Grand because of the unique nature of the goods.	○	○	○
B. Axle is required to purchase substitute goods (cover) and is entitled to the difference in cost from Grand.			
C. Axle is entitled to punitive damages because of Grand's intentional shipment of nonconforming goods.			

Task-Based Simulation 6 Solution

Analysis		
	Authoritative Literature	
		Help

	(A)	(B)	(C)
1. A. The contract between Grand and Axle was a shipment contract.	●	○	○
B. The contract between Grand and Axle was a destination contract.			
C. The contract between Grand and Axle was a consignment contract.			
2. A. The risk of loss for the 85 custom cabinets passed to Axle on April 15.	○	○	●
B. The risk of loss for the 100 cabinets passed to Axle on April 15.			
C. The risk of loss for the 100 cabinets remained with Grand.			
3. A. The contract between Grand and Axle was invalid because no delivery date was stated.	○	●	○
B. The contract between Grand and Axle was voidable because Grand shipped only 85 custom cabinets.			
C. The contract between Grand and Axle was void because the goods were destroyed.			
4. A. Grand's shipment of the standard cabinets was a breach of the contract with Axle.	●	○	○
B. Grand would not be considered to have breached the contract until Axle rejected the standard cabinets.			
C. Grand made a counteroffer by shipping the standard cabinets.			
5. A. Axle is entitled to specific performance from Grand because of the unique nature of the goods.	●	○	○
B. Axle is required to purchase substitute goods (cover) and is entitled to the difference in cost from Grand.			
C. Axle is entitled to punitive damages because of Grand's intentional shipment of nonconforming goods.			

Explanations

1. **(A)** The terms of the contract were "FOB seller's loading dock," which is a shipment contract. Answer (B) is incorrect because a destination contract would state terms specifying FOB buyer's location. Answer (C) is incorrect because a consignment is treated as a sale or return. That is, the owner of the goods delivers them to another party to attempt to sell them. If this other party, known as the consignee, does not sell the goods, they are returned. Such is not the case in this fact pattern.

2. **(C)** Risk of loss would normally pass to the buyer, Axle Co., under this shipment contract. However, since the seller, Grand, breached the contract, risk of loss remains with Grand. Since the cabinets are "custom designed, kitchen cabinets" for a luxury condominium complex, they would need to match. Therefore, the 100 units could be construed as a commercial unit and the risk of loss for the entire 100 cabinets remained with Grand. Answer (A) is incorrect because the 100 cabinets were a commercial unit and thus the risk of loss of the entire commercial unit remained with Grand. Answer (B) is incorrect because even though the terms were "FOB seller's loading dock," the risk of loss remained with the seller, Grand, because of Grand's breach of contract.

3. **(B)** The contract between Grand and Axle was voidable because Axle may at its option choose to accept or reject all or part of the cabinets. Answer (C) is incorrect because if the contract were void, neither party would have the option of remaining in the contract. Answer (A) is incorrect because under the UCC, if the delivery date is not stated, the time becomes "within a reasonable time."

4. **(A)** Once Grand ships nonconforming goods, a breach of contract has occurred. Answer (B) is incorrect because the breach has occurred even without Axle needing to reject the shipment. Axle then has the right to accept all, part, or none of the shipment. Answer (C) is incorrect because the shipment of nonconforming goods acts as a breach rather than a counteroffer.

5. **(A)** Since the cabinets are unique and custom-designed, specific performance is allowed if Axle so chooses. Answer (B) is incorrect because Axle is not required to cover, especially because the cabinets are unique. Answer (C) is incorrect because punitive damages are generally not allowed for a breach of contract even if the breach is intentional.

Debtor-Creditor Relationships

Rights, Duties, and Liabilities of Debtors, Creditors, and Guarantors: Suretyship—Rights of Parties

Task-Based Simulation 7

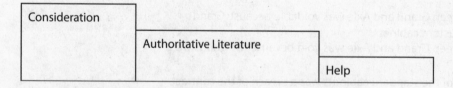

For each of the numbered words or phrases, select the one best phrase or sentence from the list, A through J. Each response may be used only once.

A. Relationship whereby one person agrees to answer for the debt or default of another.

B. Requires certain contracts to be in writing to be enforceable.

C. Jointly and severally liable to creditor.

D. Promises to pay debt on default of principal debtor.

E. One party promises to reimburse debtor for payment of debt or loss if it arises.

F. Receives intended benefits of a contract.

G. Right of surety to require the debtor to pay before surety pays.

H. Upon payment of more than his/her proportionate share, each cosurety may compel other cosureties to pay their shares.

I. Upon payment of debt, surety may recover payment from debtor.

J. Upon payment, surety obtains same rights against debtor that creditor had.

	(A)	(B)	(C)	(D)	(E)	(F)	(G)	(H)	(I)	(J)
1. Indemnity contract	○	○	○	○	○	○	○	○	○	○
2. Suretyship contract	○	○	○	○	○	○	○	○	○	○
3. Surety	○	○	○	○	○	○	○	○	○	○
4. Third-party beneficiary	○	○	○	○	○	○	○	○	○	○
5. Cosurety	○	○	○	○	○	○	○	○	○	○
6. Statute of Frauds	○	○	○	○	○	○	○	○	○	○
7. Right of contribution	○	○	○	○	○	○	○	○	○	○
8. Reimbursement	○	○	○	○	○	○	○	○	○	○
9. Subrogation	○	○	○	○	○	○	○	○	○	○
10. Exoneration	○	○	○	○	○	○	○	○	○	○

Task-Based Simulation 7 Solution

Consideration

Authoritative Literature

Help

	(A)	(B)	(C)	(D)	(E)	(F)	(G)	(H)	(I)	(J)
1. Indemnity contract	○	○	○	○	●	○	○	○	○	○
2. Suretyship contract	●	○	○	○	○	○	○	○	○	○
3. Surety	○	○	○	●	○	○	○	○	○	○
4. Third-party beneficiary	○	○	○	○	○	●	○	○	○	○
5. Cosurety	○	○	●	○	○	○	○	○	○	○
6. Statute of Frauds	○	●	○	○	○	○	○	○	○	○
7. Right of contribution	○	○	○	○	○	○	○	●	○	○
8. Reimbursement	○	○	○	○	○	○	○	○	●	○
9. Subrogation	○	○	○	○	○	○	○	○	○	●
10. Exoneration	○	○	○	○	○	○	●	○	○	○

Explanations

1. **(E)** An indemnity contract is not a suretyship contract. Instead it is a contract involving two parties in which the first party agrees to indemnify and reimburse the second party for covered debts or losses should they take place.
2. **(A)** The suretyship contract involves three parties. The surety agrees with the creditor to pay for the debt or default if the debtor does not.
3. **(D)** The surety is the party that agrees to pay the creditor if the debtor defaults.
4. **(F)** When two parties make a contract that intends to benefit a third party, that party is a third-party beneficiary.
5. **(C)** When two or more sureties agree to be sureties for the same obligation to the same creditor, they are known as cosureties. They have joint and several liability.
6. **(B)** The Statute of Frauds sets out rules that require certain contracts to be in writing, such as those in which a surety agrees to answer for the debt or default of another.
7. **(H)** Cosureties are liable in contribution for their proportionate shares of the debt. If a cosurety pays more than this amount, s/he may seek contribution for the excess from the other cosureties.
8. **(I)** The right of reimbursement is against the debtor to collect any amounts paid by the surety.
9. **(J)** When the surety pays the creditor, it "steps into the shoes of the creditor" and obtains the same rights against the debtor that the creditor had.
10. **(G)** If the debtor is able to pay, the surety may require the debtor to pay before the surety pays. This is called exoneration.

Secured Transactions: Priorities in Security Interests

Task-Based Simulation 8

Analysis

Authoritative Literature

Help

Situation

On January 2, 2013, Gray Interiors Corp., a retailer of sofas, contracted with Shore Furniture Co. to purchase 150 sofas for its inventory. The purchase price was $250,000. Gray paid $50,000 cash and gave Shore a note and security agreement for the balance. On March 1, 2013, the sofas were delivered. On March 10, 2013, Shore filed a financing statement.

On February 1, 2013, Gray negotiated a $1,000,000 line of credit with Float Bank, pledged its present and future inventory as security, and gave Float a security agreement. On February 20, 2013, Gray borrowed $100,000 from the line of credit. On March 5, 2013, Float filed a financing statement.

On April 1, 2013, Dove, a consumer purchaser in the ordinary course of business, purchased a sofa from Gray. Dove was aware of both security interests.

Items 1 through 6 refer to the fact pattern. For each item, determine whether (A), (B), or (C) is correct.

	(A)	(B)	(C)
1. Shore's security interest in the sofas attached on	○	○	○
A. January 2, 2013.			
B. March 1, 2013.			
C. March 10, 2013.			
2. Shore's security interest in the sofas was perfected on	○	○	○
A. January 2, 2013.			
B. March 1, 2013.			
C. March 10, 2013.			
3. Float's security interest in Gray's inventory attached on	○	○	○
A. February 1, 2013.			
B. March 1, 2013.			
C. March 5, 2013.			
4. Float's security interest in Gray's inventory was perfected on	○	○	○
A. February 1, 2013.			
B. March 1, 2013.			
C. March 5, 2013.			
5. A. Shore's security interest has priority because it was a purchase money security interest.	○	○	○
B. Float's security interest has priority because Float's financing statement was filed before Shore's.			
C. Float's security interest has priority because Float's interest attached before Shore's.			
6. A. Dove purchased the sofa subject to Shore's security interest.	○	○	○
B. Dove purchased the sofa subject to both the Shore and Float security interests.			
C. Dove purchased the sofa free of either the Shore or Float security interests.			

Task-Based Simulation 8 Solution

```
┌─────────────────────────────────────────────────────┐
│ Analysis                                              │
│         ┌─────────────────────────────────────────┐  │
│         │ Authoritative Literature                │  │
│         │        ┌──────────────────────────────┐ │  │
│         │        │ Help                         │ │  │
│         │        └──────────────────────────────┘ │  │
│         └─────────────────────────────────────────┘  │
└─────────────────────────────────────────────────────┘
```

	(A)	(B)	(C)
1. Shore's security interest in the sofas attached on	○	●	○
A. January 2, 2013.			
B. March 1, 2013.			
C. March 10, 2013.			
2. Shore's security interest in the sofas was perfected on	○	○	●
A. January 2, 2013.			
B. March 1, 2013.			
C. March 10, 2013.			

(Continued)

	(A)	(B)	(C)
3. Float's security interest in Gray's inventory attached on	●	○	○
A. February 1, 2013.			
B. March 1, 2013.			
C. March 5, 2013.			
4. Float's security interest in Gray's inventory was perfected on	○	○	●
A. February 1, 2013.			
B. March 1, 2013.			
C. March 5, 2013.			
5. A. Shore's security interest has priority because it was a purchase money security interest.	○	●	○
B. Float's security interest has priority because Float's financing statement was filed before Shore's.			
C. Float's security interest has priority because Float's interest attached before Shore's.			
6. A. Dove purchased the sofa subject to Shore's security interest.	○	○	●
B. Dove purchased the sofa subject to both the Shore and Float security interests.			
C. Dove purchased the sofa free of either the Shore or Float security interests.			

Explanations

1. **(B)** Gray gave Shore a security agreement on January 2. Shore also gave value but Gray did not receive the goods or have rights in them until March 1. Therefore, it was not until March 1 that attachment occurred.

2. **(C)** Perfection took place on March 10, when Shore filed the financing statement, since attachment had already been accomplished. Note that the filing was needed for perfection since this was not a purchase money security interest in consumer goods but in inventory.

3. **(A)** Float gave value by giving the $1,000,000 line of credit on February 1. On this same date, Gray gave Float a security agreement. Since Gray had rights in the collateral it already possessed, attachment took place on February 1 for that inventory possessed.

4. **(C)** Perfection occurred on March 5, when Float filed the financing statement, since attachment had already taken place previously.

5. **(B)** Generally, when two parties have perfected security interests in the same collateral, the first to either file or perfect has priority. When a purchase money security interest exists in the collateral, however, the general rule may vary, depending on whether the collateral is inventory or noninventory. In this case the collateral is inventory. A purchase money security interest in inventory may obtain priority over previously perfected conflicting security interests if (1) the purchase money security holder perfects his interest in the inventory at the time the debtor receives the inventory, and (2) the purchase money security holder provides written notice of his purchase money security interest and a description of the inventory to all holders of conflicting security interests who have filed financing statements covering the same type of inventory. If the purchase money security holder does not take these steps, the general rule applies. Answer (A) is incorrect because Shore did not take the necessary steps for its purchase money security interest to obtain priority. Answer (B) is correct because the general rule applies, and Float filed first. Answer (C) is incorrect because when both security interests are perfected, priority is not based on the order of attachment.

6. **(C)** A buyer in the ordinary course of business takes goods free of any security interests even if perfected and even if the buyer is aware of the security interests. Therefore, answers (A) and (B) are incorrect because Dove purchased the goods in the ordinary course of business.

Bankruptcy and Insolvency: Distribution of Debtor's Estate

Task-Based Simulation 9

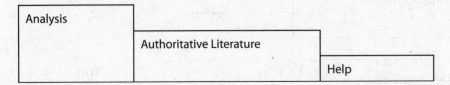

Situation

On May 1, Year 2, Able Corp. was petitioned involuntarily into bankruptcy under the provisions of Chapter 7 of the Federal Bankruptcy Code.

When the petition was filed, Able had the following unsecured creditors:

Creditor	Amount owed
Cole	$18,000
Lake	2,000
Young	1,500
Thorn	1,000

The following transactions occurred before the bankruptcy petition was filed:

- On February 15, Year 2, Able paid Vista Bank the $1,000 balance due on an unsecured business loan.
- On February 28, Year 2, Able paid $1,000 to Owen, an officer of Able, who had lent Able money.
- On March 1, Year 2, Able bought a computer for use in its business from Core Computer Co. for $2,000 cash.

Items 1 through 3 refer to the bankruptcy filing. For each item, determine whether the statement is True or False.

	True	False
1. Able can file a voluntary petition for bankruptcy if it is solvent.	○	○
2. Lake, Young, and Thorn can file a valid involuntary petition.	○	○
3. Cole alone can file a valid involuntary petition.	○	○

Items 4 through 6 refer to the transactions that occurred before the filing of the involuntary bankruptcy petition. Assuming the bankruptcy petition was validly filed, for each item determine whether the statement is True or False.

	True	False
4. The payment to Vista Bank would be set aside as a preferential transfer.	○	○
5. The payment to Owen would be set aside as a preferential transfer.	○	○
6. The purchase from Core Computer Co. would be set aside as a preferential transfer.	○	○

Task-Based Simulation 9 Solution

```
┌─────────────────────────┐
│ Analysis                │
│      ┌──────────────────────────┐
│      │ Authoritative Literature │
│      │         ┌──────────────────────────┐
│      │         │ Help                     │
└──────┴─────────┴──────────────────────────┘
```

	True	False
1. Able can file a voluntary petition for bankruptcy if it is solvent.	●	○
2. Lake, Young, and Thorn can file a valid involuntary petition.	○	●
3. Cole alone can file a valid involuntary petition.	●	○

Explanations

1. **(T)** A debtor need not be insolvent to file a voluntary petition for bankruptcy. S/he merely needs to state that s/he has debts. Thus, Able could file even if solvent.

2. **(F)** In order to file a valid involuntary petition when there are fewer than 12 creditors, a single creditor may file the petition as long as s/he is owed at least $15,775 of unsecured debt. More than one creditor may be used to reach the $15,775 requirement. However, Lake, Young, and Thorn may not file a valid involuntary petition because they are collectively owed only $4,500.

3. **(T)** In order to file a valid involuntary petition when there are fewer than 12 creditors, a single creditor can file the petition as long as s/he is owed at least $15,775 of unsecured debt. Cole may file alone as s/he is owed $18,000.

	True	False
4. The payment to Vista Bank would be set aside as a preferential transfer.	●	○
5. The payment to Owen would be set aside as a preferential transfer.	○	●
6. The purchase from Core Computer Co. would be set aside as a preferential transfer.	●	○

Explanations

4. **(T)** The trustee may set aside preferential transfers of nonexempt property to a creditor made within the previous 90 days while insolvent. The payment made to Vista Bank is a preferential transfer because it was made less than 90 days before May 1, Year 2, the date the involuntary petition was filed.

5. **(T)** The trustee may set aside preferential transfers of nonexempt property to a creditor made within the previous 90 days while insolvent. If the creditor was an insider, the time period is extended to within one year prior to the filing of the bankruptcy petition. The payment to Owen is a preferential transfer because Owen, an officer of Able Corp., is an insider, and the payment was made within one year prior to the filing of the petition.

6. **(F)** The payment to Core is not a preferential transfer because contemporaneously, Able received new value; that is, the computer. A contemporaneous exchange between creditor and debtor whereby the debtor receives new value is an exception to the trustee's power to set aside as a preferential transfer.

Task-Based Simulation 10

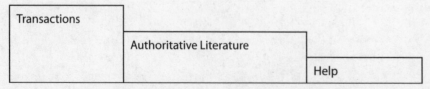

On April 25, Year 2, Rusk Corporation was petitioned involuntarily into bankruptcy. At the time of the filing, Rusk had the following creditors:

- Safe Bank, for the balance due on the secured note and mortgage on Rusk's warehouse.
- Employee salary claims.

- Year 1 federal income taxes due.
- Accountant's fees outstanding.
- Utility bills outstanding.

   Prior to the bankruptcy filing, but while insolvent, Rusk engaged in the following transactions:

- On January 15, Year 2, Rusk repaid all corporate directors' loans made to the corporation.
- On February 1, Year 2, Rusk purchased raw materials for use in its manufacturing business and paid cash to the supplier.

Items 1 through 4 relate to Rusk's creditors and the January 15 and February 1 transactions. For each item, select from List I whether only statement I is correct, whether only statement II is correct, whether both statements I and II are correct, or whether neither statement I nor II is correct.

List I

A.	I only
B.	II only
C.	Both I and II
D.	Neither I nor II

		(A)	(B)	(C)	(D)
1.	I. Safe Bank's claim will be the first paid of the listed claims because Safe is a secured creditor. II. Safe Bank will receive the entire amount of the balance of the mortgage due as a secured creditor regardless of the amount received from the sale of the warehouse.	○	○	○	○
2.	I. The claim for Year 1 federal income taxes due will be paid as a secured creditor claim. II. The claim for Year 1 federal income taxes due will be paid prior to the general creditor claims.	○	○	○	○
3.	I. The January 15 repayments of the directors' loans were preferential transfers even though the payments were made more than 10 days before the filing of the petition. II. The January 15 repayments of the directors' loans were preferential transfers because the payments were made to insiders.	○	○	○	○
4.	I. The February 1 purchase and payment was not a preferential transfer because it was a transaction in the ordinary course of business. II. The February 1 purchase and payment was a preferential transfer because it occurred within 90 days of the filing of the petition.	○	○	○	○

Task-Based Simulation 10 Solution

Transactions		
	Authoritative Literature	
		Help

		(A)	(B)	(C)	(D)
1.	I. Safe Bank's claim will be the first paid of the listed claims because Safe is a secured creditor. II. Safe Bank will receive the entire amount of the balance of the mortgage due as a secured creditor regardless of the amount received from the sale of the warehouse.	●	○	○	○

(Continued)

	(A)	(B)	(C)	(D)
2. I. The claim for Year 1 federal income taxes due will be paid as a secured creditor claim. II. The claim for Year 1 federal income taxes due will be paid prior to the general creditor claims.	○	●	○	○
3. I. The January 15 repayments of the directors' loans were preferential transfers even though the payments were made more than 10 days before the filing of the petition. II. The January 15 repayments of the directors' loans were preferential transfers because the payments were made to insiders.	○	○	●	○
4. I. The February 1 purchase and payment was not a preferential transfer because it was a transaction in the ordinary course of business. II. The February 1 purchase and payment was a preferential transfer because it occurred within ninety days of the filing of the petition.	●	○	○	○

Explanations

1. **(A)** Statement I is correct since secured creditors receive payments before unsecured creditors (up to the value of the collateral) or receive the collateral itself. Statement II is incorrect because a secured creditor gets paid first only up to the value of the security. Any debt above the value of the security is given the lowest priority along with the general creditors.
2. **(B)** Statement I is incorrect because there is no collateral backing the Year 1 federal income tax claim. It will thus not be paid as a secured creditor. Statement II is correct because taxes (federal, state, or local) have a higher priority than the general creditors.
3. **(C)** Statement I is correct because preferential transfers to insiders may be set aside when made within the previous 12 months. Thus, the January 15 repayment of corporate directors' loans are preferential transfers. Statement II is correct because the preferential transfer rule of 90 days is extended to 12 months in the case of insiders.
4. **(A)** Both transfers in the ordinary course of business and contemporaneous exchanges between creditors and debtors (whereby the debtors receive new value) are exceptions to the trustee's power to avoid preferential transfers. In this case, Rusk had purchased raw materials for use in its manufacturing business and paid cash to the supplier. These facts constitute an exception to the trustee's power to avoid a preferential transfer. Statement II is incorrect because the purchase and payment constitute an exception to the preferential transfer avoiding powers.

Government Regulation of Business

Federal Securities Regulation: Exempt Transactions and Securities

Task-Based Simulation 11

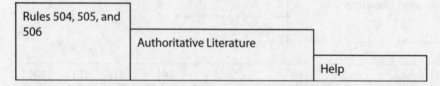

Situation

You will have 15 questions based on the following information:

Butler Manufacturing Corp. planned to raise capital for a plant expansion by borrowing from banks and making several stock offerings. Butler engaged Weaver, CPA, to audit its December 31, 2009 financial statements. Butler told Weaver that the financial statements would be given to certain named banks and included in the prospectuses for the stock offerings.

In performing the audit, Weaver did not confirm accounts receivable and, as a result, failed to discover a material overstatement of accounts receivable. Also, Weaver was aware of a pending class action product liability lawsuit that was not disclosed in Butler's financial statements. Despite being advised by Butler's legal counsel that Butler's potential liability under the lawsuit would result in material losses, Weaver issued an unqualified opinion on Butler's financial statements.

In May 2010, Union Bank, one of the named banks, relied on the financial statements and Weaver's opinion in giving Butler a $500,000 loan.

Butler raised an additional $16,450,000 through the following stock offerings, which were sold completely:

- June 2010—Butler made a $450,000 unregistered offering of Class B nonvoting common stock under Rule 504 of Regulation D of the Securities Act of 1933. This offering was sold over one year to 20 accredited investors by general solicitation. The SEC was notified eight days after the first sale of this offering.
- September 2010—Butler made a $10,000,000 unregistered offering of Class A voting common stock under Rule 506 of Regulation D of the Securities Act of 1933. This offering was sold over one year to 200 accredited investors and 30 nonaccredited investors through a private placement. The SEC was notified 14 days after the first sale of this offering.
- November 2010—Butler made a $6,000,000 unregistered offering of preferred stock under Rule 505 of Regulation D of the Securities Act of 1933. This offering was sold during a one-year period to 40 nonaccredited investors by private placement. The SEC was notified 18 days after the first sale of this offering.

Shortly after obtaining the Union loan, Butler began experiencing financial problems but was able to stay in business because of the money raised by the offerings. Butler was found liable in the product liability suit. This resulted in a judgment Butler could not pay. Butler also defaulted on the Union loan and was involuntarily petitioned into bankruptcy. This caused Union to sustain a loss and Butler's stockholders to lose their investments. As a result,

- The SEC claimed that all three of Butler's offerings were made improperly and were not exempt from registration.
- Union sued Weaver for
  ○ Negligence
  ○ Common law fraud
- The stockholders who purchased Butler's stock through the offerings sued Weaver, alleging fraud under Section 10(b) and Rule 10b-5 of the Securities Exchange Act of 1934.

These transactions took place in a jurisdiction providing for accountant's liability for negligence to known and intended users of financial statements.

Items 1 through 5 are questions related to the June 2010 offering made under Rule 504 of Regulation D of the Securities Act of 1933. For each item, indicate your answer by choosing either Yes or No.

	Yes	No
1. Did the offering comply with the dollar limitation of Rule 504?	○	○
2. Did the offering comply with the method of sale restrictions?	○	○
3. Was the offering sold during the applicable time limit?	○	○
4. Was the SEC notified timely of the first sale of the securities?	○	○
5. Was the SEC correct in claiming that this offering was not exempt from registration?	○	○

Items 6 through 10 are questions related to the September 2010 offering made under Rule 506 of Regulation D of the Securities Act of 1933. For each item, indicate your answer by choosing either Yes or No.

	Yes	No
6. Did the offering comply with the dollar limitation of Rule 506?	○	○
7. Did the offering comply with the method of sale restrictions?	○	○
8. Was the offering sold to the correct number of investors?	○	○
9. Was the SEC notified timely of the first sale of the securities?	○	○
10. Was the SEC correct in claiming that this offering was not exempt from registration?	○	○

Items 11 through 15 are questions related to the November 2010 offering made under Rule 505 of Regulation D of the Securities Act of 1933. For each item, indicate your answer by choosing either Yes or No.

	Yes	No
11. Did the offering comply with the dollar limitation of Rule 505?	○	○
12. Was the offering sold during the applicable time limit?	○	○
13. Was the offering sold to the correct number of investors?	○	○
14. Was the SEC notified timely of the first sale of the securities?	○	○
15. Was the SEC correct in claiming that this offering was not exempt from registration?	○	○

Task-Based Simulation 11 Solution

Rules 504, 505, and 506 | Authoritative Literature | Help

	Yes	No
1. Did the offering comply with the dollar limitation of Rule 504?	●	○
2. Did the offering comply with the method of sale restrictions?	●	○
3. Was the offering sold during the applicable time limit?	●	○
4. Was the SEC notified timely of the first sale of the securities?	●	○
5. Was the SEC correct in claiming that this offering was not exempt from registration?	○	●

Explanations

1. **(Y)** Rule 504 exempts an issuance of securities up to $1,000,000 sold in a 12-month period to any number of investors. Butler made the offering for $450,000.
2. **(Y)** This offering involved a general solicitation, which is now allowed under Rule 504 providing the solicitation is to only accredited investors.
3. **(Y)** This offering was sold over the applicable 12-month period in Rule 504.
4. **(Y)** The SEC was sent notice of this offering eight days after the first sale. Under Rule 504, the SEC must be notified within 15 days of the first sale of the securities.
5. **(N)** Even though this stock was sold by general solicitation, this is allowed under Rule 504.

	Yes	No
6. Did the offering comply with the dollar limitation of Rule 506?	●	○
7. Did the offering comply with the method of sale restrictions?	●	○
8. Was the offering sold to the correct number of investors?	●	○
9. Was the SEC notified timely of the first sale of the securities?	●	○
10. Was the SEC correct in claiming that this offering was not exempt from registration?	○	●

Explanations

6. **(Y)** Rule 506 allows private placement of an unlimited dollar amount of securities.
7. **(Y)** These securities were sold through private placement, which is appropriate under Rule 506.
8. **(Y)** Rule 506 allows sales to up to 35 nonaccredited investors who are sophisticated investors with knowledge and experience in financial matters. It allows sales to an unlimited number of accredited investors.

9. **(Y)** The SEC was notified 14 days after the first sale of the offering which is within the 15-day rule.

10. **(N)** Since this offering met the requirements discussed in **6 through 9** above, the SEC was incorrect.

	Yes	No
11. Did the offering comply with the dollar limitation of Rule 505?	○	●
12. Was the offering sold during the applicable time limit?	●	○
13. Was the offering sold to the correct number of investors?	○	●
14. Was the SEC notified timely of the first sale of the securities?	○	●
15. Was the SEC correct in claiming that this offering was not exempt from registration?	●	○

Explanations

11. **(N)** Rule 505 exempts an issuance of securities up to $5,000,000. Butler made a $6,000,000 unregistered offering of preferred stock.
12. **(Y)** The offering was sold during the applicable 12-month period.
13. **(N)** Rule 505 permits sales to 35 nonaccredited investors. Butler went over this limit by selling to 40 nonaccredited investors.
14. **(N)** The SEC was notified 18 days after the first sale of this offering, which is over the 15-day requirement.
15. **(Y)** This offering was not exempt from registration because it went over the $5,000,000 limit and the stock was sold to more than 35 nonaccredited investors.

Task-Based Simulation 12

```
┌─────────────────┐
│ Analysis        │
│        ┌────────┴──────────────┐
│        │ Authoritative Literature │
│        │              ┌────────┴──────────┐
│        │              │ Help              │
└────────┴──────────────┴───────────────────┘
```

Situation

Coffee Corp., a publicly held corporation, wants to make an $8,000,000 exempt offering of its shares as a private placement offering under Regulation D, Rule 506, of the Securities Act of 1933. Coffee has more than 500 shareholders and assets in excess of $1 billion, and has its shares listed on a national securities exchange.

Items 1 through 5 relate to the application of the provisions of the Securities Act of 1933 and the Securities Exchange Act of 1934 to Coffee Corp. and the offering. For each item, select from List II whether only statement I is correct, whether only statement II is correct, whether both statements I and II are correct, or whether neither statement I nor II is correct.

List II

A.	I only
B.	II only
C.	Both I and II
D.	Neither I nor II

		(A)	(B)	(C)	(D)
1.	I. Coffee Corp. may make the Regulation D, Rule 506, exempt offering. II. Coffee Corp., because it is required to report under the Securities Exchange Act of 1934, may not make an exempt offering.	○	○	○	○
2.	I. Shares sold under a Regulation D, Rule 506, exempt offering may only be purchased by accredited investors. II. Shares sold under a Regulation D, Rule 506, exempt offering may be purchased by any number of investors provided there are no more than 35 nonaccredited investors.	○	○	○	○
3.	I. An exempt offering under Regulation D, Rule 506, must not be for more than $10,000,000. II. An exempt offering under Regulation D, Rule 506, has no dollar limit.	○	○	○	○
4.	I. Regulation D, Rule 506, requires that all investors in the exempt offering be notified that for nine months after the last sale no resale may be made to a nonresident. II. Regulation D, Rule 506, requires that the issuer exercise reasonable care to assure that purchasers of the exempt offering are buying for investment and are not underwriters.	○	○	○	○
5.	I. The SEC must be notified by Coffee Corp. within five days of the first sale of the exempt offering securities. II. Coffee Corp. must include an SEC notification of the first sale of the exempt offering securities in Coffee's next filed Quarterly Report (Form 10-Q).	○	○	○	○

Task-Based Simulation 12 Solution

Analysis	
	Authoritative Literature
		Help

		(A)	(B)	(C)	(D)
1.	I. Coffee Corp. may make the Regulation D, Rule 506, exempt offering. II. Coffee Corp., because it is required to report under the Securities Exchange Act of 1934, may not make an exempt offering.	●	○	○	○
2.	I. Shares sold under a Regulation D, Rule 506, exempt offering may only be purchased by accredited investors. II. Shares sold under a Regulation D, Rule 506, exempt offering may be purchased by any number of investors provided there are no more than 35 nonaccredited investors.	○	●	○	○
3.	I. An exempt offering under Regulation D, Rule 506, must not be for more than $10,000,000. II. An exempt offering under Regulation D, Rule 506, has no dollar limit.	○	●	○	○

	(A)	(B)	(C)	(D)
4. I. Regulation D, Rule 506, requires that all investors in the exempt offering be notified that for nine months after the last sale no resale may be made to a nonresident. II. Regulation D, Rule 506, requires that the issuer exercise reasonable care to assure that purchasers of the exempt offering are buying for investment and are not underwriters.	○	●	○	○
5. I. The SEC must be notified by Coffee Corp. within five days of the first sale of the exempt offering securities. II. Coffee Corp. must include an SEC notification of the first sale of the exempt offering securities in Coffee's next filed Quarterly Report (Form 10-Q).	○	○	○	●

Explanations

1. **(A)** Statement I is correct because under Regulation D, Rule 506, the corporation may make a private placement of an unlimited amount of securities if it meets certain requirements. Statement II is incorrect. Coffee Corp. may still make an exempt offering under the Securities Act of 1933 even if it will be subject to the requirements of the Securities Exchange Act of 1934.
2. **(B)** Statement I is incorrect because up to 35 nonaccredited investors may purchase shares under Regulation D, Rule 506, if they are sophisticated investors. Statement II is correct because Rule 506 does allow sales to up to 35 nonaccredited investors **assuming they are also** sophisticated investors, that is, individuals with knowledge and experience in financial matters, or individuals represented by people with such knowledge and experience.
3. **(B)** Statement I is incorrect and statement II is correct for the same reason. Regulation D, Rule 506, has no dollar limit on the placement of securities as long as other requirements are met.
4. **(B)** Statement I is incorrect because Regulation D has no requirements putting restrictions on resales to nonresidents. Statement II is correct because Regulation D requires that the issuer take reasonable steps to see that purchasers of the exempt offering are not underwriters and are buying for investment.
5. **(D)** Statement I is incorrect. Under Regulation D, the SEC must be notified within 15 days of the first sale of the securities. Statement II is incorrect because the Quarterly Reports do not require SEC notification of the first sale of exempt securities.

Federal Securities Regulation: Purposes, Requirements, and Provisions of the 1934 Act

Task-Based Simulation 13

Analysis		
	Authoritative Literature	
		Help

Situation

Under Section 11 of the Securities Act of 1933 and Section 10(b), Rule 10b-5, of the Securities Exchange Act of 1934, a CPA may be sued by a purchaser of registered securities.

Items 1 through 6 relate to what a plaintiff who purchased securities must prove in a civil liability suit against a CPA. For each item determine whether the statement must be proven under Section 11 of the Securities Act of 1933, under Section 10(b), Rule 10b-5, of the Securities Exchange Act of 1934, both Acts, or neither Act.

	Only Section 11	Only Section 10(b)	Both	Neither
	(A)	**(A)**	**(C)**	**(D)**
The plaintiff security purchaser must allege or prove:	○	○	○	○
1. Material misstatements were included in a filed document.	○	○	○	○
2. A monetary loss occurred.	○	○	○	○
3. Lack of due diligence by the CPA.	○	○	○	○
4 Privity with the CPA.	○	○	○	○
5. Reliance on the document.	○	○	○	○
6. The CPA had scienter.	○	○	○	○

Task-Based Simulation 13 Solution

```
Analysis
        Authoritative Literature
                        Help
```

	Only Section 11	Only Section 10(b)	Both	Neither
	(A)	**(A)**	**(C)**	**(D)**
1. Material misstatements were included in a filed document.	○	○	●	○
2. A monetary loss occurred.	○	○	●	○
3. Lack of due diligence by the CPA.	○	○	○	○
4 Privity with the CPA.	○	○	○	●
5. Reliance on the document.	○	●	○	●
6. The CPA had scienter.	○	●	○	○

Explanations

1. **(C)** Section 11 of the Securities Act of 1933 imposes liability on auditors for misstatements or omissions of a material fact in certified financial statements or other information provided in registration statements. Similarly, under Section 10(b), Rule 10b-5 of the Securities Exchange Act of 1934, the plaintiff must prove there was a material misstatement or omission in information released by the firm such as audited financial statements. Actually, if the examiners wish to emphasize the phrase "filed document" in the question, then the answer would be (A). Under Section 10(b), the material misstatement may occur in information released by the firm rather than filed. Since the requirements state "...**must** allege or prove," technically the answer would be (D), since the plaintiff could allege or prove **omission** of material facts instead of material **misstatements** stated in the question. Therefore, this question depends upon how technical one decides to get on these points.
2. **(C)** Under both Section 11 of the 1933 Act and Section 10(b) of the 1934 Act, the plaintiff must allege or prove that s/he incurred monetary damages.
3. **(D)** Under Section 11 of the 1933 Act, the burden of proof is shifted to the defendant, the accountant. The accountant may then defend him- or herself by establishing due diligence. The plaintiff does not have to show lack of due diligence by the CPA. Under Section 10(b), the plaintiff must prove scienter.
4. **(D)** The plaintiff does not have to prove that s/he was in privity with the CPA under either section.

5. **(B)** Under Section 10(b), the plaintiff must prove justifiable reliance on the financial information. This is not true under Section 11, in which the plaintiff need prove only the items in item 1 and item 2 discussed above.

6. **(B)** The plaintiff does have to prove that the CPA had scienter under Section 10(b) of the 1934 Act. Scienter is not needed under the 1933 Act, however.

Business Structure: Rights, Duties, Legal Obligations, and Authority of Owners and Management

Authority of Owners and Managers

Task-Based Simulation 14

General Partnerships		
	Authoritative Literature	
		Help

Situation

In Year 1 Anchor, Chain, and Hook created ACH Associates, a general partnership. The partners orally agreed that they would work full time for the partnership and would distribute profits based on their capital contributions. Anchor contributed $5,000; Chain $10,000; and Hook $15,000.

For the year ended December 31, Year 2, ACH Associates had profits of $60,000 that were distributed to the partners. During Year 3, ACH Associates was operating at a loss. In September Year 3, the partnership dissolved.

In October Year 3, Hook contracted in writing with Ace Automobile Co. to purchase a car for the partnership. Hook had previously purchased cars from Ace Automobile Co. for use by ACH Associates partners. ACH Associated did not honor the contract with Ace Automobile Co. and Ace Automobile Co. sued the partnership and the individual partners.

Required:

For each item, determine whether (A) or (B) is correct.

	(A)	(B)
1. A. The ACH Associates oral partnership agreement was valid. B. The ACH Associates oral partnership agreement was invalid because the partnership lasted for more than one year.	○	○
2. A. Anchor, Chain, and Hook jointly owning and conducting a business for profit establishes a partnership relationship. B. Anchor, Chain, and Hook jointly owning income-producing property establishes a partnership relationship.	○	○
3. A. Anchor's share of ACH Associates' Year 2 profits was $20,000. B. Hook's share of ACH Associates' Year 2 profits was $30,000.	○	○
4. A. Anchor's capital account would be reduced by 1/3 of any Year 3 losses. B. Hook's capital account would be reduced by 1/2 of any Year 3 losses.	○	○
5. A. Ace Automobile Co. would lose a suit brought against ACH Associates because Hook, as a general partner, has no authority to bind the partnership. B. Ace Automobile Co. would win a suit brought against ACH Associates because Hook's authority continues during dissolution.	○	○
6. A. ACH Associates and Hook would be the only parties liable to pay any judgment recovered by Ace Automobile Co. B. Anchor, Chain, and Hook would be jointly and severally liable to pay any judgment recovered by Ace Automobile Co.	○	○

Task-Based Simulation 14 Solution

General Partnerships		
	Authoritative Literature	
		Help

Explanations

1. **(A)** The creation of a partnership usually may be either oral or written. A written partnership agreement is not required unless it falls within the Statute of Frauds (e.g., the partnership cannot be completed within one year). Even though the partnership actually lasted longer than one year, the Statute of Frauds focuses on the term in the partnership agreement, not what actually happens. Since no term was specified in the oral agreement, it is possible that the partnership could have been completed in less than a year so no writing is required under the Statute of Frauds.

2. **(A)** A partnership is an association of two or more persons to carry on a business as co-owners for profit. Co-ownership of property is one element of a partnership; however, the most important and necessary element of a partnership is profit sharing. Another important element of co-ownership is joint control.

3. **(B)** Partnership profits and losses are shared equally unless the partnership agreement specifies otherwise. The agreement for ACH Associates specified that the partners would distribute profits based on their capital contributions. As such, Anchor's share of ACH Associates' Year 2 profits would be

$$\frac{\$5,000}{15,000 + 10,000 + 5,000} \times \$60,000 = \$10,000$$

Hook's share of ACH Associates' Year 2 profits would be

$$\frac{\$15,000}{15,000 + 10,000 + 5,000} \times \$60,000 = \$30,000$$

4. **(B)** Since the partners agreed on profit sharing in the creation of the partnership, but were silent on loss sharing, losses are shared on the same basis as profits. Therefore, Anchor's capital account would be reduced by

$$\frac{\$5,000}{15,000 + 10,000 + 5,000} = 16.6\% \text{ or } 1/6 \text{ of the Year 3 losses}$$

Hook's capital account would be reduced by

$$\frac{\$15,000}{15,000 + 10,000 + 5,000} = 50\% \text{ or } 1/2 \text{ of the Year 3 losses}$$

5. **(B)** During dissolution, partners can bind other partners and the partnership on contracts until third parties who have known of the partnership are given notice of dissolution. Actual notice must be given to third parties who have dealt with the partnership prior to the dissolution. Constructive notice is adequate for third parties who have only known of the partnership.

6. **(B)** Under the Revised Uniform Partnership Act, the partners are jointly and severally liable for all debts of the partnership. Creditors are required to first attempt collection from the partnership unless it is bankrupt. Once ACH Associates has paid off what it can, the partners are jointly and severally liable.

Federal Taxation of Property Transactions

Property Transactions

Capital Gains and Losses

Task-Based Simulation 15

Form 8949 Schedule D		
	Authoritative Literature	
		Help

Situation

Lou Thomas (Social Security number 123-45-6789) reported the following transactions for calendar-year 2016:

- Lou sold 100 shares of Copperleaf Industries on October 20, 2016, for $4,200. Lou had acquired the stock for $2,500 on March 1, 2015.
- Lou sold 200 shares of King Corporation stock for $5,000 on November 15, 2016. He had purchased the stock on February 24, 2016, for $4,000.
- Thomas had a net short-term capital loss carryforward from 2015 of $7,300, and during December 2016 received a $1,500 capital gain distribution from the Brooks Mutual fund.
- Thomas did not receive any qualified dividends during this year.

Use the above information to complete the following 2016 Form 1040 Schedule D for Thomas.

SCHEDULE D
(Form 1040)

Department of the Treasury
Internal Revenue Service (99)

Capital Gains and Losses

▶ Attach to Form 1040 or Form 1040NR.
▶ **Information about Schedule D and its separate instructions is at** *www.irs.gov/scheduled*.
▶ **Use Form 8949 to list your transactions for lines 1b, 2, 3, 8b, 9, and 10.**

OMB No. 1545-0074

2016

Attachment
Sequence No. **12**

Name(s) shown on return

Your social security number

Part I   **Short-Term Capital Gains and Losses—Assets Held One Year or Less**

See instructions for how to figure the amounts to enter on the lines below. This form may be easier to complete if you round off cents to whole dollars.	**(d)** Proceeds (sales price)	**(e)** Cost (or other basis)	**(g)** Adjustments to gain or loss from Form(s) 8949, Part I, line 2, column (g)	**(h) Gain or (loss)** Subtract column (e) from column (d) and combine the result with column (g)
1a Totals for all short-term transactions reported on Form 1099-B for which basis was reported to the IRS and for which you have no adjustments (see instructions). However, if you choose to report all these transactions on Form 8949, leave this line blank and go to line 1b .				
1b Totals for all transactions reported on Form(s) 8949 with **Box A** checked				
2 Totals for all transactions reported on Form(s) 8949 with **Box B** checked				
3 Totals for all transactions reported on Form(s) 8949 with **Box C** checked				

4 Short-term gain from Form 6252 and short-term gain or (loss) from Forms 4684, 6781, and 8824 .	**4**	
5 Net short-term gain or (loss) from partnerships, S corporations, estates, and trusts from Schedule(s) K-1	**5**	
6 Short-term capital loss carryover. Enter the amount, if any, from line 8 of your **Capital Loss Carryover Worksheet** in the instructions	**6** ( )
7 **Net short-term capital gain or (loss).** Combine lines 1a through 6 in column (h). If you have any long-term capital gains or losses, go to Part II below. Otherwise, go to Part III on the back	**7**	

Part II   **Long-Term Capital Gains and Losses—Assets Held More Than One Year**

See instructions for how to figure the amounts to enter on the lines below. This form may be easier to complete if you round off cents to whole dollars.	**(d)** Proceeds (sales price)	**(e)** Cost (or other basis)	**(g)** Adjustments to gain or loss from Form(s) 8949, Part II, line 2, column (g)	**(h) Gain or (loss)** Subtract column (e) from column (d) and combine the result with column (g)
8a Totals for all long-term transactions reported on Form 1099-B for which basis was reported to the IRS and for which you have no adjustments (see instructions). However, if you choose to report all these transactions on Form 8949, leave this line blank and go to line 8b .				
8b Totals for all transactions reported on Form(s) 8949 with **Box D** checked				
9 Totals for all transactions reported on Form(s) 8949 with **Box E** checked				
10 Totals for all transactions reported on Form(s) 8949 with **Box F** checked				

11 Gain from Form 4797, Part I; long-term gain from Forms 2439 and 6252; and long-term gain or (loss) from Forms 4684, 6781, and 8824	**11**	
12 Net long-term gain or (loss) from partnerships, S corporations, estates, and trusts from Schedule(s) K-1	**12**	
13 Capital gain distributions. See the instructions	**13**	
14 Long-term capital loss carryover. Enter the amount, if any, from line 13 of your **Capital Loss Carryover Worksheet** in the instructions	**14** ( )
15 **Net long-term capital gain or (loss).** Combine lines 8a through 14 in column (h). Then go to Part III on the back	**15**	

For Paperwork Reduction Act Notice, see your tax return instructions.   Cat. No. 11338H   **Schedule D (Form 1040) 2016**

| Part III | Summary |

16 Combine lines 7 and 15 and enter the result . . . . | **16** |

- If line 16 is a **gain,** enter the amount from line 16 on Form 1040, line 13, or Form 1040NR, line 14. Then go to line 17 below.
- If line 16 is a **loss,** skip lines 17 through 20 below. Then go to line 21. Also be sure to complete line 22.
- If line 16 is **zero,** skip lines 17 through 21 below and enter -0- on Form 1040, line 13, or Form 1040NR, line 14. Then go to line 22.

17 Are lines 15 and 16 **both** gains?
   ☐ **Yes.** Go to line 18.
   ☐ **No.** Skip lines 18 through 21, and go to line 22.

18 Enter the amount, if any, from line 7 of the **28% Rate Gain Worksheet** in the instructions . . ▶ | **18** |

19 Enter the amount, if any, from line 18 of the **Unrecaptured Section 1250 Gain Worksheet** in the instructions . . . . ▶ | **19** |

20 Are lines 18 and 19 **both** zero or blank?
   ☐ **Yes.** Complete the **Qualified Dividends and Capital Gain Tax Worksheet** in the instructions for Form 1040, line 44 (or in the instructions for Form 1040NR, line 42). **Don't** complete lines 21 and 22 below.

   ☐ **No.** Complete the **Schedule D Tax Worksheet** in the instructions. **Don't** complete lines 21 and 22 below.

21 If line 16 is a loss, enter here and on Form 1040, line 13, or Form 1040NR, line 14, the **smaller** of:

   - The loss on line 16 or
   - ($3,000), or if married filing separately, ($1,500) } . . . . | **21** (|) |

   Note: When figuring which amount is smaller, treat both amounts as positive numbers.

22 Do you have qualified dividends on Form 1040, line 9b, or Form 1040NR, line 10b?

   ☐ **Yes.** Complete the **Qualified Dividends and Capital Gain Tax Worksheet** in the instructions for Form 1040, line 44 (or in the instructions for Form 1040NR, line 42).

   ☐ **No.** Complete the rest of Form 1040 or Form 1040NR.

Task-Based Simulation 15 Solution

Form 8949 Schedule D		
	Authoritative Literature	
		Help

SCHEDULE D
(Form 1040)

Department of the Treasury
Internal Revenue Service (99)

Capital Gains and Losses

► Attach to Form 1040 or Form 1040NR.
► Information about Schedule D and its separate instructions is at *www.irs.gov/scheduled*.
► Use Form 8949 to list your transactions for lines 1b, 2, 3, 8b, 9, and 10.

OMB No. 1545-0074

20**16**

Attachment
Sequence No. **12**

Name(s) shown on return
Lou Thomas

Your social security number
123-45-6789

Part I Short-Term Capital Gains and Losses—Assets Held One Year or Less

See instructions for how to figure the amounts to enter on the lines below. This form may be easier to complete if you round off cents to whole dollars.	(d) Proceeds (sales price)	(e) Cost (or other basis)	(g) Adjustments to gain or loss from Form(s) 8949, Part I, line 2, column (g)	(h) Gain or (loss) Subtract column (e) from column (d) and combine the result with column (g)
1a Totals for all short-term transactions reported on Form 1099-B for which basis was reported to the IRS and for which you have no adjustments (see instructions). However, if you choose to report all these transactions on Form 8949, leave this line blank and go to line 1b .	5,000	4,000		1,000
1b Totals for all transactions reported on Form(s) 8949 with **Box A** checked				
2 Totals for all transactions reported on Form(s) 8949 with **Box B** checked				
3 Totals for all transactions reported on Form(s) 8949 with **Box C** checked				

4 Short-term gain from Form 6252 and short-term gain or (loss) from Forms 4684, 6781, and 8824 .	**4**	
5 Net short-term gain or (loss) from partnerships, S corporations, estates, and trusts from Schedule(s) K-1	**5**	
6 Short-term capital loss carryover. Enter the amount, if any, from line 8 of your **Capital Loss Carryover Worksheet** in the instructions	**6** (7,300)
7 **Net short-term capital gain or (loss).** Combine lines 1a through 6 in column (h). If you have any long-term capital gains or losses, go to Part II below. Otherwise, go to Part III on the back	**7**	(6,300)

Part II Long-Term Capital Gains and Losses—Assets Held More Than One Year

See instructions for how to figure the amounts to enter on the lines below. This form may be easier to complete if you round off cents to whole dollars.	(d) Proceeds (sales price)	(e) Cost (or other basis)	(g) Adjustments to gain or loss from Form(s) 8949, Part II, line 2, column (g)	(h) Gain or (loss) Subtract column (e) from column (d) and combine the result with column (g)
8a Totals for all long-term transactions reported on Form 1099-B for which basis was reported to the IRS and for which you have no adjustments (see instructions). However, if you choose to report all these transactions on Form 8949, leave this line blank and go to line 8b .	4,200	2,500		1,700
8b Totals for all transactions reported on Form(s) 8949 with **Box D** checked				
9 Totals for all transactions reported on Form(s) 8949 with **Box E** checked				
10 Totals for all transactions reported on Form(s) 8949 with **Box F** checked.				

11 Gain from Form 4797, Part I; long-term gain from Forms 2439 and 6252; and long-term gain or (loss) from Forms 4684, 6781, and 8824	**11**	
12 Net long-term gain or (loss) from partnerships, S corporations, estates, and trusts from Schedule(s) K-1	**12**	
13 Capital gain distributions. See the instructions	**13**	1,500
14 Long-term capital loss carryover. Enter the amount, if any, from line 13 of your **Capital Loss Carryover Worksheet** in the instructions	**14** ( )
15 **Net long-term capital gain or (loss).** Combine lines 8a through 14 in column (h). Then go to Part III on the back	**15**	3,200

For Paperwork Reduction Act Notice, see your tax return instructions. Cat. No. 11338H **Schedule D (Form 1040) 2016**

Part III   **Summary**

16	Combine lines 7 and 15 and enter the result	**16**	(3,100)

- If line 16 is a **gain,** enter the amount from line 16 on Form 1040, line 13, or Form 1040NR, line 14. Then go to line 17 below.
- If line 16 is a **loss,** skip lines 17 through 20 below. Then go to line 21. Also be sure to complete line 22.
- If line 16 is **zero,** skip lines 17 through 21 below and enter -0- on Form 1040, line 13, or Form 1040NR, line 14. Then go to line 22.

17   Are lines 15 and 16 **both** gains?
    ☐ **Yes.** Go to line 18.
    ☐ **No.** Skip lines 18 through 21, and go to line 22.

18	Enter the amount, if any, from line 7 of the **28% Rate Gain Worksheet** in the instructions . . ▶	**18**	

19	Enter the amount, if any, from line 18 of the **Unrecaptured Section 1250 Gain Worksheet** in the instructions . . . . ▶	**19**	

20   Are lines 18 and 19 **both** zero or blank?
    ☐ **Yes.** Complete the **Qualified Dividends and Capital Gain Tax Worksheet** in the instructions for Form 1040, line 44 (or in the instructions for Form 1040NR, line 42). **Don't** complete lines 21 and 22 below.

    ☐ **No.** Complete the **Schedule D Tax Worksheet** in the instructions. **Don't** complete lines 21 and 22 below.

21   If line 16 is a loss, enter here and on Form 1040, line 13, or Form 1040NR, line 14, the **smaller** of:

- The loss on line 16 or
- ($3,000), or if married filing separately, ($1,500)

21 (	3,000)

Note: When figuring which amount is smaller, treat both amounts as positive numbers.

22   Do you have qualified dividends on Form 1040, line 9b, or Form 1040NR, line 10b?

    ☐ **Yes.** Complete the **Qualified Dividends and Capital Gain Tax Worksheet** in the instructions for Form 1040, line 44 (or in the instructions for Form 1040NR, line 42).

    ☑ **No.** Complete the rest of Form 1040 or Form 1040NR.

Federal Taxation of Individuals

Deductions

Itemized Deductions—Medical, Taxes, Interests

Task-Based Simulation 16

Research		
	Authoritative Literature	
		Help

In January of Year 1, Mark Smith had to have heart surgery. The total cost of the surgery was $100,000, and his insurance covered a total of $82,000. Smith paid the remaining $18,000 in February of Year 1. Which code section and subsection determines the extent to which Smith's unreimbursed medical expenses will be deductible? Indicate the reference to that citation in the shaded boxes below.

Section			Subsection		
§	░░░		(	░░░	)

Task-Based Simulation 16 Solution

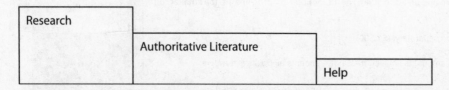

Internal Revenue Code Section 213, subsection (a) provides that the unreimbursed medical expenses of a taxpayer, spouse, and dependents are deductible to the extent in excess of 10% of adjusted gross income.

Section			Subsection		
§	213		(	a	)

Task-Based Simulation 17

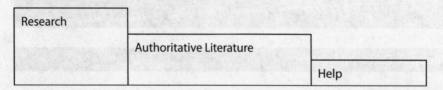

Mr. Cole is considering purchasing a new principal residence for $1,500,000, and intends to finance the purchase with a mortgage in the amount of $1,150,000. Which code section, subsection, and paragraph provides the maximum amount of mortgage indebtedness on which the interest expense will be deductible? Indicate the reference to that citation in the shaded boxes below.

Section			Subsection			Paragraph		
§	░░░		(	░░░	)	.	░░░	

Task-Based Simulation 17 Solution

Internal Revenue Code Section 163, subsection (h), paragraph (3) provides that interest is deductible on up to $1,000,000 of acquisition indebtedness, and also is deductible on up to $100,000 of home equity indebtedness.

Section			Subsection					
§	163		(	h	)		3	

Itemized Deductions—Other

Task-Based Simulation 18

Tax Treatment		
	Authoritative Literature	
		Help

During 2016 the following payments were made or losses were incurred. For **items 1 through 14**, select the appropriate tax treatment. A tax treatment may be selected once, more than once, or not at all.

Tax treatment

A. Not deductible.
B. Deductible in Schedule A—Itemized Deductions, subject to threshold of 10% of adjusted gross income.
C. Deductible in Schedule A—Itemized Deductions, subject to threshold of 2% of adjusted gross income.
D. Deductible on page 1 of Form 1040 to arrive at adjusted gross income.
E. Deductible in full in Schedule A—Itemized Deductions.
F. Deductible in Schedule A—Itemized Deductions, subject to maximum of 50% of adjusted gross income.

	(A)	(B)	(C)	(D)	(E)	(F)
1. Premiums on Mr. Vick's personal life insurance policy.	○	○	○	○	○	○
2. Penalty on Mrs. Vick's early withdrawal of funds from a certificate of deposit.	○	○	○	○	○	○
3. Mrs. Vick's substantiated cash donation to the American Red Cross.	○	○	○	○	○	○
4. Payment of estimated state income taxes.	○	○	○	○	○	○
5. Payment of real estate taxes on the Vick home.	○	○	○	○	○	○
6. Loss on the sale of the family car.	○	○	○	○	○	○
7. Cost in excess of the increase in value of residence, for the installation of a stairlift in January 2016, related directly to the medical care of Mr. Vick.	○	○	○	○	○	○
8. The Vicks' health insurance premiums for hospitalization coverage.	○	○	○	○	○	○
9. CPA fees to prepare the 2015 tax return.	○	○	○	○	○	○
10. Amortization over the life of the loan of points paid to refinance the mortgage at a lower rate on the Vick home.	○	○	○	○	○	○
11. One-half the self-employment tax paid by Mrs. Vick.	○	○	○	○	○	○
12. Mrs. Vick's $100 in gambling losses. She had $450 of gambling winnings.	○	○	○	○	○	○
13. Mrs. Vick's union dues.	○	○	○	○	○	○
14. 2015 federal income tax paid with the Vicks' tax return on April 15, 2016.	○	○	○	○	○	○

Task-Based Simulation 18 Solution

```
┌─────────────────┐
│ Tax Treatment   │
│       ┌──────────────────────────┐
│       │ Authoritative Literature │
│       │            ┌──────────────────┐
│       │            │ Help             │
└───────┴────────────┴──────────────────┘
```

For **items 1 through 14**, candidates were asked to select the appropriate tax treatment for the payments made or losses incurred by Mrs. Vick for 2016.

		(A)	(B)	(C)	(D)	(E)	(F)
1.	Premiums on Mr. Vick's personal life insurance policy.	●	○	○	○	○	○
2.	Penalty on Mrs. Vick's early withdrawal of funds from a certificate of deposit.	○	○	○	●	○	○
3.	Mrs. Vick's substantiated cash donation to the American Red Cross.	○	○	○	○	○	●
4.	Payment of estimated state income taxes.	○	○	○	○	●	○
5.	Payment of real estate taxes on the Vick home.	○	○	○	○	●	○
6.	Statute of Frauds	●	○	○	○	○	○
7.	Cost in excess of the increase in value of residence, for the installation of a stairlift in January 2016, related directly to the medical care of Mr. Vick.	○	●	○	○	○	○
8.	The Vicks' health insurance premiums for hospitalization coverage.	○	●	○	○	○	○
9.	CPA fees to prepare the 2015 tax return.	○	○	●	○	○	○
10.	Amortization over the life of the loan of points paid to refinance the mortgage at a lower rate on the Vick home.	○	○	○	○	●	○
11.	One-half the self-employment tax paid by Mrs. Vick.	○	○	○	●	○	○
12.	Mrs. Vick's $100 in gambling losses. She had $450 of gambling winnings.	○	○	○	○	●	○
13.	Mrs. Vick's union dues.	○	○	●	○	○	○
14.	2015 federal income tax paid with the Vicks' tax return on April 15, 2016.	●	○	○	○	○	○

Explanations

1. **(A)** Life insurance premiums are considered a personal expense and are not deductible.
2. **(D)** An interest forfeiture penalty for making an early withdrawal from a certificate of deposit is deductible on page 1 of Form 1040 to arrive at adjusted gross income.
3. **(F)** Charitable contributions are generally deductible as an itemized deduction up to a **maximum of 50% of AGI**.
4. **(E)** Estimated state income tax payments are deductible in full as an itemized deduction on Schedule A.
5. **(E)** Real estate taxes on a principal residence are deductible in full as an itemized deduction on Schedule A.
6. **(A)** A family car is a personal use asset and a loss from its sale is not deductible. The only type of loss that can be deducted on a personal use asset is a casualty or theft loss.
7. **(B)** A capital expenditure made for medical reasons that improves a residence is deductible as a medical expense to the extent that the expenditure exceeds the increase in value of the residence. As a medical expense, the excess expenditure is deductible as an itemized deduction on Schedule A subject to a 10% of AGI threshold.

8. **(B)** Health insurance premiums qualify as a medical expense and are deductible as an itemized deduction on Schedule A subject to a 10% of AGI threshold.

9. **(C)** Tax return preparation fees are deductible as an itemized deduction on Schedule A subject to a 2% of AGI threshold.

10. **(E)** Points paid to refinance a mortgage are deductible as interest expense over the term of the loan. Interest expense on a personal residence is deductible as an itemized deduction on Schedule A.

11. **(D)** Normally, one-half of a self-employed taxpayer's self-employment tax is deductible on page 1 of Form 1040 to arrive at AGI.

12. **(E)** Gambling losses are deductible as a miscellaneous itemized deduction on Schedule A to the extent that the taxpayer's gambling winnings are included in gross income. Since Mrs. Vick reported $450 of gambling winnings, her $100 of gambling losses are deductible.

13. **(C)** Unreimbursed employee expenses (including union dues) are generally deductible as miscellaneous itemized deductions on Schedule A subject to a 2% of AGI threshold.

14. **(A)** A payment of federal income tax is not deductible in computing a taxpayer's taxable income.

Task-Based Simulation 19

Form 1040 Schedule A		
	Authoritative Literature	
		Help

Situation

Fred (Social Security number 123-67-5489) and Laura Shaw, both age 56, provided you with the following tax return data. The amount from Form 1040, line 38 is $80,000.

Medical and dental expenses	
Medical insurance premiums	$5,600
Disability income insurance premiums	800
Prescription drugs	825
Nonprescription medicine	280
Dr. Jones—neurologist	2,250
Dentist	750
Dr. Smith—LASIK surgery	900
Insurance reimbursement for medical bills	2,000
Transportation to and from doctors	80
Taxes	
Balance of state income taxes due for 2014 paid on April 15, 2015	$225
State income taxes withheld for 2015	975
Real estate taxes on principal residence	7,000
Real estate taxes on summer residence	3,000
County personal property tax	410
Registration fee for automobiles	160
Interest	
Mortgage interest on principal residence	$5,500
Mortgage interest on summer residence	2,200
Interest paid on automobile loan	800
Interest paid on personal use credit cards	500

(Continued)

Contributions

Cash donated to church	$2,500
Stock donated to church (The Shaws purchased it for $3,000 18 months ago.)	4,000

Miscellaneous payments

Legal fee for preparation of a will	$350
Rent for safety-deposit box containing stocks and bonds	120
Union dues	600
Subscriptions to investment publications	300
Life insurance premiums	2,800
Transportation to and from work	2,400
Fee paid for tax return preparation	400
Unreimbursed business travel away from home overnight	900
Contribution to a national political party	200
Repairs to principal residence	2,000

Complete the following 2015 Form 1040 Schedule A—Itemized Deductions for Fred and Laura Shaw.

SCHEDULE A (Form 1040) Department of the Treasury Internal Revenue Service (99)	**Itemized Deductions** ▶ Information about Schedule A and its separate instructions is at *www.irs.gov/schedulea*. ▶ Attach to Form 1040.	OMB No. 1545-0074 **2016** Attachment Sequence No. **07**

Name(s) shown on Form 1040 · · · · · · · · · · · · Your social security number

Caution: Do not include expenses reimbursed or paid by others.

Medical and Dental Expenses	1 Medical and dental expenses (see instructions)	1	
	2 Enter amount from Form 1040, line 38 [2]		
	3 Multiply line 2 by 10% (0.10). But if either you or your spouse was born before January 2, 1952, multiply line 2 by 7.5% (0.075) instead	3	
	4 Subtract line 3 from line 1. If line 3 is more than line 1, enter -0-		4

Taxes You Paid	5 State and local (**check only one box**):
	  a ☐ Income taxes, **or**
	  b ☐ General sales taxes
		5	

	6 Real estate taxes (see instructions)	6	
	7 Personal property taxes	7	
	8 Other taxes. List type and amount ▶ _____	8	
	9 Add lines 5 through 8		9
Interest You Paid **Note:** Your mortgage interest deduction may be limited (see instructions).	10 Home mortgage interest and points reported to you on Form 1098	10	
	11 Home mortgage interest not reported to you on Form 1098. If paid to the person from whom you bought the home, see instructions and show that person's name, identifying no., and address ▶	11	
	12 Points not reported to you on Form 1098. See instructions for special rules	12	
	13 Mortgage insurance premiums (see instructions)	13	
	14 Investment interest. Attach Form 4952 if required. (See instructions.)	14	
	15 Add lines 10 through 14		15
Gifts to Charity If you made a gift and got a benefit for it, see instructions.	16 Gifts by cash or check. If you made any gift of $250 or more, see instructions.	16	
	17 Other than by cash or check. If any gift of $250 or more, see instructions. You **must** attach Form 8283 if over $500 . . .	17	
	18 Carryover from prior year	18	
	19 Add lines 16 through 18		19
Casualty and Theft Losses	20 Casualty or theft loss(es). Attach Form 4684. (See instructions.)		20
Job Expenses and Certain Miscellaneous Deductions	21 Unreimbursed employee expenses—job travel, union dues, job education, etc. Attach Form 2106 or 2106-EZ if required. (See instructions.) ▶	21	
	22 Tax preparation fees	22	
	23 Other expenses—investment, safe deposit box, etc. List type and amount ▶	23	
	24 Add lines 21 through 23	24	
	25 Enter amount from Form 1040, line 38 [25]		
	26 Multiply line 25 by 2% (0.02)	26	
	27 Subtract line 26 from line 24. If line 26 is more than line 24, enter -0-		27
Other Miscellaneous Deductions	28 Other—from list in instructions. List type and amount ▶		28

Total Itemized Deductions	29 Is Form 1040, line 38, over $155,650?
	  ☐ **No.** Your deduction is not limited. Add the amounts in the far right column for lines 4 through 28. Also, enter this amount on Form 1040, line 40.
	  ☐ **Yes.** Your deduction may be limited. See the Itemized Deductions Worksheet in the instructions to figure the amount to enter.
			29

	30 If you elect to itemize deductions even though they are less than your standard deduction, check here . . . . ▶ ☐		

For Paperwork Reduction Act Notice, see Form 1040 instructions.   Cat. No. 17145C   Schedule A (Form 1040) 2016

Task-Based Simulation 19 Solution

Form 1040 Schedule A		
	Authoritative Literature	
		Help

(See Schedule A on the next page.)

Medical and Dental Expenses
The disability income insurance premiums do not represent medical insurance and are not deductible. Similarly, although prescription drugs are deductible, nonprescription medicine is not deductible.

Taxes
The automobile registration fee is not deductible.

Interest
Only home mortgage interest and investment interest expense can be deducted as an itemized deduction. The interest on the automobile loan and the credit card interest are considered personal interest and are not deductible.

Contributions
The stock was appreciated and held for more than one year so it qualifies as capital gain property. As a result, the amount of contribution is the stock's fair market value of $4,000.

Miscellaneous
The legal fee for preparation of a will and life insurance premiums are nondeductible personal expenses. Similarly, no deduction is available for transportation to and from work (commuting), political contributions, and repairs to a principal residence.

SCHEDULE A (Form 1040)

Department of the Treasury
Internal Revenue Service (99)

Itemized Deductions

▶ Information about Schedule A and its separate instructions is at *www.irs.gov/schedulea*.
▶ Attach to Form 1040.

OMB No. 1545-0074

2016

Attachment Sequence No. **07**

Name(s) shown on Form 1040

Fred & Laura Shaw

Your social security number

123-45-6789

Medical and Dental Expenses

Caution: Do not include expenses reimbursed or paid by others.

1	Medical and dental expenses (see instructions)	1	8,405		
2	Enter amount from Form 1040, line 38	2	80,000			
3	Multiply line 2 by 10% (0.10). But if either you or your spouse was born before January 2, 1952, multiply line 2 by 7.5% (0.075) instead	3	8,000		
4	Subtract line 3 from line 1. If line 3 is more than line 1, enter -0-			4	405

Taxes You Paid

5	State and local (check only one box): a ☑ Income taxes, or b ☐ General sales taxes	5	1,200	
6	Real estate taxes (see instructions)	6	10,000	
7	Personal property taxes	7		
8	Other taxes. List type and amount ▶ **Personal property taxes**	8	410	
9	Add lines 5 through 8		9	11,610

Interest You Paid

Note: Your mortgage interest deduction may be limited (see instructions).

10	Home mortgage interest and points reported to you on Form 1098	10	7,700	
11	Home mortgage interest not reported to you on Form 1098. If paid to the person from whom you bought the home, see instructions and show that person's name, identifying no., and address ▶	11		
12	Points not reported to you on Form 1098. See instructions for special rules	12		
13	Mortgage insurance premiums (see instructions)	13		
14	Investment interest. Attach Form 4952 if required. (See instructions.)	14		
15	Add lines 10 through 14		15	7,700

Gifts to Charity

If you made a gift and got a benefit for it, see instructions.

16	Gifts by cash or check. If you made any gift of $250 or more, see instructions	16	2,500	
17	Other than by cash or check. If any gift of $250 or more, see instructions. You **must** attach Form 8283 if over $500	17	4,000	
18	Carryover from prior year	18		
19	Add lines 16 through 18		19	6,500

Casualty and Theft Losses

20	Casualty or theft loss(es). Attach Form 4684. (See instructions.)	20	

Job Expenses and Certain Miscellaneous Deductions

21	Unreimbursed employee expenses—job travel, union dues, job education, etc. Attach Form 2106 or 2106-EZ if required. (See instructions.) ▶	21	1,500	
22	Tax preparation fees	22	400	
23	Other expenses—investment, safe deposit box, etc. List type and amount ▶ **Subscriptions $300; safe deposit box $120**	23	420	
24	Add lines 21 through 23	24	2,320	
25	Enter amount from Form 1040, line 38	25	80,000		
26	Multiply line 25 by 2% (0.02)	26	1,600	
27	Subtract line 26 from line 24. If line 26 is more than line 24, enter -0-		27	720

Other Miscellaneous Deductions

28	Other—from list in instructions. List type and amount ▶	28	

Total Itemized Deductions

29	Is Form 1040, line 38, over $155,650? ☑ **No.** Your deduction is not limited. Add the amounts in the far right column for lines 4 through 28. Also, enter this amount on Form 1040, line 40. ☐ **Yes.** Your deduction may be limited. See the Itemized Deductions Worksheet in the instructions to figure the amount to enter.	29	26,935
30	If you elect to itemize deductions even though they are less than your standard deduction, check here ▶ ☐		

For Paperwork Reduction Act Notice, see Form 1040 instructions. | Cat. No. 17145C | Schedule A (Form 1040) 2016

Task-Based Simulation 20

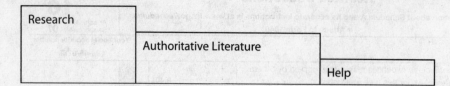

The Shaws are considering donating a painting to a state university for display in the university's library. The Shaws acquired the painting six months ago for $90,000 and believe that the painting is now worth $105,000. Which code section and subsection determines the amount of charitable contribution to which the Shaws will be entitled if they donate the painting at the present time? Indicate the reference to that citation in the shaded boxes below.

Section		Subsection	
§		(	)

Task-Based Simulation 20 Solution

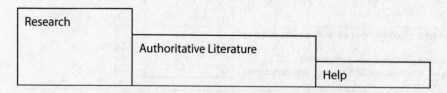

Internal Revenue Code Section 170, subsection (e) provides that the amount of the Shaws' charitable contribution will be limited to the painting's cost of $90,000, since the painting would not result in long-term capital gain if sold (i.e., it has not been held for more than 12 months).

Section		Subsection	
§	170	(	e	)

Deductions—Losses and Bad Debts

Task-Based Simulation 21

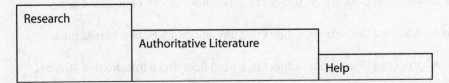

Thomas contacts you and indicates that he expects to incur a substantial net capital loss for calendar-year 2016 and wonders what the treatment of the carryforwards will be in future years. Which code section and subsection provides for the treatment of an individual's capital loss carryforward? Indicate the reference to that citation in the shaded boxes below.

Section		Subsection	
§			

Task-Based Simulation 21 Solution

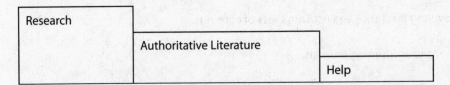

Internal Revenue Code Section 1212, subsection (b) provides that for taxpayers other than corporations, an excess of net short-term capital loss over net long-term capital gain for a taxable year shall be treated as a short-term capital loss in the succeeding taxable year. Similarly, an excess of net long-term capital loss over net short-term capital gain for a taxable year shall be treated as a long-term capital loss in the succeeding taxable year.

Section		Subsection		
§	1212	(	B	)

Task-Based Simulation 22

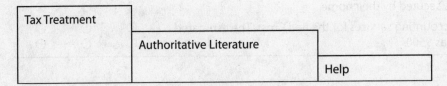

Tom and Joan Moore are married filing a joint return. During 2016, the following events took place. For **items 1 through 12**, select the appropriate tax treatment. A tax treatment may be selected once, more than once, or not at all.

Tax treatment

A. Not deductible on Form 1040.
B. Deductible in full in Schedule A—Itemized Deductions.
C. Deductible in Schedule A—Itemized Deductions, subject to a threshold of 10% of adjusted gross income.
D. Deductible in Schedule A—Itemized Deductions, subject to a limitation of 50% of adjusted gross income.
F. Deductible in Schedule A—Itemized Deductions, subject to a $100 floor and a threshold of 10% of adjusted gross income.
F. Deductible in Schedule A—Itemized Deductions, subject to a threshold of 2% of adjusted gross income.

	(A) (D)	(B) (E)	(C) (F)
1. On March 23, 2016, Tom sold 50 shares of Zip stock at a $1,200 loss. He repurchased 50 shares of Zip on April 15, 2016.	○ ○	○ ○	○ ○
2. Payment of a personal property tax based on the value of the Moores' car.	○ ○	○ ○	○ ○
3. Used clothes were donated to church organizations.	○ ○	○ ○	○ ○
4. Premiums were paid covering insurance against Tom's loss of earnings.	○ ○	○ ○	○ ○
5. Tom paid for subscriptions to accounting journals.	○ ○	○ ○	○ ○
6. Interest was paid on a $10,000 home-equity line of credit secured by the Moores' residence. The fair market value of the home exceeded the mortgage by $50,000. Tom used the proceeds to purchase a sailboat.	○ ○	○ ○	○ ○
7. Amounts were paid in excess of insurance reimbursement for prescription drugs.	○ ○	○ ○	○ ○
8. Funeral expenses were paid by the Moores for Joan's brother.	○ ○	○ ○	○ ○
9. Theft loss was incurred on Joan's jewelry in excess of insurance reimbursement. There were no 2016 personal casualty gains.	○ ○	○ ○	○ ○
10. Loss on the sale of the family's sailboat.	○ ○	○ ○	○ ○
11. Interest was paid on the $300,000 acquisition mortgage on the Moores' home. The mortgage is secured by their home.	○ ○	○ ○	○ ○
12. Joan performed free accounting services for the Red Cross. The estimated value of the services was $500.	○ ○	○ ○	○ ○

Task-Based Simulation 22 Solution

Tax Treatment		
	Authoritative Literature	
		Help

	(A) (D)	(B) (E)	(C) (F)
1. On March 23, 2016, Tom sold 50 shares of Zip stock at a $1,200 loss. He repurchased 50 shares of Zip on April 15, 2016.	● ○	○ ○	○ ○
2. Payment of a personal property tax based on the value of the Moores' car.	○ ○	● ○	○ ○
3. Used clothes were donated to church organizations.	○ ●	○ ○	○ ○
4. Premiums were paid covering insurance against Tom's loss of earnings.	● ○	○ ○	○ ○
5. Tom paid for subscriptions to accounting journals.	○ ○	○ ○	○ ●
6. Interest was paid on a $10,000 home-equity line of credit secured by the Moores' residence. The fair market value of the home exceeded the mortgage by $50,000. Tom used the proceeds to purchase a sailboat.	○ ○	● ○	○ ○
7. Amounts were paid in excess of insurance reimbursement for prescription drugs.	○ ○	○ ○	● ○
8. Funeral expenses were paid by the Moores for Joan's brother.	● ○	○ ○	○ ○
9. Theft loss was incurred on Joan's jewelry in excess of insurance reimbursement. There were no 2016 personal casualty gains.	○ ○	○ ●	○ ○
10. Loss on the sale of the family's sailboat.	● ○	○ ○	○ ○
11. Interest was paid on the $300,000 acquisition mortgage on the Moores' home. The mortgage is secured by their home.	○ ○	● ○	○ ○
12. Joan performed free accounting services for the Red Cross. The estimated value of the services was $500.	● ○	○ ○	○ ○

Explanations

1. **(A)** No loss is deductible if stock is sold at a loss and within 30 days before or after the sale, substantially identical stock in the same corporation is purchased. Here, the loss on the March 23 sale of 50 shares of Zip stock cannot be recognized because Tom repurchased 50 shares of Zip stock on April 15. The $1,200 loss not recognized is added to the basis of the newly acquired stock.
2. **(B)** Personal property taxes based on value are fully deductible as an itemized deduction.
3. **(D)** The fair market value of used clothing donated to a qualified charitable organization is deductible as an itemized deduction subject to a 50% of AGI limitation.
4. **(A)** Premiums on insurance against the loss of earnings in the event of disability are a nondeductible personal expense.
5. **(F)** Since Tom is a CPA working as an employee, the unreimbursed cost of subscriptions to accounting journals is deductible as an itemized deduction subject to a threshold of 2% of AGI.

6. **(B)** Interest on home-equity indebtedness of up to $100,000 is fully deductible as an itemized deduction regardless of how the proceeds of the loan were used.

7. **(C)** The unreimbursed cost of prescriptions qualify as a medical expense deductible as an itemized deduction subject to a threshold of 10% of AGI.

8. **(A)** Funeral expenses are a nondeductible personal expense.

9. **(E)** A theft loss on personal use property is deductible as an itemized deduction subject to a $100 floor and a threshold of 10% of AGI.

10. **(A)** A loss resulting from the sale of personal use property is not deductible.

11. **(B)** Interest on acquisition indebtedness of up to $1 million is fully deductible as an itemized deduction if the mortgage is secured by the taxpayer's principal or second residence.

12. **(A)** No charitable deduction is allowable for the value of a taxpayer's services performed for a charitable organization.

Limitations on Business Deductions

Task-Based Simulation 23

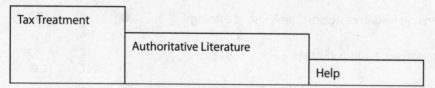

Cole, a newly licensed CPA, opened an office in 2016 as a sole practitioner engaged in the practice of public accountancy. Cole reports on the cash basis for income tax purposes and is 46 years old.

Listed below are Cole's 2016 business and nonbusiness transactions, as well as possible tax treatments. For each of Cole's transactions (**Items 1 through 20**), select the appropriate tax treatment. A tax treatment may be selected once, more than once, or not at all.

Tax treatment

A. Taxable as interest income in Schedule B—Interest and Dividend Income.
B. Taxable as other income on page 1 of Form 1040.
C. Not taxable.
D. Deductible on page 1 of Form 1040 to arrive at adjusted gross income.
E. Deductible in Schedule A—Itemized Deductions, subject to threshold of 10% of adjusted gross income.
F. Deductible in Schedule A—Itemized Deductions, subject to threshold of 10% of adjusted gross income and additional threshold of $100.
G. Deductible in full in Schedule A—Itemized Deductions (cannot be claimed as a credit).
H. Deductible in Schedule B—Interest and Dividend Income.
I. Deductible in Schedule C—Profit or Loss from Business.
J. Deductible in Schedule D—Capital Gains or Losses.
K. Deductible in Schedule E—Supplemental Income and Loss.
L. Deductible in Form 4797—Sales of Business Property.
M. Claimed in Form 1116—Foreign Tax Credit, or in Schedule A—Itemized Deductions, at taxpayer's option.
N. Based on gross self-employment income.
O. Based on net earnings from self-employment.
P. Not deductible.

Transactions	(A)(H)(O)	(B)(I)(P)	(C)(J)	(D)(K)	(E)(L)	(F)(M)	(G)(N)
1. Fees received for jury duty.	○○○	○○○	○○	○○	○○	○○	○○
2. Interest income on mortgage loan receivable.	○○○	○○○	○○	○○	○○	○○	○○
3. Penalty paid to bank on early withdrawal of savings.	○○○	○○○	○○	○○	○○	○○	○○
4. Write-offs of uncollectible accounts receivable from accounting practice.	○○○	○○○	○○	○○	○○	○○	○○
5. Cost of attending review course in preparation for the Uniform CPA Examination.	○○○	○○○	○○	○○	○○	○○	○○
6. Fee for the biennial permit to practice as a CPA.	○○○	○○○	○○	○○	○○	○○	○○
7. Costs of attending CPE courses in fulfillment of state board requirements.	○○○	○○○	○○	○○	○○	○○	○○
8. Contribution to a qualified Keogh retirement plan.	○○○	○○○	○○	○○	○○	○○	○○
9. Loss sustained from nonbusiness bad debt.	○○○	○○○	○○	○○	○○	○○	○○
10. Loss sustained on sale of "Small Business Corporation" (Section 1244) stock.	○○○	○○○	○○	○○	○○	○○	○○
11. Taxes paid on land owned by Cole and rented out as a parking lot.	○○○	○○○	○○	○○	○○	○○	○○
12. Interest paid on installment purchases of household furniture.	○○○	○○○	○○	○○	○○	○○	○○
13. Alimony paid to former spouse who reports the alimony as taxable income.	○○○	○○○	○○	○○	○○	○○	○○
14. Personal medical expenses charged on credit card in December 2016 but not paid until January 2017.	○○○	○○○	○○	○○	○○	○○	○○
15. Personal casualty loss sustained.	○○○	○○○	○○	○○	○○	○○	○○
16. State inheritance tax paid on bequest received.	○○○	○○○	○○	○○	○○	○○	○○
17. Foreign income tax withheld at source on dividend received.	○○○	○○○	○○	○○	○○	○○	○○

(Continued)

Transactions	(A) (H) (O)	(B) (I) (P)	(C) (J)	(D) (K)	(E) (L)	(F) (M)	(G) (N)
18. Computation of self-employment tax.	○ ○ ○	○ ○ ○	○ ○	○ ○	○ ○	○ ○	○ ○
19. One-half of self-employment tax paid with 2016 return filed in April 2017.	○ ○ ○	○ ○ ○	○ ○	○ ○	○ ○	○ ○	○ ○
20. Insurance premiums paid on Cole's life.	○ ○ ○	○ ○ ○	○ ○	○ ○	○ ○	○ ○	○ ○

Task-Based Simulation 23 Solution

Tax Treatment

Authoritative Literature

Help

Transactions	(A) (H) (O)	(B) (I) (P)	(C) (J)	(D) (K)	(E) (L)	(F) (M)	(G) (N)
1. Fees received for jury duty.	○ ○ ○	● ○ ○	○ ○	○ ○	○ ○	○ ○	○ ○
2. Interest income on mortgage loan receivable.	● ○ ○	○ ○ ○	○ ○	○ ○	○ ○	○ ○	○ ○
3. Penalty paid to bank on early withdrawal of savings.	○ ○ ○	○ ○ ○	○ ○	● ○	○ ○	○ ○	○ ○
4. Write-offs of uncollectible accounts receivable from accounting practice.	○ ○ ○	○ ○ ●	○ ○	○ ○	○ ○	○ ○	○ ○
5. Cost of attending review course in preparation for the Uniform CPA Examination.	○ ○ ○	○ ○ ●	○ ○	○ ○	○ ○	○ ○	○ ○
6. Fee for the biennial permit to practice as a CPA.	○ ○ ○	○ ● ○	○ ○	○ ○	○ ○	○ ○	○ ○
7. Costs of attending CPE courses in fulfillment of state board requirements.	○ ○ ○	○ ● ○	○ ○	○ ○	○ ○	○ ○	○ ○
8. Contribution to a qualified Keogh retirement plan.	○ ○ ○	○ ○ ○	○ ○	● ○	○ ○	○ ○	○ ○
9. Loss sustained from nonbusiness bad debt.	○ ○ ○	○ ○ ○	○ ●	○ ○	○ ○	○ ○	○ ○
10. Loss sustained on sale of "Small Business Corporation" (Section 1244) stock.	○ ○ ○	○ ○ ○	○ ○	○ ○	○ ●	○ ○	○ ○

Transactions	(A) (H) (O)	(B) (I) (P)	(C) (J)	(D) (K)	(E) (L)	(F) (M)	(G) (N)
11. Taxes paid on land owned by Cole and rented out as a parking lot.	○ ○ ○	○ ○ ○	○ ○	● ○	○ ○	○ ○	○ ○
12. Interest paid on installment purchases of household furniture.	○ ○ ○	○ ○ ●	○ ○	○ ○	○ ○	○ ○	○ ○
13. Alimony paid to former spouse who reports the alimony as taxable income.	○ ○ ○	○ ○ ○	○ ○	● ○	○ ○	○ ○	○ ○
14. Personal medical expenses charged on credit card in December 2016 but not paid until January 2017.	○ ○ ○	○ ○ ○	○ ○	○ ○	● ○	○ ○	○ ○
15. Personal casualty loss sustained.	○ ○ ○	○ ○ ○	○ ○	○ ○	○ ○	● ○	○ ○
16. State inheritance tax paid on bequest received.	○ ○ ○	○ ● ○	○ ○	○ ○	○ ○	○ ○	○ ○
17. Foreign income tax withheld at source on dividend received.	○ ○ ○	○ ○ ○	○ ○	○ ○	○ ○	○ ●	○ ○
18. Computation of self-employment tax.	○ ○ ●	○ ○ ○	○ ○	○ ○	○ ○	○ ○	○ ○
19. One-half of self-employment tax paid with 2016 return filed in April 2017.	○ ○ ○	○ ○ ○	○ ○	● ○	○ ○	○ ○	○ ○
20. Insurance premiums paid on Cole's life.	○ ○ ○	○ ○ ●	○ ○	○ ○	○ ○	○ ○	○ ○

Explanations

1. **(B)** Fees received for jury duty represent compensation for services and must be included in gross income. Since there is no separate line for jury duty fees, they are taxable as other income on page 1 of Form 1040.
2. **(A)** Interest income on a mortgage loan receivable must be included in gross income and is taxable as interest income in Schedule B—Interest and Dividend Income.
3. **(D)** An interest forfeiture penalty for making an early withdrawal from a certificate of deposit is deductible on page 1 of Form 1040 to arrive at adjusted gross income.
4. **(P)** The problem indicates that Cole is a CPA reporting on the cash basis. Accounts receivable resulting from services rendered by a cash-basis taxpayer have a zero tax basis, because the income has not yet been reported. Therefore, the write-offs of zero basis uncollectible accounts receivable from Cole's accounting practice are not deductible.
5. **(P)** An educational expense that is part of a program of study that can qualify an individual for a new trade or business is not deductible. This is true even if the individual is not seeking a new job. In this case, the cost of attending a review course in preparation for the CPA examination is a nondeductible personal expense since it qualifies Cole for a new profession.
6. **(I)** Licensing and regulatory fees paid to state or local governments are an ordinary and necessary trade or business expense and are deductible by a sole proprietor on Schedule C—Profit or Loss from Business. Since Cole is a cash method taxpayer, he can deduct the fee for the biennial permit to practice when paid in 2016.

7. **(I)** All trade or business expenses of a self-employed individual are deductible on Schedule C—Profit or Loss from Business. Education must meet certain requirements before the related expenses can be deducted. Generally, deductible education expenses must not be a part of a program that will qualify the individual for a new trade or business and must (1) be required by an employer or by law to keep the individual's present position, or (2) maintain or improve skills required in the individual's present work. In this case, Cole already is a CPA and is fulfilling state CPE requirements, so his education costs of attending CPE courses are deductible in Schedule C—Profit or Loss from Business.

8. **(D)** Contributions to a self-employed individual's qualified Keogh retirement plan are deductible on page 1 of Form 1040 to arrive at adjusted gross income. The maximum deduction for contributions to a defined contribution Keogh retirement plan is limited to the lesser of $53,000 (for 2016), or 25% of self-employment income.

9. **(J)** A loss sustained from a nonbusiness bad debt is always classified as a short-term capital loss. Therefore, Cole's nonbusiness bad debt is deductible in Schedule D—Capital Gains or Losses.

10. **(L)** A loss sustained on the sale of Sec. 1244 stock is generally deductible as an ordinary loss, with the amount of ordinary loss deduction limited to $50,000. On a joint return, the limit is increased to $100,000, even if the stock was owned by only one spouse. The ordinary loss resulting from the sale of Sec. 1244 stock is deductible in Form 4797—Sales of Business Property. To the extent that a loss on Sec. 1244 stock exceeds the applicable $50,000 or $100,000 limit, the loss is deductible as a capital loss in Schedule D—Capital Gains or Losses. Similarly, if Sec. 1244 stock is sold at a gain, the gain would be reported as a capital gain in Schedule D if the stock is a capital asset.

11. **(K)** Rental income and expenses related to rental property are generally reported in Schedule E. Here, the taxes paid on land owned by Cole and rented out as a parking lot are deductible in Schedule E—Supplemental Income and Loss. Schedule E also is used to report the income or loss from royalties, partnerships, S corporations, estates, and trusts.

12. **(P)** The interest paid on installment purchases of household furniture is considered personal interest and is not deductible. Personal interest is any interest that is not qualified residence interest, investment interest, passive activity interest, or business interest. Personal interest generally includes interest on car loans, interest on income tax, underpayments, installment plan interest, credit card finance charges, and late payment charges by a utility.

13. **(D)** Alimony paid to a former spouse who reports the alimony as taxable income is deductible on page 1 of Form 1040 to arrive at adjusted gross income.

14. **(E)** Personal medical expenses are generally deductible as an itemized deduction subject to a 10% of AGI threshold for the year in which they are paid. Additionally, an individual can deduct medical expenses charged to a credit card in the year the charge is made. It makes no difference when the amount charged is actually paid. Here, Cole's personal medical expenses charged on a credit card in December 2016 but not paid until January 2017 are deductible for 2016 in Schedule A—Itemized Deductions, subject to a threshold of 10% of adjusted gross income.

15. **(F)** If an individual sustains a personal casualty loss, it is deductible in Schedule A—Itemized Deductions subject to a threshold of $100 and an additional threshold of 10% of adjusted gross income.

16. **(P)** State inheritance taxes paid on a bequest that was received are not deductible. Other taxes not deductible in computing an individual's federal income tax include federal estate and gift taxes, federal income taxes, and Social Security and other employment taxes paid by an employee.

17. **(M)** An individual can deduct foreign income taxes as an itemized deduction or can deduct foreign income taxes as a tax credit. Cole's foreign income tax withheld at source on foreign dividends received can be claimed in Form 1116—Foreign Tax Credit, or in Schedule A—Itemized Deductions, at Cole's option.

18. **(O)** A self-employed individual is subject to a self-employment tax if the individual's net earnings from self-employment are at least $400.

19. **(D)** An individual's self-employment tax is computed in Schedule SE and is added as an additional tax in arriving at the individual's total tax. A portion of the computed self-employment tax is allowed as a deduction in arriving at adjusted gross income. Here, one-half of Cole's self-employment tax for 2016 is deductible for 2016 on page 1 of Form 1040 to arrive at adjusted gross income, even though the tax was not paid until the return was filed in April 2017.

20. **(P)** Insurance premiums paid on Cole's life are classified as a personal expense and are not deductible.

Task-Based Simulation 24

Tax Treatment		
	Authoritative Literature	
		Help

Green is self-employed as a human resources consultant and reports on the cash basis for income tax purposes. Green is an unmarried custodial parent with one dependent child.

Listed below are Green's Year 3 business and nonbusiness transactions, as well as possible tax treatments. For each of Green's transactions (**Items 1 through 25**), select the appropriate tax treatment. A tax treatment may be selected once, more than once, or not at all.

Tax treatment

A. Taxable as other income on Form 1040.

B. Reported in Schedule B—Interest and Dividend Income.

C. Reported in Schedule C as trade or business income.

D. Reported in Schedule E—Supplemental Income and Loss.

E. Not taxable.

F. Fully deductible on Form 1040 to arrive at adjusted gross income.

G. Fifty percent deductible on Form 1040 to arrive at adjusted gross income.

H. Reported in Schedule A—Itemized Deductions (deductibility subject to threshold of 10% of adjusted gross income).

I. Reported in Schedule A—Itemized Deductions (deductibility subject to threshold of 2% of adjusted gross income).

J. Reported in Form 4562—Depreciation and Amortization and deductible in Schedule A—Itemized Deductions (deductibility subject to threshold of 2% of adjusted gross income).

K. Reported in Form 4562—Depreciation and Amortization, and deductible in Schedule C—Profit or Loss from Business.

L. Fully deductible in Schedule C—Profit or Loss from Business.

M. Partially deductible in Schedule C—Profit or Loss from Business.

N. Reported in Form 2119—Sale of Your Home, and deductible in Schedule D—Capital Gains and Losses.

O. Not deductible.

	(A) (G) (M)	(B) (H) (N)	(C) (I) (O)	(D) (J)	(E) (K)	(F) (L)
Transactions						
1. Retainer fees received from clients.	O O O	O O O	O O O	O O	O O	O O
2. Oil royalties received.	O O O	O O O	O O O	O O	O O	O O
3. Interest income on general obligation state and local government bonds.	O O O	O O O	O O O	O O	O O	O O
4. Interest on refund of federal taxes.	O O O	O O O	O O O	O O	O O	O O
5. Death benefits from term life insurance policy on parent.	O O O	O O O	O O O	O O	O O	O O
6. Interest income on U.S. Treasury bonds.	O O O	O O O	O O O	O O	O O	O O
7. Share of ordinary income from an investment in a limited partnership reported in Form 1065, Schedule K-1.	O O O	O O O	O O O	O O	O O	O O
8. Taxable income from rental of a townhouse owned by Green.	O O O	O O O	O O O	O O	O O	O O
9. Prize won as a contestant on a TV quiz show.	O O O	O O O	O O O	O O	O O	O O
10. Payment received for jury service.	O O O	O O O	O O O	O O	O O	O O
11. Dividends received from mutual funds that invest in tax-free government obligations.	O O O	O O O	O O O	O O	O O	O O
12. Qualifying medical expenses not reimbursed by insurance.	O O O	O O O	O O O	O O	O O	O O
13. Personal life insurance premiums paid by Green.	O O O	O O O	O O O	O O	O O	O O
14. Expenses for business-related meals where clients were present.	O O O	O O O	O O O	O O	O O	O O
15. Depreciation on personal computer purchased in Year 2 used for business.	O O O	O O O	O O O	O O	O O	O O
16. Business lodging expenses, while out of town.	O O O	O O O	O O O	O O	O O	O O
17. Subscriptions to professional journals used for business.	O O O	O O O	O O O	O O	O O	O O

Transactions	(A) (G) (M)	(B) (H) (N)	(C) (I) (O)	(D) (J)	(E) (K)	(F) (L)
18. Self-employment taxes paid.	○ ○ ○	○ ○ ○	○ ○ ○	○ ○	○ ○	○ ○
19. Qualifying contributions to a simplified employee pension plan.	○ ○ ○	○ ○ ○	○ ○ ○	○ ○	○ ○	○ ○
20. Election to expense business equipment purchased in Year 2.	○ ○ ○	○ ○ ○	○ ○ ○	○ ○	○ ○	○ ○
21. Qualifying alimony payments made by Green.	○ ○ ○	○ ○ ○	○ ○ ○	○ ○	○ ○	○ ○
22. Subscriptions for investment-related publications.	○ ○ ○	○ ○ ○	○ ○ ○	○ ○	○ ○	○ ○
23. Interest expense on a home-equity line of credit for an amount borrowed to finance Green's business.	○ ○ ○	○ ○ ○	○ ○ ○	○ ○	○ ○	○ ○
24. Interest expense on a loan for an auto used 75% for business.	○ ○ ○	○ ○ ○	○ ○ ○	○ ○	○ ○	○ ○
25. Loss on sale of residence.	○ ○ ○	○ ○ ○	○ ○ ○	○ ○	○ ○	○ ○

Task-Based Simulation 24 Solution

- Tax Treatment
  - Authoritative Literature
    - Help

Transactions	(A) (G) (M)	(B) (H) (N)	(C) (I) (O)	(D) (J)	(E) (K)	(F) (L)
1. Retainer fees received from clients.	○ ○ ○	○ ○ ○	● ○ ○	○ ○	○ ○	○ ○
2. Oil royalties received.	○ ○ ○	○ ○ ○	○ ○ ○	● ○	○ ○	○ ○
3. Interest income on general obligation state and local government bonds.	○ ○ ○	○ ○ ○	○ ○ ○	○ ○	● ○	○ ○
4. Interest on refund of federal taxes.	○ ○ ○	● ○ ○	○ ○ ○	○ ○	○ ○	○ ○

(Continued)

Transactions	(A)(G)(M)	(B)(H)(N)	(C)(I)(O)	(D)(J)	(E)(K)	(F)(L)
5. Death benefits from term life insurance policy on parent.	○ ○ ○	○ ○ ○	○ ○ ○	○ ○	● ○	○ ○
6. Interest income on U.S. Treasury bonds.	○ ○ ○	● ○ ○	○ ○ ○	○ ○	○ ○	○ ○
7. Share of ordinary income from an investment in a limited partnership reported in Form 1065, Schedule K-1.	○ ○ ○	○ ○ ○	○ ○ ○	● ○	○ ○	○ ○
8. Taxable income from rental of a townhouse owned by Green.	○ ○ ○	○ ○ ○	○ ○ ○	● ○	○ ○	○ ○
9. Prize won as a contestant on a TV quiz show.	● ○ ○	○ ○ ○	○ ○ ○	○ ○	○ ○	○ ○
10. Payment received for jury service.	● ○ ○	○ ○ ○	○ ○ ○	○ ○	○ ○	○ ○
11. Dividends received from mutual funds that invest in tax-free government obligations.	○ ○ ○	○ ○ ○	○ ○ ○	○ ○	● ○	○ ○
12. Qualifying medical expenses not reimbursed by insurance.	○ ○ ○	○ ● ○	○ ○ ○	○ ○	○ ○	○ ○
13. Personal life insurance premiums paid by Green.	○ ○ ○	○ ○ ○	○ ○ ●	○ ○	○ ○	○ ○
14. Expenses for business-related meals where clients were present.	○ ○ ●	○ ○ ○	○ ○ ○	○ ○	○ ○	○ ○
15. Depreciation on personal computer purchased in Year 2 used for business.	○ ○ ○	○ ○ ○	○ ○ ○	○ ○	○ ●	○ ○
16. Business lodging expenses, while out of town.	○ ○ ○	○ ○ ○	○ ○ ○	○ ○	○ ○	○ ●
17. Subscriptions to professional journals used for business.	○ ○ ○	○ ○ ○	○ ○ ○	○ ○	○ ○	○ ●
18. Self-employment taxes paid.	○ ● ○	○ ○ ○	○ ○ ○	○ ○	○ ○	○ ○
19. Qualifying contributions to a simplified employee pension plan.	○ ○ ○	○ ○ ○	○ ○ ○	○ ○	○ ○	● ○
20. Election to expense business equipment purchased in Year 2.	○ ○ ○	○ ○ ○	○ ○ ○	○ ○	○ ●	○ ○
21. Qualifying alimony payments made by Green.	○ ○ ○	○ ○ ○	○ ○ ○	○ ○	○ ○	● ○

Transactions	(A) (G) (M)	(B) (H) (N)	(C) (I) (O)	(D) (J)	(E) (K)	(F) (L)
22. Subscriptions for investment-related publications.	○ ○ 	○ ○ ○	○ ● ○	○ ○	○ ○	○ ○
23. Interest expense on a home-equity line of credit for an amount borrowed to finance Green's business.	○ ○ 	○ ○ ○	○ ○ ○	○ ○	○ ○	○ ●
24. Interest expense on a loan for an auto used 75% for business.	○ ○ ●	○ ○ ○	○ ○ ○	○ ○	○ ○	○ ○
25. Loss on sale of residence.	○ ○ ○	○ ○ ○	○ ○ ●	○ ○	○ ○	○ ○

Explanations

1. **(C)** All trade or business income and deductions of a self-employed individual are reported on Schedule C—Profit or Loss from Business. Retainer fees received from clients is reported in Schedule C as trade or business income.
2. **(D)** Income derived from royalties is reported in Schedule E—Supplemental Income and Loss. Schedule E also is used to report the income or loss from rental real estate, partnerships, S corporations, estates, and trusts.
3. **(E)** Interest from general obligation state and local government bonds is tax-exempt and is excluded from gross income.
4. **(B)** The interest income on a refund of federal income taxes must be included in gross income and is reported in Schedule B—Interest and Dividend Income. The actual refund of federal income taxes itself is excluded from gross income.
5. **(E)** Life insurance proceeds paid by reason of death are generally excluded from gross income. Here, the death benefits received by Green from a term life insurance policy on the life of Green's parent are not taxable.
6. **(B)** Interest income from U.S. Treasury bonds and Treasury bills must be included in gross income and is reported in Schedule B—Interest and Dividend Income.
7. **(D)** A partner's share of a partnership's ordinary income that is reported to the partner on Form 1065, Schedule K-1 must be included in the partner's gross income and is reported in Schedule E—Supplemental Income and Loss.
8. **(D)** The taxable income from the rental of a townhouse owned by Green must be included in gross income and is reported in Schedule E—Supplemental Income and Loss.
9. **(A)** A prize won as a contestant on a TV quiz show must be included in gross income. Since there is no separate line on Form 1040 for prizes, they are taxable as other income on Form 1040.
10. **(A)** Fees received for jury duty represent compensation for services and must be included in gross income. Since there is no separate line for jury duty fees, they are taxable as other income on Form 1040.
11. **(E)** An investor in a mutual fund may receive several different kinds of distributions including ordinary dividends, capital gain distributions, tax-exempt interest dividends, and return of capital distributions. A mutual fund may pay tax-exempt interest dividends to its shareholders if it meets certain requirements. These dividends are paid from the tax-exempt state and local obligation interest earned by the fund and retain their tax-exempt character when reported by the shareholder. Thus, Green's dividends received from mutual funds that invest in tax-free government obligations are not taxable.
12. **(H)** Qualifying medical expenses not reimbursed by insurance are deductible in Schedule A as an itemized deduction to the extent in excess of 10% of adjusted gross income.
13. **(O)** Personal life insurance premiums paid on Green's life are classified as a personal expense and not deductible.
14. **(M)** All trade or business expenses of a self-employed individual are deductible on Schedule C— Profit or Loss from Business. However, only 50% of the cost of business meals and entertainment is

deductible. Therefore, Green's expenses for business-related meals where clients were present are partially deductible in Schedule C.

15. **(K)** The deduction for depreciation on listed property (e.g., automobiles, computers, and property used for entertainment, etc.) is computed on Form 4562—Depreciation and Amortization. Since Green's personal computer was used in his business as a self-employed consultant, the amount of depreciation computed on Form 4562 is then deductible in Schedule C—Profit or Loss from Business.

16. **(L)** Lodging expenses while out of town on business are an ordinary and necessary business expense and are fully deductible by a self-employed individual in Schedule C—Profit or Loss from Business.

17. **(L)** The cost of subscriptions to professional journals used for business are an ordinary and necessary business expense and are fully deductible by a self-employed individual in Schedule C—Profit or Loss from Business.

18. **(G)** An individual's self-employment tax is computed in Schedule SE and is added as an additional tax in arriving at the individual's total tax liability. A portion of the computed self-employment tax is then allowed as a deduction on Form 1040 in arriving at adjusted gross income.

19. **(F)** Qualifying contributions to a self-employed individual's simplified employee pension plan are deductible on page 1 of Form 1040 to arrive at adjusted gross income.

20. **(K)** Sec. 179 permits a taxpayer to elect to treat the cost of qualifying depreciable personal business property as an expense rather than as a capital expenditure. In this case, Green's election to expense business equipment would be computed on Form 4562—Depreciation and Amortization, and then would be deductible in Schedule C—Profit or Loss from Business.

21. **(F)** Qualifying alimony payments made by Green to a former spouse are fully deductible on Form 1040 to arrive at adjusted gross income.

22. **(I)** The costs of subscriptions for investment publications are not related to Green's trade or business, but instead are considered expenses incurred in the production of portfolio income and are reported as miscellaneous itemized deductions in Schedule A—Itemized Deductions. These investment expenses are deductible to the extent that the aggregate of expenses in this category exceed 2% of adjusted gross income.

23. **(L)** The nature of interest expense is determined by using a tracing approach (i.e., the nature depends upon how the loan proceeds were used). Since the interest expense on Green's home-equity line of credit was for a loan to finance Green's business, the best answer is to treat the interest as a business expense fully deductible in Schedule C—Profit or Loss from Business.

24. **(M)** The interest expense on a loan for an auto used by a self-employed individual in a trade or business is deductible as a business expense. Since Green's auto was used 75% for business, only 75% of the interest expense is deductible in Schedule C—Profit or Loss from Business. The remaining 25% is considered personal interest expense and is not deductible.

25. **(O)** The loss resulting from the sale of Green's personal residence is not deductible because the property was held for personal use. Only losses due to casualty or theft are deductible for personal use property.

Individual Tax Issues

Personal and Dependency Exemptions

Task-Based Simulation 25

Exemptions		
	Authoritative Literature	
		Help

Frank and Dale Cumack are married and filing a joint 2016 income tax return. During 2016, Frank, age 63, was retired from government service and Dale, 55, was employed as a university instructor. In 2016, the Cumacks contributed all of the support to Dale's father, Jacques, an unmarried French citizen and French resident who had no gross income.

Determine whether the Cumacks overstated, understated, or correctly determined the number of both personal and dependency exemptions.

Selections

O. Overstated the number of both personal and dependency exemptions.
U. Understated the number of both personal and dependency exemptions.
C. Correctly determined the number of both personal and dependency exemptions.

	(O)	(U)	(C)
The Cumacks claimed three exemptions on their 2016 joint income tax return.	○	○	○

Task-Based Simulation 25 Solution

Exemptions		
	Authoritative Literature	
		Help

	(O)	(U)	(C)
The Cumacks claimed three exemptions on their 2016 joint income tax return.	●	○	○

Explanation

(O) To qualify as a dependency exemption, a dependent must be a U.S. citizen or resident of the United States, Canada, or Mexico. Since Dale's father, Jacques, is both a French citizen and French resident, he does not qualify as a dependency exemption even though the Cumacks provided all of his support.

Task-Based Simulation 26

Deductibility		
	Authoritative Literature	
		Help

Mark Smith is an employee of Patton Corporation. Additionally, Smith operates a consulting business as a sole proprietor and owns an apartment building. Smith made the expenditures listed below during 2016.

For each of the following items, indicate whether each expenditure is deductible for AGI, from AGI (not subject to 2% limitation), from AGI (subject to 2% limitation), or not deductible. Assume Smith plans to itemize deductions for 2016.

	For AGI	From AGI (No 2%)	From AGI (2% Floor)	Not Deductible
	(A)	(B)	(C)	(D)
1. Smith paid the medical expenses of his mother-in-law. Although Smith provided more than half of her support, she does not qualify as Smith's dependent because she had gross income of $5,000.	O	O	O	O
2. Smith paid the real estate taxes on his rental apartment building.	O	O	O	O
3. Smith paid state sales taxes of $1,500 on a used automobile that he purchased for personal use.	O	O	O	O
4. Smith paid the real estate taxes on his mother-in-law's home. She is the owner of the home.	O	O	O	O
5. Smith paid $1,500 of interest on credit card charges. The charges were for items purchased for personal use.	O	O	O	O
6. Smith paid an attorney $500 to prepare Smith's will.	O	O	O	O
7. Smith incurred $750 of expenses for business meals and entertainment in his position as an employee of Patton Corporation. Smith's expenses were not reimbursed.	O	O	O	O
8. Smith paid self-employment taxes of $3,000 as a result of earnings from the consulting business that he conducts as a sole proprietor.	O	O	O	O
9. Smith made a contribution to his self-employed retirement plan (Keogh Plan).	O	O	O	O
10. Smith had gambling losses totaling $2,500 for the year. He is including a lottery prize of $5,000 in his gross income this year.	O	O	O	O

Task-Based Simulation 26 Solution

Deductibility		
	Authoritative Literature	
		Help

	For AGI	From AGI (No 2%)	From AGI (2% Floor)	Not Deductible
	(A)	(B)	(C)	(D)
1. Smith paid the medical expenses of his mother-in-law. Although Smith provided more than half of her support, she does not qualify as Smith's dependent because she had gross income of $5,000.	○	●	○	○
2. Smith paid the real estate taxes on his rental apartment building.	●	○	○	○
3. Smith paid state sales taxes of $1,500 on a used automobile that he purchased for personal use.	○	●	○	○
4. Smith paid the real estate taxes on his mother-in-law's home. She is the owner of the home.	○	○	○	●
5. Smith paid $1,500 of interest on credit card charges. The charges were for items purchased for personal use.	○	○	○	●
6. Smith paid an attorney $500 to prepare Smith's will.	○	○	○	●
7. Smith incurred $750 of expenses for business meals and entertainment in his position as an employee of Patton Corporation. Smith's expenses were not reimbursed.	○	○	●	○
8. Smith paid self-employment taxes of $3,000 as a result of earnings from the consulting business that he conducts as a sole proprietor.	●	○	○	○
9. Smith made a contribution to his self-employed retirement plan (Keogh Plan).	●	○	○	○
10. Smith had gambling losses totaling $2,500 for the year. He is including a lottery prize of $5,000 in his gross income this year.	○	●	○	○

Explanations

1. **(B)** Deductible medical expenses include amounts paid for the diagnosis, cure, relief, treatment, or prevention of disease of the taxpayer, spouse, and dependents. The term **dependent** includes any person who qualifies as a dependency exemption, or would otherwise qualify as a dependency exemption except that the gross income and joint return tests are not met. Therefore, the medical expenses of Smith's mother-in-law are properly deductible from Smith's AGI and are not subject to the 2% limitation.

2. **(A)** Expenses attributable to property held for the production of rents or royalties are properly deductible "above the line." Above-the-line deductions are subtracted from gross income to determine adjusted gross income. Therefore, expenses incurred from a passive activity such as Smith's rental apartment building are deductible for AGI.

3. **(B)** For 2016, an individual may elect to deduct state and local general sales taxes in lieu of state and local income taxes. The amount that can be deducted is either the total of actual general sales taxes paid as substantiated by receipts, or an amount from IRS-provided tables, plus the amount of general sales taxes paid with regard to the purchase of a motor vehicle, boat, and specified other items.

4. **(D)** Real estate (real property) taxes are deductible only if imposed on property owned by the taxpayer. Since Smith's mother-in-law is the legal owner of the house, Smith cannot deduct his payment of those real estate taxes.

5. **(D)** No deduction is allowed for personal interest.

6. **(D)** Personal legal expenses are not a deductible expense. Only legal counsel obtained for advice concerning tax matters or incurred in the production of income are deductible. Therefore, Smith cannot deduct the $500 incurred to prepare his will.

7. **(C)** Unreimbursed employee expenses including business meals and entertainment (subject to the 50% rule) are deductible to the extent they exceed 2% of AGI. Therefore, $375 ($750 × 50%) is deductible from AGI, subject to the 2% floor.

8. **(A)** An individual is allowed to deduct a portion of the self-employment tax paid for the taxable year in the computation of AGI. Normally, 50% of the self-employment tax paid is deductible for AGI.

9. **(A)** Contributions by self-employed individuals to a qualified retirement plan (Keogh Plan) are a deduction for AGI.

10. **(B)** Gambling losses to the extent of gambling winnings are categorized as miscellaneous deductions not subject to the 2% floor. Therefore, the $2,500 of Smith's gambling losses would be deductible in full since he properly included his $5,000 winnings in his gross income for 2016.

Filing Status

Task-Based Simulation 27

Filing Status		
	Authoritative Literature	
		Help

Situation

Mrs. Vick, a 40-year-old cash-basis taxpayer, earned $45,000 as a teacher and $5,000 as a part-time real estate agent in Year 1. Mr. Vick, who died on July 1, Year 1, had been permanently disabled on his job and collected state disability benefits until his death. For all of Year 1 and Year 2, the Vicks' residence was the principal home of both their 11-year-old daughter Joan and Mrs. Vick's unmarried cousin, Fran Phillips, who had no income in either year. During Year 1 Joan received $200 a month in survivor Social Security benefits that began on August 1, Year 1, and will continue at least until her eighteenth birthday. In Year 1 and Year 2, Mrs. Vick provided over one-half the support for Joan and Fran, both of whom were U.S. citizens. Mrs. Vick did not remarry. Mr. and Mrs. Vick received the following in Year 1:

Earned income	$50,000
State disability benefits	1,500
Interest on:	
Refund from amended tax return	50
Savings account and certificates of deposit	350
Municipal bonds	100
Gift	3,000
Pension benefits	900
Jury duty pay	200
Gambling winnings	450
Life insurance proceeds	5,000

Additional information:

- Mrs. Vick received the $3,000 cash gift from her uncle.
- Mrs. Vick received the pension distributions from a qualified pension plan, paid for exclusively by her husband's employer.
- Mrs. Vick had $100 in gambling losses in Year 1.
- Mrs. Vick was the beneficiary of the life insurance policy on her husband's life. She received a lump-sum distribution. The Vicks had paid $500 in premiums.
- Mrs. Vick received Mr. Vick's accrued vacation pay of $500 in Year 2.

For **items 1 and 2**, determine and select from the choices below, **BOTH** the filing status and the number of exemptions for each item.

	Filing Status	Exemptions
S.	Single	1
M.	Married filing joint	2
H.	Head of household	3
Q.	Qualifying widow with dependent child	4

	Filing Status		Exemptions	
	(S) **(H)**	**(M)** **(Q)**	**(1)** **(2)**	**(2)** **(4)**
1. Determine the filing status and the number of exemptions that Mrs. Vick can claim on the Year 1 federal income tax return, to get the most favorable tax results.	○ ○	○ ○	○ ○	○ ○
2. Determine the filing status and the number of exemptions that Mrs. Vick can claim on the Year 2 federal income tax return to get the most favorable tax results, if she solely maintains the costs of her home.	○ ○	○ ○	○ ○	○ ○

For **items 3 through 9**, determine the amount, if any, that is taxable and should be included in Adjusted Gross Income (AGI) on the Year 1 federal income tax return filed by Mrs. Vick.

3. State disability benefits
4. Interest income
5. Pension benefits
6. Gift
7. Life insurance proceeds
8. Jury duty pay
9. Gambling winnings

Task-Based Simulation 27 Solution

Filing Status
Authoritative Literature
Help

For **items 1 and 2,** candidates were asked to determine the filing status and number of exemptions for Mrs. Vick.

1. **(M, 4)** Since Mr. Vick died during the year, Mrs. Vick is considered married for the entire year for filing status purposes. There would be four exemptions on the Vicks' joint return—one each for Mr. and Mrs. Vick, one for their 11-year-old daughter Joan, and one for Mrs. Vick's unmarried cousin Fran Phillips. Although Fran is treated as unrelated to the Vicks for dependency exemption purposes, Fran qualifies as a dependency exemption because the Vicks' residence was Fran's principal home for Year 1.

2. **(Q, 3)** Mrs. Vick will file as a "qualifying widow with dependent child," which will entitle her to use the joint return rates for Year 2. This filing status is available for the two years following the year of the spouse's death if (1) the surviving spouse was eligible to file a joint return in the year of the spouse's death, (2) does not remarry before the end of the taxable year, and (3) the surviving spouse pays over 50% of the cost of maintaining a household that is the principal home for the entire year of the surviving spouse's dependent child. There will be three exemptions on the return—one for Mrs. Vick, a dependency exemption for her daughter Joan, and a dependency exemption for her cousin Fran.

For items **3 through 9**, candidates were asked to determine the amount that is taxable and should be included in Adjusted Gross Income (AGI) on the Year 1 federal income tax return filed by Mrs. Vick.

3. **($0)** State disability benefits are excluded from gross income.
4. **($400)** The $50 interest on the tax refund and $350 interest from a savings account and certificates of deposit are taxable; the $100 interest on municipal bonds is excluded from gross income.
5. **($900)** The pension benefits are fully taxable because they were paid for exclusively by Mr. Vick's employer.
6. **($0)** Property received as a gift is always excluded from gross income.
7. **($0)** The proceeds of life insurance paid because of Mr. Vick's death are excluded from gross income, without regard to the amount of premiums paid.
8. **($200)** Jury duty pay represents compensation for services and must be included in gross income.
9. **($450)** The $450 of gambling winnings must be included in gross income. Mrs. Vick's $100 of gambling losses are deductible only from AGI as a miscellaneous itemized deduction.

Alternative Minimum Tax and Other Taxes

Task-Based Simulation 28

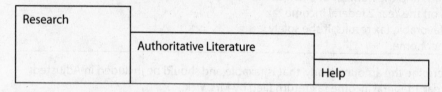

Adjustments must be made to regular taxable income in order to compute an individual's alternative minimum taxable income (AMTI). Which code section and subsection provides the adjustments that only apply to individuals when computing the alternative minimum tax? Indicate the reference to that citation in the shaded boxes below.

Section		Subsection	
§		(	)

Task-Based Simulation 28 Solution

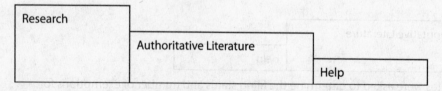

Internal Revenue Code Section 56, subsection (b) provides the adjustments to regular taxable income that are applicable only to individuals when computing the alternative minimum tax.

Section		Subsection	
§	56	(	b	)

Tax Credits

Personal Tax Credits

Task-Based Simulation 29

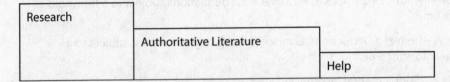

Mrs. Vick is considering making contributions to a qualified tuition program to provide savings for her daughter's college education. However, Mrs. Vick is concerned that the contributions will be considered a gift of a future interest and result in a taxable gift. Which code section and subsection provides the gift tax treatment for contributions to a qualified tuition program? Indicate the reference to that citation in the shaded boxes below.

Section	Subsection
§	( )

Task-Based Simulation 29 Solution

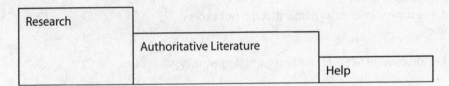

Internal Revenue Code Section 529, subsection (c) provides that any contribution to a qualified tuition program on behalf of a beneficiary shall be treated as a completed gift and not a gift of a future interest in property.

Section	Subsection
§ 529	(c)

Task-Based Simulation 30

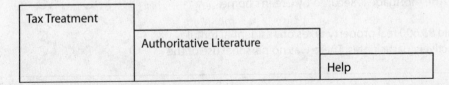

For 2016, Green, who had adjusted gross income of $40,000, qualified to itemize deductions and was subject to federal income tax liability. For **items 1 through 9**, select from the following list of tax treatments the appropriate tax treatment. A tax treatment may be selected once, more than once, or not at all.

Selections

A. Not deductible on Form 1040.

B. Deductible in full on Schedule A—Itemized Deductions.

C. Deductible in Schedule A—Itemized Deductions subject to a limitation of 50% of adjusted gross income.

D. Deductible in Schedule A—Itemized Deductions as miscellaneous deductions subject to a threshold of 2% of adjusted gross income.

E. Deductible in Schedule A—Itemized Deductions as miscellaneous deductions not subject to a threshold of 2% adjusted gross income.

F. Deductible on Schedule E—Supplemental Income and Loss.

G. A credit is allowable.

	(A) (D) (G)	(B) (E)	(C) (F)
1. In 2016, Green paid $2,000 interest on the $25,000 home equity mortgage on his vacation home, which he used exclusively for personal use. The mortgage is secured by Green's vacation home, and the loan proceeds were used to purchase an automobile.	○ ○ ○	○ ○	○ ○
2. For 2016, Green had a $30,000 cash charitable contribution carryover from his 2015 cash donation to the American Red Cross. Green made no additional charitable contributions in 2016.	○ ○ ○	○ ○	○ ○
3. During 2016, Green had investment interest expense that did not exceed his net investment income.	○ ○ ○	○ ○	○ ○
4. Green's 2016 lottery ticket losses were $450. He had no gambling winnings.	○ ○ ○	○ ○	○ ○
5. During 2016, Green paid $2,500 in real property taxes on his vacation home, which he used exclusively for personal use.	○ ○ ○	○ ○	○ ○
6. In 2016, Green paid a $500 premium for a homeowner's insurance policy on his principal residence.	○ ○ ○	○ ○	○ ○
7. For 2016, Green paid $2,000 to an unrelated babysitter to care for his child while he worked.	○ ○ ○	○ ○	○ ○
8. In 2016, Green paid $4,000 interest on the $60,000 acquisition mortgage on his principal residence. The mortgage is secured by Green's home.	○ ○ ○	○ ○	○ ○
9. During 2016, Green paid $3,600 real property taxes on residential rental property in which he actively participates. There was no personal use of the rental property.	○ ○ ○	○ ○	○ ○

Task-Based Simulation 30 Solution

Tax Treatment		
	Authoritative Literature	
		Help

	(A) (D) (G)	(B) (E)	(C) (F)
1. In 2016, Green paid $2,000 interest on the $25,000 home equity mortgage on his vacation home, which he used exclusively for personal use. The mortgage is secured by Green's vacation home, and the loan proceeds were used to purchase an automobile.	○ ○ ○	● ○	○ ○
2. For 2016, Green had a $30,000 cash charitable contribution carryover from his 2015 cash donation to the American Red Cross. Green made no additional charitable contributions in 2016.	○ ○ ○	○ ○	● ○
3. During 2016, Green had investment interest expense that did not exceed his net investment income.	○ ○ ○	● ○	○ ○
4. Green's 2016 lottery ticket losses were $450. He had no gambling winnings.	● ○ ○	○ ○	○ ○
5. During 2016, Green paid $2,500 in real property taxes on his vacation home, which he used exclusively for personal use.	○ ○ ○	● ○	○ ○
6. In 2016, Green paid a $500 premium for a homeowner's insurance policy on his principal residence.	● ○ ○	○ ○	○ ○
7. For 2016, Green paid $2,000 to an unrelated babysitter to care for his child while he worked.	○ ○ ●	○ ○	○ ○
8. In 2016, Green paid $4,000 interest on the $60,000 acquisition mortgage on his principal residence. The mortgage is secured by Green's home.	○ ○ ○	● ○	○ ○
9. During 2016, Green paid $3,600 real property taxes on residential rental property in which he actively participates. There was no personal use of the rental property.	○ ○ ○	○ ○	○ ●

Explanations

1. **(B)** Interest expense on home equity indebtedness is deductible on up to $100,000 of home equity loans secured by a first or second residence regardless of how the loan proceeds were used.
2. **(C)** Contributions in excess of applicable percentage limitations can be carried forward for up to five tax years. Here, the $30,000 of charitable contribution carryover from 2015 is deductible as an itemized deduction for 2016 subject to a limitation of 50% of AGI.
3. **(B)** Investment interest expense is deductible as an itemized deduction to the extent of net investment income. Since Green's investment interest expense did not exceed his net investment income, it is deductible in full.
4. **(A)** Gambling losses (including lottery ticket losses) are deductible as an itemized deduction to the extent of the gambling winnings included in gross income. Since Green had no gambling winnings, the losses are not deductible.
5. **(B)** State, local, or foreign real estate taxes imposed on the taxpayer for property held for personal use are fully deductible as an itemized deduction.
6. **(A)** A premium for a homeowner's insurance policy on a principal residence is a nondeductible personal expense.

7. **(G)** Payments to an unrelated babysitter to care for his child while Green worked would qualify for the child and dependent care credit. For 2016, the credit may vary from 20% to 35% of up to $3,000 ($6,000 for two or more qualifying individuals) of qualifying household and dependent care expenses incurred to enable the taxpayer to be gainfully employed or look for work.

8. **(B)** Interest expense on acquisition indebtedness is deductible on up to $1 million of loans secured by the residence if such loans were used to acquire, construct, or substantially improve a principal residence or a second residence.

9. **(F)** Expenses incurred in the production of rental income (e.g., interest, taxes, depreciation, insurance, utilities) are deductible on Schedule E and are included in the computation of net rental income or loss.

Task-Based Simulation 31

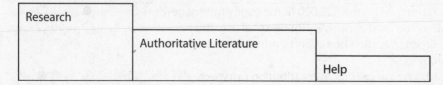

Mr. Green paid $5,000 during Year 1 to an unrelated babysitter for the care of his child while he worked. Which code section and subsection provides the maximum amount of employment-related child care expenses that qualify for a tax credit? Indicate the reference to that citation in the shaded boxes below.

Section	Subsection
§ ▓	(▓)

Task-Based Simulation 31 Solution

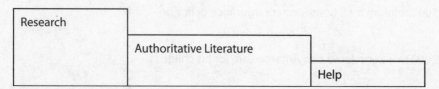

Internal Revenue Code Section 21, subsection (c) provides that the maximum amount of employment-related expenses that qualify for a credit is limited to $3,000 for one qualifying individual.

Section	Subsection
§ 21	(C)

Estate and Gift Taxation

Federal Gift Tax

Task-Based Simulation 32

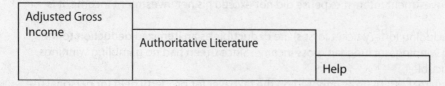

Situation

Frank and Dale Cumack are married and filing a joint 2016 income tax return. During 2016, Frank, age 63, was retired from government service and Dale, 55, was employed as a university instructor. In 2016, the

Cumacks contributed all of the support to Dale's father, Jacques, an unmarried French citizen and French resident who had no gross income.

For **items 1 through 10,** select the correct amount of income, loss, or adjustment to income that should be reported on page 1 of the Cumacks' 2016 Form 1040—Individual Income Tax Return to arrive at the adjusted gross income for each separate transaction. A tax treatment may be selected once, more than once, or not at all.

Any information contained in an item is unique to that item and is not to be incorporated in your calculations when answering other items.

Selections

A. $0	D. $3,000	F. $4,000	I. $10,000	K. $30,000
B. $1,000	E. $3,500	G. $5,000	J. $25,000	L. $125,000
C. $2,000		H. $9,000		M. $150,000

	(A) (F) (K)	(B) (G) (L)	(C) (H) (M)	(D) (I)	(E) (J)
1. During 2016, Dale received a $30,000 cash gift from her aunt.	○ ○ ○	○ ○ ○	○ ○ ○	○ ○	○ ○
2. Dale contributed $3,500 to her traditional Individual Retirement Account (IRA) on January 15, 2016. In 2015, she earned $60,000 as a university instructor. During 2016 the Cumacks were not active participants in an employer's qualified pension or annuity plan.	○ ○ ○	○ ○ ○	○ ○ ○	○ ○	○ ○
3. In 2016, the Cumacks received a $1,000 federal income tax refund.	○ ○ ○	○ ○ ○	○ ○ ○	○ ○	○ ○
4. During 2016, Frank, a 50% partner in Diske General Partnership, received a $4,000 guaranteed payment from Diske for services that he rendered to the partnership that year.	○ ○ ○	○ ○ ○	○ ○ ○	○ ○	○ ○
5. In 2016, Frank received $10,000 as beneficiary of his deceased brother's life insurance policy.	○ ○ ○	○ ○ ○	○ ○ ○	○ ○	○ ○
6. Dale's employer pays 100% of the cost of all employees' group-term life insurance under a qualified plan. Policy cost is $5 per $1,000 of coverage. Dale's group-term life insurance coverage equals $450,000.	○ ○ ○	○ ○ ○	○ ○ ○	○ ○	○ ○
7. In 2016, Frank won $5,000 at a casino and had $2,000 in gambling losses.	○ ○ ○	○ ○ ○	○ ○ ○	○ ○	○ ○
8. During 2016, the Cumacks received $1,000 interest income associated with a refund of their prior years' federal income tax.	○ ○ ○	○ ○ ○	○ ○ ○	○ ○	○ ○
9. In 2016, the Cumacks sold their first and only residence for $400,000. They purchased their home in 1996 for $50,000 and have lived there since then. There were no other capital gains, losses, or capital loss carryovers. The Cumacks do not intend to buy another residence.	○ ○ ○	○ ○ ○	○ ○ ○	○ ○	○ ○
10. In 2016, Zeno Corp. declared a stock dividend and Dale received one additional share of Zeno common stock for three shares of Zeno common stock that she held. The stock that Dale received had a fair market value of $9,000. There was no provision to receive cash instead of stock.	○ ○ ○	○ ○ ○	○ ○ ○	○ ○	○ ○

Task-Based Simulation 32 Solution

Adjusted Gross Income		
	Authoritative Literature	
		Help

	(A) (F) (K)	(B) (G) (L)	(C) (H) (M)	(D) (I)	(E) (J)
1. During 2015, Dale received a $30,000 cash gift from her aunt.	● ○ ○	○ ○ ○	○ ○ ○	○ ○	○ ○
2. Dale contributed $3,500 to her traditional Individual Retirement Account (IRA) on January 15, 2015. In 2015, she earned $60,000 as a university instructor. During 2015 the Cumacks were not active participants in an employer's qualified pension or annuity plan.	○ ○ ○	○ ○ ○	○ ○ ○	○ ○	● ○
3. In 2015, the Cumacks received a $1,000 federal income tax refund.	● ○ ○	○ ○ ○	○ ○ ○	○ ○	○ ○
4. During 2015, Frank, a 50% partner in Diske General Partnership, received a $4,000 guaranteed payment from Diske for services that he rendered to the partnership that year.	○ ● ○	○ ○ ○	○ ○ ○	○ ○	○ ○
5. In 2015, Frank received $10,000 as beneficiary of his deceased brother's life insurance policy.	● ○ ○	○ ○ ○	○ ○ ○	○ ○	○ ○
6. Dale's employer pays 100% of the cost of all employees' group-term life insurance under a qualified plan. Policy cost is $5 per $1,000 of coverage. Dale's group-term life insurance coverage equals $450,000.	○ ○ ○	○ ○ ○	● ○ ○	○ ○	○ ○
7. In 2015, Frank won $5,000 at a casino and had $2,000 in gambling losses.	○ ○ ○	○ ● ○	○ ○ ○	○ ○	○ ○
8. During 2015, the Cumacks received $1,000 interest income associated with a refund of their prior years' federal income tax.	○ ○ ○	○ ● ○	○ ○ ○	○ ○	○ ○
9. In 2015, the Cumacks sold their first and only residence for $400,000. They purchased their home in 1996 for $50,000 and have lived there since then. There were no other capital gains, losses, or capital loss carryovers. The Cumacks do not intend to buy another residence.	● ○ ○	○ ○ ○	○ ○ ○	○ ○	○ ○
10. In 2015, Zeno Corp. declared a stock dividend and Dale received one additional share of Zeno common stock for three shares of Zeno common stock that she held. The stock that Dale received had a fair market value of $9,000. There was no provision to receive cash instead of stock.	● ○ ○	○ ○ ○	○ ○ ○	○ ○	○ ○

Task-Based Simulation 33

Generation-Skipping Tax		
	Authoritative Literature	
		Help

Determine whether the transfer is subject to the generation skipping tax, the gift tax, or both taxes. Disregard the use of any exclusions and the unified credit.

Answer List

A.   Generation-Skipping Tax
B.   Gift Tax
C.   Both Taxes

	(A)	(B)	(C)
Martin's daughter, Kim, has one child, Dale. During 2016, Martin made an outright $6,000,000 gift to Dale.	○	○	○

Task-Based Simulation 33 Solution

Generation-Skipping Tax		
	Authoritative Literature	
		Help

For this item, candidates were asked to determine whether the transfer is subject to the generation-skipping tax (A), the gift tax (B), or both taxes (C).

	(A)	(B)	(C)
Martin's daughter, Kim, has one child, Dale. During 2016, Martin made an outright $6,000,000 gift to Dale.	○	○	●

Explanation

(**C**) Since Martin made an outright gift of $6,000,000 to Dale, the transfer is a gift of a present interest and is subject to the gift tax. Since Dale happens to be Martin's grandchild, the gift also is subject to the generation-skipping tax. The generation-skipping tax on the transfer of property is imposed in addition to federal gift and estates taxes and is designed to prevent individuals from escaping an entire generation of gift and estate taxes by transferring property to, or in trust for the benefit of, a person who is two or more generations younger than the donor or transferor. The tax approximates the transfer tax that would be imposed if the property were actually transferred to each successive generation.

Task-Based Simulation 34

Gift Tax Treatment		
	Authoritative Literature	
		Help

Situation

Scott Lane, an unmarried U.S. citizen, made no lifetime transfers prior to 2016. During 2016, Lane made the following transfers:

- Gave a $14,000 cash gift to Kamp, a close friend.
- Made two separate $10,000 cash gifts to his only child.
- Created an **irrevocable** trust beginning in 2016 that provided his aunt with an income interest to be paid for the next five years. The remainder interest is to pass to Lane's sole cousin. The income interest is valued at $26,000 and the remainder interest is valued at $74,000.
- Paid $25,000 tuition directly to his grandchild's university on his grandchild's behalf.
- Created an **irrevocable** trust that provided his brother with a lifetime income interest beginning in 2018, after which a remainder interest passes to their sister.
- Created a **revocable** trust with his niece as the sole beneficiary. During 2016, the niece received $15,000 interest income from the trust.

For **items 1 through 7,** determine whether the tax transactions are fully taxable, partially taxable, or not taxable to Lane in 2016 for gift tax purposes after considering the gift tax annual exclusion. Ignore the transfer tax credit when answering the items. An answer may be selected once, more than once, or not at all.

Gift Tax Treatments

F.	Fully taxable to Lane in 2016 for gift tax purposes.
P.	Partially taxable to Lane in 2016 for gift tax purposes.
N.	Not taxable to Lane in 2016 for gift tax purposes.

	(F)	(P)	(N)
1. What is the gift tax treatment of Lane's gift to Kamp?	○	○	○
2. What is the gift tax treatment of Lane's cash gifts to his child?	○	○	○
3. What is the gift tax treatment of the trust's income interest to Lane's aunt?	○	○	○
4. What is the gift tax treatment of the trust's remainder interest to Lane's cousin?	○	○	○
5. What is the gift tax treatment of the tuition payment to Lane's grandchild's university?	○	○	○
6. What is the gift tax treatment of the trust's income interest to Lane's brother?	○	○	○
7. What is the gift tax treatment of the $14,000 interest income that Lane's niece received from the revocable trust?	○	○	○

Task-Based Simulation 34 Solution

Gift Tax Treatment		
	Authoritative Literature	
		Help

For **items 1 through 7,** candidates were asked to identify the federal gift tax treatment for each item by indicating whether the item is fully taxable (F), partially taxable (P), or not taxable (N) to Lane in 2016 for gift tax purposes after considering the gift tax annual exclusion.

	(F)	(P)	(N)
1. What is the gift tax treatment of Lane's gift to Kamp?	○	○	●
2. What is the gift tax treatment of Lane's cash gifts to his child?	○	●	○
3. What is the gift tax treatment of the trust's income interest to Lane's aunt?	○	●	○
4. What is the gift tax treatment of the trust's remainder interest to Lane's cousin?	●	○	○
5. What is the gift tax treatment of the tuition payment to Lane's grandchild's university?	○	○	●
6. What is the gift tax treatment of the trust's income interest to Lane's brother?	●	○	○
7. What is the gift tax treatment of the $14,000 interest income that Lane's niece received from the revocable trust?	○	●	○

Explanations

1. (**N**) There is no taxable gift because the $14,000 cash gift is a gift of a present interest and is fully offset by a $14,000 annual exclusion.
2. (**P**) The $20,000 of cash gifts given to his child would be partially offset by a $14,000 annual exclusion, resulting in a taxable gift of $6,000.
3. (**P**) The gift of the income interest valued at $26,000 to his aunt is a gift of a present interest and would be partially offset by a $14,000 annual exclusion, resulting in a taxable gift of $12,000.
4. (**F**) Since the remainder interest will pass to Lane's cousin after the expiration of five years, the gift of the remainder interest is a gift of a future interest and is not eligible for an annual exclusion. As a result, the $74,000 value of the remainder interest is fully taxable.
5. (**N**) An unlimited exclusion is available for medical expenses and tuition paid on behalf of a donee. Since Lane paid the $25,000 of tuition directly to his grandchild's university on his grandchild's behalf, the gift is fully excluded and not subject to gift tax.
6. (**F**) Since Lane created the irrevocable trust in 2016 but his brother will not begin receiving the income until 2018, the gift of the income interest to his brother is a gift of a future interest and cannot be offset by an annual exclusion. As a result, the gift is fully taxable for gift tax purposes.
7. (**P**) The creation of a revocable trust is not a completed gift and trust income is taxable to the grantor (Lane). As a result, a gift occurs only as the trust income is actually paid to the beneficiary. Here, the $15,000 of interest income received by the niece during 2016 is a gift of a present interest and would be partially offset by a $14,000 annual exclusion.

Federal Estate Tax

Task-Based Simulation 35

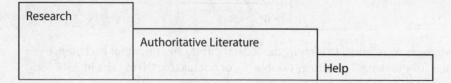

Situation

Glen Moore inherited stock from his mother, Ruth. She had died on February 1, 2016, when the stock had a fair market value of $150,000. Ruth had acquired the stock on May 15, 2014, at a cost of $120,000. Ruth's estate was too small to require the filing of a federal estate tax return. Moore wants to know how much gross income he must report because of the receipt of his inheritance in 2016. Which code section and subsection provides the rule for determining whether Moore's inheritance must be included in his gross income? Indicate the reference to that citation in the shaded boxes below.

Section	Subsection
§	( )

Task-Based Simulation 35 Solution

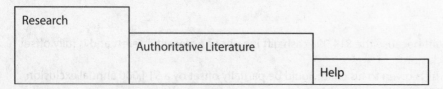

Internal Revenue Code Sec. 102, subsection (a) provides that gross income does not include the value of property acquired by gift, bequest, devise, or inheritance.

Section	Subsection
§ 102	(A)

Task-Based Simulation 36

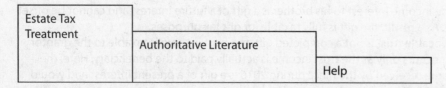

Situation

Remsen died on January 9, 2016, and was survived by his wife and only child, both of whom were U.S. citizens. The Remsens did not live in a community property state.

At his death Remsen owned:

Cash	$ 650,000
Marketable securities (fair market value)	1,900,000
Life insurance policy with Remsen's wife named as the beneficiary (fair market value)	2,500,000

Under the provisions of Remsen's will, the net cash, after payment of executor's fees and medical and funeral expenses, was bequeathed to Remsen's son. The marketable securities were bequeathed to Remsen's spouse. During 2016 Remsen's estate paid:

Executor fees to distribute the decedent's property (deducted on the fiduciary tax return)	$50,000
Decedent's funeral expenses	12,000

The estate's executor extended the time to file the estate tax return. On December 3, 2016, the estate's executor paid the decedent's outstanding $10,000 medical expenses and filed the extended estate tax return.

For **items 1 through 5,** identify the federal estate tax treatment for each item. A response may be selected once, more than once, or not at all.

Answer List

G.   Deductible from Remsen's gross estate to arrive at Remsen's taxable estate.
I.   Deductible on Remsen's 2016 individual income tax return.
E.   Deductible on either Remsen's estate tax return or Remsen's 2016 individual income tax return.
N.   Not deductible on either Remsen's estate tax return or Remsen's 2016 individual income tax return.

	(G) (E)	(I) (N)
1. What is the estate tax treatment of the executor's fees?	○ ○	○ ○
2. What is the estate tax treatment of the cash bequest to Remsen's son?	○ ○	○ ○
3. What is the estate tax treatment of the life insurance proceeds paid to Remsen's spouse?	○ ○	○ ○
4. What is the estate tax treatment of the funeral expenses?	○ ○	○ ○
5. What is the estate tax treatment of the $10,000 of medical expenses incurred before the decedent's death and paid by the executor on December 3, 2016?	○ ○	○ ○

Task-Based Simulation 36 Solution

Estate Tax Treatment		
	Authoritative Literature	
		Help

For **items 1 through 5,** candidates were asked to identify the federal tax treatment for each item by indicating whether the item was deductible from Remsen's gross estate to arrive at Remsen's taxable estate (G), deductible on Remsen's 2016 individual income tax return (I), deductible on either Remsen's estate tax return or Remsen's 2016 individual income tax return (E), or not deductible on either Remsen's estate tax return or Remsen's 2016 individual income tax return (N).

	(G) (E)	(I) (N)
1. What is the estate tax treatment of the executor's fees?	○ ○	○ ●
2. What is the estate tax treatment of the cash bequest to Remsen's son?	○ ○	● ●
3. What is the estate tax treatment of the life insurance proceeds paid to Remsen's spouse?	● ○	○ ○
4. What is the estate tax treatment of the funeral expenses?	● ○	○ ○
5. What is the estate tax treatment of the $10,000 of medical expenses incurred before the decedent's death and paid by the executor on December 3, 2016?	○ ●	○ ○

Explanations

1. (**N**) The $50,000 of executor's fees to distribute the decedent's property are deductible on **either** the federal estate tax return (Form 706) or the estate's fiduciary income tax return (Form 1041). Such expenses **cannot** be deducted twice. Since the problem indicates that these expenses were deducted on the fiduciary tax return (Form 1041), they cannot be deducted on the estate tax return.

2. (**N**) A decedent's gross estate is reduced by funeral and administrative expenses, debts and mortgages, casualty and theft losses, charitable bequests, and a marital deduction for the value of property passing to the decedent's surviving spouse. There is no deduction for bequests to beneficiaries other than the decedent's surviving spouse.

3. (**G**) Generally, property included in a decedent's gross estate will be eligible for an unlimited marital deduction if the property passes to the decedent's surviving spouse. Here, the life insurance proceeds paid to Remsen's spouse were included in Remsen's gross estate, because Remsen owned the policy, and are deductible from Remsen's gross estate as part of the marital deduction in arriving at Remsen's taxable estate.

4. (**G**) Funeral expenses are deductible only on the estate tax return and include a reasonable allowance for a tombstone, monument, mausoleum, or burial lot.

5. (**E**) The executor of a decedent's estate may elect to treat medical expenses paid by the estate for the decedent's medical care as paid by the decedent at the time the medical services were provided. To qualify for this election, the medical expenses must be paid within the one-year period after the decedent's death, and the executor must attach a waiver to the decedent's Form 1040 indicating that the expenses will not be claimed as a deduction on the decedent's estate tax return. In this case, the medical expenses qualify for the election because Remsen died on January 9, 2016, and the expenses were paid on December 3, 2016.

Task-Based Simulation 37

Estate Tax Treatment		
	Authoritative Literature	
		Help

Situation

Before his death, Remsen, a U.S. citizen, made cash gifts of $7,000 each to his four sisters. In 2016 Remsen also paid $20,000 in tuition directly to his grandchild's university on the grandchild's behalf. Remsen made no other lifetime transfers. Remsen died on January 9, 2016, and was survived by his wife and only child, both of whom were U.S. citizens. The Remsens did not live in a community property state.

At his death Remsen owned:

Cash	$ 650,000
Marketable securities (fair market value)	1,900,000
Life insurance policy with Remsen's wife named as the beneficiary (fair market value)	2,500,000

For **items 1 through 5,** identify the federal estate tax treatment for each item. A response may be selected once, more than once, or not at all.

Answer List

F.	Fully includible in Remsen's gross estate.
P.	Partially includible in Remsen's gross estate.
N.	Not includible in Remsen's gross estate.

	(F)	(P)	(N)
1. What is the estate tax treatment of the $7,000 cash gift to each sister?	○	○	○
2. What is the estate tax treatment of the life insurance proceeds?	○	○	○
3. What is the estate tax treatment of the marketable securities?	○	○	○
4. What is the estate tax treatment of the $20,000 tuition payment?	○	○	○
5. What is the estate tax treatment of the $650,000 cash?	○	○	○

Task-Based Simulation 37 Solution

Estate Tax Treatment		
	Authoritative Literature	
		Help

For **items 1 through 5,** candidates were asked to identify the federal tax treatment for each item by indicating whether the item was fully includible in Remsen's gross estate (F), partially includible in Remsen's gross estate (P), or not includible in Remsen's gross estate (N).

	(F)	(P)	(N)
1. What is the estate tax treatment of the $7,000 cash gift to each sister?	○	○	●
2. What is the estate tax treatment of the life insurance proceeds?	●	○	○
3. What is the estate tax treatment of the marketable securities?	●	○	○
4. What is the estate tax treatment of the $20,000 tuition payment?	○	○	●
5. What is the estate tax treatment of the $650,000 cash?	●	○	○

Explanations

1. **(N)** Generally, gifts made before death are not includible in the decedent's gross estate, even though the gifts were made within three years of death.
2. **(F)** The gross estate includes the value of all property in which the decedent had a beneficial interest at time of death. Here, the life insurance proceeds must be included in Remsen's gross estate because the problem indicates that Remsen was the owner of the policy.
3. **(F)** The fair market value of the marketable securities must be included in Remsen's gross estate because Remsen was the owner of the securities at the time of his death.
4. **(N)** Generally, gifts made before death are not includible in the decedent's gross estate.
5. **(F)** The $650,000 cash that Remsen owned must be included in Remsen's gross estate.

Task-Based Simulation 38

Type of Gift		
	Authoritative Literature	
		Help

During 2016, various clients went to Rowe, CPA, for tax advice concerning possible gift tax liability on transfers they made throughout 2016. For each client, indicate whether the transfer of cash, the income interest, or the remainder interest is a gift of a present interest, a gift of a future interest, or not a completed gift.

Answer List

P.	Present Interest
F.	Future Interest
N.	Not Completed

Assume the following facts:

Cobb created a $500,000 trust that provided his mother with an income interest for her life and the remainder interest to go to his sister at the death of his mother. Cobb expressly retained the power to revoke both the income interest and the remainder interest at any time.

Items to be answered

	(P)	(F)	(N)
1. The income interest at the trust's creation.	○	○	○
2. The remainder interest at the trust's creation.	○	○	○

Kane created a $100,000 trust that provided her nephew with the income interest until he reached 45 years of age. When the trust was created, Kane's nephew was 25. The income distribution is to start when Kane's nephew is 29. After Kane's nephew reaches the age of 45, the remainder interest is to go to Kane's niece.

	(P)	(F)	(N)
3. The income interest.	○	○	○

During 2016, Hall, an unmarried taxpayer, made a $10,000 cash gift to his son in May and a further $12,000 cash gift to him in August.

	(P)	(F)	(N)
4. The cash transfers.	○	○	○

During 2016, Yeats transferred property worth $20,000 to a trust with the income to be paid to her 22-year-old niece Jane. After Jane reaches the age of 30, the remainder interest is to be distributed to Yeats' brother. The income interest is valued at $9,700 and the remainder interest at $10,300.

	(P)	(F)	(N)
5. The income interest.	○	○	○
6. The remainder interest.	○	○	○

Tom and Ann Curry, U.S. citizens, were married for the entire 2016 calendar year. Tom gave a $40,000 cash gift to his uncle, Grant. The Currys made no other gifts to Grant in 2016. Tom and Ann each signed a timely election stating that each made one-half of the $40,000 gift.

	(P)	(F)	(N)
7. The cash transfers.	○	○	○

Murray created a $1,000,000 trust that provided his brother with an income interest for 10 years, after which the remainder interest passes to Murray's sister. Murray retained the power to revoke the remainder interest at any time. The income interest was valued at $600,000.

	(P)	(F)	(N)
8. The income interest.	○	○	○
9. The remainder interest.	○	○	○

Task-Based Simulation 38 Solution

Type of Gift

Authoritative Literature

Help

For **items 1 through 9,** candidates were asked to determine whether the transfer of cash, an income interest, or a remainder interest represents a gift of a present interest (P), a gift of a future interest (F), or not a completed gift (N).

	(P)	(F)	(N)
1. The income interest at the trust's creation.	○	○	●
2. The remainder interest at the trust's creation.	○	○	●
3. The income interest.	○	●	○
4. The cash transfers.	●	○	○
5. The income interest.	●	○	●
6. The remainder interest.	○	●	○
7. The cash transfers.	●	○	●
8. The income interest.	●	○	●
9. The remainder interest.	○	○	●

Explanations

1. (**N**) Since Cobb expressly retained the power to revoke the income interest transferred to his mother at any time, he has not relinquished dominion and control and the transfer of the income interest is not a completed gift.

2. (**N**) Since Cobb expressly retained the power to revoke the remainder interest transferred to his sister at any time, he has not relinquished dominion and control and the transfer of the remainder interest is not a completed gift.

3. (**F**) Kane's transfer of an income interest to a nephew and a remainder interest to a niece are completed gifts because Kane has relinquished dominion and control. Since Kane's nephew was 25 years of age when the trust was created, but income distributions will not begin until the nephew is age 29, the transfer of the income interest is a gift of future interest and does not qualify for the annual exclusion.

4. (**P**) Since Hall's gifts of cash to his son were outright gifts, they are gifts of a present interest and qualify for the annual exclusion.

5. (**P**) Yeats' gift of the income interest to her 22-year-old niece is a gift of a present interest qualifying for the annual exclusion since Jane has the unrestricted right to immediate enjoyment of the income. The fact that the value of the income interest does not exceed $14,000 does not affect its nature (i.e., completed gift of a present interest).

6. **(F)** Yeats' gift of the remainder interest to her brother is a completed gift of a future interest since the brother cannot enjoy the property or any of the income until Jane reaches age 30.

7. **(P)** Tom's gift of $40,000 cash to his uncle is an outright gift of a present interest and qualifies for the annual exclusion. Since gift-splitting was elected and Tom and Ann would each receive a $14,000 annual exclusion, Tom and Ann each made a taxable gift of $20,000 – $14,000 exclusion = $6,000.

8. **(P)** Murray's gift of the income interest to his brother is a completed gift because Murray has relinquished dominion and control. It is a gift of a present interest qualifying for the annual exclusion since his brother has the unrestricted right to immediate enjoyment of the income.

9. **(N)** Since Murray retained the right to revoke the remainder interest transferred to his sister at any time, the transfer of the remainder interest does not result in a completed gift.

Federal Taxation of Entities

Corporate Taxation

Corporate Income

Task-Based Simulation 39

Schedule M-1		
	Authoritative Literature	
		Help

Aviator provides the following information for 2016:

Net income per books (after tax)	$310,000
Federal income tax liability deducted per books	104,150
Retained earnings at January 1, 2016	425,000
Interest income from municipal general obligation bonds	20,000
Cash dividends paid to shareholders	60,000
Life insurance proceeds received on death of Aviator's president (Aviator was the owner and beneficiary of the policy)	100,000
Premiums paid on policy insuring Aviator's president	5,000
Excess of capital losses over capital gains for 2016	7,000
Employee entertainment expenses reimbursed by Aviator	6,000
Dividend income received from 5%-owned taxable domestic corporation	10,000
MACRS depreciation for 2016 in excess of straight-time depreciation deducted per books	9,000
Retained earnings at December 31, 2016	645,000

Prepare Schedule M-1, which will reconcile Aviator's income reported per books for 2016 with its income reported on its 2016 tax return Form 1120.

SCHEDULES M-1 and M-2 (Form 1120-F)	Reconciliation of Income (Loss) and Analysis of Unappropriated Retained Earnings per Books	OMB No. 1545-0123
Department of the Treasury Internal Revenue Service	▶ Information about Schedules M-1 and M-2 (Form 1120-F) and its instructions is at *www.irs.gov/form1120f*. ▶ Attach to Form 1120-F.	20**16**
Name of corporation		Employer identification number

Schedule M-1 — Reconciliation of Income (Loss) per Books With Income per Return
Note. The corporation may be required to file Schedule M-3 (see instructions).

1	Net income (loss) per books		7	Income recorded on books this year not included on this return (itemize):	
2	Federal income tax per books				
3	Excess of capital losses over capital gains		a	Tax-exempt interest $	
4	Income subject to tax not recorded on books this year (itemize):		b	Other (itemize):	
5	Expenses recorded on books this year not deducted on this return (itemize):		8	Deductions on this return not charged against book income this year (itemize):	
a	Depreciation . . . . $		a	Depreciation . . $	
b	Charitable contributions $		b	Charitable contributions $	
c	Travel and entertainment $		c	Other (itemize):	
d	Other (itemize):				
			9	Add lines 7 and 8	
6	Add lines 1 through 5		10	Income—line 6 less line 9	

Task-Based Simulation 39 Solution

Schedule M-1		
	Authoritative Literature	
		Help

Schedule M-1 of Form 1120 is used to reconcile a corporate taxpayer's income reported per books with income reported on the tax return. Generally, items of income or deduction whose book and tax treatment differ result in Schedule M-1 items. However, since Schedule M-1 reconciles book income to taxable income before special deductions (line 28, page 1), the dividends received deduction and net operating loss deduction, which are special deduction, will never be reconciling items on Schedule M-1.

The beginning and ending balance of Retained Earnings and cash dividends paid to shareholders are neither deducted per books nor on the tax return and are not Schedule M-1 items. Instead they will be included on Schedule M-2, which provides an Analysis of Unappropriated Retained Earnings per books between the beginning and end of the year.

SCHEDULES M-1 and M-2 (Form 1120-F)	Reconciliation of Income (Loss) and Analysis of Unappropriated Retained Earnings per Books	OMB No. 1545-0123
Department of the Treasury Internal Revenue Service	▶ Information about Schedules M-1 and M-2 (Form 1120-F) and its instructions is at *www.irs.gov/form1120f*. ▶ Attach to Form 1120-F.	20**16**
Name of corporation		Employer identification number

Schedule M-1 — Reconciliation of Income (Loss) per Books With Income per Return
Note. The corporation may be required to file Schedule M-3 (see instructions).

1	Net income (loss) per books	310,000	7	Income recorded on books this year not included on this return (itemize):	
2	Federal income tax per books	104,150			
3	Excess of capital losses over capital gains	7,000	a	Tax-exempt interest $ 20,000	
4	Income subject to tax not recorded on books this year (itemize):		b	Other (itemize): **Insurance proceeds 100,000**	
					120,000
5	Expenses recorded on books this year not deducted on this return (itemize):		8	Deductions on this return not charged against book income this year (itemize):	
a	Depreciation . . . . $		a	Depreciation . . $ 9,000	
b	Charitable contributions $		b	Charitable contributions $	
c	Travel and entertainment $ 3,000		c	Other (itemize):	
d	Other (itemize): **Insurance premiums 5,000**				9,000
		8,000	9	Add lines 7 and 8	129,000
6	Add lines 1 through 5	429,150	10	Income—line 6 less line 9	300,150

Line 2. The federal income tax of $104,150 deducted per books is not deductible for tax purposes and is added back to book income.

Line 3. Since a corporation is not allowed to deduct a net capital loss, the $7,000 net capital loss deducted per books must be added back to book income.

Lines 5c and d. Since only 50% of business meals and entertainment are deductible for tax purposes, 50% of the $6,000 of business entertainment expense deducted per books must be added back to book income. Additionally, the life insurance premiums of $5,000 on the president's life that were deducted per books represent an expense incurred in the production of tax-exempt income and are not deductible for tax purposes.

Lines 7a and b. The $20,000 of interest income from municipal bonds included per books is tax-exempt and must be subtracted from book income. Similarly, the $100,000 of life insurance proceeds received on the death of Aviator's president included in book income is not taxable and must be subtracted from book income.

Line 8a. Since Aviator's MACRS depreciation deductible for tax purposes exceeds the depreciation deducted for book purposes, the excess of $9,000 must be subtracted from book income.

Task-Based Simulation 40

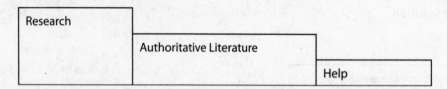

Aviator's gains from the sale of stock investments totaled $20,000, while its losses from the sale of other stock investments totaled $30,000. What Internal Revenue Code section and subsection limits the deduction of a corporation's capital losses? Indicate the reference to that citation in the shaded boxes below.

Section			Subsection		
§			(		)

Task-Based Simulation 40 Solution

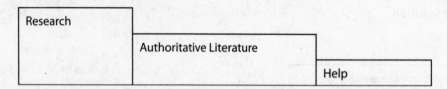

Internal Revenue Code Section 1211, subsection (a), provides that a corporation's capital losses are allowed only to the extent of capital gains. As a result, a corporation cannot deduct a net capital loss.

Section			Subsection		
§	1211		(	A	)

Task-Based Simulation 41

Schedule M-1 Adjustments		
	Authoritative Literature	
		Help

Reliant Corp., an accrual-basis calendar-year C corporation, filed its 2016 federal income tax return on March 15, 2017. The following two responses are required for each of the **items 1 through 6.**

- Determine the amount of Reliant's 2016 Schedule M-1 adjustment.
- Indicate if the adjustment increases, decreases, or has no effect, on Reliant's 2016 taxable income.

Selections

I.	Increases Reliant's 2016 taxable income.
D.	Decreases Reliant's 2016 taxable income.
N.	Has no effect on Reliant's 2016 taxable income.

	Schedule M-1 Adjustment	(I) (D) (N)
1. Reliant's disbursements included reimbursed employees' expenses in 2016 for travel of $100,000, and business meals of $30,000. The reimbursed expenses met the conditions of deductibility and were properly substantiated under an accountable plan. The reimbursement was not treated as employee compensation.	_____	○ ○ ○
2. Reliant's books expensed $7,000 in 2016 for the term life insurance premiums on the corporate officers. Reliant was the policy owner and beneficiary.	_____	○ ○ ○
3. Reliant's books indicated an $18,000 state franchise tax expense for 2016. Estimated state tax payments for 2016 were $15,000.	_____	○ ○ ○
4. Book depreciation on computers for 2016 was $10,000. These computers, which cost $50,000, were placed in service on January 2, 2015. Tax depreciation used MACRS with the half-year convention. No election was made to expense part of the computer cost and Reliant elected not to use bonus depreciation.	_____	○ ○ ○
5. For 2016, Reliant's books showed a $4,000 short-term capital gain distribution from a mutual fund corporation and a $5,000 loss on the sale of Retro stock that was purchased in 2014. The stock was an investment in an unrelated corporation. There were no other 2016 gains or losses and no loss carryovers from prior years.	_____	○ ○ ○
6. Reliant's 2016 taxable income before the charitable contribution and the dividends received deductions was $500,000. Reliant's books expensed $15,000 in board of director authorized charitable contributions that were paid on January 5, 2017. Charitable contributions paid and expensed during 2016 were $35,000. All charitable contributions were properly substantiated. There were no net operating losses or charitable contributions that were carried forward.	_____	○ ○ ○

Task-Based Simulation 41 Solution

Schedule M-1 Adjustments		
	Authoritative Literature	
		Help

NOTE: Schedule M-1 is the schedule of the corporate income tax return that provides a reconciliation of net income (loss) per books with the corporation's taxable income before the net operating loss and dividends received deductions. If an item's treatment per books differs from its treatment for tax purposes, an M-1 adjustment will result.

	Schedule M-1 Adjustment	(I) (D) (N)
1. Reliant's disbursements included reimbursed employees' expenses in 2016 for travel of $100,000, and business meals of $30,000. The reimbursed expenses met the conditions of deductibility and were properly substantiated under an accountable plan. The reimbursement was not treated as employee compensation.	$15,000	● ○ ○
2. Reliant's books expensed $7,000 in 2016 for the term life insurance premiums on the corporate officers. Reliant was the policy owner and beneficiary.	$7,000	● ○ ○
3. Reliant's books indicated an $18,000 state franchise tax expense for 2016. Estimated state tax payments for 2016 were $15,000.	$0	○ ○ ●
4. Book depreciation on computers for 2016 was $10,000. These computers, which cost $50,000, were placed in service on January 2, 2015. Tax depreciation used MACRS with the half-year convention. No election was made to expense part of the computer cost and Reliant elected not to use bonus depreciation.	$6,000	○ ● ○
5. For 2016, Reliant's books showed a $4,000 short-term capital gain distribution from a mutual fund corporation and a $5,000 loss on the sale of Retro stock that was purchased in 2014. The stock was an investment in an unrelated corporation. There were no other 2016 gains or losses and no loss carryovers from prior years.	$5,000	● ○ ○
6. Reliant's 2016 taxable income before the charitable contribution and the dividends received deductions was $500,000. Reliant's books expensed $15,000 in board of director authorized charitable contributions that were paid on January 5, 2017. Charitable contributions paid and expensed during 2016 were $35,000. All charitable contributions were properly substantiated. There were no net operating losses or charitable contributions that were carried forward.	$0	○ ○ ●

Explanations

1. **($15,000; I)** The $100,000 reimbursement for employee travel is deductible for both book and tax purposes and no adjustment is necessary. However, since only 50% of the $30,000 of reimbursed business meals that was deducted per books is deductible for tax purposes, an M-1 increase adjustment results in the amount of $15,000 ($30,000 × 50%).
2. **($7,000; I)** The $7,000 of term life insurance premiums on corporate officers that was deducted per books is not deductible for tax purposes because Reliant was the policy owner and beneficiary. As a result there is an M-1 increase adjustment of $7,000.
3. **($0; N)** The $18,000 of state franchise taxes and $15,000 of estimated state tax payments are fully deductible for both book and tax purposes and no M-1 adjustment is necessary.

4. **($6,000; D)** Since the computers are five-year recovery property and Reliant used MACRS and the half-year convention, depreciation would be computed using the 200% declining balance method (i.e., twice the straight-line rate) and the tax depreciation for 2015 would be ($50,000 × 40% × 1/2) = $10,000. The tax depreciation for 2016 would then be ($50,000 − $10,000) × 40% = $16,000. Since book depreciation was only $10,000, the book-to-tax difference in depreciation would result in an M-1 decrease adjustment of $6,000.

5. **($5,000; I)** Since only **long-term capital gain distributions** from a mutual fund pass through as capital gain, the $4,000 of **short-term capital gain distribution** from a mutual fund corporation must be reported by Reliant as ordinary dividend income, and cannot be netted against the $5,000 capital loss from the sale of the Retro stock held as an investment. As a result, Reliant's sale of the Retro stock results in a net capital loss of $5,000 for 2016. Since a corporation cannot deduct a net capital loss for tax purposes, the $5,000 of net capital loss deducted per books results in a book to tax difference and an M-1 increase adjustment of $5,000.

6. **($0; N)** Since Reliant had taxable income before the charitable contribution deduction of $500,000 for 2016, Reliant can deduct a maximum of ($500,000 × 10%) = $50,000 of charitable contributions for tax purposes. Reliant can deduct the $35,000 of contributions made during 2016, as well as the $15,000 paid on January 5, 2017, because Reliant is an accrual-basis taxpayer, the $15,000 contribution was authorized by Reliant's board of directors, and the $15,000 was paid within 2 ½ months after the end of 2016. Since Reliant is deducting $50,000 of contributions for both book and tax purposes, there is no M-1 adjustment.

Task-Based Simulation 42

Schedule M-1 Adjustments		
	Authoritative Literature	
		Help

Situation

Capital Corp., an accrual-basis calendar-year C corporation, began operations on January 2, Year 1. Capital timely filed its 2015 federal income tax return on March 15, Year 4.

The following items each require two responses:

- For each item below, determine the amount of Capital's Year 3 Schedule M-1 adjustment necessary to reconcile book income to taxable income. On the CPA exam, a list of numeric answers would be presented for the candidate to select from.
- In addition, determine if the Schedule M-1 adjustment necessary to reconcile book income to taxable income increases, decreases, or has no effect on Capital's Year 3 taxable income. An answer may be selected once, more than once, or not at all.

Selections

I.	Increases Capital's Year 3 taxable income.
D.	Decreases Capital's Year 3 taxable income.
N.	Has no effect on Capital's Year 3 taxable income.

	Amount of Adjustment	(I) (D) (N)
1. At its corporate inception in Year 1, Capital incurred and paid $40,100 in organizational costs for legal fees to draft the corporate charter. In Year 1, Capital correctly elected, for book purposes, to expense the organizational costs and to amortize the organizational expenditures over the minimum allowable period on its federal income tax return. For Year 3, no organizational costs were deducted on its books.		○ ○ ○
2. Capital's Year 3 disbursements included $10,000 for reimbursed employees' expenses for business meals and entertainment. The reimbursed expenses met the conditions of deductibility and were properly substantiated under an accountable plan. The reimbursement was not treated as employee compensation.		○ ○ ○
3. Capital's Year 3 disbursements included $15,000 for life insurance premium expense paid for its executives as part of their taxable compensation. Capital is neither the direct nor the indirect beneficiary of the policy, and the amount of the compensation is reasonable.		○ ○ ○
4. In Year 3, Capital increased its allowance for uncollectible accounts by $10,000. No bad debt was written off in Year 3.		○ ○ ○

Task-Based Simulation 42 Solution

Schedule M-1 Adjustments		
	Authoritative Literature	
		Help

	Amount of Adjustment	(I) (D) (N)
1. At its corporate inception in Year 1, Capital incurred and paid $40,100 in organizational costs for legal fees to draft the corporate charter. In Year 1, Capital correctly elected, for book purposes, to expense the organizational costs and to amortize the organizational expenditures over the minimum allowable period on its federal income tax return. For Year 3, no organizational costs were deducted on its books.	$2,340	○ ● ○
2. Capital's Year 3 disbursements included $10,000 for reimbursed employees' expenses for business meals and entertainment. The reimbursed expenses met the conditions of deductibility and were properly substantiated under an accountable plan. The reimbursement was not treated as employee compensation.	$5,000	● ○ ○
3. Capital's Year 3 disbursements included $15,000 for life insurance premium expense paid for its executives as part of their taxable compensation. Capital is neither the direct nor the indirect beneficiary of the policy, and the amount of the compensation is reasonable.	$0	○ ○ ●
4. In Year 3, Capital increased its allowance for uncollectible accounts by $10,000. No bad debt was written off in Year 3.	$10,000	● ○ ○

Explanations

1. **($2,340; D)** $5,000 of Capital's organizational costs of $40,100 would have been deducted in Year 1 with the remainder amortized over 180 months (15 years) for tax purposes. As a result, the tax amortization of organizational costs results in a tax deduction of $35,100 × 12/180 = $2,340 for Year 3. Since no organizational costs were deducted per books for 2015, a Schedule M-1 decrease adjustment is necessary for the $2,340 difference.
2. **($5,000; I)** Only 50% of reimbursed employees' expenses for business meals and entertainment is deductible for tax purposes. As a result, an M-1 increase adjustment of $5,000 is necessary to reflect the fact that 50% of the $10,000 of reimbursed business meals and entertainment that was deducted for book purposes is not deductible for tax purposes.
3. **($0; N)** The $15,000 of life insurance premiums treated as reasonable compensation is fully deductible for both book and tax purposes and no M-1 adjustment is necessary.
4. **($10,000; I)** The reserve method of accounting for bad debts is not allowed for tax purposes. Instead, a bad debt deduction can be taken only when a specific debt is determined to be uncollectible. Since no bad debt was written off during 2015, an M-1 increase adjustment is necessary for the $10,000 addition to the allowance for uncollectible accounts for Year 3.

Task-Based Simulation 43

Taxability | Authoritative Literature | Help

Sunco Corp., an accrual-basis calendar-year C corporation, timely filed its Year 1 federal income tax return on March 15, Year 2. Determine if the following items are fully taxable, partially taxable, or nontaxable for regular income tax purposes on Sunco's Year 1 federal income tax return. An answer may be selected once, more than once, or not at all.

Selections

F.   Fully taxable for regular income tax purposes on Sunco's Year 1 federal income tax return.
P.   Partially taxable for regular income tax purposes on Sunco's Year 1 federal income tax return.
N.   Nontaxable for regular income tax purposes on Sunco's Year 1 federal income tax return.

	(F)	(P)	(N)
1. In Year 1, Sunco received dividend income from a 35%-owned domestic corporation. The dividends were not from debt-financed portfolio stock, and the taxable income limitation did not apply.	○	○	○
2. In Year 1, Sunco received a $2,800 lease cancellation payment from a three-year lease tenant.	○	○	○

Task-Based Simulation 43 Solution

```
Taxability
        Authoritative Literature
                        Help
```

	(F)	(P)	(N)
1. In Year 1, Sunco received dividend income from a 35%-owned domestic corporation. The dividends were not from debt-financed portfolio stock, and the taxable income limitation did not apply.	○	●	○
2. In Year 1, Sunco received a $2,800 lease cancellation payment from a three-year lease tenant.	●	○	○

Explanations

1. **(P)** Dividends received from a 35%-owned domestic corporation would be eligible for an 80% dividends received deduction. As a result, only 20% of the gross dividends received would be included in taxable income.
2. **(F)** A lease cancellation payment is treated as rent and must be fully included in income when received.

Special Corporate Deductions

Task-Based Simulation 44

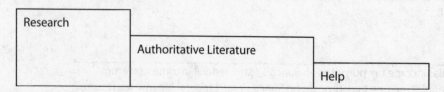

```
Research
        Authoritative Literature
                        Help
```

Dividends received from taxable domestic corporations are generally eligible for a dividends received deduction. What Internal Revenue Code section provides a special restriction on the dividends-received deduction if the stock investment is financed with debt? Indicate the reference to that citation in the shaded box below.

Section	
§	

Task-Based Simulation 44 Solution

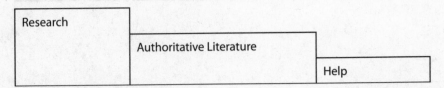

Internal Revenue Code Section 246A provides that a corporation's dividends received deduction will be reduced to the extent that its stock investment was financed by debt (e.g., if 40% of its investment was financed by debts its dividends received deduction will be reduced by 40%).

Section	
§	246A

Task-Based Simulation 45

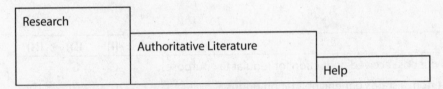

What Internal Revenue Code section, subsection, and paragraph limits a corporation's deduction for charitable contributions to a percentage of its taxable income before specified deductions? Indicate the reference to that citation in the shaded boxes below.

Section		Subsection			Paragraph		
§		(		)	(		)

Task-Based Simulation 45 Solution

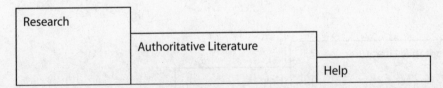

Internal Revenue Code Section 170, subsection (b), paragraph (2), limits a corporation's deduction for charitable contributions to 10% of its taxable income before certain specified deductions.

Section		Subsection			Paragraph		
§	170	(	b	)	(	2	)

Corporate Alternative Minimum Tax

Task-Based Simulation 46

Alternative Minimum Tax		
	Authoritative Literature	
		Help

Indicate if the following items increase, decrease, or have no effect on Reliant Corp.'s 2016 alternative minimum taxable income (AMTI) **prior** to the adjusted current earnings adjustment (ACE).

Selections

I.	Increases Reliant's 2016 AMTI.
D.	Decreases Reliant's 2016 AMTI.
N.	Has no effect on Reliant's 2016 AMTI.

	(I)	(D)	(N)
1. Reliant used the 70% dividends received deduction for regular tax purposes.	○	○	○
2. Reliant received interest from a state's general obligation bonds.	○	○	○
3. Reliant used MACRS depreciation on seven-year personal property placed into service January 3, 2016, for regular tax purposes. No expense election was made, and Reliant elected not to use bonus depreciation.	○	○	○
4. Depreciation on nonresidential real property placed into service on January 3, 2016, was under the general MACRS depreciation system for regular tax purposes.	○	○	○
5. Reliant had only cash charitable contributions for 2016.	○	○	○

Task-Based Simulation 46 Solution

Alternative Minimum Tax		
	Authoritative Literature	
		Help

	(I)	(D)	(N)
1. Reliant used the 70% dividends received deduction for regular tax purposes.	○	○	●
2. Reliant received interest from a state's general obligation bonds.	○	○	●
3. Reliant used MACRS depreciation on seven-year personal property placed into service January 3, 2016, for regular tax purposes. No expense election was made, and Reliant elected not to use bonus depreciation.	●	○	○
4. Depreciation on nonresidential real property placed into service on January 3, 2016, was under the general MACRS depreciation system for regular tax purposes.	○	○	●
5. Reliant had only cash charitable contributions for 2016.	○	○	●

Explanations

1. **(N)** The dividends received deduction is not an adjustment in computing AMTI before the ACE adjustment. However, note that the 70% dividends received deduction is an increase adjustment in computing a corporation's ACE.
2. **(N)** The tax-exempt interest on a state's **general obligation** bonds is not an adjustment is computing AMTI before the ACE adjustment.
3. **(I)** Generally for seven-year property, the 200% declining balance method would be used under MACRS for regular tax purposes, while the 150% declining balance method must be used for AMT purposes, resulting in an increase adjustment in computing AMTI prior to the ACE adjustment for the year placed in service.
4. **(N)** For real property placed in service after December 31, 1998, the AMT adjustment has been eliminated because for AMT purposes, the recovery period is the same as that used for regular tax MACRS depreciation (e.g., 39 years or 27½ years). On the other hand, for real property that was placed in service before January 1, 1999, an AMT adjustment is necessary because for AMT purposes, real property must be depreciated using the straight-line method over a 40-year recovery period, rather than the 39-year or 27½-year period used for regular tax purposes.
5. **(N)** Allowable charitable contributions do not result in an adjustment in computing AMTI or ACE.

Penalty Taxes

Task-Based Simulation 47

```
┌─────────────────┐
│  Deductibility  │
│       ┌─────────┴───────────┐
│       │ Authoritative Literature │
│       │        ┌───────┴───────┐
│       │        │     Help      │
└───────┴────────┴───────────────┘
```

Quest Corp., an accrual-basis calendar-year C corporation, timely filed its 2016 federal income tax return on March 15, 2017. Determine if the following items are fully deductible, partially deductible, or nondeductible for regular income tax purposes on Quest's 2016 federal income tax return. An answer may be selected once, more than once, or not at all.

Selections

F. Fully deductible for regular income tax purposes on Quest's 2016 federal income tax return.
P. Partially deductible for regular income tax purposes on Quest's 2016 federal income tax return.
N. Nondeductible for regular income tax purposes on Quest's 2016 federal income tax return.

	(F)	(P)	(N)
1. Quest's 2016 taxable income before charitable contributions and dividends received deduction was $200,000. Quest's Board of Directors authorized a $38,000 contribution to a qualified charity on December 1, 2016. The payment was made on February 1, 2017. All charitable contributions were properly substantiated.	○	○	○
2. During 2016 Quest was assessed and paid a $300 uncontested penalty for failure to pay its 2015 federal income taxes on time.	○	○	○

Task-Based Simulation 47 Solution

Deductibility		
	Authoritative Literature	
		Help

	(F)	**(P)**	**(N)**
1. Quest's 2016 taxable income before charitable contributions and dividends received deduction was $200,000. Quest's Board of Directors authorized a $38,000 contribution to a qualified charity on December 1, 2016. The payment was made on February 1, 2017. All charitable contributions were properly substantiated.	○	●	○
2. During 2016 Quest was assessed and paid a $300 uncontested penalty for failure to pay its 2015 federal income taxes on time.	○	○	●

Explanations

1. **(P)** Since Quest is an accrual method corporation, it can elect to deduct contributions authorized by its board of directors during 2016, so long as the contribution is actually paid no later than 2½ months after the end of the tax year. Thus, to maximize its deduction for 2016, Quest can elect to treat the $38,000 contribution as a deduction for 2016 subject to the 10% of taxable income limitation that applies for 2016. Since Quest had 2016 taxable income of $200,000 before the charitable contributions and dividends received deductions, Quest's 2016 deduction for the $38,000 charitable contribution is limited to $200,000 × 10% = $20,000.
2. **(N)** A penalty that is paid for a failure to pay federal income taxes on time is not deductible.

Distributions from a Corporation

Task-Based Simulation 48

Concepts		
	Authoritative Literature	
		Help

Given below are terms appearing in the federal income tax code, regulations and explanations

A.	Accumulated earnings tax	J. Dividends received deduction	S. Personal holding company tax
B.	Capital assets	K. Earned income	T. Personal service corporation
C.	Capital contribution	L. Exchanged basis	U. Portfolio income
D.	Claim of right	M. Excise tax	V. Regulated investment company
E.	Consent divided	N. Fair market value	W. Sec. 1231 assets
F.	Constructive dividend	O. Head of household	X. Surviving spouse
G.	Constructive receipt	P. Nontaxable exchange	Y. Taxable exchange
H.	Deficiency dividend	Q. Passive income	Z. Transferred basis
I.	Dividends paid deduction	R. Personal holding company	

Indicate your choice of the **best** term applying to each of the statements below. Each term may be selected once, more than once, or not at all.

1. A corporation whose income was derived solely from dividends, interest, and royalties, and during the last six months of its year more than 50% of the value of its outstanding stock is owned by five or fewer individuals.
2. The basis used to determine gain on sale of property that was received as a gift.
3. The trade-in of production machinery for new production machinery by a corporation, when the corporation pays additional cash.
4. An unmarried individual whose filing status enables the taxpayer to use a set of income tax rates that are lower than those applicable to other unmarried individuals, but are higher than those applicable to married persons filing a joint return.
5. If income is unqualifiedly available, it will be subject to the income tax even though it is not physically in the taxpayer's possession.
6. A special tax imposed on corporations that accumulate their earnings beyond the reasonable needs of the business.
7. The classification of income from interest, dividends, annuities, and certain royalties.
8. The classification of depreciable assets and real estate used in a trade or business and held for more than one year.
9. This deduction attempts to mitigate the triple taxation that would occur if one corporation paid dividends to a corporate shareholder who, in turn, distributed such amounts to its individual shareholders.
10. Sale of property to a corporation by a shareholder for a selling price that is in excess of the property's fair market value.

	(A)	(B)	(C)	(D)	(E)	(F)	(G)	(H)	(I)	(J)	(K)	(L)	(M)	(N)	(O)	(P)	(Q)	(R)	(S)	(T)	(U)	(V)	(W)	(X)	(Y)	(Z)
1.	○	○	○	○	○	○	○	○	○	○	○	○	○	○	○	○	○	○	○	○	○	○	○	○	○	○
2.	○	○	○	○	○	○	○	○	○	○	○	○	○	○	○	○	○	○	○	○	○	○	○	○	○	○
3.	○	○	○	○	○	○	○	○	○	○	○	○	○	○	○	○	○	○	○	○	○	○	○	○	○	○
4.	○	○	○	○	○	○	○	○	○	○	○	○	○	○	○	○	○	○	○	○	○	○	○	○	○	○
5.	○	○	○	○	○	○	○	○	○	○	○	○	○	○	○	○	○	○	○	○	○	○	○	○	○	○
6.	○	○	○	○	○	○	○	○	○	○	○	○	○	○	○	○	○	○	○	○	○	○	○	○	○	○
7.	○	○	○	○	○	○	○	○	○	○	○	○	○	○	○	○	○	○	○	○	○	○	○	○	○	○
8.	○	○	○	○	○	○	○	○	○	○	○	○	○	○	○	○	○	○	○	○	○	○	○	○	○	○
9.	○	○	○	○	○	○	○	○	○	○	○	○	○	○	○	○	○	○	○	○	○	○	○	○	○	○
10.	○	○	○	○	○	○	○	○	○	○	○	○	○	○	○	○	○	○	○	○	○	○	○	○	○	○

Task-Based Simulation 48 Solution

Concepts		
	Authoritative Literature	
		Help

1. A corporation whose income was derived solely from dividends, interest, and royalties, and during the last six months of its year more than 50% of the value of its outstanding stock is owned by five or fewer individuals.
2. The basis used to determine gain on sale of property that was received as a gift.
3. The trade-in of production machinery for new production machinery by a corporation, when the corporation pays additional cash.
4. An unmarried individual whose filing status enables the taxpayer to use a set of income tax rates that are lower than those applicable to other unmarried individuals, but are higher than those applicable to married persons filing a joint return.

5. If income is unqualifiedly available, it will be subject to the income tax even though it is not physically in the taxpayer's possession.
6. A special tax imposed on corporations that accumulate their earnings beyond the reasonable needs of the business.
7. The classification of income from interest, dividends, annuities, and certain royalties.
8. The classification of depreciable assets and real estate used in a trade or business and held for more than one year.
9. This deduction attempts to mitigate the triple taxation that would occur if one corporation paid dividends to a corporate shareholder who, in turn, distributed such amounts to its individual shareholders.
10. Sale of property to a corporation by a shareholder for a selling price that is in excess of the property's fair market value.

	(A)	(B)	(C)	(D)	(E)	(F)	(G)	(H)	(I)	(J)	(K)	(L)	(M)	(N)	(O)	(P)	(Q)	(R)	(S)	(T)	(U)	(V)	(W)	(X)	(Y)	(Z)
1.	○	○	○	○	○	○	○	○	○	○	○	○	○	○	○	○	○	●	○	○	○	○	○	○	○	○
2.	○	○	○	○	○	○	○	○	○	○	○	○	○	○	○	○	○	○	○	○	○	○	○	○	○	●
3.	○	○	○	○	○	○	○	○	○	○	○	○	○	○	●	○	○	○	○	○	○	○	○	○	○	○
4.	○	○	○	○	○	○	○	○	○	○	○	○	○	○	●	○	○	○	○	○	○	○	○	○	○	○
5.	○	○	○	○	○	○	●	○	○	○	○	○	○	○	○	○	○	○	○	○	○	○	○	○	○	○
6.	●	○	○	○	○	○	○	○	○	○	○	○	○	○	○	○	○	○	○	○	○	○	○	○	○	○
7.	○	○	○	○	○	○	○	○	○	○	○	○	○	○	○	○	○	○	○	○	●	○	○	○	○	○
8.	○	○	○	○	○	○	○	○	○	○	○	○	○	○	○	○	○	○	○	○	○	○	●	○	○	○
9.	○	○	○	○	○	○	○	○	○	●	○	○	○	○	○	○	○	○	○	○	○	○	○	○	○	○
10.	○	○	○	○	○	●	○	○	○	○	○	○	○	○	○	○	○	○	○	○	○	○	○	○	○	○

Explanations

1. (**R**) To be classified as a personal holding company, a corporation must meet two requirements: (1) the corporation must receive at least 60% of its adjusted ordinary gross income as "personal holding company income" such as dividends, interest, rents, royalties, and other passive income; and (2) the corporation must have more than 50% of the value of its outstanding stock directly or indirectly owned by five or fewer individuals during any time in the last half of the tax year.
2. (**Z**) The transferred basis, equal to the basis of the donor plus any gift tax paid attributable to the net appreciation in the value of the gift, is the basis used to determine gain on sale of property that was received as a gift.
3. (**P**) A like-kind exchange, the exchange of business or investment property for property of a like kind, qualifies as a nontaxable exchange. Thus, the exchange of production machinery for new production machinery when boot (money) is given is a nontaxable exchange.
4. (**O**) Head of household filing status applies to unmarried persons not qualifying for surviving spouse status who maintain a household for more than one-half of the taxable year for a dependent. The tax rates applicable to the head of household status are lower than those applicable to individuals filing as single, but are higher than rates applicable to married individuals filing a joint return.
5. (**G**) Under the doctrine of constructive receipt, income is includible in gross income and subject to income tax for the taxable year in which that income is made unqualifiedly available to the taxpayer without restriction, even though not physically in the taxpayer's possession.
6. (**A**) Corporations may be subject to an accumulated earnings tax, in addition to regular income tax, if a corporation accumulates earnings beyond reasonable business needs in order to avoid shareholder tax on dividend distributions.
7. (**U**) Portfolio income is defined as income from interest, dividends, annuities, and certain royalties.
8. (**W**) Section 1231 assets include depreciable assets and real estate used in a trade or business and held for more than one year.
9. (**J**) The dividends received deduction was enacted by Congress to mitigate the triple taxation that occurs when one corporation pays dividends to a corporate stockholder who, in turn, distributes such amounts to its individual stockholders.

10. **(F)** A constructive dividend results when a shareholder is considered to have received a dividend from a corporation, although the corporation did not specifically declare a dividend. This situation may occur when a shareholder/employee receives an excessive salary from a corporation, when there is a loan to a shareholder where there is no intent to repay the amount loaned, or when a corporation purchases shareholder property for an amount in excess of the property's fair market value. Constructive dividends often result when a transaction between a shareholder and corporation is not an arm's-length transaction.

Task-Based Simulation 49

```
Deductibility
        Authoritative Literature
                        Help
```

For the following, indicate if the expenses are fully deductible, partially deductible, or nondeductible for regular tax purposes on Reliant Corp.'s 2015 federal income tax return.

Selections

F.	Fully deductible for regular tax purposes on Reliant's 2015 federal income tax return.
P.	Partially deductible for regular tax purposes on Reliant's 2015 federal income tax return.
N.	Nondeductible for regular tax purposes on Reliant's 2015 federal income tax return.

	(F)	(P)	(N)
1. Reliant purchased theater tickets for its out-of-town clients. The performances took place after Reliant's substantial and bona fide business negotiations with its clients.	○	○	○
2. Reliant accrued advertising expenses to promote a new product line. Ten percent of the new product line remained in ending inventory.	○	○	○
3. Reliant incurred interest expense on a loan to purchase municipal bonds.	○	○	○
4. Reliant paid a penalty for the underpayment of 2015 estimated taxes.	○	○	○
5. On December 9, 2016, Reliant's board of directors voted to pay a $500 bonus to each nonstockholder employee for 2016. The bonuses were paid on February 3, 2017.	○	○	○

Task-Based Simulation 49 Solution

```
Deductibility
        Authoritative Literature
                        Help
```

	(F)	(P)	(N)
1. Reliant purchased theater tickets for its out-of-town clients. The performances took place after Reliant's substantial and bona fide business negotiations with its clients.	○	●	○
2. Reliant accrued advertising expenses to promote a new product line. Ten percent of the new product line remained in ending inventory.	●	○	○
3. Reliant incurred interest expense on a loan to purchase municipal bonds.	○	○	●
4. Reliant paid a penalty for the underpayment of 2015 estimated taxes.	○	○	●
5. On December 9, 2016, Reliant's board of directors voted to pay a $500 bonus to each nonstockholder employee for 2016. The bonuses were paid on February 3, 2017.	●	○	○

Explanations

1. **(P)** The cost of the theater tickets qualifies as a business entertainment expense, which is only 50% deductible for 2016.
2. **(F)** Indirect costs that do not directly benefit a particular activity or are not incurred because of a particular activity may be currently deducted and are not required to be capitalized as part of the cost of inventory. Indirect costs that can be currently deducted include such costs as marketing, selling, advertising, distribution, and general and administrative expenses.
3. **(N)** Since the proceeds of the loan were used to purchase municipal bonds that generate tax-exempt income, the interest expense on the loan is not deductible.
4. **(N)** No deduction is allowed for the penalty that results from the underpayment of estimated income tax.
5. **(F)** An accrual method taxpayer can deduct compensation for nonstockholder employees when there is an obligation to make payment, economic performance has occurred, the amount is reasonable, and payment is made not later than 2½ months after the end of the tax year. Here, the amount of bonus was determined on December 9, 2016, and was paid February 3, 2017.

Partnership Taxation

Formation and Basis

Task-Based Simulation 50

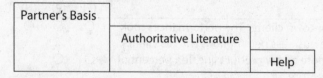

Situation
During Year 1, Adams, a general contractor; Brinks, an architect; and Carson, an interior decorator, formed the Dex Home Improvement General Partnership by contributing the assets below.

	Asset	Adjusted Basis	Fair Market Value	% of Partner Share in Capital, Profits, and Losses
Adams	Cash	$40,000	$40,000	50%
Brinks	Land	$12,000	$21,000	20%
Carson	Inventory	$24,000	$24,000	30%

The land was a capital asset to Brinks, subject to a $5,000 mortgage, which was assumed by the partnership.

For items 1 and 2, determine and select the initial basis of the partner's interest in Dex.

	(A)	(B)	(C)
1. Brinks' initial basis in Dex is A. $21,000 B. $12,000 C. $8,000	○	○	○
2. Carson's initial basis in Dex is A. $25,500 B. $24,000 C. $19,000	○	○	○

Task-Based Simulation 50 Solution

				(A)	(B)	(C)

Partner's Basis / Authoritative Literature / Help

	(A)	(B)	(C)
1. Brinks' initial basis in Dex is	○	○	●
A. $21,000			
B. $12,000			
C. $8,000			
2. Carson's initial basis in Dex is	●	○	○
A. $25,500			
B. $24,000			
C. $19,000			

Explanations

1. **(C)** The requirement is to determine Brinks' initial basis for his 20% partnership interest received in exchange for a contribution of property subject to a $5,000 mortgage. Generally, no gain or loss is recognized on the contribution of property in exchange for a partnership interest. As a result, Brinks' initial basis for the partnership interest received consists of the $12,000 basis of the land contributed to the partnership, less the net reduction in Brinks' individual liability resulting from the partnership's assumption of the mortgage. Since Brinks received a 20% partnership interest, the net reduction in Brinks' individual liability equals $5,000 × 80% = $4,000. As a result, Brinks' basis for the partnership interest is $12,000 − $4,000 = $8,000.

2. **(A)** The requirement is to determine Carson's initial basis for his 30% partnership interest received in exchange for a contribution of inventory. Since partners are individually liable for their share of partnership liabilities, an increase in partnership liabilities increases a partner's basis in the partnership by the partner's share of the increase. Carson's initial basis is the $24,000 adjusted basis of the inventory contributed, increased by the increase in his individual liability resulting from the partnership's assumption of Brinks' mortgage ($5,000 × 30% = $1,500). Thus, Carson's initial basis for the partnership interest is $24,000 + $1,500 = $25,500.

Task-Based Simulation 51

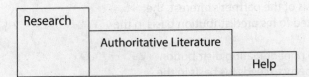

Research / Authoritative Literature / Help

The Dex Home Improvement General Partnership is planning to adopt a fiscal year ending September 30, while Brinks (a 20% partner) uses the calendar year as his taxable year. Research the Internal Revenue Code to determine how Brinks should determine the amount of income and other partnership items from the fiscal-year partnership that must be reported on Brinks' 2015 calendar-year tax return. Indicate the section and subsection from the IRC in the shaded boxes below.

Section	Subsection
§	( )

Task-Based Simulation 51 Solution

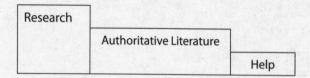

Internal Revenue Code Section 706, subsection (a), provides that in computing the taxable income of a partner for a taxable year, the partnership items of income, gain, loss, deduction, or credit that should be included should be based on the taxable year of the partnership that ends with or within the taxable year of the partner. Therefore, Brinks' calendar year 2015 tax return ending December 31 should reflect only Brinks' distributive share of partnership items for the Dex Partnership fiscal year ended September 30, 2015.

Section			Subsection		
§	706		(	a	)

Distributions

Task-Based Simulation 52

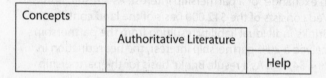

During 2015, the Dex Partnership breaks even but decides to make distributions to each partner.

For items 1 through 6, determine whether the statement is True or False.

	True	False
1. A nonliquidating cash distribution may reduce the recipient partner's basis in his partnership interest below zero.	○	○
2. A nonliquidating distribution of unappreciated inventory reduces the recipient partner's basis in his partnership interest.	○	○
3. In a liquidating distribution of property other than money, where the partnership's basis of the distributed property exceeds the basis of the partner's interest, the partner's basis in the distributed property is limited to his predistribution basis in the partnership interest.	○	○
4. Gain is recognized by the partner who receives a nonliquidating distribution of property, where the adjusted basis of the property exceeds his basis in the partnership interest before the distribution.	○	○
5. In a nonliquidating distribution of inventory, where the partnership has no unrealized receivables or appreciated inventory, the basis of inventory that is distributed to a partner cannot exceed the inventory's adjusted basis to the partnership.	○	○
6. The partnership's nonliquidating distribution of encumbered property to a partner who assumes the mortgage does not affect the other partners' bases in their partnership interests.	○	○

Task-Based Simulation 52 Solution

Concepts		
	Authoritative Literature	
		Help

	True	False
1. A nonliquidating cash distribution may reduce the recipient partner's basis in his partnership interest below zero.	○	●
2. A nonliquidating distribution of unappreciated inventory reduces the recipient partner's basis in his partnership interest.	●	○
3. In a liquidating distribution of property other than money, where the partnership's basis of the distributed property exceeds the basis of the partner's interest, the partner's basis in the distributed property is limited to his predistribution basis in the partnership interest.	●	○
4. Gain is recognized by the partner who receives a nonliquidating distribution of property, where the adjusted basis of the property exceeds his basis in the partnership interest before the distribution.	○	●
5. In a nonliquidating distribution of inventory, where the partnership has no unrealized receivables or appreciated inventory, the basis of inventory that is distributed to a partner cannot exceed the inventory's adjusted basis to the partnership.	●	○
6. The partnership's nonliquidating distribution of encumbered property to a partner who assumes the mortgage does not affect the other partners' bases in their partnership interests.	○	●

Explanations

1. **(F)** A partner can never have a negative basis for a partnership interest. Partnership distributions can only reduce a partner's basis to zero.

2. **(T)** Partnership distributions are generally nontaxable and reduce the recipient partner's basis by the adjusted basis of the property distributed.

3. **(T)** A liquidating distribution of property other than money generally does not cause the distributee partner to recognize gain. As a result, the distributee partner's basis in the distributed property is limited to the partner's predistribution basis for the partnership interest.

4. **(F)** Gain is recognized by a distributee partner only if the amount of money distributed exceeds the partner's predistribution basis for the partnership interest. Distributions of property other than money never result in the recognition of gain by the distributee partner.

5. **(T)** Generally, a nonliquidating distribution of inventory is not taxable, and the adjusted basis for the inventory carries over to the distributee partner. As a result, the distributee partner's basis for the inventory cannot exceed the inventory's adjusted basis to the partnership.

6. **(F)** Since partners are individually liable for partnership liabilities, a decrease in partnership liabilities will decrease the basis for a partner's partnership interest by the partner's share of the decrease. Thus, if a distributee partner assumes a mortgage on encumbered property, the other partners' bases in their partnership interests will be decreased by their share of the decrease in partnership liabilities.

Task-Based Simulation 53

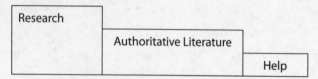

In 2015, Madison is considering making a proportionate nonliquidating distribution of shares of stock that it owns in CDE Corporation to its partners. Research the Internal Revenue Code to determine the basis that the partners will have for the CDE stock that they receive. Indicate the section and subsection from the IRC in the shaded boxes below.

Section		Subsection	
§		(	)

Task-Based Simulation 53 Solution

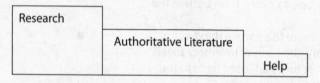

Internal Revenue Code Section 732, subsection (a) provides that the basis of distributed property to a partner is generally the same as the adjusted basis of the property to the partnership immediately before the distribution.

Section		Subsection	
§	732	(	a	)

S Corporation Taxation

Income and Basis

Task-Based Simulation 54

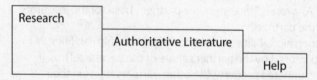

Mr. Perry is the sole shareholder of Arrow, Inc., a calendar-year S corporation. Due to the pass-through of losses in previous years, Perry's aggregate basis for the Arrow stock and debt that he owns has been reduced to zero. For its calendar year 2016, Arrow expects to incur another large loss which Perry wishes to deduct on his 2016 Form 1040 tax return. What Internal Revenue Code section and subsection limits a shareholder's deduction of an S corporation's losses to the shareholder's basis for stock and debt? Indicate the reference to that citation in the shaded boxes below.

Section		Subsection	
§		(	)

Task-Based Simulation 54 Solution

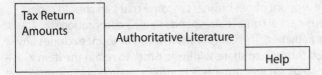

Internal Revenue Code section 1366, subsection (d) limits a shareholder's deduction of an S corporation's losses to the shareholder's basis for stock and debt.

Section			Subsection		
§	1366		(	d	)

Distributions and Special Taxes

Task-Based Simulation 55

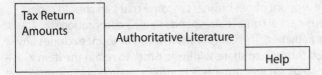

Situation

Lan Corp., an accrual-basis calendar-year repair service corporation, was formed and began business on January 6, 2016. Lan's valid S corporation election took effect retroactively on January 6, 2016. Since the question requires a numeric answer, a list of numeric amounts would be provided for the candidate to select from.

For **items 1 through 4,** determine the amount, if any, using the fact pattern for each item.

1. Assume the following facts:

   Lan's 2016 books recorded the following items:

Gross receipts	$7,260
Interest income on investments	50
Charitable contributions	1,000
Supplies	1,120

   What amount of net business income should Lan report on its 2016 Form 1120S, U.S. Income Tax Return for an S Corporation, Schedule K?

2. Assume the following facts:

   As of January 6, 2016, Taylor and Barr each owned 100 shares of the 200 issued shares of Lan stock. On January 31, 2016, Taylor and Barr each sold 20 shares to Pike. No election was made to terminate the tax year. Lan had net business income of $14,400 for the year ended December 31, 2016, and made no distributions to its shareholders. Lan's 2016 calendar year had 360 days.

   What amount of net business income should have been reported on Pike's 2016 Schedule K-1 from Lan? (2016 is a 360-day tax year.) Round the answer to the nearest hundred.

3. Assume the following facts:

   Pike purchased 40 Lan shares on January 31, 2016, for $4,000. Lan made no distributions to shareholders, and Pike's 2016 Schedule K-1 from Lan reported:

Ordinary business loss	$(1,000)
Municipal bond interest income	150

   What was Pike's basis in his Lan stock at December 31, 2016?

4. Assume the following facts:

On January 6, 2016, Taylor and Barr each owned 100 shares of the 200 issued shares of Lan stock. Taylor's basis in Lan shares on that date was $10,000. Taylor sold all of his Lan shares to Pike on January 31, 2016, and Lan made a valid election to terminate its tax year. Taylor's share of ordinary income from Lan prior to the sale was $2,000. Lan made a cash distribution of $3,000 to Taylor on January 30, 2016.

What was Taylor's basis in Lan shares for determining gain or loss from the sale to Pike?

Task-Based Simulation 55 Solution

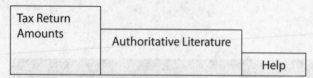

For **items 1 through 4**, candidates were asked to determine the amount for Lan Corp. (an accrual-basis calendar-year S corporation), using the fact pattern for each item.

1. **($6,140)** The requirement is to determine the amount of net business income that Lan should report on Schedule K of Form 1120S. The term "net business income" corresponds to an S corporation's "ordinary income (loss) from trade or business activities." The computation of this amount excludes any item that must be separately stated and passed through to shareholders in order to retain the item's special tax characteristics. Here, the interest income on investments is portfolio income and must be separately stated and passed through to shareholders as interest income. Similarly, the charitable contributions must be separately stated and passed through to shareholders in order to apply the appropriate percentage limitations at the shareholder level. As a result, Lan's net business income consists of its $7,200 of gross receipts reduced by the $1,120 of supplies expense, or $6,140.

2. **($2,700)** The requirements is to determine the amount of net business income to be reported on Pike's 2016 Schedule K-1 from Lan. If there is no election to terminate the tax year following the sale of stock, the income of an S corporation for the entire taxable year is allocated per share, per day to anyone who was a shareholder during the year. Lan was formed on January 6, 2016, and its tax year consists of 360 days. So its net business income per share, per day would be $14,400 ÷ 200 shares ÷ 360 days = $.20. Since Pike purchased his 40 shares on January 31, he is considered to own his stock for a total of 334 days during the year (counting February 1 as the first day). Thus, the amount of net business income to be reported on Pike's Schedule K-1 is (40 shares × 334 days × $.20) = $2,672. Since the instructions indicated that the answer should be rounded to the nearest hundred, the correct answer is $2,700.

3. **($3,150)** The requirement is to determine Pike's basis for his Lan stock at December 31, 2016, assuming that he had purchased the stock for $4,000. An S corporation's items of income and deduction pass through to be reported on shareholder returns even though no distributions are made. As a result, a shareholder's S corporation stock basis is increased by the pass through of all income items (including tax-exempt income), and is decreased by all loss and deduction items (including nondeductible expenses). In this case, Pike's beginning basis of $4,000 would be increased by the $150 of municipal bond interest income, and decreased by the $1,000 of ordinary business loss.

4. **($9,000)** The requirement is to determine Taylor's basis in Lan shares for determining gain or loss from the sale of stock to Pike. Taylor's beginning stock basis of $10,000 must be increased by his $2,000 share of the ordinary income from Lan prior to the sale, and must be decreased by the $3,000 nontaxable cash distribution that Taylor received. Recall that distributions by S corporations without accumulated earnings and profits are treated as a return of stock basis and are excluded from gross income.

Index